MW01049482

FAR-OUT, SHAGGY, FUNKY MONSTERS

FAR-OUT, SHAGGY, FUNKY MONSTERS

A WHAT-IT-IS HISTORY OF BIGFOOT IN THE 1970S

Daniel S. Green

COACHWHIP PUBLICATIONS
Greenville, Ohio

Far-Out, Shaggy, Funky Monsters, by Daniel S. Green
© 2018 Daniel S. Green
All Rights Reserved.

Thanks to western Pennsylvania investigator Brian Seech (and the Center for Cryptozoological Studies, visit their Facebook page for more details) and Harford County (MD) naturalist Bob Chance for providing access to 1970s-era track casts pictured in the texts.

Historical texts are used strictly for the purposes of criticism, comment, education, and research, per Title 17 of the United States Code (USC Title 17 § 107), and are fully cited.

Cover design by Holly Green

CoachwhipBooks.com

ISBN 1-61646-457-7
ISBN-13 978-1-61646-457-8

CONTENTS

PREFACE

The 1970s, the years Tom Wolfe called the "Me decade," was the time of Watergate, the end of the Vietnam War, a crippling oil crisis, and the last manned moon landings. They were also years in which the idea of a hairy hominid roaming practically every state in the country gained widespread popularity. Incredibly, this idea was to be no short-lived fad or passing trend; pet rocks and 8-tracks proved transitory, but Bigfoot exerted a resilient grip on our collective mindset. The historical course Bigfoot traveled in the Groovy Age is the subject of this book, a period in which the hirsute enigma became a part of our cultural fabric.

There is no mystery for me and I do not need to invent some high-sounding reason for delving into this subject. I think Bigfoot is fun—and believing history is a tool for illumination as well as explication, my hope is that between these covers readers will be both entertained and informed. Succinctly, the following pages seek to share a focused history of Bigfoot's explosive break-out in the 1970s, offering material to both hardened skeptic and long-standing devotee alike that is infrequently encountered. Bookending Bigfoot's journey through the '70s is a brief foundation of precursory import as well as a passing glimpse of what was to follow in the '80s and beyond. Bigfoot's soaring ascension in the '70s owed its blastoff ignition to the former and its enduring stratospheric reign powers it through the latter into the present day.

Any topic, argument, or field of study, when broken into discrete time periods, will have stories to tell. Though anecdotes alone do not make science, they are necessary to history. Recognizing that our views are shaped by what we consume, the ensuing selective aggregation of Bigfoot stories and accounts derived from newspaper accounts, magazine articles, books, and movies is intended here to show the scope and scale of what people *did* consume. Upon panning back and finding that consumption on a mass scale, we see the impact to our culture in the '70s and appreciate its continuing resonance.

It is easy to describe Bigfoot superficially—large, hair-covered, manlike, and often smelly. A nomological description of Bigfoot, however, is evasive; the subject defies clinical scrutiny and seems consigned to reside on the other side of the garden wall, always unknown, visible and understandable only in snatches, glimpses, and peeks through a miasmic veil of mystery. This book's intention is not to answer the question of what Bigfoot is—biological specimen awaiting classification, paranormal creature, supernatural entity, or *other*. Digging into Bigfoot's history reveals that such questions have been clinging to the hairy giant since its first stories started circulating. Arguments frothily debated some forty years ago during Bigfoot's heady heyday sound familiar to contemporary conversations.

On July 30, 2016, I was privileged to sit down with Loren Coleman, Director of the International Cryptozoology Museum in Portland, Maine. The author and noted cryptozoologist generously gave his time for an interview followed by a tour of the museum. Coleman recalled that in 1965, Ivan Sanderson told him that he was one of five people then into Bigfoot, a number which would expand exponentially in a handful of years. Coleman said Bigfoot research in the '70s, an effort he was part of, contained periods of "high strangeness," and were a time of cream-of-the-crop localized creature reports which have become legendary in and of themselves. In conquering all media, Bigfoot became accessible, and to a degree, accepted. We offered Bigfoot a home within our cultural landscape and he moved in to stay. This book will try to share that story.

My deep gratitude to Vaughn Bryant, Loren Coleman, Stan Gordon, John Mionczynski, Daniel Perez, Brad Steiger, Bruce Harrington, Billy Willard, Ray Pierotti, Dave Coleman, Gerry Mulligan, and my editor, Chad Arment for sharing their important perspectives and key insights on Bigfoot in the '70s—the research, the mystery, and the fun.

CHAPTER 1. BACKSTORY—PART I
BURNS, DAHINDEN & GREEN

Native American traditions and early European settlers' accounts of hairy giants bespeak the historical presence of large, tall, manlike, and hair-covered creatures in North America. Newspapers have for centuries carried stories and broadcasted accounts of people interacting in some form or fashion with creatures that sound like the modern conception of Bigfoot. In 1934, the United Press described these creatures, first popularly called Sasquatch, as "hairy giants, nine feet tall, with a ferocious appearance and demeanor." The same article shared a Bigfoot encounter experienced by Mr. and Mrs. James Caulfield who lived on a farm close by Harrison, B.C.

> Mrs. Caulfield relates that she was washing clothes in a river when she heard a buzzing sound similar to that made [by] a humming bird.
>
> "I turned my head," she said, "but instead of a bird there stood the most terrible thing I ever saw in my life. I thought I'd die for the thing that made the funny noise was a big man covered with hair from head to feet. He was looking at me and I couldn't help looking at him. I guessed he was a Sasquatch so I covered my eyes with my hand, for the Indians say that if a Sasquatch catches your eye you are in his power. They hypnotize you. I felt faint and as I backed away to get to the house I tripped and fell. As he came nearer I screamed and fainted."[1]

Rushing toward the sound of his wife's screams, James Caulfield ran out of their house in time to see the Sasquatch run off into the bush.[2]

J. W. Burns

John W. Burns (1888-1962) is credited with coining the name *Sasquatch* after either a mispronunciation or corruption of a First Nations term and for promoting Sasquatch as an indigenous creature of British Columbia. Reporter Alex MacGillivray wrote in 1957, "The name Sasquatch is also a Burns' product, borrowed from the Indian. It means hairy giant."[3] Burns spent several years as a teacher on the Chehalis Indian Reserve along the Harrison River, some 60 miles of Vancouver. During the 1920s and 1930s, Burns raised public awareness through several stories he authored in *MacLean's* magazine and for newspapers like the *Vancouver Daily Province;*[4] his writings publicized First Nations' hairy giant beliefs and traditions from British Columbia and made Sasquatch a household word. Thanks to Burns, hairy hominids in North America had an "official" appellation, no longer to be referred to as merely "wild men" and "whazzits."

The following article printed in 1935 does not directly credit its authorship to Burns, but its occurrence at all recognizes a debt to Burns' sponsorship of the subject and his impact to the resulting popularization of Sasquatch.

> VANCOUVER, B. C.—(UP)—Sasquatch men, remnants of a lost race of "wild men" who inhabited the rocky regions of British Columbia centuries ago, are reported roaming the province again.
>
> After an absence of several months from the district of Harrison Mills, 50 miles east of Vancouver, the long, weird, wolf-like howls of the "wild men" are being heard again and two of the hairy monsters were reported seen in the Morris valley [sic] on the Harrison river [sic].
>
> Residents in the district tell of seeing the two giants leaping and bounding out of the forest and striding across the duck-feeding ground, wallowing now and again, in the bog and mire and long, waving swamp grasses.
>
> Reported Agile as Goats—The strange men, it was reported, after emerging from the woods, came leaping down the jagged rocky hillside with the agility and lightness of mountain goats. Snatches of their weird language floated on the breeze across the lake to the pioneer settlement at the foot of the hills.
>
> The giants walked with an easy gait across the swamp flats and at the Morris creek [sic], in the shadow of Little Mystery

mountains, straddled a floating log, which they propelled with their long, hairy hands and huge feet across the sluggish glacial stream to the opposite side. There they abandoned the log and climbed hand over hand up the almost perpendicular cliff at a point known as Gibraltar and disappeared into the wooded wilderness at the top of the ridge. They carried two large clubs and walked round a herd of cattle directly in their path.

Indian's Story Retold—The return of the giants to the legendary stronghold of the Sasquatch monsters recalls the narrow escape of an Indian at the same spot last March. A huge rock narrowly missed his canoe while he was fishing and looking up, he said he saw a huge and hairy monster stamping his feet and gesticulating wildly. The Indian escaped by cutting his fishing tackle and paddling away. The same Indian declares the Sasquatch twice have stolen salmon which he tied in a tree outside his house out of reach of dogs.

The latest appearance of the monsters was peaceful. They avoided the trails usually used by the people of the valley and molested neither cattle nor human beings.

People who have reported seeing the giants on their rare appearances described them as "ferocious looking wild men, nine feet tall and covered from head to toes with thick black hair."[5]

Burns' interest and nimble pen extended Sasquatch's exposition and explication in the following lengthy *MacLean's* article from 1937. This exemplar piece limns several Native peoples' stories about and experiences with Sasquatch.

["As told in *MacLean's Magazine* by J. W. Burns"] Persistent rumors led the writer to make diligent enquiries among old Indians. The question relating to the subject was always, or nearly always, evaded with the trite excuse: "The white man don't believe, he make joke of the Indian." But after three years of plodding, we have come into possession of information more definite and authentic than has come to light at any previous time. Disregarding rumor and hearsay, we have prevailed upon men who claim they had actual contact with these hairy giants, to tell what they know about them. Their story is set down here in good faith.

X Y lives on the Chehalis Reserve. I believe that he is a reliable as well as an intelligent Indian. He gave me the following thrilling account of his experience with these people.

"One evening in the month of May some years ago," said the hero, "I was walking along the foot of the mountain about a mile from the Chehalis reserve. I thought I heard a noise something like a grunt nearby. Looking in the direction in which it came, I was startled to see what I took at first sight to be a huge bear crouched upon a boulder twenty or thirty feet away. I raised my rifle to shoot it, but, as I did the creature stood up and let out a piercing yell. It was a man—a giant, no less than six feet and one-half in height, and covered with hair. He was in a rage and jumped from the boulder to the ground. I fled, but not before I felt his breath upon my cheek.

"I never ran so fast before or since through brush and undergrowth toward the Statloo or Chehalis river, where my dugout was moored. From time to time I looked over my shoulder. The giant was fast overtaking me—a hundred feet separated us; another look and the distance measured less than fifty—then the Chehalis and in a moment the dugout shot across the stream to the opposite bank. The swift river, however, did not in the least daunt the giant, for he began to wade it immediately.

"I arrived home almost worn out from running and I felt sick. Taking an anxious look around the house, I was relieved to find the wife and children inside. I bolted the door and barricaded it with everything at hand. Then with my rifle ready, I stood near the door and awaited his coming."

X added that if he had not been so much excited he could easily have shot the giant when he began to wade the river.

"After an anxious waiting of twenty minutes," resumed the Indian, "I heard a noise approaching like the tramping of a horse. I looked through a crack in the old wall. It was the giant. Darkness had not yet set in and I had a good look at him. Except that he was covered with hair and twice the bulk of the average man, there was nothing to distinguish him from the rest of us. He pushed against the wall of the old house with such force it shook back and forth. The old cedar shook and timber creaked and groaned so much under the strain that I was afraid that it would fall down and kill us. I whispered to the old woman to take the children under the bed."

The Indian pointed out what remained of the old house in which he lived at the time, explaining that the giant treated it so roughly that it had to be abandoned the following winter.

"After prowling and grunting like an animal around the house," continued the Indian, "he went away. We were glad, for the children and the wife were uncomfortable under the old bedstead. Next morning I found his tracks in the mud around the house, the biggest of either man or beast I had ever seen. The tracks measure twenty-two inches in length, but narrow in proportion to their length."

The following winter while shooting wild duck on that part of the reserve Indians call the "prairie" which is on the north side of the Harrison river and about two miles from the Chehalis village, X once more came face to face with the same hairy giant. The Indian ran for dear life, followed by the wild man, but after pursuing him for three or four hundred yards the giant gave up the chase.

Old village Indians who called upon X to hear of his second encounter, nodded their heads sagely, shrugged their shoulders, and for some reason not quite clear, seemed not to wish the story to gain further publicity.

On the afternoon of the same day another Indian by the name of Paull Paul was chased from the creek where he was fishing for salmon, by the same individual. Paull was in a state of terror, for unlike the other Indian he had no gun. A short distance from the shack the giant suddenly quit and walked into the bush. Paull, exhausted from running, fell in the snow and had to be carried home by his mother and others of the family.

"The first and second time," went on X, "I was all alone when I met the strange mountain creature. Then, early in the spring of the following year, another man and myself were bear hunting near the place where I first met him. On this occasion we ran into two of these giants. They were sitting on the ground. At first we thought they were old tree stumps, but when we were within fifty feet or so, they suddenly stood up and we came to an immediate stop. Both were nude. We were close enough to know that they were man and woman. The woman was the smaller of the two, but neither of them as big or fierce-looking as the gent that chased me. We ran home, but they did not follow us."

One morning some weeks after this, X and his wife were fishing in a canoe on the Harrison river, near Harrison bay. Paddling around a neck of land, they saw on the beach within a hundred feet of them the giant he had met the previous year.

"We stood for a long time looking at him," said the Indian, "but he took no notice of us—that was the last time I saw him."

The Indian remarked that his father and numbers of old Indians knew that wild men lived in caves in the mountains—had often seen them. He wished to make it clear that these creatures were in no wise related to the Indian.

Charley belongs to a hamlet near Chilliwack. In his younger days he was known as one of the best hunters in the province and had many thrilling adventures in his time.

Did he know anything about the hairy ape-like men who were supposed to inhabit the distant mountains? The old warrior smiled, and answered that he had had a slight acquaintance with them. He had been in what he thought was one of their houses. "And that is not all," said he, "I met and spoke to one of their women, and I shot . . ." But let [Charley] tell the story himself.

"The strange people, of whom there are but few now—rarely seen and seldom met—" said the old hunter, "are known by the name of Sasquatch, or the hairy mountain men.

"The first time I came to know about these people," continued the old man, "I did not see anybody. Three young men and myself were picking salmonberries on a rocky mountain slope five or six miles from the old town of Yale. In our search for berries we suddenly stumbled upon a large opening in the side of the mountain. This discovery greatly surprised all of us, for we knew every foot of the mountain, and never knew nor heard there was a cave in the vicinity.

"Outside the mouth of the cave there was an enormous boulder. We peered into the cavity but couldn't see anything.

"We gathered some pitchwood, lighted it and began to explore. But before we got very far from the entrance of the cave, we came upon a sort of stone house or enclosure; it was a crude affair. We couldn't make a thorough examination, for our pitchwood kept going out. We left, intending to return in a couple of days and go on exploring. Old Indians, to whom we told the story of our discovery, warned us not to venture near the cave again, as it was surely occupied by the Sasquatch. That was the first time I heard about the hairy men that inhabit the mountains. We, however, disregarded the advice of the old men and sneaked off to explore the cave, but to our great disappointment found the boulder rolled back into the mouth and fitting it so nicely that you might suppose it had been made for that purpose."

Charley intimated that he hoped to have enough money some day to buy sufficient dynamite to blow open the cave of the Sasquatch and see how far it extends through the mountain.

The Indian then took up the thread of his story and told of his first meeting with one of these men. A number of other Indians and himself were bathing in a small lake near Yale. He was dressing, when suddenly out from behind a rock, only a few feet away, stepped a nude hairy man. "Oh! He was a big, big man!" continued the old hunter. "He looked at me for a moment, his eyes were so kind-looking that I was about to speak to him when he turned about and walked into the forest."

At the same place two weeks later, Charley, together with several of his companions saw the giant, but this time he ran toward the mountain. This was twenty years after the discovery of the cave.

"I don't know if I should tell you or not about the awful experience I had with these wicked people some years ago in the mountains near Hatzie."

The old man rubbed his knee, and said he disliked recalling that disagreeable meeting—it was a tragedy from which he had not yet fully recovered.

"I was hunting in the mountains near Hatzie," he resumed. "I had my dog with me. I came out on a plateau where there were several big cedar trees. The dog stood before one of the trees and began to growl and bark at it. On looking up to see what excited him, I noticed a large hole in the tree seven feet from the ground. The dog pawed and leaped upon the trunk, and looked at me to raise him up, which I did, and he went into the hole. The next moment a muffled cry came from the hole. I said to myself: 'The dog is tearing into a bear', and with my rifle ready I urged the dog to drive him out, and out came something I took for a bear. I shot and it fell with a thud to the ground. 'Murder! Oh my!' I spoke to myself in surprise and alarm, for the thing I had shot looked at me like a white boy. He was nude. He was about twelve or fourteen years age."

In his description of the boy, the Indian said his hair was black and woolly.

"Wounded and bleeding, the poor fellow sprawled upon the ground, but when I drew close to examine the extent of his injury, he let out a wild yell, or, rather a call as if he were appealing for help. From across the mountain a long way off rolled a booming voice. Less than half an hour, out from the depths of the forest came the strangest and wildest creature one could possibly see.

"I raised my rifle, but not to shoot, but in case I would have to defend myself. The strange creature walked toward me without the slightest fear. The wild person was a woman. Her face was almost negro black and her long straight hair fell to her waist. In height she would be about six feet, but her chest and shoulders were well above the average in breadth."

The old man remarked that he had met several wild people in his time, but had never seen anyone half so savage in appearance as this woman. The old brave confessed that he was really afraid of her.

"She cast a hasty glance at the boy. Her face took on a demoniacal expression when she saw that he was bleeding. She turned upon me savagely, and in the Douglas tongue said:

"'You have shot my friend.'

"I explained in the same language—for I'm part Douglas myself—that I had mistaken the boy for a bear and that I was sorry. She did not reply but began a sort of wild frisk or dance around the boy, chanting in a loud voice for a minute or two, and, as if in answer to her, from the distant woods came [a] sort of chanting troll. In her hand she carried something like a snake, about six feet in length, but thinking over the matter, I believe it was the intestine of some animal. But whatever it was, she constantly struck the ground with it. She picked up the boy with one hairy hand, with as much ease as if he had been a wax doll."

At this point of the story the Indian began to make fantastic pictures in the sand with his maple stick, and paused or reflected so long that we thought he had come to the end of his strange narrative, when he suddenly looked up and said with a grin: "Perhaps I better tell you the rest of it, although I know you'll not believe it. There was a challenge of defiance in her black eyes and dark looks. She faced and spoke to me a second time and the dreadful words she used set me shaking."

"You remember them?" I asked.

"Remember them," he repeated, "they still ring round my old ears like the echo of a thunder-storm. She pointed the snake-like thing at me and said:

"'Siwash, you'll never kill another bear,'"

The old hunter's eyes moistened when he admitted that he had never shot a bear or anything else since that fateful day.

"Her words, expression, and the savage avenging glint in her dark, fiery eyes filled me with fear," confessed the old man, "and I felt so exhausted from her unwavering gaze that I was no longer able to keep her covered with my rifle. I let it drop."

The old hunter has been paralyzed for several years past, and he is inclined to think that the words of the wild woman were the cause of it.

The Indian told how his "brave dog that never turned from bear nor cougar," lay whimpering and shivering at his feet while the Sasquatch woman was speaking, "just," said Charley, "as if he understood the meaning of her words."

"Indians," confided Charley, "have always known that wild men lived in the distant mountains."[6]

Sasquatch Days, May 23-24 (Monday—Tuesday), 1938

As Gold Rush fever spread north from California in the mid-nineteenth century, it transformed Harrison Lake, British Columbia, into a Coast Mountains gateway to the northern regions of the province such as Fraser Canyon and the Cariboo hinterland. Newcomers soon discovered what the Salish First Nations already knew: several hot springs fed into Harrison Lake.[7] The transcontinental Canadian Pacific Railway improved access to the area and helped cement Harrison Hot Springs' destiny as a popular resort.

In 1938, Harrison Hot Springs, then called the "Spa of Canada," and the District Improvement Association put on a two-day event called Sasquatch Days. Sasquatch Days was originally proposed to become an annual celebration, but this intention failed to materialize in succeeding years. The occasion involved 2,000 Native Americans from British Columbia and Washington state participating in historical and educational features including sports, handcraft, and traditional dances. Games and events included competitions of slahal, canoe racing, ceremonial performances, tree felling, and log bucking. The dominion fisheries department sanctioned torchlight spear-fishing. Many of these events had never been seen by the general public.[8] At night, a six-piece swing band provided the music for ballroom dancing in the Harrison Hot Springs hotel and, accompanied by the crackle of the campfire, attendees were treated to evening recitations of traditional Sasquatch lore.

> The bold fellows of Harrison have arranged a Sasquatch Festival for May 24. I say bold fellows, because they may be looking for a lot of trouble. Sasquatches are a temperamental lot. If they don't like this festival idea—then look out!
>
> I hope the committee is preparing to make proper libations to the giants of the Harrison hills. If thunder comes rolling down out of the hills, if the beautiful lake foams in anger, they'll have a pretty fair idea that the Sasquatch are annoyed.—Province.[9]

The AP called the event "Sasquatch Indian day" and described the "grotesque" native masks and costumes brought by attendees. A temporary village of 20 lodges was erected near the waters of Harrison Lake, decorated with traditional ochre drawings and totem symbols.

> You either take the Sasquatch or leave them alone. There is no middle course.
>
> Many Indians take them straight. To hear tell the Sasquatch were great hairy legendary creatures that maintain their reputation with an occasional present-day swoop from the mountains to peek in windows or smack down a lone tribesman.[10]

Reporters were on hand to record J. W. Burns' description (given in the past tense) of the celebration's eponymous guests of honor. "Despite their great size—about seven feet in height—the Sasquatch were timid and harmless," he said. "They were believed to be covered with a growth of hair and to live in caves and hollow trees. The legend probably came down from the actual existence of some primitive race." Burns added his own credence of the legend: "I believe in them myself,"[11] he stated, personally affirming the very idea of holding the event at all.

An ermine-trimmed cape fashioned in a native Canadian ritualistic style was presented to Honorable A. "Wells" Gray, minister of lands, when an honorary chieftainship of the Chehalis tribe was conferred upon him by Chief Michael Peters.[12] J. W. Burns wrote of the event:

> In a brief but impressive ceremony at the "Sasquatch Days" sports celebration at Harrison Hot Springs yesterday, Hon. Wells Gray, provincial minister of lands, was elevated to the rank of "Siam Chee'quets Sasquatch" or, chief of the forests of the Sasquatch by Michael Peter [sic] of the Chehalis Indians, under the auspices of the Harrison Hot Springs Improvement association, who had charge of the arrangements.
>
> Sasquatch Wells Gray's regalia consisted of a blanket, gorgeously decorated with crests and symbols, magic apron ornamented with little bells which tinkled bewitching sounds, and a native copper headgear. The ceremonial dress is of Chilcat [sic] design and was worn by one of the British Columbia coast hierarchy Indian Chiefs at the Coronation ceremony of Edward VII. The regalia is valued at $500 by the Alert Bay Indians from whom it was borrowed for the occasion.

Burns further introduced one of the Chehalis songs sung during the ceremony honoring Hon. Gray:

> One of the songs told a pointed and wonderful story. It said: "For thousands of years, long before our time, the Sasquatch guarded the forests and kept watch over them. He saw them grow and clothe the rocks and naked earth. And then came the deer and other animals that live in these forests. Rivers and streams meandered through these woodlands in which fish swarmed. Today the big timbers are gone, the rocks are naked, the deer have fled and fish are few. As Chief of the forests of the Sasquatch, we have faith you'll protect the forests for the common benefit of everybody. In so doing you'll become a great Sasquatch and people will invite you to many potlatches and your name will become great in the land. On great occasions and in critical times we suggest that you remember that you're an honorary Chief of the Sasquatch, the most exalted title we have to confer, a title which has never before been conferred upon anybody in the land and in honoring you with this mark of our esteem and respect we are also doing honor to ourselves. May the great power of the Sasquatch descend upon you."[13]

On Monday, May 23, disaster struck in the form of a spark from a planer which started a $10,000 fire at the Merritt Tyler mill on Harrison Lake and caused a bush fire that officials had to contend with for two days. Some of the participants from the Sasquatch Days festival answered the call and assisted in bringing the fire under control. When the mill fire was finally controlled, some 40,000 feet of railroad ties had been destroyed.[14]

Sasquatch Days demonstrated Sasquatch had promotional value and the hairy giant could be seen popping up in supporting or cameo appearances in other events through the years. Cultus Lake Regatta committee member Lacey Fisher promised the 1941 regatta would be graced with an appearance by Sasquatch partaking in the high belly flop contest.[15]

Three years after Sasquatch Days an incident occurred which entered modern Bigfoot lore as a canonical encounter between people and large, hairy bipeds. George Chapman, a railroad maintenance worker, his wife Jeannie and their three children lived in an isolated house near Ruby Creek, British Columbia. In September 1941, while George was away at work, Jeannie Chapman and the children were scared away from their home by a creature which some came to believe was a Sasquatch. One of the Chapman children, who saw the approaching creature, ran to his mother and reported a "big cow" was coming toward them. When Jeannie

Chapman witnessed for herself the advancing, hairy, manlike creature, she corralled the children and ran down the railroad tracks toward her husband's worksite. George Chapman and a group of men returned to his home to investigate, finding several 16-inch tracks (see chapter 3 for John Green and Esse Tyfting's description of the Ruby Creek incident as shown on *Bigfoot: Man or Beast*).

As author Joshua Blu Buhs points out in his book *Bigfoot: The Life and Times of a Legend*, J. W. Burns' original take on the Chapman family's antagonist at Ruby Creek was, mundanely, a large bear.[16] But Burns evidently changed that position upon the arrival of three canoes to Harrison Hot Springs manned by Native Canadians from Fort Douglas. The canoes' occupants, as reported, were in fact fleeing from monsters and they breathlessly told of the reappearance of the hairy giants, who, as it happened, were on a rampage. Jimmy Douglas and his family were among the group escaping Fort Douglas. Douglas said that a giant Sasquatch, 14-feet tall, entered his family's home forcing the family to beat a hasty retreat. As noted in the *Chilliwack Progress*, "Authorities here [Harrison Hot Springs], including J. W. Burns, one of the world's greatest living experts on the Sasquatch, believe that the huge wild-man seen at Ruby Creek is the same one which this week sent Jimmy Douglas and his family fleeing to Harrison Hot Springs."[17]

The publicity for Sasquatch, and by association for British Columbia, broadened through Burns' articles in *Liberty* magazine, as noted by the *Chilliwack Progress:*

> We don't know whether you believe in those hairy giants called Sasquatches or not—we're keeping out of this—but most residents of Harrison-Agassiz-Chilliwack will admit that the recent article appearing in *Liberty* provided the district with some mighty fine publicity.
>
> The Sasquatch was dug up, resurrected and publicized by J. W. Burns, who a short time ago came over from Chehalis to teach school at the Landing reserve. Mr. Burns, an Irishman, is a firm believer in the Sasquatch. As we said, he is an Irishman, and a good one to boot. Perhaps, just the same, his national background accounts for some things.
>
> Be that as it may, through *Liberty*, a nationally circulated magazine, this district gained wide prominence. Proof of the fact that people of the district appreciated the story is that they bought every copy available.

To Mr. Burns, whose writings appear frequently in *The Progress* and to his Sasquatch, congratulations.[18]

Changing of the Guard—Transition from Burns to Dahinden & Green

Large, hirsute, forest-dwelling giants were, by mid-century, securely and regionally ensconced in western Canada. Arguably, if the hairy giant concept was to flourish and spread continent-wide, new champions would needs be called upon to take up the mantle and carry on the work started by Burns. Two men located in the hotbed of Sasquatch's realm were about to do just that.

John Green was a Canadian journalist, politician, and author whose interest and energy as a prominent Sasquatch researcher spanned some sixty years. As the owner of the *Agassiz-Harrison Advance* (circulation 700), Green began investigating Sasquatch in the 1950s. He had heard the stories of Sasquatch since his childhood but had never given them serious attention. In 1955, Green ran an April Fools' Day story in the *Agassiz-Harrison Advance* concerning a young woman's abduction from the Harrison Hot Springs Hotel. But by the late 1950s, Green became increasingly aware of several respected people's accounts of their encounters with Sasquatch, including the Ruby Creek encounter in 1941. In 1956, Green met a Swiss émigré named René Dahinden who had stopped in to visit the offices of the *Agassiz-Harrison Advance*, seeking any information on Sasquatch Green and his newspaper might provide. For Green, the meeting with Dahinden made a good story, yet he remained, initially, unpersuaded that there was anything definite to the hairy giant legends. Such was not the case with Dahinden.

Straddling the Reuss, the city of Lucerne occupies an important location in central Switzerland for business and commerce as well as for the enjoyment of tourists. Travelers stopping at Lucerne are treated to the majesty of the Alps across the Lake, including views of snow-capped Mount Pilatus and Mount Rigi. Lucerne was the birthplace of René Dahinden, an illegitimate baby, on August 23, 1930.[19] Speaking in 1985 with interviewer J. Richard Greenwell, editor for the International Society of Cryptozoology's *Newsletter*, Dahinden described how his birthplace and early years impacted his mettle: "You know, I come from a part of Switzerland where, when you start something, you finish it. And anybody who stands in your way, or the scientist who doesn't want to go any way, you just wave goodbye to him."[20]

After several foster family experiences during his childhood—including a four-month reunion with his biological mother—Dahinden ended up fostered to a farming family for several years of hard work. Of that experience he said, "But you know, later I wrote and thanked those people because from there I went out into the world—when I was about fifteen—and compared with life there, everything I met with was just a joke."[21]

Dahinden spent several years travelling Europe, which included reaching Stockholm where he met Wanja Holmstrom, his future wife. Fulfilling a long-held dream of emigrating to Canada, Dahinden arrived in Quebec City in 1953. From there he obtained employment with farmer Wilbur Willick near Calgary, Alberta Province. On the evening of December 3, 1953, Dahinden listened to a radio program discuss the *Daily Mail's* Yeti expedition to the Himalayas. When Dahinden expressed interest in the subject, Willick told him similarly-described creatures were seen time to time in British Columbia. To speak colloquially of something "clicking" inside someone to describe an epiphany is to capture the moment Dahinden's life-direction achieved realization. Something indeed clicked inside him. Willick was able to answer Dahinden's eager inquiries by re-telling several stories he had heard while working on the western coast of Canada. Dahinden was taken by the similarity of the Sasquatch creatures in Willick's stories and the Asian Yeti. If such creatures were given credence for living in the Himalayas, why not in Canada?

In the Spring of 1954 Dahinden left Willick's farm and moved to British Columbia. As Dahinden dealt with new jobs, new locales, and new people, the idea of the Sasquatch kept floating around in his head. Despite an oft-encountered, dismissive attitude of "those stories are just Indian legends," Dahinden undertook research when he could at museums and libraries. By 1956, Dahinden had enough material to counter contemptuous perspectives and convince himself that Sasquatch was an extant creature and was something worth pursuing. "I just thought to myself, 'Hell, it seems as if there's something out there; I'll just go and collect a Sasquatch. Tallyho!' I really wasn't equipped at that time to evaluate what I was reading and hearing. I accepted—probably because I wanted to—the word of those people who said the thing existed and who pointed to stories that had never been investigated."[22]

If a sometimes-blithe disposition characterized Dahinden's initial approach to studying Sasquatch, he had begun acquiring the more serious attitude to the subject which characterized his efforts in hairy hominid research for decades to come.

An early account of Dahinden's pursuit of hairy giants came from the pen of no less a Sasquatch luminary than J. W. Burns. In an article in the

Chilliwack Progress, Burns told of a field expedition to find evidence for Sasquatch's existence to be mounted by Dahinden, Wanja Holmstrom, and Frank Poll. Holmstrom was called an anthropologist and mountaineer from Sweden and Poll was referred to as a mountaineer from Austria. The planned locale for their expedition was the Chilliwack Valley, a "vast hinterlands of the Chehalis mountains, a region hitherto which has not been explored." Burns wrote that Dahinden received mountain training from the Alpine division of the Swiss army and that Poll's background and training came from his time with the Austrian Alpine Rescue service.

Their plans called for entering the mountains in the spring to establish a base camp on the Harrison River from which they would conduct their research. "We have read your Sasquatch stories," wrote Holmstrom, "in our respective countries. They gave us such a thrill that we felt we should go on the trail of the giants, and, now here we are in beautiful British Columbia to search for the mighty Sasquatch. We have in mind an exhaustive search, and if necessary spend a year exploring the reputed Sasquatch habitat . . ." Burns added the group's novel and ambitious intention to charter a helicopter to conduct an aerial survey of some of the terrain to be explored 100 miles east of Vancouver. The group also had "a moving picture machine" in case any up-close views of their quarry afforded the opportunity to film it. Much of their intended exploration would be conducted on foot and to track Sasquatch, two dogs, a bloodhound and a great German shepherd, had been obtained. In his article, Burns indulged in a brief dog-and-Sasquatch anecdote:

> But the use of dogs in the past has proved a failure in corralling Sasquatch, a Mr. Smith found out some 20 years ago.
>
> Smith on the trail of the Sasquatch took two hunting dogs with him, when suddenly, declared Smith, they flushed a wild man sitting on a rock. But instead of the dogs staying put with their quarry, one of them keeled over and dropped dead on the spot. The other went yelping through the forest at top speed.
>
> The wild man got up, looked at Smith for a moment and without saying a word walked away. Smith hurried home, where he found his brave, but now terrified dog in a state of collapse. This writer, who knew the dog could never be induced again to venture into the forest.[23]

Burns raised a common question that has transcended the years: "Does it not seem strange that remains—skeletons—of any of the giants have not been found. How do you account for this?" Burns proceeded to supply an answer:

> It's a good question! The fact is and we are telling it for the first time, that the skeleton of one of the giants was accidently discovered some years ago by a white man and his wife, whom this writer interviewed and got documentary proof from them, which we still have.
>
> The skeleton was found in a shallow grave in a good state of preservation. The discoverers were amazed because of its huge size, measuring 7 feet 6 inches in height. The head was enormous. The teeth were in perfect condition, but twice as large as those of either white or Indian. Some 50 Indians who saw the skeleton, declared it was a Sasquatch. There was a deep dent in the skull, apparently the result of a heavy blow, which Indians thought was the cause of his death.
>
> The skeleton was crated on the spot by the discoverers, and unfortunately shipped to a museum outside Canada, where I believe, it is still preserved.
>
> The curator of the museum, commenting on the skeleton, declared it had the largest head of either man or beast he had ever seen.[24]

Before Dahinden entered the wilderness, the *Chilliwack Progress* reported in early May on his receipt of the widely-circulated (and likely encouraging) story of Stan Hunt, an auctioneer, who claimed that while driving toward Vancouver, saw two Sasquatch while on the road west of Hope. Hunt described the creatures as upright, seven feet tall, with gray complexions and gangly builds. One crossed the road on two legs from the Frazer River side. The other creature was partially hidden in the bushes near the road, though Hunt could make out its head. At first Hunt thought he was seeing a bear, "only it wasn't that big around." The hair covering the creature's body seemed "thinner" than a bear's, "not matted like an animal."[25]

Burns had moved to San Francisco about 1945. During a return trip to the Harrison area in June 1956, Burns hoped to meet with Dahinden and Anton Ruesch, Dahinden's new Sasquatch research partner. But Burns missed the adventurous searchers by about a week while the men finalized their plans and equipment for a forthcoming field expedition. In a dispatch carried by the *Chilliwack Progress*, Burns noted the ominous presence of heavy mists shrouding the Chehalis and Morris Valley areas during the end of June which could hinder any search. Burns wrote he was maintaining a correspondence with the explorers to keep abreast of their plans.[26] When the pair returned to Lumby, Dahinden reported the poor weather had indeed created unfavorable searching conditions.[27]

Centennial Sasquatch Hunt

In early 1957, British Columbia officials were well into their planning for the centennial celebration in honor of British Columbia becoming a British Colony in 1858 (the commemoration of British Columbia becoming the sixth province to join Confederation was celebrated in 1971). The *Winnipeg Free Press* article below focuses on Dahinden's aspiration to leverage the centennial to advance Sasquatch field research.

> René Dahinden, 26, says he is convinced the Sasquatch is no myth and he will go to Victoria to ask the B. C. centennial committee to help him organize an expedition into the Harrison Lake area of the interior.
>
> The Sasquatch is reputed to be an eight-foot-tall, hairy giant. It is known as "big man of the mountain" to Indians of the Lumby-Vernon area, who have passed down the story of its existence for generations.
>
> Dahinden says he has talked to three persons who claim to have seen the Sasquatch last year. But the evidence comes from "ordinary, unknown people," and the "experts" won't believe them. "If only Premier Bennett saw one everybody would believe him."
>
> Dahinden's theory is that the Sasquatch is a descendant of a tribe which lived near the Gulf of Mexico centuries ago.
>
> "Bones have been found [to] prove there were giants close to the Gulf of Mexico hundreds of years ago—some descendant of promitive [sic] man, Indians of that area say that these people disappeared around 1800 and later were seen in Idaho."
>
> Dahinden said a Hudson's Bay Co. trader near Harrison Hot Springs, B.C. saw a similar creature in 1846.

"I have spent a long time studying such evidence as we have and also evidence of the so-called Abominable Snowman or Yeti in the Himalayas, which I believe is closely allied to the Sasquatch."[28]

About a week after Dahinden's interest in combining Sasquatch and the centennial was written of, a Fraser Valley village that was no stranger to Sasquatch and its drawing power took up a similar position. On the evening of March 14, 1957, the commissioners of Harrison Hot Springs, then a village of 500, voted to devote their centennial efforts to the capture (or annihilation) of a Sasquatch. With one dissent among the five members of the council, it was voted to seek permission to divert its entire centennial grant—given by various sources to be $600 to $800—to finance a Sasquatch search. Provincial governments made grants to centres to financially assist their centennial celebrations. Clerk Paul Trout was instructed to formally forward the commissioners' request to the British Columbian centennial committee in Victoria.

The motion to conduct a Sasquatch search was made by commissioner John Johnson; during the discussion, Commissioner Mel Geyer reminded Johnson of the occasion when Johnson and a party trekking in the mountains were followed by something that stopped when they stopped. The lone opposition came from Commissioner Robert Gill. "I don't want people to think I am a fool. I have been here for 50 years and I've never seen anything like a Sasquatch," he said. "The provincial government won't approve it. They are not such fat heads as that."[29] The Centennial committee had in fact already stressed the desire for centres to place emphasis on folklore and local color during the regional observances. Rounding out their discussion the commissioners also agreed on René Dahinden as the proposed hunt's leader.

Harrison Hot Springs' move to involve Sasquatch proved a publicity bonanza. The same kind of attention, even notoriety, which the *Daily Mail* expedition had heaped on the broad shoulders of the Abominable Snowman, was given over to the Canadian and international media's coverage of the suggested search for British Columbia's Yeti-like kin. Exponentially expanding awareness of Sasquatch appeared to benefit Harrison Hot Springs and the region writ large. "Now everybody's getting in to the Sasquatch act!" claimed the *Chilliwack Progress*.[30] The Chilliwack Centennial committee, recognizing the value of Harrison's Sasquatch hunt proposed both sides of the Fraser River collaborate on a Sasquatch-slanted golf tournament with trophies to be bedecked by the hairy giants. "General feeling was that since

Sasquatch have been reported on both sides of the Fraser, there is no reason why Chilliwack cannot garner some of the publicity that Harrison is getting." It was probably a hard thing to avoid associating with the proposed Sasquatch search and thereby miss out on the guaranteed headline and assured publicity. Take for example W. T. Clark, Assistant Manager of Harrison Hot Springs Hotel, who said the hotel had considered putting up a $10,000 reward for capturing a Sasquatch.[31]

> Reeve James Fraser, Kent municipality, moved that the board's manpower and the financial resources be used to back the expedition if the B.C. centennial committee fail to allow centennial funds to be used for the project. He commented: "I would like to make it clear this thing is real and not mythical."[32]

The British Columbia centennial committee in Victoria received Harrison Hot Springs' request to use centennial funds to search for Sasquatch and the proposal was put under consideration.[33] The very suggestion of a sponsored, sanctioned Sasquatch hunt had its champions and opponents, and some looked upon the notion with a dose of humor. Back in the village, Tony Burger, chairman of Harrison Hot Springs' commissioners, discovered a fur hat perched on the hood of his car on Sunday, March 31. Reaching for the hat he saw an accompanying note: "The Sasquatch have been here."[34] Harrison Hot Springs' own Jack Kirkman, one of 350 professional guides in British Columbia, provided his guiding services over a 2,700 square-mile territory including the watershed of Harrison Lake and the land along the Lillooet River to the borders of Garibaldi Park. His experience in the wilds of the surrounding area made him a logical candidate from whom to solicit an informed opinion on the Sasquatch's veracity. "Well, I have never seen one," he said. "I have checked for signs of them often enough, but haven't found any."[35]

The commissioners of the Provincial Department of Lands and Forests received pro-Sasquatch search correspondence which included a letter addressed "in confidence" to Commissioner R. Gill. The writer stated the object of the proposed search could be found within three days and claimed to have sighted the giants through binoculars. The missive also contained a warning: Sasquatch are dangerous, and although their sight is not very acute, their sense of smelling and hearing is excellent.[36]

Peggy Sloan [also given in articles as Peggy Owen] from Virginiatown, Ontario, was twenty-one years old when she wrote to the commissioners asking to be included in Harrison's proposed Sasquatch search. She wrote, "There are few frontiers left to conquer and this one sounds like a stimulating adventure which I don't want to miss out on." With a flourish of modesty she wrote, "I've no sex appeal but I bet I can attract a Sasquatch."

> The Sasquatch are legendary giants reputed to inhabit the mountains around the south-eastern British Columbia resort centre of Harrison Hot Springs.
>
> Peggy Owen, of Virginatown, Ont., said in a long-distance telephone interview that while she has no sex appeal—"as a matter of fact I'm a little bit on the dumpy side"—she is willing to try to lure a Sasquatch if one can be caught.
>
> The young typist, who stands five-feet-eleven, wrote to the Harrison Hot Springs centennial committee this week offering to help in the village's proposed expedition to hunt Sasquatch as its project for B. C.'s 1958 centennial year.
>
> She said Thursday she wants to help in the search because it promises to be exciting.[37]

As the request for an official and subsidized hunt was under consideration, Dahinden bustled to generate interest and support for his Sasquatch research.

> Meanwhile would-be Swiss explorer René Dahinden is reported to have returned to his home town of Lumby following a trip to Eastern Canada. While there he is said to have contacted film companies in an attempt to interest them in making a motion picture of the Sasquatch search.[38]

In an article titled, "Immigrant Defies Scorn to Seek B. C.'s Lost Race," the charged atmosphere in which Dahinden found himself was colorfully described: "Raised eyebrows, knowing smiles and even open derision have not discouraged a young Swiss mountaineer from his plans to look for a 'lost' race in western Canada." Dahinden had his sights set on Harrison Hot Springs. "Wouldn't it be fabulous to produce a completely primitive race living right in our midst," he told an interviewer. "There is too much evidence of this creature to disregard it," he said. "The Sasquatch is right at your door. He is a living being and I'm going to prove it."[39]

By this point Dahinden's research had already satisfied and convinced him of the Sasquatch's extant reality and he was at ease rolling out First Nation stories as well as modern sightings of hairy giants roaming the hinterland of western Canada. One of the stories told to Dahinden came from Chief Pierre Louis of the Okanagan band, who when about 80 years old, told Dahinden a tale from his youth concerning an Okanagan woman who came upon a sleeping Sasquatch which promptly disappeared. "I saw his footprints," Chief Louis recalled to Dahinden. "They were twice as big as a man's." Dahinden repeated another story, this from Chief August Jack of the Capilano Indians in Vancouver. Chief Jack told of the capture of a nine-foot-tall female Sasquatch in the late 1880s. The creature was subsequently exhibited in Victoria, where Chief Jack saw it, for ten cents a peek.

> Probably the outstanding authority on the Sasquatch is the man who named them, a former teacher at the Chehalis Reserve school. J. W. Burns, now retired and living in San Francisco, told Dahinden he believes in the existence of the Sasquehava, meaning wild men, which he coined into Sasquatch.
>
> Mr. Burns taught the Chehalis for 16 years, starting in 1925. The Sasquatch, he wrote to Dahinden, "are there."
>
> "They do not use bows or arrows or other weapons. They hypnotize their game, such as deer and birds."
>
> He said he himself has come across their footprints but has never seen the Sasquatch in real life.[40]

His perseverance paying off, Dahinden was signed up Monday night, April 22 to lead the Harrison Hot Springs Centennial committee's search for Sasquatch.

> Dahinden made it clear that the search will not involve an army invading the mountains—he felt the job could best be done by three or four men. But he also insists that the hunt go to some kind of a decision—either the finding of a Sasquatch or collapse through depletion of funds.
>
> The leader of the exhibition is convinced that the Sasquatch are human beings, and he doesn't plan to shoot or even capture them. He [merely] wants to take pictures to prove they exist.
>
> In order to have some results well before the 1958 B.C. Centennial, the centennial committee has engaged Jack

> Kirkman, a licensed game guide and trapper, whose area takes in the Harrison Lake watershed.
>
> With the assistance of Cascades Airlines Ltd., Kirkman will establish several base camps in Sasquatch territory as soon as possible.[41]

As will be seen in future chapters, Dahinden later concluded that pictures alone would be insufficient to prove Bigfoot's existence. A body would be needed for an unequivocal writ-large acceptance, particularly on the part of scientists.

The Chamber of Commerce in Whitehorse, Yukon Territory, could well see the publicity that Harrison was getting from the proposed Sasquatch hunt. The CP article below is a comical but still meaningful way one city found to glom onto Sasquatch for commercial and community benefit.

> The Sasquatch—if there are any—will have a home to go to.
>
> Tears in their eyes, members of the Chamber of Commerce in this Yukon city voted to put this resolution on record Monday night:
>
> "Sasquatch, come home. All is forgiven."
>
> The members had been reading about a plan to capture a Sasquatch, legendary, hairy and perhaps man-eating primitive giant, for B.C.'s centennial year. This is the aim of René Dahinden, Swiss mountaineer, who is convinced the Sasquatch do exist in the hinterland northeast of Vancouver.
>
> The Jaycees voted to invite the hairy giants to the Yukon "where their presence would be appreciated."
>
> They say a Sasquatch would pass unnoticed in this territory because "the Yukon way of life allows for individual differences and personal character development." The Sasquatch "might well become a lovable part of our community life."
>
> Commented one Jaycee: "A Sasquatch wouldn't do nothing up here."
>
> There's just one problem about the Jaycees' new interest: What do Sasquatch like to eat besides people?[42]

Herbert Lambert's article in the April 24, 1957 *Montreal Gazette*, given in part below, cites the interest of another woman to join Dahinden on the hunt for Sasquatch. Juliette Legare's idea for a Sasquatch "TV play" is an early and prescient notion of North American hairy hominids' future in film and television.

> I never saw a [S]asquatch,
> I never hope to see one;
> But I can tell you anyhow,
> I'd rather see than be one
>
> (With apologies to Gelett Burgess' purple cow)
>
> Somewhere in the dense bush north of Vancouver is British Columbia's answer to the "Abominable Snowman" of the Himalayas, and a young Swiss mountaineer, René Dahinden, hopes to track the hairy giant to its lair.
>
> If Mr. Dahinden is lucky, he'll find the legendary [S]asquatch. If he's luckier still, one of the members of his expedition will be Juliette Legare, of Montreal, a very attractive 23-year-old miss, who is counting on her hunting experiences and woods lore to earn her a place on the expedition.
>
> "I've been hunting since I was seven years old," Juliette said in an interview last night, "and spend at least five months every year camping out in the bush on hunting and fishing excursions."
>
> Last Friday Juliette wrote requesting permission to join the venture after reading a newspaper account of a bid by an Ontario woman, Peggy Sloan, of Virginiatown, to join the hunt.
>
> "I don't know her reasons for wanting to go along, but three years ago, when I first came across the legend of the [S]asquatch, I thought the subject would make an interesting TV play," Juliette explained. "I've done all the research on the subject that I can here in Montreal. Now I want first hand accounts of the legends and want to absorb the geographical background.
>
> "If we find a real, live [S]asquatch, so much the better, but I don't really believe we will."
>
> "Juliette has an adventurous spirit," her mother said. "I guess in that respect she takes after me. We're the Dianas of this family. We get out hunting and fishing together whenever possible."
>
> Juliette laughed. "I've been lucky, I guess. I've inherited my love of the outdoors from Mother, and my love of writing from Dad." . . .

> At present her attention is equally divided between writing and painting, but the many-talented Miss Legare leans toward playwriting for television.
>
> "I've also started a comedy script," Juliette said, "but I do hope that I'll be able to get to British Columbia so that I can finish my [S]asquatch play.
>
> "Sasquatch means 'wild one', you know, perhaps he'll tame down if there's a woman along. In any case I'm looking forward to the experience," she said.
>
> Her request is now before the village committee of Harrison Hot Springs, the British Columbia resort where the expedition will be launched if the B. C. Centennial Committee in Victoria approves.
>
> "If they don't accept my application," Juliette declared, "I'll just arrange a vacation for myself to Harrison Hot Springs, and perhaps go up the trail a bit alonc. In any case, I'm determined to be there when the expedition returns, even if I have to get my background color through interviews with expedition members."
>
> When not busy hunting, fishing, writing or painting, Juliette works as a photographer's model and actress. In 1954 she reached the finals of the Miss Canada contest.
>
> "It's just as well I didn't win though," she said. "I wouldn't have time to do all the things I love to do—including the cooking."[43]

The growing fame of Sasquatch in 1957 was added to by Walter Lilley, former manager of both the Strand Theater in Chilliwack and the Sasquatch Inn near Agassiz. Lilley resided, during the fame generated by Harrison Hot Springs' Sasquatch expedition, in Port Coquitlam, British Columbia. Over the years, Lilley had heard several Sasquatch stories, a couple of which he shared with the *Chilliwack Progress:*

> Two young Indian braves were walking by the Chehalis river [sic] when a large boulder fell in front of them. Looking up they spied a huge hair-covered monster with a smirk on its face. It disappeared immediately.
>
> An Indian and his squaw were awakened one night when their tepee began to shake. Looking out they saw two hair-

> covered monsters playfully pushing at their tent flap. They both screamed and the giants ambled away.
>
> Many years ago an Indian maiden was abducted by a band of Sasquatch who sealed her eyes with fir pitch and carried her off into the upper reaches of Chehalis mountain.
>
> One of the younger Sasquatch took her for his bride, but the frail bride was unable to stand up to the strenuous life of the Sasquatch. Subsequently they took pity on her, and after sealing her eyes again, led her down the mountain and back to her people.
>
> The Indian girl never regained her health. Her baby, fathered by the young Sasquatch, was still-born and she herself died.[44]

As has been seen, attention was often called to the enterprising, convenient, and profitable means expressed and employed to, at least in some superficial perspectives, cash in on a local legend.

> The people of Kamloops, British Columbia, are to be congratulated on the acquisition of a fine, full-grown monster. The Sasquatch (fierce-eyed, 8 feet tall, fur-covered) appears to meet the requirements for membership in that tight little fraternity of the Abominable Snowman, the Loch Ness beastie, et al. It certainly won't hurt the tourist business in Kamloops.[45]

Victoria Daily Times editor Bruce Hutchison believed the publicity (expressed both in general popularity and resourceful commercialism) of Sasquatch was more metaphorical and romantic than mere crass opportunism.

> No, the spate of free publicity which has carried the Sasquatch into headlines all over the continent wells up from springs—much deeper and hotter than those of Harrison. He represents the British Columbia people's desperate eagerness to conceive an image of themselves. Sasquatchery is the apotheosis of the biggest boom in Canada.[46]

In the same year that his *Canada: Tomorrow's Giant* was published, Hutchison editorialized that Sasquatch was surely a powerful regional, if not national, icon. "But all this news from Harrison quite misses the point, for it is a very subtle point indeed and no one outside British Columbia can hope to understand it. At the risk of oversimplifying a complex phenomenon of the spirit, it can be said that British Columbia requires a big, striking and unique symbol of its progress, its opulent society, its system of government. Hence the quest for the hairy monster."[47]

Dahinden stated for the *Chilliwack Progress* that for a Sasquatch search to be conducted properly, necessary costs could amount to 10 to 15 thousand dollars. Equipment-wise, said Dahinden, a party should be outfitted with first-class cameras; Dahinden himself wanted a 16 mm movie camera plus a telephoto lens for bringing a Sasquatch some distance away into sharp focus. Dahinden sounded irritated by critical barbs aimed at Sasquatch. "A leading anthropologist in B. C. told me plainly they don't exist," he said. "What kind of statement is that from a man of science?" Dahinden said his research led him to the belief that the case for the Sasquatch was stronger than that for the Himalayan snowman. "The American Indians are supposed to have come across the Bering strait," Dahinden told the *Chilliwack Progress*. "Why couldn't the Sasquatch have come over during an earlier age?" he asked. Dahinden believed that Sasquatch were migratory, resulting in many sightings and encounters in the Spring and Fall timeframes. Was Dahinden doing it all for publicity, he was asked. "I spent $1500 on it [searching for Sasquatch] last year—would I do that just to get my name in the papers?" he countered. Dahinden added he was "100 per cent convinced" of Sasquatch being real. Ever lauding Harrison Hot Spring's proposed Sasquatch search, Dahinden waited like many others on final word from the B. C. Centennial committee. "In the United States, they have mountains and lakes and beautiful scenery. But there's one thing they don't have . . . and that's the Sasquatch." Dahinden further declared, "We can wait around for aid from B. C. for just so long. If we went to the East, I am sure that in two days I could get a sponsor."[48]

It took about two months for a decision to be made. First arriving through unofficial channels, word came that centennial funds, after much debate, discussion, and publicity, would not be allocated to ferreting out a Sasquatch from its wilderness abode. B.C. Centennial Committee members in Cranbrook having denied the use of funds for Sasquatch-searching decided instead to offer a $5000 reward if positive proof of the giants' reality could be brought before the committee. As the Harrison Centennial committee prepared to meet on Thursday, May 9 to receive the official decision from Cranbrook, Dahinden was busy in the field northeast of Harrison Hot Springs looking for Sasquatch evidence between Kamloops and Salmon Arm.

A glimmer of hope remained for a financed expedition however, through the auspices of Vancouver book publisher, Robert Noel. Noel's project at the time was production of a book celebrating the centennial. Noel reportedly considered funding a Sasquatch search should the B. C. Centennial directors fail to allocate funds to that cause. "Positive knowledge that the Sasquatch exist would mean world-wide publicity for B. C. in advance of centennial year," he said.[49]

The growing eminence of the Sasquatch brought forth comment from the subject's original enthusiast, J. W. Burns. "They have been referred to as monsters," he wrote in a letter to the *Vancouver Sun*, "but they have committed no monstrous acts. It appears our veneer civilization does not hesitate to even use monsters for commercial purposes." According to *Sun* reporter Alex MacGillivray, Burns by this point had authored over 50 articles on Sasquatch.[50]

A meeting between area centennial committees and the B. C. Centennial committee was the setting for comments and admissions by Reeve James Fraser of Kent municipality: "I am not going to say whether the Sasquatch are there or not—I think they are. There is all the evidence they have been seen." Fraser urged the B. C. committee to reconsider its decision to not support the Sasquatch hunt. He noted that especial publicity had resulted from Harrison's *proposed* search. "Not only Harrison and Agassiz benefitted," Fraser declared, "but the whole of British Columbia." News outlets worldwide had given their attention to the hunt for Sasquatch. "Why, it has even been in the *New York Times*, the *London Times* and other European newspapers," Fraser said. E. H. Fox, the B.C. Centennial Committee's public relations specialist, offered an admission of sorts, acknowledging the Sasquatch had indeed provided valuable publicity, "not only for the centennial committee but to the province as a whole." Despite the committee budgeting $5000 for proof of Sasquatch's existence, Fox said the committee didn't expect to have to pay out. "When the proposal was placed before us I was the tyrant who upped and moved that it be turned down," Fox said. "The members of the board felt that it could not conceivably be classed as a permanent project within our terms of reference," he stated.[51]

Dahinden, back in the Harrison area and ever willing to enter the field, trekked four miles downriver from Harrison Hot Springs to a cave for evaluation as a possible Sasquatch lair. Dahinden stated that an unnamed Vancouver businessman (possibly Noel) was willing to sponsor a hunt for the mysterious giants. Dahinden at this time estimated the cost of a properly kitted expedition would be $7,500. Dahinden was also looking for the services of a color movie photographer to accompany his search for Sasquatch, an effort Dahinden maintained properly done would take months.[52]

By July, Dahinden was in the *Chilliwack Progress'* pages again, stating that the search for a reliable sponsor was proving as difficult as the hunt for the Sasquatch. He was in Vancouver, according to the *Progress*, "trying to tee up satisfactory backing." Several North Shore merchants, it was reported, had pledged financial support. Dahinden suggested a satisfactory search would cost at least $5000.[53]

For Dahinden, the other shoe was about to drop. The Harrison Hot Springs village commission voted down the idea of $1000 to sponsor a local centennial Sasquatch search. Dahinden lost no time in accusing the commission members of lacking resolve. The B. C. Centennial Committee still had its $5000 prize, according to the *Winnipeg Free Press*, to be awarded to anyone who could produce a Sasquatch, "[dead] or with tongue in cheek."[54]

Against the backdrop of a Centennial Sasquatch search's publicity, stories of past Sasquatch encounters and experiences continued to rapidly surface. A canonical Sasquatch account was that of Albert Ostman, who claimed to have been kidnapped and held captive by a family of Sasquatch for several days. At 65 years old, Ostman appeared at the annual banquet of the Agassiz-Harrison Board of Trade on Saturday, March 22 to tell his story through the auspices of a question-and-answer format administered by John Green. One of the guests, Thomas Ainsworth, curator of Vancouver City Museum stated, as reported by the *Chilliwack Progress*, "The creatures might exist—frankly, I don't know." Ainsworth said he had accumulated a large file on Sasquatch and offered the scientific name, *giganticus aggassiz harrisonii*, should Sasquatch be satisfactorily proven to exist.[55]

As newspapers had reported, Dahinden's cost estimate for a Sasquatch search kept going down during his pursuit for financial backing: $10,000-$15,000 in May, $7,500 in June, and by July he reckoned an amount of (at least) $5,000 could get the job done. The iteratively smaller estimates may have been voiced with the hope of finding a threshold in officials' decision-making processes.

The following account from the British royal couple's 1959 trip to Canada proved that monarchs, too, were hard-pressed to avoid exposure to Sasquatch.

> The strangest story Queen Elizabeth and Prince Philip heard during their Canadian tour was the tale of the mysterious

> Sasquatch, hairy giants who inhabit the mountains of British Columbia.
>
> The royal couple were told the story one night while vacationing near here at a remote mountain lake. Outside their fishing lodge the occasional howl of a timber-wolf or an owl's hooting disturbed the wide silence over countryside which Indians believe is the roaming ground of this North American cousin of Tibet's Abominable Snowman.
>
> The Queen and Prince Philip heard how reports of these giants and their 16-inch footprints have kept recurring for 75 years. Several living white men and a number of Indians swear they have seen the monsters. Plaster casts have been made of the great footprints.[56]

The stories of hairy giants and the casts made of their footprints were too good to resist sharing with the visiting Queen Elizabeth and Prince Philip. But a year before the royals listened to Sasquatch tales in a fishing lodge, and while British Columbia enjoyed its centennial celebration, 1958's transformative discovery of giant footprints in California was transmitted over news wire services across the world. With a new decade looming, the hairy giant-epicenter was about to undergo a geographic shift, and Bluff Creek was the new stage of prominence. A coronation of sorts was in the offing—Bigfoot was about to ascend into pop culture royalty.

CHAPTER 1. BACKSTORY—PART II
JERRY CREW TO ROGER PATTERSON: SPREADING THE WORD

Ivan Sanderson

Ivan Sanderson, born in 1911 in Edinburgh, Scotland, participated in several naturalist expeditions between his studies at Eton and Cambridge University, collecting data and specimens for the British Museum. As a biologist, Sanderson appeared on several radio and television programs and hosted the first regularly scheduled color broadcast, "The World is Yours," for CBS in 1951. After World War II service in the Caribbean with British naval intelligence, Sanderson settled in Columbia, New Jersey where he continued a career as a prolific writer,[57] authoring nature books and articles for magazines like the *Saturday Evening Post.*

Sanderson became an enthusiastic author and researcher of Fortean subjects; he started collecting Abominable Snowmen material in 1930.[58] Sanderson produced influential feature articles on North American hairy hominids for *True* magazine in 1959, 1960, and 1961 and authored *Abominable Snowman—Legend Come to Life* in 1961, a significant book on hairy giants based on his research, interviews, and investigations.

True, one offering in a crowded men's magazine market of the time, focused on audacious drama and daring adventure. Beginning its 37-year run in 1937, *True* featured escapist stories and profiles of tough-guy exploits, sports, and daring; a pretension-eschewing *Esquire* for the rugged hardset. The post-World War II men's magazine market had its origins in the pulp mags of the 1920-40's. One pulp title, *Argosy* claimed its founding as a children's publication back to 1882. Many American servicemen read these slick men's magazines after the end of World War II and *True*, published by Fawcett Publications, was one of the most successful of the group (*True* at the time of Sanderson's 1959 article boasted a readership of over a million).[59] By

ABOMINABLE SNOWMEN:
LEGEND COME TO LIFE
THE STORY OF SUB-HUMANS ON FIVE CONTINENTS FROM THE EARLY ICEAGE UNTIL TODAY.
IVAN T. SANDERSON

the late 1950s, *True* had fully fashioned itself into a magazine designed to appeal to a gritty, macho ethic.

Ivan T. Sanderson's article "The Strange Story of America's Abominable Snowman," published in the December 1959 edition of *True*, had a profound effect on promoting the idea of hairy hominids in North America and specifically within the west coast region of the United States. The editorial intro for the story stated: "Somewhere in the wilds of California there is a gigantic creature which walks on its hind legs, leaves huge human tracks, and is scaring hell out of everybody. What is it? Nobody knows—yet." Sanderson's articles acted as catalysts for future high-profile researchers like Roger Patterson, propelling them to probe the depths of the Bigfoot enigma.

As Fortean and paranormal subjects absorbed more of Sanderson's time and energies, Sanderson applied a traditional epistemological construct to the phenomena of UFOs. Sanderson stated that the UFO field up to 1967 was still in the collecting phase, or the province of *What?* Sanderson states that this does not mean that only analyzing reports is possible. "If we had waited until we 'captured' an electron, we would never even have suspected that they exist."[60]

> Science, which the dictionary defines as the pursuit of knowledge, proceeds by three major states—the *What?*, the *How?*, and the *Why?* Put in other terms, this means that first there is a collecting stage that leads to a classification system. Second, a period of testing replicated observed facts with a view to establishing theories as to how the facts should be organized. Finally, we inevitably ask, "Why?"
>
> There is another way of putting this that is today regarded as rather old-fashioned but which is still quite valid. It goes as follows: You can't know anything to be a fact until you have proved it. You can't prove it until you have tested it. You can't test it until you know what you are testing. You can't test anything until you have found it. And, you can't find anything until you know what you are looking for.
>
> In other words, the pursuit of knowledge starts with *imagination*, proceeds to *search*, which should give rise to *research* upon which an *hypothesis* may be erected. From hypotheses come *theories*, which in turn have to be tested—that is, repudiated, on demand, by experiment—before they can be proved. Only then can any fact or body of facts be accepted

> with any degree of assurance. Now, you will doubtless say, and quite rightly, where does this lead us with these phenomena?[61]

Imagination and hypothesis-formulation are necessary qualities and pursuits to advance a line of inquiry; imagination applied to that which is observed can lead to closing in on the question of *How?* Sanderson's 1967 observations on the state of contemporary UFO study was applicable to conditions in Bigfoot research and provided, straight from Sanderson's pen, encouragement and advice on how to *know* Bigfoot.

Jerry Crew

In the article, "The Strange Story of America's Abominable Snowman," which appeared in the December 1959 edition of *True*, Sanderson recounted Gerald Crew's experiences from August 1958 culminating in his discovery of large, human-like tracks. As an operator on a tractor for the Granite Lumber Company, Crew had been hired to build a timber access road up Bluff Creek in an area 50 miles northeast of Eureka.[62] Logging operations comprised an important part of the northern California economy and this logging road that Crew worked on stretched back from the Klamath River and paralleled Bluff Creek along Lonesome Ridge.[63] Sanderson's account in *True* enforces the point that the area was a remote, mountainous wilderness. North of the Bluff Creek watershed are the Siskiyou mountains and to the east are the Klamath and Salmon mountains. The area is bounded on the south by the Hoopa Valley Indian Reservation, and on the west by Pacific coast mountains. The Bluff Creek headwaters originate in mountains in Del Norte County from whence they travel southward into neighboring Humboldt County. In Humboldt County, Bluff Creek flows through a V-shaped valley before finally joining the Klamath River.[64]

In her 1974 book, *On the Track of Bigfoot*, author Marian T. Place wrote directions explaining how to get to the mouth of Bluff Creek:

> Turn west off the central California I-5 Freeway onto State Highway 96, a few miles north of Yreka. Immediately cut your speed to 35 miles per hour, and follow the narrow winding paved road along the Klamath River for seventy miles to Happy Camp, a village frequented by sportsmen and loggers. Another long drive brings you to the confluence of Bluff Creek and the Klamath River where the U.S. Forest Service maintains

> a fine campground. Highway 96 continues southward over a difficult mountain pass, then drops down across the beautiful Indian reservation to Willow Creek. There you may turn west onto much improved State Highway 299 to Eureka on the Pacific coast, or drive east along the southern perimeter of the Trinity Alps wilderness to Redding, where you rejoin the I-5 Freeway.[65]

Ray Wallace, a sub-contractor to the firm Block and Company, which had contracted with the Public Works department on behalf of the National Parks Service to build the road, had the contract to the Bluff Creek section and employed about thirty men for the job, including Crew. The road was started in 1957, beginning with cutting down and hauling out trees, then gouging out stumps and boulders with bulldozers' blades, followed by men and machinery laying in the actual road. Ten miles were completed in 1957 before work halted for the winter. With resumption of work in 1958, Gerald "Jerry" Crew, employed as a heavy machine operator, was among the new hires.[66] Crew, like other workers on road construction, typically spent the week near his jobsite camping in portable or temporary accommodations. The return to their homes at Happy Camp, Weitchpec, Willow Creek, and other nearby towns,[67] occurred at the week's end.[68] As the road pushed farther along, trailers were brought in so workers could be closer to their families and these eventually occupied a semi-permanent emplacement.[69]

Sanderson provided a rich description in "The Strange Story of America's Abominable Snowman" of the area's wide, wild expanse: "The area where this road was being built is, surprisingly enough, an almost trackless wilderness. It is bordered by the Pacific Ocean on the west and Oregon on the north: Highway 299 runs along its southern border, and it stretches some 130 miles inland to highway 99. It is crossed by one winding blacktop road and some lesser roads, plus an assortment of logging trails and 'jeep-roads' which are used very rarely. While California is thought of as a heavily populated state, this particular section—encompassing some 100,000 square miles—had no or few known inhabitants at all. Almost anything could be living there, and nobody would be the wiser."[70]

Bigfoot researcher Don Davis has studied the history of large footprints in this wilderness, especially in areas where new roads were being put in. Crew himself, prior to his own firsthand experience with mysterious tracks, recalled a track discovery by another road crew working eight miles from Korbel on the Mad River. Workers were reluctant to publicly broadcast their discoveries for fear of being labeled crazy, perhaps jeopardizing their standing in the community, and risking their employment. But they did tell their wives when home on weekends; *Humboldt Times* contributor Betty Allen heard about these strange tracks from the workers' wives.[71]

At the end of a long workday on August 24, 1958, Jerry Crew was the last to leave the road site, having worked his bulldozer over a quarter-mile section beyond the rest of his crew so they could get directly to work come Monday. When finished, he drove the bulldozer down the mountain a short distance to his parked pickup truck. In front of him stretched a two-and-a-half-hour drive to Salyer, a small town southeast of Willow Creek situated on the southern bank of the Trinity River.[72]

After the weekend in Salyer, Crew returned Monday morning to the Bluff Creek job site. At the campsite, down from the advancing road head, Crew saw a job foreman standing outside the shack used as living quarters and office who told Crew he didn't need to stop. The foreman returned a wave to the beep of Crew's truck horn and he continued up the mountain to his parked bulldozer.[73] Place described the moments preceding Crew's first glimpse of large footprints:

> Before Crew left his truck he kicked off moccasins and laced up thick-soled boots. He was clad in khaki work pants and shirt, his head protected with a light-weight aluminum hard hat. Since he was a little early, he took time to enjoy the forest quiet. At the moment the air was clean and fragrant with the scent of pine and cedar. He inhaled deeply, savoring every breath because soon choking clouds of dust would churn up under the bulldozer, and the noise and stench from its engine would pollute the mountain air. As he strolled toward the machine he noticed a large track or two on the ground. But, already intent on deciding where he would operate during the day, he dismissed them as bear tracks. Not until he climbed up onto the seat of the big rig did he observe a line of footprints approaching the dozer, circling it, and continuing down the outer edge of the raw roadway. Puzzled, he leaned over and from his high seat gazed straight down onto the nearest tracks.[74]

The prints, in the analogous form and shape of a human foot, were startling for their size—16 inches long, and 7 inches wide.[75] Crew's initial reaction was annoyance at what he considered a prankster's hijinks. His suspect was an outsider; the road-building job left him and his fellow workers too tired to pull such antics. Whoever it was had to have been crafty; it would not have been easy to get past the workers' camps farther down the road without being noticed. Crew started his tractor to ensure the prankster, or worse, a vandal, had not tampered with it. To Crew's relief, the engine started fine and nothing otherwise seemed amiss.[76] Crew turned his attention back to the footprints. One startling feature was their maker's weight as evinced by their sunken depth; Crew noted the prints were depressed two inches into the ground where his own booted foot depressed only half an inch.[77] The soil had been soft on Friday but had dried over the weekend with a crusty top layer.[78] The tracks could be traced down a slope of about 75 degrees before they proceeded along the road, circled his machine, and then went off back down the road in the direction of the camp. The stride ranged from 46 to 60 inches, nearly twice that of Crew's.

With a Eureka byline, an AP story from October 6, 1958, carried Crew's remarks on his find. "I don't know what this thing is," he said. "Nobody does." Crew stated the track maker, already being called Bigfoot (or Big Foot), was apparently curious about loggers' machinery. "It can't be a bear," said Crew. "No claw marks."[79] The original publication of Crew and his casts occurred in the *Humboldt Times*, whose editor Andrew Genzoli instinctively knew it was a good story, too good not to put on the front page of his paper with a picture of Crew in a button down holding up a cast for the camera.

Andrew "Andy" Genzoli was born in Arago, Myrtle Point, Oregon, on the Coquille River. He was the grandson of a logging camp cook. "If they didn't have good food," Genzoli recalled, "the logging company would have a strike on their hands."[80] Genzoli took pride in both his Northern Californian roots and in the area's rich past. "The lumberjacks were gentlemen. They washed and there was no rough stuff. If a man pinched a waitress, he'd be thrown out on the street."[81] Genzoli started school in 1921 at the Grizzly Bluff School and from there he attended schools in Ferndale. In the seventh grade, Genzoli received his yeoman's start in newspapers when Dan Fletcher offered him a job on the *Ferndale Enterprise* for $1.50 a week to keep the office swept and clean and to wash the type. It was during this period that Genzoli discovered within the archived files of the *Enterprise* his passion for history. In high school, Genzoli covered Ferndale news for the *Humboldt Standard* from 1929 to 1933, and his lifelong love for journalism was well and truly underway.[82]

After graduation from high school, Genzoli got a job with the *Humboldt Times* under the eye of Editor Jack Crothers. After four and a half years with the *Times*, he went to Santa Cruz and worked for several newspapers including the *Salinas Californian*, the *Watsonville Morning Star*, and the *San Jose News*.[83] In July, 1943, Andrew joined the U. S. Army and spent over three years in the Pacific Theater where he used his press experience training men to write up press releases. "I was sent to small islands to cover news where the major correspondents would not go." Genzoli contributed stories to the *Stars and Stripes* and *Yank*;[84] his write-up of Sergeant James Burgess, who single-handedly took on 100 enemy soldiers, killing 20, and trekking alone through the jungle for four days to return to his base, was picked up by the Associated Press and published nationally.[85]

After the war Genzoli returned to Ferndale and after a stint in the family sporting goods store, returned to the *Humboldt Times*. Don O'Kane, publisher of the *Times* and the *Standard*, asked Genzoli to come up with a rural-focused column in 1948 which Genzoli would title "RFD." After the newspaper changed hands to the Brush-Moore enterprise, the column's name changed to "Redwood Country."[86]

"RFD" gave Genzoli a platform to indulge his love of history which often engendered nostalgic reactions from readers. "My column," Andrew mused after his retirement from the *Times-Standard* in 1979, "seemed to reach out to people, and people contributed. I got letters entitled 'Dear Andy' as if they knew me after reading my column, and it was a nice feeling."[87] Genzoli served for ten years in state historical advisory capacities, including the California History Month Commission under Governor Edmund Brown, Sr. and the Commission on California State Landmarks for Governor Reagan.[88]

"Bigfoot was simple and exciting," mused Genzoli. "I got a letter from Mrs. Jesse Bemis about a big-footed character in the Bluff Creek area. I wrote about the news in my column, and I received many phone calls. Editor Scoop Beal sent the news-release off, and over 200 letters poured in from all over the world. Some persons looked for new hope and wanted to come to live in our western wilderness. People pounded at my door with rifles and dogs, wanting to find Bigfoot. At times my wife Betty and I had to leave town to get some rest."[89]

The letter Genzoli had received from Coralie Bemis was printed in the September 21, 1958, "RFD" column in the *Humboldt Times*:

> SOMEONE, PLEASE ANSWER . . . This letter came to me in the mail yesterday from Mrs. Jesse Bemis of Salyer . . . and I beg, someone, please give us the answer—quickly . . .

> "I am writing regarding a queer situation my husband has encountered while at work. I have read your column for a long time and have noticed that you often dig into things of various natures. This happened when my husband recently took a land clearing job up on Bluff Creek, near Weitchpec.
>
> The rumor started among the men at once of the existence of a 'wild man'. We regarded it as a joke and even added fuel to the story by passing on bits of information. It was only yesterday that my husband became convinced that the existence of such a person (?) is a fact—
>
> On their way to the job, the men found tracks going down to the road—the tracks measured 14 to 16 inches in length. The toes were very, very short, but there were five to each foot. The ground was soft and the prints were very clear. In soft places the prints were deep, suggesting a great weight. The tracks were quite wide as well as long—things such as fruit have been missed by the men camping on the job. There are at least 15 men that will swear this is true, among them, my husband. Have you ever heard of this wild man?"
>
> Well honestly, no! I wonder if anyone else knows about this . . . Please help . . . maybe we have a relative of the abominable snowman of the Himalayas, our own Wandering Willie of Weitchpec.[90]

After this letter's publication, the *Humboldt Times* reported the Jerry Crew track discovery. But first, Crew reached out to taxidermist Bob Titmus from whom he learned the techniques to cast tracks. Upon the appearance of fresh tracks at the road site on October 3,[91] Crew was ready with a supply of plaster and know-how. Crew made a series of casts of both right and left prints. The casts captured a foot of distinctly human appearance, with small round toes, and arranged more squarely to the long axis of the foot than an average person. Crew carried a plaster cast to the *Humboldt Times* office in Eureka and showed it to Genzoli[92] who made Crew and Bigfoot a *Times* cover story the next day replete with photographs. This was the first published story of Crew and his casts and it subsequently exploded into wide distribution across the country's broadsheets as well as within the international press.

> Back in 1958, when the story of Bigfoot came my way, I little knew what I was letting myself in for, as I prepared the yarn for the Sunday issue of The Humboldt Times . . .
>
> A few days earlier I had published a letter in RFD from Mrs. Jesse Bemis, concerning the presence of a big-footed individual in the Bluff Creek area of the inland country of Humboldt and Del Norte counties . . . The column brought in Jerry Crew of Salyer, who had with him, a plaster-cast proof of the tracks.
>
> Rather hesitatingly, the story was placed on the Associated Press wires. This was like loosening a single stone in an avalanche, letting go a torrent of earth and snow . . .
>
> Editors from many parts of the United States demanded more, more, more about Bigfoot . . . and we, in turn tried to satisfy this demand.[93]

Subsequent to the attention-grabbing headlines Crew's story generated across the country, another significant article threw gasoline on the fire by publishing the claim of two men who declared they had actually seen Bigfoot. Ray Kerr and Leslie Breazeale reported an "ape-like" creature bounded across a Bluff Creek timber access road on October 12. *Humboldt Standard* staff writer Bill Chambers and photographer Neil Hulbert traveled to the scene to inspect a row of footprints said to have been left by Bigfoot before settling in around a campfire to hear the Kerr and Breazeale's story.

Kerr was driving when the thing first appeared, the sighting lasting all of three or four seconds. The creature cleared the road in two bounding leaps while maintaining an upright posture and swinging its long arms. "It all happened so fast it's hard to give a really close description," Kerr recalled, "but it was all covered with hair and didn't have clothing of any description." When asked, Kerr ruminated for a moment on the creature's height. "It looked eight or ten feet tall to me," he said. Whatever it was, Kerr was convinced it wasn't a bear. "I was raised in the brush, but I've never seen anything like it." Breazeale was awakened by Kerr's stomping on the brakes and just glimpsed the creature leap off the road into the brush. "I don't know what it was, but it wasn't no man—that's definite," Breazeale said over his coffee.

> How are they so sure it was the same animal that made the previous tracks in the vicinity?

> Tracks in the dusty road were identical with those seen in the construction area. Both men inspected them with the aid of a flashlight. Their sighting took place about a mile and a half below the construction camp, which is only half a mile from the older tracks.
>
> Kerr said an Indian, Charlie Beach of Trinidad, told him he saw such tracks while trapping in the area 20 years ago, but that nobody would believe his story.[94]

As President Eisenhower celebrated his 68th birthday at the White House, the October 14 *Humboldt Standard* carried the front-page headline, "Bigfoot Tracks Through Ages Says UC Professor." Dr. Theodore D. McCown, professor of physical anthropology at the University of California, said giant footprints such as those found in Humboldt County had been reported for ages and from all over the world. McCown came from a family of anthropologists and gained notoriety a few years later as one of the experts examining physical remains attempting to resolve Amelia Earhart's fate. McCown suggested the maker of the Bluff Creek footprints could be a man suffering from acromegaly, or gigantism. The same article alerted readers to one of the first mentions of Tinseltown's interest in Bigfoot.

> From Hollywood this morning came the announcement that Harvey Waterman, 19, a University of California junior and anthropology student, has been selected as a contestant on a "Truth or Consequences" program to try and track down "Bigfoot."
>
> The Ralph Edwards program is offering $1000 reward for the first person who submits positive proof, in a sealed envelope, as to the identity of Bigfoot.
>
> If the mystery is solved before next Monday morning at 10 o'clock and announced other than in one of the sealed envelopes to the "Truth or Consequences" program, [then] the offer will be cancelled.
>
> Letters must be submitted to the contest through the Eureka Newspapers, Inc. and will be received, time stamped and put in a safe by either "Scoop" Beal, *Standard* editor, or Elmer Hodgkinson, *Times* editor.
>
> The letters will be opened next Monday morning at 10 o'clock in the offices of the Eureka Newspapers, Inc.

The UC student and representatives of the "Truth or Consequences" program will be present for the opening.[95]

Betty Allen's October 31, 1958 article in the *Humboldt Times* started, "Almost every conversation one hears around here, either begins on the subject of [B]igfoot—or soon swings around to him. We presume [B]igfoot is a 'him.'"

> In this northern area of California, there is considerable speculation as to just what or who is making the great tracks. "They say"—is a favorite expression, and the "they say" authorities are filled with theories.
>
> Many of those who have actually seen the tracks taking off down the roadway are split into two camps. There are those of the "confirmed school of thought"—that the whole thing is a hoax. A wonderfully conceived hoax.
>
> On the other hand, there are those who have been "converted" to the side of the room which believes that the tracks are real as the shoes they have on.
>
> So far the whole thing is fraught with mystery—those who believe in a hoax and those who think the tracks are real—are in deadlock.[96]

Andrew Genzoli and *Humboldt Times* photographer Neil Hulbert traveled to Bluff Creek where they found and photographed more tracks as well as feces of human form, but in their words, of monumental proportions. In *True*, Sanderson mentioned other reports and sightings in northern California including a sighting of a humanoid creature by a couple flying a plane and a series of tracks, hairs, and feces found by John Green and Bob Titmus about 20 miles from the road Crew was working on.

Sanderson argued that a machine could not have produced the Crew tracks at Bluff Creek; the maker of these strange prints had varied its stride on uneven terrain, dug its toes into inclines when climbing, and pounded its heel into the earth when descending. Something moved heavy pieces of equipment from their known resting spots, deposited unusual feces, and produced a high-pitched whistling. Sanderson discounted a man making the tracks—there was no plausible scenario of a missing, lost, or runaway person of huge stature and 750 pounds in weight roaming loose in the Californian wilderness. Sanderson found a bear easy to rule out; though a bear print has some similarities to a human's, an ursine foot does not conform so analogously in shape to a man's.

Sanderson's candidate was a humanoid, a so-called intermediate between man and animal. *Gigantopithecus* of southern China, a massive gorilla-like creature known from the fossil record and later championed by anthropologist Grover Krantz, was Sanderson's choice to explain Bigfoot's identity. For *Gigantopithecus* to have survived into the modern era implied a natural milieu supplying sufficient resources for a species' population densities necessary for propagation. But as Bigfoot (often referred to derivatively as a "snowman") first cavorted onto the world stage, there was a tendency to treat the subject as a singular entity instead of as a representative from a larger group.

Tom Slick Expeditions

After the Jerry Crew publicity, Genzoli enjoyed reading people's letters about Bigfoot and even responded to some of the general inquiries received at the office of the *Humboldt Times*. What gave him pause was the expressed desire from some quarters to learn more about Bigfoot in order to hunt the creature for profit, a concept antithetical to Genzoli's sensibilities. "Tom Slick was an exception. He called me from Texas, and I met him at the McKinleyville Airport in his private plane. He put thousands of dollars into an expedition to Bluff Creek, and later he wanted me to work for him."[97]

Though Genzoli never entered Tom Slick's employ, several other notable names in the Bigfoot field did. Slick was a businessman and oil entrepreneur from San Antonio, Texas, who supported several research organizations. In the fall of 1959, Bob Titmus, René Dahinden, and John Green (with contact facilitated by Sanderson) met Slick in Willow Creek, California, and came to an agreement on funding for an expedition dedicated to searching for Bigfoot. Initial funding was $5,000 and the effort was officially named the Pacific Northwest Expedition. Peter Byrne had worked with the Slick-funded Himalayan Yeti Expedition in 1958 and came to Willow Creek to participate in Slick's Pacific Northwest Expedition to hunt for Bigfoot.[98]

The December 23, 1959, *Beckley Post-Herald* ran a story of the Pacific Northwest Expedition's progress.

> The hunt is headed by John La Pe and George Gatto, both of Eureka, and included ten other men, all heavily armed. They have pack mules and have set up a base camp and outlying trail

> camps. They were joined by Charles Burgans, helicopter pilot, with Robert Titmus of Redding, taxidermist and amateur anthropologist.[99]

In this article, La Pe reported the expedition had found more than 400 huge footprints by a creature with an 80-inch stride and recalled an instance where tracks were discovered ascending an almost perpendicular 150-foot cliff.

> Le Pe reported also the party has found places where the brush was trampled by a huge animal which walked upright, had heard a huge creature moving in the darkness, smelled a nauseating "barnyard" odor, and had found droppings which definitely were not those of a bear [or] any other identifiable animal.[100]

A particular discovery intrigued Byrne: a one-foot thick, 9-by-4-foot "bed" of moss in the underbrush nearby a creek. "The moss had been pulled from trees up to a height of 12 feet," Byrne said. "Around the bed were hundreds of bones. We also found the remains of two wild goats and a large deer." One of the titillating aspects of the supposed bed was the lack of discernable human presence associated with it. "There were no signs of man, such as fires or scraped bones. It doesn't seem likely that it was a bear because the bones had not been sucked for the marrow, and a bear would not have dragged so large a deer." An indistinct impression by the creek, which could have been a footprint, was also found.[101]

By the summer of 1960, Green, Dahinden, and Titmus had departed the expedition which continued on with the search. Dahinden reportedly left the auspices of the expedition after only a few days due to disgust with some of the team dynamics and characteristics of the expedition's search. Titmus left in order to get back to his taxidermy business. Green spent about a month with the expedition in the spring of 1960.[102] But ultimately, the Pacific Northwest Expedition produced no definitive sightings of their quarry. Titmus and Green remained in contact with Slick and along with Clayton Mack they received Slick's financial backing for the "British Columbia Expedition" to investigate Bigfoot in Klemtu, British Columbia. Slick died in a plane crash in 1962 and the funding through Slick's foundation supporting Bigfoot-related expeditions came to an end.

Bigfoot Stomps Around Again

The June 23, 1960, *Humboldt Standard* told the Bigfoot story involving Dr. Charles Johnston, orthopedic surgeon[103] from San Jose, his friend George Amann, and their families. The group was camping in the Klamath River region north of Weitchpec and the circumstances of their experience there led the men to believe Bluff Creek's "wily Bigfoot" might have been involved.

> "I was awakened in the night by the sound of moving stones," Amann said, as he recalled the incident. His camping party slept without having pitched tents because of the pleasant conditions that night. "I sat bolt upright and it died away. I figured it was an animal. There was no scent. The thing had gone right through our camp, as we discovered in the morning. It was as authentic as anything possibly could be, as far as I'm concerned. We got only four good footprints. The rest were distorted. They were within 70 feet." Curious, Amann attempted to follow the prints' trail as they led away upstream. "There is a cave across the stream," Amann recalled. "I don't care what anybody thinks, he couldn't have gotten into that cave from the water because it was too deep. I couldn't get across without ropes, but we could clearly see the prints over there. As far as I'm concerned, we definitely found footprints on our side made by a person or something very human. They weren't camouflaged, or fashioned. The toe and heel marks were perfect and he was walking leisurely." Amann, described as possessing a trapper's experience, stated his firm position on one particular point: "Those tracks weren't there the day before," he stated. "I talked to a government engineer up there and he saw the prints. He was as impressed as we were."[104]

Johnston set the scene of their arrival at their camp about a half mile from the confluence of Bluff Creek with the Klamath River. "We pitched camp Monday evening on the way home," he recalled. "We were down fairly near the main road. When we first found the tracks, they stepped about 3 and a half feet. They were from 16 to 18 inches in length. The river there is about 75 feet wide and the current is very swift. Amann couldn't make it, but we saw other tracks on the far side. Later, Michael, my six-year-old son, walked across one of the tracks. He stepped directly in the center and his print was lost in it." Johnston's wife and their other children David and Leland rounded out their family camping party. Johnston's profession gave him insights into what he was seeing, and left him thoroughly perplexed. "We lost him at the rocks. Amann is a woodsman and a trapper. He remarked on the way the heel and toe marks showed up and the way the tremendous toes gripped," he said. "I am a bone and orthopedic surgeon. I'd say definitely these were the prints of human feet with huge toes. The feet were narrow in proportion to the length and whatever it was walked flat-footed."

"I hope our photographs come out as clearly as the prints showed," Johnston said. "It was a remarkable experience. Whatever it was, the thing was peaceful. None of us except Amann heard anything in the night. One of the shots [photographs] we took shows Michael's hand as he kneeled over a print. We wanted to get the contrast for size," he added.[105]

> Dr. Johnston offered one possible shadow of doubt about the discovery, but hasted to add that it was "almost impossible."
>
> "In the evening when we camped," he said, "a big man approached us in his car. He said he wanted to get a nap—he'd been driving all night before.
>
> "He went on about a block distant and parked. We could see him in the car, where he apparently fell asleep. He had left when we awakened. At first, I thought he had decided to bathe in the river in the night. But on reflection, that seems to be beyond reason. He was a big man, but I scarcely believe anyone would have gone into the stream that night and I can't believe he had feet to match the tracks we found."
>
> The doctor and the trapper concluded that the stranger had taken his nap and pushed on. The only other conclusion was that Bigfoot might have had a yen for the car and scared the big man out of the area in high gear.[106]

In a non-digital, internet-less age, the remarkable wildfire spread of Jerry Crew's experience and Bigfoot's unfolding story fueled an explosion of interest as demonstrated in part by Genzoli's continued inundation of letters and inquiries in the first 15 months following the publication of Bemis' letter.

> A Bearish Attitude—Bob Sands, "state licensed bear guide" of Manhattan Beach, California, is looking to new fields . . . especially where Bigfoot might be concerned . . .
>
> He wrote, and said he'd like to know a little more about our wandering friend in the Bluff Creek country . . .
>
> Sands joins around 500 or more letters that I have received since Christmas, 1959, concerning Bigfoot . . .
>
> We'll try and help the bear hunter out with some information . . .[107]

Writer Glen Wright observed in November 1972: "But the *Times-Standard* publisher, Don O'Kane, was so well known as a practical joker as well as a zealous promoter of tourism in the bailiwick of his newspaper that his campaign to authenticate the legend was disregarded by serious anthropologists."[108] To a large measure, Bigfoot was from the start measured by the company he kept. Extant relic hominid or mere Hodag-esque myth . . . the public body decided they would take notice either way and the burgeoning *idea* of Bigfoot registered a healthy pulse.

Bigfoot Daze

Willow Creek, nestled northwest of Redding in Humboldt County, advertised itself as "The Gateway to Bigfoot Country."[109] Acknowledging the attention Bigfoot brought to the area, many townspeople in 1960 considered an event celebrating Bigfoot was in order. Members of the initial planning committee included chairmen Gloria Hayden and Mary Placido; Barry Carroll of the Chamber of Commerce served as publicity chairman.[110]

Bigfoot Daze (later renamed Bigfoot Days) became an annual Labor Day Weekend event and by 1970, ten years after its inception, new events including a golf tournament and the Native American sport called the "stick game" had been added to the celebration's agenda. The 1965 edition of Bigfoot Daze was known for hosting the premiere performance of Max Gilroy's musical comedy, "Bigfoot," which presented the exploits of Professor Harold Bloomgellan and his search for Humboldt's eponymous monster.[111]

Bigfoot Jamboree

Happy Camp, California, is located on the Klamath River within the Klamath National Forest and is the birthplace of the Bigfoot Jamboree which started in 1966 and continued on as an annual Labor Day weekend event excepting cancellation in 1987 due to forest fires. Two of the original founders of the Bigfoot Jamboree were George and Luella Swem. The Swems moved to Happy Camp in 1959 and George worked as a logger before opening the U76 Union Station and Tire shop in 1960. George Swem was chairman of the first Bigfoot Jamboree.

In the inaugural 1966 edition, Ms. Wanda Black was crowned Queen of the Jamboree by Swem during the Saturday square dance. The chairman of the Capture Bigfoot Committee, Charles Edson (more on Edson in Chapter 10), said that his hunters had successfully tracked the elusive Bigfoot and confidence abounded they would successfully lure it into a cage for the parade. With a degree of showmanship, Edson added he hoped the cage would be strong enough to contain the creature. The first Jamboree attracted hundreds of people who lined the streets to watch the parade's floats highlighted by the eponymous Bigfoot, safely ensconced, undoubtedly to Edson's relief, within a cage which proved equal to securing the costumed mascot. The parade also featured American Legion and Boy Scouts' marching units, the Fire Department's truck, and Smokey the Bear. A highlight of the square dancing was Bigfoot and Smokey the Bear joining with dancers for a few "fancy steps." The Jamboree remained healthy at the start of the '70s as shown in the following article whose remarks associated Bigfoot with Native American culture (precisely the manner by which Burns first introduced the Sasquatch into the modern 20th century).

> For the fifth year, over the coming Labor Day weekend, Happy Camp will be holding its "Big Foot Jamboree" (should be Bigfoot"). There'll be Friday, Saturday and Sunday events—the latter, topped off with a grand parade.
>
> In the program designed by Bob Schmidt, and produced by the Happy Camp Coordinating Council there is a version of the Bigfoot story which may be of special interest to Redwood Country readers:
>
> "The full blood Karok Indians believed in a 'Ma'-Ruk-'Ara-Ra', the word meaning 'Giant Mountain Person' in their language. The Indians tell of how this giant could be heard at certain times of the year as he traveled back and forth along high mountain ridges. The Chinese, too, believed in there being a huge ape-like man when a work gang sighted the

giant between Happy Camp and Thompson Creek during the Gold Rush.

"And so finally, the whiteman is becoming a believer and reports numerous sightings of giant human tracks in 'logging shows' in the mountains between Happy Camp and Willow Creek, a distance of about 100 miles.

"We do not ask that you become a believer, we merely state, briefly, some of history and legend behind 'Our Bigfoot'."[112]

The Apes of Mt. St. Helens

"The legend of the Apemen of Mt. St. Helens returns, like hay fever, with summer weather." In between the inaugural celebrations of the Bigfoot Jamboree and Bigfoot Daze a UPI story published in 1964 told a new generation the story of several miners who endured an attack in 1924 by what they claimed were giant apes near Mt. St. Helens. The original 1924 news story led to the great "ape hunt" that same year. "The sheriff took a posse from [Kelso] on a trip into the area. The armed searchers fired at anything that moved, it was reported. Huge footprints were found, but no apes."[113] Notoriety followed after the miners' story was made public and the area where they had built their cabin earned the name "Ape Canyon."

The Apes of Mt. St. Helens found a welcoming environment in the 1960s as the public exposure to Bigfoot steadily increased. "The story of the Apemen of the beautiful conical mountain in the Cascades is a favorite in the area," the article stated, "but it may have some basis in fact. There is more evidence to support it than Nepal's Yeti or northern California's "Big Foot," and probably as much as Loch Ness' monster."[114] Continental separation led to a logical delineation between anomalous anthropoids in the Himalayas and in Cascades. But the regionality expressed in the article (the title chosen by *The Daily Messenger* of Canandaigua, New York, was "Western Mountain 'Ape' Legend Growing") makes a difference between the Mt. St. Helens Apes and Bigfoot, thus compartmentalizing hairy giants into their local contexts. As we shall see in later chapters, regionality matured into the '70s as practically prideful promotion of small town and county hairy monsters became normative.

Fred Beck, one of the miners that experienced the attack in Ape Canyon, self-published a small booklet in 1967:

> First of all, I wish to give an account of the attack and tell of the famous incident of July, 1924, when the "Hairy Apes" attacked our cabin. We had been prospecting for six years in the Mt. St. Helens and Lewis River area in Southwest Washington. We had, from time to time, come across large tracks by creek beds and springs. In 1924 I and four other miners were working our gold claim, the Vander White. It was two miles east of Mt. St. Helens near a deep canyon now named "Ape Canyon"—which was so named after an account of the incident reached the newspapers.

Beck proceeded to write of one of the more extraordinary track finds made by the miners. "Early one morning Hank came back to the tent. He was rather excited. He led us to the moist-sand bar, and took us almost to the center. There in the center of the sand bar were two huge tracks about four inches deep. There was not another track on that sand bar!" The position and dearth of other tracks startled the men. "No human being could have made these tracks," Hank said, "and there's only one way they could be made, something dropped from the sky and went back up."[115]

"We had been hearing noises in the evening for about a week," Beck wrote. "We heard a shrill, peculiar whistling each evening. We would hear it coming from one ridge, and then hear an answering whistling from another ridge." Whistling calls are commonly attributed to Bigfoot, which is also believed capable of creating booming noises from clacking rocks, hitting trees, or even thumping chests. "We also heard a sound which I could best describe as a booming, thumping sound—just like something was hitting its self on its chest."[116]

Suggesting safety in numbers, Hank asked Beck to go with him on a trip to the spring which supplied the miners' water.

> We walked to the spring, and then, Hank yelled and raised his rifle, and at that instant, I saw it. It was a hairy creature, and he was about a hundred yards away, on the other side of a little canyon, standing by a pine tree. It dodged behind the tree, and poked its head out from the side of the tree. And at the same time, Hank shot. I could see the bark fly out from the tree from each of his three shots. Someone may say that that was quite a distance to see the bark fly, but I saw it. The creature I judged to have been about seven feet tall with blackish-brown

> hair. It disappeared from our view for a short time, but then we saw it, running fast and upright, about two hundred yards down the little canyon. I shot three times before it disappeared from view.[117]

Back at the cabin, Hank and Beck told the others about sighting and shooting at one of the creatures they had heard in the evening time. All in Beck's group came to an agreement: the miners would leave the canyon the next morning. The prospects of trying to leave during darkness interested none of them and they eventually settled down to sleep in their pine log cabin.

> We had built the cabin ourselves, and had made it very sturdy. It stood for years afterward, and was visited by many sight seers until a few years ago when it burned to the ground—the circumstances of the fire, I do not recall.
>
> In the cabin, we had a long bunk bed in which two could sleep, feet to feet—the rest of us sleeping on pine boughs on the floor. At one end of the cabin, we had a fireplace, fashioned out of rocks. There were no windows in the cabin.[118]

Sometime about midnight, Beck and the others were awakened by a thud from something striking against the cabin with force enough to knock chinking loose from the walls. There arose a commotion outside which sounded like "feet trampling and rattling over a pile of our unused shakes." By squinting through the spaces between the logs where the chinking had come away, the miners could see up to three of the creatures at one time, but Beck relates that the commotion outside made it sound like there were many more present.

> This was the start of the famous attack, of which so much has been written in Washington and Oregon papers through out [sic] the years. Most accounts tell of giant boulders being hurled against the cabin, and say some even fell through the roof, but this was not quite the case. There were very few large rocks around in that area. It is true that many smaller ones were hurled at the cabin, but they did not break through the roof, but hit with a bang, and rolled off. Some did fall through the chimney of the fireplace. Some accounts state I was hit

> in the head by a rock and knocked unconscious. This is not true.[119]

The men fired their weapons (Beck had a 30-30 Winchester) in defense. At least one of the creatures got on the roof and the men found they had to take a pole from the bed to brace the door when the creatures tried to push against it. Through the night the creatures pushed against the walls of the cabin as if they were trying to push the small building right over. With only short intervals of peace, the attack against the cabin and the miners huddled within lasted through the night.

> The attack ended just before daylight. Just as soon as we were sure it was light enough to see, we came cautiously out of the cabin.
>
> It was not long before I saw one of the apelike creatures, standing about eighty yards away near the edge of Ape Canyon. I shot three times, and it toppled over the cliff, down into the gorge, some four hundred feet below.
>
> Then Hank said we should get out of there as soon as possible; and not bother to pack our supplies or equipment out; "After all," he said, "it's better to lose them, than our lives." We were all only too glad to agree. We brought out only that which we could get in our packsacks. We left about two hundred dollars in supplies, powder, and drilling equipment behind.[120]

Beck wrote his booklet in 1967 to, in his words, "set the record straight," regarding the creatures' attack on the miners' cabin. He also set the conditions for Bigfoot and other paranormal phenomena to not only be spoken together in the same breath, but hint at their possible active association. At the time Beck wrote of events at Ape Canyon as he experienced them, he was aware of ongoing efforts to find Bigfoot. For Beck, those who were then engaged in hunting answers to the Bigfoot mystery were likely unclear on precisely what it was they were searching for. "I hope this book does not discourage too much those interested souls who are looking and trying to solve the mystery of the abominable snowmen."

> No one will ever capture one, and no one will ever kill one—in other words, present to the world a living one in a cage, or find a dead body of one to be examined by science. I know there

are stories that some have been captured but got away. So will they always get away.[121]

The Abominable Snowmen are from a lower plane. When the condition and vibration is at a certain frequency, they can easily, for a time, appear in a very solid body. They are not animal spirits, but also lack the intelligence of a human consciousness. When reading of evolution we have read many times conjecture about the missing link between man and the Anthropoid Ape. The Snowmen are a missing link in consciousness, neither animal nor human. They are very close to our dimension, and yet are a part of one lower. Could they be the missing link man has been so long searching for?[122]

Samuel Brewer

If Samuel A. Brewer, Jr., seems slightly preoccupied in his Spanish classes in McLane High School this fall, it could mean his thoughts are roving along a stream bank in the Siskiyou Mountains in Northern California, and not on verb declensions.

Brewer, a serious minded teacher and a former paratrooper, found this summer what he considers to be pretty strong evidence that many of the stories about a creature living in the piney woods of the Siskiyous are true.

His was not exactly a chance discovery. He had been searching for what he found and when it came, he experienced a thrill which he said was unlike any he ever had before.

The find was a footprint in soft, wet sand alongside Bluff Creek. It was not an ordinary footprint, since it measured 15 ½ inches from toe to heel. It obviously had been made a day or so before by a human like creature of immense size and weight.

In short, Brewer had found more evidence of Bigfoot, the almost legendary creature which is supposed to be stalking the woods of the north country and whose alleged presence is scaring people into fits.[123]

So began *Fresno Bee* staff writer Karl Kidder's September 1964 article on Samuel Brewer, a post-Jerry Crew Bigfoot enthusiast. "I'm convinced," he told Kidder. "People laugh at me, and I laugh, too. But I have what I consider proof—at least to me—that such a creature does exist." Brewer talked about his interest in North American hairy hominids which had been stoked from reading a book on the Abominable Snowman. "The more I read, the more intrigued I become," Brewer said. "This summer, to be near the spot, I got a job on a highway project in Del Norte County and spent weekends looking."

> He delved into newspaper files and talked to woodsmen and townsfolk in Willow Creek, Highway City, and other nearby towns. To most of them Bigfoot is a living creature, a natural part of the woods in which they themselves live. Some even have grown quite sentimental about the big whatever-it-is.
>
> One weekend Brewer worked his way up the creek, hacking through the waist-high brambles and other underbrush with a machete. He was looking for sandbars in a jungle of underbrush and slaty rock. The area lies amidst one of California's largest [wilderness] areas and one seldom visited by recreationists.

Brewer spent every available weekend searching in the woods for Bigfoot evidence. He recounted to Kidder the moment of discovery: "I saw a five foot log suspended on a ledge leading to the creek bank," he said. "It was high enough for me to crawl under it. I did. On the other side were two immense footprints in the wet sand. My heart flipped! This was part of what I'd been searching for." Brewer made subsequent track finds and created plaster casts to bring back to Fresno.

> His search has only started. As soon as school closes next summer, if he can get the proper backing, he wants to return to the Siskiyou country with an expedition equipped to establish camera traps and to take photographs from the air. He thinks infrared photography at night would be productive.

"These seem to be nocturnal creatures," Brewer stated. "The few who claim to have glimpsed them skulking through the woods say they are large creatures, man like, but covered with heavy hair. No one has yet captured one, although reports dating back to 1849 tell of finding signs of their presence." Like researchers who came after Brewer, the idea that some tracks could be hoaxed was not lost on Brewer. "Sure, it's possible some of the tracks are phonies," he admitted. "But the ones I found were in an area too rugged and too remote to have been put there as a joke."[124]

Roger Patterson

As the '60s waned, the popular idea of Bigfoot painted a picture of a large, hair-covered creature, which for the most part, was an enigmatic creature constrained to North America's Pacific Northwest. Bigfoot walked upright like man, sported long arms, and possessed little or no neck. For the interested, a growing willingness to share and digest Bigfoot information created a burgeoning quantity of sources to explore the subject, and with the '70s dawning on the horizon, this boon of Bigfoot information quickly included serious and non-serious movies, articles, and books. Cultural consumption of Bigfoot included older stories as well as new accounts. Bigfoot's historical framework predating 1958 was reprinted for an eager and growing audience in newsletters, books, and film documenting Native American legends and canonical stories such as Ostman, Roe, and Ruby Ridge. But generally, Bigfoot was perceived as mostly a modern phenomenon. So far, the public had been exposed to a picture of a somber and earnest-looking Jerry Crew holding a footprint cast—a reinforcement of clean cut honesty endorsing Bigfoot's presence in the Pacific coast wilderness. It was "evidence" sufficient to plant seeds of wonder and mystery. Near the end of the '60s, another image of Bigfoot emerged thanks to a certain film taken at Bluff Creek by two men named Roger Patterson and Bob Gimlin. The Patterson-Gimlin film gave the public a picture, albeit a grainy one, of Bigfoot that could not be ignored nor easily discarded. Wonder ensued, the mystery deepened, and Bigfoot officially became a pop culture star.

Like Samuel Brewer, Patterson first became interested in Bigfoot after reading about the subject, and in Patterson's case it was Sanderson's "The Strange Story of America's Abominable Snowman" in the December 1959 issue of *True*. Patterson found tracks in 1963 about 15 miles from the spot where he and Gimlin would, four years in the future, capture their famous footage. Patterson traveled to Canada, Oregon, and Washington to talk with Bigfoot witnesses and record their stories. "To me it's been one series of finding after another," he said. By the latter part of the '60s, Patterson had collected 300 sightings he felt were legitimate, some of which he included in a 172-page collection of investigations, newspaper reports, interviews, and

DO
ABOMINABLE
SNOWMEN
LATEST FACTS!
OF AMERICA
REALLY EXIST?
BY ROGER PATTERSON

drawings (by Patterson) published in 1966 titled, *Do Abominable Snowmen of America Really Exist?* Writer Dick Kirkpatrick wrote of Patterson's book, "It serves best to update Sanderson's 1961 book [*Abominable Snowmen: Legend Come to Life*] for interested readers."[125]

A concise rendition of the Patterson-Gimlin film's genesis begins with Patterson and associate Robert "Bob" Gimlin riding horseback along Bluff Creek on Friday, October 20, 1967, while working on a documentary about searching for Bigfoot. Rounding an overturned tree, they encountered a dark figure beside the creek. Patterson's horse reared, throwing him out of the saddle. He finally managed to get his camera from a saddlebag and began filming the subject, later affectionately named "Patty." The creature walked away from the men, looking back once producing the famous pose captured by frame 352 of Patty in mid-stride with head and upper body turned toward the camera. The time preceding and following the filming of the creature has been subject to exhaustive telling and re-telling and attention is invited to sources that go into far greater depth on the subject than is the purpose of this work. The film was made, developed, and shown to scientists and, particularly on the West Coast, to the public. Anthropologist David Daegling provides a concise description of the Patterson-Gimlin footage:

> Most people seeing the film for the first time get the impression that something very odd is going on. The camera stays still only momentarily in a few instances during the encounter; the rest of the film is punctuated by a series of wild jerks and pans recording Patterson's pursuit of his quarry. When Patterson did manage to steady his hand somewhat, the gait of the film subject is apparent, and it is not the walk of a typical human pedestrian. The body is thickset, although not unrecognizable as a human form.[126]

Naturalist David Hancock, founder of Hancock House Publishers—a significant publisher of Sasquatch-themed books—and founder of the Hancock Wildlife Foundation, was one of the early viewers of the Patterson-Gimlin film and his subsequent *Weekend Magazine* article described his thoughts and impressions:

> As a zoology graduate of the University of British Columbia with a layman's interest and a scientist's skepticism of the

Sasquatch story, I watched—in the company of other scientists—the Patterson film. In three minutes, it shows the two men [referring to Patterson and, mistakenly, Al De Attey] traversing the Northern California forest country on horseback. They are in Bluff Creek country northeast of Eureka (in Greek meaning, I have found it!) when suddenly—in the last half minute of the reel—the action starts.

From scenes of pack horses working up the fall-colored logging roads the film suddenly changes. The setting remains the same but the film starts to jump around as Patterson rushes forward, panting and excited (probably the understatement of the century), to get closer to a strange looking creature moving away up the creek, as they came around a bluff. At the same instant the horses smelled its strong odor—reportedly like a wet dog that had rolled in something dead—and bucked Patterson off. The strange beast was about 30 yards away on the opposite side of the creek. By the time the camera was extracted from a saddlebag on the downed horse the target was nearly 50 yards away. And all photography was with a normal lens.

Understandably (the second understatement of the century) the film jumps around as Patterson tries to follow. Moving left to right across the screen and away we see a dark brown (reportedly reddish in real life with color tones probably lost in duplicating the film) hairy creature, walking swiftly on two legs, with a long swinging stride. Its arms, about knee length, swing gracefully in a wide arc balancing the steps. The beast sidesteps several logs rather than going over them. It is aware of its observers but never actually turns to face view while being filmed. The jumpy movie makes observation of detail impossible. However, the film was run through the projector frame by frame, allowing detailed examination. Many frames were still blurred beyond recognition but some gave good detail. The animal had a very erect carriage. It possessed buttocks like a man, and such balancing structures are absent in the apes. The hands were indistinguishable, though a flash of light color suggested they may have been hairless like the soles of the feet.[127]

Ivan Sanderson and Patterson collaborated on an article about the Patterson-Gimlin film published in *Argosy's* February 1968 issue. "The issue sold out completely in the first week it was on the newsstands,"[128] noted Dick Kirkpatrick in the April-May edition of *National Wildlife* magazine, cover-dated two months after Sanderson's *Argosy* article. Patterson went on *The Joey Bishop Show* and *To Tell the Truth* and he said ABC and CBS had contacted him expressing interest in doing documentaries about Bigfoot.

> To capture Big Foot once and for all to prove his existence, Patterson formed about four years ago the Northwest Research Association with Gerald Olson, of Eugene, Ore., as his assistant. He has worked fulltime on Big Foot research, he says.
>
> Who's footing the bill? An hour and 20 minute film sponsored by the British Broadcasting Association that features Patterson's film of the beast has been netting money for the group, as well as the sale of Patterson's book. The film will be shown here at the Orpheum Feb 5-9.
>
> Asked if he wasn't really out to make a fast buck, Patterson replied that the money will be used for research expeditions.
>
> "I don't ridicule people for not believing in this thing," Patterson said. "But people should keep an open mind."
>
> From Pocatello, Patterson is scheduled to go to Idaho Falls, Montana, Spokane, Wash., Portland, Ore., and Seattle, Wash., to raise money for his search for the Big Foot. He believes he'll capture it. And when he does, "I think it's gonna shake up the scientific world pretty badly," Patterson says.[129]

Phillip Youngman, chief mammologist at the Canadian Museum of Natural Sciences in Ottawa unequivocally condemned the Patterson-Gimlin film as a man-in-a-suit capering across the creek bed. "There is no question in my mind that it is a hoax," Youngman said after a screening of the film put on by John Green at the museum.[130] Bill Fritts of the *Bakersfield Californian* found a degree of (comparative) persuasiveness in the film footage.

> I must say, in all fairness to Sanderson and the scientists who have studied the film and who cannot build a case for hoax, that if I had to choose between belief in flying saucers and Bigfoot, I'd put my money on Bigfoot.

> I wouldn't give two cents for a flying saucer claim, but Sanderson makes it almost impossible not to believe that "there's something out there" in those California and Canadian wilderness areas.[131]

The Patterson-Gimlin film became a pillar of the Bigfoot experience and a key catalyst for an explosion of interest in the hirsute subject, not just in the Pacific Northwest, but throughout the country. The film showed a large man-like creature walking erect, covered in dark hair, heavy buttocks, drooping pendulous breasts, "a peak of hair at the rear of the head," wide shoulders, and 15-inch feet. The peak of hair was evidence of a possible sagittal crest, more commonly found on large, male apes. Such crests permitted the attachment of powerful jaw muscles necessary to chew fibrous plants. But was Patty sporting a true sagittal crest, some would wonder, or was it only a tease of the subject's hair "blowing in the wind"?[132]

In his *Weekend Magazine* article, Hancock sketched a vivid description of the Patterson-Gimlin film subject:

> Footprints measured 14 ½ inches long. From this the creature was estimated to be at least six-feet-nine inches tall by Dr. Ian McTaggart Cowan, dean of graduate studies, University of B. C. Both from the photos and the plaster footprints it was evident the foot was human-like. The footsteps were 41 inches apart according to Patterson. Interestingly, this is exactly my own pace measured when walking briskly. I'm six-feet-two-inches tall.
>
> The belly was tight like a human's and while the body was heavier than human, I did not get the impression of excessive weight or strength. Certainly the weight, strength, height proportions were balanced to give easy fluid motion. Short dark hair covered most of the body. The face was never seen clearly, though in a blurred profile it was not greatly protruding and appeared flat. Heavy brow-ridges were not suspected. The head shape was most conspicuously pointed at the back and was covered only by short hair.
>
> The most striking anatomical features were the large and distinctively human breasts indicating the creature was female. They were lower on the chest than in humans, and a lighter

> overall color suggested they may have possessed less hair than the rest of the body.
>
> Were we watching the real thing or a hoax? My first impression was, "Oh God! How corny. It's nothing more than a man in a monkey suit."
>
> But the frame-by-frame analysis wasn't as easily dismissed. If it was a hoax, then I join with most of the other observers in saying it was a very clever and sophisticated one. Less believable are the plaster casts of footprints taken in the area. There are similarities in the position of the pressure points. They suggest a smaller foot (size eleven and a half) within a larger print nearly 15 inches long—perhaps a foot within a rubber, foot-shaped shoe. The toe prints could even have been added separately.
>
> Such a technique would permit a man carrying a heavy packsack (to help deepen the footprint) to move with relative freedom over the countryside. The burden of the pack could be easily overcome by the satisfaction and enjoyment of a job well done.[133]

Daegling argues that had the Patterson-Gimlin film not been, Bigfoot may have been fodder for the junk heap of American folklore. The film is absolutely seminal; while Jerry Crew's story supplied a firm foundation for Bigfoot, the Patterson-Gimlin film completed the metaphor by building the whole house, the indispensable superstructure for Bigfoot's ensuing endurance.

"If that film's a fake—and it could be—then it's a masterpiece," said Peter Byrne.[134] But perennial Bigfoot commentator Andrew Genzoli was largely unimpressed with the film. Writing after Patterson's death in 1972, Genzoli revealed his reservations regarding the film's veracity.

> There seems to be the always nearby suspicion, when the subject of Bigfoot is brought up. The suspicion of fakery is created when "oddities" like strips of motion picture film are circulated allegedly depicting the "real Bigfoot." The late photographer, when pinned down for facts, was unable to present anything resembling credibility. Things of this nature spoil the scene for the serious Bigfoot researcher.[135]

After the Patterson-Gimlin Film

"I have been investigating this thing for 14 years and now I'm going to find them," said René Dahinden in 1967, days after the Patterson-Gimlin film had been made. Dahinden and his son Erik flew over the Harrison Lake region, 60 miles northeast of Vancouver to survey the area and drop supplies. The pair later drove on logging roads as far as they could and then trekked to a snowy field where the supplies had landed. The *Medicine Hat News* reported Dahinden's intention to set up a camp in the high country to continue his search for Bigfoot. Footprints remained a key piece of the evidence for Dahinden. "There are thousands of examples of footprints that no one can explain," he said. "They have the same characteristics; actual movement of the toes can be traced."[136]

Peter Mutrie, nicknamed the "Sasquatch Sleuth," saw the Patterson-Gimlin film and was impressed by the correspondence between descriptions of Bigfoot and characteristics displayed by the film subject. "I've seen the movie. We've had it stop-framed and enlarged. As far as I'm concerned, the thing that walked across that screen was genuine."[137]

Like Green, Mutrie found a consistency in witnesses' reports: "The Sasquatch is anywhere from eight to 14 feet tall," he told reporter Joe Wiesenfeld at Mutrie's home in Manitoba, "and the estimated weight is 600 to 2,000 pounds." Detailed accounts provided steady and constant points of similarity. "It's very thick set, with heavy limbs, and arms that hang below the knee," Mutrie explained. "The body is covered in glossy fur, black to reddish brown to white, in some cases. There is no fur on the palms or the soles of its feet, or around the eyes and nose. It seems to have no neck." Mutrie participated in a three-man, 70-day expedition in the hills of British Columbia to look for evidence of Bigfoot with Dennis Primmett and René Dahinden. "The three of us got together and planned a trip," Mutrie told Wiesenfeld. "Our expedition this summer was the first full-scale expedition since the 1958 northern California expedition (known as the Pacific Northwest expedition)."[138]

The trio armed themselves with two movie cameras and three still cameras, "and as a last resort," with rifles. The group set out on August 2 for an undeveloped area some 45 miles north of Saint Boniface. Basecamp was set up in a mountainside cave from which they managed several four-day treks "up this range or that valley." They were prepared for a lengthy effort. "We had decided to stay until the food ran out or until the weather drove us out." Mutrie said at one point he was buried under an estimated six feet of snow after caught by an avalanche near the mouth of their cave. "But

René was able to dig me out right away, so there was no problem," Mutrie said. "After that, we walked out to a logging camp Oct. 15, and then back to Vancouver."[139]

Mutrie reported the men found no signs of Bigfoot, but their determination and confidence in the creatures' existence was never shaken. "This doesn't necessarily mean they're not out there, of course. It's a big country." Mutrie's confidence was further boosted by a September 1968 *Winnipeg Free Press* article recounting a Bigfoot sighting at Easterville, Manitoba.[140]

Mutrie justified Bigfoot's existence in part by invoking creatures that had been mere rumor until proven to science to be fact, a technique used frequently through the '70s. "Personally, I think the Sasquatch, is just an undiscovered species [of] primate," he said. "For example, a species of mountain gorilla in the Upper Congo remained undiscovered until 1912. Previously, it had been a legend. Similarly, there had been legends and sighting of the giant panda bear in the Orient for centuries. No one believed in it until in 1934 someone went up and shot one and brought it back." Mutrie had no doubt about the difficulty in fixing a secretive creature like Bigfoot for prolonged observation or photo opportunity. "That's wild rugged country. It could remain hidden indefinitely."[141]

Dahinden said the trip north of Garibaldi Mountain with Mutrie and Primmett met with bad weather. Incessant rain finally "made life too miserable to continue." But inclement conditions did not deter Dahinden's motivation. "The more I'm out there, the more convinced I am the Sasquatch exists," he said. Dahinden said the group left their equipment in the bush so the search could be continued without lugging it again into the backcountry.[142]

Dahinden's 1969 plans were largely focused on Canada, including a two-month Sasquatch search in the Nordegg area, 12 miles southwest of Edmonton. Like Mutrie, Dahinden's interest in a given search area was spurred by a report—this one from five workers at the Big Horn Dam who reported sighting a large, Sasquatch-like creature. "I want to be prepared to follow one of the creatures when the snow comes to the area," he said.

> Mr. Dahinden, who said he operates a contracting business in British Columbia six months a year to finance his Sasquatch hunts, bases most of his belief in the creatures on tracks.
>
> "On one occasion in California, I saw a total of 1,200 separate tracks."

> Also, he said there are historical references to Sasquatch from Indian carvings and a movie film of a large humanoid creature taken in 1967.
>
> "I wouldn't place the activities of Sasquatch hunters in the same category as UFO sighters.
>
> "We here are dealing with the fact that something makes tracks which we have recorded in plaster casts and have been seen with great consistency."
>
> Mr. Dahinden said the creatures may or may not exist and the evidence warrants further consideration.[143]

The 1,200 tracks Dahinden mentioned above would be rivaled by his close inspection in late 1969 of 1,089 tracks in northeastern Washington (see chapter 2).

Searching for Bigfoot—Tocchini Expedition

"Back in the 1960s" wrote columnist Bill Soberanes, "Petaluman Dan Tocchini led a local expedition on a search for Bigfoot in the San Antonia Creek area." Word of the expedition spread around Petaluma and during the night Tocchini and his party, including columnist Soberanes, were joined by several carloads of curiosity-seekers. Writing in 1976, Soberanes recalled that several people became convinced they saw "the shadowed figure of a giant creature—and at the same time a giant size rock came hurtling in their direction."[144] Revisiting the subject in a 1986 column, Soberanes wrote that "the nighttime adventure in the hills of Marin County was an unforgettable experience."[145]

Searching for Bigfoot—Klobuchar Expedition

Author and journalist James "Jim" Klobuchar wrote a daily column for Minneapolis' *Star Tribune* for 30 years. In 1968, under his paper's auspices, he led a four-person expedition into northern California to investigate Bigfoot.

> EDITOR'S NOTE: For generations legends about giant half-man, half-beast creatures have persisted in remote regions, from the glaciers of the Himalaya to the rain forests of northern California. They have attracted hoax-peddlers, fascinated adventurers and anthropology experts. Into the Six Rivers

> National Forest of California, in an area penetrated only by lonely logging roads, Jim Klobuchar of the *Minneapolis Star* led an expedition in search of some trace of the Abominable Snowman of the Siskiyou Mountains—or Bigfoot, the loggers' term of endearment for the creature. This is the first of six reports on his findings.[146]

That Editor's note preceded Klobuchar's first *Minneapolis Star* article describing the events he and his three fellow expeditioners experienced at the onset of their adventures. Joining Klobuchar was John Fletcher who had been senior zookeeper at Woodland Park Zoo in Seattle when he became in 1957 the first director of St. Paul's Como Zoo, a position he maintained until 1985.[147] Was there a chance, Klobuchar posed to Fletcher, of a large undiscovered hairy hominid roamed the wild country of the Pacific Northwest? "As the old baseball man Dizzy Dean would have said," answered Fletcher, "there are two chances of that—slim and none." But Fletcher did bring along a tranquilizer pistol to anesthetize their hirsute quarry if, "on the one-in-a-thousand chance," the party could get close enough to their definitive goal. "I make no such assumption," Fletcher coolly stated. "And even if it does exist I don't think we ought to be thinking about trying to bring it back." Fletcher pondered what a subdued, tranquilized specimen would really mean. "You know what would happen if we pinned one down. The first thing, every museum director in the world would come running here to try to claim the thing, bone him and stuff him and stand him in a box someplace in a corner."

> The others, businessman-adventurer Monte Later of St. Anthony, Idaho, and the globular but quick-witted Minneapolis lawyer Jerry Singer, disbelieved the Snowman story but with less acidity than Fletcher.
>
> I shared their disbelief, partly on grounds that if there really was a seven-foot giant of massive stride and strength, weighing 500 pounds and yet furtive enough to escape entrapment, he surely would have gone on the first round of the National Football League draft.
>
> And so we headed up the greening Hoopa Reservation valley toward the Bluff Creek canyon where, according to the reports, fables and gossip of decades, the big-footed snowman spends much of his time.[148]

The expedition stopped at Hoopa where they sought a "dispassionate estimate of the situation" from Pritchard Jordan. "For years and years they been talking about it around here," he told them. "A lot of the merchants down in Willow Creek want to believe it because it's good for business." Leveraging a local legend for community benefit seemed harmless enough to the expedition team. "I know where some of the tracks came from, and it wasn't from any ape-man. Still, I don't claim to know all the answers. Indian kids around here years ago used to grow up being scared by stories about big goblins. Then again, maybe some of the tracks was made by bears, or something else." The unspoken suggestions behind the "something else" were not lost on Klobuchar and company. "I'll tell you about the country where you're goin'. Up beyond Lonesome Ridge out there up the Bluff Creek, once you get past the logging roads, it's the thickest, biggest wilderness you ever saw in this country. Like that forest ranger up there in Orleans will tell you, you can go for days and days without coming close to another soul." And it was the reality of the vastness of those wildlands that Jordan tied back to the aforementioned *something else*. "My friend, there are a lot of things in there that I don't suppose many of us have seen," he said. "There could be anything in there, if you came right down to it."

Klobuchar eloquently described the timbered wilderness his party entered and which would host the expedition for several days of Bigfoot-searching:

> There is a hostile, desperate solemnity about the fir and alder jungle of the Bluff Creek forest.
>
> When the loggers and stray miners leave, no man lives there.
>
> This is a country for cougars, bear, bobcat and deer, of random mergansers fishing the unvisited streams. But even the wildlife is sparse, because only rarely does an alpine meadow interrupt the precipitous timbered slopes, and foraging animals know that the land to the south is more hospitable.
>
> Anchored to the 60-degree slopes are great Douglas firs in thick congregation, fragile-trunked madrone trees with sheeny and elegant leaves, cedars, salal bush, alder, sword fern and wild raspberry.
>
> The country should be beautiful but it is not. It is ravined and canyoned and it has high-angled forest bluffs, but it does not have the nobility of mountained height. The government allows selective logging here, and thus the drainage canyons

> are a chaos of huge boulders, log snags created by timber-cutting and flooding, the galloping whitewater of the creeks and rivers, and perpendicular walls of rotting rock.[149]

A ranger told Klobuchar, "I don't believe there is a Bigfoot in there. But if there is one on this continent somewhere, this is where he would go when everything else fell to the road-builders and the real estate salesmen." This same official also commented on the great size of the area the *Star Tribune* team was preparing to enter. "You can go for a month without seeing anything civilized in there, if you know where you're going, you just are not going to see anything again, period."

At Willow Creek, Klobuchar asked Bob McLellan, manager of the Pacific Gas and Electric office, why anyone could believe Bigfoot actually existed. "Well, the way some of the tracks are distributed, mostly. Yes, there were some fakes. But there are a lot of them that seem absolutely real, like the ones in the cast down at Al Hodgson's variety store." Some tracks had been found in locations that would seemingly preclude the efforts of a prankster. "There have been tracks, for instance, found in places no hoaxster would ever go into, 17 ½ inches long, five inches wide across the ball of the foot, and appearing in series that indicated a 54-inch stride." Subtle changes seen track-to-track weighed against a static model of a foot. "The thing is that a lot of these tracks show minute changes in indentation, depending on the terrain. In other words, where the tracks go up hill, you find more pressure on the front of the foot, a delineation of the toes, a shortening of stride. It isn't as though somebody just came in there and planked a bunch of fake prints down helter-skelter."

Klobuchar believed that perpetuation of the Bigfoot legend was an irresistible temptation for civic authorities and had led to the creation of at least some of the discovered prints. "And about that," said McLellan, "if the Chamber of Commerce bunch in this town was really scattering prints around the back country, how long do you think we're going to keep the thing secret from the rest of the townspeople, who don't care about the Bigfoot one way or another?" McLellan didn't proffer doubt or acceptance of the Patterson-Gimlin film, but Syl McCoy was not as reticent. A locally-based forest ranger, McCoy told Klobuchar he was one of the first people to encounter Patterson when he came out of the woods with the famous film. "I saw Patterson when he came out of the woods that night," he said. "I never seen a man so excited when he told me 'I saw it, I saw it.'"

> And so we stuffed provisions for a week into our packs, strapped in a couple of tents and a sleeping bag for each, and slogged eight miles into the wilderness beyond the point where a landslide and crevasse made further auto traffic impossible along the Bluff Creek logging road.
>
> We arrived at an unused loggers' campsite at near twilight on a Sunday afternoon. The recklessly bounding creek, white and emerald, poured down the canyon a few yards away and an 800-foot fir slope angled up to a high ridge behind it.
>
> Our plan was to track the drainage creeks and the fringe wilderness of the crude roads, where nobody logged right now. It was useless to charge the steep, slick forest slopes, which wouldn't have appealed to a Snowman anymore than they appealed to a lawyer from St. Louis Park. In any case, no tracks were likely to be discernable there among the matted leaves.
>
> For food we leaned on dry cereals, prepared soups, three or four rolls of salami for meat, rye crackers, dried apricots and raisins, a small amount of chocolate and a prudent portion of brandy and Canadian Club for a civilized warming additive against the 30-degree evenings.[150]

The four men split into two search teams and Singer and Klobuchar trudged lonely dirt roads where they found no sign of recent human activity. Near Laird Meadow, Klobuchar noticed Singer stop and point to a vague set of tracks near a culvert. "They're big," Singer said, "but I suppose they could be our own tracks from the morning, distorted by the mud." Klobuchar joined his companion and regarded the tracks. "They could," he began, "except for one thing. We were headed south this morning. The tracks you're looking at head north."

Klobuchar recalled the "skepticism and alarm" he read on his friend's face. "One of two things," Singer began, "either I'm imagining that this track and the ones there in the mud around the culvert were made by a big animal, or they really were, and if the second is correct, tell me what I'm doing on this lonely logging road without another soul around?"

> We examined the evidence up close, but there was not enough definition in the track to bring us to any kind of working hypothesis. We were intrigued by the recollection that this was

> the specific site, on the road to Onion Lake, where hundreds of Bigfoot tracks had been reported some time ago.
>
> "One thing about it," I noted, "if it's really a track it's no forgery, I mean something planted recently by Bigfoot promoters in that little town.
>
> "If they were going to play games, they would have done a better job than this. You can see where toes are supposed to be, but the only thing you can tell from this is that whatever made it has got terribly flat feet, and pretty big ones, because the track you're looking at is a foot and a half long."
>
> However unclear, it was impossible to view the imprint in the mud, and the even less distinct prints around the culvert, without momentarily conjuring an image of some shaggy, furtive zoological freak, doomed by the accidents of evolution to rove the dark forests, evading the reach of man.[151]

Conversation round the campfire after that first day of trekking an estimated 16-miles turned to other enigmatic footprints—the ones cast and on display in Willow Creek. "There's this about those plaster casts back at Willow Creek: Unless the track was fabricated," said Fletcher, "it was made by something enormous, with fallen arches at that. And judging by the description of the tracks seen in series, they couldn't have been made by a bear, because there's no bear I know of that would have a stride four-feet long." Fletcher's examination of those casts had given him the opportunity to see up close a part of what the Bigfoot mystery hinged upon. "One thing notable about the cast is that there seems to be a second joint print made in the area of the big toe, of a kind you don't see made by a human toe. And of course, it just doesn't look like a bear print and is too big in any case."

> "And so," he said, "if you believe the stories and film and tracks, if there is something in here, it's humanoid rather than anthropoid, meaning it's just about a human being. But we haven't seen anything or heard anything out here yet that makes you do too much speculating."
>
> Monte Later, silent during much of the conversation, now interrupted.
>
> "There was something, John," he said, "in the ravine."[152]

Klobuchar described Later as an experienced outdoorsman who pursued climbing, skiing, photography, and amateur botany, amongst other hobbies. Over the low hiss and spit of the campfire, Later continued his story. "I suppose," he said, "I ought to keep my mouth shut because this is how people get reputations, and the last thing I want to be is some kind of Baron Munchausen of St. Anthony."

Klobuchar eyed his companion. "You have delivered yourself of what the lads in my trade call a disclaimer," said Klobuchar, "and I suppose you are going to tell us you saw something on that hike you took up the Bluff Creek ravines that you cannot explain." Klobuchar noted Later's face was a mask of seriousness. "Yes," Later said, "that is what I'm going to tell you." Fletcher placed another log onto the fire and all leaned in to listen to Later's tale.

"I didn't say it was an Abominable Snowman," he began. "I can't even say it was a bear. I know it wasn't a deer or cougar, because it seemed to be too big and dark for that." Klobuchar asked Later what he thought he had seen. "I honestly don't know," Later responded. "But I'll tell you what happened."

> "It was about 2:30 in the afternoon not far from where that big landslide has torn away a couple hundred feet of the old logging road. There are hanging ravines below there where the woods slant down to the creek."
>
> The site was familiar. The aldered and huckleberried gulches, carved by spring floods from the snowfields above and disarrayed by the tangled foliage of wilderness, lie in almost permanent shadow. In a similar ravine, Singer and I had spent 10 minutes staring at the exact spot where we knew a deer to be standing—without being able to make it out.
>
> "I was walking not far above the creek," Later continued, "and there was the crack of a limb breaking down in the ravine about 50 feet away. I looked down and saw the branches of a bush moving, and then I saw a large, dark form moving in the cedar and alder.
>
> "In a couple of seconds it was gone behind the wild thicket.
>
> "In Idaho, if the circumstances would have been the same and that's all I saw, I would have said 'bear,' and let it go at that.[153]

At the time Later sighted the dark form, he had been thinking how good it would feel to rest his feet. He recalled that no one in the party had seen any bear for four days and the form he had seen had some height to it and he knew bears didn't commonly go about on their hind feet.

> "All I saw was this big, dark form, for just a moment.
>
> "So I went down there, and I could hear something moving away in the brush, and suddenly I got excited and I was really moving, but I didn't hear anything else.
>
> "I looked in the thicket where I had seen the form, and the underbrush was broken a little, all right, but the leaves were so thick and matted in there I had no way of making out a track.
>
> "I moved a little deeper into the woods. And then I remembered, 'Okay, what if it's something that might come at you if you surprised it?' because I didn't know what to think, and I'm in there alone in the bush without protection. So I went back up on the logging road, although I did take another look around for about five minutes."[154]

One of the group asked Later directly if he thought he had seen Bigfoot. "No," he said. "But, I didn't say it couldn't be, either. Every time the experts and the ultimate dispensers of truth convince us they have all the answers, somebody digs a little deeper or somebody runs a little further and all of a sudden all of the experts are a little more humble, because we really don't know all of the answers of the universe, do we, or even most of them?"

Fletcher had been musing on the prints found by the Klobuchar and Singer team. "From the alleged habits of this thing, I'd guess if you were going to find him anywhere, it would be in the kind of place where he might have some forage, some tender shoots, some accessible water, some place where it wasn't so damnably wild. If he's really supposed to be humanoid, I suppose he'd go in the same places where it would be easiest for a human. Where was it you saw the track?" Klobuchar recalled the scene of Singer's discovery. "Laird Meadow," he said. For Fletcher, the focus of their next day was clear. "Let's go for one last shot," he said, "to Laird Meadow."

The next day, Later and Klobuchar walked up the Onion Lake road toward Laird Meadow. "There were tracks here, all right," Klobuchar wrote for his April 26 installment in the *Minneapolis Star*, "deer tracks, cougar tracks, perhaps a coyote track—and 300 yards above the switchback where Singer spotted the track we found another trail of prints."

> Large prints.
>
> Again, they were old, perhaps months old, but they described a route that carried in the same direction of the earlier sightings, and this time they seemed to form a series.
>
> "How far apart were the alleged Bigfoot tracks when the hairy one was supposed to be in full stride?" I asked Later.
>
> "Somebody said 51 or 54 inches," he said.
>
> "How far apart would you guess those indentations are in the mud?"
>
> "I'd guess about four feet."
>
> There was nothing remarkable about the prints aside from their stubborn insistence on being approximately four feet for nearly 50 yards of the road shoulder.
>
> They were too old to bear any definition of the toes, assuming that whatever made them actually had toes.[155]

The tracks had endured weathering which adversely effected their worth as evidence. "But there's this," said Later as he walked alongside the trackway, "when you follow this crude trail for a while, you can start predicting where the next imprint will be. And that's where it is."

"So what we have," Klobuchar stated, "is a series of rather untranslatable mud hieroglyphics which could have been made by an animal, or by some odd coincidence of the elements and the mud, or by something we don't know about."

> Our expedition was not precisely scientific nor extensive, but it did observe the ground rules—as much, possibly, as any that has been in the [Bluff] Creek recently. In a week we covered something like 215 man miles along the creeks and in the forest.
>
> Despite the fruitlessness of most of the creek-bed hunt, I cannot say it was a wasted interlude. The country is strange and possessive, but it aroused one. It invested him subtlely [sic] and surprisingly with a sense of discovery—a jeweled little waterfall around the canyon bend where he had expected only another log snag; a lone redbud bush in full bloom amid the sterility of the black canyon walls.
>
> Yet this was the kind of outcast wilderness that never allowed one to forget he was an intruder. The creeks were

still noisy and frothing although relatively tame when we forded them. A few weeks ago they were stampeding and ruthless, so strong that the flooding Bluff Creek itself plowed a canyon 80 feet deep, in three weeks, through the defenseless serpentine rock.

In there are animals big, wild and unmolested. What else is in there depends on your theory, your fantasy, your luck.

Man's legends do not vanish quickly nor does his wish to move one stride beyond what is demonstrable truth. This is why he looks at the stars, or into the jungle, or the Douglas fir wilderness of California.

Could there be some kind of Abominable Snowman of the mountains?

Your mind tells you no, but when you are sitting about the campfire and a vagrant breeze stirs the pines, and the fire ebbs—in this reference you may conclude:

Yes, Virginia, there could be.[156]

Klobuchar's article's prompted a letter from children in which they expressed obvious concern regarding the treatment of Bigfoot. Klobuchar ran the letter in his May 3, 1968, column along with his response.

"We are 10-year-olds who believe that there is a Bigfoot. Therefore you should not call him by such names as Abominable Snowman, or monster or myth. We think he should be addressed in the correct manner, and if some day you do capture him, Mr. Klobuchar, I would like for you not to treat him roughly or hurt him and, after tests, he should be freed."—The Believers.

I could not be more in accord with your suggestions, Believers. When you view the Bigfoot's properties—seven feet tall, 500 pounds, hairy features and the strength to smash 55-gallon fuel drums as though they were thimbles—you are encouraged to treat him with extreme courtesy. In other words, you may call him many things, but if you really came face-to-face with him, the first thing you would call him is "sir."[157]

In a 2016 interview with this author, the retired journalist said he and his companions had undertaken their adventure to find any physical trace to match the creature described in the growing body of reports. "When I took a group to California, it was with reasonable skepticism," Klobuchar said. "For me, it would be exciting to actually believe there are or were such creatures."[158]

Heading Toward the '70s

In the pages of *Pursuit* magazine, Ivan Sanderson touched on the prolific number of Bigfoot-hunting efforts occurring in the Spring of 1968.

> A film is not conclusive proof of the existence of anything. Only a dead or stunned specimen, or a skull, will prove the matter and convince the scientists and other skeptics. Roger has to get back into the field to obtain such. Meantime, we know of no less than nine other seriousminded [sic] and in some cases fully financed outfits that are going into the field this spring.[159]

Kenny Silver and Alan Singer, both students at City College in New York City, were drawn to Humboldt County to search for Bigfoot. Silver and Singer had been interested since childhood in science fiction and the unknown and the young men became fascinated by Sanderson's February 1968 *Argosy* article describing the events of the Patterson-Gimlin film in Bluff Creek. "With a great adventure in California and none in New York, we decided to put our hand in the pot and experience and, hopefully, witness what we had read," they said to *Times-Standard* (Eureka, California) reporter Janice Rylander. They arrived in California via airplane, touching down in San Diego. They proceeded to hitchhike to the Klamath River and earned their fare on a jet boat up the Klamath to Bluff Creek. From their base camp at the junction of Bluff Creek and Notice Creek, they trekked logging roads and hiked creek beds. The two young men carried no weapons save for a highway flare kept on hand to ward off animals. After a short time spent in the area they had read about in the pages of *Argosy* magazine, Silver and Singer disputed Sanderson's description of the area as a trackless wilderness. "When we arrived at the Bluff Creek site we found the nearest road 100 yards away and a group of loggers living in house trailers three miles away," they said.

> When asked why they are searching for Bigfoot, they answered in a way that seems to reflect the ideas of many young Americans. "We would like to see Bigfoot because it signifies the dreams that there are things possible in this world that people don't recognize."

"The area seems to be at a stand-still in Bigfoot activity and our plans for the future include an expedition to Oregon south of Mount Hood, where the most recent tracks have been spotted," Singer stated. If necessary, the two New Yorkers would take a leave of absence from their studies to resume the search. "All we want is to find our dream," they said.[160]

The motivation of Singer and Silver was emblematic of a can-do attitude that was propelling America in the '60s toward putting people on the Moon by the decade's end. A flourishing fascination with hairy hominids in the North American hinterlands was translated into action. As the last years of the decade whisked by, people who were excited by the concept of Bigfoot had the Patterson-Gimlin film image as a new, compelling frame of reference. A raw energy propelled this new wave of sleuths—amateurs with respect to training and credentials—into the wilderness to discover for themselves just what was going on with Bigfoot. Writer John Seginski provided advice in a March 1970 article titled "Bigfoot: Man or Ape?" for these new excursions:

> Most of the expeditions included two or more persons who were trying to capture the animal or to photograph it. I believe that a solitary man, walking slowly and quietly through the forests has a better chance of seeing and photographing one of these creatures. Also I believe that a person's best bet would be to concentrate on the ground and look for the bones of these animals. If he were to find a bone or a skull of one of these creatures he could name a price or even agree to become a paid member of the expedition when the anthropologists and scientists returned to collect the remainder of the bones. Because much of the scientific world doubts the existence of the bigfoots [sic] (they need proof) a few bones of the animal are required to prove that it really exists.[161]

While camping in Idaho in the summer of 1969, Seginski asked road crew workers and forest rangers if they had heard of Bigfoot. Not only had people heard of Bigfoot, but Seginski learned a pair of such creatures had been sighted near French Creek in central Idaho. Reports said the hair was lighter than the darker colors commonly reported from Northern California.[162] Seginski had participated in several forays into California attempting to track down the elusive Bigfoot.

> I've made two trips to the Klamath River area of Northern California in search for some hard evidence of a [B]igfoot. In September of 1968 I camped for four days on the Eastern edge of the Marble Mountain Wilderness area just south of the Klamath River. The mountains in this area are steep and rugged and almost impossible to climb. The only way a person can claw his way up one of these steep mountains is to work his way along a game trail. I made the trip alone because I wanted to be quiet while I searched. My camera was set and ready at all times.[163]

After some hard hiking Seginski took a seat on a rock to catch his wind and drink water. Brushing the mat of pine needles covering the ground, he was surprised to find a large rib bone about two feet in length. Feeling his pulse quicken, Seginski searched the ground uncovering several additional bones including an upper jaw bone, which to his dismay, looked disappointedly like it belonged to a horse. A tooth he kept from the bones confirmed his initial suspicion, it was later determined to be that of a horse.[164]

Newspaper articles continued to churn out the latest news on Bigfoot sightings and track finds.

> Skamania County, where strange things just have a habit of happening, is now looking for the foot that made the footprint.
>
> The "footprint," measuring a full 22 inches in length and seven inches wide, is stashed away safely in the Skamania County Sheriff's office.
>
> The "thing" that made the print—Bigfoot, mountain ape, or whatever—is still roaming the mountains, according to the theory.[165]

Sanderson's Consultancy to the Montreal Pavilion

In 1969, the city of Montreal moved to open new pavilions on the grounds that had hosted the successful 1967 International and Universal Exposition.

When Expo 67 closed in October 1969 most of the pavilions continued as an exhibition called Man and His World, which remained a tourist attraction until 1984. One of the new pavilions focused on scientific enigmas. Shortly after Sanderson's article "Living Fossil" came out in the May 1969 edition of *Argosy*, he traveled to Montreal to meet with Michel Lambert, the pavilion designer. Sanderson's assistance and suggestions helped create the "Strange, Strange World" exhibit which included musical rocks of Pennsylvania, the miniature coffins of Scotland, little boats of Borneo, sea monsters, flying saucers, and Abominable Snowmen (ABSM). The impressions of Yeti and Bigfoot footprints were imprinted into the cement of the pavilion floor.[166]

Print & Film

John Green stopped in Lynnwood, Washington, in July 1969 to promote his 78-page book, *On the Track of the Sasquatch*. Lynnwood's Highline Plaza Book n' Card Shop reported Green's book as one of the shop's best sellers. The promotion tour allowed the 42-year-old Green to share how his interest in Sasquatch had been truly piqued when a man in his home town, "someone I knew and respected and who was known to be reliable" claimed to have seen one of the creatures. Green started keeping track of Sasquatch sightings and personally investigated many locations where Bigfoot had been spotted.

> With this growing body of evidence, Green did his best to interest the scientific world in the phenomenon, and when none of the scientists would pay attention, "I just got stubborn about it," he says.
>
> He's been on the track of the Sasquatch for about 15 years now, not with the idea of proving there is such an animal but investigating the tracks and trying to collect such evidence that the scientific community will be obliged to commit itself.
>
> During this time he has not worked alone but has met and worked with other "stubborn and determined" investigators in the field such as René Dahinden of B.C. and Roger Patterson of B.C.
>
> During these years Green has run into the easy explanations for the reported sightings and footprints of the big animal. These have been variously, "lies, bears, and hallucinations." None of the easy explanations however, take into consideration the footprints that have been reported over and over again,

> up and down the coast, nor the eyewitness reports by men of generally good reputations.[167]

Green believed the Patterson-Gimlin film had sparked a wave of scientific interest and at the time of his stop in Lynnwood, Green said the film was being shown to Anthropology students at the University of Washington. Green maintained that scientific acceptance and study of the subject was important for real breakthroughs to happen. Because Bigfoot was a creature which closely resembled humans, Green believed the serious study of Sasquatch could provide insights into the study of man with his environment, "particularly if the Sasquatch should hibernate during the winter, as would seem a probability," Green said.[168]

As reported by Dave Davies in the *Winnipeg Free Press*, by November 1969, *On the Track of the Sasquatch* had sold 10,000 copies. Green told Davies he was impressed by the quantity of Bigfoot accounts he had accumulated over the years both from people who had experienced encounters and from articles in yellowing North American newspapers. "It wasn't a gradual thing. The more I dug, the more I found. There was a lot in the way of old newspaper stories of people finding these things over 40 years ago. And I started to come across information accumulated by other people." Green believed Sasquatch were likely solitary creatures and the chances of the giants turning out to be human as opposed to ape were very slim. "Sasquatches seem to resemble humans in that they have adopted the upright posture. But if only for that reason they would be of interest to scientists."

> When talking, Mr. Green speaks as a man who feels he has been unjustly hurt. His sincerity is obvious as he speaks of an important part of his life.
>
> He admits he has never seen a [S]asquatch and that undoubtedly some reports are false. But he criticizes the scientific community for refusing to admit the possibility or even examine the evidence.

Green acknowledged the growing record contained several reports, generally older stories, describing attacks perpetrated by Bigfoot on people. If someone were attacked, Green stated, it would be unlikely they would live to tell the tale. By the end of the '60s, Green perceived a shift in the public's palate for Bigfoot. The Patterson-Gimlin film had helped enormously to publicize the creature—though the scientific community still gave the subject the cold shoulder. By the time Green's second book *Year of the Sasquatch* (1970) was published, he had noticed an unmistakable increase in the number of reports coming forward.

> What amounts almost to an explosion of information is happening not because more has been going on, but because there has been a great improvement in communications and because public and even scientific attitudes are changing. As a result people who saw something themselves or who heard reports from others in former years, as well as those involved in things happening now, have been getting in touch with investigators.[169]

In *On the Track of the Sasquatch*, Green stated he had 250 reports of sightings on hand in 1968 after 15 years of research. Two years later, Green reported in his second book, *The Year of the Sasquatch* (1970), that he had collected an additional 250 reports of track discoveries and Bigfoot sightings. Still, hinting at the idea there were many more reports to come forward, Green believed one of the biggest challenges remained convincing people to divulge their sightings. "Most people who report having seen a [S]asquatch will drop the matter when they find it exposes them to the ridicule or pity of their friends."[170]

During his promotional tour, Green dropped off a review copy of *On the Track of the Sasquatch* ($2.95 original price) to the *Brandon Sun* in Brandon, Manitoba, whose Wayne Boyce scribed a review. "As an adventure story it is a bizarre and fascinating mystery. It has many stories and much evidence, too varied to be thrown aside by a sceptic's shrug," Boyce wrote. "The author has taken care to be responsible and accurate about the evidence available to him." Boyce called the book "a collector's item if your tastes run along the lines of detective mysteries and the slightly bizarre."[171]

Author Brad Steiger used the pseudonym "Eric Norman" for his book, *The Abominable Snowmen* (1969). The alias was developed by Steiger and Warren Smith which they used for several collaborations. Steiger explores several sightings from across America, including within Michigan, New Jersey, and Pennsylvania. The book's eighth chapter, "California's Bizarre Bigfoot" is devoted to sightings in The Golden State. In Chapter 9, "Canadian Giants," Steiger relates the legend of Nahanni Valley, Northwest Territories, Canada.

Perhaps the most eerie tales in all ABSMery are grouped around Canada's mysterious Nahanni Valley, located in the southern end of the Mackenzie Mountains. Hot sulfur springs keep the valley's two hundred fifty square miles verdant during the entire year, even though the Nahanni is situated above sixty degrees latitude.

The Indian tribes in the area have avoided the Nahanni since the time of their forefathers. Even today, the Indians will not follow fur-bearing animals into the valley's warm mists. To both the Indians and the white men who live near the Nahanni, the mysterious valley is known as "The Valley of Headless Men."

Too many prospectors and fur trappers who have managed to escape the valley's headhunters and return with valuable bundles of lush furs have said that they would not enter the valley again under any circumstances.

"It's that damn mist," complained one fur trapper. "It swirls around a man all day long and pretty soon it starts to make you see things that you know—or you hope—cannot be there. My partner and I were just plain spooked by the time we left the Nahanni. We got so we had the feeling that something was watching us, spying on us, all the time.

"Hell, you can't find an Indian who'll go with you into the Nahanni," he went on. "They say that the valley is filled with evil spirits. You know, I think they just may be right!"

Could it be that a tribe of ABSMs have developed hostile attitudes toward outsiders? Or could it be that the [S]asquatch of the Nahanni have begun to collect the skulls of men for use in primitive religious ceremonies, just as Neanderthal Man severed the skulls of the cave bear to use as totems? Whatever may be the reason and whatever or whoever may be responsible, more than a dozen prospectors and fur trappers are known to have been decapitated in the eerie mists of the Nahanni Valley. And although the giant footprints near the skeletal remains constitute only circumstantial evidence, it is evidence of a most uncomfortable sort.[172]

In response to dozens of sightings from Lake Worth, Texas, in 1969, Sallie Ann Clarke authored *The Lake Worth Monster of Greer Island, Ft. Worth, Texas.* (1969). Police investigated the reports but found no evidence to

THE LAKE WORTH
MONSTER
OF GREER ISLAND,
FT. WORTH, TEXAS
BFB
BY
SALLIE ANN CLARKE

support the descriptions of a half-man, half-goat, furred and/or scaled creature, some seven feet tall. Clarke noted that her work was "semi-fiction," a variable description after Clarke saw the Lake Worth Monster for herself. "When I wrote it, I hadn't seen the monster," Clarke said in 1989 upon the 20th anniversary of her book's publishing. "After that, I saw it four times. If I'd seen it before I wrote the book, the book would have been quite a lot different. It wouldn't have been semi-fiction. It would have been like a history."[173] Clarke stated the book sold 280,000 copies.

Bigfoot: America's Abominable Snowman

Patterson parlayed the footage taken at Bluff Creek into a BBC-produced movie that broke ground as the first documentary to feature Bigfoot. After a lengthy opening monologue (and sales pitch for the Northwest Research Association) by his brother-in-law Al DeAtley, Patterson explains his interest in Bigfoot, briefly describes the creature's longstanding tradition in North America, and includes interviews with several witnesses. The movie ends with scenes of Patterson, Gimlin, and others searching the wilderness for Bigfoot, the consummation of which was the Patterson-Gimlin footage.

In 1970, reviewer Gerald Wade called *Bigfoot: America's Abominable Snowman* "low-grade baloney" in which the eponymous creature's film sequence ran for "31.5 seconds, according to my stop watch."

> The rest of the movie is of people talking about 'Bigfoot.' There are three or four persons who think they saw such a creature and there are some scientists who don't know what to think.
>
> "Bigfoot" starts with a 10-minute sales pitch in which you are shown copies of magazines which have run articles about the creature.
>
> Then you're offered membership in what amounts to a sort of "Bigfoot" fan club. For $6 you get a 5-7-inch photo of the thing, a membership card and four bulletins a year all about the latest "Bigfoot" doings.[174]

Ted Mahar's article, "'Bigfoot' Presents Only Known Film" in the March 13, 1969 *Oregonian*, gave a brief historical overview of the film.

> Roger Patterson, founder of the Northwest Research Association which is presenting the film "Bigfoot" in Memorial Coliseum

BIGFOOT

AMERICA'S ABOMINABLE SNOWMAN

150 Year Old Legend Comes To Life On The Screen!

Showing At:

- **SUPERIOR, FEB. 17** Strand Theatre
- **ST. IGNATIUS, FEB. 18** Park Theatre
- **RONAN, FEB. 19** Gayety Theatre
- **HAMILTON, FEB. 20** Roxy Theatre
- **POLSON, FEB. 21** Lincoln Auditorium

Admission: Adults $1.50
Children 12 and under 75c

All weekday show at 7:00, 8:30 p.m.
Sat.-Sun.—2:00, 4:00, 7:00, 8:30 p.m.

Northwest Research Ass'n Presents

BIGFOOT

North America's Abominable Snowman

Showing At Conrad

MONDAY, FEBRUARY 17

At The Orpheum Theatre

2 SHOWS — 7:00 and 8:30 P.M.

— *ADMISSION* —

Adults $1.50 *Juniors Under 12 75c*

ADVERTISING EXAMPLES FOR 'BIGFOOT: AMERICA'S ABOMINABLE SNOWMAN'

> Thursday and Friday, became interested in the Bigfoot phenomenon on the basis of one article in *True* magazine and has been involved in the search ever since. That was eight years ago. It was not until last year, he claims that he saw one of the creatures called Bigfoot for the first and only time—so far.
>
> He had a movie camera along and filmed what he says is one of the creatures, and his footage is included in the film at the Coliseum. The film was made by the British Broadcasting Corp., Patterson said. . . .
>
> The BBC was contacted by Napier. The BBC film team flew around the country interviewing people claiming to have seen Bigfoot and filming places where sightings have been made. The only footage of one of the creatures known to exist, however, is that made by Patterson last May.[175]

The issue of research funding, which in large measure is the focus of Al DeAtley's opening monologue in *Bigfoot: America's Abominable Snowman*, was spoken of often by Patterson and would remain a regularly-revisited topic amongst various researchers through the '70s. "A lot of people have been interested, but nobody is willing to help finance it unless you come up with a live creature or a skeleton," Patterson said. "Grants would help us, but we've reached the point where we can still get along without them."[176]

Jim McClarin

In the aftermath of the Patterson-Gimlin film's publicity, Green pointed to two mutually supporting characteristics of the burgeoning field of anomalous hominid study: a noticeable attitude shift in the aggregate regarding Bigfoot and the ensuing "explosion of information," made available to researchers. As Green readied his first book for publication, the first edition of George Haas' two-page, mimeographed *Bigfoot Bulletin* was rolled out in January 1969. The *Bulletin* was published for the next two and a half years and reached a total of 26 issues; it provided interested researchers the latest in accounts and sightings, editorials, and articles on Bigfoot behavior and ecology.

Jim McClarin emerged at this time as one of the new Bigfoot enthusiasts and became a frequent contributor to the *Bigfoot Bulletin*. McClarin was born in January 1946 in Buffalo, New York. By the third grade, his family moved to New Mexico and McClarin's first memory of having heard of

Bigfoot was during a family camping trip to White Sands National Park when his father talked of Bigfoot around the family's campfire.[177]

> After high school I attended American River Junior College where in the first week, browsing through the zoology section of the campus library, I discovered a book that would have a profound impact on my life: Ivan T. Sanderson's "Abominable Snowmen: Legend Come to Life." It was the first I realized that Bigfoot was more than a campfire story. After devouring the book I began to make plans and to correspond with Sanderson and Canadian John Green, both of whom gave me entre to others in the budding field of Bigfoot/Sasquatch research, including Roger Patterson. My choice of Humboldt State to continue my zoology major was not unreasonable since it had a well-respected marine biology program, but the truth is that its campus in the redwoods lay close to the Bluff Creek area from which so many of the early reports had issued, and that was the basis for my decision to go there.[178]

In 1967 McClarin carved the 14-foot Sasquatch redwood statue at the junction of Highways 299 and 96 near Willow Creek, which became a favorite landmark in what many considered the heart of Bigfoot country. "I carved the statue because I believe these wild, manlike creatures live in the wilderness," McClarin said.[179] Amongst his regular contributions to the *Bigfoot Bulletin* were summaries of his research and forays into the woods searching for Bigfoot. Green said McClarin "broke new ground" with his calculations on weights of erect bipeds from their height and build (found in the March 20, 1969, *Bigfoot Bulletin*). And McClarin gave public talks on Bigfoot as demonstrated by the article below which provides insight into McClarin's deep involvement in Bigfoot pursuits.

> Jim McClarin, who is organizing an expedition this winter to try to capture "Bigfoot," North America's Abominable Snowman, will speak on "The Search for Bigfoot" Thursday in the [Sacramento City College] auditorium at 1 and 8:15 P.M.
>
> McClarin, 22, is a senior zoology student at Humboldt State College and president of Bigfoot Fund, Inc. He is getting together a 15-man expedition to go into the Bluff Creek Region, 70 miles northeast of Eureka, for the possibility of

> locating "the greatest zoological and anthropological find in history."
>
> He has spent four-and-a-half years studying reports of "Bigfoot" and last summer headed a small expedition in search of the creature.
>
> McClarin hopes to equip himself and 14 other men with hypodermic-dart equipment, snowmobiles, and four-wheel drive vehicles.
>
> Financing for the project will probably come only after frames from his film showing "Bigfoot" have been published.
>
> The public is invited to attend. There is no admission charge.[180]

Joining McClarin in a new wave of enthusiastic pursuit for Bigfoot was Dick Grover who counted among his prized Bigfoot evidence a street sign that had been bent, purportedly, by a distracted Bigfoot. The back side of the sign showed what Grover considered scratch marks left by a Bigfoot's finger nails. The sign had been standing eight feet off the ground at an intersection on Fife Heights Drive in the Tacoma suburb of Fife, Washington. Grover interviewed two teenagers, Dick Hancock and Gary Johnson, who witnessed the event. As they approached the intersection at about 4 A.M. on September 20, 1969, they saw a large, hair-covered form dash across the road in front of them before it collided with the sign which left it bent and vibrating. A month later the sign was replaced at the intersection and Grover was successful in obtaining the original one.[181]

David Hancock concluded his *Weekend Magazine* article in which he described his viewing of the Patterson-Gimlin film with an expression of skepticism. His several questions distill to the simplest reservation of Bigfoot: *How can it be?*

> However, even if the [Patterson-Gimlin] film and plaster casts are a hoax, they could not negate the records suggesting such an unknown animal existed.
>
> From the scientific point of view the existence of a large primitive primate in Northern California or coastal British Columbia is most difficult to justify (the third greatest understatement of the century). No tangible evidence or even part of a specimen has ever been found. The type is only known in the old world where it is believed to have evolved.

How would such a beast make a living out of the coastal rain forest? Surely one of the darkest, least diversified habitats in the world? Just what would it eat? If it were humanoid and presumably reasonably intelligent where is its home, its art, its fire? With so few reports of Sasquatches, it is difficult to imagine there being enough individuals on the entire coast who could find each other for reproduction.

And over and over again returns that self-centered question. If they are there, why haven't I seen one, or at least more sign?[182]

Mainstream science appeared disinterested in Bigfoot, generally giving the Patterson-Gimlin film little official scrutiny and attention. Bigfoot study and research from the start was necessarily undertaken by amateurs, but if they were laymen in lacking credentials and degrees, they were paragons of passion and devotion. Heading into the '70s, their zeal and optimism could best be summed up by Roger Patterson, the man who wielded the camera at Bluff Creek: "In closing might I remind you that Bigfoot's Day is close at hand. It will be a day of Scientific upheaval—of rewriting textbooks—a day of astounded public—of religious soul-searching– but nevertheless, a day that is as sure in coming as life and death in our universe."[183] This prevailing spirit would meet head on with the first major Bigfoot story of the 1970s, and in the resulting tumult and churn, find itself tested.

REWARD!
$2500

to anyone with information regarding recent sightings of BIGFOOT or his tracks.

Kindly contact Mr. Al Hodgson at the Willow Creek Variety Store.

Information is desired by Stephen M. Pauley, M.D. (Pauley Bigfoot Expedition for the scientific inquiry into reports of giant primates in the Northwest and Northern California).

1969 REWARD OFFER FOR BIGFOOT SIGHTINGS OR TRACKS

CHAPTER 1. BACKSTORY—PART III
SELECT PRE-1970 REPORTS

Some hairy hominid encounters have become Bigfoot canon: Ape Canyon, Ruby Ridge, Albert Ostman, and William Rowe. Attention to these specific accounts will be touched on in this volume as concerns their reference and dissemination in the '70s. This section presents several other stories as exemplars, less frequently recorded than the preceding iconic accounts, to shed light on Bigfoot's historical context and, at least in part, flesh out cultural perceptions and reactions prior to Bigfoot's halcyon ascendency during the 1970s. Of these stories, all excepting two occurred before the Patterson-Gimlin film became public, and they are culled from a massive collection of accounts, reports, tales, articles, and stories. John Green, Roger Patterson, René Dahinden, and Peter Byrne gathered and assembled numerous accounts into a robust portrait of interaction between Bigfoot and mankind extending across centuries.

1867: Katie Flynn and the Bear

In 1951 the *Ludington Daily News* reprinted a series of nearly 40-year-old articles originally published in the *Ludington Chronicle* by W. E. Barry which described the triumphs and travails of Michigan lumberjacks. The fifth installment of this series featured the remarkable story of young Katie Flynn.

Katie was the daughter of Henry "Hank" Flynn and the logging camp he ran was on the Pere Marquette River near Weldon Creek, close by Custer. Along with stands of trees, the area had a large marsh which loggers turned their oxen into for green feed.

> "In the fall of 1867 a new logging outfit put in a camp about three miles above our camp. The owner's name was 'Hank'

Flynn. He moved his family up to the camp. He was a great hunter. A great many black bears were in the woods at this time and he was killing them, both old and young, for their hides.

"One old hunter at our camp made the remark that this man would be sorry for killing the young cubs some day, and it was not long before this prophecy came true. This man sent part of his crew out to a large lake and hay marsh to cut hay for the coming winter. He decided to go out and see how they were getting along. As he was saddling his horse, his little two-year-old daughter Katie came out and wanted to go with him. Of course he refused, but consented to let her ride to the top of a hill nearby, a distance of 500 yards from the camp. The mother put her on the horse in front of her father, kissed her and told her to come straight home. They started, and arriving at the top of the hill he put her down and told her to run home as fast as she could. He went on his way to the hay marsh and attended to his business there, then returned home. He arrived home about 8:30 P.M. and the first words his wife said were, 'Where's Katie?' He told his wife what he had done in the morning and had not thought any more about it until now. His wife by this time was screaming and soon in a faint.

"The whole camp was aroused and with lanterns and pine torches were soon on a search. Our camp was notified and we all turned out to join in the search. We searched all that night and all the next day until about 5 P.M., when a part of our crew, who were about two miles above camp and close to the river and were thinking of crossing over to the other side, had started up the river to a log jam to cross on.

"When they came to the jam they saw a big black bear crossing on three feet. They thought at first the bear was wounded, but just at that moment when one of the men had his gun to his shoulder to shoot, one of the men cried: 'For God's sake, don't shoot!'

"In watching the bear he had seen a part of a dress hanging down and dragging on the logs. The bear still kept hopping along, hugging something close to his breast. After crossing the jam he went about five yards, then dropped the child and made off through the woods. The men did not shoot, they were so filled with joy to find the child alive and well, with but a few scratches on her caused by the bear going through the bushes.

"The child was carried home and handed over to her mother, who shed tears of joy to find her lost daughter. Bells were rung, and horns blown to notify the other searchers that the child had been found.

"In answer to questions, the child said that, after her father had left her, she had played a little while in the sand when a big black thing came along and played with her. Then it held out its paw and she caught hold of it and it had walked away with her. Just before dark it had left her for a while and when it came back its paw was full of wintergreen berries, and she ate some. Then it scraped a big pile of leaves close to her and lay down close to her, and during the night had tried to cover her with its body.

"The old hunter at our camp said that the hunter had killed two cubs about a week before that, and that the bear had thought the child was one of the cubs. The father never shot any more bears after that."[184]

1929: Great Ape Only Small Monkey

Women Near Freeport Lock Doors and Telephone for Help When Story Goes Abroad That Great Ape Roams the Woods—Posse Fails to Find Even Little Monkey—Freeport, Ill., July 26—The great anthropoid ape hunt is ended.

Farmers and bloodhounds who scoured this district and near Elizabeth, Ill., returned empty handed today.

Authorities today learned that a very small monkey was missing from a carnival.

"Moonshine and a monkey started that ape story," said the chief of police. "I'm looking for the human ape who originated the yarn now."

The "great ape hunt" was started yesterday when it became reported that women of the countryside were in a state of panic over a story that a great hairy ape was roaming the woods. The story was sent out of Freeport and appeared in the morning papers. It said: "Posses of farmers, armed with shotguns, continued to beat through the timberland near here and northward for a reported huge anthropoid ape which is alleged to have terrified farmers' wives and children in this vicinity.

"Several farmers' wives have telephoned authorities that they had seen the ape, which they said was unusually large."[185]

1952: Orr's Bigfoot Tale

Included in Roger Patterson's *Bigfoot: Volume 1 (*1968), his second book on Bigfoot (published after the Patterson-Gimlin film was shot), are several letters written to Patterson by people willing to share their encounters. One such letter sent in by J. C. Orr depicted an encounter with an aggressive creature.

> Dear Sir, December 20, 1966
>
> In regard to a story in the *Tribune* about an investigation in the matter of the Bigfoot stories: I probably may be of some *small* help in locating one of these primitive species of humans. The place where I had a peculiar and frightening experience occurred between Happy Camp and Orleans, California, on a detour one night in 1952. I will give you definite directions on how to find this detour, but would first like to tell the story of what happened. I even sent this story to "True" magazine, but although they said it had considerable merit they couldn't publish it, (probably because they thought I was nuts), naturally.
>
> The story in short form that I sent them went like this.
>
> I had been reading a story written by Ivan T. Sanderson about a Bigfoot monster that people had seen in Northern California. As I was reading the story I suddenly had the eerie realization that I, too, had had a similar experience. As the story came snaking its way out of my subconscious, I began to remember more and more of what happened. I had me a bad case of the jitters as the memory uncoiled.
>
> The first part of the story took me back to 1952, when I had gone down to Orleans to start preliminary work on a logging operation with two men by the names of Lee Vlery and Josh Russel.

One evening Josh told me Lee had gone up to Happy Camp, but not having transportation back, wanted me to take the Mercury and go up and get him. I had driven the extremely crooked and dangerous road up there, but not being able to find him started back alone to Orleans.

It had been raining very heavily and after going back a few miles I found there had been a slide across the road. There was a man with a flashlight there who told me I could still get back to Orleans by way of a detour across the river. He said it was a dirt road that went through Bear Valley and would come out at the mouth of Bluff Creek a few miles below Orleans.

I had been driving slowly down this road for about twenty miles I guess, sort of daydreaming, when I saw it . . . dimly in the headlights and the rain was the shaggy orangutang-like [sic] apparition of a human. For an instant I had the impression the shaggy hair of the creature was a hoary blue grey in the headlights. An ogre! I remember thinking, but the thing swiftly back-pedalled [sic] off the road and behind a tree. I automatically passed it off as imagination and drove on by the spot.

Suddenly, without warning, the car went into a violent and unreasonable skid. I brought the car back under control, but for some reason glanced into the rear view mirror. In the dim light of the tail lights and license-display bulb, I thought I could see a savage looking face looking through the rear glass. I continued on, and when I looked again there was no face, so again concluded it was imagination.

I had gone another quarter mile I guess, when across the road was a small six-inch sapling—I stopped the car and got out, intending to drag it aside if possible. Suddenly I heard the swift thud of flying feet of something coming down the road. Reality was upon me and I remember cursing myself for not paying attention to what I had previously seen. It was the shaggy human-like monster I had seen in the headlights.

It at once started circling around me, snarling and acting very menacing. It kept this circling up for some time and once came up quite close, and I could see its face reflected by the headlights much better. The eyes were round, and rather luminous, the hair on top of its rather low and rounded head pretty short. Its eye teeth were far longer than a human's, also the chest and upper part of its torso was rather bare of hair, and also leathery looking. It wasn't too tall—not much more than my own 5 feet 9 inches, although it had a stooped, long armed posture.

Then it suddenly changed tactics—it would stalk off down the road but would come charging back, like a bat out of hell, when I started toward the car. The hour was late, the thing was becoming more and more menacing, and I was almost paralyzed by this time, paralyzed by fear.

Suddenly a plan of escape, born out of desperation, popped into my mind. Since the monster seemed to think I couldn't get away, why not, when it went down the road again, playing cat and mouse, try and get in the car and smash through the sapling. This I did, and sprang for the door of the car a dozen feet away. No sooner was I inside when there it was, trying to claw through the window. I jerked the car into gear, floored the accelerator, and can vividly remember the wet sapling glistening whitely in the headlights as the car slashed it aside.

I remember then the scream of rage and frustration it then gave. It was a curious trumpeting sound like the scream of a stallion and the roar of a mad grizzly. (I can imitate this scream myself pretty good, as I often practice it when off alone in the woods.) the car then felt as though it were being held back by something half riding and attempting to stop it, but the powerful Mercury proved too much for it, and after a couple of hundred yards I felt no more resistance.

To top this unbelievable experience off, believe it or not, I promptly forgot the whole experience. Then and there it went out of mind. Not even the next day when Lee asked me if I had seen anything unusual on that road last night did I remember. (He had come late from Happy Camp with another man he hired to take him to Orleans.)

A few days later an incident happened that should have brought the experience back but didn't, Lee noticed a big dent in the grill of the car and asked me how it got there. I told him I didn't know. Incidentally, Lee told me that something had tried to push them off the road, when they came through on the detour. He said there's something strange going on around here and let the matter drop.

Not until I was reading Sanderson's article in 1959 in "True" did I start remembering, oddly enough.

Was this a trick played on me by a man in a monkey suit? I don't think so. Anyway I went back down there in 1959 looking for it.

Walk that detour alone, at night, equipped with a .44 magnum, a flashlight, and a camera and you might have an experience. I've been thinking of it.

Sincerely yours, J. C. Orr[186]

1960–1961: Braxton County Monster

Shades of the Braxton County monster!

He has returned.

Or something like him anyway.

The wife of a bakery truck driver reported today that her husband came home last night with his hair standing on end.

He told her he had seen a "weird, hair-covered monster in the shape of a man" last night as he drove along a lonely, backwoods road near Hickory Flats, between Braxton and Webster counties.

Mrs. Charles Stover, whose 25-year-old husband is a driver for Dutch Oven Bakeries, said he was returning home from his route shortly before 11 P.M.

As he rounded a curve, he said "the monster, standing erect, with hair all over his face and body," glared at him from the edge of the road. He estimated it was six feet tall.

Stover told his wife he almost hit "the thing" and stopped his truck a short distance away, took another look, saw it still standing by the road, then roared off.

He didn't stop until he reached a restaurant-filling station where he went in for a cup of coffee.

"But I was so scared and shaking so badly that I spilled it all over me," Mrs. Stover quoted him.

He told his story to a group of men in the restaurant and they immediately armed themselves with shotguns and rifles and went back with Stover to the spot he reported seeing the strange being.

There, they found rocks upturned and marks on the ground. The ground was frozen otherwise.

"The men told my husband that there had been reports of weird cries for several weeks coming from the woods in the area," Mrs. Stover said.

"My husband hardly slept a wink last night, he was so upset by it all. He's still shook up."

Mrs. Stover said she knew that if the report had come out on New Year's Eve that everyone would think her husband had been drinking.

"But he wasn't," she said. "I believe him. So does his boss. So do the men who live in the area. They're going to continue their hunt for whatever it was Charles saw."

The Braxton County monster story first broke on Sept. 12, 1952, when Mrs. Kathleen May of Flatwoods said she saw a mysterious object near her home.

She said her sons and some other boys had been playing in a field near her home when they said they saw a large object pass overhead.

She accompanied them and reported she saw a mysterious "monster about 10 feet tall, with a face of fiery red, a green body and a headpiece which looked like the ace of spades."

Her report rocked the country.

From New York, a note [sic] naturalist and science writer, Ivan Sanderson, came to investigate. He said the Braxton County monster was a spaceship, one of five which flew in formation across central West Virginia that night.

Her report drew 10,000 to 15,000 visitors to view the area where the "monster" reported had been sighted.[187]

The Braxton County "monster" is back again and apparently is branching out.

A Clay County man says he saw the "thing" last week in Webster County and now a Kanawha County man says he saw it recently in Pocahontas County.

The "monster" was first sighted Sept. 12, 1952, by a resident of nearby Flatwoods. However, it has either changed appearance or there's a new one around.

W. C. Priestly of Alum Creek, Kanawha County, said he saw the monster and it was quite a "shocking" experience because it stalled his car by raising its hair. He described it as hairy. The 1952 version was not described like that.

No one is going to tell Priestly that it was a bear. He says he knows a bear from a monster and this was a monster. He said he spotted the creature on a backwoods road along the Williams River in Pocahontas County.

"My car started to miss and sputter and completely stopped," he said. "Then I saw it. To my left, beside the road, stood this monster with long hair pointing straight up toward the sky."

Priestly said another approaching car caused the "thing" to "drop his hair and my car started to run again." But he added, "the points completely burned out a short time later."

Charles Stover, a bakery truck driver, said he recently saw the monster, too. He said he rounded a curve and saw the monster, "standing erect, with hair all over his face and body."[188]

1962: California Creature

FT. BRAGG (UPI)—Two men and a woman said today they were chased by a huge, hairy creature answering the description of Northern California's fabled "Bigfoot."

They said the creature chased them into a house and let them close the door only after one of the men threatened to start shooting.

Tales of "Bigfoot"—the California equivalent of the Himalayan abominable snowman—have circulated in Northern California for years. The creature is usually described as big, hairy half man-half ape with enormous feet.

Sightings of the creature or its tracks are usually reported to have occurred in the remote mountain and forest land bordering the Pacific in Mendocino and Humboldt counties or in inland Siskiyou County.

Today's report came from Mr. and Mrs. Bud Jenkins and Robert Hatfield, a Crescent City logger visiting the Jenkins home about four miles from Ft. Bragg.

Hatfield said he stepped outside the house about 5:30 P.M. last Wednesday when he heard the Jenkins' dogs barking.

He said he saw a creature standing "chest and shoulders above a 6-foot high fence" at the back of the property.

"It was much, much bigger than a bear," he said. "It was covered with fur, with a flat, hairless face and perfectly round eyes."

Hatfield ran into the house and called Mr. and Mrs. Jenkins to join him in a search for the creature. Going around the side of the house, Hatfield said, he bumped into it. It knocked him to the ground, then chased after the Jenkinses.

They and Hatfield ran into the house, but the creature wouldn't let them shut the door, they said.

Jenkins finally started to get a gun, saying, "I'm going to shoot the damn thing."

It was then, they said, that the door closed.

Afterward, they found a 16-inch footprint outside the house and an 11-inch dirty handprint on the side of the building, they said.[189]

1963: Lode Monster

Calaveras County sheriff's deputies searched for the "Monster of the Mother Lode" yesterday—and found "nothing but cow tracks and deer tracks,"

However, deputies said, "We're not discounting the boy's story," referring to the report by David Marsh, 11, of Stockton, that he was confronted by a huge half-man, half-animal creature last Saturday near Camp Connell, three miles above Big Trees.

The Calaveras sheriff's department said it would give any assistance necessary to a Stockton search party that plans to scour the area with hunting dogs tomorrow.

Sheriff's deputies, while "not discounting the boy's story," suggested explanations of what the "thing" was that frightened the boy:

Campers in the area have been harassed lately by an extra-large reddish-brown bear, which might be taken for a "monster."

A hermit who had two shacks on the Mokelumne River in Calaveras County disappeared two years ago and has not been seen since, but may still be around the area.

Nevertheless, the boy's step-father, Raymond Clark, is more convinced than ever that David was not exaggerating.

"I know doggone good and well when my children are telling the truth or not," Clark told the *News-Sentinel*. He said that the child has awoken crying at the memory of the beast every night since last Saturday. "I saw it," the boy told his father, "and if nobody else believes me, me and Jesus know that I saw it."[190]

1964, 1965: Monster of Sister Lakes

A police report filed on the morning of June 10, 1964: "CREATURE, IDENTITY UNKNOWN. ABOUT NINE FEET TALL. ABOUT 500 POUNDS. ALL HAIR UP TO ITS NECK. HAS BLACK FACE. SKIN LOOKS ABOUT A HALF-INCH THICK. HAS VERY LARGE EYES THAT GLOW LIKE AN ANIMAL'S WHEN SHINED ON AT NIGHT. MAKES NOISES LIKE A TAME GOOSE ALSO LIKE A BABY CRYING." The previous night Mrs. Utrup had checked on her barking dogs at her Sister Lakes, Michigan, farm home. She claimed something in her yard chased her to her house. Rushing inside, she locked the door and phoned for help. When Deputies Sheline and Behrman arrived at the scene, it was raining, but they found rapidly-deteriorating tracks which resembled human footprints measuring six inches across the ball of the foot and nearly four inches across the heel.

"I know it sounds crazy—like we're ready for the bughouse," Mrs. Utrup said, "but with this thing around here for 2 ½ years, it's getting on our nerves." The possibility of negative judgements and opinions did not dissuade Mrs. Utrup from sharing her unease with the local monster's presence. "We've been afraid to tell anyone about it before for fear of ridicule. But this is getting to be too much. Whatever this is has not bothered anyone. It doesn't seem to be vicious, it just looks at them and moves off when confronted." It turned out 'The Thing' had been a regular visitor to the Utrup farm. "My dogs chased it one time—but that was the last. One—a shepherd—came back with his right eye faded into a pale blue ball. But three weeks later, the pupil became visible and now the eye is back to normal. But he's scared now. We know the Thing is in the woods back of our house when the dogs start barking and it's getting so that we're afraid to go out of the house."[191]

Gordon Brown, from the neighboring town of Dowagiac reported seeing the creature in his headlights on Tuesday, June 9. Brown watched the creature dash across the Swisher Road not far from the Utrup farm. "It was no bear!" Brown emphatically declared. "It had a face like a human."[192]

> Two workers at the Harold Utrup farm on Garret road, near Topash street, Cass county, say they have seen the "monster" of Dewey Lake. Gordon Brown and Joseph Smith told of seeing the "thing," described it as hairy and walking upright, much larger than a reporter who stood where the monster was allegedly seen.[193]

> The "Monster of Sister Lakes" caused a mammoth traffic jam Wednesday [June 10] night in southwestern Michigan.
>
> Area residents have been on edge in recent days since reports began circulating that the "monster" is back in the area. Cass County sheriff's deputies said the presence of the mysterious creature has been reported off and on for about two years.
>
> Mrs. John Utrup of nearby Dewey Lakes, Mich., told sheriff's deputies the beast chased her into her home Tuesday night and she said she was saved when her dogs barked and drove the "monster" away.
>
> Mrs. Utrup said he was nine feet tall and weighed 500 pounds. Other descriptions said it was covered with black hair up to its neck and had eyes that glowed like an animal that had a light shined in its eyes.
>
> Various witnesses said the creature made noises "like a tamed goose" and "a baby crying."
>
> Cass County Deputy Sheriff Ernest Kraus said deputies were dispatched into the area in which the "monster" had been reported. They were armed with deer rifles and would stake out the area "until we solve this."
>
> But, deputies said the area was crowded with a flow of curiosity seekers and all the officers were forced to direct traffic.
>
> "We had all the men we could spare up there and had to get some help from Van Buren County" to take care of the traffic,

> a spokesman said. He said many cars were loaded with up to six people.
>
> "We don't know what it is. We don't even know if it exists," the sheriff's spokesman said. "But there have been complaints by about 10 reputable persons and we have to check them out."[194]

When darkness fell on the evening of June 10, the sheriff's men set out to search the backroads, which turned out that evening not to be the lonely variety; an estimated 200 carloads of "auxiliaries" clogged the rambling country byways. Every Cass County lawman and some from neighboring Van Buren County were called out to help control the volume of people and traffic. "Somebody's going to get killed out here!" said a deputy. "These half-wits have deer rifles!"[195]

On June 11, three girls walked along a wooded road in Silver Creek Township only a few miles from the Utrup farm when they encountered something that looked "like a big bear on its hind legs except for the face" suddenly emerge from its concealment.

> Joyce saw him first and promptly fainted. Patsy got a good look at the creature before it ducked into the woods. Gail was too far away to see it.
>
> After the "monster" fled, the girls revived Joyce and they ran to a neighboring home and telephoned police. Sheriff's deputies armed with rifles rushed to the area.
>
> Joyce said the creature "didn't look like a man." Patsy, who said she saw it at close range, said it "looked like a bear." She said it was about seven feet tall and "had a black face."[196]

Deputy Sheriff Kraus said a gorilla had not been ruled out to explain the mysterious creature in their midst. "Whatever it is," Krause said, "it could have been in that swampy and wooded area for some time." A large bear was also proffered by authorities for the creature's identity.[197]

> It was the noisiest night the Sister Lakes area had ever known. Horns were sounding incessantly where automobiles had been left blocking the narrow byways. Men were pounding on the doors of the scattered farmhouses to demand directions and were shouting back and forth in the darkness as they swarmed

> through orchards and over fences. Tires were spinning shrilly on cars stuck in the sand, while police radios whistled and crackled. Not until 3 A.M. were the sheriff's men able to get the roads cleared and dawn found armed hunters still wandering about everywhere, while others waited at all-night diners.[198]

A man from Kalamazoo was said to have entered an orchard where he proceeded to produce a drum and bugle cacophony. When a beleaguered farmer came to investigate the man stated, "I figured the monster would come to see what the racket was."[199]

Other people came forward with their stories of seeing or hearing "something strange" during the nighttime. "People have been reluctant to call," Deputy Sheriff Kraus told reporters, "because it's a fantastic story, and they're afraid of ridicule. There's definitely something out there! I think there's a logical explanation, though. I think it's an animal of some kind."

With no new creature sightings, the effects of the curious and volunteer monster-hunters seemed obvious: any sensible self-respecting monster would leave the immediate area for a quieter, calmer location. "Whatever that thing was," said one exasperated deputy, "it's been spooked halfway to Canada by now." Warmer climes were also suggested as more desirable stomping grounds. "If I was that monster, I would have left for Cuba for now," a farmer quipped.[200]

> Before Thursday, June 12, was over, once-desolate Swisher Road was deeply rutted and littered with beer cans and bottles, and the owners of taverns and gas stations were welcoming the invasion with such delighted grins that the entire affair might have been passed off as a promotion stunt, except that all the reports had come from farm and cottage people who were far from delighted, who were in fact furious about broken fences, trampled crops and debris.[201]

That weekend, Cass County flaunted the trappings of a monster-hunting mecca. Local businesses touted "Monster Sales," the Dowagiac Theater billed a double-feature horror show, eateries featured "Monster Burgers," and a variety store had assembled "Special Monster-Hunting Kits," which retailed at $7.95 and included a baseball bat, a mallet, net, spear, and a flashlight. In the pages of *True* magazine, Gene Caesar wrote of hoaxes perpetrated all over the state, "as teen-agers, singly or on each other's shoulders, draped themselves with old fur coats and pranced about busy highways." But juvenile larks aside, by Sunday, June 14, no new, bona fide monster sightings had occurred, and the frenzy quickly wound down.[202]

Michigan's Frenchtown and Ash Townships witnessed a spate of sightings the following year culminating in a dramatic encounter whose aftermath recalled the monster-frenzy of 1964. On Friday evening, August 13, 1965, Ruth [also reported as Rose] Owens was visiting her mother and her husband, Mr. and Mrs. George Bush, in Monroe. *Detroit Free Press* reporter Stan Putnam wrote that the Bushes had been "living in terror" of the creature roaming the area. "We had gone there to keep them company that night," Owens told Putnam. "A lot of people were there. My mother and her husband aren't well, and we've been keeping an eye on them."[203]

At about 11:30 P.M., Owens and her daughter, 17-year-old Christine Van Acker left the Bush residence on Mentel Road and headed north toward Nadeau Road.

> What weighs more than 400 pounds, smells moldy, growls like a mad dog and dislikes automobiles? Answer—the Monroe County monster.
>
> That is the latest on the "thing" which has been sighted here and there in Monroe County during the last two months by at least 16 persons including Christine Van Acker, a 17-year old blond.
>
> Miss Van Acker, who goes to a beautician school here, has a black eye which she said was inflicted by the monster. State policemen are checking her story and patrolling the area at night northeast of this southern Michigan city.
>
> Miss Van Acker gave this story of the encounter:
>
> "I was driving mother (Mrs. Rose Owens) home. Suddenly there was this bump and a hairy arm grabbed me by the hair. It wasn't human or anything. I tried to go faster but the car stalled."
>
> The girl fainted. Mrs. Owens, who jumped out of the car and ran for help, described the ordeal like this:
>
> "The first I knew there was this bang and an arm came through the window. Christine yelled 'Mommy, help me! Oh, my God, help!'
>
> "I told her to get going, get the car going . . . but it stalled. The monster had its paw entwined in her hair and kept banging

> her head on the side of the car. I decided the best thing to do was go for help.
>
> "When I got back with other people, Christine was semi-conscious and the monster was gone.
>
> "The monster was at least seven feet tall, weighed about 600 pounds and it had a long reach. It was all covered with black, bristly hair, towards the end of the hair it was silver. You couldn't see its face, there was so much hair.
>
> "And it growled. It had a real growl, and definitely it was not a bear."
>
> Christine said she is sure it was not a bear "because bears have fur and this thing had prickly hair like thorns." She also said she is sure it was not a prankster "because nobody human would do anything like that."
>
> The monster sightings have occurred in Frenchtown and Ashe Townships within the last 60 days. One man reported the monster climbed onto his car and thumped on the roof and fenders before disappearing into the woods. A woman reported she saw the monster and it smelled moldy.
>
> Monroe County officers said they are not investigating any monster reports. However, a state police spokesman said they are taking official notice and troopers are patrolling the areas at night.
>
> "The monster has grown," a trooper said. "When first reported it was five feet tall and now it's more than seven feet. Our file on the case is still open on whatever it is."[204]

Van Acker told Putnam she believed the creature was more afraid of her than she was of it. "I think it had jumped on the car and its hand got caught in my hair and it was simply trying to get loose."[205] Men who came to assist found Christine unconscious and scuff marks in the gravel. Christine had a visible shiner on her left eye. Reminiscent of the Cass County affair of the previous year, responding police were dubious. "No tracks have been found," reported the Michigan State Police. "There is absolutely nothing definite to show that there is a beast." But the Van Acker encounter was more than enough to further stoke the coals of monster-hunting passions. The area was almost immediately flooded with curiosity seekers and self-styled monster hunters. The Consumers Power Company required a doubling of its guard to safeguard the Enrico Fermi power station from probing vigilantes. A hard rain Monday night, August 16, did not deter the droves as some 20 men were reportedly jailed for carrying concealed weapons. Caesar wrote that upwards of a thousand people, many armed, tromped about in the drizzly darkness.[206]

> Ravaged and littered, fences broken and crops trampled, the Mentel Road area had become a gigantic outdoor lunatic asylum; and the residents who'd originally claimed to have seen the creature were remaining in darkened homes behind bolted doors. New stories of encounters with the beast were still being heard, but none were believable. One cute little brunette told of being attacked and showed the monster claw marks on her arm to prove it. "Whatever attacked her," a state trooper commented dryly, "those welts are poison ivy."[207]

David Thomas, 23-years old and a relative of Van Acker, had been certain the creature was merely the work of a human hoaxer, that is,

> until he'd come face to face with thing and saw it was "three heads taller" than his six-foot self. After being "thrown around like a rag doll," he'd escaped into his car; and two strange-looking hairs, dark and apparently boasting light roots an inch-and-a-half long, were taken from the grillwork of that car and offered as evidence. But they turned out to be paint-brush bristles, and the young man changed his story drastically and began talking about a human hoaxter [sic] again when the police began talking about polygraph tests.[208]

"This thing has gone so far," said Detective Sgt. Pat Lyons, "that we want to prove, once and for all, that there is no monster, or discover exactly what it is that's out there." Radio station WFOB in Fostoria, Ohio, hired a polygrapher, who proceeded to interview Van Acker, Owens, and several others on August 20. "The tests proved they were telling the truth," he reported. "That is, they saw something—something that frightened them very badly." The Michigan State Police administered their own polygraph test to Mrs. Owens and Van Acker on August 23.

> The dreadful Monroe Monster, a hairy black creature, is no more. The beast was slain by a police lie detector.

> The story of the seven-foot-tall monster was dismissed by state police as a hoax after a teen-ager and her mother flunked a polygraph test Monday. The ladies, however, are sticking to their story.
>
> Mrs. Ruth Owens, 37, and her daughter, Christine Van Acker, 17, said they had taken another lie detector test last week which proved they were telling the truth when they reported being attacked by the monster.
>
> Their story began on a lonely road outside of this rural town Aug. 11. Christine said she and her mother were driving along when the beast popped out, grabbed their car and struck her.
>
> Mrs. Owens said her daughter finally fainted and the monster ran off.
>
> "It is our opinion that they were lying," said state police Sgt. Frank Barkman, who administered the test Monday.
>
> "I know what I saw and no one can change my mind," Christine retorted.
>
> Both women said they have seen the beast five times since June. Police have received reports from other area residents claiming the monster has been pestering them too.
>
> The reports resulted in civilian search parties which, one night last week, brought out more than 1,000 hearty souls to join in the hunt through wooded areas surrounding the town.
>
> The monster was a boon to merchants in the area. Business was brisk at restaurants, service stations and motels.
>
> One drive in is still serving "monsterburgers."[209]

Conflicting lie detector tests aside, Caesar aptly captured the effects of the Sister Lakes-Monroe Monster when he wrote "All that can be intelligently said is that a mystery exists, where every attempt at explanation has raised far more questions than were answered. And a mystery the matter will most likely remain, as long as men react to it with antics far stranger than any attribute to the unknown creature itself." One Mentel Road farmer offered his sentiments about the affair: "I don't know whether that thing's still around here or not," he said, "but if I saw it again, I wouldn't say a word. Not to anyone! Whatever it is, I'll take my chances with it anytime, before I'll go through any more nights of having a bunch of damned, drunken fools with high-powered rifles on my place."[210]

1964: Caddo Critter

Harvey Russell and Floyd Rodgers, two men from Breckenridge, Texas, owed their arrival in Caddo to simple curiosity. "We came down to have a look." The object of their interest was on the minds of many residents of Caddo, Texas—a *thing* locals had come to call the Caddo Critter. One man actually claimed to have gotten a shot at the creature. Charlie Gantt insisted the Critter "looked like a gorilla." Gantt recognized some people were skeptical of his claim. "I feel like I risked my life for the community," Gantt told reporters from as far away as Abilene and Fort Worth. "That's G-A-N-double-T." Gantt said he fired nine or ten shots on the night of Saturday, July 18, at the critter while it prowled outside his home.

> A neighbor, John Mitchell, 40, has a "big .30-.30" waiting for the critter. "Looks like we're gonna' have to kill it and put it under their noses to convince them," he said of the non-believers.
>
> A neighbor boy, Gene Couch, 9, said he saw the critter 200 yards from his home Saturday, on his way fishing.
>
> Mrs. Couch hasn't seen it, but disclosed that "something has been fighting the dogs at night."

There were Caddo residents who didn't hold to the notion of a creature in their midst. "Mr. Gantt probably saw a buck deer," one offered. Mrs. Rex Carey stated that monster-hunting folks were unwanted on her property. "It was a black car with spotlights on both sides. They started shining the lights all over the place and began stampeding her cattle over the fences," she said.[211]

1965: They Saw the Man-Animal

> THEY SAW THE MAN-ANIMAL by George Draper.
>
> The belief that several hundred giant man-animals are roaming the wilderness areas of California, Oregon and Washington was expressed yesterday by the owner of a Fresno lock and safe company.
>
> "There is absolutely no doubt in my mind that they exist," said O. R. Edwards, "and I know they are extremely strong and very intelligent."

Edwards, 56, a legitimate safe cracker with an uncanny knack for twirling the dials of the most formidable strong box, also believes these man-animals are "extremely dangerous" and "capable of mutilating a human being."

"I wouldn't be here today if I'd shot at those I saw," he said with disarming frankness.

Edwards is one of a dozen or more people who claim to have had face-to-face encounters with the hair-covered giants that they say stand between seven and 10 feet tall and weigh more than 500 pounds.

Another terrifying face-to-face encounter with a man-animal had been reported by Don L. Hunter, head of the Audio-Visual Department at the University of Oregon.

Hunter caught a glimpse of a giant taking enormous strides across a meadow at Todd Lake in the rugged Three Sisters Wilderness Area of Central Oregon.

"Even now the back of my neck gets all cold when I think about it," Hunter said while sitting in his comfortable home on a hill overlooking Eugene.

The University official said he and his former wife, who was with him and who also saw the creature, became so petrified that they spent the night in their car after driving 10 miles away from the scene.

Hunter said he has been trained in the scientific method of testing everything he sees and hears.

"I can't believe it was an hallucination. Two of us saw it. My wife was just as scared as I was," he said.

Edwards, who said "he was raised in the woods and used to be a good mountain man" was hunting with his friend, Bill Cole, when he encountered a man-animal in the southern Siskiyou Mountains during World War II.

This is Edwards' account of the meeting.

"We were both moving slowly and silently around this patch of brush. Bill went around the left side, I went around the right.

"I was sweeping the area ahead with my eyes. On one sweep, I caught a glimpse of what seemed like an apelike head sticking out of the brush.

"Dashing back to the end of the brush I saw a large manlike creature covered with brown hair. It was about seven feet tall and carrying in its arms what seemed like a man. I could only see legs and shoes. It was heading straight downhill on the run.

"I was about 30 feet away and the opening in the brush was only 10-15 feet wide. At the speed he was going it didn't leave me much time to make observations.

"I, of course, did not believe what I had just seen. So I closed my eyes and shook my head to sort of clear things up.

"I looked down the hill again in time to see the back and shoulders and head of a manlike thing covered with brown hair. It was disappearing into the brush some 70 or 80 yards below."

To confirm his recollections of what happened that day, Edwards wrote a letter to Cole at Grand Island, Nebraska last year.

"I guess I should have started looking for you. I don't know why, but I didn't," Edwards wrote. "Maybe I was afraid of the creature. Maybe I was afraid I'd find you dead."

Cole replied, acknowledging the incident, but saying, "I don't think it carried me at all. I was conscious all the time. I didn't hurt any place."

Cole said that after he "quit rolling," he went back up the hill and got his rifle. "I stood there some time and just looked and listened. I had a feeling I was being watched and hunted," Cole added in his letter.

Sitting in the back room of his Fresno lock and safe shop. Edwards says he has heard many stories about the Bigfoot giants from men who claim to have seen them.

"But Cole," he said, "is the only man I know who has had physical contact with a giant."

Edwards mentioned one other thing in his letter to Cole—that for 20 years "I would not believe what I had seen."

And to this Cole replied:

"Funny, neither of us has the guts to say what happened to us."

Prior to the exchange of these letters, it would seem, Edwards and Cole never discussed what took place on that unusual day.

Edwards also said he saw two more man-animals in the brush at the bottom of the ravine as he worked his way back to the logging road where their car was parked.

"Then came the darndest whistling scream that I ever heard from right behind me," he said.

"My hackles went up as I whirled around just in time to see a flash of something brown disappear behind the tree."

Other observers have described the man-animal's strange cry as "a vibrating sound" or like the sound of a steam locomotive's whistle or the sound of metal tearing.

"All I can say is that it's one of the weirdest sounds I ever heard in my life—a vibrating wail, like a person in great pain," said R. A. E. Morley, a geologist.

Morley, who believes it was a giant that hurled a boulder at him while he was swimming in a mountain stream, said he heard the man-animal scream one night in the Siskiyous southwest of Grants Pass.

The sound unnerved and completely deranged his dog, Morley said, and caused the animal to froth at the mouth and hide under the cabin mat.[212]

1966: Bush Beast

Two, teenage girls' story of seeing a "hairy monster" in the Lytle Creek wash north of here has turned into a no man's land of monster hunters.

Jumpy deputies from the San Bernardino County sheriff's [sic] Fontana station said 250 to 300 persons, many of them teenagers, are swarming nightly over the barren foothills, filling the night with wild gunfire.

One deputy said he took two .22-caliber automatics, a rifle and another pistol away from one adventurer.

The girls whose story set off the hunt of a "bush beast," seven feet tall, with brown hair, covered with moss and slime, which, or who, stood up beside their car.

Deputies said the hunters appear at dusk, since it is presumed that the "monster" walks by night.

A Marine on leave from Viet Nam set out to stalk the beast, but was driven out of the area by amateur trackers.

He was Don Pierce, 21, who set out with weapons, ammunition, flashlight and poncho, intending to stalk the monster the way he said he stalked the Viet Cong at night.

Pierce gave up. "It's too noisy out there," he said.[213]

1967: Florida Green Humanoid

The two teenaged couples were supposed to be attending a dance in New Port Richey, Fla., on that romantic moonlit night in January of 1967, but because of their youth and because of the still beauty of the night, they had decided not to come back after intermission but to take advantage of the seclusion of a lovers' lane near Elfers, Fla.

They had not been parked long when one of the girls complained of a disagreeable odor. Her date teased her that she should inhale deeply of the wondrous, untainted aroma of the heavy woods that surrounded their automobile. Mother Nature would be displeased to learn that some sensitive young thing had implied that she should use a deodorant.

"Look," the girl insisted. "There is a terrible smell around here. I'm as much of a nature girl as anyone here. Can't you smell it?"

By this time, all of the teenagers had to admit that they had become aware of a powerful, stifling, nauseating odor. But before anyone had time to speculate concerning a possible source of the unpleasant smell, an animal about the size of a large chimpanzee leaped onto the hood of the automobile.

"Then we panicked!" the teenaged driver told Mrs. Joan Whritenour, editor of *Saucer Scoop*. "The thing looked like a big chimp, but it was greenish in color with glowing green eyes. I started the motor and the thing jumped off and ran back into the woods. We tore like blazes back to the dance that we were supposed to be attending."

The teenagers told their story to a policeman from New Port Richey who was on duty at the dance. The officer checked the hood and found a green, sticky substance, which he scraped off with his pocketknife.

Mrs. Whritenour interviewed each of the four teenagers and found that their stories checked on all major points. None of the young people seemed interested in embellishing the tale and their strange narrative was recited simply and directly.[214]

1968: Zoo Woods Werewolf / Monster of Riverside Cemetery

"It's eight feet tall and covered with hair," declared William Schwark, of Parma who said he had a close encounter near the Cleveland Zoo with a strange creature. "I chased it Monday night and it knocked me down a slope." His cousin, Dale Schwark related another story of the creature's aggressiveness. "It's a big black thing and it grabbed my buddy, Ron, by the shoulder, ripped his jacket and shirt and left big scratches on his shoulder," he said.

With some people calling the thing a werewolf, several area teens armed themselves with plastic clothesline, and flashlights. Grace Lewis, manager at Stone's Open Grill on W. 25th Street, had a theory regarding the creature, she believed it could well be "the monster of Riverside Cemetery. I've seen him myself. He's a big hairy man weighing 400 pounds who's been living like Tarzan for 25 years. I-71 destroyed his tunnel home back of the cemetery and he's been displaced to the woods back of the zoo."

Riverside Cemetery Monster or Zoo Woods Werewolf, a reporter from the *Plain Dealer* followed area youths into the woods. The reporter was shown a broken sapling the boys believed was snapped as the creature chased several boys.

> . . . Bill Schwark had a white sheet with burn marks on it, a red flannel blanket and two white feathers.
>
> Schwark contended the blanket and sheet were part of the werewolf's costume. The white feathers were all that remained of the werewolf's chicken dinner.
>
> The *Plain Dealer* left the werewolf hunters as the moon rose over the Zoo deerpens [sic]. A white-haired housewife asked what all the excitement was about.
>
> "We're looking for a monster. Have you seen any in the woods there?"
>
> "The only monsters I've seen," said the housewife, "are the teen-agers."[215]

1968: Holton and Keitch Encounter

On a brilliantly sunny day in May, 1968, Eric Holton and Don Keitch were squatting around a campfire, frying up a couple of brook trout they had caught that morning. Don and Eric were San Franciscans, and they were in the second day of a week of camping and fishing in the Siskiyou Mountain Range near Mt. Ashland in Oregon. Except for some jays screeching, and the crackling of the fire, the campsite seemed unnaturally quiet.

Suddenly, from a rocky outcropping on the face of a cliff that rose above them, a number of rocks about the size of baseballs began to rain down on them, barely missing them and their fire.

"It really scared the hell out of us," Eric later said. "We both stood up quickly, knocking the pan and the lunch into the fire. We looked up at the ledge and saw this *thing*. That's the word that came to my mind in that first instant, *thing*. It looked about 10 feet tall, although I realize now that it only seemed that big because we were looking up at it. And it appeared to be huge, maybe eight or nine hundred pounds. A *thing*."

Both men thought it was a grizzly bear at first. And they thought it must have deliberately kicked rocks down on them as some prelude to attack. Don went for his rifle, a .300 Weatherby Magnum, an expensive gun with an expensive scope. He took a bead on the thing and was about to squeeze the trigger when Eric shouted: "No!" and pushed the barrel up into the sky.

"That's not a bear," Eric cried. "My God, that's more like a gorilla. Or a man!"

Don sighted through the scope now. Not to shoot it, but to get a good look at the thing standing 50 feet above them.

"I was able to study it for at least a couple of minutes," Don later said. "It just stood there, as if it was studying me. It was between seven and a half and eight feet tall and probably weighed about seven hundred pounds or a little more. It was covered all over with hair, its entire body except for the area around the nose, cheeks and lips. And it was hair, not fur. I've shot a couple of bear in my time, and a lot of other fur-bearing animals. This was not fur. It was a bluish-black hair, pretty long and straight on the head and then growing curly like body hair from the shoulders down.

"This thing had a pretty big head that went right into its shoulders. No neck at all. I'm sure of that, because when it turned to look from one point to another it moved its entire upper body in order to move its head. It was like the time my brother broke his neck in an auto accident and had it in a cast; he had to move around as if he didn't have a neck when he wanted to shift his line of vision. The thing moved just like that.

"It also had eyes that appeared close to human from where I was standing. There was a lot of white surrounding what appeared to be a brown iris, with a small black pupil in the center.

"And it was standing erect. It didn't look like a gorilla or chimp, that stands up with its arms dangling and has to support itself on its knuckles when it moves. This thing was standing like a human being. It moved on that ledge like a human being.

"Its shoulders were enormous. I'd guess they were close to four feet across. The body tapered down only slightly into a waist, but very definitely a waist. Then it flared out again in large hips and very large buttocks. They looked like the buttocks of a very large and obese woman, except that they were totally covered by this hair.

"I couldn't tell you what sex it was. I know I thought of it as a man, and I realize now that was because it had no breasts. But I couldn't see testicles or penis. There was an awful lot of hair in that area, and I just couldn't tell for sure although I had an impression of male sex organs.

"And I'll tell you one thing. As I watched it through the scope, I was thinking to myself that I was damned glad I hadn't taken a shot at it. Because that thing was human. Or close enough to it to make me happy I didn't shoot it."

While Don was studying the Hairy Giant, as they later began to call it, Eric had run to his pack to get his camera. He had with him a Minolta Autocord, a good Japanese twin lens reflex. He decided to try to get closer before taking a picture.

Don continued watching through the scope as the Hairy Giant moved away. Although the hill leading up from the ledge to the peak about 50 yards higher was an extremely steep incline, the Hairy Giant walked up it without having to get a hand-hold on any of the pines or hollies that covered the entire hill.

"That surprised me," Don said. "I took a good look at his feet and I could see he was digging in with his toes. They must have been damned strong toes and feet, and legs, to enable him to get up that hill like that. Because when we recovered from our surprise we tried to follow it up there, and we had a hell of a time making it to this top."

By the time Eric and Don had started after it, the Hairy Giant had vanished into the thick forest of trees. Just before moving out of sight it stopped and turned to look at the two men.

"I didn't even know what lens opening it was at, and I didn't even think about light conditions, light meter, anything like that," Eric said. "I simply started shooting, taking a guess at whether I was in focus for the first couple of shots. By the time I calmed down and started moving the focus knob, the thing began moving away. As a result, the pictures aren't too clear. They're pretty badly out of focus in fact.

"It stood there for a couple of minutes, just watching to see what we were going to do, apparently. Then it let out a weird sound. It wasn't like anything we had heard before. The best I can describe it is that it was a high, shrill whine. Something like the screech you get when you overload a tape recorder or accidentally put the line jack into the mike connection, or something like that. But it changed tone, and it changed pitch, deliberately. As if it was communicating in some way. I actually think it was a kind of speech; at least it seems possible to me."

The two men started up after the Hairy Giant. Don carried his rifle. Human or not, he wanted the protection of his Magnum is case they were attacked by this thing, or by a tribe of them.

"We never saw it again," Eric says. "But we saw plenty of evidence of it. And smelled it. All over the area at the top of the hill were large fecal droppings, huge masses of the stuff. About the size you'd expect from a big horse. It stunk like hell, the most God-awful smell we'd ever encountered. But it looked human. Except for the size and the overwhelming odor, it was as if a human being had defecated up there."

"We thought about scooping up some of it and bringing it back to have it analyzed," Don interrupted. "But it was a long way back to where we'd left the car. At least a full day's hike. So we thought better of it."

"We also found a number of footprints the thing left at the top of the hill," Eric continued. "There's a little bit of a pond there, a small pool of water fed by some underground stream I'd guess. The thing walked at the muddy edges of this pool and left a very clear and distinct set of prints. They were human in form—five toes, with the big toe sticking out like on a human foot, unopposed to the other toes; you know, not turned so that it could meet the other toes for gripping, like in a monkey's foot. Not opposed, but straight out in the same plane, just like my toes and yours.

"We didn't have a ruler. But I measured it with my boot. It was exactly one-and-a-half times my boot, and when we got back I measured my boot. Twelve inches heel to toe, so this print was 18 inches long. And it was about six inches wide at the ball.

"The fantastic thing was the length of its stride. It was maybe 60 inches long—twice as long as mine when I walk fast. That was the average stride of the couple of dozen prints we saw. They ranged between four feet and six feet long, as if the thing was hurrying, then slowed down, then started to move quickly again."

The two campers cut their vacation short and drove back to San Francisco to develop their film and report what they had seen. They had thought about going to local newspapers with their story but by the time they reached San Francisco they had decided against it. Instead, they contacted the editors of *MALE* and offered their story and pictures on the understanding their real names would not be used.

"We realized we'd probably be the targets of ridicule, that people would figure we're a couple of crackpots and give us a hard time," Eric explained. "Or we'd be called publicity seekers, and that would mess things up for us. Because we're going back up there as soon as we can arrange a couple of weeks off, and we're going to try to get one of those things alive. Or at least capture it on film. So for the time being, until we can gather more proof of what we've seen, we'd rather stay anonymous."

"We want our story printed in the hopes that other people who've had similar experiences will contact us through *MALE*," Don added. "Maybe if we generate enough interest we'll have a better chance of proving the existence of these giant men."[216]

1970 ADVERTISEMENT FOR 'BIGFOOT: AMERICA'S ABOMINABLE SNOWMAN'

CHAPTER 2
1970-71

> There have now been allegations of the discovery of such tracks in nearly every state in this Union, even to such unlikely places as Texas, Pennsylvania, and Massachusetts! Several dozen different plaster casts have been offered, together with dozens more photographs of same, several piles of excrement, two films of the creatures allegedly making said tracks, and a corpse in an ice-filled coffin. The creatures have been nicknamed Bigfeet, Sasquatches, The Iceman, Yetis, or ABSMs, and a whole cult has grown up around them with all manner of people from high school youngsters to college professors going charging off to hunt them with gun, rod, and camera as in the good old days of Poona-Poona. Literally millions of dollars have been spent on this endeavor.[217]
>
> "Tracks on Mt. Etna," *Pursuit* (January 1971).

As one decade bowed before the advent of the next, the Patterson-Gimlin film had instigated Bigfoot's rocket-like ascendency into the voguish stratosphere of mainstream appeal, presaging the pop culture heights hairy forest giants would occupy through, and beyond, the 1970s. With its beginnings at the end of the '60s, the Cripplefoot affair from northeastern Washington, though not as penetrating as the Patterson-Gimlin film's promotion proved to be, became an important event in Bigfoot's modern history with consequential ramifications. Bossburg, Washington, gained international fame in 1969 for the presence there of remarkable footprints—hundreds of them—revealed in a fresh blanket of November snow. The newswire-fed story of the tracks' discovery and the subsequent actions of investigators displayed the breadth of parochial impropriety baked into the search for Bigfoot.

Many of the biggest names and personalities involved in the Bigfoot enquiry descended upon Bossburg, and inevitably clashed. For the more serious-minded researchers, the amazing affair was capped by the discouraging realization that the quest to answer foundational questions of the phenomenon could so easily be consigned to Bigfoot's exploitation for steel-cold profit.

Bossburg & Colville

René Dahinden had been working at the Bighorn Dam site in Alberta in the late autumn of 1969 when he received a call from John Green who relayed the news that Ivan Marx had information on the whereabouts of a Sasquatch—a crippled one. Dahinden called Ivan Marx (a fellow-member in Slick's Northwest Expedition) to discuss the circumstances. Dahinden took three days to consider his conversations with Green and Marx before departing for Bossburg.

November 24 marked the tracks' discovery in snow near the Bossburg community trash dump by James "Joe" Rhodes, a Colville butcher. The large footprints suggested a bipedal creature, the right foot of which gave the impression of a crippled or malformed appendage. This malformity was woven into a theory for the creature's presence in Colville: the animal's mobility had become so impaired it was forced to scrounge at human dump sites for scraps of food. The area had had several Bigfoot sightings earlier in the year; Green wrote that several track reports had come to Marx's attention during the previous months (Marx had, with apparent fortuitous timing, moved from Burney, California, to Bossburg, Washington, in 1969).[218] By the time Dahinden arrived at the scene, many of the tracks Rhodes had discovered had been badly damaged by curious people desiring their own first-hand look. One print had been protected by a box placed over it; it was the print of the creature's apparently deformed right foot. Dahinden photographed this print and made a cast of it. During the next few days Dahinden remained in the area making notes, talking to people and absorbing the atmosphere and mood of the place. Bob Titmus, at the time living in Kitimat, B.C., soon arrived and as Don Hunter put it, "the actors were gathering," for a performance that would become one of the indelible events of Bigfoot history. Dahinden said of Titmus:

> "He went out and bought an eight-pound slab of beef and hung it in a tree. I believe he was sitting out there at night in his panel truck, watching the meat, and thinking that if this

> *was* a cripple and *was* living off the garbage dump, when it came along he would just grab it by the arse and throw it in the truck and run off home with it."[219]

A basket of fruit was later added, suspended six feet off the ground in a tree by Norm "Dickie" Davis, owner of the Colville radio station (KCVL). Hunter wrote that Dahinden thought these attempts to lure a Sasquatch were "frivolous." After three days and no sign of the creature, Titmus departed for home in British Columbia. Dahinden was still intrigued by the crippled print, the likes of which he had never encountered before. He made a deal with Davis—Dahinden could remain in the area living in a trailer owned by Davis (later moved onto Ivan Marx's property), and in return Dahinden would give showings of the Patterson-Gimlin film to local service clubs and other interested groups. Dahinden was by now working with Marx and on December 13 their efforts paid off.

> Several inches of snow had covered the ground that morning when René and Ivan Marx and a young local named Jim Hopkins set out in Marx's car to check an area along the banks of Roosevelt Lake, the reservoir for the Grand Coolie dam. They checked the bank for about four miles, examining spots where meat scraps had been dropped by René earlier in the off-the-beat locations, but found nothing. Near a railway crossing, where the railroad and the highway run close to the Columbia River, they stopped and Marx climbed out to check a small meat cache a little way along a side road. Just before stopping, they had passed a jeep parked by the roadside. Marx was away from the car only seconds before he came racing back:
>
> "Bigfoot tracks!" he shouted.
>
> René was filling his pipe. He kept on filling it, peering over the bowl at Marx, waiting for the kicker, the grin that would say, "Okay, joke over." It didn't come. Instead Marx jumped into the car, whipped it round, and headed back down the road, rapping out in his excitement that he needed photographic equipment.[220]

Later, the Sasquatch-hunters found and spoke with the jeep's occupants who admitted they had also seen the enigmatic tracks, whereupon they decided to leave the scene quickly. Dahinden, Marx, and Hopkins soon returned to the tracks, bringing cameras and, in Dahinden's case, a loaded gun. This was Dahinden's first opportunity to see a fresh spread of cripple tracks, which were judged to be only about 15 hours old. The left "normal" footprint measured 17 ½ inches long, 6 ½ inches across the ball of the foot, and 5 ½ inches across the heel. The right foot was bent: 16 ½ inches long, 7 inches across the ball, and 5 ½ inches at the heel. The right foot's impression in the snow gave scant evidence of the third toe. The track-maker was heavy enough that compressed snow in the bottom of the tracks could be picked up as a solid chunk (a result of both compression and weather conditions). The three men followed the trail, eventually counting 1,089 tracks. The track-maker had walked away from the river, crossed the railroad, a main road, and apparently stepped over a 43-inch-high wire fence. Managing to get themselves over the fence, the men found a depression in conifer needles under a thick cluster of pine trees. One of the nearby cows could not be discounted as having made the depression, but its location in the line of the trackway and the fact that within its shape a clump of snow compressed in the familiar shape of the left footprint conjured to some minds the creature stopping for a bit of respite. By this stage in his Sasquatch-hunting career, Dahinden had learned to exercise care and caution. But his next words belie the enthusiastic feeling the men must have shared: "Now we're going to get that hairy sonofabitch!" The trail ascended up a hill and it was the flattened terrain beyond the crest upon which Dahinden expected to run his quarry to ground. But the prints eventually went back down the hill, paralleling the ascending path. At one point the men found two side-by-side prints where the creature had apparently stopped to relieve itself. The prints continued back to the wire fence, crossing over it again only 50 feet from where the men had followed it earlier in the opposite direction.

> From there the tracks led the hunters across the road and back and over the fence several times, and eventually across the road and the railroad, through a patch of bush and to the edge of a steep part of the river bank, about one hundred and fifty feet above the water. There the bank was overhanging. The tracks turned and went upstream for approximately two hundred feet, to a point where the bank sloped gradually down to the river, and there they stopped. All the way down the bank was a deep groove, as one made by a heel and a foot acting as a brake for an upright body "skiing" down the bank. Below that there was just rocks; no further markings.[221]

Careful inspection revealed the tracks could be traced to and from Lake Roosevelt. A cautious Dahinden became apprehensive in accepting the tracks as authentic. But after further scrutiny and study his dubious wariness gave way to acquiescence. John Green in *The Year of the Sasquatch:*

> In the beginning René was rather suspicious of those tracks. For one thing he didn't like them appearing in a place where he or Ivan was sure to see them in checking the bobcat bait. He took the best part of a day, therefore, to study them one by one. At the end of it he was thoroughly satisfied that they had been made by living feet capable of toe movements and adjustments to the terrain. The most puzzling thing about them was the way in which they returned to the lake. The bank there is very steep and perhaps 100 feet high. It is made of gravel and that day it was frozen. Whatever made the tracks had slid down the bank, gouging a trough not only in the snow, but in the frozen gravel, then had jumped clear, into the water several feet above the edge.[222]

Several questions came to Dahinden. It seemed very convenient that the tracks were found in a place known for his frequent presence as he canvassed the area. He spent the best part of the day walking the trail of the tracks seven times, examining each and every print, focused on gleaning every scrap of information they revealed. The tracks were discreet and localized, they gave no specific answer to where the creature had come from or gone to. Dahinden noticed what appeared to be significantly more compression in the right track compared to the left, leaving him to conclude the right leg of the creature was shorter than the left. Further speculation proposed the creature may have met with an injury dislocating the shin bone. Dahinden ultimately became satisfied that the prints were made by a living foot displaying toe movements; his analysis convinced him the creature weighed about 800 pounds judging by the four-inch depth of the prints in the snow around Colville. "The prints," said Dahinden, "were too deep to have been put there by a human dressed up as an ape."[223]

Dahinden remained puzzled, however, as to the print-maker's return to the lake at a location where the bank was very high—about 100 feet.

> At that point the Columbia River is backed up behind Grand Coulee Dam and is known as Lake Roosevelt. The tracks began at the edge of the lake, and returned to it.

> Of course the fact that the tracks came out of the water and went back to it does not establish that the creature was spending its time in a hole in the bank. It probably swam from somewhere else. No more tracks were found in a search of that side of the river, but across it, on the west bank and some miles upstream, the same tracks were reported seen, made on about the same day, headed away from the river.[224]

Dahinden's focus on the known prints caused a rift between himself and Davis, the latter convinced that emphasis should be placed on finding new tracks. In that belief, Davis contacted Titmus, pleading for him to come back and get the hunt for new signs back on track. Meanwhile the fame of the tracks was spreading. A bus driver on a British Columbia to Spokane run stopped his bus, and according to Hunter reversed his vehicle 100 yards. He told his passengers that the activity they could see outside was due to Sasquatch prints, which he just had to see. Grabbing a box camera, he left his passengers staring out their windows, and he photographed his own souvenir of the event.

Within a week, a U.S. border patrol officer found new tracks on the other side of the river. The area was off-limits to the public and frequented only by logging company personnel. When discovered, the prints had been washed out to a degree by recent rains but enough detail remained to convince some they were a match to Cripplefoot.

> By this time René had been joined by Roy Fardell from B.C. and Roger St. Hilaire, a young zoologist from San Francisco. Together they considered the question of faking: on this side of the river the prints were perfectly located for discovery; on the other side they were in a spot virtually never used, where all the access gates were kept locked by the logging company. If the prints on this side had been faked, surely whoever had made them would have planted the ones on the far bank in an equally accessible place, to complete the hoax. (The persistent reversion into pessimism over tracks and other evidence is as much a constant of the serious Sasquatch hunter's character as his determination to resolve the mystery.) The consensus—while it remained firm—was that the tracks were genuine.[225]

Roger Patterson arrived and had an intermittent presence, but his colleague, Dennis Jensen, remained in the vicinity. The December and January months were spent hunting the crippled Bigfoot, using trucks, snowmobiles and planes. As Hunter noted, the longer the search went on, the grimmer became Dahinden's suspicion that the whole thing was the result of a hoax.

An assistant professor of physical anthropology, and one of the few scientists to make Bigfoot a central point of his academic interest and study, Grover Krantz had arrived at Washington State University in 1968. Krantz went on to become inextricably involved with Bigfoot thanks to the Bossburg tracks. After classes let out for the Christmas holidays in mid-December, Krantz traveled to Bossburg. Author Brian Regal picks up the story from his book, *Searching for Sasquatch:*

> Once there, Krantz met John Green who had only just arrived himself. Krantz admired Green's book, intrigued by his use of *Gigantopithecus*. Green liked the idea of finally finding an academic sympathetic to his ideas. Luckily, someone had protected one of the better tracks by covering it with a cardboard box and newspapers. The anthropologist and the journalist went to see it. Finding the spot and carefully removing the protective covering, the anthropologist leaned down to examine the first live Sasquatch track he had ever seen. As Krantz squatted there in the snow with his wool cap and rubber boots, staring into a foot-shaped destiny, Green took out his camera and snapped a picture, recording the moment for posterity. Krantz may have not realized it at that moment, but he had just turned permanently from skeptic to believer. In that moment an obsessive career he had never dreamed of began in earnest.[226]

In January, while Dahinden was occupied showing the Patterson-Gimlin film on a circuit of the Calgary area, two men arrived on the scene: Joe Metlow and Bill Streeter. The visitors had a simple question—how much would one pay for a Sasquatch? Dennis Jensen explained that money would hardly be a consideration given the monumental importance of a Sasquatch for scientific study. When Metlow said he had one and it was for sale, a bidding frenzy ensued. Metlow explained he had spotted a cream-colored Bigfoot on January 27 while he had been checking his claim lines. Metlow had come up from behind the creature which remained oblivious to his presence. As Metlow watched from about 80 yards away, the creature engaged itself in some activity, possibly digging ferns from the snow and eating the roots. Streeter's role in the meeting was apparently to confirm his companion's story as told to Jensen was the same one Metlow had told him. Afterwards, amid the ensuing drama, Streeter appears to have drifted away and out of the story. Metlow avoided specifics but gave the impression that he had immobilized the creature in an old mine shaft.

> He [Metlow] said nothing more about how much he had been offered, or by whom. Jensen was sold. He stressed to Metlow that the only source of any money worth considering among the Sasquatch hunters was at Northwest Research Association (another name for Roger Patterson) in Yakima, and that he would contact his principals immediately. He did, and Patterson directed him to keep the talking going, and to keep the Dahinden crowd out of it. Schism.[227]

Dahinden, Roy Fardell, and Roger St. Hilaire pieced together the story which led them to Metlow. With Metlow identified, Dahinden and company deduced the general area he would have been in on January 27, a few miles to the north on Frisco Standard.

In the meantime, Patterson had been in touch with his backer Tom Page, an Ohio businessman. Page flew out to Washington and he and Patterson huddled with Metlow. After this meeting the Patterson camp lifted and shifted operations to a hotel in Colville. As Don Hunter put it, "the divorce was final." A doleful Dahinden explained to Hunter, "I thought it had been all for one and one for all before this, but that's not the way it worked out." Dahinden, who was in Calgary, was able to talk with Metlow by phone but was unable to determine to his satisfaction that the prospector actually possessed what he claimed. Page, in the meantime had put a helicopter on alert at the Colville airport, ready to extract a Bigfoot. Danny Striker from the Colville *Statesman Examiner* reportedly staked out the Patterson hotel anticipating crucial events were in the offing. Ivan Marx attempted to stay neutral. "If you tell me anything," Marx is reported to have said, "and the other guys ask me, I'll tell them, so better not tell me anything." Page offered Metlow $1,000 to confirm the location of the Bigfoot in a mine, but though no money is known to have swapped hands, Metlow eventually confirmed the site was on Frisco Standard. Page, Patterson, and others in their group traveled to the top of Frisco Standard and started their tromp down on snowshoes. The Dahinden group were airborne themselves, flying in a fixed wing plane around Frisco Standard, wagging their wings at Patterson's party. Metlow did not officially accept any offer but was still stoking the coals to raise the competitive bidding. Bids kept increasing: $35,000, $40,000, and $50,000. As news came in, Dahinden's group would relay the info back to him, sometimes by excited phone calls at 2 A.M. Dahinden had a simple strategy: top the last bid. Dahinden called Green and asked him to go to Colville and look after their interests. Green is said to have traveled between the two camps, as Hunter coyly put it, "seeing where the best deal lay for himself."

> René's final bid, made as he recalls, "from a motel in Calgary where I was without a pot to piss in," was for $55,000. It was enough to call Metlow's bluff. The prospector walked away from the affair, still uncommitted as to the truthfulness or otherwise of his story. Whether René could have raised the $55,000 remains academic—but chances are that he couldn't.[228]

On a visit back in Bossburg, Dahinden, accompanied by Jensen, visited Metlow at his home. In their conversation, Metlow mentioned he was in possession of a Sasquatch foot stored away in his freezer. Immediately, Dahinden offered $500 for a look at it. Metlow raised the price to $5,000.

> The excitement brought Dickie Davis to the scene, antennae quivering. Before you could say, "Bigfoot," Davis had a contract sketched out. It would include John Green to write the book, Bob Titmus to skin and dissect the foot's owner—presumably stashed in a cave somewhere above the snow line—and anthropologist Grover Krantz to introduce it to science. René was out, so was Patterson.[229]

The *Montana Standard* ran a story on the Metlow proceedings which indicated the broad level of interest and participation amongst the involved Bigfoot hunters and researchers.

> An estimated 50 men were combing the rugged country of northeastern Washington Saturday for signs of a shaggy, cream-colored, man-like beast known as a [S]asquatch or "[B]igfoot."

> This latest of a number of searches for the legendary [S]asquatch was touched off Tuesday when prospector Joe Metlow of Valley, Wash., reported he had seen one of the creatures feeding near his mining claim in northern Stevens County, near the Washington-British Columbia border.
>
> Metlow said the beast was about nine feet tall and weighed an estimated 1,000 pounds. The prospector claims the hairy beast, standing erect like an ape, was scraping snow away from ferns with its front "hands" and eating the plant roots.
>
> The report was picked up by a large number of dedicated [S]asquatch, or "[B]igfoot" hunters in this northeastern Washington community and relayed to others who have pursued sighting of giant tracks, supposedly belonging to the animal for years.
>
> Two professional [S]asquatch hunting groups were spearheading the latest search. One group is the Northwest Research Assn., headed by Roger Patterson of Yakima, Wash., and a Canadian group headed by René Dahinden of British Columbia. Another of the searchers is an unidentified Washington State Game Dept. inspector.
>
> The search was not started until late in the week because Metlow refused to divulge exactly where he saw the live [S]asquatch until someone pays him what he considers a proper price for the information. One report is that he has rejected a $55,000 offer.
>
> But on Friday, groups of hunters left Colville by plane, helicopter, in various vehicles and on snowshoes in an attempt to find the beast on their own.[230]

At this point Metlow began to change his story: he didn't have the foot stashed in his freezer, instead it was in his sister's freezer, near Portland. Davis footed the bill for two tickets to Portland—one for him and one for Metlow. Just before getting to the airport, Metlow slipped on ice and claimed his ankle was injured. Metlow told Davis to go on, he would get his ankle fixed right up and no-kidding catch the next flight to Portland. Davis went ahead and stayed two days in Portland, waiting. Davis tried frantically to reach Metlow but after two days returned to northeastern Washington. "I was real sick, Dickie," Metlow reportedly said, "I couldn't make it." The Metlow affair was exhausted and the gathered Bigfoot hunters took stock of the situation, packed their bags and left. "It's a pity it happened; it was stupid and it gave the business a bad name," Dahinden said of the affair. "But then in a way I'm not sorry it happened. It taught me a lot about the people I had been working with." But the Metlow business aside, there were still the crippled footprints. Back in Vancouver, Dahinden kept a finger on the Bossburg pulse by remaining in touch with Marx. Marx was reporting a string of successes during these calls—a new track here, a handprint over there, a bedding site discovered. Bossburg offered every indication that it remained a Bigfoot hotspot.

In October 1970, during one of these calls with Dahinden, Marx shared the news that he had filmed the crippled Bigfoot. As noted by Hunter, Danny Striker wrote up the story of the film for the *Statesman-Examiner*:

> On the night of Oct. 6 an unidentified person called the Marx home, leaving a vague message that either a car or train had struck a large upright creature on the highway about seven miles north of Bossburg. Marx was away at the time but when he received the message . . . he left immediately for the area with a hunting dog he hoped would follow the spoor of the Sasquatch, if indeed that was what it actually was.
>
> Marx was armed with nothing more than a Bolex 16mm movie camera with a 17mm lens, a 35mm Nikon and a two-way radio with which he had contact with rancher Don Byington, who was in the area by the time Marx's dog had located the creature.
>
> The day was heavily overcast with smoke . . . when Marx jumped the creature in the bottom of a dense draw and began filming. The initial footage shows a large black upright figure moving stealthily but rapidly through the dense growth, but only in silhouette.
>
> Marx pressed the pursuit with his hound, forcing the Sasquatch into a clearing where, with his movie camera set at f2.8 he took the remarkably clear footage of an impressive looking creature.
>
> On the screen the Sasquatch is shown moving from right to left at an angle of about forty-five degrees away from the photographer. Distance from the subject according to Marx ranged from twenty-five feet to more than a hundred feet as it made its way into the heavy underbrush on the far side of the clearing.

> Probably the most impressive part of the film, besides its extreme clarity, is the fact that the Sasquatch is visibly injured, holding its right arm tightly to its chest and using its long muscular left arm for compensating balance.
>
> Also, both ankles of the creature seem badly skinned, the wounds showing plainly raw against the black hair of the legs and feet.
>
> In watching the frames singly, the injured or skinned area appears to extend onto the bottom of one foot, and possibly on both feet, which would account for the apparent pain-filled movements of the frightened creature.
>
> As the Sasquatch is nearing the far side of the clearing, a twisted tree limb is stepped on, bouncing up and striking it above knee level. Marx, the following day, photographed this stick which was ten feet long. In comparison the creature photographed would have stood about nine feet tall and Marx estimated its weight as that of two large bears, or around seven to eight hundred pounds.[231]

"This movie should prove to everybody, once and for all, that Bigfoot does exist. The only thing that could offer more proof will come when we capture him. That I hope will come before this time next year," Marx told the AP about a month after the film was alleged to have been made.

> Only a handful of people, including two newsmen, had seen the colored movie as of Friday [November 13, 1970]. But if Marx is successful in his selling effort, the film will be shown publicly, likely by an adventure film promoter.
>
> About two minutes of the film are footage of the Bigfoot, taken from about 100 feet away.[232]

Marx elaborated for reporters on the steps he had taken leading up to filming something which he called a Bigfoot. "We'd heard reports that Bigfoot had been hit by a train or something like that. We had an idea of the general area where he was and it didn't take long for my dogs to sniff him out," Marx said. "When we spotted him, he was on all fours in this real thick stuff (underbrush)," he said. The barely discernable creature crawled on all fours in the thick underbrush before it hobbled through a sunlit clearing, twice looking back at the camera. A reporter noted the fleshy ankles of the creature, a point which Marx addressed: "This shows wounds against his black hair," which Marx postulated had been caused by the creature's brush with civilization.[233]

Finer facial features were not captured by the film. As the creature made its way across the clearing it glanced back twice at Marx. The first time it looked back Marx reported it uttered a "weird scream" which Byington reportedly heard from his position on an adjacent ridge. Marx said he tailed the creature until dark and picked up its trail again the following day. The discernable path of the creature through the rough and rugged environment finally terminated at a body of water.[234]

"We wanted to continue the hunt for him, that's why we didn't release the word right away," Marx said. Marx claimed to have "found several thousand" tracks belonging to the creature "and spots where he has had a good time rolling in the dust." Marx stated several plaster casts were made from some of the larger, better defined prints. "I'd say there are about five of them living up there. And I think this one we photographed is young and I'm sure he's a male," Marx announced.[235]

"We know his habits and what to look for. I think he's holed-up for the winter now. There just hasn't been any more tracks to speak of and if they were there I'd seen them cause I'm out with hunters everyday." At this point, Marx thought about his further involvement in Bigfoot matters. "I don't want to kill him, so this winter I'll be taking my dogs back in. I'm sure they'll be able to find where he's hibernating, just like other dogs find lost skiers buried by avalanches," Marx said. Marx believed that Bigfoot spent the winter sheltered under boughs of trees weighed down by snow.[236]

"If we get him this winter, we'll tie him up just to get a good look at him. Then I don't care if they pass a law outlawing hunting and killing of Bigfoot," Marx said. "I've seen him, so I'm sure it's not," [a gag or hoax] he stated. "If somebody was going to try and pull a gag, I don't think they'd be walking 20 and more miles back into the woods to make tracks." In common with many Bigfoot researchers, Marx came back to the enigmatic footprints. "Besides," he added, "the tracks are just too real."[237]

Dahinden arrived in Bossburg and was prosaic on Marx's claims: "Ivan has a movie and that leaves only two choices. Either it is real or it is not. That's what I'm here to find out." As Don Hunter wrote, the "second siege of Bossburg" began shortly thereafter. Hunter noted Ivan Sanderson phoned on behalf of *Argosy* magazine and Tom Page offered Marx a check for $25,000 for a copy of the film. But Marx apparently was unwilling to confirm or deny his film's authenticity which Hunter suggested should have called its legitimacy into question. Dahinden did not dismiss the film, at least in part for the corroboration provided by Marx's wife of her husband's story. John Green arrived and pronounced the film authentic, offering Marx $800 for a copy of the film. Green sent an update to George Haas for the *Bigfoot Bulletin*.

> The movie is of the crippled creature. He [Marx] tracked it with a dog after it was reported hit on the highway. The movie is several times as long as Patterson's and is of professional quality. It shows a creature 9-10 feet tall and quite thin, with both heels stripped raw of hide, hobbling painfully away. Unfortunately the sun was already down and while the light was sufficient for every other color it shows no details at all of the black creature, just a sharply outlined black shape. There are hundreds of good frames, however, and careful study of individual frames may show a great deal.[238]

In the same edition of the *Bigfoot Bulletin*, San Francisco zoologist Roger St. Hilaire wrote:

> Presently we (myself and René Dahinden) are living in a house next door to Ivan Marx. We have been searching the area where the film was made and also adjacent areas within about a 10-15 mile radius of the film site. Since there is no snow at the lower elevations and since the ground in most places is frozen, it is going to be very difficult to find any tracks of the creature. Right now we need about 2″ of snow! I intend to remain here until about mid-December and I believe René expects to be here about the same length of time. Of course if anything significant is found we will stay longer.
>
> Both of us have seen most of Ivan's pictures and other evidence. The general thought is that everything is authentic. Of course as you well know there will always be some question until the creature is caught or killed.[239]

Amongst the buzz at this time was talk of certain individuals knowing the precise location Marx obtained his Bigfoot footage. Don Byington, the rancher who had been in radio contact with Marx on the day of the filming, had two children who were rumored to know the film site's location, but no one apparently paid them much mind. Following Marx's trumpeting of his sensational film, Peter Byrne extended an unusual offer to Marx.

> Then on the scene came Peter Byrne, a British adventurer and hunter who had been part of the Tom Slick-sponsored expeditions in the Himalayas and in Southern California. Byrne still had a source of financing and he and Marx came to an arrangement: Marx would be paid a monthly retainer as a Sasquatch hunter of $750, and his film would be placed in a bank safety-deposit box as security.[240]

Along with the monthly retainer Byrne outfitted Marx with new Bigfoot-hunting equipment. Marx claimed "five helpers and several hunting dogs" worked for him during this arrangement which lasted into the spring of 1971. Funding was reportedly provided through the International Wildlife Conservation Society, Inc., of Washington D. C. Marx went on to create 640 slides from his Bigfoot film shot in October which he found had commercial value.

> Marx said his pictures of the animal have been purchased by the National Wildlife Federation, which plans to document the capture of the first [S]asquatch.
>
> "But first we have to catch it," [Marx] said.[241]

Marx's lucky streak continued as an amazing track discovery engendered strong reactions from skeptics and believers alike. A UPI article with dateline of Arden, Washington, from February 1971 stated thousands of tourists flocked to the small lumbering in northeastern Washington to see some of the thousands of 16-inch-long Bigfoot footprints.

> They come to gaze at more than 5,000 of the big footprints said have been made by the hairy, apelike animal who weighs an estimated 800 pounds and has a stride of 50 to 55 inches.
>
> Ivan Marx, a veteran hunter and guide who has been tracking the Sasquatch for two years, said the creature walked all around Harvey Hall's grocery store in this tiny northeastern

> Washington community last week, went to the city dump and then returned to the wilderness.
>
> He said dogs were unable to pick up the scent and follow the huge monster because rains, which fell soon after the Sasquatch appeared, washed away any scent.
>
> "If we can get to where my dogs can pick up its scent, we'll take it," said Marx. "Plans are to heavily tranquilize the Sasquatch once we capture it. Then we'll photograph it and scientifically document as much about the animal as possible before releasing it."[242]

W. W. Wendt examined tracks left in semi-frozen mud at the dump; the left print showed a possible malformation or injury. "They're definitely not bear tracks, or that of any other known animal," said Marx.[243] "This animal weighs about 500 pounds," he explained. "It's not nearly as big as the one I photographed." Among those named as on hand to examine the tracks were William J. Harper, U.S. Border Patrolman.[244] Marx traced the Arden visitor's journey: it had trekked around Harvey Hall's grocery store, visited the city dump and then headed off into the wilderness. Upon examining the tracks and reading the sign, Marx declared he'd encountered them before. The creature was missing the little toe on its left foot which Marx believed was lost to a trap several years previously.[245]

The first footprints in Arden were discovered on Monday, February 15th, near a grain field. Local farmer Ernie H. Sackman said, "I hadn't seen the tracks, but they definitely weren't made by a man using a board to make the prints" an assertion Sackman may not have been in a position to accurately make. "He had been jollying around here," said Marx indicating the scattered pattern of the tracks. Near the banks of the Colville river, Marx said he had found additional tracks about five days old in otherwise undisturbed snow.[246]

Again, Bigfoot was drawing tourist and curiosity seekers to the area. Sasquatch was selected as the mascot of the Spokane Community College and bumper stickers proliferated proclaiming, "Save our Sasquatch." Norm Davis guessed 40-50 per cent of the residents believed that Sasquatch existed. John Green had a note for the doubting cynics: "In my opinion there can be little value in a skepticism that questions things almost no one accepts. It is the skeptics that question general beliefs who have a contribution to make."[247] Boons to tourism made some people take notice and editorialize on the benefits of a local monster:

> It's said that the tourist business has picked up in Washington since the bulabaloo about the Sasquatch began which gives me a small idea which I offer, without charge, to Lysander Dudley and the [West Virginian] tourist commission. While West Virginia doesn't have a Sasquatch we do have the Braxton County monster and Mothman. They aren't as well known as Sasquatch simply because they haven't received as much publicity. But with the proper promotion they could become tourist attractions rivaling the Sinks of Gandy. Get busy up there, Lysander.[248]

Agreements and collaboration could be a fickle quality in the early days of Bigfoot-hunting; rivalries seemed just as common (perhaps more so) than cooperative efforts. Byrne's association with Marx underscored by the monthly retainer paid him was about to run into its own unique problems, with familiar consequences of a broken trust.

> This arrangement carried through to the spring of 1971, Marx being comfortably subsidized to pursue his hunting while at the same time Peter Byrne was considerably less gullible than might have seemed. The Byington children kept harping, as kids will, about how they knew exactly where the film had been shot, and Byrne listened to them. The children led the hunters to a spot at the back of the Byington property immediately recognizable as the film site.[249]

Peter Byrne studied the film location and made comparative analysis with the film itself. His diligence informed him the Bigfoot in the film was only a human dressed up in a furry costume.[250]

> Byrne said a group of area residents who have been close to the Sasquatch story for several years, compared slides from the film with the physical features of the area photographed and determined the creature is less than 6 feet in height.
>
> The man said to have made the color film, Ivan Marx, a professional big game guide, claimed the furry beast to be 8-feet-six inches.
>
> "The film was not made north of Bossburg," said Byrne. "It was made northeast of Evans, about 10 miles from where Marx claims it was."

> Byrne also said a camera equipped with a telescopic lens mounted on a tripod was used to take the film. Marx claimed his camera was at close range when he filmed the Sasquatch.
>
> Marx could not be reached for comment Thursday. A sign reading "Gone Fishing" hung on the door of his nearby Bossburg home.[251]

The April 1971 edition of *Pursuit* magazine stated "we have received reports and visits from several members who have seen Mr. Marx's film and still pictures. These members are the best informed on 'sasquatchery' that we have; are hard-nosed investigators, two of them with police training; and all lean to the sceptical [sic] though retaining an open-minded approach to the problem. All of them state that they could find no evidence of fraud, nor could they think of any way in which what is shown in these pictures could have been 'set up' to perpetrate a fraud." The write-up went on to state film rights had been optioned by a company in Salt Lake City, though a contract had not been drawn up at the time of the article's writing. The article ended, perhaps hopefully and based upon a phone call between Marx and Ivan Sanderson, that Marx agreed to travel east in June or July to present his material to a closed session of Society for the Investigation of the Unexplained (SITU) Scientific Advisory Board members.[252]

But *Pursuit's* optimistic tone on Marx quickly changed. Peter Byrne had sent the following missive to SITU which was published in following (July) issue of *Pursuit*.

> "I am sending you half a dozen slides taken from the Marx film of the '[S]asquatch.' For your interest, the 'creature' in these pictures, which is either Ivan Marx or another man in a fur suit, is no more than six feet in height. The lowest branches of the locust tree, under which he passes in picture No. 273 are between 6 ft 1 in and 6 ft 2 ins from ground level. You will also notice in the picture a white 'glimmer' in the left background. This is water, a small lake in the trees. Marx claimed that he took these pictures at a distance of between 20 and 30 ft with an ordinary lens. However, if this had been done the water would not show in the picture. The water can only be seen from a higher elevation and this elevation can only be obtained by backing up a small hill (which does not show in the foreground) and shooting the scene from this hill with a

> telescopic lens. This is what Marx did. He used a telescopic lens, with a tripod. But he did not have a tele(photo) lens with him on the day that he supposedly photographed the [S]asquatch (Oct. 7th)."[253]

Byrne's letter provided points of qualified "proof" pointing to the Marx film as mere hokey fabrication. These points include an Evans man who claimed to have seen Marx purchase old fur coats from a Goodwill Store in Spokane in August of 1970 and Don Byington's son's identification of the location of the filming which happened to be on Byington's property, not the location where Marx claimed the film was to have been made.[254]

As the whole story unraveled, Marx left the area. Hunter noted that when Byrne went to the bank, he found only a roll of exposed film. On Wednesday, March 31, another befuddlement came to light. Ray L. Pickens of Colville stepped forward to say that he had made fake Bigfoot tracks around Colville because "I just wanted to show that anybody could fake them."

> There are those who say our Bigfoot is just one big hoax. And, there are those who feel there is a lot of truth in the old fellow. Some people know he exists because they say they have SEEN him.
>
> For all those who are serious about Bigfoot, there are those who goof up the work by pulling a "funny stunt." Nothing serious, nothing harmful—but it is enough to make a true believer turn to drink.[255]

Pickens, a bricklayer from Colville, said he had made Bigfoot tracks in and around Colville from several pairs of oversized wooden feet which he affixed to the soles of boots. He fabricated the sets of wooden feet from 2 x 10 lumber and each weighed about 11 pounds. "I wore the first set just after I made them," said Pickens, "February 13." This was two days before the tracks were found in a grain field. "Then the Sasquatch hunters around here started saying there was a family of creatures. So besides Bigfoot, we made a Middle Foot and a Little Foot."[256] The three sets of feet measured 16, 14, and 12 inches long.

Pickens went on six forays into the woods to place his faux footprints. "The stride I made was about 54 inches, not at all hard to make. You can do the same—just trot." Pickens said two other individuals wore the Middle Foot and Little Foot apparatuses, and though he declined to name them, Pickens confirmed they were an adult and a child. Pickens said many people knew he had hoaxed tracks and "they've encouraged us to keep doing it." Pickens was well aware of the Bossburg tracks. "I think someone else made those," he told a reporter. "I've never denied making tracks. If someone asked me, I'd say, 'You bet' and then they'd want to know more," Pickens stated. "I'll give up on it now because I've proved my point."[257]

Bossburg; Colville; Arden—northeastern Washington had been an epicenter of Bigfoot investigation, attracting a host of luminaries in the Bigfoot research field—Byrne, Patterson, Dahinden, and Krantz among them. Amateurs, professional scientists, and enthusiasts engaged in the hunt, and, too, the frenzy. Several alliances were tested and eventually broken over the first set of 1,089 tracks and subsequent events. The influence of the Colville experience and the cripple foot tracks was far-reaching; as Brian Regal notes in the case of Grover Krantz, "it marked the point at which an American academic scientist began to take the Sasquatch phenomenon seriously and pursue it actively and publicly over an extended period."[258]

Into the 1970s—Movers and Shakers

Grover Krantz

Grover Sanders Krantz was born on November 5, 1931, in Salt Lake City, the son of Swedish immigrants. His childhood was divided between Salt Lake City and Rockford, Illinois. In 1949 he began his undergraduate study at the University of Utah which was postponed for 18 months upon his entry into the United States Air Force in 1951. After honorable discharge, Krantz matriculated at the University of California, Berkley where he earned his undergraduate and master's degrees in Anthropology. He earned his doctorate in physical anthropology in 1970 from the University of Minnesota.[259]

During his career, Krantz was considered an expert on hominoid evolution and primate bone structure. From 1968 to 1998, Krantz was a professor of anthropology at Washington State University in Pullman, Washington. Counted among his areas of interest were gender identification of skeletons, early human immigration into North America, and a public attentiveness paid to cryptozoological matters—notably Bigfoot.[260]

Krantz' fascination with anomalous primates began as early as high school when he read accounts of the Himalayan Yeti. Soon he became aware of Yeti-like creatures roaming the North American wilderness through authors like Heuvelmans and Sanderson. Krantz visited Bluff Creek in 1964 and went to the location where Jerry Crew had made his footprints discovery. The idea of undiscovered primates in the Pacific Northwest intrigued Krantz despite finding the available evidence wanting.[261]

At the start of his involvement in the subject of Bigfoot, Krantz vacillated in his acceptance of giant anomalous primates in North America. That equivocal position began to perceptibly resolve following the Patterson-Gimlin film's publicity. The first grainy photos published in *Argosy* magazine left him remaining skeptical, but his first viewing of the full film captivated him. Krantz saw a high degree of realism in the creature's movements and he began the shift from sideline interest to active participation in research.

The Cripplefoot tracks at Bossburg, Washington, gave Krantz his first occasion to see Bigfoot-attributed footprints *in situ* and tracks attributed to hairy hominids would remain, throughout his career, the lynchpin to his belief of Bigfoot as an extant creature. The efficacy of genuine tracks was a point made (among others) in his letter to Roger Patterson, dated September 22, 1970.

> Dear Mr. Patterson:
> For your information, the following is a brief outline of my interest in, and conclusions regarding, the Bigfoot or Sasquatch phenomenon.
>
> In 1953 I first heard about reports of this giant man-like creature in Western North America, and have been gradually accumulating information on the subject since then.
>
> Thus far I have examined plaster casts of footprints of 17 different individuals, observed and cast one print myself, and have seen photographs of tracks and track casts of at least 50 more. I have also talked with six people, besides yourself, who have seen a Sasquatch, and have received second-hand reports of several more.
>
> A careful analysis of the tracks has led me to infer a not-quite-human anatomy of the foot. This anatomy also corresponds quite closely with my deductions of how an otherwise human foot would have to be modified to carry a body weight of 500 to 700 pounds or more. Because of the agreement between these two sets of observations I have come to the conclusion that the tracks (or at least most of them) must be genuine. Even if no Sasquatch had ever been seen, the nature of the tracks would indicate their existence.

Admittedly, I am still bothered by the fact that no Bigfoot has ever been captured for study, nor any proven physical remains of one discovered. Only its presumed rarity, nocturnal habits, shyness, and its disturbingly man-like appearance would explain why many of them have not been killed.

Prehistoric remains of this type of Hominid (near human) may already be known. Fossilized jaws and teeth known as *Gigantopithecus* found in South China and India are from primates about as large as the Sasquatch and may well be early specimens of the type. It is also possible that the Sasquatch is a form of *Australopithecus*, or still another type which is not known from the fossil record. One of my main interests in this matter is to settle the question of exactly what it is. Its discovery will go far in solving several problems concerning the origin of man.

My plans for future investigations include both field explorations and contacts with people who might have new information. I expect to continue frequent trips into areas where Bigfoot presence is likely, with particular emphasis on trying to find their bones. I will remain in close contact with you regarding new evidence, especially for identification of physical remains which might be uncovered.

Although it took 250 years for the first report of the Gorilla to its final proof, let us hope the Sasquatch story will be settled in a somewhat shorter time.

Sincerely,
Grover S. Krantz
Assistant Professor[262]

Krantz believed that faked footprints were easy to spot: an impression left by a hoaxer was often simply an enlargement of a human foot and wood-shaped feet left static impressions in the ground. "Such an attempt not only leaves an imprint of a larger foot, but also usually leaves an imprint of the grain of the wood," Krantz affirmed.[263] "Only a person with detailed training in human anatomy, a vivid imagination and an organization of very secretive members could have planned the thousands of footprints throughout the Northwest and Canada since the 1920's," Krantz said.[264]

René Dahinden

Andy Russell, the naturalist and author, had spent his life wandering around mountains, hiking through wilderness, and deciphering animal signs. Based on his experiences, he concluded, "You can't tell me there's such a thing as a Sasquatch." Russell's opinion on the Patterson-Gimlin film settled upon a hoaxer in a costume enjoying his greatest performance. Citing familiarity with the terrain in which the Patterson-Gimlin film was shot, Russell stated, "you can't see 10 feet ahead of you. An animal as big as the Sasquatch would have trails. It wouldn't charge through the underbrush holus-bolus."[265]

Russell believed some so-called Bigfoot prints could be misidentified bear tracks. "If there's an animal [Bigfoot] like that living in the areas where I've been, I must be going blind." Russell drew a comparison between Bigfoot and the Abominable Snowman saying, "The whole thing was a hoax by the lamas, to draw tourists and entertain themselves with on cold, winter nights." Russell added, "Mr. Dahinden may be sincere, but I think he's got himself talked into it."[266]

"I'll never stop searching for it," Dahinden said of Bigfoot in an interview given in Calgary in the early days of 1970. "I intend to prove that it does exist if it takes me a lifetime." Dahinden was convinced he had just missed an encounter with Bigfoot on several occasions. "Sightings of the Sasquatch have been made in Alberta, British Columbia, Washington State and California. We have film and still photographic shots that give absolute evidence that the creature does exist."[267] Dahinden made his living at this time by recovering shotgun pellets from shooting ranges and selling them to munitions firms.[268]

Dahinden famously had little patience with scientists dismissive of Bigfoot without, at least in Dahinden's opinion, giving the evidence due attention and scrutiny. Commenting on such experts Dahinden said, "They're not really scientists. They refuse to do any investigating. And if they won't examine the facts on this, how many facts on other subjects are they sitting on?"[269] The implications of a momentous discovery made without the involvement of mainstream scientists was not lost on Dahinden, who personified the amateur in the layman-versus-scientist divide. "If we ever catch a Sasquatch, who'll need them?"[270] he asked.

"I have yet to see a Sasquatch," Dahinden readily admitted, "and I haven't even come across the tracks of one on any of my own expeditions. But I've talked to too many people who have seen the beast. I may be stupid, but I don't think I'm so stupid that I been letting my leg get pulled for 14 years." Dahinden's long experience pursuing Bigfoot allowed him to reflect on the time and effort he had invested in the hunt. "I was being torn apart, between looking for the Sasquatch and attending to family and business affairs," Dahinden told reporter Joan Bowman in 1971. By 1971 Dahinden was divorced.

> Once Dahinden had set his heart on proving the existence of the Sasquatch, neither marriage nor the birth of two sons could keep him off the scent. Faced with the problem of providing for his family and still having time enough to hunt Sasquatches, he came up with an ingenious solution.
>
> "At the time, my wife Wanja and I were operating a boat rental service at Harrison Hot Springs in B.C.," he explained. "One day, when I was watching the skeet shooting, I noticed that all the lead pellets were falling in the lake. I got an option from the hotel to recover the lead, took out ten tons with a dredge, and made a profit of $2,500."[271]
>
> Since that time, Dahinden has extracted lead from gun-club lakes and ponds all over the U.S. and Canada. In fact, he might well have made his fortune by now had he devoted all his energy to this curious enterprise. However, working only enough to meet living expenses, Dahinden devoted much of his time to trekking in the wilderness for his furtive prey.

That devotion to looking for Bigfoot culminated in the breakup of Dahinden's marriage.

> Inevitably, Dahinden's long absences from home put a great strain on his marriage. "One day Wanja just told me I was going to have to stop this Sasquatch thing or else," recalls Dahinden. "I answered that if it came to choosing between her and the Sasquatch, then she was the one who would have to go. So we split up. Of course I miss her and our two sons, but I couldn't knuckle under to an ultimatum like that. If you're not doing what you like to do, you're a prostitute, not a man, and your kids will realize it."[272]

"I ask myself every day if it's worth it," Dahinden said ruminating on his years invested in the hunt for answers. He looked for the fake angle in the Patterson-Gimlin film every time he viewed it but found little to recommend a hoax: Patty's hands opened and clenched, the leg and arm musculature is evident—impossible with a suit, Dahinden maintained—and Patty's motions were fluid, natural. "But if you want to reject the film, you still have to deal with the footprints." Many footprints had been found in areas so remote and practicably inaccessible that a hoaxer had little reason to expect the faked prints would ever be found.[273]

"I am not on any campaign for the advancement of human knowledge. I just want to know whether I am right or wrong. I have many doubts about the existence of Sasquatch and I suppose we will never really know if they exist until we obtain one." As Dahinden would himself readily admit, he was incapable of letting the subject simply drift away without a definitive answer. "But we don't have a Sasquatch and in the meantime," he said, "I want to find out whether these prints were made by an animal or whether they are fakes." By 1971, Dahinden estimated that he had spent some $20,000 since he started earnestly searching for Sasquatch in the late 1950s. "In 1968, I spent 68 days in the bush in back of Stave Lake, B.C., looking for Sasquatch. In 1969, I spent the summer searching forests in Northern California and in 1970, I spent 45 days north of Pitt Lake, B.C."

Dahinden's designs for a European Bigfoot tour first surfaced in October 1971. Dahinden, then 40, said his planned itinerary included England, Holland, Germany, Denmark, Sweden, Finland, the U.S.S.R., and Switzerland for meetings with scientists and experts. These mini-summits were designed as opportunities to put Bigfoot materials and evidence in front of European scientists; Dahinden had a suitcase brimming with six plaster track casts, tape recordings of witness interviews, and other material including a copy of the Patterson-Gimlin film. "I have about 100 pictures and several casts of footprints which as far as I'm concerned show the movements and different pressure points which indicate the footprints were not made by an artificial foot," said Dahinden describing some of the evidence he intended to put in front of scientists during his European trip.

"I am going to get an answer and I am going to all the persons who are qualified to give me an answer." Dahinden said. "Scientists in North America have both rejected and ridiculed us. But if we have to go to Europe to have our work evaluated, I am willing to pay the price." Amongst the scientists Dahinden had made arrangements to meet with was Boris Porshnev of the U.S.S.R. Academy of Sciences in Moscow. "Professor Porshnev has spent a lifetime studying the evidence of the snowman of the Pamirs and Siberia," Dahinden stated. "He is the leading authority in this field and we have been corresponding with each other for the past two years." Dahinden was well aware of the differences in academic attitudes on hairy hominids between North America and Europe. "Scientists in Canada and the United States totally reject the mere idea of the Sasquatch being real," Dahinden said, as quoted in reporter Renee Baert's UPI article. "They are smug, self-satisfied and totally indifferent. It's okay to say there's something in the Himalayas, but not in our own backyard."[274]

Dahinden was optimistic about European scientists' willingness to give the evidence its due appraisal. "I want scientists to examine this material and give their view. I will also contact Scotland Yard and hope I might find an expert on footprints there, a man who could give a technical opinion as to how artificial feet and live feet behave under certain conditions and on certain materials." Though Dahinden failed to find evidence of hoaxing in his study of the Patterson-Gimlin film, he appreciated *any* film, as good as it appeared, could conceivably be hoaxed. But thousands of enigmatic footprints? "It's an indisputable fact that something is making these footprints. My basic question is, are they real, made by a creature like this or are they artificial, made by a man with artificial feet of some kind?"[275]

"Thousands of dollars were spent on expeditions in search of the Abominable Snowman of the Himalayas based on evidence that wouldn't make me walk across the street," Dahinden said. "We have 100 times more evidence of the Sasquatch than was ever collected in the Himalayas. The material is here, we're only asking scientists to examine it. Whatever conclusion they reach we're going to accept." Dahinden maintained that if the European scientists showed the film to be a hoax, he would accept it. "But if I can establish the possibility or probability of Sasquatch," he added, "I will start looking for a sponsor on a business or financial basis to hunt for the animal."[276]

Dahinden's European odyssey occurred between November 4, 1971, and March 12, 1972. Jim McClarin's first *Manimals Newsletter* gave Dahinden's completed European itinerary:

> London, 12 Nov. 1971, at Queen Elizabeth College, University of London. Present: Dr. John Napier, Director of Primate Biology; Dr. Don Grieve, Department of Anatomy, Royal Free School of Medicine, biomechanics; Prof. Garth Chapman, Head of Biology, Q. E. C.; Dr. Garth Gardiner, vertebrate paleontologist.
>
> Stockholm, 1 Dec. 1971. Present: Prof. Carlsoo, Department of Anatomy, Karolinska Institute; and four others.

Helsinki, 8 Dec. 1971, at the Zoological Museum. Present: Dr. Byorn Kurteen, paleontologist, U. of Helsinki; Dr. Bergman, zoologist, U. of Helsinki; and about 20 other people from the museum.

Moscow, 13 Dec. 1971. Present: Prof. Boris Porshnev, History Institute, USSR Academy of Sciences.

Moscow, 14 Dec. 1971, Boardroom of *Izvestia* (newspaper). Present: 2 deputy editors and about 55 others.

Moscow, 15 Dec. 1971, at the Writers' Club. Present: editors of several magazines and 50 others.

Moscow, 16 Dec. 1971, at the Darwin Hall of Evolution Museum. There were about 60-80 people. This was the monthly meeting of all the people from Moscow who have done work and are interested in Snowman research.

Moscow, 17 Dec. 1971, at the *Technical Youth Magazine*, circulation 1.5 million. Present: Vassily Zskchartchenko, editor, and all the staff.

Moscow, 17 Dec. 1971, at the Ethnographical Institute. Present: Prof. Zubov, anthropologist; Prof. Urisson, anthropologist, U. of Moscow; Prof. Chebocsarov, Ethnographic Institute, USSR Academy of Sciences; Prof. Bounak, USSR Academy of Sciences; Prof. Alexiev, V.P., Ethnographic Institute; and about 40 other anthropologists and zoologists.

Moscow, 18 Dec. 1971, at the Writers' Club, sponsored by V. Zakchartchenko, *Technical Youth Magazine*. About 300-400 were present.

Moscow, 24 Dec. 1971, at the Geographical Society. Present: Dr. Marie Jeanne Koffman, member USSR Snowman research team, gave speech on the Snowman; Igor Bourtsev, member USSR Snowman research team, also gave speech; Dmitri Bayanov, member USSR Snowman research team, also gave speech. About 125 others present.

Moscow, 28 Dec. 1971, at the Geological Institute. Present: Prof. Gromov, V. I., paleontologist, USSR Academy of Sciences; Prof. Reshetov, Yuri G., paleontologist, USSR Academy of Sciences; Prof. Urisson, anthropologist, U. of Moscow; Prof. Boris Porshnev, USSR Academy of Sciences. B. Porshnev gave a speech on this matter. About 200 others were present.

> Moscow, 6 Jan. 1972, at the Central Scientific Research Institute of Prosthesis and Prosthesis Construction, of the Ministry of Special Equipment of the R. F. R. Present: Dr. Slavutski, Jacob, Chief of Physiology Dept.; Dr. Vitenzonn, physiologist; Dr. Baskakova, Nina, biomechanic; Prof. B. Porshnev; and about 150 other members of the institute.
>
> Moscow, 11 Jan. 1972, at the Zoological Museum, U. of Moscow. Present: Dr. Vladimir Flint, zoologist, U. of Moscow; and about 150 members of the Museum and University mostly zoologists.
>
> Stockholm, 19 Jan. 1972. Present: Prof. C. Carlsoo, Dept. of Anatomy, biomechanics, Karolinska Institute; and about 20 others.[277]

An account of Dahinden's meeting with Dr. John R. Napier, director of primate biology at the University of London, was carried by Alberta's *Lethbridge Herald:*

> A London scientist undertook Wednesday [November 10th] to look into the existence of Sasquatch, the legendary hairy giant of the woods in British Columbia and the northwestern United States.
>
> René Dahinden of Richmond, B. C., who has spent his spare time and money for the last 17 years trying to prove whether or not Sasquatch exists, delivered a load of material to the University of London.
>
> Later he said Dr. J. R. Napier, director of primate biology, had agreed to get analyses of hundreds of photographs of huge footprints, some casts of the prints and a color movie film showing a huge ape-like figure that was taken in 1967 in northern California.
>
> This month Swiss-born Dahinden goes to Moscow where he has a similar date with Prof. Boris Porshnev of the history institute of the Russian Academy of Sciences.
>
> Dahinden, who makes his living rescuing expended shot at a Vancouver gun club four months of the year, said he is spending $1,500 on this trip.
>
> "I got interested in Sasquatch soon after reaching Canada in 1953 and now I can't let go," he said.[278]

Dr. Napier said he was inclined to believe that some form of giant creature existed in the north western Canadian-U.S. region. "I have been studying the possibilities of existence of a Sasquatch for some 20 years and I am convinced that something like this creature does exist. In any case, I believe we should keep an open mind and go on investigating what evidence there is." Napier concluded scientists' reticence to seriously study the creature stemmed from the lack of concrete evidence.[279]

Dr. Don Grieve of London Royal Free School of Medicine thought the Patterson-Gimlin film subject had a human gait, but that singular quality alone did not necessarily mean the film was a hoax. "I would say that if the film is a fake, then it is a very clever fake," Grieve said during an interview. "In my opinion if the film was shot at a speed of 24 frames a second, then the gait would be man-like, made by a person or creature standing about six feet six inches high and weighing about 300 pounds," he said. "If the camera speed was slower, say, about 16 or 18 frames to the second, I would say the gait would not be compatible with that of a man. The trouble is that we don't know the speed."[280] Dahinden handed out postcards during his tour which described the subject of the 1967 Patterson-Gimlin film as a creature standing about seven feet five inches high and weighing some 800 pounds, more than twice the weight estimated by Grieve from his study of the film.

The Soviet Union had its own distinct experiences with hair-covered man-like creatures, making that leg of Dahinden's journey exceptional. Some five years prior to Dahinden's arrival, Major General Topilski told a 1966 symposium that while commanding a Soviet army unit in 1925, he and his troops believed a creature they shot was "a counter-revolutionary dressed up but the doctor of the unit and I examined him (or it) and I became convinced he was some kind of a very strange being resembling a human being but all covered with thick wool."[281] In Russia, Dahinden found supportive and even like-minded scholars and specialists. "They are skeptical, but open-minded," said Dahinden of the scientists he approached. "They are willing to look, to listen, and they will analyze the evidence to see if there is anything there. This is all I ask."[282] Dahinden pinned his hopes upon Professor Boris Porshnev of the Academy of Sciences. Porshnev had the distinction of sitting on the snowman committee set up by the Kremlin to investigate reports of hairy hominids.[283] "The reception was good all over and the scientists have undertaken to make studies but there are no firm conclusions," Dahinden stated.[284]

Byrne (1970-71)

After his involvement with Tom Slick's "Pacific Northwest Bigfoot Expedition," Byrne returned to Nepal to resume his guiding career with his own outfit, Nepal Safaris, until 1968. That year, Byrne moved to Washington D. C. and with four native Washington D. C. men, M.D.s Karl Jonas and Roy Lyman Sexton, and attorneys Leonard A. Fink and Scott C. Whitney, founded the International Wildlife Conservation Society, (IWCS) Inc. Byrne returned to Nepal later in 1968 and worked with the national government to establish the 50,000-acre Sukla Phanta Tiger Sanctuary.[285]

Lured again by the Bigfoot phenomenon in America, Peter Byrne left Nepal in 1970 for Evans, Washington. "In November, 1969, I was in New York when I got a call from a one-time associate of Tom Slick's named C. V. Wood. He was staying at the Waldorf Astoria and he wanted me to come and see him and discuss the possibility of opening up a new phase of the research on the work that Tom had started."[286] Wood told Byrne about the Patterson-Gimlin film and asked him if he would be interested in visiting the men and viewing the film.

> In the end three things persuaded me to accept the challenge. One was the fact that I was at a kind of interim stage in my personal life. Among other things, I was a bit shattered by a separation from a dashing young Australian beauty who had been my companion for the last three years and psychologically needed something to occupy my mind, a new interest that would fill the void caused by her departure. Two, I had just finished working with the Government of Nepal on a one-year project that converted my old, big game hunting concession into a wildlife reserve and was looking for something new to do. Three was, simply, that I have never been able to resist a good challenge.[287]

Byrne first visited Patterson at his home in Tampico, Washington. Byrne found he had to persuade Patterson his inquiry into the film was serious and that Byrne's interest was sincere and impartial. Patterson was won over.

> He ran a copy of it [the Patterson-Gimlin film] for me in his house, using an old projector that he had borrowed from a neighbor and for a screen, a bedsheet pinned up on the [wall] of his living room. He projected it half a dozen times and

> I was intrigued by what I saw. I thought that if the subject of the footage was a man in a fabricated suit, then firstly he was a hell of a big man and secondly the suit was the work of very skilled craftsmen who had managed to make something that actually showed things like the rippling muscles on the creature's arms as it walked. I did not think this to be possible with a fabricated suit, regardless of the material.[288]

Byrne next visited Gimlin who by that point had experienced a falling out with Patterson over income derived from the film. Byrne's next step was to report back to Wood, that he had met Patterson and Gimlin and had seen and was intrigued by the Patterson-Gimlin footage. Byrne accepted Wood's financial backing for a Bigfoot research project which would launch Byrne on a nearly decade-long search for the hairy giant.

> On January 1st, 1971, I and a two-man Bigfoot project crew, Don Byington, of Marcus, WA and Dennis Jensen, of The Dalles, OR, rolled out of Spokane, Washington, with three, brand-new International 4x4 Scouts and a ton of equipment. Our destination was northern Washington and while I did not stay there very long, moving south, to Oregon in early 1971, suddenly I was back in the search.[289]

This research effort shortly collapsed, according to Byrne, when his chief sponsor insisted that his research efforts be directed at a specific goal: the acquisition of a *dead* specimen. "This was something that had never been discussed in the original planning. That it had not been brought up may have been my fault; I simply presumed that our new approach to the phenomenon was to be the same as our old one, benign, and with the intention of just finding one of the creatures, but not harming it."[290] Finding that Byrne was adamant that their effort not include the killing of a Bigfoot, Wood soon pulled his financial backing "leaving the project high and dry," Byrne wrote, "with, among other things, three thousand dollars' worth of pending bills."[291]

Byrne was devasted by Wood's decision and he traveled to Evans, Washington, to break the news to Byington and Jensen. Byrne found himself at another crossroads in his life, and he thought hard on what his next course of action would be.

> I took the project staff to dinner in Colville, the nearest little town to Evans and we all had a few snorts as we commiserated with each other on what might have been. Later that night, lying on my camp cot in the little house I had rented in Evans, a wood stove fighting against the bitter, biting winter cold, I weighed everything together and made a decision. In the morning I called the staff and told [them] that I had decided to keep the project going. I would finance it myself.

Byrne could jumpstart the effort with his own savings, but he also solicited backing from other interested parties. With the benefit of financial backing from Tom Page and Mrs. Allen Rosse, Byrne launched his investigation into the Bigfoot phenomenon by establishing a base of operations in The Dalles, where, in the early summer of 1971, eight persons, on four separate occasions, had reported seeing a Bigfoot on the city's outskirts.[292]

Betty Beale, social columnist for the *Washington Star*, framed Rosse's financing and involvement in Byrne's summer 1971 expedition as well as Rosse's own fascination with the subject in an article which also mentioned Byrne's "unsuccessful" hunts for the Himalayan Yeti. According to Beale, Byrne's own interest in hairy giants was born after watching a film of an Abominable Snowman eating rhododendron buds in a friend's Nepalese garden. Another piece of footage, the Patterson-Gimlin film, was used to help sway Rosse's support for Byrne's Oregon venture. "I have also seen a film of this creature crossing a clearing in northern California about five years ago taken about 30 feet away by a man named Patterson," said Rosse. "It was black and hairy with a face like a gorilla. The amazing thing about it was that it did not walk with arms down like a gorilla but it walked upright and its arm movements were those of a man. It was walking very fast and obviously it was not a hoax because you could see the ripple of the muscles in its enormous arms and shoulders. The picture was reproduced in a magazine a couple of years ago, but people just don't believe it."

> Another remarkable thing about the creature, which Mrs. Rosse thinks "could be one of the earliest examples of primitive man—the link between ape and man," is that its "footprint is not that of a primate. In the primate the big toe is separated and on the side of the foot. This one is like a man's footprint, only it's 18 inches long."

Byrne, who founded the International Wildlife Conservation Society to establish tiger sanctuaries in Nepal, believes the creatures might have crossed over the land mass between Asia and the western hemisphere "thousands of years ago, probably 200 or so, and still exist in isolated remote spots in the Northwest, Canada and Alaska."

When Allen broke the news of her trip at a Washington cocktail party just before leaving, there was a lot of smiling and kidding, naturally. Everyone thought the charming divorcee was simply looking for a lark. In a way she is, because she will only be out there for three weeks and she thinks it won't be found for a year. But she didn't raise the money and pack her chic safari outfit from Saks Fifth Avenue just for the fun of it.

"This is a project to evaluate the evidence of an unidentified species of primate in the Pacific Northwest which the American Indians called Sasquatch," reeled off Allen in a scholarly manner. "Other people call it 'Bigfoot.' According to Indian lore they have had battles with it."

The knowledgeable Washington charmer said that "there have been 480 sightings in the past 50 years in America's Northwest either singly or in pairs or in threes with young."

In a letter to your correspondent Byrne writes: "The last authentic sightings were in Oregon in June of this year when nine people saw one of the creatures seven times. They all gave the same description, about ten feet tall, grey in color, massive in build, walking upright. If you wish to verify this, call the sheriff's department. The Dalles, Oregon."

He has talked to 29 people who have seen the nocturnal creature that apparently turns whiter in the winter and blackhaired [sic] in the summer.

Does Allen have any fear of this giant primate that she might possibly run into?

"Oh no! I think it would be so marvelous to see this thing!" she exclaimed. But she doesn't really expect to "because it has always been sighted by sheer accident. This animal has only survived because it has avoided man. It is also only by accident that no man who has seen it has had a rifle. Peter's fear is that somebody might come across one and shoot it." There is a

> Canadian group currently hunting it who have announced via newspapers and radio they intend to shoot one if they get the chance.[293]

The penultimate goal for Byrne was the collection of sufficient evidence to establish Bigfoot as an extant creature. To delineate the procedures for acquisition and study of a living specimen, Byrne developed a catch-and-release protocol early on in his Bigfoot search. First, Byrne wanted to get close enough to a Bigfoot to immobilize it using a tranquilizer gun. The Bigfoot would then be transported to a secure location for about six weeks' scientific study (Byrne also told reporters that a Bigfoot should only be tranquilized "for about five hours—just long enough to take some samples")[294] before its eventual release back into the wild. "Side show" aspects to the creature's containment and study were to be prudently avoided. "We want some hair samples, blood and urine specimens, among other things."

> Byrne apparently feels he has already cracked the mystery of the Sasquatch but he is keeping it a secret because of the would-be "hoaxsters." Last winter there was much ado about footprints found in the snow [reference to Washington state's Cripplefoot tracks] but Byrne recognized them as a hoax, and the man who perpetrated it eventually admitted it. But because of the man's statements that he had been making all of the tracks discovered, Byrne's California backers for this summer's expedition pulled out. If he can get the backing he needs he will continue his search next winter.
>
> Mrs. Rosse's 16-year-old son Colin has been participating in the summer search in Washington state and in Oregon since June and has already seen footprints.[295]

Colin Rosse found himself in the spotlight again the following year as the steady beau of 17-year-old Mary McGovern, the only unmarried daughter of the Democratic nominee for president, with whom he attended primaries and the Democratic convention in Miami.[296]

Ohio businessman and former Roger Patterson backer Tom Page provided a portion of Byrne's sponsorship in 1971. So interested was Page in the sightings coming out of The Dalles that along with his attorney Wayne Newton, Page flew to The Dalles to meet and interview witnesses himself. Byrne joined Page and Newton and they talked to two of the owners of the

Pinewood Trailer Court [also given in some articles as Pine-Wood Mobile Manor]. Jim Forkan and Dick Ball (Frank Vérlander declined to be interviewed) spent several hours with the three investigators (Byrne stated in *The Search for Bigfoot* that Newton did most of the questioning). Later, Byrne, Page, and Newton discussed the interviews and reviewed the tapes they had made. The investigators were impressed by the witnesses, the truthfulness of what they believed they saw, and agreed they had indeed witnessed something extraordinary—an unidentified creature sporting a large man-like appearance, erect posture and gait, and grey to dark grey in color.[297]

These infamous sightings took place in the last week of May through early June, 1971. Joe Mederios, a trailer court maintenance man, was in front of the trailer park's brick office building when he glanced across the road to a cleft in a 100-foot rocky bluff. Mederios quickly forgot all about the morning's task of watering flowers as his attention was riveted to a tall, grey-colored creature he saw in the distance. "He went on to say it looked like an overgrown ape. He stated it was not a bear," Deputy Rich Carlson reported. Astonished, Mederios observed the thing in clear morning light, later estimating its height to be about 10 feet tall.

The next day Mederios with Forkan, Ball, and Vérlander saw something in a field below the rock bluff. "All of the above were in the office when they spotted 'Bigfoot' come down from the rocks across the road and walk along an open field there," the sheriff's report stated. "It stopped near a small tree and was described as being somewhat larger than the tree (checked later and found the tree to be about 8 feet tall)."

"I went to the area where the creatures had been sighted to look at the prints they had found. The ground was dry and covered with grass, making it hard to find a good print," Deputy Carlson said after his investigation. "One print was photographed, that being in the dry grass. The print resembled a large, bare foot being about 20 inches in length. The stride between 'prints' was more than I could stride myself without running." One of the trailer park owners commented, "It looked like a great big man in a furry sweater." At this point with corroboration provided by other witnesses that something unusual was in the area, an emboldened Mederios offered his earlier sighting. He had not said anything previously "in fear that I'd be called a nut."[298]

"If it was somebody running around in an ape suit," said James Weekes, managing editor of *The Dalles Gazette*, "he was willing to take a chance on being shot. We all wonder enough about it (Bigfoot) from time to time."[299]

> Two nights later, Richard Brown, a junior high school music teacher, was returning with his wife to the trailer court about 9:30 P.M. when their car lights caught the outline of a gray figure standing under an oak tree in the field.
>
> Brown ran to his trailer and returned with a hunting rifle on which was mounted a four-power scope. The creature conveniently froze for about four or five minutes while Brown studied it through the scope. Later he furnished the sheriff's department with a drawing.
>
> A few nights later a woman resident of the area called the sheriff's office. She screamed hysterically that something with a "flattened nose and large round eyes" was staring at the rear of her home over a 6-foot fence.[300]

Brown had never seen anything like the creature he confronted that June 2 evening. "It wasn't an ape or a bear," he stressed. Before the creature disappeared up a bluff Brown felt his finger squeeze the trigger, but he found himself unable to fire his weapon. "I just couldn't motivate myself to shoot it. It seemed more human than animal."[301]

"We have examined all the people involved and concluded that they did see something. But we don't know what," Byrne said of The Dalles sightings. "It could be a man in a gorilla suit but he would need to have an awfully long stride and risk being shot."

From the onset of his research, Byrne applied his wildlife experience to formulation of Bigfoot theories. "The whole life of all wild creatures is centered around the search for food. The whole idea of an animal going through an area is dietary migration," Byrne explained.[302] And as Genzoli comments below, people who saw Bigfoot, like those witnessing the creature reported in The Dalles, were the biggest proponents of something real and tangible behind the story.

> There are those who say our Bigfoot is just one big hoax. And, there are those who feel there is a lot of truth in the old fellow. Some people know he exists because they say they have SEEN him.[303]

Some local residents watching the influx of Bigfoot researchers and investigators had an air of seeing it all before. "They come every three or four years, regularly," a farmer from The Dalles said. "It's never the same people.

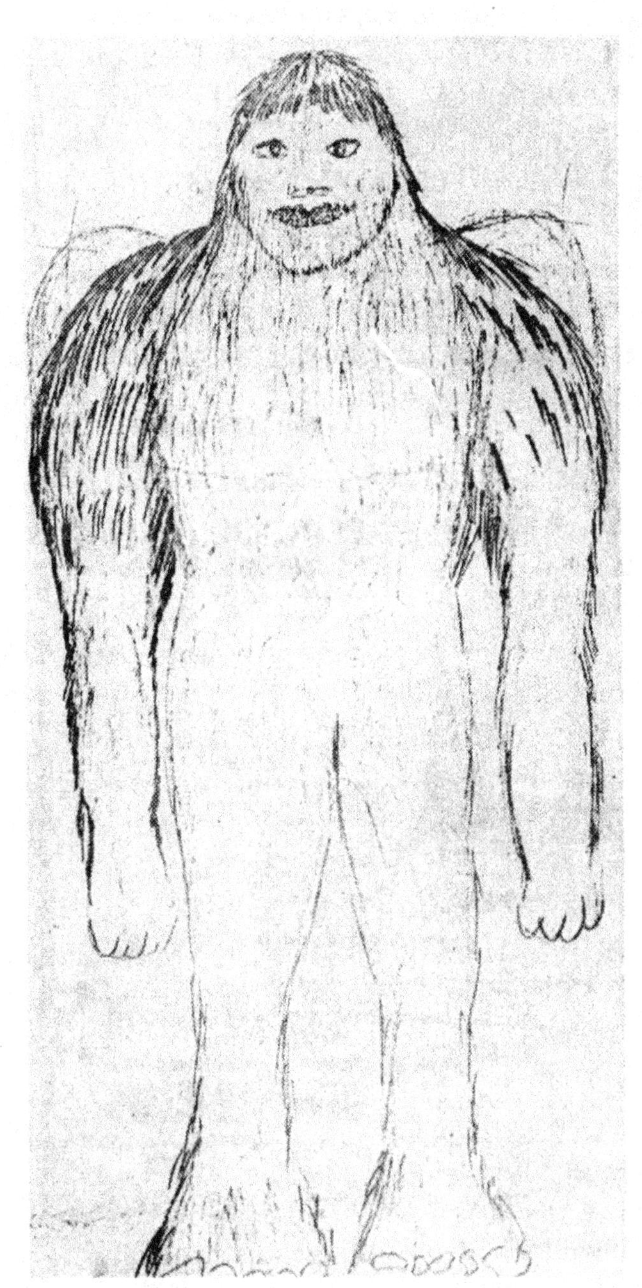

HERE'S HOW MONSTER APPEARED TO ONE VIEWER
Sketch Was Made by Teacher Richard Brown

EYEWITNESS SKETCH BY RICHARD BROWN, JUNE 1971

One hunt is probably, convincing. They come, they hunt, they leave and we never see or hear from them again."[304]

In early 1971, Byrne thought a specimen could be had within 12 months with the right effort. "I believe the animal to exist and to be a new specie of primitive similar to the huge primitive subhuman whose bones were discovered in China. These bones were estimated to be 20,000 to 25,000 years old," Byrne said, referring to *Gigantopithecus*.[305]

Copley News Service wildlife writer Bill Hill looked into the IWCS organization for his 1971 article on Byrne.

> Hunt-director Byrne has not made himself available to discuss his organization or any details if the hunt. But inquiries to Washington, D.C., revealed that the IWCS did not have a telephone number, and conservationists there were not aware of the group's existence. The organization listings in The World Almanac have never included IWCS.
>
> But the Recorder of Deeds in the nation's capital acknowledges that the IWCS is a non-profit organization and lists Leonard Fink, a lawyer, as corporation attorney.

"This hunt is a scientific and conservation operation that is dealing with fact," Fink said in an interview with Hill. "God knows there have been enough half-truths about these creatures."[306]

Like several other prominent researchers in the '70s, Byrne opted for a conservative estimate at Bigfoot population size. Byrne said "it would just be a wild guess without any scientific support, but there could be as many as 200 or 300 of the hairy, ape-like beings" living in northeastern Washington.[307]

George Harrison

George Harrison, managing editor of *National Wildlife*, took part in a Bigfoot expedition in which he reported that he and other expedition members found six-inch-wide tracks of naked feet during their search through the Washington State forest. The evidence the expedition uncovered made Harrison "85 percent" certain of Bigfoot's existence.[308]

> "One thing is sure," Harrison wrote, "reputable scientists agree there is no biological reason why Bigfoot cannot exist." Harrison concludes by stating that he feels that increasing

> evidence and the abundance of tracks and sightings have made it appropriate to face up to the next obvious question in Bigfoot investigations—that a leading scientific group, perhaps with the aid of the Federal government, should take up the search.[309]

In 1970, *National Wildlife* agreed to co-sponsor the American Yeti Expedition 1970, led by Robert Morgan of Miami, Florida. When Harrison headed west to join the expedition in June, he privately thought the whole thing was likely bunk and, charitably put, the fanciful product of overactive imaginations. In 1968, the April-May edition of *National Wildlife* printed photographs of the creature captured on 16mm film by Roger Patterson and Bob Gimlin at Bluff Creek, in northern California. Harrison wrote that before publishing the photographs, a *National Wildlife* editor flew to California to interview Patterson. In October 1970, Betty Burroughs wrote in her "One Upon Paper" *Morning News* column, that the results of a lie detector test to which Patterson submitted convinced editor John Strohm that Patterson was telling the truth about the film.[310] Harrison believed the creature on the Patterson-Gimlin film was "enormous," and based upon the 17-inch long tracks it left at the scene, weighed between 350-400 pounds. Harrison acknowledged the film had plenty of detractors, but he asserted many experts had examined the film and could not prove it to be simply a hoax perpetrated by a man in a suit. Harrison said that there had been 37 sightings of Bigfoot in 1969 and that his readership's interest kept *National Wildlife*, even peripherally, interested in the subject. When the opportunity to provide what was tantamount to a follow-up story, *National Wildlife* agreed to support American Yeti Expedition 1970. Harrison explained the fundamental reason for his personal interest:

> Honest curiosity. If you have ever seen the magnificent scenic beauty of the Pacific Northwest, you know why I was intrigued by the chance to go there, whether we found Bigfoot or not. Admittedly, the expedition was not strictly "scientific" in the sense that purists use the word, implying many people, large financial backing, and months of exploration. But its purpose was serious, based on honest curiosity, and there were certainly more than enough mystery for any enthusiastic outdoor sleuth.
>
> The first phase of the expedition was designed to look for signs of Bigfoot, test various devices for attracting it, and bring

> back enough evidence in the way of photographs, droppings, hair, and anything else that would help launch Phase Two—which hopefully will be climaxed by a Bigfoot capture.[311]

Robert Morgan

After an encounter with an unexpected creature in 1957, Robert W. Morgan went to the Sheriff's office in Washington state's Mason County. He described "the biggest, most man-like looking gorilla that I'd ever seen." Morgan stated he sought to understand what exactly he'd encountered. "I still wasn't certain what I had seen," he said. "I called around to some zoos and asked if any gorillas had escaped. They were polite, but said no. So I did what any red-blooded American boy about to be discharged from the Navy would have done. I shut up. But somewhere inside I decided as so many people do in their moments of dream—someday. Someday I'm going back out there."[312]

Morgan read a *Reader's Digest* (January 1969) article that connected him with his 1957 encounter and helped him find answers to his experience. The article explained Roger Patterson's claim to have filmed a Bigfoot, and a frame of that film reproduced in the article triggered something inside Morgan.

> "When I looked at that film," Morgan enthusiastically said, "I knew what I had seen. That was it. It came back on me like a flood that I was free, had a few dollars, and there was no reason I shouldn't do something I wanted to do, something worthwhile. I decided to go into the mountains—immediately."[313]

Robert Morgan led a three-person team into the Cascades in 1969. Morgan claimed they discovered a well-defined trackway in deep snow and a set of distinct tracks in the bottom of a mountain stream. This initial success fueled Morgan's desire to continue field research.

Morgan organized the 1970 expedition with better equipment, more qualified observers, improved planning, and an invitation extended to *National Wildlife* editor George Harrison. The full title of the search was, "American Yeti Expedition 1970 (Phase One)." Yeti is a term based upon a Nepalese word for a primate of the Himalayas, also called the Abominable Snowman in Western culture. "It may sound far-fetched," Morgan said prior to the team's deployment, "but I can assure you this is a very serious scientific expedition."[314] Morgan saw strong parallels between the North American Bigfoot and the Yeti. "So closely do they resemble what is termed *Homo Erectus* we have tentatively concluded that these beings are related," stated Morgan. "The oldest term is 'Yeti' and until proven otherwise we will attach the word Yeti to the American primate."[315]

Morgan described the Yeti Expedition's method of operating in the field: "If we can't carry it on our backs we can't take it with us," Morgan said. "Luckily most of this stuff is light. We plan to run a number of tests, including a test of the creature's mentality." The team planned to use "several selected lures" to draw a Bigfoot in close enough to photograph. If all went well, then Phase Two of the Yeti Expedition would occur later in 1970 when the group would endeavor to temporarily capture a Yeti for study under the hoped-for auspices of the Smithsonian Institution. "I can't tell you what these lures are at this time," Morgan said. "If it should work, then the mountains would be full of people trying to catch themselves a Yeti. And on that last expedition I saw men armed with high-powered rifles with telescopic sites, ready to kill one." After study and analysis of the detained specimen was complete, the Yeti would be released at the point of its capture. "If rapport has been established with the specimen," Morgan maintained, "the person most friendly will attempt to accompany him into the wild."[316]

The American Yeti Expedition 1970 team members included: Robert Carr, an archaeologist and journalist, at the time a student at the University of Miami; Douglas Jackson and Allen Facemire, the expedition's photographers, the latter also engaged to create a documentary of Phase One; George Harrison, managing editor of the *National Wildlife;* and Laymond M. Hardy, a biologist and zoologist acting as the expedition's key scientific adviser who did not accompany the group but had agreed to examine evidence. Hardy would explore the local environment's capacity to support such a creature. One of Carr's interests was the exploration of caves and lava tubes: "Carr will be after archaeological evidence to support claims of the relative intelligence and semi-advanced existence of such a creature," said Morgan, "whose appearance recalls the actions of the *Pithecanthropus Erectus*, a prehistoric manape thought to be extinct."[317]

> I did not know what to expect as our heavily loaded microbus headed for our base camp in the Cascades. I soon learned, however, that we were already in Bigfoot country when we stopped in Stevenson, Washington, a quiet one-stoplight town

> on the north bank of the mighty Columbia River. More than anywhere else, Stevenson has been a nerve center for Bigfoot sightings. Nearly everyone in town and half of Skamania County believes, at least a little, in Bigfoot—or in something that lives in the nearby mountains and looks like a huge hairy human being.
>
> Sheriff Bill Closner showed us a casting he made last year of one Bigfoot track. "I would find it hard to duplicate this track. I feel that it's authentic." And when pressed for an answer if he really believed in Bigfoot, he replied, "I lean in that direction awfully hard."
>
> County Commissioner Conrad Lundy sponsored an ordinance to protect Bigfoot. There's a $10,000 fine for anyone breaking that law. He told us: "I am a believer to a certain extent, and that's why I brought the ordinance before the county board to protect this creature."[318]

Harrison favored the sentiment expressed by Ed McLarney, a United Press International stringer who said, "by training I'm dubious, after seeing the tracks and hearing the stories from people who have seen Bigfoot, I'm 90 per cent sure that something exists which is beyond my own experience." Harrison came very close to McLarney's quantified certainty by the end of Yeti Expedition 1970 (85% for Harrison) and he garnered a new appreciation for both Bigfoot and those who searched for it.

The Yeti Expedition at one point came across an old hunter whom they asked about Bigfoot. "I been hunting in here two years now," the hunter said, "and I ain't seen nothing like that."[319] Base camp was in the northern Cascades on the southwest slope of the "White Lady," snowcapped Mount St. Helens. Team members spent two days looking for tracks, driving as far as possible along logging roads before searching on foot. The team focused on creek bottoms, logged-over fields, and snowbanks. Bob Carr explored the caves in the area. (The U.S. Forest Service later developed one of these, called Ape Cave, the longest continuous lava tube in the continental United States and the third longest lava tube in North America.)

> The third night, we made a smaller camp higher up Mt. St. Helens to save traveling time and to seek new listening posts. The sounds of the night were eerie and a little frightening. One high-pitched barking sound really puzzled me, and at first

> I thought it must be a coyote or fox, but it continued for hours. Perhaps it was one of the western owls. One night we heard what sounded like deep groans and muffled sniffing—bears probably.[320]

According to Harrison, the first day in which tracks were found started out like any other during that trip. The morning provided nothing of particular interest and following a lunch of dehydrated fruit and crackers, the search moved to a creek which flowed into a nearby small lake. "Hey, come quick," Morgan said suddenly. "I found a track." Harrison hurriedly joined Morgan. His first reaction of the fresh, large human-like footprint was skepticism, wondering if perhaps Morgan could have made the track himself. Harrison tested the dirt with his thumb and jumped up and down. No, Harrison decided, after his boots hardly left a mark, the substrate was too hard for Morgan to have fabricated the track. Further searching revealed other tracks both in the water and on the opposite bank. The impressions of the toes were nearly a half-inch deep in the hard mud. "A man of 170 pounds made no impression," Morgan reported. "Other tracks, less clear, were found in the water, indicating the creature wandered about for several minutes in water too cold to stand in."[321]

Two days later, more tracks were found about three miles south of the lake, ascending an embankment parallel to a logging road. As with the earlier track find, further searching revealed more tracks in the area—about 10 distinct, 16-inch, well-defined tracks. It was at this site that fecal matter was discovered which Hardy later commented upon as, "Not cow, not elk. It has to be bear or what we are looking for." Supplemental laboratory analysis was planned for the specimen. Harrison detailed Morgan's evening experiments with acoustics.

> An astonishing thing happened that night. Morgan decided to try his sound device at the scene of the 10 tracks. Eventually he plans to trap Bigfoot, employing devices covering sound, scent and sight. (Morgan is reluctant to have his sound device described in detail, except to say it has a high-pitched bell tone. He says he is fearful that in the wrong hands, the device could attract Bigfoot to a home or campsite and lead to serious trouble for the inhabitants.)
>
> Morgan placed it near the string of tracks and then returned to camp. At daybreak, he was astonished to find new tracks,

> clear and well defined. All of us were awed by the feeling that Bigfoot was probably near.[322]

The audio device, "designed to attract and stimulate primary curiosity" apparently succeeded. One track was found within 10 yards of the device. "A profusion of pine needles, dead bark and wood refuse prevented a clear track. However, a distinct impression was made that measured 16 inches long, 6 inches wide at the ball of the foot, and 3 ½ inches at the heel. Elk bones were scattered about the area in great numbers."[323]

> Though we thoroughly searched the entire area, no further signs appeared. Moving on two days later, we found still another set of tracks some six miles north of Carson, Washington. A sighting had been reported in that area a week before, and Sheriff Closner had passed on the tip to our group.
>
> Allen Facemire discovered two sets of tracks leading up a bank, one 16 inches long and the other 13 . . . all bare-footed and anthropoid.
>
> With all the track finds, the droppings and the response to the noise device, the group felt it had accomplished the objectives of Phase One. Facemire had shot 5,000 feet of color film. Carr had searched numerous caves and planned further exploration for Phase Two. I was convinced there could be a Bigfoot, though its precise nature, of course, still remains a mystery.[324]

Morgan said the success of Phase One warranted future expeditions. "Based upon accumulated data," he averred, "the group has detected that enough tangible evidence exists that warrants a second full-scale scientific expedition to attempt to contact or live capture of the legendary Abominable Snowman."[325] Harrison described the key steps to the Yeti Expedition's "Phase Two," the ambitious goal of capturing a Bigfoot: after luring a Bigfoot to drugged bait, the sedated creature would be followed, perhaps by the aid of trained canines, with further drugging by tranquilizer dart as necessary. Harrison stated the thoroughly immobilized creature would be flown to the Smithsonian Institution in Washington, D. C., for a full range of scientific study. When research on the prototype was complete, the creature would be flown back to the Pacific Northwest to be released back into the wilderness.

Morgan's expedition impacted Harrison and his beliefs on the whole Bigfoot business. "The Patterson photos have not been proven to be a fraud," Harrison said, "and after this trip my belief that there is something there has been reinforced."[326] For Harrison, his participation in field research and the party's findings and experiences increased the probability of hairy hominids existence in North America. "I'd say I was a 50 percent believer before joining the American Yeti Expedition 1970. And about 85 percent now."[327]

In 1971 Morgan led another expedition into the field to search for Bigfoot, this time under the organizational name of Vanguard Research, Inc. Under Morgan's direction his team combed the hills of Skamania County in search of positive proof of Bigfoot's corporeality.

> Morgan says the search team has been covertly operating out of Cougar, Wash., near Mt. St. Helens, for the past three weeks. He says that if enough positive proof is found of the creature's existence, it will be possible to obtain additional funds for purchase of sophisticated capture gear.
>
> Morgan explained that Vanguard members are primarily using their own funds for the search.[328]

Lee Trippett

The April 1971 edition of *Pursuit* carried an article concerning the July 1970 *Oregon Outdoors* (formerly *Gun and Creel*) write-up on Lee Trippett's search for answers to the Bigfoot mystery. Trippett, a 1959 graduate from the University of Oregon, became interested in Bigfoot in the early '60s. His methodology followed simple precepts: go alone into the wilderness, establish a camp in an area likely to contain Bigfoot, and then wait.

> He thinks Bigfoot has a sort of extra-sensory perception and seems to know when a man is there to harm him. He knows a gold prospector who has gained the trust of the creatures, and has even exchanged food with them by putting Trippett's theories into practice. The prospector, according to Trippett, has seen as many as 14 creatures at a time, and has watched them hunt. Since Bigfoot is nocturnal, Lee stays awake at night watching for him. He feels that over a period of time he has gotten to know Bigfoot, and that Bigfoot knows him. 'We are sort of waiting for a chance to shake hands' he says.[329]

Trippett started Flora-Fauna Research Corp., a Eugene, Oregon-based non-profit organization which aimed to "categorize available data and coordinate research," to include soliciting scientists to advise and consult on an overall Bigfoot study-program.

> Maybe Lee Trippett has the best idea of how to bring this seemingly everlasting business to a successful conclusion. Let us face this problem frontally: either such things as Sasquatches exist, or they don't. If they are only the product of Myth, Legend, and Folklore, let them be examined as such. If, on the other hand, they might be real, then anyone who has any idea as to how to come up with them should be assisted. Lee Trippett, I know, leans very strongly to the notion that such living entities exist but also to the idea that they are so "human" that they may be maintaining themselves by a combination of what we call straight "bushcraft" plus an equally inborn expertise in what we have come to call "ESP," meaning frankly a combination of super-sensory abilities and (to us) super-perceptive abilities.[330]

Trippett's patient technique of observation suggested a relatively composed and calm examination of one's surroundings, essentially "to shut up and go out in the field and see if any such 'thing' might come by." The *Pursuit* article concludes, "Considering the now dozens of so-called expeditions that have gone out west—from northern California to the Canadian Yukon—during the past decade, to look for this oddity and have found nothing, we frankly believe that Lee Trippett's idea is not only as good as anybody else's but probably more worthwhile."[331]

Government & Law 1969-70

The Regina, Saskatchewan, Junior Chamber of Commerce, aware of the public relation benefits from the right kind of hype and attention, declared it would pay $100,000 for a Sasquatch. As hunting Bigfoot began to take on serious tones and give every indication it was serious business, a growing concern over Bigfoot's protection became apparent. Commissioner Conrad Lundy of Washington's Skamania County sponsored an ordinance in 1969 to protect anomalous hairy hominids which imposed a $10,000 fine for the killing of a Bigfoot. Ordinance 69-01 (later amended in 1984) was the first official county law of the year.[332]

> The ordinance was signed by Commission Chair Conrad Lundy, Jr., and Prosecuting Attorney Robert K. Leick. The fact that it was adopted on April 1 did not escape notice. However, the commissioners insisted they were completely serious. "Although this ordinance was adopted on April 1, this is not an April Fool's Day joke," Commissioner Lundy told the [Skamania County] *Pioneer* at the time. "There is reason to believe such an animal exists."[333]

National Wildlife magazine editor George Harrison, at the time of his involvement with Robert Morgan, made the technical point that there was no legal hunting season on Bigfoot which made the creature protected by default. "Bigfoot is already protected. Though this ordinance emphasizes the need to protect Bigfoot, he is already protected by state game laws which cover all wild creatures unless a hunting season is opened on them."[334]

Interestingly, René Dahinden was not sanguine over the passing of the Skamania Ordinance. Don Hunter wrote of Dahinden's reaction:

> "It's amazing," he says. "Here they are laying down ten thousand dollar fines and five-year jail sentences for the shooting of something that most authorities say can't possibly exist. What the hell is the point of protecting something that we haven't found yet?"
>
> His tart response may be linked to speculation that the Skamania County authorities had their ears tuned much more to the music of a publicity bandwagon than to any song of distress from the mountains when they signed the ordnance.[335]

Richard Lancefield, an Assistant Attorney General in Washington's Temple of Justice, pursued making Bigfoot a protected animal throughout the Evergreen State.

> Richard Lancefield thinks it's time somebody stood up for the rights of the Sasquatch, the huge man-bear creatures sometimes reported lurking along dark roads in rural parts of Washington.

> So he's organizing a party for the creatures Wednesday [August 26, 1970] night on the steps of the state capitol building here.
>
> Lancefield, who is director of the newly founded Pacific Northwest League for the Protection of the Sasquatch, doubts there will be a Sasquatch present for the event. But he wants to bring the plight of the huge creatures to the public's attention.
>
> "Recent reports indicate the encroachment of civilization threatens the continued existence of the Sasquatch," he said Monday.
>
> Lancefield is an assistant attorney general with the State Board Against Discrimination.[336]

Jim McClarin also put energies into securing legal protection of Bigfoot in California.

> Hunting Bigfoot under California law is a misdemeanor, according to Jim McClarin, a Bigfoot fan who carved the Bigfoot statue in Willow Creek, and he is circulating petitions in Humboldt and Trinity counties which ask that it be made a felony.
>
> McClarin said the Skaminia [sic] County in Washington has passed an ordinance which makes the killing of Bigfoot a felony, punishable by a fine of not more than $10,000 and or imprisonment for not more than five years.
>
> "There are some people in Humboldt and Trinity counties," McClarin said, "who feel their counties could do with similar legislation. They don't all believe in Bigfoot, but they feel if there are such creatures they should be protected, with severe penalties at stake for any who propose a barrage of bullets as a suitable greeting for the shy, shadowy giants."[337]

Genzoli, Haas, and Student Searchers

George Haas had a life full of interesting jobs and pursuits: a gunner on escort ships providing convoy protection in World War II, a former head ranger at Calaveras Big Trees State Park, and an official for the National Park Service in Yellowstone National Park. Later in life, Haas turned his Oakland apartment into a "Sasquatch clearinghouse filled with voluminous but carefully ordered files on sightings throughout the continent—and the world."[338] Andrew Genzoli, always interested in a good Bigfoot story, wrote of Haas in a February 1970 "Redwood Country" column:

> George F. Haas of Oakland publishes a monthly bulletin in which news concerning Bigfoot and the country is collected. It has limited circulation, since the task is one of love rather than profit.
>
> Apparently Haas enjoys all angles, for in the last bulletin [January 31, 1970] he has a story by Robert Barbour Johnson of San Francisco, writer and former circusman and animal trainer. He disclaims the idea that Bigfoot could in anyway be an escaped gorilla. If you remember, that was one of the theories first advanced.
>
> "Only one American circus has ever exhibited gorillas, in the entire history of the business! The so-called 'gorilla sideshows' of circus and carnival lots contain only old chimpanzees, grown too large and vicious for performing and retired as 'gorillas' to a public that has never learned the difference between them."
>
> Gorillas, he says, are the shortest-lived of all animals, and by far the most expensive, costing as high as $20,000 each. "None of them has ever escaped." The gorilla is a delicate animal and must be protected by zoos. "They are displayed in specially built, glass-sided, air-conditioned cages, and if one of them had ever gotten out, it could not have lived more than a few hours!"
>
> He adds: "With Bigfoot records going back well over a hundred years, it's a rather feeble hypothesis! Nor has any grown gorilla ever reached a height of more than six feet. Adults cannot stand upright; and walk on all fours like dogs, which they much more closely resemble, than 'Bigfoot.' Probably the misunderstandings are due to circus movies, which for decades have depicted them as walking like men, and growing to the height of 'King Kong.' These roles, however, were always played by human beings, wearing ape costumes. Several actors have made a lifelong specialty of playing them. No live gorilla has ever appeared in a Hollywood film, being too dangerous to control on a movie set. So, the 'gorilla theory' of 'Bigfoot' is completely impossible and need not distract us, in the search for the fascinating original."[339]

Haas' *Bigfoot Bulletin* would last 26 issues; 24 issues published monthly between January 2, 1969 and December 31, 1970 and two quarterly appearances in 1971.

Bigfoot's promulgation throughout the cultural fabric fed into an emerging interest from within the college crowd. A special Bigfoot display, for example, was a newsworthy event when featured at the Humboldt State College Library in 1969.[340] In certain circles and under certain lenses, this interest imparted a scientifically-inclined acknowledgement and academe-sanctioned gravitas to Bigfoot research. Through Haas, Genzoli noted in 1970 the plans by a contingent of students set to embark on a Bigfoot-inspired trek.

> Haas reports via Ken Krasney of Los Angeles: "As of this time, approximately 15 to 20 UCLA students and graduate students (including several doctoral candidates in anthropology and geography) plan a month-long expedition into northern California. They may spend part of that time in the Orleans Bluff Creek area, and part of the time in the area below Wildwood in Trinity County. The group has submitted a proposal asking for financial backing from the L. S. B. Leakey Foundation (an anthropological foundation with headquarters in Los Angeles). They are now awaiting word as to whether or not the foundation will support the expedition. If they receive no independent support, they will pay the expenses out of their own pockets. They hope to establish a routine that will involve scouting trips to look for tracks, hair, feces, bones (or whatever), a nighttime lure (with either trip-wire cameras or someone watching at night), and a base camp situation (which would serve as a rest area and secondary lure).
>
> They will be taking up good photographic equipment, and hope to get a good shot of one of the creatures." (Tentative dates: Aug. 22 to Sept. 32[sic]).[341]

Mary Buckley, a student at the University of Rhode Island, wrote Genzoli, who printed her letter in a 1971 "Redwood Country" column. Using her anthropology background, Buckley commented on Bigfoot's import and impact to the modern world.

> "On a recent visit to California a story reached me from a former native of the Trinity Mountain region concerning the legend and pursuit of 'Bigfoot.' It recalled for me the childhood tales I heard of the 'Sasquatch,' long-feared by the Indians of the Northwest.
>
> "As an anthropology student, the possibility of 'Bigfoot' has a special fascination for me. Modern anthropology assumes that men just did not evolve from any lower anthropoid forms in the New World. This is feasible, since no living or fossil apes are known in the Western Hemisphere, as they are in the old Old World, nor are more primitive examples of the genus *Homo* believed to [be] present in the Americas.
>
> "In the light of this, 'Bigfoot,' if an authentic, undocumented, unclassified species, could complicate many an issue, including that of New World aborigines."[342]

Five students from Defiance College in Defiance, Ohio, traveled over 2,000 total miles to undertake a two-week search for Bigfoot. "We had our doubts when we first left, but as time went on we were sort of overwhelmed by the evidence," said Bill Brampton, one of the students. The other expedition members included Kevin McTeague, Gary Scharff, John Corns, and Doug Dayne. The search was conducted as part of Defiance College's month-long session, called an "inter-term," for special studies whose successful completion provided students credit equal to an ordinary course.

The Defiance students said their opinions changed after interviews with eyewitnesses and people who made a living out of investigating Bigfoot. They obtained a 17-inch footprint given to them by a Californian grocer (possibly Al Hodgson).

Corns was the catalyst for the trip; his interest in Bigfoot sparked after reading a book on the topic. Their search on the West Coast started in Weaverville, California. "We went into a small café, a bar," Scharff said. "John sat down next to a refrigerator and there was this sticker—just a big foot." As they approached locals, they learned that not everyone was keen to discuss the topic. "The man at the gas station said it was just a bunch of Indians trying to scare people," McTeague said. The group then drove north to Willow Creek where they found few people willing to admit having seen Bigfoot. Corns said of those who would talk of their Bigfoot sighting, they generally "weren't saying a lot. The fear of ridicule was really strong." Back at Defiance College, the students said they were considering studying the commercialization of Bigfoot and its consideration as a marketable property.[343]

Bigfoot was central toward younger kids' activities as well. "It's the greatest way any boy could start his summer vacation this year," said East Valley YMCA Director Bill Danch. San Jose's East Valley YMCA started a popular "Bigfoot Caravan" in the late 1960s for boys 12 to 15 years old. The first of two caravans in 1970 departed after school let out on June 22, and returned a week later on June 30; the second outing was advertised for July 6 to July 12. A few of the caravan's points of interest included Mt. Lassen, Shasta Lake, Reno, Lake Tahoe, and the California Gold Country. One whole day was allotted for Humboldt County, billed as the "home of the legendary Sasquatch—Bigfoot Monster—where caravaners will spend the day looking for signs of the famous half-human missing link."[344]

During the trip, boys took turns preparing meals and engaged in camping, fishing swimming, hiking, and exploring wild areas of Northern California. But there is little doubt as to the main leverage and promotion the YMCA relied upon. Director Danch said, "Bigfoot is a must for any adventurous junior high school boy. It's the kind of caravan that makes kids repeaters, as is shown by the number of boys signed up for this year's trip who came in '68 and '69."[345]

The YMCA Bigfoot Caravan took boys into Bigfoot country, but Noah Fredericks' truck brought Bigfoot information to people. Fredericks and his specially modified truck bedecked in Bigfoot art toured, according to the *Red Bluff Daily News*, to entertain and educate the public on Bigfoot.[346]

Print & Film

John A. Keel, who had given much attention to UFOs, wrote an article titled "Incredible Monster-Men Sightings in the U.S." published in the August 1970 *Male* magazine. Bigfoot articles via men's magazines proliferated in this period, often invoking lurid and garish tones and recycling canonical Bigfoot stories (Ruby Ridge, Ostman, etc.) with newer stories. The legacy of hairy hominid stories in *Sir!* during the '50s, in the early '60s' *True*, and in *Argosy* in the latter '60s, continued with assorted and sundry men's magazines in the early '70s. In this particular piece, Keel focused (with a certain mordant humor) on Bigfoot encounters occurring in swamps.

> The swamp creature is not necessarily a special breed of monster, though. In most cases the descriptions are very

> similar to our mountaineering Abominable Snowman. We shall call him the Abominable Swamp Slob, or A.S.S., for short. While the ABSM thrives in forests and high places, the A.S.S. prefers low-level marshes and bayous. There's hardly a respectable swamp in the Deep South that does not boast at least one A.S.S.[347]

Keel's article included 20 accounts describing encounters in 14 states to "demonstrate our theory that these events tend to recur in the same 'window' areas year after year and even century after century."[348] Such fixed centers of activity were veritable playgrounds of events strange and incredible and became a lynchpin to Keel's approach to the subject of paranormal doings.

Keel's 1971 book, *Strange Creatures from Time and Space*, which the author dedicated to Ivan T. Sanderson, is a collection of unusual creatures and monsters, including the Abominable Snowman and Bigfoot. Keel found relationships between strange events witnessed in our world, one of which was the assertion that Bigfoot and UFOs shared a nexus: "Even more incredible is the steadily accumulating evidence which strongly suggests that the hairy ABSMs are connected in some peculiar way with the phenomenon of unidentified flying objects."[349]

By 1970, both Patterson and Green had each published two books. Their collected sightings and stories were in large measure regionally focused and attentive to the Pacific Northwest. Keel's "Incredible Monster-Men Sightings in the U.S." provided several synopses of Bigfoot sightings east of the Mississippi. As acceptance of reports dispersed over a broader geographic area entered the public's consciousness, Bigfoot expanded beyond a micro-level fixation to an appreciation of continental scale; with each giant stride Bigfoot was indeed going macro, ever conquering new terrain. Step outside your home practically anywhere in non-urban North America and Bigfoot could possibly be lurking just out of sight. Town and county-named monsters, whose similarities made them analogous to Bigfoot, spread in frequency, publicity, and popularity. With respect to American geography, several of the biggest Bigfoot stories in the nascent '70s were well out of the northwest's bounds: Momo, Knobby, and the Florida Skunk Ape to name only a few. The ubiquitous Bigfoot could show up next in your county, your hometown, your backyard.

Referencing the research of Gordon Nicholson, Warren Smith wrote several conclusions explaining Bigfoot behavior in his book *Strange Abominable*

Snowmen (1970), which suggested Bigfoot form family units, they live in the mountains, employ a language, have highly developed senses, and may live to 200 to 500 years old. "I owe this theory to Roger Patterson," Nicholson stated. "He said that the reason we don't find carcasses or skeletons is the possibility of their long life. It is fascinating to consider that these enormous forest creatures may have been peeking from the woods when the first white men stepped onto the North American land mass."[350]

On January 18 and 19, 1971, the Jubilee Theater in Edmonton showed, as the second half of a double bill with *Yukon Safari*, BBC's *Bigfoot*, titled *Legend of Sasquatch* for Canadian audiences. René Dahinden was on hand with several footprint casts. In 1970 the same double bill played to three capacity crowds during a five-night run in Calgary, with a thousand disappointed patrons turned away at the door during the first few nights.[351]

Bigfoot made one of its first forays into '70s children's programming on *Scooby Doo* with the episode, "That's Snow Ghost." The Mystery Inc. gang visits Wolf's End Lodge where they encounter a white-furred Yeti-like creature who attempts to scare people away from a jewel-smuggling operation. Fred emerges from this episode with having voiced the most brilliant deduction: "Wait a minute! If the Snow Ghost didn't really turn (Shaggy) into a ghost, maybe he's not a ghost either!"[352]

Dave Simms, staff writer for the *Palm Beach Post*, wrote an unfavorable review of the Saul David-produced film, *Skullduggery*.

> The banality of the first half of "Skullduggery," the movie that opened at the Carefree yesterday, is matched only by the crassness of the second half.
>
> That is not to say that "Skullduggery" doesn't have its moments.
>
> It has one long moment, from beginning to end, of apartheid mentality.
>
> It has shorter moments of soap opera mentality at its worst.
>
> It has what I suppose is one truly funny line said by a bit player who is supposed to represent the movie-makers' version of a Black Panther.
>
> And it has one line of perverted wisdom, at movie's end, that purports to tell us we have the authority to decree who is human and who isn't.[353]

In this, one of Burt Reynolds' lesser known movies, a tribe of hairy hominids called Tropis are discovered in New Guinea and promptly exploited as veritable slave labor in a mining enterprise.

> "Skullduggery" is one of those dread and baleful instances in which the intention (guessed from small, crumb-sized traces) and the realization are so incredibly far apart that you do begin to wonder if the various creative forces involved were ever in touch with each other at all.
>
> What producer Saul David had in mind, I do believe, was a satire, in the guise of a derring-do exploration story, which would deal with the slippery question of what makes man different from the animals. (What, if anything.) The satire could have—was to have—poked unkindly fun at racist attitudes as arising in the hue of your choice, at the acquisitive instinct, at cheap sentiment and at bleeding-heart liberalism and at smugness in any form.[354]

Upon its initial release, *Skullduggery* was panned by critics and ignored by moviegoers; faulted for coming up short in its courtroom denouement of race relations by giving equal time to humanist conservationism and man's right to exploit nature's resources.

Another lackluster hairy hominid film from this period was John Carradine's *Bigfoot*.

> After the Christmas deluge theaters traditionally suffer an acute shortage of product. That's got to be the reason why "Bigfoot" was booked into 39 drive-ins and hardtops.
>
> An utterly unconvincing "missing link" monster movie, it's one of the low-budget affairs boasting a large cast of has-beens, never-weres and stars' untalented offspring. "Bigfoot" leaves a small imprint indeed.
>
> Somewhere in the Pacific Northwest (and, all too obviously, on a Hollywood set) there's this tribe of half-man, half-ape creatures—in fact, they're a couple of motheaten-looking Central Casting simians—led by one especially large beastie dubbed Bigfoot by the Indians.[355]

Thus began Kevin Thomas' caustic review for the *Los Angeles Times* upon *Bigfoot's* rerelease in 1972. Of note is James Craig's presence in the cast as the sheriff. Once upon a time, Craig had been signed by MGM as competition for Clark Gable.

Trog has the distinction of bucking the general trend in Abominable Snowman and Bigfoot movies by making its starring hairy hominid more on the diminutive scale than one of hulking, towering stature. Gene Siskel's October 1970 review (Siskel had just passed the year mark writing movie reviews at the *Chicago Tribune*) provides a capsule synopsis of the movie and unmistakably captures his poor opinion of the movie:

> The primitive man was found in a cave by three young spelunkers. Upon hearing their description of the beast Dr. Brockton, the author of "Social Structure and Primates," concludes that Trog, as the little fellow is affectionately called, may be The Missing Link.
>
> The film is as ludicrous as anything you'll ever see. Because the movie is essentially a monster picture, consider the monster. If Joan Crawford, dressed in a beige pants suit, can go in to the cave and capture Trog, how tough can he be? Moreover, Trog, who resembles Joe E. Ross dressed up as a Hell's Angel, is the shortest member of the cast.[356]

Siskel gave *Trog* the ignominious rating of zero stars.

SIGHTINGS 1970-71

Bigfoot on Mill Creek Road (1970)

After a hard day of work in the harvest fields, Rich Myers drove his motorcycle along the Mill Creek Road, Walla Walla, Washington. As Myers neared Camp Kiwanis, darkness overtook the day's last light. He told "roving reporter" Vance Orchard that he wasn't sure why he turned his head to the left, unless perhaps a just-perceptible movement caught his attention. "There . . . at a low point in the brush," Myers began, "was a huge, shadow-like form which at first I thought might be a couple of guys from Camp Kiwanis playing a prank, one on the shoulders of the other. It was 10-12 feet tall. Then it made a weird, screaming sound, high-pitched, with its arms outstretched. . . . I immediately put the motorcycle into high gear and shot out of there and down the road."

Myers was uncertain whether the thing he saw was hair-covered or not. Having heard the screech of mountain lions before, Myers was able to rule that animal out. Myers recalled that the creature's hands were lighter in color than the rest of it.

> Of what he saw . . . and what he heard . . . Myers is uncertain.
> He definitely heard and saw "something" though, and he is also certain what he saw and heard was not man or beast of the well known variety![357]

Benton Monster (1970)

About fifteen persons reported seeing a hairy, white-furred, ape-like creature, which they couldn't explain or identify, romping about Benton, Wisconsin, in the late summer of 1970. Some witnesses estimated it weighed 300 pounds and its height at around seven feet. One woman said "It's not a laughing matter. I saw it down there Sunday night [August 30] and I'm scared. I didn't sleep at all last night."

Town marshal Jerry Bottomley sounded decidedly unconvinced. "It's just a hoax," he said. Others, especially those who had spied the creature in its passing, expressed the matter differently. "I seen it," stated 12-year-old Robert Dixon matter-of-factly. But Robert's twin brother Richard was in Bottomley's camp: "I think they're making it up." Robert's encounter with the Benton Monster placed him in fairly close proximity to the creature. Robert closed to within only 25 or 30 feet as he and some friends gave chase to the thing, "but it got away," he said.

Mayor Eugene Redfern thought the matter was harmless; "it's just some kids having some fun," he said. As reports of the monster mounted, some remarkable claims were made including an account of a motorcyclist clocking the creature at 90 m.p.h. "I just can't put too much faith in those reports," said John Schleifer, a local attorney.

What was undeniably true was that the sightings had unnerved some of the residents. Search parties, some upwards of 50 people, went through the area around the town dump and the high school's football field, but no clues were uncovered. A local woman said the creature was in her yard and smelled "like a deer, only stronger." Another woman said the creature's presence at her home bothered her dogs, setting them to "barking like mad and then something bumped hard against the side of the house and it shook the windows." All in all, Sheriff Ken Pratt felt the matter would blow over. "It might be just someone with a white sheet trying to scare some kids," he said. "Anyway, there is no such thing as monsters. Is there?"[358]

Bowers Family (Vader, Washington) (1970)

Mrs. Wallace Bowers couldn't have guessed what she would see when she answered the summons from her children. It was Monday, December 4, 1970, when Bowers stepped outside her door and stood transfixed by the huge footprints in the inch-deep snow in the Bowers' yard. The tracks measured fifteen inches long and upon close inspection, Mrs. Bowers saw that the prints sank down through the snow and had pressed the crushed gravel underneath about an inch and a half. Mrs. Bowers called the sheriff.[359]

Lewis County Sheriff William Wiester and a deputy came to the Bowers residence and took pictures of the footprints. Bowers said Wiester told her to call his office back if anything unusual should happen again. Though not because of another set of unusually large tracks, Bowers did call the police again when she and her son witnessed a strange light in the sky. Bowers also called a neighbor, Mrs. Clarence Hoven. Alerted, Hoven and three of her children looked out a window and saw what "looked like a bright star" moving in the sky. Mrs. Bowers said she saw the object at 7:15 and described it as "about the length of a car." She estimated she watched the moving object for about ten minutes. She thought the object had a central dome around which spun a larger circle. It was orange in the center, with the light diffusing toward the outer edge.[360]

Three days later, Mrs. Bowers again heard the cries of her children beckoning, "Mommy, come look!" She joined her children at the window to watch what at first "looked like a bright star," but it appeared to get closer to the home and the Bowers were able to watch it for about ten minutes.[361] She noted that "it appeared to be centered by a dome around which a larger circle seemed to be revolving."[362]

Bowers said the object seemed to be tipped sideways, and then appeared to hover briefly over the nearby Brownville power lines. As the Bowers continued to watch, the object left the vicinity of the power lines, changing from its orange color to a bright, clear light as it moved in the sky. It seemed to approach closer one last time, again changing color back to orange. The children claimed they saw a "grey shape" leave the flying object and descend to the ground before it vanished from sight. During the observation of the aerial anomaly, Mrs. Bowers noticed that the home intercom was giving off a peculiar sound. "And the funny thing is," she said, "we tried to use the intercom the night before and we got that same sharp sound." Later that week, while placing a log in the fireplace, Mrs. Bowers noticed the curtains moving in her boys' bedroom. "All the children were in the living room with me," she said. "And all I could think of was getting them safely out of there. So I loaded them into the car and we left, but I definitely saw a shape in the bedroom as we drove away." Mrs. Bowers and the children only returned to their home when Mr. Bowers returned from work. "I feel sure that was probably a prowler," Mrs. Bowers remarked. "We've had trouble in our neighborhood and I don't think it's related to the others [incidents at or observed from the Bower residence]. But the footprints and the saucer—I don't know . . ." Upon later inspection, the Bowers didn't find anything missing from their home. The prowler incident—added to the other events—reminded researchers Jerome Clark and Loren Coleman of what John Keel called, "bedroom invaders."[363]

"There's been so much excitement. So I've told the kids it was just Santa Claus checking on them. My husband works for Weyerhaeuser up on St. Helens and they're teasing him that he just brought home one of those Abominable Snowmen. Since this happened I keep running into people who have seen similar things—only they don't report them because they thought they'd just be laughed at."[364]

Lawton Wolfman (1971)

Several people claimed to have seen a "wolfman" on Friday and Saturday, 26-27 February, 1971, in different parts of west Lawton, Oklahoma. Donald Childs was reported to have suffered a heart attack after his encounter with the creature Saturday night when he observed it on all fours drinking water out of a homemade fishpond. Police Officer Clancy Williams said Childs described the creature as "tall, with a lot of hair all over his face, and dressed in an indescribable manner." Police received the first report of the creature on Friday night when an individual in West Lawton saw something described as resembling an ape. Police officer Harry Ezell said other witnesses claimed the creature was running in and out of traffic, dodging cars, and hiding in bushes.

Childs stated the creature sported long hair all over its face. "Maybe he had a beard too, I don't know. It was dark and I couldn't tell for sure. He was wearing dark-colored pants that were way too little and a plaid jacket that was kind of too small. His legs, what I could see of 'em, seemed hairy, but like I said, it was dark and I couldn't swear to it."

"All of a sudden he saw me and he was as scared of me as I was of him. He didn't even stand up or get any kind of running start—he just sprung from his squatting position and jumped clear over the pond. The next day I measured it and that pond is 12 feet across!" The creature's speed also struck Childs as unusual. "He could really run—awful fast. He ran kind of hunched over like an ape in a Tarzan movie. He wasn't running on all fours. It was definitely a man. I'm sure he was somebody—you know—mentally off. I've heard that people like that have strength that normal people don't have."

Childs, who had a history of heart trouble, suffered a heart seizure from the excitement of the encounter. The *Ada Evening News* reported Childs believed the spasms around his heart were caused by nerves "and could have led to a heart attack." Childs entered a hospital and was released Sunday.[365]

Three blocks away and a quarter hour later, soldiers from Ft. Sill reported an encounter with something resembling the creature seen in Lawton. Maj. Clarence Hill of the police patrol division had the Lawton patrolmen on alert Monday for further creature sightings. "It's watchful waiting," Hill said. Police looked for footprints left by the creature but found the ground too hard to register tracks.[366]

"Something weird is going on in Oklahoma," were the opening words of Jerome Clark's story in the September 1971 edition of *Fate* magazine. The better part of his article dealt with the strange creature seen in Lawton in 1971. C. Edward Green and his wife were driving along Lake Avenue late at night on February 26, 1971, heading toward home. At about 11:00 P.M. the couple saw a figure walking beside the road. "He was walking bent over like a gorilla," Green said, "but not on all fours. He wore black pants that were cut or torn off at the knees and he had a big beard—it began higher up on his face than beards usually do—and long hair, very unkempt." When the Greens arrived home they notified the police, believing they had encountered a "mentally disturbed person."

Shortly after, at about 11:15 P.M. a sound like a siren brought Green to the window of his second-story apartment. Looking out he found himself staring right in the face of the figure he had seen about fifteen minutes before on the road. "He was crouched down on the walkway," Green said, "and while I was startled myself, I noticed that the person, or whatever, was either extremely frightened or not oriented to his surroundings. There was a glazed expression in his eyes as if he didn't quite understand where he was." Green went on to describe the physical characteristics of the creature. "His hair and beard were very black and he himself was dark-complected. He was barefooted—his feet looked normal—and he stood at least six feet tall. Nothing about his body seemed disproportioned." Green witnessed the creature evince an interesting capability: "When he saw me he jumped to the gravel below. Now that's about a 15-foot jump but it didn't seem to bother him. He must have been very strong. I didn't stay to watch him run away." And what were Green's thoughts on what he had seen? "I think—or rather I like to think—he was some mentally deficient person."

Clark wrote that the police department received about 20 calls reporting a similar person or animal between Friday and Monday. Childs further stated he had heard from a farmer a few miles south of Lawton who had during the previous year experienced several disturbing incidents. On several occasions, the farmer had found a calf or cow dead with one of its legs ripped off. The remaining carcass was unmarked, the only visible injury being the missing leg. No footprints were ever found in the vicinity to suggest what could have perpetrated the mutilations.

By Wednesday, March 3, Captain Crawford Hawkins explained that three youths had confessed they played "ape" in the area where Green and other witnesses had their encounters over the weekend. "They told me," said Hawkins, "that one of their mothers had given them a mask to play with and they were cavorting around the yard acting like apes." The mask was recovered after a telephoned tip alerted police where to find it. The rubber mask was described as having dark hair and dark facial features.[367] At least one article stated parents of one of the teen-aged pranksters turned in a wolf mask to police on Tuesday night. Juvenile officer Pat Vickers said the incident was "just something that got built up all out of proportion." The whole affair had been the result of a prank that had genuinely scared folks. "There were some people that believed there actually was a monster, but there wasn't," she said.[368]

That the matter could be labeled a prank did not persuade Green. "I talked with the kids and I saw the mask," Green explained. "It bears no resemblance to what I saw. The mask was grotesque. The man's face was not. And it would have been pretty evident if the man had been wearing a mask. Furthermore, I didn't even see any kids around." Clark noted Green and Childs both seemed to have described the same creature as well as observed agility and inferred power. Lawton's Wolfman, Clark noted, came right on the heels of the Abominable Chicken Man (see below).[369]

The *Ada Evening News* pointed out the penchant to ascribe monsters to mundane causes. If not one of the below monsters is an exemplar of a Bigfoot entity, the illustrative point is clear: the weird and strange can be conveniently explained away.

> "Even those who are pure at heart
> And say their prayers at night.
> May turn to a wolf when the wolfbane blooms
> And the vernal moon is bright."
>
> Ran across this little bit of poetry somewhere while reading up on lycanthropy. (Look it up yourself if you want to know what it means.)
>
> Anyway, Lawton had its wolfman. The mask was found and the affair was disclosed as a ruse by Lawton teenagers. But they really had everyone going for a while.
>
> A newspaper is a fascinating sort of beast. And one of the fascinations is this sort of thing . . . the bizarre . . . the strange . . . the unexplained sounds and objects that are reported.
>
> After the initial and "mysterious" encounters there almost always turns out to be a rather mundane explanation.
>
> But for a while, Oh boy.

Here the editorial elaborates on several additional oddities, including:

The mystery of the "floating lights" out by the Busby Ranch:

> But they were dandy lights. In truth, they were flashlights operated by a group of imaginative young men from Allen. The lights did come and go. They did drift eerily about. (The boys would direct the beams this way and that.)

The Lion of Ahloso, Oklahoma:

> It turned out to be a pretty good-sized animal.
>
> It was "Bo."
>
> And "Bo" was a Great Dane, fawn-colored, who liked to ramble around. A reporter-photographer team from the NEWS got a bit of that strawlike packing material and wrapped it around Bo's neck and darned if he didn't make a pretty decent looking lion.

"Monster" throwing dirt up in a woman's yard:

The armadillo may be something of a nuisance but he won't hurt a flea.

Reports of big, skulking cats:

A family of ocelots was in business in the southeastern part of the county.

Lake monster:

Well, it turned out to be a strange animal. It was a nutria and it was a refugee from the fur business.[370]

Chicken Man (1971)

In the mid-'60s a strain of humor called "camp" became de rigueur, epitomized by the scene-chewing Adam West starring in TV's *Batman*. A high-camp character named Chickenman, created by Dick Orkin, started life in 1966 at a Chicago radio station. Philip McCombs, writing in *Stars and Stripes,* called Chickenman, "supercamp in the sense that it even parodied Batman." Chickenman and the brand of humor it embodied eventually faded, "to be replaced by the turned-on 'Laugh-In' neurotic socio-political horseplay." Chickenman enjoyed a resurgence of popularity among U.S. troops in Vietnam when AFVN played one of the 150 episodes each day, five days a week.[371] In 1971, Chickenman, minus the campy trappings, careened into the public spotlight again. This time styled "Chicken Man," it left a mystery of strange foot and handprints, a broken screen door, and one bemused zoo director.

An account of Oklahoma's Abominable Chicken Man was written of in *The Spokesman-Review* on March 1, 1971:

> An El Reno farmer walked out to his chicken coop one day in December and found its door on the ground, apparently thrown there after being ripped off the wall.
>
> On the surface of the door, and inside the coop on the walls, were a number of strange hand prints—like none he'd ever seen before. They were about seven inches long and five inches wide.
>
> The farmer called a state game ranger. The ranger had never seen anything like it either and he sent the door to the Oklahoma City Zoo to see what experts could make of the prints.

> The experts were baffled too. Zoo Director Lawrence Curtis says the prints appear to be like those of a primate. A primate is an animal like a gorilla or a man that can stand erect.

The thumb of the print was considered unusual; it crooked inside, resembling a deformity or injury. "It resembles a gorilla," Curtis said, "but it's more like a man." Additional strangeness found at the scene included barefoot tracks found outside . . . in December. "It appears that whatever made the prints was walking on all fours. There were some footprints on the ground outside," Curtis said. Since the first report from El Reno, 30 miles west of Oklahoma City, Curtis said he had received a report from a man in Stillwater and a woman in McAlester both of whom had discovered prints appearing similar to the El Reno case.[372] "We've shown [print photos] to several mammologists and several wildlife experts in Oklahomas [sic] and some passing through. All agree it is a primate," he said. "These prints were made by some sort of a man, perhaps one looking for chickens."[373]

Curtis deliberated on which indigenous animal to Oklahoma could have made the tracks—bears, mountain lions, or humans. Ruling out bears and mountain lions left Curtis with the conclusion a man-like creature was responsible, but further than that he withheld speculation. Reporter Dennis Montgomery's article dubbed the creature the "Abominable Chicken Man" in an article which acknowledged the fame the creature had accrued. "A tremendous amount of material has come in," Curtis told him, referring to letters which contained accounts of footprints in other parts of the country, mainly the Pacific Northwest. Curtis only had "Chicken Man" handprints to deal with; the footprints discovered around the chicken coop were not preserved.

> The most interesting report Curtis has had [came] from a man in Springdale, Ark. "He gave a detailed sighting of three similar animals," said Curtis. "All of them were hairy and about 6 feet tall, and extremely strong. One of them pushed over a tree."
>
> The writer also reported that cattle in the area had been dying for no apparent cause.
>
> Curtis said he is surprised that the creatures are such a popular subject.

Back in El Reno with winter on the wane, the Chicken Man laid low, dealing no more mayhem to area chicken coops and no further sighting reports were publicized.

> But he has given birth to a sort of heir.
>
> Last weekend several persons in Lawton, Okla. observed a seven-foot "hairy creature," in pants several sizes too small, which reportedly could jump 15 feet, straight up.
>
> One man, who looked out his second story window to see the creature staring back at him suffered a mild heart attack.
>
> Two days later an anonymous phone call directed local police to a Halloween mask, apparently used in the hoax. Two youths later admitted being responsible for the episode. One was 6-foot 1 and neither was hairy nor an especially good jumper.
>
> "It does indicate how people exaggerate what they see," says Curtis.[374]

When asked for his professional opinion on the Chicken Man, Curtis said "I'm an optimistic skeptic. I wouldn't reject the possibility that such an animal exists." After all, Montgomery's article concluded, something did leave those tracks.[375] Commenting on the distance between the locales of creature reports, Curtis stated, "If there is one there is more than one. There has to be more than one unless he's hitchhiking." Reporters who interviewed Curtis couldn't help but notice the El Reno chicken coop door present in his office. It was there "for reference," Curtis said, "and one supposes, for conversation."[376]

Jerome Clark provided another angle on the Chicken Man in the pages of the September 1971 *Fate* magazine:

> In its February 28 issue *The Oklahoma Journal* announced in a front page story: "Hen House Terror Just Monkey Stuff." Staff writer Jane Berryman wrote that Howard Dreeson, who operates a sawmill in Calumet 13 miles west of El Reno, had seen a chimpanzee in the woods several times and tried unsuccessfully to catch it. The reporter quotes zoo director Curtis' suggestion that a chimp may have escaped from a psychology laboratory at the University of Oklahoma at Norman. (Curtis told *Fate* in early April that "these prints are definitely not from a chimp.")

A check with the laboratory in question (run by Dr. Bill Lemon of the University's psychology department) elicited amused assurance that no chimps were missing.

Dreeson himself believes the animal escaped from a circus train wreck or derailment near Mulhall some years ago. (Mulhall is about 50 miles northwest of Calumet in central Oklahoma.) *Fate* was able to determine, however, that the "wreck" was a minor one and no animals got away.

How does Dreeson know it was a chimp?

"I've seen 'em on television," he says. "You ought to see this fella—actually I think it's a female. It's about, oh, 30, 31 inches tall and it's got a face that looks like a prune. Cute little fella. Sure would like to catch it."

Dreeson regularly leaves food for the animal, which he has seen three times, always at dusk.

"I always leave out oranges and bananas," he says. "They're gone in a couple of days and I never find the skins.

He keeps a heavy net in his pickup truck hoping one day to snare the animal. "I have a good idea where it might be spending the night now and if I can't catch it," he observes, "maybe at least I can get a picture of it. I keep a camera with me all the time these days."[377]

Pemiscot 'Monster' (1971)

One of the first sightings of a three-eyed, 10-foot-tall monster haunting Pemiscot County, Missouri, took place at Steele during the Spring of 1971 with later reports occurring south of Bernie. Five different colors describing the creature were reported to the Pemiscot County's sheriff's office. Some reports conveyed relatively simple descriptions: on one occasion the creature was black and shaggy; at other times it was given a more elaborate portrayal: the body of a human and the head of some ferocious monster, between seven to 12 feet tall, and as many as five legs and three eyes.

In time, the Sheriff's department received calls asking, "Have you caught the thing yet?" One of the department's officers said, "Some of these little children around here have really been frightened by the rumors. I told them I would catch the 'weary wolf' and put him in my jail, and they clapped their hands with joy." Some reports suggested the monster was dog-like from the waist up and the body of a woman the waist down.

James Chandler, Pemiscot County's Conservation Agent, thought the monster is really just a black bear. Like the sheriff's department, Chandler had also received calls, including one from a man who was a confessed monster-story investigator. On Saturday [May 22], a woman reported seeing the thing in Bernie and investigating officers discovered tracks in a nearby field and indications of a spot where the thing "wallered down."

"It could have been a dog or a bear," said one of the investigating officers, "but there were some awful big tracks left by it if it was," he concluded. That it could all just have been a hoax or prank was not lost on many locals. "I think it's just a big joke," said one local man. One of the first official acts of the new Pemiscot County Sheriff Thad O. Shelly was the investigation of the monster reports. Said one officer, "If we catch it, I'm going to put a chain around its neck and there will be some changes made around here. We may even let it be the bailiff in court."[378]

Lee Township Monster (1971)

Based upon an area's history with inexplicable creatures, localized monster sightings could engender nativistic nods to homespun monsters from the past. Stories of the Lee Township Monster in Calhoun County, Michigan, stirred many residents' 10-year-old memories of another local monster which romped some six miles to the south: The Wilder Creek Green-Eyed Monster. That monster's mollifying exposure as the work of young pranksters probably put some residents' minds at ease as the Sheriff's department received several reports of "large, hairy monsters," in the first full week of October 1971, occurring within a "monster-zone" around 19 ½ Mile road and P Drive north (the junction of these roads is just east of Lake of the Woods).

> But the results aren't in yet about the Lee [Township] case. Is that too just a couple of kids out for lark, or are there real, live, black hairy beasts roaming wistfully through hill and dale?
>
> Whichever is the case, one thing is for sure: there IS indeed something in Lee [Township]. Something.[379]

The sheriff's office received several calls asking for information on the sighting. On Thursday, October 8, reporter Suzy Gust (whose byline was accompanied by 'Monster Reporter') went out to the area but reported nothing extraordinary. Gust interviewed people in the community for their thoughts on the monster matter. "We've got plenty of two-legged variety," said one woman, "but this is the first I've heard about the other kind." Mr. Oral Hogle, a resident on 19 ½ Mile Road, said he only learned of the creature from reading its account in the newspaper. "It's probably just someone dressed up in an old bearskin or something," he said. "I don't think it's anything else." Another woman in the area said she had noticed increased traffic along the roads. "Probably looking for that monster," she suggested. This same woman also observed probing flashlight beams in nearby fields she supposed belonged to monster hunters. Yet another woman said she received a call from her sister, who upon reading of the monster had called her sibling to warn her of threat to life and limb.[380] Gust concluded her article with a wry observation: "So, then, if there is a monster in Lee [Township], he's (or she's?) probably snickering up her hairy coatsleeve [sic] right about now, laughing about making all those stupid little humans run around in circles."[381]

Martin's Bigfoot Tale (1971)

Wildlife artist Bernard Martin wrote about his interest in Bigfoot and his own experience looking at possible evidence in the field.

> Now let's get on with the tale. The spark for my search for the Abominable Snowman was ignited when young Dan Reandeau, a park aide at Sequim Bay State park near Port Angeles, Wash., entered my trailer, slumped into a chair, propped up his feet and began to unravel a yarn that would match any told by his illustrious grandparent.
>
> "You ever see a Sasquatch?" he asked, studying my eyes intently for a telltale flicker.
>
> "Nope. Have you?" I responded, aware that I was being had.
>
> "Sure. An enormous brute with thighs thicker than second-growth fir and feet 18 inches long."
>
> Dan settled back. Having set me up, he decided to see if I'd rise to his bait. "Get on with it," I snapped.
>
> "Well, my girl friend, Jodi Germeau, and I were spending a pleasant afternoon at an old abandoned pioneer farm in the mountains a few miles above Port Townsend. We wandered about barefoot, exploring the old buildings and marveling at

the skill of the one who hand-split the cedar and fashioned the structures.

"After wandering about the buildings we walked into a nearby meadow surrounded by a growth of cedar trees. As we stood in the clearing enjoying the sun, we were startled by a sharp snap as though a tree branch had been broken by a hoof of a heavy animal.

"There were no farm animals here. We waited, expecting the appearance of an elk. Moments later a second twig snapped like a report from a pistol. Then I saw it. 'Look, Jodi, look! Bigfoot!'

"Terror leaped into Jodi's eyes as she stared into the shadows where the huge form lurked. Shrouded by cedar boughs, the creature studied us intently. Then apparently to gain a better vantage point, it side-stepped into deeper shadows. A shaft of sunlight spotlighted the heavy, hairy legs of the beast.

"'Run, Jodi, run!' I shouted. Terrified, we raced to our car. Jumping in, I pressed the starter and shoved the gear to 'drive.' The car lurched forward, then promptly settled in a bog that edged the old skid road.

"We jumped out and ran madly down the road. Rocks, like knives, jabbed into our barefeet. Blackberry thorns ripped our shins and tore at our clothing as we raced away. We did not stop until we reached a farmhouse two miles distant.

"There we panted our story, borrowed a tractor and armed with the only weapon we could find—a pressurized can of windshield cleaner—returned and yanked the car back into the road."

I roared with laughter as Dan finished his yarn. The vision of the young man and woman racing barefooted down the road to escape an Abominable Snowman struck me as hysterically funny.

"O.K., so you don't believe me," snarled Dan. "Tomorrow is my day off. Jodi and I will pick you and Maxine up about 9 A.M. and take you to the lair of the Sasquatch. You'll see the animal's paths. You may even see the critter. If you do, you'll run, too."

So the following morning, my wife and I piled in the car with our two friends and whizzed away to the land of Bigfoot.

Arriving at the old farm, I uncased my camera and we started poking about.

My lens pried into and about the old, old buildings. We saw and photographed paths that Dan claimed were fashioned by the beast's feet. Departing the clearing, we explored the surrounding forests. Following a path we emerged in a small clearing.

"Look," yelled Dan as he pointed to the earth. There pressed in the dirt of a freshly dug gopher mound was what appeared to be a portion of a print left by an enormous foot.

I snapped several frames of the footprint, then asked Dan, Jodi and Maxine to gather around the gopher mound for a final shot. Just as the camera clicked I saw a branch in the background swing sharply. I rushed to the spot but found nothing. However, I was jubilant. I knew my film, when developed, would reveal anyone or anything lurking in the background of the group picture.

The following day I rushed to town to have the film developed. When the prints were returned I came down with a thud. Only four or five frames shot inside the old building with a flash were good. None of the shots made with available light developed. Apparently, after using the flash, I failed to reset the shutter-speed dial.

Was Bigfoot there? Was he watching as I snapped the shutter? Your guess is as good as mine. Frankly, I'll always wonder.[382]

Tom Tiede Sighting (1971)

Tom Tiede was a syndicated newspaper columnist and a newspaper owner and publisher in Georgia, California, and Utah. In 1971, he wrote an article in which he admitted to having seen something in the woods that fit the description of Bigfoot. While a young sports writer for a newspaper out of Kalispell, Montana, Tiede decided to seek out and interview a hermit who lived in the woods northwest of Kalispell. Tiede admitted to getting off course during his trek in the woods and realized he would not, on that outing at least, be visiting with the hermit. He sat down for a rest before starting his return journey.

> Suddenly, and I swear by the Abominable Snowman, I saw it. About 50 yards away. Coming down off one of the interconnected hills, passing at moderate speed through the woods, disappearing and reappearing in the trees. I don't remember feeling anything. I could see plainly that it was not like anything I had ever seen before. It had swinging arms, like a B-grade gorilla movie, a gray coat of hair, and a small head which I could not make out. And it was moving parallel to me.
>
> Now, to be honest, I don't know if it saw me. But it stopped. And seemed to look in my direction. As it stopped, so did its song. I raised my rifle, forgot to take the safety off, but did nothing anyway. The thing paused for just a moment, then moved, silently now, off in a direction my shaky compass said was north.[383]

Minnesota Iceman

The July 1970 edition of *Saga* magazine contained a story enigmatically titled, "I Killed the Ape-Man Creature of Whiteface" by Frank Hansen. The referenced creature, which has come to be called the Minnesota Iceman, was male, human-like, hair-covered, and entombed in ice as a travelling exhibit that Hansen displayed at fairs, carnivals, and malls in the late '60s through the mid-'70s. Ivan Sanderson and Bernard Heuvelmans studied the creature (through the ice) and concluded it was an authentic, genuine specimen of a once-living creature. John Napier determined to his satisfaction the Iceman was simply a model, fit for the purpose as sideshow exhibit. Sanderson, then science editor of *Argosy*, wrote an article on his examination of the creature in April 1969, but it was Hansen's *Saga* article which first gave the public his side of the story, including the tale of how he obtained the creature, itself a malleable history that Hansen changed over time as he saw conditions warrant. The saga of Hansen, the scientists, and the Iceman was one of the most unusual Bigfoot stories of the '70s and begins below with Hansen's recounting for the *Saga* audience the events of the fateful 1960 day after he and his hunting buddies left a small resort on the shores of the Whiteface Reservoir and he came face-to-face with the creature.

> We left the cabin a few minutes after six on the second morning and, although I had not spotted a deer on the opening day, I

was confident that a narrow neck of swamp where I had hunted was one of the best locations in the area. I sat motionless on a hillside overlooking this pine-crested thicket for almost two hours. I was about to leave for another location when a movement at the edge of the swamp caught my eye. My pulse quickened as I thumbed for the safety catch on my customized 8mm Mauser. A large doe, partially obscured by a cedar tree, was staring directly at me.

Suddenly, a shot echoed from the other side of the swamp. With one frightened leap, the doe dashed out of the thicket and headed straight toward me. I raised my gun into firing position just as she spotted me. Making three great leaps broadside, she scrambled back toward the swamp. I fired just as she reached the edge of the trees and she fell, headlong, onto the ground. I bolted my rifle and tried to get off another shot but she was up and out of sight into the heavy brush before I could take aim.

I walked toward the thicket where I located large spots of blood on the frozen grass. I also discovered that the wounded doe had left a clear trail that led straight into the swamp. There was no snow on the ground and my borrowed compass proved to be useless. It was against my better judgement but I decided to follow the trail for s short distance into the swamp.

I pushed slowly along following the doe's bloody trail, expecting her to be lying just beyond the next bush. After an hour, however, I realized that it would be impossible to pack the deer out even if I did find her. I checked my bearings and decided to take just a few more steps before retracing my trail out of the swamp.

Stepping over a small cedar log I heard a strange gurgling sound just ahead. Startled, I raised my gun and listened to the noise for a moment concluding that the deer was down and strangling in her own blood. Cautiously, I eased my way toward the sound.

Suddenly, I froze in horror!

In the middle of a small clearing were three hairy creatures that at first looked like bears. Two of these creatures were on their knees, tearing at the insides of a freshly killed deer. The deer's innards were scattered around the clearing and the "things" were scooping blood from the stomach cavity into the

> palms of their human-like hands. Raising their cupped hands of fresh blood to their mouths, they swallowed the liquid.
>
> The third creature was about 10 feet away, on the edge of the clearing, crouched on his haunches. It was obvious that he was a male of similar stature as a man. Absolute horror gripped every muscle of my body as I stared at this frightening tableau before me. I felt as if my body had turned to stone.
>
> Without warning the male leaped straight into the air from its crouched position. His arms jerked upward, high over his head, and he let out a weird screeching sound. Screeching and screaming, he charged toward me. I cannot remember aiming my rifle nor do I recall pulling the trigger, but a bullet must have slammed into the beast's body.
>
> As blood spurted from his face the huge creature staggered, seemingly stunned by this unexpected happening. I do not recall ejecting my spent shell nor do I recall firing my rifle again. In many sweat-drenched nightmares however, I have vividly envisioned the blood-covered face lying on the ground beside the mutilated deer. I have absolutely no recollection of ever seeing the other two creatures again. They seemed to have vanished into "thin air."
>
> Blind with fear, I started to run. I dashed over the swampy terrain not knowing or caring in which direction I ran. My only thought was to get away from those horrible "things." I stumbled, fell, picked myself up, and fell again. I thought they were right behind me. Finally, I fell onto the frozen marshland completely exhausted, not caring if the creatures caught me. I lay there waiting for the attack.[384]

Having apparently blacked out, Hansen woke with no idea how long he had been unconscious. Deciding his compass was all but worthless, Hansen concentrated his efforts on leaving the area. He raised his rifle and fired three shots into the air, a signal that a hunter is in danger, and eventually he heard a response. When back with his hunting companions, Hansen felt the urge to unload his experience and share the incredible events of that day. But each time he considered his military retirement only five years away. Hansen wrote that he was a member of the 343rd Fighter Group, out of Duluth, Minnesota. Concerns over being found mentally unfit and medically discharged prevented him from divulging the day's remarkable events.

So, Hansen bore it all alone and wondered exactly what the creature could have been.

> My mind reeled with the possibilities. If I returned to the swamp what would it prove? Had I killed the creature? Was it an escaped gorilla? Or was it a man dressed up for some deer-hunting prank? Except for being completely hair-covered, the "thing" seemed to have every feature of a human being. What about the two creatures that had disappeared? Or, had the whole thing been the product of my imagination? Everything was unreal and totally incomprehensible.[385]

A month after the incident and amidst the throes of wrestling with his conscience, chronic migraine headaches hampered Hansen's desperate attempts to rationalize the experience. He realized his performance at work was in jeopardy until he determined what exactly he had experienced; the mystery, he understood, had to be solved. Hansen started watching weather conditions closely, waiting for a good snowfall that would permit him to hike back to the scene and allow him to backtrack confidently. The weather forecast on November 29 was propitious: five inches of snow fell in the Whiteface area. On Saturday, December 3, Hansen, his dog Mike, his shotgun, several rounds of double-O buckshot, and his swamp buggy hooked to the back of his pickup, headed north to Whiteface Reservoir. After passing Ranta's Resort he headed to the east side of the lake and unhitched his swamp buggy. Trundling along on 54-inch DC-3 aircraft tires, he drove the buggy down a logging trail looking for where his party had previously parked. Hansen excitedly anticipated what he might find, not the least of which included the possibility of encountering one of the creatures again. After making what Hansen referred to as several lucky guesses at Ys in the trail, he at last came into a clearing he recognized as the former parking spot. Confident in his bearings, Hansen and Mike headed out on foot for the scene of the encounter. Mike flushed out a browsing doe that made Hansen's heart race. "Mike, old friend, we'll be lucky to get back to the bug," he said to his dog. "Let's get out of here."

> It was almost two o'clock when I started to retrace my tracks in the snow. I wanted to get out of this devil swamp and back to civilization. My legs moved faster and faster as I swore to never set foot in the swamp again. I tripped over a large snow-

> covered log. When I tried to get up, horror flashed over me. *I had fallen directly on top of a frozen, human-like form.*[386]

Mike started to dig in the snow and Hansen fully realized the events from his hunting trip had been real: he had literally stumbled upon the creature's body. Hansen started brushing snow from the body and saw amidst much frozen blood that one of the eyes seemed to be missing. The creature's face was not hair-covered but much of the rest of the body was covered in long, dark hair. Comparing one of its hands with his own revealed it was twice as large as Hansen's. Hansen's fears began to subside the more he inspected the creature. He became convinced he had not shot a man but something man-like, perhaps even a freak of nature. Its preservation seemed perfect. Inspecting the surrounding area, Hansen found the remains of the deer carcass which had been predated upon, but these same scavengers had not touched the creature.

> I decided that the creature should not be left in the swamp. I was still concerned with the scandal that could jeopardize my retirement from the Air Force. It was impossible to dig a grave in the frozen earth. If the creature was left in the swamp, a wandering hunter might stumble over the body in the spring. An investigation by law officers might lead the authorities to me.[387]

Hansen hatched a plan. Concealing the buggy, Hansen returned to Duluth in his pickup and claimed the buggy was stuck. Gathering tools—pick, shovel, ax, and chainsaw, he returned to Whiteface Reservoir and drove the buggy to the creature's remains. Chopping and cutting the creature from the ice Hansen loaded it onto the rear platform of his buggy and secured it with cargo straps. Hansen managed to shift the form from his buggy to the back of his pickup. It was after dark when Hansen returned to his home in Duluth.

His wife became alarmed at the sight of the creature's frozen body. "What do you plan to do with the thing?" she asked. "I can't dig a grave, the ground is frozen solid," Hansen replied. "Maybe we can keep it in the freezer until spring?" Hansen offered, referring to the large freezer he and his wife had purchased only two weeks prior. "But the freezer is full of meat," his wife Irene said. "Then we'll have to give the meat away," Hansen said. "My retirement is more important than a few dollars' worth of meat," he concluded.

Irene finally agreed to the plan and waiting until after their three children were put to bed, managed to move the frozen form from the pickup to the freezer in the basement. "We'd better keep the thing covered," Irene said. "I'll keep the kids out of the basement tomorrow and clean out the freezer." The next day Hansen returned home to find his wife had cleaned out the freezer but was still apprehensive about the creature. "I don't know what it is, but it smells terrible and the odor is all over the house." Hansen and Irene worked at bending and working the creature into their freezer, after which they scrubbed their hands several times, washed their clothes, and opened basement windows to give the space an airing. "Let's not tell a single person about this," Irene implored. "We'll just leave it there until Spring."

> The creature remained in our food freezer for almost a month. Then, my curiosity drew me into the basement. Man or animal? A mutant human or a cross between the ape and man families? There were a hundred different explanations. I opened the freezer and discovered the creature's body was dehydrating. Certain parts of the body looked like a piece of dried-up meat.[388]

"If we bury it in the spring it won't make any difference," Hansen told his wife. "But if we learn what it is and decide to keep it then it should be properly preserved. I don't know how to keep it from drying out." Irene thought a moment. "Remember those Canadian lake trout that we kept for two years," she asked. "We froze them in ice water and they stayed fresh. Perhaps the thing could be preserved that way. It's worth a try." The couple poured 20 gallons of ice water into the freezer every day for a week after which the creature was totally encased in a block of ice.

> When the spring thaw arrived I was faced with another dilemma. It would require several days to melt the ice around the creature's body, and, in the process, the basement of our home would be filled with an odorous stench. I was also concerned about the danger of burying the "thing." A passer-by might see me digging a grave and alert the police. Transporting the body from my home to a grave site was equally dangerous. I envisioned a traffic accident, with the smelly creature tossed out on the pavement and a policeman staring at me as I fumbled for some rational explanation. My wife was now accustomed to

> having the creature in the freezer so I decided to leave it in the basement and not press our luck.[389]

In the summer of 1961, the Hansens purchased a retirement home, a farm, near Rollingstone, Minnesota. The family took up occupancy prior to Hansen's retirement and he finished his career commuting to Duluth. Not willing to risk a moving company to handle the freezer, Hansen rented a U-Haul truck and moved it himself. Friends were enlisted to help shift the "meat-packed" freezer from the basement to his pickup. The trip from Duluth to Rollingstone took seven hours and the top layer of ice started to melt. After the freezer was finally situated in a utility room on their Rollingstone farm Hansen finally permitted himself a sigh of relief. To prevent loss of power from an outage, Hansen purchased a generator for standby operation. Now, the "thing" could be buried at his convenience at a location of his choosing somewhere on his "back forty." Retirement came for Hansen in November 1965 culminating 20 years of military service, but he found himself disillusioned by the relative inactivity. He occupied himself in reading up on the Abominable Snowmen and he became convinced his ice-encased specimen was a derivative form of such creatures. Hansen also made discreet inquiries into the statute of limitations on murder and learned that the state of Minnesota had no time limit, so he decided to sit tight with his specimen for a little longer. In December 1966 Hansen met up with a showman who convinced Hansen to relieve some of his boredom by exhibiting a rare, old John Deere tractor Hansen had acquired. After a loan to the Smithsonian Institution, Hansen began showing the tractor on a selective basis. "Take your tractor on a full-time circuit of major fairs. You won't get rich but you'll have fun and discover a whole new world out there," his friend told him. "Would some sort of a frozen hairy creature resembling a prehistoric man make a good attraction?" Hansen asked. "It's a great idea," Hansen's showman friend said, "but where would you ever get a specimen like that?" Hansen likely had a knowing look as he contemplated the question. "Perhaps I could get one made," he said. The exhibit which came to be known as the Iceman had been from its first design meant for the titillation of fair goers.

> I returned home with only one thought in mind and immediately consulted with my attorney concerning the legalities of exhibiting the creature. He listened with amusement until I drove him to my farm and opened the freezer. He stared

> down into the cloudy ice with horrified fascination. Later, we discussed the legal aspects.
>
> "There's always the possibility of a murder charge if this thing is judged to be human." He informed me. "There are also laws concerning the transportation of dead bodies. I can see all sorts of legal difficulties."
>
> "I'm convinced the creature would make a great exhibit," I said. "Isn't there any way to do it by creating a model?"
>
> He lit another cigarette and thought a moment. "You have the original body. The authorities will be after it because this thing is the scientific find of the century; however, it might be possible to create a model as you suggested. Maintain a record of the model's construction but show the real creature instead. If the officials pressure you, it's a small matter to produce photos of the model taken during different phases of fabrication."
>
> "Better than that," I replied. "I'll even exhibit the model for the first year so that it will be accepted by carnies as a 'bogus' show."[390]

In January 1967 Hansen produced sketches of the creature and "went to Hollywood to confer with the men who make models for the motion picture industry." He talked with Bud Westmore, the director of make-up at Universal studios. Westmore's cost estimate to create a model based upon the sketches was $20,000. Further asking around led Hansen to Howard Ball, an independent artist who was making elephant models for displays at the La Brea tar pits. Hansen was able to engage Ball to make a sculpture of the creature and create a mold of the body. John Chambers from 20th Century Fox suggested a small wax studio in Los Angeles which possessed the technical expertise to implant the hair in accordance with Hansen's specifications. This led Hansen to Pete and Betty Corral who agreed to do the work and emplaced each hair on the model individually with an open-ended needle.

As the work neared completion, Hansen worried about the money-making potential of such an exhibit on the fair circuit. Hansen had invested "several thousand dollars," some of which he had borrowed. Hansen enlisted the aid of a friend in Pasadena and together they added the finishing touches to the model: bloody eyes, blood-soaked hair, and broken arm—all duplicated to match the prototype. Hansen froze water around the model in a cold storage room in Los Angeles which created some humorous moments. "W-w-w-w-where are you going with that thing?" an executive at the ice plant asked as Hansen brought in his model. "I've rented a storage room for a few days," Hansen said. "In our company?" The executive stared at the model. "My gosh! Was that a living 'thing'? This is a food processing plant. Get that thing out of here before a government inspector sees it." Hansen was able to secure a privately-owned locker that had recently closed and proceeded to ice down his creation. The frozen model was placed in a refrigerated coffin designed especially for the exhibit and was transported to Los Banos, California, for its first showing with West Coast Shows, opening to the public's scrutiny and pleasure on May 3, 1967. When people asked where the creature came from, Hansen replied with a stock answer of it discovery by Chinese fishermen in the Bering Straits. The last 1967 display on the fair circuit occurred in November at the Louisiana State Fair. By March 1968, as preparations for the new season of fairs were underway, Hansen felt the time was right to swap the real creature for the model.

> I cut off refrigeration to melt the ice from both specimens and made the switch using my farm tractor loader and an "I" beam. I worked the creature into position closely resembling the model by cutting the tendons in the arms and legs. I then started the difficult task of creating ice around the specimen. "This will be the greatest exhibit to hit the fair circuit," I said after the job was completed. "Even a trained scientist would be shocked to see this."
>
> The 1968 season was one of the most remarkable in our history. Physicians, professors and college students came from everywhere to see the exhibit. All pondered on the possibilities of a true "missing link."
>
> At the Oklahoma State Fair one prominent surgeon visited the exhibit on nine separate occasions. Each time he brought a different colleague. Even a high official of the State of Oklahoma tactfully suggested that we were not promoting our exhibit to its fullest extent by showing it on the fair circuit. At the Kansas State Fair the county pathologist was so intrigued that he sent many of his associates to see the "creature."[391]

Author Brian Regal calls the Iceman saga an example of "mainstream" scientists tendering initial seriousness followed by prolonged interest.

In December 1968, Sanderson's SITU was contacted by naturalist Terry Cullen who reported seeing a hominid-like creature encased in ice at the Chicago International Livestock Exposition. As chance would have it, Bernard Heuvelmans' *In the Wake of the Sea Serpents* had just been released in an English translation. Heuvelmans was conducting a publicity and promotional tour in New York and at the time of Cullen's contact he was staying at Sanderson's farm in northwest New Jersey. Sanderson and Heuvelmans traveled to Minnesota to see the Iceman. Hansen was initially reluctant to show his exhibit to the scientists but eventually relented, explaining his possession of the creature came about after he received it from an unidentified millionaire who himself had acquired it from Asia.

The scientists' inspection through the ice which was translucently clear in spots and obscured by milky opaqueness in others steered both men to accepting the Iceman as genuine. *Pursuit* magazine wrote: "Dr. Heuvelmans and the Director [Sanderson] went to inspect the specimen and saw immediately what it was."[392] Discussion followed between Hansen and the scientists about the intent to publish articles on the Iceman.

> However, the caretaker [Hansen] requested that the latter [Sanderson] not publicize his findings until specific permission was given by the owner who was alleged to be a "very prominent but eccentric man on the west coast." Dr. Heuvelmans gave no such assurance. The director later obtained permission to publish, but the parties concerned with the ownership of the specimen refused to answer half a dozen most pertinent questions as to its origin and history.[393]

Sanderson and Heuvelmans did write articles detailing their respective Iceman examinations and theories. Sanderson's account of his examination of the Iceman appeared in the May 1969 edition of *Argosy* where he served as contributing science editor.

> I must admit that even I, who have spent most of my life in this search, am filled with wonder as I report the following!
>
> There is a comparatively fresh corpse, preserved in ice, of a specimen of at least one kind of ultra-primitive, fully-haired man-thing, that displays so many heretofore unexpected and non-human characters as to warrant our dubbing it a "missing link."[394]

Sanderson shared with readers several of the Iceman's features that had struck him as highly significant: a long, slender thumb, wide (more than 10 inches) feet, a "pugged" nose likened to that of a Pekingese dog, the absence of lips, and covered in 2-4-inch hair. "Let me say, simply, that one look was actually enough to convince us that this was—from our point of view, at least—'the genuine article.'"[395]

The creature in the ice looked smaller than most descriptions of Bigfoot and far more proportional to a human; this observation supported a theory suggesting Bigfoot was derived from *Gigantopithecus* and that the Iceman was more in line with descriptions of the Almasti and closely fit with the scientists' expectations for a Neanderthal.

Some *Argosy* readers took exception with certain pronouncements bestowed upon the Iceman, as the example letter-writer below puts forward to the editor:

> I read Ivan Sanderson's "The Missing Link" (May) and found it interesting. But this time I think you have gone too far in saying this is the real thing.
>
> From the pictures in the article, it is impossible to tell what is in the ice block. How you arrived at all the particulars listed in the article is beyond my scientific knowledge. Merely by looking at "Bozo" through six inches of ice is no proof that the thing is real.
>
> Ruling out the possibility of a fake at this time is absurd. And until scientific studies are made after "Bozo" is defrosted no one will know if the so-called missing link has been found. Until such time, I believe that your magazine should refrain from making a flat statement that "Bozo" is the "genuine article."[396]

A convinced Sanderson immediately sought to interest his fellow scientists in the Iceman's inestimable value.

> Ever the hustling author, Sanderson whipped up some extensive notes on what he referred to as the "Hansen Case" and sent them to his old monster hunting cronies, asking them for their opinions. Carleton Coon, George Agogino, William Charles Osman-Hill, and John Napier all provided comments he would later use for an *Argosy* magazine article. Coon received

> his copy first, as Sanderson personally brought it to his Massachusetts home. Hoping to bring the full weight of the U.S. government to bear on the Iceman, Sanderson also sent copies of his memo to the Bureau of Customs, Department of Agriculture, Department of the Interior, Health, Education and Welfare, and the FBI. He immediately began scheming to get the carcass for himself or for some reputable institution so he could study and also parade it.[397]

In what became known as the "Hansen Case Memo," Sanderson wrote 15 pages of analysis and included his complaint against a scientific establishment's scant regard paid to subjects that would shake their very foundations. Sanderson sent his memo to contacts and scientists he deemed would be interested in the creature. Rather than dismissing the Iceman out of hand, Sanderson may have been surprised at the initial reaction generated within the scientific establishment he had railed against in his memo. Napier acquired a copy of Heuvelman's article describing his observations of the creature and contacted the Smithsonian Institution to inquire what avenues were open toward acquisition of the body. Dillon Ripley, then secretary of the Smithsonian, and who in the past had been contacted by mountaineer Eric Shipton to discuss procedures for a Yeti search, also read Heuvelman's memo. Regal reports that an informal Iceman Committee was formed within the halls of the Smithsonian owing to the initial reaction and buzz created within those hallowed halls. Regal writes:

> Excited about the possibilities of the find, William Charles Osman-Hill wrote Ripley about doing something. He asked the Smithsonian Institution's secretary, "Can you bring any influence to bear on the problem, either directly or through the legal channels?" Carleton Coon also contacted Ripley to put his two cents in. He hoped the Smithsonian would be able to get the body for proper study because "if it turns out to be what it seems to be, this could be a major breakthrough."[398]

Ripley sent a letter to Hansen inquiring directly about access to the body for scientific study. In the growing excitement, Hansen responded to Ripley in a letter dated March 20, 1969, that he no longer had possession of the body as the eccentric owner had come to Minnesota and reclaimed it.

However, Hansen noted, a replica, or "illusion" of the body would be available for the touring circuit next fair season. From the April 1969 *Pursuit:*

> It later transpired that the original (which we have code-named "Bozo" incidentally) is now alleged to have been hidden for a year. This information was given in writing to certain authorities. This exhibit had always been billed as a curiosity and probably a fake, but it had the subtitle on its exhibit truck of "Possibly a medieval man (sic) left over from the ice age (again sic)"! yet, the owner went to great lengths to ascertain what it was when he first got it, and then to even greater lengths to hide it and all trace of its origin when confronted with a proper request to allow it to be examined scientifically.[399]

Napier appreciated the bad publicity that could befall the Smithsonian if the Iceman turned out to be only a contrivance for carnival exhibition, but he remained wary, if in fact it was genuine, of letting it slip through the Smithsonian's fingers. Both Sanderson and Ripley reached out to J. Edgar Hoover and the FBI. Hoover's position was that unless a crime had been committed there was nothing for the Bureau to investigate and nothing to entice his organization's involvement.

Regal notes that at this point, Sanderson wrote his *Argosy* article:

> To give readers a better look at the creature, Sanderson had the photos he had taken and drawings he had done converted into appropriate color magazine illustrations by science fiction and wildlife artist John Schoenherr. These "artist's interpretations" showed details Sanderson believed the ice covering obscured from view on the magazine page. An experienced wildlife artist, Schoenherr made his first renderings chimplike. Sanderson rejected them because he wanted the creature to look more human. Schoenherr told Sanderson and the *Argosy* art director that the photos did not say to him human, but chimp. Determined to have a humanlike rendering, Sanderson insisted Schoenherr make the revisions. Needing the money more than he needed a fight with a past, and hopefully future, employer the artist relented and dutifully reworked the illustrations. The

> Iceman as the public would see him now looked more like a man than a chimp.[400]

Sanderson scrutinized photos of Hansen's (professed) replacement published in the Rochester *Post Bulletin* and wrote a letter to Napier stating why he thought the body as pictured in the *Post Bulletin* was the same he and Heuvelmans had previously studied. Sanderson posited that Hansen had repositioned the body and had it refrozen. Napier appeared to have lost patience with the proceedings and took up the position the Iceman was likely only a fake for carnival exhibition, a fact he stated in a June 1969 letter to Ripley, presenting a sort of denouement to the subject. Sanderson went on to write another article for *Genus*, an Italian journal. Of Sanderson's second article Regal writes, "This article ran somewhat longer, but toned down the drama of the *Argosy* piece and the Hansen Case Memo. For a 'scholarly' article, however, it contains no footnotes or citations."[401] Bernard Heuvelmans wrote *L'Homme Neanderthal est Toujours Vivant* concerning his investigation of the Iceman and Napier wrote of the Iceman affair in his own book, *Bigfoot: The Yeti and Sasquatch in Myth and Reality*.

Upon later reflection, Hansen realized that Sanderson and Heuvelmans' involvement had thrown a monkey wrench into his operations. Hansen said permitting the scientists' scrutiny and study of the Iceman "was a grave mistake on my part." According to Hansen, (and in contravention to what was published in *Pursuit*) Sanderson and Heuvelmans did not tell him of their intent to publish scientific reports. The articles of their Iceman examinations ushered in a wave of calls and inquiries to Hansen from all over the world from parties desiring to study and verify the creature's authenticity for themselves.

> Heuvelmans had stated in his article that it appeared that the creature had been shot. Newspapers began to speculate on the possibility that law enforcement authorities should investigate the manner in which I obtained the creature. ". . . If the body is that of a human being, there is the question of who shot him and whether any crime was committed," an article in the *Detroit News* reported.
>
> With these events swarming into my life, I became a regular visitor to my attorney's office. His advice was clear-cut and direct. "Frank, you had better substitute the model for the real specimen and then take off for a long vacation." This sounded

> like good advice, so I made arrangements to make the transfer in a cold storage warehouse. The original specimen was put into a refrigerated van and sped to a hiding place away from the Midwest. Refreezing the model took several days and it was during this period that newspapers carried accounts of both me and the creature vanishing.[402]

In an article titled, "Ends 'Bozo'—We Think," the July 1969 edition of *Pursuit* summarized the Iceman drama at the time the Sanderson and Heuvelmans-inspected specimen was allegedly replaced by a copy:

> This request [The Smithsonian Institution requested permission to inspect and X-ray the Iceman] was flatly refused by Mr. Hansen in a letter in which he also stated that the specimen which Heuvelmans and ITS [Ivan T. Sanderson] had inspected had been removed by the owner and would never again be exhibited, while a manmade copy was being prepared for the coming show season. Why such was needed when a copy was allegedly already on hand is not clear. However, the Smithsonian was led to a professional model-maker who stated that he had made just such a copy in April of 1967. Meantime, we had traced another professional model-maker who stated just as categorically, and for the record, that he had made another in April of this year [1969]. Both parties asked that their names not be divulged, but our man did say that he had been so requested by Frank Hansen! Hansen then turned up with the new model on exhibit in St. Paul, Minn. with a new truck containing a "something" in ice. This, however, did not resemble the thing we saw, and in five essential points. Further, the new signs on the trailer called the exhibit "SIBERSKOYA CREATURE"—A Manmade Allusion (sic); and it had a large notice saying "As investigated by the F. B. I."[403]

Odette Tchernine called the Iceman a "probable hoax," and in a chapter titled, "An Ice Mystery, or Murder?" of her book, *In Pursuit of the Abominable Snowman*, she discussed the Iceman puzzle including whether a model maker had been employed in its fabrication.

> George Berklacy of the Smithsonian, stated that he had been in touch with a Californian wax museum owner who told him that one of his employees had worked on the Iceman in the spring of 1967 inserting hair into the latex rubber body. This tallies with the time Frank Hansen began showing his "prehistoric" specimen at fair grounds. The museum owner would not disclose the name of the man who had performed the exhausting task of covering the shape with millions of hairs. The indication of decay escaping from the Iceman's glass case does not constitute a contradiction. A non-human substance like rubber can be equally objectionable when deteriorating.[404]

In Pursuit of the Abominable Snowman's consequent (and unflattering) review in the July 1971 issue of *Pursuit* magazine, is not wholly surprising given Tchernine's stance on the Iceman as a probable fake. *Pursuit's* review avers Tchernine "makes the most frightful muddle of it," calling Tchernine's research methods "odd" and taking issue with an Iceman illustration in her book labeled as an "artist's drawing of the Iceman" and attributed to Heuvelmans in her text. *Pursuit's* review clarified the drawing was actually made by Sanderson after lying atop the exhibit for six hours.[405]

Brad Steiger wrote that Hansen wrestled with second thoughts about whether his alleged act of self-defense had been against an animal or a subhuman.[406] And Hansen remained inscrutable in his *Saga* article, ending it on an obscure, murky note.

> During the past few months I have been pressed for the conditions or circumstance under which I would consider giving the specimen up for scientific evaluation. There are two conditions that must be met before I would even consider such an action. One: A statement of complete amnesty for any possible violation of federal laws. Two: A statement of complete amnesty for any possible violation of state and local laws where the specimen was transported or exhibited during the 1968 fair season.
>
> There will surely be skeptics that will brand this story a complete fabrication. Possibly it is, I am not under oath and, should the situation dictate, I will deny every word of it. But then no one can be completely certain unless my conditions of amnesty are met. In the meantime I will continue to exhibit

a "hairy specimen" that I have publicly acknowledged to be a "fabricated illusion," and leave the final judgement to the viewers. If one should detect a rotting odor coming from a corner of the coffin, it is only your imagination. A new seal has been placed under the glass and the coffin is absolutely air tight.[407]

Skunk Ape (1971)

As seen, conceptions of Bigfoot in 1970-71 expanded, giving giant hair-covered creatures a wider geographic range and the public's mainstream consciousness accepted Bigfoot as a creature existing outside the Pacific Northwest region. Florida's Skunk Ape, as a Bigfoot or Bigfoot-analogue, helped plant the ever-growing idea that Bigfoot's territorial milieu was as expansive and pervasive as the nation was large.

A flurry of newspaper articles during the summer of 1971 brought national attention to Florida's Skunk Ape by relating the encounter shared by members of the Peninsular Archaeological Society (PAS). Their story was told and retold several times in the 1970s, sometimes with differing details. The initial announcement of the encounter coincided with, and part of the publicity for, a PAS membership drive.[408] H. C. "Buz" Osbon, described as an electronics engineer, amateur archaeologist, board member of the Miami Museum of Science, and president of PAS[409] claimed he and four other PAS members, witnessed a 7-foot-tall, 700-pound creature in February 1970 while investigating an Indian mound in the Big Cypress.[410]

Indigenous cultures in the southeastern United States had a long history of mound building. Huge earthen pyramids were constructed in Florida and Georgia around 200 A.D. The tallest such earthwork in Florida is located at a site called the Letchworth-Love Mounds; the earth pyramid here is 46 feet high. In Georgia, an even larger earthen pyramid at Kolomoki Mounds stands at 57 feet high and has a base larger than a football field. Most mounds in Florida are relatively smaller sand and shell mounds and far less complex in scope than the Letchworth-Love Mounds.[411] PAS members were investigating such a mound located within Big Cypress Swamp when they encountered an ape-like creature "that came within seven feet of us," Osbon stated. "It's made a believer out of me," he added.

"There were five of us at the time, and for years we'd heard rumors about some kind of apeman running loose in the swamp. I never paid much attention to the rumors, but I believed them after seeing that critter last spring,"[412] Timothy Green Beckley's article "America's Abominable Swamp Man" appeared in the March 1975 edition of *Saga*. Beckley provides additional and sometimes differing details compared to the first iteration of the PAS' Skunk Ape encounter which emerged in 1971. A new detail Beckley adds to the tale is the appeal which ancient mounds hidden away in the Big Cypress had on PAS' members.

> Asked to comment on why at least one family of yeti has settled in Florida's Everglades, Buz told a rather lengthy but fascinating story. "The swamps here abound with strange stories and legends of lost cities, hidden treasures and so forth. Many of those who had wandered into this area have come out of it with incredible tales.
>
> For years, pyramid-like structures have been found and then lost again—all in the area known as Big Cypress Swamp where we have been carrying out our archaeological activities. "It is said that some years ago an escaped convict from a Florida chain gang made his way into this swamp to avoid being captured. While wandering through the murky mud, thick foliage and dense underbrush, the fugitive came across a pyramid-like structure. Within it, he found a secret room where he hid, and in the silence and darkness plotted his future, which at the time didn't look very bright.
>
> "Why he finally left his well-hidden sanctuary is not known, but the convict turned himself in, telling authorities that something very odd forced him to abandon his refuge."
>
> Osbon's close relationship with the swamp man came about when his organization decided to check out the claims that such a pyramid-like structure really existed. We found two such pyramids after searching for a number of weeks," Buz told me. "The more complete of the pair is a 12 ½ foot tall structure and for the life of me it's impossible to tell how the blocks were fitted together since they're so tightly packed. The pyramid has a fantastic amount of writing on its surface in what I can best describe as symbols or hieroglyphics. The second pyramid remains covered by a good ten feet of water but its upper portion is jutting out of the swamp.
>
> Speculation has it that these structures were built by a civilization long gone from the face of this planet. "This could

> well be part of Atlantis, the Lost Continent we have heard so much about," Buz speculated. "But we have no positive proof nor are we offering any conclusion at this time."
>
> In addition to the pyramids, a wall with a hard, smooth surface, 6-8 feet high has also been uncovered approximately five miles from the site of the pyramids running along for about six miles. This poses a real challenge.
>
> "We are keeping the exact location closely guarded, it's known only to a handful of people now and we want to keep it that way so that the area will not be trampled on by curiosity seekers or by those not equipped to help us in our work."[413]

As the group's encounter became known in 1971, newspapers transmitted accounts of their February 1970 experience to a public ready and willing to digest stories of hairy, humanoid swamp creatures. "It was about three in the morning when we heard something moving around outside the tent," Osbon recalled in the *Miami News*. "We went out and there it was, just standing there looking at us while we stared at it. It didn't stay very long and ran before we could recover our surprise."[414] Adding a few new (and slightly differing) details to the *Miami News* account, the following excerpted *National Observer* article by Dick Bothwell based upon his interview with Osbon was published a week later:

> "There were five of us camped on top of this big shell mound—three in a large tent, two in a pup tent. About 2:30 A.M. one of the two heard a sound like an elephant walking on this shell mound. The vibrations woke him up.
>
> "He looked out the tent flap and saw what appeared to be a big man, standing about eight feet away in the moonlight. He thought it was one of the party. He lay back down, then heard what sounded like a number of people all talking at once.
>
> "So the two of them in the pup tent got up and woke us up—told what he'd seen. We looked around but saw nothing. But in the morning, we found these huge tracks.
>
> "Footprints just like a man's, three different sizes. The largest 17 ½ inches long, 11 inches across. I've got plaster casts of it. . . ."[415]

Beckley's *Saga* article rendered another interpretation of the group's encounter. "We had all gone to bed," Osbon recollected, "when around three o'clock in the morning, one of the members of the expedition was startled awake by weird sounds coming from just beyond the perimeter of our camp. At first he thought it was a wild beast and thinking the fire would eventually chase him off, he turned over and tried to go back to sleep. All of a sudden there was a thundering noise that sounded as though a wild bull elephant was thrashing about amidst the thick trees and bushes. We all were awakened at this point and we were on our hands and knees trying to get ourselves together—enough at least to see what was causing the commotion."

Peering out from their tents into a clearing softly lit by a flickering campfire, the men received a shock. "There, directly in front of us, not more than ten feet away was a creature which was for all intents and purposes only rumored to exist. He stood in the middle of our camp looking back and forth as if searching for something. His huge seven-foot frame was covered from head to toe with thick, matted white hair and he kept swinging his long powerful looking arms from side to side. It didn't take us long to realize that this was no bear in our midst, no escaped gorilla, nor any other known animal. To think it was any of these would have been sheer folly."[416]

The men quickly discovered the animal gave off a pungent odor. When their shock subsided, the group decided to remain at their site and attempted to go back to sleep, hoping the creature would move off into the swamp and not pay another them visit. Erring on the safe side, a guard was posted to keep watch, just in case. "Our minds were going a mile a minute," Osbon told Beckley. "What had we seen? What did all this mean? Indeed, our scientific curiosity was more than slightly aroused."[417]

As the sun rose above the horizon, Osbon and his associates canvassed the area for clues to their nocturnal caller's identity. "We found its tracks the next morning," he said. "They are very man-like. I have plaster casts we made from them. The thing we saw that night had a foot 17 ½ inches long and 11 ½ inches across at the toes. In later trips, we found smaller tracks, indicating there are at least three of them in that section of the swamp." Osbon said he had learned that the Skunk Ape had been seen by trappers and fishermen in the Big Cypress since the 1920s.[418]

According to Beckley, a subsequent encounter occurred one week later when the group resumed their archaeological digging at the shell mound. This occasion however, they returned prepared for the possibility of another nocturnal visitation. "The first thing we did after setting up camp was to lay an electric wire around the camp's entire perimeter," Osbon recalled. "This in turn was connected to an ultra-sensitive electronic device which would immediately sound an alarm if anything crossed the wire. Needless to say, we had plenty of camera equipment with flash attachments and portable lighting. About midnight we heard something with heavy, sluggish steps sloshing through the water in the nearby swamp and our instruments started beeping. Knowing that 'something' crossed the wire and was on the edge of our camp, we excitedly searched the area with heavy floodlights, but we saw nothing." From Osbon's account one imagines another restless and anxious night for the group. The arrival of dawn brought the opportunity for a more thorough canvass of their surroundings. "The next morning however, we again found large footprints around the outer edge of our campsite and we knew then that we were being observed. A complete search of the area revealed footprints of three distinctively varied size footprints, our first indication that a family truly existed and was not far away."[419]

Frank Hudson, a member of PAS, said the group considered the trove of Skunk Ape stories and legends following their experience. "We've talked to many old-timers in the area who were afraid to talk to anybody about it, for fear they'd be laughed at or put in the insane asylum. But we've seen too much evidence to think it's just somebody in a monkey suit. I don't think it's a hoax."[420] Beckley's article hints at the possible linkage between PAS' digging activity at mound structures and the appearance of Skunk Ape creatures.

> Although he can't prove it, Buz Osbon believes "the Everglades Yeti and his family, are using the region around the ruins as their home," and says "the entire locale is dotted with old Indian Mounds and the remains of structures dating back to—we can only guess how long. The digging we do always seems, for some reason, to attract the creature. Perhaps it's the physical activity. We've seen them eight times during the past three years while working here. Sometimes, it takes four or five trips before we see one, but other times they turn up every trip. One of our men spent four weeks out near the diggings and saw him more than that."[421]

Instigated by Osbon's story, publicity for the Sunshine State's Skunk Ape encouraged gumshoe sleuthing to corroborate or discredit the notion of manlike hairy hominids in Florida's swamps and wild areas. "I've never heard of anything like it in any of our legends," averred Dania resident Betty Mae Jumper, a former chairman of Florida's Seminole Indian tribes. "I've lived out there in the Big Cypress off and on for a long time, and I never heard any Indian talking about any apeman," she said. "The Indians on the Big Cypress Reservation know that area pretty well, too."

The chief photographer for the Central and South Florida Flood Control District said he had never heard any "Skunk Ape" stories over his nearly 40 years of work in both the Everglades and the Big Cypress Swamp. "I've been fooling around the Florida wilderness since the 1930s, the early '30s," said Earl Diemer. "I won't say there's no such thing, but I'd have to run into it before I'd believe it." Diemer added, "The Florida black bear might be mistaken for an ape under the right combination of circumstances. Of course when it stands on its hind legs it's only about five feet tall, but they can look 20 feet tall if the circumstances are scary enough." When informed about Osbon's intention to conduct a dedicated expedition to learn more about the Skunk Ape, Diemer didn't hesitate in expressing his interest. "If they're looking for a photographer, tell them I'm game," Diemer said. "I'd love to photograph something like that."[422]

Great Everglades Ape Hunt

On Thursday, August 12, rabies control officer Henry Ring was dispatched by the Florida Highway Patrol to Kings Manor Estates trailer park in Davie, west Broward County, in response to a report that children had been frightened by two apes. According to Ring, the children told him, "it was something really big, hairy, small eyes, with a monkey face, long arms, and grey splotches over the body."[423] Ring said one of the girls had seen a creature on her patio. Her scream brought her brother and both witnessed a second creature join the first before both unknown animals ran into a nearby orange grove. The girl told Ring that the larger creature was about six feet tall, "it was bigger than Daddy," she said, adding that "one was white and one was black."

"When I arrived, half the park was running around carrying guns. They were going to start a war, I think," said Ring. "We found nothing but a bunch of strange tracks, like someone was walking around on his knuckles."[424] Ring examined deep 12- to 14-inch-long tracks, describing them as "farther than four or five feet apart with knuckle prints interspersed between them." The tracks appeared to have double-backed before eventually disappearing.[425]

"Another man at the trailer park said he heard something scratching around outside his trailer the night before. When he went out, he said, something shot off into the woods. And different people tell me that the dogs in the park have been raising Cain out there for the past few nights," reported Ring. "That park's too big for one human walking through to set those dogs off. It would have to be something they could smell."[426]

"We found tracks leading into the grove," said Ring. "It wasn't the kind of track a kid would make going into the woods. It was like something went into the underbrush and kept on going." Ring mulled over the tracks. "At first, it looked as if the thing had dug in its heels and then dragged its toes. Later, we found other tracks that looked a little like deer tracks," said Ring. "But they definitely weren't deer tracks. It was just like you'd taken your knuckles and pressed them into the ground."[427]

Ring and Kings Manor Estates security guard Tom Anderson led up to eight other searchers on Thursday night in a fruitless search to find the creatures. Ring said the creature-hunt was "really out of my jurisdiction, but we're going out tomorrow night to see if we can get a look at it." Ring said he had heard the stories of Florida's odoriferous entry into the catalog of Bigfoot creatures. "I read that story about the Skunk Ape the other day, and I didn't believe it," Ring said, adding, "but when I got out there tonight, though, I got to wondering."[428]

"There was a peculiar odor, like a monkey house in a zoo, I have no doubt those children were telling the truth," said Anderson. During the Thursday night search, the area around the children's trailer was examined. "I could see where something had gone through the bushes back of the trailer. I don't believe it was a man because it was too big and too wide."[429] At one point during their search, Ring heard the passing of something through the underbrush. "I'd nearly give two months' pay to be able to swear I heard it," he said. "I swear I heard a kind of grunting sound."[430] Neither Ring nor other members of the posse ever glimpsed the creatures. "We never got to see it, but I don't think it was somebody pulling a hoax. No hoaxer would take the time to carefully leave those foot and knuckle prints with an armed posse on his tail."[431]

Ring had started out thinking the reports of ape-like creatures were merely a hoax, but his investigation convinced him that "some king of animal's running loose out there." He soberly realized that "those people were scared and when they got scared, they got guns. If it was a hoax, I wanted to expose it before somebody got a .30-.30 bullet through his hairy ape suit."[432]

Ring's investigation at Kings Manor Estates included talking with multiple witnesses. "It turned out that a bunch of people had been hearing big things moving around their trailers at night for some time," said Ring. "And when we checked with police in the area, we found several people had reported sighting big, apelike animals as long as a year back."[433] The next night [Friday, Aug 13] "we stayed out until six A.M. Again, nothing. Then I talked to a Mrs. King, and she said she not only saw the critter but had fed, petted and been scratched by the smaller one."[434]

> Mrs. Elda King, her husband Rob and their two toy poodles live in an $18,000, custom-built trailer on the eastern edge of the park. She drives a catering truck; he drives a freight truck. She is excited by the apes; he is bored with them. "Every time I come home there's some kind of jazz," he says. "Now it's apes and orangutans. I'll get a gun and shoot the bums."
>
> Describing the encounter, Mrs. King said she thought someone was at the door of the trailer early one evening. She opened it and found herself confronting a large, hairy beast. It was three feet away. She closed the door. "Then I rolled open the window and looked at it. It was about six feet tall; gray, with splotches and sores all over it. Wow." Arming herself with a plate of food and a .22 revolver, Mrs. King decided to lure the animal within range. About 7:45 P.M. the small one showed up.[435]

King estimated the animal was only about two feet tall. While feeding on the fruit, vegetables, and raw hamburger King offered it, the creature tolerated gentle petting strokes on its arm. "It was cute," she said. "I sat down beside it while it was eating and petted it. But the third time I touched it, there was this deep growl, like a big bullfrog, from the bushes. It made the little one mad. It reached over and dug its nails into my ankle and took off. I was thinking about grabbing it and running for the trailer—but I figured no trailer would stop its mommy or daddy."[436]

More stories from Kings Manor Estates residents surfaced. One park resident confirmed she had heard and smelled something quite strange around her home since the talk of apes in the area had surfaced. Another trailer park resident, Gladys Scarpulla, said the nighttime grunting and groaning from a supposed ape creature as it wandered around her trailer had kept her family awake.[437]

> "People think we're all nuts or something," Mrs. Scarpulla said. "I don't know what the animal is, but it sure makes a lot of noise."
>
> She said the late-night visitor "smelled bad, like skunk cabbage," and could be heard "moving through the underbrush breaking limbs on the trees."[438]

Well into the next week, the events at Kings Manor Estates ushered in a wave of additional reports and sightings as people came forward to share their experiences with ape-like creatures in the area.

> The Great Everglades Ape Hunt seems to be sharpening the teeth of the old saw that says the only things weirder than fiction are the factual doings of man.
>
> Literally hundreds of sane, sober people have crawled through underbrush and sawgrass in hopes of seeing huge, apelike creatures other people say have been hanging around a trailer park west of Fort Lauderdale.
>
> Each day turns up more reports of ape or ape print sightings, even though naturalists say there are no wild apes in South Florida and it is next to impossible for an ape to have escaped from captivity without somebody knowing about it.
>
> The first suggestion that a giant primate was on the loose in the Sunshine State came from a Miami man, H. C. Osbon, who said he and four companions ran across the beast last February while hunting for Indian artifacts deep in Big Cypress Swamp.[439]

Professional advice was solicited to explain the witnesses' unusual reports. While discounting a large primate living in Florida's swamps, some experts conceded that a smaller monkey loose in the wilds could contribute to some people's beliefs in a Skunk Ape on the prowl.

> Several animal experts said they did not believe it possible for a big ape to be on the loose in South Florida, but three of them offered explanations, "that might explain what it could be—just from a conjectural standpoint, of course."
>
> None of the experts would permit his name to be used. One said, "If you tie me in with that Everglades Ape, I'll deny it. In fact, I'll deny I've even heard of Fort Lauderdale."

He then offered an intriguing theory that would explain the Skunk Ape story, assuming an ape were running loose.

"I don't think there's an ape out there," he said, "but if there is, I'd pick one of the smaller ones—say a chimpanzee.

"A 4-foot-tall chimpanzee could damn well look 7 or 8 feet if you ran up on it in the dark when you weren't expecting it.

"Now as for the smell, that angle had me for a while, but I think I can even explain that. An animal like a chimp would be susceptible to any number of skin diseases. Now say it came down with a good case of mange. If you've ever smelled a mangy dog, you'll know that Skunk Ape wouldn't be too bad a name," he said.

Ring said he wanted to wait for the furor to die down before attempting any further searches for the elusive animal.

"I'd like to bait an area for a few days and check each morning to see if anything's eaten the food. If the food is taken, then we'll settle down some night and try to get a look at it.

"I kind of go for the little-monkey-in-the-daylight, big-monkey-in-the-dark bit," he said. "But even if it's just a little monkey, we should try to find out for sure."[440]

Fouke Monster

The farming community of Fouke, Arkansas, had a population in the early '70s just shy of 400 souls. The "old Crank" home sat off U.S. 71 and became infamous as the location at which Bobby Ford, after having lived in the house for less than five days, claimed he was attacked by a large, hair-covered animal with fiery-red eyes. Ford was so terrified by the incident, one of the seminal encounters of the '70s, he ran right through the front screen door. "I was moving so fast I didn't stop to open the door, I just ran through it," Ford said.

The events started about midnight on Saturday, May 1, not long after the Ford and Taylor families had moved into the old Crank home. Mrs. Ford, who had been asleep on a couch in the living room, said a big hairy arm came in through a window and menaced her. "I saw the curtain moving on the front window and saw a hand sticking through the window," said Mrs. Ford. "At first I thought it was a bear's paw, but it didn't look like that. It had heavy hair all over it and it had claws. I could see its eyes. They looked like coals of fire . . . real red," she said. "It didn't make any noise, except you could hear it breathing."

The Fords caught a glimpse of the creature running toward the woods. It was shot at and then the Fords sought out Fouke's Constable Ernest Walraven. Walraven, who had been a constable for twelve years, arrived at the Ford's home and conducted a search around the house. He did find some tracks which he said were big and similar to a cat's.

Ford said the creature returned to the house two more times. It was while Ford climbed up the front steps when the monster grabbed Ford and pulled him down. Frantically extracting himself, Ford got away and ran through the screen door. Ford's wife reported he was "out of his head," when he bolted into the living room. Walraven said Ford was "out" when the family arrived at his home. He was revived soon after at a nearby hospital where it was confirmed Ford had not been drinking.

Since it rained on the morning of Monday, May 3, the prints seen and described by Constable Walraven had been washed out. As word spread, curiosity-seekers clogged the roads and tramped over the property. They gaped at marks on the side of the house, attributed to the creature's claws, and examined the damaged screen door. Missing strips of tin plating from the side of the house were also attributed to the creature's auspices. But as the early stories pointed out, since it was an old house, it was hard to say what had fallen off with age and what damage could have been rendered by a resident monster.

Ford said the animal was around 6 feet tall and hairy and moved on its hind legs at a speed that effectively discounted a known animal, like a bear. Ford bore three scratches from the encounter—two on his arm and one on his side. Stating flatly that he was of no mind whatsoever to remain at a house where monsters reached out and attacked people, Ford declared he was moving.

The Miller County Sheriff's office issued warnings to curiosity-seekers to keep off the premises, their concern underscored by a fear of someone getting shot. "We're trying to get people to stay away," said Deputy H. L. Phillips. "The place is becoming a real traffic hazard." Phillips said the Sheriff's office had announced that anyone caught with a firearm near the Ford home would be arrested.

Norman Richardson was State Editor of the *Shreveport Times* from 1957 to 1974 and, along with hurricanes, a favorite subject he enjoyed writing about, and had covered for many years, was "It."

> "It," of course, is the reportedly shy "monster" which has been spotted off and on for some 20 years in various spots from Jefferson, Tex. to Fouke, Ark.

> Some are quick to ridicule the idea of a monster, others adopt a "maybe so," and there are those who don't even want to know. But to Bobby Ford of Fouke, the thing is alive and well regardless of what anyone says about monsters being only in fairy tales.
>
> Up until this past weekend, "Hairy" got his kicks by simply scaring the daylights out of folks, sometimes chasing them for a bit before giving up, tearing up traps set for it, or just popping up from behind a bush, growling and then disappearing.[441]

Area newspapers reported more sightings, like the following *Arkansas Gazette* report: "Three Texarkana motorists said something like a 'giant monkey' with long, dark hair crossed the highway in front of their automobile near Fouke [on] May 22."[442] The three motorists were Mr. and Mrs. D. C. Woods and Mrs. R. H. Sedgass, all from Texarkana. The party said the creature had a stooped posture but ran upright. Woods described it as a "giant monkey" and he estimated its weight at about 200 pounds. "It was really moving fast across the highway, faster than a man," Woods said. "[Its] arms were swinging kind of like a monkey's. The thing didn't act like it even noticed us. It didn't look at the car." Mrs. Woods admitted that prior to her sighting she didn't put a lot of stock in the monster. "Now, I know it's true," she said.[443]

Photographs of three-toed prints taken for the *Texarkana Gazette* on Tuesday, June 15, were examined by Dr. Frank Schambagh, resident archeologist at Southern State College. "There is a 99 per cent chance the tracks are a hoax." Schambagh said. "All the primates have five toes," he continued. "Also the monkey family is not nocturnal and is like humans or daytime creatures." Schambagh noted the absence of primates in the archeological record. "I don't think a monkey could survive a winter here," he said. "There are, and have never been, monkeys native to North America, so that rules out anything that could have been left over from times past."

> Miller County Sheriff Leslie Greer thinks, however, that the monster may be either a large monkey or a small ape.
>
> Greer, along with several of his deputies and residents of the Fouke area, searched a wooded area about four miles southeast of Fouke for several hours Tuesday after the creature was reportedly sighted by two men Tuesday morning as it crossed a road in front of their car. The men said it walked across the

> road and into a wooded area adjoining a soybean field where dozens of tracks were found Sunday. The tracks were about 13 ½ inches long and indicated three large toes.
>
> In conflict with previous reports, those who saw the creature Tuesday described it as about four feet tall and standing in a crouched position.
>
> Dogs were used in the search for the monster Tuesday, but were unable to pick up a trail. Officials said it was too hot and the woods were too dry to hold a scent.
>
> Greer said another attempt would be made to find the creature if the weather cools off and it rains. He said his department probably would try to use a tranquilizer gun on the beast.
>
> Some area residents fear that there may be more than one of the monsters, since several differing descriptions have been reported.[444]

Schambagh added an oft-expressed sentiment during the '70s, echoed frequently in response to the large armed search parties—official and unofficial—that scoured the countryside where monster sightings occurred. "I certainly hope someone does not get hurt," he said.[445]

Reporter Richard Allin wrote for the *Arkansas Gazette* for forty years. In his "Our Town" column of June 21, 1971, Allin responded to Schambagh's pronouncement that a lack of evidence left little in way of support for an extant creature haunting southwestern Arkansas. "A college professor has called him a hoax. That indicated that he has outwitted everybody, including the smart people." Allin further touched on the Fouke Monster, more as concept than creature, romanticizing its presence and hope for its future.

> I do, in fact, hope there IS such a creature as the Fouke monster. It could mean much to the community, to Miller County, and to Arkansas. If we are lucky it will continue to be sighted over the next fifty years. it will leave footprints for us to marvel at, and occasionally "authorities" will release bloodhounds in an effort to track it down.
>
> And if we are REALLY lucky, we will never catch it. It will haunt and entertain our imaginations for years. it will run free through the ages, intriguing us and scaring the daylights out of the community.

> Perhaps, one day, the "monster" will be named Miller County's most famous resident. It is already Fouke's. Indeed, it has raised the little town in the eyes of the nation.
>
> And even if one day the monster decides to let himself be captured—either because he is tired of the game or is getting old—then it is incumbent on the authorities to refuse to capture him. For a captured monster is no monster at all. Fouke will then sink back into obscurity.[446]

Walraven and Johnny Carey, the latter a Fouke resident and area hunter, felt the creature was a panther or a wolf. Walraven said that soon after the family reported their attack, another resident living down the road reported hearing something screaming in the woods. Phillips said that panthers occasionally do roam as far north as Fouke. Whatever attacked Ford, Walraven believed the animal had made its den under the house when the Fords moved in.[447]

The notoriety gained by the Fouke Monster reminded people of another Arkansas monster, the White River Monster. The White River flows out of the Ozark Mountains and courses in a diagonal across the state towards the Mississippi. This river monster was known for making its appearances about every 40 years. Near Newport the river grows to a width of about 75 feet where old timers tell of a "bottomless pit" in the middle of the river—the supposed den of the White River Monster. In the summer of 1971, many area residents claimed to have seen flashes of a huge, white bulk in the river. "It was over 40 feet long and weighed way over a ton and it looked like it could eat anything, anywhere, anytime," said Ernest Dinks, a "sighter" of the monster's surfacing that summer.[448]

> The Fouke Monster, as he is called, is a mere upstart in monster lore when compared to its venerable White River cousin.
>
> But many residents of Fouke, the small southern Arkansas town from which the monster took its name, believe staunchly in their monster, which has been seen in the area for the past 18 years.[449]

CHAPTER 3
1972

The incredible number of tracks—in 1972 alone—is worthy of note: 102 were found on beaches or creek banks; 88 on mountainsides; 88 on cleared lands; 30 on trails or old abandoned roads; 16 in or near water; 12 in or near swamps; and seven in other varied locations.

The matter of the creature's color is also of interest: brown is most frequently reported (58 times) and shades range from light to dark. Black was reported 40 times; another 45 were described merely as "dark" (understandable since most sightings are at dusk, at night in moonlight, or near dawn). There exist 26 sightings of gray Sasquatches, 20 of white ones, and eight "silver-tipped" or "light."

Most authorities say Bigfoot eats berries, roots, and rodents, making the beast omnivorous in his dietary habits. Some "juvenile" Sasquatches have been seen (and one shot but not recovered), but female Sasquatch sightings are rare. There have been hundreds of adult male sightings.[450]

William Childress. "The Most Sensational Pictures of Bigfoot Ever Taken," *Saga* (December 1973).

I have had a number of inquiries lately, about Bigfoot. Letters have arrived from Syracuse, N.Y.; from Los Angeles, Seattle, Miami, Fla; Boise, Ida; and Detroit, Mich.—mostly from students. Most of them receive their clues and my name from a book, "The Abominable Snowman," by Ivan Sanderson.

Interest continues in Humboldt's favorite living-legend. I haven't had any reports for several months about Bigfoot.

> Surely, he must be still enjoying his old Bluff Creek haunts—or, has the searcher traffic driven him to a new haven?
>
> Have you been chatting with Bigfoot, lately? We'd like to know.[451]
>
> Andrew Genzoli. "Redwood Country," *Times-Standard* (July 21, 1972).

Leaping and bounding toward phenomenon-status and becoming an increasingly understood term of common usage and reference, Bigfoot's presence rapidly expanded through American mainstream culture in the early 1970s. Mass media exposure assured Bigfoot's entrenchment in the public's psyche through its indulging transmission of the phenomenon's intimate, visceral, and bedrock essence—reports of ongoing encounters between people and large, anomalous, hairy giants. Perhaps this icon-approaching status explained the popularity of hirsute livery for Halloween in 1972. Gorilla costumes were all the rage for Halloween, according to Chicago costume rental shops. "What the fascination is about gorilla suits, I just don't know," said Ed Roman, manager at the House of Roman. Marcella Hentschel at Marcella's Costumes & Party Supplies agreed with Roman. "It's always the same, gorilla-gorilla. We were out of gorilla suits the second week in October," she said.[452]

Fouke Monster and *The Legend of Boggy Creek*

Bobby Ford and the Fouke Monster serve as an especial and unique exemplar of Bigfoot sightings at the time: immediate experience; report to authorities; ensuing regional popularization fed by local media; sensationalized national story; a movie achieving breakout success . . . culmination: immortality. Though the Fouke Monster achieved astronomical fame on many levels, it is not so much its or any individual town or regional monster's notoriety that is noteworthy, but the success of Bigfoot writ large as an elemental opus of man's internal projections. Bigfoot more than made up for its deficiencies in known manners, studied habits, and understood ecology by providing a slate upon which anyone could imprint their fears, hopes, and dreams. The Fouke Monster exaggerated the generic pattern other Bigfoot stories followed (personal encounter; involvement of bureaucratic, objective authorities; ensuing publicity), but the celebrity it achieved owed much to the stratospheric level that the shared idea of Bigfoot had risen to in the cultural body. The stage was set for a hairy monster from the Sulphur River bottomlands to caper across the silver screen and through the national imagination.

In early February 1972, the working title of Charles B. Pierce's film was "Tracking the Fouke Monster"[453] and it was initially slated for a Spring release (which would be missed by several months). Pierce lost no opportunity to state his movie would not take the subject lightly. "I believe that the people in Fouke are fine Christian people," he said. "Most of them would not tell you a story." Pierce acknowledged Fouke's residents had borne a ridiculing response from the wider public. "There has been a lot of humiliation and joking because people are laughing about it," said Pierce. "We intend, under no instances, to humiliate those people. We are going to tell it as they tell it to us, with them on the set."[454]

The Ford encounter (discussed in the previous chapter) and the prospect of Pierce's movie helped recall and retransmit the local history of hairy hominids in the area. Jefferson, a small town in eastern Texas, is about 60 miles from Fouke, Arkansas. *Shreveport Times* writer and State Editor Norman Richardson covered several 1965 sightings in and around Jefferson of "It," a tall hair-covered creature.

> Is a seven-foot monster roaming the wilds around Jefferson?
>
> Some residents here ridicule the idea, others say "maybe so," and still others don't even want to find out. But to 13-year-old Johnny Maples, the thing is there regardless of what anyone says about monsters just being in fairy tales.
>
> According to the youngster, the creature was at least seven feet tall, covered with long, black hair, something resembling an ape or gorilla, had long arms that hung down below its knees . . . and did not have on any clothes.

Johnny had been walking toward Lodi Community when he heard something moving in the growth along Farm Road west of Jefferson. Peering into the underbrush, Johnny was startled to watch a large, hair-covered creature emerge from the bracken and brush. "As I turned to run, the huge creature started climbing over a fence and started after me . . . after I had run for a long ways, one of the soles on my shoes came loose and I had to stop and take my shoes off so I could run faster," Johnny said. As he stopped to remove his shoes, he realized he couldn't see the creature any more. Johnny's mother stated her son arrived home in a state of near shock and his feet were blistered after running without his shoes on.

> A search of the area revealed no signs of such a monster. However, an unusual footprint was discovered under a bridge in the area and officials said it did not resemble that of a human or any type of animal normally found in this area.
>
> The print was about eight inches in length and four inches across.
>
> Also, two stacks of neatly folded clothing were found in the creek bottom.
>
> The latest report of the monster marks the second in recent months in the area.[455]

Richardson kept *Shreveport Times* readers up-to-date on the latest news of *It*, including insights into local reaction.

> "It" likes pears.
>
> "It," of course, is the reported shy "monster" claimed to have been spotted roaming the wilds around here recently.
>
> And what's more, he has six toes on each foot. It has already been "established" that he's about seven feet tall, has a black, hairy body, likes to growl and probably isn't very fast on his feet.
>
> Oh . . . and he probably has long claws or else his toenails need clipping badly.
>
> These and a few other bits of information are some of [the] slowly emerging "evidence" being gathered since "the thing" was first seen at a bridge near Jefferson.
>
> Most Jeffersonians are quick to put the skids under such a thing existing, others are not so quick and are simply waiting to see what "it" turns out to be, a few are firmly convinced something is out there, and there are those who just plain don't want to know either way.[456]

Several days after Johnny Maples arrived home breathless and in shock, footprints turned up near a bridge close by the spot of his encounter. Dwaine Dennis, publisher of the *Jefferson Jimplecute,* said the footprints showed six toes, roundish in shape and larger than a man's hand. Marion County game warden Bill Belote wasn't impressed with the tracks saying, "there's nothing to it. I think someone has baited those [tracks]. Things are getting out of hand and I wish people would go on and forget it." Belote stated a heartfelt concern and warning that would be echoed many times in the '70s. "We have too many people going in there with high-powered rifles and shotguns and that presents a danger plus it's a violation of the law. There is no monster and no bear . . . there's simply nothing to it." A local café owner echoed Belote's sentiment that, "with all these people tromping through the woods hunting this 'thing' and with all the traps and the usual trigger happy folks, somebody could easily get hurt out there."[457]

While visiting the Lodi Cemetery in mid-September, Mrs. Herbert Manning said she heard three distinct, very loud growls from the woods. She described the sounds as "long, low and loud growls, with a snort or blow at the end of each one. It growled three times and by the end of the third one my daughter and a friend and I were back in the car." Manning believed she discerned a note of surprise in the sounds stating the "low growling was like a bear. He, or she, didn't sound mad, more startled, like he was walking along and looked up and there we were. We figure it's two bears, a male and a female." Manning placed a sack of pears behind the cemetery and checking on them the next day found them eaten. "I just don't know what it is," she said. "But I wish the whole thing would end and we can see what 'it' looks like."

As the fame of their discovery spread, people visited Jefferson's environs to see for themselves the six-toed tracks *in situ*. Several folks who had (and several more who had not) examined the prints theorized they had been left by a bear. Another camp thought they had been left as a kind of joke. "But the gag has gone far enough," said the owner of a local business. "It isn't fair to some of the elderly persons who are disturbed by all this." Of course, as a businessman he could appreciate some of the commercial benefits the creature's fame had brought to Jefferson. "Sure," he said, "it brings the out of town people in here every day and for the economy that part is good, but overall it isn't fair to the older folks."[458]

The G-rated *Legend of Boggy Creek* premiered in August 1972. Pierce's movie rapidly gained widespread popularity, and by consequence expanded into a growing number of theaters nation-wide. By 1975, the Strange, Strange World pavilion at the Man and His World exhibition in Montreal showed clips of *The Legend of Boggy Creek* as part of its SITU-inspired ABSM presentation.[459] Chapter 4 will look closer at *The Legend of Boggy Creek's* rise during 1973 to the status of unqualified box-office success.

In movies and TV, hairy-humanoid cryptids appeared in diverse fare such as *Horror Express* (starring Christopher Lee, Peter Cushing, and Telly Savalas) in theaters and *Scooby Doo Meets Laurel and Hardy* for small

1972 ADVERTISEMENT FOR 'THE LEGEND OF BOGGY CREEK'

screen-viewing on Saturday mornings. In the footsteps of 1968's *Bigfoot: America's Abominable Snowman*, *Bigfoot: Man or Beast*, like fellow 1972 docudrama entry *Legend of Boggy Creek*, sought to bring a serious, informing tone to the subject while not discounting its tangible and inherent entertainment value. *Bigfoot: Man or Beast* was produced by American National Enterprises Inc., a Salt Lake City-based company known for producing outdoor films. This 20-minute film featurette was frequently billed with other American National Enterprises family-friendly films such as *North Country*. *Bigfoot: Man or Beast* was used later in the decade to augment a longer movie called *In Search of Bigfoot* which focused on Robert Morgan's 1974 Bigfoot expedition (see Chapter 6). Certain Patterson-Gimlin film rights had been acquired by American National Enterprises Inc. and that famous piece of footage was incorporated into *Bigfoot: Man or Beast*. Ron Olson, 30-year-old scion of American National Enterprises Inc., founded North American Wildlife Research Association in Eugene, Oregon, to carry on the investigation of Bigfoot (see Chapter 4 for additional material on Olson, including his thoughts on *Bigfoot: Man or Beast*).[460]

Narrator J. English Smith conducts a scripted interview with Olson to create the feel of a documentary-style movie. Other filmed interviews include segments with Fred Beck, Albert Ostman, and other witnesses who relate their Bigfoot experiences in their own words.

Fred Beck Ape Canyon Encounter

Beck: "They was big, big shoulders . . . and small hips. And hairy. And they was, I'd call them black turned brown by the sun; outside hair, that's what I'd call them to be. And muscular. And they looked like they was about 8-, 9-foot-tall, no way to tell. . . ."[461]

Albert Ostman Abduction

Ostman: "Well, they was four of them, and not all of them look alike. There was what I called the Old Man. 'Course I had no scale or any rules for measurement, but he was at least 8 feet tall, and must of weighed at least 800 pounds. What I call The Old Lady, she couldn't have been over 6- to 700 pound, she was probably 7 feet tall. And, they were all covered in hair."[462]

Chapman Encounter at Ruby Creek

John Green: "When I first came here in 1957, it was still pretty well open, but all this has grown up since then. What happened at that time was Mrs. George Chapman lived in a house down by the river, behind me here. She

1972 ADVERTISEMENT FOR 'BIGFOOT: MAN OR BEAST'

was in the house and the children were outside. One of them came in and told her there was a cow coming out of the woods. She looked out and saw this man-like thing about eight feet tall and completely covered in hair like a bear. She knew it to be a Sasquatch. This was quite a well-known thing to the Indian people. She was frightened so she took the children and ran down to the river and then to the graveyard which is behind me here and then came out about here onto the track and ran on down to Ruby Creek. Now, she'd really only had one quick look at the thing, so it wouldn't be that convincing a story except that a lot of people immediately went back there and saw these enormous tracks. Mr. Tyfting, course, was one of them, and can describe just what the tracks were like and what they did."[463]

Esse Tyfting: "Well he came through the bush into the shed, of the lean-to of the house. And there was a barrel of dried fish with smoked salmon. And he broke the barrel and there was some fish eaten there and thrown around. And then he went down the river bank and apparently took a drink. And then come back up on the other side of the house, through the garden patch and up to CPR [Canadian Pacific Railway] fence, and stepped with one foot on outside of fence and one foot on this side of the fence. Walked right over it. And the footprints was about 18-inches, like. And then he went across there and over to the next fence there and went right up the hillside, and that was as far as we could follow it, see."[464]

William Roe Bigfoot Sighting

Myrtle Walton (née Roe; William Roe's daughter): "My Dad come and ask me to draw a picture of this animal or human for him, he called it a Sasquatch, so he could send it to this John Green. And I drawed the picture for him just exactly the way he told me he wanted it drawed; there was a few things he changed on it. Like the . . . he made the arms a lot heavier and the head was different and the breasts were different, and the back part was different. Between the two of us we patched it all up and we sent it to John Green."

Mrs. Walton and her husband also discussed a strange woodland noise they had heard, suggesting it could have been a Bigfoot's scream.

Narrator: A few years after Mrs. Walton made the sketch for her father, she and her husband had a personal experience with a Bigfoot. This is what they report.

Mr. Walton: "Well, I think my wife and I have heard the Sasquatch. There's a swamp fairly close to the house here where we can walk of an evening and quite often we go down and watch moose. One night we were down there and there wasn't any moose around which was strange because in the summer every night there's moose in the swamp. And just before dusk when across the swamp we heard this screaming cry."

Mrs. Walton: "There were three cries, screams, horrible screams or whatever they was, one after the other, there was silence between and everything was just dead quiet afterwards, just made the hair crawl on the back of your neck."

Mr. Walton: "We didn't see anything. But I've heard every animal that lives in the locality at different times and it wasn't any of those. If I was asked to describe the sound, I'd say it was kind of a screaming cry, and it seemed to have anguish in it, anguish was the thing that stuck with me."[465]

Fife Heights (Tacoma, Washington) Incident

Richard Grover: "This is the sight of the Fife Heights Incident. One morning approximately four o'clock, Dick Hancock and his friend came along this road stopping the car right here when they saw a huge creature behind that sign over there, it was so tall it's head was above the street sign. The creature took approximately three steps crossing the road. It was blinded by the headlights and it almost bumped into this sign. As it side-stepped it caught this sign before it went down over the hill. This is the sign that the creature struck, and it bent it like this leaving these indentations or scratch marks. It has been estimated by experts that it took five hundred foot pounds to bend this material."[466]

Dr. Charles Guiguet, Curator of Birds and Mammals, British Columbia Provincial Museum provided his opinion on cryptozoological creatures like the Sasquatch, the Yeti, and the Abominable Snowman: "All of these animals belong in the realm of folklore and mythology and my reason for saying this is simply that there is no concrete proof, evidence, that any of these creatures ever existed on the face of this planet. No one has ever produced a specimen—complete or incomplete—to prove that any of these animals have ever lived."[467]

René Dahinden: "No scientist ever came out in the bush to look at the footprints which we found. No scientist ever studied these tracks. They are saying they are fake without ever having seen the footprints in the area where we found them. No technical evaluation was ever made. In my opinion, after having seen 3,000 footprints myself of six different sizes, I came to the conclusion these tracks to be made by a living foot, a creature with a foot like this, a Sasquatch, rather than a man with artificial feet."[468]

Grover Krantz: "As a physical anthropologist, I've decided that these creatures do, in all likelihood, exist. The evidence of the footprints is what I find the most convincing. This is an example of one footprint, this is a plaster cast, which shows a crippled individual [Krantz holds a cast taken from a Colville, Washington print; see Chapter 2]. The foot was twisted. And two bulges appear, calloused structures on the outside edge of the foot and correspond to gaps in the bones which I've reconstructed here. If this was faked, the person doing it had to be an absolute expert in human anatomy."[469]

Patterson-Gimlin Film

Janos Prohaska: "The movement was the only thing that threw me a little bit because he moved a little bit more than a mammal, like a man than an animal. You could see all the muscles on the body and the whole movement; it didn't move like a costume at all. And the size of it was an enormous-big size, so I don't think they would find a big man like that."

Narrator: "Mr. Prohaska, you mentioned that the creature did not move as if it were a costume. Do you think it would be possible to create such a costume?"

Prohaska: "That would be a difficult . . . I don't think so. Because that costume, if it would be a costume, that would have taken such a long time to put the hair, and you should put the hair by glue, glue it on, that would take about ten hours the whole makeup job, and it looked to me very, very real. I'm doing this now since 1939, and if that was a costume that was the best I have ever seen."[470]

Patterson: "As it walked across the sandbar I was able to get some fairly good footage of it. It turned a couple of times, and looked at it, and as it turned it seemed to give me the impression that it didn't want anything to do with us, it didn't run, it didn't act scared, but yet it acted leery of us."

Ron Olson: "Well this footage proved to me that these creatures are real and that they do exist."

Smith: "Now how tall would you estimate that one [Patty] to be?"

Olson: "This creature was estimated by scientific methods, to be about 7 ½ to 8 feet tall. It was taking a stride of about 47 inches to 65, after he became spooked or more scared he stretched to 65."

Smith: "Now how does the length of that stride compare to, well let's say the average stride of a man?"

Olson: "Well the average stride of a man is about . . . maximum stride of a man would be about three feet."

Smith: "Now that arm appears to be proportionately longer than say a human arm. Have there been any estimates worked out on that?"

Olson: "Yes, there has. The arm is and always has been in all sightings and all cases definitely longer than a human's. Here the creature shows large pendulous breasts, indication here of course is that it is a female creature."

Smith: "Do you expect to capture one of these?"

Olson: "Well this is of course our, I'd suppose you'd call the finale of our whole program, is to make a capture. We want to make a live capture, and with this we are using tranquilizing equipment. We hope to bring one of these things in with a live capture, live and unharmed, to prove once and for all that this does exist. And since it does exist, maybe then there can be laws and things passed to protect these creatures so that they'll never become extinct."[471]

A recurring topic that emerged during the '70s was the beneficial applications technology brought and would bring to hunting Bigfoot. Olson became one of the earliest proponents of computers' analytical power applied to Bigfoot sighting data and Smith ended the original 20-minute featurette version of *Bigfoot: Man or Beast* by explaining that computers would help correlate and disseminate important information to Bigfoot researchers.

Smith: "In the past two years there has been a new undertaking by all concerned investigators to consolidate all of their data, all new sightings are investigated and reported on a lengthy questionnaire and this information is programmed into a computer. These computer reports and correlations are available to all the participating investigators upon request. In this way, each investigator can carry on his own work with a much more complete source of data. Along with the computer reports, the most modern equipment is now being used, as it is here in this camp. Procedures have been worked out to cover every aspect of a capture. In the past, many sightings went unreported, for fear of ridicule. Law enforcement officers got most of these reported sightings and most of the people who did the reporting were considered some kind of a nut. Now a central reporting system has been developed and all sightings can now be reported to our Portland headquarters by simply dialing 'Bigfoot,' Portland, Oregon. Other information can be obtained by writing 'Bigfoot,' Portland, Oregon."[472]

In an interview with reporter Doug Bates, Olson said he knew of more than 600 sightings on record, the oldest dating to the early 1800s. Confirming Smith's pronouncements from *Bigfoot: Man or Beast,* Olson claimed 300 sightings had been programmed into a computer in order to pinpoint trends and associations. "We're also beginning to work with some of the best bear dogs in the country," Olson added. Olson's use of data processing was a component of increased sophistication in Bigfoot research during the '70s, realized through the adoption of high-tech gear and tools including computers, light and sound amplifiers, and infrared film.[473]

Like several other investigators at the time, Olson lamented the problem of funding for serious search efforts. Olson augmented the estimated $3,000 he received from regular backers each month through the sale of Bigfoot novelties like ash trays duplicated from a plaster cast of a Bigfoot track. The lack of scientific acceptance was the commonly-attributed factor, posited by Olson as well as several other researchers, which prohibited the flow of funds toward earnest Bigfoot field study.[474]

Olson–Kliewer Split

Shortly after production of *Bigfoot: Man or Beast,* Olson and fellow researcher Gordon Kliewer disagreed over the veracity of a large footprint found near Salmon Creek in Lane County, Oregon, which resulted in a falling out between them. This schism led Kliewer, formerly a member of North American Wildlife Research Association, to form his own group, Pacific Coast Primate Research, based in Eugene.

The 17 ¼-inch foot-shaped impression was discovered by two fishermen on Saturday, April 29, in the mud near Salmon Creek east of Oakridge. Following publicity of the track's discovery, Kliewer led a 13-member band of hunters armed with tranquilizer guns and 16mm movie cameras in a search of the surrounding area. "We are definitely convinced that this is an authentic print made by the creature," said Kliewer, the organizing force behind the weekend's search.

"We have determined that about 95 per cent of all sightings turn out to be hallucinations or hoaxes," said Olson. "Because there is so much of this hoaxing, it unfortunately tends to discredit the 5 per cent which are legitimate sightings based on fact." This sentiment highlighted the difference between Olson and Kliewer's groups, namely, the North American Wildlife Research Association was considered more conservative in its investigative approach. Olson believed Bigfoot researchers should exercise all due caution to prevent acceding to possible hoaxes. An investigative practice gaining traction at the time called for researchers to eschew revealing a sighting or trackway's location until it could be thoroughly checked for possibility of fraud.

Regarding the Salmon Creek print, Olson's opinion was it had been inadequately checked for chicanery. "You probably remember the 'Colville Fake.' . . . It made a lot of people look like fools," Olson recalled to Bates, referring to Ivan Marx's claim to have filmed an injured Bigfoot. "When the film was finally blown up and stop-framed, investigators found the so-called creature was a man in a costume," said Olson. "You could see the seams, skin showing beneath the hide and no muscle movement whatsoever." Olson recalled the surge of adventurous glory-seekers into Colville and Bossburg armed with rifles to hunt down the creature before the film was exposed as a hoax. "It's a miracle nobody got shot," Olson declared. Ray Pickens, a bricklayer from Colville, had cheerfully admitted to making faux Bigfoot tracks with plywood feet. Olson maintained that Bigfoot investigators weren't so much angry at falling for hoaxers' efforts as they were troubled at the damaged credibility to the investigation of legitimate sightings.

Further harming the effort to authenticate the Salmon Creek print was the sensationalism surrounding its discovery, which Olson believed marred the opportunity to conduct a reasoned investigation. Like Colville, Olson thought an over-hyped atmosphere brought pranksters out of the woodwork. "I think we've got a sensationalism thing going on right here in Oakridge," he told Bates. "You can't go out and find one or two tracks and say with honesty that they're true Big Foot tracks. . . . It takes a thorough investigation of the entire area, plus extensive interviewing before you can label such a finding as either fact, fraud or question mark."

Kliewer felt differently about the discovery at Oakridge; following his examination of the scene, including casting the print, Kliewer went straight to the media. "There is no doubt in my mind that we have the real thing," Kliewer said. "The size is right, the stride is right and there is no evidence of a hoax." Kliewer maintained that an investigation of the scene gave no indication of how the print could have been faked and the fishermen who discovered the print were not the type, in Kliewer's opinion, to perpetrate a hoax. Kliewer noted no human footprints were near enough to the Bigfoot track to create concern or stoke suspicions of a setup. A companion print—a partial heel and toe impression was found seven feet, six inches away. Kliewer stated the stride was simply too long for a prankster to pull off. "The creature apparently came across the river," Kliewer said, "made the two tracks in the muddy soil, reached a rocky area that wouldn't record prints and then climbed a hillside leading to the Box Canyon area."

Olson and Kliewer's divergent approaches and attitudes were mirrored by the organizations they respectively led. Olson had been actively involved with Bigfoot research for the previous four years and had been associated with Roger Patterson and his Northwest Research organization until Patterson's death on January 15, 1972. After Patterson passed away, Olson, according to Bates' *Register-Guard* article, was chosen by Patterson's widow to continue his research. With access to Patterson's research, records, and contacts, Olson claimed his was the largest Bigfoot investigating network in the country.

Kliewer and Olson claimed they remained friends and planned to cooperate in the mutually-held goal of sharing a noncommercial Bigfoot capture with the scientific community. Both men said their organizations were non-profits, with all contributions channeled into the search for Bigfoot. "Our plan is to capture this creature alive," explained Olson. "When we do, there will be no sensationalism. We will take it to an isolated, secluded holding area, unknown to the press, while scientists are bought in to conduct tests." After a thorough scientific inquiry, the hirsute subject would be turned loose.[475]

Two days after Bates' article ran, the *Register-Guard* printed a letter from a concerned reader who singled out and chided Pacific Coast Primate Research for its objective to capture a Bigfoot.

> I am a 14-year-old reader of the *Register-Guard*. I am writing at this moment to express my feelings concerning "Big Foot." I feel Man should leave Big Foot alone. He has been around since 1884, and this or these "Big Foots" haven't harmed anything or anybody.
>
> If society goes in and tries to capture Big Foot, he could turn on Man and become very destructive. Then Man would have something to regret. Whatever Big Foot is, human or animal, it should not be penned up.

> If Man should capture Big Foot, I think it would be very inhuman on their behalf. Man doesn't like to be captured or held prisoner, and I'm sure Big Foot doesn't either. I feel if Nature wanted him found, he would live in more populous areas. I think the Pacific Coast Primate Research Corporation should use their time on more important things, such as the problem of pollution and the solution for it. I only wish more people could hear my views. Because I'm sure other people feel the way I do about this situation. . . .
>
> Kathy Fitzpatrick[476]

Ivan Marx

Ivan Marx resurfaced in the Fall of 1972, appearing on the revival of the *You Asked for It* television show. The series had originally aired in the '50s and was an early example of reality and interactive programming (viewers wrote in to propose story segments they were interested in seeing on air). One of the original hosts from the '50s, Jack Smith, was back for the 1972 incarnation. Marx appeared on the show as both a segment requester and a subject of focus. Marx carried a canned movie he claimed had come straight from his camera and contained footage of a Bigfoot he filmed during a snow storm in northern California. Smith explained to the audience that the film would be printed under the strictest controls and be examined by an expert to determine its veracity. After a commercial break (and fast-forwarded into time) the film had been processed. The show's producers had a primate expert examine the film and, fully unimpressed, he stated the subject looked like a man in a suit. For the wider viewing audience, the apparently costumed subject—a white Bigfoot this time—left little doubt that either Marx had been duped or he had indeed hoaxed the footage himself. Tim Cahill wrote in *Rolling Stone*, "To my layman's eyes, the film seems an incredibly clumsy fake. Peter Byrne said it was 'ridiculous.' In it, the creature is seen white in a heavy snowfall. It walks manlike, toward the camera, jumps aimlessly, and gives us a view of his front and back sides. The white gorilla suit bags and wrinkles in the ass."[477]

Rescue of Bigfoot Researcher (1972)

In the late autumn of 1972, 35-year-old Jim Barry searched for clues to the existence of Bigfoot near Six Rivers National Forest. Tom Willholte and George Hoover were themselves hiking and compiling research for a planned book on the Bluff Creek area when they met Barry. The three men combined their efforts into a joint expedition and established a base for their operations near the Humboldt–Siskiyou–Del Norte county junction north of Orleans.

Willholte and Hoover left Barry at their camp near the confluence of the Bluff and Notice Creeks to return to civilization for supplies. As they were about to undertake the return journey back to camp laden with food, a record snowstorm blanketed the area. Willholte and Hoover tried to reach Barry on December 10 but their attempt failed. They knew that Barry was not dressed for the weather and was running low on essentials, namely food. A Civil Air Patrol flight piloted by Mervyn Selvage was unable to reach the camp due to inclement conditions. Selvage reported no smoke in the area or other obvious signs of human activity.

On Friday, December 15, Willholte, Hoover, and Fred Holsclaw of Hoopa started out at the end of the Bluff Creek Road in Humboldt County on snowshoes, beginning what was estimated as a three-day effort to reach Barry, before turning back in the face of deteriorating weather. Snow conditions in the area were reported to have been between three to five feet and up to ten feet in spots. Their rescue attempt was counter to Sheriff Tom Lawry's orders, who was wary of good intentions to aid Barry confounding and complicating official extraction efforts.[478]

Taking advantage of rains that had washed away some of the snow, Howard Ames from Hoopa guided a rescue effort mounted in a four-wheel drive truck on Tuesday, December 19, via Onion Mountain. One may imagine the relief Barry felt upon hearing the roaring engine approaching his cabin. Ames' group and a rescue party from the Forest Service reached Barry within minutes of each other. During his stay at the camp, Barry shoveled snow and chopped wood to stay warm during some of the heaviest winter snowfall on record. Barry spent a total of four weeks outfitted in a light gabardine jacket at the snowbound camp; he lost 15 pounds during his experience and was down to his last morsels of food—homemade fudge. "He was very elated to see us," said Willholte. Willholte and Barry planned on returning to the camp later that week to reengage their search for Bigfoot.[479]

Manimals by McClarin

The first issue of *Manimals Newsletter*, dated 12 August, 1972, stated it was carrying on from George Haas' *Bigfoot Bulletin*, which had published 26 total issues: monthly from January 1969 to December 1970 and then quarterly for two issues in 1971. Editor Jim McClarin explained his title choice: "This word [Manimals] was chosen over 'Sasquatch,' 'Bigfoot,' 'Abominable Snowman,' 'Humanoid,' etc. because it is a relatively self-explanatory contraction of 'man' and 'animal,' used to mean a man-like animal, or an 'animal-like' man, and it seems to carry no other special occult, humorous, or ethnic connotation. Because people report entities whose descriptions fall outside the general Sasquatch, Bigfoot or Yeti categories, etc., and because these too should fall within the realm of our interest, I feel a very general easy-to-handle name like Manimals is ideal for application to this nebulous quantum of the unknown."[480]

"The chief immediate goal of *MN* is to re-establish an operative exchange among Manimals investigators the world over," McClarin wrote. *Manimals'* premier issue mentioned the Fourth International Congress of Primatology (15-18 August, 1972, in Portland, Oregon); "Many speakers and participants will receive issue one of *MN* as it is felt many serious primatologists may wish to keep abreast of the Manimals subject."[481] McClarin's ambition was the resolution of questions of Bigfoot's behavior and habits. "The chief long range goal will be the acquisition of information which may clearly reveal the nature of the Manimals phenomenon." In the second and last issue of *Manimals*, McClarin commented on Haas' termination of the *Bigfoot Bulletin* and his appreciation of the elder researcher's belief that time, energy and money going into the *Bulletin* could be better applied to conducting his own personal field research.

Pursuit magazine's complimentary review of *Manimals* described its contents as "general articles and letters of interest, and an extensive bibliography of both magazine and newspaper articles, with a very brief abstract of each." A feature of the short-lived subscription policy involved an exchange of information: anyone sending in a self-addressed stamped envelope (stamps were 8 cents in the early '70s) and at least one informative article, dispatch, or news clipping) would receive the following edition of *Manimals Newsletter*. If one had nothing informative to exchange, then a self-addressed stamped envelope plus 25 cents obtained the current issue of *Manimals*.[482]

Peter Byrne

Peter Byrne (46 years old in 1972) wore the mantle of having pursued evidence for both Bigfoot and the Himalayan Yeti; he believed the case for Bigfoot was the stronger one. "I give it a 95% chance of existing," he said of Bigfoot. "For me it is the ultimate hunt." Byrne, a believer in seasonal nomadism, told *Los Angeles Times'* reporter Philip Fradkin that one year after Mederios and other witnesses had seen Bigfoot in The Dalles, Byrne and three assistants rotated crewing a blind atop Crate's Point hoping, ultimately without success, to spot the creature. Byrne believed in a subdued, stealthy approach to the Bigfoot hunt. "We only whisper out here," he told a companion during a climb along the ridge south of Mt. Hood. "Voices carry too far."[483]

> Byrne and his helpers spend most of the time checking out past reports of the animals in an attempt to piece together a pattern of behavior and determine if they are true sightings or hoaxes.
>
> They are also out in the field at the same places and at the same time as previous sightings to see if the creature duplicates his movements. But since The Dalles sightings, things have been slow.
>
> About $75,000 has been budgeted for the three-year search, which began in early 1971. The principal backer is Tom Page, a Mentor, Ohio, businessman.[484]

Along with support from Page, Byrne reportedly supplemented his Bigfoot project with his own income while on leave from his position as director of the International Wildlife Conservation Society of Washington, D.C.[485] Fradkin wrote that though Byrne's funds were decreasing, he remained optimistic and undaunted. "Oh, you know it is that old business about wanting to climb a mountain that has never been climbed before. For a layman like me there is not too much left to conquer."[486]

> To the small town scene of The Dalles, Byrne adds a certain amount of class with his British accent, turtleneck sweaters and penchant for good quality Scotch without ice.
>
> Local residents chuckle at Byrne's ordering "porridge" for breakfast and Byrne snorts at the crassness of the word "Eat" emblazoned on signs advertising the presence of cafes.
>
> Byrne has gotten in trouble with the local planning commission for parking his mobile home in a sylvan meadow setting, far away from other such prefabricated structures.
>
> "Now, where's a man to pitch his tent?" lamented Byrne, who is divorced.[487]

In response to a news and articles solicitation from McClarin for *Manimals Newsletter*, Peter Byrne wrote:

> "I'll get something to you in due course, but in the meantime you could say that International Wildlife is at The Dalles, Oregon, P. O. Box ___, zip 97058, has been there since the beginning of the year, intends to be there to the end of the year and possibly longer, and a) has found/seen/heard no conclusively supporting evidence of Bigfoot/Omah this year to date, b) is still not 100% convinced that the things actually exist, c) regards all of the evidence produced to date, from all states by all of the people concerned, as quite inconclusive and in many cases flimsy, d) will continue to explore and examine and investigate whatever 'evidence' is forthcoming, and e) will not hesitate to expose, without regard to consequences, any hoaxing that is perpetrated in the Bigfoot/Omah field (including footprint making, films, gorilla suit 'acts') as well as the people involved in it." Peter Byrne, 21 July 1972 (edited).[488]

Byrne was known to share a friendly competitive relationship with Tim Dinsdale, a kindred spirit of Byrne's who investigated the Loch Ness Monster. "Just proving that one of them [Bigfoot or Loch Ness Monster] exists will help break down the prejudice of the scientific community against the existence of the other," Dinsdale said in 1972.[489]

Manimals Newsletter's second issue included an article by Byrne in which he described a "Bigfoot bed" in Del Norte County, California he and René Dahinden examined. This article provides insights into how Byrne formatted his data and catalogued evidence:

> Considerable excitement was occasioned recently by the finding, in northern California, of what was believed to be a Bigfoot bed, or lair. With Rene Dahinden, I traveled to the scene of the finding and made an examination of what was there. Here, for *MN*, is my report.
>
> FINDER . . . three US Foresters from Orleans Range, Orleans, Humboldt, Co.
>
> AREA . . . about 800 feet above the upper end of Scorpion Creek, which flows into Bluff Creek, in Del Norte County, northern California.

DESCRIPTION OF AREA . . . steep hillside; principle growth Douglas Fir; undergrowth, Rhododendron and Madrone.

SITUATION OF "BED" . . . on the ground, in a level place made so by the growth of a large Douglas Fir. "Bed" was built against the fir tree.

SHAPE . . . rounded, slightly elongated, like a misshapen bird's nest.

SIZE . . . six feet long, four and a half feet in width.

MATERIALS OF CONSTRUCTION . . . leaves, sticks, some moss, rhododendron shoots from the top ends of rhododendron bush branches, and bear grass.

FINDINGS . . . In the bed, 27 hairs, black, some with brown tips, all less than 3 ½ inches in length. Much curling "underhair," short (less than ½ inch), soft, black or brown in colour. Faeces, one small pile, in rhododendron bushes five feet from edge of "bed," shape and substance similar to that of common Black Bear, weight 5 ounces. Very small, thin scratch marks in bark of Douglas Fir to a height of 18 inches. Large, deep scratch, or claw marks, in bark of madrone tree, eight feet from "bed" to a height of 9 feet.

OPINION . . . The finding has every appearance of being the nesting bed or lair of a female bear of the species Ursus americanus, i.e., the common American Black Bear. The small claw marks in the lower part of the fir appear to be those of newly born cubs. The deep scratches in the madrone are most probably those of a mature bear; they are typical of the territorial "declaration" of the Black Bear. The hair appears to be bear hair. The faeces is very bearlike in shape, size and contents. The teeth markings on the stems found in the "bed" indicate the impressions normally made by the incisors of bear. (In breaking these stems the bear uses only the incisors and the stems are broken off with a single upward or vertical snapping movement.)

AUTHORITIES CONSULTED . . . Steve Matthes, Eureka, California, professional hunter (20 years) California Department of Fish & Game. Gus Lanergen, Eureka, California, professional hunter (over 20 years) who, in his hunting career, took more than 3000 bears (according to official records,

State Archives, Sacramento). Roger Caras, North American Mammals, Vol. I, (Meredith Press) pges. 56 to 60.

Peter Byrne 6 Sept. 1972 (edited).[490]

It was hardly surprising to Byrne that Bigfoot was infrequently encountered since, after all, Bigfoot wasn't the only seldom-seen animal in the wilderness; very few people ever spy a wolverine, black-footed ferret, or a Sonoran Pronghorn. Bigfoot became as extant to Byrne as the aforementioned uncommonly-met mammals and was likely, Byrne would contend, rarer and smarter. "People have spent their entire lives in the hills here and have never seen a cougar," Byrne said. "Primates are known to be shy and to be constantly alert," he added. Byrne believed if Bigfoot wished to operate unseen, they were creatures suitably adapted to do so and remain hidden.[491]

Writer James Bylin brought Bigfoot to the *Wall Street Journal* in an article titled, "Does 'Bigfoot' Stalk Wilds of Northwest?" which touched on Byrne's capture and release protocols:

> When and if a Bigfoot is found, most investigators want it taken alive. Peter Byrne has unsuccessfully asked Wasco County, which includes The Dalles, to outlaw Bigfoot shooting to protect the creature itself as well as hunters. Only Skamania County in Washington, to the northwest, has such a law on books, enacted after a spate of sightings there in 1969.
>
> Mr. Byrne doesn't plan to slay Bigfoot if he has the chance. Rather, he's equipped his expedition with tranquilizing gear, which, he claims, can knock the creature down in two or three minutes and completely immobilize him in nine minutes. Bigfoot, he says, would be studied and then released back into the wilderness, possibly with an electronic implant to permit tracking and further study.

Bylin discussed the opinions held by several prominent researchers regarding the kill/no-kill debate, which asked if emphasis should be directed toward Bigfoot's capture or should the goal be to bring in a body to satisfy scientific study.

> This approach has stirred debate among some other investigators, however. Ron Olson agrees that tranquilizing is the "humane" way, but writer John Green argues "this simply

doesn't make sense." The tranquilizing weapons "aren't very accurate," he says, and even if a Bigfoot is shot, it could fast disappear into thick brush before falling, making the "chance of finding it poor," Bigfoot, he says, isn't human and "not entitled to greater protection than any other animal. He's not endangered—we can't even find one. There's no reason not to kill one."

In any event, Mr. Green thinks the first catch will probably be accidental, "most likely by a hunter stumbling on one."[492]

John Green

Green accepted Bigfoot as corporeal in part from the general concurrence common across hundreds of witnesses' descriptions. Too, Green resolved the worldwide phenomenon of man-like giants by the existence of several types of creatures.

> "Most of the reports are almost identical, although there have been variations, in heights ranging up to almost nine feet, and weights, which run as high as 700 or 800 pounds," Green said in an interview.
>
> "Some people have mistakenly lumped the Sasquatch or Bigfoot with the so-called 'Abominable Snowman,' or Himalayan Yeti, reported for centuries in Nepal and throughout Asia, but they're not the same.
>
> "The Bigfoot appears to be some sort of primitive human-like animal, while the Yeti is probably a species of mountain climbing ape.
>
> "The two are distinguished by their footprints. The Bigfoot has an unopposed big toe, similar to the human foot, but the Yeti has an opposed big toe, more closely related to the ape."[493]

"Is there an unknown species of animal that is very heavy, has human-like feet and walks erect? The very idea is ridiculous," said Green. "Is there, then," he went on, "a person or organization that has been using specialized equipment to make giant footprints over an area of hundreds of thousands of square miles, for the best part of a century without being detected? That, too, is ridiculous. The only comfortable explanation is that the tracks don't really occur at all, but the plain fact is that they do."[494]

Washington State University's Grover Krantz wondered what a scientist from ages past thought upon listening to a description of a giraffe. "Now, there's an unlikely creature. He probably denied its existence until one stepped on him."[495]

Grover Krantz

Phyllis Dolhinow served as the anthropology department director at the University of California at Berkeley and was in part known for starting an on-campus langur monkey colony at Berkley in 1972. Dolhinow was also a Bigfoot skeptic. "It's a question of the number of animals necessary to maintain any living species," she said. "Taking the fact you need a lot of them, it's very unlikely we wouldn't have found one, especially in an area like the U.S."[496]

Counter to skeptics' arguments that Bigfoot was simply a myth, or perhaps a hoax, Krantz believed he had helped *prove* the existence of Bigfoot. With some variation amongst prints, he had discovered remarkable features of the creature's foot, specifically the appearance of collapsed arches and a distinctive spread to the foot's width. These findings, Krantz maintained, were fairly consistent over diverse geographic regions and was a natural adaptation to support Bigfoot's great weight.

> But he has also concluded that the bones in front of the feet are relatively short while "the bone of the heel is very, very long," making the design of the foot different from a human one. This is logical, he argues, because if the leg and foot of Bigfoot were hinged the same as a human's, they couldn't support the creature's tremendous weight, estimated at up to 1,000 pounds. The weight would have to be carried further forward on the foot; hence, elongated heels.
>
> Mr. Krantz's conclusion: The tracks correspond correctly to the size and shape he thinks would be needed. "So," he said, "our Sasquatch foot-faker, who has made so many tracks in so many areas during the last 50 years or more, would now have to be an expert on the human anatomy."
>
> Mr. Krantz, who spends about a month on the road each year in a camper searching for Bigfoot or at least some bones, says he recently viewed the Roger Patterson film frame by frame. In only two frames, he notes, could the foot and ankle

> be seen, but in both instances the front of the shin came down to the midline of the foot, compared to about the rear third of the foot in a human. "It was just exactly as I described it," he says, adding that he thinks he not only supported his theory but helped authenticate the film.[497]

For Krantz, footprints were front and center as exemplary Bigfoot evidence. "The footprints are NOT just giant human feet. They are structurally designed to support a 1,000-pound animal and nobody playing a joke could have figured out that foot."[498] By 1972, Krantz had effectively honed his theory on Bigfoot footprints citing the logical anatomical characteristics observable in (authentic) prints, while faked prints, lacking such considered detail, were easily adjudged to be hoaxes.[499]

> The theory focuses on Sasquatch's long-heeled, double-balled, collapsed-arch footprints.
>
> They're inhuman, Krantz concludes, and too sophisticated to be a hoax.
>
> Any eight-foot-tall creature that walks erect—some reports have been of Sasquatch 11 feet in height—weighing more than 500 pounds necessarily would have collapsed arches and its footprints would be flat-footed, Krantz argues,
>
> The heel marks would be elongated and the front part of the foot would be shorter—as the weight on the foot would be displaced forward (as compared to a *homo* [*sapiens*]) because of the awkward creature's massive body.[500]

Faked tracks stood in stark contrast to this reasoning. Krantz explained to *Seattle Times'* reporter John Bell that Pickens' hoaxed tracks left near Colville were identifiable as such, in part for their long stride—as much as eight feet—accomplished by the hoaxer running downslope wearing static wooden feet. Genuine Bigfoot tracks usually evinced a five-foot stride and commonly revealed a double ball near the big toe, a logical bone development, Krantz contended, for such a massively built creature.[501] "The conclusion I've been forced to make," Krantz said, "is that if these tracks are fakes, they are being faked by a highly skilled anatomist who has been secretly working in the most inaccessible places at least since the 1930s." That possibility staggered Krantz' imagination. "This fakery is quite beyond the capability of any human being . . . it's impossible. So I'm stuck with having to accept something for which there yet is no concrete evidence." Deductively, since Krantz had eliminated the impossible—human agency hoaxing all reported Bigfoot sightings and track finds—he was left with the simple conclusion that it was an extant creature leaving behind Bigfoot tracks.[502]

Krantz had also worked out a hypothesis regarding Bigfoot's hands:

> The 12-inch-long handprints seen by Krantz reflect a "non-opposable" thumb, such as the thumb of an animal that digs into the ground and cannot easily grasp things with one hand or climb trees. The human hand with its opposable thumb (which extends perpendicularly out from the base of the hand) is particularly suited for grasping.
>
> The thumbprints, however, are flat and wide, very dissimilar to the claw-marks of a bear, Krantz points out. And there is no trace in the prints of the bulging thumb muscle found in a hand with an opposable thumb.[503]

Advice and social commentary columnist Margo Coleman (later Margo Howard), herself the child of advice columnist Eppie Lederer (Ann Landers), wrote a syndicated column "Margo," in the 1970s. Coleman wrote about Krantz in a December 1972 "Margo" column which began with several examples of her friends' fertile imaginations filling the void of their obliviousness. When Coleman posed the question, "What is a Sasquatch?" they responded with disparate and colorful answers:

> A sex deviate
> A cousin to the duckbill platypus
> A new cleanser
> An argumentative person
> A polecat
> A sassy kid
> The major ingredient in tapioca
>
> I don't know what your answer would've been, but a Sasquatch is a giant ape-like creature said to be in the Pacific Northwest whose existence is becoming as hotly contested as the abominable snowman or the Loch Ness monster.[504]

"Nobody wonders why the bison or the elephant has survived," Krantz told Coleman, "so why couldn't the Sasquatch have? I think it is a rare animal that people choose not to believe exists because of its controversial characteristics. It upsets people that the Sasquatch affects a human posture."

Coleman asked Krantz who would go to the trouble of dressing up in an ape suit to perpetrate a hoax. "There are always kooks who fake evidence," Krantz explained. "They do it for kicks—to see it in the newspapers and know that they're responsible," he said. "I know there's faked evidence," he conceded, "but once you discard that, there is real evidence. Why is a piece of genuine information not believed? Frankly, I think I'm the only one who's got enough guts to stick my neck out."

> The whole business, of course, is not easy on Dr. Krantz. I mean, how would you like to be among a small minority of PH.Ds who believed in a giant ape?
>
> I asked Dr. Krantz if he were planning to organize an expedition to hunt for the Sasquatch. "Oh, no," he said. "He'll know that you're there and never come out."
>
> What he is hoping for, however, is that someone may have shot a Sasquatch and kept quiet about it thinking he had done something "immoral." If this person would come forward and lead Dr. Krantz to the skeleton, he would be vindicated.
>
> Dr. Krantz says one of the reasons he would love to get his hands on a skeleton is to "rub a few people's noses in it. I don't expect any financial gain . . . but you never know about that."
>
> Poor Dr. Krantz. Now that he's on record as crediting the Sasquatch, he's hearing from the flying saucer buffs, too. "But they're not winning me over," he states. "I just don't believe in that stuff at all!"[505]

By 1972, Krantz had casts and slides ready for use in a travelling exhibition and lecture. Reporter John Bell considered Krantz's judicious disposition toward Bigfoot: "Simply, he is a university professor who will believe totally in the Sasquatch sensation only when he can view a captured specimen or examine the bones of a dead one. And he's been looking—every chance he's had for the past three years."[506] But diligent track analysis and reflection on other evidence brought some people, if few credentialed scientists such as Krantz, to an energized confidence: Bigfoot necessarily *had* to be. But only a body, a *corpus delicti*, could answer questions, shatter doubts, silence critics, and fully exonerate the ardent proselytes like Krantz. For Sasquatch research, Krantz traveled when he could, using his own funds and resources. Krantz generally visited forested areas of Washington State where he conducted interviews with witnesses, five of which, by 1972, Krantz could find no flaws with and thusly earned his acceptance as genuine sightings. Krantz was married at the time and with his wife Evelyn traveled when possible to look at tracks or talk with witnesses. "I go up and down about Sasquatch," Evelyn Krantz told Bell. "I'll believe in this whole thing when I see one on the road or somewhere. But the chance is very high that Sasquatch exists, I'm convinced."[507]

Bell shrewdly interviewed Dr. Robert Ackerman, acting Department of Anthropology chairman at Washington State University and an expert in Arctic prehistory. "We're all for this sort of research. It's very valid and Dr. Krantz is going about it in a very professional manner," he said. "But thus far, the Sasquatch or whatever you want to call it doesn't exist for the scientific community. And it won't until someone comes up with certain evidence—like a bone—that is unique to the creature." The prospects of official funding for Krantz's singular interest remained hinged to the question of scientifically verifiable support for Bigfoot's existence. "There'll be no departmental or foundation money available for the research until that evidence is found," Ackerman concluded.[508]

John Mionczynski

An encounter in 1972 in the Wind River Mountains convinced a budding biologist and naturalist he may have come very close to a Bigfoot. The event would prove an important one in John Mionczynski's life, leading to his search for additional evidence in the '70s and following decades.

An entomology book, a present from his grandfather, spurred a young Mionczynski's interest in science and natural history. He attended Southampton College on Long Island and graduated in 1969, majoring in marine biology. Mionczynski was hired by the U. S. Forest Service to track radio-collared bighorn sheep in the early 1970s. "These sheep had been fitted with radio collars, and my link to them if they decided to migrate was my receiver. No one had ever done radio-telemetry studies on bighorn sheep before, so most of what I was doing was experimental." In the mid-1970s Mionczynski was part of the Interagency Grizzly Bear Study Team live-trapping grizzlies to attach radio collars which tracked their movements in and around Yellowstone.

Emilene Ostlind interviewed Mionczynski in 2011, noting the track casts in his possession. One cast was not of a footprint but made from the

1972 BOY SCOUT PATCH, REDWOOD AREA COUNCIL, CALIFORNIA

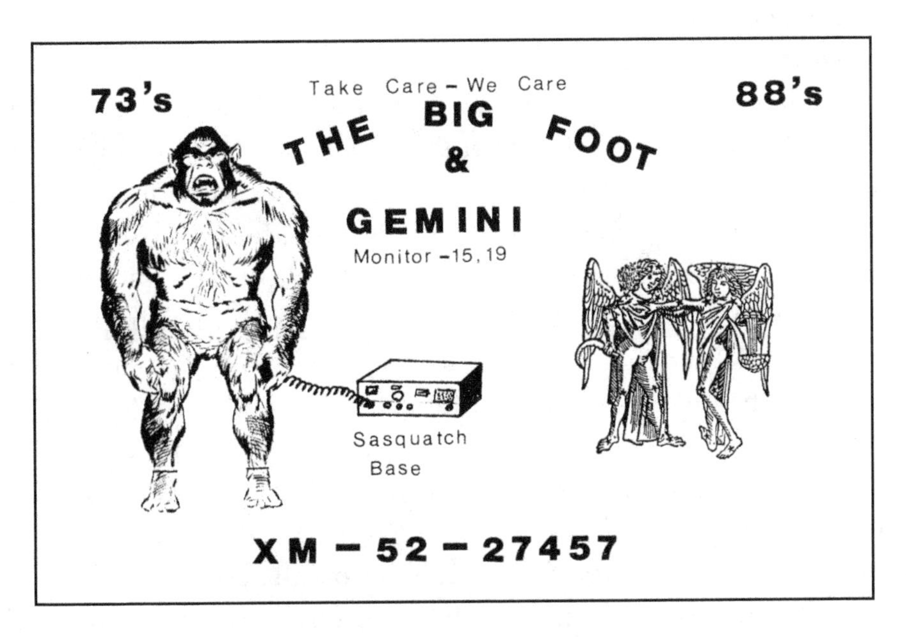

A 1970S BIGFOOT-THEMED CB RADIO QSL CARD

impression of a large hand, originally found underwater in a pond. The hand cast had especial meaning to Mionczynski, because the shape and size conformed to what he saw backlit by the moon against the top of his tent in 1972 in the Wind River Mountains.

He had been camping alone when he awoke to see the large hand pressing against the top of his 6-foot-high tent. At first thinking it to be a bear, Mionczynski realized he could distinguish fingers, not a clawed paw. The creature collapsed the tent and fell across Mionczynski's legs. He scrambled out of the tent as the animal disappeared into the nearby forest. Mionczynski started a fire and stayed awake through the rest of the night. He could hear the animal breathing and moving nearby for two and a half hours and during a stretch of about 45 minutes it threw pinecones at him, leaving no doubts with Mionczynski that it wanted him to leave the area.[509]

Ever a keen observer of details in his natural surroundings, Mionczynski told this author that he had found several examples over the course of his career, while conducting field studies, of deer which had been killed by having their necks twisted back, a method inconsistent with bear kills.[510]

SIGHTINGS 1972

Idaho's Ape Canyon

The Patterson-Gimlin film and its star, Patty, provided a dynamic, if grainy, portrait which the public could point to and identify as a Bigfoot. The sustainment of Bigfoot in the '70s' cultural mindset was effected by witnesses' continued encounters with hairy hominids and the subsequent promulgation of those stories and reports. After 1967, Bigfoot had both form and life. Conceptually, Bigfoot was approachable in the absence of concrete, unassailable evidence; a lack of personal experience did not impair personal receptiveness to either the entertainment or the mystery. Bigfoot the creature was just as beguiling as Bigfoot the idea.

Idaho State Journal editor George Neavoll's article "Bigfoot's Home in Ape Canyon" introduced readers to Justin "Judd" Phelps and his direct observations of Bigfoot. The St. Charles resident claimed to have seen a hair-covered, man-like creature in Idaho's so-called Ape Canyon located "somewhere" in Bear Lake County. A fireman-engineer on the Union Pacific Railroad, Phelps claimed not just one, but three Bigfoot sightings, the first of which occurred in 1970. Because Phelps was reluctant to reveal the precise location of his sightings, the place name "Ape Canyon" was fabricated by Neavoll for his *State Journal* article. The article contains Phelps' inferences on Bigfoot's seasonal movement patterns and use of shelters during inclement weather.

> Others have seen the animal, Phelps says, and think it's a bear.
>
> He has seen it closer than anyone though, and he swears it is not.
>
> It walks like a bear, he says, though a bear doesn't walk more than a few steps on its hind feet. This creature habitually stands erect, and swings abnormally long arms at its side.
>
> Its tracks are similar to a bear's but slimmer, and are about a Size 12 in length. They sink about a foot into the snow.
>
> Each time the creature has been sighted, it stomps its feet and shakes its head, like a child in anger.
>
> Measured against a nine-foot tree, it stands five-and-a-half to six feet tall.
>
> Phelps left his St. Charles home on a snow machine last Jan. 2 [1972], and arrived at the place of his previous sightings of the creature about noon. It was bitter cold, and he built a fire.
>
> He had been there about two hours, and the fire was getting hot, so he decided to "put a little snow on the fire—then I got this feeling." It was the same feeling he had had before, that he was being watched, and that something was about to happen.
>
> It was between 2 and 3 P.M.
>
> He looked up from where he had been resting, stretched on his snow machine, and saw, just 100 yards away, an ape-like creature covered with grayish-brown hair, returning his gaze.
>
> It was standing by a young pine tree, and when it saw Phelps looking, it "waved its arms and stomped its feet" and headed for the deeper woods.
>
> When Phelps had seen the creature the first time, he had fired above its head with his rifle. The second time he didn't shoot, but spoke to it soothingly.
>
> This time he tried to take a picture. But he only had an older model Polaroid, and his hands shook badly. When he pulled the self-developing film from the camera, there was no figure to be seen.
>
> The snow was six to eight feet deep at the site, he says, about two feet of it being new snow. The tracks the creature left sank about a foot into the loose snow.

> He did not follow the tracks.
>
> Phelps tried two days later to make contact with the creature again. He waited for it as usual, but it did not appear.
>
> The St. Charles man speculates the animal lives in a "kind of shelter" erected near an old mining claim at the site, in severe weather.
>
> He says coyotes and other wildlife he has seen in the vicinity avoid the spot where the creature lives.
>
> The sightings all have occurred within eight to 10 miles of U.S. Highway 89, on the eastern flank of the northern end of the Wasatch Range.
>
> Phelps thinks the creature moves to lower elevation in the winter, which is when it has been seen each time, so it normally may live much higher in the mountains.
>
> He also believes there is more than one. While the first one he sighted was six feet or more in height, the one he saw this year may have been only four-and-a-half feet. It did not otherwise give any indication of being an immature specimen.

Neavoll makes a geographically-based assertion that most Bigfoot reports come from British Columbia, the Cascades of Washington and Oregon, and the Coast Range of southern Oregon and northern California. "To my knowledge," Neavoll wrote, "this is the first reported sighting in Idaho." If this restricting of Bigfoot's territorial range to within the Pacific Northwest was sometimes reported, it was also often challenged throughout the '70s, buried under an avalanche of Bigfoot reports from practically everywhere.

Neavoll asked Leon V. Howell, principal of Bear Lake Junior High School, for his thoughts on Phelps' story. During the summer months, Howell served as a U.S. Forest Service guide at Minnetonka Cave (the cave attracted over 10,000 visitors in 1971, and was only a few miles from the spot where Phelps' Bigfoot sightings occurred).

> "I have worked summers in St. Charles Canyon for the past six years," Howell replied on Jan. 4, 1972, "and to date I have not heard of or seen anything like you describe.
>
> "I live in Fish Haven . . . and have spent much time for many years in the mountains fishing, hunting, and snowmobiling, if there was anything up there I feel I would surely have seen evidence of this creature.

"I have asked the people in the Forest Service office if they could give me any information. They are completely in the dark on the subject.

"Personally, from my personal observations and information I have gathered from others, I really doubt the validity of the claim of such a creature in these mountains."

So there you have it.

Are Bigfoot and the Yeti real, perhaps related species whose ancestors crossed the Bering land bridge to inhabit the wilderness regions of the New World, much as the ancient Indian tribes did?

Were they pushed back from the coastal areas by the dominant tribes, giving rise to the Indian legends of today? If so, were they pushed as far as the southeastern corner of present-day Idaho?[511]

Sasquatch Cave

Dave Stockand's article, "Sasquatch Cave Sealed by Water," in the September 6 edition of the *Vancouver Sun* described Simon Fraser University student Paul Griffiths' cave discovery and raised a possible connection between subterranean worlds and Bigfoot. Griffiths' discovery of the limestone cave resulted in a detailed geographic survey of the area intended, in part, to quell suggestions of their association with anomalous hairy bipeds.[512]

Paul Griffith's (sic) wonderland limestone cave in the Cariboo not only has grizzly bear sentinels but—based on the evidence of a fresh track—may have Sasquatch tenants as well.

And Paul has returned from a new voyage of discovery to Grizzly Bear Cave more convinced than ever that "it is a caver's cave—not a tourist cave."

He also reported that rising waters and the approach of winter in the high country have put the cave's just-glimpsed-at secrets under lock and key until next year.

"So it's safe until next spring," said the 21-year-old University of Victoria oceanography student and amateur cave explorer.

Paul found the cave 14 months ago while he was working for the provincial parks branch.[513]

Griffiths related his trek to the cave to Stockand, undertaken with Blake Killins: "We left at 3 o'clock on a Saturday afternoon and got up there (the cave) around two in the morning," recalled Paul. "You have to cross Bowron Lake, end to end, and then you go up the Bowron River." On the way, the pair surprised a bear and her cub. "Well, the salmon are spawning and the grizzlies are just infesting the area, because they feed on the salmon. No one in their right mind wants to go there except us crazy nuts. But we were just rounding a corner and, since the canoe is so silent, we surprised a grizzly, a beautiful silvertip, and her cub." Griffiths was impressed by both the beauty and the power of the adult bear. "The sow just stood up, you know, wondering what was going on. Luckily, she just took off."

Reaching the cave, Griffiths and Killins slept on a ledge near its entrance and headed into its depths at 7 A.M. the next morning. "But there was more water than the last time I was up there and we didn't get very far. We didn't have much time because Blake had only the weekend off. So basically we spent our time taking pictures, including the one of the track."

"You can go down a distance of about 200 yards when the water is low with no problem at all," Griffiths said, describing access into the cave. "If the water is really low, you can get around this bypass and continue down the river for just over a mile," he said. "I have a feeling it connects with a series of caves in the next valley over, which would make it extremely long." The rising waters provided the young men an impetus to learn as much about the cave as possible.

As for the footprint, it was 13 to 14 inches long and discovered about 100 feet inside the entrance. Griffiths snapped at least one photo of the print. "The picture of the track I got is different from the ones we took in the cave before. This one is recent—because the other footprints had been washed away."

That a Sasquatch could have been the print-maker was not dismissed by Griffiths. "I ran into what I think was a Sasquatch about three years ago," he said hearkening to an expedition by members of the University of Victoria Caving Club in central Vancouver Island. "We were exploring a cave at night and came out about three in the morning; it was snowing lightly," Griffiths recalled. "I was walking up to a fork in the road, to find a place to turn the truck around, and I spotted these two legs. I raised the flashlight, and it's this thing about seven feet high. Its eyes reflected in the flashlight—just like a cat's eyes—and it had a sort of flat face," he said. "It wasn't a bear or anything," Griffiths asserted, "and it was walking towards me. Its arms extended past the knees." Griffiths admitted that at the time he was not cognizant of Bigfoot. "At that time I didn't know anything about Sasquatches or any of this business. I just ran back into the truck, into the camper, and shut the door. That was it." As fate would have it, Griffiths had one last glimpse of the creature. "We backed up the truck. As we left, I shone the flashlight beam back through the back door of the camper and it was still standing there. When I came back up there two weeks later, I found tracks in the snow, exactly the same tracks I found in this (Cariboo) cave."

The strange experience evidently had a profound impact on the student. "In second-year university I did a quarterly report on Sasquatches and just about got kicked out of the university for it. It was a 48-page report, in a completely scientific format, and in it I correlated limestone area and Sasquatch sightings . . ."

> Now on the basis of his research, Paul is writing a book called The Abominable Snowmen of B.C., and another book called Exploring B. C. Underground.
>
> He has found that cave areas and sighting of Sasquatches generally correspond. He believes that Sasquatches winter in caves because the temperature inside caves remains relatively constant at about 47 degrees Fahrenheit.[514]

Bigfoot in *Salmon Trout Steelheader*

The bulk of Bill Mack's article "The Silent Companion," in *Salmon Trout Steelheader* takes the form of a general overview of Bigfoot. Mack opens in an interesting way, putting the reader looking through the scope of a weapon at a hairy man-like creature and debating the option of pulling the trigger. "Your shot might alter the basic tenets of evolution, boggle the learned minds of conventional anthropologists, zoologists and archeologists and will automatically land you in the nearest jail with either a whopping game violation or with a murder rap tacked neatly to your frame." The following account from an uncredited editor (*Salmon Trout Steelheader* listed seven editors counting Publisher and Editor Frank W. Amato), supplemented Mack's article.

> Many sightings by responsible people have been reported, but still no hard proof. The day after I received this article I went fishing with a scientist who told me he had seen a Bigfoot on the Grande Ronde River in eastern Oregon while he was

fly fishing for summer steelhead! When he told me I couldn't believe my ears. I asked him to tell me more.

Early in the morning he hiked down the river to a riffle. He started fishing and happened to glance across the river where he noticed something very large sitting on a rock watching him. He kept on casting all the while keeping a fairly steady eye on his neighbor who continued to stare back. My friend definitely decided that it was not a bear. He didn't know what it was. Anyone else in this situation would have moved quickly on, but not a steelhead fly fisherman, at least not until the water was all covered. But my friend confessed that if the "thing" started across the river, he would have been on his way. After about 15 minutes the object stood up and walked upright up the canyon. My friend estimated its height at about 8 feet.

I asked my friend if I could use his name but he respectfully declined. I believe his story, I have no reason to doubt it.[515]

Wallace Court Monster

The Wallace Court Monster of San Bernardino County, California, was described as a bearlike creature that spooked animals and people for several nights in the Wallace Court residential area close by the Santa Ana River and east of Norton Air Force Base. A helicopter search was conducted Friday night, August 4, with high-intensity lights, but no creature was spotted. Mrs. Barbara Sikes called deputies after her daughter, Donna, ran screaming into their home. "The story made me sound like I'm out of my mind. What I'm telling you is true. Others have seen the thing, too."

Donna had been out removing laundry from a clothesline when she saw the creature standing on its hind legs near a fence. One neighbor told Sikes that he saw something evade the helicopter's searchlight and run away into a field. "It's too big to be anything but a bear," Sikes' neighbor told her. Another neighbor said her horse required veterinary care to stitch an unexplained gash on its neck.

Wallace Court resident Kenneth Corbin caught a glimpse of the creature. "I've seen every kind of animal you'd ever want to see between Ft. Worth and Great Falls, Montana. I'm six feet two and that thing is taller than I am. I caught him in my truck lights." Corbin spotted the creature near his fence as he departed for work at about 3 A.M. As far as Corbin was aware, the creature hadn't harmed anyone. "And it doesn't leave any footprints,"

Corbin claimed. "At least I couldn't find any." Corbin's animals—horses and a Doberman pinscher—"have a fit" during every reoccurrence of the creature. "He doesn't like dogs, I can tell that," said Corbin, who estimated the creature's weight at 500 pounds. "I hope it's not a prank. I mean, I hope it's not some guy in a bear suit, he might get shot in two." Corbin understood that monster-related notoriety could aversely shape outsiders' perceptions of himself and his neighbors. "People think we're full of bull, I know."[516]

Skunk Ape

The Florida Skunk Ape remained a media darling in 1972, grabbing headlines across the country and building upon the previous year's coverage of Buz Osbon's encounter with ape-like creatures in the Big Cypress.

St. Petersburg Times reporter Bethia Caffery chronicled a creature hunt in October 1972 after a "Monster With Light Green Eyes" had been seen near Jungle Prada in St. Petersburg.

> But He's There . . . Monster Search Fruitless—"Youuuuu better get home for dinner. MAMA SAID." This carried into the mini-wood opposite the Jungle Prada where some number of us stalked The Monster With Light Green Eyes the other day. It wasn't quite dark, however, so nobody really expected to find it. Small sized Carol Ann Garner says The Monster bumped right into her the day before. . . .
>
> Two boys said they saw it too and when one of them bumped into The Monster, it was like bumping into a tree trunk. The Monster, said Bill, Dave and John Cherry, who live right there practically in the woods, have seen it too. They say it is 7 feet tall . . . no, 8 . . . no 5. And it is more like a big hairy man. Or a giant monkey. Or a bear. But, definitely, its eyes are light green and they glow in the dark.
>
> The police searched the woods twice, said the kids, but The Monster wasn't dumb enough to hang around waiting. We couldn't find it, looking up in all the trees, to make sure it wasn't hiding up there in a clump of leaves, and we poked around the Indian Mound. There was a hole under the fence to Harold and Frances Anderson's yard but it looked like it was dug a long time ago. We might all go back and look again on Halloween.[517]

Wind River Indian Reservation Sightings

In Wyoming, Wind River Reservation police said they received several reports in August of a 12-foot-tall hairy creature roaming the Lander woods. Teenagers Curt Laninger and Tom Hernandez told police the creature had chased them while they were on horseback near the reservation. The tall creature, all 12 feet of it, took long, four-foot strides and had one arm bent up as if it was injured. Wind River Reservation Police Chief Bill King said searchers found "fair prints" in the area of the sightings which indicated a large foot with a high instep and only two toes. King said most sightings had taken place at night and near water.[518]

For his part, King did not believe Bigfoot was roaming the Wind River Indian Reservation, calling some of the witnesses "unreliable sources." Tracks and associated anecdotal accounts of a giant creature were not enough to sway King. "That's all they've been doing is talking about it," King said. "I can't find anything that would substantiate their story."[519]

Two Campers see Bigfoot

Randy Norton and Steven Gillespie reported seeing not just one but a pair of Bigfoot in northern California while camping on Clear Creek in Shasta County during a rainy October 8, 1972. Showers drove the men to seek shelter under the Placer Street Bridge. At about 4 A.M. they noticed a sound like "thump, thump, thump, coming across the bridge—whatever it was sounded heavy and tossed rocks over the side." Curious, the men decided to find out what was traversing the bridge above their heads. Armed with a flashlight and a pistol the pair readied themselves. "That's when the real fun started," Norton said. "We rushed out from under the bridge and shined a spotlight toward the railing on top." They saw a large shape only fleetingly before it retreated back from the side and out of view.

"Then suddenly there was a rousing noise across the river," Gillespie said. "Randy shined the light over there and I whirled around with the pistol ready. We could see this thing standing there, next to the water tank—I didn't know what to think. It might have been a man in a funny suit or something, but I called out and it wouldn't answer." Norton dropped the light and fired a shot. The creature ran under the bridge and disappeared. "With daylight, we could see this creature on the hill looking down on us—it seemed to move from tree to tree watching us," Gillespie said, adding, "It was definitely not an ape because it was too much like a man and when it ran it bent its knees."

"The other one was watching us from across the river, pacing back and forth between trees," Norton stated. The men attempted to follow the creature, but it ran from tree to tree, "almost like he wanted us to track him," Gillespie said. "We tried to follow, but he was really smart. He'd stay on the rocks so we couldn't see footprints. Just when we'd think he was gone, there he'd be again looking at us from behind a tree. He never made a sound, but at times I know he was laughing at us." Norton and Gillespie resigned themselves of the futility of further pursuit and gave it up. "I wasn't really scared. Excited maybe, but it was like chasing a space man or something," Norton said. The next morning the men found deep tracks in sand along the river, the finer details of which had been obliterated by rain.[520]

Mid-West Monster Craze

From Werewolves to Momo, the Mid-Western states proved to be a hotspot for Bigfoot activity in 1972.

> "Folks Still See Monster," *Blade* (Toledo, Ohio) (August 10, 1972)
>
> The werewolf craze is on. Ohio residents are claiming to see the big, hairy monsters all over the state, despite reports from policemen that nothing is to be found in the areas.
>
> The latest monster was reported sighted by a woman motorist in northern Wyandot County Wednesday. Sheriff's deputies checked for the big, black thing she said that she saw, but no luck locating the monster.
>
> The same goes for Defiance police, who said they have heard no more reports of the famed werewolf who appeared before two Toledo railroad workers there last week.
>
> The craze was started last month when a 7-foot monster which smelled like limburger cheese was reportedly seen in Marion County.[521]

Defiance Werewolf

Citizens of Defiance, Ohio, held mixed reactions to the reports of a werewolf in their midst during late July; opinions ran from person or persons playing a joke to an unhinged perpetrator who was "just some nut running loose." The encounters with the furry entity occurred in the morning hours between one and four A.M. in a two-block densely populated area that was close by the Norfolk & Western (N&W) depot and near the Defiance police station.[522] One of the werewolf encounters contained violence: while switching trains, a train crewman reported he was approached from behind and struck on the shoulder with a piece of 2x4 lumber.

"We don't know what to think," said Donald Breckler, Defiance's Police Chief from 1966 to 1977. "But now we're taking it seriously. We're concerned for the safety of our people." Chief Breckler said the witnesses' descriptions were similar but also "vague."[523] Police were called to one woman's house in a neighborhood adjacent to the train yard; she hadn't seen the creature but the reports had put her "in a state of shock."[524]

> "Very hairy" is the first description given by each person who saw the "werewolf." The chief said that he thinks that a person is wearing some disguise such as a mask. "But there is a lot of natural hair, too," he said.[525]

"I'm inclined to think it might be a local person," Breckler stated. "None of the other area towns have had anything like this. And in each case he has been seen in the same area of our town." Reports generally described a 7-to-9-foot tall creature sporting fangs and wearing dark clothing. "But that was a little exaggerated," Breckler said. "If his motive is robbery then he is not picking on the type of person that would have a lot of money," Breckler suggested, adding, "and he hasn't approached any women."[526] Any rational impetus to don a costume and scare folks was lost on the staid police chief. "We don't know what his motive is." Robbery and dark humor seemed poor answers to explain the goings on. "We don't think it is a prank," Breckler said. "He's coming at people with a club in his hand. We think it's to the safety of our people to be concerned."

Ted Davis and Tom Jones, two N&W crewmen on the local freight, were interviewed at the railroad's Summer Street yard by reporter James Stegall. The men said they had encountered a creature which "had huge hairy feet, fangs and ran from side to side, like a caveman in the movies." They stated the creature had been seen on two occasions, the first of which occurred Tuesday, July 25. "I was connecting an air hose between two cars and was looking down," recounted Davis. "I saw these huge hairy feet then looked up and he was standing there, with that big stick over his shoulder. When I started to say something, he took off for the woods." Davis had his second encounter, this time with Jones present, on Sunday, July 30. The blue jean-clad creature was standing in some weeds close by the main track. "At first I thought the whole thing was a big joke, but when I saw how hairy and woolly it was, that was enough for me," Jones said. Jones had laughed at Davis' tale earlier in the week, but after accounting for his coworkers and realizing none of them could have been the creature, he began thinking the affair was something more serious than a prank. When the thing took off, Jones and Davis heard a scream from a car on the road. "That thing's going to hurt somebody someday," Jones said.[527]

"It just doesn't sound like something that would happen in this neighborhood," said neighborhood resident Kathy Kehnast. "This is probably the safest neighborhood around." Another local said the neighborhood children were keeping a keen eye open for a possible appearance by the monster. "I don't think the adults are scared, but it has scared a lot of children," he said. "I live in the neighborhood and I've got children. They're on the lookout for him and anything suspicious." One neighborhood man sounded a definite rough-and-ready tone on solving the mystery of the creature. "If I see (the werewolf) the police are going to find out who he is," Rupert Figg said. "That's because they'll have to take him to the hospital to get the buckshot out."[528]

Roachdale Monster

Town Marshal Leroy Cloncs looked back on the Roachdale Monster affair and ever with a skeptical view of it all said, "I talked to a lot of people but I never came up with anything that could be substantiated. I'm sure that it was just a prank that snowballed. People's imaginations just got carried away, that's all. Some of 'em were probably full of liquor and they just started shootin' away when they heard something. My main concern was that some poor soul might get his head blown off."

The sightings reportedly drew in curiosity-seekers and bona fide gun-toting monster hunters from miles around Roachdale, Indiana. Writer and researcher Jerome Clark reported that several residents had turned to scripture after the sightings became public, believing the final reckoning would be presaged by hairy, half-human creatures cavorting across the land.

Clark records Mrs. Lou Rogers as the first to see the Roachdale Monster. Her sighting occurred in early August at the farm she and her husband Randy rented. Late one cloudy evening as a light rain fell, Mrs. Rogers and her toddler son Keith stepped outside to roll up the car windows. She suddenly heard a growl-like sound. "You hear all kinds of strange noises in the country," she said and thought nothing untoward or amiss regarding the unusual noise. When she heard the noise again, a "boo" or "oo" sound, she took notice. The growl was "real deep," Rogers recalled, and it had a human quality. Her son became frightened and Rogers experienced the unwelcome feeling of being watched from close quarters. Scanning the darkness around the yard and seeing nothing, she retreated with her son back inside her home.

> She was unaware of it then but about 90 minutes earlier a luminous object had hovered briefly over a cornfield separating the Rogers' house from a neighbor's and then "just sort of blew up." Among those who saw it was one of Mrs. Rogers' brothers who happened to be looking out the window of a farmhouse near Ladoga, a few miles north of Roachdale. Later he mentioned this to his sister and her husband, saying he thought a plane had exploded. None had. Whatever exploded, it left no trace except—possibly—the creature that for the next few weeks seemed to have taken up residence in that very cornfield.[529]

More strange activity occurred during the next few nights. "It sounded as if someone was going around the place pounding on the siding and windows," Rogers said. The family noted with alarm that the pounding seemed to get louder each night. As the banging on the house started, Rogers would rush outside but could only catch a fleeting glimpse of six-foot, broad-shouldered creature running away on two legs, disappearing into the cornfields.

> "It would always come around at a certain hour—between 10:00 and 11:30 at night," Lou Rogers recalled. "You could feel it coming somehow. It's hard to explain. The feeling would just keep getting stronger and stronger and when it got strongest you knew something had to happen. Then the knocking would start. This happened every night for two or three weeks. Another thing—it smelled *rotten,* like dead animals or garbage."
>
> Randy and Lou Rogers never saw the creature clearly because it appeared only in the darkness but they were able to observe that it was hairy and black. Once while Mrs. Rogers was washing dishes she saw it ducking up and down outside the window above the sink.

> "But I was never exactly afraid of it," she said. "If it was going to hurt me it would have that first night. I had no awareness or fear of it in the daytime. I'd even leave the doors open. Sometimes I'd put out garbage and later it would be gone. My husband thought I was crazy, trying to make friends like that. But I was pretty curious about it."[530]

The Rogers tried to rationalize the bizarre events they were experiencing. "We sort of thought it might be a gorilla," Lou Rogers said. "It stood like a man but ran on all fours—and even on all fours it was as tall as my husband who is five-foot-nine. It was real broad." One of the perplexing features of the creature's presence was the absence of any trace of its passing. "And what was weird was that we could never find tracks, even when it ran over mud it would run and jump but it was like somehow it wasn't touching anything. When it ran through weeds you couldn't hear anything. And sometimes when you looked at it, it seemed you could see *through* it." One added oddity was a plastic toy flying saucer that showed up near the house one day. It did not belong to Keith and after he showed no interest it was placed out with the trash. When Lou Rogers went to look for it, she discovered it was gone.

The Roachdale Monster story hit the *Crawfordsville Journal and Review* on August 22 under the headline "What is It?" "Residents of this small Putnam County community are concerned about some unidentified creature which has been stalking the surrounding area for the past two to three weeks." The article continued by indicating the multitude of witnesses to the creature's presence: "Some three dozen persons say they have seen someone or something wandering about on the east side of town."

> Conservation Officer William Woodall of Crawfordsville had arrived in Roachdale on Monday the 21st to investigate and found Roachdale residents near panic.
>
> He listened sympathetically to their stories, even the wildest ones, and on the first day interviewed five persons from four different families who said they had seen the thing. Among those he talked with were the Rogerses, who reported the creature had left their farm after Randy and several friends had set out one night to try to capture it. One of them (a young man from nearby Bainbridge whom FATE has since interviewed but who has asked that his name be withheld)

> encountered the creature when it stepped out of a roadside ditch. The man yelled, "Stop or I'll shoot!" It didn't and he did but it got away.[531]

One report, which Woodall called the strangest he had learned of, came from a woman who on Monday, August 14, had sat on her porch with her husband and daughter on the east side of town. Suddenly, the woman noticed two fiery balls of light, about four to six inches apart, shining in a field across the road. "From time to time the 'balls of fire' would turn and watch a passing car, then turn back toward us," she stated. Soon, a second pair of fiery lights joined the first. "We watched for a good little bit. None of us wanted to go over to see what it was."

> The family went indoors and watched from there. The "balls of fire" continued to stare at them. At 2:00 A.M. the husband and daughter retired but the wife stayed up watching as the thing behind the glowing balls, whatever it might have been, seemed to go "down on all fours feeding like a dog. Then at times it would stand up and peer around." When she finally went to bed at 3:40 it—or they—were still there. The next day they were gone.
>
> The woman confirmed the story for FATE but refused permission to reveal her name. She says she is tired of being ridiculed. "I don't care what they say," she said. "We know what we saw."[532]

Another strange experience involving the Roachdale Monster concerned the Burdine family. On Tuesday, August 22, Carter Burdine called Town Marshal Cloncs to his farm after the discovery there of 60 chickens ripped apart and strewn along a 200-foot path from the coop to the front yard of Burdine's house. The trail of chickens appeared to end near a bucket full of cucumbers and tomatoes that Burdine had planned to feed to his hogs. Inspecting the bucket revealed it was only half full. After Cloncs' arrival, he stood surveying the carnage with Carter Burdine and his uncle, Bill "Junior" Burdine, when all three heard a noise that seemed to come from a spot somewhere between the coop and the road. Cloncs got into his car and began driving slowly up the road with Junior Burdine walking behind. Suddenly something emerged from the ditch and darted across the road only some six feet ahead of Junior but its speed (and his surprise) prevented his getting a good look at it. The men stopped to inspect the spot of the creature's passage and found where it crossed a fence. "That fence was just mashed to the ground," Burdine said. "That thing was *heavy*."

> Within a matter of hours the creature revisited Carter's farm. This time he and Junior were returning to the farm in the early morning hours after having dropped off Carter's wife with relatives in town. In the headlights of their car they caught sight of the creature standing in the chicken house door.
>
> "This thing completely blocked out the light inside the chicken house," Junior said. The door is six by eight feet and its shoulders came up to the top of the door, up to where the neck should have been. But this thing didn't have a neck. To me it looked like an orangutan or a gorilla. It had long hair with kind of a brownish cast to it—sort of rust color. I never saw its eyes or its face. It was making a groaning racket."
>
> The creature dashed for the barn and leaped into the haymow. Carter and his father Herman Burdine approached the barn, guns ready. Junior went around the building and a moment later Herman and Carter heard him yell, "Bring me a light!"
>
> Herman said, "By the time Carter and I got out of the barn and around the corner my brother was firing at something across the field. I didn't see a thing but I pulled up and started firing in the same direction."
>
> "I shot four times with a pump shotgun," Junior said. "The thing was only about 100 feet away when I started shooting. I must have hit it. I've killed a lot of rabbits at that distance."[533]

The men found no sign that the creature, whatever it may have been, had been hit by their gun fire. Checking the flock, the men discovered that a total of 110 chickens had been torn apart. Woodhall returned to the Burdine property, determined to understand what had killed the chickens. "I never could find any concrete physical evidence," Woodward said in a later interview. "All I ever had to go on were a lot of people's stories of what they saw. I think I couldn't find any tracks because the ground was hard and the vegetation high."

Officials intended to search the area but found that the throngs of curious people and would-be monster hunters hampered their efforts. Marshall Cloncs put a halt to the search idea. "There were just too many people out there," he recalled. "If the thing had been out that night it probably would have been run over by one of the searchers' cars because so many people were out looking for it."

Parke County Bear Hunt

Parke County (Indiana) Sheriff's Department authorities were on the lookout for a monster: a large, furry creature reportedly 10-feet tall which left behind 21-inch footprints. From the witnesses' descriptions, officials surmised they were searching for a bear. Most of the reports came in on Tuesday night, September 19. A solitary report the next day was dismissed by officials as a hoax after Parke County Sheriff Gary Cooper could find no one in the area by the name given by the caller.

The creature sightings occurred in the heavily wooded and sparsely populated northern part of Parke County in Liberty Township's Lodi, Howard, and Tangier areas. Reports surfaced of locals attributing the deaths of two dogs and one hog to the monster; Deputy Sheriff Rufus Finney said he had not seen any of the animals reportedly killed. The animal deaths and the creature sightings recalled for many the scores of chickens mysteriously killed near Roachdale in neighboring Putnam County.[534]

"We have to check out these reports and we will. We've had a lot of burglaries recently so maybe there is a connection," Cooper said.[535] Searches conducted by the Sheriff's Department did not produce any evidence of a monster but did yield a possible bear track. "If the monster is a bear," said Finney, "I am sure it has escaped from a zoo or circus." This view was seconded by Wayne Machan of the Indiana Department of Natural Resources. "If the monster does turn out to be a bear, I feel positive the animal has escaped from a zoo or circus in the area," Machan said. "Bears are not native wildlife to Indiana," he added. Interestingly, before the bear track was identified, a novel theory posited a misidentified badger as responsible for the monster sightings. "Badgers are more of a prairie or grasslands animal," Machan said, explaining that badgers, like bears, were not native to Indiana, though occasionally one would be seen within the state's boundaries. "They are not usually seen in areas of heavy timber." Most of the badger sightings Machan's office had received occurred in northern counties of Jasper and Pulaski. Machan said badgers weigh about 20 pounds when fully grown, with very large specimens attaining 35 pounds. Given those facts, Machan effectively quashed the badger speculation: "Badgers definitely are not monster size," he said.[536]

Cooper later changed his thinking on the cause of the sightings, moving away from a burglar toward "definitely a bear." Several Vigo County deputies traveled to Parke County on Thursday, September 20, and assisted Cooper in a search for the creature. The group found footprints near the Wabash River which left little doubt as to what they were hunting. "We referred to books on animals, and a volunteer searcher from Vigo County who has had experience with bears identified the prints as those of a bear," said a Parke County Sheriff's office spokesman. An unnamed official added, "People have been scared to let their children out to play because of all the monster talk. We've been telling people that the monster is apparently a bear and it's on the loose in the far northwestern corner of the county."[537] Cooper planned to ask a local farmer to donate a sick or dead farm animal to bait the creature. "We'll have to kill it if we do find it," Cooper said.[538]

Zoo Denies Ownership

A Cleveland Zoo spokesman confirmed that all their animals were accounted for and couldn't have been responsible for the sighting of a "monster animal" made on Saturday, August 12, by eight people. The creature was described as seven feet tall and over 350 pounds. Metropolitan Park rangers and Cleveland police conducted searches of the Brookside Park and Cleveland Zoo grounds. Patrolman Richard Brindza said bushes were matted down just north of the zoo's grounds behind a fence on the south end of West 39th Street as if something large had been there.

Wayne Lewis, himself six feet tall and 360 pounds, said he saw a creature covered in black hair and bigger than he was. "I ran into the house for my shotgun when I saw it," Lewis said. "I didn't want to call police because it would sound like I was some kind of fool. But on the other hand, I didn't want to take any chances." Michael Taub, another witness, reported the creature's standing posture was straighter than a gorilla's. Cleveland Zoo spokesman Richard Merrill said the zoo's two gorillas, Yogi and Timothy, were locked up and accounted for. Merrill discounted the idea that the creature's alarming presence owed to its seeking out fraternal companionship at the zoo. "These people are very sincere about what they saw," admitted Officer Brindza. "They are scared."[539]

UFOs—Those Saucers in the Sky are Coming Back Once Again

Stuart Nixon was executive director of the National Investigating Committee on Aerial Phenomena (NICAP) in 1972, a year marked by an increase in UFO reports. The upward trend was sure to interest UFO researchers as the reports had fallen off after 1969 when the Air Force called off its 20-year analysis of reports and the year a University of Colorado group issued a report that suggested UFOs were a figment of people's imagination. "Right now we have about 100 pending sighting cases. That's three times what we had in 1970. And some of the cases are very interesting." An encouraging sign Nixon took from the increase in reports was that many came from "re-liable" sources. "Oh, we still have the nuts around," he said. "There's the mystic barber from Brooklyn, who wears a propeller on his head and says he's from another planet. There's that guy in California who offers, for a fee, to get medical-legal advice from his space friends. But these people are exceptional today. I find that more and more we are hearing from the solid citizen."

> As it happens, Nixon adds, the solid citizens are the real hope of serious UFO watchers. There may or may not be men from Mars, but Nixon says the solid citizens are definitely real.
>
> "I'm 29 years old. I've never seen a saucer. But I sincerely believe we can't just turn our backs on the people who say they have. NICAP has gathered well over 10,000 UFO sightings in the last 15 tears. We've pretty well disproved about 80 to 90 per cent of them. But, there are hundreds which we can't explain. And I think we should explain them. I just don't think it's very scientific to simply ignore the unexplainable."
>
> Others agree. Northwestern University's Dr. J. Allen Hynek, chairman of the school's astronomy department, has set up a UFO information gathering bureau, pledging anonymity to anyone who wishes to confide. The American Institute of Aeronautics and Astronautics has, after three years of UFO probing, recommended renewed research. Even the Ugandan delegate to the United Nations has recently cited UFO evidence as one reason members should take a more urgent look at the possibility of extraterrestrial life.[540]

John A. Lutz, head of the Odyssey Club (about 20 members in 1972), believed UFOs were "extraterrestrial vehicles that have this planet under surveillance," and despite researchers' best efforts, "they are always one step ahead of us."[541]

Several Patterns Apparent in UFO Sightings

Dr. David Saunders, a psychologist at the University of Colorado, author of *Our Haunted Planet*, analyzed 18,000 reports and postulated several patterns he had concluded were part and parcel with UFOs. The majority of sightings occur on Wednesday. Dr. Saunders narrowed it down even further—the best time to see a strange event in the sky was 10 P.M. on a Wednesday. In April 1972, an "outbreak" of unusual aerial phenomena occurred in several states and by midsummer the sightings were occurring worldwide. In 1972 formations of objects were reported over Ferry, Youngwood, and Carbon, Pennsylvania. They were blamed for dropping "space grass"—metallic strips of aluminum and silicon. This material was found to follow in the wake of several UFO sightings and was likened to metallic "chaff" which U. S. Air Force planes released to deceive ground radar.

Along with an uptick in UFO reports, 1972 also witnessed an outbreak of "fairy circles"—perfect circles burned into fields and the ground, many appearing in Kansas and Iowa. Plant life would fail to regrow in these areas and some claimed dogs would not set foot in them. In the Monster arena, the Loch Ness monster got off on rocky footing when pranksters placed a sea lion's carcass on the Loch's banks on April Fool's Day. For Bigfoot, 1972 would witness one of the subject's most significant connected series of sightings, spanning weeks and lashing together several paranormal phenomena. Momo surfaced in July and entered the growing lexicon of named small town hairy hominids and, as happened repeatedly through the '70s in areas across the country, coincident with Momo's appearance were several reports of strange lights in the sky.[542]

Missouri Monster (Momo, Pike County Monster, East Peoria Monster, Cole Hollow Monster)

Set on bluffs overlooking the Mississippi, the town of Louisiana, Missouri, is set amongst the hardwood forests of the rugged Lincoln Hills and is known for its business district's rich architectural heritage replete with antebellum homes and Victorian era buildings. Located 30 miles downriver from Hannibal, Missouri, Mark Twain's boyhood home, Louisiana had a population of 4,400 in the early 1970s. Nestled underneath the Mississippi Flyway which is traveled by about 40% of American waterfowl during their migrations, Louisiana's environs are studded with caves.

Louisiana was ground zero for "Momo," one of the most extensively reported Bigfoot stories in the 1970s—with its many events recorded by such luminaries as Jerome Clark, Loren Coleman, and Brad Steiger. As Steiger mentions, many considered the 1972 Momo affair as merely another entrant in that summer's "silly season," a time where people are apt to make outlandish claims and journalists are more prone to give these stories media exposure.[543] *Independence Examiner* staff writer Kim Sexton visited Louisiana in late July to look into the Missouri Monster ("Momo") sightings. Expecting to find nothing more than rumor and exaggeration, she made her way to the town's second oldest business, the offices of the *Press-Journal* to speak with news editor John Gillis. Gillis said several reports had been made of a large, hair-covered man-like creature in or near town and several unusual tracks had been found. Asked for his own opinion Gillis stated he framed the monster flap as one rumor begetting many more until "everyone panicked." Gillis firmly believed that no hairy ape-like creature roamed the rugged environs of Pike County. "Those first two kids [Doris and Terry Harrison] were scared by pranksters, I believe," he said. "Then several persons got upset, stories were exaggerated and this thing was blown out of proportion." Gillis wasn't alone in thinking that the Momo affair had been overdone. "We have no evidence," Patrolman John Whitaker said. A waitress at a local restaurant said, "It's all a joke. I'm from Missouri, you've got to show me." A water department clerk at city hall told Sexton she thought the monster tales were bunk. But one of her coworkers disagreed, telling Sexton she had heard from people she held as reliable that they had seen strange objects hovering in the sky, even seen the hairy creature itself, had heard weird guttural cries, and had smelled a horrid odor attributed to the creature.[544]

To her surprise, Sexton encountered genuinely frightened and concerned residents during her two days in Louisiana. "I believe those I talked with did see, hear, and smell something unusual," Sexton wrote. "I talked to nearly 100 persons, and most of them convinced me there is something in those hills of Pike County that is strange to our country. It wasn't so much what they said that convinced me. It was the way they said it."[545]

> Because the Louisiana folks convinced me that something is roaming in those hills, I want to believe it is some slightly kooky individual who gets his "kicks" by scaring people. But from the speed the animal is said to travel, I don't see how that theory can carry any weight. I don't rule it out, nevertheless.[546]

Amongst Clark and Coleman's several collaborations during the '70s is an article on Momo which supplied a history of strangeness in northeastern Missouri.

> Along River Road, which stretches north from Highway 54 along the Mississippi River and past the mouth of the Salt River, there is a longstanding tradition about a phantom man who walks across the road and vanishes. In the 1940s travelers and residents repeatedly heard what sounded like a woman's screams emanating from the general vicinity of an abandoned lime kiln. The screams came always around midnight and were never explained.
>
> In addition to recurring reports of fireballs or "swamp gas" there have been a number of mysterious deaths. The strangest of all occurred during the winter of 1954, when a man and a woman were found dead in a car along the roadside. The woman sat on the passenger side and seemed to be asleep. The man lay crouched under the steering wheel completely nude, his clothing piled neatly 20 feet behind the car. The coroner listed the deaths as caused by "asphyxiation" even though the window on the driver's side was open all the way—this in ten-degree-below-zero weather.[547]

As Momo events received increasing attention in the summer of 1972, more stories came forth hinting that experiences with hairy man-like creatures were not, regionally and explicitly speaking, new phenomena. "I know they're telling the truth about that monster in Missouri because I saw one of those things myself," said Glenn Varner of Kingsport. Varner recalled for *Kingsport Times News* reporter Mary Kiss that on a September evening in 1964 or 1965, he spotted a large hairy creature peering through a window of his mother's house in Garrison, Pennsylvania. "I was coming up the lane to the house, and at first I thought it was a peeping tom. Then it turned around and I could see the light on it. I'm five feet seven, but this thing was taller than Wilt Chamberlain—seven and a half or eight feet tall."

"It caught me off guard, and I spoke to it. I know it wasn't a bear because it didn't have a long schnoz; its face looked more like a human being's," Varner said. "It took off on the side of the hill and cleared three fences at least five or six feet high. I could hear the sound of it bouncing along. I've studied a little bit about zoology and the action and mobility of animals and I know a man or a bear couldn't bound over fences the way it did. It was making 25 miles an hour within a matter of a few yards," he said. Varner's sighting gave him a good view of the creature's movements and form. "It didn't climb on its hands or crawl on its knuckles like an ape would have. It looked like it might have been related to an ape, but between the apes and man." Varner nicknamed the creature "Hairy." About a week after the his Hairy incident, a neighbor told Varner of being knocked down in his yard by "something that whizzed by in the dark." The next morning Varner found a puzzling track he attributed to the creature.[548]

In their article, Clark and Coleman included a letter published in the August 2, 1972, *Decatur Review* which further explicated the history of hairy hominids in the area.

> "To the Editor:
> "In reference to the creatures people are seeing, I am 76 years old. My home used to be south of Effingham. My two brothers saw the creatures when they were children. My brothers have since passed away.
>
> "They are hairy, stand on their hind legs, have large eyes and are about as large as an average person or shorter, and are harmless as they ran away from the children. They walk, they do not jump.
>
> "They were seen on a farm near a branch of water. The boys waded and fished in the creek every day and once in a while they would run to the house scared and tell the story.
>
> "Later there was a piece in the Chicago paper stating there were such animals of that description and they were harmless. This occurred about 60 years ago or a little less.
>
> "My mother and father thought they were just children's stories until the Chicago paper told the story."[549]

In July, 1971, Joan Mills and Mary Ryan drove along Highway 79 looking for a picnic spot. Highway 79 runs north/south through Louisiana, and parallels the River Road (Pike County 118). Finding a suitable-looking spot, they turned off the highway, spread out a blanket and laid out their food. "We were eating lunch," Ryan said, "when we both wrinkled up our noses at the same time. I never smelled anything as bad in my life." So strong was the odor, Mills suggested to her friend that a family of skunks was nearby.

Then Ryan pointed to something behind her companion. "I turned around and this thing was standing there in the thicket," Mills said. "The weeds were pretty high and I just saw the top part of this creature. It was staring down at us." Ryan gave her impression of what they saw: "It was half-ape and half-man. I've been reading up on the Abominable Snowman

EYEWITNESS SKETCH OF MISSOURI MONSTER, 1972

since then, and from stories and articles, you get the idea that these things are more like gorillas. This thing was not like that at all. It had hair over the body as if it was an ape. Yet, the face was definitely human. It was more like a hairy human." Mills added, "Then it made a little gurgling sound like someone trying to whistle under water."

The creature emerged from the brush and started to walk toward the women, who wasted no time in running to their Volkswagen and locking its doors. The women watched as the creature advanced toward the car and stroked the hood. Then, in what must have been an admixture of horror and amazement, the thing proceeded to try to open the door. "It walked upright on two feet and its arms dangled way down," Ryan said. "The arms were partially covered with hair but the hands and the palms were hairless. We had plenty of time to see this . . ."

The chilling realization that escape was impossible gripped the women when they learned the car keys were in Mills' purse back at the picnic site. "Finally," Mills said, "my arm hit the horn ring and the thing jumped straight in the air and moved back." Mills kept beeping the horn. "It stayed at a safe distance, then seemed to realize that the noise was not dangerous," Ryan said. "It stopped where we had been eating, picked up my peanut butter sandwich, smelled it, then devoured it in one gulp. It started to pick up Joan's purse, dropped it and then disappeared back into the woods." Sensing the coast was clear, Mills dashed outside, retrieved her purse and darted back inside the car. The women raced down the highway and once back in St. Louis, submitted a report with the Missouri State Patrol. "We'd have difficulty proving that the experience occurred," Mills wrote, "but all you have to do is go into those hills to realize that an army of those things could live there undetected."[550]

> "Momo" was not the only monster to frighten Middle America that summer. In the extreme northwestern part of Arkansas, a state which borders Missouri from the south, the summer brought several reports of an imperfectly-observed, vaguely-described "creature." It first appeared, according to an article in Fayetteville's *Northwest Arkansas Times*, some time in January, when on two occasions Mrs. C. W. Humphrey of Springdale heard dogs barking loudly, looked out the door of her trailer home and saw a "creature" strolling on by. In the following months several other persons in the neighborhood caught a glimpse of the thing, but only in the dark, and so they did not

get a good look at it. Early in July Pete Ragland shot at the creature with a .22 pistol.[551]

John F. Schuessler, Assistant Director of Midwest UFO Network (MUFON), and MUFON technical artist Lawrence Hanna visited Louisiana and produced research which revealed several additional contemporaneous creature reports outside Louisiana's immediate area.

> "Much background data is available to demonstrate that Momo is not something new and imaginary, but, rather, is a well-established creature, roaming the Midwest. Missouri Monster sightings date back as far as 20 years ago, perhaps much further than that. Keeping with fairly fresh reports, however, we must consider that something is going on, based on the number of Missouri and Illinois sightings.[552]

Missouri's outdoor recreational venues enjoyed a tremendous growth in interest and use during the post-World War II national boom in overnight camping. In 1955, 78,700 visitors paid a modest fee to spend the night in one of the state's parks. In 1960 that number jumped to 404,771—growth that may have been constrained by the number of available accommodations. Through the 1960s, the number of visitors to Missouri's State Parks increased each year by more than a million. By 1970, a total of 14,539,415 people flocked to state parks, more than three times the state's population of 4,677,300.[553] Situated in the midst of rich farming country, Cuivre River State Park boasted camping facilities and miles of wooded trails. The park's Lake Lincoln was known to anglers for its channel cat and black bass fishing. Predating Momo's Louisiana premiere by a handful of days, Cuivre River State Park, 40 miles south of Louisiana, hosted its own creature sighting.

> "About June 30, 1972, two Troy (Mo.) fishermen were spending an afternoon on a secluded section of the Cuivre River near Cuivre River State Park. They had fished this section of the river for the past five days with better-than-average luck. This particular afternoon was clear and bright, the area quiet, and the river flowing slowly. The curve in the river at this point creates a situation where the current is so slow and the surface of the water is so smooth that it is hard to tell which way the water flows.

"About 250 feet upstream, a tree had fallen two-thirds of the way across the river. This created a situation which caused a silt accumulation on each side of the river and formed gently sloping banks. Noticing a splash, V.M. looked up to see someone, or something, wading into the middle of the river. The someone was big and hairy.

"'Hey, Tim, look at that silly hippie wading and fishing,'" V.M. said.

"Then, almost immediately, they both noted that the intruder was not a hippie, but a large creature wading armpit-deep across the river, estimated to be five and a half feet deep at this point. The creature waded with ease, appearing to be extremely strong by the way it crossed the river. As it came out of the water, Tim scrambled away to climb the rock hillside.

"V.M. held his ground, apparently unseen by the creature, while it turned to walk along the river bank straight toward him. When the monster was about 150 feet away, V.M. panicked and started to run. When he looked back, the obviously frightened creature was also scrambling up a hillside.

"V.M. and Tim left their equipment and went to report what they had seen. The conservation officer and the policemen all thought the incident was a big joke. Later, V.M., his brother Bob, Tim, and a conservation officer returned to the scene so the fishermen might recover their fishing gear. The men found a fresh, partial, three-toed footprint about an inch deep. It was located in the area where the creature had come out of the river. Some smaller and older three-toed prints were also found in the general area.[554]

MUFON members gathered for their annual picnic at Carlyle Lake on Sunday July 23[555] and listened to a summary of the Momo sightings experienced up to that point. John Schuessler of O'Fallon, Missouri gave a presentation suggesting the Cuivre River creature seen on June 30 was similar to Momo. Schuessler had made a recent inspection of the spot where V.M. and Tim had their sighting and he retold their story to the MUFON group, adding another strange occurrence which happened at almost the same time as V.M. and Tim's experience.

> About five minutes earlier, another couple who were fishing 250 feet upstream, heard "grunts and groans, like a man in pain" and were so unnerved by the sounds that they stopped fishing also and hastily left the woods. They too reported the incident, and a search party was organized. However, nothing was found except a large 3-toed footprint; and no one took a plaster cast of the impression.
>
> The sighting of the monster at Quiver [sic] River Park may be related to the Louisiana case, which Walter Andrus, MUFON Director, says is "definitely not a hoax generated by children." Andrus had just returned from Louisiana, after interviewing the Edgar Harrison family; and he displayed a sketch done by Doris Harrison, 15, one of the children who saw the creature. From the drawing, it looked quite similar to the Quiver River animal.[556]

The "Louisiana case" referred to Momo and the first people to encounter that creature were three children—Terry, Wally, and Doris Harrison. Edgar Harrison and his family had been long-standing residents of Louisiana; Harrison himself was employed by the city's board of public works for over 20 years. Momo's fame started with a sighting made in the Harrison's backyard on Allen Street.

Momo Calendar

11 July 1972, Tuesday

Kim Sexton of the *Independence Examiner* (Independence, Missouri) produced several articles on the Momo affair that shed light on the Louisiana Police Department's involvement in the case. Sexton's article, "Many See the Missouri Monster," carried by the *Nevada Daily Mail*, contains notes on the Momo affair as written up by the local police.[557] This article states the first sighting by the Harrison children was made on July 10, 1972; the preponderance of other reports, articles, and Momo commentary state the first sighting occurred early in the morning of July 11.

At approximately 3:30 P.M. on July 11, Terry Harrison aged 8, his 5-year-old brother, Wally and their dog Chubby were playing in their backyard at the end of Allen St. near some old rabbit pens. Suddenly Terry saw "a big, hairy thing with a dog under its arm." Wally did not witness the creature his brother saw.[558] Terry ran to the house and hollered for his older sister, Doris, who looked out a bathroom window and saw the creature which would later be dubbed Momo. "It was right by the tree," Doris stated, "six or seven feet tall, black, and hairy. It stood like a man but it didn't look like a man to me."[559] For a fleeting moment she entertained the thought the creature could be a bear. "That's no bear," Doris quickly concluded.[560] Doris frantically dialed her mother who was working at the family's business. The children's father, Edgar Harrison, arrived home at 4:00 P.M. and searched the area where his children had seen the creature, noticing spots where brush had been beaten down. During his search Harrison found faint footprints as well as some black hairs.[561] Glenn McWane, Research Director of Other Dimensions, a paranormal investigative organization, interviewed Edgar Harrison in the presence of Louisiana Police Chief Shelby Ward.

> Edgar Harrison: The boy (Terry) ran into the house and hollered at my daughter (Doris, 15). She got on the phone to her mother at our café, and Betty called me. Then Doris looked out the bathroom window. The thing was standing up the hill from the house. It broke some brush completely 'round in a circle where it stood.
>
> Glenn McWane: About 20 yards up the bank?
>
> Harrison: Yes. Every little stick was broke in a circle.
>
> Chief Shelby Ward: Yes, you could see where it stamped the weeds flat where it stood.
>
> McWane: Press reports said that Terry saw the creature holding a dog in its arms.
>
> Harrison: Right, and he said the dog had red stuff on it. Now I said, "Son, why do you say this was a dog?" And he answered, "cause it had four legs . . ." And he said it was black, the same as the other thing was black.
>
> McWane: But it was only seen to have "something" in its arms when it appeared near the top of the hill.
>
> Harrison: That's right. When Terry first saw it standing up, he could see between its legs. It was big and it was weaving back and forth. It had long, black hair hanging down all over. He could not see its face.[562]

Shortly after the creature sighting in back of their house, the Harrison's dog got sick. Chubby's eyes became red and it vomited for hours; it fully recovered after a meal of bread and milk.[563] In his Momo article for *Saga* magazine, Steiger wrote that a neighbor of the Harrison's corroborated that the children had seemed affected by something.

> Mrs. Clarence Lee, who lives in Louisiana, remembers that she had been watering flowers on that Tuesday afternoon when members of the Harrison family, who live a short distance away, came running past her house. A short time later Edgar came home, and she learned that Terry and the other Harrison children had seen "something like a big bear."
>
> Mrs. Lee had also heard some kind of animal "carrying on something terrible." Later she talked to a farmer on Route 2 who claimed that a dog that he had recently given to his daughter as a gift had disappeared. The man wondered whether or not the monster might have been seen carrying the remains of their dog.[564]

After Chief Ward walked through the immediate area around the Harrison residence, he "concluded that the children had probably been frightened by a large dog and that imagination had played a large part in the report of a large hairy object."[565]

12 July 1972, Wednesday

> Shelby Ward, Louisiana's chief of police, said yesterday that the police received a call about 1:30 A.M. Wednesday [July 12] morning from Harrison, who said there was a prowler in the neighborhood of his house. Harrison said he had heard the popping of brush, as if something were running through the woods.[566]

Sexton wrote that Officers Condon and Floyd responded to Harrison's call and proceeded to his residence on Allen Street. Assuming the incident was a routine prowler call, Officer Floyd approached the house on foot from the northwest while Officer Condon drove up to the front of the residence in Patrol Car No. 1.

> When Floyd arrived at the house there were seven or eight people, mostly young children, standing in a group and one

> of the persons stated that it ran in a South Westerly direction from the Harrison residence. Floyd and Condon searched approximately 100 yards in this direction and found no evidence of anyone or anything.
>
> Officers then talked to the Harrison children and one of them, probably Doris Harrison, stated at that time that the hairy object had been back to the house. This person was asked how long it had been and she stated at that time that it had been there all evening. She was asked why she had not called the Police earlier and she said that she did not feel it necessary until she thought this object might try to get into the house.[567]

News of the unwanted visitor near Harrison's home spread quickly through the town. On July 12, a group of hunters with 15 dogs reportedly tried to trail the creature, but the dogs refused to enter the woods.[568]

14 July 1972, Friday

Harrison was serving as a deacon in the Pentecostal Church. On July 14, the Harrisons hosted a Pentecostal evening prayer service at their home for a gathering of 30 people. The service concluded at about 8:30 P.M.; at 9:45 P.M. Harrison conversed with a small group in his back yard when their collective attention was drawn to the sky. "About 12 of us were left when balls of light, moving east to west, fell over the trees in the next yard." Harrison said. "Two more came over Lincoln School. One was white, the other green, both about a foot in diameter. Then there was a loud growling sound, getting louder and louder, closer and closer." Preceding the growling, Clark and Coleman noted that Harrison heard noises sounding like stones being thrown at a metal, million-and-a-half-gallon reservoir at the top of Marzolf Hill, a favorite hangout for local kids.[569] In New Canton (11 miles away), UFOs were reported in the night sky of July 14.[570]

In his *Saga* article Steiger noted additional details from Harrison concerning the unidentifiable noises he and others heard that Friday night. "About 50 people heard the thing roar that Friday night when we had the church meeting at our house. I was standing outside and it scared the hell out of me. It sounded like a real low growl. All at once, you could hear this growling getting closer and closer. Pretty soon you could hear the trees and brush cracking up in there. Then there was a loud, piercing scream. And that was the end of it. About five minutes later, it did the same thing over again, three times in a row. Then that was it for the night."[571]

"At that time my family came running from the house. They began urging me to drive off," Harrison said. "I wanted to wait and see what it was that was making this noise. My family insisted that I drive away and so I drove down Allen Street across the Town Branch."

As the family drove down Allen Street they met a group of curious people heading toward their home. "Over 40 people were coming toward my house, some carrying guns. They had heard the same noise we did," Harrison continued. "I stopped the car and my wife told them: 'Here it comes!' And those 40 people turned around and ran down the street."[572]

> "On July 14, 1972, Officers Whitaker and Floyd on duty in Car No. 1 were stopped by Edgar Harrison in the 200 block of North 7th Street and Mr. Harrison at this time stated that he had heard a noise described as a growl coming from the area immediately behind his house. Officers went to the Harrison residence with Mr. Harrison and listened. It was immediately evident that someone was on the hill above Harrison's house throwing rocks onto a metal reservoir owned by the City. Officers in Car No. 1 drove to the top of the hill and observed three car loads of young persons who stated that they had driven to the top of the hill to look or listen for whatever had been reported by Harrison and his family.[573]

The police notes in Sexton's article do not explicitly connect the several youths seen by authorities at the top of Marzolf Hill with the sounds people heard at the Harrison residence, though a linkage was implied. Harrison and several others explored the hill later that night. The city owned about 40 acres of Marzolf Hill, also called "Star Hill" by residents because town elders erected a star on its summit every Christmas. Edgar Harrison's property included six acres of the hill and "nobody's gonna keep me off," he said.[574]

During their search they came to an old building from which a strong, unpleasant odor emanated. Harrison called it "a mouldy [sic], horse smell or a strong garbage smell." Harrison would encounter this smell "like a dead horse"[575] on several occasions, assaulted by its foulness whenever he approached an area from which strange noises emanated.[576] Harrison concluded the malodorous odor, which he believed came from Momo, provided a diversionary function for the creature.

Betty Harrison took her seven children and slept at the family restaurant on South Main Street in downtown Louisiana, while Harrison kept vigil at the family home on Allen Street. Harrison took a leave of absence from his position with the water works to devote his full time and energy to discovering exactly what was causing the uproar in his family's life; he reportedly camped behind his house at the foot of Marzolf Hill for twenty-one straight nights.

15 July 1972, Saturday

In what may be traced as Momo's first weekend, creature sightings increased. At about 5:00 A.M. on July 15 Pat Howard of Louisiana saw "a dark object" walk like a man across a road near Marzolf Hill. "I spend my noon hours with some of the fellas looking in the woods," Harrison said. "I'll look under every piece of brush, every piece of rock. I won't stop until I find out what it is."

> "The next night, July 15, 1972, at 11:30 P.M. police were summoned to the George Minor residence on 1102 Dougherty Pike which is just below and to the Northwest of the Harrison residence. Mr. Harrison had been standing in the roadway outside of his house and had heard strange noises coming from behind the Minor residence. [Officer] Floyd at this time, determined to find what had been making noise or put a stop to rumors of such occurrence, walked from the Harrison residence to the top of Star hill. Floyd found nothing unusual. The only audible sound being a rock and roll band playing about a quarter of a mile northwest of the Harrison and Minor properties.[577]

Mrs. George Minor complained that searches for Momo should be conducted at night. She reported hearing the creature growl on several occasions—always between 10:00 and 10:30 P.M. The noise would begin as a low growl and end in a high-pitched scream.[578]

18 July 1972, Tuesday

Monster-hunting became a popular pastime for many Louisiana residents. "I hope this thing quiets down," said State Conservation Department official Gus Artus, "and we don't get a whole lot of adventure-seekers here from all over the country."

> As with other monster flaps, the town was invaded by throngs of gun-toting monster hunters. "This place is starting to look like an armed camp," remarked a deputy sheriff. "Everywhere you look there's a carload of men going by with a load of guns. They're looking for instant fame by being the person to shoot down 'Momo.'"[579]

According to Steiger, the July 18 *Louisiana Press-Journal* carried a warning from Artus against the inherent dangers posed by gun-toting monster-hunters on Marzolf Hill. "Whatever it is, it runs from people," Artus said. "My advice is that people in that neighborhood should go inside their homes. If they are frightened, they should lock their doors. If something comes around their houses, they have plenty of time to call the police, or a neighbor. They can defend themselves from inside their houses, if necessary. They should ask the outsiders to go home."[580]

One week into Momo's official existence and the strange experiences had begun to pile up—a resident reported seeing Momo north of Marzolf Hill stride across Highway 79 (Frank Ford Road) with a sheep or dog in its mouth (similar to Terry Harrison's account from July 11); several residents reported seeing red eyes stare at them from the darkness; three-toed tracks were discovered, confusing "the question of the number of digits on Momo's feet."[581] Chief Ward said he had heard several rumors explicating Momo; one line of gossip suggested the creature was a "monster bigfoot bear."[582]

19 July 1972, Wednesday

Before starting off on his planned vacation, Chief Ward instigated an official search of Marzolf Hill on the morning of July 19 to resolve the matter of monsters in the neighborhood. Vic Meyer raised Australian sheep dogs and quarter horses in Clarksville and participated in the hunt as a member of the Pike County Rescue Squad. "There were maybe a hundred people at City Hall when we got together for the hunt," Meyer stated, "and many of them had guns. I was glad when Shelby held it to law enforcement officers and members of the rescue squad. I wouldn't have gone up there if he hadn't."[583] During an election year, amongst those taking part in the search on July 19 were four candidates for county sheriff "showing their devotion to duty."[584]

> "On July 19, 1972, a search of the Marzolf hill area was ordered by Chief Shelby Ward of the Louisiana Police Department.

> Along with State Conservation Officer Artus, about 20 officers from around Pike County took part in this search. A line was formed and each man walked within 15 feet of the next and in this way the whole area of Marzolf Hill was thoroughly searched. The searchers were instructed to look for footprints, hair, to look into the trees, and to observe anything unusual or unordinary. Ward concluded at the end of the search, which lasted for about three hours, that nothing unusual had been found and there was nothing in the area to search for.[585]

Harrison would never see the creature himself, but along with others, he did hear sounds and smell odors on multiple occasions which were beyond his normal experience. "The odor is worse than any old goat you'd ever smell," said Edgar Harrison's brother-in-law. "It growls like a bear, but it runs on two feet."[586] His wife concurred. "It sounded like a gorilla," she said. "That's what it is—a 'Big Foot.' I heard they've got one in California and up in Canada."[587]

> Harrison: To me, it smelled just like a moldy old horse pen. It burnt your nose, like sulphur.
>
> Glen McWayne [sic]: Did the odor last long?
>
> Harrison: No, I only detected it when the thing came. Twelve reporters came from Chicago to spend the night in my front yard. My dog took off right up the ridge and up on top of the hill. They took off after the thing when they heard it. Boy, you should have had a recording of those men when they hit the smell! I was with them, and it stank so bad that you would've thought you were walking in horse manure. It was that strong.
>
> McWane: Chief Ward, did you smell anything when you came up to investigate?
>
> Chief Ward: No, I didn't smell a thing.
>
> Harrison: When my dog chased it that night, it went right up a hollow and we followed. The dog went 300 feet up there, then he came back with his tail between his legs. He laid right down in back of the house and just got sick as can be. His eyes got bloodshot and he lay there for over an hour throwing up. Finally, he became O.K., but now I can't get him to go back in there. He just won't go.

(Harrison then told McWane that he had been setting out fish at night to bait Momo).

Harrison: You can see right where it reached up to get that fish. That's about 12 ½ feet high. That's why I figure the thing must be at least seven and a half feet tall in order to reach those fish. If it had arms that hung about its knees, it could easily reach 12 feet high.[588]

20 July 1972, Thursday

> Louisiana's monster replaced politics as the top topic of talk yesterday. One gagster managed to combine the two by reporting that the Marzolf Hill creature had been identified—as "one of McGovern's hippies." Which was promptly countered with another gag that it had been identified as Nixon's choice to replace Spiro Agnew. As far as the actual Louisiana situation is concerned, Police Chief Shelby Ward there told his brother Bill Ward last night that strenuous search had found no tracks, no traces, no nothing.
>
> And a non-political gagster said it must have been a "six-foot-tall, shaggy, beer can."[589]

Pike County Sheriff James Marshall attempted to close the door on the story of a hairy monster cavorting in northeastern Missouri on Thursday, July 20. "As far as this office is concerned the whole thing is a big hoax and rumor," he said. "This creature story has been thoroughly investigated throughout Louisiana, Mo., and Pike County and there's been no evidence of a monster anywhere."[590]

Richard Crowe, a reporter for Chicago's *Irish Times* and a contributor to *Fate* magazine, arrived in Louisiana on July 20 along with Skokie, Illinois, attorney Loren Smith. After stopping by the police station, they were escorted to the Harrison home at about 9:30 p.m., where Harrison and his daughter Doris' fiancé Richard Bliss were camped in the back yard. After Harrison related recent events to Crowe and Smith, the men set out together into the night to explore Marzolf Hill. Near a tree where the creature was first seen by Doris, the party found a spot of evident disturbance. "There was a circular spot in the brush where leaves and twigs had been stripped away from the branches." It was not clear if this was the same disturbed area noted by Harrison almost nine days prior. Not far from that spot Crowe found evidence that something had dug in an old garbage dump. Harrison discovered what appeared to be disinterred dog graves with the unearthed bones strewn about. The further up Marzolf Hill the party hiked, the steeper and wilder the land became. The group proceeded to examine two tracks.

> As we continued up the path we came to the first of two tracks Harrison and Bliss had discovered earlier that day. The first track resembled a large human footprint. Even with the heel impression incomplete it measured 10 inches long and five inches wide.
>
> The second track farther up the hill was less distinct. It was five inches long, curved and showed three or possibly five toes. It might have been the print of a hand. There had been no rain in the area for 10 days and it was estimated that more than 200 pounds of pressure would have been necessary to make prints in the hard soil.[591]

Descending the hill, Harrison pointed out an abandoned shack to his visitors which he believed served as a refuge for the creature. Crowe looked inside and saw a pile of leaves and litter in one corner which resembled bedding or an animal's nest. It was outside the shack that Harrison had hung fish and a strip of ham skin in a nearby tree as lures for Momo, but these were found to be undisturbed. After investigating the hovel, it was noticed that Chubby, Harrison's dog, had left the party. It was then about 10:30 P.M. when the men encountered a terrible stench. Crowe wrote, "We smelled an overwhelming stench that could only be described as resembling rotten flesh or foul, stagnant water."

"That's him, boys!" Harrison shouted. "He's around here somewhere." The men heard the rising cacophony of neighborhood dogs barking along Dougherty Pike. About five minutes later, the odor diminished.[592] The four men returned to the Harrison home and stayed up to 3 A.M. but nothing of note happened.

On July 20, George MacArthur of Other Dimensions interviewed Mrs. G. R. of Boonville, Missouri who had reported seeing a "ugly-looking thing" while driving near New Haven on Highway "C."

> Mrs. G. R.: It was walking in a field. It was very tall and it had what looked like silver or white fur.

George MacArthur: Fur or hair?

Mrs. G. R.: At that distance, I couldn't really see. I could tell it was tall. I stopped and watched it walk away, then it turned around and started to come back. That's when I left. Terribly fast, I can tell you!

MacArthur: Did it make any noise?

Mrs. G. R.: Not that I heard. I had my window closed. When I got to my father's house in New Haven, I was shaking. My father thought I was stupid for stopping the car. When he pointed out that the engine could have died or something, I really got scared. I didn't see any features, because I left too fast. My estimation of its height was about nine feet. And it was a very clear day.

MacArthur: Did it act like it was hostile, or curious?

Mrs. G. R.: It acted curious, I would say. It didn't come charging at me. It just kind of nonchalantly started walking back toward the car, like it wanted to see what I was all about, too. Like my father said, I was probably stupid for stopping the car. This has given me a few bad nights, especially when I am here at home alone.[593]

21 July 1972, Friday

By July 21, an estimated 50 residents of Louisiana, population 4,400, claimed to have seen the monster.[594] During the evening of July 21, Kathy Hickman from Fulton's *Kingdom Daily News* spent the evening searching for Momo with Edgar Harrison, several members of the Harrison family, and two women from UFO Research Associates, Inc. of Kansas. Steiger wrote that Hickman thought Edgar Harrison sincere and not perpetrating a hoax. Hickman's reporting included the negative side of monster hunting on Harrison's wallet: "I've already lost $90 since this thing was seen," Harrison said. "My wife and kids have moved out and say they aren't coming back. And we've worked hard for this house and land." Hickman reported she heard a loud sound like a branch cracking as she sat on the steps of the Harrison home. "The night sounds in the woods stopped for a brief period. We saw nothing more but Harrison and Kietha Fish [Fish edited *The Kansas Newsletter*, a publication devoted to UFO studies] of the UFO Research Associates, remained longer and said they had caught a whiff of some foul-smelling odor."[595]

On July 21, "grizzled, toothless fisherman"[596] Ellis Minor, a resident on Pike County 118 (River Road), was home alone in his cabin when his dog suddenly began to growl sometime between 10:00 and 10:30 P.M. "I'm 63 and lived here since I was 6," said Ellis Minor who at the time of the sightings spent his summers at his cabin on the river. "I was sitting right here in front of the house, the rest of the family were at a fair at Pleasant Hill," he said. "My white bird dog started to growl. He's usually quiet. And I shone a light, right there about 20 feet up the road. It was standing there, hair black as coal. I couldn't see its eyes or face—it had hair nearly down to its chest. As soon as I threw the light on it, it whirled and took off thataway," Minor said, indicating the creature's path toward railroad tracks and on into the woods. The railroad tracks in Louisiana were owned by the Gulf, Mobile and Ohio which became the Illinois Central Gulf in 1972. "It's the first time I ever seen an ugly-looking thing like that. If that dog hadn't growled, it might have walked right down into my yard. It was headed for the water. I don't know which would've run faster—me or the dog. We tried to track it the next day, but couldn't 'cause it was so dry," Minor said. "Besides, a person would be a damn fool to try to catch that ugly thing. He's absolutely the damndest looking thing I've ever seen in my life." Patrolman John Whitaker listened to Minor's account. "I've known Ellis Minor all my life and I've never known him to make anything up," Walker said. "Something just might be up in these hills."[597]

As Steiger details, July 21 witnessed another incident of strange aerial phenomenon:

> Can one make a connection between UFOs and Momo? On the evening of July 21st, shortly before Edgar Harrison and several witnesses heard Momo emit "a big, loud, screaming noise" from the hill, two lighted objects had been seen falling from the sky.
>
> Edgar Harrison: Just before the sound came from the hill, there were two lights that came out of the south and went to the north and fell behind the Lincoln school.
>
> Glenn McWane: Would you say they fell, or just disappeared?
>
> Harrison: They glowed and went right across the top of those trees (he pointed to a stand of trees south of the Harrison property, around the abandoned schoolhouse). Now there were two coming from this way (southeast) and glowing over the top of those trees.
>
> McWane: How fast were they going?

> Harrison: They weren't moving real fast. They were moving slow enough so you could see them real good and tell approximately how big they were.
>
> Chief Shelby Ward: That was the same night a report came in from Fulton (Mo.) telling me that people had seen three lights over King City.
>
> Harrison: Up at the bowling alley, two doctors said they saw a flying saucer last Saturday (August 12th). The same night, Ernie Shade, his wife, and my wife and kids saw a thing on top of this big hill up there, and it was just sitting there blinking on and off. I went up there at 11 P.M. that night, and I watched it. Some people who saw it said it had square-looking windows in it, approximately two feet in diameter. Some say it shot red lights out of it.
>
> McWane: What color were the window openings?
>
> Harrison: Kind of yellowish-orange. The guy that runs the filling station up there on river road said they saw the thing on the same night. It was coming down the Mississippi. It was up high and it went south down the river.[598]

In his *Saga* article, Steiger wrote of another unusual event occurring on July 21. A pregnant housewife in Bowling Green, eleven miles southwest from Louisiana, reported she watched two balls of light land in a cow pasture near her home that evening. Later, she said she smelled a nauseating odor and her family heard strange grunting and screaming sounds "like nothing we'd ever heard before." She claimed her landlord threatened her with eviction if the location where the lights touched down was divulged.[599]

22 JULY 1972, SATURDAY

> The Louisiana, Missouri Police Department has received many calls and reports of sounds and smells and [sights] which persons have thought unusual. Most of these have been investigated by the Department and have been found to have a logical explanation or the report has been so vague that investigation was impossible. Due to a lack of undisputable evidence, it must be concluded by the Police Department that nothing unusual or out of the ordinary as regards the reports of hairy objects, smells, tracks, and sounds exist in this immediate area.[600]

Hayden C. Hewes, founder and director of the Unidentified Flying Object Bureau, came to Louisiana with his wife and Daniel Garcia on Saturday, July 22, to interview residents and investigate their reports of encountering a huge, smelly, hairy monster. "I am convinced something has been observed," Hewes said. "Just what it is I don't know at this time." After talking with Edgar Harrison, Hewes made plaster casts of footprints found near the Harrison home. Hewes said the casts were of "average to poor quality because the soil was quite dry." The casts were nine inches long by seven inches wide and they appeared to show a foot that had "four or five toes coming out from a palm-like base."[601]

Hewes and others camped out in the woods of Marzolf Hill Saturday night with cameras and tape recorders but failed to turn up any evidence of Momo. "It was 9:35 Saturday night when a neighboring farmer heard a loud, growling noise on the other side of the hill," Hewes said. "There's always the possibility of a hoax," Hewes acknowledged, but he was impressed with Harrison as a genuine witness to strange events. "I believe, however, that Mr. Harrison is very sincere. He's scared and he wants to know what's on his farm and then get whatever is on it off the property."[602]

Momo, Hewes averred, might be a classification of extra-terrestrial creatures called giant hairy bipeds (GHB). Hewes' organization claimed they had compiled a file of about 300 reports of extra-terrestrial creatures. GHBs, Hewes said, were described as having large pumpkin-shaped heads, glowing orange eyes, hairy bodies, large feet, clawed hands, long knee-length arms, and the intelligence of a chimpanzee. Hewes stated some UFO enthusiasts believed GHBs were experimental animals sent to earth from another planet.[603]

> Researchers in the field of flying saucers believe the hairy bipeds might be experimental animals sent to earth by alien masters on another planet, Hewes said. While earthbound, the hairy biped would carry out robot-type duties, he said.

Hewes said Momo descriptions aligned with descriptions of creatures seen in the Florida Everglades and near Vader, Washington, in 1971. GHBs were one of four creature classifications the UFO bureau advocated for. "They range in height from the 2-foot small hairy biped to the 7-foot tall giant hairy biped." Hewes said. Hewes suggested the terrible odor associated with the creature was typical of the sulfur-like odors described in other encounters across the country. As far as anomalous hairy giants went, Hewes made a distinction between Bigfoot and GHBs.

> "A female biped was filmed in California," Hewes said. "The motion picture footage was featured in the film 'Big Foot.'" Big Foot, another hairy creature reportedly has been sighted near lumber camps in northern California and Oregon.
>
> If Momo is not a biped, Hewes said, it might be a troglodyte. A troglodyte is an ancient cave dwelling creatures which some believe is the missing link. He explained there are caves in the Louisiana area where such a creature could live. The abominable snowman of the Himalayas is said to be a troglodyte, Hewes added.[604]

23 July 1972, Sunday

As mentioned earlier in this section, MUFON members picnicked on Sunday, July 23, and listened to several presentations on Momo. MUFON Director Walter Andrus had interviewed the Harrison family, and he displayed a sketch by Dorothy Harrison depicting her rendition of Momo.[605] John Scheussler received credit in the July 24 *Centralia Sentinel* for dubbing the monster "Momo."

During an appearance on a St. Louis television program discussing Momo, Scheussler received word of another creature incident. A woman caller described a year-old incident when, while her husband was fishing at Foley, Missouri, he was startled at the sight of a shaggy monster emerging out of the water. "We've been teasing him about it," the caller told Scheussler, "but now we're not so sure." Andrus, Scheussler, and other MUFON members were no novices when it came to strange, unusual, and improbable stories.[606]

As seen, the events in Louisiana attracted many researchers grounded more in UFO studies than in hairy hominids. Coral Lorensen, a Tucson authority on UFOs and cofounder of the Aerial Phenomenon Research Organization, stated there was no connection between Momo and UFOs, but she did urge additional research into the Momo sightings.[607]

> By now [late July, 1972] national publicity was drawing visitors from near and far. Among them were 12 sailors from Texas and a carload of students from Chicago. Harrison's home became

"monster outpost," his phone rang constantly and the strain began to tell on him. He lost weight and took a leave of absence from his job.

> Although Harrison heard and smelled the monster on many occasions he never saw it. He said the terrible smell would come just when the searchers were onto something. He speculated that it might be stink gas used to distract the searchers. On one occasion the group of sailors saw a small glowing light that silently exploded and was followed by the stench. Harrison said he had observed the same thing himself on other nights.[608]

Ivan Sanderson told the *Tucson Daily Citizen* that "three members of our society have gone to Missouri" to investigate the July 17 reports from the Harrison family. "They reported to me that the original reports of Harrison and his daughter seem to hold water," Sanderson said. Sanderson shared some additional thoughts with reporter S. C. Warman regarding Momo:

> "One, these monsters are not a variety of apes but some sort of primitive human being because they leave human footprints and there is no evidence that apes ever roamed in North America.
>
> "There's no connection with monster reports and UFOs, for they are some sort of primitive humans of this earth," he added.
>
> Sanderson said he founded the "Society for the Unexplained." Members of the society investigating MoMo are Rich Crowe of Chicago, Hayden Hewes of Oklahoma City, and Eugene Austin of University City, Mo.
>
> He explained "There have been wild stories" originating in the Hannibal-Louisiana, Mo., area "for the past 10 years." Both are Mississippi River cities, upstream from St. Louis.
>
> He also cited instances of "monsters" reported in northern California, and the states of Washington and Alaska in recent years.[609]

Clark and Coleman wrote about the seemingly disparate paranormal topics which appeared to be associated in the Momo matter.

> "We are confronted with three presumably separate questions: mysterious anthropoids, UFOs and, perhaps most important, psychic phenomena. Clearly, to us at any rate, the answers do not lie in conventional flying saucer buff theorizing, and Hayden Hewes' much-publicized theory that Momo and his relatives might be experimental animals dropped by extraterrestrials from their saucer-spaceships proves only that there is much of which many ufologists are unaware.
>
> For example, there is the Russian folk tradition about "Wild Women." The legend reminds us unmistakably of our anthropoids—up to a point—when suddenly we discover that the other half of the tradition is just as unmistakably out of the fairy-faith. Using Hewes' logic, might we then assume that anthropoids are a kind of fairies? Of course not. Not any more than we can assume, because in recent years Irish countryfolk have reported viewing "leprechauns" stepping out of flying saucers, that fairies are really UFO beings.[610]

Crowe also considered the Momo-UFO association, citing several additional reports of unusual lights seen in the sky and their possible connection to Momo.

> Many students of monster lore like Hewes postulate some connection between monsters and unidentified aerial phenomena. Both monsters and UFOs share the distinction of being widely observed by numerous witnesses yet never yielding to scientific confirmation. Although news accounts from Louisiana played down any mention of UFOs I found the local residents had a different tale to tell.
>
> The most interesting UFO reports come from River Road where Minor spotted the monster. On the night of July 26 a fireball was seen to land in the top of a large cottonwood tree at the first railroad crossing on River Road. Two red spurts of light shot out from it; then it took off into the night.
>
> On the following three nights small blue and red lights, like flashlights signaling back and forth, were seen atop the limestone bluff at the north end of River Road. Members of the relocated Harrison family were among the witnesses. Another

> witness, Mrs. Lois Shade, Edgar Harrison's sister, described the lights as being about the size of an apple.
>
> Mrs. Shade's seven-year-old son Rossie went outside to play and returned home with two pieces of good-quality white linen paper upon which cryptic messages had been written with a blue ball-point (see box). Mrs. Shade and Edgar Harrison believe these messages relate directly to the intelligence behind the monster and the UFOs.
>
> Shortly after these notes were found the small lights were seen again—on the night of Sunday, July 30, about 9:00 P.M. A lighted object was spotted in the thicket at the top of the limestone bluff just above a house that was vacant at the time. Ernest Shade Sr., described the UFO as an "orange-looking color" resembling a car light. Later the color changed to red and gray and a definite shape could be made out. Mrs. Shade said it was disc-shaped with what "looked like little bitty windows all lit up."
>
> The object stayed atop the bluff from 9:00 P.M. until about 2:00 A.M. when "the lights went out." The UFO then gave off a "red glow" and "went straight up into the air and disappeared," according to Mrs. Shade.
>
> This same morning a glowing UFO was sighted heading north along the Mississippi. After this alleged UFO landing activity in Louisiana ceased.[611]

Sexton's reporting turned up more than a half-dozen witnesses admitting to seeing, hearing, or smelling something strange during the Momo affair. Sexton's own assessment, based upon her conversations with townspeople, left her to conclude half of Louisiana's residents believed there was something behind the reports, a fourth who didn't believe any of it and the rest were unsure or perhaps unwilling to admit the creature could be possible.[612] Sexton wrote:

> Unidentified Flying Object experts spent a few days in Louisiana. Most said they were unsuccessful in obtaining evidence that a hairy bi-ped was in the area, but one man claiming to have [seen] the monster said it resembled sketches of the hairy bi-ped which UFO experts say is an experimental robot-type animal.

> He has affectionately been called Momo.
>
> The UFO experts may have said they didn't find any evidence, but there is another reason they might have left. Their presence was creating quite a stir among the people.
>
> Police ordered them off private property on several occasions. Many observers said their presence seemed to add reality to the monster stories, and rumors of UFO sightings ran rampant.[613]

The July 23 *Bonham Daily Favorite* (Bonham, Texas) repeated the report Momo had been seen crossing a highway with a dog in its mouth (some accounts say the animal was a sheep). An undecided Police Chief Shelby Ward stated, "The more I keep hearing about it from people the more difficult it is for me to be skeptical." Hewes found congruity between Momo sightings and creatures seen around the country. "We have talked at great length to witnesses. They told us things in the interview that fit in with other sightings made around the country," he said.[614] In the July 23 *Jefferson City News*, Sheriff Ward remarked that two different kinds of footprints were found in areas where the creature had been seen. One set of footprints was eight to ten inches wide according to Ward; the other set of footprints was smaller, four to five inches long, curved in the middle, and showed three toe prints.[615]

24 July 1972, Monday

John Scheussler researched several creature sightings in and around Louisiana. "Two teenaged girls from O'Fallon, Mo., saw a bear-like creature walking upright near the edge of a wooded area just a few miles out of town. This occurred near sundown on July 24. Two days later, a young boy saw a similar creature nearby."[616]

25 July 1972, Tuesday

Police and authorities, it was true, were far more concerned with the public's antics and behaviors than entertaining the possibility of a local monster. Those concerns were stoked after groups of searchers had swept over Marzolf Hill's 100 acres carrying high-powered rifles. "Someone is likely to get shot," Gus Artus observed with concern. Indeed, reports of a shot heard from the wooded prominence drove officials to action. By July 25, Louisiana police had blocked off Marzolf Hill, right up to Harrison's property. After Chief Ward left for vacation on Saturday, July 22, Assistant Chief of Police Jerry Floyd became the acting head of the department. "If you ask me,"

Floyd said, "Harrison has got a still behind his house and must have had a bad batch. . . . We don't think there is anything around here, but we'll continue to investigate whenever we get a report."[617]

> Harrison says he's had over 700 curious visitors at his home since Momo was supposedly seen by his daughter and son in their back yard. He is obviously delighted with the publicity and notoriety and recounts the various area episodes for hours. He has also seen flaming balls pass over his house, fall to earth and leave no trace of their presence.
>
> Harrison and his neighbors claim they have heard siren-like noises and have pursued "something" through the woods. Asked to describe Momo, Harrison said, "I can't repare (sic) it with anything." He says the report it picked up a small foreign car is untrue. Trade people seem to be benefitting from the rumors: they're even selling monster-burgers in Bowling Green. The Louisiana Pizza parlor is offering monster pizzas. And Harrison, who closed up his hole-in-the-wall restaurant a few days ago, wishes he had stayed in business. "I'd sell 'em feet burgers."
>
> Harrison has chairs out in the yard for visitors to sit in, but he says "I don't want to talk to nobody that don' believe in it." There is apparently no shortage of those willing to believe in Momo's existence.
>
> A middle-aged lady carrying an old Reader's Digest opened to the article "Is There an American Abominable Snowman?", high school kids playing Sherlock Holmes, families out for a Sunday drive—all types show up, scoff, speculate, scan the woods and leave.[618]

According to Coleman and Clark, whose research shed additional light on the scope of creature sightings experienced in the Midwest, the July 25 Pekin [Illinois] *Daily Times* stated, "Creve Coeur authorities said a witness reported seeing 'something big' swimming in the Illinois River."[619] Leroy Summers of Cairo, Illinois, located at the confluence of the Mississippi and Ohio Rivers, said he saw a 10-foot, white hair-covered created near the Ohio River levee on the evening of July 25. Coleman and Clark wrote, "The Cairo police found nothing when they came to investigate and Police Commissioner James Dale warned that henceforth anyone making a monster report would have his breath tested for alcoholic content."[620]

26 July 1972, Wednesday

Police in Joplin, Missouri, received a call on Wednesday afternoon from a woman who reported a "thing" walked through her garden and across her yard. The woman said the thing resembled a man wearing a cape, but she was stumped as to exactly what it was. Joplin police searched the area but found no evidence of the entity that crossed the woman's property.[621]

On Wednesday night, authorities received a report of a gorilla sighted on the abutment of the Cuivre River bridge on Highway 54 between Scott's Corner and Laddonia. Deputy Sheriff Russell Wilkes said deputies and farmers searched the area around the bridge but didn't turn up any sign of the creature.[622] The July 29 *St. Joseph News Press* reported an elderly Louisiana lady said she saw a seven-foot, black-haired, smelly creature on July 26.[623] The East Peoria Police Department reported more than 200 calls concerning monster sightings jammed their switchboard on July 26.

> Crowe's investigation uncovered a number of Louisiana UFO sightings which did not make the papers, presumably because reporters were already busy enough running down monster stories and rumours [sic]. Nonetheless, on the night of the 26th, a "fireball" alighted on top of a large cottonwood tree at the first railroad crossing on River Road. It shot out two spurts of red light and then zoomed out of sight. On the following three nights coloured [sic] lights were observed along the top of the limestone bluff at the northern end of River Road. The witnesses, the Harrison and Shade families (Mrs. Shade is Mrs. Harrison's sister), thought the lights were signaling back and forth to each other. Sunday night, the 30th, at 9:00, an orange, glowing UFO with lighted "windows" landed in the thicket at the top of the bluff and sat there for five hours before it "went straight up into the air and disappeared," in Mrs. Lois Shade's words.[624]

27 July 1972, Thursday

Three Chicago students were amongst those joining in on the hunt for Momo. "We're curious about this thing," said Jack Clegg. "I'd just like to get a chance to see it if it's still down there." The Chicago Daily News Service reported that Clegg's group, which included Clegg's brother and a friend, intended to leave Chicago on Thursday, July 27, and make way to Star Hill where they would camp out and look for Momo. "We're mainly interested in just seeing it," Clegg said. "I have a lively imagination and I have read about a lot of these things, but I've never gotten a chance to see one before." Clegg added that not all of his family considered hunting a hairy monster a productive effort. "My dad thinks my brother and I are just idiots for wanting to do this, but what would you expect parents would think?"[625]

Police found a costume "with a dragon-like body, a frog-like head and bulging eyes," in a wooded area in New Canton, on the eastern side of the Mississippi and about 18 miles northeast from Louisiana. Two off-duty officers, William Earles and dispatcher Larry Forgey, were driving on Illinois 96 about a mile south of New Canton on Thursday when they encountered something quite unexpected. They witnessed a "green, long-tailed, strange-looking," creature cross the road in front of their vehicle before plunging into the woods. Earles, the driver, turned around and parked so the pair could inspect the area where the creature disappeared. During their investigation of the scene, the men heard screams. Earles and Forgey rushed to the spot and found two unoccupied cars. Friday morning, state police went to the area and found the costume.[626] On Sunday, July 30, police said there was no connection between the dragon costume and Momo.[627]

> On the night of the 27th "two reliable citizens" told police they were startled by a ten-foot-tall something that "looked like a cross between an ape and a cave man." A United Press International account describes it as having "a face with long gray U-shaped ears, a red mouth with sharp teeth, [and] thumbs with long second joints . . ." It smelled, said a witness, like a musky wet down dog." The East Peoria Police Department reported it had received more than 200 calls about the monster the following evening.[628]

28 July 1972, Friday

The article, "Gruesome Missouri Monster Sets Sleepy Hamlet Agog," published in the *Pittsburgh Press*, recounted the experience of a woman who smelled a terrible odor, saw unusual aerial phenomenon, and heard something unidentifiable.

> At City Hall, the town's bars and the A&W Root Beer stand people are buzzing with tales of "it," "the beast," "the creature," or, as they have nicknamed it, "Momo"—Missouri Monster.[629]
>
> About 11 miles southeast of Bowling Green, Mo., a young, pregnant housewife stood angered and embarrassed in front of a small, two-story frame house.

> She had been harassed by skeptical neighbors and her landlord threatened to throw out her family because of her report of what she saw in a field the night before.
>
> She refused to give her name, although it was stenciled neatly on the mailbox in front.
>
> "We're church-going people," she said. "We got no need to lie. I'm not crazy and I'm not afraid of those who'll say I am. I know what I saw."
>
> She said she had been washing the dishes last Saturday night and smelled "something dead." She said she went outside where she saw two balls of fire and thought one of them landed in the cow pasture.
>
> "Then we heard grunts and like a scream," she said. "We've got coyotes around here and I've heard wild hogs—but never anything like that."[630]

29 July 1972, Saturday

The July 29 *St. Joseph News Press* reported that more than 100 people armed with guns and other expedient weapons prepared to hunt for Momo on Saturday night,[631] an evening that was the first of two occasions in which disembodied voices were added into Momo's melting pot of strangeness.

> On the night of the 29th Harrison and a group of college students, standing on top of the hill, heard what sounded like a shot from near the road. They rushed down the hill until they got near the road, where they all distinctly heard an old man's voice saying, "You boys stay out of these woods."
>
> The voice seemed to have come from a nearby clump of trees no more than 20 feet wide by 50 feet, but an immediate and thorough search failed to turn up anything.
>
> A week later, on August 5, another evidently disembodied voice spoke to Pat Howard and a friend, who were camped out in Harrison's back yard. The two were drinking coffee when someone or something said, "I'll take a cup of your coffee." Again a search produced no results.[632]

31 July 1972, Monday

When reporter Kim Sexton arrived in town police were at Noix Creek near downtown Louisiana investigating a woman's report of a gorilla cavorting near the bank of the river. A neighbor of the witness said she didn't see a gorilla or any other creature but had caught a whiff of something malodorous. "It smelled like bad urine multiplied by six," she said, insisting the extreme odor "lingered."[633]

Even the FAA became involved in Momo, according to Pennie Sue Thurman's reporting in the July 31 *Lewiston Morning Tribune*, when a large, hairy creature was sighted near a private landing field close to Louisiana and again at Haerr Field in Taylor. "In our profession you have to check everything," said Philip Maxted, an official at the Quincy, Illinois, flight station. "The general opinion is that the monster is a joke, but one never knows."[634]

East Peoria Monster

An estimated 100 people armed with guns and other weapons stormed the woods around East Peoria, Illinois, on the hunt for a 10-foot-tall, hairy, smelly monster that in time was called the Cole Hollow Monster. Though their efforts failed to turn up a monster, one man reportedly shot himself in the leg when his .22 caliber pistol went off unexpectedly. A 48-year-old woman who requested anonymity as she talked with the press, said she and her family had been in the woods at about 6 P.M. Wednesday, July 26. "We saw some tracks," she said, "and then we heard—oh, I don't even know how to say it—kind of a low growl, like a dog would make only much deeper and from something much bigger." Unnerved by the sounds, the family left the scene. "Anyway, we didn't look for more tracks," she added, "but made tracks of our own right for our car." East Peoria patrolman David Madsen said the police came out to the woods along Coal Hollow Rd., "to try to get the people out before they hurt themselves," he said. "When it started to get dark with all those people in there anything's liable to happen." Madsen said a single monster report had come in to police officials about a month ago. "Some kids supposedly made pictures of the tracks, but we've never seen any," he said.

> The description of the monster matches that of a beast reportedly seen in Louisiana, Mo., 120 miles southwest of East Peoria. Reports of the monster have circulated widely in the last week and a similar creature was reportedly seen standing at the Ohio River levee Tuesday evening near Cairo, Ill.[635]

Steiger wrote of the Cole Hollow Monster description given by Randy Emert, 18, of Peoria, Illinois, to Nancy Willavize of Peoria's *Journal-Star*. On July 26, the same date as the family's encounter mentioned above, Emert and several of his friends saw a large hairy creature in the woods near Cole Hollow Road in East Peoria. He said several three-toed footprints had been seen "all around" Cole Hollow. "By the pressure of the prints," Emert explained, "it looks like it's pretty heavy." Among his friends, Emert appeared to be alone in willing to discuss his experience. "I'm kind of a spokesman for the group," he said. "The only one who has guts, I guess." The Cole Hollow Monster was said to be between 8 and 12 feet tall, with white hair, and a scream "like an old steam engine whistle, only more human," and several accounts mentioned an offensive, sulfur-like smell. Emert stated he had heard descriptions of the Missouri Monster and averred that what he saw resembled "Momo."[636] Willavize's article included remarks from Ann Kammerer of Peoria who, while appreciating the story's outré quality, said all her children had seen the monster. "It sounds kind of weird," she admitted. "At first I didn't believe it, but then my daughter-in-law saw it," she explained.[637]

August 1972

The Rockford, Illinois, *Morning Star* contained a playful editorial on Momo in its August 1 edition wherein given the number of regional monster sightings, the name "Il-Mo" was pitched.

> Now it's the "Il-Mo" monster.
>
> Don't scoff.
>
> The thing actually exists. We have it on the best authority that this monster, first seen in a woods near Louisiana, Mo., since strayed into Illinois.
>
> That makes it an Il-Mo monster (Illinois-Missouri) instead of just a Momo.
>
> And it's grown.
>
> Seven feet tall before, it's now been estimated at 10 feet by the folks around Cairo, Ill. Also, its shaggy black hair is supposed to have turned white. It now wears a red band around its repulsive middle, a la Mick Jagger. And, befitting a monster, it can be monstrously frightening.
>
> Police Commissioner James Daley of Cairo says anybody else who reports seeing the monster will have to take a test to prove his sobriety.
>
> At East Peoria, 100 miles from Cairo, patrolman Patrick Quinn says, "Reports of this thing are completely unfounded.

> There is absolutely no evidence there is a monster. I hope it goes back to Missouri."
>
> We don't.
>
> Stick around, monster. Make a legend. Be the object of search parties, speculation, and TV talk shows.
>
> Be as famous as the Loch Ness monster of Scotland.
>
> You can do it, Il-Mo.
>
> Do you bite?[638]

By the start of August, creature sightings in Louisiana had largely tapered away from their July highs. For a brief period, Momo still garnered attention; the aggregate of reports drove conjecture and comparison.

> The description of the beast given by two Harrison children, who saw it, is very close to that of our Big Foot. But our Sasquatch had five toes, according to plaster casts made of his tracks. The Missouri monster had five toes on one foot, but only four on the other. Maybe Big Foot lost a toe crossing the Rockies last winter.[639]

Sometime in the morning of July 23, something made three-toed tracks on Freddie Robbins' farm eight miles south of Louisiana. Protection was given to one of the better tracks by a large tin container which was later lifted off by Edgar Harrison and his hunting partner Clyde Penrod. Putting the container to the side, the men regarded an oval-shaped, slender-toed track pressed into the earth.[640]

On August 3, Betty Suddarth noticed her dog acting oddly right before she and her husband Bill Suddarth heard a loud howl in the yard of their farm just northwest of Louisiana. Investigating, the couple found three-toed tracks pressed into mud smack-dab in the center of their garden. Suddarth called Clyde Penrod, who drove to the Suddarth home and made a plaster cast of the best track. "It was 20 to 25 feet from the tracks to anything else," Penrod said. "I can't understand how they were made." A check of the rest of the property didn't reveal any additional tracks. "It looked as if the three-toed visitor had flown down," Crowe wrote in *Fate*, and "deliberately planted four perfect prints and then flown off again." Clark and Coleman noted that the Suddarth prints were both narrower and longer than the Robbins prints. A copy of Penrod's cast went up on display at Penrod's Louisiana Auto Parts on Fifth and Georgia Streets.

Momo Wrap Up

The last known prints attributed to Momo were those found at the Suddarth farm. As August wore on both UFO and monster sightings trickled away and Momo's time in the limelight essentially came to an end. Harrison went back to work and with his family later moved into a new home.

Jerry Floyd, the assistant chief of Louisiana's six-man police force, said at the end of July he would be very happy to dump the monster matter back into the lap of Police Chief Shelby Ward when Ward returned from his Michigan vacation. "We've investigated in hopes of ending the rumors," Floyd said. "I walked up and down Marzolf Hill with a flashlight and found nothing but three carloads of kids looking for the monster. It could be a combination of things. People don't have much to do in the summertime. They might let their imaginations run away with them. Or it could be kids. Most of the people are disgusted with the whole thing. They think it's ridiculous." When asked about other reports that hadn't made the papers, Floyd said, "In all fairness, we have had other people say they've seen this thing. Most at a distance of about 20 feet and at night. Some good, reliable citizens, I just don't know." Hayden Hewes camped out one night with an assistant in Harrison's backyard, but they didn't encounter anything unusual. Hewes said, "We did not see or smell or hear anything. But from the several reports, it's apparent that something [has] been sighted."[641]

As monster-fueled hype and excitement began to wane, some venues found in Momo a convenient source of humor. From the *Pittsburgh Press:*

> Some are amused. One resident cracked, "from the description, I'd say it was the guy dating my oldest daughter."
>
> Another, dubious about the national publicity, muttered, "they probably think we're a bunch of country bumpkins."[642]

"Louisiana Jokes About its Monster" was title for the *Mexico Daily Ledger's* July 21 article combining mirth and Momo.

> "The city of Louisiana hasn't had this much excitement since the centennial," a writer to the open forum column of the Louisiana Press-Journal said, and called for the hill to be turned into a tourist attraction.
>
> An editorial in the paper said "It sort of tickles our vanity that a will o' the wisp has turned us into the most notorious place in the United States between conventions. But, like

> the Democratic convention, we don't know yet what kind of monster we've given birth to.
>
> "In the meantime, for the information of the innocents abroad, we are not sitting behind locked doors with guns at the ready. We are going about our daily business, right in the shadow of the hill, mind you . . . wishing our Chamber of Commerce could devise a way, as effective as this but not as harrowing, to bring such nationwide attention to Louisiana. And now, let's get ready for the Republican convention."[643]

And from the *St. Joseph News-Press:*

> Albany Ledger—We will not hasten to make any jokes about Momo the monster. Described as seven feet tall, hairy all over, possessed of an evil odor, and with immense orange eyes—he could turn out to be one of our relatives with a hangover. Whoever Momo is, he sounds like he would make one helluva pulling guard.[644]

The seriousness that resounded with witnesses' convictions in the veracity of their respective experiences, continued after the Momo sightings ended. For Edgar Harrison especially, thinking about the events that so rattled his family and consumed him for weeks was an effort to understand what exactly had transpired that remarkable summer in Louisiana. During his interview with Steiger, Harrison mused about the possible number of creatures involved.

> . . . But, you know, I've been wondering whether or not it was really a dog that Terry saw. What I mean is, it didn't have anything in its hands when it ran up the bank, but when they looked out the bathroom window and saw it at the top of the hill, it held this something. I was home within 30 minutes and standing where it had been standing. There was no red stuff, no blood or anything on the ground around the stamped-down circle where it stood. I wonder if the thing might not have picked up its young one, then set it down again so they could run away from my place.
>
> Chief Ward: Now, Edgar, don't go saying things like that. I have my hands full looking for one. Now don't go getting me looking for two![645]

Harrison crafted a theory that several or perhaps a family of the creatures had been in the area. He told McWane that he had noticed a black, soot-like substance in areas of suspected creature activity. The abandoned Lincoln schoolhouse, Harrison noted, had an old coal bin in its basement, a potential source of the sooty spots. Harrison further stated that the swell of Momo publicity helped uncover an anecdote of a local boy who had encountered a "big, tall, black, ugly thing" near the Lincoln school in July 1971. The school's basement, Harrison concluded, could have served as a refuge used by the creatures.[646]

Exploring the possibilities of what Momo could be, McWane asked Chief Ward if people could have misconstrued bears for a monster. Ward stated he thought one could simply "just rule a bear out." Any answer to the mystery would have to take into consideration the strange sounds and howls people had heard. "A bear will let out an awful roar, but I will still rule out a bear after all these people heard it. There is a livestock auction barn about five blocks over, and the owner said that on the same Friday night (July 14) that Edgar and others heard the growl, people heard the roar clear up there."[647]

"If there's a bear up in those hills," Harrison added, "you're going to find bear tracks. We've looked these hills over, practically inch by inch, and we've found no bear tracks," he said.

> Chief Ward told Glenn McWane that the first print cast they had made was far too big to be a bear. Edgar Harrison mentioned the names of several people in the area who had discovered footprints on their property.[648]

The idea of a misidentified bear was also commented upon within the pages of the September 1972 *Skylook* magazine, suggesting that a bear may have been seen in a Louisiana neighborhood.

> Shelby Ward, chief of the Louisiana Police department said no bears have been sighted in the county in recent years. However, your editor [Norma Short was *Skylook* Editor & Publisher] heard on a Sedalia, Mo. TV news report that a woman in Louisiana reported seeing a brown bear near her garbage cans, just two blocks from the latest creature report.[649]

Oklahoma City Zoo research director Dr. Hobart Landreth announced on August 3 that the alleged Momo hairs sent to him from Hayden Hewes and Dan Garcia for analysis were "normal looking hairs," explaining that "one is from a dog and the other is either from a bear or a raccoon." Landreth expounded further on the analysis of the hair samples. "It is fairly easy to classify (hair) within an animal group, but pinning down the actual species is a bit more difficult. And the other hair is not in the best shape possible, but we can narrow it down to one of the two animals (bear or raccoon)." The hairs in question had originally been found by Harrison near tracks believed left by Momo.[650]

First it was The Chicken Man which had engaged Lawrence Curtis, now it was Momo's turn. On July 25, the Oklahoma City Zoo's director pronounced casts of Momo tracks as less than inspiring. "It does not seem to be an actual print made by a natural living animal," Curtis said. "It appears to have been made by one of those rubber-type gloves women use to wash dishes with—either that or a snow mitten."

> As to the prints having been made by a rubber glove, in the words of Chief Shelby Ward: "I can't see for the life of me how anyone could tell from a cast whether it had been made from rubber or not."[651]

Ultimately, Curtis deemed the prints he examined as fakes, "and not very good fakes, at that."[652] Curtis' humor that had been evident during the Chicken Man publicity came again to the fore. "We have a cage all ready for him [Momo], and we're willing to put him on exhibit. If he wants to turn himself in, he should know he'll have a nice place to stay, cool in summer and warm in winter, and we'll be glad to feed him whatever he eats. But it really would be better if we could get two. We'd like to raise a few little monsters, too, if we have a chance."[653]

"I think this whole thing in Missouri will turn out to be a hoax," was the assertion of Saul Kitchner, assistant director of Chicago's Lincoln Park Zoo. "A lot of these things turn out that way." Kitchner recalled a certain incident at a zoo in Oklahoma upon the temporary escape of a wallaby. Kangaroo reports started coming in that same day, the small creature's size increasing to "menacing proportions." Kitchner conceded that new animals were continually being discovered but had little confidence in anything left hidden from science on the scale of an 8-foot-tall man-ape. Most new creature discoveries come from the sea, are insects, or new variations of birds, Kitchner maintained. "Look at the Loch Ness sea monster," he said. "With all the money available to spend on it we don't have one good picture of it." Like many who commented on Momo, Kitchner did not disparage the witnesses' sincerity. "I'm quite sure that these people in Missouri believe what they have seen. If you want to see something like this, you will."[654]

Glenn McWane's own visit to Louisiana had convinced him that something had affected the townspeople who witnessed Momo, strange lights, eerie sounds, and repugnant odors. "I don't believe the people in Pike County were suffering from over-worked imaginations. I believe they did smell an odor foreign to them, that they did find unfamiliar footprints, and that they did see an animal alien to their environment." He added, "The majority of these men and women are extremely well-acquainted with the wildlife of their section of Missouri. If the creature had been an animal that belonged, someone surely would have identified it."[655]

Whatever the strangeness that affected the area, McWane believed it was important to explore and explain the events. "I don't know if the Bigfoot-type creatures are deposited here by extraterrestrial UFOnauts to test our environment in the same manner that we might deposit chimpanzees on a planet whose atmosphere we wanted to evaluate in terms of a potential landing. I don't know if Momo is some kind of prehistoric man that comes up from the caves from time to time. (And there are a lot of caves in Pike County, Missouri!) But I do believe that these Bigfoot-type creatures exist and we must discover what they are—and quickly."[656]

Momo, 1973

In an epilogue to 1972's strange events, eastern Missouri, still flush with memories of Momo, experienced a UFO flap in 1973 which recalled the "balls of lights" mentioned by Harrison and others during the previous July. The first sightings of unusual aerial phenomenon came from Piedmont in early 1973. UFOs were reported in April by several Bernie, Missouri, citizens including police officers and the county sheriff. The Bernie UFOs were described as changing color from white to red to green as they moved steadily westward in the sky. Norman Swafford, a professional photographer with flying experience, witnessed and photographed one of the Bernie UFOs. "It has depth, it moves in an irregular manner as if starting and stopping and it changes speeds," he said. Like the lights witnessed in Piedmont, the UFOs spotted in Bernie were seen between 10 and 11 at night.[657] Stoddard County Deputy Sheriff Helen Triplett also saw the lights and described them as moving across the sky in an irregular fashion while they changed colors. Police Chief Gene Bearden believed that declining numbers of reports meant people were getting used to the lights.

Bearden said numerous investigators had visited the Piedmont area representing several UFO study groups, including scientific researchers from SEMO [Southeast Missouri] State University and Dr. J. Allen Hynek, astrophysicist from Northwestern University, Evanston, Ill.

"People have really appreciated the interest Dr. Harley Rutledge from SEMO University has shown in the light," the police chief said. "We hope he can come up with some solution for us."[658]

The August 1973 *Skylook* carried a story titled, "Is Mo Mo Still Around," which focused on a July 13, 1973, article in the *Salem* [Missouri] *News:* "One tall and skinny beast has been reported to be scavenging for food in a brush covered area near Wayne-Dale Trailer Court." Eunice Sutton stated that while talking with her mother and a friend in their front yard on Roosevelt Street about 11:30 Wednesday evening they suddenly noticed a movement in a nearby field. It appeared to Sutton's mother to be an unusually thin bear. Sutton estimated the height of the animal as six feet and she said it was covered with hair. A steak placed in the field where the creature had been sighted was reported gone the next morning.[659]

CHAPTER 4
1973

> In our October 1973 issue (Vol. 6, No.4) [*Pursuit*] I gave an indication of the great numbers of huge, hairy bipeds that have been sighted in the United States during 1973. Since writing that, there have been many more reports which read like something out of some old book on "spooks, hobgoblins and demons!" Have these creatures always been with us—but stayed away from man?[660]
>
> Allen Noe. "And Still the Reports Roll In," *Pursuit* (January 1974).

Print & Film

Sasquatch by Don Hunter

Published in 1973, Don Hunter and René Dahinden's *Sasquatch* is an important period resource that describes Dahinden's quest for truth concerning giant hairy hominids in North America. Hunter explores Dahinden's first searches for hairy hominids in British Columbia, his investigation of the Bossburg tracks (see Chapter 2 for this book's description of Dahinden's role in the Bossburg Cripplefoot tracks), and his presentation of Bigfoot evidence to European officials. Hunter's portrait of Dahinden captures an open and honest man who acknowledges his passionate feelings toward the subject he had utterly devoted his life to:

> "I have my doubts all the time about what I'm doing: I've always had them. It's a lonely place to be, on one side of the fence with the rest of the world on the other side. But it's where I have to stay.

SIGNET•451-Y6642•$1.25 

BIGFOOT,
THE ABOMINABLE SNOWMAN
—AN ANCIENT MYTH...
OR THE "MISSING LINK" IN
MAN'S EVOLUTION?

SASQUATCH

DON HUNTER
with
RENÉ DAHINDEN

8 PAGES OF ASTONISHING PHOTOS,
INCLUDING FRAMES FROM
THE FAMOUS BLUFF CREEK FILM

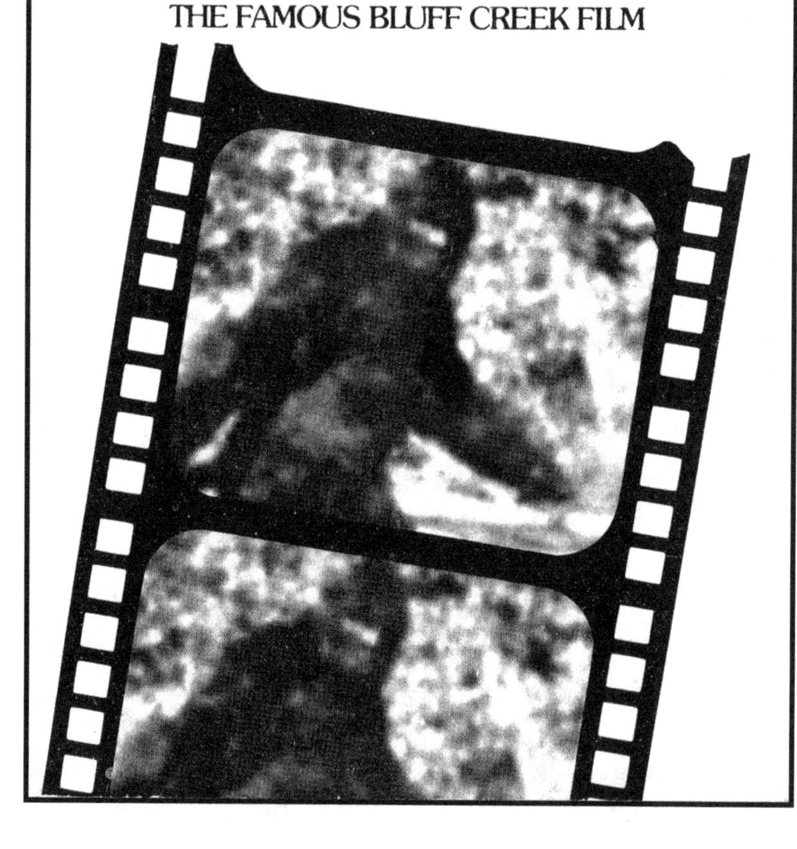

> "I know I won't be able to convince the world by argument, because it doesn't want to be convinced. I just have to keep on going—and I will do—until one of these creatures is collected dead or alive."[661]

Canadian author and outdoorsman Andy Russell described *Sasquatch* as a "fascinating and probing book," in a positive review. Russell added his own thoughts about the enigma, specifically regarding the tracks ascribed to Bigfoot.

> Although my own experience across a wide stretch of what is supposed to be Sasquatch range has revealed nothing, I was not really looking for it with any enthusiasm. Then there were those tracks people were finding from time to time. Were they fakes? If so no individual could have done it, for the casts of the tracks came from widely separated places. They would have to have been made by a secret and well organized group with considerable financing, as Don Hunter points out—a group dedicated to an expensive and elaborate hoax. Something else bothered me as well as other people. All the photos of the casts and tracks that I have seen showed remarkable similarities. All had flat arches and distinctively shaped heels, details of structure that would be highly unlikely if individuals had manufactured them by one means or another. After all, tracks 18 inches long in six-foot strides in ground requiring the pressure of much weight, over widely separated locations on rugged country, would require some elaborate preparations and mechanical aids that would have drawn attention. Furthermore in some locations they would have been impossible.[662]

BIGFOOT: THE YETI AND SASQUATCH IN MYTH AND REALITY, BY JOHN NAPIER

Primatologist John R. Napier was one of the first scientists to regard Bigfoot as more than a simple hoax or waste of time. Napier had a significant role in the BBC's *Bigfoot: America's Abominable Snowman*, he was involved in the Iceman affair (see Chapter 2), and with other European scientists was visited by Dahinden (see Chapter 2) during his European tour presenting his evidence in support for Bigfoot.

Early in his career, Napier developed an interest in functional hand and foot anatomy which led him to author, collaboratively with other scientific luminaries such as Louis Leakey, taxonomic monographs on paleoanthropological topics. As he undertook the writing of *Bigfoot: The Yeti and Sasquatch in Myth and Reality*, he reached out to his contemporaries who were also interested in the Bigfoot enigma. Grover Krantz responded to Napier and provided "transparencies" of hoaxed footprints for Napier's consideration. On August 17, 1971, Napier wrote Krantz with both thanks and praise for a fellow scientist willing to look at the evidence.

> Dear Dr. Krantz
> It was most kind of you to send me the three transparencies of fake footprints. I hear from Jim McClarin that you are currently engaged on an analysis of Bigfoot prints. As perhaps you may know, I have been interested in feet, footprints and walking patterns for years but I must admit that Bigfoot prints have really given me a headache. I see three kinds, which I have called the 'Hourglass,' the Backscratcher' and the 'Humanoid' (e.g. Bossburg). The Backscratcher has 5 toes of *equal* width and the hourglass has a high lateral arch and toes which all appear to flex at take off; it also has high energetic kink behind the big toe. To me, none of the footprints suggest heel-toe walking which is one of the reasons why I find Patterson's film so unacceptable; his creature *was* heel-toe striding.
>
> My book (called "Bigfoot" will I hope be published in the U.K. in the spring of 1972 and in the U.S. a few months later), deals with the idea of giant hominoids rather than, specifically, Sasquatch. If anything, I have concentrated more on the Yeti.
>
> Your transparencies, I must say, are more convincing than some of the fake footprints I have seen but, of course, they lack the dynamic quality of a real print. This criticism applies to many of the Bluff Creek, Onion Mountain and Blue Creek pictures too. I am not convinced about the Sasquatch although I certainly couldn't prove its non-existence. I am not a "scoffer" but equally I am not a "believer."
>
> Sincerely, with thanks,
> John Napier[663]

One of the first things noticed about Napier's book is the prominent use of the term Bigfoot, subsuming other common appellations like Yeti and Sasquatch; the name Bigfoot was becoming the go-to, one-stop title

BIGFOOT
THE YETI AND SASQUATCH IN
MYTH AND REALITY
JOHN NAPIER

for North American, and particularly American, bipedal and hairy man-like creatures. "Bigfoot, the living animal, if it exists must be part of nature," wrote Napier. "Bigfoot, the legend, which undeniably exists, is part of human culture."[664] Napier looked at both the physical evidence and the cultural record of Bigfoot. There are grainy photographs of Bigfoot, yes; a controversial film, granted; and an ever-growing body of eyewitness testimony, all true. But Napier pointed out the physical evidence is not corroborated by a body or skeleton. "Cultural evidence concerns what people think, write and say about Bigfoot. The material components are the eyewitness accounts which are the real lifeblood of the Bigfoot phenomenon. Without this type of human involvement, the affair would never have got off the ground."[665]

For Napier, footprints ranked high in the catalog of physical evidence; the historically important tracks included in *Bigfoot* were those discovered by Eric Shipton in the Himalayas in 1951 and the Bossburg prints whose authenticity remained unsubstantiated, but in Napier's consideration, still feasible. The cultural evidence consisting of written records, stories, and legends was certainly expanding with an acknowledged constraint: people write and talk and think in known and understood terms. Bigfoot, so inscrutable a subject, was often consigned to nebulous descriptions and shadowy tales.

Consideration was given in *Bigfoot* to modern events in America's hairy hominid experience. Napier discussed Frank Hansen's Iceman which had garnered so much attention and notoriety and which Napier labelled a "Hollywood-made fabrication of synthetic materials."[666] At the onset of writing his book, Napier contacted British primatologist William Charles Osman-Hill, who suggested Napier contact the Tom Slick estate for a report relating to findings and results from the Slick-funded expedition, which, Osman-Hill was aware, had never been published. Napier reached out to the estate, assuring trustees that as a researcher, "my feet are—by upbringing—firmly on the ground." A return letter from the Independent Executor for Tom Slick's estate was sanguine but when a follow-on package of materials followed, the report alluded to by Osman-Hill was not part of its contents. Napier wrote the trustees, bringing to their attention the omission of the desired report. Their response contained in part, "We regret we cannot furnish the information requested." Napier replied and asked for specific photos. The trustees responded that due to interests of other participants in the Tom Slick expedition, Napier's request could not be fulfilled. Napier wrote back,

> The late Mr. Tom Slick, like so many other enthusiasts of this phenomena, often expressed his disappointment that scientists

> in official standing did not bother to interest themselves in the Abominable Snowman or Bigfoot affair. Yet when I, as a reputable, internationally known scientist in the field of primate and human evolution, request simple *factual* information you deny it to me. [Napier's italics][667]

The requested materials never arrived, leading Napier to exclaim with signs of exasperation, "It has proved difficult to find out exactly what the Slick Expedition *did* [Napier's italics] find."[668]

Despite the absence of data from the Slick foundation, Napier persevered with writing *Bigfoot: The Yeti and Sasquatch in Myth and Reality* and its publication in 1973 generally earned positive reviews, many of which acknowledged that a credentialed scientist took the time to give the subject serious attention. Excerpts from two admiring reviews follow:

> Napier's romp through Bigfoot lore and his thoughtful analysis make this little book hard to lay aside without finishing. He may alienate Yeti buffs with his jab at their favorite myth and his open-mindedness about the Sasquatch may leave skeptics unconvinced, but there is no more intelligent or rewarding discussion of such matters available today.[669]

> "Bigfoot" is the most authoritative book yet written about the creature for whom no bones have been found. Napier relates its history from discovery of the first footprint in America in 1811, and in Asia in 1832, to the many prints and sightings in recent years. He sifts the evidence with careful scientific analysis.[670]

Books targeted at younger readers became popular works at libraries and bookmobiles, frequently enjoying checked-out status. Hal G. Evarts' *Bigfoot* (1973) and the previous year's *A Darkness of Giants* by Allan Bosworth were both set in the northwest woods exploring the experiences of kids on expeditions to answer the Bigfoot mystery.

Bigfoot on TV

Children's television fare through the '70s proved a reliable source for Bigfoot content, featuring hairy hominids as either a main or supporting character. Starting in 1973, a cooperative effort between the Council of

Better Business Bureaus and the National Broadcasting Company produced a series of 30-second children-oriented TV spots dealing with a variety of topics. "It is self-evident that today's children are tomorrow's consumers," said William Tankersley, Executive Vice President of the Council of Better Business Bureaus. The spots featured the Ritts Puppets, including the Abominable Snowman who starred in a spot devoted to the benefits of saving money as an alternative to spending.[671] Another hairy hominid starred in *Zoo Robbery*, a British children's television show about a group of kids on the Regent's Canal in London trying to rescue a Yeti kidnapped from the zoo.

Schlock!

Independent film companies proved the mainstay for Bigfoot movies in the '70s. A case in point is *Schlock!* which is not only John Landis' directorial debut, but in which he also donned costume and makeup to portray the Shlockthropus, a last-of-its-kind creature that emerges from its cave to explore the modern world of the early '70s. One moment goofy and the next murderous, Landis' monster repeatedly breaks the fourth wall to cast a knowing nod to the audience in this convention-breaking, low-budget guerrilla comedy.

The Legend of Boggy Creek

By far the most successful and influential movie from the early '70s' Bigfoot film canon was first-time filmmaker Charles Pierce's *The Legend of Boggy Creek*. Opening in late 1972 (see Chapter 3) the movie continued to conquer box office records and scare audiences into and beyond 1973 with its portrayal of Louisiana's Fouke Monster. Re-released several times during the rest of the '70s, *Legend* inspired, frightened, and entertained a generation. Bigfoot researcher and scholar Daniel Perez told this author that his introduction to Bigfoot was "entirely due" to Boggy Creek which he saw with his older brother and sister when he was about ten years old. "To say it had a huge impact on the direction of my life would be an understatement."[672]

Pierce apparently didn't know the numbers behind filmmaking in the U.S., and as it pertained to one of the seminal Bigfoot films of the '70s, or any decade, it was probably for the best. When he took his cameras and crew to Fouke, Arkansas, only 11 percent of motion pictures released in America ever showed a profit. Pierce said he wasn't aware of such facts and the concomitant risks. "If I had," he bluntly admitted, "it would have scared me to death and I probably would have laid an egg."

Reportedly made at a cost of $160,000, *The Legend of Boggy Creek* grossed between $10 and $11 million in its first two months in 1972. Toward the latter half of February 1973, *Legend* had been shown in 117 cities and in 111 of those *Legend* broke first-run box-office records. On March 7, *Legend* was slated to open at 62 theaters in Los Angeles County—the largest opening day in L.A. history.[673]

Pierce described his film as, "not quite a documentary, not quite a horror film. . . . I guarantee that we'll bring the people up out of their seats a few times and make their hair stand on end. It scares the kids in a good way, and it's funny in places. It's a good, wholesome audience participation film." Pierce believed the runaway success of his movie centered on virtues ingrained in both approach and final product. "It proves," he said, "that you can still make a film that entertains the entire family, without sex, violence or blood, and still make an honest dollar. A fellow named Walt Disney did pretty well with this type of film." Pierce received lavish praise for the sumptuous cinematography in the film; he called the Fouke area, "incredibly beautiful . . . one of the last great wildernesses in this country."[674]

Pierce, a native of Hampton, Arkansas, had been exposed to stories of the area's mysterious hominid creature. "I'd heard about the Boggy Monster for 15 years," he said, "and motion pictures had always fascinated me, so I asked a friend to put up the money to do a film on the subject." That friend was L. W. Ledwell, a wealthy truck trailer manufacturer from Texarkana, Texas, whose financial backing, it was reported, garnered him a 50 per cent interest in the film. "We thought maybe we might get our money back," Pierce stated. "We had no idea at all that it would take off like it has." Earl Smith, writer of the screenplay, also did well, earning five per cent of the gross. Though Pierce had heard tales and yarns about the Fouke Monster for years, inspiration for the film came during a serendipitous and propitious moment when he realized just how widespread the Fouke Monster's fame had spread.

> Pierce was running an advertising agency in Texarkana four years ago when he began listening to stories of a man-like creature spotted near Fouke, about 14 miles from Texarkana. He scoffed at the stories and didn't think much about them.
>
> When a friend, Earl C. Smith, told Pierce he had written a low-budget western, he and Pierce traveled to Los Angeles in search of financing and actors. As they were driving down an

> L.A. boulevard, they spotted a teen-ager wearing a T-shirt with the inscription: "Save the Fouke Monster."
>
> "We stopped the car and got out and talked to the kid," Pierce said. "And I told Earl, 'Let's head back home. If this thing has attracted this much attention, that's what we'll make our movie about.'"[675]

Pierce said his initial total cost estimate of $25,000 "didn't even pay for the raw film." Shaving costs where he could, Pierce borrowed a camera in Jackson Hole, Wyoming, lights in Texarkana, and other equipment in Shreveport, Louisiana. As a production technique, Pierce's use of actual Fouke residents in the cast immediately became famous. "Not one of them had ever seen a movie camera before," Pierce recalled. "People asked me how I was going to get these people to act, but of course the secret was that they didn't act at all. We weren't Hollywooding it up, so we were able to get them to behave naturally."

Novice if not novel approaches to filmmaking extended to post-production. Pierce recalled for the *Spartanburg Herald's* Tom Butler that he "didn't have a clue about how to get it shown anywhere. . . . I called a theater in Texarkana to ask if they'd run it, but their headquarters in Shreveport wouldn't agree unless they could see it. And I didn't have enough money to fly there on spec."[676] This introduces the subject of the movie's premiere date and location. Butler continued his record of Pierce's early efforts to get the movie in front of audiences: Pierce stated that after searching for a venue to show his film, he finally found a 500-seat Dallas theater rentable for $3,600 a week. As mentioned above, it appears at some point Pierce intended *Legend's* premiere to occur in Texarkana. Local advertising coincident with hometown openings spawned several claims of the movie's premiere. The "world premiere," according to Baton Rouge's *State-Times*, was to occur on August 18, 1972, at Shreveport's Strand Theater, as announced by the Shreveport-Bossier Convention and Tourist Bureau.[677] A movie advertisement in the August 24, 1972, *Ruston Daily Leader* stated the "World Premier Engagement" for the *Legend of Boggy Creek* started that day. Nearly two weeks prior, an article in the August 12 *Camden Daily News* began, "'The Legend of Boggy Creek,' a sensitive action documentary, of an alleged 'monster' who terrorizes the area around Fouke, Ark., will have its world premiere in Texarkana August 17, prior to national distribution."[678] Copley News Service writer Ruby Sexton seconds this: "The movie had its 'world premiere' in Pierce's home town of Texarkana, 14 miles from Fouke, in a newly reopened theater which he rented for showing his single print."[679] In the authoritative book by Lyle Blackburn, *The Beast of Boggy Creek*, the movie premiered on August 18.[680] What is not in contention is the incredible success the movie met with. "In two weeks," Pierce fondly recalled, "we grossed $55,000. Then we moved on to Shreveport and grossed $49,000 in two weeks there. I saw people eat sack lunches while waiting in line to see it."[681]

"Every setting," Pierce said of the film's locations around the Sulphur River bottom near Fouke, "has been close to Boggy Creek or one of its tributaries." Pierce believed the 45-square-mile wilderness surrounding the river bottoms, lush with honey locust, mesquite, eastern and red cedar, wild plum, and hickory, was prime habitat for the creature. "I think he lives in the Sulphur River bottoms and periodically works his way up Boggy Creek. It is usually in spring and late summer when the Sulphur River is flooding that the creature is [sighted]," he said.[682]

Though Pierce had never seen the shadowy hominid beast himself, he suggested he may have heard its wailing scream. "I didn't much believe in the Fouke creature when I started making the picture. I got about half way through and actually heard him scream and started believing. The more we studied the creature and worked on the movie, the more firm my beliefs became that there was something there," he said. Pierce shied away from calling the creature a 'monster,' stating, "I don't believe in monsters." Monster or not, Pierce did acknowledge that the stories, rumors, and testimonies pointed to something quite tangible. "There is something there," he said. While conducting research, Pierce heard of only one account of a dog chasing after the creature. More often, hunting dogs brought to the area refused to track the beast. "This proves a point. The only thing a good hunting dog won't track is a man," said Pierce.[683] When asked for his thoughts on what the creature's identity could be, Pierce said, "The people in Fouke don't believe in the Fouke monster. They believe as I do, and as scientists and mammologists believe . . . that there is a wild man living in the Sulphur River bottoms. We believe that he is from a generation of a Wildman family that has lived in there for years. We think he's one of the last left."[684]

While gathering background material, Pierce said he collected information from about 250 sightings which provided a fairly uniform description of the creature: it stood about six feet tall and weighed 250 pounds. Always bipedal, its chest and shoulders were wide, the hips were narrower, and it was completely covered in a coat of hair. "This massive amount of hair on his body may make the creature look heavier and larger than he actually is," Pierce suggested.[685]

One playful critic, skeptical of a monster haunting the Fouke countryside and the Sulphur River bottomlands, suggested the monster hoopla resulted from an escaped linebacker from Frank Broyles' University of Arkansas Razorbacks. Freelance writer Fred Wright wrote a positive review for *Legend of Boggy Creek:*

> Several hundred screaming youngsters can't be wrong.
>
> Yet one is hard put to label and identify the success factors in Charles B. Pierce's "The Legend of Boggy Creek."
>
> Pierce, with years of TV production experience, makes his first film a near one-man effort. He produces, directs and photographs this home-spun story of [a] rural monster.
>
> The monster hails from Fouke, Ark., and folks thereabouts have been seeing, sometimes shooting and generally running from this monster for some time now.
>
> Pierce pointedly avoids any time factor in his film; we don't know how recent all these events are supposed to be.
>
> But by using Fouke folk and some stunning bayou photography, Pierce makes a movie we somehow feel compelled to watch.
>
> There is very little acting here, and some sloppy staging.
>
> The monster is never fully seen, and its roar is nowhere near as blood-chilling as radio advertisements would have you believe.
>
> But doggone it, a hairy hand thrust through a broken window does make us start, and scream, and since the monster tends to go visitin' houses full of skittery females, there's much screaming indeed.
>
> Pierce and company do build suspense, and while we know all along no one's going to get really hurt by the Fouke Monster (else how could the film have that G rating?), we know he's going to keep popping up and scaring the bejabbers out of people.
>
> Even the repetition of situations—hunters caught unawares, women alone at night, etc.—work in the film's favor.
>
> The monster comes close to becoming a folk hero (but not a Fouke hero), because he's big, shaggy and mysterious.
>
> In all of us there's that element of curiosity and fear about the unknown, and a holdover from every childhood, that fear of unseen, unknown, unimaginable monsters.

So here we have a real, honest-to-goodness monster, and we can go right ahead and scream along with hundreds of others, exorcising, perhaps, those primordial fears that may somehow still lurk in the corners of our minds.

Truly, the monster of Boggy Creek boggs the mind. He comes creeping out of the bottom lands around Fouke, and while our sophistication makes us a bit unbelieving, we want to believe, we want to be scared.

There's something about the thought that there may really be a creature without a name or label, like the Loch Ness monster, out there somewhere avoiding man and civilization.

Pierce deserves credit for tapping this reservoir of potential empathy, and for some really outstanding photography that helps overcome the camera shadows, and wagging mikes that otherwise mar the professionalism of this film.

It's a credit, too, that "The Legend of Boggy Creek" is such a one-man effort, shot for around $160,000.

More of this type of film-making certainly should be done, and perhaps will be, judging from the box office success Pierce's effort is having.[686]

In contrast to Wright's appraisal, Tommy Toles, City Editor at the *Rome News-Tribune* (Rome, Georgia), provided a different take on *Legend:*

Movie, *The Legend of Boggy Creek;* theater, Desoto; violence, very little; sex, none; nudity, none; language, clean; code rating, general audiences.

The producers of "The Legend of Boggy Creek" have ruined a good 10-minute documentary with a 1 ½ hour movie. It's [sic] only redeeming feature is that it is clean. But who's interested in clean vapidness?

As nearly as can be determined, the "true" movie is about a legendary "monster" in the vicinity of Fouke, Ark. Specifically the Boggy Creek bottoms. The hairy beast, which resembles an over-weight King Kong, is recreated for the movie.

And since many of the people who actually are supposed to have encountered the beast play themselves in the movie, the quality of acting is horrible with the exception of a couple of spots.

> Viewers receive a graduate-level education in identification of tree limbs. Each time the action lets up—which is most of the time—director-photographer-producer Charles B. Pierce turns the camera lense [sic] on twigs, flowers, bees, birds or limbs.
>
> Generally, the photography is poor and the film quality it worse. There are a few fairly good shots of scenery around Boggy Creek but they are indeed few.
>
> The exaggerated narrative is another low point of the film. The songs are simply atrocious, especially the one about "Travis Crabtree."
>
> The only really exciting part of the movie is near the end, which, is sad because most viewers are already asleep. The nocturnal visit of the "monster" to a lonely house containing two couples and a couple of visiting relatives is not frightening—albeit exciting—as was intended, but merely ridiculous.[687]

The State Editor of the *Shreveport Times*, Norman Richardson, long an interested party in local monster sightings and a dependable chronicler of "It," (see chapter 2) chose to see for himself if he could coax his own encounter with the area's legendary denizen.

> I drove on roads that haven't seen a car in years and I walked through woods which I'm sure no human foot has never stepped. I even called out to Big Foot, explaining I was his friend and was well acquainted with his monster cousin "It" that roams the woods near Fouke . . . but all I received in return was a curious look from a scared bunny rabbit.
>
> This adventure began to take shape a few weeks ago when I figured that maybe Big Foot, which has been "seen" around DeSoto Parish for some 15 years, was probably related to "It" in some way. Too, I figured the odds of a friendly meeting were in my favor since I have been following the varied career of "It" for so long.
>
> So, loaded with camera equipped with a telephoto lens, and a pistol (why a weapon I don't know since I can't hit anything with it anyway) I set forth.
>
> Suffice it to say that the whole thing was a waste of time outside of getting a first hand look at Mother Nature slowly changing her colors.[688]

In the wake of the movie's fantastic popularity, many people, like Richardson, wanted to learn more about the Fouke Monster. *The Legend of Boggy Creek* touched a collective nerve and instigated a flood of inquiries sent to Fouke, the natural epicenter of monster inquest. Fouke's tourism boomed as both the curious and the deadly serious visited the town to learn more about the monster and maybe even catch a gander of it for themselves.

> One year after the movie premiered residents of this small community [Fouke], population 506, are beginning to realize that the movie could have bolstered the town's economy if they only had acted sooner.
>
> "Lots of people here in Fouke have missed the boat by not taking advantage of the publicity we have received and expanded on the monster theme," said Mayor J.D. Larey of Fouke. "A novelty shop might have been the thing to bring in more money from tourists. But the people here just didn't realize what they had when the iron was hot." . . .
>
> One man who was involved in financial arrangements for the movie shared Larey's opinion. "None of us dreamed that the darned thing would make the money that it did," he said. "The man who made the movie had never made a movie in his life. The guy who backed the movies had never backed a movie in his life. The people who acted in the movie had never acted before in their lives. I don't think you could have foreseen anything happening on it."[689]

In August 1973, Mayor Larey stated he received several long-distance telephone calls and 3 to 12 letters each day concerning the monster. Sometimes a letter was addressed directly to the Fouke Monster itself. The volume of mail demanded certain protocols which resulted in all monster mail directed to the mayor.

> One such letter addressed to the "Boggy Creek Monster, Fouke, Ark." was from a young girl who said the film was "a real neat movie."
>
> Another letter, addressed to the "Mayor—Or any City Official, Fouke, Ark." was from a member of the volunteer fire department in Martinsburg, W. Va.

> The man inquired about the monster's habitat, size and identity. The fireman said he also would "like to have some pictures of the monster." He promised to keep the information "confidential."
>
> Fouke residents say it is not unusual for a tourist to stop in their town to hunt for the creature in the swamp along Boggy Creek.[690]

Soaking in the monster mood in Bill Williams' Boggy Creek Café, reporter Debra Hale listened to a customer's tale of a man wandering through the swamps conspicuously armed with a knife. He said he was hunting for the beast and mentioned he had recently discovered claw marks on a tree which he attributed to the creature. "I just laughed at him," the customer recounted. "He got mad."

Larey told Hale that one of the recent phone calls he received was from three Green Berets from Virginia asking if they could search for the Fouke Monster during their summer leave. Larey's advice to them was to wait until deer hunting season. "I was afraid the game warden would pick them up," he said. Hale reported the Miller County sheriff's department forbade hunting the Fouke Monster with guns, except during deer season, thus limiting the possibility of an accidental shooting.

The Boggy Creek Café offered "Boggy Creek Breakfast," "Three-Toed Sandwiches," and a dessert of waffle cone and ice cream called the "Boggy Creek Delight." If not Larey's envisioned novelty shop mentioned above, the Café did have assorted items and knickknacks for sale including money clips, key chains, and bumper stickers with "Home of the Fouke Monster" written on them. The jukebox even offered a Bobby Picket version of "Monster Mash." Interested patrons could obtain a reproduced print of the monster's foot. Though smaller than the monster's actual 5-inch-wide, 14-inch-long track, the souvenir version came autographed by both Willie E. Smith, owner of the Fouke garage and on whose property tracks had been discovered, and Fouke resident Smokey Crabtree, who starred in *The Legend of Boggy Creek* and authored *Smokey and the Fouke Monster* published in 1974. Mrs. Williams estimated 20-25 tourists stopped by the Café daily. "I believe there's something out there. From the way the people I have talked to described it, I think it's a gorilla-like animal," she said.

"Smith," an insurance salesman, told Hale he had seen the creature several times near his house close by the bank of Boggy Creek. "First time I saw him back in 1955, I thought he was a man. I shot at him 15 times with an

SMOKEY and THE FOUKE MONSTER

A TRUE STORY
BY
SMOKEY CRABTREE

Army rifle, but missed him," said Smith. "Next time he came up behind the house throwing chunks at my dog," Smith recalled. "So, I shot through the brush and missed him again. The third time my wife was working on the TV when I heard him. He slapped my dog across the porch into the screen door." Smith shot again and again, and missed. Two weeks before Hale interviewed Smith, locals had heard what they believed was the creature. "He was roaring and cutting up and sounding like a crazy man," Smith said. Smith told Hale he believed the creature was a vegetarian and shared his theory about the monster: "I believe it is a Sasquatch," Smith stated. "It's the next thing to a human."

The gas station next to the Café also sold souvenirs. Proprietors claimed they received more monster-based questions each week than gasoline sales. A young Fouke resident who saw the monster's revenue potential was 12-year-old Perry Parker, whose family owned the house Bobby Ford and his family occupied when the monster attacked Ford. "Back when that happened to the Fords, cars were lined up with people hunting for the monster," the youth said. Parker told Hale that his family had to put barbed wire around the house to keep out unwanted trespassers lured to the location by *The Legend of Boggy Creek*. "I make a lot of money off it," Parker said. "I'm going to put a sign up for guided tours and charge about a dollar per carload."

> Perry and his brother, Richard, 15, live with their mother and step-father, Mr. and Mrs. Joe Simmons, who own the 79-year-old house.
>
> Perry said in the past most tourists voluntarily had paid him—some up to $5—for a look at the house and swamp behind it.
>
> The house in the movie, however, was not the real one, but a similar one in Texarkana. The Simmons refused to allow the house to be filmed because, according to Perry, they didn't think $2,000 was enough money for such a project.
>
> Behind the white and green house is a vegetable garden.
>
> "People see the corn knocked down in the fields because the coons got in and ate it," Perry laughed. "They think the monster ate it!"
>
> Perry said he makes about $20 per week on the guided tours. "I hate to take the money," the youngster said, but conceded that he probably would continue taking it.

> He said he had met tourists from as far away as Montana and Ohio.
>
> Just as he was accepting a dollar from one tourist, in fact, two carloads of sight-seers drove up.
>
> The group said they had driven 178 miles from Monroe, La., to get a glimpse of the legendary house.
>
> As Perry said, "The movie has put Fouke on the map."[691]

In Pierce's estimation, if there was a downside to the spotlight the movie cast upon the creature, it was the swarms of people that descended upon Fouke and the surrounding area who styled themselves as monster hunters hoping to bag the ultimate catch. "I believe there is a strong possibility that he will be killed because all the people in the area are on the lookout for him and most of them carry guns," he said. With perhaps a hint of romanticism, Pierce hoped the riddle to the creature would one day be definitively answered. "Sometime in the future I would like to go back in there and find out the truth of what he really is," Pierce stated.[692]

The Legend of Boggy Creek placed not just Fouke, but also the surrounding region on the map as a hotspot for hairy giants. While the movie broke box office records, several area Bigfoot sightings, such as in Pine Bluff, Arkansas, added to the Boggy Creek monster's notoriety. And additional creature sightings continued to emanate out of Fouke.

> "It," as most everyone familiar with monster hunting knows, is supposed to be a big [hairy], man-like creature standing 7 to 10 feet tall, has glowing red eyes—has been spotted in the Fouke area for years, and is possibly a relative to a monster dubbed "Bigfoot" who has been "seen" in DeSoto Parish for some 15 years.
>
> Anyway, there may be two of them now around Fouke since a smaller version of the legendary Fouke monster was reportedly seen over the weekend [24-25 November].[693]

> Orville Scoggins, a farmer who has scoffed at tales of a Fouke monster, now believes that something—maybe not a monster—but something stalks the woods near Fouke.
>
> Scoggins, 67, said he, his son, and grandson saw the creature in his field Sunday morning [November 25]. He said the "monster" was about four feet tall, stood upright and had "long pitch black hair."

> A spokesman for the Milller County Sheriff's office said Monday that the report is not being pursued.
>
> Scoggins told Fouke constable Ernest Walraven that the three were helping one of his cows deliver a calf about 7:30 A.M. when he heard several cows bellowing.
>
> "I looked up to see what the noise was and there it was about 100 yards away, walking to the east," he said.
>
> The owner and manager of Boggy Creek café [sic] in Fouke, Billy Williams, who is a friend of Scoggins, said, "Orville was always one of our worst believers. He always made fun of the Fouke monster"—before Sunday, that is.[694]

Grover Krantz (1973)

A March 1973 AP article stated Grover Krantz stopped short of considering himself a myopically-devoted believer in North American hairy giants; he openly acknowledged that at least on the surface, the very idea of Bigfoot as an extant creature of North America sounded silly. "But there is too much evidence," he said, "that can't be explained any other way." But scientists gave little to no credence to hirsute hominids coexisting alongside modern man and largely avoided examining the evidence. Krantz pointed out he *did* spend time on Bigfoot evidence.[695] "Several hundred people have reported sightings just in the last century alone," Krantz said. "Possibly 10 times as many have failed to report sightings to newsmen or law officers, for fear of ridicule. But if this animal really exists, it would probably be man's closest living relative and a member of the zoological family Hominidae."[696]

Enjoying a correspondence with others interested in the study of the Bigfoot enigma gave Krantz a special look into his contemporaries' views and opinions. From a letter dated January 24, 1973, Bernard Heuvelmans, who assigned credibility to Frank Hansen's Iceman, shared with Krantz his less-than sanguine regard for the Patterson-Gimlin film.

> To justify my opinion on the Patterson film I am sending you herewith enclosed a summary of my reasons. And there is a lot more to say, but unfortunately I do not own a copy of the film, but if you do, you could check some of the following points.
>
> *First.* There is something unusual (or new?) in the hair pattern of the face (apes and monkeys never have the whole

face covered with hair, except around the eyes, and men never have hair on their foreheads). This might of course be the case in ape-man (how would we know?), but this creature looks exactly like a man wearing a nylon-fur mask with just a slit showing the eyes and the upper part of the nose.

Secondly. Please check whether the palm of the hands is as naked as it should be.

Thirdly. Please check whether the fingers can be seen as separate units, as they are normally seen in apes or men when moving along. If they cannot be, this would confirm my suspicion that they are enclosed in mittens.

If the hair pattern of the face looks normal to you, if the palms are naked and if the fingers show, this would not mean that the depicted creature is a real Omah. But if one or more of these three points turns out to be negative, it would add more weight to the evidence con, which in my opinion is already sufficient.

I would be very pleased to have your own comments on all this. I keep an open mind, and I am quite ready to change my mind if you can help me to sweep away my doubts.[697]

Krantz regarded the Patterson-Gimlin film quite differently from his colleague, assessing the footage genuinely captured a living Bigfoot striding across a creek bed in 1967. Krantz wrote back to Heuvelmans with his points in favor of the film's authenticity. A chastened Heuvelmans responded in a letter dated September 13, 1973:

Dear Dr. Krantz
Everything you say about the Patterson film is so sensible that I now have doubts about my doubts. I cannot say that I am quite convinced, but at least I will from now on refrain from labelling the film as a blatant hoax. When Dr. Marie Joanne Koffman spent several months in France we met very often and have had long conservations about our research, and she also made some good points in favour of the film's authenticity. So I will provisionally consider it just as a dubious document, possibly based on a real Bigfoot, possibly based on a faked one. Let us keep an open mind.[698]

Heuvelmans likewise also endeavored to champion his beliefs and positions, one of which was very pro-Iceman (based upon his examination and study of the Iceman, Heuvelmans co-authored *L'homme de Néanderthal est Toujours Vivant* with Boris Porchnev*);* he wrote to Krantz:

> Nobody understands better than I your reluctance to accept the Neanderthal hypothesis. I have been thinking just like you for years: I have had endless arguments with Porshnev about this. You should see the letters we exchanged! But when once I was faced with a frozen specimen of a Neanderthal Man, I had to change my mind. I examined it very carefully for three days, and later on spent two whole years studying the numerous photographs I took of the corpse. I will not try to convince you now—it would take me several hundreds of pages, in fact the book that I just wrote—but until you will have a chance of reading this book, you can take my word for it: there cannot be the slightest doubt that there is a Neandethal Man of a very specialized type.[699]

Ron Olson

"I believe in it," Ron Olson said. "I believe in it as firmly as I believe that I'm sitting here saying it. It's like a religion to me." By 1973, the 31-year-old Olson, head of the North American Wildlife Research Association (also referred to as the North American Wildlife Research Organization (NAWRO)), had dedicated five years of his life to the study and promotion of Bigfoot. Sitting down with reporter Doug Bates, Olson discussed his eagerness to use automation and computer power to analyze Bigfoot sightings. This interest characterized an emerging and growing application of technology in the quest to study Bigfoot.

> The computer is being used to search for Bigfoot by spotlighting longitudes and latitudes where sightings seem to be occurring with greatest frequency. It has enabled NAWRO to identify certain areas where there seem to have been many more or less reliable observations and assign men to stand by to see whether pictures or actual specimens of Bigfoot might be obtained. The computer has analyzed the sightings as related to time of the year as well. There were high hopes last June because Bigfoot

> has been reported every June for four years in a certain area. A whole group of watchers went out last June, but, alas, no Sasquatch.[700]

Olson's computer-driven data analysis joined such innovations as Biscardi and Findley's employment of a thermal detection device (more on this device below) and, as popularly proposed by several researchers, the use of radio telemetry devices to track a transmitter-tagged Bigfoot.

> Olson and a team of several dozen volunteers throughout the Northwest are cooperating with Big Foot hunters in British Columbia in programming a computer with data collected since the early 1800s, when white settlers began hearing the legend from Northwest Indians. By weeding out hundreds of apparently fraudulent or mistaken Big Foot sightings, Olson says, the researchers hope the computer study will spew out a pattern indicating the creature's migratory behavior, feeding habits, population density and so forth.

"I might be able to tell you someday that we figure on June 1, 1976, or some such specific date, that at this certain point on the map, at this longitude and this latitude, there's going to be a Sasquatch pass through," Olson said.

Bates described Olson as a man who "dresses conservatively, goes to church, votes Republican, keeps his lawn mowed and lives in a typical house in a typical Springfield neighborhood." At the heart of Bates' article was why and how a man of Olson's age and attributes pursued something that many people believed did not exist. Olson first heard of Bigfoot as a 12-year-old student at Goshen Elementary School, in Eugene, Oregon, where he read a newspaper story about enormous human-like tracks discovered around a diesel tractor left on a forest road.[701] "I was really intrigued, but I didn't think much about the story and I didn't pursue it," Olson recalled. "At that time I don't really feel I could say I was a believer." Bigfoot remained a tale, a backwoods fable as Olson went on to Pleasant Hill High School.

Olson attended Southwestern Oregon Community College for a few terms before he did a year at the University of Oregon. He pursued liberal arts courses, Olson recalled, "hopefully to find a field I really wanted to pursue, but it just wasn't there." Leaving college, Olson served in the Army between 1964 through 1966, including time in Vietnam.

While Olson was in the Army, his father became involved in a film distribution company, American National Enterprises, Inc., of Salt Lake City. "When I came back from the Army," Olson said, "I went right into the family's film business." Olson traveled throughout the country, showing family-oriented wildlife documentaries like *Alaskan Safari* and *Cougar Country*. Beginning in 1966, Olson's income came primarily from the distribution, promotion, and showing of films. "It was in 1968," Olson recalled, "I was on the road showing *Alaskan Safari*, when an odd coincidence occurred. While my brothers were showing the same film in Ohio, I was working up through the Carolinas. All the way through North Carolina, I talked with the man who was company president at that time about how rough the competition was getting. Finally, he said to me, 'Ron, what kind of a wildlife film could we pick out that nobody could compete with?' Then I remembered those stories I had heard in Oregon, and I suggested the subject of Sasquatch to him. He said 'What's that?'—and we got to talking about it." Olson and the executive decided to make a Sasquatch documentary if any footage of the creature should become available.

Not long after that decision was reached serendipity presented Olson his golden opportunity. "My brother called me in February from Cincinnati and said, 'Ron, pick up the *Argosy* magazine.' So I went out and bought one, and there it was: The whole story of how this guy in Yakima, Wash., made a film of a Sasquatch in Northern California. I got right on the phone, called him up and arranged a rendezvous in Yakima to set up a deal."

Olson wasn't necessarily a hairy hominid believer as he hammered out details with Roger Patterson; his motivation was to market a profitable documentary film. "A lot of things went up and down for a while—problems with company board members saying, 'Gee, this thing is too far out and we don't want to put the money up for that kind of film.' But I tested Patterson's footage on movie audiences and found the subject to be as strong as I predicted it would be," Olson said. The Patterson-Gimlin film worked well not only on test audiences but on Olson himself. "I don't think I was even near the point of believing in it until I saw Patterson's footage," Olson stated. "Not until I had seen the film and had worked with him for a while did I start coming to the point of thinking in my own mind that there was really something out there."

"I think that in four years of knowing Roger, that if there had been a flaw in the guy's personality, that if he even had the possibility of faking something like this, I believe I would have detected it," Olson said. "He was a congenial, quiet guy who would just as soon not talk about his film and who never made a penny off it in his life."[702] Olson said that during Patterson's last days in 1972, he reassured Olson that the film was authentic.

> While Patterson lived, Olson worked with him gathering data on Sasquatch sightings and trying to get backing for the production of a major feature-length documentary film on Sasquatch. Proceeds from the enterprise would have financed a year-long expedition in which Patterson and Olson planned to hunt for the creature in the wilderness of Northwest California, Oregon, Washington and British Columbia.
>
> Instead, there has been only disappointment. Patterson's footage has been ignored by the scientific world, the documentary has never materialized and the big expedition has been indefinitely delayed.

In 1972 Olson was devoted nearly full-time to North American Wildlife Research and Bigfoot activities. The organization's Eleventh Avenue office in Eugene contained displays of tracks and literature, featured a life-size oil painting of Sasquatch, and whose walls were adorned with maps pinpointing sighting locations. The organization even had the services of a full-time secretary. "At one time last year we had six small expeditions out, led by six full-time guys, paid through contributions we were receiving that amounted up to $4000 a month," said Olson. The expeditions turned up no tangible evidence and were eventually halted as contributions slowed. Olson helped put bread on the table through the sale of items such as Bigfoot-themed books and plastic ash trays made from the mold of a Bigfoot print. He laughed at any suggestion his motivation was fueled by an easy-money angle. "I would be ashamed, in fact, to have some of my friends know how little I made last year," Olson said. "It's a matter of pride, I guess. Some of my friends make a thousand dollars a month, and that's not the greatest pay in the world but it's a hell of a lot more than I make. We're hanging on by a shoestring."

Olson said he could have advanced up in the film business, if not for his interest—passion—in Bigfoot. "I think a guy should know when to quit, but I just can't. It would just kill me to turn my back on this after all I've put into it in the past five years. I've had some great business opportunities, but I've turned them down because there is still a slight glimmer of a chance that this Big Foot thing might jell into something where I have the financial backing, an expedition in the field, a movie under way and all these things put together. I think we've got to keep this thing in front of the people to keep it alive. If we keep it out there long enough, somebody sooner or later is going to come up, with something really great—a sighting, or maybe a film. We always will have this hope that somebody out there with their Instamatic is going to get a picture for us."

American National Enterprises produced an inexpensive, 20-minute documentary film titled *Bigfoot: Man or Beast?* (see Chapter 3) which ultimately under-produced in terms of what Olson believed was possible. Olson was not only critical of his 20-minute featurette but also looked disapprovingly upon the quality of the British Broadcasting Company's 1968 film, *Bigfoot: America's Abominable Snowman*. In both efforts, Olson sensed that limitations stemming from poor production techniques engendered more harm than good in the final product. "There's an extremely fine line between fact and fantasy when you're dealing with this subject," Olson stated. "If you don't stay on the factual side of that line, the people will throw rocks at you." Perhaps Olson hadn't had to literally dodge rocks, but he admitted to receiving a fair share of ridicule. "I used to get a lot of people laughing at me all the time," Olson admitted. "But lately, they don't laugh so much. In fact, people seem to be getting a little more open-minded about Big Foot. It's really funny about people. If you can just get enough data out in front of a person over a period of a year or so, he'll end up admitting, 'Heck, there's probably something like that.' If a person can stay involved as long as I have and go through all the garbage that I've been through, talking to idiots and talking to good people, and still come out and say he doesn't believe in Sasquatch, then I believe he has an honest reason to say so," Olson affirmed. "But if that person doesn't give himself a 100 per cent opportunity to look into the subject then I don't believe he has the honest right to say he does or doesn't believe in it."

Olson told Bates he wanted to make it impossible for people not to believe in Bigfoot, and he realized the surest way to do that was with the capture of a specimen. "As far as a capture goes, well, right now it depends largely on coincidence," Olson admitted. "With good fortune, a capture could come tomorrow—if it happened by accident. But a planned capture is at least another year down the road." But Olson indicated he had thought out the procedures and protocols that would follow a North American Wildlife Research Bigfoot live-capture. "The minute that creature is captured, we will begin a well-rehearsed procedure. We've got an all-terrain vehicle available so that if we can't fly the thing out—which would be the number one priority—then we can take it by ground vehicle to a secret and secluded holding area. We have several such areas available. The ideal areas are on private land, have one road in, no roads out and gates blocking entrance and exit. We have permission to go in and set up a chain link fence holding facility which will take five men approximately 6 ½ hours to set up. We've already made contact with the Smithsonian Institution, the Yerkes Primate Center of Atlanta, Ga., and the Craighead brothers tracking team from Missoula, Mont.—the same outfit that tracked Grizzly bears in a project for National Geographic not long back."

Olson described to Bates one of the earliest thought-out and deliberate protocols for the capture-and-release of Bigfoot. "What we will do immediately after the capture is bring in the appropriate scientific people to study the creature, make the necessary tests, take blood and bone samples, and then release the creature with a transmitter implanted behind its neck. Then we would track it for the next two years, probably recapturing it every six months to recharge the battery in the transmitter. We would set up big directional tracking equipment to keep watch on the creature over a 20-mile radius," said Olson. Olson further explained to Bates that his group was interested in studying Bigfoot interacting with its own environment; a dead specimen was neither the intended nor desired outcome of Olson's capture protocols. "The creature will be protected. It will not be killed. By tracking it, always knowing where it is, we'll answer all the mysteries: How far does it migrate? Does it hibernate? What does it do? Why the hell can't you see it? Roger Patterson wanted to use the creature in a sideshow—have the thing ride around in a cage," Olson recalled, "but I strongly disagree with that."[703]

Olson commissioned a box-like Bigfoot trap with a 150-pound steel bar gate built in the Siskiyou Mountains at a spot where an old miner had lived alone in for 50 years. According to Olson, this miner regaled him with tales of large creatures appearing in a clearing across the canyon from his mine. With that information in hand, Olson hired a man to live on site and follow the daily routine the old miner had followed. Armed with a tranquilizer gun and a camera, the stand-in's duties included the maintenance of both the Bigfoot trap and an electric wire sensor that encircled the project area.[704]

> "There was something around all last fall," said the hired mountain man. "There were howls that carried up these canyons and bounced off the hills. It wasn't bear and it wasn't coyotes. My dog will howl at a coyote but when he heard this he was quiet. He just listened with the hair standing straight up on his back."[705]

The trap would become an iconic fixture of the Bigfoot landscape. Stepping on a spring mat located one foot inside on the floor released a heavy door that dropped down and bolted shut. "And nothing, not even Bigfoot, can break out," Olson said.[706] The exterior frame of the trap was made of seven-inch diameter poles sunk three feet into the ground and spaced three feet apart. Two-by-twelve boards made the walls. Experiments with varying types of bait hung inside the trap were carried out in hopes of enticing Bigfoot's entrance.[707]

Ivan Sanderson Dies

Ivan Sanderson's first wife, Alma, died from cancer on January 18, 1972.[708] Ivan married Sabina W. Sanderson in May 1972. In September 1972 he was involved in a minor auto accident after which "he was never quite the same again." Later in the year he suffered double pneumonia followed by a bout of "London flu," and toward the end of 1972 he suffered from pain in his right arm that eventually prevented him from typing.[709] Sanderson, founder of the Society for the Investigation of the Unexplained, and author of key Bigfoot articles that helped promulgate hairy hominids into the cultural mainstream, lost his battle with cancer and passed away at age 62 on February 19, 1973.

Geoffrey Bourne

Geoffrey Bourne, director of the Yerkes Regional Primate Center thought large, hairy hominids in North America could at least be possible. "But there's not enough evidence to make a search worthwhile. If we could get some unequivocal evidence, such as a really convincing picture of a footprint, it would be worthwhile." Regarding the Patterson-Gimlin film, Bourne commented: "I've seen that film and I'm not impressed," he said. "It looked like a man dressed up in a monkey suit."

Atlanta-based reporter Charles S. Taylor interviewed Bourne for the primatologist's opinion on the possibility of Bigfoot's existence. "It certainly looks like there's something in all these reports of a giant man that existed in the northern parts," of the world, Bourne acknowledged. "I don't deny that a number of these people ever existed," he said. "But there is not enough evidence to convince me" that they exist in the modern world. The fossil evidence was there for giants, Bourne said, citing *Gigantopithecus*. "It is possible some survived up to recent times in isolated areas perhaps not in the same form as *Gigantopithecus* but not very much different from it." Bourne surmised a Bigfoot would be a living fossil. "It would be the first whole specimen of man's evolution," he added. Bourne said he placed the possibility of Bigfoot in the category of flying saucers—evidence existed, but no definitive proof.[710]

Peter Byrne / KACI, The Dalles

According to Bob Walters, who operated radio station KACI in The Dalles, Oregon, hundreds of people had searched the area's hills in June 1971, trekking over the rimrock in the wake of several Bigfoot sightings. Deputy Sgt. Richard Carlson had expressed his relief that no one had been shot during the spate of Bigfoot searchers and curiosity seekers who had converged on The Dalles.[711] That publicity had also lured Peter Byrne to The Dalles who designated the area a prime hotspot for Bigfoot activity and established his headquarters near the Columbia River starting what eventually became a multi-year study of Bigfoot encounters primarily occurring in the Pacific Northwest. During an interview conducted in The Dalles, Peter Byrne told writer William Childress that he was 95% certain that Bigfoot existed, and he cited four key factors underpinning that high confidence: the history of Bigfoot sightings going back over centuries, the footprints, similarities in sighting reports, and the Patterson-Gimlin film.[712] Interestingly, Dahinden outlined these same four points "to understand what the Sasquatch investigation is all about" for the pseudo-documentary *The Force Beyond* later in the decade. Dahinden was one of Byrne's greatest critics but it appeared that the two men agreed on several bedrock elements of the Bigfoot enigma.

Childress acclaimed Byrne as one of the serious Bigfoot hunters in the field. "I and a small team have been in the field now, full time, for two years and five months on a search and investigation of the Bigfoot phenomena, and have learned a great deal . . ." According to Childress, Byrne said the work coordinated from The Dalles "has produced some very convincing evidence within the last few years."[713]

Ivan Marx (1973)

> Marx has been a Bigfoot hunter since 1960, when his dogs tracked one of the creatures near Willow Creek for Tom Slick, the late Texas oilman and Bigfoot hunter. Marx still carries a lavishly-tooled Swedish-made Husqvarna 30.06 rifle given him by Slick's son, Tom Jr.
>
> A well-credentialed big game hunter and one-time U. S. game warden in Alaska, Marx has authored numerous men's magazine hunting articles and says he has guided Alaskan expeditions for newsman-adventurer Lowell Thomas Jr.
>
> "I've caught every animal I've wanted to," Marx says. "There isn't an animal in the world I can't catch."[714]

Following his appearance on *You Asked for It* in the previous year, Ivan Marx avowed he could spot a phony Bigfoot witness based on the creature's reported description which, if in conflict with Marx's own construction, emphatically indicated an outright hoax or a falsified report. "There's hair all over his face," Marx offered as example. "Old Sasquatch is a cold weather animal and nature wouldn't leave him out in the cold with a bare face."

> In Alaska, where the creature beats a drum, Marx says, the Indians, too, beat drums to show "Bushman" that they are unafraid.
>
> One of Marx' mementos of his years of Bigfoot hunting is a red, seal-skin drum given him by an Alaskan Indian from the upper reaches of the Yukon River.
>
> Marx says he has beat the drum for Bigfoot in Washington and California, but so far without results.[715]

In the *Fairbanks Daily News-Miner* story below, Marx comfortably flits between motorcycle gangs, the Marx's travelling Bigfoot exhibit, and theories of Bigfoot breeding.

> The Marx's trail [B]igfoot on their own and check out sightings of the animal.
>
> "You wouldn't believe the number of people who put somebody in a monkey suit and parade him around for photographers and hunters." Marx said.
>
> He went on to tell a story of a whole gang of motorcyclists who put on monkey suits and terrorized a town by showing up under street lamps and climbing up and down nearby hills.
>
> But still there is enough real evidence, hair left on rocks and trees, footprints and real sightings to make a few people believe in his existence.
>
> Marx and his wife have a wildlife farm and an exhibit of their finds concerning [B]igfoot that they show as they travel and that is how expenses are met.
>
> Marx has a theory that the arctic is a breeding [ground] for the [S]asquatch, but he has no idea exactly where it might be. Since he believes the animals are mainly migratory, traces of them could be found almost anywhere.
>
> "I've got to see for myself if he is real or not," Marx said.[716]

In addition to the traveling exhibit, Marx also worked as an expert tracker assisting and advising Tom Biscardi and Gene Findley in a cooperative pursuit of Bigfoot . . . and profits. Bigfoot had eluded capture, mused Marx, because of its nocturnal and nomadic habits. "He's always moving, never going anywhere, but always moving," Marx said. Other than espousing the creatures' general rarity, Marx had no clear handle on how many could be living in the wilderness. "Maybe 15, maybe 1,500," he said.[717]

Biscardi & Findley and the Infrared Device

Carmine "Tom" Biscardi stated his exposure to the Patterson-Gimlin film helped instigate a decades-long involvement with Bigfoot. "I was watching Johnny Carson in 1967, and I saw the first 8mm footage that Roger Patterson took of the Bluff Creek finding Bigfoot sighting. I said to myself, 'How the hell can we send a man to the moon, but we can't find this creature.' I went to the library and researched Bigfoot and my predecessors, to see what kind of mistakes they had made, so that I could do better. I then started my own Bigfoot research company to stage expeditions to find the creature."[718] Biscardi's first Bigfoot-oriented company, Amazing Horizons Corporation, was established in 1971 with the ostensible goal of representing Ivan Marx's Bigfoot films. But it was his association with Gene Findley that propelled him into the public spotlight.

Biscardi and Gene Findley formed B-F Enterprises in February 1973 formalizing their Bigfoot-investigating business venture. By May 1973, Biscardi had concluded Bigfoot utilized migratory routes from the northwestern United States to Mexico. He told the *Ledger-Gazette* (Lancaster, California) that the Bigfoot migration, as of late May, was about ended in the Antelope Valley, an area Biscardi visited (accompanied by Ivan Marx) after California Bigfoot Organization members reported Bigfoot sightings there. "In any area where there are sightings some are bound to be hoaxes," Biscardi said. "But in talking to members of the California Bigfoot Organization headquartered in Palmdale, it appears that not all of the sightings have been hoaxes."[719]

In 1973, 24-year-old Biscardi and 25-year-old Findley proclaimed the field-readiness of an infrared device capable of monitoring an animal's body heat and transmitting its image onto a screen. By flying at low altitudes, this scanning device would, its makers hoped, snoop out Bigfoot. Should Bigfoot be detected by their device, the men would radio their base camp where a specialist in ESP and an expert tracker (presumably Marx) would be waiting, ready to go into action and pursue the creature (see below for B-F Enterprises' further involvement of ESP in the hunt for Bigfoot). The infrared device's purported capabilities exceeded military-grade analogues according to Findley, the machine's inventor; the device provided the exact temperature of any monitored creature and indicated its general shape.

Biscardi had quit a sales job with a clothing manufacturer to become a full-time Bigfoot hunter. "It shouldn't take more than a couple of months," he said providing one of the most sanguine estimates of Bigfoot's imminent capture, exceeding prognostications that Olson or Byrne would likely suggest to a reporter. "We've got everything going for us. Every angle covered."

Biscardi and Findley reported they had finalized a survey of proposed study areas and upon the start of their forthcoming expedition, their team of about ten members would focus their efforts on mountainous areas hosting the most recent and creditable sightings. Biscardi and Findley's analysis had pared the list of potential expedition areas to three mountains: two in Washington and one in Northern California. "We can't be more specific," said Biscardi, "because 25,000 people will come if we publish the area. It'll be like a Bigfoot convention." What did Biscardi think of Bigfoot naysayers? "Listen, we've been ridiculed already," Biscardi said. "But they ridiculed the Wright brothers, too."[720]

Lassen Peak Expedition

Reporter Richard Harris of Eureka's *Times-Standard* spent the weekend of June 1-3 on a special assignment for the newspaper, participating in a B-F Enterprises-sponsored Bigfoot expedition led by Biscardi and Marx.

> Bigfoot—fact, fiction, or flim-flam?
>
> This is my big question, after spending the weekend in the wilds at the foot of Lassen Peak volcano with an expedition in search of the legendary giant hairy ape man of the Pacific Northwest.
>
> Another newsman and I were promoted along on the adventure by fast-talking Tom Biscardi, 24-year-old Bigfoot impresario and partner in B-F Enterprises, a Santa Clara firm formed in February and dedicated to capturing the mythical monster.
>
> Biscardi told us last Friday that his tracker, tobacco-chewing Ivan Marx, was hot on the trail of the elusive Bigfoot. "Just hours behind," I was told. Capture might be imminent.

> Sunday, UPI reporter Carrick Leavitt and I were shown a series of about 20 alleged Bigfoot tracks, 15-inch-long human-resembling right and left foot prints sunk inch-deep in the Lassen loam, but Bigfoot was not to be found.
>
> The tracks, nearly six inches broad at the toe joints and four inches at the heel, we saw at three separate locations in a mile-long southeasterly line. The [standard] strike was about 66 inches, but the strides varied.
>
> Conveniently, the tracks were all within 50 feet of the gravel logging roads which honeycomb the area and within 50 miles of Marx's "Bear Ranch" at Burney, a two-mill mountain lumbering town 50 miles east of Redding.
>
> The tracks looked good to me, but I'm no outdoors expert. I could see no signs of print fakery and am left wondering how those big prints were driven one inch into the ground.
>
> Marx concluded that the Bigfoot—a 6′ 6″, 400-plus pound, partially-blind female, he hypothesizes—returned to the safety of the national park after venturing to the logging roads on the park border, where we saw the tracks.[721]

The prints were the second significant track find Marx made for B-F Enterprises. Coincidentally, both had occurred relatively near Marx's house. Marx had been stung by ridicule, Harris wrote, amidst allegations of hoaxing Bigfoot prints and film. The derision fueled what Harris called Marx's obsession to find Bigfoot and thereby clear his name. "I just want to tie that thing up in my truck and drive it into town and stick it in their faces and make them recognize that I got it," he said. Harris linked Marx's desire for exoneration with his association to Biscardi.

> Marx thinks that his best chance to capture Bigfoot may come later this summer, when special electronic night-time sensing devices are perfected for B-F Enterprises' scheduled late-July Bigfoot hunt.
>
> Leavitt and I were supposed to get a look at the B-F night scope last weekend, but were told that the batteries had gone dead. The scope, an 18-inch red metal tube with a telephone camera lens screwed on the end, is said by its inventor to be twice as powerful as the scopes used by U. S. Army snipers in Vietnam.[722]

Findley at the time was a 25-year-old, pipe-smoking shop foreman for Applied Technology Inc., a Sunnyvale defense contractor. Findlay told Harris that he and Biscardi had been high school chums and shared an interest in Bigfoot since their exposure to the Patterson and Gimlin.

> Spot From Air—The balding, blond-bearded Findley says he is now making final refinements on an airplane-mounted infrared sensor which will be able to spot Bigfoot from the air at nighttime on a television screen. But this machine, also, was not demonstrated for me, so I cannot vouch for its effectiveness—or even its existence.
>
> While Findley fine-tunes his electronics gadgets and Marx hunts, showman Biscardi beats the promotional drum.
>
> Brooklyn born and doubleknit-dressed, the stocky Biscardi is a non-stop talker, on subjects ranging from the Mafia to fast women, to Bigfoot.
>
> "He's going to be caught this year and it' going to be worth $4 million to whoever catches him," the promoter claims.
>
> "Are you an investor?" the answering service girl asked B-F callers until newsman Leavitt raised the issue with Biscardi. The B-F answering service is also designed to take calls (at 408-248-[xxxx]) reporting Bigfoot sightings throughout the Pacific Northwest.[723]

Biscardi admitted his Bigfoot-hunting interest was not sustained solely by potential scientific benefits. "There's money in it for us even if we don't get Bigfoot," he said, envisioning a lucrative payoff from various promotions like movie and TV rights. Still, one had to be practical; Biscardi confided to Harris that should no Bigfoot turn up by October 1973, he intended to find another "money-maker." But what if B-F Enterprises actually captured a Bigfoot specimen, Harris asked. "I'd bring him in, let people see him for three days so they'd know he was real, they I'd let him go again and I'd be really happy," Marx said. Marx maintained he held onto some hunters' superstitions. Indians, he told Harris, would not kill a Bigfoot for fear of retributions from the creature's kin.

Biscardi had slightly different ideas. B-F's chief promoter said that after a brief period for scientific observation, a captured Bigfoot would go on the auction block, to be sold off to the highest bidder. "Museum, zoo, traveling circus, I don't care," Biscardi stated.

And Findley's position? "Scientifically neutral," Harris wrote. "Frankly," Findley added, "I don't care what they do with it. Ivan's the hunter, it's his problem." Findley withheld holding sentimental reservations pertaining to Bigfoot. "I regard it the same as I regard a bear—if you kill it, you kill it," he stated. "And besides," he added with a puff on his pipe, "how can you seriously worry about killing something that doesn't even exist yet?"

Harris also wrote on the state-of-play then in force amongst the Bigfoot hunters:

> Biscardi, Findley and Marx are not alone in the quest for the Bigfoot.
>
> Funded by an Ohio businessman, Irish adventurer Peter Byrne, an ex-World War II RAF pilot, is reportedly using night scopes and infra-red devices in his Bigfoot hunt centered at The Dalles, in north-central Oregon.
>
> Bigfoot hunters are also active at Colville, Wash., Medford, Ore., and Palmdale, Calif., among other places and Marx says there is a mad scramble among the rivals to be the first to nab the mythical monster.
>
> "They really want to catch the darned thing," he says. "If they hear you've got something, then here they'll come.
>
> "This thing is worth so damn much money that they'll hijack you," Marx says, "but I'm not going to fool with them—I've told 'em that if they get near me, I'll shoot their legs off."
>
> He was insistent that I not print the exact locations of his track sighting near Mt. Lassen or his picture-taking northeast of Spokane, for fear that rivals will jump his claim.
>
> The different Bigfoot hunters strive to discredit each other's sightings and Marx has alienated Bigfooters in Palmdale and Colville by pooh-poohing their claims to track sightings.
>
> Movie Footage—Near The Dalles, Marx says, he took movie footage of a supposed monster with its arms straight up in the air. The arms shot up, Marx says, after he fired a bullet over the bogus Bigfoot's head.
>
> Marx has more than once been accused of phonying his Bigfoot sightings and in a May article in a national counterculture newspaper [*Rolling Stone*], Marx was blasted for perpetrating "an incredibly clumsy fake" film account of a supposed Bigfoot jumping up and down in a California snow storm.

> Marx acknowledges that he shot the phony film, but says that he did not stage the incident. He can't explain why anybody would be jumping up and down in a white gorilla suit in a California snow storm.[724]

Harris' article is an early and extensive interview of Biscardi who kept his energetic Bigfoot showmanship and promotion going into the 21st century. In the end, an incredulous tone seeps through Harris' writing of his weekend spent learning about B-F Enterprises and the men behind it.

> B-F Enterprises—adventurers or con-men?
>
> The questions stick in my mind.
>
> "The only way to know what's inside (the monkey suit) is to catch him," says Marx.
>
> And the odds on capturing the maybe-beast?
>
> "I'd say about three in a hundred," Marx says, with a spit of tobacco juice.[725]

Tom Biscardi & Findley Continue the Search

The December 1973 *Saga* ran an article by William Childress on Marx, Biscardi, and Findley's continuing efforts to bring in Bigfoot.

> The deep, throaty hum of the Cessna 172 cuts through the pitch-dark night. Hunched over the controls, his nerves strung like barbed wire, blond-bearded Gene Findley tries to master the powerful mountain currents that buffet the tiny plane.
>
> It's 3 A.M. on a cold, gray morning, somewhere over the wilds of Alaska. It is no time for a pleasure flight. "O.K., hold her steady now," says Ivan Marx, a veteran hunter and tracker. "I'm starting the electronic sweep."
>
> Tanned and toughened, famed as an outdoors man who knows the wilderness like the palms of his hands, Marx keeps his eyes glued to a flickering blue-white screen. Though it looks like a television receiver, the device converts animal heat into an image of the beast being pursued.
>
> In this case it's Bigfoot—the legendary half-man, half-monster that has haunted North America for almost 200 years.

> "If he's out there," Findley mutters grimly, eyes straining to spot jagged peaks in the inky darkness, "we'll find him!"

Findley's oft-written of infrared sensor was rigged to a camera and designed for attachment to the belly of a plane. "It works on a heat-seeking principle," Findley said over the Cessna's roaring engines. "We think Bigfoot will have a body temperature different from most animals. The device—I call it simply my BF Analyzer—will pick up his body heat and transform it into an image on the screen. Reading that image will tell us whether we've got a moose, a bear—or Bigfoot." The basic principle sounded familiar to Childress. "Sounds like infrared light," he offered. "Infrared is used in my machine," replied Findley. "The entire theory would take too long to explain." That enigmatic statement was not lost on Childress who realized technical secrets would not be divulged during his interview. "Suffice it to say we're onto something, and with it we mean to prove or disprove the existence of Bigfoot."

Childress interviewed Biscardi in the Bigfoot-pitchman's San Jose apartment.

> "I'm the drum beater," Biscardi says. "Hell, somebody's got to do it. I've sunk so much money in this thing now—so has Gene—that I have bad dreams at night. There's this huge bill collector dressed up in a Bigfoot suit . . ."
>
> He pauses, grinning, and takes a gulp of red wine. "The more interest we can get in finding this creature, the better. It takes a lot of cash to keep a specially-equipped plane flying over some of Alaska's roughest country."

"We lived in sleeping bags," said Biscardi reminiscing of time spent on the trail searching for Bigfoot. "And snakes? Man, we were wrapping blankets around our legs and feet to guard against bites by timber rattlers. That terrain up there is so bad, so rough, I'm amazed someone hasn't fallen into a crevice or canyon!" Childress asked Biscardi the whereabouts of his current search efforts. "Can't tell you that," he responded. "The place would be a Bigfoot circus in a matter of hours. Maybe you don't know it, but there are thousands of people trying to find this creature all the time. The reason we've had better luck is because we're better organized to stay in the field longer. This last time, we spent almost a month. I had to come back to raise some money. The others are still up there, still on the alert. We're close, too—damned close! Here, take a look at these."

> Two large, glossy color photos encased in plastic with the bluish tinge that comes from dim light were placed before me. The blowups, taken from 35mm color slides, showed a dark, furry creature remarkably resembling a man resting himself on—or perhaps climbing down—a cliff ledge. The cliff was almost sheer and composed of great, vertical slabs of stone.
>
> "Ivan Marx took those early one morning, near dawn," Biscardi said. "He shot them at 280 yards with a telephoto lens. What do you think of them?"
>
> "Could be a . . ."
>
> "A man in a monkey suit?" Biscardi smiled. "I knew you were going to say that. It's one of the first comments we get. People are afraid not to be skeptical; they're afraid of being laughed at."
>
> He paused, and finished his glass of red wine in a gulp. "But I agree—it could be. But it's not. You're looking at the clearest pictures of a Sasquatch ever taken." His eyes sparkled with the importance of his discovery. It was easy to see that Biscardi was convinced of Bigfoot's existence. "Only one other photograph has come as close," he went on. "And that was Roger Patterson's 12-second film. That got folks pretty excited, especially when they blew up one of the frames and distributed it to the newspapers."[726]

The 52-year-old Marx claimed he took telephoto pictures in April 1973 of a gray-colored Bigfoot close to the Washington-Idaho border northeast of Spokane and 100 miles east of Marx's Bossburg, Washington, home. A Washington cattle rancher had alerted Marx to the possible presence of Bigfoot in the area. Reporter Richard Harris discovered Marx had a hard time pinpointing the exact date the pictures were taken. "Maybe it was April Fool's Day," he offered.[727]

The lesson from the Patterson-Gimlin film's publicity guided Marx's actions; his photos were distributed and printed in numerous newspapers throughout the country, fueling a burst of attention and notoriety for the BF Enterprises team. An article in the December 12 *Reno Evening Gazette* revealed the photos may have indeed been a lucrative asset: "Biscardi and

Findley who were able to sell their photos for $25,000 now plan to capture one of the creatures."[728]

On the trail, Biscardi had seen a diverse spectrum of people drawn to the Bigfoot scene, from serious researchers to spirited hoaxers. "We scared hell out of one faker," Biscardi told Childress, his dark eyes likely grinning at the memory. "Some clown in a hair suit came leaping out of his skin when we fired a shot over his head," likely referring to the shot Marx allegedly fired at a hoaxer near The Dalles. By the early 1970s, many Bigfoot researchers acknowledged Bigfoot had been sighted in nearly every state, not just the states of the Pacific Northwest. "We've pushed it one farther," Biscardi mused, "into Alaska. We think it's much more wide-ranging than previously thought."

Childress wrote that the most common Bigfoot footprint length found was 16-inches long, located in all kinds of substrate—snow, mud, and soft earth. Biscardi took up some of the familiar arguments about Bigfoot. "We get asked why no Bigfoot bodies are ever found," he said. "The reason is simple: how long would a dead human body last in the woods? It would rot, or be scattered by animals. The same is true of Bigfoot corpses." Findley held the opinion that Bigfoot bury their dead, raising the tantalizing possibility of someday finding a Bigfoot tomb or larger graveyard of Bigfoot interments. "If we can find million-year-old fossils of our ancestors," Childress asked, mindful of some scientists' reservations on hairy hominids in North America, "why can't we locate a few Bigfoot bones—if indeed there are any?" It was a cool logic that ran up against others' pessimistic conclusions. "We know the creatures are out there," said a hunter from the shade of his camper, "and we think we'll eventually see one. You have to realize, these beasts walk only at night. And they've eluded man for decades! It's easy to be a skeptic, but I've seen proof enough for me, and that's all I care about." Biscardi claimed the creature employed natural night vision. "How else would it get around, leaping fallen logs and boulders, without some sort of cat-sight?"

What was the *full* price of hunting Bigfoot? For Biscardi, securing funding, identifying research areas, and procuring equipment were not the least travails to be suffered by Bigfoot researchers. Could a certain karmic malignity be connected with the pursuit of hairy hominids? "I'm not saying bad luck accompanies those who hunt the beast," Biscardi ruminated. "But it's a little odd that no less than five people who were hot on Bigfoot's trail have died?" Childress added to Biscardi's thought: Not only did these men die, but except for the Russian investigator Porshnev and Ivan Sanderson, the other three were under 46 years old: Roger Patterson, Tom Slick, and Dr. Clifford Carl, head of British Columbia's natural history museum. Biscardi thought the spate of deaths had sinister hallmarks. "You take Patterson and his movie," he said. "The man had experts view it and analyze it. He was getting too close—and he was struck down." Did this line of thinking extend to Biscardi's own Bigfoot-hunting operation, Childress asked. "We've talked with hundreds of people, uncovered fakes, and explored hundreds of square miles of territory. All I can say is that when Ivan Marx took these pictures early one morning, and showed me the results, I had a feeling of foreboding." Did this foreboding compel Biscardi and his associates to give up Bigfoot? "No way," Biscardi said confidently. "First, our expedition isn't a charitable one. Why should it be? We want to be the first to find Bigfoot because he will be worth millions to the finder. For that kind of potential wealth, I'm willing to take a few risks—and so are the other members of my expedition."

"I want to prove my machine," said Findley of his heat-seeking sensor. "That's my big reason for hunting Bigfoot. I also fly the plane on these searches. The only time we can get good, clear readings on the screen is when the earth is cool. Remember we're trying to track a creature by its body heat. Now, a man's heat and an animal's heat are different. Animals—large ones—usually run several degrees higher."

While Biscardi was indisputably the entrepreneur and showman, Findley was BF Enterprises' technically-minded scientist. "Our biggest problem," Findley maintained, "is waiting for the earth to cool. Rocks, trees, anything that receives light gives back heat. That's an elemental rule. It means our best flying time is in the wee hours of the night." Findley flew his Cessna at the relatively low altitude of 600 feet. "The scanner can cover a wider area from a higher altitude," he said. Findley went on to explain that his device's lens expanded its coverage area the higher the altitude but at the cost of decreasing granularity. "Trouble is, for details we must get down closer to the target—much closer. Add to that our flying times—2 A.M. to about 6 A.M.—and you get a pretty good picture." The low altitude flying could be dangerous. On one occasion, Findley's Cessna 172 unexpectedly found itself flying toward a mountain. Findley pulled up in time and averted disaster. "That one shook us up a bit," he recalled.

"If we spot him from the air," said Findley, "we won't shoot him. We're setting up an elaborate network to surround the area and capture him, if possible without harm. We plan to use a new type of tranquilizer gun. Our sole aim is capture, not kill. A dead Bigfoot is of no scientific use whatsoever." Findley had apparently ameliorated his tone regarding "something that doesn't even exist yet" since Richard Harris' June *Times-Standard* article on BF Enterprises' doings.

Biscardi was willing to try out various techniques, including use of an ESP expert. "This guy is convinced he can communicate with the creature and assure it we mean no harm," Biscardi said grinning in perhaps a self-deprecating awareness. "Who am I to doubt it? Hell, J. B. Rhine of Duke University proved the existence of ESP decades ago! I'm giving him a crack at it, and gladly. Maybe he'll turn up some data on the creature's thought processes that will astound the world." Biscardi evinced zero reticence with envisioning the results he was working toward. "I'd love to be the one to astound the world!"[729]

The subject of Bigfoot has always begged for speculation of the creature's identity: ape, man, alien, troglodyte, or other. Childress wrote of true human giants who, if not the catalyst for Bigfoot reports, could be viewed as type-analogs to Bigfoot, such as Robert Pershing Wadlow who upon his passing in 1940 weighed 491 pounds and had shoes 18 ¼ inches long. Childress also noted acromegaly, a disease causing the enlargement of the hands and feet, as additional correspondence between people and the over-sized appendages which had been part and parcel of many Bigfoot reports.

Carrick Leavitt, who had joined Richard Harris to cover the BF Enterprises team's June expedition, authored an article printed in Eureka's *Times-Standard*, under the title, "ESP Hunters Pay to Track Bigfoot," which fleshed out Biscardi's incorporation of extrasensory perception (ESP) in his Bigfoot expeditions. Prospective expedition members cum Bigfoot hunters were offered an experience involving no soap, deodorant, or shaving lotion, and no teeth brushing. Shoes were to be soaked in ammonia. Those and other field measures were prescribed by Biscardi, whom Leavitt described as a "Bigfoot impresario," and by Bob Miles of Safespace Foundation, an organization Miles formed after he experienced a UFO encounter in 1968.

> A classified section ad in the San Francisco newspapers says, "Bigfoot anthropological expeditions need exped. members. No exper. neces. World authority will lead. Not a hunting party."
>
> Safespace is an organization with two additional major projects under way—creation of the world's largest trimaran and an island kingdom off the coast of Honduras. "Our business is creating dreams," says director Bob Miles, 32.

The impetus for the search was a photo claimed as the first to capture Bigfoot's face taken in July 1973 in Alaska. The going price for a spot in the expedition? $750. The expedition's plan was to follow the migratory route of the creatures starting out at Arctic lava tubes and guided by a series of ESP operations. Ivan Marx was slated to lead the expedition members through the maze of lava tubes in Lassen National Park. The expedition's ad drew 11 people to an introductory session.

> "The trail looks pretty hot," Miles told the prospective ESP hunters.
>
> He laid out the program. "There will be a qualification period to get to go, it's included in the package. We must learn to communicate with each other before we can communicate with Bigfoot," he said.
>
> The ESP training will be done at Safespace facilities during a two week period. It includes four steps. Learning too [sic] focus your thoughts; separating from your thoughts; focusing for 10 minutes on just one thought, and practicing "vacancy of mind, making you a perfect receiver."
>
> "A lot of people have looked for Bigfoot and they've never been able to find him. Our technique is to ask him," Miles said.
>
> Biscardi passed around a photograph—a head shot—of a hairy creature with marble red eyes, no discernable nose and streaks of grey through brownish black fur.
>
> The picture was taken by "one of our trackers with a telephoto lens," Biscardi said. A telephone call to Marx elucidated a slightly different story.
>
> "That came out of the north," he said. "They [sic] guy that gave me that is half Eskimo. If they offend him (Bigfoot) in any way, they have to pay the consequences. In the Arctic he's a now thing—he's not a legend of the past."
>
> The picture was made in July, 1973 by the man who is also a bush pilot. "I can't tell you his name," Marx said.
>
> What about the ESP hunters?
>
> "That's Tom's side. We'll see what they can come up with. Maybe they'll surprise me," Marx said.
>
> Marx will lead the EXP [sic] hunters, shepherded 300 miles north from San Francisco by Biscardi and Miles, through the

maze of lava tubes in and around Lassen National Park. It is here, averred Marx, that numerous signs of Bigfoot have been found.

Biscardi laid down the rules to his prospective hunters. "There will be no toothpaste, no cologne and no soap during the expedition. We'll put ammonia in cotton on our shoes so it smells like cougar urine. The wild animals are the friends of Bigfoot and we must erase human smells in order to get close enough to contact him."[730]

By that autumn, Biscardi and Findley claimed more success: sighting and photographing a gathering of Bigfoot in Oregon. That resulting publicity for BF Enterprises was consequently responded to by a concerned Bob Neville of Reno whose open letter to the Bigfoot entrepreneurs was published in *Grit*.

A Reno man is protesting the plans of two adventurers who say they have sighted the legendary man-beast, "Bigfoot," and now propose to tranquilize, bind and carry it off for scientific study.

The article on the adventurers' findings appeared in the Dec. 2 issue of *Grit*, a Williamsport, Pa., newspaper. Bob Neville, an astronomy instructor for the Western Nevada Community College, has written an open letter to *Grit*, protesting the King Kong-like tactics planned to catch "Bigfoot."

The adventurers, Tom Biscardi, 24, and Gene Findley, 25, claim they have "concrete proof" of the existence of "Bigfoot," also known as Sasquatch.

The pair took an aerial expedition into dome [sic] rugged Oregon mountains and claim they sighted and photographed not one, but a congregation of the creatures. A consensus of reports, beginning with the first sighting of the creature in 1811 described "Bigfoot" as about 10 feet tall weighing 1000 pounds with gray fur broad shoulders and long arms.

Biscardi and Findley who were able to sell their photos for $25,000 now plan to capture one of the creatures.

"They could be hit with a tranquilizing dart" Findley said in the article, "and while unconscious, bound and carried off for scientific study."

In his letter to the hunters, Neville asks, "Are we to treat this 'lesser' species, the Sasquatch, as we have the other animals on this planet, which we have hunted, caged, tortured and slain?"

In an interview, Neville said he believes the Sasquatch probably does exist.

"But whether he does or not is not the point. The basic point is we suffer from a misplaced conceit," he said. "We feel that we have to take, by way of example the Bible, that the universe was built for us and therefore, we can manipulate it any way we want to."

"Through such an animal as Sasquatch," Neville said, "we can see ourselves as one step in an ascending intelligence. We can realize the same consideration that we would want to receive, were we at the low end of the meeting, is what we should be willing to extend to other creatures who we consider lower than ourselves."[731]

CBO & Antelope Valley

Students at the Eastside School in East Lancaster were treated to a Bigfoot presentation by California Bigfoot Organization (CBO) members Rich Grumley, president; Floyd Smith, vice president; Lonnie Smith, secretary-treasurer; and team member Bill Darch. The CBO members talked about the club's purpose and significant findings in their recent searches for Bigfoot evidence. Grumley, of Palmdale, told the students about Bigfoot tracks he found on February 15, 1972. The tracks were 17-18 inches long and discovered about 90 miles from Lancaster. Whatever made the tracks, Grumley explained to the students, had a seven-foot stride. Color slides and plaster footprint casts complemented the presentation. Grumley talked about the CBO's future plans to equip and mount a substantial expedition oriented toward a live capture. The CBO's motto was, "We do believe, we search to prove."[732]

One of the CBO's investigations involved footprints discovered by a woman and her son near an old reservoir in eastern Antelope Valley. The prints measured 5 ¾ inches across the heel and were eight inches wide and revealed a large, 15-inch long human-like footprint. Other footprints found near the woman's house were not as distinct and proved more difficult to make out. Grumley, Smith, Darch, and seven other CBO members canvassed the area and discovered several additional footprints in a nearby cave.

Describing this finding Smith said, "there was a pile of sticks in the center of the footprints but no evidence of paper or a fire being started, or anything else that would aid in starting a fire." These prints were eight inches across the toe, six inches at the heel, 16 inches long. This particular investigation occasioned a possible CBO Bigfoot sighting as Smith and Darch glimpsed a dark object running through the area.[733]

Following a tip, Smith and CBO member Fred Adams traveled to Nine-Mile Canyon in May 1973 to a location near Lake Isabella where both men subsequently reported seeing something "big and furry." They believed, in contrast to Biscardi's migratory theory, at least one Bigfoot creature remained at large in the Antelope Valley. Chuck Wheeler's article below gives a glimpse of a recurring friction between the two Bigfoot camps:

> CBO members were perturbed with Biscardi for two reasons. One, he said that he and Ivan Marx, who has been hunting the [B]igfoot creature for more than 20 years, did not believe that CBO reports were valid, and two, Biscardi's members in a safari purportedly once shot one of the creatures.[734]
>
> Smith said that the man who saw the creature in Palmdale saw it running around his house. Evidently, the creature likes to run around houses and leaving footprints. That is its MO in the East Lancaster area where footprints were found around several houses recently. One woman reported that the creature ran around her house and scratched at the door. A small boy sent to tell his father supper was ready was found hours later crying near the corral. When asked what happened to him, he answered that a big, furry man would not let him pass.
>
> Droppings from an animal believed to be [B]igfoot were found by CBO members near 279th St. East and Ave. J. It was near 100th St East and Ave J that the two most credible sightings were reported, the first two, in fact. Those sightings were by two marines whose auto skid marks were found the next morning and then a week later a nineteen year old girl who came home from babysitting in the early morning hours.
>
> When Smith and Adams spotted the creature recently at Nine Mile Canyon, Adams saw the bottom part of it as it ran from them through the bush and it emerged momentarily at the spot where Smith was breaking camp. He saw just the upper part of the body. The creature was running up a steep

> incline when first spotted by the two men. They described it as being seven to eight feet tall. They intend to go back there and to keep searching close to home.[735]

The CBO maintained a file of local sightings, prominent of which was the Lancaster *Ledger-Gazette's* account of three Marines who entered the Lancaster Sheriff's office after 1 A.M. on March 14 to report a "dark creature of human shape and about eight feet tall," which ran in front of their car on Avenue J near 110th Street causing the Marines to run their auto off the road into alfalfa fields. *Ledger-Gazette* reporter Chuck Wheeler suggested the hit movie currently playing at the drive-in, *The Legend of Boggy Creek*, may have suggestively influenced the Marines' perceptions of what they thought they had seen.[736] But Wheeler's own skepticism was shaken when a week after the Marines' encounter, he spoke with a man who owned a crop dusting company; he told Wheeler his teenage daughter was frightened badly late one night while returning home, only about a mile from the Marines' sighting. Believing she had heard a whining dog when getting out of her parked car, she walked toward the sound. Suddenly, rising up from the grass in front of her, was a seven-foot tall creature covered all over with hair except its face. The creature ran off and the girl ran to her trailer. Wheeler went with Grumley to her residence where the latter found a large footprint.[737]

Another Wheeler-reported CBO Bigfoot-hunting anecdote covered a nighttime field outing when Grumley and several companions got shot at in the eastern Valley by people who Grumley assumed were likewise hunting for Bigfoot.[738] Smith said that the sightings from the area, including the mid-March report from the three Marines, had brought many curious folks to look for themselves. One night while searching for footprints, a woman's scream overpowered the CBO's walkie-talkie chatter. Her scream was followed by a man's shouted warning, "There is something big coming at us!" Smith recounted he did not see anything himself, but shortly after the shouts startled the CBO searchers, bullets started to fly. Smith said that following the gunshots the next sounds heard were the roar of jeep and motorcycle engines fading into the desert. "We stayed down behind the rocks for 45 minutes," said Smith, "before we went back to town."[739]

In all, Wheeler is credited with writing at least nine Bigfoot stories between March and November 1973. Wheeler and *Ledger-Gazette* staff photographer Jack Overlade accompanied Grumley in November 1973 to a Sycamore Flats campground on Big Rock Creek in the Angeles National Forest.

The newspapermen observed the CBO investigate a woman's report of hearing strange grunts and screams. "While Grumley showed us this footprint and that footprint and this faded print and this pretty good print and another that might have been a footprint, it was Overlade who found the only print I would say showed great definition and looked authentic," reported Wheeler. "The print definitely was not made by a bear. It appeared as if the owner of the foot was surprised and slipped. The foot itself was possibly twice the width. It looked like a real footprint, of some huge animal." A man told Wheeler he was convinced the whole Bigfoot hullabaloo was bunk and the footprints had been fabricated. In 30 years of roaming the valley this man said he had never seen Bigfoot. But, the man confided to Wheeler, he was now prone to take a weapon with him when he entered the hills. "Sometimes even a lunatic thing just might prove real," he said.[740]

Cincinnati, Ohio—UFOs & Ape-like Creature

Canadian UFO Report retold an incident originally reported to Dwight Connelly's *Skylook* concerning a Mrs. R. H. who lived in western Cincinnati. On the night of October 21, 1973, she and her 13-year-old son were home in their trailer when unsettling events which included strange lights and a hairy humanoid began.

> "Mrs. R. H. relates that she awoke sometime around 2:30 A.M. because of intense thirst, and on arising from her bed was attracted to a bright light coming through the drawn curtains. She pulled the curtains apart and was startled, initially, by a row of individual lights forming an arc about two yards from her window.
>
> "Each light source was as large as a 'hand with the fingers spread out.' The lights, 'maybe six' she recalled, were about 4 feet off the ground and alternately vividly blue and silver 'like stars as beautiful as Christmas lights,' each 'lit up inside' (self luminous), casting no radiance to the ground or onto a nearby storage shed. The lights were in a fixed position and did not pulsate. She did not open the window. No sound was audible, nor odor.
>
> "While the 'Christmas lights' still attracted her attention, the witness said her eyes were drawn next to a strong bright

> light further out in the asphalt parking court beyond her trailer, which partly obscured the bottom portion of the light source in which an 'ape-like creature' appeared.
>
> "Terrified, she watched this area of light for about two or three minutes and thought the creature appeared to the rear of the parked car 'maybe doing something to the car.' (It was at this time she ran to her son's bedroom and tried to awaken him. She yelled, 'My God, Carl, get up . . . get up and look at that thing out there!')
>
> "When she returned to the window, Mrs. R. H. relates, 'The creature appeared to be further away from the car, maybe 35 feet away.' This time it was inside a 'shield of light,' the light looking like a light in an 'operating room.' The shield was shaped like a lady's umbrella, 'the kind that comes down over the head' (often referred to as a bubble umbrella). The bright light was within the shield. There was no glow of light beyond the shield.
>
> "The creature 'stood out clearly,' looking like 'an ape' with a big waist and no neck. There were no distinguishable features in the head, but Mrs. R. H.'s description indicated it was a side view of a head of prognathic configuration with a snout, which tapered downward. The head and body were facing the Swallen's warehouse building, which was to the left of the witness' mobile home. The body was entirely gray and was also featureless. Only the arms on each side of the big waist were moving 'very slowly' alternately up and down."[741]

Mrs. R. H. demonstrated the creature's movement by holding her outstretched arms in front of her and moving them in an up and down motion in robot-like caricature. Describing the object's shape, Mrs. R. H. held up a bell jar, saying the object was about seven feet in diameter and like glass with a bright light inside it. No instruments or indicators within the object could be seen though Mrs. R. H. suggested the occupant's arm may have been moving an invisible lever. Mrs. R. H. said the creature was in view for four or five minutes.[742]

$10,000 for Living Space Alien

Bigfoot happenings in Pennsylvania found their way across the country and turned up in interesting venues. Bob Houglum, owner of KLOO in

Corvallis, Oregon, co-hosted that station's popular morning show "Toast and Coffee" for over 30 years. Days after Houglum made an on-air offer in 1973 of $10,000 for a living space alien, he reported that KLOO had been flooded with so many calls he considered installing a special UFO telephone line to handle the volume. Some people called inquiring if moon rocks or moon dust would satisfy the requirements for the $10,000 reward. One of the most promising calls, Houglum noted, was from a caller from Pennsylvania who played a recording of a moan he said was made by a nine-foot hairy creature with red eyes roaming through the woods of Sharon, Pennsylvania.[743] It was intriguing, but not enough by itself to win the money.

Little Monster and Fisherwomen

Something strange happened in the vicinity of the Illinois River Bridge in Benton County, Arkansas, at dusk on Saturday, May 26. Two women engaged in evening fishing were understandably startled as a monster—on the smallish side as monsters go—emerged out of the water near the bridge. Washington County sheriff's deputies received the report 9:30 Sunday morning. The thing, thought to be about four feet tall, proceeded to bite not only a boat's propeller, but also one of the women's fishing poles. The creature was described as green and black with long black hair and large yellow-glowing eyes.[744]

SIGHTINGS 1973

Sykesville Monster

About 20 miles north of Baltimore in Carroll County, the town of Sykesville, Maryland, could boast a population of 1,400 in the early 1970s. On Tuesday, May 29, resident Anthony Dorsey, a volunteer fireman, encountered a creature in a section of town known as Oklahoma Hill. Dorsey at first thought he was seeing a bear but it ultimately proved to be something he couldn't identify. In the publicity of ensuing sightings, the creature entered the rolls of '70s parochial horrors as the Sykesville Monster. Dorsey was watching television that Tuesday night when he heard his dog, Rex, howling from the woods behind his house. "I went to investigate," Dorsey recalled, surprised that his dog had ventured so far into the woods that late at night. "Then I heard a kind of heavy sound," he said, "something like a bear going through the bush." Dorsey gave chase until the thing reached a clearing. "I shined a light in its face and I saw that it had two eyes, the size of jumbo marbles and they were about five inches apart! And when it stood, it looked to be at least seven feet tall!"[745] The news broke in the *Baltimore Afro-American* and that paper remained the Sykesville Monster's primary champion, printing several follow-on stories as additional events unfolded.

As word of Dorsey's sighting spread, residents exhumed several half-forgotten monster terms for this latest creature in their midst. The following article from Hagerstown's *Morning Herald* includes history and lore of previous monsters in the region:

> Maryland State Police are continuing a search in this rural Carroll County community for a huge, hairy monster described by residents as a cross between a "Dwayyo" and a "Snallygaster."
>
> Police pressed a helicopter and searchlights into service last week after Anthony Norris[746] reported finding footprints in his backyard measuring 13 ½ inches long and almost six inches wide.
>
> At the same time, several residents reported sighting the beast described variously as from seven to ten feet tall and very hairy.
>
> State Trooper Donald Higgins, assigned to investigate the case, says he's getting "a lot of [hearsay], but the sightings seem genuine."
>
> About eight years ago, nearby Frederick County was the scene of several incidents involving a mysterious creature described as "about six feet tall, with a big bushy tail and black hair."
>
> A person identified as John Becker told State Police at that time that he had battled the beast—which he called a "Dwayyo"—in his backyard, located near Gambrills State Park.
>
> An Ellerton woman said she had heard it "cry like a baby and then scream like a woman."
>
> Like the Frederick monster, the Sykesville creature is said to have killed several dogs and a cow, and residents refuse to be put off with explanations that it's either an escaped circus gorilla or a deformed bear roaming the area.
>
> "Snallygaster" is defined by Webster's Third New International Dictionary as a "mythical, nocturnal creature, half bird and half reptile, chiefly reported in rural Marland [sic], which preys on children and poultry."
>
> The exact origin of the Snallygaster remains locked in rumor and mystery, but some reports indicate the creature came into being to scare moonshiners around the Middletown area.

> Snallygaster tales continued to flourish through the early 1930's but the sightings finally stopped when a Middletown newspaper published a story saying the winged creature had drowned in a moonshiner's mash barrel in the mountains west of Middletown.
>
> Later, the "Dwayyo" was said to have been hatched from one of the Snallygaster's eggs.
>
> Although police and armed civilians say they'll continue their nightly searches for the monster, Sykesville Police Chief Omer Herbert says the real danger comes from the searchers themselves.
>
> "They don't know what they're looking for. They're jittery. If one comes over one ridge with a rifle and one comes over another ridge well . . . ," Herbert said.[747]

Dorsey wasted little time in calling the Sykesville Police Department and he was soon joined by police office Charles Rupp. Dorsey took Rupp to the location where he saw the large eyes and both men heard a loud crashing noise in the brush in front of them. Dorsey told Bigfoot researcher Mark Opsasnick in 1986 that the men debated their next move. "Officer Rupp told me to go in and check it out," Dorsey told Opsasnick, "and I said no way!"[748]

Rupp made his way into the woods and could hear something in the underbrush. Rupp yelled, "Halt, or I'll shoot." Dorsey recalled to Opsasnick that the men next heard a large tree snap and their unknown quarry moved off into the woods.[749] Rupp was admittedly baffled by the reports. "I don't know whether it was man, critter, or a combination of both," he said. "We've had several prowler reports, but to my knowledge, no official has seen it—as far as I'm concerned, it's all unsubstantial." Rupp was concerned about actions from folks he styled as "latter day Daniel Boones,"—people acting in a vigilante role to hunt the monster, and thusly becoming a danger to themselves and others.

Dorsey's aunt, Mrs. Dorothy Cross of Baltimore, called the offices of the *Baltimore Afro-American* on Wednesday, May 30, prompted by concerns "for the safety" of her loved ones in the community. Wednesday was also the day Chief of Police Omer Hebert and Dorsey searched the area behind Dorsey's home. Approximately 50 yards from the house Herbert discovered three footprints, the best of which he later cast. One of the footprints measured 13 ½ inches long and six inches wide. A right-footed print was found six feet away from a left-footed print, suggesting a very long stride. The *Baltimore*

Afro-American posed the question of hoax or fakery. "Minimal," according to Officer Hebert who noted that since the prints showed their maker's weight was evenly distributed, the chances of hoaxing were slim. While Dorsey and Officer Rupp checked the area both men heard something move away from them into the woods. "Whatever it was didn't respond to command to halt and upon pursuit, it outdistanced us. It was about 6 ft. tall and seemed to be a man."[750]

Amidst the growing hype of a strange creature lurking in the environs around Baltimore, Miss Carolyn Tyson told the *Baltimore Afro-American* that she had experienced Fouke Monster-hype when she lived in Missouri during the previous year. She explained the hairy, human-like creature of the Fouke River bottomlands was "a large walking figure, with long shaggy hair and a weird odor,"[751] reported by several residents. S. Stover was told a story by Patricia Fergeson of an encounter she and her husband experienced with a strange creature in Leakin Park, 20 miles east of Sykesville.

> According to Mrs. Fergeson she and her husband were having a picnic in Leakin Park on a hot summer day in June of 1961. As dark approached, they went to their car to leave. Mrs. Fergeson was going to drive, they got into the car, closed the doors and were talking, when Mrs. Fergeson glanced at the right rear window and saw two huge eyes staring back at her. She screamed and the creature ran down into the stream bottom next to the road. Mr. Fergeson got out of the car and followed it, whereupon the animal pulled back a tree limb like a slingshot and started growling. Mr. Fergeson ran back to the car and he and Mrs. Fergeson left the area quickly. Mrs. Fergeson described the creature to me as being tall and with a large body and a hairless face.[752]

Charles Edward Patterson added further historical perspective as he recounted for the *Afro-American* his story of a creature he had seen in Druid Hill Park in late May or early June, 1968. He recalled the sighting took place late at night, stating, "When that particular section of the park hadn't been closed in, back of the amusement area, my wife and I were coming in my car up behind the Monkey House. It was dark, really black. We were driving toward the lights and that's when I saw the 7-ft. monster they are talking about." Patterson and his wife were completely startled by the creature. "He was about 7 ½ feet and weighed from 265 lbs. He walked fast. He was very swift. He seemed to be leaving some kind of danger. I stopped the car. My wife said, 'Oh my God.' I stepped on the gas. I locked the doors. I stepped on the accelerator peddle [sic] hard and we got out of the area as fast as possible."[753]

> "The way he walked you could tell he was wild. The way he looked, you could tell he was wild. When he turned and looked at the car, I got a good look at him. He was heading to the Monkey House. That's when I took off. Before this, I didn't think anybody would believe me. I said nothing. Last week, I was talking with my wife about the picture in the AFRO. I knew they had it pinned down to a tee. I hope they don't kill him because they could find out more about the thing if he is alive when they catch him."[754]

A truck driver requesting anonymity reported seeing something on Friday, June 8, which was dark brown in color and stood between seven and eight feet tall. The truck driver noticed that the thing appeared to be caked in mud from the waist down and was first seen in the sitting position before it stood upright and quickly disappeared into the woods.[755]

The Sykesville Monster's wildfire publicity inspired a paranormal research group called Odyssey Scientific Research (also referred to in newspaper articles as Odyssey Club, Odyssey Research and Odyssey Scientific International) to investigate the encounters. Over the course of the '70s, John Lutz, director of Odyssey's (then) 14-person organization, claimed his group investigated upwards of 480 claims of unusual phenomenon.[756] Lutz and the Odyssey group had been engaged in investigating UFO reports in Maryland which had been experiencing a resurgence in the Old Line State. Lutz said between September 1971 and February 1972, "we have followed up eight sightings—three on the Eastern Shore and five in the Baltimore metropolitan area."[757] While investigating the Sykesville case, Lutz stated that Dr. Grover Krantz of Washington State University, Dr. J. Allen Hynek, chairman of the Department of Astronomy at Northwestern University, and Dr. Ted Roth, assistant director of the Baltimore City Zoo were all Odyssey consultants.[758]

Reporter John Sherwood's article, "Sykesville Beastie is Still Mystery" in the June 13 *Evening Star and Daily News* described Lutz's investigation of the matter.

Sykesville's antagonist is rumored to have harmed nothing and looks like a skinny eggheaded gorilla, not bird or reptilian at all. And it has human feet, sort of, and in at least one sighting wore trousers.

So yesterday, a strange-looking duo in search of the snallygaster arrived in these hills from the lowlands of Baltimore; Dr. Ted Roth of the Baltimore Zoo, a small, bearded man dressed in an African bush outfit with his Great Dane 'Loki' and a tranquilizing rifle; and a pale, thin man with wispy hair, squeaky voice and a secretive nature.

The pale man was John A. Lutz, 32, an "investigator of local phenomena" and director of the 14-member "Odyssey Scientific Research Association" in Baltimore. In his less adventuresome moments he is a traffic communications dispatcher.

Also there were the skeptical police.

Dr. Roth said he was just there to try to determine if there was a large animal about. (People are talking about gorillas and bears.) One natural resources officer said it was all "an insult to our intelligence." A state policeman said, "I don't know. I just don't know." Another thought "this whole thing is growing out of proportion."

Lutz, caught up in the excitement of a phantom chase, brought out his maps and laid them on a car trunk. There were little X's marking the "sightings" around Sykesville. Slipping on a canteen belt, a packet of snake-bite serum, high rubber boots and a green cap, he noted the area where he wanted to go. . . .

Roth, Lutz and Loki waked across the railroad bridge near the tunnel and down along the banks of the south branch of the Patapsco. Swatting bugs and trudging through a rocky area infested with poisonous copperheads, they looked for any kind of hair snagged on bushes, for droppings, for footprints. They only found days-old deer tracks, and Loki the Great Dane tracker found no scent at all.

Lutz, his canteen belt dragging and his round shoulders sagging, was still puffing from the hot hike. He drank a soda pop, while Dr. Roth tossed down a beer.

"We are suspending the investigation indefinitely," Lutz said, stern and serious, all in his official capacity as Odyssey

> founder and director, "until we hear more reports. We have found no solid evidence of anything."[759]

Following several witness interviews, Lutz suggested they had likely seen "an unidentified prowler,"[760] or had been the victims of pranksters. According to the *Baltimore Afro-American*, "Mr. Lutz added that tape recordings are being made of each [witnesses'] account in order to form verbal records which will be studied by veterinarians, zoologists and biologists." On Sunday, June 10, residents in and around Oklahoma Hill revealed the levels of concern and anxiety many felt. "They should have gangs of men out looking for it," said Mrs. Agness Dorsey, mother of Anthony Dorsey. "I hope it's caught!"[761] Anthony Dorsey stated the monster had also been seen in the surrounding communities of Woodstock and Marriotsville.

Leaving little in the way of even the most obscure stones left unturned, the *Baltimore Afro-American* solicited comment from Dr. Fred Pokrass, Superintendent of Springfield State Hospital, who stated for the record that Springfield had not incurred an unusual number of escapes,[762] and none of mention with particularly big feet. "We always have a certain number who leave without permission," he said, adding nothing unusual "has come to my attention."

The June 30 *Baltimore Afro-American* carried a depiction of the Sykesville Monster with the caption: "Movin' Down the Line is the infamous Sykesville Monster, shown here as described to AFRO artist Thomas Stockett by an excited Sykesville citizen. Although residents in Sykesville say they haven't seen the 'thing' in two days, the AFRO has received numerous calls from Baltimore citizens claiming they have seen some unworldly looking creature in this area. Fiction or Fact? Only time will tell!"[763]

An update from Lutz on Odyssey Scientific Research's revived investigation appeared in the *Baltimore Afro-American* on July 3. The aggregate results from Odyssey's research and interviews led Lutz to reason away prowlers and pranksters. "There's a 95 percent possibility that this Sykesville monster isn't a joke. There is definitely something out there! We're convinced that everybody saw something." Lutz said. "My personal belief is that the monster is a Bigfoot or a Sasquatch, the American counterpart of the Abominable Snowman in the Himalayas."[764]

Lutz added his voice to the cadre cautioning the public against forming groups or posses to hunt the creature. "This thing is more afraid of humans than humans are of it," he said. "Leave your guns at home, don't try to look for something without knowing what you are looking for, let us do it!" Lutz

1970S TRACK CAST BY JOHN LUTZ, SYKESVILLE, MD
COURTESY BRIAN SEECH AND THE CENTER FOR CRYPTOZOOLOGICAL STUDIES

added a final warning: "Like anything, however, it could become dangerous if cornered."[765] But so far in the investigation, there was no cause for alarm. "There have been no confirmed reports of dead animals or dead people. The Sasquatch is not a meat eater, it only eats vegetables and wild berries," Lutz added.[766]

Leroy Byrd of Oliver Street, Baltimore, was skeptical of a monster in his midst. Getting to the bottom of the mystery required some patience, a 30-30, a box of ammo, and a map. "I don't think it's a beast," said Byrd. "I think it's someone dressed up in hides, but whatever it is, give me a rifle and some shells and we'll all find out!" Mr. Byrd's opinion was the entity behind the creature-buzz could be brought in alive, if not unharmed. "I just want to know the general area it's supposed to be in and I'll go there without anybody knowing who I am or what I'm there for, that's the key," Byrd affirmed. "I hope I see him," said Byrd, "then, everyone will know what has been going on. I wouldn't kill him though," Byrd vowed, "I'd just wound him so we could see what the hell it is!"[767]

The reliable *Baltimore Afro-American*, in its July 14 edition, carried a mold-breaking sighting which occurred on Sunday, July 8 of *two* Sykesville Monsters.

> According to the unidentified grandmother, one of the monsters was grizzley [sic] and shaggy and looked like death on crackers. The other monster was much taller and was content to passively stride about his business.
>
> "He (it?) was on his way somewhere and cut a path through Leakin Park like a truck," she said
>
> "I watched from my porch and saw the trees go down as he crashed through," she continued, and it was at this time that grandma realized that she was not witnessing an ordinary occurrence.[768]

Several Sykesville Monster inquiries and reports received at the *Baltimore Afro-American* offices were explored in its July 14 edition, one of the last nods to the Sykesville Monster which that paper entertained:

> One caller said the monster was in East Baltimore around Pulaski Highway and was walking in between two telephone poles looking, "really bad!"

The caller stated some dog howled and barked at him and then dashed away, tail tucked between his legs.

Following closely behind was the caller who said the monster snapped at them, just as she blew into the house.

Another caller reports the monster was out Govans way and looked at her with two sets of eyes at the top of its head.

Like the other two callers, this young lady dashed into the house and didn't touch the ground until she was well inside!

"He went right on by the house," she said, "walking from side to side and stepping high."[769]

Renee Allen Sighting

Renee Allen of Vilda, Oregon, told Lane County sheriff's deputies she glimpsed Bigfoot while she was hiking near Linton Lake in the High Cascades on May 24. Allen told a deputy she and her two-year-old daughter were alone on a trail when she heard a noise. Allen watched what she took to be Bigfoot, about 40 yards away, run up a hill before it quickly disappeared into the forest. In total, Allen stated her sighting of the creature lasted about 90 seconds, adding it ran on two legs and parted the brush with its hands like "a swimmer's breaststroke motion." The face, hands and feet of the creature were a dark brown in color and the hair covering its body was about four inches long. Allen said she wasn't a believer in Bigfoot previous to her sighting.[770]

Bigfoot Hunt Slated

Dean Seaman, assistant director of the Medical Lake, Washington, Parks and Recreation Department, promoted a Medical Lake backpacking program which featured a weekend search for Bigfoot evidence. Eight backpackers had signed up for the trip designed with the "sheer purpose of protecting Bigfoot, because the Department of Natural Resources refuses to acknowledge he exists," Seaman said.[771]

Oberlin Monster

One of the first reports of a red-eyed, gorilla-like creature traipsing through the Huntington woods along Ohio's Lorain-Ashland county line came from a group of Oberlin coon hunters who encountered such a creature on Friday, August 3.

> The first time Randy Reinhold and Jim Chandley saw the 'monster,' most of their viewing was done over their shoulders as they ran out of a swamp in southern Lorain County.
>
> The two, running their dogs, became the first of several people who reported sightings in that area this year of what is becoming a local legend.
>
> Others have reported seeing something seven feet tall and weighing about 400 pounds.
>
> Its eyes, seen only by flashlight, glow red.
>
> It screams, say Reinhold and Chandley. They describe the sound as something between a bear's growl and a woman's scream.
>
> The two, both Oberlin residents, have gone back to the marshy area near Ohio [State Route] 511 and have seen the creature again at distances near 100 yards. They do not want to get closer.[772]

Oberlin Police Chief Lawrence Nowery described the coon hunters as "pretty reliable persons," and officials theorized the monster was a bear or a large dog. Bears are rare in northern Ohio. "These fellows were quite earnest in their story," said one of the investigating policeman. "I've checked these reports out before, and I know that they usually turn out to be a large dog or something," he said. "And I know that a lot of animals, their eyes do glow reddish in the light," he added.[773] Cleveland's *Plain Dealer* reported that the hunters' description was "similar to that of a hairy monster reported in the Oberlin area last August. Friday's report was the first for this year."[774] A similar description to the one offered by Reinhold and Chandley was given to authorities by a 13-year-old Oberlin youth who saw the creature while picking blueberries.[775]

Larry Wickham, an Oberlin police sergeant as well as a wildlife ranger advocated capturing the creature to find out exactly what it was. "Too many people have seen it—there's something there," he said. Wickham had searched for the creature, as a private citizen, in areas he refused at the time to disclose. People living there, Wickham said, were close to shooting anything they saw that moved. "It could be the food prices," Wickham offered.

"These people have had chickens and piglets come up missing for the last six weeks."[776]

Wellington police seemingly solved the monster mystery after several motorists reported a "red-eyed, hairy monster" in a local cornfield on Tuesday, August 7. The investigating officers discovered the "monster" was a white sheet tied around cornstalks with two soft drink cans swabbed with fluorescent paint for its eyes.[777] But the prospect of a prank hadn't dimmed the view of officials, however; Oberlin police hadn't dismissed the earlier reports. "They saw something, all right," said a police spokesperson. "The only question is what."[778]

Honey Island Swamp

The Honey Island Swamp Monster was the subject of a 1978 episode ("The Swamp Monster") of the Leonard Nimoy-hosted *In Search of . . .* television series. "Swamps inspire fears in many minds," intoned Nimoy in the episode's introduction. "Dark and damp, they are full of mystery and creatures that slither in the mud. An experienced guide entered Louisiana's Honey Island Swamp one Fall day in 1973. The outing would become the stuff nightmares are made of. Normally, the trek held few terrors for the guide, even the lethal alligator was rarely a problem for an experienced outdoorsman. The guide would discover something else lurking in these quiet waters, something that struck his boat."[779]

Honey Island Swamp, located in eastern Louisiana between the Pearl River and West Pearl River, is a natural wilderness held in high esteem for its hunting and fishing. A large portion of the Honey Island Swamp area is within the boundaries of protected lands—the Bogue Chitto National Wildlife Refuge contains 40,000 acres and the Pearl River Wildlife Management Area encompasses nearly 36,000 acres. Evoking for some observers a natural cathedral as light shafts downward through cypress and tupelo trees, the Honey Island Swamp is a sanctuary for plants and wildlife.

Greg Faulkner, at the time an occasional guide in the Honey Island Swamp, said he hit a strange creature with his boat while on an outing with his girlfriend. "I rolled over it, the motor kicked up and I realized I hit something," Faulkner said. "I stopped and looked, but I kept going up the bayou a ways." When Faulkner looked back he saw "coming out of the water was it, was the animal. It was about five foot, it was black, and I couldn't tell if it was hair or skin." Faulkner didn't know what he was witnessing. "It was running, it was on two legs. It run up on the bank and disappeared" into the foreboding swamp. Faulkner examined the tracks the creature left behind. Faulkner said he was familiar with bear tracks, deer and wild boar prints, but the creature's prints were none of those. "There was a size ten foot with five toes, and there were a dozen or so prints where it ran along the bank before it disappeared into the swamp," he said. "And it looked like there was some sort of flesh or webbing between the toes," he added.[780]

Stan Gordon

Investigator Stan Gordon, who by profession was an electronics technician with a specialty in radio communication, traces his first foray into exploring and investigating UFOs, Bigfoot, and a host of other unexplained phenomenon back to about age 10. His birthday occurred during Halloween and spooky stories always held his interest. His frequent trips to the library started him on his journey of conducting research and he started cutting out articles from newspapers and magazines to put into scrapbooks.[781] Starting in 1965 and extending into the 21st century, Gordon conducted thousands of on-scene investigations of mysterious encounters across Pennsylvania. Throughout the '70s, he was one of the most active researchers into Bigfoot and unusual events. Gordon gained eminence in part for his paranormal investigation into a series of Bigfoot encounters and UFO sightings that occurred throughout Pennsylvania in 1973.

A 1973 Gallup poll revealed that 15 million Americans had seen UFOs and 51% of the population believed UFOs were "real"—both large increases since Gallup's previous poll taken in 1966.[782]

Stan Gordon was director of the Westmoreland County U.F.O. Study Group (WCUFOSG), which he had organized in September 1970, and which later became the Pennsylvania Center for UFO Research in 1975. Gordon also served as a State-Section Director for the Mutual UFO Network (MUFON) during the '70s.[783] By 1972, the WCUFOSG had 40 members. "Our main goal is to be able to send out field investigators who know how to gather physical evidence and collect data," Gordon told the *Greensburg Tribune Review*. "We try to find a logical explanation for the things people see," he stated. "And 95 percent of the time we do." The WCUFOSG's Monitoring Station, WDX3GHF was, during different periods in the 1970s, staffed 24-hours a day.[784]

In the February 1974 *Skylook*, Gordon said his 24-hour UFO clearinghouse, staffed by as many as five people at once, investigated close to 600 reports during 1973—truly a banner year. Regarding Bigfoot, Gordon said, "there is some evidence that some of these creatures are UFO-related. I think that the creature data is extremely important for all serious UFO investigators to be aware of."[785]

A hallmark of Gordon's approach was not to discount, and indeed probe the possibility that some of the anomalous events his group investigated could be linked. "There is a great deal more involved in it from the puzzle we are beginning to put together. This data will be released as soon as possible," he said in the February 1974 *Skylook*.[786] Gordon told the *Uniontown Evening Standard* about an incident which demonstrated a possible connection between UFOs and Bigfoot that occurred at Presque Isle State Park in July 1966. Observers witnessed a UFO land on a beach and a hairy creature was spotted moments later.[787] The raw quantity of Bigfoot sightings convinced Gordon the phenomenon was widespread, noting that "these creatures are apparently showing up all over the country." Gordon said the typical Bigfoot was eight to nine feet tall, hair-covered, walked upright on two legs, sported long arms, had orange-red eyes, emitted a foul odor, and made sounds like a crying baby. Gordon's study of myriad reports had convinced him that creature sightings increased as UFO sightings increased. During several of WCUFOSG's investigations of ostensible UFO sites, enigmatic footprints and other evidence of Bigfoot turned up.

Bigfoot Shook Couple's Car

Wanting to experience a sighting of Bigfoot, Anne and Jay Hancock (pseudonyms) certainly got their wish. The Hancocks arrived at Jumonville (a United Methodist camp and retreat center in Fayette County, PA) in July 1973 with their four-year-old son and German shepherd. They had heard that if anyone parked near the Great Cross of Christ, a Bigfoot would approach the vehicle. Deciding to test if this was true, the couple drove toward the Fayette County landmark. Approaching the Cross, the Hancocks met two teenaged boys and soon after noticed a fog descend onto the area. "My husband thought he heard something so he turned the car lights on," Anne said. "There it was. A huge creature about eight feet tall with long, dark matted hair from head to toe."

"As soon as my husband turned the lights on, the creature slid down over a cliff, which would be about 35 feet." The Hancocks were excited and intrigued and decided to remain in the area on the chance they might get a second look at the creature. Suddenly their dog started whining. "Our German shepherd is attack-trained, but is usually very gentle," Anne said.

"But he jumped toward the back of the car and started barking at the rear window.

"Suddenly, the dog started biting at the window as though he was trying to grab something. I was quite frightened when I saw the white teeth of his mouth, so I grabbed my son." Holding her son close, she strained to catch sight of what was outside the car. "When I looked through the window, I could see a pair of red eyes peering at me and a huge pair of hairy hands clawing at the window. Then the car started shaking." Mr. Hancock lost no time in starting the car and driving back down the mountain.[788]

Greensburg, Pennsylvania, Sightings

The Washington, Pennsylvania, *Observer-Reporter* reported that on a foggy morning in early summer several residents of Greensburg, a town of 17,000 in southwestern Pennsylvania, gathered around what they thought was a three-toed, 18-inch-long footprint. Several more townspeople subsequently reported seeing what may have left the alleged print—an ape-like creature topping out at an estimated 8 feet in height. Police became concerned following reports of bands of vigilante-like hunters driving backroads with guns at hand while scanning the woods for Bigfoot. "What started out as being kind of funny has turned into a sickening situation," commented a state police dispatcher.

Police commonly referred reports and queries they received to the then 23-year-old Gordon. "Stan's a good kid, not a screwball," said Greensburg Fire Chief Edward Hutchinson. "Some reports came to us even before the publicity began," said Gordon. "We have a number of hair samples and waste material we hope to have analyzed." Gordon, whose uncle once headed the county detectives, stated he operated with a healthy skepticism, but maintained "there always is a possibility . . ."

Not all evidence measured up. One solitary print was found and one official who viewed it said, "It could have been drawn in the mud with a person's finger." Hutchinson took two trained bloodhounds to the scene of a sighting but the dogs didn't pick up a scent. "A couple of days ago a police department nearby got called to a farm by a woman who said she saw a black object in her field," said Hutchinson. "When they got there, she had a bead on the object, which turned out to be a man in a dark sweatshirt training his bird dog."[789]

John Chedrick Jr., a steelworker, reported he had smelled "something like rotten eggs," late one night. Chedrick turned to a window which was eight feet above the ground. "I glanced out the window and saw two shiny eyes," he said. "They were reddish, like a dog's when you shine a light in them at night. I got so scared I jumped into bed." Chedrick was taken from his job to the hospital the following day. "I have a bad heart," he said, "but I don't know if seeing that thing had anything to do with going to the hospital." Chedrick's wife reported her son had found large tracks along railroad tracks near their home. "Ah, it's just a damned joke," said Hutchinson. "Eight-foot is awful god-damned big to be walking around the countryside without leaving but one footprint here and there," he said. "Find me a couple of prints and I'll bring out the dogs. I don't want to discount it, but get me some concrete evidence." Hutchinson's skepticism was mirrored by a local paper, the *Tribune-Review*, which, until the spate of Bigfoot activity started, had only given scant attention to the subject. The *Observer-Reporter* of Washington, Pennsylvania, took the *Tribune-Review's* skepticism a step further:

> "One last word about Bigfoot: Unless or until someone leads this creature or thing into the newsroom, with or without a leash, this is the last time the word will appear in this newspaper's news columns, even in jest.
>
> "As for you true believers, please contact the newspapers, radio stations, TV stations and neighbors and friends who started this nonsense, with your tips and questions. We have more serious things on our minds."[790]

Blairsville

> Residents throughout a wide area of Westmoreland County have been seeing (or hearing) a lot about a big (9 foot tall), hairy, sulphur-like smelling monster known as "Big Foot" for several weeks now.
>
> The monster apparently is afraid of humans and must be harmless because no one has suffered any more than the "loss of a year's growth" after seeing the "big one."
>
> In the most recent encounter with humans, Big Foot supposedly scratched on the side of a mobile home along Route 982 in Derry Township, and when the couple went outside, the woman screamed and Big Foot took off. Police arrived in minutes and found three large footprints near the mobile home.

> According to searchers, including an off-duty Latrobe policeman who photographed the prints, the creature was running over and knocking down small trees in its haste to depart.
>
> Depending on who tells the most recent story about Big Foot, the monster is described as standing about nine feet tall, has long, hairy arms, a human-like face, and emits a sulphur-like smell from its body. Some say the monster makes sounds like a crying baby and others say it sounds like a man screaming.
>
> Reports have even come in from Glassport and the Mon Valley areas in addition to reported sightings at Herminie, Hillside, Latrobe, and other areas.
>
> The director of a group handling calls concerning Big Foot, Stan Gordon, urges reports of sightings be mailed to his 6 Oakhill Ave., Greensburg address complete with a report of details. Mr. Gordon is a member of the UFO Study Group.[791]

As Pennsylvania Bigfoot reports continued into September, one stood out for a reported personality change for one of the witnesses, a feature similar to the later Kowalczyk encounter in October.

> Perhaps the most interesting case thus far publicized concerns a reported creature sighting in a wooded area by two girls about 9:30 P.M. on Sept. 27, 1973. The two reported that they encountered a white, hairy creature about seven or eight-feet tall, carrying a luminescent sphere in its hand. Both girls were reportedly white with shock when they returned to their house.
>
> The father of one of the girls went into the woods (he owned the property), according to the daughter, and stayed for over an hour. However, in an interview the father denied having gone into the woods, and he stated that there were some things that shouldn't be discussed. He added that he didn't want anyone tramping around in his woods. The man reportedly experienced a personality change following the episode. After the incident described by the girls, a "plane" was reportedly seen shining a bright light down into the woods.[792]

Yothers Encounter

While visiting their son in Naples, Florida, over the '74 Christmas holidays, Mr. and Mrs. Chester Yothers of Whitney, Pennsylvania, read several accounts concerning the Everglades' Skunk Ape in local newspapers. The stories struck them like a revelation, marking the moment they realized there could be an explanation for what they saw in Pennsylvania 15 months previous. Hoping to compare notes with anyone who could help explain what he'd seen, Mr. Yothers checked with the sheriff's department for recent Skunk Ape reports but was unsuccessful in obtaining witnesses' names.

> Anonymity is usually followed in monster sightings, Yothers said, because eye witnesses want to avoid hounding by the curious or ridicule by the skeptical.
>
> Yothers followed the same procedure but he, and some of his Western Pennsylvania neighbors, have since publicly told the story of their monster sightings.
>
> The Western Pennsylvania monster is known among the residents as Bigfoot and has been sighted off and on for several years, Yothers reports.

Yothers' experience with Bigfoot took place in the early morning hours of September 3, 1973. The events began with a resounding thump on the outside of his mobile home. Yothers' first thought was someone was trying to break into his garage. After throwing open his bedroom curtains Yothers received a most unexpected sight. Standing only twelve feet away was a veritable monster which Yothers described as "huge, a two-legged thing with a human posture about it. Its arms went below its knees. It was all hairy and didn't seem to have a neck. I didn't believe it even after I saw it." Yothers woke his wife and she also glimpsed the creature. The couple called the police but by the time they arrived the creature had secreted away. The police found a bent awning and a large footprint was located right outside the Yothers' front door. A substance which *Naples Daily News* reporter John Tippins suggested could have been blood was found smeared on side of the trailer.

Yothers said examination of the footprint revealed it was 14 inches long and 7 ¾ inches wide. Its depression into the ground indicated the creature weighed 350 to 400 pounds, Yothers stated. Further investigation of the premises yielded a smudge on a window which was surmised to have been left by a nose. The distance between the imprint on the window and the ground was 8 ½ feet. According to Yothers, others had seen the creature in the area and their reports added that the beast growled and smelled like sewer gas. Yothers possessed pictures of the footprints found on his property.

> Yothers said he was very skeptical of the Bigfoot stories some of his neighbors told him until he saw the beast himself. Footprints, believed to be those of Bigfoot, have been found around his mobile home on occasion since the sighting.
>
> Since he saw the beast, others have become interested in monster sightings around the nation. There appear to be several Bigfoots roaming isolated parts of the country, he says.
>
> Although several theories have been advanced on the origin and purpose of the beasts, Yothers doesn't have any solid explanation for what he saw but adds, "I keep two loaded cameras and a loaded gun in the trailer with me now."[793]

Westmoreland County Bigfoot Sighting

"I wasn't more than four feet away from that 'thing'," Shyla Kemper (pseudonym) told researchers with the Pennsylvania Center for UFO Research on September 9, 1973. The 'thing' was a Bigfoot-like creature that several people had seen during the summer in Westmoreland County, PA. Kemper related how she had gone to bed about 1 A.M. but awoke from her slumber with the feeling that someone was looking at her. She glanced at her clock and noted it was 2 A.M. As she started to roll over to go back to sleep, she noticed something at her bedroom window which was nine feet off the ground. Her curtains, which she maintained had been closed when she went to bed, were now open permitting the view of an inhuman face at the window. "It looked like a gorilla," Mrs. Kemper recalled with emotion. Her bed was only four feet from the window. Determined to close the window, she slipped out the opposite side of her bed, but having been painted recently by her husband, it stubbornly remained stuck in the open position. "I moved to the back of the bed and all it did was stare at me. I called to my daughter to come and help me because that creature was at my window, but she was so scared she couldn't move. I sat there trying to think of what to do. Finally, I had nerve enough to run over and close the curtains," she said.

Kemper reported the creature had deep set eyes under which were pronounced wrinkles. Its eyes were more oval than vertical, she said. "The strange thing of it is that they were not the same size. I wish you could have seen the reddish glow they seemed to give off. The eyes were all dark inside. There was no white as there is in our eyes." The creature's eyes were the definite feature Kemper fixated on. "I can't believe I was looking directly into its eyes," she said. "The only thing I can tell you is that the skin was shiny and leathery with many wrinkles," she said describing the creature's forehead. The nose was short and flat resembling a gorilla's. The sides of the creature's face were dark and could have been hair. Regaining her composure, Kemper managed to crawl from her room and joined her daughter. The mother and daughter later saw a shadow passing across a window but didn't see the creature again. Later investigation at the Kemper residence was unable to discern any tracks in the hard ground but did locate spots of flattened grass.[794]

Kowalczyk Affair

Based upon his research, Gordon concluded Pennsylvania Bigfoot sightings usually occurred at night and contained a single creature, though he did have multiple-creature reports in his files. By 1973, Gordon knew of at least three creatures which had been shot at.[795] One of those incidents was the Kowalczyk Affair, an unusual UFO and Bigfoot sighting occurring along Vances Mill-Road in North Union Township, Fayette County, that brought media attention to Bigfoot in Pennsylvania and to Gordon as the foremost researcher in the state.

> While some of the Pennsylvania "Big Foot" creatures bear some resemblance to the Fouke Monster of Arkansas, the Sasquatch of the Northwest, the Missouri Momo, the Everglades "Skunk Ape," the Maryland Sykesville monster, and [others], there are also differences in the descriptions given by Pennsylvania witnesses, probably based in part on variations in the creature, and possibly in part on pre-conceived ideas of what monsters are supposed to look like.
>
> For UFO investigators, the relationship of the monsters to UFOs is more important than the similarities of the creatures to each other. An Oct. 24 incident near Uniontown, Pa., represents another in a series of apparent UFO-creature tie-ins

> which intrigue UFO investigators like Gordon. About 15 persons claim to have witnessed the landing of a huge reddish ball-like object, but the view of the incident reported by George Kowalczyk is of most interest.
>
> Kowalczyk was driving when he saw an orange light in the sky over his father's field. He parked his truck, and took his .30-16 rifle and two neighbor boys to investigate. The object slowly descended apparently to the ground. "This time it was completely white. It was about 100 feet in diameter, as big as a house, with a dome on top. It was very, very bright," Kowalczyk reported to investigator Gordon. The object sounded like a large lawnmower.[796]

Gordon said the Kowalczyk Affair was like other reports involving multiple, unusual phenomenon in southwestern Pennsylvania which his organization had looked into. "We've had eight confirmed sightings from reliable sources of low level UFO activity minutes before or minutes after Bigfoot was seen," he said. Gordon had already been busy investigating Bigfoot reports near Greensburg in late September and the first part of October. WCUFOSG was particularly interested in the sighting because of the details it shared with other reports. "There haven't been any sightings of Bigfoot since the first week of October in western Pennsylvania," Gordon said, "but the creature described in this incident fits those creatures identically." Gordon; David Smith, a physics teacher and a civil defense radiation expert; student Dennis Smeltzer, a sociology major; George Lutz, Jr., ex-Air Force and co-director with Gordon of the WCUFOCG; and photographer David Baker,[797] interviewed witnesses and thoroughly investigated the site. Though no footprints were found, Gordon reported that farm animals in the area, including dogs and cows, would not go near the spot where the UFO was observed to land and the creatures were seen.

Of the 15 persons who said they observed the landing of a huge, red, ball-like object, 22-year-old George Kowalczyk had perhaps the best view of both the UFO and the two hairy creatures in a field on his father's farm. Kowalczyk's encounter started when he watched an orange light in the sky over his father's field. He grabbed his .30-06 rifle and with two neighbor boys went to the field to investigate. "He said he watched the thing descend slowly to the ground," Gordon stated. "This time it was completely white. It was about 100 feet in diameter, as big as a house, with a dome on top. It was very, very bright," said Gordon, echoing Kowalczyk's testimony. The object made a noise compared to a lawnmower. One of the boys spotted movement along a fence and the group subsequently saw two creatures, one eight feet tall, and the other slightly shorter at about seven feet tall. Both walked stiff-legged, were hair-covered, possessed long arms, and were making crying sounds likened to an upset baby. An odor like sulphur was smelled which Gordon noted was a recurring detail from many Bigfoot-like creature reports. One youth ran away in fear, and Kowalczyk fired a warning shot into the air and then leveled a shot at the creatures when they began to advance toward him. The *Uniontown Evening Standard* related Kowalczk's testimony of what happened next:

> "The larger creature made a moaning sound, raised his right hand and the light in the field disappeared and the sound stopped. The two creatures then slowly walked away."
>
> Mr. Kowalczyk, who stated his eyes began to bother him at this time and that lights on his pickup truck dimmed, then got into his truck and called the State Police.
>
> Both Mr. Gordon and a trooper at the scene acknowledged that Kowalczyk was visibly shaken by the incident.
>
> No physical signs of a landing were evident, but Mr. Gordon said the grass in the pasture was cropped low by grazing cattles [sic]. In addition, no footprints were found, but the investigation is continuing.
>
> "We've had dozens of sightings all over the state in the past few weeks," Mr. Gordon said, "of large luminous objects hovering near the roofs of cars. The headlights would dim and the radio would be filled with static when this happened," he added.
>
> Mr. Gordon noted that over a dozen UFO sightings were reported in western Pennsylvania on Thursday night.
>
> His office has reported over 400 sightings already this year.
>
> "I never believed in any of this," said one eyewitness, "but I know what I saw. And I saw that thing."[798]

The similarity of physical characteristics and mannerisms between the creatures in Kowalczyk's sighting and the creature descriptions given by other Greenburg witnesses impressed Gordon: long dark hair all over the body, long arms, eight-feet tall, and a sulphur-smelling odor were qualities present in many sightings.[799]

Hynek

In 1973, the outbreak of UFO hysteria in the years following World War II was some 20 years in the past and a new wave of public interest in UFOs in 1973 recalled that earlier period. Dr. Josef Allen Hynek had served as science advisor for three U.S. Air Force UFO-related projects: Project Sign, Project Grudge, and Project Blue Book. His thoughts on UFOs, by extension, can be applied to other paranormal subjects.

Hynek told reporter James Quinlan that science's provincialism on fact was temporal in nature. "We've arrived at the final point. The guys before us were dumbbells." And here Hynek advised a measure of caution against hubris. "We forget that we're going to be the dumbbells to those who come after us." Quinlan remembered an 1895 quote from philosopher and psychologist William James, "There is included in human nature an ingrained naturalism and materialism of mind which can only admit facts that are actually tangible. . . . Our science is but a drop, our ignorance a sea. Whatever else be certain, this at least is certain; that the world of our present natural knowledge is enveloped in a larger world of some sort, of whose residual properties we at present can frame no positive idea." Hynek said he neither believed nor disbelieved UFOs; he contended *belief* was a proper term for the auspices of religion.

> This is the role the bearded, gentle man who gives the impression of a stereotyped television father, has assumed. Like the suggested "bit of undigested pork" in Scrooge's belly he has been giving the scientific world dreadful nightmares. To the cultist and "nuts" as he calls them he has steadfastly refused their emotional demands for acceptance of the UFO phenomena.
>
> "Allow for the unknown," Hynek tells his fellow scientists.
>
> "Proof, where is your proof?" he demands from the UFO "believer."

Hynek told Quinlan that people—witnesses—were central to the study of UFOs.

> At the heart of the total mystery for Hynek are both the people involved in most UFO experiences and the strong emotional reaction to the whole thing by men and women from many different disciplines.
>
> By and large the majority of sightings are made and reported by rational people.
>
> "The most coherent and articulate UFO reports come from people who have not given much thought to the subject and who generally are surprised and shocked by their experience."

Upstairs in his Evanston, Illinois home, Dr. J. Allen Hynek leaned back in his office chair, puffed on his pipe and explained his thinking on the theoretical presence of UFOs in our world to Quinlan.

> "Between the nucleus of the atom and the outside electrons there is relatively as much space as between the sun and the planets. There is a lot of space in matter. Matter is almost a vacuum really."
>
> "There could be interlocking universes. The cultists have been saying that for centuries but that's not science.
>
> "If I had to be pressed to the wall for a hypothesis I would say we live in a multi-dimensional spacetime continuum and the typical world we see around us represents a cross section through that.
>
> "Look at the evidence that these things are reported to do. They appear very suddenly and disappear very suddenly. The question is where are they right now? Where is this thing that visited these two in Mississippi [Pascagoula Abduction] right now physically?
>
> "Time and again I've had reports of where sort of a fuzzy cloud appears around them and then the whole cloud disappears. Almost like ectoplasm disappearing into another dimension. They violate gravity. They take off with enormous acceleration without any sonic boom. A physical object can't do that. They make right angle turns. Any object with any appreciable mass can't do that.
>
> "They behave more like holographic images, like projections, more than physical things. Yet they produce real

physical effects, stop cars, frighten animals, break branches, leave marks on the ground, and in that sense they are almost like the poltergeist phenomena. Nobody knows what they are but they're pretty well documented.

"That is why I say think the UFO phenomenon is a signal of another domain of nature that we haven't explored yet."[800]

Enfield Monster

Enfield, Illinois, was the scene of a lot of strangeness in 1973. Enfield resident Henry McDaniel, a disabled war veteran, reported two possibly related incidents: he saw a gray, hairy, three-legged monster four to five feet tall with pink reflecting eyes on April 25 and he discovered six-toed tracks near his home three to five inches across.[801]

Greg Garrett, a boy in McDaniel's neighborhood was the first to experience what was to become known as the Enfield Monster. Playing in his own yard about half an hour before the events on McDaniel's porch, Garrett claimed an unknown creature attacked him, stomping on his feet and tearing the boy's tennis shoes to shreds. Garrett managed to escape to his home crying hysterically.

McDaniel stated events started about 9:30 P.M. on the Wednesday night in question when he heard scratching at his door. Checking on the noise, he was startled by a creature on his porch which he described as having "three legs on it, a short body, two little short arms coming out of its breast area, and two pink eyes as big as flashlights. It stood four-and-a-half to five feet tall and was grayish-colored. It was trying to get into the house."

"When I first saw it, I thought it was an animal. I went back (inside the house) and got a gun and flashlight," McDaniel said. Kicking the door open, he found the creature still on his porch. "It was right about three feet from me. I wasn't scared. Then I saw those pink eyes shine at me like a reflector on a car. It had pink eyes, a large head and was a kind of dirty-ish gray color . . . hairy . . . about four or five feet tall. Standing right in front of the door on three legs just like a human being." McDaniel said he shot at the creature four times.[802] "I knew I hit it once," he said, noting the creature "hissed like a wildcat." The creature proceeded to cover about seventy-five feet in three bounds and disappeared into underbrush bordering railroad tracks near McDaniel's house. McDaniel called police to report the events. Law enforcement investigated and found some fur as well as several four-inch tracks "like those of a dog, except they had six toe pads."[803]

Almost two weeks after McDaniel shot at a creature on his porch, he encountered the unexpected animal a second time. On Sunday, May 6, at around 3 A.M., McDaniel was awakened by neighborhood dogs' howling. Looking outside he saw the creature again. "I didn't shoot at it or anything," McDaniel said. "It started on down the railroad [B&O] track. It wasn't in a hurry or anything." The creature was about 75 feet away. "I wasn't scared," McDaniel said. "I'd like to have it as a pet and charge admission. It's something that's there and we've got to accept it."[804] White County Sheriff Roy Poshard Jr. was concerned for the public's safety. Five young men were arrested by Deputy Sheriff Jim Clark on Tuesday, May 8, for discharging their weapons in the neighborhood after they opened fire on something gray and hairy they had spotted in the underbrush. Three Elwood youths were detained for not possessing valid hunting licenses and carrying uncased guns. Game Warden Donald Hall fined each of the youths $30. The idea for their "monster hunt" started when the youths heard stories of the Enfield Horror on the radio. The "hunt" provided some excitement when half the group saw a grey, hairy creature run through underbrush faster than a man could have. One youth fired a .22 rifle at it and others fired their shotguns.

> White County Deputy Sheriff Jim Clark said the guns carried by the youths were confiscated but would be returned.
>
> "Nothing I know of is in season now, especially monsters," Clark said. "Anybody we know of out hunting monsters, especially with guns, will be put in jail. We're afraid they'll kill somebody."[805]

Rick Rainbow, then of radio station WWKI in Kokomo, Indiana, spent two days in Enfield looking into the matter of unknown creatures in the area. With three others he spied something he described as five feet tall, grayish-black and stooped over, near Springerton, north of Enfield.[806] Rainbow was credited with obtaining a tape recording of its wailing. Cryptozoologist Loren Coleman, who also investigated the Enfield sightings, likewise heard sounds attributed to the creature.[807]

"I hate to dispute somebody's word on something like that," said a waitress at the Ecko Café and Motel located a mile south from town at the intersection of routes 45 and 460, as she pondered McDaniel's monster sighting, "but I doubt it," she concluded. Reporter Chris Dettro, did a follow-up story in August on Enfield's strange events; he asked the waitress if the creature's notoriety had brought in business. "Nah, not a bit," she said. "You'd think it would've though, wouldn't you?" Perhaps as an afterthought she added, "I think it's about all over now, anyway. I heard the sheriff told him [McDaniel] he'd better not be seein' any more monsters out there or he'd be off to the funny farm. And somebody said he's left town." So, the creature, whatever it was, hadn't been caught? "Nooo," the waitress said, "but if we do we're gonna butcher him and eat him."

Dettro described White County Sheriff Roy Poshard Jr. as young, with muscular arms and thick chest. "No, there ain't a damn thing to it," he responded emphatically when asked his opinion on the matter of local monsters. "I let all that stuff go until he [McDaniel] got people with guns out there. Then I went out and told him, 'If I hear any more from out here, I'm haulin' you in.'" Heading into town, Dettro sought out other opinions on the matter. Reba Trapp owned Reba's Café which shared a building with the Gulf gasoline station. Dettro ordered from a menu posted above the counter which ended with "No Swearing Aloud—B-Good or B-Gone." One of the patrons, a trucker, was aware of the monster-doings which had transpired in Enfield earlier in the year. "I think I'm going to apply for hazardous driving pay every time I come to Enfield," he said playfully.[808]

Dettro interviewed McDaniel for a retrospective on the Enfield Monster.

> McDaniel, a disabled World War II veteran, has two guns in the house, a little .22, which he says makes "a pretty good hole," now sits by the door—just in case.
>
> The other one is in the bedroom, where McDaniel once shot a hole through his wall at something that was fooling around out back of his house. "It might have been that thing then, I don't know."
>
> Anyway, about 9:30 [P.M., April 25] Henry heard the scratching outside his door and looked out and saw something. He thought it was an animal—maybe a bear, "We have bears down here sometimes."
>
> He got his gun and a flashlight and went outside, where the wind was blowing strongly.
>
> He spotted something between two rosebushes to the left of a big maple tree in his front yard. When he got to within about eight feet of the thing, he shined his light right in his eyes. That's when the light came back pink at him, and that's

> when Henry fired his gun. Four times. And he's sure he hit the thing once.
>
> "It just hissed. Did you ever hear a cottonmouth hiss? Well, that's how it sounded.
>
> "And then it jumped into those weeds over there," Henry said, pointing to some thick growth. "And then it jumped again, over that ditch, and then a third time onto the tracks. I never did see it turn. It just jumped."
>
> The total distance from the rosebushes to the B&O tracks is about 75 feet. All around the tracks is scrub brush and undergrowth so thick you could dump a body in it and they'd not find it for a year.
>
> Then Henry jumped the ditch and got on the tracks and shined his light. By the time Henry had gone about 80 feet, the thing had gone bootin' and a scootin' a good 440 yards down to where the tracks curved.
>
> "The state police had somebody here in a hurry," says Mrs. McDaniel. But they didn't produce any monster. His tracks and some fur on the bushes were all that were left McDaniel said.[809]

Myrtis Fields, the Enfield town treasurer and stringer for the *Carmi Times* and radio station WROY, said she received a letter addressed to the publisher of the Enfield newspaper, and owing to no newspaper in Enfield, Fields opened it. The letter was from Alan Yorkshire of Elyria, Ohio, who thought the Enfield monster could be his pet kangaroo, Macey, which had been missing—either a run-away or stolen—for over a year. Yorkshire offered a $500 reward for information leading to the capture of his pet. McDaniel was dismissive of the kangaroo angle. "I used to have one as a pet myself," he said, "until I sold it to this fella that had an animal show. And kangaroo tracks have claw marks, and a kangaroo has a narrow face. This wasn't no kangaroo."

McDaniel and his wife admitted they had borne some public disapproval because of their encounter with the creature. "They think I'm crazy," he said. "I can't help what I saw. But it's not my problem. If that thing kills somebody, it just isn't my problem. If I see it again, though, I'm gonna call the FBI, not the sheriff. There's other people that's seen it too. They just ain't saying anything." Dettro ended his visit to Enfield bemused that the events from April and May had caused such long-lasting exasperation. "I just wish all this was over," Mrs. McDaniel said.[810]

Author Troy Taylor traveled to Enfield to interview people who had experienced the Enfield Horror in 1973 for his book *Monsters of Illinois: Mysterious Creatures in the Prairie State*.

> I visited Enfield in the summer of 2004 and spoke to a number of people about their memories of April and May 1973. Many that I spoke with had never heard of the encounters at all, but several others spoke guardedly of that spring, usually talking in a low voice as if they didn't want anyone else to hear what they were saying. An older woman that I met in one of the local gas stations explained that most people were embarrassed to talk about what had occurred. "Things were in such an uproar around here at the time," she said. "There were people coming into town looking for monsters. It was all really kind of silly considering that hardly anyone saw the thing anyway. We were locking our doors at night, though, and not letting the kids play outside after dark. Thinking back, we probably overreacted, but most everyone I knew was pretty scared."[811]

Taylor asked her for her thoughts as to what the Enfield Monster could have been. "No idea," she replied, "and I can't even say for sure that it was real. I never saw anything and don't know anyone who did. I had a neighbor who heard some weird noises one night but that could have been a stray dog, I don't know. I've got no idea what that thing could have been—but I sure wouldn't have wanted it scratching on my door in the middle of the night."[812]

Mojave Desert

Jerome Clark and Loren Coleman wrote in the January-February 1973 *INFO Journal* that "Fairies, anthropoids, UFOs: in a sense all are the same, each no more and no less real than the others, and all are part of a vast riddle whose answers do not wait on another planet but much, much closer to home."[813] The following events took place amidst the northern Mojave Desert's rolling foothills, broad mesas, Joshua trees, and native yucca in the summer of 1973. Author Peter Guttilla had worked for Stanton Friedman's California UFO Research Institute in the early 1970s by designing, editing, and typing newsletters. Several reports and clippings from late 1972 helped Guttilla decide that a connection between UFOs and Bigfoot could be possible.

His article "Bigfoot: 3 Tales of Terror" in the October 1976 *UFO Report* explored a series of events Guttilla had a personal hand in.

> On July 18th [1973] our group, The Western Society for the Explanation of the Unexplained, received an urgent telephone call from Marvin J__ reporting that local residents had witnessed a low-flying UFO jettison "something" to the ground. Marvin seemed extremely upset by the incident and asked us to look into it. The society, which is a type of "Invisible College," consisting of an aerospace scientist, a college professor, a university student, and myself [Guttilla], consented and, after some fast and furious preparations, arrived at the location late that afternoon.[814]

At about 10:00 P.M. on July 17, three individuals watched a glowing, torpedo-shaped object in the sky descend close to the ground where it seemed to hover and several dark objects dropped from the object to the ground. Guttilla's group interviewed the witnesses separately and found that despite the inability to provide a description of the dropped objects, the witnesses agreed the objects were animate forms that ambled off upon reaching terra firma.

> As the shapes fled into the night, the UFO silently swiveled on its axis and shot off into the distance and disappeared. One of the eyewitnesses, a Ms. S__, theorized the dark "figures" were living things and suspected that the glowing dots were eyes permitting the entities to see in the dark. When asked why she thought this, she said as the masses changed direction the dots appeared to grow closer together and widen respectively, "Just as if they were looking around when they moved." Ms. S__ pointed out that she could not sleep after the sighting, and her eyes burned severely for several hours afterward. She had also awakened abruptly from light sleep in the early morning hours muttering, "No union now . . ." A meaningless phrase but one that left her with the impression that the whole incident was to be forgotten before she could get any rest.[815]

Guttilla and his group found tracks in the area, but none proved suitable for casting. The Society's investigating members systematically widened their search and discovered several additional sets of tracks, these only a few miles north of a U.S. Air Force facility. One set of well-defined, 18-inch long tracks displayed five toes, seven inches wide at the heel, and showed a six-foot stride. An interesting peculiarity of these tracks was that the foot that made them was twisted and the toes were contracted into a cluster as if fused. The middle toe appeared enlarged, and the fourth and fifth toes seemed practically joined, the same condition as the big toe and the second. The effects of the toe arrangements were graphically depicted by the extrusion of soils forced up between them.

> On July 25th we returned to the area hoping to find some answers to a few of the questions. We had received a frantic telephone call from the wife of another professional rancher who lived close to where the original sighting took place. Mr. L__, a former newspaperman, wrote the following report of the events of the preceding night.
>
> "We set out on foot along a ridge to the north of the ranch. We walked about two miles along an old rutted service road that wound its way through dense overgrowth. Armed only with flashlights, we followed the road through a veritable jungle of creosote bush and manzanita until it ended in a clearing on which stood the ruins of an old adobe corral. On several successive nights we had heard high-pitched wailing sounds from the surrounding foothills. Our dogs cowered and livestock panicked when the shrieks began, and even our neighbors were becoming alarmed. As the minutes passed each of us had a growing feeling of apprehension. We walked about a mile when suddenly an awful moan floated out from the darkness ahead of us. The cry resembled that of a sobbing man—yet it was different. It seemed resonant and bellowing.[816]

They waited for ten minutes to hear the cry again but all seemed still and calm save for the gentle susurrus sigh of the wind. Taking the dirt road linking the main highway and the military reservation, the group headed back to the ranch. They again felt awe at the silence surrounding them. "Was there a Bigfoot nearby? The Indians said that when the Mountain Devil was near, his looming presence blankets the countryside."

> "As we walked, Mr. C__ noticed that a distant shanty situated to the east of us was strangely dark. Usually, the owner, whom

the local people considered a hermit, kept a bright light on throughout the night. Passing the hermit's shack, we inched our way along and discovered that the northern gate to the military access road had apparently been torn from its hinges. The hermit's dogs were quiet, too. This was odd since they usually erupted in violent fits of barking upon a stranger's approach. We had heard complaints about them before and were making enough noise to raise the dead—yet there wasn't even a whimper from the dogs. We continued along the base of the foothills for about another mile, sweeping the ground with our lights in a wide arc searching for telltale tracks. We were in luck for there ahead of us were several sets of three-toed prints not unlike the casts we'd seen earlier. As we huddled around one of the better prints, we discussed the odd twisting of the foot that was special to the Mojave Bigfoot.

"As we knelt on the ground examining the tracks, a member of our party, Ms. S__, kept saying that she was beginning to feel uncomfortable. 'I think we better leave,' she said, 'I don't know why, but I get the feeling we shouldn't be here.'

"When we hiked in the desert before, especially at night, we had the feeling we were being watched. Not by kit fox or coyote as Edward L__ (A Forest Ranger) explained, but by something whose stare seemed to blanket you like so many cobwebs. And this night was no exception. With little discussion we agreed that the silence coupled with the apparently fresh tracks, was ample reason to head back to the ranch. Ms. S__'s discomfort was turning into obvious alarm. The tracks, the ominous quiet, and the feeling of dread in the air, added up to something she didn't like. Heading back, we exchanged a lot of small talk to help keep the anxiety from building to the panic point . . .[817]

The group suddenly realized that two members of their party had fallen behind. Aware of the treacherous nature of the terrain—steep canyons and gullies—they hurried to find their missing friends. Approaching a sharp decline, the absent members were found intently focused on something toward the east. The rest of the party were motioned to be quiet and turn off their flashlights.

". . . Suddenly, a wave of excitement surged through our little group. There, against a backdrop of Joshua trees, were two, dim, orangish-yellow lights. The two members both said they noticed the lights earlier but thought them a distant camper's lantern and had dismissed them. At first glance the lights seemed to be fixed, but were in fact slowly bobbing. Reaching an indeterminate height, the lights stopped and seemed to methodically blink. There was something strangely alluring about the lights . . . transfixing. . . . Suddenly Ms. S__ blurted out, 'That's it, that's one of them.'

"Our attention momentarily distracted, we jolted back when someone else yelled that we were looking at 'eyes.' We moved closer to the open field separating us and the lights by an approximate distance of 300 feet. It was then the lights dropped to what appeared to be a few feet above the ground, all the while remaining equidistant from each other. We stood there dumbfounded for what seemed like an eternity. Without uttering a word we simultaneously threw our spotlights in the direction of the lights and were shocked by what we saw. Behind and slightly to the right of the Joshua trees, was an ape-like figure leaning on its side with its head tilted upward looking directly at us!

"The lights were indeed the creature's eyes—self-luminous eyes. No, not reflecting light, but actually glowing. When we turned off our lights the eyes took on a deep reddish glow that gradually faded to a yellow-orange. The glow seemed to wax and wane in intensity giving the impression that the creature was blinking. The whole thing was incredible! What kind of creature has self-luminous eyes?

"We stood there for several minutes trying to gather our wits. What could we do? Our camera was useless; even in the light of our torches it was unlikely we could get photos of the creature. We were too far from civilization to get help. Suddenly, as we stood whispering among ourselves, and gazing at the thing, a swarm of lights appeared from the direction of the military access road. The rumble of heavy equipment shattered the silence. The trauma of seeing the unbelievable coupled with the fear that we might be in added jeopardy caused us to bolt back up the hill in search of hiding places. We had changed positions considerably and moved up about 1,000 feet before we collected everybody in a group and regained our composure. Hidden by a clump of shrubs, we had a clear view of the shallow valley and the Joshua grove.

"We watched in utter amazement as a virtual convoy of blue trucks descended on the grove and the glowing-eyed thing. We cursed ourselves for not having field glasses. A hard pill to swallow considering what was happening . . . but rather than reveal ourselves, we stood back helplessly and merely watched.

"The trucks which, from our vantage point, seemed to bear no identifiable markings, drove almost directly to the Joshua grove and the figures of men surrounded the area. A figure, apparently that of a man, was carrying a powerful light and moved in a hurried manner toward the creature. He seemed to make a violent back and forth motion with the light as if directing the creature to come to him. Suddenly, the creature stood up, its silhouette plainly visible against the bright lights, and lumbered in the direction of the smaller figure. Our later estimates placed the creature at about eight to 10 feet tall, since its head seemed to reach midway on a 20-foot Joshua tree. As the creature walked toward the smaller figure, its silhouette showed the unmistakable shape of a man-like entity.

"In what seemed like an eternity, the creature walked slowly past the man toward a large truck. At that moment it let out a desperate, anguished cry, the same moan we had heard earlier several miles away. Minutes later several men swept the outlying fields with a flood light as though looking for something. We decided that someone may have either heard or seen us. At that point, we started running back over the crest of the hill in the direction of my ranch, a good five miles away. Ms. S__ was terrified. She kept repeating that we saw something we 'shouldn't have.' Someone else wanted to know if those were military people we had seen, and why were they keeping the 'things' secret? We had nothing but questions, and even though we wanted to storm the bastions and demand an explanation, our nervous indecision prevented any such notions . . .

"When we returned to the ranch we just sat there and said nothing for nearly 15 minutes. None of us had the energy

> to speak. We kept thinking what now? Something awful, incredible, was going on right under our noses, but what did it all mean? No knowing what else to do, I had everyone write down his or her impression of what we had seen. Everyone agreed that if it took the rest of our lives, we'd find out what was going on . . ."[818]

A search conducted of the area the next day yielded track finds (which were cast) and photographs taken of the Joshua grove and of tire tracks leading to the military access road. Subsequent to these events, Guttilla wrote that strange events in the area continued, including appearances of glowing-eyed Bigfoot-like creatures.[819]

Murphysboro Monster

Smack in the period when local, small-town Bigfoot-like creatures of the 1970s gained widespread, and at times national fame, Illinois' Murphysboro Monster went on to attract international interest and attention. The Murphysboro Monster, or a similar creature, was first encountered just after midnight on Monday, June 25, by a couple parked near the Big Muddy at a boat ramp in the southwestern edge of Riverside Park. That couple, Randy Needham and Judy Johnson, heard a roaring yell from nearby woods. They both saw a large shape about seven feet tall standing on two legs covered with matted hair which was streaked mud from the river. The creature howled as it lumbered toward them and as the creature closed the distance to about twenty feet, the couple hurriedly left, heading immediately to the police station to report the encounter. In sedate understatement, the ensuing "Unknown Creature" report noted the pair "left the area."[820] The police took the matter seriously because Johnson was married—but not to Needham. "They wouldn't risk all that if they weren't really scared," said an unnamed official.[821] "They were absolutely terrified," police officer Ron Manwaring later recalled. "I'm convinced that they saw something that night. . . . I can't tell you what it was that they saw, whether it was a bear or something else. But something was definitely there."

Officers Meryle Lindsay and Jimmie Nash were dispatched to the scene and during their investigation at the boat ramp they found several footprints ten to twelve inches long and about three inches wide. At 2:00 A.M., the officers were joined by Randy Needham and Jackson County sheriff's deputy Bob Scott, and their further scrutiny of the area turned up additional tracks. While Lindsay left to get a camera, the remaining men followed the newly discovered tracks. A scream from the woods a hundred yards away pierced the early morning darkness. "I was leaning over when there was the most incredible shriek I've ever heard," Nash said. "It was in those bushes. That was no bobcat or screech owl and we hightailed it out of there."[822] The three men retreated back to a patrol car.

The next monster report occurred on Tuesday, June 26. Four-year-old Christian Baril told his incredulous parents he saw "a big white ghost in the yard," as he was chasing fireflies with a glass jar. Their incredulity notwithstanding, Christian's parents were compelled to take his story seriously when an encounter with a creature matching Christian's description occurred in a neighboring yard. Two of the Baril's neighbors on Westwood Lane, 17-year-olds Randy Creath and Cheryl Ray, were talking on a darkened porch when something stirred in the nearby brush. Cheryl turned on a light and Randy went to investigate.

> Towering over the wide-eyed teenage couple was a creature resembling a gorilla. It was eight feet tall. It had long shaggy matted hair colored a dirty white. It smelled foul like river-slime.
>
> Silently, the trio stared at each other 15 feet apart then, after an eternity of perhaps 30 seconds, the creature turned slowly and crashed off through the brush back toward the river.
>
> It was the Murphysboro Monster, a strange creature that has baffled and frightened police and residents for weeks now in this southern Illinois town on the sluggish Big Muddy River.
>
> It is a creature that has brought a real kind of Halloween to Murphysboro's 10,000 citizens. And although the hobgoblin is so far benevolent, no one here is taking any chances. Many have armed themselves and a good number of God-fearing families curtailed traditional Halloween trick-or-treating rounds.[823]

Cheryl insisted that the creature's eyes, instead of reflecting light from another source, actually generated their own glow. The youths described the creature as possessing a roundish head and long arms like an ape's.[824] Creath told police the creature was "covered with mud," and weighed "300 to 350 pounds."[825]

"That did it for Chief Berger," wrote *New York Times* columnist Andrew H. Malcolm. "He ordered his entire 14-man force out for a night-long search. And Jerry Nellis, a dog trainer, brought [Reb], an 80-pound German shepherd."

> Officers discovered a rough trail in the brush. Reb found gobs of black slime, much like that of sewage sludge, on a direct line between the river and the Ray house.
>
> Reb was off down the hill, around the pond and into the woods toward the old Bullar farm.
>
> There, Nellis and Officer Nash, his .357 Magnum drawn, approached an abandoned barn. At the door the dog yelped and backed off in panic, Nellis threw it in the door. The dog crawled out whining. The man radioed for help.
>
> Fourteen area police cars maneuvered the mile-long, rutted, overgrown road. But the barn was empty.

Police reported Riverside Park during the last week of June was a "beehive of cars," noting hundreds of vehicles drove the park during the night and several overnight campers had set up in the area.[826]

> "These are good honest people." Said Chief Berger. "They are seeing something. And who would walk through sewage tanks for a joke?"
>
> "I know it's out there," said young Randy Creath. "It would be fascinating to see it again and study it. But, you know, I kinda hope he doesn't come back. With everyone running around with guns and sticks, he really wouldn't have much of a chance, would he?"[827]

Reports circulated that a white bear, ostensibly the "monster," had been killed over the weekend. "That's the first I have heard of it," said Murphysboro Police Chief Toby Berger Jr. on Monday morning, July 2, when asked about the rumor. After hearing some of the stories making the rounds, Berger said anecdotal reports suggested a large white bear had been killed in the Gorham-Grand Tower area over the weekend. "We did get one report someone had seen the creature Friday night, but a check showed it was a cow in the field," Berger said.[828]

The monster was seen again on July 7 when traveling Miller Carnival workers said the creature's presence agitated the carnival's Shetland ponies used for children's rides at Riverside Park. The creature reportedly stood near the ponies' enclosure but did not attempt to molest them. Three carnival workers walked around a truck to investigate the ponies' alarm and they saw a 300- to 400-pound hairy creature standing about 8-feet tall. The creature appeared to harbor menace to neither pony or human, but instead seemed curious about the ponies. The carnival operators delayed filing a report for fear of harming their business.[829]

> Police finally invited [following the sighting near the carnival ponies] Harlan Sorkin, a St. Louis expert on Big Foot, down to the town to help the investigation.
>
> According to Mr. Sorkin the descriptions of the creature matched the hundreds of previous sightings over the decades.
>
> Typically, he said, these creatures were very shy and favored river bottoms for their ample vegetation and were generally placid.[830]

Sorkin's absorbing hobby collecting information about Bigfoot had naturally focused his attention on Murphysboro. On July 7, Nedra Green heard a piercing scream from a shed on her farm as she was preparing for bed. "It's it again," she said. Green's description of the cries appeared to match the reports from Needham and others.[831]

> They [Murphysboro Police Department] received letters from hunters and trappers who offered to track down the monster and kill it or capture it. Two men from Oregon offered to do the job and wrote that they "would be willing to take on this adventure at only the cost of expenses and materials for doing so." Some writers suggested that the police use bait to snare the creature. A Florida man suggested, "Why don't you put bread and cheese and eggs out for your creature? You would have a splendid attraction if you could have it in a little hut, to show people."
>
> Assistant professor Leigh Van Valen, from the University of Chicago's biology department, also wrote a letter to Chief Manwaring. "I have heard of your creature," the letter stated, "which could be of considerable scientific interest. There have been many reports of such animals but no real specimens have been available for scientific study." Professor Van Valen went

> on to explain how the creature, if circumstances required shooting it, should be properly embalmed or "preserved in good condition." The professor agreed to cover the necessary expenses to procure the monster for scientific study; it wouldn't matter, though, for the monster never returned to Murphysboro.[832]

Van Valen published "A New Evolutionary Law" in 1973, a paper which introduced his "Red Queen Hypothesis," a model for evolutionary interaction which suggested no species pulls ahead in a constant arms race for very long.[833] If Bigfoot existed, it (and all organisms) must continually adapt in concert with and in response to environmental changes and to ever-evolving competing species. Van Valen's hypothesis might interpret Bigfoot's 20th Century survival, in part, as owing to exemplary skills at successful hiding, concealment, and avoidance of people—necessary adaptations in the face of mankind's encroachment into its habitat.

Authors John Lee and Barbara Moore wrote about the Murphysboro Monster in their book, *Monsters Among Us: Journey to the Unexplained*. Lee and Moore mention Sorkin's findings after he interviewed witnesses and visited the scenes of encounters. Upon his review of the evidence, Lee and Moore write, Sorkin concluded the Murphysboro Monster "was probably from the Shawnee National Forest, a moderate-sized, protected wilderness which straddles Illinois about 400 miles south of Chicago, or some cave down-river from the forest. Ordinarily, Sorkin says, creatures like the Murphysboro visitor are very shy and prefer to remain out of sight, hovering near river bottoms where there is ample vegetation to feed them, but this creature may have been forced out of its home by heavy flooding that occurred last year."[834]

In 1979, C. W. Gusewelle of the *Kansas City Star* recalled his part in a Murphysboro monster investigation in the autumn of 1973 which Gusewelle had named the "Sasquatch I" expedition. After convincing his editor at the time to underwrite the endeavor, Gusewelle started making arrangements.

> We prepared carefully. If one goes looking for a monster, one has to deal seriously with the possibility—however slight—that a monster might actually be found. Otherwise it is nothing but a stunt, a fool's errand.

Gusewelle recruited a writer and a photographer from the *Kansas City Star*, and easily convinced a lawyer friend with a penchant for adventure. Sasquatch I's official advisor was Harlan Sorkin.

> In Murphysboro we first spoke with the witnesses, and found them impressive. Then, in darkness and pelting rain, we descended by Jeep into the wilderness below the town to make our first night's camp.
>
> You would expect to find no such desolate and forbidding terrain in this part of the country. Sometime in antiquity the Mississippi shifted its course, and there in the river's primordial bed has evolved a tangle of forest hammocks and bamboo thickets and peaty bogs some 10 miles wide and 40 long—400 square miles in all—bounded on the east by a steep bluff, atop which sits the town of Murphysboro.
>
> Hunters do not follow their lost dogs in there. The only visitors are herpetologists collecting poisonous snakes. It is a place no one spends the night.
>
> Our consultant's theory was that floods earlier in the year had routed Sasquatch from his lowland fastness and up onto the bluff where, like a suburban raccoon, he had found happiness for a time in the garbage cans of Murphysboro subdivisions. But now, after the commotion he had caused, he likely had retreated again to the bogs.

The party pitched their camp in this foreboding place, ringing their perimeter with gasoline lanterns and maintaining a watch throughout the night. That first night their only visitor was a bedraggled opossum. The group called the place Mud Camp and off-and-on rain remained the unwelcome constant of their stay. Log platforms were constructed to keep feet out of the muck but these soon sank into the mire after usage and as careful as they were, their tents still filled with slimy mud.

> The second night it turned bitter cold. The St. Louis man [Harlan Sorkin] and I were standing the graveyard shift together, and as we huddled over the fire in damp and smoky misery, I think that not even he really believed in Sasquatch anymore. Or much cared.

> Then, at some awful hour of morning—3 o'clock or maybe 4—the first cry came.
>
> We had rehearsed it all. One man would operate the tape recorder. The photographer would stand his ground with strobe lights flashing. At a range of 20 steps or so, a third man would activate a fire extinguisher whose sudden hiss and burst of vapor would slow or turn the beast.
>
> Whereupon, backed up by the fifth man with a heavy gun in case of a determined charge, I was to fire a tranquilizer dart into some fleshy part. (The one drawback was that the potion needed 20 minutes to work—promising what might be the longest, most vigorous and possibly the last 20 minutes of a lifetime.)
>
> That was the plan.
>
> What happened instead was that the two of us careened stumbling and shrieking through the mud in mindless terror, crying the camp awake.
>
> My lawyer friend remembers lying in his underwear in his wet sleeping bag, wondering irritably at the commotion that had snatched him out of the mercy of sleep.
>
> Then the second cry came from the woods, much closer and much louder—a piercing scream that descended through several octaves to a great resonant, guttural roar.
>
> It filled the mind. It seemed to fill the world. My friend's next memory, without any elapse of time, is of standing fully dressed beside the fire, gun loaded and aimed out into the night.

But no other cries came from out of the surrounding darkness. The group, all awake and all huddled close together by the stoked fire in Mud Camp waited until daylight to venture into the area where the cries had emanated from. They found "a single area about the size of a living room, the trees had been freshly broken—living saplings, some of them as big as your arm, not gnawed off, but torn off and partly peeled of bark, flung about as if in a giant's frenzy."

Sasquatch I would last one additional night, this time removed out of the bottomlands to a bluff where the remaining members (the lawyer had returned to Kansas City after the second night) were able to put their backs against stone and place their fire to their front. The third night appeared to pass without incident, excepting the notions and thoughts capering through the men's minds. Over the years, Gusewelle revisited the cries and commotion of their second night and found no solution to identify what had been lurking in the darkness, just out of reach of Mud Camp's firelight.

> I won't presume to tell you what made the cries we heard, or what it was that did such unexplainable violence to that area of woods. Any firm conclusions I might have reached while cowering there against the cliff have softened now.

Gusewelle assured his present editor at the time of his 1979 reminiscing article that just because there had been a Sasquatch I, he, Gusewelle, wouldn't be lobbying to instigate a Sasquatch II. His participation in investigating the Murphysboro Monster, he said, brought him close to "something I still hesitate to name" which "seemed much too close to stepping into the open and becoming truth. I have driven it back now into some deeper, safer region of my mind. I mean to keep it there."[835]

Bigfoot in Ohio

Pursuit magazine published a letter dated October 15, 1973, from a woman residing in western Ohio:

> I've been following with great interest the happenings in Greensburg and Derry, Pennsylvania. The reason for this is that for a great number of years there has been a similar animal-man around where we live. Over the past ten years it has been heard and recently seen. The location is about one mile south of (deleted) on a deserted farm road that dead ends into Interstate 75. I myself have seen this animal, can tell you he's very real. I have numerous friends who have heard him and know he exists.[836]

Intrigued, Allan Noe gathered additional details of the letter writer's sighting. She saw the creature at 12:30 A.M. during a moonlit night on the farm road mentioned in her original letter. At that early hour the creature was close enough to I-75 to have its eyes reflect a red glow from cars' headlights.[837] She described its face as human-like, and the body was hair-covered, its arms were very long, down to about its knees. The creature's height was estimated at an impressive ten feet, judged in part by the observation of its step over a five-foot fence. From time to time the letter-writer heard cries she attributed to the creature which she described as "a cross between the cry of a man in pain and the high pitched howl of a wolf." The woods from whence the cries emanated were described as dying, littered with numerous fallen trees and absent of normal bird and animal life; an adjacent wooded spot was lush in growth and full of animals and birds.[838]

Durham Gorilla

The following section describing the Durham Gorilla concerns a Bigfoot-like creature seen in and around Durham, Maine, in 1973 and is taken from this author's book, *Shadows in the Woods: A Chronicle of Bigfoot in Maine* (2015).

In the *Lewiston Daily Sun* of April 20, 1973, an article noted a gorilla costume had not been returned to Drapeau's Costume Shop of Lewiston. It had been rented on March 15, apparently under false pretenses.[839]

> Residents are asked to keep an eye out for a suspicious-looking person who might be seen making an extremely large purchase of bananas, or swinging from tree to tree.[840]

The missing gorilla costume preceded a rash of reports which became known as the "Durham Gorilla." The costume was reported as realistic in quality and designed to fit a large person.[841]

The Durham Gorilla events started in the Shiloh-Lisbon Falls Road area in Brunswick, a half-mile from the Huntington home, in Durham. The three Huntington children Lois, (13); George Jr., (10); and Scott, (8); and their friend Tammy S., (12) were bicycling along the road on July 25, where they reported an encounter with a creature resembling a chimp. Mrs. Huntington told reporters: "My 13-year-old daughter fell off her bike about three feet from him and all he did was cock his head and look at her." It was described as upright and chimpanzee-like. Lois told the *Maine Sunday Telegram,* "I fell right down in front of him and all he did was look at me. I would have known if it were a hippie or something. But it had a regular monkey face. You have seen a monkey before, haven't you?"[842]

Also on July 25, the gorilla was seen near the Jones Cemetery, close to the Durham Road in Durham. A gorilla-like animal standing on its hind legs was observed two or three times by James Washburn. A subsequent search of the area by officers found moose and deer tracks.[843]

The following encounter occurred on the Shiloh Road,[844] near the Durham-Brunswick line. Mrs. George (Meota) Huntington, 33, of Lisbon Falls Road, was driving home Thursday evening, July 26, from a baseball game when she saw the "ape" peeking out from the bushes on the Durham Road. It was twenty feet away and made a "mad dash" on two legs into a heavily wooded area. The "ape" was described as a little over five feet tall, with a shaggy, black coat, and weighing about 350 pounds.[845] Mrs. Huntington reported the creature had a "monkey face." Mrs. Huntington had the opportunity to spy the creature twice, the second occasion during a return to the area with neighbors. During this latter incident she remained in her car as others searched the woods. While sitting in her car she saw it again, peering at her from behind a tree. Reportedly over thirty officers searched for the animal for two hours, involving the Androscoggin Sheriff's Department, the Cumberland County Sheriff's Department, the Maine State Police, and State of Maine Game Wardens. Tracks found near a cemetery had the appearance of human-like prints but had claws—likely those of a bear.[846]

A beast resembling an ape or gorilla was reported to be prowling through Durham on Thursday night, July 26. The Androscoggin County Sheriff's Department dispatched several units to look for the beast which was reportedly seen by several residents. A spokesman for the department said similar reports originated from Brunswick on Wednesday, 25 July, but local police hadn't found any trace of the beast.[847]

On Friday, July 27, several witnesses came forward saying they had seen "it" at the Durham-Brunswick line. Peter and Jean Merrill found a footprint behind the Jones Cemetery, the scene of several of the Durham Gorilla sightings. The Merrills stated the track looked like a chimpanzee print. Androscoggin County Deputy Sheriff Blaine Footman examined a series of prints, casting one of them described as "rather deep." Footman said it was about five inches wide with "the thumb part broken off. Whatever made it weighs 300 or 350 pounds and I can't tell you much more. It's definitely not a bear track. I don't know what's going on here and I'd rather not express an opinion."[848] The Durham Gorilla's witnesses descriptions said the creature resembled a gorilla, a bear, and a big chimpanzee. Auburn Dog Officer Louis Pinette joked with a reporter that it could be "a hippie out looking for a free meal."[849]

Robert Huntington, a resident on Shilo Road in Durham, reported to the Androscoggin County Sheriff's Department that someone wearing a gorilla costume Saturday night, August 11, scared his wife and daughter while brandishing a knife. Huntington said he chased the creature into the woods and thought that its face mask fell off during the pursuit. He tried unsuccesfully to find it in the fast-approaching darkness. Deputies Dufresne and Footman and Dog Marshal Louis Pinette were dispatched to the scene, but they were unable to find any trace of a mask or the creature.[850] During the rash of sightings, the critter earned the moniker, Osgood the Ape,[851] from locals. As the gorilla's fame spread, so did the interest in finding the creature. The August 15 *Lewiston Daily Sun* reported that the County Sheriff's Department said that persons seeking the creature were causing a significant amount of property damage. The Department said that the creature, which officials believed to be a man in a gorilla costume, had scared residents in Durham, Lisbon and Brunswick.[852]

> Gorilla Spectators Cause Durham Property Damage—Spectators were in the news in Durham Tuesday, being the cause of complaints to the Androscoggin County Sheriff's Department.
>
> A spokesman for the department said the complaints stated persons seeking to pick up firsthand any clues in the so-called "gorilla" case are trespassing on private property and causing damage. According to one complaint, these persons are tramping over lawns and breaking down shrubs and other ornamental plants as they roam about the Shilo Road area where the "gorilla" reportedly has been seen.[853]

About the middle of August 1973, the Durham Gorilla sightings abruptly stopped.[854] Conceptually, the possible donning of a gorilla suit in Durham may have inspired a political protest which occurred later in the decade at the seemingly coincidently named Durham, New Hampshire. A man in a gorilla costume mocked President Ford and his main challenger, Ronald Reagan, during their University of New Hampshire addresses. When Ford was there the gorilla was called "Bozo", a nickname some liberal editorial writers had given to Ford. At Reagan's appearance, the gorilla was dubbed "Bonzo" for obvious cinematic associations with the former actor.[855]

Skunk Ape (1973)

Speaking with members of the Yeti Research Society in St. Petersburg, Florida, in August 1977, Bill Allen recalled the experience of a 1973 camping trip he undertook in the Everglades with the express intent of photographing a

Skunk Ape. Allen and five others had set up camp on an Indian mound in an area close to where large tracks had previously been discovered. On the sixth day of the expedition, at one o'clock in the afternoon, a group of up to eight hairy bipedal creatures of varying size converged on the campsite. The creatures pelted Allen and the other five team members with conch shells, branches and rocks. Rifles were fired into the air hoping to scare off the creatures, but this only seemed to enflame the creatures' negative dispositions. The men were eventually chased down to their boat which was readily used to make their retreat. Returning to the abandoned campsite the following day, Allen and his fellow campers found little left undamaged—broken tent poles, twisted cots, smashed glass. Two cans of food had apparently been twisted apart. "I still don't know what we did to rile them up," said Allen.[856]

Gordon Prescott, president of the St. Petersburg Yeti Research Society, explained, "We want to settle down once and for all and try to find one of the things," as the reason for Society's genesis back in December 1972. Prescott's group found frequent outlets in Florida newspapers to espouse their latest doings and investigations. For bona fide Skunk Ape aficionados, the Yeti Research Society produced the *Yeti Newsletter*.[857]

A mid-September AP story stated that Prescott was in the throes of planning an expedition into the Big Cypress Swamp to look for the Skunk Ape. "We're not saying exactly where they are, because we don't want the place overrun by curiosity seekers," he said. "We think there are five of them in two family groups near where we were working." Prescott claimed to have glimpsed a Skunk Ape once through the trees at about 100 yards. He estimated the creature's height and weight as eight feet and up to 1,000 pounds. "But we heard and smelled them regularly while we were working out there," Prescott said. "Apparently, they'll eat anything that's left around, including people's lunches. We had that happen many times. They'd sneak up, grab a lunch bag and run." Prescott's expedition was to include two anthropologists who had requested their names not be mentioned, "for obvious reasons," Prescott said. "They're in scholastic circles, and you can get an awful lot of ridicule by just suggesting it's possible the things might exist."[858]

Ultimately, the Big Cypress Swamp expedition fell through but Prescott undauntingly planned a late October trip to Brooksville[859] based upon "some hot leads in the area." A creature lurking in the area had been dubbed the Brooksville Beast and was described as 8 feet tall, weighing 700 pounds, timid in nature, with light green eyes and a disgusting smell. Prior to seeing a Skunk Ape himself, Prescott had been a skeptic; but after his own sighting he formed the theory that Bigfoot was a kind of pre-Neanderthal, positing the creatures as an evolutionary link between apes and man. To convince the world, Prescott wanted his group to photograph one and if possible, bring one out of the swamps alive.[860]

> Yeti stories are almost as hard to believe as the animals' existence, and some tales even connect the creatures with UFOs. In the recent Brooksville sighting, Prescott said several children saw a female Yeti with a younger animal beside her. The young Yeti played with a wheel on one of the children's tricycles, but finally retreated with the older Yeti to the swamp.[861]

Reporter Bruce Estes supplied several stories for the *St. Petersburg Independent* describing Skunk Apes and the people who hunted them. In the following excerpt, Estes foreshadows an increasing association between the Skunk Ape and UFOs. B. Ann Slate would delve deeper into this combination in the following years, but Prescott provides an early notion that somehow Bigfoot and UFOs shared a connection.

> The space Yeti is a theory supported by several reports, Prescott said. One sighting was made in southern Florida by a night watchman at a telephone company. According to Prescott, the watchman saw a Yeti standing by a truck and when the Yeti saw the watchman it vaporized, leaving a sulphur smell in the area it had been standing. The animal presumably traveled to a UFO, according to some theorists. Other space Yeti sightings report similar occurrences and are usually reported in areas around high-tension wires, radio antennas and other high-power sources, Prescott said.[862]

Ecology held popular interest in the 1970s thanks to the environmental movement that began in the previous decade. The assumed pressures on Bigfoot from dwindling natural resources and disappearing living space was an oft-repeated theme in the '70s.

> Prescott maintained that Bigfoot liked the backwoods because they were shy creatures. But they were being seen with greater frequency because of dwindling wild areas. Despite their aloofness from humans, they were prone to frequent camps

> and lonely abodes in the hopes of absconding with something to eat, especially salt.[863]

By November, the Yeti Research Society believed they had uncovered concrete evidence that the Brooksville Beast roamed an area eight miles north of Brooksville. "We've seen their tracks, heard them and witnessed a pair of pinkish, reflective eyes staring at us," stated Prescott. "We just weren't able to get a photograph." Yeti Research Society secretary, L. Frank Hudson said, "We were close, but apparently not close enough."[864]

Reminiscing in 1974 back to the Brooksville-area search, Prescott said, "About 10 or 12 of us were consistent in going out. We set up camp northwest of Brooksville near a garbage dump where we were pretty sure the yeti foraged periodically. We baited the area with bread and pretty soon it got to be a nightly stop. During those winter weekends three of our members saw five distinct individual Yetis, and we heard five others."

> Prescott described the swamp ape's call this way: "They have three distinct speech patterns. One is a little like a squirrel chatter—only it's much louder and deeper. Another is a barking sound, somewhat like that of a dog. The third is a whistle that has a very distinct rise and fall in pitch. By the pitch and tone we think it may indicate a very primitive form of communication."[865]

Recalling the area's conditions, Prescott wasn't surprised by the general inability to produce a photograph. "We never could get close enough to get any pictures," he recalled. "The undergrowth always seemed to be too dense. The Yeti's ability to stay out of close range scrutiny, and the way it has thwarted all attempts to capture it lead us to believe it's far more intelligent than most animals."

Prescott was a guest on KMOX's "At Your Service" radio program on Thursday, December 13, for a show entitled "The Great Yeti Hunt in Florida," which gave him the opportunity to review The Yeti Research Society's findings and conclusions from Brooksville and other research areas.[866]

CHAPTER 5
1974

I still get letters about Bigfoot—some come from school children who are doing "essays," while others are from high school and college students working on "papers." They all want to know the same thing, and I do my best to oblige.[867]

Andrew Genzoli. "Redwood Country," *Times-Standard* (February 20, 1974).

Beliefs in monsters are a universal element in the history of human cultures, and the [S]asquatch has all the typical characteristics: He is big, he is ugly, he dwells in the wilderness and he remains mysterious. Such beliefs developed, apparently, as an expression of man's insecurity with the rationality of the civilization he built, and there is good reason to argue that Americans retain that insecurity in some degree—perhaps now more than ever. Some believers in the [S]asquatch seem as fanatical as some believers in unidentified flying objects. Wayne Suttles, a professor of anthropology at Portland State University, says: "When we were little kids, we learned about strange creatures and monsters, and then as we grew up, we learned that they weren't real, that we had to give them up. When we find out again, it's like finding your Teddy bear in the attic."[868]

David C. Anderson. "The Mystery of Big Foot," *Courier Journal & Times Magazine* (February 24, 1974).

Portraits of hairy hominid researchers studded newspaper articles, magazine stories, and documentaries in the '70s almost as frequently as the latest encounters with hairy hominids themselves. Writer and *Outdoor Outlook* editor Ken Castle's article, "The Search for Bigfoot," published in Daily Review Publications' February 1974 *Outdoor Outlook*, lays an important foundational understanding of the Bay Area Group, one of the most significant assemblages of Bigfoot researchers active in the '70s.

> Arthur ["Archie"] Buckley swears that he saw one.
>
> George Haas says he's tracked hundreds of large, humanoid footprints and heard bizarre screams at night in the wilderness.
>
> Warren Thompson is not yet a believer, but he has invested a small fortune in electronic surveillance equipment to find out "if something is out there."
>
> Barbara Wasson, a clinical psychologist, has interviewed people who claim to have made sightings, and she is convinced that at least some of them are telling the truth.
>
> What these Bay Area residents all have in common is their quest for something that science in general is not quite prepared to accept—the existence of a huge, manlike creature that roams the mountain ranges and forests of the western United States and Canada.[869]

By 1974, Willow Creek, California, in wooded Humboldt County had a population of 1,050 and advertised itself as "The Gateway to Bigfoot Country."[870] Castle wrote that in 1969, San Francisco native Warren Thompson motorcycled into Willow Creek, California, where he spent the fifty-cent charge to view a short movie being shown in town. The feature turned out to be the Patterson-Gimlin film. Fascinated and enthralled, Thompson plopped down two more quarters to watch the film again. René Dahinden obligingly took his money and ran the film a second time. That was it for Warren Thompson, the moment he became enthralled with Bigfoot.[871]

Thompson went to Al Hodgson's store to look at casts of Bigfoot tracks on display there. Hodgson and Thompson took up a conversation and Hodgson told his visitor he should contact George Haas when back in San Francisco. Haas, Thompson, and other Bigfoot luminaries such as Archie Buckley, would go on to form one of the decade's most influential Bigfoot research groups—the Bay Area Group. From the organization's charter:

> This is an informal group of people interested in solving the Bigfoot mystery. There are no dues, no membership cards and no party line except the protection and preservation of the Bigfeet which we feel already are an endangered species. We have no grants, no funds, nor do we seek any. Members pay their own expenses, we have no profit motive in this Bigfoot research and investigation; we are out to obtain knowledge and information only.[872]

The main aim of the group was the protection and preservation of Bigfoot resulting from studying Bigfoot in its environment. "At the present state of the investigation *we do not know what they are*." The group was against killing a Bigfoot to obtain a specimen for scientific scrutiny. Along with Thompson, Buckley, and Haas, other early members of the Bay Area Group included Ray Pierotti, Dalhousie University Ph. D. and later associate Professor of Ecology and Evolutionary Biology at the University of Kansas; Steve Sanders, zoologist and veterinarian; Mike Ward, University of California undergrad; and Tucson writer Joel Hurd.

Archie Buckley was born at the Alameda Sanatorium on August 15, 1917, and graduated from Chico State University in 1941 with a degree in education. During World War II, Buckley joined the Army and became a medical administrative officer. Buckley rose to become the Chief of Physical Reconditioning at McCloskey General Hospital in Temple, Texas, and through this experience he became a pioneer in the new field of physical therapy. After the war's end, he accepted a position at the Veteran's Administration in Oakland to assist in the physical rehabilitation of recovering veterans. Based on his experience there, Buckley contributed to the article, "Follow-Up Study on a Group of Older Amputee Patients" published in the *Journal of the American Medical Association* in July 1959. His professional experience gave Buckley a background for evaluating *in situ* Bigfoot prints discovered during Bay Area Group expeditions. At times, Buckley differed with other prominent Bigfoot researchers on conclusions drawn from footprints.

Starting with his analysis of the Colville Cripplefoot tracks (see Chapter 2), Grover Krantz had emerged as the significant representative from the scientific establishment to propose some Bigfoot prints pointed to an extant, unknown hominid. Krantz's Bigfoot track analysis indicated, to him, that Bigfoot possessed certain podal characteristics: a flat foot, no arch, a long heel, and short forefoot. Study of tracks as well as the Patterson-

Gimlin film led Krantz to construe Bigfoot's ankle position differed from that found in humans.

> Some of his [Krantz's] conclusions about the tracks are challenged by Archie Buckley of San Leandro, who is a member of the Bay Area group. Buckley for over 20 years was coordinator of medical rehabilitation programs for injured military men at the former Veterans Administration Hospital in Oakland (now located in Martinez). While with the VA he also performed research in ambulation—the science of physical movement.
>
> Buckley says he has studied in detail both the Patterson film and footprints of at least a dozen Bigfeet. His analysis of fresh tracks points to the conclusion that the creatures are more humanoid than ape-like or anthropoidal.
>
> In contrast with Krantz, Buckley said the imprints he's seen definitely show signs of arches. "They are both longitudinal and transverse, just as in a human foot," he said. "The toes point straight ahead and there is little or no eversion (outward pointing feet).[873]

Buckley's contention with Krantz centered on the latter's suggested podal structure for Bigfoot which Buckley argued made little sense for a creature of such great size and inferred capacity for speed over rough and mountainous terrain. "These characteristics indicate to me," said Buckley, "that Bigfoot is a superb bi-pedal walker because of his anatomical similarity to man. Apes, by contrast, cannot functionally walk upright because their pelvis is long and legs are short."

"When you see a footprint you also have to consider the type of soil in which it was made," said Buckley. "If it is hard ground, you would get virtually no hint of an arch because the foot would not have pressed far enough into the ground." Buckley's physical therapy experience informed his opinion that flat-footed people tended to be inefficient walkers due to a propensity for their feet to point outwards. "And Bigfoot certainly is not a poor walker." Buckley maintained that casts imperfectly reflected the subtle contours and features of a foot's disturbance of a given substrate, let alone more obscure but noteworthy features present in the prototype. "You have to examine a set of tracks in the field to really see the details," he averred. Buckley encouraged folks to get out into the field to see for themselves what was going on, an activity being taken up in the early '70s by an increasing number of people, mostly laymen. For Buckley, first-hand track inspection trumped musings over a cast; as he explained to Castle, a foot sliding in a soft substrate could lead some researchers to overestimate the size of the foot and consequently the body size of the track maker. While interviewed by Castle, Buckley recalled a particular trackway which numbered about 24 prints in the Trinity forest ranging in length from 16 to 24 inches; the size of the print had been dependent upon the substrate and terrain conditions. "The smaller print would really be the more accurate one," Buckley stated.

> A short, bearded 57-year-old man, Buckley is no newcomer to the Bigfoot search. In fact, for the past 35 years he's had periodic encounters with something in the wilderness.
>
> While a college student at Chico State in 1937, he and a companion were hiking in the Trinity mountains when they surprised what he now believes was a family of Bigfeet.
>
> The hikers never saw the creatures but could hear them scampering up a mountain crevice. "When we tried to climb up after them, they threw 50-pound rocks down at us," said Buckley. "We also heard them jabbering," he added.
>
> The two youths later found tracks and what he now considers to be a Bigfoot bed—a "mattress" of boughs from a white fir tree. The creatures, theorizes Buckley, break off these branches from the lower parts of the trees.[874]

At the time of Castle's interview, Buckley claimed to have experienced a total of 37 distinct incidents with Bigfoot, from which he singled out one as his most memorable and auspicious encounter. In May 1970, Buckley with his brother Delmas and brother-in-law Jim Whalen, set up a campsite in the Trinity forest, a half mile from a ranger station. Hoping to lure in Bigfoot, they put out a bait of salmon on top of a garbage can. At about 3 A.M. one morning, the group was awakened by raucous dog-barking coming from a nearby ranch. Over the patter of a light rain, the men heard dull thuds, about a dozen of them or so, like the tread of a heavy creature. Scanning the darkness they saw nothing. With the morning's sunrise, Whalen found over 20 clear footprints about 50 yards from their campsite. The prints showed the creature was apparently making toward the salmon bait before suddenly veering off. About June of that year, Buckley learned from an Indian friend that a geologist discovered another set of prints in an area that naturally divides one watershed from another—a natural passageway for local fauna, which Buckley believed would innately include Bigfoot as well.

> Alone, Buckley returned to the Trinities and set up another camp, arranging more fish baits on a tree limb. He then ventured out daily into the surrounding countryside, carrying a fish on his back and calling out in a friendly, encouraging voice.
>
> Often, when he returned to camp, he found the fish bait gone.
>
> One night he sat in his Volkswagen to wait. At 4 A.M. on June 17 [the date of this encounter is also listed as June 18]—during a cloudy, moonless night—"I was suddenly cognizant of something outside."
>
> "I reached over for the flashlight and turned it on the bait," he recounted. "It was still there, so I scanned the light around the area. That was when I saw him, about 25 to 30 yards away. He was standing in the dirt road looking right at me.
>
> "I had the light on him for three minutes and I was talking to him, trying to get him to come closer. Finally, he took three or four steps toward me and then stopped. I reached for my flash camera but when I turned around he was gone," said Buckley.
>
> "The next day I examined his prints and found that he had moved from one tree to another as he approached. But what really got me was that the tracks led right up to my car—to less than four feet from where I was sitting," he said.[875]

According to Buckley, the creature he encountered was over 7 ½ feet tall, weighed 750 to 800 pounds and left 15-inch footprints. Buckley spent parts of the next two summers in the same area but he didn't find sign of Bigfoot activity, possibly, Buckley believed, due to increased logging activity nearby.

Another member of the Bay Area Group, Warren Thompson, invested $300 in a Navy surplus infrared scope which could illuminate an area 50 feet wide up to 150 feet away. Also in Thompson's technical arsenal was a 250,000-candlepower spotlight. Thompson combined inexpensive box cameras with flash attachments to create homemade camera traps which the Bay Area Group employed in the field. "I still cling to my skepticism," admitted Thompson. "I really won't be convinced that Bigfoot exists until I see for myself. I've talked to a number of people who have reported sightings. It seems like 50 percent of them are dead serious and the others just don't make sense. It's really maddening to go up to the mountains year after year and not know whether I'm wasting my time."[876]

During his interview with Castle, Haas stated, "I have over 2,000 newspaper and magazine clippings and card files on 500 to 700 direct sightings," and perhaps with a bit of pride he confided, "I've been told that I have the largest collection of Bigfoot information available." Haas' voluminous correspondence truly took off after his publication of the first issue of *Bigfoot Bulletin* in January 1969. This newsletter's length reached up to 12 pages before Haas stopped its publication in 1971. Castle called Haas the unofficial leader of the Bay Area Bigfoot group in 1974, which then numbered about 12 active members.

Haas admitted he had never seen a Bigfoot during his forays into the Shasta-Trinity National Forest but had experienced several unusual events while in the field. One of these strange episodes happened near a creek in Shasta County in August 1970. Five people from Red Bluff were camping on a Saturday night when at about 2 A.M. they were startled by piercing screams coming from a nearby hill. Subsequent investigation of the area revealed the front half of a fawn's neatly severed carcass. Haas and other members of his group noted the entrails appeared to have been scooped out of the body cavity and the fawn's backbone appeared ragged suggesting it had been broken via violent twisting. Near the carcass was a pile of dung and at least five suspected Bigfoot tracks. More large tracks were found in the vicinity of a deer trail.

"We believe the creature waited here and ambushed the fawn as it came along the trail," Haas said. Only a year before the discovery of the fawn carcass, Haas and a companion discovered, in July of 1969, an estimated 400 large human-like footprints while hiking near the south fork of the Trinity River in the Trinity National Forest. Haas' companion could not create an imprint in the ground next to the tracks, despite weighing 220 pounds. Those prints evinced a stride of 36 inches and examination of the immediate surroundings revealed some reddish-brown hairs snagged in nearby trees which Haas dutifully collected.

With frustrating results, Haas had submitted some suspected evidence collected by the Bay Area Group to scientists. Hair samples which Haas sent to the University of California at Berkley found no one interested in examining them. "Most of them [credentialed scientists] don't believe us, or maybe would rather not have their traditional beliefs challenged," Haas maintained. In 1970, Haas was successful in getting suspected Bigfoot fecal matter examined at California State University, Hayward. That testing showed the material was heavily comprised of manzanita berries, but proved unable to identify the animal that deposited it. "We have had help from a number of college students who were studying zoology, biology and anthropology," Hass said, underscoring the importance of young, open-minded people's involvement.[877]

"Most of us in our Bay Area [Group] feel that we are dealing with a creature that is more than a 'mere animal': that we are dealing with a being very close to man, a subhuman perhaps, or even a sub-species of the genus *Homo*," Haas said. The closeness shared between Bigfoot and people conferred certain responsibilities upon the latter, Haas believed. "However, whatever the Bigfeet turn out to be we feel that they already comprise an endangered species. Considering the current rape of our national forests, the continued shrinking of our wild areas and the increasing invasion by backpackers and others of what used to be true 'wilderness' areas, we hope that eventually we can see laws passed, preferably on a national level, to stringently protect them and to have areas set aside for their preservation."[878]

The Bay Area Group's espoused no-kill position was predicated on moral grounds, concluding that Bigfoot should only be studied in its natural habitat. "It would be nice to have a body for examination and dissection but we feel strongly that there can be no justification whatever for killing one of the creatures for that purpose," Haas stated. "It is to be hoped that such a scientific examination could wait until the body of one that has died naturally, or been killed by accident, had been found. Sooner or later that will happen."

Both John Green and Grover Krantz maintained at this time an opposite and contrary position with the Bay Area Group—killing a Bigfoot was justified to unambiguously settle the question of its existence. From Green's *The Sasquatch File* (1973): "Science will keep its eyes tight shut until someone produces a body, or part of one, and the more quickly it is done the better. The successful hunter should find it very profitable as well. . . . Gun it down, cut off a piece you can carry and get out of there."[879] Krantz agreed: "It's kind of absurd to say you can't shoot something that is not even certain to exist. That's like prohibiting the killing of unicorns. Let's prove that Bigfoot is real first, by any means necessary."[880] Krantz' view may have been self-mollified by his estimate of several hundred creatures residing in the Pacific Northwest and that the population's diminishment by one would not adversely affect the viability of the species. Haas considered killing a Bigfoot as a bloodthirsty proposition, an irrational stance against a species which, Haas maintained, evidence indisputably suggested was peaceful in nature. "We do not feel that Bigfoot is a hostile or dangerous creature and we think that most, if not all, tales of hostile man-killing Sasquatches are either hoaxes, downright lies or simply tales cooked up by sensational writers for a fast buck."[881]

"We in our group advocate a quiet approach to investigations," Haas said. "We go into the woods completely unarmed in small groups. We try to blend into the landscape and entice the creatures to look for us rather than the other way around. And we try to project a relaxed, friendly attitude, purged of the hate—fear that provokes hostility and aggression." Haas was one of the best-connected people in the Bigfoot-following world and he had likely been aware of episodes of infighting and internecine struggles since the Patterson-Gimlin film. Certainly "relaxed and friendly attitudes" had not converged on Bossburg, Washington, after the publicity of Bigfoot tracks and sightings had blossomed there. Castle posed to Haas the classic question: what would you do if you came face-to-face with Bigfoot? "I really don't know," Haas replied. "I've asked myself that question for a long time. But one thing I do know—I'm getting too old to run."[882]

Andrew Genzoli wrote a 700-word précis of Haas in "Redwood Country" which captured some of the heartfelt beliefs and positions on Bigfoot shared between Haas and members of the Bay Area Group.

> George F. Haas of Oakland, a former Humboldter to begin with, is one of those people who, whenever he can heads up into Bigfoot country.
>
> "Even if we don't see anything, the group I go with, have the pleasure of being in the wilderness. But, we have this year, had an opportunity to study the source of food supplies, which could sustain a big creature," he says.
>
> This year, George says, a special study was also made of the nomadic travel habits of Bigfoot. Various travel routes were studied, to determine if this is the same Bigfoot who makes the rounds of Trinity, Humboldt and other northern California

areas, and travels now and then into Oregon. "So," George says, "even if there was no sighting of Bigfoot, this summer, we make good use of our time."

He adds, "This year, while we found no evidence of Bigfoot, I can remember when 1970-71 were filled with quite a few incidents, after which he disappeared, which gives me reason to believe Bigfoot is nomadic."

George Haas says attention has been turned to South Fork Mountain, which is the world's longest mountain—some 35 miles in length, and extremely flat on top. It is interesting to view from the air.

George says it is the feeling of his Oakland group, that Bigfoot has made good use of South Fork Mountain as one of his "pathways." "It is possible for a person," George says, "to travel from this area all the way to Canada and not be seen by a human being, so why not Bigfoot in his travels?"

No, he says, his group isn't discouraged with not finding evidence of Bigfoot, this year. Next year, he says, a graduate in biology plans to join the search; while an English anthropologist has expressed his desire to join the group next summer.

George has the same experience, I have had since the search for Bigfoot began, of receiving letters from school kids and high school students and others for information on the monster. Well, it isn't always easy to comply with their wishes, but we try. The excitement has caused young people to spend more time in the field of anthropology, geography and history—which, of course, is good.

While in Eureka, the other day, George was on his way to see his 93-year-old father, Fred Haas, a former sheep rancher in Mendocino who now makes his home here.

Looking back to his earlier Humboldt years, George says last June it was 50 years since he graduated from Fortuna Union High School. He says he came to this area when he was six years old, and remembers making the trip to Fortuna by horse stage from Bell Springs.

George understands this area, and he says, Bigfoot, the giant hairy Wildman of the western forests, is rapidly becoming a folk hero to the youth of our land. Hundreds and hundreds, undoubtedly thousands of high school and college students across the country are writing term papers and science reports on him . . ."

"Until recently, Tarzan has been the folk hero of the Wildman type. In the fall of 1912 the short novel 'Tarzan of the Apes' by Edgar Rice Burroughs appeared in the October issue of 'All Story' magazine. Although that was 62 years ago, and I was only six-and-a-half years old, I recall as vividly as if it were yesterday my mother reading that story to my stepfather and me. It took her all day to do it, we wouldn't let her stop. That was my introduction, not only to fantasy literature—which was to become a life-long interest—but to apemen."

Now George sees Bigfoot joining the "hero league" with Tarzan. George says, "Unlike Tarzan, a fictional hero, Bigfoot is for real . . . Bigfoot is free, he roams the wilderness in perfect freedom, but does not harm it . . . he has all of the virtues now held in esteem by today's environment-conscious youth."

George has a fear. He says Bigfoot's range is decreasing due to encroachment on the wilderness by man, and he sees those who would if they could, kill the free spirit for personal purposes of exploitation, fame or fortune. "Surely we can do better by a folk hero than that," George Haas says.[883]

Joel Hurd had been on the trail of Bigfoot for five years when he was interviewed by reporter Paul Brisso for the *Eureka Times-Standard*. Joel and his wife Tina traveled throughout the western United States, Canada, and Mexico interviewing people and investigating locations where Bigfoot had been spotted. "I'm very much inclined to believe that they're real," Hurd said.

Hurd was another Bigfoot enthusiast whose interest flourished after seeing the Patterson-Gimlin film in 1969, the same year Thompson viewed the footage. Hurd had been confronted with a couple of choices—travel to Alaska for work or begin serious in-depth research into Bigfoot. "Bigfoot was far more important and intriguing to me than making money," he told Brisso.

Shortly after embarking on his research, Hurd found fresh Bigfoot tracks in a remote area of southern California where a man had reported three large creatures had roamed about his property. Hurd collected witness reports and secondhand accounts of encounters with Bigfoot; one of his prized possessions was an audio recording made by a Washington man of an enigmatic scream he heard one morning. Hurd liked to played the tape for other witnesses and often found they had heard the same scream. Hurd's efforts were supported by the sale of his wife's artwork—charcoal drawings and oil paintings.

> Describing himself as a "budding writer," Hurd hopes to use the material he has been collecting for two books, one on Bigfoot, designed to answer questions about the reports of the creature, and another on the men who have made looking for Bigfoot a major part of their life.
>
> "I thought it would be a good idea to write a book about the men looking for Bigfoot because they have a rugged individualism that seems to be dying out," Hurd said.[884]

Like other Bay Area Group members, Hurd placed himself firmly in the no-kill camp. "If Bigfoot's existence is proven, it will be incredible that such a huge creature could go undetected in such an advanced society. You have to come to the conclusion that it is because our society has become very blind to the environment," Hurd said. "Yurok Indian lore depicts Bigfoot as the Traveler or Patroller, a creature half-man, half-animal sent by the Great Spirit to keep men and nature in harmony," Hurd stated. The attainment of this harmony between nature and man was as important to Hurd as the discovery of Bigfoot.[885]

Hurd theorized that Bigfoot could be a relation of Neanderthal man that broke off, became isolated, and failed to evolve any further. Bigfoot was smart enough to be able to avoid man easily, Hurd maintained. He invoked a 1966 monster hunt (Hurd likely refers to the Monster of Sister Lakes, Michigan; see Chapter 1—Encounters) to reporter Glen Wright as a reason why Bigfoot would want to steer clear of man.

> A small farm town in Wisconsin was overwhelmed by hunters in 1966 after a "hairy, man-like creature" was publicized.
>
> "They were armed men in a crazed state of mind," Hurd says. "They converged on a farm, a 6-pack of beer in one hand and a rifle in the other. There was a traffic problem for miles around. Police had to come in to break it up."
>
> For this reason, says Hurd, he will not tell the exact locations of his "finds," many of which have been made in the state of Washington. However, he will permit his tapes of

> alleged [S]asquatch noises to be heard. They were recorded in woods near where [S]asquatch were suspected to be. They are an astonishing variety of whoops, screams and hyena-type laughter.[886]

Hurd brought his recorded Bigfoot calls and other evidence he had collected to *Santa Cruz Sentinel* columnist Wally Trabing who featured Hurd in his "Mostly About People" column, a daily piece he penned from 1962 to 1994.

> Joel Hurd sat at my desk jabbing at his portable tape recorder, searching for the scream—then he found it.
>
> The chilling, eerie, bark-whoop echoed from the forest depth, haunting, almost pleading growing in threatening intensity, then fading.
>
> Was it Bigfoot?
>
> Was it the giant, hairy upright human-ape, as illusive as flying saucers, and in various parts of the world also known as Sasquatch, Yeti and Abominable Snowman?
>
> Joel Hurd is a lay researcher of this mystery. He's from Sells, Arizona, and spent last summer in the Trinity Alps country and Washington state searching out clues which he hopes to compile into a book.
>
> Those screams. He recorded them from a tape made by a man living in a new subdivision bordering thick woods in northern Washington. The man had heard the calls before, as others did, but authorities could give no answers.
>
> Then, one July morning 1973, while shaving, he heard them again and held his tape recorder by the window. Joel also taped an interview with a policeman in the area who claims he saw the hairy giant that looks so human. He's compared the sounds of the call with those made in the Trinity. High pitched, scary screams.
>
> Joel, a slight, bearded, earnest man, is reluctant to pinpoint the sighting locations.
>
> There is always the fathead quick to grab his rifle and a sixpack of beer and set off in search of cheap heroics. It has happened several times before.

> Now, scientifically, Hurd is not saying specifically that Bigfoot exists. But he speaks as if he does, as if families of them do.
>
> So intent is his belief that the expansion of civilization is forcing their exposure, he feels that these creatures should be officially placed on the endangered species list through legislation. That's a mind blower, all right.
>
> Hurd has been collecting evidence for the past two years.
>
> He showed me a packet of hair he is taking to the University of Arizona to have analyzed, some blood samples given him and some leaves he gathered form a supposed Bigfoot nest.
>
> The footprint cast he carried was made from another cast taken in the Trinity Alps.
>
> I measured it—15 inches in length and 10 inches across the toe area.
>
> Hurd said the Indians have always claimed that such a creature existed.
>
> Well, it either does or doesn't.
>
> The worthy of mankind will always chase rainbows to prove that they exist.
>
> His subspecies waits in the wings to destroy.
>
> It is just as well if Bigfoot is never found out.
>
> For Bigfoot's sake.[887]

Andrew Genzoli wrote of the Bay Area Group's Mike Ward after receiving a clipping from *California Monthly* titled, "What Has Big Feet, Many Scoffers and a Few People in Hot Pursuit?"

> The story is about University of California senior, Mike Ward, who has been looking for Bigfoot.
>
> "When senior Mike Ward visits some of his departmental professors to talk about his favorite anthropological topic, he has to gird his loins.
>
> "'My usual reception,' he says, 'ranges all the way from skepticism to getting laughed right out of the office.'
>
> "Ward's problem is that he wants to conduct field studies on a giant North American bipedal primate which most of his professors insist does not exist.

"Conclusive physical evidence of Bigfoot so far has failed to appear, but there's no shortage of sightings," the article states. There is reference to Sasquatch, who may interest Pacific Northwest people, but somehow old sasquie doesn't have the appeal for us that Bigfoot has.

Ward is apparently a cheerful individual and doesn't mind being ridiculed by his professors. "He spent all of last August in the southern Trinity Alps in pursuit of his quarry," the article states.

"With George Haas, an experienced Sasquatch researcher from Oakland, Ward established a base camp in an area said to be frequented by Bigfoot. No one has been able to track the creatures, so Ward and Haas sought contact with them by appealing to their curiosity. They set out a salt block and rigged four tripwire flash cameras along likely routes. At night they stalked the forest with flashlights, hoping to see the usual red reflections of Bigfoot eyes. In the morning they checked dirt roads and deer trails for footprints. Everywhere they went they carried a cassette machine to catch on tape Bigfoot screams, said to be loud and high-pitched and disconcerting.

"For all their diligence, however, Ward and Haas saw nary a reflection, heard not a scream. This was disappointing, because tracks, screams and other evidence had indicated Sasquatch activity in the area during the three previous years. They speculate that atypically hot weather, heavier-than-normal logging and construction operations, and perhaps their own presence may have kept the animal away or made them stealthier . . ."

In the past all this did not bother Bigfoot, for he is recorded as having entered the camp perimeter to help himself to tractor tires, 50 gallon gasoline drums, and make a nuisance of himself.

Mike Ward has hopes of returning to continue his investigation, and one day find some evidence—be it skeletal—to prove his point there is a Bigfoot. "Ward wants to keep working to improve the odds that evidence will turn up. If it does—Ward uses 'if' and not 'when'—he'll already have the foundation for a fascinating life of study."[888]

Barbara Wasson, another high-profile member of the Bay Area Group, was also profiled in Castle's treatment. Wasson and her husband lived in a home overlooking Lake Berryessa in Napa County. Watching for inconsistencies as well as for shared congruities, Wasson assiduously reviewed over 600 reports—many of which had been collected by researchers John Green and Ron Olson. She followed-up on several reports and conducted tape-recorded interviews with witnesses. Wasson concluded that some people who claimed sightings had "a need to see something different," and many witnesses were sincere and earnest. "There must be a number of valid observers who have not come forward because they do not want to credit their own faculties," said Wasson. "They may try to rationalize that what they saw was a bear, because they don't want to run the risk of ridicule." Wasson attributed an increase in people stepping forward to report sightings as a result from increased public exposure to Bigfoot.[889] She was engaged, at the time of Castle's article, in working out predictive conclusions to questions such as what are Bigfoot's movements, what defines its geographical niche, and what are its feeding habits? "We want to collect enough statistical data so we can draw up a formal proposal for research and submit it to some agency for funding," she said.[890]

Ron Olson (1974)

> "The first person to bring a Bigfoot in could become rich if he wanted to. Right now, that's not our goal. We just want to prove they exist and learn more about them. We want to know what Bigfoot is—a manlike ape or an apelike man or a monster."—Ron Olson[891]

Ron Olson was 31 in 1974 and openly matter-of-fact about never having laid eyes on Bigfoot. Reporter Bob Downing interviewed Olson in the latter's office of the non-profit North American Wildlife Research Association (NAWRA) in a Eugene shopping center, nestled between an insurance company and a laundromat. The office was full of Bigfoot paraphernalia: a glass case housed casts of footprints, maps of the Pacific Northwest hung from the walls with colored pins marking report locations. A life-size painting of Patty, the star of the Patterson-Gimlin film, adorned one wall and dominated the space.

"The only Bigfoot evidence is based on pure coincidence—nothing more," Olson said. "Someone driving home at night sees a large, hairy figure cross the road in front of his car. Berry pickers see one briefly before the creature disappears into the brush. A pattern is beginning to emerge but right now it is too sketchy that it is almost useless," he said. Downing followed Olson's gesture toward the outsized painting. "A large animal like that could very easily exist unknown in this country—the Northwest's so damned big and so sparsely populated," he said. "You can leave one of the handful of roads through the mountains and walk 100 yards into the forest. You'll find an [impenetrable] wilderness."

Olson believed in capture and release, holding a drugged creature only long enough for scientific study. "We just want to learn something more about the Sasquatch," Olson said. "We're trying to do something different, something out-of-the-ordinary. In a sense, we're a different kind of explorers, dealing with something that is almost totally unknown. The mystery and the unknown are disappearing from our society. Heck, if (Christopher) Columbus would have needed extra crew members, I probably would have been one to sign on, sailing off into the unknown."

Olson hadn't seen a Bigfoot but he had come "awfully close—twice." As a road was being built in Oregon's McKenzie Pass wilderness in mid-1971—a situation, Olson pointed out, similar to the footprint finds in northern California of the late 1950s—one of the workers caught a fleeting glimpse of Bigfoot during the first week of June. Olson described the sighting to Downing: "The guy was out about 7:55 A.M. with his huskie. Suddenly, the dog just froze in its tracks. Looking down the hill, the surveyor saw the Bigfoot hunkered down low about 55 feet away. Looking over its shoulder, the creature saw the surveyor and the dog and, in the words of the surveyor, 'just exploded through the brush, parting the brush with its hands.'"

Olson admitted that initially he had been unconvinced by the story. Arriving at the scene himself, Olson was shown the area by the witness accompanied by his dog. "The dog, its hairs still bristling, went sniffing down the hill. After the guy described the route of the Bigfoot, the dog then sniffed out the same route. You can tell any number of stories but you cannot fool a dog which just sniffed out the exact route described by the surveyor two minutes before. That convinced me."

Searchers with dogs entered the area to find the creature. "Nothing came of the efforts. In order to seal off the area with all the forests and the mountains, we would have needed hundreds of men. And even if we had all that manpower, we probably couldn't have kept the creature from slipping through the net. It's a problem of limited manpower and the terrain working against you," he said.

With Downing taking notes, Olson described the second situation Olson thought may have placed him in close quarters with Bigfoot. It was 1972 and Olson and another man were in McKenzie Pass, Oregon, employing a wounded rabbit call, hoping to attract a Bigfoot. Olson continued the story: "We gave the call a couple of times. Suddenly we could hear something tromping through the brush at the far end of the canyon, moving towards us." Olson told Downing that it sounded bipedal. "Whatever it was was obviously very large. Then the tromping stopped. We gave the call again and waited. The thing again started moving toward the sound. Then it stopped. We repeated the call and it came again, stopping in the woods at the far side of a meadow where we couldn't see it."

Olson was prepared just in case they were able to lure a Bigfoot into range. "I had the (tranquilizing) gun ready—I just had to get the creature out into the meadow and it would be in range. We gave the call again. We could hear it tromping around, back and forth at the edge of the meadow as if it couldn't make up its mind whether it wanted to come out into the open." With the tranquilizer gun at the ready, Olson began to appreciate the situation. "We gave the call again and the tromping continued. When the realization hits you that something you've been looking for for four years, devoting all your time and money, is right across a meadow from you—just out of sight and out of reach, by gosh, that feeling is something.

"Suddenly, whatever it was—and I'm sure it was a Bigfoot although I can't prove it—turned and went tromping through the brush, down the canyon and away from us." Olson held up two fingers for Downing, with two inches' space between them. "We had come so close—and failed."

The most successful public outreach undertaken by Olson was the production of the 20-minute film titled, *Bigfoot: Man or Beast*, the second movie to use clips of the Patterson-Gimlin film. Below, Downing writes about the impact that short featurette had on audiences.

> Olson's group has taken advantage of the only known Sasquatch photographs, turning an 18-second film-clip into a 20-minute nature film which has been seen nationally (including the Akron area), in order to finance its field work.
>
> The movie—"Bigfoot: Man or Beast"—resulted in 20,000 letters and 17,000 phone calls a year to the Eugene office,

> according to Olson who says the contributions kept the operation going strong for nearly four years.
>
> A Salt Lake City film company, which set up Olson's NAWR group, purchased the film rights from the late Roger Patterson, a former rodeo rider from Yakima, Wash. Patterson, who died of cancer in 1972, spent eight years searching for the Sasquatch before he stumbled upon fame and controversy in late-1967.[892]

Olson placed full faith in the Patterson-Gimlin film's authenticity. "The thing that really clinched it for me is that Roger fell over a log while rushing toward the creature on foot. He fell head over heels which you see at the beginning of the film." Those 18 seconds of film shot in 1967 were the impetus Olson needed to pursue Bigfoot himself. "It is unlikely that it could be faked. Remember, this was 40 miles from anywhere. It was hunting season, making faking tracks or running around in a gorilla suit a pretty risky venture. And 40 miles from anywhere, the odds against seeing anyone else out in the brush or finding any tracks are very, very remote." Believing himself to have been close to Bigfoot, Olson remained in awe of the film's accomplishment. "Can you imagine the feeling? Looking for something you're convinced is out there for eight years without finding a thing. Suddenly you walk right into it. Jeez. Roger became unglued and excited when he saw the Bigfoot. I know Roger and he couldn't have faked anything like that. Besides, up to the time of his death, he was sinking every penny he had into another expedition—always another expedition—trying to prove the creature exists."

> Financed by contributions from movie viewers and by the sale of Sasquatch memorabilia like ashtrays shaped like life-size Sasquatch footprints, Olson's NAWR spent almost $40,000 in 1972. The money turned into a trickle last Spring, turning Olson and the others associated with the NAWR into unpaid volunteers. (He, his wife and two children had been receiving $700 a month from NAWR.)[893]

One of Olson's ardent endeavors was leveraging computer analysis to tease out behavioral patterns from of over 750 Bigfoot reports. This meshing of computer power to Bigfoot reports (prominently mentioned in *Bigfoot: Man or Beast* (1972)) reportedly cost $20,000 and identified areas with a high density of reports at certain times of the year. Olson told Downing that conclusive results were dependent upon the raw data. "Part of the problem is that we have to get all the reports we can in order to feed the computer," he said. "People see Bigfoot or find tracks but they're afraid to tell anyone, fearing that no one will believe them. That, by itself, is the major obstacle that we have to overcome."

Olson stated that an estimated 5 percent of Bigfoot reports were genuine, an additional 5 percent were likely hoaxes, leaving 90 percent as questionable. "It's easy to figure out what to do with the first 5 percent and the last 5 percent. What do you do with the middle 90 percent?" The computer analysis had pinpointed several promising areas for Bigfoot research including: The Dalles, Oregon (Byrne's home base); McKenzie Pass–Willamette National Forest area of Oregon; and the Mount St. Helens area, Washington.

Olson's Bigfoot trap, built in 1973, remained an attention-grabbing project. Olson chose to locate the trap at a spot in the Siskiyou Mountains along the boundary between California and Oregon. Downing reported the weight of the trap as 150 pounds and Olson proudly proclaimed it was "strong enough to even keep a Bigfoot in." The trap was constructed of wooden beams with 2 x 12-inch wooden planking on the sides and was anchored to supports set three feet into the ground. A steel gate came crashing down when an unsuspecting Bigfoot sprung the track by stepping onto a spring mat inside the door. The exact location was selected based upon an old prospector's reports that Bigfoot used to watch him work at that spot. Olson hired a prospector to be on site. "Wire-sensing devices," located about six-feet off the ground, surrounded the area about the trap.

At the time of Downing's interview with Olson, two bears had been caught inside the trap. Olson also confided to Downing that the hired prospector stand-in had told him of strange screams emanating from a canyon over several days in the autumn of 1973, stating it "wasn't a bear and it wasn't coyote. The hairs on my dog's neck just stood straight up."

With his computer analysis underway and producing analytics, Olson's fund-raising was focused toward field investigative work. As Downing reported, Olson had sights set on a new Bigfoot movie [this would become *Sasquatch, The Legend of Bigfoot;* see Chapter 7] to help sustain his organization's work. "He says the key to raising the money may be the current negotiations with a Denver film company for the full-length feature film script which Olson has written on the Sasquatch."

Downing also interviewed Edith Olson, Ron's wife. "I've been behind Ron, mostly because he is so involved in the project. I'm not terribly enthused about the time he has spent away from the family. We've had to make some sacrifices—with Ron being away and the money that isn't there. But that is what Ron is all about—why should I ask him to change?" she asked. "If bears can live in the mountains out here, why can't Bigfoot?" Edith and Ron Olson shared a similar judgement on Bigfoot's existential reality. "Mountain lions are back in the mountains and are almost never seen. Yes, I'm a believer, too."

"I don't know what Bigfoot is, nobody does," stated Olson. "But many of the scientific reports show a similarity of size and physical characteristics of the bones found in China. It's a logical answer that may or may not be correct. Until we capture a Bigfoot to find out once and for all, I think the 'Gigantopithecus' is as good an answer as you'll find for our mystery creature." With Downing taking notes, Olson added, "If I ever see one, I'm going to get it and then maybe the mystery will end."[894] Olson's protocols for a live-capture of Bigfoot incorporated the attachment of a tracking device to the creature prior to its release.

Dick Grover (1974)

Dick Grover, who hosted the "Fife Heights Incident" segment in *Bigfoot: Man or Beast,* was a commercial fisherman from Everett, Washington, who used much of his spare time researching Bigfoot sightings and camping out in areas he believed were hot spots for Bigfoot activity. Grover was the founder of Project Discovery. "Our interests are strictly scientific," Grover explained to reporter Martin Heerwald. "Our goals are to bring together sincere investigators from all parts of the state to solve the mystery of the Big Foot, to coordinate and disseminate information and to develop a rapport between our group and people living in Big Foot regions." Though Grover had never, at the time of Heerwald's article, seen a Bigfoot himself, he was sure the creatures existed based largely upon the numerous reported encounters people claimed with hairy giants. Grover told reporter Heerwald that Project Discovery kept members' names confidential, including two members who were scientists and university professors, but who were not ready for their names to be associated with Bigfoot research. Project Discovery, Grover stated, was interested in "extremely hard core evidence, something you can put your finger on." Photos capturing clear images of Bigfoot could be sufficient evidence. "We hope one day to be able to come up with close-up photographs, including close full-face views."

Grover explained that though not all of Project Discovery's membership believed that Bigfoot was an extant creature, the skills of believers and skeptics alike were welcomed to evaluate and explain evidence.

> The Sasquatch that Grover and most of the 30-odd members of Project Discovery believe in is "highly intelligent, but more animal than human, living in heavily wooded areas, but not necessarily remote, uninhabited mountain country." He says they could be as tall as 8 feet and weigh up to 800 pounds.
>
> He believes only 150 to 200 of the creatures exist in all of Washington state. "That's perhaps why so few have seen one."

Grover believed more evidence collection could convince the general public that hairy giants roamed sections of the nation's hinterlands. "This kind of information comes along very slowly," he said. "You need a lot of patience."[895]

Byrne Dispatch to *Pursuit*, April, 1974 [Morgan is mentioned as heading up an expedition]

Peter Byrne submitted a report of Bigfoot happenings in and around The Dalles, Washington, to *Pursuit*, published in that journal's April 1974 edition. Byrne's conservative approach to evidence acceptance is on display and near the end of his letter is an early mention of the museum and information hub which Byrne's group operated through most of the decade.

> Here in the Pacific Northwest, the western front as we Bigfoot searcher-investigators call it, it has been a very quiet time. Through 1971, 1972, sightings averaged two a year and footprint findings averaged three. Then came 1973 and a long dry spell broken only by one sighting—by four commercial fishermen, Bute Inlet, B. C., in March—and a footprint finding by myself in B.C. in the fall. There were no other sightings in 1973 of which we can write and it was not until last month that another sighting was reported. The incident took place in Florence, a small town on the Oregon coast, where a young boy (age 14) said that he saw one. A search of the area revealed almost no evidence but intensive questioning of the boy convinced me that he was telling the truth and that he probably did see a medium-sized (about six feet) young male Sasquatch. I spent three days in the area and then returned later to look at what might have been old tracks.

In 1973 I and my associates made a total of twelve field trips, each lasting from one to four weeks. Three of these were in the coastal ranges of Oregon and Washington. Four were into British Columbia, and of these latter four, one was by plane with Explorers Club writer-photographer Russ Kinne, the remainder by chartered boat. Several of the deep inlets were explored (some of which go back 80 or more miles into the mountains), including Bute Inlet, the scene of the March sighting. An interesting discovery was made at the head of Bute: Sasquatch Pass, a high pass out of the Homathko Icefield. It is so marked on the Canadian geological survey maps.

In the full-time search and investigation field here, there is presently only one group, and that is the group which I operate from The Dalles, Oregon. Various individuals make temporary sorties into the mountains, and among these the Colville, Washington searchers are probably the most active. Principal among these are Bob Hewes and Dwane Scott, Don Byington and Norm Davis. In other areas, mostly in northern California, serious searching is done during the summer months by George Haas and his colleagues. Haas is based in Oakland and each year spends a total of about 100 days in the field. There are no other fulltime or seriously interested searchers at present in the Bigfoot field.

This situation, however, is soon to change. In mid-May the National Wildlife Federation, of Washington, D. C., the foremost and most respected wildlife conservation society in this country and one of the biggest in the world, is to sponsor a serious, well organized, long-term scientific search. Leader of the expedition will be Bob Morgan, explorer and adventurer and one of the few men who has actually seen one of the objects of the search, as well as the leader of the 1970 expedition to the Mt. St. Helens area, which found footprints on two occasions. I shall be working with this group, probably for a period of at least a year. General areas of search are at present confidential but this information will probably be released for *Pursuit* readers in the coming months. The approach that Morgan and the NWF are taking is one I personally support. None of the group will carry guns, and the object of the expedition is a humane temporary capture and release of one of the giant primates. A few misguided people still think that a Sasquatch should be shot, simply to prove that they exist. (A small boy said to me recently, what if the one they shoot is the last one?) Morgan and his team think otherwise and I personally believe that his approach is one that will pay off.

What else is happening in the Bigfoot field? Here in The Dalles, to open on May 1st, a scientific and educational museum/exhibition based on the theme of the Bigfoot. Presently under construction by myself and designer Celia Killeen, the exhibit will contain panels depicting the search and investigation to date, using both colour and black-and-white photographs: the Himalayan searchers (as a comparative phenomenon), various groups of prehistoric men that might have been related to the Sasquatch, the Loch Ness investigation (again as a comparative phenomenon), old newspapers dating back to 1842 that contain references in various form to the Sasquatch, drawings and photographs of footprints of bear, man, gorilla, [S]asquatch, etc. and in glass cases, 3-D maps of the Pacific Northwest showing where the various findings have been made, edible plants of the Pacific Northwest of the type that a Bigfoot would eat, plaster casts of the various footprints (man, apes, bear, [S]asquatch, etc.) and fossil skull reproductions of some of the prehistoric men, including *Gigantopithecus*, etc.[896]

Green Response to Byrne Dispatch to *Pursuit* (October 1974)

Byrne's missive in April's *Pursuit* garnered a response from John Green in the October edition of that magazine. Green started out advising *Pursuit* readers "to disregard the report on the subject in the April issue of the magazine, as the writer apparently knows very little about it, either regarding the reports of the creatures themselves or the activities of those looking for them." Taking obvious issue with Byrne's report, Green raised the point of Byrne's acknowledgement of 13 reports starting in 1971 through March of 1974. Green told *Pursuit's* readers his own data revealed 13 sightings in the state of Washington alone, . . . just in the calendar year 1972.

There are a few individuals who use the Sasquatch as a means of raising money and to this end devote much of their "full-time"

> activities to the task of publicizing themselves so that they will be able to line up new sources of support when the current contributors find out some of the facts of the situation. Of course there are probably as many potential contributors around as there were in Barnum's day, but something is needed to attract their attention.
>
> The people who do the real digging for information and the real hunting are seldom publicized, as is usual in most lines of activity, and most of them spend their "full time" in working for their living.
>
> Of course there are quite a few people searching just for the satisfaction of seeing one of the creatures, a pastime with which one would hardly quarrel. It seems rather disrespectful to Ivan Sanderson's memory, however, to publish disparaging comments on those who would shoot a Sasquatch—especially such comments from a man who made a business of helping exterminate the tiger.[897]

Green further recounted a few of the reports from 1973-74. A June 1973 account by a B.C. logger featured a grey-furred creature which he observed ambling about on recently cut logs near Selma Park. A footprint was later photographed. The creature was erect and appeared larger than a man. In late November 1973, two Washington State University students reported their discovery of Cripple Foot tracks in an area southwest of Colville.[898]

The Donskoy Analysis

Pursuit, the house organ of the Society for the Investigation of the Unexplained (SITU), was "devoted to the investigation of 'things' that are customarily discounted" and an important specialty publication for Bigfoot-related information as the preceding missives from Byrne and Green attest to. Dr. Dmitri D. Donskoy was the Chief of the Chair of Biomechanics, Physical Culture Institute of the USSR, in Moscow and his report on the Patterson-Gimlin film appeared in the October 1974 edition of *Pursuit*. Donskoy's analysis of the film and photograph stills left him with the impression of a "fully spontaneous and highly efficient pattern of locomotion shown therein," presenting a smooth system of ambulation.

Donskoy noted the cross-limb coordinated movement of the arms and legs (e.g., a forward swing of the upper right arm accompanied by a forward swing of the left leg)—a natural gait construct for man. The leg strides were energetic, the swinging movement of the arms indicated muscular limbs. Each heel strike was accompanied by a bent knee which took on the full weight of the body and gave the creature's step a smooth impact. Donskoy could see muscles in the leg become tense in preparation for the pending "toe-off."

To compare his film-based observations with a human activity, Donskoy described the machinations of the creature's gait as analogous to cross-country skiing. The subject's knee flexion indicated the creature was very heavy and its robust toe-off contributed to its speed. The leg swing itself showed considerable flexion in the joints; the movement of the foot is behind the shank, which itself is behind the hip. Donskoy saw this movement as indicative of massive limbs with "well-relaxing muscles." The subject's movements evinced the use of muscle resilience in a fluid and easy gait that is not typically or ordinarily used by humans. Donskoy called the creature's gait "confident" and its strides "regular." The movement of the creature during its turn to the camera was achieved by a turn of the torso, noted Donskoy, which might indicate a limited mobility of the head. During its look back at the camera, the creature spreads its arms which likely increased its stability during the torso turn.

The toe-off phase revealed the sole of the foot which in comparison to a human's is large given the supposed height of the creature. Donskoy noted the absence of a recognizable longitudinal arch and the hind foot, formed by the heel, extended farther back than in humans. These observed anatomical characteristics "facilitate the work of the muscles that make standing postures possible and increase the force of propulsion possible and increase the force of propulsion in walking." Donskoy wrote that the lack of an arch could be attributable to the great height of the creature.

> Since the creature is manlike and bipedal its gait resembles in principle the gait of modern man. But all of its movements indicate that its weight is much greater, its muscles (especially) much stronger and its walk swifter than that of man. The movements (of the filmed creature) are harmonious and repeated uniformly from step to step, a provision of "synergy," i.e., the combined operation of a whole group of muscles.
>
> Lastly we can observe certain characteristics of the creature's walk which defy actual description. These could be described as "expressiveness of movements." In man this quality is manifest

> in a goal-oriented sporting or labour activity which impresses one with an economy (and accuracy) of movement. This characteristic can be noted by an experienced observer even if he does not know the specific given activity. "What needs to be done is neatly done" (with economy and efficiency) is another way of describing "expressiveness of movement." In the particular case (the creature in the footage) the motor system characterized by this quality is well adapted to the task that it is called upon to perform. In other words neat perfection is typical of those movements which through regular use have become habitual and automatic.

Donskoy concluded that he saw no "artfulness" in the creature's natural-looking movement, a gait that "is absolutely non-typical of man." *Pursuit* added an Editor's note affirming its position that the subject of the Patterson-Gimlin film was not a man in a costume. "The manufacturer of the "monkey suit" would have to have (in addition to a great deal of money and time) a rather phenomenal knowledge of biomechanics and an incredibly adept actor to wear the suit and maintain a non-human gait with such finesse that it fools a skeptical expert."[899]

Sanderson's Composite Reconstruction of Sasquatch and Yeti

Ivan Sanderson composed separate drawings of both the Yeti and Sasquatch in 1970 based upon "all the reports that we know of by alleged eye witnesses of both of these creatures," including the Patterson-Gimlin film and the examination of Frank Hansen's Ice Man exhibit which Sanderson had undertaken with Bernard Heuvelmans. Sanderson concluded that several types of "Abominable Snowmen," or ABSMs endured worldwide. Sanderson described the so-called original ABSM, the Yeti, as a rock-climbing variety of ape; other ABSM creatures were primitive hominids. The reconstruction of the Sasquatch and the accompanying text appeared in the October 1974 edition of *Pursuit.*

> Frankly, while the composite of the Yeti seems to make good zoological sense, that of the Sasquatch (i.e. Bigfoot, Hun-Guressu, or Dzu-the) looks to me utterly 'ridiculous.' No wonder not only skeptics but those anthropologists sincerely interested in the matter said that Roger Patterson's film looked

IVAN T. SANDERSON'S SASQUATCH RECONSTRUCTION

IVAN T. SANDERSON'S YETI RECONSTRUCTION

like "a man in a monkey suit (no one has ever come up with any proof that the film is not genuine). There have been those who have drawn or modeled their conceptions of this Sasquatch but all appear to have made it much too bestial and much more like the Yeti. It now transpires that the Sasquatch is in every way a hominid but that (as seen in the original specimen that was exhibited by Hansen (not the model exhibited after April 1969)), it has some very specialized characteristics. Most notable among these are facial. First, the face is naked and there is no beard, but a thick submandibular fringe (under, not on, the chin). Second, there is no brow ridge; third, the nose is excessively retroussée and the nares (nostrils) point straight forward; fourth, in place of a mustache there appear to be a few sparse, stiff hairs on either side above the angle of the jaw and then a vertical line of much smaller but more profuse bristle-like hairs running up the septum from the top of the upper lip almost to the tip of the nose.

The other extraordinary feature described by everybody is that while there appear to be no eyebrows, the hair across the forehead forms a forward, upward, and backward curling fringe. Upon this point old Mr. Ostman (kidnapped by a Sasquatch) was most insistent and we have his original sketches. While the torso is extraordinarily massive, its dimensions can be matched by modern human beings of all races but in particular professions such as wrestling, freight moving, and so forth. It turns out further that neither the arms nor the legs are either excessively long nor excessively short, though it does appear that the hands are very large. The final and perhaps most interesting fact that emerges from this analysis is that the feet of the Sasquatch would appear to be exactly in proportion to their stature. However, there is now cumulative evidence that their feet are short but very broad but that their toes are extremely long and webbed up to the proximal end of each phalange.

I cannot refrain from stating once more that I think the poor Sasquatch looks utterly 'ridiculous,' and as two professional artists, one an ex-Walt Disney cartoonist, said on viewing it: "It's altogether too theatrical." I agree; but in any endeavor such as this one cannot deviate either way from what facts we

> have. It would be very easy to, on the one hand, dramatize this reconstruction, or on the other hand to make it look even more human than it is. However, I am afraid we are stuck with this, even if it does look like a huge and robust Mongol wearing a peaked cap and a fur coat![900]

In 1974, *Pursuit* encouraged its readers to send suspicious hair and other physical specimens to *Pursuit* accompanied by a full report providing data on when, where, and how it was found and retrieved.[901] In October 1974, *Pursuit* published an article on findings from sample analysis from the "Western Pennsylvania 'monster'":

> As promised, we publish here the full report on hair samples and feces analyzed by Frederick A. Ulmer, Jr., formerly with the Philadelphia Zoological Gardens.
>
> "Here is the report about the hair and feces samples of the Western Pennsylvania 'monster.' I regret that it is not more conclusive, but these things are not easy to work with and present no end of knotty problems.
>
> Hair Sample #1—24 Aug. 1973—Monongahela, Penna.—Tentatively identified as human hair.
>
> Hair Sample #2—3 Sept. 1973—Glassport, Penna.—Positively identified as human hair.
>
> Hair Sample #3—26 Aug. 1973—Latrobe, Penna.—Found near mine shaft. This bunch of hairs intrigued me no end [sic] and I spent much time on them. Result—They are the hair of a cow, probably Holstein. Not much luck on immune-techniques.
>
> Hair Sample #4—21 Sept. 1973—St. Anne's Home, Greensburg, Penna.—This matted mass of light colored hairs had a strong fecal odor about it and I am certain that it was part of some feces. I positively identified it as cat and suspect that it was a domestic cat, for the pigment was too light for a bobcat. A serum protein test was tried on cat antiserum but there was no reaction. A positive reaction would have made it cat beyond the shadow of a doubt. However, I still feel that it is cat and the cellular struction strongly resembles that of the domestic cat.
>
> Feces Sample #3—This highly comminuted (pulverized, powdery) sample contained a claw bone and some meta-tarsal

> bones that I tentatively identified as coming from a chicken or a pheasant. There were also a great many chitinous remains of unidentified insects. The stool suggested that of a skunk or a raccoon.
>
> Other Fecal Samples were inconclusive."[902]

Jim Klobuchar (*Minneapolis Star*) mentioned by Genzoli (1974)

Writer Jim Klobuchar revisited the 1968 *Minneapolis Star* Bigfoot expedition in his January 28, 1974, column. His reminisces were presented with a tone of dubiety and rejection that surpassed his original disposition to the subject of six years prior. "Every so often man feels the urge to prove he can function independently of the rules of logic. At these times you can expect another outburst of sightings of 7-foot [S]asquatches."[903]

Andrew Genzoli, always willing to revisit the topic of Bigfoot in his own column, wrote about and commented on Klobuchar's recollections of his foray into the northern California environs.

> Another Bigfoot 'Aficionado'
>
> Now, Jim Klobuchar, columnist for the Minneapolis Star, turns out to be an old Bigfoot fan—with some reservations.
>
> Klobuchar opens his heart to reveal a secret or two: "Six years ago I led a four-man expedition into the rain forests of the Siskiyou Mountains in northern California, a mysterious land said to abound with giant footprints, suggesting a half-man, half-ape creature weighing 700 pounds.
>
> "Our exploration, sadly, was uneventful. The only improbable creatures available were members of the nearby (Willow Creek?) Chamber of Commerce. They evidently were planting the rare prints by moonlight and then calling the wire service with scientific findings." (Sort of a low blow, methinks.)
>
> And Klobuchar says: "Each time I voiced skepticism about the [B]igfoot story, I was met by fresh salvos of rage and denunciation. Man's yen to believe the unbelievable overpowers all pale rebuttals of reason. It accounts for the sudden comeback of the devil,[904] and probably our willingness to accept the oil industry's statistics."[905]

Robert Morgan 1974 Expedition

Writer-photographer Penelope McPhee wrote a lengthy article on Robert Morgan's 1974 American Yeti Expedition. She started her article, which appeared in the September 8, 1974, *Spokesman-Review Sunday Magazine,* with a narrative of Morgan's first encounter with a Bigfoot in 1957.

> The hunter sat alone on the edge of the canyon. Exhausted from the morning's fruitless hunt, his head began to nod; his heavy eyelids fought sleep.
>
> It was good to be in the mountains again; good to feel the fresh, clear air; good to remember the exhilaration of the hunt and the chase—the anticipation of the kill.
>
> A noise! Danger? He was instantly alert for his quarry. But something wasn't right. Something about that sound was all wrong. It sounded more like . . . like what? Like a man. But how could a man walk through that thick, tangled brush? And why? Danger!
>
> "Hello! Who's there?"
>
> Nothing.
>
> A bear would have run for it. Instead there was only silence. Even the cold mountain breeze stopped, momentarily being suspended—as though Nature herself held her breath.
>
> An uncharacteristic hush drowned out the bird chirps, the animal scratchings. Silence. Dead silence in the forest is discomforting—strange, forboding [sic]. The unnaturalness stimulates adrenalin—and imagination.
>
> "Hey, you there! Who are you?"
>
> The heavy crunch of dry, trampled brush. The hunter's trained ear followed the crackling leaves. Through the rifle sight, he tracked whatever was there as it smashed straight through the brambly thicket. In the same instant, eye and animal reached the clearing and stopped—cold.
>
> The two stood staring at one another. Seconds slowed to eons, as each kept a steady eye on the presumed intruder—the other.
>
> Curiosity stayed the animal. Shock stayed the hunter. Too paralyzed to act, he felt his highpowered [sic] rifle shrink to a toy.

> The animal made no effort to move, no indication of advance. The creature's look was clear, cool, intelligent. It was not the state of a wild animal. It was an almost human expression of surprised interest. A mirror of the hunter himself.
>
> If the animal was afraid, he never showed it. Nor did the hunter. Each was mesmerized by the presence of the other. Each was curious. Each felt, perhaps, the tickle of an old memory—the familiarity of something at once known but unknown, remembered but forgotten over many intervening millennia.[906]

For Morgan, that hunting trip laid the foundation for what became one of his life's passions. As Morgan said, he hadn't initially made a conscious decision to leave the rat-race behind; "I'd never liked it, and I didn't want anything to do with it, but I never made a deliberate decision—until I tried to go back."[907]

The "going back" followed on the heels of Morgan's first foray into the wilderness to seek out and understand what he had encountered in 1957. In 1969 Morgan went to work for Scientific Control Corp. in Dallas, Texas. "I sat there with this funny little thing around my neck, trying to figure out why cuffs were on pants; why I had to wear a jacket to meet someone. You know, the dance of society. Finally, I asked myself, what the hell am I doing here?"[908]

Up to his 1974 expedition on the Washington-Oregon border starting that May, Morgan had supported himself in construction, as a logger, a film writer, and a dog trainer—all jobs taken to maintain his pursuit of Bigfoot. Morgan's stated goal was to conduct scientific expeditions and to that end he had solicited and garnered financing through a grant from a "renowned family," administered through the National Wildlife Federation. McPhee provides the following description of Morgan:

> Morgan is, by anyone's estimation, an unusual man. His physical presence belies his 5 feet 8 inches. His romanticism reaches deeper than his [Yul] Brynneresque bald head and his Mephistophelean mustache and beard. Although his clear azure eyes and his easy, perfect smile are attractive to women, Morgan is a man's man. He radiates adventure, strength, ego. He is energy. He is raw muscle, tensed and ready for action.[909]

"If we find a primate—an unknown species in North America, it is going to alter anthropology from A to Z, and to find them still alive and prospering is going to shake an awful lot of minds," Morgan said. "There are going to be a lot of scientists horribly red-faced because they simply do not want to accept the possibility that there is something beyond their expertise."[910]

Enlisting the help of biologist Laymond Hardy and botanist Donald Blake, Morgan conducted an ecological survey of candidate research areas in 1974—credited as being an early, if not the first environmental study completed with Bigfoot as a specific point of interest. Morgan and his associates concluded that the studied ecosystems could feasibly support a large primate. They also identified what they believed were three migratory routes with associated feeding patterns in areas of Washington and Oregon.

> His team will monitor these areas and act accordingly. His approach resembles that of anthropologist Jane Goodall in her chimpanzee studies. He continually places himself in Bigfoot's path, between him and food, between him and his shelter.[911]

Similar to Olson and Byrne, a component of Morgan's ambition was the temporary capture of a Bigfoot specimen, detaining the creature for eight hours or less. A tranquilized Bigfoot would be subjected to a number of tests including X-rays, blood samples, tissue samples, and extensive photographs and filming. Following this examination and study, the creature would be returned to the wild.

> To Morgan, the creature's safety is the primary consideration. Over the years, he has become an ardent conservationist. He no longer hunts for sport, and he has nothing good to say about the Bigfoot "researchers" who go out "armed to the teeth."[912]

In late September, Morgan stated that strands of suspected Bigfoot hair found near Mt. St. Helens in August had been identified as human hair. "It's something we're very excited about." Mary Joe Florey, a microbiologist from Portland, Oregon, concluded the hair was human, probably from an ankle or leg, Morgan said. Morgan told McPhee that hair analysis was then ongoing, including comparison to other hair strands which Morgan had found two years previous on a fence near a spot where deer and cattle had been killed and large footprints discovered. "If it was a Bigfoot, then it opens up many new doors," said Morgan.[913]

American Yeti Expedition members also found a trackway in August which gave the impression their maker had heard searchers approaching.

"And if it was a human, why would he want to hide from two other humans?"[914] Morgan asked. The researchers had been walking along a trail which brought them to a stream. As the group started to cross the stream, they noticed a fresh scuff mark on moss-covered rock. Further scrutiny led to the discovery of the hair strands eventually submitted to Florey and the trackway, composed of huge footprints, was found close by. The prints followed the stream for about 20 yards, then circled above the trackers. "That is exactly the movement a primate would make if it wished to observe while not being observed," Morgan said. "I'm not saying it was a Bigfoot, but it's very unlikely a barefooted human would be running around in that area."[915] Morgan stated his search for Bigfoot in 1974 would continue in the southwestern Washington area "until the snow flies."[916]

A group of loggers found 161 footprints on October 7 in southwest Washington's Lewis River Basin. The creature responsible for them was thought to be an eight-foot tall Bigfoot which, according to Morgan, regaled the loggers with "strange, chirping whistles."[917]

"It's the longest string of Bigfoot tracks ever examined by scientists to my knowledge," Morgan said. "Field measurements indicate the footprints were a whopping 18 inches long, seven inches across at the ball of the foot, and 5.5 inches across the heel. The average stride was well over 50 inches." At Morgan's request, Grover Krantz examined casts of the tracks. "It is overwhelmingly probable that they (the tracks) are real," Krantz said. "I've seen some pretty sophisticated fakes. I don't think these could have been done with fake feet." Krantz estimated that the creature that left the tracks weighed about 800 pounds.[918]

Morgan interviewed the loggers who told him they had heard the sounds of a stump being ripped apart. Elizabeth Moorman, a biology student affiliated with the American Yeti Expedition, said the tracks were found "within a few miles of a report we received in July when a boatyard owner saw a Bigfoot near one of his boats." In August, Moorman said she received a report "from a logger's wife who saw it across the road just across the river from where the tracks were found."[919]

In contrast to Peter Byrne's more favorable opinion of Morgan expressed in his *Pursuit* dispatch from April, Byrne delivered up a most unenthusiastic reaction to Morgan's October announcement of the discovery of a supposed Bigfoot trackway numbering some 161 prints. "Not again," said Byrne whose direct experience with members of the American Yeti Expedition went back to the summer of 1973. Referring to his cooperation with

Morgan from the previous summer, Byrne said, "It was growing ridiculous. Morgan was claiming new finds at the rate of one a week."[920] Such apparent success was counter to Byrne's conservative approach to evaluation and evidence acceptance. Byrne said, in fact, it was possible that "years can go by without any advance in our knowledge of Sasquatch." According to Byrne, by October 1974, he and Morgan had ended their cooperative efforts.[921]

Print & Film

Bigfoot's use in film and TV remained varied in tone. The long-lasting Canadian comedy-drama show *Beachcombers* featured a Bigfoot hoax in the episode "The Sasquatch Walks by Night." In the film *Shriek of the Mutilated*, a clan of cannibals uses a man dressed as a Yeti-like creature to scare away people from their island where the cannibals hold their feasts. A group of college students defy warnings and travel to the island anyway, only to be mercilessly torn to pieces by the Yeti-costumed fanatic. In *Beauties and the Beast*, Bigfoot terrorizes hippies and nudists in the woods, taking several young nubile women back to his cave; the film has very little plot to speak of and rather a lot of gratuitous nudity.

Kolchack: The Night Stalker lasted only two seasons on ABC but its durable influence made it one of the inspirations for future shows like *The X-Files*. In the first season's "The Spanish Moss Murders," Kolchack realizes that two murder victims shared the oddity of Spanish moss draped on their bodies, suggesting a linkage between the murders. Richard Keil plays a towering swamp monster called a Peremalfait which Kolchak confronts in the sewers.

Sid and Marty Kroft's *Land of the Lost* live-action Saturday morning television show featured a Yeti in two episodes: "Ancient Guardian" and "Abominable Snowman." The series also featured the Pakuni, advanced hominids that make regular appearances during the show's run.

Monsters! Mysteries or Myths (1974)

Rod Serling narrated NBC's 1973 television documentary *In Search of Ancient Astronauts* (based on the bestselling book *Chariots of the Gods* (1968) by Erich von Däniken), which asked if certain phenomena on Earth could be ascribed to extraterrestrial visitors. In 1974 Rod Serling was back narrating a Smithsonian television special, *Monsters! Mysteries or Myths?*, which aired on Monday, November 25, at 8 P.M. on CBS. The special was written, produced and directed by Robert Guenette for Wolper Productions, with George Lefferts as executive producer. Coordination for the Smithsonian Institution was done by Nazarel Cherkezian, William Grayson, and Carl Larsen.[922] The segments of Robert Morgan were filmed in the summer of 1974, about a month before Yeti Expedition footage shot by Bostonia Film Co. The latter footage would be seen in the 1975 re-release of *Bigfoot: Man or Beast* as the longer, Morgan-dominated *In Search of Bigfoot. Monsters! Mysteries or Myths?* proved to be an unqualified success for CBS and revealed the depth of public interest and appetite for monsters in our midst.

> The Nielson viewership ratings remained unmatched for decades, with literally tens of millions of Americans having watched this one-hour examination of the cryptozoological phenomena (the first real introduction to this burgeoning field for many).[923]

"I resent the dream-busters," said the six-time Emmy Award-winning writer and *Monsters! Mysteries or Myths?* host, Rod Serling. "You know the kind of people who insist on telling you that what you saw wasn't really a flying saucer." Serling represented a natural choice as host for such a special as he harbored an interest and fascination in some of the world's biggest mysteries. "I've used comparable legendary 'monsters' in scripts I've written," Serling said, "and frankly, I'd like to believe that they're real. These legends have lasted so long because most of us want to dream about what is possible." Serling suggested that despite lacking creditable evidence for scientific acceptance, there remained compelling, tangible support for the world's mystery monsters. "Even though scientists have never found evidence to prove that the Abominable Snowman, the Loch Ness Monster and Bigfoot are real, they don't debunk the possibility," he said. "The legends are a subject worthy of investigation, and, luckily, they give us a frontier that allows us to dream a little."[924]

Win Fanning, who for 25 years reported on television for the *Pittsburgh Post-Gazette*, shared a positive reaction to the special; describing it as an "engaging, if somewhat overtalkie, hour," and well worth viewing.

> Led on by narrator Rod Serling, a host of scientists, dedicated observers and just plain folk described their contacts—or

> imagined contacts with the beasties in question [Bigfoot, Yeti, and the Loch Ness Monster]. The pros and cons seemed about evenly divided, except that in discussing the two manlike giants the expert opinions came down harder against their existence than they did in the case of the Scottish sea serpent.
>
> However, in his closing comments, Serling noted that in the absence of conclusive, hard evidence the Smithsonian scientists "do not endorse the reality of such creatures as Bigfoot, the Abominable Snowman or the Loch Ness Monster."[925]

Dr. S. Dillon Ripley, then Secretary of the Smithsonian Institution, wrote about the importance of myths shortly after the airing of *Monsters! Mysteries or Myths?* According to Ripley, in certain instances myth and science could be at odds and in others they could be complementary, suggestive that phenomenon like Bigfoot would neither be easily dispelled or accepted.

> Through the ages, man has manifested a need to believe in scientifically unproven facts as a way to reinforce his other beliefs. Such myths have become part of the traditional folklore of many civilizations, both old and new, as humans seek to explain somehow a practice, a belief, or a short or long-lived phenomenon.
>
> What is fact? What is fiction? The scientific method often can be used to ferret out the truth. Mythology, however, still confronts modern science with some animal legends that offer challenges to those who seek to explain them.[926]

Marian T. Place—*On the Track of Bigfoot*

With an original hardcover price of $4.25, Marian T. Place's *On the Track of Bigfoot* gives the reader a wide assortment of Bigfoot stories and provides a look at some of the key people involved in searching out answers to the mystery of giant man-like creatures in North America. Place's book was intended for a younger evidence but remains readily readable and informative for adults. The author wisely presents the stories and evidence objectively, and leaves any conclusions to the reader. Genzoli was so impressed with the book he devoted most of one of his "Redwood Country" columns to covering its merits:

ON THE
TRACK OF
BIGFOOT
ARCH
29944-1
$1.75
Marian T. Place
"...an engrossing story of those who
are trying to get close to the
legendary man-beast"
—Publishers Weekly

> Now, there is another Bigfoot book ready for the market. "On the Track of Bigfoot," is by Marian T. Place of Jacksonville, Ore., and published by Dodd, Mead & Co. ($4.25). It is neatly printed along with a bountiful supply of photographs.
>
> The book, while targeted for the younger—the juvenile—reader, can be enjoyed by the adult. All the facts are there, you'll even find things from the old "RFD"; references to a lot of people you know. There is the story of how the news about Bigfoot reached the "outer world," and the furor it caused.
>
> There are historic accounts about Bigfoot, some of which I had unearthed from the old files of *The Humboldt Times*, others from the *Del Norte Record*, and other useful sources. Mrs. Place has taken all these things, plus her own research and succeeded in weaving a readable story. It has good sense and humor, and stays within the bounds of reason, which some authors in the past have exceeded.
>
> She features all sides of the Bigfoot story, even the controversial photo by Roger Patterson, who claimed what he had filmed was Bigfoot. I agree with other Bigfoot "aficionados" (some are anthropological experts), the strip of film is a lot of hokum. Looks just like something which ran away from a Hollywood costume party.
>
> Don't let this comment turn you from the book, for it is worth having and reading. The kids will love it, and so will you.
>
> Now, about Marian T. Place: she has authored over 30 books for children and young people, specializing in the American West. She is the recipient of four Golden Spur Awards given by the Western Writers of America, as well as awards for Best Western juvenile novel and Best Western juvenile nonfiction title.
>
> She has worked as a newspaperwoman and a children's library, and has published over 200 articles. She and her husband live in Jacksonville, in the Oregon portion of Bigfoot country.[927]

On the Track of Bigfoot won the 1977 Garden State Children's Book Award.

Another general overview of Bigfoot, including historical sightings to the early '70s, is the 64-page booklet from Beau Davis titled, *Bigfoot is Alive!*

Davis devotes short chapters to the Abominable Snowman, hairy hominids in Russia, Skunk Apes, the Fouke Monster, and Momo. Davis relates his own Bigfoot encounter from October 21, 1959, when he and a companion encountered a giant hair-covered creature in Redwood Forest while driving from Los Angeles to Crescent City. "With a sudden impulse—I opened the car door; got out and went in pursuit of the creature. It then began to run. I was no more than an arm's length from the creature." The creature disappeared into the forest leaving a shaken Davis behind. From that transforming moment he became fascinated with Bigfoot.

> His kind generally exist mostly in the vast and often impenetrable forest, or in inaccessible rock gorges where unexplored caves are numerous. He only ventures on open slopes when necessity, such as the hunt for food, or a new lair, drives him to open ground where he leaves tracks, before disappearing into the forest. Bigfoot would seem to be carnivorous, though frequently resorting to berries, shoots, and other plants or roots which he tears up during his progress on mountain slopes. With all of our technological knowledge and devices, it is only a question of time before modern man will have all the answers as to the diet, habits, life span of our primate man.[928]

In the back of the booklet are several Bigfoot items for sale from Tambarlee International, Inc., including posters, prints, decals, sweatshirts, and a 40-inch long rug in the shape of a foot for that special room or as an eye-catching wall decoration.

SIGHTINGS 1974

Ron Bailey

Ron Bailey lived in Palmdale, California, with his wife Margaret and their son, Brian. Bailey was employed at Rockwell International. B. Ann Slate interviewed him for an article published in the June 1976 edition of *Saga* magazine. The Bigfoot-related incidents that Bailey experienced spanned the early '70s and included elements (e.g. "the mind grab"), which up to that point had not been commonly associated with Bigfoot.

> In 1972, Bailey had never heard of a Bigfoot or cared less whether they existed or not. It was a hot summer evening

and as he pulled into his carport Bailey was instantly on the alert. His special jungle tracking experience from the Force Reconnaissance Marines in Vietnam and Cambodia had given him the background to observe the smallest details. Bailey sensed something was extremely different and wrong about that night.

What bothered him at first was the silence. Normally the neighborhood dogs would be barking at the approach of a car. The crickets should have been chirping but the night was strangely quiet. The light from the house next door illuminated his yard, casting shadows on a large bush behind the carport. The bush appeared to be swaying slightly in the wind but there was no trace of any breeze. A rotten odor which Bailey compares to "sewage or spoiled apples" was emanating from somewhere near the swaying bush.

"I'm not the scary type and I don't get frightened easily but I made a beeline for the house in no uncertain terms!" the veteran said. Within the safety of his home, Bailey put the kitchen lights on, pulled up the blinds, and looked into the back yard. He saw nothing except the big bush which was no longer swaying.

"So I thought to myself, it's as plain as day . . . I'm losing my marbles!" Bailey said. "I started to let the blinds down when something grabbed me mentally. I don't know what it was. It's beyond description but whatever it was literally hypnotizing me. I'm not a dramatic person, or an imaginative one. You could say I'm about as down-to-earth as a door knob but I felt like something alien and outside myself was trying to control me!"

As Bailey stood transfixed at that kitchen window—unable to move his muscles but being commanded from somewhere in that courtyard to continue looking—*he saw it.* Standing next to the telephone pole in the center of the yard, about 50 feet away, stood a nine-foot-tall, black, hairy form, standing motionless and relaxed. While shadows obscured the creature's face, Bailey knew it was looking directly into his eyes, telepathically and hypnotically urging him to come outside to it.

The veteran, who has a tremendous amount of self-control, broke out in a profuse sweat as he fought the terrible compulsion

> that was not his own. For a few tense moments, suspended in time, the two stared at each other. The gigantic dark form mentally urging, Bailey mentally resisting but weakening with each passing second.
>
> Abruptly, as if tired of the game, the hairy form walked across the courtyard and disappeared into the blackness of the night. Bailey collapsed with fatigue and relief against the kitchen cupboard. The nightmare was over. It was gone, whatever it was, Bailey thought to himself as he wiped the beads of sweat from his forehead. But he couldn't have known it was just the beginning. While his "normal" life style would remain the same on the outside, Bailey would be a man possessed with the fires of curiosity to again see this man-like creature who had tried to mentally control him, and had very nearly succeeded.[929]

Palmdale is located on the western edge of the Great Mojave Desert in Antelope Valley. Once, prehistoric megafauna such as mastodons roamed this space in earth-shaking herds. To the south are the San Gabriel Mountains and the area is bordered on the north by the Tehachapi Mountains—snow-capped peaks replete with caves and abandoned mines.

This area experienced industrial expansion in the '70s. Lockheed turned out the Tri-Star jetliner and Rockwell International was involved in work on the space shuttle project. Palmdale also sat in a location increasingly popular with vacation-minded folks from the greater Los Angeles area and beyond. Motor-homes seeking their vacation-haven wound their way through the area toward the many campgrounds in the Angeles National Forest. The growing popularity of dirt bikes and dune buggies could be seen and heard as riders enjoyed their motor sports recreation in the high desert.

To some, it may have seemed an unlikely choice of habitat for Bigfoot, yet multiple-witness sightings since 1972 established, to some researchers' satisfaction, that Bigfoot creatures migrated through the region annually. Slate asked if perhaps Bigfoot was a form of prehistoric man, bypassed by evolution and surviving on highly-developed senses of animal cunning and hypnotic techniques, qualities abounding in Indian stories and legends. Slate invoked civilization's inexorable creep into the wilderness as the cause behind an increase in Bigfoot sightings; an upsurge owing as if from a defiant protest against mankind's intrusion.

Along with Bailey's unusual experiences, Slate's article included her research of other sightings from the region. In the summer of 1973, Mike Pense was riding his 450 Honda motorcycle on his day off, racing through the sands and buttes of a park. Attaining the top of a ridge, Pense turned off the engine and enjoyed the view out across a valley. A rock suddenly landed near his back tire and as Pense turned to look he saw above him a black-haired figure with its arms held above its head, ready to throw a boulder at Pense and his motorcycle. Wasting no time, he started his engine and hastily retreated down the side of the ridge. Pense later joined Ron Bailey in nighttime expeditions to search for answers to the events each had separately experienced. These men formed the nucleus of the High Desert Sasquatch Research Team. John Baylor of Lancaster, California, joined the team after an incident that occurred to his son Bret in the summer of 1973 at the Baylor residence on the edge of the desert. In an interview, Bret shared the following account of his experience:

> "My sister Stephanie and I were walking down this dirt road about 10 o'clock in the morning. We were just talking and looking around. I happened to glance up on the butte and I yelled 'Guy'! He was looking down at the road and he turned his head and looked at us . . . this huge thing behind the boulder just looking at us! He was brown. I thought it was an ape. The hair around his face was white and his head was kind of pointed. The hair all over his body was brown. We started backing up and then ran about 15 yards and I had to pick Stefanie up because she couldn't run fast enough. When we got to the road, I turned around and it was gone."[930]

Joyce Baylor appreciated that whatever her children encountered, they had experienced something truly terrifying. Later she and John drove through the buttes but saw nothing.

Antelope Valley became known for three-toed tracks periodically found there. During the spring of 1973, Bailey and several friends were out in the desert at night, searching for Bigfoot in a location known for several previous Bigfoot sightings. As the group ascended a tall butte, Bailey's flashlight beam illuminated a 12-inch long print, freshly-made and displaying only three toes. "It wasn't made by any animal that I'd ever heard of," Bailey told Slate. "It wasn't human and it wasn't made by someone faking a hoax way out there. The tracks were plain, fresh, and made by something which had passed that way just a few hours before." The tracks were lost in rocky terrain, and after turning up no further evidence the men returned to their respective homes. In the early hours of the following morning, Ron set his head against his pillow in bed when a thumping started up at the rear of the Bailey's recently-purchased house. "It sounded like someone was stomping," Bailey said. The thumping continued as a neighbor dog began yelping as if it were being harangued or beaten. Bailey got dressed and grabbed his gun. Visibility was too poor from his bedroom window so he went outside, just in time to catch a glimpse of something moving away. "It was pretty good size moving at a pretty good pace. Whatever it was, was heading for the hills. Margaret and I stayed up the rest of the night and when morning came, we checked the sage field to the rear of our home. The footprints were three-toed and well sunk in like it had deliberately stomped over and over again in the same spot," Bailey stated.

> Why are the creatures searching for Ron Bailey? Is there something in his background, his military training perhaps, which has developed certain animal instincts such as the old mountain men possessed? And does Bigfoot sense this and moves in closer, even to follow him to his home in an effort to communicate? Or could it be that Bailey represents a threat to them?[931]

Bailey told Slate he disavowed possession of any psychic affinity but did attribute a certain sensitivity to Bigfoot as simply "feeling vibes," by which he could tell not only if a Bigfoot was near but how many were hidden in the shadows. One of the creatures Bailey's group came to know they named "Big Ben,' a colossal Bigfoot about 12-feet high which left tracks 24-inches long and nine-inches wide at the heel. Incredibly, Big Ben seemed at times to affect a stride exceeding 20 feet. Bailey's vibes on Big Ben had led him to conclude that the massive creature was well aware of Bailey and his friends' interest. Bailey's wife Margaret was terrorized during an incident in August 1973, convincing Bailey that Big Ben had turned the tables on the researchers. The scene was a canyon leading to the Mojave which ended in a sandy area known as the Buttes. The canyon offered a natural lowland area in which springtime fruit and alfalfa fields prospered. The High Desert Sasquatch Research Team assessed the location as a logical travel route for Bigfoot.

> On this particular summer night, the search group included John and Joyce Baylor. The women remained in one of the cars parked at the base of the mountain trail while Bailey and the men climbed the steep, narrow canyon. As they climbed higher, they could hear scuffling sounds ahead of them in the darkness.
>
> "Whatever was up there was big—and there was more than one of them!" Bailey said. "Then the rocks started coming down at us from behind the bushes and trees, thrown at us like we were getting too close to them. I was armed. Apparently they didn't like it. Of course they didn't know it was for my own protection."
>
> The men decided to retreat and began picking their way down the trail. It was a dangerous situation. The rocky ledge on which they walked was extremely narrow and still the rocks continued to come at them from above. As one hit at Bailey's right heel, he lost his footing, fortunately falling on the seat of his pants rather than over the side of the mountain. But now he was mad. As he scrambled to his feet, his eyes were narrowed with anger.
>
> Turning to look with defiance in the direction of the attackers, something he calls "the mind grab" began. "It was happening just like before, this over-powering feeling cutting into my own thoughts and trying to take control," the veteran said. "It wasn't exactly in words; more like a feeling. It was telling me to put down my gun and walk to it!"[932]

Bailey found himself in a fugue-like state, obeying the telepathic urging by laying down his weapon and walking up the dark canyon. Finally, his willpower prevailed and his self-control reasserted itself. "I grabbed myself back to myself and caught what I was doing. At the moment when my mind was released, I was instantly back to being mad again so I picked up some rocks at my feet and started throwing them back at the creatures." Bailey went back down the canyon where the cars had been parked. He discovered only John Baylor's car remained . . . Bailey's auto was gone, as were the two women. Checking the scene carefully, tire marks from Bailey's car were found, indicating a hasty departure. The anxious men drove back toward the Bailey residence. While on the way, Ron contacted Margaret via Citizens Band (C.B.) radio and learned she was waiting for him at their home. "We saw something," she told her husband, "but I'll tell you about it when you get home." Slate wrote an account of her experience.

> As the men had hiked in the upper canyon, the two women sat quietly in the darkened car. Suddenly, from out of the bushes a gigantic, bulky silhouette emerged which passed right in front of the vehicle. Its size was out of a nightmare. The young sycamore trees in the area stand at a height between 10 and 12 feet and the head of the creature was clearly outlined above the tops of those trees. It moved with no apparent haste. Across the road, campers were parked in a motor-home. "I could see its form outlined against the trailer and it was head and shoulders over the top of it!" Margaret said.[933]

Ron was convinced it was none other than Big Ben. Returning to the canyon the following morning, several giant footprints validated his suspicions. But Big Ben was not alone that night; near the spot where the Bailey car had been parked, several smaller prints were found revealing the presence of at least two other creatures. "They put prints in a lot of places that didn't make any sense," said Bailey. "They were facing all different directions and then a group of them would trek off into a flat area and then stop completely for no reason. There were footprints helter-skelter all over the place!"

> While the patterns didn't seem logical to Bailey, certainly not those of animals simply following a trail, what if Ben and his friends weren't animals but another form of Man simply evening the score on the tracking expedition that night? As the men drew closer to Ben's companions high up in that canyon, the hairy leader moved swiftly to the bottom of the trail and the cars, knowing full well what kind of a response the sight of him would produce in the two women![934]

On September 15, 1974, Richard Engels and Neil Forn, both high school students, encountered a Bigfoot and experienced telepathic warnings while camping in the Buttes. It was a moonless night as the boys searched by flashlight for a spot to pitch camp. The boys climbed a ridge and saw a small, pyramid-shaped pile of rocks. Neil was first to approach the pile when a strange feeling came over him. "I could sense a hostility, like something didn't want us there," he said. "It was like we were just being tolerated yet something was telling me that if I touched those rocks, it was going to kill me!" Richard was also experiencing uncomfortable feelings, particularly the unnerving surety that he and his friend were being held under close inspection by something both close by and unseen. Richard joined back up with Neil as the latter was making his way back down from the ridge. "Where are you going?" Richard asked. "I'm getting a bad feeling," Neil replied. "Let's get away from those rocks!" As Richard asked what pile of rocks his friend referred to, he turned and his flashlight shone upon a dark form standing above the boys up on the hill. The man-like figure was lean and covered in dark hair and sported a conical-shaped head. With the light upon it, it shied behind nearby rocks and Richard and Neil wasted no time in running back to their car.

> Later measurements ascertained the creature as being over seven feet tall. The three-toed, 15-inch footprints found in the sand nearby were in keeping with the description of the height and weight of the creature. If, as [John] Green cites, the Sasquatch will pick up rocks to smell them for scent of small animals they eat, then neatly stack them in a little pile, it is probable that the boys had inadvertently infringed on this Bigfoot's hunting grounds. This particular area of the Mojave abounds with desert chipmunks and kangaroo rats.[935]

In 1973, one of Ron Bailey's friends, Kent Lacy, formerly a newscaster at Palmdale's KUTY station and by the mid-'70s working at KAFY in Bakersfield, joined Bailey's team for a stakeout of a shallow cave in the Buttes where Bigfoot prints had been found.

> During that night, a figure covered with hair was seen moving across the valley, its form outlined against the light-colored rocks by the full moon. The characteristic foul odor of the creature momentarily filled the air. Attempts to follow it proved futile and near daybreak, the trackers disbanded. As Kent drove alone on the dirt trail out of the desolate Buttes, the sound began; faintly, almost imperceptibly. At first the newscaster thought it was the desert wind, rising in pitch as it rushed across the sagebrush and Joshua trees.
>
> The high-pitched sound increased in intensity, a plaintive wail much like a woman moaning in pain. It came closer and

> closer to his Volkswagen until, as Kent puts it, "I thought the thing was standing right on top of the car!"
>
> Dawn was still too far away to provide any light so Kent lost no time in driving out of there at top speed, tearing across the rocky terrain with the creature's screams ringing in his ears. (A tape recording of a Sasquatch scream, sent to the author by Stan Gordon of the Westmoreland County UFO Study Group in Pennsylvania, was played for Kent Lacy who identified it as the cry he had heard!)[936]

Slate wrote about Jim Mangano's inexplicable compulsion that made him walk away from his fellow hikers and leave their San Gabriel Mountain campsite, trekking upstream through the night of October 19, 1974. After walking for a period of time he sat down on a rock. He felt a "weird feeling," as if he were to wait upon something to happen. In this state he became increasingly frightened. Eventually, he was able to return to camp, perplexed at what had induced him to walk away from his companions.

> The others had already gone to sleep and Jim tossed restlessly in his sleeping bag, wondering about the strange compulsion. The screams started about midnight, screams which the boy compares to "sounding like a child being murdered." Over and over, the frightening cries were repeated, coming from the same direction upstream where Jim had felt mentally called to go earlier that night. He had the feeling to get up and help that person who was screaming but his terror overrode the impulse.[937]

In the morning, the hikers found human-type footprints over 20 inches long near the rock Mangano had sat upon.

William Bosak UFO & Creature Encounter

"I don't know if I should even be talking about it now," said Bill Bosak of Frederic, Wisconsin, while talking with interviewer Dewey Berscheld. "I know if I tell anyone I'm going to get a lot of ribbing. I've decided to talk now so that anybody else who sees something similar to what I saw will know what to do and maybe even try to communicate with it."[938] *Canadian UFO Report* printed Bosak's interview about his encounter with a creature which appeared just as unnerved by Bosak's presence as Bosak was of the Bigfoot-like entity.

> "I was coming home from a co-op meeting at about 10:30 P.M. It was the early part of December [December 02, 1974[939]] and very mild for the time of year. There were patches of fog on the road so I was driving slowly with my car headlights on low beam.
>
> "When I was about one half-mile from home I noticed something in the left hand lane of the road, so I slowed up nearly to a stop. When I was only a few feet from this vehicle I could see it very plainly. I could only see the top part of the vehicle and the occupant from the waist up.
>
> "The strange being in the vehicle had his hands up as if to show he was surrendering or to show that he meant no harm. His eyes showed intense fright.
>
> "He was a very strange looking man. His hair on the sides of his head stuck straight out about an inch, but he did not have hair on his face like a beard or whiskers. I tried to see what clothes he was wearing but I believe the fur that covered his body was really his skin and not a fur suit because I could not see a seam down the front or a collar around his neck like there is on a shirt or jacket. The fur was a sort of reddish brown or a bit darker than what we know as Guernsey color. His ears were more like a calf's ears than like human ears and they stuck straight out at least three inches.
>
> "This person was slender and I think that he was about six feet tall but he seemed much taller because I suppose the floor of the vehicle was about two or more feet up off the road. I could not see the lower part of the vehicle because it was in the fog.
>
> "He seemed to have quite a flat look to his face, so with the strange ears and hair sticking straight out it made it pretty frightening. Besides he seemed so tall. I also noticed his arms as he stood there with his hands up, and there was hair sticking out on his arms. I could not see any end of a sleeve so I do believe the fur was really his own skin. I did not see his hands very well but he held them right together as he held them up.
>
> "When I got right alongside of the vehicle which was about six or eight feet away, he was watching me. As I passed, it

> seemed the object came right toward my car, and it became very dark in the car. I was looking back as I passed him and I do not know if the car lights dimmed or what caused it to become so dark in the car.
>
> "When this object did take off as I passed, there was a sort of swish and it seemed as though something brushed against the car. It did definitely seem as though it came right at me and there seemed to be a tremendous surge of power.
>
> "I did not tell you at the start that the first thing I thought of when I saw the object was, now what in the hell is that? I also knew that if I ever told of this, or even dared to tell, I'd have to describe it very thoroughly."

Upon concluding his account, *Canadian UFO Report* posed several questions to Bosak which elicited additional details of the encounter.

> "I could not say what color his eyes were but they were eyes like that of any man," wrote Bosak. "I could not remember the exact shape of his mouth and nose but his neck was moderate in length and like a man's neck. His head was about the size of an average man's head."
>
> Asked for more details about the object enclosing the creature and how he fitted into it, Bosak replied:
>
> The transparent enclosure was about six feet across. No, he did not fill the container. He was about six feet tall and slender. The container was standing upright (or hovering?) in the left lane on a blacktop road. I could only see the object above the fog which was about at the occupant's waistline. He did not move toward me but stood there with his hands up and looking possibly as frightened as I was."[940]

Canadian UFO Report asked if extraterrestrial visitors had employed humanoid animals for unknown purposes or if it was merely coincidence that such creatures figured prominently in many UFO reports.

> Speculation along these lines inevitably leads to a subject that we consider related to the UFO question, that of Sasquatch or the Bigfoot. Observers of the Sasquatch are usually not inclined to see a connection. But to many ufologists, including ourselves,

> cases in which sightings are adjacent to strange animal forms—and their smells—suggest there is a connection. Some sort of relationship might also explain why ape-like creatures are seen suddenly in places where they have not been seen before, though they may be described in local legend.
>
> Understandably Sasquatch-watchers do not try to explain this puzzle of sudden appearance in unlikely places. Instead they prefer to concentrate on wild mountain areas where the creatures are seen and where they could conceivably live and breed through the ages without being imported from anywhere. But the anomalies remain and, following up on the idea that our space visitors may be responsible, let's look at a few recent cases. In doing so we emphasize that, to our knowledge, no sighting of strange craft was involved. These are simply more Sasquatch-type incidents, but they are incidents in an area where no such creatures were previously reported except perhaps by the local Cree whose legends tell of the Weetekow and Saulteaux and the Wendago.[941]

Peter Guttilla visited Bosak's story in an article published in the July 1978 *UFO Report*: "I was so scared I was afraid to go out at night for a few days. I'm over the shock now," Bosak said, "but I was pretty shook up for a couple of weeks. I'm sure a lot of people are going to be skeptical even after hearing what happened to me, but if people don't believe me, I'll take a lie detector test to prove this isn't something I made up."[942]

ESPER & the Plum Canyon Monster

> SANTA CLARITA VALLEY—Could the legendary Sasquatch (Big Foot) and the hairy monster of Plum Canyon be one and the same?
>
> The California Society for the Exploration of the Unexplained (ESPER) thinks so.
>
> Peter Guttilla, ESPER spokesman, said his organization is so convinced that there is something to the reports of a nine-foot-tall hairy creature lurking in the area that it is negotiating with a private landowner near here for use of a portion of his property for an around-the-clock observation post.

> In addition [Guttilla] said ESPER plans to contact the Sheriff's Department and U.S. Forest Service to arrange a program under which strange sightings and unusual activity could be forwarded to the group.
>
> Guttilla said the steps are being taken following a month-long investigation in the area which included interviews with residents as well as independent field study.
>
> "What we are learning from residents," Guttilla said, "is that whatever is spooking livestock or upsetting nerves is similar to events surrounding Bigfoot sightings in Northern California."
>
> Guttilla said one of the phenomena is a strange sound heard at night which sounds like a child crying.
>
> "Such sounds," he said, "have been recorded up north and identified by local residents as the same they have heard. We have a rancher in the area who is tape recording what she describes as unusual night sounds."
>
> Guttilla said that while combing the rugged canyons surrounding Santa Clarita Valley members of ESPER have "found what we think might be the vestiges of old footprints, in sequence, indicating they were made by something with a six-foot stride." However, he noted that rain has ruled out any possibility of full identification.
>
> Guttilla said that the planned observation post observers would use infrared viewing equipment to scan the area at night.[943]

Cascade Mountains' Hidden Cave

Peter Guttilla's article, "Bigfoot: 3 Tales of Terror" in the October 1976 *UFO Report*, included a story whose events' temporality were not precisely indicated, but which took place no later than 1974.

> The state of Oregon is an ancient and mysterious place blanketed with more than 30 million acres of woodlands and dormant volcanic-scarred wilderness territory which is virtually inaccessible. The following narrative was sent to the author in 1974. A trip to the location in 1975 yielded no substantial evidence, and efforts to locate the principals—

who were skeptical of outsiders to begin with—proved futile. However the report has a "ring" of authenticity and includes some amazing features. While on a summertime excursion in search of Indian artifacts in 1969, the witnesses discovered a hidden cave. They wrote:

> "After locating the cave about 150 feet from where we were, we stopped and carefully looked over the area around the cave. We didn't see anything unusual. We went closer, and in front of the cave was a pumice formation making it very dusty. In the dust leading from the cave was a human footprint. In fact there were several, showing that this ground had been walked upon quite a bit—and recently. These were the largest footprints I had ever seen. Some of them looked as if they had been made within the last day or two. I will admit I was scared. . . . We wanted to go inside the cave but it was getting late and we didn't care to be in this part of the country after dark.
>
> "A couple of weeks later we had a chance to go back there again. We arrived at the place . . . (and) . . . found it much easier going than the first trip. . . . We tried not to make too much noise by watching our step and not talking, hoping to slip in and possibly catch a glimpse of the man at the cave. We circled around to the place we had picked on our last trip . . . and we were in a position where we could see anything or anybody before they got to within 75 feet of the cave. Sitting there waiting for a couple of hours, we suddenly heard a noise to our left . . . it kept coming closer. I practically froze on the spot. Finally a large deer appeared. The doe passed and we calmed down. About three o'clock we decided to leave, but I went over the tracks one more time, some had been made since we were there before. Having a metal tape measure in my pocket I measured the clearest track and found it to be just shy of two feet long, and almost 10 inches wide. From the looks of the print the foot was heavily calloused across the ball of the foot with several cracks in the heel and the ball of the foot.[944]

About a month later the group returned to the cave and coming upon its entrance, they caught a glimpse of something emerging out of the darkness. "It looked to be about seven feet tall, maybe more, and covered with black hair." After a period of initial shock, the group cautiously approached the cave mouth. "Seeing and hearing no movement of any kind, I noticed something shaggy lying on the floor, and as my eyes became accustomed to the darkness of the cave, I saw that it was the hides of animals that had been spread out, as if they had been used for a bed." A foul odor permeated the cave.

> "I then got enough courage to enter the cave. Off to one side there were numerous animal bones that had been stripped of all flesh. On the other side of the cave was a freshly killed deer, with part of the flesh gone. The hide had been rolled back revealing that the flesh had been gnawed or torn with some crude tool of some kind.
>
> "As I approached the spot where I had seen the hides the odor became stronger. I noticed that the hides had been used for a bed, these hides had not been tanned and still had hair on them . . . they were real shaggy and looked like they had been used for a long period of time. There was no sign of fire. After taking some pictures of the cave and footprints, we went back to the car and started for home. If we had told anyone else of this location it would have started a stampede and this could have ruined everything. We decided that after we got all the information we wanted, we might tell others. . . .
>
> ". . . Starting up the hill (several months later, on the fifth and final trip to the cave), the going was steep and there were lots of loose rocks. If any of these rolled down the hill they could have rolled close to the mouth of the cave and scared him (the creature) out of there before we were ready (to snap a picture). We slipped over a little father to the right so that if he did hear us, he would have to go through a spot where the brush wasn't so thick, but if he moved as fast as he had before, we wouldn't be able to get a picture of him. We heard a noise toward the opening . . . he started toward us . . . we froze right there. We had always come in from the other side before. He took off on the regular route he had always used . . . he didn't see us until he was almost on top of us . . . but he was going so fast he ran within three feet of us, we could have touched him. We were so startled that we forgot all about taking pictures.
>
> "It was the most gruesome thing I've ever seen. It looked to be over seven feet tall and resembled a giant ape, or gorilla,

> entirely covered with short shaggy hair, his face fairly smooth. It would take a lot more nerve to stand there and get a picture than I had at that moment. I looked at my friend, I never saw anybody so pale and trembling so badly. It was quite a while before I could quit shaking. We continued down the hill, and stopped at the cave only long enough to get the measurements of his long strides. These measured five feet. . . ."[945]

Guttilla noted the witnesses continued their spring and summer visits to the cave for the next two years and his efforts to contact them proved futile. A landslide was said to have buried the mouth of the cave and Guttilla wrote that his own search of the general area turned up nothing.[946]

Estelle De Voto

In the June 1977 *UFO Report*, Peter Guttilla wrote of Estelle De Voto of Saugus, California, and the strange experiences she had three years earlier in 1974.

> It was in October 1974, I had just gotten my son off to school that morning when my husband called my attention to an article in the *Saugus-Newhall Signal*. Under the headline, "Does Bigfoot Roam the Santa Clarita Valley?" the story told of two teenaged boys named McBride who reported to police that they had seen a strange creature running and carrying a pig away under its arm.
>
> I'm a member of a local club interested in reports of that kind, so I contacted the owners of the ranch where the sighting took place and went to investigate. I learned that only one of the McBride boys actually saw the creature on the grounds. While his brother glimpsed the monster as it ran off with the pig. What really interested me was that both boys said the creature had a "glowing blue belt" around its waist. I mentioned the blue belt to other members of my club but no one had heard of such a detail before—this was a new one.
>
> After making a detailed report to my group, I decided to issue a press statement to the *Signal* in hope that someone would come forward with more information or at least another report. Well, after the statement was printed there was the

usual amount of joking and ribbing from my neighbors, and my husband got a great kick out of calling the McBride report a "bunch of hogwash." I don't know how many times I heard that pun. But my kids felt differently, they claimed that their friends at school—whose parents had farms near the McBrides—told them of similar stories that weren't publicized for fear of ridicule.

Anyway, several weeks after my press statement appeared in the newspaper, I received a call from some people who said they saw a UFO near a place called Texas Canyon. They described the object as disc-shaped, glowing white, and hovering silently near the east end of the canyon. I was interested in that report since the McBride sighting was just south of that area.

One night in late November, about 11 P.M., I received a telephone call from a group of teenagers who had been driving late at night near Texas Canyon. The only way into the canyon is a passable dirt road used mainly by weekend campers. I asked them to come to the house. My husband protested saying he didn't want a "bunch of weirdos" coming to the house that late, but I convinced him of the importance of talking to them.

Minutes later six of the most frightened kids I've ever seen were sitting in my living room. What they told me was that shortly after the high school football game, they decided to drive through Texas Canyon to Sierra Highway and head back into town. They entered Texas Canyon at the northwest end and had traveled about three miles when they noticed a cloud of dust on the road ahead of them. Thinking it was a motorcycle or car kicking up the dust, they drove on. As they approached the spot they were shocked by a "herd of the weirdest looking animals we'd ever seen . . ." They described the three animals as tall, hairy creatures with dog-like faces, the bodies of a human and eyes that glowed. As they passed them, the creatures threw dirt and stones at the car and screamed in what the kids thought was "monkey chatter." Several of the witnesses said they saw more "points of light" coming down off a hill, giving them the impression that more of the creatures were approaching.[947]

De Voto straightaway contacted several friends with whom she undertook a late-night drive to Texas Canyon. Her husband, who had grabbed a shotgun, "just in case," joined the group. De Voto and the others searched the site for signs to corroborate the teenagers' report. Though no tracks were discovered, the group could not help but notice the smell of rotten eggs hanging heavy in the air. They also noticed a large amount of dirt and rocks had apparently been thrown out into the road.

> As we stood discussing the situation, one of our group yelled out and pointed to the sky. Above us a small plane seemed to be having engine trouble. It circled several times, almost directly above us, and its motor sputtered. Suddenly we heard a loud sound from somewhere farther down the canyon. It sounded like a helicopter but more muffled. While our attention was focused on the sound, we noticed that a hill across the canyon was illuminated by an off-white light. At that moment the plane, which was apparently still circling above us, started running smoothly and with that an enormously bright light blinked on just to the right of the plane. The light made a sharp turn and disappeared to the east with an incredible burst of speed. We stood there dumbfounded. My husband dropped his binoculars and one of our group snapped a picture with a Polaroid camera but nothing came out on the film . . . the plane, which seemed to pick up speed, disappeared over the horizon.
>
> As the bright light vanished, the strange helicopter sound grew louder and then stopped. But though we couldn't see a thing we could still hear the sound of rushing wind—as if there were a helicopter out there somewhere.[948]

After the party returned from Texas Canyon, members drank coffee and filled out reports on what they had experienced. The next day De Voto attempted to ascertain from the local airport if any pilots had reported seeing a UFO but "as usual," her call was simply transferred from one person to another. Later that day after De Voto parked at her supermarket she noticed two men sitting in a white car parked next to her. She took them at first for police officers due to the unflattering "hard stare" they leveled at her, glowering in an undisguised, "pin-you-to-the-wall" way.

De Voto went about her shopping and at the checkout line noticed a friend, "Ed C___." She knew his wife from PTA meetings and was aware that Ed had served a stint in the Army. As De Voto was leaving the store

Ed approached her, introduced a friend with him and asked if she could talk. De Voto took note of his serious tone and became curious about what was on Ed's mind. Ed explained he'd become aware of De Voto's interest in strange events upon reading a newspaper story about her investigation of the McBrides' Bigfoot report. Once in the parking lot, Ed stopped her with a grip on her arm and began his story.

Ed had been attached to a military intelligence unit stationed in southern California during 1967. His unit, he told De Voto, had been engaged in investigating UFOs. Ed looked seriously at De Voto and asked if she believed in UFOs, perhaps gauging whether it was worth unpacking his story to her. De Voto said she retained an open mind on the subject. Satisfied enough to continue, Ed did provide this caveat: if De Voto were to reveal what he was about to say, he would deny ever having said a word.

Ed's next utterance exposed the ostensible reason for his need to trust De Voto. In 1967 he was taken to a remote desert location which just so happened to be the site of a UFO crash. Ed knew that several military trucks drove to the site, some containing "special devices." (At this point, De Voto noticed again the two men in the white car, their attention still on her. She thought of asking Ed about them but as her "stomach was doing cartwheels," she decided against it.

When he arrived at the site, Ed recalled a pungent odor which permeated the air. The actual object itself had broken into two sections. Four bodies of the occupants lay about the scene. Ed described them as "hideous-looking creatures you can't imagine." They were about nine feet tall and covered in fine hair. The occupants' faces were hairless, "Mongoloid" in appearance and sported pig-like noses. Fang-like teeth were exposed by lips pulled back in death.

In her recounting of these events to Peter Guttilla, De Voto admitted Ed's story had to this point frightened her; she could not come up with a reason why Ed would lie to her. Ed had continued, telling De Voto about the examination of the bodies conducted at the crash site. One of the creatures, investigators soon learned, was still alive. One of the men tried to offer it water. The creature reached up its hand, grabbed the man's shoulder, gasped and died. Each creature wore a copper-colored belt adorned with a large "buckle" sporting several small buttons. Their feet were shod in sandal-like boots with thick soles. Apart from the belts and footwear, the creatures had no other clothing. Reading of the McBrides' blue-belted creatures worried Ed. As related by De Voto, Ed said: "Estelle, these beings are dangerous. They have no compunction about killing people. They've been turning up in recent years in growing numbers. Stay away from them . . . have I made myself clear? You're in over your head. There are other animals, too, which are vicious . . . we don't know where they come from . . . but I don't want you to get in trouble over this. I wouldn't tell you what I know if I didn't think you were in danger. . . . I've been in this business a long time and know what I'm talking about."[949]

In conclusion, Ed said the crash victims had been put into plastic bags and shipped off; their whereabouts and their crashed vehicle's disposition was unknown to him. The gentleman with Ed didn't say anything during this time but seemed intent in gauging De Voto's reactions. De Voto realized the conversation had taken some fifteen minutes, in which time, the two men in the white car had discreetly driven away.

Guttilla recorded De Voto's lingering concerns appeared to have been vindicated, albeit in unfortunate circumstances. In April 1975 her home was broken into on three occasions. Doors had been left wide open but nothing appeared to have been taken.[950]

> On several successive nights the family was terrified by "horribly loud" pounding on the roof and sides of the house. The clincher came in June of that year when more than a dozen school children watched a tall, "hairy, white-faced ape" stare fixedly at them from an adjacent hillside. The De Voto children were among them and later said they had the feeling it was looking at them! Estelle De Voto needed little prodding to end her investigation of the blue-belted Bigfoot of Texas Canyon—she decided not to take the chance.[951]

Guttilla notes two other unusual stories from Texas Canyon in the Spring of 1975. A sheep rancher reported a glowing, oval-shaped object flying low to the ground. A narrow beam of light seemed to emanate from the object, sweeping over the terrain. At about the same time, telephone repairman Patrick Macey, himself a Bigfoot enthusiast, decided to do a little late-night hunting with a friend in Texas Canyon. The pair noticed two points of light only a few yards off to the left of their car at about 1:30 A.M. The men decided the lights were attached to something large which seemed to stoop behind a thicket. The men got out of the car and heard heavy footfalls in the brush behind them. They rushed back to the car and sped off down the road. After about fifteen minutes, their courage and curiosity regained, they drove back to the scene. There they encountered a dark form which was described as "very large, on two legs, covered with gray fur, and had a dark stripe running down its back. The eyes were very large and appeared to glow orange . . ." The men also noticed at that time a high-pitched humming noise suffusing the area.[952]

> In April 1975, two officers from the Foothill Division of the Los Angeles Police Department observed a large ". . . glowing, orange ball float out of the sky and land near the Vasquez Rocks State Park." Two weeks later a sheep rancher named Harlin Campbell discovered several sets of big tracks which can only be described as those of a giant ostrich, on the western slopes of the San Gabriel Mountains and near Vasquez Rocks State Park. Several members of the Western Society for the Exploration of the Unexplained found a set of enormous, man-like, barefoot tracks at a place called Mystery Mesa a few miles south of Vasquez Rocks wilderness area and within view of Texas Canyon.[953]

Frisbees-Shaped UFOs & Bigfoot

Terrance Mitchell, whose research into UFO phenomenon started in the early 1970s, spoke to a University of Minnesota class about some aspects of UFO studies. Mitchell's own interest in the subject began with forays into the mountains of the Pacific Northwest looking for Bigfoot creatures before branching off into UFO investigations. "In my studies I noticed that a large portion of UFO sightings occurred in remote, desolate areas like the mountains of the Pacific Northwest," he said. "And boy, is it desolate in some of the areas there." Mitchell's presentation was full of theorizing and qualified language, being careful of what he asserted. "Is it possible," asked Mitchell, "that a branch of humanity (the [B]igfoot) could have survived apart from civilization in those remote areas?" Mitchell then provided a possible linkage between UFOs and Bigfoot. "And if extraterrestrial beings—also seeking remote areas—arrived, is it possible they decided to contact the most primitive humans (the [B]igfoot)?"[954]

Hilton Head, S.C., Track Sightings (Reported in 1974)

Bigfoot's popularity meant it was hardly ever an ill-timed affair to narrate past Bigfoot-related anecdotes. The emergent conception of Bigfoot could explain historic sightings of shadowy forms glimpsed in the woods as well as past discoveries of large, mysterious footprints. Published in the July 8, 1974, *St. Petersburg Times*, reporter Red Marston wrote of large footprints discovered several years prior by hunters.

Dean Poucher, a former Clearwater radio announcer, had grown up in the Seminole-Clearwater area and claimed to have twice seen the mysterious tracks. "There were five of us, all experienced hunters, who went to a certain island near here, the name of which I cannot mention," Poucher told Marston. "We had gained special permission from the owner who warned us that the interior was so thick it would be impossible to penetrate, not even by trained Marines from Camp LeJeune. We had been informed that the year previous some other hunters went to the island and certainly did find the interior impassable. But that hunting trip was really spoiled because the dogs absolutely refused to hunt.

"Well, on our trip, we had two boats and two of the finest dogs in all Beaufort County [South Carolina]. We landed on a narrow, sandy beach and gathered to lay out our battle strategy." As the men got ready they took satisfaction in the evident indication of game. "The sand in which we drew our plans of dispersing was rutted with deer tracks. There was no question of plenty of game on the island." Plans solidified, the party made ready to move out. "We proceeded to implement the game plan and it was then we noticed the strange behavior of our dogs," Poucher said. This was their first indication that something was not quite right. "They wouldn't get out of the boat they were in. They sat shivering miserably with their tails between their legs. The owner who had been popping off about his great deer dogs was both embarrassed and mad.

"He finally dragged them out by the collar, hauled them up the beach to the tree line and jammed their noses into fresh deer tracks. Then he turned them loose but the dogs turned tail and ran back to the boat. Both leaped in and sat there shivering." The hunters entered the woods but did not encounter any deer. Poucher and another companion separately saw something that each decided to keep to himself until a chance meeting a few days later provided the opportunity to compare notes.

"At opposite ends of the islands, we had come across tracks," said Poucher. "I had no opportunity to see these tracks other than those buried up in a foot of blue marsh mud, but I will never forget their size, nor the depth to which they were sunk. My boot alongside, a size 11, was hardly half as large as the track. To compare, I put my full weight on one boot but I sank less than an inch into the mud. My guess is that our big-footed friend would tip the scales at three to four times my weight, placing him somewhere between 600 and 800 pounds. The tracks on the north end of the island, where my hunting companion came upon them, were in hard sand. They were about 18 inches long, 7 to 9 inches wide. There was no instep; the animal was flat-footed. The tracks were likewise packed so deeply into the hard sand that our weight estimates checked out."

If not for the chance conversation's revelation that one of his companions also saw the tracks, Poucher admitted he would likely have remained silent. He didn't go back to the area for three years, at which time Poucher and his wife were walking along a dock on one of the uninhabited islands. "Ann and I were just standing there enjoying the view," recalled Dean. "The view was of the island we had tried to hunt and the same place where the dogs instinctively cowered. I happened to look down at the mud bank alongside the dock. It was low tide. There were the tracks! They came up out of the creek and disappeared into the thickness of the island." Poucher admitted he was incredibly curious, but this interest was tempered by his idea it was perhaps best to leave well enough alone.[955]

Jimmy Sumner Sighting

George Fawcett's article, "On the Trail of Big Foot," for the September 13, 1974, *Mount Airy News* gave readers an overview of Bigfoot and told of a local encounter which occurred just north of Mount Airy, North Carolina, earlier in the year.

> In early January (date unknown), 1974 Jimmy Sumner, a college student from Mount Airy, while driving on the Pipers Gap Road near Pauls Creek at the Smith Bridge, about 4 miles North of this city encountered what appeared to be a local 'Bigfoot' that jumped "only twice" to clear the road in front of his car at between 11:30 P.M. and midnight. The animal-like creature when seen through his glaring headlights appeared to be about 6 feet tall and was covered by gray or black hair all over. Recovering from his initial shock, twenty year old Sumner cautiously opened his car door and turned on his car spotlight in the direction where he had last seen the "creature" move, but was unable to see it again. Several moments later, two of Jimmy's friends (who were also interviewed, but preferred anonymity) who were driving south on the same road towards Mount Airy found the badly-shaken Sumner on the highway

> moving his car spotlight back and forth in a nearby field, as if looking for something. Jimmy told them his story. His friends told this writer that Jimmy looked "scared to death" and was "white in the face" and "shaking all over, like he'd seen a ghost." Later Jimmy provided this investigator with his own sketch of the creature and picked out one sketch from among others that best depicted what he had seen. To date, no explanation has been forthcoming. But the pursuit for knowledge concerning the experiences of many on a global basis . . . On The Trail of Bigfoot . . . continues.[956]

Parkdale, Oregon, Encounter

Jack Cochran, a 49-year-old logging foreman from Parkdale, Oregon, became a Bigfoot believer in 1974. Some newspaper articles state Cochran's encounter occurred in April 1974 but Al Stump's *True* article on Peter Byrne placed Cochran's Parkdale experience on May 13, 1974.[957] During the morning in question, Cochran was operating a Link-Belt logging crane on Fir Mountain. He turned off his machine as he waited for catskinners to chute another load of timber his way. Chancing to look under the crane's boom, he just made out, about 50 yards away, a broad-shouldered creature with a massive torso and long legs walking across a clearing toward the tree line in an effortless, gliding-like movement. "I asked myself, 'What's Tom doing out there.' Then I looked again and I saw it. I told myself, 'This is something else,' and a cold chill went up the back of my neck." Cochran surmised the creature was easily over seven feet tall and when it turned to look at him, Cochran could see its large, human-like eyes. As the thing remained visible for two minutes returning Cochran's awe-struck gaze, he realized it was not a bear; there was no snout on the flat, hairless face. When it raised a hand Cochran could see its thumb and fingers.[958]

"I told the other boys, 'You know, I think I saw Bigfoot out there,' but they told me I had had too much sun, so I dropped the subject." But inspection of the clearing showed trampled grass and vegetation where Cochran saw the creature and a man was dispatched down the mountain with the news. On May 14, Cochran became the 83rd person to report a Bigfoot sighting to Peter Byrne.

According to Cochran, and only a day after his chance encounter, a co-worker, Fermin Osborne, reported seeing what he described as "some kind of monster." Osborne gave chase as it moved off toward the timber. Cochran stated Osborne followed the creature to a point where it descended a hill. Osborne rolled down rocks after the retreating form, hoping to catch a glimpse of the thing's face when it turned around. But it moved quickly away and didn't look back. "Fermin saw me later and said, 'Jack, I guess you weren't crazy because I saw it too,'" Cochran said. Peter Byrne joined Cochran at the location of Osborne's sighting and they found dislodged rocks at the bottom of a hill which Byrne took as support for Osborne's account; verifying the detail of tumbled-down rocks helped satisfy Byrne that Cochran and Osborne had seen Bigfoot.[959]

Youth Director Spots Sasquatch at Harrison Lake

Casts were made of 15-inch long footprints at Harrison Lake, British Columbia, left by what was described as a huge hairy creature. The prints were six inches wide and each had the appearance of five toes. Wayne Jones, who saw the creature on July 18, said only prints of the right foot were found.

"It had a well-rounded head with long ears and arms," claimed Jones, the director of the Dunbar-West Point Grey Youth Project at Harrison Lake. Jones' relatively lengthy five-minute viewing of the creature began as he noticed something come around a corner of a camp building about 25 feet away from him. "It was big, something between seven and eight feet tall—it was huge. My first reaction was, 'My God, what is this?' It was quite wet and I could make out that it was covered with hair, not fur."

Jones said the seven- or eight-foot-tall hairy creature had a closer resemblance to a human than a beast. The creature left after apparently being alarmed by campers' flashlights. Word of the sighting had been slow to spread because Jones was reluctant to share it, worrying that the camp would suffer a deluge of curiosity-seekers and serious hunters, all looking for the creature. Jones enlisted the aid of 30 young campers, swearing them to secrecy to keep the word from spreading. "A few of them saw it then and all of them heard it crashing through the bush," Jones said. "I have never believed in things like this and I always promised myself that if I ever did see something I would keep it to myself," he said. "I saw the thing and there is no mistaking what I saw."[960]

Watova Monster

Summer nights during 1974 kept the citizens in the southern Nowata County town of Watova, Oklahoma, on edge. Descriptions of the unknown (and unwanted) creature said it looked "bearlike," "tall and slender," was a "fast runner," and possessed the ability to "jump a high-wire fence."[961]

> The creature was first reported as a "guy with long hair and a beard" standing on a front porch. Two other peeping Tom reports trickled in and last Sunday two deputies spotted a "six-footer running like a deer" and who was thought to be a prowler.
>
> The two fired warning shots but failed to stop the fleeing form, which then jumped a four-strand barbed wire fence "at speeds you wouldn't believe possible," said undersheriff Buck Fields.[962]

Nowata County Sheriff Bill Sutton said the Watova Monster reports began in late July and by the start of August he had received 15 calls from the town of 100. Farmers reported something was agitating their livestock and several people in the community said they had heard strange noises at night coming from their porches and around their windows and doors. Sutton said one of the calls he received had come from a frantic teenage girl; she had been babysitting a younger sister at the time of the call and something had ripped the upper screen from a window.

The sheriff had his own theory to explain the Watova Monster: a timber wolf known then to be prowling the area coupled with a bona fide Peeping Tom. Sutton believed the timber wolf had come from the Oologah River bottomlands seeking opportunities for food around Watova.[963] A wolf had been seen by a resident one morning in late July near the edge of town and it was posited as the likely malefactor which had been spooking farm animals. The second part of Sutton's theory was bolstered by an undersheriff's late-July nighttime apprehension of a young man caught prowling around a house.[964]

SITU Expedition to Pennsylvania

During the summer of 1973, SITU tracked the "flap" of UFO and creature activity which occurred in western Pennsylvania's Westmoreland County. SITU knew of some 145 reports from 250 witnesses involving UFOs, creature sightings, footprint finds, and a recording of a purported Bigfoot scream. The police received so many reports they began to regularly turn them over to the Westmoreland County UFO Study Group (WCUFOSG) under the direction of Stan Gordon. In September 1974, SITU launched its first official ABSM expedition to Westmoreland County to investigate and determine if the creature sightings supported the presence of an Eastern species of Bigfoot.

SITU expedition organizers developed four possibilities for what could explain the creature sightings: a hoax or hallucination; a mundane "terrestrial animal"; an extra-terrestrial UFO-related creature; or a type of hologram capable of interacting with its immediate environment. Each of these possible explanations provided some answers and explanations to some of the collective sightings' puzzling details. While expedition members agreed to keep their minds open, the expedition went forward under the assumption they were dealing with a terrestrial animal.

Members' availability for participation as well as securing the necessary funds were two of the problems the expedition confronted during its planning phase. According to the expedition write up done for the October 1974 *Pursuit*, the team made their foray into western Pennsylvania full of enthusiasm but not with all desired gear and equipment.

Camp was made north of Latrobe, Westmoreland County, in the midst of where several sightings had taken place in 1973. From camp, members searched westward along Chestnut Ridge for approximately ten miles. Old mine areas around Latrobe and Deery and several caves and swampy areas nearer the group's campsite were investigated. Thanks to team member Dick Laing, a scuba diver, the bottoms of area lakes were explored. Searching kept team members out in the field at all hours. Baiting was attempted, and tracking techniques tried out. The expedition lasted eight days and no ABSMs were seen or evidence collected. Robert Jones also wrote about the expedition and his article in the January 1975 *Pursuit* included a tantalizing story of something which had scared some nearby campers.

> The closest we may have come to it [an ABSM] was one night when we returned to the campsite and were told by two frightened campers (who knew nothing about Bigfoot or of our purpose in being there) of an incident that had occurred ten minutes before we arrived. While asleep in their tent they were awakened by a shrill scream, followed by heavy footsteps of a 'man' crashing through the brush off the hill behind them. When near the tent the 'animal' stopped and emitted a series of grunts and growls, apparently became frightened by the noise

> inside the tent, and fled back up the hill. The campers were adamant that the gait was bipedal and not that of a quadruped. Ray Naugle (one of our communications experts) and I [Jones] searched the area thoroughly but aside from some trampled underbrush found nothing definite to corroborate their story.[965]

Jones' post-expedition wrap-up noted the presumed lack of a sufficient food supply in the searched area for a terrestrial animal the size of Bigfoot. The location was, however, "underlain by a very complex network of caves, whose ends, in some cases, have not been found." Caves, suggested Jones, could be used by the creatures for movement and perhaps explain why Bigfoot sometimes popped into view and then disappeared as quickly.[966]

Mill Race Monster

Trick-or-Treaters were still tucking into their candy on Friday, November 1, as police in Columbus, Indiana, received the first report of a "large green beast" in Mill Race Park. Authorities actually closed the park to the public at night starting on November 9 for fear someone—either a monster hunter or the presumed monster impersonator—was headed toward injury or worse.

> They swear it's true. Six young women told city police Friday in two separate reports that they had seen a "Mill Race Monster"—once in broad daylight.
>
> And whatever it is, the six are agreed, it is: (1) Green, (2) Hairy, (3) Large, about six feet tall and walking upright, and (4) Has claws.
>
> Four of the women, whose names police did not list, said they saw "the thing" about 3 P.M. Friday near the paved boat ramp in the park along White river [sic] at the west end of Fifth street [sic]. The other two said it jumped on the hood of their car, leaving scratch marks in the paint. That was about 11:45 P.M. No one was hurt, only frightened, police said.
>
> Officers searched the area on both occasions but found nothing. They are hoping it's only a misguided hobgoblin who lost its sense of timing and doesn't know Halloween is over for another year. But, just the same, they warned other residents to take care and keep an eye out for the "monster."[967]

Four days later the Columbus, Indiana, *Republic* printed another Mill Race Monster sighting.

> The Mill Race Monster has returned, apparently stepping out of the shadows Tuesday [November 5] long enough to scare two park-goers and possibly cast his vote in local elections.
>
> County police reported two men in their 20s saw a large, hairy "thing" hiding behind trees near the covered bridge about 4 P.M. and again shortly before midnight.
>
> The men, who did not give police their names, said after seeing the monster Tuesday afternoon, they returned with binoculars that evening for a closer look.
>
> They told police the monster was found, and eventually chased them from the park.
>
> One of the men suggested an explanation for the newly-found monster, that it had been left here in the early fall by visitors from another planet. At that time, Columbus and much of the Midwest was flooded by sightings of Unidentified Flying Objects (UFOs).
>
> One political know-it-all when hearing about the monster sighting Tuesday night, suggested it was a publicity-seeking candidate trying to begin an early campaign for office in 1976.[968]

Monster-hunting in Mill Race Park grew into a nocturnal pastime, popular enough so that authorities began contemplating closing the grounds to the public at the end of the day to prevent folks falling victim to over-zealous hunters.

> Warnings to would-be "hunters" of the so-called "Mill Race Monster" were issued today by police and the city park director. Robert Gilligan, after a night in which authorities counted dozens of individuals in cars and on foot searching the park at the west end of Fifth street [sic] along White river [sic].
>
> Some were armed with knives and one carried a club, and authorities fear the prankster who dresses as a "monster" may get hurt if the "hunters" don't first hurt themselves or another "hunter."

> Gilligan said it may become necessary to close the park to the public at night, not because of the "monster" but because of the public. Twenty-eight cars were counted in the park at 11 P.M. Thursday.
>
> First sighted last Friday [November 1] night, the "monster" was described as large, hairy and green by six young women.
>
> Latest appearance was reported by the city dog catcher, Rick Duckworth, who told police he saw it early today while on a routine patrol. His description was hardly as dramatic as others, however.
>
> He said the "monster" looked to him like a person wrapped in blankets and wearing a mask.[969]

As quickly as it appeared, the Mill Race Monster abruptly vanished. However, in 1975, the Columbus Jaycees planned a special creature cameo for its annual haunted house. Along with Dracula, Frankenstein's Monster, the Wolfman and bug-eyed space invaders, the Jaycees intended to have the Mill Race Monster as part of their macabre menagerie.[970]

Chalmers Sighting

Andrew Genzoli, who was obviously proud of his part in the early promulgation of Bigfoot, often engaged a playful tone with the subject . . .

> The other day, Roger Chalmers on his way to visit with his aunt, Anne Victoria of Allon, says he had a real surprise near Willow Creek, when he saw a hairy figure in the nearby [bushes].
>
> He said it made enough movement to catch his eye. Now he is wondering if it was a figment of imagination, a bear, or Bigfoot. He feels it is too real to have been nothing and it isn't necessarily news that Bigfoot has been seen in the area concerned.
>
> Chalmers is in the U.S. Airforce near Reno, and was enroute to Eureka when the incident occurred. It jarred him a bit, so he didn't go back to investigate—not at night—and he headed on west.
>
> Is it possible old Bigfoot was out roaming around to find a place to hang his oversized Christmas sock.[971]

Carol Stream Bigfoot

Writing for the *Chicago Tribune,* Dave Schneidman reported that by early October about a dozen sightings of a creature in and around Carol Stream, Illinois, had been reported.

> As far as monsters go, the Carol Stream apparition ranks far down on the scale. Maybe 7 feet tall and weighing a tad more than 500 pounds, it isn't very big, and it's a total dropout when it comes to raising havoc thruout the countryside and making brave men's blood run cold.
>
> But don't knock it—it's the only monster the Chicago area has.
>
> First sighted about a month ago by several youths in a Carol Stream cornfield, the monster, described as black with a gray-tipped head and with eyes the size of golfballs (a fiendish red color, those eyes), has been scaring a lot of people but has done remarkably little damage.
>
> It has also brought itself to the attention of the Yeti Research Society headquartered in St. Petersburg, Fla., an organization devoted to the study of such monsters.

According to Schneidman, Gordon Prescott of the Yeti Research Society believed the Carol Stream sightings represented an especial situation. "The closest a Yeti has been to Chicago before this was in the Murphysboro, Ill., sightings." Prescott shared some advice for Carol Stream residents:

> First, don't panic. Yetis are docile souls, and if you leave them alone they'll leave you alone.
>
> Second, the next time one happens to cross your path, report the incident immediately by writing the Yeti Research Society, . . .
>
> Third, keep in mind that the male Yeti, fully grown, can weigh close to 1,000 pounds and is strong enough to topple an auto. He also has great curiosity about humans. So, if he stares at you, don't fight him, just let him stare. He doesn't mean you any harm.

Prescott further related that a Bigfoot could make three distinctive sounds: a sharp, high-pitched bark; a growl ending in a loud, high-pitched scream; and a whistle. And rounding out his article, Schneidman included Prescott's response to the oft-asked why a Bigfoot had never been captured.

> Well, there was a capture of a Yeti in 1934 in Arcadia, Fla., according to Prescott. A Yeti was destroying cattle, and finally ranchers, fed up with the nuisance, tracked the Yeti—a female—and captured it.
>
> Not knowing what else to do with the thing, the ranchers locked it up in the Arcadia jail, but that plan lasted only a month or so.
>
> Seems that other prisoners and jailers couldn't tolerate the smell—similar to rotten eggs—or the sound of the thing longer than that, so the ranchers took the Yeti back to where they found it and set it free.[972]

Wooley Park Monster

The Wooley Park Monster was seen by several residents of Wooley's Mobile Home Park in Lakeland, Florida. Descriptions said it was covered in black fur and it was heavy enough to leave 18-inch footprints pressed deep into sand. Up to late November, only children had reported seeing the creature, but that changed when Larry Southwood said his dog started barking late at night on Friday, November 29. Curious as to what the disturbance could be, Southwood looked out and saw the figure of the monster—all seven to eight feet of it—standing in a grove and backlit by the moon.

Examining the grove on Saturday, Southwood and others found two footprints, one full and one partial print depressed into sandy spots. Additional scrutiny of the area produced a freshly broken tree limb. "It had to be something strong," Southwood said, "because the limb is green." Other trees were festooned with orange skins, the fruit's pulp "chewed out." Melvin Kincaid said he and some of his friends had seen the monster, stating it walked like a man, sported a scar by its nose, had large hands, and one shoulder was higher than the other. Earlier that fall, the creature made its debut when it chased a group of children out of a grove.[973]

> Other children in the park say they have seen it since then and adults say they have seen evidence that it had been near their trailers. Some said they [hear] noises at night around the park

> and find the lids of their garbage cans on the ground in the morning.
>
> They said the creature must know to be as quiet as possible as it sifts through their garbage cans.

Other evidence included a damaged barbed wire fencing in a nearby grove. Southwood said the manager of Wooley's Mobile Home Park had found a few pieces of hair on the barbed wire but threw it away.[974]

Richard Lee Smith Collides with Skunk Ape

Motorist Richard Lee Smith claimed an unusual animal almost collided with his vehicle on State Road 820. "It jumped out at me. I swerved to miss it and almost hit another car headon," [sic] Smith said. "I thought it was a big black man with no clothes on. It was hairy (and) looked to be about seven to eight feet tall." Smith, described by the UPI article as "a big, rawboned resident of a truck stop on an Everglades highway," telephoned the Florida Highway Patrol at about 12:40 A.M. from Saler's Truck Stop at the junction of Krome Avenue and State Road 27. Back at the scene on 820, Smith amazingly experienced a second run-in with the creature. "This time it jumped across the (highway) guard rail right in front of me and I just couldn't avoid it," Smith said. "I hit it on the leg with my right front fender. It didn't scream or make any sound when I hit it. I've never seen anything like it before."[975] State trooper M. E. Johnson, one of the investigating officers, said Smith "was very, very scared and he was sober."[976] Johnson could find no evidence of a hard collision on Smith's car, and nothing noteworthy (no blood or hair) other than "a kind of brush mark" on one fender.[977]

About three hours later, another motorist contacted the Dade County Highway Patrol detachment and reported "a large seven to eight-foot thing limping" along U.S. 27 and Okeechobee Road near the Dade-Broward border and about seven miles south of the location Smith claimed to have had his experience. Patrolman Robert Holmeyer of the Hialeah Gardens police investigated this second report and had his own sighting: "It looked like a man, except it was an extremely large man—about eight feet," he recalled. In utter amazement, Holmeyer watched the creature's hasty retreat. "It was running, beating out a path in the sawgrass. I didn't want to go in after him in the dark," he explained.[978]

> A Coast Guard helicopter [other articles mention a Dade County sheriff's office helicopter] searched with powerful floodlights, then a dozen state and county officers joined Hialeah Gardens police in a systematic hunt over a large area of sawgrass and hammock swampland after dawn.
>
> They found nothing except the trampling of a large area of brush. . . .
>
> A few animals have met mysterious deaths in the areas of the reported sightings, but otherwise the swamp creature has done little harm.[979]

With the start of a new day, officers at the scene turned up some mysterious findings: a large swath of brush had been trampled, as if by a bear or other large animal; a holly tree had been freshly uprooted, its sap still running; and a whimpering mongrel dog turned up with four fresh puncture wounds to its throat. The dog had been seen in the area for about two weeks, loitering around a couple of the fishing camps. Danny Fernandez, a camp operator, described the dog as "terrified," and said he thought the puncture wounds looked like they "had been made by a large-jawed human rather than some wild animal."[980]

Robert Morgan appeared on the scene during the investigation of Smith's Skunk Ape encounter.

> In one of the helicopters over the area this morning was Robert Morgan, local member of the American Yeti Expedition. Yeti is the Nepalese word for the Abominable Snowman.
>
> Morgan, who said he also is affiliated with the National Wildlife Federation, said he was convinced the creature reported today was similar to the Yeti.
>
> He said the hunt would continue in an effort to capture the creature for study and later release. He said the creature was probably traveling through the vast Glades with its family and had been injured by the [Smith's] car.
>
> He appealed to the general public not to try to catch it. It is not aggressive, he said, unless it feels threatened.[981]

"I'm sure he saw something, but I don't know just what." said Trooper Johnson. "We found no physical evidence to prove anything," he said. "We were afraid at first it might be a human. That is primarily why we were searching." That morning at least one local radio station ran with a facetious story that the animal struck by Smith had been located and surrounded by law enforcement officers; its capture imminent. "We never saw it," said Johnson. The search was called off at around 7 A.M.[982]

"This happens annually," said Stewart Wallace, a patrol dispatcher. "You know, it's a full moon." The flavor bestowed by the *Pocono Record* upon Smith's experience was revealed by its choice of story subtitle: "A Walking, Eight-Foot Cookie Monster."[983] Wallace appeared to have taken the whole matter in stride. "It seems we get one of these wild goose chases every year," he mused. "We saw nothing but that's par for the course."[984]

> The *News-Herald* Candid Comment reporter asked the public, "What do you think about the skunk-ape—is he real?"
>
> "Yes, I think it is a possibility. I think this creature could be preserved in the swamp area because there are not that many people in that area. If I saw it, I'd try to take a picture of it to do research and find out more about it." Wendell Branum; student; Panama City.
>
> "I don't know what it is, but it must be real. The troopers said they saw it, and a man said he hit it with his car. If I saw this creature I would try to get away from him and report it to the officials. According to what it is I think it ought to be put on exhibition in some zoo if it is caught." Danny Pinkard; produce manager; Panama City.
>
> "It could be! I saw a recent movie about one in Arkansas. In it they were talking about an animal that was similar to the skunk-ape in size and build. If I saw the skunk-ape close-up I'd probably take off as fast as I could. I think it ought to be preserved. There is no point in killing it. It is probably innocent." Mrs. Paula Gibbs; housewife; visitor.
>
> "It could be real. But I think this thing is about like the UFO's. People believe in UFO's and claim to have seen them. But, none [sic] is sure about them. I believe it is probably true. If the creature was near me I would try not to panic, then get away to contact the police or somebody!" Leonard Williams; student; Panama City.
>
> "I think it is probably an escaped pet gorilla that has grown to full size. However, I don't conjecture much about the Yeti.

Yet, there have been too many reports about responsible people seeing a large silhouette at night in the woods, so there must be something. If I saw this creature, I'd run as fast as I could in the opposite direction. I am sure it would out-weigh me, whatever it is." Dorothy Fawcett; bookkeeper; Panama City.[985]

In the immediate wake of Smith's encounter, a slew of other Skunk Ape reports and stories surfaced. "I've seen him three times," said George MacLean, executive director of Miami's Dinner Key Auditorium. "I call him the Abominable Swampman." MacLean, who used to have a camp in the Everglades off SR 27 and Griffin Road in Broward, further stated he knew many hunters and fishermen that had also glimpsed "The Thing."

"I saw it once in 1967 and twice in 1969," explained MacLean. "It was always at sunset. It just came quietly out of the swamp water and stood levee [sic] for a few moments before it loped off. It was about 80 yards from me each time. It was eight feet tall and furry. It was a light brown color." Its facial features, according to MacLean, were "like those of a man with hair all over his face." MacLean said the creature was quiet and never appeared aggressive or threatening.[986]

Brooksville Beast

The Kelly family lived on the Lucky K Ranch outside Brooksville in Hernando County and in December 1973, with a simple and very earnest request in mind, they called the St. Petersburg Yeti Research Society and asked for help.

Up to that point, the Kellys had endured several months of having "company" on their ranch. Unearthly screams punctuated the night and several small animal cages behind the family's home had been torn into and a wet-dog smell lingered about the place. Soon after the Kellys moved to the ranch in 1971, an animal—which the Kelly's came to believe was a Bigfoot, tried to get their rabbits by bending their sturdy metal cages, a feat which Kelly could not duplicate. Small animals, torn violently apart, had also been found around the Kelly property suggesting an agent possessing great strength and manual dexterity.

The Kellys began carrying firearms while outdoors at the Lucky K but as they became more familiar with the goings on around them they slowly accepted the idea of what might be doing it. Following this acceptance weapons were left inside. "You think you'd be frightened the first time you see one, but actually the first thing you think is, 'My God, how big it is,'" said Mrs. Kelly. "And if you see one alone, you try to talk yourself out of it."

In mid-December 1973 members of the St. Petersburg Yeti Research Society met at the Kelly's ranch house and finalized plans for a stakeout on the property. At about 1 A.M. during the first overnight of the stakeout, dogs were heard howling in the distance and, on the ranch, the family horses whinnied in apparent agitation. "They were all standing in a circle, rump to rump, which is a sure sign they sense imminent danger," stated Ramona Clark, of Jacksonville, who participated in the stakeout. Suddenly a giant hair-covered creature was spotted in the pasture. By using a nearby tree to gauge its size, the creature was estimated to have stood about eight feet tall. The sounds of baying hounds were coming closer and the dark figure retreated into the darkness.

In the morning, Clark and Randy Singer, a professional photographer from Punta Gorda, found an 18-inch long, five-toed footprint and what they took to be a shelter comprised of branches and Spanish moss. The Spanish moss had been draped and placed over a fallen tree's upended roots. Inside was a "hollowed out area smoothly packed down."

Gordon Prescott, president of the Yeti Research Society and English teacher at Northeast High School, said that the concentration of sightings in Brooksville over a two-year period had prompted the area's selection for their first field study. "Residents of wooded areas near Brooksville have been literally scared to death by Yetis," reported Prescott, "and we feel that it is an excellent possibility that at least one, if not several, [Skunk Ape] families are located in the area." Several unusual events occurred during an all-night vigil conducted by the Society in 1973. "At about two in the morning, heavy footsteps were heard, heavier than any animal could make," Prescott said. Society members tried to flank around the whatever-it-was hidden in the darkness. "The entire group tried to encircle the sounds, but the creature outsmarted them and fled. At one point, a loud, high-pitched scream was heard, one characteristic of Yeti sightings in British Colombia and Oregon." A good view of the creature remained elusive. "Somewhat later in the night, two of the group reported seeing a pair of reddish, reflecting eyes staring at them from across a nearby river. Spotlights were flashed all around, but nothing was seen."[987]

Prescott was aware that a lot of data was being collected on Bigfoot in the Northwest, "but so far no one has done any serious work on the Yeti in the southeast states, especially Florida." This lack of serious attention was detrimental to research and ultimately, to producing answers. "We want to spread our knowledge around as far as possible and remove the Yeti from legend to reality," Prescott stated.[988]

Allen Carter joined the Society for some field outings. Carter was a private detective, on whose property, a few miles north of Brooksville, two Skunk Apes were seen in 1972. The Carter children were the first to see the creatures while playing in the yard of their mobile home. The children rushed inside the house in a state of obvious terror. Their mother went to the front door to see a five-foot, brown-haired female creature closely watching a smaller, supposedly younger creature spin a wheel on a tricycle. Noticing it was spotted, the Yeti youngster ran toward the embrace of the larger animal. This caretaker creature held the smaller one close and glared aggressively at Mrs. Carter. The creatures then exited the scene by a fire trail. Later that day Allan Carter returned home and tracked the creature's prints for several hundred yards before losing them in thick brush.

Several additional sightings of Bigfoot creatures on the Lucky K ranch occurred between January and March 1974. These hairy forms left several prints, the largest of which measured 19 inches long, as they moved between the ranch and a stone quarry, less than a mile away.

> "Caves provide the clue to the Yeti habitat," Ramona [née Clark] Hibner wrote for the January 1974 issue of the Yeti Research Society's Newsletter. "This is the only feasible answer to their sudden disappearance and to the areas they have been observed in. Florida had numerous caves formed of limestone, created by ancient rivers and ocean currents when Florida was once the ocean floor. Sea shells are still visible in the roofs and floors of these caves.
>
> "These occur in sinkhole areas in all sections of Florida, from the northern portion to the Everglades. Some are shallow and easily entered; some are deep holes extending several hundred feet down before the bottom can be reached. They may extend from a few feet to several miles in length, usually running north and south. Most river beds and creeks in these regions also run north and south."[989]

Calling to mind the Kliewer–Olson rift in 1972, the Skunk Ape-hunting community also experienced a schism as several members from the St. Petersburg Yeti Research Society decided to strike out independently and pursue the Skunk Ape in Hernando County by their own methods. "We disagreed with the way the other group was doing it," Kelly said. Kelly and others like Clark and Duane Hibner advocated patient acclimation as the best approach to inure Skunk Apes to observation by researchers.

> George Kelly, owner of the Lucky K Ranch, and his family recently split from the St. Petersburg-based Yeti Research Society to form a new study group that he says is using more scientific methods to study the man-beasts that he and many of his neighbors believe inhabit the thick woods of Hernando County.[990]

Kelly and his team attempted to habituate local Bigfoot by maintaining a near-constant presence in the field. "The St. Petersburg society confines much of its work to weekends, and sends large groups into the field to use loud music and campfires as lures for the Yeti. Kelly's researchers—known as the Yeti Evaluation and Technological Investigators [YETI]—'think small and quiet' and try to conduct the study continuously."[991]

The YETI team strove to keep someone continually in the field every night between the hours of 6 P.M. and 6 A.M., considered prime time for Skunk Ape interactions. "We've gotten closer to them this time than we ever have before," Kelly said. His team believed they had a Bigfoot family in their research area with whom the researchers had become so familiar with they considered giving them names. As the investigators broke down barriers, the creatures, according to Kelly, continually decreased the distance between them and YETI members.

> The Kelly's neighbors also have reported yeti coming in close.
>
> A yeti reportedly chased one frightened woman into her house, and another woman "has one appearing regularly at her cookouts," Mrs. Clark said.
>
> Another neighbor reported seeing a yeti playing with the wheel on a child's tricycle in her yard.
>
> Women seem to see yeti more frequently than men do, the Kellys say.
>
> "Maybe they think men are more competitive," Mrs. Clark theorized.[992]

At the time Susan Denley wrote her article for the *St. Petersburg Times* on the new team, the YETI investigators were seeking financial backing to continue and expand their field research efforts. The group was not solicitous for the involvement of casual sightseers but was disposed to accepting creditable and earnest researchers into their ranks. "If a science professor from the university in Tampa called, we'd be glad to have him come out," YETI member Mason O'Neil said.[993]

Ramona Clark originally traveled to the Lucky K to work with Kelly and satisfy her curiosity about Bigfoot. Clark and fellow researcher Duane Hibner married and eventually made their home in Brooksville. Together, they became two of the most prominent Skunk Ape researchers in Florida. B. Ann Slate wrote, "Their files of hundreds of sightings spill over from each available nook and cranny of their Brooksville residence." Slate's description of the couple: "Duane Hibner is an easy-going, blond, well-conditioned man who stands over six feet tall, while his red-haired petite wife is a bundle of boundless energy." The Hibners opted to not carry guns on their stakeouts, swapping firearms for sound recording devices.[994]

> They also bring to their unique undertaking certain inborn sensitivities that lure the creatures in for that closer, curious look at the humans. Documentation from many episodes, and from a variety of locales, has indicated that if a Yeti approaches man, it is because they want to and not the other way around. This writer feels that there is something in the very nature or personality of Bigfoot trackers which contributes to the success or failure of any expedition.[995]

Duane Hibner's first experience with Bigfoot happened long before he settled in Florida, during his 1946 Christmas vacation on the Hibner family farm in Iowa. Duane's father, Frank Hibner, was a farmer who had grown up in Canada where he acquired hunting and trapping skills. One day, recounted Hibner, his father discovered a hollowed-out area under a large oak tree. The space was large, indicating a sizeable creature had made it, and the senior Hibner set one of his double-spring bear traps nearby. During this Christmas break, Duane accompanied his father on the rounds to check his traps. Crossing the then-frozen Big Cedar River, the pair were on their way to the hollowed-out space when they came across 16-inch human-looking footprints with an approximately three-foot stride between them. Duane asked his father if a bear had made the huge tracks which dwarfed his father's size-11 boot. His father didn't think so, since the tracks had been deeply compressed into the snow by something moving on two legs.[996]

> Upon reaching the trap site at the oak tree, a wide circle of ripped up ground and dislodged rocks indicated that whatever "animal" had been caught had torn itself free using amazing strength. The bear trap, bent completely out of shape, was now a useless piece of junk. Large boulders had been torn from the embankment and thrown out onto the river's ice. The thick steel wire attached to the trunk of the tree [securing the trap] was broken, and where it had been wound around the four-inch thick oak tree roots, it had been chewed through.
>
> Enormous five-toed footprints led away from the site to the south, and while the youngster excitedly asked to follow them, his father would not permit it. With the spring came rumors of a naked wild man living along the river in a swampy area, but this seemed inconceivable. The biting cold of the snow thaws would rule out any human living nude or without shelter in that region.[997]

In her story "Man-Ape's Reign of Terror" printed in the August 1977 *UFO Report*, Slate wrote about one of Ramona and Duane's 1974 experiences involving both a Bigfoot and mysterious lights in the sky. At the time, early in the calendar year, the couple still operated under the auspices of the St. Petersburg Yeti Research Society.

> In late January 1974, the Hibners took up a position on what was called the old mine put road [sic] while two friends from St. Petersburg kept in contact via walkie-talkies from the Lucky K. Near midnight, strange, lonely screams echoed from the woods near the Hibners' outpost. The couple froze, alert and listening for any movement. From the direction of the screams came a large golden-colored ball of light, silently bobbing and weaving at a low level through the trees. Drifting over the road, it headed toward the Lucky K Ranch. Their walkie-talkie suddenly came alive with the excited voices of the two men stationed at the ranch, watching the UFO pass overhead.
>
> Ramona wondered, "Had the UFO been there to pick-up or discharge the Yeti? Was the screaming a message, a plea to the UFO—or anger? We didn't know, but a weird feeling persisted!"

> Now early February, Duane Hibner was preoccupied in a business deal with his construction company so Ramona took up the solitary vigil. The night was chilly. The woods seemed strangely quiet . . . until a huge dark body moved from behind a tree—*only 40 feet from the small woman.* Ramona quickly switched on her flashlight.
>
> "I was covered with goose bumps and knew absolute, unadulterated fear," she said. "Every nerve was strung so tight I couldn't move or speak for several moments. It was seven to eight feet tall and covered with dark brown hair. The head sat on the shoulders with a large bulge behind the head, like a muscle. The back of the head sloped downwards toward this bulge. The side of the head was visible and the profile had what appeared to be a large lantern jaw or maybe whiskers."
>
> Paralyzed with fright at the nearness of the creature, Ramona watched the Yeti walk slowly past her, step out of the woods, and cross the road. It had never turned to look in her direction but continued on about its business. In the dust on the road, she found footprints measuring 19 inches long and 11 inches wide.[998]

According to Slate, a few weeks later and in that same area, the Hibners encountered a female Bigfoot that chattered loudly and, in what was perceived as irritation at the Hibners' presence, threw rocks and stones at them. When they illuminated her with their flashlights, the Bigfoot's eyes had a greenish glow. Another Bigfoot the couple became familiar with was an immense, gray-haired male. "He squatted down in the woods and just made vocal threats. We heard barks and whistles when he was around, and once a scream which sent cold shivers down out spines. We've never heard anything like it before or since; a lonely, sad sound no human could duplicate."[999]

> Soon the fear of the Yeti creature subsided, to be replaced by something akin to an inner awareness. Ramona Hibner tried to describe it: "It's difficult to express to others that the knowledge you have *inside* yourself is more of a feeling rather than an actual sensory awareness. It's a feeling one gets and I am aware of the creatures long before I hear or see them. I just *know* when they're about. It's as if everything in the woods stops breathing when the Yetis are around."[1000]

Slate wrote several articles on the Skunk Ape research conducted at Brooksville. Below she describes a standout encounter story from the Lucky K ranch.

> The strangest of all the Yeti encounters on that ranch, which was under almost constant surveillance, was later told to researcher Ramona Hibner—an incident that occurred on March 26th under a full moon at about 10 P.M. The ranchwoman, together with her son, age 17 at the time, had walked to the laundry shed a short distance from their trailer to get the clothes from the dryer. The night was cool and strangely silent. There was that familiar, overpowering sensation that the Yeti were again nearby.
>
> Straining her eyes in the darkness, the woman thought she saw someone standing near the livestock catch pen. There was a distinct mental image of thin, leathery-looking hands and the feeling of a desperate need for food.
>
> Suddenly, as if someone were speaking directly to her mind, a voice said; "*What is to become of my people?*"
>
> The woman instantly thought back in response, "What is to become of *my* people?"
>
> The total feeling projected in that question brought sudden fears of compassion and the woman ran back to her trailer, consumed with grief and pity for that solitary, shadowy figure which she was certain was a female Yeti.
>
> *What is to become of my people?* A rather sophisticated thought coming from what is believed to be only an animal![1001]

Reporter Michael Marzella wrote that the Yeti Research Society had 40 active members after Kelly and others split off to form YETI. Brooksville obviously remained a focal point for both groups.

> It will happen near Brooksville, Gordon Prescott figures, where the pines and palmetto thickets huddle so closely there's not room to swing a cat. That's where they'll catch the Yeti.
>
> At night probably, after days of baiting the trap with dainties and at last getting photographs of the elusive quarry, building its confidence, the weighted net will drop. Tranquilizer darts, needles jabbed through stinking, matted fur, will pacify a

> thousand pounds of shrieking monster, seven feet tall and frighteningly man-like.[1002]

"I'm sure they are out there," Prescott said. "I've seen them. Four years ago, we were excavating for artifacts in the Great Cypress Swamp. From the bottom of the hole, someone looked up and shouted 'My God, what's that?' Just for an instant, we saw a big hairy head peering down at us, before it ran away. That was the first time I'd seen a Yeti." Prescott said that first sighting was of a large male. "Since then I've seen them twice, but only briefly," he said. "Now the Yetis are more known than even a few years ago. We get reports from all over the world, and we're trying to collect as much information on the Yeti as possible."

The Yeti Research Society held that about 300 of the creatures lived in Florida grouped into family clusters. "I've seen footprints 17 inches long and 10 wide at the toes near Brooksville. That's not a bear, or anything else we could use for an excuse. But we haven't had a report in eight or nine weeks of any sightings. The dry season, I think, makes them migrate up deeper into the forest," said Prescott.

"They're an endangered species, even if we haven't recognized them yet. His (the Yeti's) living areas are being condominiumized. He may phase himself out before he is understood," Prescott said. And it was this belief which catalyzed the Yeti Research Society's readiness to shift into quick action to capture one of the creatures . . . a creature viewed not merely as a missing link, Prescott maintained, but a separate branch of life, primitive in its design. "There's no way to protect them, as long as there are any left in the world, unless we know more about them," Prescott said. "A few have been captured, including one in Arcadia about 40 years ago [Arcadia, Florida, is about 130 miles south of Brooksville], but no one there will talk about it."[1003]

Yeti evidence in Florida is almost non-existent—no fossils, skeletons, skins or photographs—because the Yeti is clever and elusive, Prescott theorized. Just the sight of a giant, stinking beast striding upright down a trail freezes the most fearless photographer, he maintained.[1004]

"What we need though is a live specimen, not just a photograph," Prescott said, convinced pictures alone would be insufficient to settle the issue and prove the creature's existence. Prescott believed sometime after October and continuing through May as the best time to hunt Skunk Apes. Marzella wrote that the Yeti Research Society intended to put several four- or five-person teams into the woods on stakeouts during the fall and spring. "Once the Yeti is drugged, we're not sure what we'll do with it," Prescott admitted. "They apparently travel in family groups, with the biggest male doing the scouting. If he gets in trouble, he'll call for help, and four Yetis are more than we'll be able to handle."[1005]

Kanter Shoots at Skunk Ape

In September, Cary Kanter, employed by Burns International Security Services as a security guard, was sitting in his jeep and watching over an unfinished housing development off Highway 441 which connects to the southern end of Lake Okeechobee. At about 1:30 A.M. he saw a shadowy form which he took to be a possible vandal. Flicking on his jeep's lights, he cried, "Hey what are you doing there?"[1006]

> Cary Kanter describes himself as "a relatively calm person," and he doesn't want to make a big affair out of the thing he says he saw the other night—a creature that resembled what other reputed witnesses to it call the Skunk Ape.
>
> Like others in Central and South Florida, Kanter claims not only to have sighted it; he also scented it.
>
> "It smelled like it had taken a bath in rotten eggs," he is reported to have said. "it made my eyes water and my nose fill up."
>
> Kanter, 24, was at his post at the unfinished Wellington housing development off Southern Boulevard west of U.S. 441 early Tuesday, sitting in a Jeep and watching over the development in his job as a Burns security guard.
>
> He reportedly saw something move in some bushes, and when he saw it move again, trained his jeep lights on the spot. He got out of the Jeep and ordered what now appeared to be a dark form to tell what it was doing there.
>
> The hulking form moved toward him, and he pulled out his service revolver and told it to stop, but it kept coming, he told Palm Beach County Sheriff's deputies later.
>
> "It was huge, about seven feet tall—was real hairy and was either hunched over or had no neck at all," he reportedly said, and also described its awful odor.

> When it got to less than 30 feet away, Kanter, a former military policeman in Vietnam, fired all six rounds of the highly lethal kind of ammunition that fragments and spreads when it hits. He said that he was positive he hit the form twice, but that "it grabbed his chest and ran like you can't believe—like a track star."
>
> Sheriff's Department spokesman Frank Messersmith confirmed part of the incident, saying, "He reported a large object and that it smelled bad." But the sheriff's report contained no reference by Kanter to its being hairy, Messersmith said.
>
> "He said he shot at it six times with his service revolver, and it fled south," the spokesman said.
>
> The incident occurred about 1:30 A.M. and Kanter called the Sheriff's Department. Deputies came, searched and found nothing.
>
> "He probably did see something, there's no doubt about that—whether it was a bear, a Florida panther, or whatever it was," said Messersmith. "I'm not suggesting what it was."
>
> The place where it was seen, he said, "is a quite woodsy area."
>
> Kanter declined to return a call to confirm a report of the incident. An [employee] of Burns international Security Services said he preferred not to talk further about it.[1007]

Having weathered the fragmentation of departing members who started their own Skunk Ape investigative group, Gordon Prescott and the St. Petersburg Yeti Research Society was back in the news in September as they prepared for weekend expeditions into Hernando County later in the fall. Writers and columnists like Randy White of the Ft. Myers' *News-Press* usually covered the basics of Florida's hairy hominids in their stories—Skunk Apes smelled bad, Bigfoot was most often seen in the Pacific Northwest, two cowboys purportedly filmed a female Bigfoot several years prior, and hairy hominids appeared to be a worldwide phenomenon. These stories also provide insights into local researchers' ideas and views, making them invaluable resources.

Prescott believed large tracts of heavily wooded areas were where "you have your share of swamp apes. They need large wilderness areas in which to roam." Prescott took a conservative view when estimating Skunk Ape population size. "According to one London anthropologist," he said, "there is an estimated world Yeti population of around 3,000. We feel there are probably 250 to 300 living in Florida."[1008]

"Here in Florida," Prescott continued, "we call them swamp apes or skunk apes. In some northern territories, they're known as 'Big Foot' or the 'Sasquatch' or 'Windigo.' Down in the Bahamas they're called 'Yahoos.'" Prescott, like many other researchers recognized the uphill struggle he and others of his ilk were up against: not only finding the Skunk Ape in the haystack—or swamp—but also the dismissive Ivory Tower of academia which largely ignored their efforts and findings. "It really does bother me scientists think of the Yeti as a sort of fairy tale," Prescott said. "But I imagine the three or four anthropologists around the world who study them serious [sic] are even more disturbed by it. I think the Yeti should not only be accepted by scientists, but it should be placed on the endangered species list too."[1009]

The capture and study of a Skunk Ape remained a priority for the Yeti Research Society, though the precise protocols to be followed post-capture had still not been fleshed out. "If we caught one now," he said, "we wouldn't know what to do with it. We're bickering with two southern universities to see which can provide the best equipment to study a Yeti under laboratory conditions. From correspondence with people in Washington and British Columbia who have experience with the Yeti, we think it is probably docile enough to be civilized and undergo experiments without trouble."

One of the questions reporter Randy White likely thought his "Sketchbook" column readers would like to know was, in precise terms, where does one go to find a Skunk Ape? "Actually," Prescott began, "you don't find them. They find you. We maintain watches when we're on expedition, hoping one will wander by. Because they are reclusive and nocturnal, you are most likely to see a Yeti in a densely wooded area. And oddly enough trailer parks are pretty good areas, too. The Yeti seems fascinated by trailers. There's a trailer park near Brooksville where it's pretty common for Yetis to come and rub themselves. It's getting so the rubbing doesn't even bother the residents. They just keep right on watching TV or whatever else they're doing."[1010]

Skunk Ape Festival

6,000 people attended the first annual Skunk Ape Festival held on Saturday and Sunday, December 14-15, at the Oasis Airport off US 41 on the Tamiami Trail three miles east of Monroe Station. The event was held to raise funds for a new fire engine for the Ochopee Volunteer Fire Department.

Mainly attracting folks from South Florida—Collier, Monroe, and Dade Counties—the festival was a rarity for the area. "This is the only time people here have had something like this," said Joe Perez of the Ochopee Volunteer Fire Department. "Whoever heard of a carnival and festival in the swamps?" Estimates suggested as many as 3,000 people attended the fair on Saturday. Permutations and variations over time have kept the Skunk Ape Festival an annual event.

> Perez admitted he used the skunk ape, the smelly, hairy, half-man, half-beast myth of the swamps, as the theme of the festival because "I figured I needed to draw people."
>
> As a publicity stunt Perez said he lured the skunk ape "in person" onto the highway during the morning and called sheriff's deputies and highway patrolmen to the scene.
>
> Whether the furry beast that paraded on U.S. 41 was The skunk ape or just an imposter will probably never be known.
>
> Whether there actually is a skunk ape or not will also probably never be known.[1011]

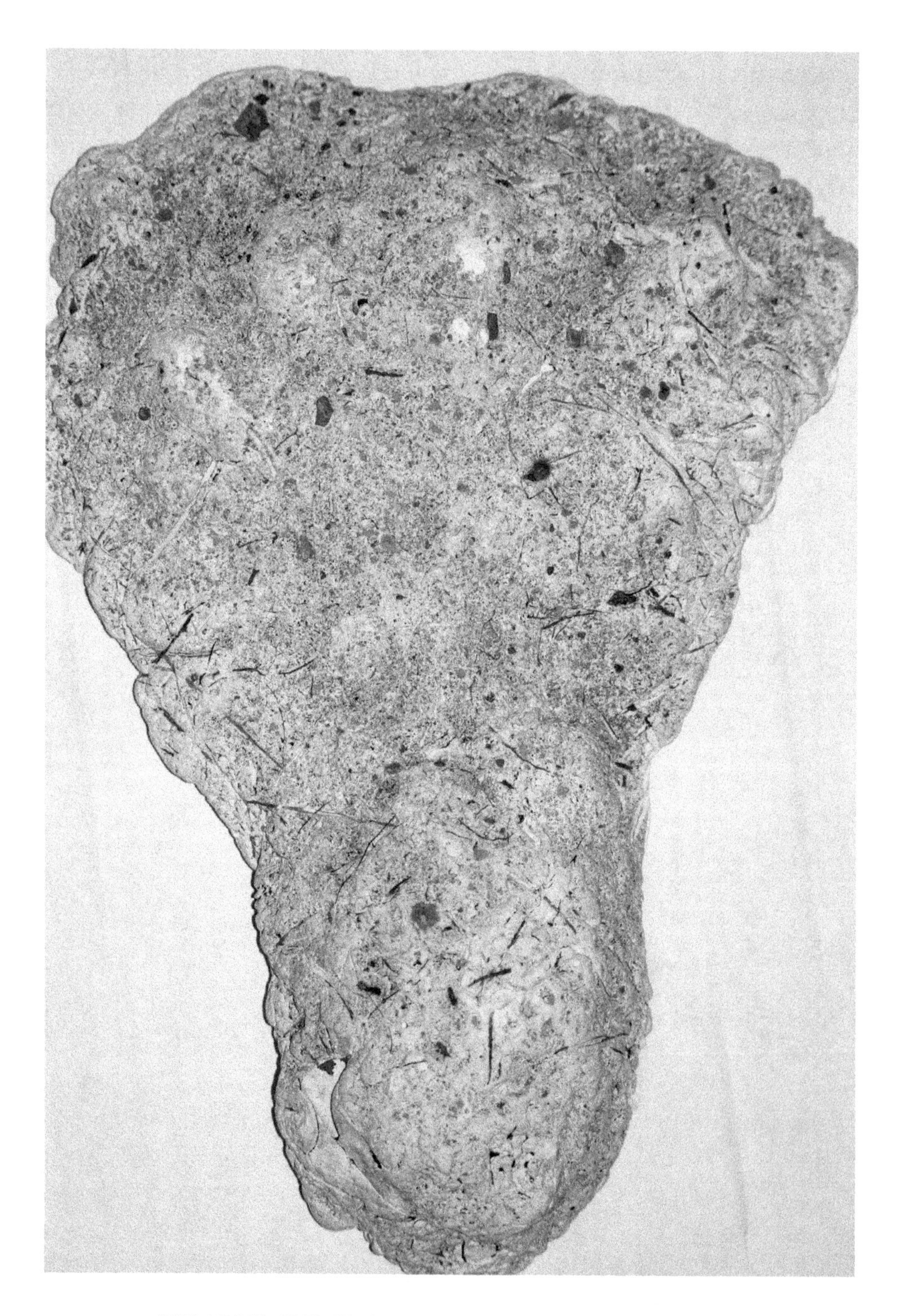

1974 TRACK CAST FROM ALLEGHENY COUNTY, PENNSYLVANIA
COURTESY BRIAN SEECH AND THE CENTER FOR CRYPTOZOOLOGICAL STUDIES

1974 EYEWITNESS SKETCH, OREGON

1975 ADVERTISEMENT FOR 'THE MYSTERIOUS MONSTERS'

CHAPTER 6
1975

While the number of expeditions and their degree of sophistication in searching for the Sasquatch is increasing every year, all the fuzzy film, recorded screams, bits of fur and plaster casts of footprints they bring back will not convince the great majority of people that what they are seeing and photographing is anything more than bears, shadows in the woods or perhaps clever hoaxes.

Only one thing will convince everyone: Bring one of the creatures in, dead or alive.[1012]

Hall Leiren. "It's Sasquatch Time Again in B.C.," *Ottawa Journal* (November 15, 1975).

The interest in Bigfoot has been greater this past summer than at any time since his "discovery" in the Bluff Creek area. All through the years the dear old critter has been good for news stories, and his continuing "presence," has a way of inspiring the dreamy and the desperate would-be locators of the old fellow. (It has a way of attracting the rather unstable, too.)

Most of the letters want back clippings, files, etc. about Bigfoot, which of course, are impossible for Redwood Country to provide. All one has to do is go to a library and do their own digging. If they object, it is because they are plain lazy about doing research, or aren't really serious. For those who appear to want to really know something, we try and answer a letter or two—but these have been quite numerous of late.

The kind of letters we don't like, are those safari-conscious birds who are planning an army to capture Bigfoot, dead or

> alive. One letter said he would like to know the best kind of gun he should bring along. We informed him to bring any kind of a gun he liked, if he intended to use it on himself—but nothing for Bigfoot, because in a wild moment he'd likely kill some innocent bystander.
>
> Bigfoot no longer needs the attention of the casually inquisitive—only the serious are welcome to try and decide just what makes up our fine living legend.[1013]
>
> Andrew Genzoli. "Redwood Country," *Times-Standard* (September 17, 1975).

By 1975 it was clear Bigfoot was not skulking off into the desolate wilderness of fringe pop culture. A widely demonstrated appetite for Bigfoot information and entertainment sustained the subject's conventional, mainstream popularity. If physical evidence of its extant nature remained elusive, a conceptual essence of hairy hominids had distilled across and infused into the cultural landscape. An example letter to the editor printed in the *Daily Inter Lake* and shown below intimates the expanding interest in Bigfoot at the time:

> Editor: I am an anthropology student here at the University of Montana, and for some time have been gathering data on the possibility of unknown hominid creatures inhabiting North America.
>
> These creatures are generally known by the popular names of Bigfoot or Sasquatch. My reason for writing is to inquire if it is possible to have this letter published in your paper's letters to the editor section. In this way I hope to contact people who have information on the subject.
>
> Although the subject traditionally has been ignored by scientists, more and more are being convinced that the present evidence warrants further investigation.
>
> Any person who contacts me will not be ridiculed or ignored and their name will remain confidential if they so desire.
>
> It is only through public awareness and cooperation that this enigma shall one day be solved.
>
> Tim Church, Missoula.[1014]

Ivan Marx

Ivan Marx was busily engaged in promoting his film, *The Legend of Bigfoot*, in the latter months of 1975. Marx gave the appearance of enjoying himself while regaling reporters, including Jim Scott writing for *Argosy*, with stories and yarns from his experiences with Bigfoot. Scott's *Argosy* article presents a colorful portrayal of Marx, created from the controversial Bigfoot hunter's own words.

After Marx's discharge from Navy service in World War II, he moved to northern California where he became a professional hunter and trapper. He told reporters that from time to time he was hired by game wardens to track down man-killing bears in national parks and in the mid-1950s he was hired by the Department of the Interior to work on a five-year study of Alaskan brown bears.[1015]

Marx claimed October 1951[1016] as his first direct exposure to Bigfoot. At that time Marx supported himself and his wife Peggy as a hunting guide and wildlife photographer; he had taken several hunters on a bear-hunting excursion near Mount Shasta, but he turned up no fresh bear tracks. He decided to steer the hunting party towards Burney in hopes of finding bear sign near the wallows of Dead Horse Summit close by Highway 89. Reaching the wallows, an astonished Marx found tracks twice as long as any bear print he'd ever seen. "For the life of me, I couldn't figure out what it was," Marx told Scott. "I figured someone was playing a joke on us. But how could he fake those footprints? I took my lead dog out of the truck to see what he would do. He started sniffing. And then, suddenly, he bolted in terror for the pick-up. I had no idea then that it was Bigfoot." An intrigued Marx found himself more constrained than restrained. "I would have liked to have followed those tracks but I was hired to find bear."

According to Marx, finding those mysterious tracks was but the first of his many Bigfoot experiences. As recounted in *Argosy*, on one particularly memorable occasion Marx came across a hairy creature carrying a tombstone. When the creature noticed Marx, it dropped the tombstone and beat a hasty retreat. Curious, Marx said he approached the stone and saw it had "1865" chiseled on it. Describing another incident for Scott, Marx recalled a deputy who, after looking up Marx at his cabin asked, "Will your dogs trail a gorilla?" His curiosity piqued, Marx sought more details. "We really don't know what it is," explained the deputy, "but the farms and ranches between Mount Lassen and Mount Shasta have been visited by this beast. It likes to roam around in the cattle herds." The deputy flatly admitted to Marx the "beast" was something beyond his experience. "It's too tall, really, for a gorilla," the deputy said. "Everyone says it must be over seven feet tall." Ultimately Marx decided against extending his services to the deputy, explaining to Scott, "My dogs had no experience with gorillas."[1017]

During the ensuing weeks after meeting the deputy, Marx heard recurring stories of the "towering" creature and how it terrified the area's cattle herds. People who glimpsed the beast said its arms hung to its sides as if they were injured. Then Marx received a call from a café owner in Round Mountain, California, who explained a large hairy creature haunted the local environs. Marx decided to investigate these claims for himself. "This time I agreed to go," he told Scott. "I found large tracks around a mud hole near Round Mountain. I was stunned. The tracks were exactly the same size and shape as the ones I had found earlier."[1018]

Marx began to form an idea of what it was he was confronting: a prehistoric man with short toes designed to grip jagged rocks when climbing rough, uneven terrain. In February 1969 Marx was living on the Columbia River just a few miles south of the Canadian border. "I spent the summer photographing wild animals there, much the same as I have done all my life. Then, in the spring, I found a small, muddy, spring-fed animal wallow. It was about 60 feet across and 70 feet long," Marx recalled, foreshadowing his encounter with a Bigfoot he would call, "Old Cripplefoot." Marx's assignment at the time was to film bear and he decided the wallow was a perfect location to build a blind and wait for the animals to come in.

The cool mud had a depth of about four feet and was an ideal spot for animals to get rid of ticks and pests. "It was a hot, dry summer, and forest fires ravaged the parched land. Some days the smoke along the lake was so thick I could not take photographs. However, with my Rolex 16-mm movie camera and Nikon 35-mm still camera, I made my blind. The movie camera on a tripod fitted with a telephoto lens and the 35-mm hung around my neck, I waited for the animals to come in. Through my lens, I could tell a huge animal had been using the wallow, so the next morning I waited, but no animals came in," Marx said. At about 5 A.M.[1019] on what would prove to be a fateful morning for Marx, he remembered he "fumbled around with my exposure meter, trying to find the camera setting, the light got better—and then I saw it. There, lumbering through the willow bushes, heading for the wallows, was a tall, hairy creature with one crippled arm and skinned up feet."[1020] Marx admitted he was apprehensive and shocked by the sight of the beast. "It scared the heck out of me. But if the world was blowing up I will get my camera on it, so I started filming it," Marx said.[1021]

"I quickly turned the movie camera on him and started taking pictures. The beast heard the camera and whirled to face it twice as he limped through the bushes. My camera ran down. I quickly wound it as the creature darted into the thicket. I jumped from the blind, and got a few feet of pictures as he ran toward the rocky cliff. Then I snapped six still pictures."[1022] In other accounts Marx stated the creature shrieked at him during its backward glances.[1023]

Thoroughly excited, Marx returned to his cabin and told Peggy about the incredible creature he'd seen: tall, skinny, with chocolate brown hair all over its body including its face.[1024] Marx and Peggy returned to the mud wallow and searched for tracks. Marx said they found footprints made days before as well as fresh prints whose distinctive characteristics undoubtedly marked them as left by the limping creature Marx had just encountered. Marx procured plaster and made casts which showed there were only four toes on its right foot—the center toe was missing. Growths on the outside of the foot suggested a crippled appendage, a state of affairs that appeared to have been endured by the creature for some time. "I measured the tracks later. It had a 52-inch stride and was very long-legged, not at all like an ape with short legs and long arms."[1025] The mud hole also yielded hand prints from which Marx deduced the creature sported a half-paw, half-hand.[1026]

Marx's inspection of the broken foliage led him to conclude the creature's height was seven feet four inches. Stool found in the area of the mud hole which Marx attributed to the creature revealed no signs of meat or hair but instead showed that chokeberry, Oregon grapes, and elderberry seeds comprised the bulk of the creature's dietary habits.[1027]

"The next day I followed Bigfoot's tracks. I called in several other men to help in the chase. I took one of my young dogs along on a leash. He was helpful in finding the tracks but, strangely, he didn't bark. In a few minutes he came back, and pointed to the way the trail led. We came to a heavily entangled patch of vine, and the dog let out a strange cry." Surveying the scene Marx spotted his quarry. "Then I saw the monster lying face down in the thicket. I turned my camera just as he got up and galloped off through the dark, dense brush. The dog took off after him when he emitted two long piercing screams of fear. Cautiously I followed," Marx recollected, "crawling through the entanglement."[1028]

"The smell was terrible, for apparently the beast was vomiting. Several times I almost turned back, as I knew it would be curtains for me if he turned to fight. But the urge to photograph him spurred me on. Hours passed. I used my walkie-talkie to call my associates. One of the men had been near enough to hear the screams of the distressed animal. I told them the creature was heading down the mountain and that we should try to head him off. But soon the sun sank behind the mountain, and darkness forced us to give up the chase."[1029]

By this point, Marx had filmed and photographed, or nearly so, the Cripplefoot Bigfoot on two separate occasions and taken plaster casts of its footprints. "For the next few days I drove around the lake following trails. If I could but capture the injured Bigfoot, the world would be electrified by the news. But again I lost the trail, and could not find his carcass. I looked for buzzards, hawks and magpies that might lead me to the spot, but saw none." Whether consciously realizing it or not, Marx was devoting significant time and energy to studying Bigfoot and its habits. One conclusion he reached was that Bigfoot was migratory, taking a route all the way to Alaska. "I have found tracks in eastern Washington through the Rocky Mountains via Dawson Creek area to the Ross River-Keno Hill region to the Yukon Territory," Marx stated.[1030]

"Near Keno Hill, two friends of mine in their snowmobile saw 14 of the monsters," Marx told Scott, revealing a sighting encompassing an unusually large number of individuals. "They were bedded down in the snow. When the snowmobile approached, the things raised up and lumbered off into the brush." As Marx invested increasing effort into looking for Bigfoot, he found his experience as an outdoorsman useful in conjecturing, beyond the migration theories, on far-ranging aspects of Bigfoot's ecology and behavior. "In the animal kingdom, scent plays an important role. Knowledge of animal scent and how to use it has helped me in my research on Bigfoot. But, as yet, we have no trained animals that will track him. I believe the strong stench of Bigfoot serves to warn away other animals and tell fellow beings of his whereabouts." Bigfoot's cognitive ability alone elevated it far above other animals, placing it in a superlative sphere. "Bigfoot is the only animal, in my estimation, that has a mind. I believe he has a memory and has reasoning ability."[1031]

Determined to learn all he could, Marx told Scott that he and Peggy packed up for Alaska to further their understanding of Bigfoot and after a long drive, a plane flight, and a two-mile walk, they arrived at a location pre-selected to provide the best opportunity for finding evidence. "It was a beautiful place, this rolling slope of the arctic tundra. The berries lay like a lush carpet as far as you could see. The foliage consisted of caribou moss and berry bushes, no more than six inches high, but loaded down with fruit."

"The first two nights, although short, seemed an eternity, but nothing happened. I had the tape recorder and walkie-talkie with me so I took them about 200 yards out, locked the walkie-talkie to the transmit position and put the receiver in our tent. The very first night we heard a series of deep-throated grunts, then the rustling of the tundra, and eventually nothing." Huddled in the tent, Marx was thrilled the location appeared to have Bigfoot present. "When daylight finally arrived, I found the walkie-talkie 20 yards from where I had it propped up, laying in the tundra unbroken. The tape had been loosened from the transmit button. Whatever released the transmit button caused the unit to go on the receive pattern and, in doing so, it made a crackling sound, probably scaring the animal away. As I headed back to camp the next night, I heard my wife in a screaming whisper, say, 'They are here, hurry!'"[1032]

Marx warily closed the distance to camp, senses alert, ready for the possibility of danger. "I moved cautiously the few hundred feet to the tent, and then I saw it! It looked to be some 400 yards away. My blood ran cold while I tried to figure out what it was, and see at the same time that my wife didn't panic. She had stood her ground many times in the path of charging grizzly bears and helped back me if I needed it, but this was something else. This was so eerie my hair stood on end. My ever-present movie camera, loaded with extra high-speed film, reminded me I had work to do, so I turned it on and recorded the phenomenon. Peering through the view-finder, I could see something raise slowly up and down, then one glow would go out and reappear again. All of a sudden, it appeared to walk up out of the low spot in the tundra and materialize in my viewfinder. It then moved back to the low spot and vanished."[1033]

"In my heart," Marx recalled, likely evoking a sense of vindication, "I knew it must be the Bigfoot. Winter was closing in. The temperature was down and snow the size of quarters was falling. We packed up and made our way out while the trail was still visible."

From consultations with Alaskan and Canadian Indians concerning their knowledge of and experience with Bigfoot, Marx learned the creatures would freeze when in the presence of humans. From a distance of only a few hundred feet, Bigfoot would become practically invisible, resembling a tree stump and blending seamlessly into its environment. Native Alaskans told Marx several stories of Bigfoot stealing children from Eskimo villages. When some of these children made their way back to their villages, they told of being made baby-sitters for Bigfoot young, and so allowing the adult females to be free to reproduce.[1034] "The Indians call it 'stickman' and it's easy to see why, it's so skinny," Marx said.[1035] Marx told Scott a story he had collected on one of his Alaska expeditions. An elderly Eskimo shot at what he thought was a bear. The creature leapt up and ran away clutching its chest and the hunter realized the creature had not been a bear but instead was a Bigfoot or "Bushman." Returning to his village, he candidly described his encounter. He was ordered to leave the village, Marx said, for if he remained, the Bushman would bring evil upon all of the community. Driven into the tundra he expired after a few days, alone and abandoned.[1036]

As noted by Scott, Marx found his experiences led to bona fide expertise and he adopted the guise of a Bigfoot expert, ever ready to confidently tick off his conclusions concerning Bigfoot's habits and anatomy.

> The head is shaped much like a gorilla's, yet with some features of prehistoric man. Nature designed it as a cold weather animal. The ears have no external flaps. They look like small canals that lead into each side of the head, and they are covered with thick hair to keep out the cold.
>
> The eyes are rather small, also to evade damage from the cold. The pupils are heavily colored red to prevent snow blindness. The iris of the eye has the ability to dilate wide, like an owl, for night vision.
>
> The nostrils are two large chambers, covered inside and outside with thick hair. The function of the nostrils is nearly the same as a human, except that they are designed to handle a larger volume of air.
>
> The mouth is rather small for such a large animal. The lips are thin and hair-covered. When the creature's mouth is shut, the hair blends together so that the slit of the mouth is hardly visible.
>
> The hands are half-hand, half-paw. The thumb sits far back toward the wrist. The fingers have hair on the back and in between the digits. The palm is heavily padded with calluses.
>
> The creature is not able to use its hands like a human, but they are tough as leather and are not easily torn while climbing on jagged rocks or frozen ice packs. The feet are protected in the same manner as the hands. However, it has more trouble with its feet than it does any other part of its body. It just doesn't watch where it is stepping because it is too interested

> in scanning the horizon for trouble. So many of the creatures have toes missing, broken feet and often growths on them. Traps for bear, wolf, coyote and lynx are powerful enough to jerk the toes off Bigfoot.
>
> Marx believes the body is freeze-proof. It can quickly adapt to warm weather by controlling hair growth. The legs are long from constant walking. The plume on the head can be raised or lowered to control temperature. The organs are well covered in fatty tissue and hair to protect them from weather, thorns, sharp rocks and ice. The arms are extremely powerful, as are the legs.[1037]

Promoting *The Legend of Bigfoot* allowed Marx to espouse many of his views and thoughts on Bigfoot. Bigfoot was incredibly rare, only about 150 specimens total[1038] (which made Marx's claimed seven sightings[1039] all the more remarkable). Bigfoot was not human, according to Marx, though very intelligent. Bigfoot emitted a musky odor, buried their dead, tended to be unaggressive, and preferred to run from a confrontation. "It doesn't consume great amounts of food. Just plants and a few fish—no [red] meat that I know of," Marx stated in the December 19, 1975, *Kansas City Times*.[1040] Bigfoot was incredibly strong according to Marx, who once found a brown bear's head nearly twisted off. "It broke the third vertebrae of the bear's neck. It just wound it up until it snapped."[1041]

> Tracks nearby showed that the bear had attacked a Bigfoot that was stooping over to drink from a stream. Marx took hair samples found in the dead bear's mouth to University of Washington scientists who said the hair belonged to no known species of animal.
>
> It was the hair samples, among other evidence, that prompted the Washington state legislature to pass a law declaring the Bigfoot an endangered species and prohibiting the killing of the animals.[1042]

On a swing through Albuquerque, Marx said *The Legend of Bigfoot* encompassed his and Peggy's last 10 years of their 24-year search for Bigfoot. Marx played up the New Mexico venue by associating the area with local Bigfoot lore; he told *Albuquerque Journal* reporter Carol Cohea a legend concerning a Bigfoot trapped within a cave by Native Americans where the creature's desiccated corpse remained sealed in the Mountainair region southeast of Albuquerque.[1043]

His longest and most important sighting, Marx said, had occurred during the spring of 1975 at a secret location he called Beaver Swamp. On this occasion while hidden behind a blind, Marx filmed two of the creatures for nearly 12 minutes. "Apparently they breed in the north during the slow period of winter," he concluded. "The young are born in the spring and they migrate south. However I don't think the young migrate until they are 12 to 13 years old because there have been no reported sightings of young ones much farther south than Alaska," he said.

> To finance these investigative trips along the Pacific Coast the Marxes took their projector and nature films, putting on shows in small towns which did not have television and which were hundreds of miles from the closest movie theater.
>
> He learned how to spot phony reports and after several years discovered a pattern to the Bigfoot sightings. In the summer the animals apparently migrated south to northern California, and by winter had retreated almost to the Arctic Circle.[1044]

Marx stated he did most of his filming from elevated positions using disguised blinds in trees and he employed household ammonia which he said smelled like urine to animals. Marx hoped future breakthroughs would include successfully approaching a Bigfoot to within 100 feet. "I'm not afraid of it at all. It's one of the meekest, most timid things in the world," he said.

Marx used a soothing voice in his field investigations to verify what he termed an animal's "pressure point," the proximity a wild animal will tolerate before it panics, flees, or attacks. "With bears it's 20 feet, with mountain lions, it's seven feet." Marx estimated it would require five years to achieve his goal of closing the tolerable physical distance between himself and Bigfoot. "I don't want to move it from the wild. The idea is to move the people into it," he said. "It is in no way human. It's a species all its own. I don't believe it could strike up a conversation. It's an animal, a very cunning animal with a memory and ability to think ahead," he said.[1045]

At this point in his Bigfoot-hunting career punctuated by the achievement of a theatrical movie release, Marx's future plans centered on a return to Beaver Swamp, where he intended to capture a young Bigfoot specimen, fly it to a base camp for intensive study, and then return it unharmed to Beaver Swamp. Despite those designs, Marx professed he had no interest in exploiting Bigfoot, but rather, he and Peggy looked upon *The Legend of Bigfoot* as a vehicle to finance their Beaver Swamp sortie and ultimately prove Bigfoot's existence. "It'll be so nice to get one of them by the leg and prove it's true," said Marx. "Even if I do get my head bashed a little."[1046]

Print & Film

In kid's television fare, Bigfoot made a couple of appearances on live-action format shows common to the era. On *Isis*, two unnerved students were frightened by an indistinct presence in the woods during a class picnic.

> *Cindy*: Something's out there! I don't know what. It really frightened us, a big, hairy . . .
>
> *Andrea* (*Isis*): Calm down now. What do you think you really saw?
>
> *Cindy*: I don't know, maybe a bear.
>
> *Lee*: No, no it wasn't a bear it was just too big. Aw, I wish I'd gotten a picture of it. Wait a second, maybe it was Bigfoot.
>
> *Mickey*: Bigfoot?
>
> *Rick*: Bigfoot . . . it's supposed to be a large man-like creature that lives in the woods. People report seeing them everywhere. Of course, that's just a legend.
>
> *Cindy*: Well, it sure describes what we saw.

The shadowy figure in the woods turned out to be a large hermit who ultimately saves Lee from plunging down a cliff. The students learned lessons in tolerance and appreciating people's differences.

The *Ghost Busters'* episode "The Abominable Snowman" featured mad scientist Dr. Centigrade and his hard-of-hearing minion, the Abominable Snowman, tangling with the bumbling Ghost Busters—a trio (one is a gorilla) of occult investigators. This live-action children's show was rife with slapstick and screwball comedy. The Abominable Snowman costume was a bulbous layering of fur sporting a rounded head but featureless face.

In the *Kolchak: The Night Stalker* episode, "Primal Scream," Carl Kolchak, intrepid reporter and investigator of things weird and strange, sleuths a series of savage murders. Kolchak's investigation leads him to an oil corporation where organic matter held in a freezing unit mutates into a murderous hominid beast. It all culminates in an underground showdown between Kolchak and the creature.

Written and directed by Walerian Borowczyk, *Beast* strives to be taken as a work of arthouse fare but is recalled now mainly as an infamous relic of '70s trash cinema. *Beast* stars Sirpa Lane as a woman set to marry a scion from an impoverished upper crust family which has a troubled history involving a hominid monster with a wolfish face. This pornographic film has attained some measure of critical attention in the DVD era; it is opinionatedly a lurid and uncompromising product of its time.

Sasqua

Sasqua was an independent film shot in Lowell, Westford, and Dracut, Massachusetts, and in Pelham, New Hampshire. The plot involves a young man, played by Jim Whitmore, who being fed up and dissatisfied with city life, moves to a rural setting and recruits like-minded folks to join him to create a commune. The eponymous *monster* enters the picture and wreaks havoc on commune members and townsfolk alike. The story is developed against conflict between the commune and the local community, each group blaming the other for the series of brutal killings occurring in their midst.

Like 1979's *Revenge of Bigfoot*, the shot-in-color, 83-minute long *Sasqua* has become a lost movie. The movie was lensed for $186,000 from a script written by Channon Scot who intended to establish a movie company in the Lowell area focusing on film processing and editing as well as set-creation. Scenes for *Sasqua* were filmed with coordination and cooperation from the Lowell police, area merchants who permitted filming on their premises, and from property owners who allowed filming on their land. Many cast members were local talent.[1047]

The world premiere of *Sasqua* occurred at the Chelmsford Cinema Theater on August 13, 1975. Attendees arrived in dungarees and in tuxedos. Children in the audience were delighted by a Sasqua-monster that leapt out of a cardboard closet and ran up and down the aisles. Movie reviewer Pat Mitchell from Boston's WBZ-TV Channel 4 was given five-star treatment. "I came here to work. I didn't expect such a wonderful welcome. How many of you are in it?" she asked the audience; about 50 hands shot up in response. "It is very rare to get to come and review a world premiere of a film in your locality," Mitchell said, "especially one in which you see local talent and backed by local money." She reviewed the film in her 11 P.M. news report as suggestive of great promise ahead for Scot, calling the film "not an epic" but definitely "a start." Children were quick to grab up posters in the theater's lobby and the audience applauded nearly everything, particularly during known individuals' appearances on screen.

One of the biggest audience reactions during the film came when Scot, portraying a hippie, woke up the film's lead James Whitworth, exclaiming, "It was in the window. It was big and hairy." Nobody believed him and the film's hairy antihero proceeded to vent cinematic mayhem—much to the audience's delight.[1048]

THE MYSTERIOUS MONSTERS

The Mysterious Monsters aka *Bigfoot: The Mysterious Monster* is essentially a re-editing of *Monsters! Myths or Mysteries?* Host and narrator duties were undertaken by Peter Graves, replacing Rod Serling who had passed away in 1975. Writer and director Robert Guenette is also credited with authoring a companion paperback book. Guenette and his son were founders of the International Documentary Association, a non-profit organization promoting nonfiction filmmakers and the documentary genre. *The Mysterious Monsters'* distributor, Sunn Classic Pictures (also known as Schick Sunn Classic Pictures), was an independent motion picture and television company perhaps best remembered for 1974's *The Life and Times of Grizzly Adams*. In addition to *The Mysterious Monsters*, Sunn produced several additional paranormal ventures including *The Outer Space Connection* (1975) and *In Search of Noah's Ark* (1976).

Publicizing the film, one of the producers, 31-year-old[1049] Charles E. Sellier Jr., said of Bigfoot, "He's the only monster we Americans have got." *Tucson Daily Citizen* Entertainment Writer, Chuck Graham, wrote of the "hype and hoopla that barraged Tucson" in the days prior to the film's opening in two area theaters on November 5. "We've proved everything and done everything short of actually capturing a Bigfoot, but still the scientific community is skeptical," said Sellier. "In a court of law, all the testimony presented in this film would be considered conclusive evidence that Bigfoot exists."

Sellier thought there were as many as 200 Bigfoot creatures roaming the wilds of the United States, placing him in company with Ivan Marx for espousing a relatively low population estimate. "What many people don't realize is that there are many so-called riddles of nature that could be answered scientifically if someone would just put up the money for proper research.

When we started gathering material for Bigfoot, we found any number of Bigfoot-related studies that scientists have been proposing for years but never have received funds for. So we funded a number of those." As an example of scientific application shown in the movie, Sellier pointed out the voice print analysis of a recording of a supposed Bigfoot call. Without benefit of knowing the sounds' source, analysts concluded they were produced by an animal 9-feet tall that was incapable of making the long 'E' sound.[1050] Sellier stated apes can't make the 'E' sound due to the construction of their jaws and tongues.[1051]

Film reviewer Ron Perkins added a movie morsel at the end of his article on Sun Classic Pictures at the time of *Bigfoot: The Mysterious Monster's* release:

> Short Subject: Fellows, next time you feel too much is being spent on clothes, be glad you're not in the movie business. The costume for the recreations of Bigfoot cost $25,000. For one outfit . . . plus tax: Think it over.[1052]

Some commercials for *The Mysterious Monsters* aired during children's programming; they proved disturbing enough for one Maple City, Michigan, parent for her to call several local television stations and express her concerns.

> 'Big Foot' ads—Dear People: I wonder how many other parents are concerned about the effect on their children of the TV commercials for the 'Big Foot' monster movie. They have severely frightened our preschooler.
>
> The ads are shown all day and even during cartoon shows. The movie is rated 'G' which shows what's wrong with the rating system!
>
> I admit I myself was unnerved when home alone at night and the ad came on, showing a woman home alone at night and a huge hairy arm comes crashing through the window! No wonder my kids have bad dreams!
>
> When I called the TV stations to suggest they use these ads after 9 P.M., Channel 7 was abusive and hostile. Channel 9 was indifferent, and Channel 29 concerned enough to promise to screen the ads. I hope other concerned people will call soon.
>
> Margaret Valentine[1053]

Channel 29 president Thomas Kiple responded to Ms. Valentine in an open letter published in Traverse City's *Record Eagle*.

> 'Bigfoot' Action—(Editor's note: The following letter is in response to an open letter from Mrs. Margaret Valentine of Maple City, which was published Nov. 15)
>
> Dear Mrs. Valentine: I would like to follow-up after your telephone call of last week regarding WGTU's carriage of the advertisements for the movie, "Bigfoot: The Mysterious Monster".
>
> After receiving your suggestion that we screen the ads which the movie's producers scheduled in the WGTU children's programming we held several meetings. The discussion centered around the actual ad (the hairy arm through the window) and the producer's rating (G). The advertisements had been cleared for telecast in children's TV programs. However, after carefully reviewing this ad we agreed with you and not with the movie's producers.
>
> After discussion with the producers, however, they agreed to allow WGTU to reschedule the ads and broadcast a substitute ad in all of our children's programs. They agreed that their intentions were not to scare any children, but to spark interest in their movie.
>
> We thank you for bringing this to our attention and we are equally pleased to be able to help.
>
> Thomas W. Kiple
> President, WGTU[1054]

Columnist John Sinor wrote daily columns for the *San Diego Tribune* and later the *San Diego Union-Tribune* from 1965 until his retirement in 1992 which were distributed nationally by Copley News Service. From time to time he wrote about Bigfoot and repeatedly claimed he directly had a hand in creating the sensation Bigfoot became (see Chapter 10). In 1977, Sinor wrote about his indirect association with *The Mysterious Monsters*.

> Monsters such as Bigfoot and, I suspect, the Loch Ness thing in Scotland are not created in the lower rooms of rain-lashed castles amid a laboratory of bubbling test tubes and cracking machinery.

> No, Virginia, these monsters are created out of illusion, imagination, practical jokes, hysteria and lonesomeness, among other things.
>
> And the machine that gives them life is a newspaperman's typewriter.
>
> Last year at a luncheon with Peter Hurkos, the psychic and seer, I scoffed at the idea of Bigfoot when he told me he was working on a documentary movie [*Mysterious Monsters*] about the monster.
>
> He gave me a strange kind of look and then led me to believe that [B]igfoot really existed.
>
> But that's OK. He also led me to believe that Ronald Reagan would be the next president of the United States.[1055]

The Mysterious Monsters by Robert and Frances Guenette complements the movie of the same name, which was basically a re-editing of the incredibly successful *Monsters! Mysteries or Myths?* A short section of the book is given over to the Loch Ness Monster, however most of its pages are devoted to hairy hominids. Robert and Frances Guenette had examined the Bigfoot legend during the '70s, and in the opening pages, Robert captures the essence of that investigation with one of the most convincing pieces of evidence he came across—an interview with a former law official:

> At the time [July, 1974], I was preparing a television documentary for the Smithsonian Institution series to be broadcast on CBS, a show entitled: "MONSTERS! Mysteries or Myths?" I was in the Pacific Northwest compiling film and data on the 8-foot, 500-pound hairy, man-like monster known as Bigfoot. I had been talking to a wide variety of people who claimed to have seen Bigfoot, or tracked its mysterious footprints. I had interviewed and accompanied an investigative team on an expedition looking for the creature. For almost a year, I had immersed myself in Bigfoot lore, running down every clue as to the possible existence of the creature. And after one year, I was still uncertain about its possibilities, more prone to rejecting it than accepting it.
>
> Then I met Oliver Potter.
>
> Straightforward, honest, reliable, Oliver Potter told me a story he had never publicly told before. "I don't want any

A SCHICK SUN CLASSIC BOOK
1548 * $1.75 *
PROOF!
There are giant creatures living at the edge of our civilization. Astounding new evidence and facts!
the
MYSTERIOUS MONSTERS
By ROBERT and FRANCES GUENETTE
Plus 32 pages of startling photos of Bigfoot, the Loch Ness monster, and many more.
NOW A MAJOR MOTION PICTURE

attention," he said. "I want no publicity." What he was saying was for no personal gain.

This is what he said: "I'm born in the woods, the Cascade Mountains. I know the animals that are here. This was something different, that I had never seen before. A large creature, 8 feet tall, grayish black in color, walking as a man would walk, on its hind legs. It moved away at quite a rapid speed. I know that it wasn't a bear or some other animal, because I know what those animals look like. And besides, I looked at the footprints the creature made. They were not the footprints of bears, they had no claws. They were larger and looked more like a man's."

I had an unsettling experience that night, flying back to Los Angeles, alone with my thoughts, for the interview with the former sheriff had registered in a way the others had not. Not that the others weren't credible, because some of them were, as you shall see in the later pages of this book. But this one statement, so clear and so uncomplicated, so motiveless, made by such a responsible citizen, seemed impossible to contradict.[1056]

Keel's *The Eighth Tower*

John Keel's book *The Eighth Tower* got its start from material cut from his book *The Mothman Prophesies*. "Today one group of pragmatic scientists is investigating BHM [Big Hairy Monsters] while they scorn, even laugh at, the psychic investigators and UFO enthusiasts. Another group is bent on trapping sea serpents. Still others are chasing ghosts and poltergists [sic]. None of these groups seems willing to examine the evidence of the others. Yet they are probably all pursuing the same intangible force." Keel argued that paranormal phenomena are essentially unknowable. They can't be caught, pinned down, caged, or fenced in. Quasi-physical, they leave tantalizing evidence of their passing—like a shadowy materialization, a foot-shaped depression in the soil substrate, an anomalous howl emanating from the woods.[1057]

Keel had concluded that conventional methods of investigation were useless as applied to paranormal phenomena. Taking hairy hominids as an example, a creature can be seen one moment and gone the next. Keel referred to a "shadowy world of energies" as the source of paranormal events; a "super-spectrum" which is apart from our world but quite capable of influencing it. Bigfoot, by its very nature belonged in Keel's sphere of paranormal events and by extension resided within the superspectrum.

> Each month, somewhere on this planet, a monster appears briefly. It leaves huge footprints behind. Then it vanishes. For a short while it was real, a physical entity seen by one person, or ten, or one hundred, and then it ceased to be. These monsters take many forms and have been observed by millions of people over the past several thousand years. So far as we know they have no sexual system, but they do operate according to a set of specific rules. Rules that could only have been invented by a mad scientist.[1058]

In *The Eighth Tower*, Keel provided the mechanics of how his theory worked:

> Since energy masses in the superspectrum can alter their frequencies and move up and down the electromagnetic spectrum, we can assume they can also manipulate atomic structure and enter our plane of reality by creating atoms compatible with our atomic structure. The ancients called this process transmogrification. Heavier, tightly compacted atoms with a dense field of orbiting electrons dissipate their energy quickly. Plutonium is a very unstable element, prone to spontaneous combustion. Let's imagine that when energies of the superspectrum vibrate down into our reality, they change into very short-lived atoms of unusual density. In the early stages of creation, the transmogrified entities are relatively harmless to us, but when deterioration begins to occur, they throw off electrons and radiation that can harm humans and animals in the same way that flying saucers harm us.[1059]

Keel contended that the presence of a being of the superspectrum within our space-time continuum was ephemeral in nature as the transmogrification of energies that allowed its entrance to our world inevitably faded away.

> Some of our funny monsters remain in an area for several days and are seen by many people before they finally disappear. Token attacks on domestic animals occur throughout the period,

> because the monster is somehow replenishing its diminishing energies with earthly animal matter. But it is a losing battle, and the monster must ultimately melt away leaving nothing but a terrible stench behind.[1060]

Keel believed that some Forteana failed to receive appropriate media coverage because the police and other officials asked reporters not to print or publicize such stories. Keel encouraged would-be investigators to remain aware of rumors or stories and to be prepared to investigate them. Such intrepidness would unfailingly turn up events and stories that had been ignored by the media. "All of us must learn," wrote Keel, "to track down such stories to their original sources before we can hope to trail a wandering Bigfoot or wave our Geiger counters around an alleged UFO landing site."[1061]

> A Sasquatch could conceivably stroll through Times Square, overturn a taxi, stomp a policeman into the pavement and fly off in a disc-shaped object without ever receiving notice in the New York press. If, however, our hairy friend should carry a picket sign and give a fiery political speech he might manage to make the six o'clock news.[1062]

Keel believed that any scientists coming into a field of paranormal field of study would have to begin from square one, given the dearth of scientific attention the subject engendered.

> New scientists lured into Ufology will have to start from scratch since even at this late date very little scientific data has been published on the subject. They will have to go through all the bewilderment and theorizing of the newcomers to the amateur scene.[1063]

Byrne, Baumann, and More

The Search for Bigfoot by Peter Byrne had its hardcover release through Acropolis Books in 1975. The paperback from Pocket Books was released in 1976. "I also sat down and in twenty-eight days, wrote a sixty-thousand-word book, *The Search for Bigfoot*," Byrne wrote in his 2017 autobiography, *A Fortunate Life*. "It did well, selling, in six months, ten thousand copies in hardback and over the following year probably 250,000 in paperback."[1064]

The Search for
BIG FOOT
Monster, Myth or Man?
Startling new evidence that a gigantic—
but extremely shy—primate unknown to science
still lives in the Pacific Northwest!
by Peter Byrne
A Founder, International Wildlife Conservation Society
Foreword by Robert Rines
President, Academy of Applied Science
80442 • $1.75

Byrne, known for preferring the term *Omah* in the '70s, went with the more commercial "Bigfoot" for his book's title.

> The historical and updated accounts of the exciting search for the Bigfoot or Sasquatch that Peter Byrne here provides in his own inimitable and refreshing writing style, should delight the reader, and bring to the Byrne camp an ever-increasing army of well-wishers and believers, so necessary for the lonely pioneer who must defy convention and the mainly unimaginative and usually self-appointed custodians of our current scientific "knowledge."
>
> Robert H. Rines, President
> The Academy of Applied Science
> Boston, Massachusetts[1065]

In *The Search for Bigfoot*, Byrne explored the historical context for hairy hominids including Leif Erickson's encounter with creatures described as "horribly ugly, hairy, swarthy and with great black eyes," Northwest Fur and Trading Company agent David Thompson's diary entry describing his discovery of large human-like tracks in 1810, and the tale of Muchalat Harry, a native Nuu-chah-nulth (Nootka) who claimed (in a story with some similarities to Ostman's claim) to have been kidnapped and temporarily held by a group of Bigfoot.

Byrne also discussed the Patterson-Gimlin film and included reports on that film's analysis from Dr. Don Grieve, Dr. Dmitri Bayanov, Dr. Igor Bourtsev, and Dr. Dmitri Donskoy.

> I am inclined to give the 1967 footage a 95% chance of being genuine and the subject of the footage a 95% chance of being a real living creature. I base this belief on my own examination of the evidence that the footage supplies, of the footage itself, which I have viewed probably a hundred times, and of the site. I am inclined to disregard statements such as "nothing walks like that, therefore it is a fake," in spite of their learned scientific origin.[1066]

Two appendices in *The Search for Bigfoot* reprint Ivan Sanderson's "Preliminary Description of the External Morphology of What Appeared to be the Fresh Corpse of a Hitherto Unknown Form of Living Hominid," describing Sanderson's observations of the Ice Man, and the Sasquatch section from the U.S. Army Corps of Engineers' *Washington Environmental Atlas*.

The Corps of Engineers, an unexpected source for taking Bigfoot seriously, listed the Sasquatch in a section of their *Washington Environmental Atlas* called "Some Important Wildlife of Washington." The atlas, intended for use by civic planners, developers, and the interested public, included treatments on Washington wildlife and their habitats and lists more than 5,000 Washington features of environmental significance including native plants, archaeological sites, geological features of public interest, rivers, and lakes. The atlas is an over-sized publication with large, nearly two-by-three-foot folio pages. Copies were originally available for order priced at $48 and the Corps of Engineers furnished copies to state libraries.

The atlas was part of a national program to "support the environmental information needs of planners at all governmental levels," according to a Corps spokesman. Along with Washington, other states in the pilot environmental atlas program included Vermont, and North and South Carolina.[1067]

Jean McManus, editor of the atlas, said Bigfoot was included because "there is so much overwhelming evidence that points to such a creature." The *Washington Environmental Atlas* describes Bigfoot as an ape-like creature, eight to twelve feet in height and capable of reaching a weight of 1,000 pounds. "The details about the creature were gathered from many sources —anthropologists, writers and genuine Big Foot hunters," McManus said. "A great deal of time and effort has gone into hunting this creature, and it seemed only right to include it in the book."[1068] A map accompanying the text showed locations of track reports and Bigfoot sightings across Washington state.

Hiking the Bigfoot Country is a guide to exploring the hinterlands of northern California and southern Oregon. "The man-ape Bigfoot is not the exclusive property of the Klamath region," notes author John Hart. Hart focuses on those areas considered in most danger of being lost forever. "The trails are chosen to acquaint you with places which, five or 10 years from now, will not necessarily be there to be enjoyed." Hart describes 700 miles of trails in precise step-by-step detail: "Pass a big mossy boulder. Cross a fallen log. Then the trace becomes more obvious." Topographic maps marked with the described routes complement this Audubon Society guidebook.[1069]

IT EXISTS!
Startling eyewitness accounts of America's mystery man...or animal!
BIGFOOT
AMERICA'S ABOMINABLE SNOWMAN
DELL • 90555 • 1.25
BY ELWOOD D. BAUMANN

Elwood D. Baumann was a prolific writer for young readers in the '70s. Among his books' subjects were vampires, the Loch Ness Monster, the Devil's Triangle, and extraterrestrials' involvement on Earth (*They Came From Space* (1977)). Baumann's *Bigfoot* recounts the Jerry Crew track discovery and the subsequent publicizing of that news by Andrew Genzoli. Canonical and significant Bigfoot stories are given due treatment including the Ostman kidnapping, Roosevelt's Bauman tale, the attack on miners at Ape Canyon, Roe's detailed sighting, the Jacko tale of a captured juvenile Bigfoot, as well as George Haas' *Bigfoot Bulletin* and the story of the Patterson-Gimlin film. Bringing the subject into the '70s, Baumann includes several contemporaneous encounters, notably the 1973 story of the Murphysboro Mud Monster. *The Legend of Boggy Creek* movie is mentioned, though Baumann refers to the film as "The Legend of Foggy Bottom."[1070]

Mid-decade marks the approximate transition point when Bigfoot articles in UFO-related mags (*Canadian UFO Report*, *UFO Report*, etc.) outnumbered those written for and appearing in what Byrne referred to as the "glossier magazines,"[1071]—hardscrabble, gritty Men's interest magazines like *Male*, *Argosy*, and *Saga*. The more lascivious of the lot like *Male* and *Man's World* had all but vanished from the stands; *Argosy* and *True*, whose Bigfoot articles from the previous decade helped promulgate and instigate broad attention for the subject, would not survive to the '80s.

Peter Guttilla

Peter Guttilla wrote on Bigfoot and UFO connections in the Antelope Valley, an arable desert 45 miles northeast of the Santa Clarita Valley in southern California. Antelope Valley is bordered by the Sierra Nevada on the north, the Tehachapis on the west, and the Sierra Paloma Mountains to the south. The area was dotted by a few isolated farms and cattle ranches and was plagued with reports of UFOs and Bigfoot during the 1970s. At times enormous tracks were found resembling large, human-like prints; but there were other tracks that showed three toes, evocative of a large bird. Another variety of track was cloven-shaped, "circular tracks of huge, heavy four-legged animals."[1072]

Guttilla wrote in *UFO Report* that while leaving Pearblossom on the night of January 5, 1975, three truck drivers watched an "orange-colored, globe-shaped light streak through the sky," which appeared to land near Lake Los Angeles. Two weeks later three children heard heavy footfalls and growling noises while they were playing on a hill overlooking the eponymous, shallow lake. An adult heard the children's story and went to the location where large five-toed "Bigfoot tracks" were found pressed into the soil.[1073]

> Throughout the years 1971 to 1975, rural areas of southern California experienced an unprecedented wave of UFO and Bigfoot sightings. However in the spring of 1968, 150 miles south of Antelope Valley in California's desolate Anza Borrego Desert, prospectors Ed Sampson and Bill Johnson claim to have had a positively ghoulish experience.
>
> While sleeping one night near their dwindling campfire, the two men were jolted awake by an incredible explosion. Suddenly, the sky was filled with a red light that slowly faded. To the west, a series of brilliant flashes erupted from somewhere in the valley below.
>
> During an interview in 1973, Ed Sampson explained that he and his partner scurried out of their camp and climbed a few hundred feet to the crest of a hill. In utter amazement they watched "a red, circular flying saucer" hover silently while several entities with "glowing red eyes" moved in single file near the ridge of an adjacent canyon. Sampson explained that the sound of a "bell, like a church bell" rang out intermittently and the clanking of "heavy machinery" could be heard. The two prospectors beat a hasty retreat when they spotted "two of the things standing right behind us, they just stood there, looking at us with those glowing eyes . . ."
>
> Sampson said he and his partner fled the scene in panic. They did not return for their gear, and both vowed to say nothing to authorities for fear of being called "crazy."[1074]

Oliver

Two members of the Society for the Investigation of the Unexplained (SITU), Robert Jones and Jim McGrath, spent five hours in Tuxedo, New York, as guests of Frank Burger and his ape, Oliver. When not hunting animal specimens or guiding game hunters in South Africa, Burger performed with his dog and chimpanzee "animal acts" on the U.S. circuit. Jones' article in the October 1975 *Pursuit* stated Oliver was part of the chimpanzee act, but Burger was aware Oliver possessed several unusual characteristics, most notorious of which were his odd physical appearance and precocious behavior.

> Oliver is an ape, and in a general way he resembles a chimpanzee. But when he is placed next to a chimpanzee the differences are immediately obvious. To begin with, Oliver is said to be a biped. According to Berger, [sic] in the seven years of Oliver's life he has never "gone on all fours." Whether one can credit this statement fully is one thing, but I can testify that during our limited observation Oliver remained upright. There are pads on his knuckles for the "normal" quadruped mode of walking, but the pads appear to be unused.
>
> The physical appearance of Oliver is quite unusual. He does not have pronounced buttocks as do humans. There is an extreme lack of hair on the top of his head and very little hair on his chest, a condition that makes him susceptible to sunburn. His lower face does not have the typical roundness found in chimpanzees. Instead, it is squared off both in the area of the chin and along the jaw line. The eyes and the ears are also not chimp-like, but here the differences are more subtle. And finally, his head is slightly domed, with the top of the skull having an egg shape.[1075]

What impressed Jones and McGrath most, however, was Oliver's evinced intelligence. The SITU team listened as Burger described Oliver as two-to-three times smarter than a fully developed chimpanzee. Burger stated Oliver was toilet trained and could operate a coin-fed, can-dispensing soda machine. Jones and McGrath felt Oliver was very comfortable interacting with humans. Burger informed them that Oliver was slated for a series of tests at a university in New York (unnamed in Jones' article) in order to determine why Oliver was so advanced.

> The question boils down to this: is Oliver a new species of ape? Could he be a cross between two different types of ape? The specialists at the university who will be testing Oliver have suggested tentatively that he might be a mongoloid chimpanzee. This hypothesis seems difficult to accept in view of his very high intelligence. We tend to favor the crossbreed concept, though this too presents considerable difficulties, and we would suggest that he might be a cross between a chimpanzee and a Sehite (or Agogwe), the pygmy ABSM reported for many years in Central Africa.[1076]

It is possible that Jones and McGrath's article is what caught the attention of a Manhattan appellate lawyer named Michael Miller. Miller became fascinated with the idea of meeting Oliver and tracked the Burgers down to their New Jersey home and straightaway asked if he could meet Oliver face-to-face. The Burgers hosted Miller to dinner in December 1975. After their meal, Burger led Miller into a barn and shortly brought out Oliver on a tether. Oliver cocked his eye when inspecting Miller up close and finally reached out to shake the lawyer's hand. "It was a transforming experience," Miller said in an interview for a 2003 article. "I thought I was seeing the missing link. I was seeing *Australopithecus*. And I felt a terrible sense that if this creature was so important to science, he shouldn't be with a carnival guy."[1077]

What's in a Name

In his article, "Notes from a Member" published in *Pursuit,* Ron Marsh inquired into the term *Bigfoot* and explored its linguistic usage.

> What is a Bigfoot when it brings a friend?
>
> Are there two Bigfeet standing there? Or does a group of Bigfoots walk across your lawn?
>
> In question is that least consequential aspect of science, but the one where tempers wear thinnest: nomenclature. *Bigfoot News* (Dec. 1974, p. 3) tells about "three Bigfeet." Well, I prefer "Bigfoots," emphasizing that it is creatures and not a variety of foot I describe. English puts –s at the end of a noun to show plural, except for irregular words. Foot is such a case; Bigfoot is not. If a hyphen separated Big and foot, only then, it seems to me, could the word be pluralized by changing foot to feet.
>
> Anyway, why isn't it called "a Bigfeet" instead of "a Bigfoot?" Both feet are big, right? For, tho we know it has two feet and always did, we still use this singular of the twin body parts noticed, which is consistent: waxwing, redwing, pronghorn, bluegill.
>
> The word is a unit, plainly enuf: not a big nor a foot, but a BIGFOOT. Two Bigfoots. Twelve Bigfoots. I never have discussed more than one Sabertooth at a time, but Saberteeth sounds more of dentistry than animal science.
>
> The indigenous names were here first, and I favor them, in particular, the pneumatic "Oh-Mah," with a sound like a

> drawn breath. I suggest that the first Bigfoot that is examined by science should be called Omar (Oh-Mah), respecting the Indians, to whom he was not a beast, but another man.[1078]

Bigfoot in New Jersey: Jersey Devil Kin to Bigfoot?

New Jersey was the most densely populated state in 1970. But despite the density of people, there remains a wild side to the Garden State: a 2,000 square-mile area of virtually uninhabited wilderness called the Pine Barrens. This was the home of the Jersey Devil. Writing in the July edition of *Pursuit*, Robert Jones referred to the many facets of the legend as a "jungle of fantasies," noting that disparate Jersey Devil descriptions contained wide variations in the creature's size and abilities. The flying variant of the Jersey Devil resembled a so-called Thunderbird and another commonly-described terrestrial species sounded quite like Bigfoot. Jones summed up several of these latter reports in *Pursuit* as regularly describing a "6-8 foot, hairy, man-like biped with a forlorn cry or bellow."[1079]

Jones wrote of a Sussex County, New Jersey, resident who had, on two separate occasions within an area known as Bear Swamp, witnessed a large, hair-covered creature cross the road in front of his car. The sighting came out in a local newspaper in February 1975 and was followed by an additional story of another Sussex County resident who claimed to have shared a similar experience. Jones, intrigued by the possibility of Bigfoot in northwestern New Jersey, some 60 miles from New York City, decided in late February to look into the stories.

Jones contacted the two witnesses, which led him to interview a total of 18 people during three months of investigation. Their descriptions of what they'd seen formed a composite description; it seemingly couldn't be anything "other than our old elusive friend, Bigfoot!"

> Nor does this appear to be a new phenomenon in Sussex County. A little diligence in following up clues has led to the discovery of a report of a sighting here approximately 60 years ago, and other sightings have been uncovered from every decade since the late nineteen-forties. Other older sightings have been brought to my attention, but because I have not yet been able to interview the witnesses or document these in any other way, I am not including them in this discussion. In any event, ten of the accounts have described an animal crossing a road. In the remainder of the sightings the animal

> has been seen in a variety of circumstances, for example, by hunters in the woods, by a game warden on patrol, by rangers at a campsite, and by boys playing in the woods. Most of the sightings have occurred at night or at dawn or dusk. However, five witnesses, in three separate cases, have reported sighting the animal during the day time.
>
> One outstanding aspect of the accounts so far has been the consistency of the descriptions of the animal. It is by all accounts the typical Bigfoot, and the descriptions of size, shape, face, color of eyes, and so forth are virtually alike. One remarkable aspect of these descriptions is the color of the animal's hair or fur. About one third of the witnesses spoke of the "greyish" hue of the fur. As one witness put it, this was "sort of grey and brown fur mixed together." This is not unique in the North American Bigfoot reports, but it is rather rare.[1080]

Jones' research uncovered an encounter (undated in his article) involving a game warden who one day took a friend along with him on his rounds. The warden heard "a loud ruckus" emanating from a nearby swampy area and climbing to a higher spot overlooking the swamp, the men took in a startling sight. Below them, about 50 yards away, was "a huge, hairy, ape-like yet man-like creature standing in about three feet of water. The animal was apparently occupied in a serious dispute with a large snarling mongrel dog." By the warden's estimation, the two men watched this standoff for about half an hour. It appeared the creature and the dog were fighting over something—the dog would never get too close during the melee and the creature would roar and occasionally pound its fists against a tree stump. The men's amazement eventually changed to fear and they decided to leave and report the creature to a State Trooper office about six miles away. As the men returned with armed troopers they spotted the same dog running off but didn't find any sign of the creature. A search of the swampy area produced a freshly killed deer with its chest ripped open. The State Troopers' conclusion, Jones wrote, was the game warden and his friend had witnessed a life-or-death fight between a deer and a wild dog. Jones dismissed this conclusion outright, asserting a game warden was perfectly qualified to identify a deer, observed for half an hour, at only 50 yards distance.

> Is the Bigfoot living in Northern New Jersey? I have yet to see one, and the evidence in favor of its existence here is

> nearly all in the form of personal accounts by eye witnesses. Nevertheless, most of these witnesses seem to be competent and reliable people, with nothing to gain and perhaps much to lose (their reputations) by telling of their encounters with the creature. The area in which these many reports originate is really quite wild, dotted with lakes, mountainous, heavily forested and thinly populated. There is abundant wild life, and it is conceivable that a small group of Bigfoot-type animals could survive there undetected. Undetected, that is, in the wider sense of the term. In my three month investigation I have uncovered a wealth of fascinating evidence, and few if any "natives" of the area in question have any conception of the extent to which the animal has been seen there. This fact underscores the need for painstaking, long range study of this and similar phenomena. Naturally, my investigation has been carried out in a very quiet, publicity-shy manner. Names and locations have been kept in the strictest confidence. Only when witnesses know that they can tell their stories without incurring ridicule at the hands of newspaper writers or neighbors will they come forward with the vital details.[1081]

By the time Jones wrote again of Bigfoot's presence in The Garden State for a short *Pursuit* article in the October 1975 issue, he had collected 28 eye-witness reports occurring in northwestern New Jersey alone. His October article revealed Jones was then in the midst of organizing a field investigation to go beyond the collection of people's Bigfoot encounters to explore first-hand Bigfoot's possible manifestation in New Jersey. Jones viewed the study of regional topography and geographic data as necessary to inform vigorous field research. The planned makeup of field teams was based upon SITU members' indication of interest on their Membership Participation Questionnaires to participate in such activity. The SITU Board of Governors approved the expedition and allocated funds to purchase needed gear.[1082]

Magical, Mystical, Mythical Sasquatch

Scientists Not Interested

Vancouver journalist Clive Cocking penned an article titled "The Magical, Mystical, Mythical Sasquatch" in which he sought and collected several scientists' viewpoints on Bigfoot. Cocking discussed the subject with Dr. Ken Burridge of the University of British Columbia (UBC) anthropology department, as the professor "reluctantly" gave him ten minutes. "Most scientists wouldn't give you the time that I'm giving you, they'd just say that Sasquatches don't exist and they'd put down the receiver," Burridge said. "Ninety-nine percent of scientists say it doesn't exist, they believe it's an evolutionary impossibility and therefore won't be caught discussing it."[1083] Audrey Hawthorn, a curator at the UBC's anthropology museum, considered Bigfoot a non-starter from the get go. "The Sasquatch is just not a matter of interest to anthropologists," she said. "Nobody believes in it, so they're not interested in it."[1084] Dr. Wayne Suttles, professor of cultural anthropology at Portland State College in Oregon, suggested misidentification or misinterpretation could explain sightings of Bigfoot. "There have been far more sightings of the animal than footprints, which is the reverse of bears—you find more tracks than you see bears and this is true of other animals," he said. "This, I think, means many of these sightings are illusions, imagined—people are deceiving themselves."[1085]

On the other hand, Cocking recorded quick impressions from scientists ensconced in the camp supporting, or at least not entirely dismissing, the Patterson-Gimlin film. Dr. Dmitri Donskoy, chief of the chair of biomechanics at the USSR Central Institute of Physical Culture in Moscow, had told René Dahinden the film subject did not walk like a man. Dr. Don Grieve at the London's Royal Free Hospital, analyzed the creature's movements on the film and said its authenticity depended on the speed at which the film was shot: if 16 frames per second, then the creature's walk was inhuman, but at 24 frames per second, the subject walked like a man. (Cocking mistakenly switches the conclusions derived from consideration of the film's speed.) "If it is a fake," Dr. Grieve added, "it is an extremely clever fake."

Serious consideration and analysis of the Patterson-Gimlin film and other Bigfoot evidence suffered from hoaxes—including, Cocking wrote, several hoaxed films by Ivan Marx. But Cocking concluded there were too many sightings for them all to be hoaxes. He reiterated analysis conducted by Grover Krantz on Bigfoot tracks: the stride lengths often surpassed what a person could do, imprint depth (sometimes up to three inches) could only be made by great weight, many tracks demonstrated independent toe movement, and Bigfoot's inferred biomechanical foot was perfectly adapted for a creature weighing over 500 pounds.

Both Krantz and John Napier thought the cripple footprints at Bossburg would require a "super genius" to conceive and fake. "It is very difficult,"

Napier wrote in *Bigfoot*, "to conceive of a hoaxer so subtle, so knowledgeable—and so sick—who would deliberately fake a footprint of this nature." Cocking quoted the British primatologist from his book: "I am convinced that the Sasquatch exists, but whether it is all that it is cracked up to be is another matter altogether. There [is] something in northwest America that needs explaining, and that something leaves manlike footprints. The evidence I have adduced in favor of the reality of the Sasquatch is not hard evidence; few physicists, biologists or chemists would accept it, but nevertheless it is evidence and cannot be ignored."

René Dahinden

After meeting with the venerable Bigfoot hunter, Cocking wrote that Dahinden's eyes lacked a "wild glint of fanaticism." Cocking soon learned, as he and Dahinden sat in the lounge of the Vancouver Gun Club, that talk of scientists' generally dismissive attitudes toward Bigfoot provoked a strong reaction from Dahinden. "Those clodhoppers!" he blurted out to Cocking. "Science is the pursuit of the unknown. Now, maybe the scientists think there's nothing unknown, since they know it all, and therefore they don't have to pursue it. I don't know, it looks like the scientists get up every morning and pray, 'Please, God, let me go through another day without a new thought.'" Dahinden showed Cocking the 24 feet of 16 mm shot by Patterson. After Dahinden doused the lights the "sandy-orange-green" blur of Bluff Creek flickered to life followed by the shaky image of the ambling creature.

> It's obviously phony—just a man in an ape-suit, is my immediate gut reaction. But then Dahinden puts it through another sequence in slow motion, with blow-ups and stop-frames, explaining what Hollywood experts had said of how difficult it would be to fake and what biomechanics experts in Britain, Sweden, Switzerland and Russia pointed out about the creature's walk, when he (fed up with North American scientists' indifference) brought it to them for analysis in 1971. When it was all over, the film didn't seem so easy to reject out of hand: it remains an intriguing question mark.[1086]

It was from a "sense of adventure" Dahinden said, that in 1955, and only a couple of years after his arrival in Canada, he began his pursuit of Bigfoot. "I thought at that time I could just go out there and grab him by the rear end and bring him home to mother. And here I am, 20 years later, still holding out my hand to grab something that may or may not exist. But it's just so bloody fascinating." Dahinden who referred to himself as a "Sasquatch investigator," lived rent-free at the Vancouver Gun Club collecting and then reselling shot back to the club and earning about $4,000 to support himself and his research. Dahinden's field kit included binoculars, movie camera, two 35mm cameras and a rifle. At the time, Dahinden told Cocking he favored Pitt Lake, a rugged and mountainous area northeast of Vancouver as a promising locale for Bigfoot hunting. "You tend to try everything. You don't really know what will work." Dahinden's summer plans for 1975 included sailing up the coast to search around Bella Coola, about 250 miles north of Vancouver.

Investigating with John Green

> It was eight o'clock on a sunny Sunday morning and my head was still foggy with sleep when I stumbled to the phone.
>
> "How would you like to do a little Sasquatch hunting today?" the voice asked.
>
> "What?"
>
> "I've just had a report of three people seeing something big troubling some cows in a pasture near Bellingham." It was John Green calling from his home in Harrison Hot Springs; I had interviewed him two days earlier. "It looks pretty reliable, there are three witnesses—I'm going down now to check it out."
>
> It was with a mixture of curiosity and skepticism that I headed down the freeway to Bellingham, about 50 miles south in Washington, where I met the group at the home of a local Sasquatch buff. Green, a tall, bony, quiet-spoken man, asked questions from a special form. Jim Watts, 48, a millworker, said he had picked up his son, Jim Watts, Jr., 19, and Mark Engels, 21, from a farm where they were working and was driving them home along the Mount Baker highway late Wednesday afternoon of that week, when Engels suddenly got excited about something big and hairy he saw in a pasture 200 yards off the road.
>
> Engels: "The cows were just going dingy. They were all jumping around, twisting their heads and staring at something

over on the other side of the fence. That's when I just saw it standing there still."

Watts Sr.: "The first time we went by Mark saw it, then I came back on the other side and I saw it on the way. Then we made the third pass going back and I parked on the right-hand side of the road and at that time we saw the majority of it."

Watts Jr.: "It just towered above the cows quite a ways. He seemed kind of heavy-set in the shoulders and in the stomach and lower hips. It was just like a black blob."

Engels: "You could see shoes on a guy from that distance, but there was none. It was all one black object. So I figured it's no guy. It was just standing there at first, then it walked away to the next bunch of woods, a casual, slouchy walk like it owned the land."

We checked out the fields but there were no signs; it had rained since and the muddy sections were chewed up with cow tracks. But the three witnesses were convincing: they either saw what they said they saw, or they were consummate actors. "That was," said Green, "pretty much an average report. People swear they saw something—but there's no hard evidence."[1087]

It was clear that Green wanted to impart an especial point to Cocking concerning attitude and belief: "Let's get this business about belief straight," Green said. "The believers are the scientists, they're the ones who are clinging to a belief. The people who think that there are Sasquatches are the ones who are investigating, the ones who have become convinced on evidence. The scientists are the ones going on pure faith and don't actually know much about it and make darn sure they don't know anything about it."[1088]

Al Stump Interviews

Peter Byrne

When author and sportswriter Al Stump (known for writing Ty Cobb's biography) decided to interview Peter Byrne, he learned the Bigfoot investigator was camped at 8,000 feet in the "Kinskini River" area of western Canada. Stump finally found his man and after several lengthy conversations produced an indispensable exposition on Byrne printed in *True* magazine. Upon their first meeting, Byrne set down certain guidelines: "If you're open-minded on the matter of a live humanoid biped not in the science books, I'll talk to you. Otherwise, don't waste my time. I've been called crazy by so many so-called experts that my ass aches. I want no more of it."

"When you track the *Omah*, you accept a couple of conditions," Byrne told Stump. "One is that you go without women, because you're usually in the wild. The other is the weather. You're never warm. Where the *Omah* goes, it's colder than charity." Byrne said he had investigated sightings submitted by cattlemen, timbermen, trappers, hunters, roadbuilders, and fishermen. "More than 350 Sasquatch-*Omah*-Bigfoot sightings have been made," Byrne said (by way of comparison, this was well below the 1,000 sightings Green had on record at this time), "dating in North America from 1811." The International Wildlife Conservation Society of Washington, D.C., and the Academy of Applied Science were important sources of funding for Byrne. One day while at the Academy's Boston offices, Byrne was cornered by a visiting primatologist who couldn't wait to engage him: "You're wasting everyone's time on this fool's chase! Why don't you give up?" Byrne sized up the man for a simple retort: "For the same reason Captain von Beringe didn't give up," Byrne countered. "I presume you know who I mean?" Von Beringe had discovered the mountain gorilla in 1902—after shooting two specimens and donating them to Berlin's Natural History Museum.

By 1975, Byrne had put 125,000 miles on two International Scout vehicles, climbed countless cliffs, had withstood sub-freezing temperatures during isolated lookouts, and had used hounds, radios, and tranquilizers in his quest for Bigfoot. Byrne had even endured being shipwrecked and marooned on an islet in the British Columbian straits. This occurred in 1973 when Byrne set off alone in a small powerboat into the Queen Charlotte Straits westward of Vancouver Island. Byrne intended to explore his theory that Bigfoot are excellent swimmers by examining the shoreline for tracks and other signs. Byrne ended up running out of gas and was at the mercy of the currents for over twenty miles. After beaching on the islet his food lasted for three days; it took five days for a costal patrol launch to see smoke from his campfire and rescue him. The experience gave Byrne some perspective on food sources. "They claim the regional food is too scanty to support a big eater. But I never went hungry—I made a spear and caught flatfish and found a clam bed and some crabs. Oysters were plentiful, also berries. I could have stayed a month or two without suffering."

To continue their conversation with good food, Byrne took Stump to Spooky's, a local eatery. Stump took note of Byrne's garb: "padded jacket, wool cap and trail boots," attire Byrne habitually maintained while at headquarters in case a called-in Bigfoot "contact" demanded immediate investigation.

"Of course, very great subhumans *do* exist from a known boundary of Prince Rupert in British Columbia to the Humboldt County highlands of the California-Oregon border—just as they exist in the Himalayas. The Asian species is given the godawful name of the Abominable Snowman and joked about by idiots, scientists included. The proper name is the *Yeti*." Byrne, who had the distinction of having pursued hairy hominids on two continents, comfortably discussed aspects of hominid behavior and physical characteristics. "*Yetis* are smaller than *Omah-Bigfeet*, perhaps considerably so. Here in the U.S.-Canadian outback, they're probably 200 or more scattered in small families or colonies. They're cunning and mobile and very shy, which are among reasons why they've never been captured. They see man as a threat, but case evidence is that they're not belligerent. That is, they've never torn anyone's head off. But I wouldn't approach one without heavy net equipment or a tranquilizer gun. He could crush me easily."

Byrne proved optimistic when contemplating the inevitability of irrefutable proof furnished to a skeptical scientific establishment. "And when we do bring in an *Omah*—a stiff injection from a dart of Amytal or chloral hydrate should take care of that—we'll shake up some very big scientists as never before. Proof will change the shape of natural history. It'll open a new door to man's origins and evolution."[1089]

> On the way back to his operations center, Byrne offered to screen the Patterson footage for me in blown-up stop action. With a show of emotion, he said, "Know why I keep on with the hunt? It's such an incredible damned proposition. It's beyond belief and yet I know it's *out there*. Nothing could be more fascinating. It's something I've got to solve."
>
> Packed into his $20,000 operations trailer is enough gear to equip a small polar party—rope, freeze-dried food packs, axes, pitons, binoculars, raingear, radio, zoom cameras, NOD (Night Observation Device), rucksacks, fuel and what resemble single-barrel shotguns, but are tranquilizer-dart projectors. A photo of the celebrated Ishi is included.[1090]

Byrne regaled Stump with several Patterson-Gimlin film details that he found compelling, as well as an anecdote of the man behind the camera. "In the movie you see the *Omah's* leg muscles in play and—it's a female—

you see well-defined breasts. It should end all doubt, but as some philosopher stated, incredulity is the product of a constipated brain," Byrne said. "Notice the fingernail on the left hand . . . now see how the arm action is like a human's . . . notice the arms are hinged from the shoulders, not from the chest, as with bears." Byrne switched from film subject to film shooter. "Before Roger Patterson died of cancer in 1972," Byrne told Stump, "he told me he wished to God he'd shot and killed it, so the world would have believed him."[1091]

Grover Krantz

Byrne told Stump to visit Krantz. "Go talk to Dr. Grover Krantz at Washington State University. Krantz specializes in this field and knows the truth because he goes out personally and finds it." Stump took the advice and interviewed the over-six-feet-tall, 210-pound Krantz in the professor's Pullman office.

Stump asked Krantz if he was persuaded Bigfoot was an extant creature, walking through the hinterlands of the Pacific Northwest. "That's right," he readily replied. "I was highly skeptical for years, but now I'm reasonably certain the species is roaming about. There's too much credible information to ignore. Those in my field think I'm half-cracked . . . I'm known as a mammoth freak, second only to friend Byrne." Krantz went on to offer one of the biggest divides between his and Byrne's approach: "I disagree with Byrne. He feels we're dealing with an intelligence, a *homo sapien's* relative, and that to destroy one would be murder. He wants it drugged and incapacitated. I don't. I'd kill it without hesitation."

When Krantz conducted his own forays into the backcountry of the Snake River territory his Swedish-made .358 magnum was always at hand. Krantz argued that due to unknown aspects of Bigfoot physiology, a tranquilizer dart could leave it in agony. If a dart didn't render Bigfoot unconscious, it might cause aggressive behaviors, causing an overt menace to people. One dead body, Krantz said, would give scientists practically all the information they would need. "I may be wrong. Peter Byrne was widely known for his tiger and rhino safaris during his years in India. He understands big game and might be correct not shooting it. In Skamania County, Washington, they go along with him. In Skamania it's a $10,000 fine and five years in jail for manslaughter for killing it."

Krantz referenced Project Snowman from 1958, describing to Stump the search into the Russian Pamir peaks funded with $2 million in Soviet government funds and led by ethnologist Professor Boris F. Porshnev, a scientist who was convinced the Yeti was an extant species. The unfavorable attitudinal contrast Krantz educed between the U.S.S.R and United States governments was evident.

Getting to the essence of the phenomenon, Stump asked Krantz for his thoughts on exactly what was Bigfoot. "I've concluded it isn't human in any sense of the word," Krantz said. "No cultural apparatus has been found near it—spears, pottery, eating tools, for instance. So I have to say that it's a bipedal ape. Possibly a cross between anthropoid apes and successors of Neanderthal Man. A few scientists see a faintly possible connection with *Gigantopithecus*, who lived 500,000 years ago in Central China. His excavated jawbone classes him as an aberration or mutation. *Gigantopithecus* was larger than a gorilla and might have crossed the Asia-North America land bridge before or after the Ice Age." Stump asked how one could explain Bigfoot's durability through the ages. "We have no idea and that's what drives science up the wall. One can guess that it emerged from the Andean massif or Mato Grosso of South America at a much later period and moved north. Old Indians legends around here tell of tribes fighting with *Sasquatches*."[1092]

> Krantz is caretaker of a remarkable set of handprints,[1093] removed from eastern Washington mud in 1970. He says they're Bigfoot's. The largest measures 300mm in length and 185mm in width, or more than 12 inches by 8 inches, twice the span and half again as long as Krantz's large mitts, which are the size of George Foreman's. "The structural detail eliminates any chance they're fakes," the professor stressed. "I've also studied similar anatomically complete footprints of from 18 to 23 inches long, meaning Bigfoot could go over nine feet tall. A 1,000-pound weight is possible. Just imagine his power."
>
> Krantz said he was sorry he couldn't pour me a new drink on the market—the "Abominable Snowman," made with sloe gin.
>
> "Peter Byrne doesn't think the gags going around are funny," I said. "For a joke, one guy made a girl Bigfoot of plywood. She had 70-inch knockers and buttocks to match and he put her in the forest and called her the 'Adorable Woodswoman.'"
>
> Krantz chuckled, saying he could see where Byrne wouldn't fall down laughing. "He's obsessed with what he's doing. By

next summer he'll have given five years of his life to it. He goes without sleep and into some of the wildest places in the country. When someone comes up with the answer—if I don't do it—I hope it'll be Peter.

"But he'd better be careful. This thing could destroy him."[1094]

Back to Byrne

Byrne told Stump, "I haven't yet reached the age of myopia, this side of senility, and with an amount of luck, I'll bring in the creature. I'm betting he'll be the closest thing yet to man in thinking ability."[1095]

> At 4 P.M. on January 9, 1971, veteran road construction foreman [William] Taylor, of Pemberton, British Columbia, was driving a spare parts truck down a paved forest road. He slammed on the brakes and grabbed a shotgun he carried in case of grizzlies. Confronting Taylor was a brown-black monster—with a fish in its hand.
>
> Interrogation by Byrne follows:
>
> Q. Could you see the features?
>
> A. Enough to notice a small nose and large black eyes. The face had little hair.
>
> Q. How long was it visible?
>
> A. Fifteen seconds or so. It crossed 100 feet of road in a few jumps and went up a vertical bank no man could climb.
>
> Q. How about the hands?
>
> A. Very large hands—and in one of them it was carrying a fish. It looked like a small salmon or trout.
>
> Q. You have no doubt you experienced this?
>
> A. I'll know it happened as long as I live. I resent any other implications.
>
> Climbing 1,000 feet down from the road, Byrne reached the Checkamuth River, which was enjoying a steelhead run, and barehandedly caught fish snagged along the bank. Conclusion: Taylor—widely respected thereabouts—told the truth. His shotgun was poised and he may have come closer than anyone to slaying a Bigfoot.[1096]

Byrne told Stump he used the services of two trackers and one photographer, Nick Bielemeier. Byrne and his team made regular sweeps into suspected areas of Bigfoot activity and into specific locations of reported sightings; Byrne was known for keeping a lonely vigil for up to twelve hours in lookouts built on tabletops in the Cascades. These timberline lookout stations were sunken with an advantage of 360-degree viewing. Byrne did not leave food offerings, thought by some to be an enticement to bring a Bigfoot in. "We think the *Omah's* too smart for that," said Bielemeier. "From a lot of signs we think he has nocturnal vision."

Byrne felt technology, like ground sensors then used by the U.S. Forest Service to detect forest fires, offered an opportunity for Bigfoot research. Such sensors, Byrne reasoned, could be adapted to detect Bigfoot's body temperature and allow fixing its position so researchers could rush to the site and take photographs; Byrne hoped to add such sensors to his Bigfoot-hunting stores.

"This character is extremely shifty and lives in caves or undiscovered glacial pits, of which there are many thousands," Byrne told Stump. "He has reasoning power and can camouflage himself better than anything in the woods. For elusiveness, I rate him with the Giant Panda of the China-Tibet border. The great Pandas were suspected to exist and were hunted for nearly 100 years without result and not verified until 1937."[1097]

As researchers like Sanderson and Olson had done, Byrne created a police-like Ident-A-Kit composite of the creature. "Assembling what Cochran, Pittenger, Parry, Brown, Patterson, Taylor and more than 70 others tell us," Byrne explained, "we know it has a backward-sloping forehead rising to a conical top, a lipless mouth and no neck. The eyes were expressive. The ears are medium and the arms are manlike in length, not monkeylike. The torso is about as thick as it is wide. The fur grows bluish-grey with age. The sound the *Omah* makes has been described by many. It's a high-pitched, penetrating, whistling scream, unlike any native animal's."[1098]

On the subject of tracks, Byrne rejected hoaxing as a wholesale answer. "It would take a team of pranksters financially able to travel to hell and gone just to get to these places," Byrne told Stump while shaking his head at the implausibility of the thought. "And even if they went to that length, they couldn't duplicate the prints without an expert knowledge of anatomy. Not even a Hollywood special effects unit, working for months, could reach the unmapped places where tracks up to 22 inches have been found."[1099] Byrne likewise had little time for the explanation that Bigfoot tracks were prints left by smaller animals in snow which later expanded and distorted due to weathering. "It is preposterous to assume that one could follow a line of humanoid tracks with clear toe prints for seven miles, as I have done in Asia, and not find blurred or misshapen tracks." Byrne added that persuasive tracks left in other substrate, like mud or sand, could not have become enlarged by the sun's effects.[1100] "Yet those who think the *Omah* is a myth go on saying that our print evidence is manufactured."[1101]

Stump solicited the protocols established for bringing in a specimen for study. "That," Byrne replied, "I will not discuss." A source told Stump that Byrne would seek, in similarity with Olson's plans for a Bigfoot's capture and release, to confine the creature in a secure containment area, study and liberate it with an electronic device implanted to permit its tracking.[1102]

> Peter C. R. Byrne is a man trapped in a preternormal enigma. Sitting in one of his lookout pits in the snow-mountains, his thoughts turn to the dozens of people who swear by all they honor that they have looked upon the giant. He stares into the distance. The hell and the irony of it is that never—not once in nearly 60 months—has he personally heard the cry of Bigfoot or seen him.[1103]

More from Byrne

Los Angeles Times writer Jim Stingley interviewed Byrne in October. One of the things that first impressed Byrne when he arrived in the Pacific Northwest, he told Stingley, was the overall vastness of its size. "A case in point," he told the reporter, "is that since I came to the Pacific Northwest, no less than six airplanes have been lost in the tangled wilderness of the coast ranges. Now, massive searches involving many people, planes and much money have yet to result in one airplane find." The promising implication of such a vast expanse, large enough to consume airplanes, as the possible home range for giant, secretive creatures was obvious to Byrne. "And since it has been determined that the Big Feet do not wish to be found—and they inhabit the same area. . . ."[1104]

Stingley asked Byrne about the motivation and drive required for pursuing an enigma like Bigfoot. "It sounds fanciful, I know, but I'm very interested in communication with those who would bring a means of studying them, and, above all, providing protection for them. You'd be surprised at the number of people who run through the woods out there hoping to see

Big Foot, blow his head off, take it into town and sell it," Byrne said. "But, you see, once we establish he is there, once we get a sharp piece of film . . . then it would be very, very easy to get an executive order protecting them." Stingley surmised it would be difficult to enact and enforce wildlife legislation protecting Bigfoot. "Yes, I have thought about that a great deal, because I do believe that the Big Foot is a harmless, primitive man who should really be left alone," Byrne said. "But they do have that enormous area of protection. You could put 10,000 people in there tomorrow looking for a Big Foot and they won't find one. It's not as though every family is going to jump in their car and go out and interfere with the Big Foot."[1105]

Robert Morgan

Robert Morgan was interviewed in Miami, Florida, in January and again by telephone in April by Marty Wolf, whose article on the Bigfoot researcher appeared in the July 1975 issue of *Pursuit*. Morgan had sent two "scouting" teams to northern California, Washington, and Oregon in June and Morgan planned to follow with a full expedition in the summer of 1975 based upon feedback from these teams. Wolf described Morgan as "a dynamic person," and "an aware and sincere individual who wants the creature he is after to be accepted into the world of science without death." Along with the summer expedition Morgan was planning, *In Search of Bigfoot*, a Bostonia-produced film about Morgan's 1974 Bigfoot expedition was close to its release. Morgan also spoke about Bigfoot at schools and universities. "When I go and lecture to colleges and particularly to schools, I always preface everything with 'I didn't come here to convince you of anything; I merely came here to advise you of what we are doing with regard to a new type of research.' I don't try to convince them of anything, but I find it intriguing that the young kids are so fascinated by something that is in their realm," Morgan said, noting the enthusiasm prevalent in younger ages for a subject like Bigfoot. "These kids get interested in these things because they are overwhelmed by the books that are thrown at them, by the amount of knowledge that has already been accumulated. They sit there and they look around and they say 'This is overwhelming to me. I can't go to the moon. I'm Johnny Nobody. What am I going to do?' And here I'm saying to them this: There are things that are outside the textbooks. Be aware of what's around you."

Musing over the state of Bigfoot research, Morgan told Wolf, "as long as the profit motive is there, it's a cancer." But aside from commercialism or pursuit of personal gain, solving the mystery of Bigfoot had massive ramifications for all people, Morgan believed, and all related knowledge gained should be shared. "What I want to do is donate all scientific data to all nations throughout the world regardless of political affiliation. I feel that this is knowledge for Mankind; that includes all colors, races, creeds and political affiliation. Otherwise, let's stop the nonsense."

Morgan was adamantly opposed to killing a Bigfoot for scientific study: "I want this thing (Bigfoot) accepted into the world of science without death. This has never been done. Well, hell, that doesn't mean it can't be done, it means only that it hasn't been done." Wolf noted Morgan's affiliation with a scientific advisory board, reportedly comprised of seventeen members, several with doctorates, representing a breadth of complimentary disciplines. "I have found that there are very few serious investigators in the field. There are a lot of Bigfoot hunters, but very few researchers."

After years of experience dealing with people who had encounters or had evidence to offer, Morgan reached a quantified conclusion: "I've found that there is a formula in Bigfoot research: 40% of the people who come to see me are either alone and need some pats on the butt, or they need to have someone hold their hand, or they are crying out, 'Please, someone, recognize me.' Either that or they are doing it deliberately as a joke. Another 40% are actually mistaken. The remaining 20% consists of facts." Wolf followed up on this point by asking for some of the "facts" Morgan had alluded to and for reports then coming out of Florida.

> "On February 2, 1975, at two o'clock in the morning, a young man by the name of Richard Davis, of Cape Coral, Florida, responded to his dog acting up and what he thought was a recurrent visitation from an unseen prowler that had been upsetting his household for a period of about three weeks. He went outside by way of the garage and turned loose his German shepherd, a young aggressive female; she ran out of the house and around the corner into the spotlights, and in a few moments turned around and ran back. Her eyes were wide and her mouth was open. She was not barking, but she ran past Mr. Davis and into the garage and under the car. It is my understanding that there has been an altering of the dog's character and demeanor since that time.
>
> "Mr. Davis, who had a .22 caliber pistol in his hand, walked outside and saw a creature move. He said it was very tall, perhaps nine feet tall, had graying to brown hair, a flat

profiled face with no distinguishable chinline, [sic] and did not have a snout-like nose. He said it looked like something that had been hit in the face with a frying pan.

"It was about fifteen feet from Mr. Davis. As it took a step toward him, Davis fired one shot into the chest and he saw the bullet hit just above the paunch. The creature grunted, turned and ran away.

"Now, for your information, something rather intriguing came out in the interview: Davis said that after firing the first shot, his intention was to fire the entire cylinder of the revolver. He could not fire the second shot. And he does not know why . . ."[1106]

Upon questioning from Wolf, Morgan clarified Mr. Davis' inability to fire his weapon again.

"He could not mentally pull the trigger again, and he finds this almost unexplainable. He does not understand why he was not able to shoot a second time.

"Now this gentleman lives on an outskirts of the town of Cape Coral. There are canals on two sides of the house which is in a rather isolated area. There are trees within a mile or so of the area and there are also truck farms. It is an area that would be easily accessible for a creature that can move quickly at night. Also, within five to eight miles of that area, to the north of it, is a very wild area in which there are bears.

"Mr. Davis, after firing the shot, went back into the house and called his father and then called the police. He then went back outside, where he could hear the creature thrashing around in the weeds quite some distance away, and then he heard a distant splash. The police came but were extremely skeptical and were very, shall we say, slow to respond. There was hair retrieved from the eaves of that house and it is under analysis in Portland, Oregon, and we do have a drawing of the creature made by Mr. Davis.

"Now within a half mile of Mr. Davis' house was the home of John and Betty Michalowski. Mr. and Mrs. Michalowski, in my interview with them, indicated to me that they had had, over a three week period, a problem of very odd or terrible smells near their home. This would only occur between nine and eleven at night, and it would come from one side of the house only. And about fifteen minutes later it would go away.

"Now going back for a minute to Mr. Davis. There were smudemarks [sic] of a large footprint on his air conditioning unit, which is an exterior central air conditioning type unit. Mr. and Mrs. Michalowski had whorl-type white fingerprints on the top of their air conditioning unit, and that unit is on the same side of the house where they had smelled the strange odors, which leads us to wonder what the attraction was to these air conditioners.

"There are truck farms nearby, and I spoke with a gentleman who told me that it is rather common for them to have the edges of their truck farms torn up. They assume it is done by animals."[1107]

Richard Davis' encounter attained a measure of local publicity and the *Fort Myers News-Press* Outdoor Editor, Bill Miller, offered his advice for firearm choice should Davis find himself staring down a Skunk Ape in the future.

> Right here and now I want to laud the bravery of the young man who stood face-to-face with that awesome critter and plunked a little .22 pellet somewhat above its navel—assuming it has a navel of course. Ordinary men have been known to advance and strangle an opponent after having been shot as many as five times with a small bore handgun.
>
> Being a somewhat semi-expert in sporting arms, I would recommend the guy obtain either a double-barreled, full choke shotgun loaded with double ought (00) buckshot, or perhaps a .338 Winchester Magnum with a 300-grain bullet, just in case the Skunk Ape makes a return call.[1108]

Morgan also related the details from a March collision between a car and a hairy hominid.

> "Another report that came in is this one: on the sixth of March, 1975, in Martin County, Florida, near Lake Okeechobee, a man by the name of Steve Humphreys and his wife were traveling

> in their car. At about 11:20 P.M., as they approached a small bridge, a large hairy creature that they could not identify came out from beside the stream next to the bridge; they swerved into the other lane of the road to avoid it, but the creature was traveling rather fast, and they collided.
>
> "The aerial of the car was torn off, the front fender damaged, and the door on the passenger's side was dented to the extent that it could not be opened. Mr. Humphreys came to a stop and backed up, thinking that he had hit a cow or horse. There was nothing in the highway. The one unusual part of the story is that he did find, when he opened the car door, that his two dogs would not leave the car and they acted very, very oddly. Hair was obtained from the front fender, and again, was sent off for analysis. I went up to the area and spent some time there, studying the point of impact, etc. I did find fresh hominid feces, although not of a very large size, and there were human footprints in the area; I don't really know what happened there, but we should know more when we get the analysis of the hair. The incident was reported to the Fort Pierce station of the Highway Patrol."[1109]

As a locally known Bigfoot authority, if not outright celebrity, Morgan was prevailed upon to deliver authoritative pronouncements on sightings and validity of evidence.

> "Then again we had another report, and I examined a cast that appeared to be authentic, taken by teachers at the Redland Elementary School in Homestead and Rangers of the Everglades National Park, of tracks of a barefooted, large hominid creature that had come out into a truck farming area, tracked around, and torn up plants. They did make casts of these tracks, and the tracks do appear to be Bigfoot. The tracks came out of the Everglades National Park and went back into it."[1110]

The weight of evidence left Morgan to consider Bigfoot as an extant hominid, perhaps a giant ape. "I think the supporting evidence is very much swinging in behalf of Bigfoot. What we're dealing with is not an animal at all. I think this creature is *Gigantopithecus*, perhaps. Perhaps. He certainly fits the physical structure," Morgan told Wolf. "I had made an earlier speculation (which was endorsed by Dr. Carleton S. Coon) that these creatures may also be an earlier or previously unclassified form of *Homo Erectus*. Something very interesting on *Homo Erectus*: supposedly *Homo Erectus* died about five hundred thousand years ago, and yet we've discovered (and this was published three years ago in *Nature Magazine*) in Australia, that *Homo Erectus* had been alive and well, walking around in the swamps of Australia, as little as ten thousand years ago. This tells me that there are big holes in our knowledge of anthropology. Now when some kids can pick up a textbook and read there that *Homo Erectus* lived 'X' amount of years ago to five hundred thousand years ago, he's going to take it as fact, and dammit, this is a dynamic science, it's a science that's learning, that's moving! I think all of these statements must be prefaced with 'to-the-best-of-our-knowledge.'" Morgan also had something to say about people in general, their acceptance of new ideas, and their unwillingness to entertain the incredible. "My hypothesis is very simple: if *Homo Erectus* lived as little as ten thousand years ago, why not *Gigantopithecus?* There is no reason why not. Except that we don't know it! And our damned egos keep getting in the way. And I swear, the more I learn about science the more I learn about the layman in general. I don't care what their color or what their creed is, they get up in the morning with the same essential prayer: God, Budha, Allah—Whoever, please let me get through this new day without a single new thought!"[1111] Interestingly, this is nearly the same statement that Dahinden had spoken to Clive Cocking.

Michael Polesnek

Michael Polesnek of Anchorage (listed as vice president of the American Anthropological Research Foundation in Miami) talked to a reporter about plans for his next expedition. "This is a scientific study," Polesnek said. "We're very level-headed and don't make fun of anyone who thinks he's seen it." Polesnek was back home in Anchorage following 1975's 10-person expedition to Mt. St. Helens which, Polesnek stated, produced interesting results. "We found hair samples and footprints," he said, adding, "but lost him when the hunting season opened."[1112] Polesnek said the hair samples were analyzed by scientists at the Oregon Regional Primate Center and found to be "close to human but not human," and were not determined to be from any known primate species.

> Polesnek said during his six months in Alaska he will search libraries and other research centers to determine locations most likely to nurture the Yeti. He also plans interviews of hunters and others who may have seen the creature, he said. . . .
>
> "When you get involved with this, it becomes an obsession," Polesnek said. "He's been sighted hundreds of times and if he's here on earth you're going to find him."[1113]

Speck Films Bigfoot

Joseph M. Speck of San Rafael claimed he not only saw Bigfoot in Samuel P. Taylor State Park (Marin County, CA) but was able to capture it on film. Speck said he was strolling along a creek filming inspiring scenery at 9 A.M. one September morning, when an unusual noise across the creek attracted his attention. "It made a weird, neighing kind of sound," he said. Pointing his camera toward the sound, Speck claimed he captured a few seconds of a huge creature disappearing into the tangle of growth and brush. Speck reported it was about the size of a horse, black in color and hairy, but he hadn't clearly seen its arms or legs during the brief encounter. Speck crossed the creek and examined the area where the creature had faded from view but found no footprints or other trace of its passing. Speck took his film to Los Angeles and allowed Wolper Productions to examine the movie.[1114]

> Date: August, 1975 [conflicts with newspaper account above stating Speck's film was shot in September] Jon Eric Beckjord reported seeing this super-8 film shot in Marin County. It was out of focus and at extreme zoom but showed a large, gray-black bipedal figure striding over some logs, partially hidden by leaves.[1115]

Alan Berry

Supposed vocalizations from Bigfoot had been recorded and pressed as 7-inch, 33 1/3 rpm phonograph records available from Bigfoot Records, Redding, California. The screeches, gibberings, and howls would become known in Bigfoot circles as the "Sierra Sounds." Writing in the November 1975 *Probe the Unknown,* Alan R. (Ron) Berry gave an account of his involvement with the recordings and his efforts to get them professionally evaluated.

> The utterances are mighty sounds, mighty weird sounds too. Hair-raising in their flesh-and-blood resonance, they nonetheless provoke smiles and wonderment due to their primitive character.[1116]

The vocalizations were first recorded by a group of hunters in 1971 at their hunting camp in a remote region of California's middle High Sierra Mountains. By the time journalist Berry arrived on the scene in October 1972, the hunters reported a dozen encounters with the creatures and they had collected several hours of odd and sometimes frightening sounds.

> Except to appeal for scientific help, the men, fearing ridicule, had kept their story secret. They knew that if the camp's location were ever publicly disclosed, the area would be overrun by curiosity-seekers and trophy hunters. Today, they still fear ridicule and, justifiably, want to keep the seasonal Bigfoot retreat secret.[1117]

Berry's lead on the hunters' strange experiences came to him by way of Peter Byrne, who, Berry said, had felt the story was too far-fetched to pursue. Berry took on the story in a light-hearted way. "Good offbeat feature material," he explained to smiling colleagues; surely the hunters were simply engaging in a kind of jest, even prank. Berry would go along with the fun, get the story, and join in a good laugh at the end of it, right along with the hunters.

> In preparation for the trip, I studied up on infrared photography and how to snare, photographically, various kinds of creatures, including the human type, in the wild. I also raided every camera shop within reach, buying up special film, flashbulbs, remote shutter releases, used cameras and an assortment of miscellaneous equipment—not the least of which was a quantity of bailing wire.[1118]

Berry's photography gear filled several boxes and weighed about 100 pounds. This was in addition to approximately 20 pounds of stereophonic recording equipment. Berry accompanied the hunters on the 15-mile, 3,000-foot uphill trek to the camp, itself an 8-foot-high, 15-foot-wide shelter built like a "beaver lodge" of branches and logs within a framework of a small stand of trees.

> We slept inside it when sleep was possible. When sleep was not possible, we used it as a fortress.
>
> During my second trip, "Biggie" finally came around. Still convinced the hunters were taking me on a grand snipe hunt, I played along in my jolly best and was bent on having the last laugh. The sudden presence of the *thing,* unseen but heard in the darkness just outside the shelter, was a heart-stopper. My knees trembled so violently that even long after I had recovered my voice, which had cowered somewhere in my throat, I could barely get up off my sleeping bag to have a look outside.
>
> Announcing its presence were two sharp whistles, spaced about a minute apart. Then, like a nightmare-come-alive, the enormous, thoroughly awful-sounding voice reported from a short distance away uphill. It was a wild, almost human-sounding gibberish interspersed with long, drawn-out, but empathic, snarls. To my amazement, one of my companions was calling out in a calm voice, "Aw, come on big fella, *that's* not nice!" Frankly, to me, the thing sounded like it was going to storm the shelter. I wondered what in God's name had ever possessed me to get involved with these people and their weird tale. They carried guns, and had insisted that I carry one, as well. Now the reason why seemed all too clear.
>
> Then almost as if the thing were responding to the hunter's voice, it seemed to calm down a bit. In rough syllabic, this is how it carried on, "Ah-na-owww. UummmMMM-WAUGH! Rah! Nah . . . nuh-nuh-nuh . . . ruh. Nah-naughhh-na-owWW! Oy-yoy-yoy-yoy!"
>
> They were emotional, some of them even humorous, sounds delivered rapid-fire. Some seemed to be uttered as the breath was inhaled, a humanly-difficult feat. Others came at humanly impossible speeds.[1119]

Shocked and terrified at the prospect of what could be out beyond the piled and stacked stick-and-log walls wore off as it became evident the creature was sticking around. Berry said that he later learned there were at least two of them, a larger one with a 20-inch foot and a smaller one, owning a commensurately "smaller" voice and a 14-inch long foot. As the initial astonishment subsided, he found his skepticism returning. "How ingenious!" Berry thought. "Somebody is out there in the trees with a portable amplifier. It's only a joke, after all!"

> About this time, however, the thing hurled a few sour-sounding epithets, then suddenly roared and slapped its chest. I could hear its jowls shaking and the hollow reverberations of the chest being slapped. *That* couldn't be any man![1120]

Wedging his feet between logs for purchase, Berry forced his head and shoulders through a narrow opening in the camp's roof, hoping to get a picture of the noise-maker. Losing his foothold, Berry found himself supported only by his elbows resting on the roof, his legs dangling free. Fear gripped him as he realized how his precarious situation rendered him practically helpless. As his feet frantically sought for support, Berry was certain he was hearing something creep up behind him. Inside the camp, one of his companions resumed talking to the creature. "Now that isn't nice, big fella. Come on down here and let's be friends!" Berry at last found his footing which precipitated the return of his composure. By the end of this night, his first night hearing and experiencing the vocalizations for himself, Berry asserted he began to feel like a veteran Bigfoot hunter.

> The following night, I even ventured forth from the shelter with two of my companions briefly—perhaps insanely, in retrospect—to chase the creatures on foot. It was wildly exciting. I couldn't wait to tell my friends about it and to play for them the tapes I'd made.
>
> But it was just the beginning for me. After recovering from the initial shock and those few moments of anxiety and "lost cool" when the reality of the creature seemed absolute, though I wanted to believe, I couldn't help questioning the hunters, the big, five-toed footprints we found and the sounds issuing from the darkness. In daylight, everything was cool, so I spent long hours looking for what I imagined to be the real evidence—shoeprints other than our own, a hidden amplifier, electronic gear other than that we'd packed in, extraneous batteries, wires, whatever. I repeatedly searched the shelter and even went through the other men's belongings while they were away hunting deer. I found nothing suspicious, but still I

> wasn't satisfied. I knew I had to come back, again and again if necessary, until I found what I sought.
>
> I did go back, many times. Since that first meeting, there have been many close encounters and brushes with the Bigfoot "people." I still look for the conclusive evidence which hides or shelters them from us, but the hunters are now trusted friends. I have known for a long time that they are "clean" and as thoroughly stumped and mystified by the phenomenon as I am. All of us agree that even today the story still has only beginnings.[1121]

Sierra Sounds

By the flickering flames of a campfire at the Drizzly Creek campground near Fortuna, California, a vacationing family listened to Alan Berry, John Meltzer, and Max Cantowine talk about searching for Bigfoot in the High Sierra near Sonora, California. "The more they talked, the more we half believed them," Lucile Huckle told the *Daily Sentinel* of Le Mars, Iowa. "The kids were so enthused about it." Following their camping trip and after returning home to Iowa, the Huckles received a record of the remarkable sounds which were purported to have made by Bigfoot. "It was an unbelievable experience," said Lucile about her family's visit with Alan Berry.

> Sounds on the record taken from a tape made by Mr. Berry on Oct. 21, 1972, are something like "Ahn, na, owww. Ummmm-MMM-WAUGH! Nah. Nuh-nuyh-nuh . . . ruh. Nah-nau-GhhnaowWW! Oy-yoy-yoy-you!"
>
> There's a pause and then an horrendous 7-second snort: ". . . Nnnnnnnnn-naaaaugugugugggggasssssNUK-Hungh-TT!"
>
> That's the way a *Sacramento Bee* staff writer wrote it in the April 5 interview story about Berry.
>
> Berry and the hunters with him actually saw Bigfoot reeling around the brush just beyond the camp.
>
> "A shape, a shadow, a fleeting blob in the woods," was Berry's description of the creature.

The uncredited story appearing in the July 9, 1975, *Daily Sentinel* stated Berry had been a reporter for the *Redding Record-Searchlight* for three years, a job Berry said he quit after his October 1972 experience at the hunters' camp. By 1975 Berry was selling records and posters of Bigfoot to support his family and had become a full-time researcher supplementing his teacher-wife's income.[1122] The 1975 copyrighted vinyl record (of which about half of its audio content was devoted to actual Bigfoot sounds) was titled "A Living Legend: Bigfoot Sounds Off!"

After coming face-to-face with the phenomenon and with his recordings in hand, Berry solicited interest in and evaluation of the audio evidence from private and academic experts. He reached out to Dr. Edwin W. Snider of the National Geographic Society's Committee for Research and Exploration. "Well, what are your credentials?" he asked Berry. To the response of 'reporter,' Snider replied, "Well we're usually only interested in people who are recognized in a particular science field, people who've achieved . . ."

> It was but the first of many failures to create even a ripple in establishment waters. But I [Berry] learned not to be surprised, and I now suspect that the story is an old and familiar one to anyone who has ever tried to elicit scientific interest in a scientific unknown.
>
> Among the few letters of inquiry ever answered was the one requesting financial backing and participation sent to George H. Harrison, managing editor of *National Wildlife* magazine. In response, Harrison wrote that yes, *Wildlife* might wish to participate and that in exchange for "a very small token . . . we would merely request that we accompany you and report what we see and photograph." To this reporter-photographer, however elated by a show of interest from *someone,* the offer was less than a rose.[1123]

Berry sent a record, hair samples and photographs of footprints to Dr. Vaughn Bryant Jr., Texas A&M University anthropologist and botanist. Bryant was a recognized authority in prehistoric diet, pollen and fecal analysis. Berry's evidence joined other samples previously collected from two separate locations in the Pacific Northwest which had been under scrutiny at Texas A&M. Bryant's reaction upon listening to the 15-minute record was the vocalizations seemed similar to known primates.[1124]

Berry said that Dr. William Mason of the Yerkes Primate Center at the University of California-Davis, called the sounds "definitely primate" and recommended further analysis. Recordings were also shared with Syntonic

Research Inc., a firm that gained notoriety for having conducted analysis on the Nixon tapes during the Watergate investigation. According to Berry, Mike Kron a research associate at Syntonic said, "In my opinion, the sounds recorded have been spontaneous in nature and seem to have taken place at the time of the original recording." Berry had maintained the creatures were only 30-50 yards from his hidden microphone, but the recorded sounds appear to be generated from right on top of the microphone which caused some reservation on the part of Syntonic. Berry concluded the remote volume control of the unit, plus the enormously powerful projection the creatures were capable of, accounted for the phenomenon of their apparent close proximity to the microphone.[1125] I. S. Teibel, president of Syntonic, Inc., wrote to Berry in December 1973:

> ". . . we have been in correspondence with several people whom we thought might have interest in pursuing this matter on the basis of scientific interest alone. As we have been unable to obtain any positive response . . . we are herewith returning the four tape cassettes. . . . I would suggest . . . submit the recordings . . . to a university acoustics laboratory which might undertake a thorough examination on the basis of scientific interest."[1126]

A recording was sent to the Naval Weapons Center in California which returned it after six months without comment. Jane Goodall, visiting professor at Stanford University, wrote Berry in 1975 before her departure for a year in Africa: "I am fascinated by the phenomenon. . . . I wish you the best of luck!"[1127]

Berry concluded his *Probe* article with comments on the feasible—though he believed very remote—possibility of a hoax.

> In the pursuit of any funding source, scientific or professional, one driving force has been the possibility of hoax—perhaps a hoax too sophisticated and refined for even a trained investigator to expose single-handedly. And, of course, if the Bigfoot creatures are real, what financial backer, scientist or professional in the field would not want to share in the discovery?
>
> It is the very risk of a hoax, in fact, that has been a stopper in this bottled mystery. I pull it out now only because the Bigfoot

sounds themselves seem too remarkable. Even after spending more than two years acquainting myself with the High Sierra locale, its flora and fauna, the handful of people who frequent it and, yes, at a distance, the Bigfoot "family," many questions remain. But, there is one scientifically irrefutable certainty—the sounds and footprints associated with the sounds' occurrence are real and are the result of "something." And, that something, I am convinced, is worthy of public understanding and scientific interest.[1128]

Iceman

Frank Hansen's Minnesota Iceman remained on tour into the mid-'70s housed in a 6,000-pound[1129] exhibit appearing at fairs and in malls. Articles in small market newspapers during these years catalyzed bursts of publicity for Hansen and his frozen specimen. Perry Fulkerson, staff writer for St. Petersburg's *Evening Independent,* wrote that during open exhibition times, Hansen usually stayed near the Iceman. Perhaps with conscious showmanship, Hansen told Fulkerson he never strayed far because the FBI wanted to confiscate the Iceman and scientists wanted to conduct unauthorized studies. Articles at this time (and Fulkerson's was no exception) typically included a recounting by Hansen of how, at a time he was showing an antique tractor at state fairs, he had come into possession of the Iceman. Hansen by this time had changed the story of his introduction to the Iceman from the account he authored for the July 1970 edition of *Saga*.

"I was at the Arizona State Fair when this fellow came up to me and said how impressed he was by my exhibit, how I was attracting so many people with this old tractor," Hansen said relating how his relationship with the Iceman got started, "and he said 'I wonder what you would do if you had what I have.' What do you have? I asked. 'I don't know,' he said.

"The gentlemen took me to a warehouse where this specimen was frozen in a huge block of ice," Hansen recalled. "This man didn't know what to do with what he had. He thought it might be a seal or a large fish, but we couldn't tell because of the thickness of the ice." An ice carver was engaged to chip away ice so the thing inside could be more visible. A sight was presently revealed that startled both Hansen and the carver—reposing within the ice was a humanoid figure. The "apelike man or manlike ape" was about 7 feet tall and covered in dark brown 2-inch hairs which stood straight up off its skin, tipped by tiny crystal caps of frost. "These crystals are one of the reasons scientists say this cannot be a completely manufactured thing," Hansen affirmed. "The condition would be impossible to duplicate."

Hansen said he and the creature's owner drew up an agreement. "He turned it over to me for two years. I was to furnish all necessary equipment and materials, show it throughout the United States, charge no more than 35 cents so that about anyone could afford to see it, and return the specimen to him in two years," said Hansen. "As part of the contract, I was told I could never reveal the owner's name, but I can tell you he is a prominent person in the entertainment industry," he stated.

"It was brought into the United States illegally," Hansen continued. "So I decided to clear myself legally by having a model of it made by several artists, including some who had worked with 'Planet of the Apes.' These artists didn't know what it was they were making, they did it from drawings I gave them, and they thought it was for an illusion show." The copy was put into storage, ready to be called upon if Hansen felt it was necessary to affect a switch. Hansen proceeded to exhibit the real thing at state fairs in the same trailer as had exhibited his tractor, replete with new Iceman banners attached to the sides.

After the original contract expired, Hansen explained to Fulkerson, he had gone home to Minnesota to await word from the creature's owner. On a cold December night the phone rang, and instead of the owner Hansen found himself talking with Ivan Sanderson of the Society for the Investigation of the Unknown. Sanderson said he and Dr. Bernard Heuvelmans of Belgium wished to come and examine the creature. "I told them they could come look, but nothing could be published," said Hansen.

Sanderson and Heuvelmans drove all the way from New Jersey to Minnesota, finally arriving during a snowstorm. Sanderson and Heuvelmans were amazed by the Iceman; they conducted their analysis, took measurements, and snapped photographs. A piece of lighting equipment placed on the glass broke it and a bad smell wafted out. "This smell, this putrescene, convinced Dr. Heuvelmans it was no fabrication, that indeed this was an animal decomposing, and he said 'I am a scientist first, a gentleman second.' I reminded him of our agreement but he didn't heed it," Hansen said.

Heuvelmans and Sanderson did indeed go on to write and publish articles on their observations. Heuvelmans, who called the creature a *Homo-pongoides* (apelike man), suggested that during the creature's freezing, the hardening ice compressed the creature's hairs thus forcing air bubbles from them resulting in the frost crystals at the follicles' tips.

Phone calls came rolling in, Hansen said, and he denied everything and suggested the learned scientists should be discredited. "The third day, the local sheriff came out and said he had instructions from the FBI, that Hoover himself was interested and wanted to know was I in violation of a federal law and could they confiscate? I contacted the owner and he said to get out. My wife and I pulled out in the middle of the night with the specimen," Hansen said. "We were gone for 10 days during which time I made some changes in the exhibit, and you can draw your own conclusions as to what I mean," Hansen said.

Hansen received a letter from the Smithsonian asking if their representatives could come and study the form in the ice. Hansen recalled for Fulkerson that he wrote them back saying his "specimen" was just a fake and not to waste their time. Hansen later booked his Iceman exhibit for three fairs in Canada. The last fair he visited on this swing was in Regina, the capital of Saskatchewan, which was not on his official itinerary with the customs office. He planned to pull out of Canada days ahead of official schedule "in case somebody were to try anything." Which is exactly what happened.

Coming back into the United States, Hansen told Fulkerson, he was stopped by irritated customs officials who believed he was breaking the law by transporting a cadaver without proper credentials and authorization. "I told them it was merely an illusion show and not a cadaver. They said I'd have to prove it was an illusion. I said they'd have to prove it was a cadaver. So they said they would call in a biologist. And I said no they wouldn't." Hansen rung up the creature's owner, called a federal judge, and called a "friendly senator in Minnesota."

Gears turning, Hansen retreated to an around-the-clock vigil over the creature. In the morning he received apologies from seemingly chastened customs officials. "The owner was so infuriated over this obvious attempt to seize the specimen that he decided he would never allow government scientists or the Smithsonian or anyone do a biological study," Hansen said. "We decided to redo the display and put it back on the road for the people to see, because if the government ever got it no one would see it again."

A platform was built and the exhibit started to do bookings in shopping centers and malls. Instead of the exhibit generating a profit, all proceeds went to charities, said Hansen, such as the American Cancer Society. "I sent photos of the model being made to the government and said what I am showing is a fake," Hansen stated. "That got them off my back. But you'll have to decide for yourself is it the real thing? Or what?" Hansen wasn't saying for sure. "When we started showing the creature, the ice was 6 inches thick," said Hansen. "Now it is 2 inches. We figure that in two years or less, it will be completely dissolved, at which time the owner will permit a biological study."[1130]

In Gadsen, Alabama, Hansen and the Iceman stopped at the Gadsen Mall for a week-long display.

> The [*Gadsen*] *Times* interviewed some of the curious onlookers peering into the frozen coffin and found that most of them believe the creature is real.
>
> Phil Cossey, 18, of Chicago, said, "I've read about these things before and I've seen some remains in museums, but I've never seen a frozen one before."
>
> Jeff Marbut, 16, of Hokes Bluff, described the creature as "a hairy man." He said, "It looks real to me. I believe [it's] something in the ice, but I don't know what."
>
> One lady who asked that her name be withheld said: "It made me just sick to look at it. It looks like an ape or something. I just don't know, it was so sick-looking I didn't look too long. It's terrible."
>
> Randy Vice, 10, of Wellington, said "It looks like a man from the Planet of the Apes."[1131]

Hansen repeated to *Gadsen Times* reporter Jerry Harris what he had had told Fulkerson: the exhibit's ice was slowly melting despite efforts to keep the ice-coffin at six degrees. Hansen said he was concerned that adding and freezing new, fresh water would not work because it would not freeze as clearly as the original ice. Hansen told Harris that he was unable to prevent the slow process of decomposition surely going on at the time of their interview. Foul odors permeated the display area when the glass lid was lifted off for defrosting. "We may not have much longer," Hansen teased.[1132]

The Society for the Investigation of the Unexplained also revisited the Iceman in 1975 through the pages of *Pursuit*. The April and July editions reprinted Sanderson's "Preliminary Description of the External Morphology of What Appeared to be the Fresh Corpse of a Hitherto Unknown Form of Living Hominid" as originally published by *Genus* in 1969. Also in *Pursuit's* July edition was a short piece titled "Epilogue on Bozo" by Robert Durant which provided a denouement of sorts on the matter from the Society's perspective.

> The Bozo affair was an agonizing experience for Heuvelmans and Sanderson. Both men had devoted an enormous amount of their time to the study of so-called unknown animals, and in the process had committed their professional reputations in a manner that is both rare and dangerous in the scientific world. It may be that the Psychological result of this commitment was a predisposition to believe in the reality of what some have called an obvious hoax. On the other hand, both men were really extraordinarily well qualified professionally to examine and judge such a specimen, and even the most severe critics of the authenticity of Bozo have been careful to note the technical competence of these two observers.[1133]

SIGHTINGS 1975

Indianola Monster

In mid-September, in reports that bore a striking similarity to accounts from northeastern Oklahoma earlier in the month, residents in Indianola (Pittsburg Co., OK), claimed they were catching glimpses of a "monster" which resembled a monkey. Several Indianola residents formed a search party on Saturday night (September 13) but did not turn up anything monkey-like. Anthony Ketchum said he and two others saw the creature as they drove to a fenced-in enclosure where hogs and horses were kept. "We heard something when we first stopped the car," Ketchum said. "We got out and saw the animals making a funny noise. When we were walking back to the car it jumped out of the bushes and started after us."

The group saw the creature in the car headlights and "it looked big. It had hair all over it. It looked like a big monkey and it made a grunting noise," Ketchum stated. "It hopped like a kangaroo when it started chasing us. It seemed taller than a man, but it's easy to exaggerate when you're scared." McAlester police took another report from an Indianola couple who reported seeing the "monster" and also received a claim the creature had peered into a woman's window.[1134]

Fitzgerald Desires Protection for Bigfoot

When Jean Fitzgerald encountered enormous footprints in Roseburg, Oregon, she knew just what to do: rub them out. "We destroy them so some

'Bigfoot' hunter won't stumble across them," she said. Fitzgerald unsurprisingly advocated for legislation to protect Bigfoot. Fitzgerald had written to Governor Robert Straub to seek his backing of legal safeguards for Bigfoot. "I would like to see the governor step in and help make it illegal to capture or kill one," she stated. Fitzgerald said she and her family had been privileged to see Bigfoot on multiple occasions over the summers of '75 and '76, including one instance of seeing nine creatures together at the same time. "They proved to us they don't mean any harm," she said. "Each time we saw them, they were as curious about us as we were about them." Her husband Steve left a candy bar conspicuously out for a Bigfoot and then hid. Fitzgerald said a Bigfoot came to investigate, took the candy bar and ate it, wrapper and all.

Fitzgerald described Bigfoot as covered in short black hair except for the face, hands, and feet which were "weather-beaten." It sported high cheek bones, a flat nose, and could reach a standing height of nine feet. Those weather-beaten hands were like a human's, but the thumb was the same length as the rest of its fingers. "He could have killed us many, many times over the past two summers if he so desired," Fitzgerald said. "He's so huge he could have done almost anything he wanted to."

Danny, Fitzgerald's 15-year-old son, claimed to have seen six of the creatures walk leisurely across a road in order of height, tallest to shortest. Danny stated he had received ridicule from incredulous peers who put no stock in his sightings. "I'd like to see somebody bring one in," he said in obvious contravention to his mother's position, "so it could be proven once and for all."[1135]

Metcalf Expedition

The front page of the April 6, 1975, *Tuscaloosa News* carried the story of University of Alabama student Michael Metcalf who was then organizing an expedition for the summer of 1975 to explore the Pacific Northwest to determine if Bigfoot was a flesh-and-blood creature or merely apocryphal stories.

Metcalf, an ex-Marine who served in Vietnam, entered the prospect of expedition-organizing with a bias—believing, as he did, that there was credibility to the reports of a large ape-like creature living in the nation's hinterlands. *Tuscaloosa News* reporter Milton Grishman noted Metcalf had found three men to accompany him and share the expense of the expedition. Two were former Marines who Metcalf met while in the service, the other man was a close friend, and all lived in New York, Metcalf's home state. Plans called for the group to drive to Washington in June and explore "Monkey Canyon" in the south-central part of Yakima County.

A component of Metcalf's protocol was the use of a grid system during fieldwork. In contrast to teams and researchers who espoused a no-kill approach to searching for Bigfoot, Metcalf's group would go armed. Thoughts of using tranquilizers were curtly dismissed because according to Metcalf, and similar to Grover Krantz's position, there was no certainty a selected dosage would be powerful enough to sedate a forest giant. Though killing a creature was not the ultimate goal of the group, "If the opportunity presents itself," Metcalf stated, "I don't know what the outcome will be. . . . I wouldn't fire unless I was certain I could bring it down with one shot." The team's objective was to obtain indisputable proof, and, Metcalf acknowledged, "the ultimate piece of evidence is the 'corpus delicti.'"

If successful, Metcalf maintained, "We could become very, very famous and very, very rich." At the very least, the trip would be an exciting getaway, even if no traces of Bigfoot is detected. "I do know in 25 years or so, I can sit by the fire with my grandchildren and spin quite a yarn about the summer of '75 when a bunch of my buddies and I went after Bigfoot."[1136]

Corona Monster

By the time the San Bernardino, California, *Sun-Telegram* published the story of an ape-like creature in south Corona in Riverside County, the creature had been seen off and on for twelve days. A search of the orange groves near Main Street and Upper Drive after two men made the initial sighting failed to turn up footprints or other tangible trace. A week later, a man came forward to report he had seen an ape-like monster sitting atop a block wall in a local grove. The ensuing search turned up no evidence of a monster. In the evening of Monday, August 18, a costume was found in the grove and subsequently, two youths admitted to wearing the suit to prank passing traffic. "We have no evidence there is any kind of strange beast in the area. There have been no reports of animals being killed. We even checked with local zoos and Lion Country Safari," said a police spokeswoman. "They said they weren't missing any large animals, just a few small ones. But nothing like the monster described to us," she said. "We're not saying there isn't one," she continued, "just that we haven't found evidence of one, yet."[1137]

Mark Karr

"The thing that really freaked me out was just the idea that it was still there," said Mark Karr of Chico, California. "It didn't chase me or anything." Karr said he spotted a creature in his headlights while driving on a sharply curved Oroville, California, road on September 3, 1975. The creature was hairy, had gorilla-like features, and was six to eight feet tall. Karr was so startled that he crashed, hitting a tree. He left his car and fled down the road, eventually being picked up by a state trooper.[1138]

Noxie Monster

Several residents of Noxie, Oklahoma, a farming community near the Kansas border, experienced monster sightings in the summer of 1975. "I was within 10 feet of it before I saw him," said farmer Ken Tosh as he described his sighting of a seven-foot, hairy, and foul-smelling creature that came to be called the Noxie Monster. "He growled and ran one way. I screamed and ran the other."[1139]

"There haven't been any reports since the weekend [August 30-31] of anything except a bunch of idiots running around drinking beer and carrying rifles and CB radios," Nowata County Sheriff Bob Arnold said. "They're going to kill somebody."[1140] Noxie resident Marion Parret claimed to have shot at the beast three times with ineffectual results. Parret was convinced he had hit it every time, but only once did it even seem to react as if it had been shot: by swatting its arm as if at a fly.[1141] "It just walked away," Parret said.

"The eyes glowed in the dark, reddish-pink eyes," Tosh recalled. "They glow without a light being on them."[1142] Arnold thought folks had seen something, but he doubted it was a monster. "Something that big would leave quite an impression in the ground, first of all," Arnold explained, "and second, human eyes don't glow. Animals' eyes do, of course, so there's no telling what it was they really saw. In the dark, people's imaginations often make a whole lot out of nothing."[1143]

Arnold was simply unconvinced the Noxie Monster was a monster. "I don't think we have a monster problem, I think we have a people problem," Arnold said. "I had one unconfirmed report there had already been one horse and two dogs shot last night by the gun-crazed idiots running around drinking—with their CB radios and so forth," he said. "I want to give notice right here and now that anyone in that area that is caught running around with a loaded firearm in their vehicle and drinking is going to be incarcerated." Arnold himself investigated several reports, which mostly occurred between 10 P.M. and dawn. "I won't believe it until I see it," Arnold stated. "I've been looking for UFOs since 1947 and I haven't seen one yet." Arnold believed that the monster-hunting climate created a dangerous situation. "A young person in this day and age, with long hair and a lot of stuff on his face, might at night look like a wolfman and one of these guys that are drinking their beer might want to blow him to bits."

Arnold recalled another mysterious creature sighted in 1974 near Watova, Oklahoma (see Chapter 5). That beast, as reported, was smaller than the Noxie Monster but "ran upright like a man and hurdled fences like a speeding bullet or something like that," recalled Arnold. "I had a report last night citizens band radios in Oklahoma and Kansas were working on this thing," said Arnold, "and that people up there have been drinking beer and carrying guns. This information returned Arnold to the at-hand problem that human nature presented during a period of monster mania. "We're going to get some righteous people killed by some idiots running around. And you can quote me on that," said Arnold.[1144]

Undersheriff Harold Lay commiserated with the witnesses. "I don't know what they saw, but they sure saw something," he said. "One woman was almost hysterical and her husband seriously said his knees were still knocking."[1145]

The Noxie Monster hit the AP news wires and attracted the attention of Hollywood producer David Wolper. Wolper said he would pay $10,000 for home movies of the Noxie Monster to be used in the development of a Bigfoot documentary. "That's nice," said Sheriff Arnold when told of Wolper's offer. "It's gone up $5,000 since he called me last week. Now I suppose we'll be swarmed again."[1146] Arnold summed up the situation on a wry note: "Maybe we'll luck out and find a monster and a UFO both. I've never seen one of those, either."[1147]

Bigfoot in Farmville

Farmville, North Carolina, citizens had started to believe, after the mid-September rash of Bigfoot sightings had died down, that the hullabaloo had been the result of a hoax. The sightings started in the second week of September when huge footprints were found around Brody Parker's vegetable garden. The three-toed tracks were eighteen inches long and seven inches wide and were discovered by Mrs. Parker while adding fertilizer to her garden's butterbeans. Following an investigation by a sheriff's deputy and game warden, Parker said 1,000 armed citizens converged on the area to hunt for the creature. "I saw some of the finest weapons I've ever seen down there," Parker recalled.[1148] About 100 prints were found on Wednesday, August 10, to be followed two days later by another set of prints found on Friday morning. The toes shifted in their placement from step to step, initially lending the tracks authenticity.

Other unusual signs were limbs as high as 25 feet up broken from pecan trees in a nearby orchard. Parker said the prints stopped appearing after the warden promised to bring a bloodhound to the scene should the prints show up again. Game Warden A. C. Goodwin called the tracks and the whole notion of Bigfoot in the area a hoax. "If you were a game warden," Goodwin said, "you'd be saying the same thing (that it's a hoax) to keep those people from shooting each other. If it's somebody pulling a prank, they shouldn't be doing it because folks around here are taking it mighty serious." Charlie Peek, then city editor at the *Sanford Herald* said, "The authorities believe it's a hoax and they're not fooling with it much." Peek's general description of the monster-hunters was they were "looking for blood." Of the scene created by their presence Peek said it "looked like a Frankenstein movie or something." Peek suggested the broken branches were intriguing; they were up to 25 feet off the ground and of "pretty good size," he stated.[1149]

Joplin, Missouri, Hoax

Reports stated a seven-foot-tall, 300-pound hairy monster with red, glowing eyes the size of half-dollars[1150] was on the loose in the vicinity of Joplin, Missouri. After a week of sightings during the end of September, Police claimed they apprehended the monster—a young man in a gorilla suit. On Tuesday, September 30, Police Chief Bernard Kakuske said no charges would be filed against the young man or two other youths who were involved in perpetrating the hoax. In another instance of officials expressing concern for the public's safety, Kakuske, while displaying the gorilla costume for reporters, said someone dressed up in such a way was lucky not to have gotten hurt. "I find it an act of God the boys didn't get shot," Kakuske said. "We had people roaming around with guns ready to shoot the monster. It's just lucky they didn't cross the paths of one of those people. It's really kind of a dangerous game to play, some people can get genuinely scared," Kakuske said. "I sure as hell hope they'll be more relaxed now."[1151]

Three youths had rented the gorilla costume for $12 from a rental agency. "It was just a hoax, but the costume was really quite realistic," Kakuske said. "Under poor lighting conditions, I suppose you wouldn't be able to tell what you were seeing."[1152]

Before the boys' admission to their part in the prank, one person involved in the official investigation discounted the idea of a monster based upon tracks found at one scene which looked to belong to a large dog. "They're just large prints, with some of them four or five inches in length," said Donald Seneker, director of law enforcement program at Missouri Southern State College. "But there's nothing I could classify as human or primate." Seneker also stated that hair discovered in the vicinity of one of the sightings turned out to be hog bristles.[1153]

Lockridge Monster

During the late autumn of 1975, sightings of the "Lockridge Monster" occurred in the Turkey Creek area north of Lockridge, Iowa. "If I see it again, I wouldn't go up and throw my arms around it,"[1154] Mrs. Peiffer said of a large, hair-covered creature she and her husband had seen on their turkey farm.

> Lockridge, Iowa (AP)—Skeptics call it "The Lockridge Monster," but the bear-like creature with a monkey face reportedly seen in this turkey farming community is no laughing matter.
>
> "If someone's playing a joke, they're sure liable to get shot," said Mrs. Gloria Olson, a farm wife who says she saw the mysterious animal.
>
> Stories about a "four-legged, black haired thing in the cornfield" began circulating after Herb Peiffer saw it in his tractor lights while driving to his turkey pens. At first, Peiffer was reluctant to discuss it with his family.
>
> "He thought we would make fun of him," Mrs. Peiffer said.
>
> Lowell Adkins, a hunter, later found 10 inch tracks near the carcasses of four partially eaten turkeys. Some think the tracks were a bear's, possibly a black bear from northern Wisconsin or Michigan.
>
> But no one in Jefferson County recalls ever seeing a bear in the area and until the mystery is solved, some parents aren't letting their children go outside after sundown.

> "It was just before dark and I was driving past an old deserted farmyard when I saw it," Mrs. Olson said. "To me, it looked like it had a monkey's face and kind of had hair all over.
>
> "I didn't tarry too long," she said.[1155]

The Peiffers reportedly found three to four dead turkeys in a pile, their bodies partially eaten, nearly every morning before their birds were shipped to market in late October. The Peiffers had also noted several partially eaten apples still hanging from their branches about seven feet off the ground. "It looked like a bite was taken out of some of the choicest apples clear around the tree," Mrs. Peiffer said. Mrs. Peiffer related a hunter's claim, who happened to have been carrying a camera, to have spotted the Lockridge Monster on the Peiffer farm in November. "Before he got the camera focused, it was gone," she said. "He said he didn't know what it was, but it wasn't a bear."

Mrs. Peiffer stated that her teenage son was easily able to place his size-12 shoe into a track attributed to the Lockridge Monster which was discovered in a sand bar along Turkey Creek. Local hunters said the large tracks bore resemblance to bear tracks.

The Peiffers received numerous requests for more information about their sightings. Ramona Hibner, who reporter Alan Koonse said represented the "South Mountain Research Group" of Brooksville, Florida, contacted the Peiffers to solicit additional details about the bear-like creature and its behavior. Mrs. Peiffer said inquiries had been received from every state in the country except Alaska and Arkansas. "I'm kind of disappointed in Arkansas," she said. Mrs. Peiffer stated that along with calls from radio and TV stations across the United States, one group from Pennsylvania attempted, in Mrs. Peiffer's retelling, to persuade her that the creature was a lost being from a UFO. Mrs. Peiffer stated her family's lives hadn't changed much since the emergence of the Lockridge Monster. "But we keep our eyes open more than we used to," she said.[1156]

Bob Moody Sees Three Bigfoot

Bob Moody said he saw three Bigfoot at 8:45 A.M. on Thursday, October 2: a large adult and two smaller ones. Moody was engaged in trapping in the Grande Prairie (Alberta) area over 200 miles northwest of Edmonton when he saw the trio of creatures. "I'm an old bushman, there's no way that was a bear." Moody thought the larger of the group was a female and the smaller ones its young. "She was crouched but when she heard the motor she reared back," he recalled. Moody stated that as he stopped his truck at the edge of a tree line off the southbound lane of Highway 2, about 11 miles north of Sexsmith, the Bigfoot quickly faded into the trees. Moody estimated the largest was about seven or eight feet tall and all were covered in brownish hair except for their face.[1157]

Pinegrass Ridge Bigfoot Encounter

> Three shaken Tacoma youths, bear hunting south of Rimrock Lake Wednesday evening [October 1, 1975] believe they saw a creature resembling a Sasquatch.
>
> The youths' report, related to Yakima County sheriff's deputy Larry Gamache hours after the reported sighting, led Gamache to believe they had, indeed, seen "something" similar to the legendary "Bigfoot."[1158]

The trio thought something followed them on a trail as they hunted bear at Section 3 Lake on Pinegrass Ridge, Washington. Periodically shining their flashlight back up the trail failed to illuminate the source of the noises that seemed to shadow them. The youths reached their camp at about 9 P.M. and they quickly built up their fire. After hearing a noise, Earl Thomas, one of the youths, aimed his flashlight across a pond whereupon he spotted greenish-yellow eyes which were also seen by fellow-hunter Gerstmar. Gertsmar then shined his light on the spot and according to Gamache's report saw "what went with the eyes." Later, the youths each provided similar descriptions of what had been lurking about their camp: a creature eight-to-nine-feet tall, covered in black hair with a human body type. It stood upright and shied from the light.

The youths decided to use their rifles and seven shots were fired to ward off the creature. The creature responded with growls and then screamed at the group. The boys abandoned the area and retreated to Trout Lodge. Gerstmar stated he nearly wrecked his jeep in their haste to flee the camp scene. The boys telephoned the sheriff's office from the lodge and reported what had happened. Gamache and another deputy were joined by Washington Game Department agent Larry Konen in an investigation of the scene on Thursday, October 2. They found the camp undisturbed.[1159]

The following interview was conducted on October 15, 1975, between interviewer Dick Grover, Director of Project Discovery, and Thomas.

GROVER: Could you relive the experience and tell us just what happened?

THOMAS: We started up the hill and Tom was on the trail ahead of us. He was about 25 to 50 yards in front of us when something went up these rocks in front of us. It went up so fast that you couldn't even see it. If it was a bear . . . a bear wouldn't go that fast.

GROVER: Was this at night?

THOMAS: No, this was during the daytime. We all sat down to rest and smoke a cigarette, then we started back down the trail, near dark. We kept noticing that something was following us. We kept hearing these noises, like twigs breaking and brush cracking. Tom shined the light back and there wasn't a thing back there. We kept walking and walking and I just kept hearing this. I had the feeling that there was something following us and I felt sure there was. So, we got down to camp and got back to the jeep and started to light a fire. When I started to chop some wood we heard a noise and shined the light across the pond and saw those yellowish-green eyes. It was enough to kind of scare a guy.

GROVER: How far apart were they?

THOMAS: About like ours.

GROVER: Were they closer or wider apart than ours?

THOMAS: I'm not really too sure for it was a long ways. Like a guy asked us how tall it was. What do they expect us to do? Go up and measure it or something? So I yelled to Tom and he shined the light again and he seen the same thing, the eyes. He went and sat back down and I put some more wood on the fire. If you go up there you can see where I cut up a bunch of wood off this log. Tom got back up and shined the light and we seen the whole body.

GROVER: In the light?

THOMAS: Yes. Then we realized what we saw, it turned its head and that was enough to scare us right there. We wouldn't want to say paranoid, yet we started getting our gear and started to take off. Junior (i.e. Jerry Lazzar, 16. Editor) started getting the sleeping bags and lantern and just when junior started back out of the tent the thing just screamed. We just grabbed our things that were close by and took off. Before that Tom fired seven times.

GROVER: It screamed when you shined the light on it?

THOMAS: No.

GROVER: Did it scream when you were in the tent fooling around or when?

THOMAS: No. Me and Tom weren't in the tent. Junior was in the tent. We were prepared to shoot if it would have came at us.

GROVER: What do you think caused it to scream then?

THOMAS: Well we had some meat sitting there on the table. That could have been it. The next day when the sheriff went up there the meat was gone, so something ate off it.

GROVER: The bone was in the same place on the table?

THOMAS: No, it was down on the ground. Although, it could have been a squirrel . . . I'm not sure. We didn't go back up that night, we were too scared to go back that night. All I know is I won't sleep out in a tent again.

Moments later Dick Grover asked Earl Thomas to elucidate on the features of the "creature."

GROVER: Maybe you can describe to us what it looked like.

THOMAS: It was about 8, 9, or 10 feet tall, it was big, it was dark out, this thing was dark and furry.

EDITOR'S NOTE: Apparently, the estimate of size was based on a visual comparison between the "creature" and nearby tree limbs.

GROVER: What did the head look like?

THOMAS: Like I said, it was like ours.

GROVER: Did it have a neck that was stretched out?

THOMAS: No, not really.

GROVER: Did it have a head that was sitting down on the shoulders or did it look like ours?

THOMAS: It was like ours, only bigger, thick.

GROVER: Could you see the hands at all?

THOMAS: No, they were hanging down at its side . . . very long arms.

GROVER: Did you shine the light up and down the creature as you seen it?

THOMAS: When you shined the light it would show up the whole creature in the light.

GROVER: It was a real bright light then?

THOMAS: Yes, that's why we took it with us.

GROVER: What was the head shaped like?

THOMAS: Like I said it was like ours.

GROVER: Did it have any features about the top that you noticed particularly?

THOMAS: I didn't notice too much (laughter).

GROVER: About how far away do you think it was?

THOMAS: About 100 yards. Also the day we went up there we found birds all torn up and entrails in the lake like something was feeding there. The Deputy Sheriff that helped investigate said he didn't doubt this story too much, for he seen one too, standing on the side of the road a while back.

GROVER: You said the eyes were greenish-yellow?

THOMAS: Yes, they were glowing in the light, just like the eyes of a deer or elk would reflect.

EDITOR'S NOTE: It appears that this "glowing" effect may be attributed to the tapetum membrane as in cats. I make this point to differentiate this case from other reports of "creatures" reported to have eyes that glow internally.

GROVER: When you took the light off there was nothing there?

THOMAS: Yes, there was nothing there.

GROVER: How many times did you shine the light on it?

THOMAS: I think it was two or three times. Then later we turned the jeep headlights on and it wasn't there. One thing we noticed when the creature screamed, it sounded like it was all over us. That is when we decided to leave.

The witness, Earl Thomas, also mentioned having smelled a strong odor during certain phases of their "Bigfoot" experience. According to Thomas, just before they split the scene of the encounter, they began to smell a very bad odor which Thomas described as smelling like "rotten loggers sox," whatever that is. When they returned the next day with the deputy sheriff, the odor permeated the area.[1160]

Spottsville Monster

There's a creature roaming the bottomlands of Henderson County that area residents have named the "Spottsville Monster."

It was first seen two weeks ago on a Spottsville farm by some children and later by their mother.

It has been described variously as seven to nine feet tall, and either green or brown in color. One of the children said the monster was brown and white with a face "like a man's only with a lot of hair all over it."

State police were contacted and made a report but some troopers say privately they think the whole thing is a joke—"absurd" as one put it.

The Henderson County sheriff's department is not discounting the story and is presently conducting a full investigation.

"I wouldn't kid about something as scary as this," said Mrs. Sid T. Nunnelly of rural Spottsville. "It's awful. I saw an outline of this thing in the dark several weeks ago. It was dark and I couldn't see very good, but it was real big."

Five of Mrs. Nunnelly's children also have seen the monster and her husband claims he's heard the thing growl at night.

Robert D. Nunnelly, 10, saw the monster two weeks ago when he went to check on his younger sister and cousin who were playing on the family farm.

"It really scared me," Robert said. "The front of it was sort of a brown and the back was white. I hadn't ever seen anything like that in my life. It was standing up by the truck near my sister."

His sister and cousin had their backs turned to the monster. When he screamed, the monster ran away, the boy said.

The other Nunnelly children saw the monster at a distance several days later as they were waiting for a school bus to take them to Spottsville Elementary School.

The Nunnellys and nearby neighbor Ray Vibbert have talked with sheriff's deputies about the monster. Vibbert made a plaster mold of one of the monster's paw prints.

> Vibbert also gave the deputies what he believes may be part of a claw or tooth belonging to the monster. Both are being checked at a laboratory.[1161]

Deputy Charles Johnson thought the Spottsville Monster was likely something ordinary and mundane. "I don't think it's anything that we haven't seen before," he said. "It's probably a bear." Though rarely seen in the area, Johnson had learned from some Spottsville residents that a bear was seen in the vicinity about 15 years prior. "Some people may think this is a joke, but we're treating it seriously," Johnson stated. "I don't think it's a prehistoric monster though."[1162] As was often the case when crowds of people entered the woods with weapons to search for a "monster," concerns for public safety came to the fore. The Henderson County Sheriff's Department said that deputies wished to keep people out of the woods "before somebody gets shot down there."[1163]

Al and Witch Encounter Bigfoot

Reporter Thomas Love wrote that a witness he identifies only as "Al," fried potatoes over his campfire as "the summer sun was just slipping behind the wooded Oregon hills on a calm June evening," in 1975. Leaving the stress of the hustle and bustle of Portland behind, the man enjoyed the chance to spend a weekend camping in the Mt. Jefferson wilderness, accompanied by his German shepherd, Witch.

Suddenly, a low growl emanated from Witch and Al noticed her raised hackles. "She barks when there's something she understands but growls when it's something she doesn't," he said. "So I figured there must be a deer, raccoon or something like that nearby. But when I looked up, I saw something quite different straight in front of me. It was about 150 yards away from where I sat. I was scared and almost ran because at first I thought it might be a bear. But then I could see that it wasn't any bear," he recalled. "I had dreamed about Bigfoot, but I never dreamed he really existed," Al said. "But there he was, squatting down with his arms across his knees, quietly watching me."

"He seemed to be terribly curious," Al continued. "He squatted there for about 45 minutes, watching me, as if he was wondering what I was. I just sat there and watched, continuing with what I was doing—slowly stirring the potatoes. Finally I picked up the cheap little camera with a small electronic flash unit that I had then. When I tried to take a picture, the flash of light seemed to scare it. It just stood up and slowly walked off. I was sitting back in the pines while it was out in the sunlight and all I got on the film was a picture of the pine trees," Al said. He spent two nights at his campsite but never spotted the creature again.

Love wrote that Al harbored no doubts about what he saw. "None at all," he said. "I was sure that day it was Bigfoot. Now I'm more sure than ever. For the next five weekends I took a box of apples and left it where I'd seen him. For the first two weeks, the apples were gone but the box was there. It could have been anything that took them—deer, bear or whatever. But on the last three weekends, the box was gone, too. I couldn't find any trace of it, even though I searched. Now tell me, what other animal in the area would pick up a whole box of apples and carry it off? I believe it's there. I think it lives in that area. I don't think it's nomadic. When he left, it was like he had someplace specific to go, not as if he were looking for a place," Al said. "Please don't use my full name," he asked. "I don't want any more people to know who I am than do now. I didn't tell anybody about my experience for a long time. I was kind of worried about what people would say. Then, I was listening to a radio talk show where they were discussing Bigfoot and I called in. Somebody from Washington (state) got my name shortly thereafter and nearly drove me crazy trying to find out where I'd seen the animal so he could shoot it." And therein was Al's chief worry for the creature he encountered. "That's my main concern—that someone will shoot it."[1164]

Skunk Ape

Though significant commercial and residential development had occurred south of Safety Harbor and Oldsmar, these two Pinellas County, Florida, towns had remained largely rural, surrounded by woods and swamplands. *St. Petersburg Times* writer Susan Denley interviewed several residents who believed they had seen a Skunk Ape, and her resulting story was published in the May 16, 1975, *Manatee Times*. Denley found witnesses in Florida were like those from other parts of the country—they tended to evince a certain reluctance to come forward and share their observations.

> "There's something big and dark out there. I didn't see it well, but I'll tell you, I wouldn't go back."
>
> That was a Safety Harbor man talking to *Pinellas Times* reporter Susan Denley this week. Not some crackpot hermit

> who's been living in the woods too long or hitting the moonshine too often, but a respected member of the community.
>
> That's why he wouldn't talk to Miss Denley until she agreed not to use his name.
>
> His friends also made the same request before they would talk to her. They're also respected members of the community—and want to remain that way.
>
> But they know the looks they would get—not to mention the outright guffaws behind their backs and to their faces—if they publicly admitted that they had seen "something out there."
>
> What did they see? That's for the reader to decide.[1165]

Those who had witnessed the creature around Safety Harbor were left with no doubts they had seen something very peculiar indeed. Most of the local sightings occurred in a rural area around State Road 580 as well as more-developed areas near State Roads 593 and 590. "You won't find me out there again," said Frank (real name withheld) to reporter Denley. Frank admitted to scoffing at his friends' sightings of the Skunk Ape. "Me and a friend used to drive around out in the woods sometimes," he said. "We'd be driving around and come back to where we'd started and there'd be a small tree torn out of the ground and thrown in the road. We'd make a [joke], like "There must be a yeti out here," Frank said. "Finally I said to my friend Larry one night, 'Let's go find us a yeti.' We went out there and parked in the woods, and just sat there awhile with the lights turned off." Frank reported that later that night, the men heard something moving in the brush. Looking in that direction, they saw a large, lanky shape moving through the woods. The thing moved on two legs and had "two things hanging down, like arms." The shape was at least seven feet tall, he said. "I got out and went after it," Frank recalled. "I had my gun with me. You could just see the brush moving back where it had run past." Whatever he had been pursuing slipped away into the night. "I'm sure it wasn't a man," Frank said.

Another friend of Frank's, called "Bob" for Denley's article, also used to laugh at Skunk Ape reports. He went out one night expressly to look for a Skunk Ape, but not really expecting to see one. "I drove into the woods, parked and got out of the car," Bob said. "I had my spotlight with me and started shining it around. All of a sudden a friend who was with me said, 'Move the light back,' I did, and we saw it standing there, under a tree." Bob's description largely tallied with Frank's: a large, man-like figure, but

Bob stated the creature he saw was covered in silver-gray hair. "I'd planned to go up to it and see what it was," Bob said, laughing. "But as soon as I saw it, I leaped in the car and pushed that accelerator to the floorboard getting out of there.[1166]

> Another man had a closer view. He says he came face to face with the creature in a remote outlying area between Safety Harbor and Oldsmar. This time both creature and man ran. There are other things that the believers think give evidence of yeti. Outlying homeowners frequently report night prowlers—and the believers are convinced the prowling is being done by Yetis.[1167]

Pinellas County yielded few reports according to Gordon Prescott, an amateur archaeologist, English teacher at St. Petersburg's North East High School, former president of the St. Petersburg Yeti Research Society (the group was disbanded in 1975[1168]), and past editor of the Yeti Research Society's newsletter. "A couple of years ago we had a couple of reports from Weedon Island," he said, but they were not substantiated. Prescott believed Skunk Apes made their homes away from people. "You need the wide-open spaces before you'll see a [Y]eti," he maintained.[1169]

Many residents of Pinellas County remained skeptical. "Yeah, out there where they say they're seeing all these things there's a field with a big white horse; sure are a lot of people looking at horses these days," said one cynic. In the believer camp, those who thought they had seen the creature stated a fear of ridicule was enough to halt compulsions to share their encounters. "People laugh about it, they joke, you know, you don't want everybody to think you're crazy," Frank said. "I wouldn't say anything about [it if] others didn't say they'd seen it." Despite the experience of his avowed sighting, Frank appeared conscious that he had witnessed a creature that science hadn't confirmed, and the general public didn't consider as an extant, living animal. "It's like UFOs," he said. "You never know if there might really be some truth in those stories. I'm not sure I even want to know."[1170]

Steves Encounter

Ronnie Steves saw the Skunk Ape on Saturday, June 7, 1975, at his home in Venice, Florida. That night at around 10 P.M., and just as the 12-year-old was falling asleep, Ronnie heard a commotion outside at his duck pen. Looking out a window, Ronnie said he saw an unknown animal inside the pen chasing the ducks. He turned and called for his parents. When he turned back, the thing was gone.

Still in his pajamas, Ronnie went outside to investigate. "All the feathers of my ducks were all around the place," Ronnie said. Ducks had been plucked but also left alive. "When I saw what had happened to the ducks, I went to the other pen about 100 yards from the house to see if those ducks were all right," he recalled. At the pen, Ronnie noticed a section of fence bowed and bent to the ground. It was when he stepped toward it to assay the damage that Ronnie came face-to-face with the Skunk Ape, its blackish-brown hair-covered body illuminated by an outdoor light. "I looked up and there was this ape, it looked like a gorilla," recalled Ronnie. He ran back to the house screaming for help. Ronnie's parents and some neighbors chased the animal across the Lazy T Ranch before it lost its pursuers in the woods. Sheriff's deputies were called to the residence where they found tracks leading from the area and noted the bowed chain link section of fence.

"In 80 per cent of the cases, we have found that something has been at the scene," said Mike Corradino of the Florida Monkey Sanctuary in Venice who visited the Steves' home to investigate Ronnie's sighting. Corradino, a primatologist, believed the Skunk Ape did not act like a monkey and seemed to resemble a bear more than an ape. "They (monkeys) are not nocturnal like this thing is," he said. But, Corradino stated, the seven-to-eight-inch-long tracks it left behind resembled neither ape nor bear. Corradino and an associate, Rick Koplau, followed tracks from a field near the home to a fence adjacent to the Lazy T Ranch and then eastward toward the Myakka River. In their estimation, the prints bore the closest resemblance to a chimpanzee's. Reporter Jeff Stanfield wrote that Corradino speculated the creature may have been one of the chimpanzees from a nearby circus.[1171] However, the five-toed prints were dissimilar from a chimpanzee's due to the lack of a thumb-like big toe. "The ape would have to have been an unusual size and have deformed feet," Corradino said.[1172]

"I'm not going to say we have a skunkape and I'm not going to say we don't. There is just too much circumstantial evidence," he said. "Animals move around in the dry season and the skunkape seems to follow them," Corradino said, adding that the creatures move toward the coast as interior watering holes within the state dry up. As to its diet and bizarre feeding habits, Corradino admitted the creature appeared to bite the heads off its prey. "They (the heads) seem to have been gnawed-off. It doesn't seem too interested in the bodies just the heads." Corradino didn't know exactly what the Skunk Ape was, but its presence in Florida, was to him, a proposition beyond cavil. "There's no question there is something out there," he declared.[1173]

Corradino was himself attacked by a monkey. B. Ann Slate wrote of Corradino's interview published in the January 4, 1976, *Floridian:* "On Feb. 13, 1975, I was attacked by a seven-pound white-faced capuchin monkey. I had been working at the top of a 10-foot ladder, refurbishing a cage, when I felt a pain in my heel. Cecil had escaped from his cage over 500 feet away and sneaked up behind me. Most monkeys of this species will call out a warning. Cecil had slipped past our five dogs and my wife in complete silence. He slashed open my heel, narrowly missing my Achilles tendon. I jumped down from the ladder, but found I couldn't run. He was back on me in a flash, ripping open my other leg. Because I couldn't move, I was forced to keep throwing him off while trying to get any object with which to defend myself. Within seconds both legs and my left had were bleeding profusely where his three-quarter inch fangs had cut deep. I was trapped. There was no escape and I couldn't stop his relentless attacks. I knew I couldn't keep up the battle as I was getting weaker and would soon bleed to death if something didn't happen. In desperation I allowed him to get a hold of my left hand. I grasped his head in my right hand to keep him from getting free and clutching him like this I threw myself in our monkey moat a few feet from the attack site. I held him under water in an effort to drown him. For three full minutes his canines sank deeper and deeper into the fingers of my left hand but I knew if I let go he would be on me again . . ."[1174]

Gordon Prescott

Gordon Prescott said though he continually received new Skunk Ape reports, they were usually lacking in information and witnesses often requested their names not be printed. One item from the Society's newsletter, as reported by the *Star-Banner's* Patti Griffiths, told the story of a hunter walking along the Crystal River's bank who heard a noise in the bush ahead of him. Investigating, he was startled by the sight of a tall man-like creature staring back at him. The creature came at the hunter with hands outstretched over its head, giving him every reason to believe it was about to attack. Raising his weapon, the hunter shot it. The creature screamed and fled into the swamp, a trail of blood left in its wake. The hunter claimed he had another sighting of the creature which displayed no overtly violent behavior to him and promptly ran away.

Prescott told Griffiths two Boy Scout troops spied a Bigfoot in a quarry one mile southeast of Crystal River and U.S. 19. "They gave the standard description of a Yeti," said Prescott, "a large hairy creature, weighing from 600 to 700 pounds. They said the smell of the Yeti lingered in the area through the next day." Emphasizing the prevalence of odor, Prescott said the creature's smell was one of the key characteristics of a Skunk Ape sighting. "It's something like a skunk smell, but stronger," he said. "Once you have smelled it you never forget it," Prescott stated, affirming the odor's infamous potency. Prescott talked with Griffiths about the Society's investigation of the quarry sighting. "We never could nail down any evidence of the Yeti's presence in the quarry," said Prescott, "but reports from there kind of dwindled and we sort of abandoned the idea of further exploration. Since then the quarry has been officially closed down to us," he said.

As related in earlier chapters, it was during one of his amateur archaeology outings that Prescott had his own sighting. "While exploring Indian mounds several years ago I saw one," Prescott said. "It kind of sparked my interest. When you meet them they are not frightened, not angry—they act like they are more displeased because you are intruding on them," he said. "I believe they are above the intelligence of a dog or horse. They have an acutely developed animal instinct and some primitive form of communication."

Griffiths wrote that wildlife officers and biologists of the Game and Fresh Water Fish Commission, intimate with Florida's wilderness areas, had never reported sighting a Bigfoot creature. Society members, credited with having volunteered thousands of hours investigating sightings, estimated there were between 250 and 300 of the creatures making Florida's wild lands their home. Griffiths reported Dr. O. E. Frye, director of the Game and Fish Commission, had recently told Prescott the commission would aid the Society in the investigation and possible capture of one of the creatures. Prescott said plans were being developed by the Society to conduct a fall expedition for data collection and documentation of known sighting areas in South Florida.

> The group will track, photograph, study terrain and make plaster casts of footprints. A professional photographer and, hopefully, a portable darkroom, will be part of the expedition.

> Prescott said every effort will be made to photograph a Yeti but no attempt will be made to capture or harm one. The objective of the expedition is to collect and catalog data from the areas explored to be used for future magazine articles and books.[1175]

The Society's fall expedition was intended to be open to nonmembers who were comfortable in the outdoors and could pay their part of the two-week search. Griffiths wrote that L. Frank Hudson (member of the Peninsular Archaeological Society, and fellow witness with H. C. Osbon and others of a Skunk Ape in 1970; see Chapter 2) was the Society's point of contact for people interested in participating in the planned expedition. Per the *Manatee Times'* reporting in its January 1, 1976, edition that the Society disbanded in 1975, this expedition appears to have been one of the last functions for the group.[1176]

Venice Sighting

Two men found large droppings and footprints near Venice, Florida, on Friday, June 13, and both believed the sign had been left by an ape-like creature seen fleetingly in that area through the spring. One of the men said the tracks were "definite, distinct tracks between five and six inches in width and the big toe was an inch and a half across. There were (five) distinct toe marks. I'd say it (the track) was made early (Friday) morning or sometime last night." The men described the tracks as at least eight inches long but admitted it was difficult to be more precise because the heel—if there was one—was indeterminate. The front of the foot had pressed down into soft sand, and where the heel should have been was harder substrate resulting in an ill-defined shape. Inspection of the excreta left the men to conclude it contained vegetable matter and had not been left by a horse or other domestic animal; it was saved for further analyses.[1177]

Skunk Ape-hunters toting guns and nurturing hopes of bagging the elusive creature were enticed to the Venice area by the spate of sightings. Mike Corradino, operator of the Florida Monkey Sanctuary near Venice, was alarmed at the implications for public safety: "My first concern is that someone is going to be shot—possibly me and possibly some other person that is out looking for this thing," he warned. "There have been a number of search parties. It would be very easy to mistake a person for a big foot." Corradino's monkey sanctuary operated to preserve monkeys that had been rejected by their owners or had escaped. Corradino was also a Sarasota County animal control officer responsible for catching monkeys; in that capacity he had captured about 40 by 1975.

The rash of spring Skunk Ape sightings brought Corradino's skills and experience to bear on the problem. "A lot of major development is going on in this thing's territory," he said. "Hundreds of acres in the area have been cleared within the past year. This leaves much more open space and diminishes the creature's territory." Corradino said the creature's behavior did not align with typical ape behavior—the Venice sightings had almost all occurred at night, and belied a stealthy, secretive creature. Normally, apes are active during the daylight hours.

One rural Venice chicken owner said several birds had been killed, their necks "wrung." The chickens had not been eaten, atypical behavior for predators such as large cats, raccoons, and possums. A Florida Game and Fresh Water Fish Commission biologist told the *Manatee Times* that a Haitian Voodoo fertility rite involved the removal of a setting hens' head and leaving the body on the eggs, had reportedly happened in Venice during the spring. But Corradino explained such behavior could be due to natural predation saying, "it's not uncommon for animals to eat heads. Brains are tasty morsels."[1178]

Manatee Times staff writer William Braun wrote several articles on Skunk Apes, the following was published in the June 27 *St. Petersburg Times* and provides further comment on the Venice sightings and the difficulties that could be encountered while pursuing evidence in the field:

> I can understand the skeptics' point of view. One of the two men who found a footprint and some fecal matter June 13 told me that afternoon that a plaster cast would be made that evening and the stool specimen would be analyzed.
>
> Where is the cast and what were the results of the stool test, the skeptics can logically ask.
>
> There was not a successful cast and the stool specimen has not been analyzed.
>
> "Aha," the skeptics can say. "It's nothing but a hoax."
>
> That feeling is understandable.
>
> But I am well and personally acquainted with some of the people who have been involved in the attempt to find and identify the creature. And they are not hoaxsters.
>
> Mike Corradino is the man people have been looking to for help and information as the sightings have been reported.

> Corradino is one of the first people I met when I came to Florida four years ago. He is a fellow newsman and is news editor of the *Gondolier*, Venice's twice-weekly newspaper.
>
> He is honest and sincere and a credit to the business. And he has the good newsman's skepticism that means he doesn't accept things at face value if there's the slightest reason not to.
>
> In his spare time, Corradino operates the Florida Monkey Sanctuary, a non-profit refuge for monkeys that have become too mean or too old to continue as pets.
>
> Corradino is also a family man, the father of four young children and the bearer of all the responsibilities that go with being a parent.
>
> So I can understand that when two of Corradino's friends discovered a track and the fecal matter June 13, Corradino couldn't just walk out of the office and hurry on out to make a plaster cast.
>
> And I can understand how, when he finally had the time that evening, the friend who led him to the "track" got confused and led Corradino to the wrong spot and the wrong "track."
>
> When the other man who originally found the track went out to pick up the cast the next morning, he realized Corradino's cast of a wind-blown something was not a cast of the print he and the other man had found. And before Corradino could get the "real" print cast, it rained heavily.
>
> And Corradino simply felt there would be little to be gained by having the stool specimen analyzed. So it hasn't been.
>
> But Corradino's belief that people in his neighborhood are seeing something strange is unshaken. And so is my belief.[1179]

Braun speculated that the Skunk Ape could be a "wild man," a person intentionally avoiding direct human interaction. During the '70s, examples like Ishi and the Philippine Tassaday showcased the ability of humans to remain relatively unseen and unknown. Braun mentioned a closer-to-home example for his Florida readers.

> The possibility that a demented person is roaming the area is not as far fetched as it might at first sound.
>
> Just a few weeks ago, there was the case of the Chinese sailor who was caught after roaming the Green Swamp for months.

> And about 10 years ago, the sheriff's posse mounted a two-day search after a Myakka River area resident reported seeing a strange ape-like creature near his home.
>
> The hunt was successful. And deputies captured an insane man.[1180]

In an expansive *St. Petersburg Times* article published on January 1, 1976, Corradino shared his thoughts on the Venice investigation. "A year ago in the spring," Corradino recalled, "we were chasing what was supposed to be a runaway ape but it wasn't behaving like an ape. It was nocturnal. In the rainy season, it disappeared." Corradino postulated it followed waterways since almost all sightings were near a canal or other body of water and he believed the creature was very strong, capable of feats such as bending metal fence posts. And, according to Corradino, whatever it was, it typically showed no aggression toward people; in almost all cases, the creature skirted man's presence when it is aware people were nearby.

> Although good footprints were found in the area of the Venice sightings, Corradino says no plaster casts were successfully made. In one case, the footprints were washed away by rain before the casts could be attempted. In another, a property owner destroyed the footprints out of fear that knowledge of sightings on his property would hurt his business. And, Corradino admits, attempts at making the casts finally failed.
>
> "So that we don't appear like bumblers," he says, "let me explain that plaster casts are not as easy to do as it may seem." Since the frustrating failures of June, he said, he has read about making casts. If the sightings begin next spring, he'll be prepared to make the casts correctly.
>
> Most of the sightings in Venice in 1974 and 1975 were in the eastern part of town, right near a 39,000-acre wilderness that very few persons ever enter, Corradino says.
>
> "Anything could be in there," he says. "We know there's a Florida panther in there, for example, but very few people have ever seen her. The area is virtually untouched."
>
> Corradino says that based on circumstantial evidence there appears to be a Bigfoot, or Sasquatch, in Venice. "But scientifically, we have nothing," he says. Still, he believes.

> "The gorilla was only officially discovered in 1865," he says. "The giant Panda was discovered less than 75 years ago. We are always discovering new forms of plant and animal life. Why not Bigfoot?"[1181]

Jim Spink

Jim Spink, B. Ann Slate believed, represented the convergence of treasure-seeking and monster-hunting. In early 1975, Jim Spink, then 28 years old, conducted a one-man investigation into the Skunk Ape for his studies at Miami-Dade Junior College. Spink explained that his strategy was to doff clothes and wait patiently on a shell mound southwest of Ft. Myers. "What I'm hoping for is a confrontation and the establishment of some kind of rapport," Spink told Lee Butcher in the *Floridian* of July 13, 1975. "I want it to come into my tent, sit down, and let me have a look at it."

> For three months, a small orange pup tent filled with canned goods, water, books, and research equipment was the Yeti researcher's home—along with a retreat perched in the higher limbs of a gumbo tree when thousands of hungry mosquitoes decided to have dinner all over the 150 pounds of Spink's hide.
>
> Thus it was, upon returning from a routine search in the woods for tracks that the "hunters" met. A crane and bulldozer were positioned near the red-bearded student's tent. Spink, eating sparingly on scant rations and the island's wild herbs faced a well-financed, well-outfitted band of treasure-seekers.
>
> "They were ready to dig up my camp site," Spink related. "I told them that if I had to, I'd row into town and bring the sheriff back. So they didn't dig up my camp, even though they thought I was sitting on top of $150 million. I managed to keep them from doing it but it's pretty hard to argue convincingly when you're standing there stark naked!"
>
> While a mental picture of that situation might bring a chuckle, no ridicule is intended. Jim Spink's dedicated approach may seem somewhat unorthodox to the arm chair academicians who claim that no evidence of such a creature exists (and who further stay warm, dry, and safe behind polished desks), but those doing the grinding field work in the

> muck of the swamps, the baking deserts and the freezing snow-filled canyons feel otherwise.
>
> Spink believes he heard the Yeti scream from the dark bushes near his camp one night; a deep inhuman growl which rose to a crescendo of rapid chant-like tones. "Like a raccoon only much louder and with a deeper resonance."
>
> In following the trails of something enormous that plowed through the bush, a litter of decapitated raccoon skeletons were found. And then there was a pitch dark evening in his tree perch when the student swears the Yeti climbed up and sat, breathing quietly, near him.
>
> "There's no doubt in my mind that he was in the tree with me," Spink vows. "I could see this big, hairy shape and the glowing eyes. I sat very still, hoping not to scare him away."[1182]
>
> Bigfoot researchers are themselves divided when psychic factors or telepathic interplay between witnesses and hairy beings arise. And to add to still another split, there are the correlated sightings of UFOs and monsters in both time and geologic distribution.[1183]
>
> Like a subtle thread, UFO sightings wove a distinct design into the Florida Yeti tapestry in recent years.[1184]

Slate frequently illuminated a connection she saw between UFOs and Bigfoot. Slate found a case for linking them from a January 1974 UFO sighting by Mrs. Thomas Small, who witnessed a blazing orange object close to the surface of the Indian River, with Richard Lee Smith's claim he hit a Skunk Ape. Also, Slate noted a connection between the July 1974 orange-red object that reportedly crashed near Lake Okeechobee with security guard Kanter's Skunk Ape encounter. And, Slate also invoked the slew of aerial anomalies sighted over Lake Okeechobee in January 1975 with the following hairy hominid encounter from the January 1975 *Yeti Newsletter* edited by L. Frank Hudson:

> "Two cowboys recently reported seeing something large and hairy in a cow pasture about 10 miles from the northwest corner of Lake Okeechobee. They had previously found the carcasses of two cows that looked as though they had been literally torn apart by something with tremendous strength.

> The bodies had been torn in such a way that certain organs were missing, mainly the hearts.
>
> "Large, man-like footprints led away from the site. The cowboys followed these for some three miles, finding several more mutilated carcasses of other cows and one goat along the way. Then they came upon the thing. Their first impression was of its very foul odor. The next thing they knew, they were looking at what appeared to be a large, black-haired man. It stared at them briefly and then disappeared into the brush. They reported shooting at it but to no avail."[1185]

Slate made the following conclusion: "Again, it would be premature to connect the two phenomenon as yet, but like Mary's little lamb, where the one went, the other was sure to follow."[1186]

Juvenile Skunk Ape?

The *Palm Beach Post* of November 19 presented the remarkable story of a creature believed by a law enforcement officer involved in its capture to have been a juvenile Skunk Ape.

> Not deterred by the lack of evidence a Skunk Ape has never been captured—are Hialeah Gardens Police Chief Ray Bennett and Miamian Robert Morgan.
>
> Bennett firmly believes there are Skunk Apes and encourages hunters in his district near the Glades not to shoot them.
>
> What keeps Bennett going is an incident that happened seven years ago near his Glades area city of 3,000. Bennett says:
>
> "We got a call one night to go out to 20-Mile Bend, where there's a trash heap. We had to subdue a little subject about 3 feet tall. Its skin was black and furry and it wouldn't talk. It just mumbled and held on to your legs. I decided before we got it to the hospital that it wasn't completely human."
>
> Unfortunately, Bennett says, Jackson Memorial Hospital has no record of the "little subject." But since Skunk Apes have been spotted in recent years. Bennett says the creature he caught that night was "possibly a child Skunk Ape."[1187]

Sohl Encounter

John Sohl and six friends were sitting around a campfire one November evening in the Rock Crusher quarry in Citrus County, Florida. The group enjoyed singing ballads to the accompaniment of a strummed guitar. It was about midnight when sounds in the brush just beyond the light of the fire caught the group's attention. Sohl walked up a hill and from that elevation saw several upright hairy creatures, outlined in the bright moonlight. The biggest he estimated to be eight feet tall, a shorter female one "with very definite beasts," and a third, the smallest, standing at about five feet. Sohl hurried to his car to retrieve a camera, flash unit, and flashlight. Joined by one his friends, Sohl re-checked the shallow valley where he had seen the "family," but the creatures were gone.

"There were no clear footprints," Sohl told reporters. A slide mark was found showing where a foot had slid and carved a furrow in the ground. Sohl failed to recreate the effect on the same ground. Sohl concluded, "when we stepped on it, it didn't slide anymore . . . so apparently they were fairly heavy." Sohl returned to the fire to warm himself. After a time, and consumed by curiosity, he decided to stake out the scene. Finding what he thought was a good position, he sat in knee-high grass and readied his camera. As the flash built up power, the unit gave off a high-pitched squeal, which was later thought to be what brought a creature right up to Sohl's position. "Apparently this thing heard it and moved down to see what it was," he said.

Hearing a noise behind him, Sohl turned to see the large male only two feet away. He swung his camera and the flash unit blindingly dissipated the darkness. Next, Sohl felt himself airborne. "The moment I hit that flash, the next thing I knew I was in the air. The Yeti tossed me a good 15 feet." Sohl said the creature very quickly disappeared into the night. "After I was laying there on the ground was when I got scared." His friends responded to the flash of light form his camera and hurried toward him. They found his camera and helped him limp back to the campsite. Sohl was a student at St. Petersburg Junior College and was later examined and treated for several bruises at the college clinic. When asked at the clinic how he had gotten his bruises, Sohl replied dryly, "You wouldn't believe me if I told you." He interpreted the encounter as one of accidental contact; when the creature turned to flee, Sohl believed, its long arm swung out and struck him. As to the picture Sohl snapped, his camera lens had been focused for a subject up to 40 feet away and the camera, like Sohl, had been sent into blur-inducing motion.[1188] "I do know this, it got awfully darned close to me," Sohl said.[1189]

"I'd give his reports quite a bit of authenticity," said Gordon Prescott when asked his opinion on the Sohl encounter. "He's not given to exaggeration." During its tenure, the Society's newsletter had chronicled many Bigfoot reports in Florida. Prescott had received Sohl's report, who, though not a member of the Yeti Society "had done quite a bit of reporting for us up there."

Apart from being a student, Sohl worked part-time at a television service store and volunteered with the St. Petersburg Junior Achievement Program. His Rock Crusher experience had given him a yearning to learn more about hairy hominids. "Whenever I'm up there I keep my ears open for that sort of thing," Sohl said. He had heard of several additional reports from other campers using the area but tended to discount most of them. "You have to take it with a grain of salt," he said. Sohl said he explored many caves at the Rock Crusher but "there is nothing inside those caves but bats." However, on one occasion about three and a half years ago, Sohl believed he and his friends were close to a Skunk Ape. Another camper smelled something unpleasant and asked Sohl if he smelled it too. Upon opening the tent flap, Sohl was confronted with a smell he likened to being downwind from the Toytown sanitary landfill in Pinellas County—he considered this evidence of being close to Bigfoot. Sohl also heard something heavy moving through the brush in the darkness as well as "yelling sounds."[1190]

CHAPTER 7
1976

> Here in this forest, investigators have discovered a set of very strange footprints, human-like footprints about 18 inches long and seven inches wide; the footprints of a giant. A mysterious creature is roaming this wilderness, a creature that has confounded scientists, baffled investigators, and captured the imagination of millions of people. We have all heard of the reported sightings of this creature, a creature most of us know as Bigfoot. We have read about it in our newspapers and heard about it on radio and television. And some of you, like me, might have been skeptical about these reports, wondering how it could be possible for a sizeable population of 8-foot, 500-pound monsters to live among us on the edge of our industrialized society. Well I was skeptical, but I was also tantalized by what I heard, so I decided to find out for myself whether Bigfoot was fact or fiction. I did this by going out to talk to the eyewitnesses, questioning scientists, by examining the footprints, by looking at and listening to all of the available evidence. What I found out I will now show you, a body of evidence difficult to ignore.
>
> Peter Graves (narrator). *The Mysterious Monsters*, directed by Robert Guenette (Schick Sunn Classic Pictures, 1976).

Men's magazines like *Argosy*, *True*, and *Saga* were on the wane by mid-decade. In years preceding their passing they had represented a reliable platform for Bigfoot articles. Ivan Sanderson had written several articles for *True* in the late 1950s and early 1960s and he went on to become the science editor at *Argosy*—his tenure there involved breaking the story of the Patterson-Gimlin film in the February 1968 issue. In the early 1970s, almost as if a baton had been passed, *Saga* became the mainstay magazine for Bigfoot articles. By the end of 1975, *True* was defunct. *Argosy* was still going in 1976 but it too would soon cease publication. *Saga* persevered into the early 1980s. Bigfoot magazine articles in the mid-'70s had largely affected a shift from men's interest periodicals to paranormal and UFO-themed magazines.

Bigfoot Enters *Webster's Dictionary*

As a term, Bigfoot came to be applied to a broad collection of beings sharing defined characteristics: upright, large, hairy, and living in the wilds; an amalgam of ape and man, not only seen in the Pacific Northwest but encountered in the wilderness throughout the United States and Canada. The prevalence of usage led to Bigfoot and Sasquatch's entry into *Webster's Dictionary*.

> The words "Sasquatch," "Bigfoot," and "Omah" have found their way into a standard dictionary of reference by means of *6000 Words: A Supplement to Webster's Third New International Dictionary* (Kay and others 1976). The editors give this explanation for the words' presence.
>
> For all the years men have lived on earth, they have not exhausted the study of earth's natural history. It is true that discoveries of undescribed and uncatalogued animals and plants are not as frequent as they were in earlier ages, when whole continents were being opened up for scientific exploration. Nor have we yet discovered living things in our exploration of outer space. But we shall probably never feel confident that we know all the forms of life. Few new discoveries are as striking or as controversial as that, as yet unconfirmed, of a large nonhuman primate in the Pacific Northwest. Whether or not he exists, the animals' names, *Sasquatch* and *Bigfoot* are now part of our language. (Kay and others 1976: 13a).[1191]

Peter Byrne

Peter Byrne's investigative field research into Bigfoot continued into and through 1976. The page-one editorial of the May 1976 *Bigfoot News* explained that the Bigfoot Information Center's relationship with the public improved research by reducing the time between the occurrence of a Bigfoot-related event and the Center's ability to evaluate the subsequent report and place researchers on the ground to investigate. This enhanced relationship with the public was epitomized by the Bigfoot Information Center's outreach to exchange mutually useful information, what Byrne referred to as the "P.R. method."

> There are many ways in which to search for a Bigfoot. Most of them have, to date, proved only partially successful. One method, a method used by the Bigfoot Information Center in The Dalles, Oregon, is beginning to produce results and in the long run it may well prove to be the most successful method of all. It is one of the three methods used by researchers of the Center and it is called, simply, the P.R. Method.
>
> The initials P.R. stand for Public Relations and the P.R. Method is a system whereby the public is "employed" by the Center to provide information useful to the ongoing research program of the Center.
>
> Contact with the public is made by telephone and with correspondence and it is kept alive with newspaper articles, radio programs and television appearances by members of the Center. The *Bigfoot News* plays an important part in this public contact, presently being read by probably 2500 to 3000 people in the Pacific Northwest and through the US.
>
> Is the P.R. Method working and is it bringing in results? The answer is yes, it most certainly is and a clear sign of this is the visible reduction of the Time Gap, the problem child that has thwarted so many of our efforts since the Center program began in January, 1971.
>
> The Time Gap is the term that we use to describe the period that elapses between an incident—which can be a footprint finding or a sighting, taking place and our hearing about it at the Center. This, as we have learned over the past years, can be anything from a week to a month or more.
>
> But now the Time Gap is disappearing and within the last month the immediate reporting of no less than three incidents shows this to be true. The Wright Ranch, California, incident was reported within four hours. The Packwood, Wa., footprint finding, twelve hours. And the eastern Oregon report—an

> alleged sighting in the Wallowa Ranges—was received at the Center two hours after it happened.
>
> Fresh evidence—and its examination—are vital to the ongoing research of the Center. The P.R. Method is, at long last, beginning to provide us with that essential ingredient.[1192]

After a North Bend, Washington, theater's monster movie showing in January was followed by the discovery of Bigfoot-like tracks on Sunday, January 18, near the Snoqualmie River's south fork, suspicions became aroused. The tracks were discovered by Jim French, 38, a self-employed sub-contractor, and Joseph Langston, 33, a lumber mill employee, while metal-detecting for discarded and lost treasures along the river.[1193]

> French said he always believed reports of the Bigfoot "was a bunch of bunk" until he found the tracks.
>
> The four-toed tracks[1194] were 18 inches long and about 8 ½ inches wide, he said. The indentation they left, compared to those left by his own 180-pound frame, indicated whatever left the track weighed as much as 400 pounds, French said.
>
> French said he and Langston also found hair on some tree limbs along the path of the tracks. The hair was found about five or six feet off the ground.
>
> French said he made plaster casts of the footprints and intended to contact University of Washington scientists to let them analyze his findings.
>
> He added, "No man helped make those tracks. Whatever made them, made them by themselves."[1195]

The Bigfoot Information Center's Lynn McKinney was dispatched to examine the tracks, arriving in North Bend on the day after their discovery. After spending Monday night at a cabin along the banks of the Snoqualmie, McKinney examined the tracks and discovered they could be followed for about a quarter mile. The tracks appeared to show indications of slide marks and deeper indentations where the foot had found purchase moving uphill. The stride was variable: a longer stride was obvious when the creature moved across relatively flat ground.[1196]

Soon after McKinney examined the tracks, Byrne weighed in on their authenticity: "These were made with a device of some kind, like a hard board or a hard surface, probably a carved wooden foot," he said. "There's no pliability in them at all. And all of the footprints have three toes. There has never been a three-toed Bigfoot."[1197] (That is, Byrne hadn't accepted any three-toed tracks as genuine Bigfoot prints. Many unusual three-toed tracks, from several locations across America, had been found and attributed to Bigfoot by other researchers.)

Relative to Byrne's conservative approach to Bigfoot evidence, three-toed tracks served as a proverbial spanner in the works—unorthodox evidence at best and likely the result of hoaxing. Keeping with his moderate if not cautious methodology, Byrne unabashedly shared his doubts for Bigfoot's existence outside the Pacific Northwest, writing in his book *The Search for Big Foot*, that a particular Arkansas sighting (found in the May 16, 1851, edition of the *Times-Picayune*) "is the only one occurring outside the Pacific Northwest that seems to be describing a Bigfoot." Byrne's rigid conventionalism jarred with other researchers' findings and experience. In his review of *The Search for Big Foot*, Society for the Investigation of the Unexplained (SITU) member Robert Jones wrote he had in his possession not less than 145 Bigfoot reports from Pennsylvania, about 40 from New Jersey, eleven from Illinois, seven from New York, and six from Maryland. SITU files contained additional reports from Florida, Virginia, and other eastern states. Jones shared this rollup of aggregated sightings to counter Byrne's suggestion that Bigfoot was isolated primarily, if not only to the West Coast of the United States and Canada.[1198]

Another Byrne collaborator at the time was Richard (Rick) Noll who began investigating Bigfoot in 1969 and was a member of a college Bigfoot group while matriculated at Green River Community College. Noll's first opportunity to see Bigfoot tracks for himself occurred in 1975 outside Twisp, Washington, while investigating a sighting report.[1199] Noll participated in several field investigations with Byrne, including an ultimately disappointing excursion to the Wallowa Mountains in 1976.

> A report received May 1st of a sighting claim by a Sumpter, (eastern Ore) guide. Two Center researchers, your editor [Byrne] and Rick Noll of the Green River Community College Bigfoot Group, drove most of the night to reach the area at dawn. The guide, a Mr. "Sparkey" Walker accompanied the researchers to the actual place of the claimed sighting, a stream bed deep in the Wallowa Mountains, altitude about 4000 feet. After thorough questioning of the alleged witness, a search was instituted. Ground surfaces were soft after recent snow and deep

> drifts of snow still lay in many areas. The search, which lasted some six hours and covered the whole area a mile above and a mile below the incident, produced no evidence supporting the recent presence of a Bigfoot. Credit Rating, 2/10.[1200]

As he had done with the defunct *Manimals* newsletter, Byrne remitted occasional hairy hominid updates to *Pursuit* in which he described the Bigfoot Information Center's ongoing activities. Published in that magazine's summer 1976 edition, Byrne described in his missive several research tools apart from the Public Relations (PR) method actively employed by the Bigfoot Information Center, including credibility scales and Geo Time Patterns.

> Bigfoot, Homo Nocturnis, Update for 1976
> At the Bigfoot Information Center in The Dalles, Oregon, full time work on the Bigfoot phenomenon, now in its sixth year, progresses. So far 1976 has produced a fair amount of new evidence in the form of footprints, sightings (two) and historical background. The most interesting sighting was one reported in March. This sighting occurred south of The Dalles, where a woman and her two sons reportedly saw a large, dark creature climbing a boulder on the face of a steep hillside. Researchers were at the area within two hours of the sighting, where they employed night vision apparatus to scan the area in darkness. A dawn search was carried out on the following day. No definite evidence was discovered at the site.
>
> Two sets of footprints (containing from 400 to 500 prints in each set) were found in north central Washington. Photographs of these prints suggest that they are valid Bigfoot tracks, although the original prints were not fresh enough when examined by our researchers, to be positively identified. A credibility rating of 6/10 was given. (The credibility rating scale used is 1/10. High ratings are in the 7 to 8 area, moderate in the 4 to 6 range, and the lowest rating is 1.)
>
> Many people now know about the work which is in progress, and the aims which are the peaceful (non-violent) solution of the Bigfoot question by a find that will provide conclusive proof of existence, to be followed at once by protective legislation (in the US and Canada), long-term behavioral studies and, in time, communication with the creatures.

Methods

The Geo Time Pattern Method is a system that is used to determine the feasibility and potentiality of applying physical search to contained areas of probable habitat. It is, basically, a computerized form of study, the results of which indicate the most likely geographical areas for temporary habitat and the most likely time that the area may be used, as temporary habitat, by one of the giant primates. It is a method which has now been in use by Bigfoot researchers for about one year; it took more than four years of study before any usable results could be obtained. It is a method which holds much promise for the future, for it clearly indicates that these elusive giants do pass through certain geographic areas in regular time patterns.

The PR (public relations) Method is a system which, in effect, invites the general public to join in the search. The purpose of the system is to establish relations with a large segment of the general public whose work or play takes them on a fairly regular schedule into the general habitat of the primates. People are asked to write or call if they see or hear anything that looks as though it might relate to the phenomenon. In return they are promised that all reports will always be investigated regardless of how flimsy they may seem, and that complete confidentiality will be given to all persons making such reports. A long time ago it was realized that one major problem was the time gap that existed between an incident taking place or being discovered, and the report of the incident to researcher. The PR Method of research was begun to bridge this gap and (it is hoped) to eventually eliminate it. To date it has been working with ever increasing success.

This year for the first time we are accepting offers of volunteer work from suitable candidates throughout the US and Canada, in the hope that we may increase our strength from the present four to eight or ten people in the coming Summer months.

The mystery of Bigfoot is not one that is going to be solved in a few days. It is one that may yet take years of patient study and research, and for those who may find discouragement in this, we say look to men like Tim Dinsdale at Loch Ness (now in his sixteenth year of research there), and to decades of

> endurance, patience and determination which lie behind many of the great finds of history.[1201]

Bigfoot Talk at the Monessen Rotary Luncheon

The Monessen, Pennsylvania, Rotary Club's first weekly luncheon of August featured a talk by Pat Morrison, member of the Pennsylvania Center for UFO Research. About 50 Rotary Club members dined at the New Alpine Restaurant and listened to Morrison, a North Huntingdon Township mother-of-two, discuss Bigfoot as an extant creature. Morrison supplemented her talk with drawings and colored slides and explained what to expect if one should meet up with the creature (it wouldn't harm people "unless it is trapped or bothered," Morrison said).

"There is a story that one was captured in Texas in 1936 but, unfortunately, nobody got a picture even though the creature was jailed in the city jail for two months," she said. Morrison described Bigfoot as standing between 7 and 12 feet tall, had sunken red eyes, definitely not human, an able parent that actively takes care of its young until they are about five feet tall, enjoys eating apples, berries and corn, and weighs between 600 and 1,200 pounds. Morrison remarked Bigfoot had been seen practically everywhere in the nation including several locations within the Mon Valley of Pennsylvania. Proximity seemed to play a role in whether or not a witness smelled its horrid odor, likened to rotten eggs, sulfur, or bad meat. Morrison said domesticated animals, such as dogs and cats, feared the creature and would keep as far away from a Bigfoot as possible.

> The UFO volunteers [Pennsylvania Center for Unidentified Flying Objects] have made numerous casts of Bigfoot's steps, Morrison explained, and, in most cases, the volunteers have either arrived on the scene too late or left too early to spot the monster.
>
> Morrison is also convinced that there is a correlation between UFOs and Bigfoot.
>
> She said whenever the center gets calls about UFOs, immediately there are reports about Bigfoot sightings.

"I'm not saying that they came here from outer space, but there is some relationship," she said.

Several willing Rotary members entered into the debate over Bigfoot's existence. One asked Morrison if Bigfoot had indeed been captured, why wasn't it photographed at some point during its two months in captivity? Wouldn't it dawn on someone to get photographic evidence? Another Rotary member wondered about the plausibility of jailing a creature for so long that supposedly smelled so bad. Morrison stated many reports came from reliable people. In the Latrobe area, Morrison stated, Bigfoot had been reported performing such activities as eating apples, running through fields and even peeping into windows. "One gentleman even had a heart attack when he spotted the creature looking in the window," she said. Morrison played a recording of the Bigfoot's wailing cry. "Hey," one of the Rotarians said, "that late monster movie on TV can sure use that sound." Morrison told the gathering that if they ever experienced a Bigfoot or UFO sighting to call the police. Her organization, she explained, had a good relationship with the police in the area and such calls would be routed to them for investigation.[1202]

The Childress Article

William Childress' article in the November 1976 *Friends* magazine (put out by Chevrolet) highlighted several Bigfoot encounters and the author's discussions with several prominent Bigfoot researchers. "There are no experts," one unnamed interviewee (possibly Byrne) told Childress. "We are researchers. I set out with a vengeance to disprove the existence of the creature—but I've only succeeded in convincing myself that Bigfoot really does exist. When people ask me how they can live so near civilization yet not be captured, I tell them of Ishi, the last of a now extinct tribe of Indians. Near the turn of the century this amazing man lived on the very fringe of California towns, yet wasn't seen until his tribe died out and he strode from the woods to become a worldwide anthropological sensation. His story, called simply, Ishi, is available at any library." The unnamed interviewee also raised the discovery of the Tassaday. "The elusiveness of the Sasquatch does not prove it exists—it merely proves it is clever."

Childress interviewed a law officer, college-educated and trained to observe, who had witnessed something quite unusual one night while sitting in his squad car. Childress believed this man was an unlikely hoaxer and noted "the strain on the face of his young wife told me I was right, they were paying for having told their Bigfoot experience. To escape crank callers, many of them profane, they had obtained a private phone number."[1203]

> "On a clear, cold night in September 1972, a young Washington state law officer parked his patrol car off the pavement on a lonely country road. Lights from the City of Tacoma blinked in the distance. He turned on his amber warning signals, left his headlights on high beam, and began the nightly chore of writing his duty report. It was 1 A.M. and the road, though paved, wasn't much traveled. It was flanked by the dense evergreen forest this area of Washington is noted for.
>
> "I saw one vehicle pass," the officer—who asked that his name not be revealed—told me as we sat in his living room on July 7, 1976. "I went back to writing up the report. Suddenly I became aware of a strong, offensive odor, very powerful, a combination of rotten eggs, rotten meat, and Sulphur, but really impossible to explain. Once smelled though, it is never forgotten. It wasn't a wolverine, a bear, a skunk, or any other 'odorous' animal.
>
> "I glanced up and saw some shape, some shadowy form, at the timber's edge. Then to my astonishment a large, apelike animal—taking huge strides—walked directly in front of my parked patrol car, right into the headlight beams. It stopped, peered intently at me as if to say, 'You don't belong out here!' then strode across the road to a steep embankment on the opposite side. It went up the bank without hesitation, taking large unmanlike strides."
>
> The officer had just seen a Bigfoot—the all but legendary beast which, under various names, has been seen around the world. Perhaps the most famous is the "abominable snowman" of Himalayas, but it is also called Omah, Sasquatch, Dsonoqua, Giant Hairy Ape, Wild Man of the Woods, Bukwas, Seeahtik, Creek Devil, Smy-a-likh, and Bushman.
>
> Any journalist of experience is skeptical by nature, but my interviews convinced me that the interviewees were all sane, serious people with conservative occupations: a fire lookout with the Forest Service, a law officer, a reporter, a paving contractor, a store owner.[1204]

Childress called Grover Krantz, "easily the best-known and most knowledgeable scientist involved in Bigfoot research," whose opinions and thinking on Bigfoot remained consistent as the decade's years rolled on. "Bigfoot or Sasquatch," Krantz said, "is simply *Gigantopithecus*, a higher primate of great size whose jawbones and teeth were discovered in China's Kwangsi Province around 1958." Krantz invoked the coelacanth, another oft-cited example of an ancient creature that survived into modern times. "*Gigantopithecus*, alias Bigfoot, could have crossed to North America via the land bridge from Siberia. A higher primate, it is nonetheless not human—they don't make or use tools, they apparently are mainly solitary like bears, having no organized social groups, and they don't use language."

By the time Krantz and Childress talked, the Washington State University anthropology professor had collected 13 casts whose details indicated nonhuman feet. "They're differently designed," Krantz explained, "as they must be to carry a load of about 800 pounds—the usual weight of Sasquatches when fully grown. The foot bones are very strong, and the ankle joins the foot nearer the center than does the human ankle, for better leverage in taking huge strides. A few footprints are faked, but these are easy to spot.

"I'm convinced the Sasquatches are real," Krantz told Childress. "The casts of footprints is reason enough. But suppose we yell, 'fakery!' and try to prove it. Whoever the faker is, he's been around such a long time he'd be in his dotage by now. He'd have to be very strong, very clever, very ingenious mechanically, and be possessed of a great deal of anatomical knowledge to come up with such consistency in footprints. Besides, there have been so many footprints, it would require a small army to have made them.

"My conclusion is," Krantz emphasized, "the whole idea of a Sasquatch is ridiculous. But every alternative is impossible, so we're stuck with it. As Sherlock Holmes said, 'When you have eliminated the impossible, whatever remains, however improbable, must be the truth.'"

Krantz also expressed to Childress his unwavering conviction in the Patterson-Gimlin film: "It could not be a human in an ape suit," he emphatically pointed out. "I'm positive." Krantz remained in the camp advocating for obtaining a Bigfoot body for scientific study—including by means of killing one. "I know it would be sad to kill one, but I can't think of another way to convince skeptics that they really exist—and frankly I want a skeleton for further study."

After driving fourteen miles over bumpy roads, Childress arrived at the fire tower station atop the highest peak in the Colville National Forest for another witness interview. Bill Lamon told Childress about his experience in 1965 with Bigfoot. "My story isn't much," he insisted. "But I'm convinced the existence of Sasquatch is a definite possibility."

Lamon and a companion found giant tracks in the snow at the end of a fire road. "I was with a buddy," he started, "and we wanted to get an elk. We needed meat, and the cat skinner was gone for the winter, leaving his rig parked at road's end. Six inches of snow had fallen the night before, and near the bulldozer I saw several large footprints, very clearly outlined. They were the largest human-like tracks I'd ever seen. I estimated their length at 14 or 15 inches.

"We went a ways farther, and I turned to my buddy and said, 'Say, Ben, them tracks back there weren't bear tracks—they looked more like man tracks,' and Ben scoffed, 'Have you gone crazy?' So I just let it pass, but I'm certain now that what I saw were Bigfoot prints."

Childress' met with other Bigfoot researchers and people claiming encounters with hairy hominids.

> My route basically had followed mountainous areas thus far, but following my next interview—with a reporter on the *Tacoma News Tribune*—I proceeded westward down the Oregon Coast to Northern California, where many Bigfoot sightings have been made and many tracks found.
>
> The reporter, to my surprise, also refused to let his named be used. "Sorry," he said, "but I have to live around here. I've had enough cuckoo calls, which is why I got an unlisted number. But in answer to the questions you're bound to ask, yes, I think Bigfoot/Sasquatch exists, but what we have at this point are reams of unrelated phenomena which, if we can ever get it all together, will spell Sasquatch with a capital 'S'."
>
> The newsman holds high hopes for the Krantz/Green Bigfoot data file, and is pleased that a major Canadian university has donated free computer time for analysis. How did he come to believe in Bigfoot?
>
> "I was as skeptical as a man could be," he told me. "Then the contractor and police officer you just interviewed came to me and said, 'Look, we can't promise you'll see or hear anything—there are many nights when we don't—but come on out with us for a few nights and see if you get a story.' It seemed like a fair request, so I went. And the second night out, something roared like all the banshees of Hell a few hundred yards away. I vaulted into my car and locked myself in, scared silly."[1205]

Next, the reporter played a recording of an animal cry that impressed Childress for its power and its resistance to positive identification.

> The officer took a cassette tape recording, which, interrupted by bursts of static from the radio with which he talked with the contractor and the newsman (at different posts but nearby), was not easy to hear. But when the yowl of Bigfoot came on, it was instantly evident that the sound was one I had never heard. I was impressed and made a bit nervous by the sheer strident volume of the animal's cry. To me it seemed a little like the trumpeting of an enraged elephant, but much coarser and of ever louder volume. Even on the tiny cassette, it was a sonic demonstration of terrific animal force.
>
> "If you listen," the officer explained, "you can hear the animal luring coyotes to it by imitating them. It is primarily vegetarian, but will eat meat—especially in winter when vegetation is scanty."
>
> According to the patrolman, the next morning he hiked into the area the Bigfoot yowls had come from and found two dead coyotes. "They had been smashed against a tree ten and a half feet off the ground," he told me.[1206]

Further on in his journey, Childress met a couple from Florida who were fascinated by Childress' Bigfoot-writing project. "We've had sightings in Florida," they eagerly told him.

> Therein lies a curiosity. Since Bigfoot/Sasquatch seem most prevalent along the West Coast, how is it the animals have also been sighted in other states as well?
>
> Skeptics say they haven't—and indeed a recent sighting in my own State of Missouri seems evidence of this. Hulking youths in an ape suit were terrorizing Joplin citizens—and very nearly got themselves shot by nervous policemen. Such deceptions can be dangerous.[1207]

Yet another Bigfoot luminary Childress interviewed was Al Hodgson whom the author met at his variety store in Willow Creek, the town in which thousands of tourists had their picture taken in front of the carved redwood statue of Bigfoot. "I used to actively hunt the creature," Hodgson told Childress. "But there came a time when I had to choose: home and business, or Bigfoot."

> The wall of Al's variety store holds artifacts of his own hunts—casts of footprints, photos, a blown-up frame from Patterson's movie.
>
> "Roger called me from the phone that used to be beside the highway there," Hodgson told me. "He said, 'Al, I got me a *picture* of the son of a gun!' and asked me to come over and look at it with him. There is *just no doubt to my mind* that he photographed a genuine Sasquatch."[1208]

After its publication in *Friends*, Andrew Genzoli took issue with Childress' article on several points. Genzoli remained an enthusiast for the *idea* of Bigfoot but stayed incredulous concerning its reality.

> Childress even manages to drag poor old Ishi into the discussion—a total error on his part—since Ishi had no part of Bigfoot. A number of persons from whom Childress has quoted lack of credibility. Childress quotes an unnamed newsman which I feel would remain unnamed, even if Childress was invited to name him. And, I'll always question the film by the late Roger Patterson—since Patterson lacked certain credibility. I'd like to hear that someone I can believe in has really seen Bigfoot, but so far, no luck. I'd like to see old Bigfoot, too! And, if I do, I'll take a look at the last cup of coffee I had, to see if it might have been in the process of fermentation.[1209]

John Green

John Green visited Glen Rose, Texas, twice during 1976 to inspect possible human or human-like prints embedded into the limestone formation there, a location famously known for its preserved dinosaur tracks. Green's interest had been piqued after he watched *Footprints in Stone*, a film made in 1969 by Films for Christ Association. The film persuaded Green of "a convincing case that there were indeed human and giant humanlike prints in the same limestone as dinosaur prints." Green was aware that carved footprints (as well as fabrications of fossils) were sold during the Depression era and likely had the effect of scaring off any serious attention and study to the prints. Green's forays to Glen Rose occurred in March and July 1976.

During his first visit, Green discovered several of the prints featured in the film had been reclaimed by the river and were under water, covered over by silt. Cecil Dougherty, a chiropractor who made a hobby of studying the prints at Glen Rose, showed Green several exposed "tracelike marks that were exposed," all of which lacked evident detail. Green learned that there had been detailed tracks in the past which had eroded or washed away due to the violent flooding of the river. Green visited the Films for Christ office in Elmwood, Illinois, where he was shown casts of many of the tracks which appeared in the film.

During his second visit to Glen Rose in July, Green participated in an organized dig headed by Fred Beierle of Commerce, Texas, and Dick Caster, of Seattle. The organizers wished to expose new tracks by digging into the bank several yards from the river but only a small area was eventually excavated. However, Green used one of the dig's pumps to remove silt from several tracks thought to have been featured in the film. With the help of Jack Walper, professor of geology at Texas Christian University, Green was "able to clean out, dike and pump dry perhaps half the area excavated, including most of the dinosaur trail, three of five 'giant' tracks and nine of two dozen 'human' tracks."

Green decided the human-sized tracks shown in the film were not from the area the men uncovered. These "giant" tracks Green and Walper exposed were 18 or 19 inches long, seven inches wide, with a stride more than four feet long. Green realized even the best tracks lacked any clear detail, a similar feature shared with the dinosaur tracks. No evidence of claws could be discerned, a detail evident in the dinosaur tracks. Dr. Walper agreed with Green's conclusion that the tracks were made by a bipedal creature with elongated feet. "As far as I can determine, no creature known to have existed in any era would leave a similar trail, other than man or his close relative," Green wrote in *Pursuit*. "There does not appear to be any explanation that would not involve a considerable re-assessment of present theories to accommodate new information."[1210]

René Dahinden

On Tuesday, December 21, CBC-TV's investigative television show *The Fifth Estate* spotlighted René Dahinden,[1211] who had by that point devoted 20 years of his life to the Bigfoot hunt.[1212]

"I can't go to the moon, I can't climb Mount Everest, but I can find the Sasquatch," Dahinden told an audience of 400 at the National Museum of Man (later renamed the Canadian Museum of History) in Gatineau, Quebec. Dahinden said his efforts through two decades kept him poor and cost him his marriage. Dahinden spoke about the Patterson-Gimlin film and Russian scientists' acceptance of the film subject as something other than a man in a monkey suit. Experts believed, Dahinden told the crowd, that if the film was shot at 24 frames per second then it was a man in a suit. But if 16 frames per second was the film speed, then the locomotive system exhibited by the creature was entirely different to a man (a mammologist interviewed at the Museum of Man called the Patterson-Gimlin film an unequivocal hoax). Dahinden stated Bigfoot had no language, no tools, nor shelter and did not make fire. Bigfoot was non-territorial and walked in an easy, cross-country skier-like stride.[1213]

Ted Ernst

In 1976, Ted Ernst completed a two-month expedition in the Pacific Northwest with the American Yeti Expedition. Ernst was joined by Mike Polesnek of Anchorage, Alaska, for a search around Mount St. Helens, after which they journeyed to Richmond, British Columbia, to meet up with René Dahinden. The three men proceeded to investigate recent sightings in the Lummi Indian Reservation on the shores of the Puget Sound with the assistance of Lummi tribal police sergeant Ken Cooper. Cooper told the investigators the tribe considers Bigfoot to be men. "To kill one would be like killing your grandfather," Cooper stated. According to the *Massillon Evening Independent*, Ernst was secretary-treasurer of the American Anthropological Research Foundation, Inc. and Robert W. Morgan was listed as president.[1214] The AARF was an organization founded to aid research into the Bigfoot phenomenon.

Ernst and Polesnek also served as extras in Morgan's film *Blood Stalkers* which debuted in 1976. The "hixploitation" horror film centered on two couples menaced in the Florida Everglades by locals not overly keen about their presence.

Glassboro State College Students Search for Bigfoot

"There have been about 100 reported sightings of Bigfoot in that area over the past three years," said Richard Grigonis, speaking of the Paradise Lake region of Sussex County, New Jersey. "And approximately 75 dogs have disappeared, some from enclosed yards," he added. Grigonis was a journalism major and leader of a 23-person group from Glassboro State College (later renamed Rowan University) eager to conduct an overnight expedition to look for Bigfoot.

Paradise Lake is a man-made body of water located at the top of a 1,600-foot mountain in Stillwater Township. Stillwater Township is an area of rolling hills and flat valley floors located within the Kittatinny Valley in northwestern New Jersey. Paradise Lake is about 120 feet long and 50 feet wide and located a few hundred feet off the Appalachian Trail.

"We should arrive at the lake by late afternoon," explained Grigonis to reporter Peter Beck, speaking of the expedition's plans for November 11-12. "Then we'll set up three separate camps and do some exploring." Grigonis explained that the students' goal was to prove, at least to themselves, the existence of Bigfoot. "According to my research into past sightings, 'Bigfoot' is an ape-like creature which walks erect," said Grigonis. "Several Sussex County residents who claim to have seen the animal say that it has a blood-curdling scream." Joining Grigonis in organizing the trip were Doug Kirby and Jim Jordan, all G.S.C. students.[1215]

The collegians relied upon Jay Adams of Crandon Lakes, a local Bigfoot researcher for advice. In April 1976, Adams (who claimed to have seen Bigfoot six times altogether) said he saw what he took to be a Bigfoot family of five creatures, ranging in height from 4 ½ to 15 feet.[1216]

> "The creatures basically live in the Great Bear Swamp," said Adams. "There are sightings of them emerging from the swamp near Lake Owassa, crossing Route 521 and running up into the Kittatinny Mountains. The creatures use the mountain ridge as a sort of highway, running along it and then at intervals they make their way down to the lake communities, where they've been sighted foraging through garbage cans and grabbing about 75 dogs in total from backyards in the area. People use the ridge too—the Appalachian trail runs along it, near the top. Anyway, when hunting season starts, the creature goes northeast along the ridge and then down into Stokes State Forest."[1217]

Adams pointed out Paradise Lake to the group as a probable spot for strange activity. Grigonis, Kirby, and the rest of the students making up the expedition did not log any sightings of Bigfoot and decided to curtail their adventure when they realized that hunting season had started.

Another instigator of field forays, William F. Beamer, a SITU member, organized Bigfoot expeditions in southwestern Oregon and northwestern California. The 4-16-person expeditions had been advertised nationally since March 1976 and promised 22-day long forays into the wilderness to search for Bigfoot. Interested parties were invited to send inquiries to Beamer Expeditions and request a catalog of expedition dates and locations.[1218]

Oliver—Juvenile Bigfoot?

"It has a half ape, half human appearance, but we don't know what it is," said Michael Miller at a news conference held in his Manhattan office. "I don't know if he is the real Bigfoot," Miller stated referring to the enigmatic Oliver, an ape he had recently purchased. "His foot is about this big," he said, spreading his hands about 18 inches apart per one reporter' estimate.

Miller had, according to Peter Byrne, paid $10,000 for what the Manhattan lawyer believed could potentially prove to be a baby Bigfoot. "I understand he bought the thing from a circus in South Carolina because he had pity on it," Byrne said in an interview on Friday, January 2.[1219] Miller, Byrne stated, turned the creature over to a medical laboratory in Philadelphia for an examination and tests. Byrne said he thought Oliver looked like a chimpanzee and not a Bigfoot, based on two photos he had seen. The animal lacked Bigfoot characteristics, Byrne claimed.

"I am purchasing what I see to be a worthwhile investment," Miller told the press. "Whether he is a scientific phenomenon, I do not know. But I find him very fascinating. When I saw him I knew he was interesting scientifically but whether he is the 'missing link' I don't know."[1220]

Miller was indisputably impressed with what he saw as Oliver's catalog of special attributes. "Oliver's responses are also most human-like," Miller stated. "He does not have to be taught to do things. All you have to do is show what you want and he does it."[1221]

The *Oregon Journal* created a stir on Friday, January 2 when it quoted Miller saying he owned a live Bigfoot specimen.[1222] There were occasional guffaws from the press while Miller answered reporters' questions. The lawyer passed around three color photographs of the bald-headed, ape-looking animal. Oliver stood about four and a half feet, had pinkish brown skin, brown eyes and oddly-shaped ears (some compared them to *Star Trek's* Spock). Though it looked like a chimpanzee, albeit an odd-looking one,

Miller was adamant Oliver was a non-chimp. "When you look at him, you can see the obvious difference in his head which is dome-shaped when a chimpanzee's head is flat," said Miller. "He also walks on his hind legs and his spine is shaped like a human's. When he sits in a chair, he crosses his legs." Oliver had a flat face due to missing teeth, his jawline was shaped differently from other chimps, and he sported powerful shoulders.

Miller claimed he learned of Oliver's existence in December 1975 and became so fascinated with the creature he and an unidentified partner "invested" $8,000 to purchase Oliver from an unnamed animal act (Oliver was purchased from animal trainer Frank Burger, see Chapter 6). "I have promised to protect everyone involved," said the 34-year-old Miller, explaining his secrecy.

"If you tell him what a cigarette is and then ask him if he wants one, he will indicate 'yes' with his head," Miller told reporters.[1223] Oliver's age was given as seven years old, his weight at 120 pounds, and his diet as fruits and vegetables. Oliver was said to walk very erect and had "the ability to understand more than the average chimp and last but perhaps most important, his features are very human-like."[1224]

Oliver, the habitually bipedal, coffee-drinking, cigar-smoking chimpanzee, was reportedly captured in the Congo and sold to animal trainers in South Africa—Frank and Janet Burger. The Burgers were internationally renowned animal trainers. The couple were married for 38 years and later maintained a working partnership following their divorce. The Burgers trained animals for circuses, nightclubs, and television performances for nearly 50 years. One of their more dubious acts was Pepper the singing pig, which headlined an act called The Ham 'n' Egg Review for a Philadelphia 76ers halftime show in 1974. Pat Williams called the act, "the worst promotional disaster in 76ers history."[1225] After being thrust into the limelight, Oliver appeared on *The Ed Sullivan Show* and at New York's Radio City Music Hall.

A 2006 Discovery Channel documentary featured the ongoing fascination with Oliver. Test results analyzed in Japan revealed that Oliver had 47 chromosomes and might be a man-ape hybrid. One less chromosome than an ordinary chimpanzee, 47 is one more than a human being has. Dr. David Ledbetter, a geneticist at the University of Chicago conducted further detailed genetic analysis in 1997 showing that Oliver had 48 chromosomes, the full number for an ordinary chimpanzee. "So the report of 47 chromosomes was either a misinterpretation or a purposeful misrepresentation," said Ledbetter.[1226]

Oliver passed away Saturday, June 2, 2012, at Primarily Primates in Boerne County, Texas. Oliver was nearly blind in his later years, and when he moved, walked on all fours. A female companion, Raisin, had been placed with Oliver to keep him company.

Letter Concerning Bigfoot

> In regard to the letters on the subject of Big Foot. I'm a Sioux Indian and currently working at the North American Indian Alliance here in Butte. I've been able to help the Non-Indian and Indian to better understand each other and respect and accept each other's ways. It seems it is very difficult for some individual non-Indians to accept things as they are [in] the case of Big Foot and the North American Indians. It seems the Indians were of different nature and belief to the non-Indians and therefore were forced to change on behalf of this country's social conformity.
>
> My heart is sad when I think of what the majority of Native American Indians went through in the past and what they are going through now. I believe if there is a Big Foot, people should leave him alone [and] let him live his own way. He has not killed any of you or he hasn't tried to take away your land or your loved ones.
>
> If Big Foot chooses to live a life of solitude and in quietness and hiding, I believe he should pursue his happiness. If you tie a horse to a stake and compel him to stay there, do you expect he will grow fat? If you catch Big Foot and compel him to stay in one place, he will not be content nor will he grow and prosper. I hope that someday the human race will accept an individual as he is, and as he chooses to live. It does not require many words to speak the truth. Marty Cuny, North American Indian Alliance, Butte.[1227]

Bigfoot Theory and Science

William S. Laughlin, a University of Connecticut anthropologist, said in no uncertain terms that Bigfoot did not exist. "There are no living primates in North America, other than humans, and those which have been brought in for display and scientific purposes," he flatly stated.[1228] Such conclusions likely hampered broad professional scrutiny by scientists and may just as likely have had little impact deterring enthusiasts' zeal for further investigation and data collection.

The '70s were no stranger to advances in science and technology—new techniques and capabilities were evaluated for their potential use in the search for Bigfoot. One such technology and research innovation that surely excited some Bigfoot researchers for its potential applications was the study of grizzly bear habitats from space. This study started with a foundation of grizzly biology, its food preferences, social behaviors, spatial needs, and ecological considerations. "By understanding the grizzly's habitat in a specific area of wilderness," John Craighead wrote, "could we not more accurately estimate the population?"[1229] The goal of such population estimates was to improve decision-making for grizzly management.

Traditional techniques of color-marking and radiotelemetry were not ideal methods for habitat study. A solution was to harness a satellite's ability to distinguish types of ground cover. The intensity of light reflected by various types of terrain returned unique values and areas with specific vegetation signatures could be analyzed. A grizzly research project was undertaken by John Craighead, Jay Sumner, and Steve Ford (son of the President) within 81 square miles of Montana's Scapegoat Wilderness and "aided by the National Geographic Society, the National Aeronautics and Space Administration, the U.S. Fish and Wildlife Service and the U.S. Forest Service," the men "set out to map the grizzly bear's larder."[1230] That breadth of clout and support had not been (and continues to not be) afforded to areas of study considered fringe or farcical.

Landsat imaging (from the Earth Resources Technology Satellite) was preceded by two summers of vegetation sampling. The satellite image was displayed on a General Electric 100 computer's television screen, containing over 47,000 pixels, each a record of approximately 1.1 acres of terrain. By superimposing sampling-defined vegetation areas, a baseline was established for locating sample vegetation plottings, thereby instructing the computer what to "read", or "look for." Once "trained," the computer was programmed to look for other designated vegetation areas on a wider scale. Contours were added to construct a three-dimensional view of the land. The computer-generated map was vigorously tested for accuracy against sites of intense ground survey and scientists discovered an 88 percent accuracy rate.

Starting with the question, "How do animals use the land?" the map revealed centers of direct and indirect (tracks, feces, etc.) observation of grizzly activity. Grizzlies tend to favor the vegetated rock complex at 8,800 feet. Scientists knew what food grizzlies prefer; the Landsat imaging provided a picture of a broader area where the grizzly could find those food zones.[1231]

> Space technology can give greater understanding of grizzly bear numbers and habitat requirements. Now we need the wisdom to apply space science, courage to act in the interests of endangered species, and foresight to properly manage a rapidly changing national landscape where even wilderness may not be inviolate.[1232]

Grizzly studies informed officials and the public that this large animal lived in home ranges, mostly in high-altitude alpine environments. Granular details emerged on grizzly foraging, socializing, breeding, denning, and avoidance of man. Several Bigfoot researchers inferred that Bigfoot and grizzlies likely shared similar diets amongst other biological habits. Therefore, these researchers contended, an omnivorous Bigfoot's diet was likely comparable to what grizzlies ate—huckleberries, whitebark pine seeds, small rodents and larger game animals. Could environmental impacts on grizzly habits have the same effects upon Bigfoot? Many food sources experience year-to-year fluctuations in abundance—during periods of berry and nut scarcity, the grizzly must alter its diet to reliance upon grasses, sedges, and plant tubers.[1233]

In a period where it was popular to say, "We can land a man on the moon, so why can't we . . . ," technology that produced results like those from the Landsat ecological analysis was viewed with optimism by some Bigfoot researchers. The potential of new techniques and promising applications (perhaps excepting Biscardi and Findley's suspect infrared camera), were viewed as valuable means to increase knowledge about Bigfoot or, at least, refine inferences about its diet, behavior, and movement.

Terry Albright

Terry Albright of North Hollywood and four other men returned to the Valley from a Bigfoot search in the Bluff Creek and Willow Creek area. The quintet, all members of the Western Society for the Explanation of the Unexplained, brought back 11 plaster casts of large footprints which they had discovered. Albright was convinced Bigfoot spent some of its existence underground and he believed that sightings over the last 100 years followed a long, gentle "S" pattern from Alaska all the way to Mexico that roughly corresponded to earthquake fault lines. These would be relatively good places, Albright reasoned, for Bigfoot to find abodes in caves or tunnels; they could go underground to evade searchers and if they died underground it would guarantee their remains would be undisturbed.

Albright believed there could be a connection between Bigfoot and UFOs since witnesses often saw UFOs following sightings of Bigfoot, the former perhaps fulfilling some kind of caretaker role for their hairy wards. "My personal theory is that Bigfoots are in some way related to UFOs" said Albright. "The Indians in Pennsylvania have legends of Bigfoots dropped from shiny moons."

> Another possible explanation for so many Bigfoot sightings, especially around Newhall-Saugus and Palmdale, Albright said, is the bionic man the government is putting together at Edwards Air Force Base. Instead of a real Bigfoot, people are seeing Steve Austin on a training mission.
>
> "That's an extreme possibility," Albright said, "but there have been rumors about it for years. There are also stories about a UFO they have out there. But the government won't cooperate with researchers and tell us what they know."
>
> Nothing is but thinking makes it so, another adage goes. Terry Albright has all the outward signs of sanity. He pays for his Bigfoot research by working as a carpenter.
>
> "I believe in it because I can't be convinced that it doesn't exist," Albright said. "To me it seems conceited to say Bigfoot or UFOs don't exist."
>
> As with religion, apparently, one begins by either believing or not believing, and the burden of proof then rests on whichever persuasion is on the other side.

"Anyone I've talked with about unexplained phenomena is extremely interested," said Albright. "People don't think I'm nuts. Usually they have experiences of their own they want to tell me." Albright said it was easy for him to be a Bigfoot believer, because three years ago he saw one near Saugus. "I was driving along the road and it jumped out, right across the two-lane highway," Albright recalled.

"There have been more Bigfoot sightings there than anywhere else," Albright said, speaking of Bluff Creek and Willow Creek. Of his trip to that area, Albright said his group went armed with cameras, tape recorders, walkie-talkies, and a high-frequency transmitter brought to act as a lure for Bigfoot. "Down here if you talk about Bigfoot, people might say, 'Oh sure,' Albright said. "But up there it's a matter of fact. People have been seeing them for years."

"I personally don't feel that they're any threat. There has never been any account of one hurting a human being." Along with finding and casting footprints, Albright said his group heard strange noises one night on their expedition. "It was like a donkey braying, but without the hee-haw sound," Albright explained. "The sounds were coming from three different places. It was the strangest thing I've ever heard. Talk about making the hair on the back of your neck stand up."[1234]

Bigfoot Taxonomic Proposal

The July 1976 *INFO Journal* described John C. Holden as a "consulting geologist, paleontologist, artist and humorist of science." With a dose of humor, Holden proposes in the same edition of *INFO Journal* a taxonomic description for Bigfoot following the International Code of Zoological Nomenclature's convention for the establishment of animals' new scientific names.

> It is hoped that the following brief statements will act as a standard for future reports and help guide and correct the imaginations of those reporting.
>
> Class .... MAMMALIA
> Phylum .... CHORDATA
> Suborder .... CATARRHINI
> Superfamily .... HOMINOIDEA
> Family .... HOMINIDAE
> Genus .... SASQUANTHROPUS
> Species .... MEGAPEDITATUS
>
> Holden designates the holotype for *Sasquanthropus megapeditatus* as the largest living male residing near Sasquatch Pass in the Cascade Mountains, Whatcom County, Washington.[1235]

Print & Media

The success of the movie *Jaws* (1975) catapulted sharks into the vanguard of popular monsters. But Bigfoot, the quintessential American bogle, maintained a steady and firm grip on the public's interest and imagination.

> Fans of the beast and skeptics alike will find books about the man-animal at Timberland Regional Libraries. For patrons of those libraries where the supply of books about Bigfoot has already been checked out, requests will be taken and filled in order.
>
> "Since the film has been released [*The Mysterious Monsters*], we've already experienced an increase in the number of requests for books about the Sasquatch," a Timberland employee said.[1236]

Strange Monsters and Great Searches was one of those popular children's books at Timberland Regional Libraries (WA). Authored by George Laycock, a wildlife management specialist, it portrayed monsters as Nature's unsolved mysteries. Other popular books at Timberland Regional Libraries were Green's *Year of the Sasquatch* and Grumley's *There are Giants in the Earth*.[1237]

Eleven-year-old editor Jamie Keller steered an editorial board of other 8-to-10-year-olds in the production and publishing of *Monster Tribune*, a newsletter resulting from an after-school workshop at the La Crosse (WI) Public Library, whose purpose, according to assistant children's librarian Linda Kramer was to teach youngsters how to use the library as a resource and to stimulate a love for reading. A vote of the editorial board showed that the children believed Bigfoot was in fact real, but the creature seen in Cashton (the Cashton Creature, see below in this chapter) was regarded by this youthful constituency's consensus as a mere hoax. *Monster Tribune* was a mix of monster lore, scholarship, and lots of imagination.[1238]

Genzoli on Place's *Nobody Meets Bigfoot*

Marian Place's book, *Nobody Meets Bigfoot,* told the fictional story of a family's third son who considered himself a "nobody" until the day he meets Bigfoot. Andrew Genzoli, who wrote about Place's *On the Track of Bigfoot,* took on her second Bigfoot book with an expected combination of glibness and interest in the subject.

> Bigfoot will always be a good subject for writers, and since we first found the old boy in our midst he has made the world's press, has been a subject for national television, and a choice topic for book publishers.
>
> Now, Marian T. Place of Jacksonville, Ore., comes along with her second book on Bigfoot. This time it is "Nobody Meets Bigfoot," which is just about the most truthful statement ever made in print. Those who have "seen" Bigfoot, "photographed" Bigfoot, and made other claims are way out in limbo—just like the funny people who claim they have "ridden" flying saucers between Trinidad and Hoopa.
>
> The last book Author Place wrote, was "On the Track of Bigfoot," which told about the events in the past few years which remain a mystery to this day. That book, and this one, were printed by Dodd-Mead. Both are written for the younger reader, 10 years and up, of course the story is fiction, but enjoyable.
>
> If your book shop doesn't have a copy, they can order it for you.[1239]

Jan Klement's *The Creature*

Jan Klement is the pseudonym for the author of a very different kind of Bigfoot book. In the pages of *The Creature*, Klement penned one of the earliest works to focus on Bigfoot habituation. Klement was at The Diggins, his rural cabin in southwestern Pennsylvania, when after a day of hard work improving his property, he was startled to see "a large hairy creature."

> I was trained as a scientist and if I had to, I would track the creature if at all possible and study it. I would keep the incident to myself since anyone seeing "[B]igfoot" like creatures were portrayed as looneys by the news media. I take this method now to tell of my subsequent meetings with the creature and the events that followed. You may doubt me or believe me, your opinion is of no consequence to me or to truth.[1240]

Klement named the creature "Kong" and successfully entered upon a series of follow-on encounters. According to Klement, the time he and Kong spent together was often droll, if not for the reality of being in the immediate presence of a Bigfoot.

> In our many hours of just squatting and looking at each other there seemed to be no purpose on his part. He seemed to anticipate that I would devise something or do something to give him something. It does not seem strange to me that we would sit and look at each other for hours. I do that with my cat to this day.

Klement observed Kong display a fear of metallic objects, noted his love of apples, and witnessed his toilet habits. Klement effected simple communication with Kong, including STAY and GO. The author concludes his book suggesting other encounters he believed provided the public with accurate descriptions of Bigfoot and their behaviors. Among these Klement includes the report given by Chester Yothers of Whitney (see Chapter 4) whose encounter occurred in western Pennsylvania.

Wildman of the Woods

One of the more unusual Bigfoot books of the '70s, Ed Bush and Terry Gaston's *Wildman of the Woods*, subtitled "An Encounter with Bigfoot," was published upon the heels of a girl's claim she had been abducted by a Bigfoot.

Wildman of the Woods contains usual references to Bigfoot history including Jerry Crew and Roosevelt's Bauman tale. The authors asserted several points on Bigfoot behavior, among them:

- Bigfoot lives in family groups
- Pregnant females carry for fourteen months
- A baby weighs about 40 pounds at birth
- The population of Bigfoot is decreasing in our modern age

The book is divided into two sections; the first part is a fictionalized account of a young Bigfoot. The writing jarringly switches from third to first person, occasionally within the same paragraph. The protagonist was a Bigfoot who with his brother survive an attack by humans which claimed the lives of their parents. Later, the brothers befriended another group of Bigfoot—a father and his two sons. But this family were sick with a disease contracted from men. The protagonist Bigfoot picked medicinal roots to help his new friends.

> I stayed with the smallest one at all times, for it seemed like he was getting worse instead of better. The juice from the

> roots was not helping the sickness go away and I felt there was nothing more we could do for them. During a bad coughing attack, the smallest one could not catch his breath and he died there gagging for air. It was very sad for all of us when we took him out to place him under ground. We had been taught to do this with our dead so wild animals would not find them and drag them off to be eaten. My brother helped me dig the hole that was big enough to place the small body underground.[1241]

The remaining newcomers as well as the protagonist's brother later succumbed to the ravages of man's disease. Setting out on his own, the lone Bigfoot met another group, including a female named Tasha. Together they become mates and have a son they name Kumo.

The book switches from Bigfoot speculative fiction to Bush and Gaston's interest in Bigfoot and their formation of Outdoor Adventure Motion Pictures. They hired "several women that had been trained for some time previously in the art of photography and the most important of all, physical fitness."[1242] The group went into the field in northern California to investigate an area of recent sightings. They followed a technique which they attributed to the Fish and Game Department of California—female-scented baits. Bush and Gaston's goal was to lure Bigfoot in close to their cameras and film it.

Bush and Gaston then describe, from their point of view, a real-life event—the alleged snatching up of 23-year-old Sherie Darvell (also given in newspaper articles as Duvall) and her subsequent return to society.

> She was hardly recognizable to her friends as she was bruised and torn severely. She could not talk much then, of her ordeal, so her friends could only imagine her suffering. Her hair was a tangled, matted mess and she had several cracked ribs. Her fingernails had been cut back so the authorities could analyze the soil to determine the facts. They learned that her clothes and other personal belongings, such as her purse, had been confiscated.[1243]

The self-published book is illustrated with several simple drawings. Of the two copies this author owns, one has a printing error which repeats a significant portion of chapter 2.

The "Darvell abduction" story was well-covered by the media who had a field day with the purported kidnapping of a young woman by Bigfoot. The story's eventual denouement was beset with cries of hoax, which certainly remains the present opinion of the event. The details of Darvell's aspiring movie-making group's actions up to and including the point the creature absconded with her are based upon her colleagues' conversations with reporters and law officials; print media accounts do not mention witnesses to Darvell's alleged abduction other than the members of Outdoor Adventure Motion Pictures.

The purported abduction occurred on Saturday, May 22. The Outdoor Adventure film crew told authorities late Saturday afternoon that one of their party, a young woman named Cherie Darvell, had been carried off—kidnapped—by a Bigfoot while the group filmed their search for signs of the mysterious creature between Weitchpec and Orleans.[1244] Darvell reportedly hailed from Modoc County, California, and from Longview, Washington, and was described as an unemployed beautician who also used the name Cherie Nelson[1245] (in at least one account she was called Sherry D. Nelson[1246]).

The members of Outdoor Adventure Motion Pictures—Ed Bush, Terry Gaston (listed in some articles as Grafton), Cherie Darvell, Kathleen (Kathi) Bush, and Jacqueline Bush[1247]—arrived at their selected research area and began putting out scent lures in a ten-mile radius around their campsite. Below is the account by Bush and Gaston from *Wildman of the Woods:*

> Ed and Terry returned to camp first, after checking their assigned traps, then later a few more returned. The only two members that had not yet returned were Ed's Daughter, Kathi Bush and her friend, Cherie Darvell. As the crew members awaited their arrival they grouped together by the creek while Ed took pictures of one of them fishing. At about 11:00 A.M., when Kathi and Cherie arrived at the last trap within everyone's sight. All hell broke loose. A frightening scream rang out through the valley as Kathi was brutally pushed down the bank by a large gruesome looking figure that had appeared out of nowhere. Ed immediately turned his camera towards the screams as he captured on film, the hairy giant as it picked up Cherie in one arm and made its way into the thick timber. It looked to them like he carried her as if she was as light as

> a feather. Terry, looking with disbelief reached for his pistol, fastened to his hip and fired two shots in the air to try to get the thing to drop Cherie.[1248]

The account Bush and Gaston told to officials and media closely followed the abduction tale related in their book, to wit, Darvell and Kathleen Bush were walking along a trail some distance from their camp while scattering marshmallows (the medium to which human female scent had been applied). The pair were startled by a hairy creature suddenly springing from the brush; it pushed Kathleen aside, scooped up Darvell and absconded with her.[1249] Bush stated the shove the Bigfoot gave Kathleen caused her to tumble 40 yards down the steep trail and consequently she did not get a good look at the creature.[1250] An unidentified member of the group described the hirsute kidnapper to authorities as "a big furry animal, not a bear, but which looked like descriptions of 'Big Foot.'"[1251]

Responding to a potential abduction, the Humboldt County sheriff's office and U. S. Forest Service sent officers and personnel into the mountainous area 40 miles north of Eureka on Sunday, May 23, to search for Darvell.[1252] Deputy Jack Whelihan, credited as the director of the ensuing search, described the abduction: "Mr. Terry Gaston said he saw Bigfoot hover over Sherie Darvell like a big bat, and then pick her up and they disappeared up the canyon. He said it was Bigfoot. Said it looked just like the pictures."[1253] Along with a search helicopter, as many as 150[1254] searchers were on the ground looking for Ms. Darvell on Monday (May 24). A *National Inquirer* reporter told detectives he thought the whole business was a hoax and that Darvell's companions intended to make a book or movie about Bigfoot (both of which they did). Outdoor Adventures members were seen filming the search efforts of the deputies, helicopter and search dogs.[1255] Apparently not unaware of possibilities for the event's monetization, the remaining Outdoor Adventure members simply, if not innocently, kept their cameras rolling.[1256]

"We don't really know what we've got up there," said Sergeant Harold Reed of the Sheriff's Department. "A young lady is missing. Until we can definitely show it's an unfounded call, we handle it as if it's strictly legitimate." Early reports from Monday stated searchers had found a tennis shoe identified as Darvell's and discovered several footprints measuring 16 inches long and eight inches wide.[1257] "We are treating this seriously," Reed said. "We have a girl missing. None of her relatives has heard from her. We don't know what we have. Even if this is a prank, this is serious."[1258] Peter Byrne said two associates from the Bigfoot Research Center investigated the matter to determine if Bigfoot was really involved.[1259] Byrne maintained a skeptical opinion of the affair, though he was aware accounts of Bigfoot abductions were not without precedent.[1260]

An AP story in the *Spokesman-Review* quoted a Debbie Darvell of Redding, given as a cousin to Cherie: "I just think it's weird," she said. "I believe in Bigfoot, but it's strange that he would just take her. Why didn't he kill the other people or something, too?"[1261]

"We'll continue the search until we either find her or establish what the deal is," said Sgt. Harold Reed of the Humboldt County Sheriff's Department. Asked if the disappearance was a hoax, Reed said, "we never discount this as a possibility." Bear hounds were brought to the area but were unsuccessful in picking up Darvell's trail.[1262]

Late into the drama's second day, Darvell turned up at the Bluff Creek Resort, about five miles from where she had reportedly been abducted. When found on Monday, she was sans one tennis shoe and screaming hysterically.[1263] Once in a calmer state and able to relate her recent travails, Darvell said she had passed out after being grabbed up by the "big, black beast," and awoke during the night, alone, somewhere in the woods.[1264] "I don't think it meant to hurt me at all," Darvell told a reporter, "It could have if it had wanted to."[1265] Darvell struggled to recall details of the creature, claiming she never got a good look at its face. "It was just big and hairy." Darvell said she wandered aimlessly for a day and a night before finding a highway leading to the sanctuary of the Bluff Creek Resort.[1266]

"We got a report of a woman screaming at the resort," a Humboldt County Sheriff's office spokesman said. "Our units . . . found her and called an ambulance. She's been through quite a lot."[1267] Darvell was taken to the Humboldt Medical Center at Hoopa, where examination revealed she had scratches and bruises and she told a nurse her left arm hurt.[1268] Humboldt County Sheriff Gene Cox stated Darvell turned up mumbling, "They wouldn't stop and pick me up," referring to vehicle traffic on the road. Cox said when Darvell was asked if she had been abducted by Bigfoot, she began to scream.[1269] But Sheriff Cox noted that overall, Darvell seemed to be unharmed physically. "She's not in too bad a shape," Cox said.

The more he dug, the more Cox became skeptical of Bush and Gaston's kidnapping claim and Darvell's own tale of being held as Bigfoot's prisoner. Ultimately, Cox found cause to dispute the kidnapping account and threatened to press charges if he could prove Darvell's disappearance was a hoax. He noted the fresh perfume and clean clothes worn by Ms. Darvell when she surfaced. Displaying a knowledge of Bigfoot reports, Cox noted most people who claim a Bigfoot sighting report a "foul smelling odor permeating this so-called animal or human."[1270] Darvell suggested that perfume from a woman who held her consolingly at the resort had rubbed off on her and her clothes were only slightly soiled for having spent some of her ordeal on a carpet of leaves. On Thursday, May 27, Darvell was reported to have volunteered to take a polygraph test.

Bloodhounds were able to backtrack Darvell's trail from where she resurfaced back into society. Her trail was followed for several hundred yards down the road to a point where her footprints were associated with those of two other individuals. The dogs lost her scent at Highway 96. Cox told reporters that Darvell's psychiatrist had spotted her riding in a car in Redding during her alleged abduction. Commenting on the uncooperativeness of the film crew, Cox stated that officers and Darvell's associates had nearly come to blows when authorities asked for items of Darvell's clothing to give to tracking dogs. At its height, about 150 searchers looked for Darvell, including deputies, reserve officers, marines, National Guard Soldiers, Forestry Service officers, conservation camp inmates, and local volunteers.

In the days following Darvell's resurfacing, Cox said Darvell's compatriots "have been very uncooperative" since the initial abduction claim. "Their total lack of cooperation with the investigation indicates the whole thing was a fabrication and has no connection with any mystical animal they alleged kidnapped the girl," he said.[1271] "We are not satisfied with the story we are receiving from the parties involved," Cox summed up.[1272]

One of Cox's biggest suspicions rested squarely on Bush's claim he had filmed the alleged abduction. But despite the magnitude of this exculpatory evidence, Bush had refused to surrender the footage to authorities. Darvell had initially been open about her experience with officials but refused to make further comment after talking to Bush on Tuesday morning, May 25. This was followed by Outdoor Adventure personnel informing officials they were not making further statements without consulting their attorneys. At the time, knowingly making a false report of an emergency was a misdemeanor carrying a one-year jail sentence and $1,000 fine.

Sherriff Cox said that despite the claim of the circumstances surrounding Darvell's alleged abduction, his department had to take it seriously. "You can't just ignore a missing person report, no matter how flaky it is," he said. "If there's a possibility someone is lost or hurt, you have to act." Cox also admitted there had been a measure of local pressure from people who believed Bigfoot was a real creature. "I don't believe in monsters," Cox said, "but there's people around who swear by the '[B]igfoot.' If we had just ignored that report we'd have caught all kinds of flack." The tweezed implication is that context was important in the Darvell case; a report of little green men from Mars abducting someone might not have received the same amount of heightened attention in the Bluff Creek region. "Bigfoot's kind of a local favorite," the Sheriff admitted. The sheriff's office had been deluged with phone calls from news media across the nation as the incident received wide coverage in print and television. "I guess it's sort of different," Capt. Wendell Cyphers said. "Flying saucer stories are getting kind of old hat and the exorcism fad seems to have died out." Capt. Wendell added, "Bigfoot has been a local thing for a quite a while, but I guess he's sort of new out of the area." And as is prevalently recorded in the '70s, Bigfoot or the local monster-of-record is simply good for promotion and exposure. "One good thing—the county probably got more national publicity than the Chamber of Commerce could have ever dreamed of," said Wendt. "The tourist business up around Willow Creek and Hoopa should get a heck of a lift from all this."[1273]

Mac McDonough wrote several articles on Bigfoot for the *Bakersfield Californian* during the '70s. He learned of the abduction saga while listening to a San Francisco radio station and an intrigued McDonough learned the hirsute abductor was described as nine feet tall and about 350 pounds. Those proportions, McDonough noted, gave Bigfoot the physique of a pencil. "Possibly I'm wrong about Bigfoot's gentleness. Maybe in the years since I first heard about him, he has turned bad. Maybe," McDonough wrote, "he flipped his lid reading and hearing about the coming Presidential election and mistook the woman [Darvell] for a candidate's speechwriter or campaign chairperson. In that event, I can't fault the big fellow. But," he continued, "if he's nine feet tall and weighs only 350, he's emaciated—and he couldn't have carried that woman very far."[1274]

District Attorney John Buffington told the press that the Humboldt District Attorney Office would investigate possible charges in the Darvell case. Initial estimates of the search's costs topped off at approximately $15,000. Sheriff Cox had already shared his opinion that Darvell's condition, when found, was inconsistent with someone missing for 50 hours in the mountains and officials were publicly speculating that the report of abduction was all a publicity stunt for a movie Outdoor Adventure Motion Pictures was shooting. Buffington said the matter of pressing charges depended upon determining if the abduction constituted a "false report" of an emergency or felony. "A kidnapping would normally be a felony,"

Buffington said. "On the other hand, an attack by an animal obviously isn't. It might constitute an 'emergency', but the penal code isn't absolutely clear on that point." With some evidence of humor, Buffington added, "I'm not sure what section a reported attack by a mythological monster would come under." Suspicions and doubts aside, the fact was that Bigfoot had been the ostensible catalyst for an expensive search operation. "The situation may not have been envisioned by the framers of the legislation," Buffington said. "At any rate," the district attorney continued, "we're working on it. Frankly, I'm even more anxious to see the county recover some of the money we had to spend on this business."[1275] Toward that precise end, on Tuesday, August 17, the Humboldt County Board of Supervisors voted 4-0 to bill Shasta County $11,613[1276] for the Darvell search.[1277] The board's vote was instigated under a seldom-invoked state law permitting the billing of the victim's home county of residence for charges incurred from search or rescue efforts.[1278]

Ron Olson had formed a dim view of the Darvell affair. "I've got a feeling it's a hokey," he said. "Especially after finding out that they were in there to make a Big Foot movie. If you've got a camera and a thing like that happens in broad daylight, why haven't you got some pictures?"[1279] About 16 months after the abduction claim, evidence surfaced that Bush and Gaston's aspirations to create and market a Bigfoot film had in fact enjoyed celluloid consummation. The *Eurek Times-Standard* from November 16, 1977, contained the following story under the title, "'Bigfoot' Flicker Interests DA":

> Outdoor Adventures this week is presenting in Redding the 60-minute color epic "Wild Man of the Woods—Humboldt County Bigfoot Abduction," and Humboldt County's district attorney say he is interested in seeing the film.
>
> The film has already enjoyed exclusive engagements at the Birney Lions Club, the Weaverville Civil Defense Building, the Hayfork fairgrounds and Siskiyou College in Weed. And it is scheduled to be screened this weekend at the Redding Civic Auditorium, according to an ad printed in the Redding Record Searchlight.
>
> An advertising department spokesman for the newspaper said the ad lists admission as $3 for adults and $2 for children under 12. The spokesman also said the ad was paid for in advance.

> The movie was produced by Ed Bush and his film crew, which happened to have cameras loaded and ready when one of the crew, actress Sherie Darvell, was allegedly kidnapped by what filmmakers said was a large hairy creature May 22, 1976 near Orleans.[1280]

There still remained the question of which county, Shasta or Humboldt, would pay the operational costs incurred by the Darvell search. The appearance of the film reengaged the district attorney's office which still considered a criminal case against Bush and Gaston for filing a false report. District Attorney Buffington admitted that his office had only circumstantial evidence that the film crew knew there was no emergency. Prosecutor Bernie DePaoli added that the expense of a month-long trial and possible change of venue had to be balanced against the probable light sentences (conviction of making a false emergency report could carry a one-year jail sentence[1281]). Still, Buffington said he would be interested in seeing the film.[1282]

In September 1977, Humboldt County formally sought payment from Shasta County for wages and overtime, travel, food, aviation rentals, and indirect expenses including reimbursement for the Six Rivers National Forest crew's participation in the search effort. After Shasta County's refusal to pay, Humboldt County filed a suit in Humboldt County Superior Court.[1283]

> Humboldt County Counsel Raymond Schneider argued before [Judge] Peterson that state law required Shasta County reimburse to Humboldt County because the case involved search and rescue for a Shasta County resident.
>
> Shasta County Counsel Robert Rehberg countered that Miss Darvell's disappearance was at best a kidnapping, and even the Humboldt County officers' reports indicated they were skeptical about the abduction reports.[1284]

His decision ending a nearly two-year drama between Humboldt and Shasta Counties, Superior Court Judge Frank Peterson ruled on Tuesday, February 7, 1978, that Shasta County did not have to pay Humboldt County for the expenses incurred through the Darvell search.

> The search for Bigfoot is "at least an exercise in futility" says a judge who denied reimbursement for a search involving an alleged victim of the legendary creature.

> So saying, Superior Court Judge Frank S. Peterson, from Del Norte County, ruled Tuesday that Shasta County doesn't have to pay Humboldt County more than $10,000 [$11,613] for the search of a young woman that Bigfoot allegedly carried away.
>
> Peterson added, "I have hiked the hills and mountains of Northern California for almost 50 years and the biggest footprint I ever saw was my brother Bob's."[1285]

Judge Peterson said his decision was based on a county's entitlement to reimbursement from another county for search and rescue operations for lost persons or persons in imminent danger of their lives and not on grounds of investigations into alleged crimes. Peterson said the only large creatures left in the area were bears and he doubted one would hie away with Darvell.

> Rehberg said he was "pleased" with the judge's decision.
>
> But he said he sympathizes with the dilemmas faced by Humboldt County officials, ranging from whether to begin the search for Miss Darvell to trying to determine who should pay the costs of the search.
>
> Rehberg said that if Humboldt County authorities had been willing to stipulate that Bigfoot is a Shasta County resident, negotiations over the costs might have been possible.[1286]

Judge Peterson said officials in Humboldt County "in an exercise of caution, must have thought they were investigating a crime," and therefore were not entitled to the reimbursement they sought.[1287]

Judge Peterson wrote that the facts of the case led the court to conclude that "it was likely 'batman' and not 'Bigfoot' that had carried off Sherie Darvell."[1288]

Humboldt County Counsel Ray Schneider said the Sheriff and the district attorney "are not in a position where they feel they can appeal the case."[1289] Unsurprisingly, perennial Bigfoot commentator Andrew Genzoli also touched on the affair:

> We would bet old Bigfoot is sitting in a quiet spot up around Bluff Creek merrily snickering over the latest fiasco committed in his name by a ham-handed bunch of "adventurers."
>
> As an event it was one of the most clumsily handled things we have ever seen; that it had publicity in mind is apparent. The

> legal implications that may have been created by the oversized search, may provide the last laugh for Bigfoot. Motion picture companies often do strange things—this is one of the strangest.
>
> And worse than that famous old serial movie, "The Perils of Pauline," what do we have—our heroine, stumbling into camp, screaming in distress—but even so somewhat unscathed for someone who has tangled with Bigfoot. And, when someone is offered an opportunity by the Sheriff to take a polygraph test, it is "Oh, no," and something about "individual rights," or some tripe of that nature. An honest situation will never fear a polygraph—a lie test.
>
> And we'd like to know since when did a mythical figure ever do anyone any harm? Not Bigfoot, for sure—for, while he has been the center of attractions since his discovery back in the 1950s he has never carried anyone away, never hurt anyone. But, he has had fun keeping people on the chase, and the only incidents of unusual interest have been that of competing explorers attempting to "do one another in." Somehow, most of those in the numerous expeditions to Bluff Creek remind us of some of the characters in Keasey's "One Flew Over the Cuckoo's Nest." The Bigfoot legend has surely attracted a variety of people with an even wider variety of beliefs.
>
> . . . Bigfoot hasn't hurt anyone—and, he never will. No wonder some folks shy from the polygraph![1290]

Per the *Times-Standard's* account of *Wild Man of the Woods—Humboldt County Bigfoot Abduction*, the film received screenings in Shasta, Siskiyou, and Trinity counties. (Humboldt County, District Attorney John Buffington's stomping grounds, is notably absent.) This movie then, is submitted to the roll of Bigfoot filmography as a rare, and likely lost, oddity on par with *Revenge of Bigfoot*.

Creature from Black Lake

In the ensuing years following its release, *Creature from Black Lake*, about two anthropology students spending their summer in the Louisiana swamps searching for a renowned local hairy cryptid, has grown in stature as a period favorite of Ciné du Sasquatch,[1291] having been roundly panned by critics at the time of its release. *St. Petersburg Times* film critic Dorothy Smiljanich did not mince words in her fault-finding review:

> Although he is reported by assorted and sundry characters in the film to be an enormous, hulking giant of a creature, what viewers can see—and it is not much—appears to be a man in a monkey suit, who makes all sorts of moans and groans and screeches that are played almost continually on the soundtrack, even when the creature isn't around; the idea probably being to keep viewers unnerved and on the edge of their seats.
>
> As a matter of fact, I sat through the whole film not only on the edge of my seat but with my car keys in hand—in order to facilitate a rapid exit. And not, gentle readers, out of fear.[1292]

Creature from Black Lake, like *The Beast of Boggy Creek,* uses location photography to instill an aura of authentic realism; Dean Cundey performed the cinematography and *Creature from Black Lake* was an early entry in his portfolio of motion picture photography. Later films crediting his services as Director of Photography include *The Thing* (1982), *Back to the Future* (1985), and *Who Framed Roger Rabbit* (1988).

Legend of McCullough's Mountain

Its title a homage to *The Legend of Boggy Creek, Legend of McCullough's Mountain's* original footage came from 1965's *Legend of Blood Mountain,* a South-regional film that had essentially nothing to do with Bigfoot. *Legend of McCullough's Mountain* was filled out with pseudo-documentary-style Bigfoot footage to produce an inglorious jumble. The original monster from 1965 was excised in favor of a Don Davison-lensed, Bigfoot-like creature, always filmed in a miasma of obscuring fog. Davison, who had been involved in the adult film industry, went on to write, produce, and host *The Force Beyond* (1978).

Six Million Dollar Man

> *Oscar Goldman:* (indicating a giant footprint) What is it, a mountain lion?
>
> *Steve Austin:* No, it's too big. What do you think, a huge grizzly, Tom?
>
> *Tom:* No. No, not a cat. Not a grizzly.
>
> *Oscar Goldman:* Well, what is it?
>
> *Tom:* There's only one thing in the mountains that leaves a track like this. The creature of legend that roams the

> Timberline. My people named him Sasquatch. You call him . . . Bigfoot.[1293]

The country's preoccupation with unexplained hairy hominid phenomena in the '70s found an outlet in ABC's *The Six Million Dollar Man*. Professional wrestler André the Giant donned makeup and costume to portray the roamer of the timberline and met Lee Majors' Colonel Steve Austin for a matchup of pop-culture icons.

The two-part episode (originally aired on February 1 and February 4) had Majors' Bionic-enhanced Steve Austin battle André's Sasquatch, in actuality a cyborg. Along with Bigfoot, episode writer Kenneth Johnson incorporated another element of paranormal interest—UFOs and aliens—into the plot.

Jeff Bergman, a tourist from New York, was on hand to view some of the filming at the Universal Studios. "At first I couldn't believe it when the tour guide told us that hairy creature was André the Giant. I had just seen him wrestle in New York the week before, and now here he was again," Bergman said. "Of course, the makeup made it difficult to see André's face completely. But when he stood up, I could see how tall he was. Then I knew for sure it was André the Giant. It would be impossible for me to describe my feelings when I came to this realization, except to say I was a bit shocked."

The specially-designed facial makeup for André that impressed Bergman was applied in several layers. The first step was casting André's face in order to build a mold that would change the contours of André's facial features. Extra latex molding was applied to the cheeks and greasepaint was applied to effect shading. Lastly, crepe hair was added. The makeup took a total of three hours to apply, a chore André endured each morning of the ten days of shooting. "It was a lot of fun doing the show," André said in an interview conducted after filming wrapped. "I had to do my own stunts. After all, how were they going to find a stand-in who is seven foot-five inches and weighs over four hundred pounds?"

One of the action-oriented experiences from the set had tested Andre's patience: "It got a little rough for me at times. There was this one scene where Steve Austin gets the upper hand and sends me rolling down this huge wooded hill. I rolled and rolled until I finally came to the bottom and almost crashed into the lighting equipment on the set. Because of some technical problems, we had to do that scene five times," André recalled. "By the third time I was ready to murder the guy who kept yelling 'We'll have to do that scene again.'"[1294]

Bigfoot would prove a popular character in the bionic franchise, making three more appearances (portrayed by Ted Cassidy) between *The Six Million Dollar Man* and *Bionic Woman* series, all of which were written by Kenneth Johnson. An action figure based on the Bigfoot character is, in the early 21st century, a highly collectible '70s toy.

Ron Olson & *Sasquatch: Legend of Bigfoot*

Entering 1976, the year of the nation's Bicentennial, America was a cauldron of stewing social unease and political unrest as traditional conventions were being tossed out in the midst of ongoing social revolution. As its psyche was healing following the end of the Vietnam War, the Cold War remained, providing a tense and combative context for international relations. Popular fear-filled film plots in 1976 involved demonic children, nature run amuck, and Bigfoot, which swelled the horror movie genre with a plethora of ghouly, ghastly, and monstrous fare.

Sasquatch: the Legend of Bigfoot enjoyed its world premiere Wednesday, January 28, in Eugene at the West 11th Entertainment Center. The 7 P.M. showing was by invitation only and the 9 P.M. showing was for open-to-the-public tickets which had been on sale at the North American Film Enterprises, Inc. office. The *Eugene Register-Guard* claimed the film was the first feature film made entirely in Oregon with Oregon capital and talent. Olson had been involved with the movie business since 1966 when he began distributing and promoting films on an independent, "four-wall" basis. In this technique, a distributor rents a theater, advertises the movie on his dime, and the profits from ticket sales go to the distributor. The "four walls" referred to the distributor renting the "four walls" of the theater. Frank Olson of Springfield, Ron's father, is credited as being a pioneer and early practitioner of the four-walling practice. Ron Olson was engaged in four-walling when a February 1968 *Argosy* article changed his life. The story highlighted Patterson and Gimlin's movie of a Bigfoot walking across a sandbar in northern California on October 20, 1967. After reading the article, Olson knew he had to make a movie about it. Olson arranged to meet Patterson the following month, and shortly after, North American Wildlife Research was started with the purpose to document Bigfoot's existence. A segment of the Patterson-Gimlin film is included in *Sasquatch*.

From his first reactions to Bigfoot, Olson's instinct was that it was a perfect subject for a movie. In the years that followed, not only had he gathered a substantial body of knowledge and experience about the creature that would benefit such a project, but he also figured a movie would be a cinch to make money which would fund future expeditions and searches.

To raise funds to make *Sasquatch*, Olson developed several prospectuses and created a two-hour slide show accompanied by a lecture which he presented in western Oregon "from Riddle to Portland," beginning in March of 1975. Olson developed a $300,000 (1/3 for distribution and 2/3 for production) budget, with a goal to develop 300 prospective investors of $1,000 each. By the end of April 1975, Olson had 134 people come up with the necessary $300,000. Early on, before the full funding had been secured, a confident Olson hired a producer, John Fabian of John Fabian Productions, in Springfield. Fabian has made an eclectic range of films and had received awards from the National Outdoor Film Festival, the Cine Film Festival and the International Film Producers of America, among others. Ed Ragozzino, head of the Performing Arts Dept. at Lane Community College, was hired as director. Many cast members hailed from Lane County.[1295]

Principal filming began August 4 in the Bend area and resumed in Lane County the week of August 11, 1975, near Blue River where cast and crew remained about a week. In its production phase, the film was referred to as "Expedition for Sasquatch." The movie was billed as the first fictionalized, feature-length film treatment of the Bigfoot subject that dealt with Bigfoot "in the most comprehensive detail that's ever been done," Olson said. As Executive Producer, Olson took pride in the wildlife integrated into the film, primarily the responsibility of Dick Robinson of Oakley, Utah. Robinson had experience training animals for Walt Disney Productions and owned a business described at the time as "one of the largest animal compounds in North America." Plans called for him to include grizzly bears, cougars, wolves, and deer among other kinds of wildlife.[1296]

Veteran Oregon stage actor George Lauris played the expedition leader Chuck Evans. He was asked about the mounting excitement in advance of the January 28, 1976, premiere in Eugene. "I think that anxiety is heightened, though, because the whole thing is out of my hands. There's nothing I can do about it. You can do it, they film it, it's gone after that, and you have no control. You do it, and you realize that's it. You can't say, 'Let me do it again,' or 'I'll do better tomorrow night,' or anything like that." Lauris had also become aware of certain differences between stage and film work. "There's another feeling that sort of creeps in, too. You've done this forever. It's in a can now, and it's going to be shown for three years. It will be seen by an awful lot of people you don't even know. That doesn't happen with theater. The audiences there are sort of your family, but this is going to be shared with thousands of strangers, and I'll never know what they thought." Lauris stated that the actors did their own stunts. "The situation would be set up, and you'd go through it one time only, and you as an actor don't know what to expect, so you're really reacting to the event. You're no longer trying to create the illusion of something. You really are trying to regain control of your horse after he's been scared." Such situations created very unpretentious acting. "So some of the expressions of concern you'll see in the movie—or even of outright fear—are genuine."[1297]

Director Ed Ragozzino was known for his work at the Lane County Auditorium Association summer shows and other plays he had been involved with.[1298] *Sasquatch* was Ragozzino's movie directorial debut. "I couldn't really say whether I'll do more of it or not," Ragozzino told the *Bend Bulletin* while on location. "The control factor here is so much different than with theater. With a theater production, I call a rehearsal for a certain time. Now, we're stopping because a jet leaves a trail or there's no sun or there's too much sun."[1299]

Olson was guarding his control of the Patterson-Gimlin movie rights in advance of *Sasquatch's* premiere, as demonstrated in the below November 30, 1975, article in the *Eugene Register-Guard.*

> A segment of film that purportedly shows a legendary Big Foot striding through a northern California forest was in the news this weekend.
>
> This time, the film—taken by the late Roger Patterson of Yakima, Wash.—is the subject of a suit filed by American National Enterprises, Inc., of Utah, and two Oregon firms headed by Ron Olson of Springfield.
>
> Associated Press said the suit was filed in U.S. District Court for Utah and claims that a California company is illegally using the Patterson film in a movie. The suit asks $100,000 damages.
>
> In Springfield, Olson said Saturday he acquired exclusive theater rights to the film segment for his still-to-be released film title, "Sasquatch, the Legend of Big Foot." The movie was directed by Ed Ragozzino of Eugene and was filmed in Oregon last summer.
>
> Olson's companies are North American Film Enterprises, Inc., and North American Productions, Oregon, Ltd., formed to produce and distribute the movie.

> He said American National Enterprises, Inc., purchased movie rights to the Patterson film and he in turn, signed an agreement with American for use of the film segment in Olson's movie.
>
> However, Olson said Patterson's widow retained television rights to the film. He said the rival film company, Sun Classic Pictures, Inc., a Delaware firm doing business in California, has expanded what was originally a television film into a movie called "Big Foot, the Mysterious Monster," and is showing it in theaters around the United States.
>
> The suit alleges that this is an illegal use of the Patterson film, since the Utah film company holds exclusive theater rights to the original Patterson 16-millimeter color film.
>
> Olson said final editing is under way on the film directed by Ragozzino and it is expected to be released next spring. The Patterson film is spliced into the locally-produced movie.[1300]

George Lauris went to several early showings of *Sasquatch* and noted the reactions of fellow movie-goers. "I do remember going to several showings of *Sasquatch* in the Eugene area. Actually, I was sort of amazed that people accepted it as being real. I kept wanting to say, 'Wait a minute, this isn't a real expedition. It's not real.' It was satisfying when the Sasquatch creature attacked the camp and some people in the audience actually jumped up and screamed."[1301]

Leveraging the publicity from *Sasquatch,* Olson spread the word early in 1976 that his organization, North American Wildlife Research Association (NAWRA, also referred to during this timeframe as NAWR), was planning an expedition for the coming spring. Use of computer analysis, first associated with Olson in 1972's *Bigfoot: Man or Beast,* remained an important research tool for Olson.

> Okay, Sasquatch: your days in hiding are numbered. The computer is after you.
>
> Ron Olson, executive director of North American Wildlife Research, a Eugene based organization devoted to hunting the legendary Bigfoot, said a nine-man team using computerized information and electronic detection gear will go Sasquatch hunting in British Columbia in April or May.
>
> He said the object of the expedition is "to discover, once and for all, the subhuman creature who has left his giant

> footprints as enduring proof of his existence and raised unanswered questions in the mind of modern scientific man," Olsen said.[1302]

Oregonian Roy Lack, who had worked with Olson for several years, became a high-profile field investigator for NAWR in 1976. Lack started what would become a busy spring and summer by making plaster casts of prints found near Butte Falls, Oregon, a small community about 40 miles northeast of Medford. The prints were originally found by women picking flowers on April 13. Lack arrived at the scene and covered the tracks with brush and logs. The prints lacked an arch and were 56 inches apart. On Saturday, April 17, Lack and others returned with materials to make a cast of a track about 12 inches long and seven inches wide at the ball.[1303]

A wilderness area in British Columbia was chosen for NAWR's expedition because of its history of reported Bigfoot sightings and a computer study which pinpointed Bella Coola, a small town about 25 miles west of Anahim Lake, as a likely location for Bigfoot encounter.[1304] "Lack and a half dozen others in his party are there because it is a high frequency area where [S]asquatch patterns have occurred," Olson said.[1305]

On June 1, Roy Lack set out into the wilds of British Columbia to set up a base camp and spend the summer conducting a systematic field investigation. "But an actual sighting occurred when he got in there," exclaimed Olson. "He didn't even have time to set up a base camp." With Jerry Jardstrom, Lack's focus shifted to investigate the fresh report. The sighting was made by a man, described by Olson as "a British Columbia resident, an Indian fisherman. He told Roy he trailed him (the Sasquatch) for about 12 miles." As Olson related Lack's response to the sighting, the preparedness of the expedition proved prescient. "I trust Roy's judgement, and he feels very strongly that this is a good sighting. So we could be getting word at any time, maybe even this weekend. Roy's fully equipped with tranquilizing equipment and camera equipment, so I hope he's going to turn up with something."[1306]

The expedition under Lack's leadership was dramatically described as "secrecy-shrouded" and called a "secret safari." The precise and secret location of the search area was known only to NAWR members. "We don't want the news media to go charging up there and ruin everything," Olson said.

Jim Cisler [also written as Gene Sisler], named as a spokesman for NAWR, told the press that Lack, Jerry Jardstrom, and other supporting NAWR members had commenced the hyped expedition, establishing camp near Bella Coola, B.C.[1307]

Cisler said Lack and Jardstrom focused on collecting evidence to verify the fisherman's sighting.[1308] Investigation of the area revealed footprints 16 ½ inches long. "It's pretty common knowledge in that area that fishermen have seen Sasquatches come down to the edge of bays and inlets or swimming between the islands. This man said he heard grunting noises and sighted it a couple times. When Roy investigated, he found 16 ½-inch tracks," Olson said. "We're really excited about this one," he added. "We didn't expect anything to happen this quick."

According to Olson, the challenge to prove the existence of Bigfoot was the motivation of NAWR's 500-members organization. "The pioneers must have felt like this," said Olson, invoking patriotic nostalgia as the Bicentennial events and observances were in full swing. "We want to discover something that hasn't been discovered yet."[1309] If field investigation could locate Bigfoot, Olson said the same NAWR plan as had been in place for years would go into effect: tranquilize the creature, remove it to a secure area where access by the public can be controlled, bring reputable scientists to the creature to study it and authenticate it, then turn it loose again with a radio homing device to track and gather data on its movements.

Olson provided an update on Lack and his team's investigative efforts in a UPI article carried by the August 25, 1976, *Syracuse Herald Journal:*

> An expedition roaming the wilds of northern British Columbia to film or trap one of the huge-footed, hairy creatures with great black eyes hasn't found a trace of the legendary Sasquatch.
>
> "But we're not discouraged," said Ron Olson, director of the North American Wildlife Research organization, a private group in Eugene, Ore., sponsoring the expedition. It has been searching for Bigfoot for more than a month.
>
> "We know it will take time to locate and track Bigfoot," he said. "That's why we're prepared to spend a year or two in the effort."
>
> "Rain has made the terrain difficult to track or backtrack," Olson said of efforts by an expedition headed by Roy Lack of Astoria, Ore., to find Bigfoot.
>
> The search is going on near Bellacoola, Canada, close to a 15,000-acre wilderness.
>
> "Lack is checking out the sightings of Bigfoot by the Indians," Olson said. "And if he finds some presentable tracks, he will begin to set up tracking operations."

> He said Lack "still believes the Bellacoola surroundings are the best to work during fall and early winter. The weather is relatively mild, although it is rainy."
>
> "Studies show that the creature does not hibernate and travels from higher elevations to lower terrain in winter. We have reports that tracks by the creature have been seen coming down from snow county rather going into it.
>
> "Our group will stay at the lower elevations during the winter because there is no sense messing around in the snow.
>
> "We also believe we have a better chance of finding one or more in Canada because of evidence that the area is a regular habitat of the creature, and the group will not be bothered by news media exploitation," he said.
>
> "We're making a movie of the search and what it may find, and revenue from that can help keep the expedition going.
>
> "Our group has succeeded in accomplishing what it set out to do to this time. Phase One was setting up the search effort, and Phase Two consists of working high concentration areas where the creature has been seen. Our group is setting up sensing devices to not only find but keep track of Bigfoot."
>
> The expedition hopes to capture a Sasquatch, plant a radio transmitter in the animal and further trace its movements.[1310]

Along with keeping track of Lack's progress, Olson remained engaged with promoting his film, *Sasquatch*. Olson said *Sasquatch* grossed "a little over a million dollars" in the first three months of 1976 and it was headed toward a re-release to new markets when the prime movie season began again in November. Though there were no immediate plans to film a "Son of Sasquatch," Olson hinted that it might just depend on what Lack's expedition might find.[1311]

Toting several plaster footprint casts, Olson's promotion itinerary included a stop in St. Louis where he said the proceeds from the film would fund a Bigfoot expedition to British Columbia in the spring of 1977. "I've been involved in this since 1967," said Olson. As a young man, Olson said he attended a commercial showing of the Patterson-Gimlin film which helped to foster his interest in Bigfoot and the prospect of its investigation. "But growing up in Oregon, I heard tales about Bigfoot from childhood. There are Indian legends going back 200 years in the Pacific Northwest about the creature they call Sasquatch." After Olson started researching Bigfoot he was amazed at the instances of large, hairy man-like creatures found both in Native American lore and early settlers' accounts of whazzits that meshed closely with the modern picture of a Bigfoot. "I believe that these early reports have a lot more credibility than more recent ones, with our modern media.

"It is definitely true that, every time there is a story in a newspaper or on television, there will suddenly be a rash of sightings. We [North American Wildlife Research Association] check out all reports, and I would say that only about 3 to 5 per cent of the modern sightings are legitimate. But still, we have about 1000 reports going back to 1811. That is what gives it credibility."

Being in St. Louis, Olson had natural occasion to comment on Momo, a flap of sightings centered in Louisiana, Missouri, (90 miles north of St. Louis) from 1972 (see Chapter 3), which failed to convince Olson they indicated Bigfoot's presence. "For one thing, with Mo Mo you don't have the great historical record of sightings that you have with Sasquatch. How come nobody saw one until four years ago?" Olson appeared to be more comfortable with the ecological understanding of Bigfoot as tweezed from its indications in the Pacific Northwest. "Another thing is that the predominance of evidence is that Sasquatch is a mountain creature who stays as far away as possible from men and settlements. I'm not saying necessarily that Mo Mo doesn't exist, but the sightings just don't have comparable credibility."

Olson's opinion of Bigfoot's origin mirrored that held by Krantz and other prominent researchers. "In 1941," Olson began, "scientists in China uncovered the fossil remains of a huge man-like creature somewhere between an ape and primitive man. They dated the remains back about 500,000 years. The creature would have been about 10 feet tall, weighed 900 to 1000 pounds and walked upright, all of which fits with Sasquatch. They called the creature *Gigantopithecus*." In his model of Bigfoot's origins, land bridges afforded passable routes of travel between Asia and North America. "One theory is that these subhuman creatures migrated from Siberia across the Bering Strait, much as the Indians are thought to have done, and made their way down to the Pacific Northwest," Olson said.

Weren't bears a rational explanation to account for the mystery? "No. Reports emphasize that the creature walks upright like a man. A bear will get up on his hind legs to look around or to smell, but when he walks he gets back on all fours." Espousing rational explanations allowed Olson to take Bigfoot out of the realm of fantasy and monsters and present it as a cogent and comprehensible creature.

Olson believed Bigfoot, amongst North America's rarest fauna, was losing ground as humans progressively encroached into its habitat. Man's deleterious impact on the environment was a popularly expressed sentiment in the '70s, a period which saw the strengthening of the ecological movement. "The sightings often come in wild areas where new roads or logging operations have just gone in, and Sasquatch has not had time to move out," Olson said.

The promotion for *Sasquatch* gave Olson a rostrum which he used to the fullest to discuss all facets of North American hairy hominids, including his own close calls with Bigfoot, though he had never experienced a clear-cut sighting himself. "I missed a sighting by about two hours once, and another time I was in a thicket and thought I could hear one [a Bigfoot] moving around in the underbrush—crunch, crunch, crunch. I thought, 'Any moment, that thing is going to step out in front of me.' But then he went away." Olson, reiterating his no-kill position, also spoke about plans for NAWRA's next expedition. "These creatures may well be endangered and need our protection." What would the successful culmination of Olson's investigation mean to him? "I tell you this. When I finally see Sasquatch, it will be the most exciting moment of my life."[1312]

"If [S]asquatch is purely legendary, the legend is likely to be a long time dying. On the other hand, if [S]asquatch does exist," Olson proposed, "then with the [S]asquatch hunts being mounted and the increasing human population it seems likely that some hard evidence may soon be in hand."[1313]

Olson & Hoaxed Tracks

> Somewhere, the ghost of humorist H. Allen Smith is chuckling.
>
> But Ron Olson is not amused. Nor is the sheriff of Coos County.
>
> It was years ago that Smith, a chronicler of practical jokes who died recently, wrote of the Great Rhinoceros Scare in Ithica, [sic] N.Y. It happened because a student at Cornell University in Ithica had an uncle who was a big game hunter.
>
> The Uncle had bagged a rhino and—for unknown reasons—had one of the animal's huge feet made into a wastebasket, which he sent to his nephew. One snowy night, the nephew and friends were sitting around the dorm when inspiration struck.
>
> They took the rhino-foot wastebasket, attached two long ropes to it, and proceeded to make a trail of rhinoceros tracks

across the snow-covered campus. The trail extended to the shores of Lake Cayuga.

The pranksters continued the tracks out onto the snow-covered ice of the lake—right up to the edge of a big hole they chopped in the ice.

The next morning, campus and town were in a dither. Knowledgeable faculty experts pronounced the tracks to be those of genuine rhino.

Since Lake Cayuga also served as the source of Ithica's [sic] drinking water, Smith reported that half the town's population immediately quit drinking the water. The other half, he said, swore that it tasted like rhinoceros.

The scene now shifts to the present, near the Oregon coastal town of Coos Bay. It was the beginning of the Labor Day weekend, and a Coos Bay resident, Phil Thompson, was hunting pigeons in a remote area east of town called Stock Slough.

Thompson came across huge tracks in the dirt—seven of them. They were shaped like a human foot but were at least twice human size.

Thompson reported his find, and the immediate thought in everybody's mind was Sasquatch—the legendary Big Foot, a huge ape-like creature that reportedly has wandered the forests of the Northwest for centuries.

The Coos Bay World launched an all-out search, sending three reporters on an overnight expedition into the area. The newspaper also sent for Ron Olson of Eugene, who heads North American Wildlife Research, the outfit that's been looking for Big Foot for years and has produced a feature film about it.

"I went down and looked at the tracks, and I was a little concerned," Olson said. "I said, 'The stride isn't right for the length of tracks.'

"If you take a 17 ½-inch track, which is a pretty good-sized creature, it'll have a 55-to-60-inch stride. The one in Coos Bay was a 17 ½ track, but only a 33-inch stride on easy ground."

But Olson asked to be kept advised, and the World team continued its search, along with pigeon-hunter Thompson and a covey of other amateur Sasquatchwatchers. Then, a week later came the revelation.

Four Marshfield High School seniors admitted they had made the tracks. Two of them had constructed the phoney [sic] Big Foot feet out of wood and glue as part of a school project, which might cause some to ponder what kind of classes they're teaching at Marshfield High.

Coos County Sheriff Les Miller said he "isn't exactly pleased" about the hoax and the time and money spent investigating it. He even consulted with Dist. Atty Robert Brasch, but the DA ruled, "There's nothing illegal about putting footprints in dirt."

In Eugene this past week, Big Foot searcher Olson admitted that such hoaxes "make me a little bit mad—but not as much as they used to.

"I'm always irked when something's a fake," he said, "because I don't see the logic of people trying to do something like that . . . (and) I think the more of that you get, the more discredit you get" on the existence of Big Foot.

It's an existence in which Olson says he still devoutly believes. In fact, he's flying to Canada Thursday [September 23] to rendezvous with an associate, Roy Lack of Medford, who's been Sasquatch-searching the wilds of British Columbia all summer.

Back in June, you may recall, Olson reported that Lack was on the trail of a recent apparent sighting by an Indian fisherman there. But that investigation was literally a washout.

"Roy went in just about a day after it happened," Olson said. "But evidently their summer's been something like ours—they've had tremendous rain and snow up there.

"Roy spent about seven days until the storms just blew him out of there. He said there was no way. It just demolished the tracks."

But last week, Lack was checking another sighting report. So, Olson hopes to learn about that while he's in BC, in addition to doing some filming for a short documentary that'll accompany the Big Foot feature film showings when they get going in November.

And things like the Coos Bay hoax never seem to cloud Olson's faith.

"Don't throw out the fact that Big Foot is possible," he said. "Big Foot, in my opinion, does exist."

I hope he's right. And I think H. Allen Smith would feel the same way.

But he'd still get a chuckle out of the Coos Bay caper.[1314]

SIGHTINGS 1976

Alcorn County Bigfoot

Did Bigfoot show up in Corinth, Mississippi? The following UPI story from March was widely printed in southern newspapers.

> Something is lurking in the hills of Alcorn County, but nobody seems to know quite what.
>
> Whoever or whatever it is, it's been leaving monster-sized tracks around Alcorn County. The footprints—nearly 15 inches long and 6 ½ inches wide—were first found March 14 near Smith Bridge Road north of U.S. 72.
>
> Since then, other huge tracks have been reported about five miles from the bridge near Hatchie Chapel Church.
>
> Joe McKewen, local photographer and naturalist, said Tuesday the tracks are "very authentic looking," but he thinks they are a hoax.
>
> "At certain places the heel would dig in a little deeper. At some places its toes would grab in deeper," he said. "It looked just like tracks a human would make if he were walking."
>
> McKewen said for the creature to make such tracks it would have to be at least eight feet tall and weigh about 400-500 pounds.
>
> About two years ago, there were reports of a "big hairy creature" seen around Alcorn County. "Two boys said that some large hairy creature knocked their cabin door down and started in on them," McKewen said, "and they left it (the cabin)." A farmer also reported the same type creature entering his field.[1315]

Bob Lea

Teenager Bob Lea told Lewis and Clark County sheriff's deputies that he saw two hairy biped creatures on April 4. He stated the creatures had been observed that morning near his East Helena, Montana, home on the York Road close by the Lewis and Clark County pet cemetery.

> "I woke up a little before 5 A.M. Sunday morning and got up and walked over to my bedroom window and looked out. My bedroom is on the second floor so I have quite a view of the area just east of our house.
>
> "I didn't have my glasses on at the time, but I could see that someone or something was walking across the field right over there," he added, pointing to a field on the east side of the house. "I thought it was rather odd for someone to be walking in the field that early, (so) I went and got my glasses on.
>
> "It was at this point that I realized it just wasn't someone, but something." Lea said he watched the creature walk north across the field to a haystack where it joined a second creature. The second one was shorter, but had the same features—little or no neck and was hairy.
>
> "Upon reaching the stack where the other creature was standing," Lea continued, "they both proceeded to examine a large object," Lea said the object was a lot bigger than a bale of hay with something sticking out of it like a handle.
>
> He declined to say what it appeared to be, "I've taken a considerable amount of kidding about my sighting and would rather not say any more about the object," he said.
>
> After this, which took only a couple of minutes, Lea said the larger of the two started to walk back toward his house.
>
> "I really didn't realize just how big they were until the large one walked by two posts in the field that are about eight feet tall," he said. "It was much taller than the posts, I would guess that thc creature stood about 10 feet tall, according to how much taller it was than the posts.
>
> "When the hairy thing reached those two posts," he continued, "that's when I headed downstairs to get my dad up. Those posts are only about 85 feet from the house and I was really getting shook by then."

His father was slow to rousing, but eventually agreed to accompany Lea back to his room and have a look. When they got back to the window, the creatures were gone. Lea and his father scanned the field with binoculars, but no creature was seen. After discussing the whole experience with both parents, Lea's mother convinced him to report what he saw to the county sheriff's office which, about an hour after he first saw the creatures, he agreed to do. Deputies came out to the Lea house but did not turn up any trace of the creatures.

> A spokesman for the sheriff recalls that deputies "covered the field real well" but found nothing. He wrote the story off as "just the vivid imagination of a young boy."
>
> Lea was gone most of the afternoon, but when he returned early in the evening, his sister Debbie told him she had found some tracks left by the creatures.
>
> They found three huge tracks which measured 17 ½ inches long and seven inches wide. It was too late to take a cast that evening, so Lea covered the best of them with a wooded box, then made a plaster cast the next day.
>
> The casts are not too clear, which Lea said is the result of his inexperience.
>
> They appear to have three toes, with a larger toe in the center. Apparently, there are no claws on the foot.
>
> "The stride of the thing was huge," said Lea, a strapping six-footer. "It was much longer than mine, even when I stretched out my legs as far as I could from print to print."[1316]

Deerslayer

On Friday, April 23, two patrolmen responded to Caroline Morris' report of "screaming and screeching and growling" sounds emanating from a ravine below her hillside home. When the officers arrived at Morris' Mill Valley home on the north side of San Francisco Bay, they quickly found the strange vocalizations were ongoing. "When we got there," said Dan Murphy, one of the patrolmen, "we heard the sounds too. They were strange, high-pitched sounds like something was screaming or howling viciously." The sounds were enough to make the policemen draw their weapons as they carefully hiked down the wooded slopes, their flashlights probing through the darkness. "I heard this heavy breathing ahead of us," Murphy said. This was quickly followed by "crackling and rustling noises as if something was approaching through the brush." Murphy said his flashlight fleetingly illuminated a "large, dark colored thing."

"It was walking on its legs," declared Murphy. "I saw it climb an eight-foot retaining wall and disappear into the brush." With the sun up and shining on Saturday morning, the officers returned to the scene where they discovered a trail of blood. They followed it through the tangle of brush to a slain deer, its neck broken and its body mangled and eviscerated. The carcass was taken to the Marin Humane Society where some thought that the animal had come under attack from a mountain lion. "It was a weird thing all right," said Murphy, "but I never said anything about Bigfoot—somebody must have made that up."[1317]

Flintville Monster

During the spring of 1976, some residents of Flintville, Tennessee, claimed, amidst the attention garnered from ongoing Bigfoot sightings around town, that a monster fitting Bigfoot's description had plagued the area for close to two decades. Several avowed it was a dangerous creature, prone to attacking motorists, carrying off livestock, and menacing children. "That thing's so big it could easily hurt somebody," said a local farmer. "Who knows how many head of our livestock have gone missing because of it?"

E. Randall Floyd wrote that the trouble started in April when a woman told police a "giant, hairy monster" attacked her car. The creature emitted a foul odor like a skunk and left behind 16-inch footprints. When her story was made public, others came forward with their own accounts of the aggressive creature. On April 26, Jennie Robertson's 4-year-old son Gary was playing in the yard when she heard him scream. It was a cool, late afternoon when she ran outside and immediately was struck by a foul stench. Then she saw a huge, ape-like creature move around the corner of the house. "It was seven or eight feet tall," she told investigators, "and seemed to be all covered with hair. It reached out its long, hairy arms toward Gary and came within a few inches of him." Just a moment before the creature would have clutched her son within its grasp, Robertson snatched up Gary, ran back inside the house and locked the door. Looking out a window, she saw a "big, black shape disappearing into the woods." Robertson picked up the phone and called a neighbor and then called the police. Presently, a half dozen men, many of whom were armed, gathered in her yard and proceeded to search the area around the house for clues to the creature's identity.

The story quickly circulated in the area that something was lurking in Flintville's backwoods, occasionally attacking cars, pounding on sides of homes, and "filling the night air with blood-curdling shrieks." On the night of April 26, teams of hunters scoured the local countryside. No overt sightings were made but several searchers claimed they heard what they took to be the monster grunting and snorting at them. Some of the hunters felt compelled to fire their guns out of concern for their safety. At each report of gunfire, Floyd wrote, the monster would unleash a high-pitched scream and throw rocks at its pursuers before bounding away into the brush and disappearing again into the darkness. A fresh day brought the curious out to the scene and many 16-inch footprints were found, as well as hair and blood. Floyd reported the hair had been "scientifically analyzed but could not be identified."[1318]

Paranormal researcher Brent Raynes investigated the activity in Flintville in early May 1976, later writing about his time spent with residents and discussing what they'd witnessed. Raynes talked to a man who stated, that on the night of April 25, he saw a large creature about 7-feet tall, "shaggy looking," and walking upright. "There's just a silence down there when we've heard this thing," he told Raynes. "We all heard something walking down there." Signs that the creature was near included heavy breathing sounds like someone with bad asthma, cries like a woman shrieking, and a stink on par with rotten eggs. A resident described to Raynes an occasion late in 1975 when he stepped outside his home one night around 9:30 P.M. to investigate his dog's barking. The man saw a seven-foot-tall, broad-shouldered creature standing by his chicken pen. The thing was covered in black-brown long hair and the man observed it for about a minute before it walked away. Raynes met investigator Lee Frank on his first visit to Flintville and the two later had dinner at Pizza Hut where they discussed monsters.[1319]

> For over a year I periodically went back and forth to Flintville, to follow up on the stories and see what more I could learn. One very pleasant elderly lady who lived in the same neighborhood as the two families I just mentioned had also seen the creature, she told me. She recalled one personal encounter, back in the summer of 1976, which happened, she said, in the presence of other witnesses. She was in a nearby field and had slipped and fallen, which is when the creature appeared. She said she saw a 6-7-foot-tall, short white-haired creature with "real red eyes," standing a mere 25 feet or so away, at the edge of the woods, just watching her and her friends. It had an upright human-like form, but with a pointed head and eyes that looked a little bigger than a regular human's eyes. She said she and a neighbor had seen it eating potato peelings she had thrown out. She didn't seem afraid of it, and added, "Why don't you come down and see it."[1320]

Bigfoot in Packwood

Several human-like tracks attributed to Bigfoot were found three-and-one-half miles southeast of Packwood, Washington, along a trail to Glacier Lake. The tracks measured six to eight inches wide and 16 to 18 inches long. Dave Fryberger and two companions, Bill and Chris Owens, discovered the tracks on May 9 during a fishing trip to Glacier Lake. Fryberger said though weathered from rain, several of the 19-inch tracks showed the clear impressions of five toes and formed a trackway that could be followed about 300 yards. A possible deformity in the right track suggested a foot missing one or two toes. Fryberger took *Daily Chronicle* (Centralia, Washington) reporter Dennis Auvil and J.M. (Merle) Auvil back to the scene.

> Inspecting the tracks, which except for some rain Saturday evening had not been disturbed, Auvil and Fryberger seemed convinced they are genuine.
>
> This reporter, however, after examining the large tracks, concluded there is a 96 per cent chance they are faked. Except in one place, the tracks lead only a few steps and are found only in soft earth here and there along the trail.
>
> Auvil and Fryberger counter, however, that the big fellow who made the tracks probably walked up the trail, moving off occasionally to munch on vegetation.[1321]

Peter Byrne delivered a less-than-rosy opinion of the tracks, suggesting they "didn't look like real prints." Byrne also noted that the prints seem to be noticeable only in receptive substrate easily observable from the trail, not in the brush. Byrne stated "the toes were all the same size," suggesting artifice and "the shape of the feet were wrong." In one spot, Byrne believed the track hoaxer "jumped off a log to make them."[1322]

Beast of Lincoln

Reports of unusual animal activity in North Carolina's Lincoln County enjoyed a banner year in 1976. Lincoln County Deputy Darrell Jones made several trips down U.S. 321 to Gates Road on what became a familiar route as Jones dutifully followed up on the reports of strange creatures. On one occasion, Jones investigated a story told by two women concerning an unknown animal treed by dogs. As he neared the location, Jones heard cries that sounded like a woman's screams, leading him to believe the treed creature was a cougar. After he radioed for assistance, Jones was joined by Deputy Andrew White and the pair began searching for tracks and signs along the muddy banks of a creek. "I'm pretty sure it is a cougar from the looks of things," said Jones. "We could see footprints with three toe marks and the toes had claw marks on them like a cougar. But whatever it is, it is still out there."

> "We could hear growling and snarling when we were down there and we saw a couple of scared dogs running out of the woods," Jones said. "The women told us they had found a couple of half-eaten kittens and little dogs that the animal had chewed up and left. Everything we saw and heard and what they told us makes me think that this time we definitely have a cougar running around."
>
> Jones said the animal could be the same one reported to deputies a year ago by residents of the Iron Station area.
>
> "There were a couple of small pigs killed by something that got everyone stirred up, but we never found a thing," Jones said.
>
> Deputies have warned residents along Gates Road to watch for the cougar and to keep their children out of wooded play areas.

Passing by the relative mundaneness of a resident cougar stalking the neighborhood, past reports from Lincoln County residents had described Bigfoot-like creatures—known in the area as wildmen—that had lurked about their homes in the Heeps Grove area.[1323]

Ocheyedan Sighting

Dan Radunz saw a hairy man-like creature on Sunday morning, August 22, along the banks of the Ocheyedan River, three and a half miles south of the city of Ocheyedan. The sighting occurred while Dan was a passenger in the family car returning to the Radunz farm. "I was surprised and I thought it was my imagination when I saw it," stated Dan, an eighth grader, who did not immediately tell his parents. "I was too scared to say anything," he admitted.

Later, the Radunz family noticed a big change in Dan's behavior and anxious questioning prodded his revelation that he had seen Bigfoot. He described witnessing a black-haired creature about six feet tall sporting an oval-shaped head. The creature was standing alongside the riverbed with its back toward the road. Its arms were raised suggestive of drinking water from its hands.

The following day, accompanied by his mother and neighbor Dwight Glade, Dan visited the spot on the river bank where he had seen the creature. The group was astonished to find footprints spaced about six feet apart. The prints had been pressed nearly an inch into the ground and measured about 14 inches in length. The heel was narrow, and the spread of the toes measured almost seven inches wide.[1324]

Lowell Park Bigfoot

Two large tracks were found on Monday, July 5, in northern Dixon, Illinois' Lowell Park.

> Speculation continues here as to whether Bigfoot, the legendary ape-man, made a visit over the Bicentennial weekend to Lowell Park.
>
> Dwayne Norvell, Kirkland, a member of the North American Wildlife Research Association, has said he "questions" whether 17-inch-long footprints found July 5 in the park were made by Bigfoot.
>
> "But I'm not ruling out the possibility," Norvell added.
>
> It was the second trip Norvell had made to Dixon to check out Bigfoot evidence. Norvell said it is "my job as an association member to investigate Bigfoot rumors in his area, and share information with other members."
>
> Norvell said he found two incomplete footprints, showing toes of both left and right feet, on his July 5 visit. He dug up the footprints, which were in river mud near the Lowell Park shelter.
>
> The tracks measure 8 ½ inches across.
>
> Sunday [July 11] Norvell came to Dixon to view a plaster cast made of other tracks found along the Rock River north of the park.
>
> Norvell said he was less impressed with the authenticity of the tracks after viewing the cast, because the track seemed shallower than the "monster's" size would warrant. The print

also lacked the normal depression between the ball of the foot and the toes.

In the meantime, a rumor surfaced that the tracks were made by a prankster, who sawed himself some plywood feet with toes, and strapped them on for an early morning stroll in Lowell Park. The park, two miles north of Dixon along the Rock River, contains 200 acres of timber.

But the prankster, if such he is, has made himself as scarce as Bigfoot since the Bicentennial week-end.

Norvell said that among Bigfoot rumors, "the majority are hoaxes."

But Norvell is inclined to believe there is a creature behind the legend, after finding 15-inch-long footprints in an out-of-the-way spot in northern California mountains. Norvell went there in 1973 with the express purpose of looking for Bigfoot tracks.

The Kirkland man also investigated a sighting in Louisiana, Mo., where a fisherman known for honesty "definitely saw something."

Numerous sightings have occurred along the Mississippi, but none in Illinois so far, Norvell said.

Another factor that caused Norvell to question the Lowell Park footprints was that several were found in one place. "Multiple footprints are very rare," he said.

The only time they'll leave a footprint is where they have no alternative."

Norvell added that the Lowell Park area is "the type of terrain it hangs out in, in the Pacific northwest. But I'd have to question it if I didn't find more footprints elsewhere in the area."[1325]

Abair Incident

A large creature was seen on the nights of August 24 and 25, 1976, on a rural stretch of the Abair Road outside the Village of Whitehall, New York. Marty Paddock of Whitehall and Paul Gosselin of Low Hampton were the first witnesses to see the creature on Tuesday night, August 24.

> "It was about 10 P.M. when Marty Paddock and I saw a large human form standing on the side of the road. We went down to the end of the road, turning around and came back. We stopped and heard a sound like a pig squealing or a lady screaming. We drove off to the top of the hill, locked the doors on the truck, I loaded the gun and pointed it out the window. We turned around and drove to the opposite side of the road so I could have a better shot at it." [1326]

In his 2018 book, *Abair Road: The True Story*, author Brian Gosselin recounts that he was on duty as an officer of the Whitehall police force on August 24 and the first to talk to his brother Paul and Paddock following their sighting. Brian called his father, Wilfred Gosselin, who was also working on the Whitehall police force. Wilfred and other officers met Paul, Paddock, and their friend, Bart Kinney, back at Abair Road and listened to their story. After Paul and Paddock had heard the strange screams and turned their truck around a second time, they recounted for the officers that they had anxiously scanned the field in front of them.

> This time when they got to the field, they thought they saw something a few yards out by a telephone pole, so they stopped. When they shone their flashlight on it, they saw a creature that was huge. It must have stood at least seven feet tall. It was covered in dark hair and it was staring straight at them, once they locked eyes on it, it took off, straight for the truck. They hit the gas hard, laying a strip of rubber down the road.[1327]

The officers questioned Paul and Paddock about their sighting and a check along the sides of the road was made for tracks. As officers began expanding their search into the field they heard a loud scream. One of the officers shone his car's headlights out into the field and the men saw a large, dark, man-like shape walking at the back of the field. It stepped over a fence at the back corner of the field and disappeared into the night. The next day, Brian talked to his father about what he'd seen. "Brian, we all sat there and watched the same thing," he said. "It walked upright like a man on two legs. I can tell you it wasn't a bear or gorilla or anything else I've ever seen before. Whatever it was, it just don't belong here."[1328] At the end of August the *Post-Star* of Glen Falls, New York, ran a description of the creature from the group sighting of August 24:

> Whitehall Police, New York State police and a Washington County Deputy Sheriff all responded to the scene and searched the area, but were only able to spot the creature from a distance.
>
> Although descriptions vary somewhat, the creature has been widely described by both police officials and civilians as between seven and eight feet tall, very hairy, having pink or red eyes, being afraid of light and as weighing between 300 and 400 pounds.[1329]

In his book, *Bigfoot on the East Coast* (1993), author Rick Berry includes additional comments by Wilfred Gosselin: "I'm not saying this is a monster or anything else, but there is something out there, and it's no animal that belongs in the northern part of this state!" [1330] Brian Gosselin believed his father, brother, and other men involved in the sighting on August 24 were credible witnesses who had seen something truly extraordinary. On the evening of Wednesday, August 25, Brian and a friend (who happened to be a New York State Trooper) drove to the scene along Abair Road of the previous night's remarkable events.

His friend parked his car near the edge of a meadow and Brian parked his vehicle in the middle of a field. Communicating by CB radios, the two began to monitor their surroundings. Sometime before midnight, both men heard a large racket as something moved noisily through a hedgerow. Brian's friend hurriedly drove away leaving Brian alone in the field. Brian continued to hear something breaking branches as it moved through the underbrush.

> At that point, the night took on a silence like I've never experienced before. It was like being in a vacuum. There was no sound whatsoever. It was unnatural and made the hair stand up on the back of my neck.[1331]

Brian heard the sounds of movement approach ever nearer to his position. Sensing that the unknown being was very close, Brian turned on his vehicle's floodlight.

> The shock rolled over me like I was hit with a tidal wave. Nothing could have prepared me for this, nothing. . . . There it was, standing right in front of me. My spotlight shone on a 7-8 foot tall, hair-covered "creature." It was only about 30 feet away from me. When the light hit its eyes, it let out a scream

> that vibrated through my entire body and it pulled its hands up to cover its face. You really can't describe a scream like that. It just wasn't human. I only saw its eyes for a brief second but they were large, red, and bulging. To me, they looked to be about the size of a mayonnaise jar cover.[1332]

In the aftermath of his encounter, Brian recounts that he had difficulty sleeping, beset with nightmares featuring the creature he saw at Abair Road. Local researcher Bill Brann took an interest in the Abair Road sightings on August 24 and 25 and conducted interviews and on-scene investigation. Brann's professionalism and diligent attention to detail and veracity impressed Brian Gosselin who found consolation in other creature sightings made in the area. Though none of these accounts reached the wider popular audience of the Abair Road sightings, they revealed that Brian and other Abair Road witnesses were not alone.

Cashton Creature (1976)

The village of Cashton, Wisconsin, sits about 15 miles east of the Mississippi River and 20 miles east of La Crosse. In 2004, former *La Crosse Tribune* writer and editor Terry Burt recalled a local Bigfoot seen in Cashton's heavily wooded area of Brush Creek Hollow in the fall of the nation's bicentennial year.

> Bud [Cavadini] came into the *Tribune* office one day in September or October 1976 and told me an amazing story that I was able to confirm to my satisfaction before we printed anything.
>
> I always like finding news of the offbeat, weird variety but this was the strangest case I had ever encountered. Keep in mind, too, this was before television and Hollywood made commonplace the mysterious myths and unknown, sometimes otherworldly, subjects we can see almost weekly on cable television.[1333]

Burt interviewed Cavadini and consequently became convinced the affair was a credible story. *La Crosse Tribune* editor Ken Teachout agreed, and the first Cashton Creature article ran on page one, carrying the story to the Coulee Region.

Back in 1976, Bud Cavadini ran the Phillips 66 Service Station at the intersection of Highways 27 and 33. One of the fixtures of the place (aside from the dog Ringo) was the station's motley collection of cats. Cavadini was also a photographer for the *Cashton Record*. He would recall his byline occurring on the story about an "unidentified creature," a seven-foot tall Bigfoot specimen that became known as the Cashton Creature, as one of the high points in his journalistic career.[1334]

> There's a story on Page One that should get readership—if the response it got in the *Tribune* newsroom is any indication.
>
> The story on the Big Foot reportedly sighted at Cashton is the kind readers probably will be talking about.
>
> The monster, sighted by a farmer near the hamlet during the past two months is described as hairy, 7 feet tall and having a bad odor.
>
> Reading about it provided a hilarious break in what is a sometimes harried, sometimes monotonous routine of putting out a daily newspaper.
>
> There was speculation that a few people out there might be hitting funny cigarettes or moonshine.
>
> News Editor Merle Hill and staffer Pat Moore suggested political overtones.
>
> Could it be a campaign-weary politician who took a wrong turn on his final stump of the area? Or a campaign-weary voter hiding out until Nov. 2?
>
> Opinion Page editor Sandy Goltz ventured that, with a trick or treat bag in its hand, who would have the nerve to refuse it? But the best comment came from staffer Mary Liberte: 'Sounds like he could use industrial strength Right Guard.'"[1335]

The first known encounter with the Cashton Creature was experienced by a farmer and his dog. The farmer wanted to tell his story, but also craved anonymity. "It's hard to believe how many people think you are nuts," he said. Asking Bud Cavadini not to identify him, the farmer said he had gone into his fields to bring his cows in for milking. The cows had wandered into some nearby woods and as the farmer approached the tree line he saw a large creature about seven feet tall and covered with dark hair. The creature walked upright, had a flat face and gave off a strong, unpleasant odor. "The smell got stronger and the dog was barking. I was about 20 feet away from the woods when I heard a beller which sounded something like a young bull would make," the farmer told Cavadini.

The farmer's dog boldly advanced upon the creature, and in the ensuing confrontation actually bit it in the leg. As the creature brushed the dog to the side, the farmer, who was 50 feet away, saw some saliva from its mouth fall onto the dog. "By that time I'd had enough," the farmer said, and with his dog retreated to the farm house as the creature withdrew into the woods.

The farmer theorized that the creature had been circulating amongst his cows after he noticed the stink from the creature's foul-smelling effluence that besmirched his dog was the same odor noticed on his cows when they nightly returned to the barn after the day's rambles in the woods. The farmer and a nephew later reconnoitered the location of the encounter for any evidence of the creature, but the hard, dry ground made attempts at tracking it to be useless. On a later occasion, the farmer and three accomplices sat out one night in the woods with the intention to finally see the creature. Though they didn't see anything unusual, they did hear odd noises and noticed the same unpleasant smell that had been clinging to the farmer's cows and dog. "When you smell the smell you can usually hear its bellowing," the farmer said. "We can hear it many times up in the woods." The farmer confided to Cavadini that both he and his wife had smelled the strange odor on several occasions, and a neighboring family had smelled it, too. The dog, brave on its first encounter with the creature, had taken to remaining in the farm yard when the odor was present. The smell was like that of a skunk, said the farmer, "until you get closer, then the smell is different."

The farmer and a male relative armed themselves and searched the woods around the farm at night. They believed they heard the creature several times, including an occasion when something loudly circled their tree stand. The farmer's wife told Terry Burt about several inexplicable events that had occurred on the farm, which taken in context of her husband's encounter with the creature, became somewhat more understandable for the family. There were the unexplainable sounds from the hay mow: "It sounded like someone was moving hay bales around," she told Burt. "We thought our son probably got up early and was playing up there, so we didn't think much more about it." The same uncanny odor was discovered emanating from 12 feet up a pole leading to the hay loft. Terry Burt arrived weeks after it was first noticed but the spot still smelled strange when he climbed up the pole.[1336] When the odor associated with the creature was strong around their home, the farmer stated his wife was afraid to take their children outside. "We take a gun to bed with us at night," he told Cavadini.[1337]

A game warden from Sparta told the farmer he'd probably seen a bear, though the same warden admitted that a seven-foot bear was unusual. "The warden said to 'come back when you get more proof,'" the farmer recalled. One of the rumors held that the Cashton Creature was an injured bear, perhaps a specimen which had been shot by hunters. Others conjectured a bear had been malformed from a Cataract forest fire which caused burns to its paws and muzzle. These burns, so went the rumor, became gangrenous, creating a blunted, disfigured face. The burned front paws would have encouraged the bear to walk on its hind legs and the gangrene would help explain the terrible odor emanating from the creature.

Cashton Police Chief Dave Schaldach stated he was not aware of any bears in the area, injured or dead. Monroe County game warden Calvin Clark and Mike Lanquist, a state forester with the Department of Natural Resources, echoed Schaldach's contention. Burt wrote that several unmolested bee hives kept close to where the farmer saw the creature cast some doubt on the bear angle.

Burt's Cashton Creature article in the November 17 *La Crosse Tribune* carried the discovery of some intriguing tracks near the location of the original sighting.

> The wife of the farmer who saw the creature in September said Monday that for the past three weeks the area has been silent. The family has not heard the strange bellow of the creature nor smelled its vile scent.
>
> However, George Wuensch of Middle Ridge said his son, Paul, and an 11-year-old companion from Sparta were hiking in some nearby woods the last week in October when they came across a large footprint which was clearly visible in the soft dirt of a mole trail.
>
> Wuensch said the print, which showed four toes, was 18 inches long and seven inches wide at the widest point. It had a four-inch heel area and what was believed to be a deep arch.
>
> He said there were four prints in all, about 3 ½ feet apart, and that two strands of a wire fence had been broken near where the prints were found.
>
> The Wuenschs attempted to make a cement cast of the print, but the cast broke and only crumbled pieces remain.[1338]

Barrens Monster

Frank Zaworski, editor of the *St. Croix Falls Standard Press*, stated he wasn't ruling out the work of pranksters behind the October 1976 Bigfoot sightings in northwest Wisconsin. "It's the big topic of discussion in the taverns, whether it's a hoax or not," Zaworski said. "It sure beats talking about the election."

On the night of Friday, October 8, twelve teenagers from the Cushing-St. Croix Falls area rode along a gravel road on the Sam Burton property in Sterling Township. The group later admitted they had been shining their car lights to spotlight deer on the north end of an open field. Suddenly one member spied something just at the wood line. John Hanson described the strange sight: "We were out shining and spotted something different out in the field so we waited around for awhile. Someone further up the road came running back saying it had crossed the road. Everyone beat it up the hill, (a small hill on the gravel road) some were in cars. This is when we spotted Bigfoot on a sand bank on the south side of the road. He stood in one spot for about 10 seconds when me and Rodney Bystrom ran up in the woods. We heard him coming through the woods and we took off and ran down the hill. By that time most of the cars had taken off. We found a car and took off too!" Hanson told reporters the creature was about seven to eight feet tall, hair-covered except for its man-like face.

On Saturday morning, a contingent of folks returned to the scene including a group of teenagers who had been present during the previous night's encounter, several parents, and *Standard Press* reporter Pete Jensen. Jensen found several tracks that measured 19 inches long and 9 inches wide which he was able to follow for about half a mile. Along the creature's route of travel were several broken branches at the 7- and 8-foot level and a dry stump that appeared to be freshly uprooted. Zaworski said the prints could have been faked but given their depth and way the toes appeared to have dug into the ground, fakery would have required a sophisticated hoaxer. "My own personal opinion is that the kids we talked to weren't lying." Zaworski said. "But maybe somebody knew they were going to be in that area and decided to play a hoax."[1339]

"I studied wildlife management at a college in Northern California, and worked in a wilderness area for five seasons in that area," said Al Seidenkranz, a naturalist for the St. Croix National Scenic Riverway. "The most authenticated sighting of Bigfoot was made in that area and I personally would not say that there is no such thing." He further added, "It's interesting how the creatures always seem to match the same description." Seidenkranz was certainly open to the prospect of Bigfoot. "I would not discount the possibility that Bigfoot exists," he said, adding, that what the teens claimed they saw in the barrens area may not be an imaginary creation or simply a hoax.[1340]

But, a hoax it was. Four St. Croix Falls youths copped to a Bigfoot ruse that had the St. Croix Falls community buzzing. Frank Zaworski, editor of the *St. Croix Falls Standard Press,* who broke the story, maintained most local people had met the story with skepticism. "Then someone suggested that the forest fires up north may have driven such a creature south," Zaworski said, "and when a second sighting occurred, a number of people were convinced that the Barrens harbored some strange creatures."[1341]

Zaworski dug into the story and by the end of the week determined that the Barrens Monster was the result of four imaginative high schoolers playing a practical joke. "As much publicity as this got made me think the local Chamber of Commerce ought to pay the kids something for getting the city mentioned by so many news agencies," Zaworski said. The referred-to publicity included coverage via the United Press International (UPI), mention of the Barrens sightings on NBC's *Today* show, and local color segments on several Twin City television affiliates.[1342]

"Heck, we just did it for fun," said Joe Anderson, one of the prank-pullers. "It didn't really hurt anybody and it gave the town something to talk about besides the elections." Bart Larson, another one of the boys who participated in the hoax explained its idea came about after a group of kids "were startled by what looked like Bigfoot when we were in the Barrens one night looking for deer." The moment of shock was catalyzed from shadowy, anomalous shapes in the darkness. "We were flashing a light around," Larson said, "and a tall stump showed up in the dark. It looked just like one would imagine Bigfoot to look. It really scared us for a minute. Then we decided it would be fun to have a Bigfoot out there." Jim Anderson and Gene Fehlen were enlisted into the syndicate. Giant feet were fashioned out of wood and made to attach to shoes. Next, a suitable Halloween mask was purchased. "Then Jim put on the feet and left a few prints in the sand," said Joe Anderson. "We broke off some tree branches to show where the giant might have pushed his way through the brush."

A few days later the conspirators were out at the Barrens again, looking for deer with other youths not part of the prank. The uninitiated were allowed to "discover" the tracks Jim had left. On a second outing, a group of spectators saw Bigfoot standing near the woods by the side of a road. Following this second sighting, a growing number of people came to Sterling

Township to investigate and just maybe get a glimpse of Bigfoot for themselves. The 19-inch tracks were eventually found and measured but the icing on the cake was naturalist Seidenkranz bestowing a degree of legitimacy on the supposed Bigfoot activity. Talking with the *Standard Press* he said, "I don't rule it out. I lived in other areas where those things have shown up—there is a possibility of a hoax—but I believe such things exist."[1343]

Hoaxed Footprints in Agawam

Bigfoot investigator Lee Frank concluded that 27-inch, five-toed footprints made near the Westfield River in Agawam, Massachusetts, could be authentic. "The prints look good—but 'Bigfoot' tracks are a dime a dozen . . . we really need to see him," Frank said. Along with other trackers, Frank spent Wednesday night, December 29, camping near Robinson State Park, hoping to catch sight of the creature.

"Whatever the tracks are, they merit further investigation," he said. Frank had responded to Agawam resident Marianna Cascio, who requested Frank investigate after the tracks appeared on Monday, December 27. According to Cascio, the tracks were the real deal, belonging to a 1,500-pound giant which may have left the area.[1344] Local officials announced the Agawam tracks as their first monster investigation, and identification of the supposed prankster was just as elusive as an anomalous hairy hominid.[1345]

"It wasn't meant to go this far. I didn't feel too good inside," said David Deschenes who constructed 27-inch long plywood feet and used them to leave footprints in the fresh snow near the Westfield River. Frank's examination eventually concluded the prints were fake but both he as well as local police were unable to solve the mystery of who was leaving the prints until an anonymous phone tip implicated Deschenes. "I did it as a joke for the little kids around here, but it got out of hand. The next thing I knew the police were out at two in the morning looking around, taking it seriously," he said. "I didn't feel like going out to tell them I was Big Foot," admitted Deschenes. Police were holding onto the feet, at least temporarily, at police headquarters.[1346]

Following the decade's trend, investigation into an area's Bigfoot reports continued to reveal deeper layers of sightings and experiences and Agawam offered another instance of peeling the onion, as in the below letter written by George Earley to the *Springfield Union*:

> It is a fact that the 27 ½ inch "[B]igfoot" tracks found nest the Westfield River in Agawam a few days after Christmas were

> fakes, the hoax of a clever youth. However, to assume that all reports of [B]igfoot-type creatures are equally spurious would be a mistake.
>
> During my investigations, as well as those of others, into the recent footprints hoax, information was received that a number of people in Agawam feel that they have seen, from time to time over the past six to 10 years, [B]igfoot-type creatures and/or their tracks. There are reports, as yet unsubstantiated, of photographs of tracks . . . and perhaps of a creature.[1347]

Bigfoot Tracks?

Phil Thompson and a friend found several prints in the rough shape of a human-foot near Coos Bay, Oregon, during Labor Day weekend. The Coos County Sheriff's Department made casts of the footprints which measured 17 inches in length, seven inches across the toes, and five inches wide at the heel. The big toe measured two inches across. Three prints were found on one side of a ditch and four more on the opposite side. The stride between prints was over five feet.[1348]

Creatures in Cascade County

Sheriff Captain Keith Wolverton of Cascade County, Montana, looked into several unusual and strange events in the mid-'70s including UFOs, cattle mutilations, and Bigfoot. With Roberta Donovan, Wolverton authored *Mystery Stalks the Prairie* (1976) in which he detailed these events and their subsequent investigations. According to Wolverton, two sightings of hair-covered, upright-walking creatures were reported in the last half of July. Wolverton said an Ulm woman sighted a creature covered with dark hair and "very wide at the shoulders," at 5:30 A.M. on Interstate 15 on Wednesday, July 28. The woman reported the creature was only 20 feet away from her vehicle as she drove by. The seven-to-eight-foot-tall creature walked away when she stopped her car. An investigation of the scene did not turn up footprints. Another sighting had occurred about 10:30 P.M. on July 21. Four men were near Rainbow Dam on the south side of the Missouri River when they saw two creatures about 100 yards away. "We consider both these reports authentic and are investigating each one," Wolverton said. Wolverton added that the previous winter, several residents reported large man-like creatures in the area.[1349]

Hollingsworth & the Chatham County Bigfoot

By 1976, mental therapist Jim Hollingsworth had spent six years looking for Bigfoot. In September 1976 his search focused on the tobacco lands of Eastern North Carolina. Hollingsworth was looking for an animal that some locals were calling "that thing,"—a seven-foot, black-haired, ape-like creature, said to stalk the Cape Fear River area. Several people had reported hearing "deathly screams" that could make bold dogs cower in fear. Hollingsworth's time off from work at a state hospital was largely consumed looking for "that thing," a creature he acknowledged he had never seen. His efforts were concentrated in rural Chatham County, the location for several reports of Bigfoot sightings and 18-inch footprints.

"I'm not saying, 'There's a monster out there and let's prove it,'" Hollingsworth said. "My purpose is to research and investigate these reports to determine what these people say they are seeing and hearing." One of the reports came from Brody Parker (in whose vegetable garden several large prints were found in 1975) who for an estimated 20-minutes watched a seven- to eight-foot-tall creature. The Chatham farmer described the black-furred creature as "sort of hunched over and looking back at me."

Hollingsworth's interest in Bigfoot had taken him to Washington for field research on the West Coast. "The idea that some sort of relic biped could still be alive today is fascinating to me," he said. "The whole thing is unknown in North Carolina, even compared to the Big Foot case, which is also virtually unknown." Hollingsworth investigated several sightings from the Cape Fear River area, and compulsively collected as much information on Bigfoot as he could. "If these creatures do exist around here, they are very shrewd and very cunning," Hollingsworth said. "It could explain why they haven't been shot or captured, again assuming that they do exist."

Hollingsworth believed an understanding of dogs' behaviors in relation to the suspected presence of Bigfoot could yield insights—many Chatham County residents had described the cowering, whining behaviors their dogs evinced when Bigfoot was thought to be around. "It's a growly fuss somewhere between the sound of a yearling and an elephant," one farmer said, describing the supposed Bigfoot vocalizations. Hollingsworth had set up "traps" in the areas where screams had been reported, but declined to state exactly where. "Some fools are going to shoot each other hoping to kill themselves a monster."[1350]

Bigfoot in Maryland

In two articles written for *Strange Magazine*, Bigfoot researcher Mark Opsasnick makes a study of Bigfoot's presence in Maryland, detailing several encounters from the '70s. Harford County is located northeast of Baltimore and borders York and Lancaster counties in Pennsylvania and the northern reaches of the Chesapeake Bay. Harford County is about 50 miles from Sykesville.

Several Bigfoot incidents were reported in Harford between 1973 and 1975 followed by a flap of Bigfoot reports in southeastern Baltimore County in 1976. Richard and Elva Steward of Harewood Park said they had smelled a sulfur-like odor and heard a large animal moving in the woods while the couple burned brush near their home. The sounds of movement came close enough to the Stewards that Richard directed his hose into the woods. Undeterred by the spraying water the creature continued to approach the couple who were unnerved enough to leave the scene.

Opsasnick wrote that Elva Steward told the *Baltimore News American* that "I looked back and saw something about eight feet tall with two big green eyes. I was really scared. I didn't know what it was. Finally it just went back into the woods, making its own path through the bushes and small trees." She went on to recount that one night following the brush-burning incident, she heard scratching on her bedroom window. Richard investigated but didn't locate the intruder, instead confronting only a foul smell hanging pungently in the air. The following day, Richard discovered claw marks on their cellar door and nine feet above the ground on a bedroom screen. Richard further reported finding a shallow cave dug into dense undergrowth near their home.

The *News American* is quoted by Opsasnick for a report by Harewood teenager Jay Beavers. Near his home on University Drive, Beavers said he encountered a creature in May 1976 that was not a bear and which "cried like a cat." The creature was something outside of Beavers' experience. "The thing ran when it saw me. I could smell it. The animal had real long arms that sort of swung when it got away. I took some pictures of it, but the film got exposed."[1351]

Police Captain Jack Freeland told the *News American* that there had been several other creature reports that May. One of the stranger reports was noted by Opsasnick:

> Perhaps the most bizarre encounter with the Baltimore County Bigfoot during the May flap occurred when a county

> cab driver, while taking a break, reported seeing the creature behind the Hawthorne Plaza Shopping Center. What makes this report so unusual is that the shopping center is located in the residential area where Eastern Boulevard crosses over the Middle River. The *News American* quoted Captain Freeland as saying, "According to the Police Officer who took the report, the driver claimed to have seen something that was seven-to-eight-feet-tall. It was covered with dark hair. When the cabbie approached it, the thing started throwing trash cans at him."[1352]

In the second article of his *Strange Magazine* series on Bigfoot in Maryland, Opsasnick continues his canvas of Bigfoot reports occurring across the state, including several reports from the '70s. In September 1976, Ronny Williams of Riverdale was hunting in a spot adjacent to the Patuxent Wildlife Refuge, approximately 40 miles southwest of Harewood Park. Williams was occupying a 12-foot deer stand when he thought he heard the noise of another hunter moving through the woods below him. "Hey, wait for me and I'll walk out with ya." Williams called out as he climbed down. Williams next saw something, obviously not a fellow hunter, step into a clearing only 20 yards away. Opsasnick takes up Williams' account:

> "I could see it had arms and was up on two legs. It just kept going (in a southwest direction towards Rt. 197). It was big, almost eight feet tall, and it walked in a hunched-over position," Mr. Williams recently told this author. He stated that he didn't smell any odor and didn't have the time to notice any other characteristics, though the sheer size of the creature makes it unlikely that it was another human. "It was black, it was huge," Mr. Williams continued. "I saw something down there, I'm just not sure what it was. It's something I've kept to myself over the years, I guess out of a sense of being laughed at or being called crazy."[1353]

Another incident that fall occurred four miles northwest of the Williams encounter—when Francine Abell began to exit Route 198 onto I-95 South in Laurel one rainy morning, she noticed something large in the middle of the road. "It was some kind of gorilla, about six feet tall and very heavy," Abell told Opsasnick. "It was covered with greyish-brown fur and it was just standing there looking at me. Finally, it walked over to the side of the road, stepped over the guard rail, and ran off into the woods. The police didn't believe me, but I know what I saw."[1354]

Thomas Defleaugh of Glen Burnie, Maryland, didn't shoot any game, but did end his hunting excursion by shooting pictures of strange tracks he found during the week of November 7, 1976. Defleaugh had been hunting rabbits with a 12-gauge shotgun in the forests around Woodwardville in Anne Arundel County when he discovered the tracks left in fresh snow. "I was walking near an old gravel pit and I looked down and saw a bunch of three-toed tracks, each measuring about four inches wide almost eight inches long," said Defleaugh. The tracks were impressed about three inches deep into the snow. "There were four tracks," he said. "One of them was very clear because the ground was frozen. I wasn't really scared but I thought I better tell the police what I found. So I took some photos and got to a telephone." Defleaugh's pictures were scrutinized by County police. "I've never seen anything like this before," said one county policeman. Defleaugh said this was not the first time he had come across strange tracks. Defleaugh said several years previous he and his brother-in-law found three-toed tracks in a swamp area near Woodwardville. "I don't say what it is, but I thought it might be an animal maybe similar to Bigfoot," he said.[1355] Opsasnick noted that the relatively unusual characteristic of three-toed prints occurred frequently in the Old Line State. "The majority of the footprint finds in Maryland have displayed three toes, with the heaviest concentration of three-toed prints in Harford County."[1356]

Skunk Ape

B. Ann Slate penned several significant Skunk Ape articles in 1976 for the pages of *UFO Report*. Slate wrote about sightings in Crystal River, Florida, and their subsequent investigation by Duane and Ramona Hibner. Crystal River is a Citrus County town north of Brooksville whose emergence as a Skunk Ape hotspot started in February 1976.

Things kicked off as two women were assaulted by a foul odor upon exiting their car at their Crystal River home. The appalling odor was followed by the sounds of something moving about in the nearby woods. A large creature suddenly erupted into view and ran across a clearing about 30 feet away from the house. The women reported the creature performed a windmill-like action of its arms as it ran and it emitted a high-pitched yell. The frightened women ran into their house. After securing themselves inside, they ventured to look out the windows but the creature was gone.

The next morning a man, his son, and two friends were enjoying an early spot of fishing in a subsidiary creek of Crystal River. A creature they later described as eight feet tall with dark brown hair, approached them and threw back its head, giving the impression it was smelling the air. The witnesses noted the creature's very long arms and features like "lots of muscles, a face like a gorilla, and beady black eyes." "We had a hard time trying to interview them," Hibner told Slate. "They were all talking at once they were so excited as well as scared. None of them would return to the spot with us. Their fishing poles were still there when Duane and I got to the creek." Another incident in the area centered on a young woman walking to her car as she left a friend's party. The woman saw something that prompted her excited and rapid return into her friend's home, screaming in terror. Partygoers looked out windows to see a big, black shape running on two legs. In the ensuing excitement, a young man picked up a .38 pistol and fired at the shape but succeeded only in hitting car windows. The Hibners took stock of the rash of sightings, all relatively localized, and theorized logging operations south of Crystal River had pushed the creatures into residential areas. Of the Hibners' investigative findings, Slate noted that both behavioral patterns and an over-all composite picture of Florida's Skunk Ape (still frequently referred to as a Yeti vice Bigfoot) had begun to emerge from the collected data.

> The tracking team's documentation which began in 1965 had more than doubled by 1975, and now certain patterns were emerging. One was a definite migratory route traced via southern-flowing rivers throughout the state as well as the creature's use of numerous man-made canals. During 1975 and 1976, the Hibner files indicated a substantial increase in reports along these waterways which also provided thousands of uninhabited acres of swampland lending shelter and a steady supply of food.
>
> "More males are seen than females," Ramona says. "The breasts of the female are seldom noted, making me wonder if they only are apparent when nursing. In considering state-wide reports, it appears more (Yeti) young are reported in Florida. The warmer, more temperate climate may account for this.
>
> "The general description of the Florida Yeti is of a smaller type than the California version of Bigfoot," she continued. "Ours are usually six to eight feet tall and about 350 pounds.

The six-footer is mentioned more than the larger ones. Colors vary from brown to black and white or gray. The gray ones seem to smell worse than the others. The feet are flat and generally five-toed."[1357]

Slate did not shy away from exceptional and bewildering Bigfoot accounts in her articles. One such special event occurred on August 11, 1975, involving a group of three young boys who saw a five-foot Skunk Ape on an island off North Fort Myers. The boys watched it as it ate a bird and when the creature noticed it was being observed, it dropped its meal and growled at them. The creature was covered in long black hair which was bushy on the top of its domed head. Small ears, canines, and red eyes were observed and the hands and feet were described being large. It walked and ran upright as well as ambulated in a crab-like fashion. Witnesses said the creature had a high-pitched scream and a fetid, overpowering odor and an intriguing feature associated to it were *six-toed* footprints found on a nearby beach.[1358]

Slate and Hibner maintained an active correspondence from which Slate wrote of Hibner's account of an unusual discovery at the Withlacoochee River in February 1976.

> "We found something that has to be a baby Bigfoot! It looks like there has been no one in this river swamp in many moons. We could see impressions where something big with about an 18-inch foot had stood in the shallow water. Limbs about three inches in diameter had been broken off at a seven foot height on trees lining the bank. Three holes had been dug in the sand. This is where we found the hand prints. The fingers were most unusual; long, slender, curled—and webbed. All that showed on the baby footprint were the toes where it had stepped over the water plants. These were rounded and also webbed. I'll make a tracing of the casts for you."[1359]

Had the Hibners found evidence that the Skunk Ape was amphibious? One of the questions debated by Bigfoot researchers asked, could there be more than one kind of Bigfoot? The discovery of the "webbing" in certain, supposed Bigfoot tracks appeared to give reports of Skunk Apes' swimming ability credence. From this line of thinking, Slate pondered if underwater caves could be hiding spots or living abodes for Bigfoot.[1360]

Milton LaSalle's macro-analysis of Bigfoot data focused on predicting probable Bigfoot behaviors and so, perhaps, provide aids to enable successful field investigations. In the Fall 1976 edition of *Pursuit,* LaSalle wrote about the recurring theme prevalent in many reports concerning Bigfoot's apparent affinity to water. LaSalle analyzed this apparent association to determine if Bigfoot and water were correlated or simply a matter of coincidence. Citing John Green's *Sasquatch: The Apes Among Us,* LaSalle noted Green's observation that 65% of sightings occurred either in or near significant bodies of water. LaSalle combed his own file of sightings and came up with 78% and he concluded both ratios lent credence to Bigfoot and water sharing a connection.

Confident of a link between water and Bigfoot, LaSalle presented several cases in his article to explore this relationship including Dahinden and Marx's investigation of the cripple foot tracks meandering to and from the banks of the Columbia River as one example. Later investigations turned up more tracks on the opposite side of the river which LaSalle hailed as evidence of waterways serving as lines of communication for Bigfoot—navigable and exploitable travel routes.

LaSalle also wrote of a collection of sightings near Albany, Oregon, in the vicinity of a small lake. A Bigfoot had been witnessed disappearing into this lake. Concealment and evasion, LaSalle contended, represented additional uses Bigfoot could exploit from water. The report from two British Colum-bia prospectors who had occasion to observe a large, 12-foot Bigfoot in 1965 intrigued LaSalle. This particular specimen left 24-inch tracks which the prospectors followed to a frozen lake. The tracks went right to a hole in the ice and then led away giving the impression the track's maker had been dragging something. The next day the prospectors found smaller tracks leading to an ice hole on yet another lake. This second hole was some five feet in diameter.

> Why in the world did the Bigfoot break huge holes in the ice? And especially, what could he have found in this small lake to drag away behind him? One can immediately rule out the idea that he was just trying to obtain some drinking water; a much smaller hole would suffice for that. The next thought would be for food. Is there any source of food he could reach in this manner? As a matter of fact there is: there have been some observations of a Bigfoot feeding on water plants. If he was in a place where the water was fairly shallow, he could

> be reaching down and pulling up plants. The size of the hole would then depend on how hungry he was and how thick the plant growth was. But that still leaves the question of what was being dragged away. The marks described would not seem to fit a bundle of water plants. It is well to keep in mind the fact that the hole was large enough to permit the animal to have entered the water and returned through it.[1361]

As a matter of investigative protocol, LaSalle encouraged the use of maps to appreciate a report's terrain and context. Lakes, ponds, and rivers have especial geographic importance and should be investigated for Bigfoot sign, LaSalle argued; the knowledge of Bigfoot's use of waterways as food baskets, or means of travel, could lead to productive field research.[1362]

Research conducted in the summer of 1976 at the Double D Ranch outside Dunnellon, Florida, pointed to the presence of an aggressive, three-toed Bigfoot, according to the Hibners, who conjectured the incidents at the Double D Ranch involved a pair of Bigfoot which had taken up residence in the area. The Hibners maintained that high levels of aggressiveness displayed in several Bigfoot encounters was the creatures' assertion of territorial rights.

Before Donald Duncan took up the lease of the Double D Ranch's 40-acre parcel, the elderly owner had heard strange mumbling noises from his front porch in the early 1970s. Slate wrote that the man reached for his .22 rifle and cautiously opened the door. Standing on the porch and staring back at him was a tall, hair-covered creature. The man unloaded six shots into the chest area of the creature which, seemingly unaffected, simply walked off the porch and disappeared into the inky blackness of the night. The next morning a thorough search of the yard revealed several three-toed prints.

By May 1976, Duncan and his wife had taken a lease of the Double-D Ranch. In an interview with the Hibners, Duncan recalled the occasion when he and his wife arrived home at 2 A.M. After he parked in the yard, the couple got out of their car and saw two red, glowing eyes staring at them from the edge of their yard. Donald had heard tales of Skunk Apes from the ranch's elderly owner as well as from his neighbors but hadn't put much stock in them.

> Using a 30/06 rifle with scope, he shot at the eyes looking in his direction. While certain he hit the creature, it began walking away. Duncan fired again, hearing the impact of the bullet strike a solid form but it didn't bring the Yeti down nor

> halt its stride. A later inspection of the tree revealed no bullets imbedded in the trunk by faulty aim.
>
> Donald Duncan, a powerfully built man himself who weighs close to 300 pounds, did not convey his fears to the family but something about that creature was not natural; that and the fact that it was coming in too close for comfort.
>
> The male Yeti retaliated to those shots by pulling fence posts up out of the ground, tearing the Duncan children's pet rabbits from their cages and ripping them apart. Their Doberman puppy was found with its neck broken, and its stomach slashed open. Then the colt was found, alive but missing an ear and an eye. A large chunk of flesh had been torn from its flank.[1363]

Duncan's alarm increased when his children reported finding dark hair in their tree house. Duncan deployed straightedge razor blades on a limb near the playhouse as a deterrent. It was later discovered the blades had been snapped off. Unidentifiable sounds permeated the nighttime darkness—screams, howls and high-pitched whistles. A teenaged neighbor told Duncan he had seen two small baby Bigfoot and requested Duncan's help to shoot them. Duncan refused the offer. In July the family's five-year-old son came running into the house loudly declaring that he had just seen a big monster. The child wouldn't budge from the couch and his grandfather shot an air rifle outside to placate him. "There, I've chased it off, Chris," he said, but the traumatic nature of the boy's experience left him shaken for some time.

A culminating event was the death of the Duncan's thoroughbred horse, a prized and beloved animal that weighed 1,500 pounds. The horse was found dead, dragged, it was thought, by the lower jaw from the pasture into the family's yard. Three-toed prints were found stomped into the ground around the carcass. When the Hibners began their investigation into the events at the Double D Ranch, Duncan was still having difficulty discussing his horse. "He still cries over it," said his wife. "We had close to $5,000 and a lot of emotion tied up in that animal. And we had no insurance. That horse was pretty special to us."[1364]

> For Donald Duncan, that was the final straw. A monster wrecking his fences, killing his livestock, terrifying his children—a monster that couldn't be stopped by bullets—and then those strange lights in the night sky, coming so close that they shook the house and rattled the windows . . . it was a

> scene out of hell. With tears in his eyes, the burly, bearded rancher told his family that they were moving out of there.[1365]
>
> But by then, with the knowledge of the habits of the Yeti earned the hard way by hundreds of stake outs in mosquito ridden Florida swamps, Ramona and Duane Hibner had located the pits and caves high in an old mine where the Yeti family lived. This site is a well-guarded secret, as currently the tracking team is gathering the necessary equipment to capture and photograph one of the twin offspring. Should the tranquillization and confinement (an old but sturdy cement gorilla cage built by the prop department for a Tarzan movie of long ago) be of sufficient duration after photographing, medical equipment will quickly take samples of blood, skin, urine, hair, and so forth.[1366]

Slate noted the optimism the Hibners evinced in their correspondence to her, suggesting breakthrough results were near at hand.

> There will, of course, be dangers. For while the Yeti twins curiously approach man, as does any outgoing human child, as Ramona puts it, "Pa is meaner than hell's demons and you can bet Ma isn't going to be too far away. I may not have any change in my pockets out there in the boondocks so if you get a collect call, accept it. I'll have what we both want for sure!"
>
> This is an exciting prospect for any Bigfoot research-writer to say the least, and having studied the methodology and motives of all major Bigfoot expeditions that continue to turn up nothing, all bets are on the expertise of the Hibners. But there is something else. While the husband and wife team remain on the lookout for fresh tracks after the torrential rains of a recent hurricane, it looks like "someone" might also be watching them.
>
> Returning from "the site" shortly before midnight last August, a blinking aerial white light flashed in staccato beat ahead of them on the road. There was a rhythm: one . . . one, two. One, two . . . one. After several minutes, the UFO moved slowly and deliberately over the Hibner truck; a wingless craft estimated at some 200 feet in length. Three large red lights on the belly flashed from front to rear. Pulling the truck to the

02968-1 ★ $1.50 BANTAM BOOK
FOR THE FIRST TIME—
THE AMAZING TRUTH ABOUT
THE GIANT FOOTPRINTS,
AND THE MYSTERIOUS
CREATURES PROWLING
AMERICA'S WILDERNESS...
BIGFOOT
BY B. ANN SLATE AND ALAN BERRY
WITH 8 PAGES OF ACTUAL PHOTOGRAPHS

> side of the road, Duane shut off the engine. The UFO was soundless. After hovering a few seconds, it slowly moved on toward the Orlando area, remaining in sight for another four minutes.
>
> One wonders if this UFO encounter like the craft which buzzed the Double-D Ranch prior to the time the Duncan family moved out was purely coincidental. Do aliens have some special vested interest in Florida's other life form because the state is a breeding ground for the creatures? Do they acknowledge that Ramona and Duane Hibner are getting too close, and if planned capture of one or both of the Yeti twins should succeed, would it result in knowledge our "Space Brothers" might prefer to keep secret?[1367]

The Duncans' experience with the Skunk Ape, as shared by Slate, is notable for the suggestion that a young family member had a connection with a creature that visited their home. Again, Slate writes in *UFO Report* about the Skunk Ape and its more outré associations:

> July 17, 1976. Young Chris Duncan sat listlessly in his trailer home near Dunnellon, Fla. Normally talkative and energetic, the five-year-old was pale and apathetic, stunned by the memory of the "Big Monster" seen near his tree house a few days before. The family doctor would not comment on the alleged Skunk or Swamp-Ape (or Yeti) as the locals called the hairy ape-man creature. After examining the boy, he could only advise, that "whatever he saw, he is young and will get over it."
>
> As the clock ticked the minutes away and nightfall approached, Chris slowly began showing signs of extreme agitation and nervousness. Abruptly he screamed, "The monster is coming!"
>
> Family members rushed to calm him, to assure the child that he shouldn't be afraid; nothing would happen. But in their hearts, they knew their words were empty. The terrifying episodes of the past three months left no doubt that the seven-foot-tall Yeti was prowling around their ranch. Fence posts had been uprooted; pet rabbits torn from their cages and ripped apart. The "being" was destructive and potentially dangerous. Perhaps it was just cave man-type macho; a show of strength in

> front of his mate and twin offspring who had been seen nearby. Or perhaps it was because he had been shot at many times in the past. Regardless, Chris's father Donald Duncan, had to protect his own.
>
> At three A.M. that morning, the boy's predictions came true. The family Dobermans took up a howl and barked alarm warnings. Duncan grabbed his rifle, flicked on the outside lights, and headed for the porch. In front of the gate, the hair-covered creature was rolling in the dirt with three mongrel dogs. Duncan fired a shot at the ground. The strays ran for cover but the Yeti raised up slowly, unafraid, and turned to look with deliberation at Duncan. Its eyes were fire red.
>
> With his heart thumping in his chest, the rancher fired two more shots at the creature's feet. Each time, the Yeti howled like a wolf but did not break his long graceful stride into the woods. He would return to retaliate, however, leaving behind those enigmatic three-toed prints that have baffled Bigfoot researchers across the U.S. and Canada.
>
> Donald Duncan is a respected, mature, homespun type of man not given to wild imaginings. He would later describe the Yeti as having a face and body like something out of the movie Planet of the Apes—long black hair, glowing red eyes, long arms, and a stooped posture but walking upright like a man. The odor about him was "foul."[1368]

Slate referenced Herb Goldberger's article, "The Ghost of Cayo Pelau," from *Gold,* (Winter, 1974) concerning the strange atmosphere of Cayo Pelau Island in Lee County, Florida. "Maybe it is the Florida Yeti, the skunkape-like creature that roams from one mangrove island to another. Or perhaps it's just the wind howling through the tall palmetto grass," wrote Goldberger. "Whatever it is—Cayo Pelau is shrouded by a mysterious atmosphere which haunts every adventurer, treasure seeker, or fisherman who treks upon the one-time pirate island." Goldberger was aware of another treasure-hunter who suffered a series of baffling mechanical difficulties during his effort on Cayo Pelau, "I had a strange feeling I was being watched," the man told Goldberger. "As far as I'm concerned, I'll never go back to the island of Cayo Pelau. It's haunted and it's cursed. Someone else can find its treasures."[1369]

For Slate, the potential of Bigfoot's association with other unusual, if not strange phenomenon, deserved its due, and so her writing gave exposure to possible linkages between Bigfoot and other fantastic subjects. The fact that some of the more significant Bigfoot articles were published in a variety of UFO-themed magazines by the mid-'70s suggested a shift in the public's consumption of the subject. Slate's denouement of Bigfoot and other paranormal activities is best given from her writing in the July 1976 *UFO Report.*

> Yeti—Skunk Ape—Bigfoot creatures have raised much speculation by researchers everywhere. Theories range from one extreme, that they are being landed on this planet by extraterrestrials, to the other, that they are more like overgrown teddy bears. The middle ground and most logical supposition comes from Canadian journalist-Bigfoot tracker John Green who states:
>
> "As to linking the Sasquatch with visitors from outer space, I see no need to do so. But Earth could hardly be the only inhabited planet in the universe, or man the most advanced intellect in it. Since man can travel only a relatively tiny distance into space, it seems reasonable to assume that other creatures with greater capabilities may be flying in to look us over . . .
>
> "It is understandable too, that when people report seeing an animal that science insists does not exist on Earth, it should be suggested that it comes from somewhere else. But the Sasquatch, as I know them, fit very logically among the other creatures of Earth—far more so than does man himself. If they have been seen near UFOs, I would prefer to consider it a coincidence or to assume that the occupants of the UFO were just looking at the Sasquatch or vice versa . . ." (*Bigfoot* by Slate and Berry, Bantam Publishing, 1976).[1370]

Possible Skunk Ape hair found on a wire fence and described as "lice-ridden," was collected and sent on Tuesday, June 8, to the University of Miami anthropologist Dr. J. Manson Valentine for analysis. Valentine was identified by the *Tampa Times* as one of the discoverers of the "Bimini Road,"[1371] and had previously cooperated on research with the "now defunct" Yeti Research Society of St. Petersburg, contributing expertise to reports of Bigfoot-like creatures investigated by the group.

John Holley of North Fort Myers sighted a strange creature about ten feet off a dirt road he was driving on with his brother Bill and a friend on Sunday, June 6. "It was standing upright, just like you or me," Holley said.

"It looked to be about six feet tall with long black hair." Holley said he stopped his truck and got out at which point the creature retreated into the woods. "He didn't run or anything. He was just walking fast with real long strides." Charlotte County Deputy Sheriff Warren Vallier and Holley went to the site on Monday and found apparent footprints impressed two to three inches into wet dirt. The prints were followed across a ditch, to the fence where the hair was found and continued into thick brush. "If the creature did make those tracks, then it was sure heavy and I do believe something was seen by these men," Vallier said. "Now that could be cattle hair, but those sure aren't cattle tracks."[1372]

"I saw something," said Charlotte County Deputy Tom Williams. "I'm not sure what it was but it looked like an animal. Maybe more like a bear than an ape." On June 15, 1976, Williams was called to a freshwater pond at the end of Buck Creek in Grove City. The pond was the site of a Skunk Ape sighting by three teenagers—brothers Robert and Ralph Platt and Kent Hazelrigg.

"When I first saw it, it was on all four legs," Williams said. "When it left the pond, it scampered across the road. It looked about four feet tall." While at the water, the animal stood erect at a height of about 6 ½ feet tall, Williams explained. The boys had wanted to get a rifle and pursue the creature and find out exactly what it was. "It wasn't hostile or aggressive at all," Williams said. "I told them [the Platts and Hazelrigg] it doesn't bother us, so we shouldn't bother it."[1373]

Skunk Ape—Jim Spink (1976)

Jim Spink's first foray into the Everglades in search of Bigfoot turned into a six-month investigative marathon. By 1976, Spink had become a tax-exempt nonprofit organization, certified by the Internal Revenue Service. Spink had figured a list of required equipment for one-man expeditions into the Everglades; the priciest kit was infrared camera equipment with an estimated cost of $21,790, for which, he hoped, the National Science Foundation or another sponsor would provide funding. Despite his efforts, no benefactors signed on to back Spink's expedition. During Spink's 1976 six-month Everglades stay his camera (sans flash attachment) was second-hand and picked up at a flea market.

> At 30, Spink is a perpetual junior college student: "retired," he says, living off $290-a-month from the GI Bill for going to school.

> He is the research director of the Bigfoot Research Society, and he collects letters from scholars and professors.
>
> "I would be happy to collaborate," writes David E. Martin, Ph. D., Yerkes Regional Primate Research Center, Embry University. The doctor is an authority on semen evaluation. He knows about electronic microscopy of spermatozoa. He would appreciate specimens.
>
> "I would be extremely interested in seeing any casts," declares Paul R. Scherer, dean of the California College of Podiatric Medicine. "Blue dental plaster in the fastest setting."
>
> "Good luck," says Professor Digamber S. Borgaonkar from Johns Hopkins University School of Medicine. "My specialty is cytogenetics," he writes. "Collect blood samples."
>
> From Oxford Polytechnical in England, K.F. Howells, Ph. D., says, "We would be only too willing to analyze any samples of hair."

Spink, an ex-Navy quartermaster, was the author of an unpublished manuscript, "Bigfoot and Me," which told the story of his lonely expedition within a Charlotte County mangrove swamp on Florida's Gulf Coast. Excepting a handful of voyages to a marina, Spink lived isolated near an oyster mound from January 6 to June 20, 1975. Spink spent most of his expeditionary time in the buff, the better for Bigfoot to sense more in common than not. Spink acknowledged that despite the length of his stay and his best efforts, he had never caught a glimpse of Bigfoot. But, he maintained, Bigfoot most certainly watched him.[1374]

"I'm positive he was out there somewhere," Spink said. Spink believed he had experienced several close encounters with Bigfoot, all of them at night. On one occasion, Spink said something approached right up to his tent. The interloper unnerved him by "chattering and raving in a high-pitched scream." Spink sang a Gilbert and Sullivan tune, played a harmonica, and spoke in soothing tones, all to reassure and calm a particular Skunk Ape visitor, whom he named Gin. Spink believed that on some occasions Gin brought his mate close to camp, especially when the fruit ripened on a nearby ficus tree.

Spink said he had collected several feces specimens (264 grams) and he took many pictures during his 6-month stay on the oyster mound. He found one footprint which measured 11 by 5 ½ inches. Spink became convinced a Skunk Ape stole applesauce from his pan. When he dusted it for fingerprints, Spink discovered large thumb latents. Around mid-March, disaster struck his campsite. While making one of his occasional forays away from camp, "scoundrels" burned his camp destroying his journal, specimens, collected samples, even a $7 magnifying glass. As Gene Miller reported, it was fortunate indeed that Spink's girlfriend had won $660 on "Bowling for Dollars," which financed new equipment for Spink, including a "$47.63 spotlight with a 200,000 candlepower Q beam." But after the vandal's destruction, Skunk Apes never came near again. During the six-month expedition Spink lost a total of 23 pounds.

Spink submitted a $100,000 grant request to the National Science Foundation (in 1977, the Foundation had a $780 million-dollar budget). Dr. Nancie L. Gonzalez, the foundation's director of anthropology, reported Spink's request was "under consideration." Spink's proposal demonstrated his research on his equipment needs—$10,324 for parabolic microphones, a veterinarian pathologist, an airplane pilot, and assorted tranquilizer weapons. He included an expense of $28 for a new harmonica.[1375]

Spink wrote local Florida papers inquiring after their Bigfoot-related stories published in the previous five years. "Since my studied opinion is that BIGFOOT is man-like, it is quite possible that his territorial range is extensive," Spink wrote *The News Tribune* of Fort Pierce. "Just seeing or hearing or finding a footprint has little value," continued Spink. "All elements of their basic life functionings are essential to a wholistic [sic] understanding of just what and who BIGFOOT is." Spink asked that his nonprofit's contact information be printed so parties with information on sightings could write or phone him.[1376]

A year later, Jim Spink lived in a camper sans running lights or water, drove a car which served as a place to sleep when on the road, and did his scientific reading at night in a kosher restaurant which did have light and where people tended to ignore him. Spink had been going to college for nine years on the G.I. Bill studying recreational management, but his interest in Bigfoot diverted him into other subjects like zoology, biology, and anthropology. When reporter Charles Whited first met Jim in 1976, Spink had just returned from his six months in the wilds near Punta Gorda, Florida. There, Spink had been engaged in the study of a family of three Bigfoot who would prowl his campsite at night. His request to the National Science Foundation for $21,790 was ultimately refused. In March 1977 Spink sold his scuba gear for $125 to finance more cameras and a tape recorder. He returned to his previous research area to discover the family of three had dwindled to one. Spink wasn't able to get any pictures on this endeavor but did manage to tape-record some screeches he believed came from a Bigfoot which he played for reporter Charles Whited.

Spink telephoned the office of Representative Paul Nuckolls of Fort Myers advocating the creature be placed under the jurisdiction of the Governor's Council on Indian Affairs and that all sightings be reviewed. Nuckolls' office told Whited that Spink's idea would be taken under consideration. Nuckolls would go and sponsor protective measures for the Skunk Ape. The Florida House Criminal Justice Committee approved a bill in the autumn of 1977 protecting Bigfoot in Florida.[1377]

Two Women See Bigfoot from Car (1976)

Mac McDonough, a long-time reporter on Bigfoot matters, wrote of two Bakersfield, California, women sighting Bigfoot in Santa Barbara County on Monday, November 29. Carmen Lomas was the front seat passenger in a car being driven by Lucille Calvillo, while Carol Martinez occupied the backseat. About 50 miles southwest of Cuyama, Calvillo said "Look," and Lomas turned to the direction indicated. On a slope only some 10 feet from the road was a huge, 12-foot tall creature. "He had something in his hand, maybe a club, and he lowered it in a chopping motion after taking a step toward us. Lucille stepped on the gas. When Carol heard about what we saw she suggested we turn around and go back," Lomas said. "That creature was solid black in color, but I couldn't tell if he was covered with hair," she added. Darkness had descended as the women approached Cuyama when they saw a California Highway Patrol officer using a spotlight on cattle grazing on a hillside. "He turned off his light when he saw us, then turned it on after we passed," Lomas said, speculating there might have been something on the hill frightening the cows. "But it's like a bad dream and I'm still frightened when I think about that monster," she said.[1378]

And . . . Santa Claus

No less a celebrity than Santa Claus joined the ranks of Bigfoot witnesses during the '70s.

Wearing the trappings of jolly old St. Nick, Roger Hines, 19, walked into the sheriff's office (in Multnomah County, Oregon) and told deputies he saw Sasquatch while driving home from a Christmas party at his father's home.

Hines claimed the creature was eight feet tall with "lots of hair." He said it crossed the road in front of his car. "The deputies just cracked up when I told them," Hines told a reporter, "because I was still wearing the Santa Claus suit from the party."[1379]

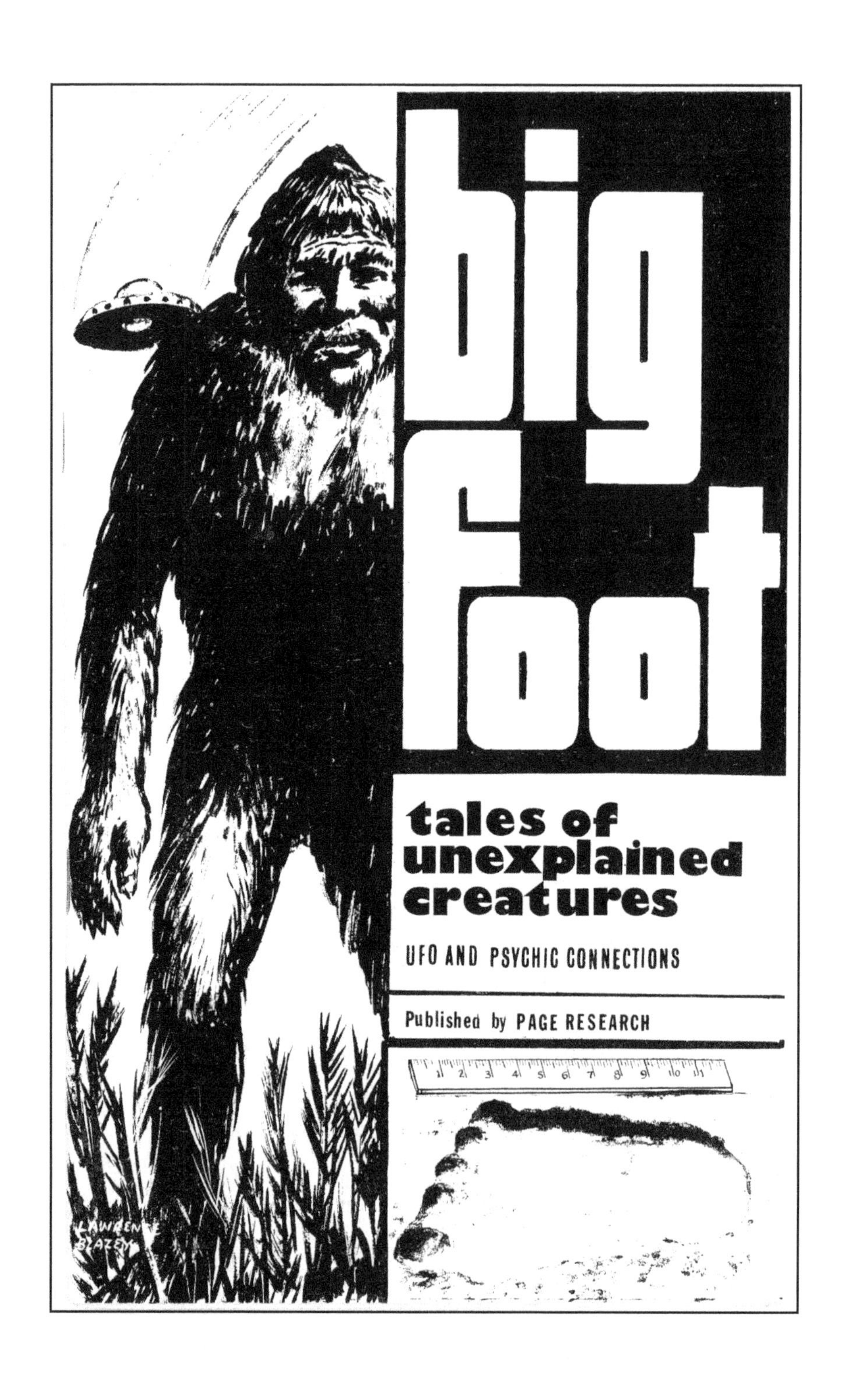
big foot
tales of unexplained creatures
UFO AND PSYCHIC CONNECTIONS
Published by PAGE RESEARCH
LAWRENCE BLAZEY

CHAPTER 8
1977

We are living in the day of the "Big Foot Syndrome."

And so some kid, or adult with nothing better to do, fashions a big footprint in the soft dirt near somebody's house. The homeowner, or resident, spies the footprint, has visions of a big, hairy creature standing on one foot in her yard, then taking off without any additional sign. The police and daily newspapers are called. The police regard it as a prank and forget about it, but the daily blows it to the sky. Pictures, feature stories, plaster impressions, etc., the whole bit. A segment of the public also falls under the spell with numerous telephone calls, tromping through the yard to see "it," and all that sort of thing.

One would think that in this year of 1977 when we are supposed to be more sophisticated and knowledgeable than ever, people would not let their imaginations run rampant in such a way.

After all, 1977 is the year of the snake, not the big footprint. Now if some idle minds fashion a big snake yarn a bit later in the year, they will be much more believable.[1380]

William R. Bradford. "No Foolin'," *Fort Mill Times* (February 28, 1977).

Know Anything About Bigfoot? It has been a time since we have last heard from out friend, Bigfoot, up around Bluff Creek. I have an inquiry from a student, David Rite, Bethlehem, Pa., asking for information.

"What has Bigfoot been doing this summer?" he asks. Sorry to say, I haven't had rumors or reports, and of course we discuss "imagination" as not useful.

> If you can help us help David—let Redwood Country know.[1381]
>
> Andrew Genzoli. "Redwood Country," *Times-Standard* (October 21, 1977).

Laymen & Scientists

Some of the figures associated with Bigfoot's origin like Crew, Titmus, and Wallace reemerged in 1977, a year in which it was said "hardly a week goes by without a sighting of Bigfoot. A week without Bigfoot would be like a week without Walter Cronkite."[1382] Bigfoot's eminence in pop culture not only depended upon the lay public's interest, but also in the researchers' investments of resources and in some cases considerable time investigating North American hairy hominids and the content that emanated from their efforts. Insights into the first generation of Bigfoot researchers' beliefs and approaches further explored the phenomenon with respect to both its conception and the trail it subsequently traveled.

Jerry Crew's interest in Bigfoot had endured for nearly 20 years when the *Escalon Times* of Oakdale, California, interviewed him. Crew was living in Escalon, California, and commuted to his job working on jet engines at the San Francisco International Airport. He told the *Escalon Times* he would like to "capture one of the crazy things to show some of the people who have laughed at the idea" that Bigfoot could possibly be a reality. "I think there's probably hundreds of them," Crew stated. Recalling the first time he saw the infamous Bluff Creek tracks in 1958, Crew upheld the profound astonishment and wonder he first felt. "I couldn't figure out what it was," he said, "and I was very curious." Crew admitted to never having seen the creature, but believed he had "smelled him and I've heard him."

> Tracking him, Crew once found where the creature had made a nest and killed and ate a deer. The 13-foot nest was layered, showing three different times it had been used. He described the sound of "Bigfoot" as "real weird." The odor, he said, was "tremendous."

Over nearly 20 years of interest in Bigfoot, Crew said he had seen "five different footprints," and had gained a healthy respect for the creature's abilities. "I can't imagine the strength of the creature," he told the *Times*.[1383]

In 1977, Bob Titmus' Bigfoot-tracking and researching interests had covered the better part of three decades, a period in which he journeyed from disbeliever to full confidence in Bigfoot as an extant creature. "I was getting sick and tired of people coming to me and describing strange tracks and asking if they were Sasquatch tracks," the 58-year-old Titmus said. "I'd never seen the tracks, so I couldn't answer, but I certainly didn't believe an animal could make the kind of tracks they were describing."

> His search has taken him from north of Fairbanks, Alaska to Mazatlan, Mexico, and he has since amassed the largest collection of original casts in the world. He admits, however, that as scientific evidence such casts are useless.

Along the trek of search and discovery, Titmus collected many samples of hair and fecal matter believed to be from Bigfoot which he had sent to "analysts all over the world," but consequent study and scrutiny proved "unable to identify the source."

"This is a giant primate, perhaps the first cousin of man, and people won't believe in it," Titmus said. "Some scientists dismiss it out of hand, without even looking at the evidence." Scientists would believe, Titmus likewise concluded along with many of his fellow aficionados, when they could be presented with cold, hard proof: nominally a body on a slab or a living specimen in containment.

Titmus' first encounter with Bigfoot was close enough for him to "see the wrinkles on its lips. But I flatly refused to believe what I was seeing." Years later, his second encounter involved three creatures climbing the face of a sheer granite cliff. "Personally, it's not a question of thinking they exist. I know positively. I'm not trying to convince anyone."

Titmus estimated there were thousands of Bigfoot on the West Coast but they were being driven into smaller enclaves from man's encroachment into their wilderness habitats. According to Titmus, Bigfoot had an opposable thumb, a trait infrequently discussed amongst Bigfoot researchers at the time. Titmus said though he had gone broke three times over the last 19 years hunting for Bigfoot, he would "always hunt the [S]asquatch, any time I am able, physically and financially."[1384]

Ranking as one of the stranger articles on Bigfoot promulgated during the '70s, a *Columbia Press* (Warrentown, Oregon) story stirs the Bigfoot stew with ingredients such as Ray Wallace, the Clatsop County Bigfoot

Information Center, the discovery of Bigfoot skeletons, and the involvement of a breathless Smithsonian employee.

> One mile past the Lewis and Clark turn-off on old Highway 202 there's a home with floats and driftwood in the yard. It would look like many other homes in this coastal community were it not for the sign that identifies it as the Clatsop County Bigfoot Information Center.
>
> Grace Gensman Hanby (G.G.) who runs the Center has new reason to be excited these days. She reports the discovery near Toledo, Oregon of a skeleton believed to be that of a Bigfoot.
>
> The bones were found about ten miles northeast of Mount Saint Helens in freshly melted snow near a lake. They were bleached out, and are believed to have belonged to an adult. The leg bones are three feet long, G. G. says, and the skull measures 20 inches from top to bottom, with an eight-inch jaw.
>
> "Instead of a hollow nasal opening as we have," G.G. commented, "this one has a bony ridge across it that is about an inch thick."
>
> Ray Wallace, a contractor who lives in the Toledo area, found the skeleton. He has been involved in the Bigfoot search for about 15 years, and was with a group of men in 1968 who found twelve skeletons. They were sent to the Pentagon, G.G. says, and they were never heard of again.
>
> The recent find has been turned over to Harvey Culver of the Smithsonian Institute. He drove out to pick the skeleton up and is personally driving it back to Washington, D.C. According to G. G., Culver kept repeating, "This is the link we've been looking for."
>
> Culver also is taking 23 teeth Wallace removed from two other skulls. G.G. describes them as chisel-like incisors with built up ridges on the back and linen like patterned enamel on the front. One molar is more than an inch wide.
>
> "Bigfoot are known to bite chucks out of trees," G.G. says. "In fact, that is one of the signs we look for."
>
> Wallace saw what he thought was a Bigfoot family this May in northern California. He watched them for an hour as they

> ate huckleberry brush and seemed to be playing with "throwing rocks." Bigfoot enthusiasts believe the rocks are used to kill small game. Wallace and G.G. both have collections of the stones.
>
> G.G. said there have been many sightings in the local area. A white one was hit by a car at Seaside. Later a young couple parked by the south jetty were attacked by a white creature. G.G. feels it was probably the same one, and that it was after the car, not the people inside.
>
> Three people saw a black one standing in Cullaby Lake. One sighted on Ridge Road by a family in a car was clocked running at 20 m.p.h. Other sightings have been reported by the Military Cemetary [sic], at Knappa, on Cedar Creek Road, Saddle Mountain, and on the road to Jewell. They have been white, grey, black or buff.
>
> This area is home to Bigfoot because it has good food and ground cover, G.G. explains. She thinks people should leave some fruit on their trees and some things in their gardens for the Bigfoot to eat during the winter.
>
> G.G. stressed that these creatures should not be shot. She says they are not violent. In fact, at least two rescues by Bigfoot have been reported. One involved a hunter who fell. When he woke, he was in a cave with some Bigfoot, and his broken leg had been set and splinted with pieces of bark.
>
> "If anyone has information on anything recent," G.G. says, "I would appreciate if they would come by and tell me." She says she's always home after 5 P.M. She also takes reports of Unidentified Flying Objects.[1385]

The above article's *coup de grâce* would seem to be the anecdote of Bigfoot's implied aptitude in field first aid. But this is followed by the inevitable mention of UFOs, which is a fitting denouement to a Bigfoot story brimming over with such varied content.

The sanction (or lack thereof) bestowed by card-carrying Ivory Tower delegates imparted (or withheld) a pipe-smoke air of serious, informed perspective to the question of Bigfoot's existence. Dr. William Montagna served as director of the Oregon Regional Primate Research Center and was an ardent nonbeliever in Bigfoot. He issued a scathing denunciation of both

Bigfoot and its adherents; from Montagna's reproof in the September *Primate News:* "Fascinated by the unknown and goaded by his imagination, man is forever fabricating devils and saints. . . . Nothing is to be gained by arguing with believers. Incapable of sifting reality from fantasy, they swear to have seen the footprints of Bigfoot or of the Abominable Snowman (Yeh-the) and to have heard their chilling roars. Even the tricksters who perpetrate these outlandish hoaxes sometimes come to believe in the reality of their creatures."

Edward W. Cronin Jr., a zoologist who searched for the Yeti in the Himalayas, arrived at his own conviction after finding evidence in the field. He concluded there had to be such creatures after awakening one morning to find clear prints in the pristine snow outside his tent. The tracks passed Cronin's tent and continued down a steep slope. Cronin wrote in the November 1975 issue of *The Atlantic,* that "based on this experience, I believe that there is a creature alive today in the Himalayas which is creating a valid zoological mystery."

Dr. Paul Simonds, senior physical anthropologist at the University of Oregon told writer Jeff Williams that it was conceivable *Gigantopithecus* crossed the Bering Strait via a land bridge. "My basic feeling is there is no such thing, but I'm not willing to rule it out," Simonds said, adding that *Gigantopithecus* may have been migratory in contrast to other primates, such as gorillas which remain relatively static. Simonds noted that chimpanzees and gorillas wear down their teeth in similar fashion, and that *Gigantopithecus* and early man appeared to have worn their teeth down in a congruous manner. "So it looks as though there is a similar jaw action," Simonds said. Williams posed a question about this dental wearing: could it mean man and *Gigantopithecus* went looking for similar food? "At least it means their dietary adaptation was not similar to the chimp and the gorilla who stayed in the tropics. But it's hard to go beyond that," Simonds stated.[1386]

Grover Krantz

Washington State University's Grover Krantz, associate professor of anthropology, remained the eminent American scientist who publicly advocated Bigfoot's existence. As a Bigfoot celebrity, Krantz received correspondence from enthusiastic writers eager for his opinions and advice:

> Dear Doctor, postmarked July 08, 1977
> My name is Robert "Crazy" Kaup. I read part of the book title [sic] "The Mysterious Monsters." I am thinking on looking

for the Bigfoot as soon as possible (moneywise). The following things are things I that I know I need for the expedition:

Guns
Camaras [sic]
Back pack
A sleeping bag
Hiking boots
Food
Box matchs [sic]
Silver wear [sic]
Plates
Knifes [sic]
A tent

Am I missing anything? If so could you please write it down.

I have never went on a expedition, would you or would you not say go by yourself. . . .

P.S. Do you know of any expeditions going on this year? And when. Thank you for your help.[1387]

Krantz gained increasing notoriety in the latter years of the '70s for his pro-kill position. "I think a Sasquatch has to be shot and killed to convince scientists that they exist," Krantz told an audience of about 400 at the Ohio State University Mansfield campus (M-OSU) Friday night, April 8, 1977. Krantz hastened to add that only one body should be enough for science—no need, literally, for overkill; Krantz estimated that roughly 200 of the creatures roamed the North American wilderness areas. After Bigfoot was proven to the scientific establishment's satisfaction as an extant animal, Krantz said it should be given the full auspices of legal protection.

Krantz brought five plaster casts to Mansfield made from what he considered authentic Bigfoot tracks. He sold a set of casts to OSU for $150; according to Dr. Richard Wink and Dr. James B. Heck the purchased casts were funded from the anthropology department's budget. Along with the set purchased by Ohio State University, a set remained in Krantz's possession and a third set resided at the Smithsonian Institute. Dr. Sherri Deaver told the *Mansfield News Journal* she would use the casts as teaching aids and intended to have them on permanent display in the Mansfield campus library.

Krantz told his OSU audience he preferred the name Sasquatch over Bigfoot. He explained the term Bigfoot was descriptive of only one part of the creature's anatomy. Why wouldn't Big Elbow or Big Ear be as equally appropriate, he asked. "Sasquatch is a legendary animal or thing that many people have described seeing and is almost universally denied by the scientific community," Krantz said. "The animals are described by quite a number of observers . . . (with) very few deviations. Basically, a Sasquatch is an animal that stands on two legs with the body more or less vertically, two arms, shoulders with some breadth, the head sitting in the center of the shoulders, and this is pretty much a description of a human being," he said. "The legs are roughly of human proportions. The arms are not used in locomotion. They just swing to the sides," Krantz added. "But the interesting part starts when you consider the size. They are usually described as being about eight feet tall," Krantz stated, estimating such a creature's weight would be about 800 pounds.

Krantz confided to his audience that after much invested time and effort investigating tracks in the field he was beginning to devote more energy into studying witness accounts, of which he had collected some 800 reports and had conducted 24 eyewitness interviews. He stated he had viewed five films of Bigfoot and assigned credibility to only one of them—the Patterson-Gimlin film. Concerning the other films which he adjudged as fake, Krantz said he had a good idea "who was in the monkey suit." Krantz reiterated for the audience that it was the Colville prints evincing a crippled foot that made him a believer. Reviewing the overlaid anatomical structure onto the cast, Krantz said it would take an expert, equaling if not surpassing Krantz in aptitude and ability, to successfully and deviously fake such a misshapen foot. Krantz also pointed out to his listeners that though there were indeed many faked tracks, he knew of two telltale factors to authenticate tracks which he had never written about or told anyone.[1388]

Jon Beckjord

Long-time *Seattle Times* writer John "Hint" Hinterberger interviewed Jon Erik Beckjord, then 38 years old, for a *Times* article published on October 15. Hinterberger sat down with the Project Grendel president at the latter's dining room table in "an ordinary neighborhood" in North Seattle. Scattered across the table were numerous photographs, documents, and drawings. On a wall hung three maps marked with Bigfoot sighting data and snowshoes occupied a corner of the room.

"Part of the problem of not being able to come up with scientific proof," Beckjord told Hinterberger, "is that scientists don't work for nothing." Beckjord knew the familiar lament shared by many Bigfoot hunters which bemoaned the lack of funding for their efforts. "And nobody is giving out grants for Sasquatches."

Beckjord told Hinterberger that he started out convinced Bigfoot owed its notoriety, its *existence*, to hoaxes and misidentifications. In 1975, he came to Seattle to do a documentary film to expose the Bigfoot bamboozle. "I intended to find the hoaxer," Beckjord said. "Instead, all I found were a lot of very sincere people."

Beckjord produced a tape recorder and played a moaning scream for Hinterberger. "That was recorded by Sgt. Kenneth Cooper of the Lummi Tribal Police," Beckjord said. "It was in 1975. He and another officer were investigating a disturbance at the orchard turnaround on Chief Martin Road. They heard the screaming, rolled down the window and this is what they got."

> The eerie cry howled for a few choruses and went silent under a wash of tape hiss. Beckjord clicked it off and snapped on a film projector.
>
> It documented the now familiar set of [B]igfoot tracks, heavily indented in fresh snow running alongside a snowmobile trail near Mission Ridge.
>
> "This was in January of this year," he said. "They were found by a Mr. and Mrs. Wain Jarvi of Kirkland, a retired couple, who ran across them while they were snowmobiling. There were more than 300 prints, 16-inches long, with a space of 5 feet between each track."
>
> But footprints in the snow, he admitted, were clues to Bigfoot's existence, not hard proof. "Snow melts; they go away."[1389]

Hinterberger raised the popular question so often posed to Bigfoot aficionados: why hadn't a Bigfoot body ever been found? Beckjord replied with a rationale just a bit off script from the usual retort that focused on explaining the rapidity with which nature breaks down bodies in the wild: "The Sasquatch is at the top of the food chain," he stated. "He is not prey for anybody. The time and place of his death is a matter of his own choosing."

By way of introducing one of his prized pieces of Bigfoot evidence, Beckjord recounted for Hinterberger the so-called "Ingalls Creek Incident," which occurred in the Wenatchee National Forest of Chelan County, Washington. A farmer named DeWeef was startled to see an unknown animal on his property. "He looked out and saw a large black creature tearing open his chicken coop. The animal killed five chickens, one at a time. Then laid each down in a row as it snapped its neck, something a bear would never do. DeWeef measured it against a post near the coop; he estimated it to be 7-feet tall. He fired at it with his shotgun and it took off—jumping a 15-foot creek in the process." With an air of drama, Beckjord then produced a "weighty, foil-wrapped package the size of a melon" to Hinterberger.

> "I have here," he proclaimed, "the only Sasquatch bleep in the city of Seattle."
> Sasquatch dung?
> "The real thing," he said. "It was recovered by one of our members after the Ingalls Creek incident."
> But where have you kept it?
> "In the freezer. Where else?"
> Well, let's have a look at it.
> "You are going to open it?" he asked.
> Of course.
> "That's what I call investigating in depth," he said.
> The specimen was unlike any bolus this reporter has encountered in 15 years of diverse American journalism; in shape it was a cross between a French roll and a softball. Its color, density and other characteristics were unmistakable.
> "Have you had this analyzed?" I asked him.
> "No money," he said. "If scientists seldom work for free, feces analysts never do."
> As soon as Project Grendel got some funds, he said, the Ingalls Creek Sasquatch pie would meet appropriate scrutiny.[1390]

As director of the Seattle-based Project Grendel, an organization of 21 Bigfoot researchers, Beckjord advocated hunting Bigfoot without weapons. Beckjord claimed blood and hair samples from three states represented the best evidence for Bigfoot's existence.

> Beckjord said he was making the information public to encourage the submission of more evidence by "closet" Bigfoot observers—those who believe they have seen the creature or possible evidence of it but have been unwilling to come forward for fear of ridicule.

> Beckjord said he has become more convinced that the Sasquatch exists as the result of analysis of clues found in the past two years in Washington, California and Maryland.[1391]

Beckjord described for *Modern People* magazine the different incidents which produced the samples.

> May 9, 1975, a motorist in the desolate Rocks State Park, Maryland, struck a black hairy creature on a foggy, pitch-dark night.
>
> The creature fit the typical Big Foot description: Large, approximately seven feet tall, with huge feet—demonstrated by the footprints and the creature walked on two legs, just like a man. The motorist saved the clues, found mingled with the broken headlight of the car.
>
> On Jan. 15, 1976, a mysterious animal broke a window on the remote Lummi Indian Reservation in Washington, when it tried to get into a food storage area. A man who believed in the Sasquatch (the Indian name for Big Foot) sent what he found to Beckjord.
>
> Most informative was an eye witness account of four teenagers who watched in horrified fascination while a nine-foot-tall creature are fruit off trees in a California orchard, and then easily scaled a tall barbed wire fence.[1392]

The hair samples were analyzed by Tom D. Moore, forensic hair expert at the Wyoming Fish and Game Laboratory. "The three samples had sufficient common characteristics as to be able to consider them as coming from the same species of animal," Moore reported. "The hairs could not be identified as coming from any animal found in the Wyoming mammal collection, nor as coming from a Washington black bear, gorilla, champanzee [sic], orangutang [sic], gibbon, siamong or languor moneky [sic], or man," he added. According to Moore, the hairs "exhibited some characteristics found in some primate hairs in general."[1393]

The hair sample found on the Lummi Indian Reservation near Bellingham reportedly contained traces of blood. In an article in the *Daily Record* of Ellensburg, Washington, Beckjord said this blood sample was tested by a University of California biochemist who determined the blood in question belonged to a mammal, though not a bear, dog, or other carnivore. Granting the analysis of the samples had not proven the existence of Bigfoot, "they do represent a major milestone for research of this type," Beckjord said, providing researchers "strong indications" that "a breeding population of such primates does in fact exist in the remoter areas of the U.S."[1394] Beckjord agreed with other researchers like Krantz that Bigfoot was descended from *Gigantopithecus*. Beckjord contended that Bigfoot was able to remain hidden from man owing to the vast wilderness areas of the Pacific Northwest. "You could probably hide a battalion of anything in those areas."[1395]

By 1977, Beckjord claimed to have seen Bigfoot three times: once on the Lummi Indian Reservation, once near Monte Cristo, and once in Ohio. Like Byrne, Beckjord drew comparisons between Bigfoot and the Loch Ness Monster. While these two cryptids were the most famous mystery creatures he studied during his life, Beckjord also explored the alleged existence of "phantom kangaroos" on the East Coast, the so-called "Big Bird" of Texas (an enormous bird with a 20-foot wingspan), as well as mysterious black dogs in England with gleaming red eyes that followed people on dark, misty nights.[1396]

Along with the Lummi Indian Reservation recording made near Bellingham in mid-1976, Beckjord also possessed recordings of suspected Bigfoot vocalizations from South Dakota and California. Beckjord granted the cries on the recordings sounded like coyotes but he suspected they were actually Bigfoot mimicking coyotes' calls. Beckjord had submitted his tape recordings for analysis to zoology professor Gordon Orians at the University of Washington. Analysis was done via sound spectrograph, which made a printed record for comparison with other known sounds. "If these are sounds of [S]asquatches then they sound remarkably like coyotes," Orians said.

Commenting on the tapes, Beckjord said a possible Bigfoot yowl from Little Eagle, South Dakota, sounded like "a coyote pack going crazy simultaneously at outrageously loud volume mixed in with monkey chatter." Orians admitted the Lummi Indian Reservation recording included a sound he had never heard before. "But I could show you bird calls that look exactly like this," he said, referring to the recording's spectrograph. Orians made a spectrograph of a coyote and then made comparisons with Beckjord's tapes. The coyote sound and the South Dakota recording were at the same pitch but the suspected Sasquatch calls were "very, very weak" and difficult to distinguish.

According to Beckjord, a Lummi Indian Reservation police officer once played a suspected Bigfoot recording over his patrol car's loud speaker and two Bigfoot emerged from the woods. Trying the same tactic himself,

Beckjord disappointedly found he could not replicate the same results. "They didn't respond to me. I won't say this won't work, but it didn't work for me. Maybe I smelled wrong to them or maybe they thought they were fooled once but not again." Orians concluded the tapes may or may not have been the recordings of Bigfoot calls. "All you've seen are what these sounds look like," Orians said. "The final proof will come from observing the organism actually uttering the sounds."[1397]

While not collecting and submitting evidence for professional analysis, Beckjord found time to petition Pacific National bank to help him lobby for Bigfoot protection legislation. Pacific National Bank had filed a federal trademark registration for its unique Sasquatch logo on May 20, 1976, which the bank used for several years.[1398] The bank appeared to be disinterested in Beckjord's efforts. "Bigfoot has helped the bank, and its name hasn't cost a cent," Beckjord said. "Now it's time for the bank to help Bigfoot."[1399]

Beckjord said he did not mind the use of Bigfoot as a promotional device. "At least Bigfoot is presented as a friend, a non-threatening image," he said.[1400] The friendly image of Bigfoot didn't last long however; as the '80s began, changes were afoot for the Pacific National Bank.

> Oh, the disadvantages of being a corporate symbol.
>
> Bigfoot, the fluffy, white [S]asquatch-like creature who promotes Pacific National Bank in the company's ads, is about to get the boot.
>
> It seems Bigfoot doesn't quite have the right image for the "common identification" program planned by the Los Angeles-based Western Bancorporation, the parent company of Pacific and 20 other national banks in the West.
>
> Western has decided to change the name of its banks in 11 states to First Interstate bank of each state. So, the current plan is for Bigfoot's Bank to become First Interstate Bank of Washington next June 1, and Bigfoot will be phased out.[1401]

Southeastern Wildlife Research Association

A group of Tennessee men formed the Southeastern Wildlife Research Association to further their Bigfoot inquiry within the Volunteer State. "It started with me," said Jim Vincent of Hendersonville, Sumner County. Reporter Max York wrote that the Tennessee investigators had fertile ground to search—Bigfoot had been reported in Henry, Cheatham, Sumner, Lincoln, and Moore Counties. Jim, a district manager for a textbook and school supply company, was convinced of Bigfoot's reality based on direct experience. "I had an encounter with this creature more than one time." Jim and his brother Dan Vincent told the *Tennessean* the details of their first Bigfoot encounter:

> "It was in Henry County in December 1973, pretty close to Christmas. I was duck hunting with my sons Stuart, who was 14 then, and Doug, who was 15.
>
> "I heard this very unusual screaming. It was a screaming and growling. It was extremely loud. It was the kind of sound that would make the hair on your neck stand up. It made this sound twice. It was about 10 in the morning.
>
> "A week later Dan (his brother) and I were duck hunting in this same area. This time it came from this same thick area. We had shot a duck and it fell into this area of thick vegetation. Dan went over to get it. He ran into this big hairy thing and it scared him pretty bad."
>
> Dan has to admit his brother was right. *He* was scared.
>
> "I was so close that rather than hear it, I felt its footsteps," Dan Vincent says. "I left quickly, what you might call a scheduled retreat.
>
> "I ran the boat out into the water in some little trees. I could hear it running over brush. I didn't see enough to tell anything about it. But it was something larger than usual. If I had stayed, I would have seen it."
>
> The Vincent brothers are experienced woodsmen.
>
> "I went and got the duck," Jim says. "The ground was all torn up. I saw nothing. Well, I did find the duck. I felt that maybe it was a bear. But I had never heard a noise like that before.
>
> "It was pretty quiet until '74. In the winter of '74, I was in the same area about 4:30 A.M. I was alone.
>
> "There is a blacktop turnaround area there and some flooded woods. There's a stand of pines up on the hill. I had been putting gear in the boat and putting the motor on the boat. It was very cold. The car lights had been on. I turned them off.

> "I suppose it had been watching me from up in the pine thicket. I heard this same noise, this high pitched scream. I could almost feel it running. I got in the boat and headed for deep water. I knew this time it wasn't a bear.[1402]

Rex North and his family attended the same Hendersonville church as the Vincents. Intrigued by their experiences, North joined them during field investigations. "Bigfoot has a large stride. We've found tracks six feet apart. We've found what appeared to be tooth marks eight feet up on trees. There was no tree limb close to it. We do know they eat young bark. We've found it in their stool," North said. "We're very serious about this. We don't want a lot of people who will be careless and shoot livestock. We're not interested in shooting one."

Like other investigative groups of the time, the Southeastern Wildlife Research Association hesitated to pinpoint precisely where they conducted their field research in order to prevent disruption from curious crowds. North believed Bigfoot had a particular effect on its immediate environment. "You know how all the birds, crickets and frogs go quiet when there is a predator in the area?" North asked. "One time we were out and they stopped for two to three hours. We found some tracks."

> If you should run into Bigfoot, you aren't likely to mistake it for anything else, the men say.
>
> "It's usually from six to nine feet tall," Jim says. "It has extremely long arms. It has a barrel chest. It seems to have no neck, but it may be that the neck is just covered with hair.
>
> "The head is rounded. Some seem to have a little peak in back. The eyes are deep set. They glow from lights at night. They have relatively long hair. They range in color from black, to brown to white or gray. They have huge hands.
>
> "It's purely theory, but we believe they progress from blond to brown to black to gray as they age. But we've heard of some gray ones that weren't so big."
>
> People in some areas consider them little more than a nuisance, the men say.
>
> "One woman near Bethpage says she has known about them in that same hollow for 41 years," Jim says. "They usually show up the same time of the year. This should help us find one."[1403]

But North averred the group was not about trophies. "We don't want to shoot one," he said. "We would like to capture one. That would prove they exist. We want to find out exactly what it is. But capturing one may be impossible." Recognizing a subdued Bigfoot as a futile pipedream was one of several ruminations North and the Vincents developed to illuminate the Bigfoot phenomenon. "Dogs are insanely afraid of them," Jim told York. "The only time we know of a dog attacking one was down near Decatur, [Alabama]. Eight hogs, three cows and several other dogs were killed in that area. It ran through two fences getting away." The Southeastern Wildlife Research Association believed Bigfoot produced a wide repertoire of noises other than the better-known howls and screams. "For 10 or 15 minutes we listened to what we thought was Bigfoot beating on a well house. It was a rat-a-tat-tat sound. We believe now it was beating on its chest." And, voicing a relatively infrequently mentioned trait, the group suggested Bigfoot employed tools to produce sounds: "They have been known to beat on a tree with a stick," Dan Vincent said.

Lee Frank

Reporter Robert Montgomery called Lee Frank a "mustachioed young adventurer, who might have been an African big game hunter during an earlier era." Following studies in political science at the University of Massachusetts (eventually graduating in 1975), Frank joined an expedition to Loch Ness, Scotland, in 1972, his first of three forays to the Loch where he manned a camera station for the Loch Ness Investigation Bureau. Frank told Montgomery he had always been interested in monsters and after searching for Nessie directed considerable attention toward investigation of Bigfoot. He started an 800-number called the "Monster Hotline" for people to report sightings of Bigfoot or other oddities.

> Frank suggested the animal eventually came in contact with primitive man, *Homo erectus*, and found itself at a decided disadvantage because of man's intelligence.
>
> "But he was man's mortal enemy," Frank said. "He was the boogey man. The animal man feared."
>
> Eighty per cent of the sightings, he said, "have dealt with people trying to shoot [B]igfoot."
>
> But that isn't the way Frank thinks man finally will verify the existence of [B]igfoot.

> "One of these days a [B]igfoot is going to be in the road," he said, "and a truck driver is going to come barreling down that road . . ."[1404]

During the evening of Tuesday, March 1, 23-year-old Lee Frank gave a talk at Saint Leo College sponsored by the college union board. *Pasco Times* reporter Jan Glidewell observed Frank "tempers his remarks with a careful distinction between what he believes and what he knows, what he can say he has seen as an individual and as a scientist—with an occasional dash of humor."[1405] In early April, Frank regaled an audience at Moore Auditorium on the Florida State University with an enthusiastic presentation on monster-hunting. On April 28, Frank gave a presentation titled, "The Loch Ness Monster, Bigfoot and Other Creatures" at the Russell House Ballroom on the University of South Carolina. [1406]

At one point during his two-hour presentation at Moore Auditorium, most of his audience signaled they believed in cryptozoological creatures after Frank asked for a show of hands. "My mother doesn't know what to make of it all," Frank said, who was based out of New York City and was then making his living talking and writing about his cryptozoological pursuits. "Whenever anyone asks her what her son does, she says he's an accountant."

> Frank joked frequently as he recounted sightings of shaggy creatures with "severe B.O. (body odor)" and large aquatic animals with humped backs, undulating necks and small heads. But his flippancy seemed more to reflect the character of the speaker than how he feels about the subject matter.
>
> "I've given up trying to prove to people the animals exist," Frank said after his speech. "It bores me." So he talks about his monsters, and has a good time doing it.[1407]

"If I thought it would work, I'd go into the woods wearing a tuxedo, carrying a bag of bananas under one arm and a tricycle under the other," Frank said. But before his research into Bigfoot got underway, Frank was a devoted Nessie-phile. In 1973 Frank joined the Academy of Applied Sciences' expedition to Loch Ness as both a scuba diver and field monitor. When the expedition left Loch Ness in 1974, Frank stayed on and set up his own camera post. "As a person, I saw the Loch Ness monster," Frank said. "I saw a wake, which was maneuvering, which was too large and was not consistent with other creatures we knew to be in the Loch. As an investigator, I saw something, I believed indicated the presence of the creature but was unable to come up with other supporting evidence at that time." Frank said equipment difficulties plagued the expedition's efforts, which nonetheless produced several enigmatic photographs that had been published in scientific publications that normally stay at arm's length from such topics. In 1977, Frank said he entertained no plans to return to Loch Ness. "There's a Loch Ness monster hot dog stand there now," he said. "I think I would prefer to remember the Loch and its beautiful desolation as it was when I was there last."

After his time at Loch Ness, Frank's cryptozoological zeal was transferred to North American hairy hominids and he became a committed Bigfoot researcher. "On one expedition I found myself being followed by two pairs of eyes, but did not have the proper film to photograph what was following me," Frank said. "I retreated hopefully to the campsight [sic], hoping whatever it was would follow me back so I could get a picture of it. But it went away." The next day, Frank calculated the eyes he'd seen were approximately seven feet off the ground.

Frank observed there was more resistance to belief in Bigfoot's potential existence than in large aquatic creatures in Loch Ness. "What you have here is your archetypal bogeyman," Frank said. "People are naturally resistant to the idea that there might be some creature on Earth or anywhere in the Universe that is as intelligent or almost as intelligent as man. I think we're dealing with an intelligent creature, that buries its dead (accounting for the fact that no bodies have been found) and who is intelligent enough to stay away from man—for good reason. Almost every sighting I have investigated has included someone, somewhere, planning or attempting to blow holes in the thing. That is not conducive to a relationship where the creatures would come around people."[1408]

In his *High Times* article, "Stalking Bigfoot in the Land of Cotton," Frank shared one of his first Bigfoot investigations, at a location named Peaceful Hollow in Davisville (in a state Frank never specifies),[1409] because, he wrote, "I wanted to see what kind of evidence there was for the creature. I wanted to search for the beast myself and learn if Bigfoot really lives."

> As it happens, monsters are my business. One day a few weeks ago I got a call from some friends who were traveling [through] the back hills of the deep South. They said they were in a town called Davisville, where a number of the local folk had met up with a massive humanlike beast that was scaring them out

> of their bejejus. My friends said these people had never heard of one, but all their descriptions indicated that the creature lurking about was a Bigfoot. I asked them how I could get in touch with a reliable eyewitness. Minutes later I was on the honker with a gentleman by the name of Huston Smith.
>
> "Well sir, there's something out here all right," he says in a Gomer Pyle voice. "Now I can't tell you what it is. I just know that there's something out there. Only five days ago this big old thing came skulking out of Peaceful Hollow, which are the woods behind my house. This thing was real gruesome. It was well over seven feet tall and hairy, and it walked on two legs. It looked like a cross between a man and a gorilla.
>
> "This thing tromped over to my neighbor's four-year-old son and waved his hands about and made like he was going to play with him. Well, his mother grabbed the boy and had him in the house before that old thing knew what happened. Now that child's daddy, a right good boy named Melvin Robertson, has seen this thing—I'm not real educated so I don't know what you'd call it—four times at close range. And I've seen it seven times."[1410]

Frank interviewed Kenneth Sons, recording a fresh eyewitness account of the creature lurking about Peaceful Hollow.

> "It was 11:30 this morning when I was down in the back woods. I was on my knees digging ginseng. Suddenly I felt something like someone was behind me, looking at me, even though I didn't hear a thing. I looked around and slowly stood up. And there the thing was. Seven-plus foot tall—well over a foot taller than me, and I'm six foot. It had black hair all over, four to six inches long anyway. It looked like it was half-human and half-ape. It had a flat face—almost like a human's, but more like a gorilla's—and a flat nose. Ears . . . the ears were kind of higher than on a person, and they were round. Hand . . . its hands were just like a human's. I couldn't see its feet because they were in the brush. Its eyes, they were just one solid color—red. The thing just stared at me through hair hanging over its eyes like it was trying to hypnotize me. I couldn't tell if it was male or female because its hair was so long around those [parts].

> "It was just standing there. And it had a rabbit in its mouth. Then it dropped the rabbit and made smacking sounds with its lips. And then it eased its hands down. It stuck its right hand out and made some different sounds like it was trying to show or tell me something.
>
> "Now I'm not afraid to admit it—I was scared. I ran and tripped and fell and just prayed to God that thing wouldn't harm me. I looked over my shoulder and saw the thing lope off. And I swear to you, that's exactly what happened."[1411]

Of the rich personalities Frank encountered and wrote about during his visit to Davisville, Stan Ingram likely ranked near the top; his beguiling tales and diverting theories surrounding the hairy hominid of Peaceful Hollow evoke wonderment and a sense of compassionate pity.

> "I've been researching this phenomenon for three years," says Stan Ingram, "and I think I've come up with some answers.
>
> "It's my belief these animals exist. They're just as big and just as horrible as people say. As a matter of fact, they look very similar to the Bigfoot of the Pacific Northwest."
>
> I ask him if he thinks this is a different kind of animal.
>
> "No question about it," he says. I notice he has a severe nervous tic in his hands. "I learned a lot in the beginning from my 17-year-old daughter, Becky. Becky came back very late one night, and she snuck up to her room so we wouldn't know how late it was. My wife and I didn't say anything. But when she came in the same late hour a week later, she was all beat-up and bruised. I sat her down and very firmly told her to tell me exactly what was going on.
>
> "That's when she said she'd been riding. She said UFO people had been talking to her for a while, and then one day they said they were going to take her up in their spaceship. They hypnotized her and made her leave school. She walked across the football field and walked into an invisible UFO. The doors went *whoomp* behind her and the UFO people said not to worry, they were going to take her riding. In a little over a quarter of an hour, they took her to the deserts of northwest Australia and back.

Since then, she's been riding lots of times and only got into trouble when the bad UFO people caught on to her. That's when they beat her up and threatened to kill her.

"Now, I've since learned that many, many people have been riding and most of them don't know it. You see, they can put you in a trance and make you forget the whole experience. And sometimes the estratellestricles don't take you up in their spaceships. Instead they take you riding in those smaller vehicles that look like golf carts and have force fields to keep the rain out. The only way to know for sure if you've been riding is by the side effects, like if you wake up in the morning with a hangover, even though you didn't do any drinking the night before. I, myself have been riding dozens of times, although each time they erase it from my memory."

"Why do you suppose they erase your memory?" I ask. Stan Ingram's arms are crossed and his hands do a tap dance of nervous tics.

"Dezezda says you're all right. I can tell you. You see, Dezezda is the monitor who was assigned to me by the UFO people who call themselves Plantos. I'm able to communicate with her through a series of signals she sends by making my hands twitch. She tells me everything. She says the creatures in Peaceful Hollow are animals from another planet who gather food and supplies for the Plantos. And she says the reason they erase my memory was because I stood to get in a lot of trouble with the government."

"I'm already in a lot of trouble with the MIB's, or the Men in Black, who are the bad UFO people. They're the ones who beat up my Becky and have offered us money for what we know. They offered us $500,000. They showed my friend Swarner the money in a suitcase. But I knew if we took it, something would happen to us before we had a chance to spend it.

"Swarner's monitors, named Sarday and Quanquat, told him the MIB's have something to do with the Red Chinese, and the leader of the MIB's goes by the name Harlu Lang Chow. Now, I don't know if they've been crossing with the Red Chinese or what, I do know that other UFO people have been crossing with folks in this country, and I've talked to many

> people they've crossed with. And I'm sure that for every one who knows he's been crossed with, there are hundreds they've crossed with who don't know."
>
> Stan Ingram says he has something interesting to show me. He goes out to his car and returns a minute later. He hands me a long, thick animal's nail. He says he believes it comes from a Bigfoot. The nail is much larger than that of a dog or wolf and looks nothing like a bear's claw or that of any animal I can think of. He wants me to hold onto it and have it analyzed. He says it was found in an area where he and others have heard the beasts wailing. The nail has a glob of flesh at the base and it's easy to see why even a feisty boojum would howl when he lost this nail. Perhaps the MIB's are in cahoots with the Reds who sent some of their boys over to extract information from the Bigfoots through an ancient Chinese method of . . . aw, forget it.[1412]

Frank investigated footprints found near the Davisville cemetery, which he described as bordered on three sides by thick woods. Examination of the area yielded two 14-inch prints of large human-shaped feet—one left and one right. One print evinced five distinct toe impressions. Frank stated the prints were not made by any known animal he was familiar with and were not overlaid fore and hind bear tracks. Frank found he could match the depth of the prints only by jumping from a height of two feet.

> It is 10:30 at night and very dark; Kenneth [Sons] and I are standing in a field by the side of the forest and listening for odd sounds. We hear an odd sound: something is stepping on branches and stirring up a ruckus 20 feet into the woods. It could be a person, but when we call, no one answers. More and louder noises like bushes and branches being crushed underfoot. This is getting very eerie. We cannot see into the dark woods, so we step back a few feet and hunker down and hope that whatever is in there will come out and has already eaten. Adrenaline jets through my body. Something is out there, and it's big.
>
> The noise continues, although there are long periods when we don't hear anything. At one point, Kenneth stands, so I

> stand. He says he feels as though the creature wants him to go into the woods, as though he is being drawn in. I say if he goes in, I'll go in with him. Then we decide that if it's so dark the beast could peck us on the cheek and we wouldn't even see it, so who wants to go into the woods anyway? Especially if that's the beast's idea of a good time. We sit down and chuck bananas into the forest instead. A half-hour later, we hear whatever it is making the commotion galumph off into the deep woods.

Through successive conversations with Sons, Frank learned additional details about his experience.

> As Kenneth gets to know me better, he feels he can open up more. He tells me something today that he was afraid to tell me before because it is so unbelievable that I might think his entire sighting is hokum. When he first turned to see the Bigfoot, the largest bobcat he had ever seen was sitting on its haunches next to the Bigfoot. It was the size of a German shepherd. And it just sat there. The cat didn't go for the rabbit when the Bigfoot dropped it. When Kenneth looked back and saw the Bigfoot lumber off, he saw the cat trail a few feet behind. It was Kenneth's impression that the bobcat was the Bigfoot's pet.

Witnesses like Allan Thompson and Jim Mattick decided to come forward and share their sightings with Frank during the investigator's stay at Davisville. "We were sitting by the creek keeping real quiet," Jim began. "Then around 10:00 at night, we saw something—about 50 yards away. We got a pretty good look at it since there was a full moon. It looked like some kind of horrible ape but it walked like a man. Hairy and between seven and eight feet tall and weighed 500 or 600 pounds. We kept still and watched for 10 minutes while it just hung around. Then one of us made a sound and it saw us and left."

Huston Smith and Melvin Robertson found suspected physical evidence (blood and hair samples as well as a branch believed to have been chewed on) left by the creature which they turned over to Mattick and Thompson. Mattick and Thompson had a friend who worked at a medical school lab. The men took the evidence to their friend and returned a week later to check on the results. Lee recounted Allan's story of what happened. "We were met by a team of scientists, which included our friend and they said they were sorry because they misplaced our samples before they had a chance to examine them. Jim, here, got so mad he almost decked one of the scientists. Then later, when no one was around, our friend came over and said, 'I can't tell you any more than what I'm about to tell you, and I shouldn't even be telling you this. You've got something there. You're on to something hot.' It's sure a good thing we didn't give them all our samples."

"A lot of people are mighty interested in that animal out there," Mattick said. "A bit too interested, if you ask me. People know me through my reputation as a bear hunter, and I've been getting anonymous phone calls all hours of the day and night offering me $500,000 for the animal, dead or alive. And one of the biggest Las Vegas casinos called to say they'd pay me $1 million if I could deliver the animal alive." Mattick and Thompson handed over a boxful of their remaining evidence to Lee so the researcher could have its contents analyzed.

> I talk with Allan and Jim until two in the morning, and then I head back to Peaceful Hollow. As I pull in, I see Melvin and Kenneth standing behind Melvin's house and watching the woods. It's the first night of the full moon, so its pretty light out. Melvin is toting his rifle. I walk over and ask what's going on.
>
> "The house is under attack by Bigfoot," Melvin said. "That thing has been shrieking and hollering all day, and it quieted down early tonight. A friend of my wife's came over and we were telling her about the thing and she wanted to hear it, too. So we brought my son outside because we figured that might stir it up. Well let me tell you. . . . That thing began wailing loud enough to wake the dead. It came charging through those woods as fast as lightning. Kenneth yelled, 'Get the kid inside quick,' and we did and I grabbed my rifle. We've been holding that thing at bay ever since."
>
> I hear hefty branches crack 25 feet into the woods. Something is out there. I step into the edge of the woods. Melvin, who has been the staunchest UFO disbeliever of anyone around, says he and Kenneth saw great glowing spheres just above the trees several times tonight. "You don't

> think there's anything to that UFO business, do you?" Melvin says, believing his most frightening suspicions.
>
> I move closer to the woods. Melvin and Kenneth darkly warn me not to go any further. I want to see whatever is in there and I want to see it bad. Another loud crash. I get the shakes. My mouth fills with the taste of coins. But I want to go into those woods and I tell Melvin and Kenneth so. Melvin aims his gun above my head and says he'll keep me covered. I determinedly walk forward, as if pushing against an elastic wall. More branches cracking, exploding. It is pitch black inside these woods. I can't see a thing. I hear something moving a few feet in front of me and I suddenly think this isn't such a hot idea and I tear out of there rabbit-quick.
>
> Melvin and Kenneth and I stand between Melvin's house and the woods for an hour and a half while we hear noises of something colossal close by. Twice, Melvin says he sees some form through the trees, but I see nothing. Then we hear the creature plod away, fading deeper into the dark woods.[1413]

Bringing closure to his experience in and around the woods of Peaceful Hollow and listening to the colorful locals, Frank concludes his article with an appraisal of his quarry and an eye toward the future . . .

> I spend the rest of the morning trekking through Peaceful Hollow, and I get to thinking that whatever is out there remains a very important discovery. We have a lot to learn from these animals. I also get to thinking I don't have any of the proper tools to make that discovery. I've learned a lot about the animal's behavior. I've also learned that its genius lies in its ability to elude people. Since the animal is nocturnal, I need night-vision instruments and camera stations that will be triggered automatically by infrared electric eyes and other equipment. I need to enlist accomplished scientists who will be part of an organized and sophisticated expedition. And I need to know that no harm will come to this creature that has managed just fine without human interference.[1414]

Peter Byrne

Peter Byrne worked with up to five associates in 1977. During a telephone interview with CDN News Service, the 51-year-old Byrne said that the evidence "indicates we're dealing with a human form, a hominid. It walks upright; its feet have five toes; the toes are aligned and not splayed out," he said. "Every other mammal walks or runs on all fours. The only biped is man." Over years spent pondering Bigfoot, Byrne had crafted a theory of what researchers were dealing with. "We're not certain yet, but all the evidence suggests Bigfoot is a 'fossil man.'"[1415]

"I hope it's not caught," said Byrne. "We just want to find one, get a picture and prove that Bigfoot does exist. Then we want to work toward legislation to protect it." Long one of his most important considerations in evaluating a Bigfoot report, Byrne continued to judge the trustworthiness of witnesses as a critical element. "The credibility of the person reporting the sighting is the most important thing to go on when investigating whether a sighting was real or a hoax." By 1977, Byrne's *Bigfoot News* newsletter, which included sightings the researcher deemed authentic, boasted a circulation of 3,000 at a $5 annual subscription.[1416] "We get hundreds of Bigfoot reports every year but only two or three are creditable sightings," said Byrne, who continued to hold a very conservative and strict line with regards to accepting reports as convincing and plausible. "We have 90 creditable sightings on our books going back 30 or 40 years."

John Mitchell's article in the February *Sports Afield* explored Byrne's beliefs on Bigfoot.

> At the geographic center of Bigfoot Country U.S.A., about 80 miles east of Portland on the Columbia River, is The Dalles, Oregon. The Dalles is an industrious and industrial city serving the needs of the larger agricultural community roundabout, and the people who live and work there have neither the time nor the inclination to dwell much on the possibility that hairy upright creatures may be lurking in the forests south of town. At the west end of town, across the parking lot from a pizza parlor, is a large white trailer that houses the Bigfoot Information Center and Exhibition. The people of The Dalles accept the center's presence with bemused tolerance, if only because, for want of other amusements, it probably constitutes the only bonafide [sic] tourist attraction in town. . . .[1417]

"There is nothing like it remaining in Africa or Asia," Byrne said of the Pacific Northwest terrain and climate. "The coastal mountain region of British Columbia alone constitutes one of the greatest wild forest habitats on the face of the earth. Food, water, cover, space. The four essential elements needed by any creature. And it's all there. In spades." Byrne argued Bigfoot was shy. "It surely isn't aggressive, like the grizzly," he said. "And look at where aggressiveness got the grizzly. Aside from Alaska and British Columbia, the grizzly is virtually gone." Byrne said of bones, "When anything dies in this country, it gets eaten. Bears coyotes, ravens pick the bones clean. Then porcupines come along and consume what's left. Even the teeth." . . .[1418]

On November 1, 1975, Leroy Lucas of The Dalles was hunting alone for elk in the Mt. Hood National Forest. It was dusk. Lucas was walking along a paved road between dense stands of Douglas fir. Suddenly, some 20 or 30 yards ahead, the hunter saw a large furry creature cross the road and disappear into the forest. Later, the incident was investigated by Peter Byrne, who believes he found ABSM tracks on the floor of the forest nearby. By Byrne's method of assessing a situation, this went into the center's files as a probable Bigfoot sighting.

Lucas, however, isn't so sure. Nearly a year after the episode Lucas and I stood on the front steps of his home in The Dalles.

"I'm not sure *what* it was," he said.

But at the same time, I asked, hadn't he said it was Bigfoot?

"I never said it was a Bigfoot. I don't even know if there is such a thing. Peter Byrne said it was a Bigfoot."

Then what had Lucas seen?

"Probably a bear."

"Walking on its hind feet across a road?"

"Must have been," said Lucas. "Couldn't have been anything else."

"Have you ever seen a black bear walk 20 to 30 yards on its hind legs?"

"No," said Lucas. "But I haven't seen a Bigfoot either. You show me one, and I'll believe it."[1419]

Byrne believed that Bigfoot was endowed, both by its character and the natural habitat (in the Pacific Northwest), with the right qualities to remain a persistent enigma. "Once you go 50 feet into these forests you simply disappear. It is as dense as any jungle. And we're dealing with a nomadic group, or individuals, who stay in an area only one day before moving on. This adds to the difficulty of finding them." Byrne, Mitchell wrote, though never having seen Bigfoot himself, had examined 16 separate sets of prints which he assessed as authentic. Mitchell asked Byrne if he was indeed convinced Bigfoot was extant, why continue the hunt? "It doesn't seem important except for one reason. We're not going to get protective legislation for something that is not proven. When it is known to exist there will be expeditions, and some scientific expeditions can be awfully ruthless. We hope there will be full protection, to the point where even a scientific expedition from the Smithsonian Institution will not be allowed to collect a specimen." George Haas, who Mitchell noted had a collection of 3,000 newspaper clippings in his extensive files on Bigfoot, agreed with Byrne on the treatment Bigfoot deserved. "The last thing we need to do is shoot or even capture a specimen," Haas intoned. "It is more than a rare animal, it may be a primitive man. To kill him would be murder."[1420]

One of the most widely-publicized Bigfoot sightings in 1977 involved several bus passengers which Byrne initially called "quite creditable." Byrne concluded, based on factors such as the witnesses' homogenous description of the creature and the fact the passengers hadn't known each other prior to getting on the bus, that the possibility of a hoax was unlikely.[1421]

This particular sighting occurred on May 15 as several passengers on a Pacific Stage Lines bus westbound on the Harrison Hot Springs-to-Vancouver run were astonished to see a hair-covered creature as it capered into their view. Bus driver Pat Lindquist was at the wheel with four passengers aboard about 35 miles east of Vancouver when their strange experience began to unfold.

"At first we thought it was a prankster in a fur suit," said Lindquist, who was also a reserve Vancouver city policeman. "But people were shouting 'what is it, what is it,' so I slammed on the brakes to have a look. The first thing I noticed was the smell," an odor Lindquist described as "a horrible smell like very rotten meat." Lindquist brought the bus to a stop, put it in park, and rushed out the door.

"To tell the truth, I thought it was someone trying to con us so I took off after it. I guess I thought I was going to pull off his hat and bawl him out. I don't know why I did it. I'm not sure I really intended to catch up with it," he said. Lindquist's chase after the creature took him away from the bus and into dense growth. The six-feet-two-inch Lindquist said the thing he chased was no more than seven feet tall and "much heavier than I am."[1422] As the distance between himself and the bus increased, Lindquist realized he was venturing outside of his element with something he had no experience with. "The bush was thick and I was pushing the branches apart when I saw it about 20 or 25 feet away. I just couldn't believe it. At first I was mad. But then I went to awe and then to fright as I began to shake. I couldn't stop shaking and then I got out of there."

Of all the people on the bus, Lindquist had the closest look at the creature. "It had flat flared nostrils like a monkey and large, wide eyes. It didn't make any sound except heavy breathing. It had a broad chest and it was heaving up and down." Lindquist described the hair color as light brown and "it appeared to have the mange; the skin underneath looked kind of white." Constable Robert Eyford of the Royal Canadian Mounted Police noted the witnesses' descriptions were "consistent, they all saw the same thing." A 15-inch long track was later found, though other tracks had been obliterated by droves of curious sightseers.[1423]

> Peter Byrne, director of the Bigfoot Information Center at Hood River, Oregon, said Canadian Bigfoot experts interviewed the unidentified Pacific Stage Line bus driver [Lindquist] shortly after the sighting.
>
> "We give the sighting a good credibility rating at this time," Mr. Byrne said. "We have also talked with the RCMP and they're quite convinced that something crossed the road in front of the bus."[1424]

"Sightseers turned out by the hundreds," was the opening line in a CP story that ran in *The Medicine Hat News* of May 17; these sightseers were essentially Sasquatch tourists, on the scene for the chance to see the footprints or perhaps a return visit by the creature itself. By the time the word had gotten out and people descended upon the area, few footprints were still visible on May 16. "They [the tracks] are 15 inches long by seven at the toe and four at the heel," said René Dahinden who'd arrived to investigate the sighting location. "The strides were 55 inches from heel to heel. That's a long stride—those tracks were like those of a natural foot."

Eminent Bigfoot researcher John Green described the encounter as "about as well-authenticated a sighting as you could get. It would be impossible to fake." Green described the tracks as a "pretty standard model" although they were smaller than typical Bigfoot prints. "The last time I saw tracks this authentic was in California in 1967," he said.[1425] Doug and Billie Lightborn arrived on the scene early on May 16 with preservation in mind. They were able to make a cast of one of the last good prints before rain washed it away. "Of course there's something there," said Mrs. Lightborn. "But whatever it is, I hope no one ever finds it. When they do the mystery will be gone and so will the fun."[1426]

By the time Dennis Gates, Bigfoot researcher and owner of the Sasquatch-Bigfoot Clippings Reproductions Service in Sedro (annual subscription at $5.00 for 12 issues), arrived at the spot of the encounter, there were, by Gates' estimate, more than 100 people at the scene. Gates, along with John Green, cast a right and left track. Suspicions about the event began creeping into Green's thinking. The men conferred the following day and Green told Gates he didn't like the look of his cast—the toes looked suspiciously too straight.[1427]

The revelation of deception was made by Vancouver radio station CKNW which reported Monday, May 23, that the Sasquatch seen by the Pacific Stage Lines' bus passengers and driver near Erroch Lake in the Fraser Valley was in actuality a hoax. Dahinden, hearing this news, said he wanted to see the suit. "If they can produce the evidence that this was a hoax I would like to see it. The hoax would be more important than a real Sasquatch sighting . . . it would teach us a lesson to smarten up." Dahinden had not dismissed the tracks and reserved doubts on the hoax angle. "CKNW doesn't know whether or not it was a hoax because it doesn't have any evidence. Let them produce the fur suit and the material used to make the foot prints."

Dahinden said he had been in Mission, British Columbia, when RCMP questioned Pat Lindquist, the bus driver. "The questioning was very professional and I cannot see how Lindquist could have mistaken a man in a fur suit for the real thing," Dahinden said. "Maybe my view was colored but if there was a hoax let's see them re-enact the whole thing." Dahinden was incredulous that Lindquist would be unable to discern if he was being duped or not. "He said he was only 15 feet away and described the flaring nostrils. He said he was close enough to see that there was no white in the eyes." Dahinden went on, "I think he was an excellent witness. I was impressed by his report. If anyone has evidence of a hoax, I would like to see it."[1428]

But the reality was the hairy creature seen by Lindquist and the bus passengers was a hoax perpetrated by four practical jokers using a monkey suit and shoulder pads to enact the faux Bigfoot encounter. "It was just a good practical joke, we thought it might fool a few people," said Ken Ticehurst, a 5-foot-11, 165-pound man who was the one in the ape costume. "I was running like O. J. Simpson."

The four pranksters used three weeks to prepare their prank. First item checked off their list was the purchase of a gorilla suit from a costume shop. Next was the manufacturing of a foot, modeled after a resin-cast print pictured in Don Hunter and Dahinden's book, *Sasquatch*. And finally, procurement of walkie talkies and careful study of local bus schedules. Planting a phony witness (Don Ticehurst) on the bus guaranteed passengers would notice. Ken Ticehurst, of Port Coquitlam, revealed the prank during an interview on a CKNW talk show. In with Ken and Don Ticehurst were fellow pranksters René Quesnel of Port Moody and Gordon Jacobi of Port Coquitlam.[1429]

Pulling the hoax on bus passengers ensured witnesses would see the costumed prankster and "to make it more believable." The group's plant (Don Ticehurst) on the bus would get things moving. "I was expecting (the Sasquatch) but I had to act pretty excited," Ticehurst said. "Some people were asleep." Constable Bob Eyford of Mission RCMP had led the investigation and was convinced the men's admission closed the case. Ticehurst said he had initially started to write his own name on the bus manifest but thought better of it and scratched it out. Eyford said the bus manifest did indeed have a scratched-out name.

"I hate a hoax, it makes every other sighting questionable," said Milton LaSalle of the Society for the Investigation of the Unexplained (SITU). "The experts would have decided that the discrepancies in the stories of the witnesses proved it to be no real Bigfoot," said LaSalle (in contravention to Byrne's assessment of the similarity in the witnesses' descriptions), but Lindquist remained convinced he had seen a hairy giant face-to-face. The implied time and money invested by the pranksters made for a remarkable story in its own right. The men stated their monkey costume was a $200 affair, a relatively cheap hair-covered "monkey suit" of the day. Philip Morris and his wife Amy started a costume company in their Charlotte, North Carolina, home in 1960. Later connected to the Patterson-Gimlin film as a potential supplier of a Bigfoot costume to Roger Patterson, Morris Costumes represented the high end of ape-looking habiliment and an advertisement from 1977 reveals the price of quality: Morris Costumes' "Gorilla Suits" were listed in *The Circus Report* of November 14 as "still only $435.00,"[1430] or $1,805 in 2017 dollars.[1431]

> And the plastic cast of a Sasquatch print was made of some strong, expensive material, because the men placed it in the dirt and then jumped on it, making the soil displacement so deep that the creature seemed to be much larger than Pat Lindquist, the bus driver, reported it, Mr. Green told [LaSalle].
>
> "And, Kent Ticehurst, 24, of Port Coquitam, Can., who wore the costume, says Lindquist never saw him and never smelled any horrible odor. . . . Lindquist must have wanted to make it a good story," Mr. LaSalle said.[1432]

LaSalle acknowledged Ticehurst and his group had been entirely successful. "It was a very good hoax," he admitted. He cautioned that it carried a lesson: investigators' judgement should be reserved until every point and question is satisfactorily resolved.[1433]

As the details of Ticehurst and his accomplices' hoax emerged, the pranksters were asked why they did it. Their reason: B.C. was due for another Sasquatch sighting. Green pointed out an unexplained component of the affair involved bus driver Lindquist. After stopping the bus, Lindquist claimed to have run some 400 yards pursuing the creature, eventually confronting it and close enough to observe body and facial details. Lindquist stuck to his story despite the clearing where the face-to-face encounter took place was only 60 or so yards away from the bus. Once out of sight of the bus patrons, Ticehurst stripped off the head portion of the costume so he could see where he was going; he claimed Lindquist never caught up with him.[1434]

> Lindquist said he was convinced that the creature was for real because "no man could have made that smell." He also said he finds it impossible to forget the incident:
>
> "I can't sleep. I have the covers up to my chin. I'm shaking and I keep the lights on."
>
> Robert Eyford, an investigator for the Royal Canadian Mounted Police, said the six passengers [other reports note only four passengers] on Lindquist's bus have consistently supported his version. Police declined to release the names of the passengers.
>
> However, two of them—Mike and Cathy Byrne—later came forward on their own, insisting they were not questioned by authorities and sharply contradicting Lindquist's account.

> According to them, what they saw did look more like a man in a monkey suit who conveniently sauntered across the road and stood shouting, just as the bus happened by.
>
> "I was so convinced it was a joke that I ran down out of the bus after it had gone across the road and shouted, 'You are not fooling us.'" said Mrs. Byrne in a phone interview from her home in Calgary.
>
> The Byrnes also said Lindquist wasn't nearly as scared as he now claims when he emerged from the thicket, that he had failed to even mention the encounter until asked about it by another passenger 10 minutes up the road.[1435]

A successful hoax, Kim Ode wrote in the *Argus-Leader,* required sufficient thought and detail in its execution to stand up to the rigors of examination.

> New reports of the creature will no doubt spark the fire in pranksters' minds, but credibility is hard to prove. Anthropologists, studying Big Footprints, have found that the creature is flat-footed and possesses a double ball, or a second fleshy pad behind its big toe. Also anatomical consideration must be made as to how much weight is exerted on the print. Clearly, a successful hoax would be the job of a professional.[1436]

But not all tricks and stunts were made to outsmart the Bigfoot doyens; sometimes pranksters' ambitions resided in the initial reaction of startled and scared targets. Bigfoot's blend of characteristics—for all intents and purposes, a monster—made it fodder for jokes, pranks, and outright hoaxes. Since it was manlike in shape (though usually reported as much larger in size), it was relatively easy to impersonate, and its footprints were similar enough to humans to fabricate crude knock-offs for the purpose of pulling off a prank. From sketchy films to dodgy footprints, 1977 saw no shortage of hoaxers' attempts to shock and frighten.

Frank White's Bigfoot Film

On Friday, October 7, 1977, Frank White and his wife Lorraine were in Washington's Mt. Baker region, filming the fall colors and also on the lookout for Bigfoot. The Whites had been camping on the Lummi Indian

Reservation after they heard of recent Bigfoot sightings occurring there. After finding nothing, the couple moved on to Mt. Baker and during a stop for lunch, and still reserving hopes they would be fortunate enough to see Bigfoot, Lorraine suddenly shouted, "There's a bear!" White hurriedly trained his running 8mm camera in the direction she indicated.

The "bear" walked out of a forest thicket and for a moment was outlined in sunlight. In a slow and deliberate gait it began walking away but stopped twice to look back at the camera, glowering with what the Whites took as menace. "We got the hell out of there," White said.[1437] "I'd call it a North American ape. You can call it a Sasquatch or anything you like," he added.[1438] White received his developed film on Saturday, October 8, and started showing it to reporters the following day.[1439]

According to one reporter attending White's film showing, "The beast matches in every way the popular conception of a Sasquatch." Another reporter confided to White that the creature looked like a person wearing a gorilla costume. "That's the first thing my kid said," replied White. "That's what it looks like," White agreed, adding, "but why would someone be up there in a monkey suit?"

Estimation of the creature's size was difficult according to White, "because I was so surprised and so busy operating the camera." The movie showed the creature putting its hand on a tree, totally covering its circumference. The tree was thought to be a foot in diameter. White was identified as the vice president of the Scientific Progress Association, which White said was dedicated to encouraging scientific interest in young people. The organization did not advocate for the existence of Sasquatch, White said.[1440]

News of White's Mt. Baker footage, with its dangling hint of a Bigfoot in the area, may have helped spark a novel Bigfoot-searching expedition. David Button, operator of Pacific Northwest River Tours of Sedro Wooley called Seattle's *Post Intelligencer* to relate strange goings-on in the area. "Deer race out of the wilderness and leap into the river, as if escaping from some terrifying creature," Button said. "There also have been strange roars heard at night." *Post Intelligencer* photographer Tom Barlet and reporter John O'Ryan joined Bigfoot researcher Dennis Gates, fresh from investigating the Pacific Stage Lines' Hoax in May for a water-borne Bigfoot expedition. "I've never seen a [S]asquatch," said Gates. "But I am 98 percent certain that they exist. When I see one, I'll make the other two percent." The group journeyed up State Highway 20 toward Mt. Baker stopping to put their towed raft into the water at Glacier Creek.

> Torrents of water poured down the creek flooding after a big storm and heavy rainfall that had swept the area.
>
> A wild ride between boulders brought us to the junction of Glacier Creek and the North Fork of the Nooksack River. Here there was a huge "rapids," with water swirling and waves leaping as torrents from the two streams met.
>
> "This raft can't go through that," I said to myself.
>
> But it did. The raft, built in Oregon to travel on the wild Rogue River, has a high bow and stern that lift it right to the top of river waves.
>
> As we raced with the swirling waters of the Nooksack, reaching apparent speeds of 20 to 30 miles per hour in rapids, I was so busy clinging to the raft I could barely watch for the [S]asquatch.

But Gates, O'Ryan noted, was very much prepared. During the journey he kept a movie camera at the ready, in case Bigfoot popped into view. Button sat in the raft's aluminum seat maneuvering the raft back and forth with oars, avoiding large rocks and trees. At a bulge in the river the group stopped to put Barlet ashore, so he could race ahead and photograph the raft coming down the river. After Barlet rejoined the raft the group proceeded down the river.

> We continued our descent, scouring the river banks for a [S]asquatch, and stopping at a mid-river island where we encountered another back eddy.
>
> Here Button said he had seen some huge footprints, but flood waters pouring over the island had wiped them out. The only footprints we saw this day were deer tracks where we launched the raft.
>
> We had been on the river four hours when we encountered a highway bridge where the journey ended.
>
> No [S]asquatch.
>
> But even if we didn't sight this hairy creature, we had a thrilling ride down a wild, wilderness river.
>
> Gates, as a longtime [S]asquatch researcher, was disappointed that we didn't sight the hairy beast, but he was inclined to see the brighter side.

> "If the [S]asquatch is human, the government would have to provide him with decent housing, schools and school buses, Medicare and food stamps.
>
> "Maybe it's just as well we didn't find him."[1441]

Grover Krantz viewed the footage and put his thoughts in a letter to White dated January 17, 1978.

> Dear Mr. Frank White,
>
> This is just to put in writing my observations on your Mt. Baker film of last year. To begin with we can eliminate any possibility of trick photography or a recognized animal of any kind. There are just 3 possible accountings for it:
>
> Someone walked by in a fur suit to fool you.
>
> You managed the hoax.
>
> It was a Sasquatch.
>
> There are problems with all three views. Anyone trying to fool you was taking his life in his hands. You or another person seeing him might have shot him instead of filming. I can find nothing in your account, or in your personality, to suggest you might have faked it. There seems no motive. As a Sasquatch, it looks too scruffy and the forehead is too high.
>
> After reviewing the objections to all these theories I find the last set of objections are the weakest—I don't know what kind of fur and forehead Sasquatch has. If forced to choose, I would presently lean in favor of the authenticity of the film as showing a real Sasquatch.
>
> Improvement of the film quality might help to settle this in my mind, and in the minds of a few others. But no film, however good, will convince the skeptics.
>
> Please feel free to show this letter to anyone interested in the subject of your film.
>
> Grover S. Krantz[1442]

Dennis Gates went on to review the White film which he unceremoniously and unequivocally decried as a phony. Gates' account provided some additional details of the film including the Whites' involvement with René Dahinden.

No doubt SITU members have heard about a new film of an alleged Sasquatch taken in the Mt. Baker area of Washington State toward the end of last year. John Green, Rene Dahinden and I have viewed the footage many times. It is an obvious fake.

Frank White, the man who eventually produced the footage, originally came to Rene last April wanting to know all about "[B]igfoot," and asking to be introduced to Ken Cooper at the Lummi Indian Reserve. He said he would like to cruise the roads at night (as Rene and I had done for six weeks the year before).

Rene took him there, introduced him, and even spent a night or two with him to show him where most of the sightings had occurred. White and his wife then spent several nights cruising around the reservation on their own.

A few weeks later, they decided to rent a movie camera and take a run up by Mt. Baker, "to film the colors of Fall." Apparently, they decided to stop along the highway (one of the most traveled tourist highways in the state) to have their lunch. As they walked about 600 feet into the woods looking for a nice place to eat, guess what stepped right in front of their rented camera!

According to them, they hurriedly left the area, but stopped a short way down the road to talk it over, then returned. But, try as they might, they were unable to find the location again. Later, at their home, Frank White told me he thought he could now re-locate the spot. Would I like to go with him to look the area over?

I told him I certainly would, and to bring along the film because I had a stop frame projector and we could therefore all study the film, frame by frame, together. By now, I already suspected the film was faked; I therefore told him we would have to take many measurements on location, explaining just what that meant: I had to know exactly where White had stood, the path taken by the creature, the height of the tree limb under which the creature had passed, all distances from each object, etc.

On the day we were supposed to do all this, he called me to cancel our appointment, claiming he had to await a phone call from a film outfit in Los Angeles—and besides, he didn't know

> if he could locate the area in question after all. What he really wanted to know was how much we thought the film would be worth.[1443]

Bigfoot Mischief in Piedmont, Alabama

"We weren't thinking about getting shot at or anything," said Bigfoot prankster Terry Humphrey. "We thought it was fun."

Driving northbound on Alabama 9 heading toward Piedmont, Clyde Young, his wife, and daughter were victims of Humphrey's lark on Saturday, August 9, shortly before 10 P.M. But the Youngs didn't realize what they had seen was simply a hoax. "If it's somebody pulling a trick, somebody could get hurt," Mrs. Young said. "If there are teen-agers doing it, they could get hurt because there are a lot of people who go through there [Alabama Route 9] with guns."

Just above Holley Cross Roads, and at the approximate spot where one Glen Smith had reported a Bigfoot sighting three months' prior, the Youngs glimpsed something traipsing at the edge of the woods on the left-hand side of the road. Mrs. Young said the creature was hairy and reddish-brown in color and about 5 feet 7 inches tall. Twice, the Youngs' car was turned around to return to the spot where the creature was spotted so the family could have another look. "At that time of the night, the reason that we turned around was that we thought our eyes were playing tricks on us. I know we were kind of crazy to do it, but we wanted to know what it was." The second time they tried to spot the creature the family heard a scream come out of the darkness. That was enough for them and they sped away. "You can imagine how we felt," Mrs. Young said. "We didn't waste any time getting out of there."

> Whatever it was, apparently, was a teen-ager wearing a red-and-green sleeping bag with the red side exposed.
>
> Terry Humphrey and two friends, Eddie Brock and Wallace Phillips, were taking turns donning the strange garb and walking about just enough to catch the glare of passing car lights and the eyes of those who were driving the cars. Brock was taking his turn when the Youngs drove by, because he tells a story similar to Mrs. Young's—the car slowing down, turning around returning twice to the scene, and moving away after he screamed.

Continuing north to Piedmont, the Youngs stopped to collect both guns and friends before returning to the scene later that same night. But after a brief search, the armed searchers didn't find anything. Clyde Young revisited the scene on Sunday and his follow-on inspection of the area turned up the red-green sleeping bag left in the woods. But at the time the Youngs had no idea how the sleeping bag played into the fright they'd received.

The youths also paraded their get up for passing motorist William Bridges, a cousin to Terry Humphrey. Bridges stopped his northbound pickup when he spotted the "creature," angled his handy shotgun's barrel to the sky and fired into the air. Bridges then drove north and stopped at the Humphrey's home, which he entered "white as a piece of cotton" and described his encounter. Bridges persuaded Joe Humphrey (Terry Humphrey's father) to get a gun and together they returned to the scene but their subsequent search didn't turn over any further evidence of a lurking monster. "He didn't know it was them (the kids)," said Joe who himself learned about the characters behind the antics about half an hour later when Terry, Eddie, and Wallace—all of whom were outside under the auspices of camping out—appeared at the Humphrey house and revealed their story. Joe Humphrey told the youths about Bridges' experience and chided the kids that such a prank could get someone shot.

Mrs. Young was certainly not amused. "You can laugh about it, but still it's not a laughing matter when you get something off [sic] your mind and can't get it off," she said. "My husband has heart trouble," she continued, "and anything like that could throw him into another heart attack." But the episode definitely instilled life in Bigfoot talk in Piedmont. "There may be something to it," said Floyd Willis, a local contractor, "but I've been in these mountains all my life. I've never run into anything like that. It's hard to believe."

The three youths were adamant they were not doing their sleeping bag stunt on Alabama 9 three months prior when the aforementioned Glen Smith reported seeing Bigfoot. Since Smith's sighting, large footprints had been painted along the highway and two unofficial Bigfoot-related signs had been surreptitiously emplaced along the route. The first sign, made of metal and anchored to two metal poles had announced that area of Route 9 as a "Bigfoot crossing." Another sign, taken down by a state road crew was also made of metal and had been hung across the road at a height of about 25 feet. Ray Garmon, superintendent of Calhoun County's highway district said, "Whoever is doing it [making the signs] is a pretty good artist." Garmon said both signs had been removed because they were un-approved by the highway department. Confiscated signs found a new home in Garmon's district office but he didn't expect anyone to come and claim them.[1444]

Monster Tracks, Beastly Joke in Dixon, Illinois

North American Wildlife Research member Dwayne Norvell's first thoughts on several large footprints found in the Dixon, Illinois, area in 1976 (see Chapter 7) leaned toward the possibility they were the "real thing." But his level-headed investigation convinced him, beyond any reasonable doubt, that the prints had been hoaxed, an announcement he made during an interview on January 20 with reporter Florestine Purnell and subsequently published in Rockford's *Morning-Star.*

> If big hairy creatures stalking through the woods are your thing, you'll have to go elsewhere to find them. Last summer's Illinois-area Big Foot scare was a hoax.
>
> A group of youngsters in the Dixon area built wooden foot print makers and tramped around Lowell park, upsetting area residents and bringing a North American Wildlife Research Association member into the area to investigate.
>
> "It was a farce," Dwayne Norvell, Kirkland, an area researcher for the wildlife organization said Thursday. "At first I thought they might have been the real thing," Norvell said of the 17-inch long prints. They were found at the edge of the Rock River a short distance north of the heavily-timbered 200-acre park two miles north of Dixon. Park benches were also thrown about in the area of the footprints.
>
> "But then I checked the plaster cast made of the prints and found they should have been a lot deeper," Norvell said.
>
> The "prints" were about a half inch deep and about 8 ¾ inches wide at the ball of the foot, Norvell said.
>
> "They should have been much deeper than that in the soft mud they were in. My own foot prints were about an inch-and-a-half deep and I weigh only about 190 pounds."
>
> Based on the size of the footprints, the creature should have been much heavier than the plaster casts indicated he was, Norvell said.
>
> Norvell said his knowledge of Big Foot prints came from castings he made in California several years ago.

"They were one to one-and-one-half inch deep."

Then, too, there was the distance between the prints. The creature would have had to have been more than the usual seven to 12 feet tall because there was "a print here, then another 100 yards away," Norvell said. . . .

Before Norvell determined the Dixon monster report a hoax, he said he speculated the monster might have come to the area along the Mississippi River, went overland to the Rock River, then followed the Rock River back to Mississippi.

He said he spent a lot of time running around and the hoax was "kind of a hassle. But I had to do it, otherwise we'd never find out anything about the creatures."[1445]

Bob Stamps & the Stilwell Incident

A family in Norman, Oklahoma, believed a series of events starting in 1976, which included thrown stones, foul odors, fruit plucked from trees, and several unusual vocalizations, indicated the presence of Bigfoot on their property. Bigfoot researcher Bob Stamps interviewed family members and made casts of several footprints during his investigation in Norman.[1446]

Stamps' regular job was vinyl upholstery repair. In his spare time Stamps was—as described in the *Southeast Missourian*—a "hunter, adventurer and scientist, dedicated to the search for the legendary ape-man creature called Bigfoot." Stamps described his quarry as a "cunning animal, about 8 feet tall, hairy, foul-smelling and built like a cross between man and gorilla." Stamps estimated he daily spent two to three hours immersed in the subject of Bigfoot; "I definitely believe they exist."[1447]

A small room in Stamps' apartment in an Oklahoma City suburb served as headquarters for Sasquatch Research Corp., a non-profit entity Stamps created. The space was crammed full of books, magazines, drawings (an 8-foot high silhouette of a Bigfoot adorned one wall), and Bigfoot-related correspondence. "I don't have to be a trained scientist to study Sasquatch," said Stamps. "I have studied this creature. You could call me a Sasquatchologist." Other members of Sasquatch Research Corp. included Stamps' brother-in-law and a childhood friend.

Stamps' correspondence included Bigfoot enthusiasts in the Soviet Union and Australia. By August 1977, Sasquatch Research Corp. had undertaken 14 expeditions through Oklahoma and along the Oklahoma-Arkansas border searching for evidence of a Bigfoot family group Stamps believed was comprised of two to six Bigfoot creatures. Stamps' field efforts also attracted other interested parties; Stamps described one such individual as a professional ghost hunter and psychic. According to Stamps, a board of unnamed consultants advised Sasquatch Research Corp.

As of his interview's appearance in the August 23 *Southeast Missourian,* Stamps had written four articles intended for magazine publication, including one given the working title, "Sexual Encounters with Sasquatch," which would eventually be published with co-author Hayden Hewes as "Sex and the Single Sasquatch" in *True's* Winter 1979 edition of *Flying Saucers and UFO Quarterly*. He also stated he hoped to write a Bigfoot book.

Stamps had gained enough of a reputation, at least within Oklahoma, to be called upon to assist the inquiry of the so-called Stilwell Incident whose investigative denouement exposed the affair as a hoax, but still had enough strangeness directly and indirectly associated to its events to convince some it was not all owing to just a prank. The Stilwell Incident (also known as the Adair County Bigfoot) centered on the claim by Brian Jones (given in differing accounts as 15- and 17-years-old) that on Saturday, August 6 (some accounts state Jones was attacked on August 5), he had been thrown through the air after his back was clawed by a 9-foot tall hairy creature near Stilwell in northern Oklahoma. Investigation by the county sheriff's department and the Oklahoma State Bureau of Investigation turned up missing calves and slaughtered goats in the area which some linked to the Stilwell Incident. "We don't know what to call it," said Adair County Undersheriff Gary Fain. "We don't know how to cope with it and we don't know what to do with it when we find it."[1448]

Ray Crow wrote about the Stilwell Incident in an article published in the August 11, 1977, *Phoenix & Times Democrat.*

> A hairy monster with eyes like fire had paused Saturday night at the bedroom window of Robert Ritchie, northwest of here on England Hollow Road, witnesses said.
>
> Jones said he felt the beast was about to reach in the window to try to jerk Ritchie's head off. Somehow he just knew. He, he only, heard the ominous pronouncement.
>
> A warning holler aroused the household. Lights seem to frighten the beast away.
>
> Jones is best-acquainted with the mystery. He's seen it for years. It jumped out of the darkness and lifted him up by the shoulders before being frightened away by lights bounced off a nearby tree, he said.

> Time stands still as Ritchie, his wife, his sister, brother-in-law, children and Jones tell of the sights, sounds and smell of a mysterious being suspected of being the devil himself.
>
> The monster or its shadow, its eyes burning like embers on the ends of two cigarets [sic], but larger, the size of quarters, has been seen every night since Saturday at or near the house, family members said.
>
> Horses bolt from their tethers, dogs cower under the house. People flee in terror, according to the accounts.
>
> And it hasn't just been in the last few days.
>
> Eerie lights in the Winter snow, mysterious hoofs clomping across the porch, prints of a giant human-like foot in the Spring garden have been heard or seen in the past year or two at or near the Ritchie home.

Jones stated he first saw the creature in 1973 and was so scared by the experience he spent several nights at a relative's house before returning home. Jones said he didn't believe the creature intended him harm Saturday night [August 6]. "I imagine I scared it as much as it scared me."

> Jones and his brother Stephen and two Ritchie boys had fixed themselves dinner Saturday night and were watching television, Robert Ritchie said. He wasn't home.
>
> Stephen went to get some bread in the kitchen.
>
> Fiery eyes peered through the kitchen window, seven or eight feet off the ground.
>
> The boy jumped over the top of a three-and-a-half-foot table, the father said, and went to the room where the others were gathered.
>
> Brian Jones went to a pickup and got a club. He went to the west side of the house. He heard breathing, he said.
>
> It stopped.
>
> Suddenly a giant figure was in front of him. Eyes ablaze, it grabbed him from the top of his shoulders and picked him three or four feet off the ground, he said.
>
> The other boys didn't hear, but were shining lights toward the back of the house. A reflection from a tree apparently frightened the monster, Jones said.
>
> The beast dropped him and headed for the woods.

> Rick Ritchie fired a rifle about 13 times into the woods, he said.
>
> Then a big rock came sailing over the house in reply. Then four more came over the house, the youths said.

Robert Ritchie and the boys claimed they experienced several additional incidents. Sunday night, while staying the night at the Ritchie's, Jones woke the household after he saw a set of eyes peering in the bathroom window. Later that night he heard a "voice from the sky."

> "It won't be stopped! It can't be stopped!"
>
> The words "came from the sky" and thundered through the mind of 15-year-old Brian Jones.

Strange events reportedly occurred on a nightly frequency to folks in the area:

> Friends and neighbors gathered Wednesday at the Ritchie house to ask what was happening.
>
> One man said a couple of hunters at Nicut, south of here in the next county, had shot at a giant creature recently and it had damaged a house.
>
> Doris Ritter, 18, of Greasy, south of Stilwell, said about a year ago she had shot at some big creature near her house.

Some locals attributed the events in and around Stilwell to the antics of bears, known from time to time to attack livestock. "I wish people would quit botherin' the bears," Associate District Judge J. T. Spray said. Mildred Kaiser of Oak Grove said a bear had attacked her dogs[1449] and other instances of bears in the area had also been reported. Some witnesses disagreed with the bear theory—they had seen the creature's bright eyes.

> Besides, there are other unexplained happenings, they said. Like the appearance of giant foot tracks in their garden last Spring, or three lights appearing in the snow last Winter, or when Sara Kear heard hoofs on the front porch of the Ritchie home and thought the horses had got loose. They hadn't, she discovered the next morning.
>
> Or one time last Winter when Mrs. Kear saw a shadow through the kitchen window. Then something pushed on the

> door from the outside, jamming it tight against the bolt. It wasn't the wind, she said.
>
> Authorities are trying to discourage sightseers from visiting the area. They said they did not want a "bunch of people with guns going out and shooting each other."[1450]

"We don't believe anyone is lying about this," Fain flatly stated. Adair County civil defense officials notified the Sasquatch Investigation of Mid-America to share information and ascertain if the unidentified beast could be Bigfoot.[1451] Stamps and 15 other Bigfoot investigators from Oklahoma and Kansas City examined the scene and upon completion of their investigations at Stilwell and Dutch Mills (which included use of a night vision device loaned by the Oklahoma City police department), Stamps stated he was "fairly convinced" that at least one of the Bigfoot creatures he believed inhabited the general area was responsible for the incidents.[1452]

Chemists at Oklahoma State Bureau of Investigation (OSBI) analyzed hair samples from the boy's clawed shirt and arrived at tentative candidate for his attacker. OSBI chief chemist Don Flynt stated he could not say "positively, absolutely, that it was a black bear hair that was analyzed. But that's the closest thing the hair resembles." Stamps was not disheartened. "Chemists say they aren't positive it was a bear hair," he said. "Who's to say Bigfoot doesn't have bear-like hair?"[1453] The AP story published in the *Big Spring Herald* (Big Spring, Texas) noted black bear sightings were rare in Oklahoma but they could be found in Arkansas. "I doubt they check borders carefully before crossing," Flynt said.[1454]

As the investigation continued, Sheriff Dan Abbot said that Jones had volunteered to take a polygraph test but failed to make his appointment.

> Some local observers say they believe most of the talk of a monster or "Big Foot" in this area began at about the same time as the movie, "Return to Boggy Creek," about a monster, appeared at the Eagle Theatre here. They believe that the movie may have appealed to the imagination of some people.
>
> After the first report of a red-eyed creature being seen at the Robert Ritchie place, four miles northwest of Stilwell, county officers and Tobe O'Neal, county civil defense director, have been actively looking for it.[1455]

"People don't act like this when they are telling tales," Under Sherriff Fain said to reporters, who was obviously taken with witnesses' sincere reactions to a monster in their midst. "These people have seen something and they are going to pack up and move if they see it again."

> The witnesses say it is seen only at night. [Its] eyes glow bright red. It grunts like a hog, and it can throw a rock the size of two fists about 75 yards. They also say it is hairy all over, smells bad, and it stands between seven and nine feet tall.[1456]

Texas oilman Jack Grimm put up reward money for the capture of the Adair County Bigfoot. Grimm showed an interest in several cryptozoological subjects and reaped attention in the 1980s for his salvage work of the *Titanic.*

> A $5,000 reward for the safe capture of an elusive creature reportedly seen in Adair County has been offered by a West Texas oilman.
>
> Jack Grimm said the bounty applies to the safe capture of the creature allegedly roaming around Adair County—or to a similar beast said to be in the hills north of Abilene, Texas.
>
> The rules are that the creature be previously unidentified and undiscovered.
>
> "I don't want to pay a reward for a bear or a gorilla that escaped from the zoo," Grimm told newsmen.
>
> The monster seen near Abilene is said to be shaggy, and about seven feet tall.
>
> Grimm said that he doubts that the beast reported to be in this area is the real thing.
>
> "I really discount that sighting. I really discount those that might be seen in the south and southwest as illusions," he said.
>
> Grimm, who has placed in world poker playing tournaments, is betting on what he calls the "big three." Those are $5,000 rewards for the capture of Big Foot, Big Bird of South Texas and the Loch Ness Monster.
>
> Grimm, an oilman, has paid the way for a news reporter and photographer to track Big Foot in the rugged mountains of the U. S. Northwest and has sent film crews to photograph the Loch Ness Monster.
>
> The newsmen looking for Big Foot found an Indian chief whose sons had seen it, said Grimm. A film crew photographed

> a fuzzy outline of what the oilman thinks is the Loch Ness creature.
>
> "I'm a geologist by profession. It's a contribution to science. I get a great deal of pleasure from pursuing these things.
>
> 'I don't belittle these sightings. I think they're worth checking out by qualified people. But most qualified people won't stick their necks out."[1457]

Grimm's reward money ultimately went uncollected. More than two weeks after the Stilwell Incident began, Brian Jones admitted to Sheriff Dan Abbott on Tuesday, August 23, that the hairy, smelly, violent monster encountered northwest of Stilwell at the Robert Ritchie home in Mulberry Hollow was a hoax he had contrived. The confession came after a polygraph test was administered to Jones in Fort Smith, Arkansas. "He told me that he had told the story to the Ritchie brothers and that they had later told their father, Robert Ritchie," Abbott said. Robert, believing his sons and Jones, told Abbott and others. In a couple of days the news of the fabricated events spread like a prairie wildfire as newspapers, radio and television picked up the story. "Brian told me that he told the Ritchie brothers about seeing the red eyes looking at him through the screen window and about being attacked by the monster because the boys were being rowdy and he wanted to scare them so they would settle down," Abbott said.

> Although Brian Jones' monster is a figment of his imagination, others have reported strange goings-on not related to the first incident.
>
> Ed Bailey, a dairyman near Dutch Mills, Ark., discovered claw marks on the screen door of his dairy barn and on nearby trees. He also found two large footprints near the barn. No one knows who they belong to, but some think practical jokers may be at work.
>
> A man living northwest of Stilwell reported this week that an unidentified animal had scratched up a rabbit house. The man said he did not wish to reveal his name or address.
>
> Mildred Kaiser, who lives in the Oak Grove Community, told officers last week that a big brown bear had attacked her dogs.[1458]

Undeterred by Jones' revelation, Stamps planned Bigfoot expeditions into neighboring states. "I'm not a publicity nut. I never have been," he said, confiding he found in Bigfoot an enigma that required explanation. "I'm a very curious individual, I love a good mystery. . . . I'm interested in getting the truth." Scoffers who denigrated Bigfoot revealed themselves to be uninformed on the subject. "Most nonbelievers haven't read a thing about it (Bigfoot)," Stamps said. "It's totally insane to say that no new animal can be discovered. It bothers me when people are willfully ignorant, when they ignore the facts." Stamps believed scientists hadn't recognized the existence of Bigfoot because "their standards are very strict. They're scared to stick their neck out . . . they want the body." But Stamps confidently maintained that the discovery of Bigfoot would be recognized by mainstream science establishment within his lifetime.[1459]

Stamps' ambition was to become a full-time Bigfoot hunter and researcher. "This is a hobby for me," Stamps said. "Other people have boats, or campers, or model planes. This gives me a chance to meet a lot of people. I like the outdoors and I like to get out. I don't spend as much time with this as a lot of people do sitting in front of a television set." Stamps wanted to obtain tranquilizer guns and ground radar to enable the first live-capture of Bigfoot, a creature he believed was "more human than ape." Obtaining a type specimen for the benefit of science would be "the ultimate," Stamps said.[1460]

Government & Law

Political observer and writer Kevin Phillips commented on Bigfoot and other "oddities" in a September 1977 newspaper column.

> Okay. We all have our little oddities, our side pre-occupations with the unusual. Jimmy Carter is interested in unidentified flying objects, having once himself reported a sighting. And when Sir Eric Gairy, prime minister of the tiny Caribbean state of Grenada, was in Washington for the Panama Canal treaty-signing, he and Mr. Carter reportedly exchanged UFO small-talk.
>
> My own escapist therapy is monster sightings, both lake and mountain variety. The president believes UFOs exist; I'd bet on the Loch Ness monster and maybe even on the Abominable Snowman.
>
> Besides, which, it's fun. . . .

> Frankly, every once in a while, I'd rather go all the way, leapfrogging the lowbrows and Neanderthals of U.S. politics to ponder the existence of genuine full-fledged apemen.
>
> There is no proof, of course. And the whole thing sounds enormously improbable. Hairy creatures, vegetarians halfway between apes and humans, seven or eight feet tall, 400-600 pounds in weight and with feet 16-20 inches long? No such animal could exist.
>
> Except that hundreds of different people have reported hundreds of different sightings. . . .
>
> Big Foot or Big Hoax? That's all from the monster front for 1977, and I leave you to your own conclusions. As for President Carter, if he runs out of unidentified green lights hovering over Americus, Georgia, there are apparently plenty of other oddities to be investigated.[1461]

As for official protection of Bigfoot, B. E. Faist, chief of the Wildlife Protection Branch, California Department of Fish and Game, said that Section 2000 of the California fish and game code protected Bigfoot, if the creature existed at all. The section read in part, "It is unlawful to take any bird, mammal, fish or amphibian except as provided in this code of regulations." Faist said, "We are not concerned with the existence or non-existence of Bigfoot, but assure you that the current California fish and game laws or penal code sections do fully protect this animal if such a creature does exist. First, any person who kills this alleged creature would be in violation of California fish and game laws if Bigfoot should be classified as an animal. Any taking of animals is prohibited in California unless such taking is authorized in the California Fish and Game Code or California Fish and Game Commission regulations. There is no provision for the taking of Bigfoot in our fish and game laws. Second, any person who kills this alleged creature would be prosecuted for murder under appropriate sections of the California Penal Code if Bigfoot is determined to be human."[1462] Depredations against Bigfoot would also be costly in Skamania County, Washington, which passed an ordinance in 1969 making the killing of Bigfoot a felony, punishable by a fine of not more than $10,000 and or imprisonment for not more than five years.

Oregon state legislator Ted Kulongoski from Lane County's Junction City, who later served as Oregon's 36th Governor, introduced a bill in 1977 to prohibit "harassing" Bigfoot. The Oregon Legislature committee approved his resolution and sent it to the House floor Tuesday, June 7. The resolution declared the legislature's "especial concern over the potential harassment of and possible extinction of one species, the creature known as Bigfoot." Kulongoski, a Democrat, said he was not decided if Bigfoot existed or not, but had decided to err on the side of caution, "I don't think anyone should be out hunting him."

Kulongoski admitted his original intent had been tongue-in-cheek, but a flood of positive responses encouraging his continued support for the bill showed "to a large number of people it is not a frivolous issue. It is serious." The measure passed by Oregon's Committee on Environment by a 4-0 vote, which noted the import of Bigfoot's existence and associated scientific significance, if proven to be alive and well in Oregon. The measure directed state educational institutions to build efforts to resolve the question of Bigfoot's existence and enjoined state employees to be protective of the creature. Citizens were urged to exercise care and caution lest Bigfoot be unintentionally harmed.[1463] On the day the measure was debated, someone dressed in a Bigfoot costume appeared on the house floor and in showmanship-fashion, ate a copy of the bill while Kulongoski tried to speak to the measure's merits.[1464]

The Oregon House went on to pass the measure, but it ultimately died in Senate committee.[1465]

During the resolution's publicity, Kulongoski received an autographed picture from Sasquatch which read, "To Ted, Thanks for caring. Love, Sas." The photo came with a collection of Bigfoot memorabilia from "the men and women of North American Wildlife Research." A letter accompanying the memorabilia stated:

> "The assorted publications are to help you in your noble quest to find a just and lasting peace for this most gentle inhabitant of our state and national forests. The (phonograph) record, from the soundtrack of the motion picture, 'Sasquatch,' filmed here in Oregon, has an authentic reproduction of a Bigfoot call on the flip side. Use it to quash opposition to your compassionate legislation. Note the plaintive, tortured, almost tormented, quality of the voice. Only quick action by our lawmakers can still that awesome plea for help."

Not all the attention Kulongoski received was as positive as that sent from NAWR. "One guy called last week [early February, 1977] and chewed me out for the resolution," Kulongoski said. "He said he spent a lot of free time hunting for Sasquatch and didn't want me to interfere."[1466]

On the other side of the country, another measure to protect hairy hominids got underway in 1977. "I felt like putting the bill through because we've got just as much of a legend to protect as Washington state," said Florida State Representative Paul Nuckolls of Fort Myers, sponsor of a protective measure for Florida's Skunk Ape. Nuckolls's office had been contacted in 1976 by a concerned Jim Spink, Skunk Ape researcher and advocate for the species' protection. Nuckolls' bill proposed a misdemeanor to take, possess, harm, or molest a Skunk Ape cleared the Florida House on Friday, May 20, with little discussion.[1467]

> Lawmakers struggling with a billion dollar budget and a sales tax hike haven't been too busy to take up such issues as the safety of skunk apes and the surliness of auto vehicle inspectors.
>
> Such tongue-in-cheek legislation lightens the serious—often tedious—job of being a state legislator.
>
> The session's most absurd bill is a 16-line measure that would make it illegal to molest skunk apes, legendary anthropoids said to lurk in South Florida swamps.
>
> One lawmaker is so taken with the bill he is expected to offer an amendment extending its protection to tooth fairies, elves, and gnomes. Legislative officials say with a knowing grin that a real skunk ape may show up soon to express his, er, her, uh—its—appreciation.
>
> "It's an important piece of legislation," Rep. Paul Nuckolls, R-Fort Myers, joked last week after his bill cleared a committee. "They're very important, but I can't get them to the polls."
>
> Rep. Dorothy Sample, R-St. Petersburg, has a bill that would require motor vehicle inspection workers to have a pleasant disposition. It's up for final House action.
>
> "This is a bill that does everything for everybody," Rep. Sample boasted last week in debate. "And it won't cost one red cent."[1468]

Within a couple of weeks, Nuckolls' bill (House Bill 1664) which had brought the Skunk Ape into Florida politics met with resistance.

> Efforts to make it a felony to harm the legendary animal known as the "skunk ape" were shouted down in the House Thursday.

> Rep. Paul Nuckolls, R-Fort Myers, tried to tack on to a cruelty to animals bill a one-year jail term and $1,000 fine for a conviction of molesting the skunk ape.
>
> Scientists have not completely verified the existence of the animal, but Miami researcher Jim Spinks recently reported seeing a family of them near Charlotte Harbor.
>
> Other [sightings] have been reported over the years, but the legislators thought the amendment was frivolous and Nuckolls admitted he suggested it in order to get publicity for Florida.[1469]

Nuckolls was undeterred when HB 1664 failed to garner support and attempted to promote a similar measure during the following legislative session. The bill, officially called House Bill 58, making it illegal to molest Bigfoot, passed Florida's House Criminal Justice Committee in the autumn of 1977. The bill's next hurdle was to pass the House Appropriations Committee before it could be presented to the full floor for a vote. The *Star-Banner* interviewed Nuckolls who explained why he sponsored the bill: "We can engender a legend in the history of the state of Florida over this." Nuckolls said he had received support from several sources including groups from Miami and the Fort Myers newspaper press who had encouraged the legislation. "If it's a hoax, somebody did a really good job in pulling it over on us," Nuckolls said. "You wonder if they were having a lucid situation or were drunk or what down in Monroe County to keep reporting these things."[1470] Like its predecessor House Bill 1664, House Bill 58 ultimately failed to pass, leaving Florida's Skunk Ape without legal protection.

The U. S. Fish and Wildlife Service suggested a Bigfoot scenario to answer, what would happen if Bigfoot was captured or otherwise thrust into the public limelight?

> Undisputed proof of a Bigfoot might cause an immediate, short-term problem no law could handle. Word of its discovery would be flashed around the world within hours. Hysteria, fear or panic might accompany the news in the area where the creature was located. The throngs of curiosity seekers, would-be captors and others wanting to find Bigfoot would not only create a serious threat to the animal itself, but to public safety as well.[1471]

"Some officials doubt whether any state or federal action short of calling out the National Guard could keep order in the area with the first few hours or days of the creature's discovery," the statement continued. "This would be necessary until a team of scientists could do the necessary things to ensure the creature's survival."

Reporter Sam Hurtz wrote an article on the Fish and Wildlife Service's statement, in which the other perennial superstar monster of the '70s, Nessie, also found mention:

> One government scientist said that if Bigfoot is ever found alive, he hopes the discoverers will quietly notify officials without publicly giving details on its location.
>
> The Fish and Wildlife Service noted the British have officially described the Loch Ness monster in scientific documents so legal steps could be taken to protect the creature if it were found.
>
> Nessie, which has been spotted periodically in Loch Ness, Scotland, over the last 14 centuries, was given the formal name *Nessiteras rhombopteryx*, meaning roughly "Awesome monster of Loch Ness with a diamond-shaped fin."[1472]

Many considered the Endangered Species Act, with its pledge to conserve animals and plants facing extinction, as the lynchpin law for Bigfoot's preservation. Should a flesh-and-blood Bigfoot be found, the emergency provisions of the Endangered Species Act could be used to prevent the property owners where it was located from killing, capturing, or exhibiting the creature. "Any movement of an endangered species, such as for scientific study, would require a permit and the harassing, killing or capture of an endangered species is prohibited," said Bruce McBride of the Fish and Wildlife Service's endangered species office.[1473]

The question 'Would Bigfoot be exploited along the lines of King Kong?' was both asked and responded to in an AP story from January 1978: "Hardly, if the Department of Interior could help it."

> "After receiving 120-day temporary protection under the Endangered Species Act, Bigfoot would undergo the humdrum processing for long-term safeguarding. The following would be considered:

> How big is the Bigfoot population? Do Bigfeet occur anywhere else? Is the Bigfoot population in danger or decline? Is Bigfoot's habitat secure? Is the Bigfoot species being exploited?[1474]

Before an animal can receive protection under the Endangered Species Act a number of formal actions had to occur. The species must receive a formal description and naming in a recognized scientific publication. The Governor of the State where a creature was found would be contacted and a decision arrived at to extend endangered or threatened status. "But for the record," said Keith Schreiner, associate director of the U.S. Fish and Wildlife Service, "I doubt we'll ever have to do anything, because I don't believe there are any of the things around to be discovered in the first place."[1475]

Reporter Mike Wyman couldn't resist juxtaposing the government's theoretical recognition of Bigfoot with the dread certainty of taxes:

> The usual approach of government is that if you ignore a problem long enough, it might go away. This time, instead, the bureaucracy is thinking about a problem before it even happens.
>
> It may be enough to make Bigfoot come out in the open. But I expect the Big fellow will wait until after April 15. If one part of government has its eye on him, or her, no doubt the Internal Revenue Service does too, and the only way to avoid income taxes for the year is to remain legendary.[1476]

Print & Film

Recurring expression in film and print proved Bigfoot's significant niche in popular culture. A zeitgeist in the media (reflective, of course, of the public ambience) disposed it to promulgate Bigfoot and thereby compare the simpler, natural trappings integral to the subject against the rapid fall of many once-normalized barriers in modern society. Jim Delay's seemingly facetious yet solemn column published in the May 26 *Boston Herald American* uses Bigfoot to contrast society's yearning for simpler times with the contemporary prevalence and appetite for violence. As he approached his car one morning, Delay wrote, he found Bigfoot sitting in it. Doing his best to ignore his passenger, Delay proceeded to drive to work, listening to the news from the car radio which amounted to story-after-story of violent murders and depraved crimes replete with full, gory details, breathless descriptions, and gruesome particulars. Delay and Bigfoot proceeded to engage in a contest of wills—Bigfoot turns off the news, but Delay finds himself unable to resist the brutal stories and turns the radio back on.

> Bigfoot is appalled. He is sobbing, deep sobs, massive, ten foot sobs.
>
> I say, "Stop that, Bigfoot. I am trying to hear the news of these grisly events."
>
> The announcer is now telling us about the gruesome murder of the school teacher in the woods near Plymouth. He describes this crime in ghastly detail.
>
> Bigfoot puts his fingers in his ears so he will not hear the ghastly detail. He whimpers softly.
>
> I turn the volume up so that I will not miss any news.

Eventually, unable to bear any more of the "news," Bigfoot kicked the car radio, silencing the descriptions of debauchery.

> Tears stream down Bigfoot's face. He crashed open the car door on the passenger side and gallump-gallumps into the woods.
>
> Only static comes from my smashed car radio.
>
> I drive to work uninformed.[1477]

If Bigfoot was indeed at odds with the 1970s brand of modernity, the subject's elemental equipage remained a key foundational element for its popularity. On the lighter side, Bigfoot was leveraged for humor and as such, a recurrent fixture for April Fools' Day antics. On April 2, the Springfield, Massachusetts, *Morning Union* summarized the pranks from the preceding day:

> In Orange, a radio manager issued a broadcast from a remote unit in his car saying, "I've just seen a big, hairy, ape-like man loping down the road toward Orange. It must be one of those [B]igfoot or [S]asquatch creatures."
>
> The fun was on. About 150 persons called.
>
> "If that creature is six-foot-six and 300 pounds," one woman caller said, "that's my husband. Lock him in a cage and hold him until I get there. He's been fishing since morning."[1478]

Among Bigfoot movies from 1977, *Yeti: Giant of the 20th Century* comes off as a cheesy and capricious Italian knock-off of Dino De Laurentis' *King Kong,* including aping an over-sized mechanical hand. Melting polar caps loose the titular frozen Yeti into man's modern world. Cartoonish and bumbling, the movie appears undecided if it is children's fare or meant for an older audience. Actor Mimmo Craig wore heavy makeup as the Yeti, but otherwise does not don a mask, making for a somewhat bizarre-looking monster. This creature is relatively over-sized—about 20 feet tall, which makes this realization of Bigfoot one of the largest entries in the Bigfoot film canon.

"What a Beast," was the introduction in *Seattle Times'* TV Today article on *Snowbeast's* triumph in luring watchers. "Viewers continue to be fascinated by Bigfoot-like monsters—that dog of an N.B.C. movie, 'Snowbeast,' wound up being last week's most-watched program, according to the Nielsen ratings for the week that ended Sunday night [May 1]."[1479]

Goliathon (aka *Mighty Peking Man*) was produced by the Shaw Brothers to capitalize on the hype of Laurentis' *King Kong* from 1976 and is about an expedition to the darkest reaches of India where it is hoped gigantic ape-men will be discovered.

> One of them [an expedition member] gets separated from the others and teams up with a girl who was raised in the jungle. Her name, while not Mowgli, seems to be either Samantha or Siddhartha; apparently the film dubber couldn't make up his mind. A tousled blonde with dirty knees and fresh coral lipstick, she looks like Deborah Harry of Blondie pumped up on steroids and poured into a Sheena of the Jungle outfit. She's obviously every Hong Kong big-game hunter's dream girl.
>
> It turns out she's best buddies with the [titular] big ape, so the hunter convinces them to come out of hiding and go with him to civilization, by which he means Hong Kong.
>
> When they get there, the Hong Kongers are so insensitive to the ape-man's needs that he stomps the city flat. The freaked-out police chief has no choice but to call in the toy helicopters and plastic tanks, and blow the big guy to pieces. The jungle girl gets wasted too. Jeez, what a bummer.
>
> At no time do they call the ape Goliathon. They call him Peking Man presumably because he likes to peek through windows at the jungle girl.

> Movies like this can be fun if you're not expecting high art. For example, when the hunter convinces the jungle girl to doff her leather bikini to wear something suitable for Hong Kong, and he has her put on a black vinyl hot-pants outfit, you get a telling glimpse into the dark minds of the moviemakers.[1480]

Fouke monster champion Charles Pierce had nothing to do with the film *Return to Boggy Creek,* produced by Bayou Productions and released by Triple Seven Studios. Filming was accomplished in December 1976 and January 1977 at Lake Dauterive near New Iberia, Louisiana.

> Several years ago the film "The Legend of Boggy Creek" capitalized on popular interest in the monster known as, Abominable Snowman, Yeti, Sasquatch, Skunk Ape (depending upon what part of the world you were in) or, as in this case, Bigfoot.
>
> In "Return to Boggy Creek," the odiferous beast reappears in a film that is strictly for children.
>
> "Return" is set in a Louisiana bayou and relates the efforts of three children to track the beast down. Hot on the trail of a local guide and a tourist determined to photograph the creature, the kids run into various dangers and end up getting a closer brush with Bigfoot than they expected.[1481]

The climax of the movie features swamp scenes during a hurricane which actors Vic Vead, who plays the sheriff, and Ray Gaspard, as "Crawfish Charlie," explained were created by air boats and water hydrants. Close-ups during the storm scenes utilized water hoses and hand-held fans. Vead stressed *Return to Boggy Creek* was no horror film. "At the end of the movie, kids will [want] to go up there and kiss the monster," Vead said.[1482]

Curse of Bigfoot centers on an ancient Indian burial ground in California out of which stalks a mummified beast in the vein of Bigfoot who comes back to life and terrorizes a small town. Movie reviewer Fred L. Smith thought the CBS-affiliate in Charleston, WCSC's "Scream Theater," could do better for its late-night horror offerings: "The word 'low-budget' was invented just to describe the late movie offered by Channel Five. It's a little number called 'The Curse of Bigfoot.' It's a curse, all right. I don't see why WCSC can't acquire better horror movies."[1483]

In the firmament of the iconic characters of *Star Wars,* Chewbacca, a seven-foot, six-inch Wookie (from planet Kashyyyk), became one of the movie franchise's indelible heroes. Played by seven-foot, three-inch actor Peter Mayhew, Chewbacca was bipedal and covered in hair. In pre-production for *Star Wars,* Ralph McQuarrie and George Lucas discussed the look for Chewbacca: "George thought of [Chewbacca] as looking like a lemur with fur over his whole body and a big huge apelike figure."[1484]

Joe Butcher and Ray Young (6-feet-seven-inches tall and 230 pounds[1485]) starred as the eponymous *Bigfoot and Wildboy* in segments of the *The Krofft Supershow '77* premiering at 10 A.M. on ABC. This Saturday morning kids' Bigfoot-fare emphasized "maintenance of the balance of nature."[1486]

The *Grizzly Adams* episode "Unholy Beast" aired on April 20, 1977. Adams, Mad Jack, and Nakoma search the woods for an unknown and secretive creature. While tracking the beast, Mad Jack muses it could be the fabled 'Sasquatch' as was said to exist on the western coast. The animal is finally cornered and discovered to be a camel, definitely an exotic visitor to their neck of the woods.

In 1967 Hiram Walker Importers started an advertising campaign for Canadian Club in which print ads provided clues to the location of hidden cases of whiskey (at the time worth $120). Between 1967 and 1979, 17 cases had been hidden, ten of which had been found. Often the whiskey was secretly cached in locations tied closely to a local legend, such as the Lost Dutchman Mine or Bonnie and Clyde's last hideout. In 1976, Hiram Walker dispatched six men, all employees of McCaffrey and McCall advertising agency, to the Pacific Northwest to hide a case of whiskey in support of the 1977 ad campaign, the copy of which, with the trademark location hints, could be found in two-page spreads in several magazines:

> Our burial party moved with caution once we learned that thousands of respected people from around the world believed in Bigfoot's existence. So with a 48-pound case of Canadian Club strapped firmly to one man's back, we deployed five other men to cover his front, rear and flank.
>
> Each man was carefully trained to spot the incredible 17 ½ inch footprints so common in the area. Each man had studied firsthand accounts of the creature's behavior, including most of the confirmed Bigfoot sightings. And yes, at times each man struggled with a special kind of fear.

> On November 5, 1976, after hours spent threading our way through this primeval forest, we found Bigfoot's feeding ground, buried the case of C.C. and quickly returned to civilization. But for the rest of our lives we will never know what some of us suspected all along . . . that Bigfoot himself was watching our every move.
>
> Directions for a few brave souls.
>
> The buried C.C. is located almost the same number of miles south of Canada's Good Hope Mountain (elev. 10,617) as it is north of Bluff Creek in northwestern California. You'll know you're on the right track when you stumble on a temporarily dormant volcano. Now proceed somewhere between 6 and 9 miles (as the eagle flies) from this mountain's frigid peak to an eerie pile of broken green rocks.
>
> Standing high on this unnatural rock pie, walk 65 paces due east to a stream. Turn and walk 70 paces due south. Then freeze in your tracks. Because exactly 11 inches below the soft, virgin forest floor 12 bottles of C.C. are resting peacefully.[1487]

Writer Ben Fulton read Canadian Club's 1977 advertisement and perceived whimsy in its conception and happily played along.

> When I saw the ad I immediately thought of Homer Hagood, a woodsman who, where this project is concerned, definitely qualifies as a consumer. I called him.
>
> "Homer. How would you like a free case of imported blended whiskey," I asked.
>
> "I'll be right over," he replied.
>
> "Hold it. Let me finish." I read the ad to him.
>
> "What a waste. Nothing about it makes any sense."
>
> "Don't be too sure. If college kids haven't changed since my day, every fraternity on the West Coast will have a contingent thrashing around in those big Redwoods looking for that box of booze. That means publicity, and publicity sells products."
>
> "Yeah, I can't argue with that," Homer said. "but I don't buy the Bigfoot story, an animal that acts like humans, indeed."
>
> "Why not? We've got humans that act like animals."
>
> "Doesn't matter. Bigfoot's a hoax," Homer persisted. "Although I do have a drinking buddy who swears he married

Bigfoot's sister. I've seen her; believe me, he has good reason to be suspicious."

"If it's a hoax, how do you account for all the documented sightings and circumstantial evidence?"

"I don't. I'll admit there have been occasions after some extended happy hours—when I have seen some strange creatures myself."

"What you're saying is that if those who find the hidden liquor don't spot Bigfoot before locating it, there's a good chance they'll see him afterwards."

"Exactly. Furthermore, if there is in fact a Bigfoot, we had better hope a searching party finds the booze before he does."

"Why is that, Homer?"

"Imagine what a conservation problem we could have in the Pacific Northwest if a tribe of Bigfoots become alcoholics after digging up a case of whiskey. It would be worse than strip mining."[1488]

In total, the "Hide-A-Case" campaign hid 22 cases of Canadian Club between 1967-1981 (with a hiatus between 1971-1975). Most of these were found over the years, including the one buried in Bigfoot's stomping ground in Oregon.[1489]

In books, *Night Shadows* by Mary Sellers is a unique Bigfoot story weaving together gothic and romantic tones.

> The Loch Ness monster, UFOs, the Abominable Snowman—products of overactive imaginations, helped along by someone with an interest in faking "evidence." Thus with the legend of the Sasquatch, Dodie was certain; one prankster had already admitted laying tracks in the snow, for hunters to discover and cry Bigfoot. Dodie grinned, she was going to enjoy poking holes in this legend, and she'd figured the best place to start was with Matt Stockdale's ranch, where the latest "sightings" had been reported. If the man didn't object to her headquartering there, she could check out sites for herself and personally look over any so-called evidence.[1490]

Mary Sellers' story involves skeptical reporter Dodie Gordon out to research Bigfoot, never supposing romance could be in the offing. Gordon meets rancher Matt Stockdale, a brooding Vietnam veteran and together they unravel a web of intrigue and mystery involving Stockdale's highly-coveted ranch property. Sellers explored the idea that Bigfoot, whatever it might actually be, was easily overshadowed by truly monstrous creatures—men overtaken by greed and avarice.

Another work of fiction was M. E. Knerr's *Sasquatch: Monster of the Northwest Woods* which pitted a Bigfoot, enraged after being mistakenly shot for an intruder, against anyone hapless to cross its path in Lodgepole County, California. Reminiscent of the fast and loose fiction-writing typically found in men's adventure magazines (*True, Male, Saga,* etc.), *Sasquatch* delves into more character development than might be expected from such fare.

Near the end of the book, Sheriff Tom Murphy was alone in the woods hunting for the creature.

> Morning came in a kind of seeping glow that didn't seem to come from any particular quadrant. It just developed, lighting up the thick-falling flakes of snow to make the eyes tired with the flickering.
>
> The whole thing was fast. Too fast.
>
> One second he had been walking through the rocks with the rifle at port arms, and the next an enormous, hairy arm reached out and ripped the weapon from his grasp. In a shocked state, Murphy watched the rifle spin through the air and crash into a lone pine, the sling catching a broken dead branch to keep it dangling.
>
> Then he was fighting a monster.
>
> The [S]asquatch was huge, coming from the rocks, the red-brown hair of his body dappled with snow. His growl was a deep rumbling sound that seemed to wrench itself from beyond the open mouth as he lunged forward, powerful arms reaching. Murphy ducked instinctively under the heavy shape and slammed the hardest right he had ever thrown into the Bigfoot's solar plexus. It had absolutely no effect.
>
> The beast howled in anger and swung a backhand lazily as though he were brushing a fly away. Murphy tried to dodge the swing entirely but the snowshoes got in the way. The heavy forearm caught him across the chest and he felt his left collar bone snap like a twig. The force of the blow lifted him, snowshoes and all, and slammed him into the rock ledge on

> the other side of the flat. The pack cushioned the blow and kept his skull from being crushed against stone, and while he somehow kept his feet, he sucked hard to regain his wind.
>
> The [S]asquatch reached out roaring, his big hands grabbing the front of the parka, and when he drew back Murphy felt himself picked up bodily and heaved into the snow as though he were a child. Pain seared through his left side. The ape-man picked him up again and threw him, stunning him.
>
> He was trying to clear his head when he felt the beast grab him by the shoulder and thigh. He was lifted again. Through the falling snow he could see the long incline of the hill below him and the trees that grew on it.
>
> The Bigfoot roared and threw him down the slope.[1491]

In his author's preface, Knerr writes, "This book is designed to show what *could* conceivably happen in the Pacific Northwest through carelessness. Searches are presently being conducted into the country to attempt to solve the enigma of the Bigfoot, or [S]asquatch, which apparently does exist. My intention is not to throw stones, but to portray a chain of events that could create a monster out of a normally timid and gentle giant."

Dave Manuel's Sasquatch Sculptures and More

Artist David Manuel, born in 1940, started a series of bronze sculptures in the '70s called "Vanishing Wilderness." The second in the series depicted a coyote family, displayed for a time at the Baker-Boyer Bank W. Main Street branch in Walla Walla. The first sculpture in the series was titled "Indian Legend of Sasquatch." The 75-pound sculpture depicted a Bigfoot and large bear squaring off. Manuel called Bigfoot "the most vanishing of the vanishing species." He said that the subject of Bigfoot was of interest to him because it was a widespread Indian legend in which many Native Americans held strong convictions. The piece was displayed at the Spokane Western Art Show, fascinating many viewers. Manuel worked in beeswax with bronzing performed at Maiden's Bronzeworks in Walla Walla. Manuel planned for 20 editions of each sculpture, each with a price tag of about $2,000.[1492]

When the Interstate 90 bypass took away traffic from Stateline, Idaho, the small village known for its massage parlors, motorcycle races, and bars felt the decline in business. That's why Ted "Tex" Cordell relocated his "Snake Pit," a roadside attraction of reptiles, to Rock Creek, about 20 miles west of Missoula, Montana. Cordell's reptile collection included Big Ben, a 27-foot, 350-pound python. Along with Big Ben and about 75 or so other reptiles was a so-called replica of a Bigfoot skeleton.

More filled-out than a mere skeleton, the 6-foot tall, nearly 200-pound statue of a black and brown-haired Bigfoot that had stood in front of Singleton's Taxidermy (of Sumter, South Carolina) was reported stolen Friday night, April 1. Jesse Singleton, owner of the statue said it was worth about $500[1493] (another newspaper account cited $5,000).[1494] On April 5, Singleton reported that residents near an airstrip in Santee, approximately 40 miles away, found the Bigfoot and alerted authorities to its location.[1495] Singleton said he created the model, noted for its 5-foot arms[1496] after an authentic Bigfoot, several years prior, was said to be present in the area slaying cattle and other livestock.[1497]

LaBrecque Bigfoot—Iowa Bigfoot

"When Bigfoot is caught," said Cliff LaBrecque, "it will be caught between the Missouri and Mississippi rivers. The habitat is right, food is abundant, and there are few forests and mountains for trackers to contend with." Bigfoot was serious business for Cliff LaBrecque, 38, of Des Moines, Iowa. By his admission, LaBrecque had been, as of 1977, seeking Bigfoot evidence for 18 years, the last 12 mainly within Iowa.

LaBrecque started Bigfoot Research, Inc. of Iowa, which he ran with Kevin Cook, of Des Moines. He became so involved with Bigfoot he quit his job as a Ford truck salesman to devote as much time as possible to his passion. Cook himself was at the time experiencing his own ardor for Bigfoot research, and planned leave of absences from his job with the Des Moines Flying Service. By his estimate, LaBrecque had invested $40,000 into his search for Bigfoot.

LaBrecque said he would classify most stories he had heard of Bigfoot as unfounded rumor or unsupported anecdote. "I can tell you a lot of things, a lot of stories about Bigfoot that are hearsay. But I don't want to tell you anything that's hearsay." LaBrecque appeared to have a preference to deal with only his stories. "I've seen Bigfoot 15 to 16 times, but never on the west coast," said LaBrecque, who spent seven years in the northwestern U.S. before moving to Iowa. "All my sightings have come in Iowa . . . all in southern Iowa . . . all within 25 miles of Des Moines." David Rhein's *Des Moines Sunday Register* article noted key beliefs LaBrecque operated under counter to some commonly held misconceptions regarding Bigfoot:

There's more than one Bigfoot. Up to 200 Bigfoot creatures roaming the North American continent. LaBrecque claimed Iowa was home to about 24 of the creatures.[1498]

Bigfoot is primarily nocturnal.

Bigfoot is vegetarian.

Bigfoot is passive. "Unless you stumble upon his home, or find him during the mating season, it's quite passive."

Bigfoot is intelligent.

"I can catch Bigfoot," LaBrecque stated confidently. "If you're a golfer, your goal is a hole in one. If you go after one of these, your goal is to bag the first one." LaBrecque told writer Dave Rhein, sounding much like a man with his eye on the prize.

LaBrecque's crowning achievement was a Bigfoot replica he had built according to his careful specifications at a cost "more than a car and less than a house." The construction was done by Neal Deaton of the Deaton Museum Studio in Newton, Ohio. Deaton had built natural history exhibits for museums all across the country. "It was the first non-museum piece we've ever made," said Deaton. "He (LaBrecque) was dead serious about it. It really turned into a fun project." Deaton relied upon LaBrecque's descriptions and pictures provided from a woman in southern Oregon. Deaton's process started with creating a small clay model. Then raw materials, including 900 pounds of clay, were worked and formed into a 7-foot-six-inch model of the bona fide prototype. After a plaster mold was made of the 33 separate clay model pieces they were cast in reinforced fiberglass. The fiberglass parts were then assembled, fastened, and finally laminated with more fiberglass. The hair covering the model was nylon tinted with dark paints. In all, the Bigfoot model took six months to construct and weighed almost 100 pounds.

LaBrecque showed his Bigfoot model at the 1977 Iowa State Fair which was accompanied by the sale of t-shirts ranging in price between $4.99 and $5.99, but no admission fee was charged for seeing the replica. "We don't want any kind of carnival light to this," said LaBrecque, "that's why no admission will be charged. We don't want any 'Hi ya, Hi ya, step right up' kind of thing. We have the only museum-quality replica of Bigfoot in the country. Other replicas are just a bunch of burlap bags. We figure if we don't charge admission, more people will come to see it."

"It's a chance of a lifetime," added Cook. "It's either going to fall flat on its face, or it's going to go great." LaBrecque intended any proceeds derived from his Bigfoot statue would help support his research. "It might not even work," LaBrecque admitted. "I don't think it's going to be a money grabber in Iowa because the people don't know much about it. But I'd be a little disappointed if people here didn't support it a little." LaBrecque planned to take the replica to other fairs in Ionia and Saginaw, Michigan; Tulsa, Oklahoma; and Jacksonville, Florida. LaBrecque's travel itinerary, with his replica carted up in a box and conveyed via a 12-foot trailer, meant his absence from his wife Betty and their two children at home. LaBrecque said it would fall to Betty to fill the t-shirt and poster orders. When the fair touring season concluded and LaBrecque found himself back in the Hawkeye State, he intended to spend November and December 1977 hunting for Bigfoot in the field.

Peter Byrne, when queried by Rhein if he knew of LaBrecque, said the Iowan researcher had come to his attention only recently. Byrne wondered if Bigfoot would find enough to eat and enjoy enough forested land to live in in Iowa. "The evidence is all there," countered LaBrecque. "The only thing that isn't there are the bones (evidentiary proof)." What did LaBrecque think about the naysayers' attitude that Bigfoot was all a joke? "It doesn't bother me," said LaBrecque. "They can believe what they want to believe."

In August, LaBrecque predicted Bigfoot sightings in Iowa would increase if a mid-summer drought that had plagued much of central Iowa persisted because Bigfoot would have trouble finding water. "I've always seen it at night," he said. "The latest was about 5:15 A.M. I've been as close to it as 40 feet. But I don't have an infrared camera, so pictures are out of the question." LaBrecque focused his searching to southern Iowa and relied on calls and reports from people in Iowa to select locations in which to track Bigfoot. "The papers report these sightings as a 'Hi ya, Hi ya' kind of deal. Naturally, people won't report sightings for fear of being ridiculed. This is hampering our search more than anything. When you go out and search for clues to where he's been, you go out and kick cans and stumps and look and look and look," said LaBrecque. "You go in the early morning to see where he's been the night before. Try to establish a pattern he follows, and then start talking to people in the area. Then you start searching those areas out."

LaBrecque demurred sharing his research locations because he wanted to extract as much information as he could from them without being hampered by the presence of serious and non-serious folks, motivated to catch a glimpse of Bigfoot for themselves. "I'll tell you one thing, they seem to spend a lot of nights under bridges. I don't mean Interstate 80, but country bridges. Whenever we hear it's been seen in an area, that's the first place we check out—the bridges." LaBrecque was intrigued by the potential live capture of a Bigfoot and claimed Bigfoot Research, Inc., of Iowa was considering the legal question of possessing a Bigfoot. "You could get $1 million cash with no problem," LaBrecque suggested, but was quick to add that the commercial windfall was not his sole motivation. "We could put on a hoax if we wanted to. We have the replica and everything. But we're not after that. We hope to write books on the subject."

So the two men—LaBrecque who had quit his job and Cook, who took time off from his employment, all in the name of pursuing their Bigfoot research—had reportedly invested $40,000 in a project they hoped would lead to establishing an educational center and full-time pursuit of Bigfoot field research. What would they do if they actually could capture a creature? "We'd have to cross that bridge at that time," said LaBrecque. "I don't know what we'd do."[1499]

"You have to know where and when to look for them," LaBrecque said. "Most people think that since he's seven feet tall, they look seven feet in the air. They don't understand that they lay down to eat and that's the best chance to see them." LaBrecque believed the Midwest had ample habitat suitable for Bigfoot to thrive in. "There's food in the Midwest all the year round. It's the obvious place for him to be." Asked how he would hunt Bigfoot, LaBrecque answered, "Quietly."[1500]

LaBrecque claimed Bigfoot attacked him in 1977. He had been monitoring a Bigfoot for about two and a half months at a location near the outskirts of Des Moines. One night at about 11 P.M., LaBrecque decided to shoot the creature. "It was about 25 feet away from where I was parked in my pickup truck," said LaBrecque. "Two of the creatures walked up from behind a hedge. One stopped but the other went to a woodpile, bent down and started to eat with [its] back towards me. I stayed in the car and waited for it to turn around but it just kept on gnawing at the wood. Finally I decided to shoot it from behind. When the animals turned and saw me, I got buck fever and couldn't shoot. As it came towards me, I couldn't get the window rolled up fast enough. It was really close."

The creature continued its advance toward the terrified LaBrecque. "It loomed over the car. It was about 8 feet tall. It reached through the window, grabbed me and shook the daylights out of me. It was terribly strong. I could feel its face about 6 inches away from mine and believe me I was in a state of tremendous fear. I could feel my whole body shaking. I felt a sensation of being twisted around and pushed down onto the floor. The creature's eyes were burning with fury. It was angry, very angry at me for trying to shoot it. Then I [passed] out. When I regained consciousness it was gone."

Following the attack LaBrecque claimed his memory of the events were disappointingly vague so he worked with Eric Elster of Knoxville, a hypnotherapist. The model whose construction he later ordered was based in part on details derived from the hypnosis. "I searched 15 years before finally meeting Bigfoot face-to-face," LaBrecque said. "The animal exists and it's thriving in great numbers and increasing all the time."[1501]

SIGHTINGS 1977

McLaughlin Monster

Little Eagle, South Dakota, perched on the Grand River and surrounded by scenic mesas, is part of the 2.3 million-acre Standing Rock Reservation straddling the border between North and South Dakota. The town is nestled amidst thick scrub cottonwoods in the Grand River Valley and is 25 miles northwest of Mobridge and 10 miles south of McLaughlin. Following a spate of Bigfoot sightings there in 1977, the moniker McLaughlin Monster was coined.

Writer Bonnie Lake visited Little Eagle where she noted many witnesses were reticent to share details concerning their respective sightings. The restraint which Lake encountered was summed up by Art Eifenbraun, office manager of the *McLaughlin Messenger:* "People are not looking for publicity," he said. "It was held down if anything. People don't want their names used so people can make fun of them."[1502]

"I don't care to talk," said Ester Thunder Shield, one of the witnesses interviewed by Lake. "They say it might come back and hurt me." But Thunder Shield eventually relented and shared her encounter; recalling the "big, ugly" creature standing amid low brush near Jim Chasing Hawk's residence. "When it run, it does not bend its legs," Thunder Shield told Lake. "And it had no neck, a head like oval. When I see it, I sweat and was scared."[1503] Lt. Verdell Veo for the Bureau of Indian Affairs in Little Eagle quickly discovered that the mounting evidence indicated there was something to the talk of a strange creature in the area.

The first Bigfoot sighting at Little Eagle occurred in late August as 16-year-old Craig Two Hearts was doing repair work on his aunt's home. He looked up from his work to see something emerge from the trees which he described as large, dark-brown in color, and hair-covered. Two Hearts recalled that the creature swung its arms when it walked on two legs and appeared to have a hunched back.[1504]

> The next sighting was reported in early September by LeMar Bear Ribs, 17, of Little Eagle.
>
> Bear Ribs had spent an evening playing cards with a friend and was walking home along a dirt road at about 10:30 P.M. when the creature appeared out of a clump of bushes 10 feet from him.
>
> He ran home. According to neighbors who were visiting at his residence, he was nearly in a state of shock when he got there. Bear Ribs began talking wildly of seeing a "big hairy man out there," and fell on a couch in what witnesses described as a state of convulsions.
>
> "We decided to take him to the CHR (Community Health Representative)," said Ester Thunder Shield, one of those present.
>
> "When we started to take him outside, he started screaming and hollering. Then we opened the door and smelled this stinking odor. . . . To this day, I get sick when I think about it."
>
> Bear Ribs was loaded into the car and Mrs. Thunder Shield began driving away.
>
> "Just as I backed out," she said, "a girl in the back seat (Adele Antelope) saw something and grabbed me."
>
> Mrs. Thunder Shield swung the car's headlights onto the road in time to see the hairy creature walking stiffly away.[1505]

On September 11, ranchers Chris Howiatow and his brother Mike Howiatow experienced a relatively lengthy sighting. "It was about 4 P.M. on a real nice Sunday afternoon," Mike recalled for reporter Tom Hasner of the *Sioux Falls Argus-Leader*. "We went out to put oats in a feeder near a creek four miles from here. We filled the feeder and then looked up through a ravine and saw him standing on a hill a half mile away." The brothers had a good view of the creature during their five-minute sighting. "He (the monster) would bend way down to one side," Chris said. "Then he would stand up and bend way down to the other side. Back and forth. Back and forth."[1506]

Rancher Paul Monselowsky and his teenage son saw something "big and hairy" while rounding up a stray bull from a pasture near the Cannonball River. On September 18, at about 3 P.M., Paul was parked on a hill while his teenage son Bob walked to the river to collect the animal. Suddenly, Monselowsky saw something unusual moving toward his son "as fast as a horse could run." Monselowsky realized his son was out of earshot. "It was a half mile from me," he recalled. "It was coal black and looked to be about eight feet tall. The thing was covered with fur. It (the fur) was so long that I couldn't even see space between its legs." When the creature and Bob came into visual contact of each other, the creature veered to the east and entered the water, apparently determined to cross the Cannonball. Bob climbed a hill to keep the creature in visual range. "He was about eight feet tall and had arms that hung to his knees," Bob said. "He was all black. it looked like he was covered with thick shaggy fur." About 500 yards separated Bob and the creature. "I yelled to get his attention and he turned and looked up at me. His face was black, too. It looked like it was covered with hair but I was too far away to tell for sure." The creature made the opposite bank and ran away.[1507]

> Reactions of other residents in Little Eagle toward the people who reported sightings of the creature continues to be disbelief and ridicule of their stories. Still, not many people drive through the community of about 60 people at night unless they have to.
>
> One resident of Little Eagle said, "It's awful. It's coming right into town."
>
> "People are scared," she continued, "but at least it hasn't attacked anyone."
>
> Attitudes of residents in neighboring McLaughlin are about the same.
>
> Betty Ficher, a young woman employed in a McLaughlin grocery store, says she's one who believes that "something" is out there.
>
> "Otherwise why would the animals behave the way they do?" she asked.[1508]

Gary Alexander, who with his wife Karen ran the Little Eagle Trading Post, found the first of many footprints that would be discovered in the area in the soft mud of the Grand River close by the Bear Ribs sighting. Alexander told Hasner the tracks were 18 inches long and eight inches wide. The stride of the track-maker was an impressive 8-to-10 feet.[1509] "Just so nobody thinks it's a hoax, we found tracks five and a half miles east of Little Eagle in such a remote area no one would ever go there," he said. "One of the guys wears a size 13 boot. He stepped beside the footprint and hardly made an imprint at all. I guess he (the man) weighs about 240 pounds."[1510] Lt. Veo made a cast that showed a human-like foot with five toes and a spur-like formation on the outside joint. Wendy Village Thunder, an officer with the Bureau of Indian Affairs, stated the tracks were impressed into the ground by something with great weight. "Something very heavy made them," she said. "They were a good two inches deep."[1511]

> Veo felt that the tracks would have been difficult to fake, a sentiment echoed by Merle Lofgren, editor of the *McLaughlin Messenger,* a Corson County weekly. Lofgren pointed out that it would have taken enormous weight to make the tracks, and the stride would have been much too long for a man. Stilts, were out, he said, "since a man would have had a hard time wallowing around on stilts in that kind of mud."[1512]

Lofgren was impressed by the mounting evidence, especially after he accompanied Veo on a trek along the Grand River looking for evidence.

> We puffed up to some tracks in the mud where the water had been sitting and then evaporated. There were some tracks which appeared to have been made by a foot like a human's except they were about two feet long.
>
> I don't think I would believe in Susquach [sic] if I saw him. I can't explain the tracks but I saw them and took a picture of them.
>
> If there had been only one track I would say it was a freak formation in the mud or the ground under the mud. There were several tracks. They were twice as big as any track made by Veo's size 12 boot.
>
> Even if by chance somebody put on a wooden foot they couldn't make the strides shown by the tracks. This thing or whatever was taking steps about 8 to 10 feet apart. Stilts? A person would have a hard time staggering around in the mud on stilts. If they were trying to carry out a hoax it would be better to do it closer to somewhere near Little Eagle where they would be more likely found. They had to walk a long ways to get to the place where the tracks were found and cattle

> grazing the area could have wiped out the tracks. Some people looking for deer tracks found the ones I saw.[1513]

Lofgren would eventually assign a "Big Foot Operator" in the *Messenger's* newsroom. "I was spending more time taking calls about Big Foot than I was putting out the newspaper."[1514]

More footprints attributed to the McLaughlin Monster were discovered a quarter-mile northeast of the Trading Post in Little Eagle on Sunday, October 2, by Alexander, Veo, and Veo's son. "They (the footprints) were across the edge of an old lake bed," Alexander said. "The length of the stride seemed to show that the monster was walking, because the prints weren't quite as far apart as others have been," he said. Alexander stated that efforts to track the creature were then ongoing. "We probably will get some more pictures of the tracks, too," he added. "There's no question in my mind that something is out there."[1515] People began toting their weapons night and day raising safety concerns. By mid-October armed groups were organized to hunt the creature.

According to Eifenbraun, most of the creature sightings had occurred during nighttime. There were no reports of anyone being harmed, Eifenbraun stated, either by the creature or in the hunt for it. Eifenbraun dismissed a report of a man suffering a heart attack after the shock of seeing the creature as only a false rumor.[1516] "There have also been stories going around of people finding animals which have been killed, but we don't have any proof of any of them," he said.

By the end of September, the growing deluge of Bigfoot reports compelled authorities to take notice. The Bureau of Indian Affairs in Fort Yates, North Dakota, took up an investigation of the area's creature sightings.[1517] On the evening of September 29, Lt. Veo had an experience that convinced him in the reality of the strangeness going on.

> "I was out with my boys (his teenage sons) here in my pickup. I had been ordered to get something done about this thing. On the road I met two other officers, Bobby Gates and Selvin Arlen." The group proceeded to Elk Horn Butte north of town, he said, a seeming "hot spot" for sightings.
>
> They parked the vehicles and sat for a while. Jeff decided to play a recording of a cry made in Pennsylvania during frequent sightings of the alleged Sasquatch or Bigfoot there.

> The men were laughing and joking, when suddenly Jeff asked his father, "Are there any Indian monuments on this side of the butte?"
>
> "I told him 'no,'" said Veo. "I looked through the scope and I could see it too . . . something on the side of the knoll on the butte."
>
> "We got out and started to walk toward what we had seen—me and officer Arlen. We got about 350 yards away from it, then stopped to watch it with the binoculars. I could see it better now . . . it seemed to be teasing me, coming forward in the moonlight and then going back into shadow. It had us sort of spellbound—you know, hypnotized."
>
> "At the time I saw him, I had a feeling or instinct, you might say, that no weapon I would have been carrying could have made any difference. Something told me—I could sense it—that I'd better just get out and leave the thing alone."
>
> Veo's exciting evening on the butte lent new credibility to the situation. Things got more seriously immediately. Shortly thereafter, the BIA and the Standing Rock Sioux Reservation tribal council called a town meeting. The small white clapboard community center was packed to capacity. BIA officials asked the people in the room exactly how many people had witnessed the creature, and were surprised to find that no fewer than 47 people raised their hands![1518]

Not everyone was a believer in a phantom-like creature haunting the wilderness. "As far as I'm concerned, this Bigfoot stuff is pure myth," said Corson County Sheriff Harry Kettleson. "I don't know where all this is coming from, but I'll bet you there's nothing to any Bigfoot or whoever he's supposed to be." By October, a composite description of the creatures had formed. "It's hard to describe . . . very tall," said Esther Thunder Shield. "It doesn't have any shoulders and doesn't bend its legs when it runs." Thunder Shield continued, "I cannot make you believe me," she said. "But I saw what I tell you."[1519]

The Alexanders' Little Eagle Trading Post became a clearing house and focal point for Bigfoot information; Gary kept an informal record of McLaughlin Monster witnesses' sightings and the shop was a reliable venue for collecting and disseminating the latest Bigfoot news. Karen took many of the McLaughlin Monster inquiries that came into the Trading Post which had one of the few business phones in town. With exasperation she told Bonnie Lake events "are turning into a nightmare around here." Publicity of the Little Eagle creature sightings had obviously ranged far and wide. "We got a call from Honolulu the other day," she told Lake.[1520]

Gary Alexander said representatives from several national magazines such as *Saga* and *Argosy* had reached out to him. "It gets a little aggravating sometimes when I'm real busy," he said. In 1981, Alexander recalled that "one morning for three hours that phone rang solid with calls from London, Hawaii, Germany . . ."[1521] during that hectic autumn in 1977. *Newsweek* gave over nearly a page to Bigfoot reports from Little Eagle including a photo of Gary Alexander holding a footprint cast. KFYR-TV at Bismarck aired a documentary on Saturday, October 29.[1522] NBC came to do a story that left a bad taste with Alexander. "NBC made a regular hoax out of it," Alexander said. "They should have shown Mickey Mouse cartoons right afterwards." A Minneapolis station did a three-part story on the events at Little Eagle following which Alexander said he received 47 calls at the Trading Post.[1523]

The *McLaughlin Messenger* was instrumental in keeping the area's creature sightings in the public attention and interest. Editor Lofgren dutifully printed the reports but generally "played the story down," in the *Messenger*. But as the total number, frequency, and credibility of reports mounted, the editorial tone became decidedly more serious. The *New York Times* called. A radio station in Texas sent a reporter who spent a week with parties going out to search for the creatures, intent on taping the strange cries and wails for the station's audience.[1524]

Many phone calls taken at the Trading Post were simply people asking questions, but sometimes callers had very definite comment or advice to impart. "We get a lot of good information that way, but we also get some weird letters and calls. Some have said it's the spirit of the devil. We get a lot of prayers said for us, and one person said we must be the people of Satan to have such a thing happen," Alexander said.[1525]

B. Ann Slate, who represented herself in a letter to Alexander as working with *Saga* magazine, told Alexander that Bigfoot creatures appear to be attracted to babies, women experiencing their menstrual period, soft music, and small campfires. "We are continuing to look for patterns" she wrote. Slate asked if there was a particular crop, timber reserve, or military installation in the area. Slate stated that Bigfoot was apparently an excellent swimmer and may rely on rivers and bodies of water for key avenues of movement. She also sent Alexander a tape of a purported Bigfoot creature's cries made in Pennsylvania. After several residents of Little Eagle listened to the tape they agreed the same cries had been heard locally. Dean Olson, of North American Films, Inc., told Alexander about his group's protocols for capturing and studying a Bigfoot. "He (Olson) told me on the phone that the first time we find clear tracks in snow, he'll come out here," Alexander said. But, Alexander added, Slate told him that Bigfoot sightings decrease in winter months. In terms of capturing a Bigfoot, there had been talk at the Trading Post of digging a pit trap or dropping a net over the creature. "The most practical offer of local assistance has come from Sam Holland, a Mobridge veterinarian, who told Alexander he will search for the creature with an airplane and a tranquilizer gun after the next sighting."[1526] A monster-spotting plane did fly in Little Eagle on Sunday, October 30, but nothing unusual was seen.[1527]

Hannah Shooting Bear reported her brush with something unusual on October 25 as she looked out the window of her daughter's mobile home in northwest Little Eagle. Police investigated but found no evidence at the scene. Some enterprising Bigfoot-baiters tried the techniques of hanging what was hoped to be enticing bait from trees as well as starting bonfires with observers set off at a distance to observe if anything approached.[1528]

On Saturday, November 5, two employees of the Bureau of Indian Affairs Land Operations Branch checked on cattle east of Porcupine when they sighted what they assumed was Bigfoot. One of the two, David Dunn, said the creature could have been a person or even a rider on horseback. Another sighting that Saturday occurred at Little Eagle. The creature was described as black, and eight-feet tall. It had been encircled by several pickup trucks in a brushy, off-road area. The creature was able to avoid the trucks' searchlights and starlight scopes. On Monday, November 7, a Little Eagle resident took a shot at Bigfoot with a .22 Magnum at a distance of 70 yards.[1529]

> There was suspicion there might be more than one Big Foot in the area after one was seen by Virgil and Ardyce Taken Alive and a younger sister along the Grand River. Ardyce said they were driving along the river in a pickup and were not looking for a Big Foot when the younger sister said she saw something on the opposite bank of the river. The creature was sunning himself and when the pickup stopped he got up and ambled off. The Taken Alives' description of the thing they saw indicated it was not as big as the ones previously seen. They said it had almost no neck and appeared to have a black face. It was apparently not frightened.[1530]

Pat McLaughlin, Standing Rock Sioux tribal chairman, and Shirley Plume, Bureau of Indian Affairs superintendent for the Standing Rock Agency, issued a joint statement expressing concern for the safety of people on the reservation and for the well-being of Bigfoot. The joint statement prohibited employees of the tribe or the BIA from hunting Bigfoot. McLaughlin said that Vance Hill, tribal judge, was ready to issue a court order prohibiting the carrying of firearms if appeals to not use them while Bigfoot hunting went unheeded. McLaughlin stated he had received calls from six reservations in a five-state area calling for action to protect Bigfoot. While announcing the joint statement, McLaughlin explained that traditional Indians believed in "Taku He,"[1531] and should he be maltreated, great harm would come to the Native Americans[1532] On Tuesday, November 8, officials announced a more stringent stance taken on hunting Bigfoot.

> Pat McLaughlin, chairman of the Standing Rock Sioux Tribe, called off all hunting of Big Foot, Tuesday afternoon.
>
> . . . Therefore, in order to insure that no harm comes to Susquatch [sic], or Big Foot, the tribe was ordering all people, all law officers, and all BIA officers, to stop hunting for Big Foot. Furthermore, he invoked a tribal law, under which he could ban hunting by anyone, Indian or non-Indian, on the Standing Rock Reservation.[1533]

Writer Ralph Katus' article describing his visit to Little Eagle appeared in the November 17 *McLaughlin Messenger*. Katus asked why this supposed Bigfoot was haunting the Little Eagle environs "so far removed from [its] original haunts" on the West Coast.

> Having done considerable research on this creature while a resident of California a few years back, I was extremely interested in all these accounts and stories, emanating from the Little Eagle vicinity.
>
> Sunday, November 13 was such a nice day, my wife and I decided to visit Little Eagle to try to get some firsthand information from someone who had either actually seen this creature or heard [its] unearthly cry.
>
> When we left home the sun was shining brightly but as we drove south from McLaughlin a cloud cover came up. As we drove down the long hill into Little Eagle, the wooded river

bottom and valleys, these clouds seemed to add to the eerie accounts I was able to get from a rancher who lives near Little Eagle.

It seems that several interested parties have spent many nights with CB-equipped vehicles in an effort to sight this Bigfoot creature. The CBs give them the advantage of being able to converse back and forth during their nighttime vigils. The story of Saturday night, November 12th goes thus:

A group of men, hearing that this ghostly creature was attracted by fire had built a bonfire just north of the Little Eagle Store.

Within an hour Bigfoot showed up in a patch of brush near the fire. This brush was about waist high to the average man and this creature towered high above the brush, it's reddish-orange eyes gleaming in the fire light. It quickly moved out of sight. About an hour later this same man heard the unearthly scream of the creature a short distance south of the store. The cry starts with a scream, sometimes ending with a whinny like a horse and at other times in maniacal laughter. The person told me this said that at first he was as skeptical of this creature's existence as the average person but now he was definitely convinced about it. I asked him what he thought it was and he just shook his head with a grin and spread his hands wide. His story continues:

About 2:30 Saturday night as he drove into his yard, he heard frantic cries and pleadings over his CB. Someone, driving north on the hill from Little Eagle had the unnerving experience of Bigfoot crossing the road in the headlights of his car. He lost control of his car, went into the ditch and was afraid to leave the car for fear the creature might return. It was from his car he gave the frantic cries for help. Upon arriving at the scene the man found the car's occupant in a bad state. He rushed around the man's pickup and climbed in. He was in a state of shock. The man said it was just a small problem to turn the car's wheels around and drive back up on the highway.

It seems that many Little Eagle residents are afraid to sleep in their homes at night. A recent BIA directive prohibits the use of firearms in the pursuit of Bigfoot on the reservation.[1534]

Katus dismissed the idea of a practical joker behind all the sightings, leaving all the footprints, and making all the nighttime screams. But practical answers seemed in short supply given the incredible events. Because it hadn't been known to bother livestock, Katus deduced the creature was vegetarian, which prompted him to wonder how such a creature could gather enough food in the Little Eagle area to sustain itself. "A strange and disturbing thought comes to mind," wrote Katus. "Is this creature, in some mysterious way attracted to humans or in some other manner trying to communicate with them?"[1535]

LeMar Chasing Hawk was one of the claimants to a close encounter with one of the creatures. The incident occurred on a path in the vicinity of his backyard. "I didn't stay around long enough to find out what it looked like," he said. "I turned around and ran for home and didn't look back." Chasing Hawk stated that after his sighting he routinely carried a rifle with him.

> Authorities have asked those who remain in Little Eagle not to carry weapons—even tranquilizer guns—for fear of injuring each other. But many ignore the pleas.
>
> "We're not out to hurt it," one hunter said. "We're all carrying .22-caliber rifles or .22-caliber magnums."
>
> Ed Meller, an unemployed gravel hauler and oil-products distributor, has set up a [mobile] camper equipped with a tape recording system on Chasing Hawk's property. The animal showed up at the van about two weeks ago, and two of them appeared twice around 4 A.M. Wednesday, he said.
>
> Milton LaSalle, a New York state soils engineer who has studied Bigfoot sightings on the East and West coasts for the past 20 years, traveled to Little Eagle last week.
>
> "There are far too many witnesses involved in the various sightings for it to be rigged," he said. "The sightings are conclusive that it doesn't fit the description of any wildlife native to the area. It's not a bear, that I'm certain of."
>
> LaSalle, however, won't commit himself without more evidence. "I won't say it's a Bigfoot, not until I see it myself," he said.[1536]

At the end of November, reporter Mark Kinders wrote that 28 sightings had been reported since September of up to as many as three Bigfoot creatures from as far away as 150 yards to as close as 10 feet.[1537] Alexander summed up the creatures' descriptions from the several area sightings: A large one, dark in hair color, stood between six and nine feet tall and weighed between 600-900 pounds; a smaller one had a lighter-hued covering of hair. A third Bigfoot, the smallest of the trio, was about six feet tall and weighed about 400 pounds.[1538]

"I couldn't stand its running around shrieking all night," said the Rev. Angus Long Elk, recalling the unnerving, strange-sounding screams. "It was doing it all the time," he said. "And about two weeks ago [early December] my wife saw it at night while she was down by the river. She's been afraid ever since and wanted to leave."[1539]

Gary Alexander experienced his own sighting, of two creatures, in the early morning of December 2. "It was a relief," he explained over the phone with reporter Sam Lowe, "I knew I hadn't been chasing butterflies. After three months of trying, I saw them." For Alexander, the power of a personal sighting, confirming for his satisfaction the creature's existence, steered his thoughts toward future contact. "I was a skeptic at first, just like everyone," he said. "But after I saw them myself, that's all I needed. I'm pretty well relaxed about it now. I'd like to communicate with him. I'd like to watch him as an individual, not as part of a group trying to capture him."[1540]

> "We left the trading post here about 2 P.M. It wasn't a good day . . . there was no snow. We went out to Lyle's (Lyle Maxon) place and got horses and snowmobiles. There was a bunch of people from Iowa with us, and we split up in groups."
>
> "We had cameras with us, but the going was rough, so we took the cameras back to the pickup truck. About ten minutes later, we were near the spring there on Lyle's ranch, when we saw 'em. Two of 'em. We looked at 'em about three or four minutes. I was so interested in seeing them that I realized later that I forgot to take off my yellow snow goggles and look through the telescope on my rifle. And I had no desire at all to shoot at the things."
>
> "They were standing up. You could tell there was nothing like clothing (some Bigfoot creatures have been seen with clothing like wraps, according to researchers), just hairy. They were dark. One was bigger than the other by about a foot and a half. And they were big," said Alexander.[1541]

A deep draw which was impassable for his snowmobile separated Alexander from the creatures, which he estimated were 600 yards away. "We didn't try to crowd them. They looked at us, didn't turn around full, but turned their heads. They didn't run, I guess, because we didn't present a threat to them."[1542]

Alexander told Lowe about some of the trace and sign left behind by the creatures. "Some droppings and hair that have been found were authenticated by a research firm in Denver as that of a primate, but not an ape or human," Alexander said. Lowe wrote that Milton LaSalle of New York had reportedly authenticated a McLaughlin Monster track cast as a bona fide Bigfoot print.[1543]

The day after Alexander saw two creatures, rancher Lyle Maxon and his eight-year-old son were sawing wood in the vicinity of the same spring visited by Alexander and his party. "Hey Dad! I think here are some of those Bigfoot tracks they've been talking about!" Maxon stopped work to investigate. "There were a good twenty of 'em," recalled Maxon. He later showed the tracks to his brother Dick. "The stride again was six to eight feet—that was plenty of proof for me. But what in the hell is making them?"

> "We'll have to live here a long time after this thing has died down," said Alexander. "I hope everybody tries to remember that, but everybody's getting up in the air and there's already been trouble here." Alexander had taken it upon himself to escort reporters around town, he said, but he added, "I'm about through. This has been taking up all my time." On one day, he said, the Little Eagle Trading Post telephone had rung no less than fifty times—starting at 4:30 A.M. and ending at 1:30 A.M. "It's hard to get much else done," he said.[1544]

Bonnie Lake would make four trips in total to Little Eagle prior to writing her article. On one occasion while in town, Lake, her husband, Karen Alexander, and the Alexander children were talking outside the Trading Post when a long, wailing moan was heard—a bloodcurdling howl that Lake averred was not coyote or anything else she was familiar with. She wrote the strange wail "seemed to be coming from an animal with a deep resonating chamber," as it echoed along the valley. "It's starting up a little early tonight," Karen Alexander said. "Usually this doesn't start up until dark."

> The sound as reported by witnesses varies in nature. Rancher Maxon, for example, described the sound he heard one afternoon on his ranch as a kind of "modulated moan, ending in kind of a whinny, and followed by what I can describe only as the laughter of a crazy man." At other times, the sound was "like someone in great pain," said Karen. "One night the dogs started up and this noise started up from back in the hills," she said. "My first thought was 'My God, what are they doing to some child.' Then, I realized that was whatever it is that's been making all these noises, it was a sound I've never heard before in my life."[1545]

Ed Meller, an oil products distributor, set up a mobile camper equipped with sound-recording equipment and volunteers willing to spend time on site investigating the mystery. One of his camper's locations was the site of the Esther Thunder Shield sighting.

> Meller's findings in studying the habits of the creatures corresponded closely with information obtained from Milton LaSalle, Bigfoot specialist who traveled to the town the third week of November. One such finding was that the creatures exhibit signs of quite a high intelligence and awareness, even to the ability to mimic words and gestures they witness among humans. Meller also found that the creature had a tendency to creep on all fours when it was threatened—which might account for its ability to hide in relatively sparse cover despite its size.[1546]
>
> Meller is also convinced that the Bigfoot creature has an all-consuming curiosity that might be its downfall ultimately. "It's pretty nosy," he told one reporter. "Anything that goes on, he just has to see."[1547]

"Nobody was interested in Little Eagle before this thing," remarked one local in the Trading Post in earshot of Lake. "That's why they say we do it—so the papers will notice us." *McLaughlin Messenger* editor Lofgren scoffed at such a notion. "You'd have to know these people like I do—these are people who'd never do this for a joke. Verdell Veo's the best. A fine policeman. I've seen him in court and no lawyer can shake his testimony. He wouldn't be out there night after night trying to figure this out if he wasn't convinced it was out there."[1548]

From an outside perspective, the frenetic level of hairy hominid activity eventually died down, but for the locals who called the area home, the subject of Bigfoot in and around Little Eagle slowed only to a simmer. *Rapid City Journal* reporter Bob Tucker revisited the McLaughlin Monster in October 1981 upon the occasion of a fresh Bigfoot sighting near Little Eagle.

> Jim Walton of Sioux Falls came to Little Eagle to take a look for himself in 1978 and never left, staying on as a teacher. He also heads up a Big Foot Research Center with two other local men. They check out sightings, collect tape recordings of the creature's primal scream and have albums filled with failed attempts to get a good picture of Big Foot.
>
> "Jim was out of work and Big Foot turned up," his wife Jo explains. "He wants to go where the adventure is and this was closer than the Bermuda Triangle. He came in and didn't make fun of the people and they accepted him."
>
> That includes the Alexanders, who often talk of the creature in human terms, referring to "him" as Frankie and speaking wistfully about establishing communications. Using the name Frankie allows restaurant conversations "without people getting their ears up so high," says Alexander. "Besides," adds his wife, "I never thought of him as a monster because he has never hurt anybody. He has had lot of opportunities."
>
> "Maybe he isn't human," Alexander says. "Maybe it's migrating through on a cycle. One guy said it was from the third dimension."[1549]

Claw Marks & Prints

Ed Bailey operated a dairy farm north of Dutch Mills, Arkansas, across the state line from Adair County. He found claw marks on a dairy barn's screen door and two 13-inch-long footprints near the barn on Friday, August 12. Additional claw marks were discovered on three nearby trees. "I stuck my head in the door of the barn and saw that the latch on the inside door had been forced open. That's when I left and went to get my gun," Bailey said. Inside the barn, a barrel of alfalfa feed had been turned over. Bailey reported that when he brought cows up to the barn they didn't appear skittish despite *something* having visited the premises. Allen Pershall, a resident in Evansville, believed one of the first theories, that a bear had visited the Bailey farm, didn't hold up given the prints left behind. "It wasn't a bear that broke in here," Allen said. "The footprints are too big." Pershall recalled a circus truck having overturned on US 71 about 35 miles from Dutch Mills some 15-20 years previous. "It may be that one of those gorillas has been prowling around here," he said.

> Two Cane Hill, Ark., skeptics visited the scene and said they believed the claw marks were made with a metal instrument by a practical joker, and that the footprints also are bogus because both prints are of the same foot. They declined to give their names, fearing the practical joker would visit their farms next.
>
> A Sasquatch Investigation of Mid-America team [Bob Stamps] from Oklahoma City searched the area this week but did not reveal its findings. Another Sasquatch team was due from Tulsa but failed to show up.
>
> The first reported incidents of a "monster" being in this area cropped up several days earlier, but were kept quiet because officers feared local residents might panic.

Bob Stamps' investigation left him "fairly convinced" that at least one Bigfoot was in the area.[1550] The week prior to Bailey's discovery, the Stilwell Incident occurred some 12 miles away in the Mulberry Hollow community north of Stilwell, Oklahoma. Article writers drew comparisons between the Adair monster and the creatures reported at Indianola in September 1975 and with the Noxie Monster earlier in August.[1551]

Wayne King

Bigfoot researcher Wayne King of Caro, Michigan, investigated a report made by Mr. and Mrs. Richard Clark who described finding 17-inch prints in the snow near their cabin on the Platte River back in 1975. "The creature must have had a very good height and size and a very good weight" to have left the impressive tracks, King said. "The tracks were bigger than my husband's, too!" as well as "deeper than we could sink," Mrs. Clark said in a telephone interview with the *Record Eagle.*

"People are always talking about bear," said King. "Now I know there are not that many bear in lower Michigan. Even a large bear will not have a print 17 inches by eight inches." Investigating Bigfoot was a family affair for King: his wife, and four of their six children actively participated with him in his field investigations. "We do everything together," Lillian King, Wayne's wife, said. She called their family's Bigfoot outings as "good for the kids" and "a good education." Lillian and 15-year-old Kathy King had collaborated on Bigfoot sculptures which King was considering patenting and marketing for sale.

In 1977 the 40-year-old King worked at the General Motors metal fabricating plant in Flint. In his spare time, King served as the director of the Michigan Bigfoot Information Center headquartered in his home in Millington. "I believe in the existence of Bigfoot," King told reporter Bill Pritchard during an interview at a Traverse City fast-food restaurant; King described Bigfoot as "a form of man that has never really cultured itself."

In a widely-shared belief amongst Bigfoot researchers for Bigfoot's presence in North America, King posited that Bigfoot arrived on the continent by crossing the Bering Straits during the Ice Age. The creature, he averred, was curious. "Don't let anybody laugh at you about this," he said, "all my life I've been after the Yeti," he said, using a term most often employed during this period for reference to Florida's Skunk Ape. King had established his Information Center in early 1977 and was in contact with the "National" Bigfoot Information Center in The Dalles, Oregon. Pritchard called the Oregon center and listened to a tinny, tape-recorded invitation to leave a message. Pritchard rounded out his *Record-Eagle* article by soliciting an official's opinion on Bigfoot.

> "What a way to start the day," commented a conservation officer this morning. The *Record Eagle* had called to ask the mysterious question . . . does Bigfoot live in the Lake Ann area swamps?
>
> "I rather doubt it," he said, but added, "There's quite likely a bear or two over there."
>
> The officer said he had never heard of Wayne King and certainly not of Bigfoot of the Platte.
>
> "Everybody has their own little thing," he said.[1552]

Lake Ann

In May 1977 King conducted a Bigfoot field expedition, involving his teenage daughter and an assistant, into the wilds of northwestern Michigan's Benzie County. The precise location owed to the Clark's 1975 track finds and was in the area where King had found a huge footprint in April pressed into snow in the woods near Lake Ann, about 15 miles southwest of Traverse City. King stated the print measured 17 inches from toe to heel and 8 ½ inches wide.

"There are probably 12 (Bigfoot) in Benzie County alone," said King. "We'll be prepared for plaster castings and immediate movie taking. We'll be looking for a nine-foot giant who weighs between 800 and 1,000 pounds."

Benzie County Sheriff Bert Higgins told a reporter that his department had never received a report of a Bigfoot creature. "It is impossible," Higgins said. "It is absolutely impossible for a Bigfoot to be running around in this area. Maybe they [the Clarks] saw a bear. We do have bear." King said he was not put off by the healthy skepticism of others. "The whole world is skeptical," he said. "But I believe I can prove the creature exists. I'm not doing this for fun. I'm doing it for science and mankind."[1553]

"I'm confident I will return with either a plaster casting of the creature's huge prints or a movie film of the creature," King said Friday, May 6, concerning his expedition planned for May 14-15 in Traverse City. King was serious enough about his Michigan Bigfoot Information Center to have his family's regular phone line removed from their home and four business phones installed. "They are placed strategically throughout the house and serve the sole purpose of collecting and disseminating information about Bigfoot," King said.

"There's no doubt about it now," declared Wayne King holding up a hunk of plaster drying in the general shape of a giant foot about 19 inches long, 10 inches wide, and 6 ½ inches wide at the heel. During his field outings in May, King had discovered several prints in the ground but the cast he held was made from the best defined of several he found around the northeast end of lower Woodcock Lake. King asserted there could be male and female creatures in the area.

Abe Roorda, a singer from Grand Rapids, claimed he had an unusual experience while fishing Lower Woodcock Lake in mid-May. Roorda noticed that everything had suddenly gone quiet around him, as if "life had stopped around me," he said. Two creatures, about one and a half miles apart "shrieked and squealed" at each other for more than a minute. "It was spooky, it really was," he said.[1554] Roorda stated he understood "how vocals work" and estimated the creatures were "more than 140 pounds" by the volume and power of their calls. "Never before in my life have I heard a sound like that," Roorda said. "It must have had lungs bigger than mine. It was almost human."

Reporter Jeffrey Sheler began his article on King by involving the reader in an exciting moment during King's field research.

> A twig snapped somewhere below the thickly wooded ridge along the river bank and Wayne King stopped dead in his tracks.
>
> Silently, he swung his 8mm movie camera into position and waited, eyes intensely searching for movement in the forest shadows.
>
> "He's out there. I can sense it," King whispered, adjusting the tripod on his camera.
>
> He stood ready to record the moment he'd spent 27 years preparing for—a face-to-face encounter with Bigfoot, a legendary ape-like creature who King believes inhabits the wilds of northwestern Michigan.
>
> Ten minutes passed with no sound, no movement, no Bigfoot. King and his three companions moved on.[1555]

"I'm not disappointed, because I know he exists," said King. "Even though I've never seen him, there is plenty of solid evidence, eyewitness accounts, proof that Bigfoot, or Sasquatch as the Indians call him, is in Michigan. And some day, I don't know when or where, I'm going to find him." King spent as much weekend time as was available in the woods, following leads, investigating recent sightings, and continuing the search. Often with him, in the later '70s, was "field man" Natham Blakemore, a fellow worker at the Flint Chevrolet plant. "I'm no Bigfoot hunter," said King. "I don't want to hurt him. I only want to prove he exists so we can get some laws to protect him."

Only a week prior to Sheler's interview, King discovered 12 large footprints spaced 7 to 8 feet apart about a half mile from Lower Woodcock. King cast one of the prints that he claimed, "clearly shows the padded foot of a 600 to 800-pound primate. Definitely not a bear. No claw marks." A year before, the Clarks from Flint, while vacationing in the Lower Woodcock area came across giant footprints that King said were "those of a large humanoid." The same couple earlier in 1977 reported to King they had heard a strange scream accompanied by a foul odor. In all, Sheler reported King had received 40 "solid pieces of evidence" of which eight were Michigan Bigfoot sightings occurring since 1973. After his investigation of the Roorda report failed to turn up any evidence, King and Blakemore propitiously drove to a nearby café for lunch. Thanks to a local radio station's promotion, the Bigfoot researcher's presence in the area was well known. Soon after he crossed the café's threshold he was handed a message alerting him to a local track find by mushroom hunters. "Look at the size of that," King said, indicating a 15-inch long impression in the shape of a human-foot. It was one of about 40 widely spaced prints that formed a 300-yard trackway trailing off into the woods. "How can you dispute evidence like this?" King asked. He scrutinized the tracks, noting their depth and shape. "A good find," he declared. "Not as good as finding Bigfoot in the flesh. Seems like I'm always a step behind him. But someday he and I are going to shake hands. I just hope I have my camera with me."[1556]

"I don't think there's a thing to it," said Rev. John Bare. Bare had lived in Michigan's Woodcock Lakes area for many years. The "it" was reference to the Bigfoot creature which King believed was in the area. "I know every foot of this land, the streams and everything else," explained Bare.

King had taken multiple trips to the area and said he had "no doubt" that one or more large creatures were in Benzie County. Some residents were "twitting me about being Bigfoot," said Rev. Bare. The minister was 6-feet, 4-inches tall, sporting at the time a size-14 shoe. "I think some of these people are just having dreams," said Bernie Lake, a Benzie County resident on North Woodcock Lake. "I've been here all my life so far," he said, adding, with conviction, there was naught but the "run of the woods" full of the normal, natural critters one would expect to find. "I know these woods pretty well," he continued. "I never seen any unusual tracks."

"Oh, back a few years ago, over towards Bendon Swamp I was tracking some calves and I ran into a bear track," said Bert Rayle, another local resident of long-standing. "That's about the biggest track I'd ever seen." Rayle said it didn't make sense that a large animal such as Bigfoot could live in Benzie County without being discovered. "It's thickly populated enough" and "enough people go hunting in the woods in the area that any big creatures would have been noticed long ago," Rayle claimed. "I roved the woods back when I felt like it, hunting deer," but had never encountered anything in the realm of being strange, he said.

The Bigfoot stories making the rounds at the time "might just upset some women and kids and all, but it don't me," said Douglas Don of Lake Ann, an inhabitant of the area since the 1930s. "I think it's probably a pipe dream," he added. Don admitted the stories had scared his grandson, but hadn't produced anything verifiable. "They're all kind of kidding about it around here. One guy says he hasn't seen it since he quit drinking," offered Don.[1557]

King believed the wilds of Benzie County in northern Michigan was home to at least two Bigfoot creatures. Standard tools of the trade in King's investigation bag included a camera, tape recorder, and smelly items for bait—sardines and mackerel amongst other malodorous morsels. King believed that his investigations would pan out and provide the world with conclusive evidence of Bigfoot's existence. "I feel I am the man who can do it," said King, adding, "I fear nothing."

"You've got to have a certain amount of bone nerve," King said. "Man gets upset when dark sets in . . . the snap of a branch or a shadow on a tree seems to draw an unnerving feeling." By July 1977, King claimed he had evidence of Bigfoot's existence. "We have proven this, we have hard evidence," King said referring to a tape recording of supposed Bigfoot vocals he said were identical to vocals made in the western United States. Unfortunately, the tape ended up as victim to a "Rose Mary Woods" incident (Woods was Nixon's secretary who claimed she accidentally erased five minutes of a taped meeting between Nixon and H. R. Haldeman), succumbing to erasure. Another piece of evidence, turned up by retired Michigan State Police Lt. Zane Gray, was purported Bigfoot feces, found along an old railroad grade in Benzie. King claimed the sample was given over to a wildlife biologist's analysis.

A Millington man named Gray, whose career as a state policeman spanned 26 years, owned and ran a farm implement dealership near Traverse City with his son Dave. During 1977, both father and son built new homes in an isolated part of Benzie County.

> The Grays, who will be Bigfoot heroes if the beast is ever found in the vicinity by King, also uncovered 25 to 30 nineteen-inch footprints outside the newly laid foundation on Dave's construction site.
>
> "They looked like . . ." said the elder Gray, pausing to chuckle the nervous chuckle chuckled by most people when forced to talk seriously about Bigfoot, ". . . They looked like they were made by something that belonged to them."

> In other words, they weren't fake so far as Gray could tell.
>
> Supporting that thesis, Gray noted: "I don't know why anybody would go to the effort to make tracks just for someone to see them."
>
> Gray's wife, [daughter] and grandson all told him they heard the howl of Bigfoot one night, Gray said, [but] he himself missed it.
>
> Despite the mysterious goings-on Gray said he is not especially fearful of the creature, if it exists.
>
> "I've never heard of anybody attributing bodily harm (to a Bigfoot), or even property damage," he said.
>
> (Just to make Gray glance over his shoulder every once in a while, there are stories of Bigfoot vandalism and worse; in fact, sometime early in this century an Oregon Bigfoot allegedly snatched two human pursuers and whomped their frail bodies against tree trunks. The bodies were a gruesome sight, or so the tale goes.)
>
> But if the Benzie episodes are just quackery—Gray is not convinced either way—that would really upset him.
>
> "It would be a dirty trick," he says. "There are some people that are really scared. They won't hardly go out of their homes."
>
> A reporter for the Traverse City *Record-Eagle*, which has done its share of Bigfoot investigating, said reports of Benzie Countyites quaking in their mukluks are "bull."
>
> "It's good copy, for us and for you, but no one is scared of [B]igfoot," he said.[1558]

Skepticism, even pessimism, did not restrain King, who remained enthusiastic about the chance to prove Bigfoot's existence to the world. "I deal only in fact—fantasy destroys," King said. "With 95 to 99 percent of all the reports taken in that are validated, when I ask 'why didn't you report this sooner?' I always get the same answer: 'I don't want to be ridiculed, laughed at, called a hallucinatory.' It's a human thing."

King had considered ways to monetize his interest and leverage the public's amusement and enjoyment with Bigfoot. As reported in the *Detroit Free Press,* he was interested in marketing a Bigfoot doll; a prototype had been fabricated and a manufacturing company contacted. King thought a doll had potential, saying "so many people asked about it, maybe it would be a hot item." King also wanted to dismiss the idea that Bigfoot was only a denizen of the Pacific Northwest and work toward national recognition and protection of Bigfoot. "This is the biggest find of mankind, once this mystery is broken," a serious King said.[1559]

Bob Kurtz—Is There Really a Bigfoot in Michigan?
King was not the only researcher looking into the question of Bigfoot in the Wolverine State.

> Is there REALLY a Michigan Bigfoot?
>
> Before you answer that with a fast "yes" or "no" give some thought to happenings of this week in the northeast portion of Mecosta County near the vast, sprawling Martiny Lake flowage.
>
> Newspaper reporters are cynics by nature and this one is definitely no exception. During the recent whirl of reports of a "Bigfoot" in the Lake Ann area of Benzie County, I scoffed to myself about even the possibility. Any kind of "proof" offered was just too flimsy, I decided, without even looking.[1560]

So wrote Gordon Charles, then the *Record-Eagle's* outdoor editor. He believed the majority of people who heard Bigfoot reports considered the subject to be some kind of joke, as he certainly had. Then his phone rang. It was the evening of Wednesday, September 7, and one of Charles' oldest friends, Gene "Gordie" Little, was on the other end of the line. Little was known for his wildlife films and Charles stated flatly there wasn't "an insincere bone in his body."

Little began, "We've got something down here that I can't figure out. George McClain and I went over to look and as far as we can tell it looks like we've got a real Bigfoot here." Charles knew Little and McClain to be familiar with bears, both having hunted bear with dogs on the Upper Peninsula. "No way this could be a bear," the men told Charles when he talked to them at Barryton the next morning. The tracks were located at Bob and Becky Kurtz's home where the family discovered them Saturday morning. More mysterious tracks were made either Saturday night or Sunday morning.

> Seeking the answer, we visited Bob Kurtz and his wife, Becky. They moved into a little house barely a week ago in a wooded

> portion of Mecosta County, not much more than a mile from where Gene Little lives. Bob finished up a hitch in the Navy recently and the young couple was waiting for promised jobs to open up in Grand Rapids. They will eventually move down there.
>
> The Kurtz home sits near a gravel road. To the left of it is a small apple orchard and a few grapevines hung with luscious purple fruit. Beyond the orchard and grapes is a field which was plowed last Friday by their landlord. The field extends around to the right side of the house.
>
> Bob and Becky have two ferocious watch dogs that are kept tied at the back door. Mandy and Tanya are mixed German shepherd and husky breed and their bared fangs left no doubt that it would be unwise to fool around with them.
>
> Behind the house is a metal trash barrel in which refuse is periodically burned. It sits on a piece of partly-bare ground. It was in that area we found some enormous footprints. I measured them carefully and found them to be 16 ½ inches long and 9 ½ inches wide at the point of greatest width.
>
> There was enough bare, though fairly firm, ground to see where the giant had walked through the yard and past the trash barrel. Most strides were 58 inches apart although there was one of 76 inches where the foot had sunk into the ground 3 ½ inches indicating the creature had lunged ahead suddenly, possibly after being startled. Most other tracks were 1 ½ to 2 inches deep.[1561]

Bob Kurtz walked barefoot through the yard—his feet sank into the earth between ¼ and ½-inches. Kurtz weighed 178 pounds which led Charles to arrive at the weight for the mystery footprints' maker at about 800 pounds. Charles got on his hands and knees and searched for the tell-tale impression of a bear's forefoot, but he found none.

> A hoax? Had a prankster put the prints in the ground with some kind of device, the obvious place to leave them would have been in the freshly-plowed field. There were none there, though. Those footprints on the harder ground would have had to be pounded into the dirt and would have probably been rather perfect. The prints behind the Kurtz home varied according

> to the soil type and it was difficult to find a completely clear, undisturbed track.[1562]

Bob Kurtz cast two tracks and Charles inspected another that had already completed curing. It showed the five toes and the great width of the footprint. The ball of the foot showed two "odd bulges" which Charles attributed to "extra-thick bones in that location." The dogs apparently wanted nothing to do with the creature. Once brought inside they resisted being put outdoors again for two days. "Up until then we have had deer coming into the little orchard in early morning and toward evening," Becky Kurtz said. "They didn't show up for a couple days, either. Something really scared all of them." Becky noted one other quality which she ascribed to their nocturnal visitor—a passion for rotting fruit. "If it's really Bigfoot, though, I know the right bait to trap it," Becky Kurtz continued. "On Friday night I tossed out some partly spoiled peaches and the next morning they were all gone, pits and all!"

> Whatever it was that walked through the Kurtz yard on two different nights left a relatively easy trail to follow for perhaps 60 or 70 feet. In addition to the bare footprints on the mineral soil, there were unmistakable spots where milkweeds had been crushed by something heavy as the visitor had headed off to the left, skirting the plowed field.
>
> Back beyond the field is a huge swamp which is used by deer as a major winter yarding area. It extends for at least 14 miles and is close to impenetrable in spots. Nearly anything could hide in there without any danger of detection.[1563]

Unusual Events in Ohio Spark Imagination

"I see it as a very natural process," said Dr. Anthony G. Greenwald. "Since we were very young children, our parents taught us that everything has to have a cause. When we become adults we conjure up causes for mysterious events that are not immediately explained." Greenwald was a social psychologist at Ohio State; his undergraduate and doctoral work was completed at Yale and Harvard respectively and in 1977 he was the editor of the *Journal of Personality and Social Psychology*.

Joe McKnight's AP article ("Unusual Events in Ohio Spark Imagination," *The Advocate* (May 30, 1977)) focused on Greenwald's reaction and explanation for the unusual events reported in Ohio in the early and mid-1970s, including a Marion County man's 1972 encounter with a seven-foot tall animal whose trailing odor smelled of limburger cheese, a hairy monster roaming the environs northwest of Columbus in 1973, UFO reports that spanned several years, and at the time of the article, the then-recent Allen County sheep kills. Of the latter event, authorities believed the culprits were wild dog packs while Lewis Caverras, an "animal expert" from Xenia, said tracks near the sheep kills were apparently those of a bear.

"I don't understand why some of the explanations become popular," Greenwald said. "Especially those that apparently are dangerous." Greenwald believed level-headed judgment provided rational answers to mysteries. But on occasions when a sensible explanation was wanting for lack of accessible and understandable evidence, people, argued Greenwald, had great capacity for crafting unusual agents to explain their experiences. "When we don't know the cause of a sheep kill we invent a cause that threatens us. Why we invent a threatening cause, social psychologists don't understand." Those threatening causes then, could give modern people meaningful and necessary doses of unease and alarm. "It adds fear to our daily lives that is more dangerous than the evidence demands," Greenwald said. "But there is nothing abnormal about people creating dangerous causes," he added. "It may be a healthy thing. It may keep us on our toes, alert to actual dangers, a reminder to not trust wild animals."

Greenwald compared adoption of unusual, even dangerous causes to conspiracy theories surrounding such events as the assassinations of John and Robert Kennedy and Martin Luther King. "We tend to believe it was a conspiracy and not an isolated incident," Greenwald said, "that the threat is more than just to one immediate victim." Greenwald focused his argument back to events in the Buckeye State: "A farmer in Ohio who decides it may be a monster killing sheep is in the same class with those who believe the King and Kennedy deaths may be a conspiracy."

Greenwald maintained that factors of education level and current lifestyles could affect people's adoption of unusual explanations for unusual events. "The more educated are more likely to come up with different types of explanations," he maintained. "The likelihood of trying to explain something more dangerous than the evidence supports is good regardless of the level of education," Greenwald said. "It may be that the more educated you are the more eager you are to find a cause. But I don't understand the kind of causes that may be invented. Some are picked up and spread by the news media and people adopt them." But what happens when the mundane agent is finally discovered? "When someone finds it is a dog killing sheep and this is documented, the rumors disappear," Greenwald said, "so the degree of belief (in rumors) is no more than moderate and it is dropped when better evidence comes along."[1564]

Believing in Monsters is Good for You

The question of what compels widespread belief in monsters was taken up in a *National Enquirer* article which aggregated responses from prominent scientists and experts including John Napier, Joseph Campbell, and Wayne Suttles.

> People need monsters—mythical creatures like Sasquatch, Nessie of Loch Ness, the Abominable Snowman and Florida's Skunk Ape—say five mythology experts.
>
> "Mythical beasts help to channel our anxieties away from disease, hunger, war and other disasters," said Dr. John Napier, professor of primate biology at the University of London's Birkbeck College.
>
> "They take our minds off things—make us forget our troubles and give us something else to be interested in."
>
> Joseph Campbell, a retired Sarah Lawrence College professor who has written 20 books on mythology and is considered one of the world's top experts on the subject, agreed.
>
> "Monsters make life more pleasant," Campbell said. "They awaken in the individual a sense of awe, even rapture, about the mystery of the universe.
>
> Dr. Gertrude Williams, a clinical child psychologist and a member of the American Psychological Assn., says monsters help to stimulate our imagination. "A belief in monsters represents an existential desire to get beyond the real, drab, predictable, plastic world," Dr. Williams said.
>
> "Whether people find the Loch Ness monster or not, it's the search that is so positive—it means people are dreaming, fantasizing. And fantasy is the seed of creativity. We need fantasies to create."
>
> Dr. Leonard Wolf, professor of English at San Francisco State University and author of books on monsters, said monsters are socially useful. "So long as people are afraid, they'll invent

monsters," he said. "Monsters help people release their fears and are symbols of shared terrors."

Wayne Suttles, a professor in anthropology at Portland State University in Oregon and an authority on the Sasquatch monster, agrees that monsters are reassuring. "When we were little kids we learned about strange creatures and monsters," he said. "Then we grew up and learned that they aren't real—so we gave them up.

"But when we find them again, it's like finding your teddy bear in the attic—it's very reassuring."[1565]

Science Group Hits 'Cults of Unreason'

A group of scientists and science writers formed the Committee for the Scientific Investigation of Claims of the Paranormal (later the Committee for Skeptical Inquiry) which called for action against 'cults of unreason,'—including astrology, the Bermuda Triangle, and Bigfoot. Paul Kurtz, professor of philosophy at the State University of New York, helped found the organization which was formed to counter uncritical support for paranormal claims in the media and in society. At a Tuesday, August 9, press conference, the group said that such beliefs can cause harm and "break down our critical judgement, it may also break down our resistance to new and unforeseen forms of tyranny."

> At its opening volley, co-chairman Paul Kurtz said the committee has filed a complaint with the Federal Communications Commission against NBC, protesting the content of what it called "quasi-documentaries" and films in prime time on Bigfoot, the Outer Space Connection and demonic possession.

NBC's primetime broadcast of *Monsters! Mysteries or Myths?* and *Bigfoot, The Mysterious Monster* had occurred earlier in 1977. Such fare poured "a steady torrent of paranormal claims into the marketplace." The Committee called for cooperation with the scientific community to offer a "more responsible balanced treatment of claims of the paranormal."[1566]

Psychic Aids Bigfoot Search

Bigfoot enthusiast Patrick Macey explored the Bigfoot phenomenon in the 1970s with an enthusiastic cadre of amateur investigators. Macey was profiled in a series of *Valley News* articles by June and Paul Hospodar in May and June 1977. "Patrick J. Macey is a talented amateur who has been on Bigfoot's trail for years and he thinks that maybe there is a link between Bigfoot and UFOs."[1567] With that introduction, the Hospodars began an obviously admiring series of stories that portrayed Macey as a proletarian and passionate Bigfoot investigator.

> Macey has no degrees to offer as proof that he knows what he's talking about, he's no scientist, he's just a working stiff like the rest of us, but he is intelligent, not given to hallucination and he is educated about Bigfoot. He knows that ordinary citizens like him can be and have been an enormous help to those leading the search for Bigfoot.[1568]

In their profile of Macey, the Hospodars wrote that he had been a Reconnaissance Marine in Vietnam.

> He was in the jungles in 1967 when Marines saw what they presumed was one of their choppers trying to come in for a landing, hovering above them, landing lights blazing, so they went to help. Suddenly the 'chopper' veered away, straight up and out of sight in seconds. That it was not a chopper was obvious. Just what it was, no one would say. Macey learned a healthy lesson. People do not like to talk about something they do not understand![1569]

After his service in the Marine Corps, Macey returned to civilian life and found employment with a telephone company and returned to school. One day at work, Macey's wife called from their Topanga Canyon home. She agitatedly complained that a hairy hippie was staring at her. Macey reassured her and headed for home.

> He found his wife quaking and shaking. Seems she had taken another look at the hairy hippie and saw that he was a bit too large to be one of their neighbors—unless they happened to be second cousins to King Kong. This gent was big! And hairy! And he stank, stank, stank! By this time, Macey had been doing some very in depth studying about Bigfoot and related phenomena and he recognized this somewhat classic description of him. Outside the house, he looked around for

> further evidence of who or what his wife had seen. There was nothing that could be called conclusive except that feeling that something extraordinary had been there, looking into his home in the middle of civilization![1570]

Macey joined together with other fans of unusual phenomena—Gary Smith, Larry Wetterland, and Jeff Perry to form "The Understanding Inc., Unit #85—Research and Investigation of UFO, Bigfoot and Related Phenomena." One of the group's first undertakings into the field was to a place called "Lost Creek Canyon" in the Los Padres National Forest and where campers had seen "apes with belts."

> After interviewing reliable witnesses Macey and Wetterland decided to go into the canyon and see for themselves. Neither young man is stupid, so they went prepared, with a good, sturdy truck, cameras, lights, sleeping gear and high powered rifles—just in case. The truck was driven into the canyon and nothing much happened until suddenly, both men became frightened, not a little scared, but very unexplainably panicked. Macey swept the spotlight of the car along the brush at the side of the road trying to find out why. All at once, the light fell across a giant shape with glowing, orange eyes. Could it be they were looking at Bigfoot? They started, scared as they were, and he stood quite still, staring right back.
>
> Macey realized that he had his rifle near at hand but fear was so real, so electrifying that he couldn't have reached for it if he had wanted to. They heard the creature breathing they were so close and they smelled that awful stench! And then, on the quiet road in the middle of nowhere, they heard another sound that compounded their fear and made sweat break out on their foreheads. The sound of heavy footfalls behind them. Another Bigfoot was coming up on them from behind and the fear they felt was overpowering. [They] climbed into the truck and took off. About a mile down the road they felt almost normal and when Macey saw a recently uprooted Yucca tree, he tossed it into the truck and they took it to a woman psychic when they got home. She described exactly what they had seen beside the road. But she added a blockbuster. The creature which uprooted this plant was not of this planet![1571]

June and Paul Hospodar called the dread the men had experienced as a "zone of fear," and speculated Bigfoot could use it for defending itself. During a subsequent field outing in Angeles National Forest the men again experienced "unreasoning panic." After an uneasy night, they woke feeling drained and discovered several three-toed prints of enormous size around their camp as they packed up their gear.

> This time there had been no smell, no sound—but there was that zone of fear. Carefully they took plaster casts of the fresh prints that had certainly not been there the evening before and knew that Bigfoot had been there, watching them that night. He had done them no harm—was he just protecting himself and his family?[1572]

Macey believed that Bigfoot could so mentally boggle a person within the zone of fear that actual "damage to the minds of those people" could occur.[1573]

Oregon had long been known as a hot spot for Bigfoot encounters. But if a group had a limited amount of time, where would the best location be to visit in the hopes of laying eyes on the creature? That was the question Macey put to a young woman psychic (The Hospodars did not indicate if this was the same woman who had pronounced upon Macey's Yucca tree) with a precedent of working with police to locate criminals. Enlisting her help in a 1977 Bigfoot expedition, Macey laid out a map of Oregon and overlaid it with a plain piece of paper, effectively masking the map underneath. The psychic laid her hands on the plain paper, and based upon her psychic cues, informed the group of the locations at which they had the best chance of a sighting. The psychic predicted a gathering storm that was driving Bigfoot down from the higher elevations.

Armed with their psychic-identified hot spots, Macey along with like-minded Bigfoot enthusiasts headed to Oregon in May to search for Bigfoot. After passing Mt. Shasta and entering Oregon, the group paused in their northward trek to visit with Jean Fitzgerald, claimant to several Bigfoot sightings and at the time reportedly engaged in writing a manuscript for publication about her experiences. The group continued on and stopped at a particular location indicated earlier by the psychic. For Macey, this was not his first foray into Oregon to search for Bigfoot. During their first day the weather turned rainy (seemingly in line with the psychic's prediction), but undaunted, the group hiked into their mountainous surroundings to search for evidence of Bigfoot. They slogged over muddy trails and through dense cover for several days before making a discovery. Bones of a recently deceased deer were found near a stream. The bones had been separated into two neat piles and cleaned entirely of their meat. Macey kept the skull and upon their return to California, showed it to their psychic friend. She "read" it and relayed a frightening tale told from the deer's perspective of being hunted. The hunter was a large shape which "blocked out the sun," she said.[1574]

Psychics could also be counted on for colorful explanations as to the nature of Bigfoot and its origins.

> Says Dr. Joseph Jeffers, U.S. seer: "Bigfoot resulted from genetic experiments by the people of Atlantis 7,000 years ago."
>
> Now, says Dr. Jeffers: "Bigfoot becomes increasingly restless as the poles of the earth shift back to the position held at the time of Atlantis."
>
> Speaking of Bigfoot, Dr. Jeffers says: "Bigfoot is very real. The people of Atlantis were very advanced in the study of genes and life at that time. They crossed the genes of the people of Atlantis who were very tall with the genes of animals and Bigfoot was one of the result."

Atlantis, Jeffers predicted, was going to return from the depths to which it sank. "The ocean floor is rising in many places. Atlantis is coming up again."

> Now, says Dr. Jeffers, Bigfoot is restless. He feels the changes in the earth's position and his ancestral memory tells him that Atlantis is about to reappear. Instinct tell this half-human creature that mankind today is bent on the same self-destructive course that sent Atlantis to its doom.[1575]

Top Psychics Comment on Bigfoot

National Enquirer psychics Clarissa Bernhardt, Bill O'Hara, and Mickie Dahne were asked in 1977 for their professional comments on some of the world's most baffling mysteries, including Bigfoot. All three agreed Bigfoot was harmless. "This creature isn't a scary monster," said Dahne. "It's just a big, big monkey. He's nothing to be afraid of." Bernhardt felt Bigfoot and science would have a coming *tête-à-tête*. "In the coming year Bigfoot will be captured and found to be a kind of ape, sensitive and not harmful." O'Hara made it a hat trick of psychics envisaging a peaceful Bigfoot: "I see nothing harmful about Bigfoot—but I have strong psychic impressions that he is of a breed similar to the Yeti or Abominable Snowman. I feel that there are many of them in high regions throughout the world, and they are simply watching us." O'Hara added, "I foresee this mystery is going to be solved very soon."[1576]

Barbara Ann Slate

Of 1,356 American Astronomical Society (AAS) members who responded in 1977 to a questionnaire from Professor Peter A. Sturrock, an astrophysicist at Stanford's Applied Physics Department, four-fifths believed UFOs "certainly," "probably," or "possibly" deserved scientific study. Only about 20 percent felt UFOs were not worthy of scientific scrutiny and attention.[1577]

Barbara Ann Slate, author of several magazine articles and the 1976 book, *Bigfoot*, did find UFOs meriting attention; she began investigating the connection between Bigfoot and UFOs as early as 1974 (see Chapter 5) in her August 1974 *Saga* article, "The Strange Link Between UFOs and Bigfoot." Her article in the October 1977 *UFO Report* included the psychic phenomena of mind-to-mind communication which she believed she had directly experienced with a female Bigfoot.

> For this writer, the introduction to the Bigfoot creature came in such a manner as to eliminate any instinctive fears I may have harbored. Also one continual question kept nagging me: What was the female creature attempting to relate?
>
> With no preconceived notions on the subject, I took off for the small town of Pearblossom, which borders the western edge of the Mojave Desert in California, to interview several Bigfoot witnesses about a recent sighting. It was early in 1974, a crisp, clear day that made the mental image that much more vivid in my mind. Not at all given to this type of contact, I can only describe it as looking at a picture on a color television set of intense clarity.
>
> The face had a yellowish-tan, wrinkled, leathery skin. The eyes were black and piercing; ape-like but gentle, they looked directly into mine. Her shoulder-length hair was unkempt and

stringy. The color seemed to blend with the skin tone. I had no doubt that the "vision" or mental transference was of a female, as she held an infant of the same species in her arms. It was pathetically thin and with that same peculiar leathery look to the skin. No words were exchanged. It was just a crystal clear image of a woman holding a child but it invoked great feelings of sorrow within me. Somehow, for some reason, she seemed to be asking me for help . . . but why?

The answer to that question has taken years of research, countless letters sent to all parts of the country, and many hundreds of hours spent in tape-recording eyewitness accounts. It was necessary to gain the confidence of those persons who would otherwise be reluctant to reveal similar experiences for fear of appearing slightly "balmy." To observe and report these hair-covered behemoths is slowly becoming acceptable and credible; to admit to having them telepathically talk for you is quite another matter.[1578]

Peter Guttilla on Bigfoot and UFOs

For author Peter Guttilla, Bigfoot and UFOs were entwined, related subjects. From the June 1977 *UFO Report:*

> The expanding list of UFO-Bigfoot sightings is much too lengthy to be contained in the space of a single article. Nevertheless, there's little doubt that the "[B]igfoot controversy" has acquired many added dimensions since Jerry Crew's 1958 discovery of giant tracks in northern California. Where there are colossal, smelly, hairy, two-legged creatures, there are UFOs![1579]

In the same article, Guttilla pedagogically poses several questions concerning the perceived relationship between Bigfoot and UFOs.

> The big question now is which came first? Is Bigfoot the desperate survivor of a bygone era whose only mistake is being in the wrong place at the wrong time? Have the elusive monsters become the unwitting slaves of ultra-advanced extraterrestrials? Are the giant anthropoids themselves from some distant or

> dying planet? Today, research files are bulging with tales of Sasquatch-like nightstalkers from the Everglades of Florida and New Jersey's Kittatinny Mountains, to the swamps of Arkansas and the deserts of the southwest. Together with the monster mania, a once murky "guilt by association" link to UFOs is rapidly crystallizing into a complicated image of complicity. What role does our government play in the scenario? What about the perennial, irresistible suggestion that the military knows more than it is revealing?[1580]

Santa Ana Register staff writer Cheryl Pruett interviewed Guttilla for an article which begins with a Bigfoot investigation which the researcher and his team was engaged in and the oddness, other than Bigfoot, that he encountered.

> It was too still. Peter Guttilla had been awakened abruptly in the middle of the night while camping in the wilderness of northwestern California.
>
> The trap he had set for whatever might move around the perimeter of his camp area had worked. The earthquake sensors picked up movement; bells were triggered by whatever moved in the wooded darkness.
>
> Guttilla ran from his tent with camera in hand and tape recorder dangling from his neck.[1581]

Reflecting on the 1975 incident, Guttilla described to Pruett what he experienced next. "I didn't like the feel," said Guttilla. "I had this feeling to look into a certain part of the darkness—like a compulsion." Looking over, Guttilla couldn't make out anything out of the ordinary. "It's as if something had been looking at me, but I couldn't see it. Then a little red light came out and hovered over me. I got three photographs. Then the light shot away—rapidly." Footprints had turned up around their campsite, and some of the sensors Guttilla had employed had been lifted and carried off. "There was no evidence of bear tracks or other animals. At that point we couldn't conclude anything. Nocturnal lights such as the red light that hovered over me constitute one form of UFO." Guttilla told Pruett the evidence hinted at a correlation between Bigfoot and UFOs. "It is an associative factor we can't ignore. This incident might infer there is a connection between Big Foot and UFOs." One of Guttilla's earliest experience with paranormal events occurred on a Wisconsin farm when he was five and he observed an object hover above a nearby hilltop. As Guttilla, then 33, told Pruett, "something clicked," and he would go on to investigate subjects like Bigfoot and write books about the unknown and the paranormal. At the time of Pruett's article, Guttilla averaged four month-long trips a year, usually with at least two companions. "I planned it out from the beginning to have time to do this, to support myself and pursue this," Guttilla said. Guttilla had worked in an industrial chemical company and in 1977 was venturing into writing and screen work with Spiegel/Bergman Productions. Pruett wrote that a book Guttilla was working on, "Far Side of Forever," would, as of her writing, soon be published. According to Guttilla there were 100 members in an organization he had formed, the Western Society for Exploration of the Unexplained. Though not necessarily scientists, Guttilla said members were professional people, with background and experience to further research and knowledge on the subjects they explored. "Reading a few books isn't enough," he said.

Guttilla explained the Western Society's purpose was not to prove things like Bigfoot and UFOs were real, but to collect evidence and attempt communication. "We want to keep track of the state of things so that eventually we might piece the puzzle together and match wits with these phenomena. So far, they've beaten us at every game." Guttilla claimed a Bigfoot sighting in 1973 while camping on Sierra Paloma in the Angeles National Forest. "It was early in the morning. There were five other people with me. Then all of a sudden, Bigfoot appeared. He was within 200 feet of us. He was about eight feet tall and dirty beige." The abruptness of Bigfoot's appearance caught Guttilla off guard. "I was completely unprepared after all the years of investigating. I stood there dumbfounded." The creature simply walked away.

Guttilla argued for an open mind and willingness to try new experiences as keys to investigating paranormal subjects. "We are conditioned to perceive the world a certain way," he stated. "It's definitely a perception problem. We see things we only think we should see." "Don't be afraid to get your shoes dirty. If you have an experience you will think twice before getting too critical of those who say they see something.[1582]

Gray Barker

Gray Barker's March 1977 *UFO Report* article contains several international incidents of "victims attacked by reptile-like slime creatures, Bigfoot, flying

'Mothmen,' and violent hairy dwarfs." Barker included the Van Acker case from 1965, writing that just before the encounter, Van Acker's car engine suddenly stopped and the headlights went out. Barker also wrote up the Wetzel case from 1958 in which 24-year-old Charles Wetzel said he encountered a monster on Saturday, November 8, while he was crossing the Santa Ana river on North Main Street near Riverside, California. "It didn't have any ears. The face was all round with two eyes shining like something fluorescent and a protuberant mouth," Wetzel reportedly said in his report to sheriff's deputies. "It was scaly—not like fish scales, but like leaves."[1583]

> As the "thing" approached the car it made a gurgling sound ("like the noise you make when you gargle") mixed with a high pitched scream.
>
> Wetzel, momentarily stunned, wondered what he should do as the creature stood in front of his car, peering at him with its luminous eyes. Then it made a grab for him, its arms reaching *the full length of the automobile hood* as if it were not aware of the windshield. Wetzel described the creature's "webbed hands" as—"Something like those of a bird."
>
> As the thing reached for him, Wetzel jerked backwards in his seat. At the same time he grabbed a target pistol he had been using earlier that day. He took quick aim but didn't fire. If he missed, the windshield, his only protection, would be shattered. He was afraid to roll down the side window. Then he took the next logical action, put the car into low gear and stomped on the gas pedal. He rammed the creature, knocking it down and under the car. He heard the bottom of the car scrape the body as he ran over it.
>
> "Did it get up after you ran over it?" I asked.
>
> "Buddy, I wasn't interested in whether it got up or not—I was only thinking of getting out of there!" was his reply, carefully quoted in my notes.
>
> Wetzel then drove to the nearest police station and reported the frightening encounter. Although reluctant to revisit the scene he accompanied two officers in a patrol car back to the site. The three inspected the road carefully but could find no signs at the spot where the creature had been run down.
>
> Then one of the officers shined his light at the edge of the highway and made a strange discovery. It was an almost

> circular depression in the soft earth, about 10 inches in diameter, with the suggestion of "toes" or appendages around the circumference, giving the distinct image of a webbed foot! Inspecting the river bank the men found three other similar indentions, though they were not as clear. The evidence indicated that whatever the unnamed horror was, it probably had emerged from the river and escaped back into its muddy depths.[1584]

Deputies were initially inclined to believe Wetzel had befallen the antics of a mischief-maker wearing a Halloween costume. However, officials received 28 calls Monday, November 10, from people reporting their own sightings of the creature. "I guess we'll have to make another search for it," a deputy said. "It seems like everybody's seen it but us."[1585]

Sheriff's Sgt. E. R. Holmes speculated Wetzel experienced a close encounter with a vulture which may have flopped down onto the hood of Wetzel's automobile. "Sometimes cars hit them when they're in the road eating rabbits cars have killed," Holmes said. Holmes searched the area of Wetzel's sighting on Sunday, November 9. "But," he said, "I didn't even find a feather."[1586]

Barker was surprised by the apparent lack of intelligence displayed by the creature. Barker asked Wetzel if he made any connection between UFOs and the creature. (Barker's research determined there had been UFO sightings in the Riverside area prior to Wetzel's encounter.) "If you think this thing may have come from another planet you're all wrong. It just didn't act intelligently. People from other planets would be smarter than this thing!"

> Thinking of other cases of physical attack, I remember Bigfoot, a huge, hairy, ape-like creature with glowing eyes which utters a pitiful, baby-like wailing. The creature has chalked up an impressive list of eyewitness appearances in recent years. These sightings have been documented by veteran UFO investigators, who have also noted the consistent creature pattern: Bigfoot is definitely UFO-related.
>
> Complementing the horror of its sudden appearance, usually when an unsuspecting housewife peers out a window on a dark night to meet its Peeping-Tom stare, is a sickening odor connected with the mysterious entity—described, almost universally by witnesses, as smelling like rotten eggs, probably

> "rotten egg gas" (hydrogen sulphide) which in concentration is poisonous and could represent an explanation of the illness of dogs that have gotten too close to the creatures.
>
> Although UFO researchers can list no substantiated reports of physical attacks by Bigfoot on humans, most of them have overlooked a little-known case from May 1956.
>
> I was intrigued by the case. To me it presented credibility for three principal reasons: 1) The victims had no opportunity to read about Bigfoot cases; 2) Their descriptions of the creature, complete with its odor, fitted perfectly with the hundreds of sightings to be reported 20 years later; 3) The late astrophysicist Dr. Morris K. Jessup had the opportunity to interview the witnesses in depth during a Michigan lecture tour and supplied me with his notes.[1587]

Barker referred to the 1956 account of the "Marshall Bigfoot," an incident which occurred near the small agricultural community of Marshall, Michigan.

> Is the Green-Eyed Monster of Wilder Creek fact or Fiction?
>
> Most reports of hairy monsters or little men from Mars are laughed at; but authorities caution skeptics, reminding them that the stranger-than-fiction tale of a half-man, half-animal was proven valid about 15 years ago in this area.
>
> And now comes the present-day story of a 10-feet-tall hairy monster with glowing green eyes "big as light bulbs."
>
> When initial reports of the Wilder Creek monster filtered out nearly a month ago, it touched off whispers which have carried across Calhoun county. The whispers have resulted in a twisting of the original report; the area where "it" allegedly was spotted has been changed; the nationality of the men who were picked up by the snarling beast has been altered, and at least one person wrote the entire tale off as a figment of some child's imagination, spurred by a TV program.
>
> But three Marshall-area young men will swear that their story is not fiction; one was so shocked by the event he broke down and cried.
>
> It happened on a Saturday night about a month ago when brothers Herman and Philip Williams, part-Indian, and their

> friend, Otto Collins, 20, a full-blooded Indian, returned home from dates in Marshall. The three stopped off at a local restaurant for a cup of coffee and then drove their 1949 model car to their home, southeast of Marshall, just past Wilder Creek.[1588]

The young men enjoyed sitting in front of their abode talking late into the night, but this night a freak thunderstorm broke and the temperature was lower than usual, and the trio decided to retire early.

> The time was about 11:30 P.M. Philip, 17, stepping outside the one-story building for a breath of fresh air, saw "something big" and ran to tell the other two. While Herman, 20, searched for a shotgun, Otto and Philip went outside.[1589]

The overcast sky after the rain made the scene very dark. A faint glow from a kerosene lamp inside the shack was their only illumination. A broken tree felled by the storm was attributed as the cause of Herman's fright and other than a peculiar odor in the area, nothing else unusual was noted.

> "Evidently, it was behind us," Philip said. He told of feeling arms wrapping around him and of thinking it was his friend "fooling around." Then he felt himself being hoisted off the ground.
>
> "We couldn't see it—it was dark. It had big green eyes, that we could tell," he said. "The eyes were big as light bulbs; they were enough to scare you to death!"
>
> Herman, who couldn't find the gun, ran to his car when he heard screams. "I was doing his (Otto's) share of screaming," Philip said, explaining that Otto "couldn't scream: It choked him."[1590]

Herman heard the yells and forgetting the search for his shotgun ran outside. "I've never heard anybody scream like that—I thought it must be the devil dragging them down to Hell!"

> Herman, running out of the building, saw the object toting the two, who have a combined weight of at least 300 pounds, down a dirt road that leads off the Homer road, past the front door of the house and through a "village" of some 22 huts.

> He flicked on the car lights and turned the car around. When the lights hit the monster, it veered from the flat stretch of ground surrounding the eastern end of the house, and brushed a table, losing its balance and its grip on Otto (tucked under one arm while the animal covered Philip's face with its other paw), who landed in an upright position.[1591]

Finding himself released, Otto's fear turned to anger, and he rushed the creature.

> Philip credited Otto who pushed the beast, causing it to lose its balance again, releasing Philip—with saving his life.
>
> "It stood there and watched us; probably wondered what we were," Philip recalled.[1592]

The creature gave the appearance of being confused and frustrated and then "ambled off in a sort of stumbling, sidewise motion" into the enveloping blackness of the forest. "We grabbed Philip and lifted him to his feet and he came to. We dragged him inside and propped a bed against the door."[1593] A pervasive rotten-egg smell clung to Otto and Philip, apparently from their contact with the creature. According to Barker, the pair would later end up burning their clothes in an effort to rid the area of the persistent smell.

> The three described their experience to their employer, who informed sheriff's deputies.
>
> So frightened were the young men that they vacated their three-room residences and now occupy one room. The day after the event occurred, the 22-hut village was deserted.
>
> "I think it just wanted us," Philip theorized. "It could have killed us if it had wanted to."
>
> Do the brothers, who have lived near Marshall for eight years, believe in monsters?
>
> "Heck, no!" But we saw something," Herman reported. "I don't know what it was but we saw something," his brother agreed.[1594]

The young men were not able to make precise descriptions of the creature, but Barker noted they agreed the thing that attacked them was covered in thick hair and stood about eight feet tall. Otto, who remained conscious during the attack, maintained the creature was remarkably strong. "It had big green eyes," Otto reported, "and they were as big as light bulbs." Those large eyes created an indelible impression. "They were enough to scare you to death!"[1595]

> The trio took a dog to the area the first part of the week following the incident. It appeared nervous when they kicked at what appeared to be footprints in the grass.
>
> Sheriff's deputies, who might be expected to scoff at reports of monsters, nevertheless sat with sawed-off shotguns in the area for three nights, but found no trace of the green-eyed monster.
>
> Following the first report, a wave of similar stories cropped up. One man told friends in the Wilder Creek area that he too had spotted "something" the previous night; an area farmer told friends his cow had been clawed to death by something mysterious, but investigating officers were unable to locate him.
>
> Is there such a monster? Some may recall a similar tale of a few years back being debunked by Charlotte police, who learned that boys had dressed up with an animal skin.
>
> But three young men, who were frightened to tears, are convinced it exists.[1596]

The astrophysicist Morris K. Jessup had interviewed several witnesses to the Marshall Bigfoot affair and subsequently shared his notes with Barker.

> Unfortunately Dr. Jessup had little time in his busy lecture schedule to gather other possible reports in the area, and none of the scientific UFO groups had a chapter in the area to investigate the incident in depth. However, a search through the files of *The Marshall Evening Chronicle*, which carried a brief news item on the case, reveals what we now know as the usual pattern: Although there was no spectacular UFO "flap," there were three reports of strange lights in the skies two days prior to the incident, and on the following day a short item briefly noted a mysterious aircraft flying low over a suburban area without sound. Although this is explained as "a prank by

> boys with kites," it is unfortunate that this explanation, which sounds so traditional from the school of UFO debunkers, was not subjected to skilled investigation.[1597]

Referring not only Bigfoot but the wide panoply of aggressive, possibly hostile creatures peppering the reports in his files, Barker asked, "If interplanetary, are the creatures coming from a number of different worlds? Do their physical structures adhere to a logical model which would indicate the most likely type to evolve successfully into machine-using civilizations?"[1598]

Rounding out his article, Barker references journalist and paranormal researcher John Keel for additional thoughts on Bigfoot and other unusual creatures' linkage to UFOs.

> John Keel has theorized that the ufonauts may release experimental animals for environmental testing, to disguise the real physical nature of the occupants, or for other unknown reasons. If Keel is correct, such lower life forms would unlikely be armed.
>
> The seemingly illogical actions of UFO "monsters" could represent, still borrowing from Keel's many creative ideas, clever ploys to confuse us as to their purposes as well as physical appearances.[1599]

Barker reveals his own, no-less creative theories touching on aggressive creature encounters, thwarted abduction attempts, and missing persons. His article paints a picture of UFOs and associated non-human creatures as complex subjects demanding attention:

> Or could some of the Ufonauts represent a group of retarded escapees from some interplanetary institution, who have somehow seized complex technological devices they do not know how to use properly? Are we being visited by dangerous ignoramuses? Or, like the late Richard Shaver's "dero," could the visitors represent a degenerate race which has discovered the ancient "mech" of a long-vanished technological society, begun pushing buttons and learned some limited mastery of the devices—in Shaver's theory, deep within the bowels of the Earth?

> Instead of incredible theories, I would prefer to give you answers—if I had them. I am not trying to explain the UFO mystery—no researcher, including myself, has been able to do that after almost 30 years of study.
>
> Dr. Donald Menzel, Harvard astrophysicist, can explain away some UFOs as natural phenomena. Avant garde thinkers such as Dr. Jacques Vallee can give us sociological and mythological data. Spiritualists can "contact" them and convince some of us the UFOs are designed by some kind of genius in the ["spirit world!"] John Keel can fit them into a sub- or supra- physical spectrum of mysterious radiations. And none of these theories should be dismissed without consideration. After all, many capable and renowned scientists have attacked the problem and failed to solve it.
>
> With these cases involving physical attacks by non-human creatures I hope that I have conveyed that there is no simplistic solution to the UFO mystery, and that it represents a vast, complex problem.
>
> Finally I urge you to view the mystery from a more personal level. I have dealt here with unsuccessful or thwarted attacks or attempted abductions by non-human creatures.
>
> . . . Every year thousands of people disappear in the U.S. alone and are never seen again. True, many of them turn up eventually; a majority are runaway kids, and some are fleeing nagging wives, brutal husbands, and interfering mothers-in-law. . . . What if Charles Wetzel had not flattened the horror with his car?
>
> Do the lists of missing persons include those living in interplanetary zoos?
>
> The next victim could be YOU—with no fortunate circumstances to ward off the horror![1600]

Members of Cleveland's Tri-County UFO Study Group, which was celebrating its 25th year in 1977, found a natural congruence between Bigfoot and UFOs as evidenced by their open-to-the-public monthly meeting on Saturday, March 12, at North Benton's Lakeside Pines Restaurant. Effie Glover, "group research co-ordinator," gave a presentation on Bigfoot. Paul J. L. Rozich described recent Bigfoot sightings that occurred on March 7 at 1 A.M. and March 8 at 9:30 P.M. on a rural road between Alliance and

Sebring. Pat Kaforey gave a slideshow presentation geared more toward UFOs but recounted a Bigfoot case from northern Ohio then under investigation concerning three youths shooting at a Bigfoot-like creature in early March.[1601]

Writing for the *Christian Science Monitor,* Robert C. Cowen referred to Sturrock's survey of 1,356 American Astronomical Society members which revealed 80% of the respondents felt UFOs deserved scientific study or possibly deserved scientific study. Only 13% of the 1,356 questioned members thought they could see a way to effectively conduct that necessary study.

> It is understandable that scientists don't want to waste time on a subject they consider unrewarding. But without the social pressure of scoffing colleagues or the off-putting gullibility of believers, some scientists might begin to think of new ways to tackle it.[1602]

Pat Morrison Talks about Strange Events

Pat Morrison, who in the previous chapter gave a talk on Bigfoot to the Monessen, Pennsylvania, Rotary Club in 1976, wrote "Adventures into the Unexplained," published in the *Oil City Derrick* on May 4, 1977. Though her article did not specifically mention Bigfoot, several characteristics Morrison described therein are shared with some Bigfoot encounters, especially those which specifically include mention of UFOs.

As Morrison relates, on August 15, 1973, a family in Greensburg were busy with fall household chores. Mrs. Grogan told her eight-year-old son, Danny, to use care while burning household trash in the back yard. Ten minutes later, Mrs. Grogan heard her son scream and fearing his clothing may have caught fire she ran toward the back yard. Arriving at his side, Danny launched into an explanation of what had terrified him.

> "I piled everything into the wire basket and started the fire. I watched it for a few minutes till it was really burning, then I looked up and saw a man standing there on the other side. He was dressed in black.
>
> "He had on a long, black coat and a black hat. He was just standing there staring at me. He didn't say anything. Then he started moving slowly toward me. But the way he looked at me . . ."

Mrs. Grogan put her arms around the child, and they went to the trailer where he repeated the story to his father. Concerned and angered over what he thought was a cruel joke, Grogan called his brother, Carl, who lived next door.

Armed with guns the two men began a search through the heavily wooded area behind the trailers. They found nothing, and they were unable to account for the lingering, nostril-burning, chemical stench that hovered over the lower end of the yard.

Mr. Grogan felt it was quite similar to that of sulphuric acid, yet not quite the same.

Later that evening, Carl noticed the odor again as he walked into the kitchen. He looked out the window, thinking perhaps the man in black may have returned. He heard heavy, labored breathing for quite some time around the window, but when he stepped out there wasn't a thing in sight.

He looked around the trailer home and noticed the grass under the kitchen window had been trampled, indicating something or someone had been there.

Immediately he called the state police who were all too familiar with such incidents and conducted their own investigation.

While there, they heard a crying sound coming from the direction of an adjacent orchard. The police looked everywhere and still found nothing.

There was no man in black, no creature and, strangest of all, not even a single print. They just shook their heads in disbelief and wrote it up as another "episode."

The next evening, Carl and his brother were relaxing on the porch when the same sound—similar to that of a baby cry—was heard from the nearby orchard.

Results of a search were the same as before—nothing.[1603]

Tom Bearden

Louisiana native and retired Army colonel Tom Bearden pursued his paranormal interests from Huntsville, Alabama, where he worked as an air defense tactician with Control Data Systems. Bearden suggested that the public's fear of ridicule prevented the reporting of about 90 per cent of unusual, paranormal incidents. Therefore the number of submitted reports suggested they were only the tip of the iceberg of a phenomena Bearden defined as "lying somewhere in between the purely physical and purely mental." Bearden aspired to develop and hone a scientific theory to holistically explain paranormal data. "UFOs have been seen by probably 40 million people in this country," Bearden said. "Most of the UFO people are trying to prove a conclusion that they have already reached. They assume that a bunch of young stalwarts on planet X which circles star Y are getting beered up on Sunday afternoons, hopping in the old space jalopy and motoring over to planet earth to jolly up the natives."

> But the extraterrestrial explanation just won't fit the facts, he argues. To incorporate such things as UFOs, bigfeet and various other psychic goings on into science, he is elaborating a new theory, much as Einstein developed the theory of relativity to explain certain observations that would not fit into the standard Newtonian physics.
>
> Most of the theoretical groundwork has already been completed by physicists and mathematicians around the world. Bearden claims that he is just using their work to explain what he has observed.

Reporter Julian Godwin's article in the *Athens News Courier* noted two groups in Alabama dedicated to the study of paranormal events, one of which had been founded by Bearden and the other by Dr. Joseph Slate:

> At least two groups have been formed for the study of paranormal phenomena in North Alabama. The Parapsychological Research, of which Dr. Joe Slate at Athens State College is the president, was formed in 1972. It includes 500 on its mailing lists with an active membership of 140, most in in North Alabama.
>
> "The basic idea is to explore, study and arrive at explanations for now unexplained phenomena," says Slate. Guest speakers to the group have included well known psychic Jeanne Dixon.
>
> The American Association of Meta-Science is a non-profit research group recently formed by Bearden, and others, among them several psychics and trained scientists.
>
> Both groups have plans to expand their investigative efforts in the area. Slate has recently concluded a successful research

> project on Kirlian photography for the U.S. Army. This is just one of a number of phenomena which may be physically detected, but for which no completely acceptable scientific explanation has yet been advanced.

Bearden, himself a holder of a Master's Degree in Nuclear Engineering at Georgia Tech, hoped to expand his group's services to provide trained investigative teams to work with those who experienced unusual events, "without harassing or ridiculing them, treating them seriously, like adults." Bearden estimated he spent about $5,000 a year purchasing books and photographs and collecting testimonies and interviews. "We're not interested in pranks or obviously unbalanced people who need psychiatric treatment," he said. Bearden believed that contributions from mainstream science, such as from physics and mathematics, could help explain paranormal occurrences. "We will bring a lot of scientific brainpower to bear," he said. "We have something going on of fantastic magnitude that none of our ordinary scientific institutions are set up to deal with."

Of Bigfoot, Bearden told Godwin there had been three independent hairy hominid reports between Huntsville and Decatur during the last six months of 1977. Bearden believed Bigfoot displayed metaphysical qualities which classified it alongside UFOs and ESP.

> Casts have frequently been taken of its footprints. It breaks branches off trees and uproots bushes as it crashes through the woods.
>
> "But you can't run it down with dogs, it can't be tracked, no one has ever found a dead or drowned one, the bones of one, or its lair," says Bearden. "It's physically real, sometimes, but of a different kind of reality than we are used to thinking of."
>
> Bearden hopes that if enough people will come forward with their stories, and their experiences are taken seriously but critically, the true nature of UFO's, ESP, clairvoyance, [B]igfoot and many other phenomena can be established.
>
> When this is done, he envisions vast new horizons of knowledge opening up to man, knowledge which may provide solutions to such plaguing questions as the energy crisis, the cold war, cancer and interstellar travel.[1604]

Vestigia

In 1976, frequent SITU contributor Robert Jones of Stanhope, New Jersey, and Dr. C. Louis Wiedemann, a dentist from Hackettstown, New Jersey, co-founded a paranormal research group they named Vestigia which they described as an organization dedicated to pursuing an assortment of mysterious enigmas, including Bigfoot.[1605] Wiedemann told the *Lebanon Daily News* the story behind the group's name: "The word vestigial is Latin, meaning 'footprint.' But it's also the root of the English word 'investigate.' We kind of liked that double meaning."[1606]

In September 1976, Robert Jones interviewed a woman in Morris County, New Jersey, for her account of the large "dark form" she saw in her yard. Jones shared the account with Vestigia member Jack Mazzuchelli who investigated the scene on September 9, 1976, and discovered 17-inch-long tracks. Wiedemann told the *Lebanon Daily News* that the prints were not quite good enough for casting, but photographs were taken to record them. Mazzuchelli followed the tracks, which showed a stride of some five to six feet, from the woman's back yard to about a quarter mile back into the brush to a point where they disappeared into a pocket of thick bramble. Mazzuchelli noted the thorny branches appeared to have been pushed apart and the underbrush was trampled down, much as if something quite large had passed through it.

Wiedemann said this was the same area where residents in September had seen strange white lights in the night sky. In Hackettstown a man and his son watched a "glowing transparent ball" on September 12 which gave the impression of "a kind of cage or bars inside." Neither the father nor his son could determine the actual size of the object or estimate its distance. According to Wiedemann, reports of glowing orbs came from "the same basic area in which the first [B]igfoot sightings occurred perhaps a month, a month and a half ago." One of these Bigfoot sightings was made by two boys, ages 13 and 5, who reported seeing a large, hair-covered creature; one of the boys said the man-like thing looked as if it "had blood coming out if its eyes." Later investigation found tracks that investigators felt corroborated the boys' report, Wiedemann said.

Vestigia members had differing views on the relationships, if any, shared between the phenomena they researched. Wiedemann was open to a possible linkage between UFOs and sightings of weird creatures occurring in the same general area. Jones maintained Bigfoot was an animal unrelated to UFOs. Jones was able to present his and Vestigia's views during an episode of *The Jersey Side* newsmagazine show. Airing on October 26, 1976, co-hosts

Marvin Kitman and Richard Reeves interviewed Jones for a segment titled "Bigfoot East," exploring Bigfoot sightings in New Jersey.[1607]

Vestigia's plans for 1977 included building teams to investigate "spook lights," the Jersey Devil, and phantom hitchhikers. Vestigia produced a newsletter with Gary Szele serving as its editor. "We can foresee it (the newsletter) as possibly growing into an actual journal of some kind," said Wiedemann. "This will be of general interest to people beyond the actual membership."[1608]

Vestigia investigated the so-called Wantage Event, a series of strange happenings that began in northern New Jersey on May 12, 1977, at the isolated Sites family farm. Wantage is in Sussex County and its northern border is the New Jersey-New York state line. "There was a very exciting Bigfoot incident. The monster invaded the Sites family farm and ripped the door off a barn, after which he entered and killed seven rabbits which were kept in cages," Wiedemann said.

The Wantage Event began to unfold just after 6:00 A.M. on May 12, as Barbara Sites put two family cows to pasture, part of her early usual morning routine. This particular morning the animals were obstinate about moving into the field. Attempting to push them through a gate she heard a noise she described as "like a woman screaming while she was being killed." The strange noise came from a swampy area just back of the farm.

After succeeding in getting the unusually reticent cows into pasture, Barbara headed toward the barn where nine rabbits were kept. Nearing the structure she noticed that a wooden sliding door was off its frame. Looking inside the barn she found seven of the family's nine rabbits were dead. "Apparently he (the killer) took one or two of them with him—or ate them on the spot—and then fled," said Wiedemann.[1609] Examination of the rabbits' cages showed some had their hatches unhooked and some cages were simply smashed. One cage had contained rabbits and guinea pigs and here Mrs. Sites found the rabbits had been removed but the guinea pigs had been left unmolested. Two pregnant rabbits were missing. Of the seven rabbit bodies left in the barn, one appeared to have had its head twisted off, another had its right hind leg nearly removed from the body. "There were hardly any marks on the other five rabbits," Mrs. Sites said. "They just looked like someone squeezed them to death."

Wiedemann told reporter Curt Sutherly that the rabbit carcasses which Richard Sites, Barbara's husband, had buried were exhumed by Jones and turned over to a veterinarian for study. "We also had them x-rayed," Wiedemann said. "While I can't tell you everything, I can say this: all the bones in the rabbits' bodies were broken—multiple fractures. In other words, the bodies had been crushed."

> Wiedemann then paraphrased the veterinarian, saying that "from the amount of [destruction] done to the rabbits, it (the killer) couldn't have been anything smaller than a dog or a wolf." However, the vet also noted that the killer must have had "enormously powerful hands or jaws."
>
> As for the heads missing from the carcasses, Wiedemann said the preliminary vet's report indicated they had been "torn, not bitten" from the bodies.[1610]

The State Police were called, and an investigation was undertaken. Officials suggested a wild dog or bear may have caused the rabbits' demise, candidates the family pointedly disagreed with. Richard Sites later noticed that several wall boards of the barn had been broken, suggesting they could mark the perpetrator's attempt to gain entry into the barn.

At around 9:00 P.M. on May 12, Barbara Sites noticed that a handle of baling twine used at another door of the barn had been removed. The board normally kept propped against this door was discovered lying on the ground. The family undertook an eyes-on vigil of the barn from behind a window of their home.

> It was not long before they witnessed a creature appear under the mercury-vapor lamp which lights up the farm yard. The oldest daughter, aged sixteen, began screaming immediately. The entire family observed the creature standing under the bright light at the corner of the shed. (It was from seeing the creature in this position that Mr. Sites estimated the height to be at least seven feet, the same as the eave at the corner of the shed.)
>
> "It was big and hairy; it was brown; it looked like a human with a beard and mustache; it had no neck; it looked like its head was just sitting on its shoulders; it had big red glowing eyes." This is how Mrs. Sites later described her observations of the creature that night. The dog went after it. The creature merely swung an arm, and the dog flew about twenty feet through the air, landed, rolled over, scrambled to his feet, and ran away (not to return until the following day). The creature,

> seemingly unshaken, casually turned and walked away on its hind legs.[1611]

The following morning, Barbara Sites delivered her children to her mother's house in a nearby town. That night, with their children safely away, Barbara and Richard determined to wait for the creature again. "This time we were ready for it," Richard stated. With the Sites was Barbara's brother and a friend; the four adults were armed with a .410, a .12 gauge, and two .22 caliber rifles and they took up positions to watch for the creature. At about the same time as the previous night, the creature appeared under the mercury-vapor light. "At first all I saw were these two red eyes staring at me from over there," Richard said, indicating an old shed. The party opened fire and the creature fled into the shed. The creature broke out through a window and stood under a tree near the structure. Richard was closest and fired his weapon. "I shot at it three or four times with deer slugs in my .410 gauge shotgun, and I know I hit it." The creature reacted by emitting a growl. "I thought the thing was coming at me," Richard said. Having run out of ammunition, Richard returned to the farm house. While the adults regrouped, the creature fled up a hill and disappeared into an apple orchard. "My husband jumped into his pickup truck and tried to chase it, but the thing ran into the fields and disappeared," Barbara said. A close inspection of the area didn't reveal any signs of blood or other indicator the creature had been struck by bullets.

SITU's R. Martin Wolf and Steven Mayne visited the Sites' farm on May 17. Wolf and Mayne interviewed the family and became impressed with them as witnesses. Examining the exact locations where the creature had been seen, the investigators found the ground hard and compacted and not conducive to registering footprints. Deep "claw" marks found on a barn wallboard suggested something had attempted to enter the structure.

Wolf and Mayne walked to the swamp, from where the strange scream-like noise had been heard by Barbara. A recent spell of dry weather created excellent conditions for getting around the area and the men crisscrossed the location several times. Several spots of flattened pasture grass caught their interest, in the midst of which appeared to be strewn the viscera from a mammal.

> The organs were strung out, with several clumps of hair scattered about the vicinity, and some hairs were actually attached to what appeared to be intestines. We collected what

> we could of the hair—mostly short, one to two inch long, brown specimens (we returned the following day in order to obtain the organs themselves).[1612]

"I'd never have believed it existed if I hadn't seen it with my own two eyes," Richard told the investigators. The rabbits were turned over to another investigative group for analysis but not before Wolf and Mayne were able to examine the carcasses on the Sites' premises. Excepting the rabbit with its head removed and another whose leg was left dangling, the other bodies seemed to evince great internal damage—broken bones and presence of blood in the throats and mouths.

Returning to the Sites home the following day, Barbara told them that shortly after their departure the previous night, the creature appeared again under the mercury-vapor light. Richard got in his pickup and chased the creature which narrowly avoided being run over. Over the course of the next several weeks, the Sites' farm received droves of interested and curious people, sometimes toting weapons. The parade of hopeful monster-seekers proved exasperating at times. "In fact," Richard said, "one group started telling me—not even asking me!—what they were planning to do, so I threw them out and told them never to come back."

> An interesting occurrence took place in the presence of *five* SITU investigators, who just happened to be visiting the farm when the following event occurred. Mr. and Mrs. Sites, two of their friends, and the five SITU investigators were standing outside the house discussing the various events which had occurred throughout the previous two months, when we suddenly heard a strange "scream" coming from some distant area behind the house. "That's it!" Mrs. Sites cried. We all ran through the fields to the edge of the woods as the sound continued, now rapidly retreating into the swamp.[1613]

Over dusty back roads, SITU members attempted to drive closer to the source of the sounds.

> The screaming was still audible, but gradually diminished as whatever made the sound moved swiftly away. A thorough check of the area failed to turn up any clues whatsoever, but it soon became apparent to us that the lay of the land offered

> an opportunity for a creature to walk (or run) for miles and miles through the surrounding woods and swamps without ever needing to pass close to a house.

If the whole affair had simply been made up—a scenario not discounted—then it was a bizarre and complicated hoax with seemingly little to benefit anyone, most of all the Sites family. "I don't care what anybody says, we saw what we saw and the only way anybody is going to believe us is to see it themselves," Barbara said. The Sites had, to all appearances, been honestly irritated and worried by the curious visitors coming to their home in hopes of seeing a monster. Many who became familiar with the Wantage Event, especially those who met the Sites, felt convinced Barbara and Richard's reactions and testimony indicated they had indeed lived through something inexplicable. Richard was asked what he would do if the creature continued to visit his farm. "Well," he said, "either capture it, somehow make it leave, or else we're moving!"[1614]

Mill Swamp Booger (Mill Swamp Booger Man)[1615]

On Sunday, January 9, a group of hunters met at Whaley's Store in southern Chinquapin, Duplin County, North Carolina, to hunt the creature called the Mill Swamp "Booger" which had been seen by Dean Maready.[1616] It was during a walk in the swamp near the Woodell Aycock home on the last day of December 1976, he had seen a creature clinging to the trunk of a pine tree. Maready said he heard what he described as bark falling from a tree and looking up saw what he described an ape-like creature about six feet tall with brown-grayish fur and claws. Maready stated the creature sported an interesting feature—a roughly three foot-long, twitching tail. Maready said he quickly left the area when the creature appeared to notice him and started coming down the tree.[1617] Woodell Aycock saw Maready hurrying out of the swamp; Aycock said Maready had looked "pale as cotton."[1618]

> Later in the day, Dean Maready and Bobby Maready went back into the swamp to check on what Dean thought he had seen. They found tracks. They said they saw where bark had been scraped off the tree where the creature slid down the trunk.
>
> They said they saw tracks. The tracks were made by something with three toes in front and two on the back of the foot. The toes measured about three inches in length with something resembling talons on the ends.[1619]

Maready and two relatives went back to the scene of the encounter with their dogs (another newspaper report reports one dog). The dogs reportedly picked up and followed a scent for a short distance before apparently losing it.[1620] The group also found five trails leading between a square of swamp thicket and nearby chicken coops and turkey houses.

> They surmised the creature may have been picking up the dead birds thrown out of the poultry houses as there was a scent of dead birds in the swamp, along with some feathers. None of the farmers reported any unusual losses of birds.[1621]

The *Wilmington Morning Star* reported that Wilton Aycock, whose home was close to the location of Maready's encounter, had noticed his dogs barking furiously at something but paid little attention to what may have been concerning them. On another occasion, Aycock said, two dogs chased after something and disappeared into the swamp. Later, only one dog returned and wouldn't leave the Aycock yard.[1622] Linda Dale and Randy Maready, both residents of the area, stated they had seen a creature similar to what Dean Maready had reported, but had been hesitant to publicly come forward.[1623]

The *Wilmington Daily Star* also added a bit of background to the mystery:

> About 24 years ago Terry Whaley, about twelve years old at the time, discovered a mysterious carcass in another portion of the swamp. The carcass was partially rotted away, but the remnants didn't resemble those of a dog, or wildcat or bear, according to local residents.[1624]

ASA Monster

The "Asa Monster" was a name coined by Marines at Quantico Marine Base in northern Virginia after shadowy figures were seen and strange sounds heard coming from a tree line near an ammunition storage area (ASA). "A few marines claim to have seen 'brown things' walking on two legs. Others say they have heard strange shrieking screams, and some claim they've heard something climbing a fence."[1625]

"I remember the night I saw it very well," said a Marine who asked not to be identified. "It was about 2 A.M., I was walking my post when I heard something in the woods. I stopped and looked in the direction of the noise." At first the Marine could only make out a vague shape. "I could see a dark figure beyond the fence just in front of the tree line, so I shined my flashlight at it. I couldn't believe what I saw. It was some type of creature that looked like a cross between an ape and a bear."

With the aid of the flashlight, the Marine sentry was able to make out some details of the six-to-eight-foot-tall creature. "The first thing I noticed was its large glaring eyes. Then I noticed it had arms and was covered with dark brown hair." The Marine decided backup was called for and told others what he had seen. The sentry returned with a sergeant but when they searched the area they "found nothing except some very large tracks with a pattern that resembled those of a dog."

Sgt. Stolpa, member of the physical security platoon, said that most of the strange noises heard by Marine guards took place in the summertime. "Occurring between the hours of 11 P.M. and 4 A.M., the noises will be there for two days and then go away for two days, in a continuous cycle." Sgt. Stolpa reported one of his sentries had heard a noise that "sounded as if someone was being mutilated." The Marines believed there had to be a rational explanation . . . perhaps the sounds came from people playing at nearby recreational grounds. But Sgt. Pultz of Quantico's public information office noted that the closest housing and recreational areas were "some distance away."[1626]

Saluda County Bigfoot Sighting

D. W. Berry was not sure if the 14-inch-long and 7-inch-wide footprints discovered on his farm in Saluda County (SC) were a hoax or not. But, he said, they looked real to him. "There are all kinds of possibilities" as to how the prints were made, he added. David P. Charles, chief deputy of the Saluda County Sheriff's Department, stated his department was not investigating the footprints. "It's more of a joke than anything else," he said. "I think it's a hoax."

Berry said the circumstances of the prints' discovery was itself unusual. "My grandson and another boy discovered them" in early February on rural property his family refers to as the "Old Homestead" about 10 miles from Saluda. "They were setting some traps down there when they heard a noise. They said it was a terrible sound, like a bobcat." The youths decided to hastily leave the area. "They were really shook up right after it happened," Berry said in a February 20 article in Charleston's *News and Courier*. Soon after the boy's frightening experience, large flat-footed tracks turned up at the Old

Homestead. Berry estimated that in the ensuing two weeks after word of the tracks had spread, some 300 persons had traveled the dirt roads leading to the Old Homestead to see them for themselves.[1627]

Gromoskes' Footprint

Helen and Leonard Gromoske found a single footprint in the backyard of their Fort Mill, South Carolina, home on Saturday, February 12. "It gives you an eerie feeling, knowing that something could be that close," said Mrs. Gromoske. "It makes you feel uneasy." Fort Mill Police Chief Floyd Foss described the footprint as just over 12 inches long, five and three-quarter inches wide, and about an inch deep. He was also decidedly of the opinion the print was a fake.

Ray Liguori, curator of natural history at the York County Nature Museum, didn't immediately concede the reported print as a prank. "It really puzzles me that there's no other print unless they came out of the sky or something," Liguori said on Tuesday after he was able to examine the print. "But it's not a human foot, I'll tell you that." Even a flat-footed person, according to Liguori, has a slight curve along the lateral edge of the foot. The Gromoske print was straight on both sides. "An animal with a foot that size would have to weigh 400 pounds, and it would make a deeper indication that that," he said. Liguori made a plaster mold of the print, which he intended to take to the anthropology department at Winthrop College. Leonard Gromoske Jr., 13, watched the cast-making process. "That's what they did on *Sasquatch* [the movie]," he said.

"Fort Mill has had, over the years, the most unusual animals found here," said Liguori, commenting that Bigfoot was not the first strange creature to have reputedly stalked through Fort Mill. "Somebody not long ago killed a coati mundi around here, and that animal comes from Mexico, Central American and South America." Mrs. Gromoske said the family had been receiving numerous phone calls since news first spread of the discovery of the footprint. About 15 people showed up at the residence on Monday, February 14, which was exceeded the following day by an estimated 50 people. Helen Gromoske said she felt it was her duty to report the footprint. "If there is a danger, I would want my child protected. I just wish it had been in somebody else's yard."[1628]

Northwest Trek Sighting

An unidentified serviceman from Fort Lewis reportedly went into shock after encountering "a big hairy thing" near Eatonville, Washington, which he believed was Bigfoot. His mid-March sighting occurred while he hiked in woods near the Northwest Trek wildlife preserve. A Madigan Army Medical Center doctor said the enlisted man came to him "extremely upset" but would not immediately disclose the reason why. "He is quite sure he saw Bigfoot," the doctor told a *Tacoma News Tribune* reporter.

"I can assure you it was no put-on by us. We have had nothing to do with any of these sightings. I did nothing and none of our people did anything," said Roger Thacker, Northwest Trek director. "The doctor called me and told me the man was terrified and in an extreme state of shock," Thacker said. A Madigan ambulance driver, Don Durden, said a Puyallup man he had met near the Northwest Trek wildlife preserve had told him of seeing something similar in September 1976. During a hiking trip, Durden came across footprints near Trek that measured 18 inches long and eight inches wide. "I'm 6-foot-4 and 285 pounds and my footprint was dwarfed in comparison with his." Following the footprints, Durden met the Puyallup man who told Durden a Bigfoot had stared at him for five minutes as he sat in his parked truck on a logging road close to Trek. "He said the animal was between 8 and 9 feet tall with black fur covering most of his body. The face was definitely not that of a gorilla, but closer to that of a human," recalled Durden.[1629] "He said it stared at him for five minutes and even leaned a hand on the truck, but never made a move toward him," Durden stated.[1630]

Thacker said he was unaware of any evidence that a large creature had entered the wildlife park. "If I could get him in here, though, I'd give him free room and board." When interviewed, Thacker allowed "it is possible" that there could have been a Bigfoot in the area near Eatonville. "I joke about these sightings," he said, "but anything's possible."[1631]

Forest Oaks Footprints

Teenager Dave McGee discovered "humongous" footprints in the Greensboro, North Carolina, neighborhood of Forest Oaks on Monday evening, March 14, the account of which was published in the *Greensboro Daily News*.

> Dave, who had watched a television special on the Bigfoot creature several weeks ago but claimed it to be a farce, said he "got nervous when I saw the footprints."

He called one of his friends and told him, but for fear "people would think I was crazy" he didn't tell many others. Some of them thought it to be a figment of his imagination.

Walking down by the lake where the footprints were spotted, Dave and two of his buddies (who still thought he was sane) Tuesday went in search of Bigfoot, hoping only to find his footprints and armed only with a yard stick and a tape measure.

There were four prints, measuring 14 ¾ inches, 16, 17 and 17 ½ inches long, 7 inches wide and stuck about 3 ½ inches deep in the mud. Five stubby toes were imprinted in the ground. The footprints led up two different paths.

Could there possibly be two of them? Or was this a four-legged monster phenomenon with a seven foot, 11-inch stride? Or possibly a long-footed Jaycee trying to attract interest for the upcoming Greater Greensboro Open golf tournament to be played soon at the Forest Oaks Country Club for the first time ever?

"There could be an adult in North Carolina with a foot that big," said Dave. "But what adult would be walking around barefoot this time of year? If it's a fake, it's a good one. I don't think it's a fake, because the toes curl up."

Since only Bigfoot's footprint could be found, Dave used a formula he conceived to estimate the invader's size.

Multiplying and dividing on a calculator, Dave came up with a creature 9.1875 feet tall. He divided his own height (63 inches) by 10 inches (his foot size) and multiplied by 17 ½ (the size of the largest foot print)—he came up with 102.245 inches. He divided that by 12 and derived a Bigfoot monster 9.1875 feet tall.

Logical, maybe. But where did the footprints go?

"With a stride that long," Dave suggested, "he could have stepped about anywhere in the bushes."

There were no signs of broken trees or branches. The good-humored monster apparently stepped around trees and branches and into the bushes so no one could track his progress.

"I think it could exist, Dave contends. "I'd like to track it down," he says, pausing. "When I get older—I've got to do a little living first."[1632]

Packwood Footprints

A Forest Service employee found footprints Friday, April 29, measuring 18-inches long and eight-inches wide at the ball of the foot at the River Bar Campground (WA). The prints formed a series that could be followed for 200 yards. According to Sam Benowitz's article in Centralia's *Daily Chronicle*, a Forest Service spokesman said several of the tracks discovered at the River Bar Campground were protected on Saturday with a plastic covering and casts were eventually made on Monday afternoon, May 2. "The casts are not the greatest in the world but you can definitely tell what is there," commented the Forest Service spokesman. "It was something bipedal that made footprints pretty deep," the spokesman said adding that photographs of the prints had been taken. The gentleman who made the casts will probably keep them, he said, "and the local district will keep the pictures." Shari Seidlitz, a member of the Bigfoot Information Center said the Center was "definitely interested in investigating the prints." She was impressed with the care taken to preserve them and the fact they were in sand suggested "they could be pretty good evidence."

> Using tables compiled by noted primatologist John Napier, doubt could be cast on the authenticity of the prints.
>
> Dr. Napier is a specialist in bipedal locomotion and former director of the primatology program at the Smithsonian Institute.
>
> Using the tables provided by Napier, a human-like creature with the reported foot size would stand nine feet nine inches tall.
>
> The usual height reported for [B]igfoot is between six and one half and eight feet although there have been occasional nine-foot sightings.[1633]

Footedale (PA) Bigfoot Sighting

> Big Foot is back in the news again. Another reported sighting of the half human animal has taken place in the Fayette County area.
>
> A Footedale couple and their three children experienced several frightening moments Sunday night [May 15, 1977]

when they confronted the creature along a dark, rural road in German Twp, about 9:30. The family members, who wish to remain anonymous, were returning from the McClelland town area when the incident occurred.

The animal, described by the wife was a large creature with shaggy hair walking upright in a slumped over position. She said it was reddish brown color. "When I first saw it, I thought it might be a deer, but it was no deer!" she said. She added, "Its hair was shaggy, not smooth like a deer and it had to be at least 6 feet tall."

The husband said the creature was standing upright at the edge of the narrow road with its back to the occupants of the car. "We were rounding a bend in the road when we suddenly saw a large animal like object about 6 feet or so tall, with reddish brown hair," he said. When the headlights of the car shone over the creature, it quickly dropped from sight over an embankment along the roadway. The husband said it was a drop from 35 to 40 feet and that it led to an open plowed field.

The three children in the car reacted differently to the Big Foot sighting. The mother said the 11 year old daughter threw her ice cream down, locked the door of the car and hit the floor. The youngest child, age 7 just sat there. The 14 year old son returned to the scene of the sighting later that night with his father after the remainder of the family was dropped off at home.

The son and father used flashlights to inspect the area. They discovered some broken branches and a fence post was pushed over, but no footprints were discovered. The family returned the next day during the daylight to check the area once again.

The wife said the grass and weeds were pushed down in certain areas. She added, "I could tell something was down there."

According to Joan Jeffers, co-director to the Pennsylvania Center of UFO Research, his was the first reported Big Foot sighting in Fayette County this year.

Last year, one sighting was reported in Smock, Franklin Twp and another occurred at Republic.

Jeffers reported two sightings took place in McKean County recently and one also at Clearfield County during February.

> Numerous sightings of Big Foot have taken place since 1967 across the country and in Canada.
>
> The Footedale family has now been added to the list of believers. "Before this happened, I never believed in anything like this," the wife remarked.[1634]

The article's mention of numerous Bigfoot reports occurring "since 1967" coincides with the inception of the Patterson-Gimlin footage into the public consciousness. The fecundity of sightings and encounter tales during the ten years that spanned the Patterson-Gimlin film's meteoric publicity and the above *Brownsville Telegraph* article was undoubtedly indebted in some part to Patty's grainy, but enigmatic image.

Stoneridge Plan Sighting

John Tiskus of Shaler Township, Pennsylvania, claimed he saw a Bigfoot drinking out of his swimming pool in the early morning on Tuesday, June 14. John Downing, staff writer for the North Hills' *North Record*, wrote of the young man's experience. "I was downstairs doing some homework," said Tiskus, a student at Triangle Tech in Pittsburgh. "It was somewhere between 2 and 3 A.M. and I decided to go upstairs to take a little break. I heard something like a gurgling sound, together with a high-pitched squeal like a rabbit makes. Then I saw what I thought at first was a prowler standing by our swimming pool. So I started banging on the window. But it wasn't human. It stood about 7 ½ feet tall and had hair over most of its body and real thick slimy skin. The back yard light was still on, so I could see." The creature scooped a handful of water from the pool and drank. Then it left the yard heading for the woods behind Stoneridge Plan.

Tiskus had almost the same experience on Wednesday, though he didn't see the beast. Tiskus explained the creature "played around the wood pile. I couldn't see it, but I heard the gurgling and squealing again. I found a lot of branches crushed and splintered." Tom Shields, a former resident of Richland and at the time living in Slippery Rock, planned to investigate the site with several fellow researchers and attempt to make plaster casts of any footprints.

Tiskus didn't describe himself as a typical Bigfoot buff and, "No, I don't watch the stars late at night," he said. "But I know what I saw out there. I know, not many people are going to believe me. But I'm telling you what I saw," he said.

Hints of Bigfoot were not unknown in the area. In December 1975 three children in Hampton found giant footprints by their home off Harts Run Road. Shields and fellow investigators visited the scene and cast of some of the better prints which were subsequently analyzed by anthropologists who, Downing reported, ruled out a hoax. Downing's article concluded with, "*News Record* has talked to many residents of the Hampton-Shaler-Richland area of North Hills who are familiar with the squealing cries of Bigfoot."[1635]

Hawley Him

Hawley is about seven miles north of Abilene in southern Jones County, Texas. Roger Downing of the *Abilene Reporter-News* wrote the first story of the Hawley Him, a creature described as a 7-foot, hairy, long-armed monster, which reportedly attacked three youths at 10:00 A.M. on Wednesday, July 6, at Bob Scott's ranch. All three youths saw the creature before it departed the scene and disappeared into thick underbrush. The alleged attack occurred while two of the boys, Tom Roberts and Larry Suggs, were clearing brush for Scott. Scott was superintendent of Abilene Boys' Ranch, where the two youths lived.

While taking a break from the hot, dusty work, the pair were startled by the breaking of tree limbs and a shower of rocks. One boy said he was hit in the leg by one of the stony missiles and displayed a bruise on his right calf to Downing. The other boy said a projectile just missed his head. The youths quickly retreated from the scene, running to the safety of Mr. and Mrs. McFarland's nearby home. "We got three good glimpses of him, I call it him—whatever it was," one of the boys said. "It was kind of an ape, but still a man," he added. "He had huge arms. They hung to his knees. You'd have to see it to believe it."

The boys soon decided to return to the work site on Scott's ranch. Going with them in the McFarland's van was McFarland's daughter Renee and her 30-30. "It's a good gun. It's got a boom like a cannon and a kick like a horse," she told Downing. After they arrived at the site, a rock was reportedly thrown at the McFarland's van and all three youths were able to see the creature standing about 40 yards away in the brush. One of the boys took up the 30-30 and fired a shot, but decided he missed his target. "She was going to shoot it until she saw it. Then she crammed the gun at me and said, 'You shoot it,'" the young marksman said. After squeezing the trigger, the weapon's recoil floored the boy and he never got off a second shot. The creature melted into the brush, as it "glided" through the mesquite and sagebrush tangle. "That stuff (the brush) is so thick you have to know where you're going and he just glided through it," one of the boys said.

One of the boys told Downing that a rotten odor was smelled prior to the attack. In the area the boys worked for Scott was near where the rancher had lost twenty-one penned goats without a trace. Several carcasses were later found in the brush. Scott told Downing that Jones County Sheriff's officials told him coyotes got his goats, a claim which he remained skeptical of. None of the goats were apparently killed in the immediate vicinity of the pen but were seemingly taken from the pen location. McFarland's daughter claimed she and two friends had seen Hawley Him in October during a slumber party. When she told her parents of the creature's presence lurking about their home they dismissed it as a "trick of the night."[1636]

Hawley Him's appearance roughly coincided with the Stilwell Incident as reports from eastern Oklahoma of a tall monster with red eyes and covered in brown hair like a bear appeared in newspapers. "The ones who've seen it say it has a flat face and doesn't appear to be a bear," said a spokesman for the sheriff's department. "We've had about five or six different calls and they all pretty much give us the same report. I guess there's something to it. We just haven't been able to get close enough to find it," the spokesman said.[1637]

Hopeful monster hunters coalesced into several groups to find Hawley Him. Scott said that he had received calls from people all over the state requesting information about the creature. A monster-hunting group of three Abilene college students and another group led by Ed Nash, who claimed he had his own face-to-face encounter with a similar creature in the woods of West Virginia in 1964, had solicited Scott's permission to hunt for Hawley Him on his ranch. Believing Hawley Him to be nocturnal, Nash said he intended to start his investigation at dawn—the ideal time to find traces of the creature's passage. One of those signs, aside from the wide trail through the brush which it leaves in its wake, was its horrible smell. "You talk about the odor. It's worse than any rotten meat odor. It will turn your stomach," Nash said; Nash was actually drawn to investigate Hawley Him when he read of the terrible odor noticed by Roberts.

> Even as amateur monster hunters are preparing to catch the Hawley Him, the Jones County Sheriff's Office sees no cause for alarm. Sheriff Woodrow Simmons said his office has received no reports of monster sightings, and that he does not believe there is such a critter roaming the brush and nettles of Jones County.

> When asked about the reported sightings Thursday, Simmons said, "Have I seen what?" After it was explained, he asked again, "The Hawley what?"[1638]

Dr. Frank Conselman was a Texas Tech geologist from Lubbock who headed the International Center for Arid and Semi-Arid Land Studies. He provided columnist Katharyn Duff with the following poem based "on his research into the Hawley Him." Hermleigh is about 70 miles west of Hawley in Scurry County, Texas.

THE HERMLEIGH HER
Or Firmleigh for Hermleigh

The Hawley Him
Is but the whim
Of man's imagination.
Now the Hermleigh Her,
Like a cotton burr,
Is no chauvinist creation.
Enough, then, of this Hawley chatter.
Hermleigh's where the action's atter.

The Hermleigh Her is no mere "sir."
Nor yet a common lady.
She comes and she goes on her tippytoes
From Roaring Springs to Brady.
But the Hawley Him, we understand,
Can't operate except in sand.

Her's family tree is no mystery,
But quite well documented;
The Spur Her was her mother
And Ben Hur was her brother
Long ere Hawley was invented.
(She also has some children dear,
But we'll repeat no scandal here.)

True, the Hermleigh gal
Had a Hawley pal,

Whom she met at a 4-H* Rally.
(*Hermleigh, Hatchell, Hawley, Haskell)
But they were never real pally.
Legends relate their only date—
A rendezvous at Roby,
Many years ago, to see a show—
Harley Sadler playing Toby.
But the Hawley Him cut it much too slim
Alas! He never made it home.
He left his bones in western Jones,
A few miles* north of Noodle Dome.
(*Several kilometers, in the metric system.)

Is he a ghost? No more than most,
Stuck out in that shin-oak wilderness.
But we must defer to the Hermleigh Her
For she still remains in business.
—by The Snide Sniper from Snyder[1639]

As often occurred with accounts of local Bigfoot creatures, Hawley Him evoked memories of other "monsters" which in their time had gained their own notoriety.

> Back in the early 1960s, Haskell County had The Thang.
>
> Porter Oakes, then the editor of the *Haskell Free-Press* spent a lot of his time chasing The Thang. It was described as an animal, perhaps a very large bear. Maybe it was a gorilla. Some even thought it was a yak. . . .
>
> Whatever it was, The Thang would run across the road in front of a motorist late at night. It was frequently sighted on lonesome roads.
>
> The Thang may still be roaming the hills of Haskell but we have not heard much about him since Porter left the *Free-Press.*
>
> But about that time when The Thang was in the news, The Caddo Critter made his appearance in Stephens County.
>
> "Oh, I remember The Critter well," said Bob Bruce, our travel editor.
>
> "One of my early assignments when I came to work at *The*

> *Reporter-News* was to go to Caddo and find out about The Critter.
>
> "I remember the tales of those who had seen him. He was an animal, too, a gorilla-type beast and a big one.
>
> "And I recall talking with a woman who was a skeptic.
>
> "'Now Honey,' she told me, 'I think The Critter was dreamed up by some drunk cedar-shoppers!'" Bob said.[1640]

Conselman's poetic offering inspired by Hawley Him was not his first foray into monster musings. Seven years prior to Hawley Him grabbing headlines and attention, Conselman penned a whimsical answer to The Thang.

> Remember the "thang" that was so much in the news? Here's a Frank Conselman poetic explanation of it: "An ocelot it's not—This varmint's so much bigger. It hasn't got a single spot. And moves with so much vigah. It's a puma or a cougar, or a panther—or a booger."[1641]

West-Central Montana Sightings

According to Air Force Staff Sergeant Fred Wilson of Malmstrom Air Force Base, a massive Bigfoot was said to have charged a group of Great Falls campers and one of them fired a shotgun at it to frighten it away. The campers' experience occurred at the end of about an eighteen-month period of Bigfoot sightings in the Great Falls area of west-central Montana. Wilson stated the incident occurred about 2 A.M. on Saturday, August 20. The group did not report it right away for fear no one would believe them.

Wilson told the *Great Falls Tribune* the camping group was made up of himself and two others—his nephew and another youth. The group had set up camp on a ridge in Belt Creek Canyon about 20 miles southeast of Great Falls. About 2 A.M. Saturday morning, a rain storm convinced the group to pack up and head home. As they approached their car, one of the youths heard a noise and trained a flashlight on the spot, back along the path they had taken. That's when the group saw the massive creature swaying beside a willow tree.

One of the them fired a shot from a shotgun to frighten the creature away and the creature retreated into the darkness. The group took advantage of its departure and raced back to the car. Wilson said when he was about ten feet from the car he saw the creature again racing toward them. Hurriedly getting into the car, the group sped away, not stopping until they reached Great Falls. As they sped away from the scene Wilson related he had looked back and saw the creature's head looking up over an embankment. "It was hideous," Wilson said. "It had small, apish-type eyes, a flattened nose and canine-type fangs which showed when its mouth was open. Its face was totally covered with hair. The head was oblong."

One of the boys with Wilson said the creature bore a resemblance to the "giant monkey" [likely Chewbacca] from Star Wars. Wilson stated he returned to the scene in the daylight and found one poorly defined track in a muddy creek bed. His inspection of the track revealed he could fit both his size 11 shoes inside it, and it was seven inches deep, while nearby cattle tracks were approximately three inches deep. Intrigued by the encounter, Wilson told the *Tribune* he planned to camp in the area again with the intent to photograph the creature.[1642]

Track Find in Vancouver

Five people from Fort St. John came across something most unexpected during their fishing trip in the Chetwynd area of northeastern British Columbia on August 8. They discovered a series of large tracks measuring 17 inches long and 10 inches wide. The supposed Bigfoot footprints were spaced about six feet apart and showed only four toes. "I laughed when I saw the prints," said Marilyn Wiles. "They were really big . . . so big that no one else could do them." Wiles' brother, John Ross, said the prints were old and located about 50 miles south of Chetwynd, and a mile away from the nearest road. The trackway started from a creek and traveled across sandy soil and disappeared into a rocky area. "They'd been rained on once," said Ross. "They weren't all that fresh. If anybody wanted to try a hoax, they would have done them near the bridge or near the road." Wiles said plaster casts from some of the prints had been made. "They weren't fresh so we didn't get scared."[1643]

Bigfoot in the Uinta Mountains

Two Bigfoot sightings within the Uinta Mountains grabbed public attention and sparked an official Bigfoot search by Utah conservation officers. The sightings occurred about 17 miles apart but their respective descriptions shared several details. The first sighting occurred in June and involved two couples who reported seeing Bigfoot near Mt. Elizabeth. They said the creatures had human-like features but animal like behaviors.

The second sighting, witnessed by eight people: two adults and six youngsters, occurred on August 22, and involved one creature. While hiking to a ridge at the head of the Weber River Drainage between Pass Lake and Cuberant Basin, they saw a large ape-like animal near the edge of a small alpine lake which was described as about 10 feet tall and covered in a mantle of white hair. It walked off after one of the party knocked some rocks loose. The party also reportedly found what they took to be a partially eaten rabbit near the sighting location.

"The people involved with this sighting were pretty credible," Conservation Officer Don Paul said. "They spend a lot of time in the outdoors." Though not dismissive, Paul took the sightings with a skeptical grain of salt. "But they saw this thing from 600 to 800 yards away in the early morning," he said. "Now a moose can be 10 feet tall and have gray about its shoulders. Of course it can't stand on its hind legs." Paul stated that grizzly bears shared some features with the creature descriptions, but none had been reported in Utah since the 1930s. "It just seems to me that if Bigfoot really existed we would see more of them," said Paul. "There would have to be some population density—a breeding population anyway."[1644]

In the ensuing weeks scores of people entered the High Uintas Wilderness looking for Bigfoot or evidence of its presence, but into mid-September no additional sightings surfaced within the press. "We're not joining the Bigfoot fans," Paul said. "But one of our people will be making a routine patrol next week into the area where it was reported. He's going to see what he can find."[1645]

Routine or not, newspapers reported that two Utah Division of Wildlife Resources conservation officers, Terry Parkin and Jerry Dahlberg, went into the area in early September searching for sign of Bigfoot. "We won't make an attempt to catch him," Parkin said.[1646] "We'll be looking for tracks or anything else to substantiate whether there is a creature or not." According to Dahlberg, some of the terrain they trekked through was "so primitive it looked like it had never before been penetrated by man." The conservation officers regarded their canvass through the Cuberant Basin as a serious matter but doubted they were entering into a dangerous enterprise. "We aren't concerned," Parkin said referring to the two attention-grabbing sightings. "As soon as Bigfoot saw the others . . . he took off. He would probably only fight if he's cornered, just like any other animal."[1647]

Mindful of the attention their patrol received, Parkin and Dahlberg shared their findings after their rounds were completed. "We covered the entire Cuberant Basin area one day and the following day searched the Bear River side of the area," Dahlberg said when he and Parkin returned from their patrol. "If such a creature is in the area," he averred, "he would be constantly on the move, but we should be able to find some evidence of existence, such as animal carcasses, torn tree bark, a form of shelter, etc. But we found none." Despite the lack of evidence, Dahlberg insisted "we are not going to just write the whole thing off." Dahlberg said he planned to look in the area of Holiday Park on the Upper Weber River. "There are miles and miles of rugged terrain up there," he said. "The two areas of sightings are very primitive, very rugged. Few people have visited the areas." Visitors coming to the Uinta Mountains were urged to bring their cameras, not only for capturing the beautiful landscape, but also "just in case."[1648]

Not a Dream

Mildred Quinn reported seeing Bigfoot while on Mount White Chuck in northern Washington. "It's not that I want to impress anybody," she said, "but I know what I saw." Quinn was camped alone in mid-September at about the 6,000-foot level of Mount White Chuck (6,690 feet). She started out as a member of a Mazama climbing party, but feeling fatigued from the hike, asked to remain at camp while the rest of the party made for the summit. It was about midday when Quinn woke from a nap and spotted the creature about 80 feet away. "I looked away for a minute hoping that I was dreaming," said Quinn, "but as I forced myself to look again, he was still standing on his two legs, like a human, looking at me and the dog that had accompanied our party.

"I closed my eyes and thanked God for loving me and told him that I loved him, and now would he please take the animal away. The dog never stirred from my side. When I opened my eyes a few moments later, it was gone," Quinn said. "It was a formidable black figure, almost human-like, with long hairy arms and legs and huge shoulders," she recalled. "It was covered with long black fur which seemed to stand out as if it were in a static electric position. It was leaning against a rock, looking at me."

Quinn was a cartographic technician with the Division of Technical Services, Bureau of Land Management. She told Jack Fement of the *Oregon Journal* she hoped to go back to Mount White Chuck and document evidence of the creature's existence.[1649]

Michael Polesnek

Michael Polesnek was Vice President in charge of field research for the American Anthropological Research Foundation, a nonprofit foundation described as managing grants and funding for the American Yeti Expedition project.[1650] *Evansville Courier and Press* editor Tom Lindley profiled Polesnek and his 10-year pursuit after answers to Bigfoot. "Every year they find (the fossil remains) of mammoths and mastodons—fantastic archeological finds—well, we think we can find something called Bigfoot," Polesnek told Lindley while in Owensboro, Kentucky, investigating the Spottsville Monster (see chapter 6). Growing up in the Everglades, Polesnek had a keen interest in wildlife and had early aspirations in becoming a game warden. Polesnek's wife and fellow Florida-native Debbie shared her husband's zeal for hairy hominid study. Polesnek told *Messenger-Inquirer* writer Keith Lawrence that he "grew up with game wardens, learning how to handle animals and track them."

> Then a few years ago, he started finding cattle on his 28-acre ranch in Florida slaughtered, many of them with their heads torn off.
>
> Polesnek and several others believed the Florida Skunk Ape (another name for Bigfoot) was responsible. And he's been tracking him since.
>
> He's luckier than many men who have become obsessed with finding Bigfoot. He's got a wife who is also hooked on the dream.
>
> Mrs. Polesnek says, "I grew up in the Everglades. Our house was right on the edge of the Everglades. It was just a part of life."[1651]

Defining Bigfoot, Polesnek explained the creature was "a walking primate with the mechanics of the human. This represents an evolutionary gap." Certain hyphenations used to describe Bigfoot fell short in Polesnek's estimation. "No man was ever an ape and no ape was ever a man." Debbie Polesnek told Lawrence that she was tired of hearing Bigfoot explained away as a bear. "If it was a bear, they (people who have reported seeing it) would know it was a bear," she said.[1652]

> There are believed to be from 250 to 2,500 of them on the North American continent, Polesnek says. The Bigfoot is related to the Abominable Snowman in the same way a Caucasian is to

> a Mongolian, he adds, they are the same species but different races.
>
> Among the things the Polesneks have learned about the creatures are: they can eat and digest raw meat, they're not fully nocturnal but they seem to move around a lot at night, they use tools, they can communicate across distances by knocking rocks together and they are dormant in winter.[1653]

Polesnek participated in Robert Morgan's 1974 American Yeti Expedition in which he was given the task to spend five days alone investigating a remote section of woods. "Some of the tracks we found were probably no more than an hour old," he told Lindley.

> His most serious attempt at making fact out of what many think is fiction came in 1974 when he hiked through the woods of the Pacific Northwest tracking "a walking primate with the mechanics of the human." Polesnek didn't see Bigfoot on that excursion, but he claims he did see foot-prints that were probably made by an up-right walking "thing" that could have measured as much as 7-foot-5, and weighed 800 lbs.[1654]

Polesnek felt that one of the hardest aspects of searching for Bigfoot was dealing with nay-sayers. "Do you know," Polesnek asked, "there are people who still don't believe we've landed on the moon?" Some doubt could be expected throughout the national aggregate, but it was the scientists that especially irritated Polesnek. "Science wants hard information. We give them hair samplings (from Bigfoot), foot prints and droppings for analysis. They say that's not enough," Polesnek averred. "Instead they want skeletal or fossil remains, or the live creature—science demands a body. They won't accept anything less than that, and neither will the public."

One of the predictable questions posed to Bigfoot researchers, 'Why hadn't remains of a creature ever been found?' was met by Polesnek with some innovative responses. "There are a number of possibilities. Are they cannibalistic? Do they eat their dead? Do they bury them? Or do they put them in caves and conceal their remains forever? Or do they just die on the forest floor where their remains are spread all over and disintegrate in the rain-forest climate which doesn't lend itself to fossilization? Or could it be a case of all three? Or are they of this earth? Are they creatures from another world?"

Having had experience with expeditions, Polesnek suggested that a properly outfitted and manned effort could cost as much as $100,000. "Science today is governed by money," Polesnek said. "People are demanding hard facts, but will they support (scientific expeditions)? Government? No. The people? No." People were understandably reluctant to put money into a venture which in all likelihood would fail. But Polesnek believed those conditions were likely in line with Government designs on keeping Bigfoot a creature of legend. "The public isn't ready, isn't prepared for that shock," of learning the potential truth that Bigfoot was an extant creature.

> Polesnek wants to find Bigfoot, examine the creature, and let it go free.
>
> Feeling that Bigfoot is "too close to reality, it's too conceivable," Polesnek claims he will never give up the search for the elusive Bigfoot. "Here's what I say: If he walks on this earth, we will find him."
>
> Maybe it is the ridicule he has faced, or the belief that the next clue he chases down might give the ultimate answer. Whatever, Polesnek appears to be a man of conviction:
>
> "All that is important to me now is just to see him.
>
> "If it would cost me my life to reach out and touch him I think I would—the final conviction."[1655]

Skunk Ape

A pattern emerged to those who studied the Skunk Ape's movements: it would leave the underbrush behind during the dry season, and thus increase its exposure to people. One of the Skunk Ape's calling signs was dead livestock and pets, some with their heads chewed off.[1656]

With results published in the November 17 *Ocala Star-Banner Impact*, 30 residents from Ocala, Dunnellon, Summerfield, Lynne, Weirsdale, Ft. McCoy, Lowell, Oklawaha, Fairfield, Anthony, Belleview, Sparr, Williston, Wildwood, Inverness, Hernando, and Lecanto were asked if they believed Bigfoot existed in North America. Almost half, 14, said "No." Two responded as doubtful, four answered that Bigfoot possibly or probably exists, three said they'd never heard of Bigfoot, and two said they believed Bigfoot did indeed exist. "I really believe there's something unexplainable out there with a big foot," said an Inverness woman. The sentiment from a Lynne man was more typical. "I think somebody making moonshine liquor spreads these rumors to keep people scared out of their areas," he said. Also in the disbelieving camp was a Weirsdale woman who said, "If there was one, they'd have finally captured one by now. There's no proof."[1657]

Mrs. Mattie Gnann of Hog Valley had an "inside" story on one Skunk Ape event, and that knowledge colored her whole perception of Skunk Ape and Bigfoot. Mrs. Gnann's story was written up by Ron Baygents in the November 17 *Ocala-Star Banner*. Mr. and Mrs. Shoup Gnann's step-daughter and husband were camping one weekend in the mid-1960s near the Pasco-Hernando County line.

> After noticing some nearby campers had temporarily left their campsite after dark, the couple decided to have some fun, said Mrs. Gnann.
>
> "They took some bed-sheets and stuffed them with moss, forming a figure with some large feet," Mrs. Gnann recalled.
>
> The Shoups stretched a rope across part of the lake and tied it to a point within sight of the nearby campsite, then sat on the bank until the campers returned, she added.
>
> By attaching their creation to the rope and tugging gently on the line, the "animal" appeared to either walk in air, on the water or wade in the water.
>
> The campers spotted the "creature" and fled the scene, said Mrs. Gnann.
>
> "I would have probably reported seeing a ghost if I'd seen that creation, but we read in the papers that some campers saw a Bigfoot," she said with a smile.
>
> "Now, every time I see something on T.V. about people spotting Bigfoot tracks, I start laughing about how these things must get started."
>
> Mrs. Gnann said the news wires picked up her story and it ran in newspapers all over the country.
>
> What about other people who give detailed explanations of their Bigfoot sightings, Mrs. Gnann was asked?
>
> "I don't believe there's any Bigfoot," she said. "The Bigfoots' seen out West are nothing more than people in costumes with big feet."[1658]

In February 1977 Dr. J. Allen Hynek gave a lecture on UFOs at the West Palm Beach Garden Center. "Hynek proposed," wrote *Palm Beach*

Post-Times writer Rafe Klinger, "that these Bigfoot/Abominable Snowman/ Skunk Ape beasts could be inhabitants of a 'parallel universe' and slip in and out of our universe through some dimension connecting tunnel."[1659] This line of thought was in line with "what many religions having been telling us for a long time," Hynek said. The hairy giants associated with UFOs could be creatures that are physical in nature, but composed of different kinds of materials than are familiar to humans.[1660]

A 7-foot-tall, ape-like creature sporting "shaggy, black hair" was seen on a Delray Beach golf course twice during early February. John Street, director of County Animal Regulation, investigated the sightings and said positively identifying the creature "could put an end to the Skunk Ape stories" that had circulated in Florida for years. During his investigation, Street learned of a sighting by a security guard at a housing development adjacent to the south side of the golf course. The guard saw a creature on Sunday night that looked like a "gorilla." Two other men on the golf course in the early morning of Tuesday, February 8, reported being "scared by something they never saw—it just raised hell in the Palmettos," Street said.

The superintendent for the golf course described for an artist what he saw at about 1 A.M. on Wednesday, February 9, near a lake near the second tee. "He was down drinking water. He was at least 7 feet tall and this wide (the man held his hands about three-and-a-half feet apart) at the shoulders. He was real hairy—long, black shaggy hair, with no clothes." The superintendent turned his pickup truck's lights on the creature which he claimed, "smelled bad, like a skunk." The creature looked at the truck and slowly left the scene, disappearing into dense woods about 200 yards away. The superintendent threw some bananas at the wood's edge where the creature had entered. He returned at around 5:30 A.M. and the bananas were gone.

The superintendent first took his story to city police but after being scoffed at, turned to Animal Regulation. Street's investigation started on Wednesday with an interview of the superintendent to whom he suggested placing additional fruit on a raked-off area near the woods edge. "I'm not that concerned unless it eats the food or makes some tracks," Street said. "I'm convinced this guy is convinced himself he's seen something."

Street believed the creature was likely a wild chimpanzee or orangutan, or even "just some damn fool in a gorilla suit trying to freak out lovers on the golf course at night." Street asked state officials to check if any local permits for pet primates had been issued. Later, Street checked the spot where the second bunch of bananas had been left. No tracks were to be found "other than human," and the bananas were gone. Concerning the bananas' disappearance, Street suggested, "Anybody could have walked by and taken them." Street learned that the golf course had been plagued by late night trespassers. Street didn't advocate disclosing the name of the golf course saying, "I didn't want a bunch of idiots with guns running here and scaring the animal away."[1661]

Dateline: "The Swamps"

On a budget of $50 from the Fort Myers' *News-Press* and with a dateline of "The Swamps," Randy White, reporter for the *Fort Myers News-Press,* led a six-day Skunk Ape expedition in late February. White wrote that the last day of the expedition found his group looking forward to getting back to civilization.

> At this moment the men are dismantling camp. They seem happy. And a little smug, perhaps—secure in the knowledge that we may have proven a hairy, gorilla-type creature could roam the Florida wilds.
>
> After all, one of our ROTC Special Forces men says he made a definite sighting.
>
> "It was tall, hairy, walked on two legs and had no neck," he said later, describing the creature to visiting experts.
>
> Immediately afterward, we dispatched a reconnaissance team to investigate. They found huge, human-like footprints. One scientist said the tracks were "interesting," three experts said they were definitely tracks of the Florida Yeti, and one expert said they were "not convincing."[1662]

L. Frank Hudson, president of the Anthropological Research Center, believed his group had heard a Skunk Ape moving through the tangle of growth near their camp. "I am convinced your men saw a Yeti of medium size," said Hudson. "A number of sightings have been made in this area, so it is not entirely surprising." Dan Gentry listened to the report and was left unimpressed. "The evidence is interesting, but not convincing."

The expedition was divided into two teams that spent nights in remote parts of an unnamed Florida swamp. Both groups reported unusual sounds; one team believed they heard something large crashing through the brush near their camp. With Hudson were William Grimstad (also known as Jim Brandon, author of *Weird America*) and John Leith who had spent time with

Peter Byrne. During the expedition Hudson regaled White's group about a close-up encounter he had experienced with a Skunk Ape. "I once got within two feet of one," Hudson said. "Leith and I and some other friends were working on an island up in Charlotte Harbor. We walked through some brush and there he was, I could have reached out and touched him. He turned around and looked right at us." Hudson was familiar with a particular Skunk Ape which haunted an unspecified area. "I call him 'Jim'," Hudson said. "Jim and I are almost friends. Whenever I go out there, I take him salt and a new transistor radio. Jim likes to listen to the radio, so I always leave one where he can find it."

Grimstad (Brandon) asked White's group if they had noticed any UFO activity.

> "It is strictly supposition at the moment," Brandon said, "but many of the Yeti sightings occur shortly before or after a UFO actually disappearing before the very eyes of the observers, and also of them walking across water. And when a UFO or Yeti are spotted together, we also usually receive reports of animal mutilation in the area."
>
> But Hudson added, "Although the creatures have been known to attack animals, they are only aggressive toward people when people react aggressively toward them. Tell people they should never try to shoot a Yeti or hurt it in any way. If you don't bother it, it won't bother you."[1663]

Don Harshman with the Cypress Lake High School ROTC program told White he knew the denouement of White's story, as published for the *News-Press,* would read: "I know how your story is going to end—with a big question mark." But for White, there had been tangible positives from having taken part in the search.

> But the best thing which came out of the expedition was the good fellowship which, surprisingly, resulted from mixing people from tremendously different lifestyles and backgrounds. Men who had spent most of their lives in or around the Florida swamps talked easily with internationally known writers and explorers. Men with excellent and long military records sat comfortably beside individuals who had found their political niche in the peace movement of the late '60s.

> Long after this journal ends, people will no doubt ask me if I think a Skunk Ape or Yeti actually exists in Florida. Let me precede my answer by saying I was a skeptic before the expedition began. I had talked to many people who claimed they saw a Skunk Ape and, while I was often convinced they saw something, I was never convinced [it] was Florida's answer to the Abominable Snowman.
>
> But the people who were impressed by the tracks impressed me. So now I like to think of myself as interested and open minded. Am I convinced a Yeti exists? No. But I am not convinced it doesn't exist, either.[1664]

Charles Stoeckmann

Charles Stoeckmann was a Vietnam War veteran and former policeman. His home sat close to U.S. 1 about a mile and a half north of Key Largo and close to a thick Mangrove forest. Stoeckmann, his wife Leslie, their son, 13-year-old Charlie, as well as a neighbor, had sighted a strange man-like creature lurking in the mangrove jungle which Stoeckmann said became "a nightmare that has seriously changed my family's life."

Sgt. Rondell Chinn from the Monroe County sheriff's office at Plantation Key investigated the scene but found no concrete evidence of an unidentified creature living there. "There is definitely a problem there. These people are truly scared to death," Chinn said. The Stoeckmanns said they had sighted the Bigfoot-like visitor several times. Other than stoking fear, Chinn said whatever folks had seen was causing no harm. "The family has rabbits in their backyard and they've not been disturbed," Chinn stated.[1665]

Stoeckmann said he seriously considered moving his family after multiple sightings of the creature. The family's first sighting occurred on July 14 while Stoeckmann and his son were out bottle-hunting in their three-acre mangrove thicket. "I think I startled it," he said. "It was way ahead—a dark, hairy patch. It sort of stayed there, like a deer does when the wind shifts and it catches your scent."

"But it stunk awful, like a dog that hasn't been bathed in a year and suddenly gets rained on," said Stoeckmann. Leslie Stoeckmann claimed she had been awakened in the early morning on July 22 by thrashing sounds coming from a brush pile in the yard. "Through a gap in the jalousie window, from where I was lying in bed, I saw these bright, colorless eyes," Leslie stated. "They must have been reflecting the backyard light, like a cat's would. They were evil-staring. I could see the silhouette of its huge shoulder and head above an eight-foot bush, 30 feet from the bedroom window. I got hysterical," she said.[1666]

Since the creature or creatures' first appearance at their isolated home, the Stoeckmanns experienced about a dozen subsequent visitations. When interviewed by reporters, Stoeckmann made it clear that his family's experience had been an ordeal of fear.

> On Friday [July 29, 1977], Mr. Stoeckmann received all the proof he needed to convince himself the skunk ape was real. That was the day he picked up a roll of film he had left for developing at Eckerds in Key Largo. The prints from Eckerds included one of a field in which Mr. Stoeckmann claims to have seen the skunk ape after dark on July 21.
>
> The color photo, taken with Mr. Stoeckmann's instamatic camera with a flash-cube from more than 30 feet away, shows the field as a mostly purple, characteristic of underexposed color film.
>
> In the center of the purple is a brownish blur, less than an inch long, with the shape of a human being, or, perhaps, skunk ape. Little detail is present.
>
> On Friday night, Mr. Stoeckmann found additional evidence of the skunk ape near his home. Three large piles of fecal droppings were present in the field of which he had taken the photograph of the skunk ape.[1667]

Ted Ernst, Big Pine Key lawyer and secretary-treasurer of the American Anthropological Research Foundation, Inc. ("an organization self-described as dedicated to the study of the Skunk Ape, or Big Foot"), advised Stoeckmann that the feces should be analyzed by proper authorities to determine if they were deposited by a known animal. Ernst had made two visits to the Stoeckmann home and said that he "sincerely believes something is out there in the swamps," lurking near the family's home. "Whether or not it is a Skunk Ape doesn't really matter to me," Ernst said. He told reporter Phillip Sloan that he believed the Skunk Ape was a real animal in Florida and was confident it had the ability to swim to the Keys.

Ernst, a frequent hairy hominid-hunting colleague of Robert Morgan, further stated it was not unreasonable that a Skunk Ape could be resident to the Key Largo area, citing several Key Largo sightings during the mid-'70s.

But could the identity of the Key Largo Skunk Ape be something other than a Bigfoot-like creature? Some long-time Keys residents speculated that the Skunk Ape sighted by Stoeckmann could in fact have been a monkey, descended from some monkeys who got loose in the Upper Keys during the past 30 years.

> Ann Miller of Marathon, formerly of the Upper Keys, contacted the *Keynoter* Monday and reported that in 1947, several monkeys got loose from their cages on Plantation Key, near the present site of the Seabreeze Trailer Park.
>
> Kenny McKenny of Theater of the Sea on Windley Key said that in the 1950's and 1960's, as many as 20 monkeys escaped from his family's tourist attraction.
>
> Bernard Russell of Islamorada says he remembers that monkeys from Theater of the Sea that got loose during the 1960 Hurricane Donna were seen and fed for several years by a resident of Windley Key.[1668]

The monkeys mentioned didn't appear to fit the description of the seven-to-eight-foot-tall Skunk Ape which Stoeckmann reported seeing, a creature he maintained was no mere monkey. The duress from the publicity and concomitant interviews and visits from investigators appeared to have taken their toll as Stoeckmann said his family would leave the Keys without a forwarding address.[1669]

Bigfoot Attack Called a Hoax

Donnie Hall, the night watchman at John's Nursery in Apopka alleged a Bigfoot attacked him Monday, October 3, as he was doing his rounds. Hall said at 3 A.M. he heard a noise coming from some tall plants and decided to investigate. As he entered that area of the nursery, Hall claimed he was grabbed from behind by a large, 10-foot-tall apelike creature whose claws scratched his back. "He had me by the shoulder and I only came up to his waist," Hall said. He said the creature was covered in long hair and "smelled like a goat." Hall managed to break away from the creature's clutches, and grabbing a shotgun, fired at his attacker. "I know I hit it twice because the creature hunched over and moaned when it was hit." Hall next turned a flashlight on the creature and the light appeared to scare it away. "It took about three steps and he was out the door," Hall said.

"This was the second time I saw it," Hall reported. "He tried to break down the door to get at me two nights before he grabbed me Monday morning." Hall was so shaken he quit as security guard at the nursery.

The Orange County Sheriff's department investigated the incident and reported they found Hall at the nursery with a torn shirt and visible scratches on his back. Footprints were found at the scene. Robert Johnson of the Florida Game and Fresh Water Fish Department said it was his opinion the footprints were made by a man trying to make human prints appear to belong to an animal. Following Hall's report, the authorities dealt with a rash of Bigfoot sightings, though none were apparently as violent as Hall's claimed encounter.[1670]

Reverend Whatley Sighting

"All I can tell you is what I saw," said Reverend S. L. Whatley, 67, a Baptist minister at Lost Haven Baptist Church in Salt Springs, Florida, who encountered something in the Ocala National Forest on October 11. The forest covers 366,000 acres and resides north of Orlando between Lake George and Lake Ocklawaha. Whatley had been engaged in cutting wood with a chainsaw on Hugh's Island, a sandy hill studded with oak trees and surrounded by pines. During a pause in his operation to put the chain back on the saw, he heard gruff, guttural sounds coming from within the tree line across a road.

Whatley looked about him but saw nothing. He put in another 15 minutes of work but the saw continued to be problematic. "So I said to heck with it and got in my truck and started home. In just a little ways I went around a curve, and standing out there in palmettos about this deep (about knee high) was an animal. It looked like a gorilla, but it had a flat face like a man. I was as close from here to that tree, about 65 feet I guess, and so I said, 'well, I'm going to look you over real good.' I switched off my motor.

"It looked to me to be seven or maybe eight feet tall. It had a dark chocolate colored face, a face that was clear of hair, and a flat nose," Whatley said. "An ape, when he stands up, you know, his backend hoops out. This thing didn't. It stood straight up." Whatley reported that the creature's breasts were visible, indicating it may have been a female. "He had kind of a pointed head and broad shoulders, and across his chest it looked like female breasts, not full, but flat. If it was a female, it didn't look like it had ever nursed."[1671]

"He just stood there looking at me, across his shoulders like this," he said. "He had big old arms on him that hung down into the palmettos, and he was standing up straight like a man." Whatley said he hunted and fished for over 30 years in the Ocala National Forest and counts encounters with deer, bears and panthers among his experiences. But this thing was entirely new to him.

"And then I thought, what if it attacks me?" That's when fear entered the equation for Whatley. Deciding he'd feel better if he had something with which to protect himself, Whatley grabbed an axe from his truck. When he looked back, the creature had disappeared. Overriding curiosity about what he'd just seen impelled Whatley to action and he went off after the creature, axe in hand. "All I saw was deer tracks," Whatley said. "I walked up this sand road thinking for sure that I'd see some tracks, but there weren't any." As he approached the spot where he'd seen the creature standing, Whatley started concentrating on finding signs, but the ground cover of grass and leaves was not conducive to holding a track's impression. "That's what kept me from telling anybody," Whatley stated, referring to the lack of evidence he found. His immediate impulse following his sighting was to "go and find the law." But with no evidence, he decided to let the matter drop. "I figured that huntin' season was just around the corner and somebody else was bound to see the thing and I'd let them tell me about it." Whatley said. "I don't know what to think it was." But Whatley allowed that if he had had the means to definitively find out what the creature was, he would have used them. "I tell you one thing," Whatley added, "if I'd had a double-barrelled [sic] shotgun, we would know for sure."[1672]

After telling some friends he had seen what might have been a gorilla, his story shot him into notoriety as press services took up his encounter and radio stations were calling. "I've had calls from all over the place," Whatley said. "Some from as far away as Hawaii, Pittsburgh, Chicago . . ." Some interviewers' questions had put Whatley off. "Somebody from Chicago asked me if it had little antenna like some sorta outer space monster," Whatley said indignantly. "And somebody else," he recalled, "asked me if I drank much. I said well, not for at least 45 years. I've been preachin' for about 40 years . . ." This reaction stunned Whatley, who had spent a lifetime advocating faith in something he could not see, only to find himself defending something he knew he witnessed. The outcome for Whatley was, in the words of reporter Al Burt, disheartening. One missive Whatley received came from a person in Colorado who took umbrage with Whatley's wish he had had a rifle with him. "I hope you go to hell," the letter ended. An old college roommate wrote, "You just happened to look into the mirror and when you turned, missed the mirror." Whatley said the LSU basketball coach said he'd appreciate being appraised of future sightings (via collect call) because the LSU team would embrace a player that size. "It got a little provoking to me," Whatley said. "I had no reason to fabricate something like that. It just happened. I've thought about it a lot. I think it was an intelligent creature, and I think maybe it was from the ape family but not like any ape or gorilla I've ever seen. They're all blacker and stooped. And it wasn't a bear. I've seen too many bears. I wasn't drunk, either. I haven't had a drink of whiskey in 40 years, not since I was about 18 years and used to drink a little white lightning."

Whatley couldn't suppress a chuckle during his interview with the *Ocala Star-Banner*. "I don't know. I guess I'm amused about it. But just one fact bothers me. Some people have already said I might be lyin' about what I saw. Well, I'll tell YOU that if I was going to LIE about something I'd make it something really GOOD."[1673] Counting his family among his supporters, Whatley told Burt that a fireman from Ocala told him he had seen either the same or similar animal. A hunter camping in the forest made a similar claim, as did two reports from Belleview, and a report from Lakeland and another from Apopka—the latter involved a security guard who said he was attacked by a 10-foot tall creature. And Burt wrote that the Lake Kerr General Store had tacked-up pictures of tracks taken at different locations within the forest, some of which were 17-inches in length.

But there were occasions when Whatley thought the attention he had received for talking about his encounter had not been worth it. "I'd wish I'd a kept my mouth shut," he told Burt.[1674]

David Humphrey

"I ain't scared of nothing—except that night I was," said David Humphrey, who believed his fellow students at New Port Richey's Gulf Comprehensive High School "will probably think I am crazy, but I know what I saw." Humphrey's encounter with a "hairy monster" occurred on Tuesday, October 18; the creature, Humphrey claimed, chased him across the bridge on Bay Boulevard in Port Richey. Humphrey said, "The only thing I heard was a hard bumping sound as it got closer to me."

Humphrey said the creature "got within about 50 or maybe 100 yards of me," which helped him make out some of the creature's details: it was grayish-brown in color, about 7 to 8 feet tall, and possessed of large arms. Humphrey stated he first heard the creature at about 10 P.M. as he walked past the unfinished section of the Old Post Apartments. "I was coming back from the Village Bowling Alley, walking by the apartments when I started hearing something running in the woods now and then," he said. "When I started walking up the bridge I heard it again and I started running over the bridge."

Humphrey said he alternated between running and walking depending if he was near homes or wooded areas. "When I got to a wooded section again I turned around and saw it," he said. Humphrey lost sight of the figure when it entered the woods on the north side of Bay Boulevard. "Up in Indiana I never heard or saw anything like that, and I've hunted just about everything there is to hunt up there," he said.

"If anybody else had told me what David did, I would say they were crazy," David's father told a reporter. "But I know my son, and I believe him." Port Richey Police Chief Steve Balog declined to speculate about what David had encountered; "but I think his story is legitimate," he stated. "This is the third report like this in the three years I have been here. But the other two reports were of something smaller—about 4 or 5 feet tall and were near the recreation area about a block north of where Humphrey saw this one."[1675]

Little Bigfoot?

> "It scared me. It kept me awake all night," said Listene Maxwell, a neighbor of some of the children who told her of seeing the "being." Mrs. Maxwell reported the sightings to the police and they are investigating the reports.
>
> Several children claim to have seen the creature "jumping up and down" in a wooded area near Booker Field. According to Mrs. Maxwell, their stories are similar.
>
> It could just be imagination, but some people wonder if it could be that a "Little Bigfoot" has decided to pay a visit.
>
> He has long teeth. He walks on two feet. He doesn't have a tail and he sits down with his hand on his chin.
>
> These are just some of the descriptions of a four-foot tall, hairy human-like creature who is reported to have visited a wooded area near Booker Field for several nights in a row.
>
> The creature nicknamed "Quicksand," because it disappears as if in quicksand, was reported Monday night [October 3] to Palatka Police.[1676]

CHAPTER 9
1978

The beaver is the animal most often pictured as a symbol of Canada. But it's the Sasquatch, however elusive, that's far better qualified to serve as the north country's national beast.

Though Bigfoot has often been sighted along the West Coast of the United States, his relatives and ancestors—both (allegedly) real and imaginary—are uniquely Canadian.

In fact, monster legends are as Canadian as hockey players, Molson's beer and Pierre Trudeau. They've been around longer, and some scholars seriously suggest that mythical beasts represent the wilder side of Canadian culture.[1677]

Joel Connelly. "The Mysterious Monsters of BC," *Post-Intelligencer* (September 17, 1978).

Indeed, sightings of Sasquatch (or Bigfoot, as it more commonly known here) in Southern California are often in some way connected to the supernatural, or to UFOs. Sasquatch hunters in the Northwest snort at their Southern Californian brethren, down there in the San Bernardinos and Sierras crashing around in the woods with their divining rods and hired psychics.[1678]

Rich Louv. "Bigfoot: To Kill or Not to Kill," *Star-News* (June 22, 1978).

George Haas

George Hass, a pioneer of Bigfoot investigation, co-founder with Archie Buckley of the Bay Area Group, and former editor of the *Bigfoot Bulletin,* passed away from cancer February 16, 1978, at age 72. Haas' *Oakland Tribune* obituary described him as an innovator in organic gardening methods, proponent of reforestation efforts, and a lover of the natural world. "More than that, he climbed mountains and, in a perfect mating of interests, also sought out the legendary Bigfoot in the Pacific Northwest." Long-time friend Don Herron said Haas "had an open, scientific attitude," and that Haas "was inclined, from what he knew, to believe in its [Bigfoot's] existence."[1679]

Peter Byrne

"The people who hunt Bigfoot with guns," Byrne said, "are a bunch of idiots. I think it's criminal. It's archaic. It is incredibly stupid of them. Here we have something which is obviously rare—possibly a form of primitive man, unchanged and in a natural state—and they want to shoot one!"[1680]

That position was in stark contrast to Byrne's temperament when, before he devoted himself to searching for Bigfoot, he led tiger-hunting expeditions. It was a fact Byrne was self-conscious of. "Like many professional hunters, I simply got very tired of hunting," Byrne explained. "I got sick of the killing and I got very tired of the type of person I was taking hunting. Some of them were very decent people who became good friends of mine. Others, however, were the kind of people you meet once and never want to meet again—true killers, uncouth and ignorant people. Also, I saw the decline of the game animals, especially of the tiger in Asia. I loved the animals and I loved working there, but I just didn't like the killing anymore. In fact, you'll find that many of the top conservationists working in Africa today are ex-professional hunters who reached this same point and switched over to conservation."[1681]

The International Wildlife Conservation Society was founded in Washington, D.C., in 1968 as a non-profit organization dedicated to creating a refuge out of part of the big-game hunting concession which Byrne operated between 1953 and 1968. The IWCS's efforts led to the creation of the Sukla Phanta, or White Grass Plains, Wildlife Reserve, located south of Mahendra Nagar.[1682] The Park has grown to 200,000 acres, encompassing large tracts of natural grassland in southwest Nepal. As with his efforts with the tiger, Byrne was interested in government recognition and legislation to officially protect Bigfoot.

> This he has found to be a rather difficult proposition. It is hard to convince legislators to protect something that hasn't even been conclusively proven to exist. That doesn't deter Byrne,

who, emphatically insists that they have yet to be proven *not* to exist.[1683]

"Basically, they are man-like in structure. Quite large—six feet and up to seven feet tall. Weight: up to 450 pounds, perhaps more than that. They have large feet and hands, the feet being about 14 to 16 inches long. They are totally covered with hair, except for the face, the palms of the hands and the soles of the feet." Byrne believed that Bigfoot's countenance bore a closer resemblance to man than to apes. "Their faces are man-like, not gorilla-like; that is, they don't have the jutting jaw and mouth and the huge nose of the great apes. The eyes are large. Coloration is black, sometimes brown and may turn to gray with age."[1684]

Byrne had proven a very conservative arbiter in accepting a given Bigfoot encounter as genuine by employing high standards for accepting evidence as genuine. "When in doubt, throw it out." Byrne had dealt with numerous misidentifications of stumps and rocks as well as misinterpreted tracks. From his vetted pool of bona fide sightings, Byrne had deduced several expected responses from Bigfoot. "When an encounter with man takes place, the pattern seldom varies. The creature just turns and walks away. They always do this. They don't run. They don't swing through the trees or scream or pound their chests. They simply turn and walk away. We have over 90 sightings, I think 92 or 93 to date, and only twice do I recall them acting otherwise."[1685] Evidence from some sighting reports suggested that Bigfoot was curious and willing to observe man on its terms. "On one occasion one of them stood and watched a man at his campfire. The man in question didn't do anything. He saw the Bigfoot and the Bigfoot saw him. They watched one another for a space of nearly an hour while the man continued to cook his dinner at the fire. In another case, fairly recently at Mt. Shasta, one stopped and looked over the top of some bushes at a man and then went on its way. Otherwise, we've never seen any variation in the pattern at all. Perhaps they are conscious of the danger of modern man in the forest."[1686]

An example of burgeoning interest in Bigfoot, Byrne said, was the increase in subscriptions ($5 per year) to the Bigfoot Information Center's monthly newsletter, *The Bigfoot News,* which had more than tripled its subscription since 1976. The newsletter provided updates on the Bigfoot Information Center's findings and investigations.[1687] Byrne was also happy to talk about the Bigfoot Information Center itself; both his headquarters and public exhibition. "We can see the rise in public belief in the number of people who are coming to our exhibit here, talking to us and telling us about the experiences they've had," said Byrne. "They tell us because they see we will take them seriously. They lose the fear of being laughed at which was what originally held them back. I think there are many sightings taking place that we don't know about, that we're going to learn about over the next few years because of the public's changing attitudes."[1688]

Byrne maintained that each day was unique at the Bigfoot Information Center. "One day may be spent totally in correspondence. We have about 1,000 letters a month coming in right now." A source of mail that gave Byrne joy was the letters he received from young men and women at college who took Bigfoot seriously. "We have a fairly heavy correspondence with people in colleges—in Idaho, California, and some of the Eastern states—who want to come out and visit. They are in anthropology and biology and they are fascinated with Bigfoot. Their minds are open to the point where they say, 'Well, there could be something there. Let's do something about it.'"[1689]

Action at the Bigfoot Information Center really took off when an encounter was called in. "Another day, supposing a report comes in in the morning of some footprints or a sighting, one or more of us will act on it. If the scene is nearby, we will go immediately into the area. If it's far away, we will check and see if we have any associate in the vicinity. For example, if the sighting is in, say, northern Washington, 300 or 400 miles away, we'll make phone calls and have that associate look at whatever it is and then call us back. If it looks good, one or more of us will go. If there has been a sighting or if there are fresh footprints, then we may spend a week or two weeks in the area searching and trying to find out what made the prints, and to see something if we can."[1690]

"I seem to be asked the same three questions over and over again—especially by skeptics," Byrne observed. "The first question raised is usually something likc, 'If Bigfoot exists, why hasn't anyone ever found skeletons or remains?'" Byrne cautioned that the discovery of bones in dense forests was a rare event. Bigfoot, Byrne pointed out, was already a relatively rare animal to begin with and it was possible that Bigfoot buries its dead. In the wet, acidic soil conditions of the Pacific Northwest, bones dissolve, proving Nature was an excellent processor of remains. "In the course of my research, I have questioned hundreds of people about finding bones of a mountain lion and only once have I talked to someone who found the bones of a black bear. Very few people have ever come across even the complete skeletons of deer and those were usually quite fresh." The second question Byrne said he was commonly asked was, 'What does Bigfoot eat, especially in winter?' Byrne contended Bigfoot were omnivorous—even carrion could be part of their diets. In Byrne's experience, the third-most asked question was "usually put to me as more of a challenge than anything else. People ask, 'Where could the things live? Where could they possibly hide? How is it that more of them are not seen with the mountains full of fishermen, hikers, hunters, timber cruisers, cross-country skiers, and snowmobilers?'" Byrne offered examples of how easy it was to remain hidden in the northwest. Since Byrne's arrival to the region, he stated, no less than six planes had been lost in the dense forests and mountainous terrain. Byrne adroitly ran through several of the '70s' commonly provided examples of people hiding in plain sight: the 1972 discovery of the Tasaday tribe discovered in the Philippines; also in 1972, a World War II Japanese soldier was found on Guam, having remained hidden for 28 years while unaware the war had ended; in 1911, Ishi, the last member the Yahi Indians in California joined civilization; and in 1969, two boys watched a man enter the bushes in Portland's Washington Park which led to the discovery of the man's furnished cabin, hidden in the middle of the 149-acre park which enjoyed the services of several full-time gardeners and maintenance men and received an average of 50 people a day, 300 in the summertime.

> Now, Byrne urges, given these examples, ask the question of yourself. How can Bigfoot remain undiscovered when there is no place to hide? They do it with ease. In his book, *The Search for Bigfoot,* Byrne elaborates. "There is a saying," he writes, "that you may find what you are searching for if you search hard enough but that you will not find that for which you are not searching. This saying can be applied to the Bigfoot. Part of the reason why one has never been found, in the fullest sense of the word, is that with the exception of my own expeditions no one has ever searched for the creature on a full-time basis. The finding of the Tasaday tribe is a case in point. This incredible stone-age group was not discovered mainly because no one was looking for them. They in turn were not really hiding. If they were, like the Yahi and, perhaps, the Bigfoot, they would have taken steps to remain hidden."[1691]
>
> With the knowledge gained about the Bigfoot over his years of searching for them, Byrne feels that he is getting ever closer to the end of his hunt. He states confidently, "I think if we had the funds now, we could probably produce a Bigfoot in two years. We've learned so much and we have studied so carefully all of the things that should be done, we could put a plan into action within a month or so. With the study of various patterns

> and the use of the various scientific disciplines, I think within two years we could come up with one."
>
> As he draws nearer to the day he meets his long-time quarry, does he ever wonder how he'll react when the moment of truth comes, when he and a Bigfoot come face to face? "I've thought about it many times," he muses, "and, as a result, I believe that I have trained myself—as I try and train my associates—to act in a proper manner. Photography is very important and none of us goes anywhere without a camera. This virtually means taking it to the toilet with you and sleeping with it. One might see one of these things for a few seconds, then never see one again for 20 years.
>
> "One's immediate reaction, of course is very important. You might be shocked by the sight or presence of a Bigfoot, but the important thing is to stand still. If the thing were walking away and it looked as though it were going to disappear into the dense brush very quickly, then perhaps try and get some pictures. But, if it were standing, then the thing to do would be to stand perfectly still and make no movement, no sign of aggression of any kind, and just observe it.
>
> "The man who saw one last year, the one who had a Bigfoot watch him cook his dinner at his campfire, sat there for nearly 50 minutes while the thing stood there about 80 yards away. This sighting was fascinating to us because it suggested the possibility of communication. The man in this incident had to leave the area shortly after it took place. If it had been us, we would have stayed in the area and tried to communicate in some way. So it is important to remember, like this man, not to panic, not to run, to make no aggressive gestures of any kind, and to keep perfectly still—which is, of course, what you do with any large, potentially dangerous animal."[1692]

"They are not numerous. There can't be very many of them because if there were, there would be more evidence. I think they are quite rare now. I wouldn't care to hazard a guess as to how many there are. But if there were something like a couple of hundred and you were to spread that number all across the northwest and into British Columbia . . ." Byrne paused. "This is an enormous area of 100,000 square miles and which could easily hide a thousand or more of the creatures. No, there aren't very many and it's highly possible that they are declining numerically. When I first came here some years ago, I talked with the Indians and they said there were many more Bigfoot in the old days. They said they caught the white man's diseases. They talked about smallpox which, as you know, wiped out thousands of Indians in the late 19th Century."[1693]

Grover Krantz

Krantz, remained as ever the staunch scientific advocate for Bigfoot: "If the Sasquatch is a hoax, the fakery must have been designed by a brilliant human anatomist at least 40 years ago, and one who ever since has been directing a large group of people placing thousands of similar foot tracks under remarkable circumstances," he said. "No matter how incredible it may seem that the Sasquatch exists and has remained uncaught, it is even more incredible to believe in all the attributes of the hypothetical track-maker."[1694]

Krantz said his study of the Sasquatch foot had revealed to him "precisely what would be expected in an otherwise human foot adapted to a body weight of 500 pounds." "If the foot of the Sasquatch were built just like a man's, the Sasquatch would not have enough strength in his calf muscles to easily lift his much greater bulk with each step. Thus, the footprints in general show no arch but do show evidence of greatly enlarged ankle bones and toes more equal in length than those of a human foot."[1695]

> Dr. Krantz says he has examined plaster casts of two reputed Sasquatch hand-prints. They are half again as big as a man's. Unlike those of man, the Sasquatch's fingers do not appear to be more mobile than his toes, and possibly even less so.[1696]

Jon Beckjord

Writing in the March 1978 *Anthropology Newsletter,* Jon Beckjord mentions his group Project Grendel, its newsletter, *Gigantopithecus Gazette,* and the then forthcoming Bigfoot conference to be held in British Columbia in 1978.

> In the last nine months following the announcement in the Anthropology Newsletter of the formation of Project Grendel for the purpose of studying the available evidence relating to the alleged nonhuman hominid genus that some residents of the northwest feel strongly is a real animal and

not the result of too many beers in loggers' taverns, we have received an unprecedented response from anthropologists all over the United States and Canada. While some of the inquiries have contained some restrained sarcasm, the vast majority have revealed themselves as closet believers, now glad that someone, somewhere, is attempting to bring serious attention to the subject, even if unfunded and without formal institutional affiliation. The response to the announcement of the publication of our newsletter, *The Gigantopithecus Gazette,* named in honor of a possible ancestor of the subject of our research, has brought not only affirmative response but also membership and subscriptions.

This response seems to indicate to me that there is a vacuum in contemporary anthropology in the area of investigating subjects for which the only evidence is "soft" evidence. As far as many fieldworkers are concerned, it seems to be "safer" to stick to subjects for which there is already a type-specimen reposing on a museum shelf. It is also, unfortunately, easier to get funding to study such safe subjects.

An encouraging note is being rung, however in the announcement of the up-coming conference, entitled "Sasquatch and Other Phenomena," at the University of British Columbia, sponsored by the UBC Museum of Anthropology and scheduled for May 9-13. Scientists such as Bayanov and Bourtsev of Moscow's Darwin Museum, Krantz of WSU, Carleton Coon, Vladmir Markotic of the University of Alberta and others too long to list, will be presenting papers and leading discussions. While there will be a number of psychological and folkloric papers given, a number of papers concerning physical anthropology and evolution in relation to the putative "Sasquatch" will also be given. Project Grendel will also present some findings, admittedly "soft" evidence, relating to blood and hair sample correlation form three widely separated (Maryland, Washington and California) "Sasquatch"/human contact incidents to an analysis of six different vocalization samples via the sound spectrograph and to a series of drawings made by persons who feel that they have made genuine sightings of this alleged unknown primate, or primate-like, animal.

> Perhaps this will herald a new series of conferences that will raise our consciousness still further, in order to hammer in more firmly the lessons of the panda bear, the golden langur, the coelacanth and the gorilla.
>
> Jon Beckjord
> Project Grendel,
> Seattle, Washington[1697]

Project Grendel claimed 45 members by early 1978. "Some scientists will scoff openly," said Beckjord, "but quietly they say there's not enough scientific proof yet."[1698]

> An extremely effective way to first determine whether Bigfoot is in the area, suggests Beckjord, is for people to begin leaving food outside. Pigs, quarters of beef, garbage or fruit will undoubtedly draw the creature's attention.
>
> Sasquatch considers salmon a real treat—either fresh, smoked or dried. In fact, says Beckjord, there have been many reports from Washington state of Bigfoot taking salmon from fishing nets along fresh-water streams.
>
> Once an individual can determine that the food is being taken, Beckjord says the area around the bait should be raked and checked frequently for signs of tracks. Once you can establish a Sasquatch is in the area, photography gear can be set up.
>
> However, Beckjord is quick to caution against the use of firearms. And, he says "people shouldn't freak out."[1699]

Beckjord, calling himself an amateur anthropologist, presented what *Herald* (Everett, Washington) staff writer Jim Haley called "slim evidence" to a crowd Thursday at Edmonds Community College. "There's little good proof and a lot bad proof," he said. The presentation included a slide show and recordings of purported Bigfoot vocals. "Tracks don't prove anything. They just show that Sasquatches might have been there," Beckjord told the group. Beckjord said some of the best Bigfoot reports came from Snohomish County. Beckjord also acknowledged the work of pranksters, which ironically had sometimes aided serious research.

> Some past hoaxes have helped his cause, Beckjord said. The publicized hoaxes have brought public awareness and encourage people to telephone [genuine] sightings to him or police agencies.
>
> He's confident that there are more Bigfoot believers today than there were a few years ago. And that, Beckjord says, will lead to recognition that Bigfoot lives and that he should be protected.[1700]

Beckjord contributed an article to *Signpost,* a newsletter started in 1966 to provide news on Northwest hiking, which was summarized in the *Montana Gazette:*

> Sasquatches are described by the writer of the article, Jon Beckjord, "not as ape-types, but rather as wild relatives of man—man-like hominids—that, while living without the benefits of Coleman stoves and rain tarps, are just as smart as we are, and choose to avoid us by coming out only when we are normally dead-to-the-world, and in off-trail areas we generally don't get to." Beckjord feels that there are many [S]asquatches in the Cascades and Olympics and that there is no need to fear them; that they in fact have a healthy respect for humans and their guns. Beckjord further recommends that if you are lucky enough to see one you shoot it—with a camera.[1701]

Beckjord Examines Marion Schubert's Photo

Marion Schubert recalled a particular morning in April 1978 during a camping trip as crisp and clear with golden beams from the rising sun slanting through the trees. Schubert paused from fishing at a quiet pool near Lake Tahoe to take a photograph of the morning's beauty. She raised her Kodak Instamatic and focused on the reflection of two birch deadfalls symmetrically paired alongside the bank near her cast fishing line.

Pinole, California, resident Schubert was 4-foot-10, 85 pounds, and employed as a cable TV representative for El Cerrito Video.[1702] She hadn't been a believer in Bigfoot before that April morning snapshot was taken. Her position after seeing the resulting photo? Schubert: "I believe." What did Schubert see when she looked at the color print after it was developed? An indistinct, oval, blonde blurry spot.

Enter Beckjord who scrutinized the photo and came away believing that Schubert had captured something remarkable. Beckjord was described by reporter Don DeMain as a part-time stagehand, odd-jobber, and anthropology student, and the catalyst behind the formation of the Society for the Identification and Protection of Bigfoot. Beckjord and Schubert had decided not to reveal the precise location for fear of hordes of curious people perhaps chasing the Bigfoot away. Schubert went back to the site with her son and friends and heard eerie sounds.

> They were strange howls and cries, but not like coyotes and wolves.
>
> Beckjord said that was because the Sasquatch uses a "rah rah" type of ritual to communicate pleasure, anger and victory.

DeMain wrote that Beckjord, by this point in his Bigfoot-researching career, claimed to have seen Bigfoot twice, the first occasion in 1975 in Bellington, Washington, while he was driving a car and the second instance in June 1977 at a garbage dump in Everett, Washington.[1703]

> Schubert, 24, who works as a cable TV firm representative, took the photo while camping in the woods surrounding Lake Tahoe. She was alone and fishing in a pond at 5:30 A.M. when she decided to photograph the water and the trees towering over it with a small pocket camera.
>
> She recalls she didn't see or hear anything unusual at the time and, until recently, thought Bigfoot was a "big joke." But when she had the film developed, she noticed a weird blur of shadows and a yellowish spot by a tree. Some friends convinced her the shadows were Bigfoot and she called a radio disc jockey with news of her discovery.
>
> A listener gave her the address of Beckjord, who flew down to the Bay Area to investigate the incident.

"I've been looking at the photograph for a while and I think it's excellent evidence of Bigfoot's existence," Beckjord declared. After a reporter examined the enlarged photograph and expressed doubts that it contained something like a gorilla form, Beckjord offered, "Everything is not apparent the first time you see it." Beckjord pointed out the specific areas where he said the creatures' eyes, noses, and ears were. He also suggested a baby or juvenile

Bigfoot may also have been captured by the camera, but "it's so vague I'm not even going to try to push it."

> University of California anthropologists who have seen the photograph are unconvinced and refuse to "waste their time" travelling to the spot where the picture was taken, Beckjord said.
>
> But Beckjord and Schubert traveled to the scene last weekend and claimed they heard "screaming that definitely did not come from a coyote" and probably was made by Bigfoot creatures that were hunting for food.

As DeMain noted, before her fateful fishing trip, Schubert hadn't put any stock in Bigfoot, but she became convinced it was a real creature after meeting the enthusiastic Beckjord. She expressed the intent to travel back to the spot every weekend until she got a clear look at Bigfoot. Asked what she would do when she had that desired sighting, she answered, "I'll give him a big hug."[1704]

"We (the Project) [Project Grendel] have been collecting photos for many years and so far, Marion's is the best," said Beckjord.[1705]

> Many blowups and computer-enhancements later, he was certain he had found evidence of up to 15 Sasquatches—mothers, fathers and babies.
>
> Bekjord asked Ms. Schubert to return to the area for more photographs, so he could see if the same objects were still visible. She complied. The second roll of film, Beckjord says, showed "still more Sasquatches, but in different places."
>
> Convinced he was on to something big, Beckjord visited the area with Ms. Schubert. He made measurements which indicated to him that the largest animal was 10 feet tall. He photographed footprints.[1706]

Beckjord submitted his photos to Alan Gillespie's GeoImages, Inc. of Altadena, California, for enhancements; Gillespie had previously worked with photographs from Loch Ness which some believed showed Nessie's flipper. As Beckjord examined his enhanced photos, he was astonished, he said, "to find still more Sasquatches in my own photographs. They had been watching us, and we didn't even see them." Beckjord was ready to aid an undiscriminating eye toward where the Bigfoot lurked in his photos. "See, right there, a distinct head. And there's a body. Oh, and that one is carrying a baby."[1707] The Bigfoot captured in the Schubert pictures revealed creatures with blond and brown hair. Darker hair is found across the top and bottom of their backs, and showed prominent brows, wide nostrils, and flat faces. Not all observers of the photos were as convinced as Beckjord of their content.

> Vincent Sarish, professor of Anthropology at UC-Berkeley, said he thought the existence of Bigfoot "about as likely as Santa Claus." He and others who have seen the picture said it looks "for all the world like a long distance shot of someone in a shiny football helmet."
>
> Alan Dundes, a folklore expert at the university, said it was "hard to see anything" in the picture. "I think you had to believe something was there," he said.[1708]

Lee Frank

By 1978, the once Nessie-hunting Lee Frank had participated in more than two dozen Bigfoot searches in the U.S. and Canada. Frank took his one-man presentation, "Monsters Are My Business," to Douglass College's Hickman Hall on Tuesday, October 17. Hundreds of students listened as Frank tried to persuade them that Nessie and Bigfoot do exist, and the Abominable Snowman and other cryptozoological creatures may indeed be extant animals also. One of his investigations that Frank described was the foray to Davisville he wrote about for *High Times* in 1977 (see Chapter 8).

> When Frank arrived on the scene, he heard a loud rustle in the bushes and followed it. He approached to within five feet of the creature—close enough, he said, to where the beast could have pecked him on the cheek if it wanted to—then turned around and ran.
>
> "The thing about looking for monsters is that you're not entirely prepared to find them," Frank said, to the cheers of the audience.[1709]

Theories About Bigfoot

With multiple explanations put forward from several different quarters to explain Bigfoot, writer Edward Loughran proposed to succinctly organize them in his article, "Notes on the Origin of Bigfoot" in the March-April 1978 *INFO Journal.*

The first theory proposed Bigfoot as the descendent of a known progenitor from the fossil record, notably *Gigantopithecus,* known from the molars found by Professor Ralph von Koenigswald in a Chinese apothecary shop in 1935. *Gigantopithecus* moved from its east Asian climes to North America via the temporary Beringia land bridge. "Bigfoot then traveled down the panhandle of Alaska through Northwest Canada and into the Pacific Northwest. His search for different food sources led him out of the northwest and into different areas of the United States. The theory allows for such different creatures as the Mississippi Swamp Monster, the Florida Skunk Ape, and the Berkshire Valley Bigfoot of New Jersey. If your mind is open enough to accept Bigfoot at all, then you can accept that these creatures have had to adapt to new environments, and these varied forms are the result."[1710]

More akin to historic ideas of wild men, the second theory suggested that some people hadn't advanced into modern society and so remained more animal then man. The third theory, which Loughran called the "Pennsylvania Effect," after Alan Berry's term, suggested Bigfoot and UFOs were linked.

The fourth theory subscribed to ideas posited by the likes of Keel, suggesting that Bigfoot as well as other paranormal creatures are "visitors from another dimension and at certain times the 'door' to this dimension opens and these beings appear. After an unspecified amount of time, the door reopens and they seem to vanish off the face of the earth." Loughran points out that the fact none of these monsters—Bigfoot, Nessie, Mothman, etc. has been captured lends the theory an amount of credence.

Lastly, Loughran's fifth theory explaining Bigfoot is the one he contends most scientists can accept: Bigfoot is all in one's mind. Belief in monsters helps channel our fears and anxieties and in the end are healthy diversions. Loughran ends his article on the point that wide-scale hoaxing cannot possibly explain Bigfoot, so he has purposely omitted it because "the scope of the Bigfoot phenomenon is much too large to use 'hoax' as a valid theory."[1711]

Two responses to Loughran's article appeared in the July-August edition of *INFO Journal.* Dr. Delwin Cahoon, professor of psychology at Augusta College, Georgia contended that Loughran's article was "excellent in all respects," excepting his last theory describing psychological origins for Bigfoot. Cahoon states it is a common fallacy to dismiss phenomena ascribed with psychological origin as "lacking substance."

> Phenomena with psychological causes may or may not have a palpable existence. Certainly it may be true, as Mr. Loughran seems to assert, that most scientists seem to think Bigfoot is no more substantial than a dream or fantasy. However, it must also be considered that some psychological causes do lead to material effects having independent existences apart from the individual mind. . . .
>
> Obviously, except perhaps in unusual cases, Bigfoot is not conjured up by a person or persons concentrating upon his image. If the psychological hypothesis is valid at all, the process must be considerably more subtle than that. Perhaps in certain times and places of human existence subconscious archetypes are projected and activated through group energy. Bigfoot's appearance (monstrous hairy humanoid, occasionally with red, glowing eyes) is certainly a Jungian archetype for the hairy wild men previously met in childhood nightmares.[1712]

J. Richard Greenwell, who would go on to help found the International Society of Cryptozoology, discussed contenders for Bigfoot's origin from the fossil record, including *Paranthropus,* which Greenwell wrote, was "a more likely candidate for Bigfoot" than *Gigantopithecus*. With respect to Loughran's fourth theory suggesting Bigfoot was a visitor from another dimension, Greenwell wrote that "the less said about visitors from other worlds and visitors from other dimensions, in connection with Bigfoot, the better." Greenwell summarized his revision of Loughran's proposals into six new theories.

> *Gigantopithecus:* a ground-dwelling ape of which very little is known. He may have been large, but was probably not gigantic as his name implies. Some believe he was in the hominid line.
>
> *Paranthropus:* the large or "robust" *Australopithecus,* believed by many to be in the hominid line.
>
> *Homo erectus:* the first species in the genus *Homo.* He used fire and tools, and if he is Bigfoot, he must have regressed.
>
> *Homo sapiens Neanderthalensis:* the first true man. He had a concept of life after death, used fire and more advanced tools, and would have had to have regressed even more if he is today's Bigfoot.

> Unknown species: the possibility of an independently evolved hominoid-hominid (*not* found in the fossil record) surviving to the present should be considered.
>
> Misidentification/Imagination/Hoax: the question here is: can these three explanations, in combination, account for all the reports?[1713]

Ron Olson

While continuing to promote *Sasquatch,* Ron Olson identified to reporter Bob Michals the event that captured his interest in Bigfoot: the occasion of his first viewing of the Patterson-Gimlin film. Olson explained that when he and Patterson first met, Olson learned there was only 29 feet of the 16mm film. "I realized that wasn't nearly enough to do a movie, but it could form the basis for one so I began doing additional research on my own." That journey of research lasted about ten years before Olson felt he had enough to begin making a movie. Olson said he was close to Patterson until his death in 1972. "It was just one of those things where he had everything going in his favor," said Olson. "He (Patterson) was in the area checking out reported Sasquatch sightings from two weeks before. He was on horseback, which helps whenever you're tracking game, and the wind was blowing just right.

"Suddenly his horse reared and he saw the creature keeling to drink at a stream, not 30 yards away. He jumped off the horse and began running towards it, shooting the camera as he went," Olson said. "That's why the first few seconds are so jumpy. If he had had his tranquilizer darts, he could have easily dropped it because there was nowhere for it to hide in the canyon."[1714] Olson's respect for Patterson's accomplishment was obvious: "I don't think I ever met a more sincere man," he said.[1715]

Michals wrote that Olson suggested 95% of all reports he received were fraudulent or imaginary in an article that brought attention, again, to the computer analysis Olson helped instigate several years prior.

> To separate such fact from fantasy, Olson was instrumental in compiling a 1970 computer study of the Sasquatch that analyzed detailed questionnaires taken from people who claim to have made sightings. From this data, scientists have been able to make some very predictable assumptions as to the creature's diet, physical limitations and behavioral patterns.

> Olson doesn't discount other sightings—such as Florida's fabled Skunk Ape or Bigfoots supposedly sighted in Kansas and Ohio. He just points out that most, if not all, of these sightings have occurred since reports of the original Bigfoot have leaked out of the Great Northwest.
>
> According to Olson, two or three footprints are not usually considered adequate proof for an official sighting. "You have to use common sense in investigating these things. Is it a straight track, or a waddling stride? Are there scuff marks indicating someone was stretching out to achieve the right stride length for fake tracks? Are the tracks deep enough to indicate a heavy creature? Is there other evidence of a large creature moving through the area, like broken brush?"[1716]

Reporter Steve Otto of the *Tampa Times* was unimpressed by Olson's surrogates who remained on hand during his interview with the NAWR director.

> Alone, Ron Olson would have been a little more acceptable, even with that briefcase full of feet.
>
> But the two flacks circling him made it kind of a mini Ringling Brothers act and a lot less believable. . . .
>
> Olson was preceded into *The Times'* newsroom by two public relations men who made it clear that Olson was not only bringing startling revelations to the Cigar City [Tampa, Florida] regarding the existence of Bigfoot-Sasquatch, but that after seeing Olson, no one would ever again dare to challenge the existence of the legendary creatures.
>
> "Wait until you see what's in his briefcase," said Flack One. "That's the real proof. You won't be able to believe your eyes."
>
> "He knows more about Sasquatch than any one man alive," said Flack Two. "You can't talk to him and not come away believing what he says. I was with him when they made the movie, and I can tell you it's authentic all the way. He's been up there in the Pacific Northwest gathering facts for years, and now he's out to clear up all the misconceptions people have about the creature."
>
> After all that you would have expected maybe a Paul Bunyan type with kind of a wild look in his eyes to come

> in. But Olson resembled more of a downtown businessman with his conservative suit and briefcase and matching dour expression and quiet manners.
>
> Maybe he had been into too many newsrooms and talked to too many skeptical people to get excited anymore. . . .
>
> Olson and his group financed an expedition to British Columbia in 1976 but came back empty after three months of hunting. "But it's such a vast territory. We hope this movie will help us finance another expedition in the spring.
>
> "We don't want to kill one," Olson adds. "We want to tranquilize a specimen, run some tests on it to prove its existence beyond doubt, and then release it into its natural habitat again."
>
> Unfortunately Flack One cut in on Olson. "Show him the briefcase Ron. He won't be able to believe his eyes."
>
> So Olson popped open the case and held up two plaster casts of footprints made in Bluff Creek. "These are from Sasquatch," he said.
>
> The big one measured 24 inches in length, which made it seem likely that University of South Florida basketball coach Chip Conner might be interested in financing his own expedition into British Columbia.[1717]

Olson maintained an unshakeable belief in Bigfoot's existence on the basis of the Patterson footage and the historical sighting record. "You need a long history of sightings to substantiate something that can't otherwise be proved," Olson said. "For instance, in 1811 David Thompson, a trapper working for the Hudson Bay Trading Company, made note in his diary of seeing tracks of a giant man-like creature. And in 1893, Teddy Roosevelt interviewed an old mountain man named Bauman who encountered one of the Sasquatch when he was a young man. Roosevelt thought enough of the man's account to include it in one of his books." With such a long record of reports made by people with no expected benefit contributed to Olson's foundational acceptance of Bigfoot as an extant creature. "There are many other references by very credible people, made at a time when there were no newspapers to get publicity in. That's why I have so much faith in those old reports," Olson stated. "They had absolutely nothing to gain from talking about their sightings but ridicule."

> Often theorized to be a distant relative of the Himalayan Abominable Snowman or Yeti, Olson suggests Bigfoot is more probably related to similar creatures unearthed in Southern China during the early 1940s since the tracks of the Yeti indicate a prehensile (grasping) foot like that of a gorilla or ape. Bigfoot's tracks are unquestionably man-like, in both design and function.
>
> While most sightings have been of solitary figures, a few "families" have turned up. Again, speculation leads Olson and other researchers to believe the single creatures may be food gatherers who venture forth from the homestead to minimize risk to the main clan.
>
> Should Olson's luck parallel Patterson's, he doesn't plan to be caught empty handed. A tranquilizer gun, capable of knocking down its target at 70 yards, is always near. If a creature is captured, contingency plans call for implanting a small transmitter and releasing it where it was captured for study at a later date.
>
> Whether the findings will substantiate the folklore of which legends are made remains to be seen. In either case, the event will undoubtedly spawn "Son of Sasquatch" and countless other sequels.[1718]

Michals reviewed *Sasquatch,* sharing with his readers a less-than-sanguine assessment of the movie.

> No one knows for sure how many tourists in that part of the country [Pacific Northwest] go out of their way to "look around" the legendary critter's stomping grounds, though the number most certainly exceeds a handful and with each new sighting the crowds are sure to grow.
>
> The only surprising thing about Sasquatch is that somebody didn't make a movie of his exploits long before this. If not the C of C, [Chamber of Commerce] at least the tourist development authority should have had the prescience to finance such a venture.
>
> The task, however, fell to Ron Olson, founder of North American Wildlife Research, an organization dedicated to

> proving Bigfoot's existence. When he's not out following down reported Bigfoot sightings, Olson is a film distributor specializing in low-budget outdoor items like "Wilderness Family."
>
> Assembling all the available data into a story form, Olson molded the information into a pseudo-documentary designed "to create a positive reaction in the public's eye." By stirring up viewer interest, he hopes to apply a portion of the film's revenue toward funding of major expeditions to the wilds of Canada in search of Sasquatch, as the Indians have named the beast.
>
> By weaving recreations of actual historical confrontations, as told around the campfire, with a wholly fictionalized storyline the viewer is left with the inescapable conclusion that there must be some basis for the legend.
>
> More like a wildlife travelog than anything else, 90 percent of "Sasquatch" could just as easily have been titled "Beaver" or "Bear." The footage is pretty, but not pretty enough to keep at least a dozen people from walking out long before the final credits rolled.
>
> Trying to find one of those few remaining specimens in an area almost as dense as the Amazon Jungle in vegetation is like looking for the proverbial needle. The only way is to have them come to you and that's exactly what Olson does.
>
> His party of seven, comprised of both researchers and trackers, eventually meets the Sasquatch on its own terms and the costumed movie version does a very credible job of imitating the creature immortalized in 1968 by the camera of researcher Roger Patterson. Or is it the other way around?
>
> No matter. Either way "Sasquatch" is nothing more than a boring, amateurish attempt to capitalize on a gullible public and provides absolutely NOTHING you haven't seen or read several times before. Since you probably didn't pay for that information the first time, why start now?[1719]

In a *New York Times* movie review, film critic Janet Maslin wrote, "'Sasquatch' is the kind of pseudoscientific silliness that manages to discredit itself entirely, thanks to an approach that might best be labeled simulated-verite."[1720] The generally unfavorable reviews did not stop crowds from flocking to cinemas to see *Sasquatch*. North American Film Enterprises claimed that in its first 10 days in New York City, *Sasquatch* was shown in 102 theaters and earned $1,210,000 ($4,543,000 in 2017 dollars).[1721] Longtime *Register-Guard* (Eugene, Oregon) writer Fred Crafts picked up the tale of Olson and his movie's success in the Big Apple.

> Although some people may find it hard to swallow, "Sasquatch" has taken a huge bite out of the Big Apple.
>
> You remember "Sasquatch." The low-budget movie about the legendary Bigfoot was produced in 1974 by North American Productions, Oregon, Ltd., directed by Ed Ragozzino, starred a host of local actors and was distributed by North American Film Enterprises, Inc. [NAFE], of Eugene.
>
> Well, that little movie has played all across the nation and in January came within a snowflake or two of setting all-time box office records in New York City. Hard to believe, isn't it?
>
> As films go, "Sasquatch" is a 90-minute visual pollutant that appeals to hard-core Sasquatch fans and low-brow moviegoers. But, as NAFE's president Ron Olson has learned, the world is full of gullible souls who are anxious to be separated from their money. Consequently, "Sasquatch" is one of the most profitable movies ever made.
>
> And it's not through yet. The film is still being shown in the United States, New Zealand and Australia and its future includes stops in Canada, Britain, France, Germany, Iran, Japan and possibly a movie-of-the-week spot on national television next year.
>
> "Sasquatch" is a remarkable success story. Its filming was slowed by frequent reports of dissension among the cast and crew. Some doubted whether the project would ever be finished. When it was, others questions whether it would make any money. When it did, backers wondered how *much* money it could make.
>
> The film grew out of Olson's interest in Bigfoot sightings. He figured the subject matter was just outrageous enough to spark the public's curiosity. He was right. To shore up his sagging story line (the film concerns a backwoods adventure by some scientists to find a Sasquatch), Olson obtained Roger Patterson's film of a purported actual sighting.
>
> So many of us are so anxious to accept Sasquatch we are willing to go to extraordinary lengths to suspend our disbelief

and to discard our aesthetic sensibilities. Consequently, the film has been a hit, earning enough money to rate it one of the three top "four-wall" films of the last two years.

What's more, most of the entertainment dollars the movie is earning are being brought back to the Eugene-Springfield area, where NAFE retains its headquarters for its 12 member staff in a small office, jammed with film cannisters and filled with ringing telephones, near the Oakway Mall.

The way "Sasquatch" is kept alive is intriguing. NAFE representatives make a deal with a theater owner to rent his facility (all "four walls") for a certain fee. The theater owner gets a certain amount, regardless of how well or how poorly the movie does. In most cases, "Sasquatch" did very well, giving its 134 backers a tidy profit. . . .

"Sasquatch" rode into the Big Apple on the crest of a mammoth $250,000 television advertising blitz that placed 1,070 ads on five stations in 16 days. Viewers could scarcely turn on their sets without being confronted by "Sasquatch."

The film opened Jan. 13 in 110 theaters in the New York area and hundreds of people lined up to get in. Every show was packed. The next day the weather turned cold. It grew even colder with each passing day. Soon a blizzard set in that eventually paralyzed the East Coast. Because no one was on the streets, the theaters closed their doors. "Sasquatch" was dead.

"We came in there so strong that the theater people told us we would have been the strongest grossing film ever to play New York City," Olson says. "We went into New York to come out with a million dollars net. We were hot enough to do that. We'll always wonder how big could we have been."

Indeed, the movie had opened so strongly that it set a new record as the largest grossing "four wall" film ever to play on Broadway (it earned $42,600 in five days), the film had paid back $800,000 investment required to play New York and was beginning to pile up profits.

That's all so much melted snow now. Olson says it doesn't pay to rerun a film anywhere (a rerun of "Sasquatch" even did poorly in Eugene), so he doubts the movie will take another crack at New York.

> "Maybe in 10 years but not a year away," says NAFE accountant Ralph Hope. "The problem is it's going to take another $250,000 to start TV advertising again. You don't want to risk the money trying to suck up what you didn't get the first shot."
>
> "'Sasquatch' was no loser," Olson says. "One theater owner told us it was one of the most enthusiastic movies he's ever seen: 'The people just go crazy when they get in there,' he said. 'They come out babbling like a bunch of geese.'
>
> "The general public like that movie. It's not an Academy Award winner. But how many Academy Award winners sell tickets? Hey, I'm not interested in awards, I want to sell tickets."[1722]

"I believe in this story," Olson said. "Just about every Indian tribe in the Pacific Northwest talks about the creature in its folklore. And the stories of witnesses contain certain consistencies that seem to indicate the sightings are true." Olson was ready for skeptics as he promoted his movie with passion for the subject. "We're talking about thousands of miles of square territory and possibly only a few hundred creatures," said Olson. "The chances of anyone stumbling on identifiable remains are infinitesimal."[1723] While promoting *Sasquatch* in Florida, Olson described the movie as "a fact-filled and accurate attempt by concerned people to give Sasquatch the recognition it deserves and that is what really counts."[1724] Some reviewers called *Sasquatch* a pseudo-documentary noting any pretext that the expedition's members were anything else but authentic explorers was dispelled when the end credits revealed the actors' names against their respective roles. Did the chosen approach hamper the film by a pretext at being something it wasn't? Some critics unhesitatingly said 'yes.'[1725] Venerable *Tampa Tribune* movie reviewer Steve Otto mentioned a promotional lure for audiences in the Tampa area: "But all is not lost. If you go to the theater you can pick up a coupon, which for only $1.50 entitles you to send away for a [long-playing] record that includes the Bigfoot scream."[1726]

Print & Film

Force on Thunder Mountain was produced by American National Enterprises and tells the story of a father-and-son camping trip and the menacing powers they encounter. In one scene, they discover six-toed footprints—the atmosphere of mysterious goings-on atop and around Thunder Mountain (including curses, Indian legends, and UFOs) appears to owe some inspiration to the Bigfoot mythos.

Sioux Falls KELO-TV's chief photographer Howard Phillips traveled to Little Eagle, South Dakota, part of the Standing Rock Reservation and location of several widely-publicized Bigfoot sightings in 1976. Phillips spent two weeks collecting Bigfoot information which he turned into a two-part "KELOland" documentary examining the sightings and lore of the Mclaughlin Monster.[1727]

Peeping Times aired on NBC January 25 in the 9-10 P.M. slot. The special depicted a satirical news magazine show which television critic Jay Sharbutt called a "reaction" to the seriousness of *60 Minutes.* Put up for parody were stories of victimless crime, religious fashion, the need for more fat content in America's diet, and a longshoreman from New York who was pursuing his dream to become a nun. One of the segments starred reporter David Letterman investigating how the fictional town of Yule, Washington, purposefully faked Bigfoot evidence to promote both the creature's existence and the town's stature as the veritable epicenter of the phenomenon.[1728]

Manbeast! Myth or Monster, was, in the words of Timothy Harper, a two-hour movie which "simulates, but does not stimulate." For its television broadcast, CBS advised viewers, "This film includes dramatizations of speculative material." Wrote Harper, "This is a glossy production, with magnificent mountain scenery backed by the sound of trumpets and strings. It's too bad the pristine sights have to be ruined by shots of actors running through the forest primeval with patches of hair pasted on their arms and legs." The film posited Bigfoot as an extant creature, even condemning the logging industry for wiping out precious habitat the creatures depend upon.

"Unfortunately, 'Manbeast' adds little to the realm of what is known about the creature. Times, dates, names and places often are omitted in the recitals of various sightings, and only one person—a Louisiana farmer—appears on screen to say he saw Bigfoot face to face," wrote TV critic Timothy Harper. One reenactment assigns the blame of a skier's disappearance on Bigfoot minus witnesses or concrete evidence. Harper decries the movie's conflation between reenactments of genuine sightings with simulations of what could have happened.

Manbeast! presents Bigfoot as a shy, gentle creature, whose harmless, innocuous nature was proven by the story of a Bigfoot's restraint from visiting harm upon a little girl after she wandered away from her family's campsite. Viewers also watched the depiction of a sympathetic hunter lowering his rifle, refraining from taking a kill shot when what he saw through his scope was Bigfoot's benign and friendly eyes. A sort of cryptozoological arms race is hinted at, showcasing the pervasive competition between the United States and the Soviet Union, with the Communists out in front in the search for definitive answers and evidence on Bigfoot (a tact similarly taken by Al DeAtley in his opening monologue to *Bigfoot: America's Abominable Snowman*).[1729]

Harper appeared to have been perplexed by the transition, at about the movie's half-hour mark, to spotlight Peter Byrne: "the film suddenly and inexplicably shifts its focus." Byrne is showcased as one of the leading Bigfoot investigators and several scenes show Byrne participating in the *Anthropology of the Unknown* conference at the University of British Columbia in Vancouver.

The world premiere of *Manbeast!* occurred in Mobile, Alabama. "We chose Mobile because it is a reasonably representative audience," said Alan Landsburg, the film's producer. "The film is for the open-minded—it is [a] phenomena, something without a pat explanation." Landsburg called the film a "search for man's most recent descendant." The film was self-dubbed "the most documented film produced about the Bigfoot sightings;" based on over 130 recorded encounters. "You've got to be careful about sightings," Landsburg told *Mobile Press* reporter Lolo Pendergrast. "We chose to dramatize 12 stories, all of which showed different encounters with the manbeast."

> The crew collected just as many off-screen adventures as manbeast stories.
>
> "It was an interesting way to put together a movie," says [Landsburg], an enthusiastic, friendly man who speaks of yetis as though they are living just around the corner. "We didn't know what was going to happen. In Nepal, we met the Llama of Katmandu. It was quite a thrill. We walked into a room and there was this 82-year-old man, sitting on a great red cushion in a red and gold robe. We asked him, 'Have you ever seen a yeti?' and held our breaths. He said, 'Oh, yeti. Many yeti,' and began to tell us yeti stories. Now, that's what I call an

> unimpeachable source. He's not the Pope, but in his part of the world he's pretty close to it."
>
> Other encounters were less enlightening. On one location, someone made fake '[B]igfoot' prints to entice the filmmakers. In the Himalayas, they were snowbound for 8 days and had to be airlifted to safety. In Russia, they were denied entrance to a region where, as local legend had it, a farmer had mated with one of the creatures.[1730]

Landsburg, whose *In Search of . . .* television series had just marked its third season, was willing to put some credence in the possibility of Bigfoot's existence. "There are three points of view here," he said. "Either you're absolutely neutral, you do or you don't believe. There has got to be the possibility of another explanation about these creatures. There are 135 verified eyewitnesses—are 135 people loons? Is every footprint phony?"

At the end of the '70s, there was a contrast to be drawn and recognized between the world's vast wilderness areas with man's ever-present ability to negatively affect it. "Manbeast is a biological dead end—big and physical enough, but not smart enough to survive. It is a form of man never seen around, that has survived out of sight, like lost cities," Landsburg said. "If you place a pin on the globe at random, there is one chance in 400,000 that you will hit a populated area. There are just so many places where we don't know what exists."

Landsburg, who had broken into producing following a career as a writer of radio and film scripts, itemized some of the necessary ingredients to make a movie about Bigfoot: 10 round trip airline tickets, log about 60,000 miles traveling to locations around the world, hire some of the best special effects and makeup artists in Hollywood and spend about $1 million. As well as suffering pranksters' antics, the production of *Manbeast!* was setback by thieves. Makeup man Bob Bottin, who would have a long career in makeup special effects, reported that two Bigfoot costumes and three pairs of artificial feet had been stolen from a Hood River, Oregon, hotel over the July 15-16 weekend. Bottin said filming of *Manbeast!* would carry on with "a lot more makeup and a little more imagination."[1731]

It is an understatement to call John Green's *Sasquatch: The Apes Among Us* detailed and thorough. Green's straight-forward writing style is clean and direct which, combined with his voluminous sighting data, creates one of the seminal and most comprehensive books devoted to the subject. One

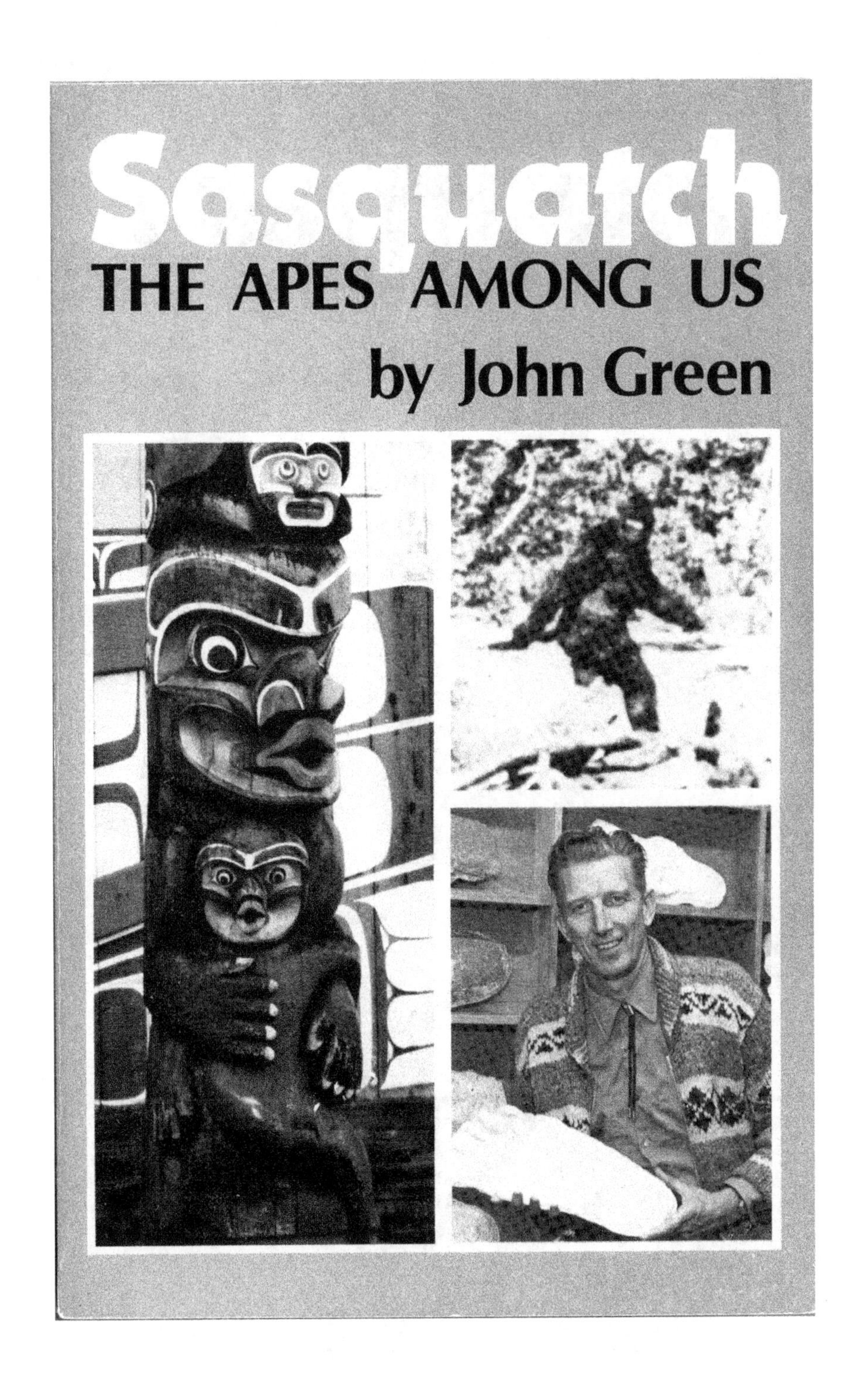
Sasquatch
THE APES AMONG US
by John Green

CREATURES
OF THE
OUTER EDGE
by JEROME CLARK
and LOREN COLEMAN
Authors of
THE UNIDENTIFIED
What
lies
behind
the Bigfoot
mystery?
WARNER BOOKS 89-150 $1.95

chapter discusses hairy hominids on the world scene, but the book's predominant focus is on North America. The tome is illustrated with maps (British Columbia, California, Washington and Oregon, Eastern United States, Florida, and Montana and Idaho) and includes a chapter on organizations and expeditions.[1732]

Creatures on the Outer Edge by Jerome Clark and Loren Coleman discusses the Bowers encounter in Vader, Washington (1970-71), the Lawton Wolfman (1971), and many other Bigfoot or Bigfoot-related encounters. Reviewer William H. Banks calls the psychic overtones connected to the Ape Canyon encounter which Clark and Coleman write of as one of the most surprising revelations in this eclectic collection of weird creatures. In his privately printed 1967 account of the Ape Canyon encounter, Fred Beck believed that the apes that attacked his mining party were supernatural in nature. Banks writes that *Creatures on the Outer Edge's* bibliography alone is worth the price. The authors dedicated their book to John Keel.[1733]

Don Worley

Staff writer Terry Burt's career at the *La Crosse Tribune* spanned 34 years. His "On the Other Hand . . ." column of October 20, 1978, was devoted to Bigfoot and the conclusions of Don Worley of Connersville, Indiana, that linked Bigfoot and UFOs.

> After researching the reports of 602 witnesses in 32 states, Worley's report draws the conclusion that the Big Foot is connected with UFO sightings which frequently have been reported in the same area, by often unrelated sources, at about the same time the hulking Big Foot was sighted. These sightings, by the way, did not come from the town drunk as often as from members of the clergy and police. Most often, however, from a cross-section of persons similar to average people anywhere.
>
> In some cases the creature was reported to have been almost transparent, many reported pumping volley upon volley of high-caliber bullets at the thing at point-blank range with little apparent effect.
>
> It isn't one or two persons who took a shot at Big Foot, it's numerous reports. Also, given the fact that these fusillades

> by even the most inept marksmen would have felled a herd of elephants, I'm at a loss for further explanation.
>
> While Worley makes a case for the UFO-connection, I will go on record as saying Big Foot is a flesh-and-blood creature.[1734]

Government & Law—1978

The *La Crosse Tribune's* Terry Burt waded into the debate over Bigfoot's legal protection and the kill/no-kill debate.

> I further believe that all states and counties in which sightings are made should follow the lead of at least one California county and place strong penalties upon anyone who would harm the creature.
>
> Killing a Big Foot may be akin to murder. It may be a subhuman species, or it may be something else. But whatever it is, it's a creature of God and probably a rare one at that. It's not something to shoot at. It may be something to learn from, not personal hygiene perhaps, but it might have some particular ingratiating qualities if we give it half a chance.[1735]

Robert Morgan back in Pacific Northwest

Michael Polesnek reported that Robert Morgan was engaged in a solitary search in Washington during August at the exact spot he had his own Bigfoot encounter in 1957. Morgan by this time touted his association (founder and president) of the American Anthropological Research Foundation (AARF) based in Miami. Polesnek listed the Foundation's other officers as: Michael Polesnek, Jr., vice-president; W. Ted Ernst, Secretary and Treasurer; and Deborrah D. Polesnek, field researcher.[1736]

Kurtz Files Complaint

Paul Kurtz, speaking for the Committee for the Scientific Investigation of Claims of the Paranormal, said his organization had filed a formal complaint with the Federal Communications Commission charging that NBC had uncritically aired several TV shows depicting paranormal subjects. The shows conformed to what Kurtz called "the new religion of the paranormal." Kurtz, a professor at State University of New York in Buffalo, editor of *The Humanist* magazine, and chairman for the Committee for the Scientific Investigation of Claims of the Paranormal, said: "Our work is to bring to public and scientific scrutiny all those alleged phenomena which are paranormal—which means anything extraordinary which has not been scientifically validated and so which may not be true." There were no shortage of subjects and their portrayal for Kurtz to take issue with. "The list of people and things we challenge is endless. It includes astrology, Uri Geller, the so-called Bermuda Triangle, thinking ivy plants, yetis and Loch Ness monsters, biorhythms, Jeane Dixon, ESP and flying saucers—especially flying saucers."[1737]

Bigfoot Scare Reported, But Nothing Bears Up

> The Legend of Bigfoot lives in Krotz Springs [Louisiana], but it may be reduced to just the bear facts.
>
> State Wildlife and Fisheries [WL&F] agents Tuesday were still puzzling over what person (?) or thing may have left a 19-inch-long track and a 15-inch-long track in the soggy earth near a swamp two miles west of Krotz Springs over the weekend.
>
> "I really believe it is a bear complaint," said WL&F Capt. Winton Vidrine. "I don't believe in it (Bigfoot) but something scared those people down there."
>
> WL&F Agent Durward McGee of Melville, who investigated the sighting of the hulking, hairy, infamous human-like legendary critter, said that what he saw was "definitely not bear tracks."
>
> McGee said that while on routine patrol he was called to investigate the sighting after Leonce Boudreaux and his family spotted the thing twice Sunday—once around 2 A.M. and again "after daylight."
>
> "I don't know what it was, but they definitely saw something that shook 'em up," said McGee. He quoted Boudreaux as describing the varmint as "between seven and eight feet tall," weighing 400 to 500 pounds with reddish brown, long hair and "he walked upright on two feet just like a man."

"There's nothing to it," said St. Landry Parish Sheriff's Office Chief Deputy Milton Hargroder. Capt. Vidrine said that although he was not with Boudreaux when he saw the creature he felt certain the frightened man had seen a bear come down from the nearby Atchafalaya Spillway. A bear was seen rummaging through trash near Melville (about 12 miles north of Krotz Springs on Highway 105) over the weekend bolstering Capt. Vidrine's confidence in his theory.[1738]

Boudreaux had the distinction of experiencing a repeat encounter with Bigfoot. Boudreaux told St. Landry Parish officials that while he and his wife were at a fishing camp near their home they saw a giant figure. Boudreaux and his wife had heard a strange noise which prompted Boudreaux to flash a light in its direction. Outlined in the light was a large, reddish-haired, creature. Plaster casts were later made of prints found at the site which measured 19 inches long. A Louisiana Department of Wildlife and Fisheries official suggested the impression should have been compressed deeper into the ground for a 7 to 7 ½ foot, 500-pound creature.[1739]

'Big Foot' Only a Big Bear (1978)

> A lab report had ruled that animal hairs found clinging to a pine sapling by a rancher's son Jan. 12 belong to a bear while nearby foot-long tracks have officials speculating "its gotta be a big one."

Cattlemen of Caesar, Mississippi, noticed that something stampeded their herds near the Catahoula Creek. While deer hunting, Karl Gross' son Grayson heard a guttural roar from an unseen creature crashing through the underbrush. "At first I thought it was two deer fighting, but it was so loud that I walked to the edge of the pine ridge to see," Grayson said. "Then [sic] is when I heard it make a sound. That was when I got real scared and got in the truck and left."

Hairs turned in for analysis had been found by Hancock County Game Warden C. J. Cameron who was called out to investigate the reports of a "Caesar Big Foot." Cameron examined several prints and found the hairs clinging to some saplings on a piney ridge. The hairs were turned over to Walter Fowler, a conservation officer for Harrison County who in turn forwarded them to the Mississippi Crime Lab in Jackson where (after a mistaken routing to the Gulf Coast lab in Gulfport) the hairs were eventually examined by Dr. M. A. Bass Jr.[1740]

"The hair was confirmed to be bear hair," Cameron said. "We couldn't confirm the track. We didn't make an impression [casting] or anything like that." Four prints had been discovered along the ridge, about five feet apart. The tracks were six to seven inches in width with four 1 ½ inch claws to each print. "From the size of the track, it would be a black bear," Cameron stated. "It sure was a big one. It was unusually large. He must have been a very old bear."[1741]

Cameron noted that bears, though uncommon, were seen from time to time in that section of the country. Cameron himself found the tracks of a mother bear and a cub along the banks of Wolf River in 1974. "This would be the place for one [bear] to be," Cameron said. "There are probably more than that one, but we just don't know about them," he added. Cameron was asked if bears would harm cattle stock: "If the occasion would arise, I'm pretty sure it could. We never know until this happens." But, he hastened to add, "Let me say, that it is strictly illegal to shoot bear in this state," he said, "I'm sure he wouldn't harm anyone or their property."[1742]

Edd Kaye and the Bigfoot Mystery Museum

> Sunday morning, 4 A.M.
>
> The phone rings, shattering investigator Edd Kaye's sleep. He reaches across the bed and snatches the receiver.
>
> "Edd Kaye," he says, untangling the phone cord. "What is it?"
>
> A hysterical voice babbles from the earpiece. Kaye kicks off the covers, fumbling for the pencil and pad on the nightstand.
>
> "Are you sure?" he says. "Now tell me exactly what you saw."
>
> After hanging up, he decides to wait till morning to relay the call to Cliff Crook, leader of Seattle's crack Sasquatch tracking team.
>
> "Basically what the tracking team will do," Kaye said, "is sit out there in there in the woods waiting for brush to move."
>
> Kaye is curator of the Bigfoot Mystery Museum in Seattle's Pioneer Square. The "mystery" refers to Bigfoot, not to the museum, he said. Kaye also answers the Bigfoot hotline, dispatching tracking teams to investigate sightings.
>
> "The problem we face is that of the detective," Kaye said, pointing out that Bigfeet are shy creatures shunning human contact. "The team always has to work after the fact, often hours after Bigfoot has been seen."

> "Since we can't predict where we'll see a Bigfoot," Kaye said, "all we can do is carefully investigate the reports we get and search out the area for ourselves."

The Bigfoot hotline allowed reports to be called in to the museum; Kaye carried a transceiver with which he could quickly respond to calls. Kaye told *The Daily of the University of Washington* he had been interested in Bigfoot since the early '60s. Though he had never seen a Bigfoot, he believed he may have smelled one of the creatures while he and his wife were driving along a country road. "It smelled rank, like nothing I'd ever smelled before," Kaye recalled. "To tell you the truth, my wife and I were a little scared. We didn't want to get out of the car and go looking for it." Monitoring the museum's hotline, Kaye had come across many stories of people having smelled something terrible, seen strange tracks, or encountered something that fit no other description but that of a Bigfoot. A composite of Bigfoot that Kaye had arrived at described its characteristics as: five to 10 feet tall, up to 1,000 pounds in weight, nocturnal and normally omnivorous but may occasionally eat meat. The Bigfoot Museum displayed casts of handprints and footprints as well as several hair samples. The Bigfoot-Sasquatch Information Service was a monthly collection of Bigfoot-related clippings edited by Kaye and billed as "another service from the Bigfoot Mystery Museum."

Kaye held a no-kill position. "Some folks are more cynical, I guess," he said. "They won't be satisfied until they put their fingers in the bullet holes in his side."

> Bigfoot Mystery Museum is run by the International Sasquatch Society (ISS). The ISS is comprised of the world's most respected Bigfoot researchers, including Cliff Crook, tracker of Bigfoot for 23 years, and René Dahinden, author of the book, "Sasquatch."
>
> The museum and the ISS work to suppress false claims and faked evidence. "Everything that goes into this museum has to stand up to scrutiny by the experts," Kaye said.

Kaye stated all evidence underwent critical vetting before being accepted. "It's easy to spot fangs that have been airbrushed onto a monkey photo," he said, "and some people bring in plaster casts that could not possibly have been made by a living creature." The museum was also wary of less-than-creditable researchers. "Some of these guys try to make money on pirated evidence. They steal or copy video tapes and films of Sasquatch and resell them, or they persuade curious people to give them money to help catch a Sasquatch." Those kinds of behaviors damage the creditability of Bigfoot research, Kaye said. Kaye referred to the Pacific Stage Lines bus hoax in 1977 (see Chapter 8), as an example of a hoax that unravels itself. "But what can you expect in a field as controversial and publicized as Bigfoot? A lot of jokers get involved for the attention they get for themselves."

> Kaye, whose job at the museum involves swapping information with visitors, will always have to remain quick to sort detail and check accuracy in Bigfoot reports.
>
> A man came into the museum last week and asked Kaye if Sasquatch had three toes.
>
> "No," said Kaye, "it's biologically impossible for a creature to stand on three toes. Why do you ask?"
>
> "I once saw a footprint on Vashon Island [Washington]," the man said, "and I wondered what it was."
>
> "Really? Did you report it?" Kaye asked as he slid the man a yellow ISS sighting report form.
>
> "Naw, I didn't think anything about it at the time," said the man.
>
> "Well, how big was the footprint?"
>
> The visitor's eyes wandered about the room and finally settled on a giant, purple, shag footprint rug beneath his feet. "Oh," he said, pointing down at the rug, "about as big as that."
>
> Kaye's eyebrows dropped and he plucked the sheet from the man's fingers.[1743]

Cliff Crook

When Edd Kaye at the Bigfoot Mystery Museum in Seattle received a tip on a possible Bigfoot sighting, his habitual contact for field research was Cliff Crook of Bothell, Washington. Crook investigated one of Kaye's leads on January 3, checking on possible Bigfoot tracks found in Kirkland.

> Reporters have searched for evidence of Christ, chased UFOs, fished for giant sharks and even hunted Bigfoot, all in the pursuit of the people's right to know and a chance to get out of the office.

So when the director of International Bigfoot Society called the other day, it was comforting to know precedent had been established.

Ed Kaye of Seattle, who also operates a Sasquatch museum, had read a story in *The Daily Journal-American* last week about the discovery of a mysterious 21-inch footprint embedded in a frozen stream near Redmond.

He was putting together a hunt. An experienced Bigfoot tracker had been enlisted.

The search began Tuesday at the spot where 27-year-old Diana Johnson of Kirkland found a clear print in the city stream while checking the water supply in her family's horse pasture Dec 31.

Located about 150 yards east of Willow Road at NE 97th Street, the track left a 1 ½-inch impression of a right foot, 10 inches wide at the ball, with the toes progressively smaller.

Bigfoot investigator Cliff Crook of Bothell said the location of the find fell in the middle of an area between Duvall and Woodinville with a history of Sasquatch sightings.

In the '50s and early '60s, Crook explained, eyewitnesses reported capturing glimpses of the legendary half-man, half-ape in the area. Dogs were found mutilated.

And every year since 1970, there has been at least one discovery of footprints and other circumstantial evidence, he said.

Crook has been on the trail of Bigfoot for 22 years, ever since he saw something in the woods near his home in Kirkland Lake that looked like the creature.

He learned to identify bear, deer, and beaver tracks while growing up in the rural area in the 1940s—and to distinguish them from the large, unexplained tracks periodically found in the United States and Canada.

Crook had made plaster casts of prints and collected hair samples and animal droppings linked to Bigfoot.

Within a half-hour Tuesday, he found a left footprint in a patch of ice several hundred yards from the other track. He soon located another possible but less-clear track nearby.

By the time he had finished a search of pastures on both sides of Willow Road, Crook had located a total of eight similar ice formations resembling footprints.

All measured 21 inches long, about 10 inches at the ball.

"Nothing is real clear," he said, "but it's possible they were made by Bigfoot."

"It's just curious that they all were 21 inches."

Crook said the tracks were larger than the average 16 to 18 inch print.

Kaye said no one, including himself, will believe there is Bigfoot until "one of the creatures is brought in, and you can pull its hair and poke it."

The best evidence to date, he said, is 30 feet of film shot at Bluff Creek in northern California in 1967 by amateur photographer Roger Patterson.

Patterson's movie showed a hairy beast, standing upright, disappearing into woods after turning and looking at the camera.

"It's the only film that hasn't been proved to be a fake," Kaye said.

He said serious Bigfoot researchers approach all evidence with skepticism.

"It's the only way," Kaye said. "People fake evidence and try to make money."

"We try to prove everything false, and if we can't, it becomes possible evidence."

Kaye has been a Bigfoot buff for 20 years. He said witnesses report the Sasquatch walks on two feet, swinging his arms to the side, unlike a bear, which holds its paws in front.

When a woman who lives in a trailer in the area said she had lived in terror for a week, Kaye assured her a Sasquatch would not likely harm her.

The woman said six unopened cans of pet food disappeared from her storage shed a week before Johnson found the track.

Kaye and Crook said that was interesting.

Anybody missing a can opener?[1744]

Friends Find Bigfoot Evidence

The *Tribune* from South Lake Tahoe published a letter written by an "accomplished woodsman," who described some of the unusual things he found while in the Knopki Creek area near the Oregon border.

> "Had a claim for placer gold up Knopki Creek and one day we parked the old pickup and were walking down the trail and [alongside] the trail in soft dirt were large manlike tracks about 18 inches long. It had come down an old skid road. Terrain here was rocky and lost sight of tracks until up the creek on a steep open hillside we saw big tracks ambling up and into dense brush. Those were the only tracks of that sort we've ever seen. So much of this country is also very rocky.
>
> "Another peculiar thing we ran into was a bed made of broken foliage behind a large Douglas fir tree. Bed was about 5 or 6 feet around and was depressed in the middle like something sleeping with the hip area pressing down. Looked the twigs [sic] broken over very carefully. They didn't appear to have been chewed or bitten off but to have been picked. There were droppings off to one side of the nest that appeared to contain tan oak acorns."[1745]

Murad's Courses Incorporate Bigfoot

Turhan Murad was an associate anthropology professor at Chico State University (CA) and in 1978 he taught an extension course at Shasta College intended to get people to think about Bigfoot and other mysterious beasts' meaning to both the biological sciences and to folklore. Murad called himself a Bigfoot skeptic and said if Bigfoot did exist, he was likely susceptible to similar conditions that were leading to the worldwide decline of all the known great apes, a leading cause of which was mankind's encroachment into their habitats. With less territory came pressures on finding enough food. Murad said Bigfoot could be impacted by this kind of encroachment because the professor averred there were few food sources for it in the Pacific Northwest. "He would probably have to spend all his waking hours foraging for food," Murad said. Murad also put value on Bigfoot accounts as stories. "There is a need to have faith in these kind of legends," Murad stated. "If you come across a footprint, you need an explanation for it."[1746]

Murad's course was titled, "Bigfoot and Other Monsters: Myth or Reality," and it examined evidence in support of and against the existence of Bigfoot as well as other cryptozoological entities. "I don't try to impose my beliefs in the class," said Murad. "What I do is to first define Bigfoot. We talk about stories and monsters in general. Why are some things considered monsters—because they're hairy and ugly? It is hard to come up with a cross-cultural definition."

After delineating hairy hominids, Murad and his students explored Bigfoot's ramifications on science and culture. "We deal with some folklore and talk about how scientists study reality. We investigate the evidence both for and against the existence of Bigfoot. I discuss the sightings, the footprints, the fossil records and primate behavior. At the end of the course I try to draw a conclusion. Does Bigfoot exist or not? It's all a question of how much one is willing to accept."

"The possibility of a Sasquatch interested me because I teach physical anthropology and deal with primate evolution and primate behavior," Murad told reporter Terri Dougherty, adding that students in his physical anthropology classes would inevitably ask questions about Bigfoot, particularly when Murad's lectures came around to discussing *Gigantopithecus*.[1747] "The fact that there have been fossils found from seven million and then two million years ago, bigger than a gorilla yet gorilla-like and possessing manlike characteristics, needs to be explained. One explanation is that they could be ancestors of Sasquatch."

When Murad arrived in Chico in 1972 he began hearing reports of nearby Bigfoot sightings: near Magalia and near Lake Oroville. "Occasionally people will call the Anthropology Department and say they have seen Bigfoot and want to know what the instructor thinks," said Murad. "I try to reach that person if I can. Lots of people don't want to talk about sightings; they're afraid of being laughed at." Murad's course was offered on campus and via televised extension classes to remote sites.[1748]

Greenwell & King Survey

Toward the end of the '70s, mainstream science noticeably crept further into the realm of Bigfoot. Cryptozoologist Richard Greenwell and Dr. James E. King, of the University of Arizona, polled 300 scientists to survey their reactions and critical comments on Bigfoot and the Loch Ness Monster. As one of their motivations for the study, Greenwell and King wrote they wanted to flesh out how new claims and theoretical frameworks challenge establishment science and "to what extent the attitude of scientists (in rejecting such claims) is related to psychological causes, such as social conformity, rather than to a critical examination and assessment of the data themselves."[1749]

The surveyed population was made up of 100 physical anthropologists, 100 biological limnologists and oceanographers, and 100 physical chemists.

Half of each group received a Bigfoot questionnaire, and a Nessie questionnaire was sent to the other half. The authors received 181 responses for a 60% response rate.

> Of the returned questionnaires, 53% were on Bigfoot (physical anthropologists 22%, physical chemists 13%, marine biologists 18%), and 47% were on Nessie (physical anthropologists 17%, physical chemists 13%, marine biologists 17%). Overall, then, the highest response rate was from physical anthropologists on Bigfoot. It is interesting to note that the control chemists responded equally on both topics.[1750]

Greenwell and King found that acceptance of Bigfoot as a living species among all three groups of scientists was lower than the acceptance of Nessie (10.6% and 31% respectively). Among all three groups, 40.4% asserted that ordinary animals, bears for example, were involved in Bigfoot reports and 69.1% believed that Bigfoot reports owed to "hoaxes, imagination, and myths (physical anthropologists 74.4%, marine biologists 78.1%)," and the lack of fossil evidence was the most cited reason respondents gave for rejecting the idea of Bigfoot as a living species.

> One of the most interesting results from our survey is the different perceptions of the impact that the discovery of such animals would have "on science." Only 3.3% of the physical anthropologists believe that the discovery of Nessie would have a "severe" impact, 36.7% believing that it would have a "moderate" impact, and 60% believing it would have only a "slight" impact. When it comes to Bigfoot, however, the reverse effect occurs: 51.3% of the physical anthropologists believe that its discovery would have a "severe" impact, 30.8% believe it would have a "moderate" impact, and only 7.7% believe it would have a "slight" impact. This consensus among physical anthropologists on Bigfoot is not shared by their scientific colleagues in physical chemistry and marine biology. Only 13% of the physical chemists believe Bigfoot's discovery would have a "severe" impact on science, 60.9% a "moderate" impact, and 17.4% a "slight" impact. Among the marine biologists, 21.9% believe it would have a "severe" impact, 53.1% a "moderate" impact, and, again, 21.9% a "slight" impact.

The authors also commented upon the extemporaneous comments they received. "There was nothing in our questionnaire or cover letter that hinted at anything but a sincere interest in obtaining their views on a controversial topic. Why, then, were we subjected to abusive comments? We can report, in this regard, that an informal Bigfoot survey conducted in 1974 by Joel Hurd among 500 anthropologists, biologists, and environmentalists, failed to elicit any abusive comments whatsoever (Hurd, King, and Greenwell, in preparation)." The promulgation of the survey seemed to suggest for many of the respondents an inherent bias on the part of the survey's creators.

Beliefs in Bigfoot

In May, the *Weekend* reported results from a poll measuring the public's perceptions of Bigfoot and other paranormal subjects. 40 percent of people thought the creatures definitely do not exist and 17 percent thought they probably don't exist. The number that believed the creatures definitely do exist came out as 9 percent. Canadians held similar levels of belief in the Loch Ness Monster and Ogopogo (though residents of B.C. expressed a higher level of belief than other Canadians) and lower belief in spirits and ghosts than Americans. Canadians did register a higher level of belief in extraterrestrial subjects (the Center for UFO Studies in Illinois stated at the time that more UFO sightings are recorded in Canada than anywhere else.) A combined 73 percent of respondents said stories about flying saucers were definitely or possibly true.

> "Do you personally believe that man-like creatures such as Sasquatch, Bigfoot and the Abominable Snowman really exist today?
>
> | | |
> |---|---|
> | Definitely exist | 9% |
> | Possibly exist | 33% |
> | Probably don't exist | 17% |
> | Definitely don't exist | 40% |
> | Did not state | 1% |

> "Do you personally believe in the existence of spirits, ghosts, demons or other such supernatural beings?
>
> | | |
> |---|---|
> | Definitely exist | 15% |
> | Possibly exist | 24% |
> | Probably don't exist | 17% |
> | Definitely don't exist | 44% |

"Do you personally think that some of the stories one hears about flying saucers are true?

Definitely exist	22%
Possibly exist	51%
Probably don't exist	13%
Definitely don't exist	14%

For some, the poll results corroborated the view that people were moving away from rational thinking. The youngest Canadians were the strongest believers in all forms of the supernatural; they were especially likely to accept stories about flying saucers—87 percent of them did, compared to 73 percent of the national sample. Skepticism generally increased with age; while only 27 percent of those 55 and older expressed some belief in beings such as ghosts and demons, 53 percent of the 18- to 24-year-olds did. Even more significant, perhaps, is that among people with higher levels of education there was greater belief in supernatural phenomena of all kinds.[1751]

A Gallup Poll published in June revealed that many Americans, particularly the young and well-educated, believed in at least some paranormal phenomena. The poll results were based on interviews with 1,553 adults, aged 18 or older, taken in over 300 selected localities across the country between February 24 and February 27. One in eight persons interviewed, or about 13%, said they believe in the existence of Bigfoot, similar to the 9% of respondents to the *Weekend's* poll who said Bigfoot, Sasquatch, and the Abominable Snowman definitely exist.

"Which of the following do you believe in?"

UFO's (Unidentified Flying Objects)	57%
Angels	54%
ESP (Extra-sensory perception)	51%
Devils	39%
Precognition	37%
Déjà vu	30%
Astrology	39%
Sasquatch (Bigfoot)	13%
The Loch Ness Monster	13%
Ghosts	11%
Witches	10%[1752]

Robert Chance

Robert Chance was described during the '70s as an environmental education high school teacher, wilderness outfitter, columnist, and a town commissioner of Bel Air in northeastern Maryland. His interest for which he earned the greatest notoriety however was his ardent conviction that Bigfoot was present in Maryland. For evidence, he ticked off instances of inexplicable slaughters of chickens, mauled dogs, and fifteen-inch tracks as supporting Maryland's own hairy hominid. A July 1978 AP story carried Chance's description of Bigfoot:

> About 7-7½ feet tall, the creature is a two-legged humanoid weighing roughly 350 pounds. He is covered with dark or reddish brown hair, except over his face. He has a flat nose and a pointed head and is a good swimmer. Most active at night, Bigfoot feeds on fish, poultry, roots and garbage.[1753]

Chance was reported to have collected 237 Bigfoot sightings in Pennsylvania going back to the 1950s. Chance himself believed he had encountered Bigfoot on two occasions. The first occurred in 1972 as he hiked an old logging trail near Muddy Creek in southern York County. Chance and four companions were surprised when several large boulders came rolling past them. Apart from the large bounding rocks, there was no further evidence of a landslide. "I've never been as scared as I was on Muddy Creek," Chance said. "I think he was just trying to scare us off. He could have hit us if he wanted to."

Chance had read of Bigfoot encounters and stories in the Pacific Northwest and the incident at Muddy Creek started him thinking Bigfoot made stomping grounds on the East Coast his home as well. In 1976, while looking into a Bigfoot report in Harford County, Chance came upon a horrid odor. "I could smell something, and my dogs were going crazy. I heard this [crash] through the thicket and this weird cry. I went and found saplings broken off waist high." Chance ascribed the incident as another close call with Bigfoot.

> There have been sightings in the county's Muddy and Codorus Creek areas, he says. Tracks have been found in outlying farmland. And a truck driver says he saw a Bigfootlike creature near the Peach Bottom power plant March 2.[1754]

Of Bigfoot's physical evidence in the East, Chance claimed hairs extracted from barbed wire had been identified as belonging to an unknown

'THREE-TOED' TRACK CAST, HARFORD COUNTY, MD, JUNE 1970
COURTESY BOB CHANCE

primate. Several prints had been cast and Chance was aware of a camper who believed he had tape-recorded a Bigfoot shrieking. Chance was unaware of any known photographs of Bigfoot on the East Coast. The very elusiveness of the creature was, he pointed out, a quality of its inferred intelligence; "You can't set a trap for it. It's too smart."

> Bigfoot perhaps has retained survival instincts humans lost thousands of years ago. Although curious and powerful, the fleeting animal is afraid of humans, Chance says.
>
> That attitude, combined with thick vegetation, makes summer a slow season for Bigfoot sightings. Winter is when incidents abound because scarcer food forces more activity by Bigfoot, thin foliage makes spottings [sic] easier and snow clearly marks footprints.
>
> The best theory Chance can develop is that Bigfoot roams the Appalachians, traveling from northern Florida to central Pennsylvania. In the [mid-Atlantic] area, Chance figured there actually are three Bigfoot animals. He guessed there may be 200 in the continental U. S.[1755]

"I don't think I could capture it because I wouldn't know what dose of tranquilizers to use. And I don't have 20 men with a steel mesh net." With the *Gettysburg Times*, Chance pursued more pragmatic musings concerning physical contact with Bigfoot. "I've thought I'd stand my ground and mimic what it'd do. Idealistically, I'd like it to communicate with me, although I admit that is a little far-fetched," he said. "I get razzed a lot. My father can't buy it (the Bigfoot notion). The commissioners and a lot of the people I teach with can't buy it. You lose some credibility. But eventually I'm going to regain it when Bigfoot is found." Critiques and comments came from many corners, however not all were worthy of consideration. "I don't mind criticism from outdoorsmen," Chance said. "But comments from a Monday morning quarterback who's never even camped out in the backwoods—I get upset when they give me grief. It's something I got to live with, I guess."

> Much remains to be learned about Bigfoot. Chance points out without hesitation researchers do not know where they come from, where they sleep, why no dead ones have been found, among other questions.[1756]

Robert Walls' Thoughts on Bigfoot

Robert E. Walls had arrived at a harsh assessment of people interested in the study of Bigfoot—researchers had not lived up to Ivan Sanderson's dispassionate and objective analysis embodied in his book, *Abominable Snowmen: Legend Come to Life*. So argued Walls in the Fall 1978 edition of *Pursuit,* positing that contemporaneous Bigfoot literature was rife with speculation and offered little in the way of unbiased examination. The results: arguments and conclusions with no firm footing. Walls stressed that queries were fundamental to science. The absence of this analytical *sine qua non* was, in Walls' opinion, part of mainstream science's negative reaction to the "pseudoscience" of Bigfoot research.

Walls' article discussed the state of the Bigfoot phenomenon in 1978 as he saw it. He offered a preface that despite the large amount of data collected from the Pacific Northwest, his theory should be applicable to Bigfoot populations existing anywhere in North America. Walls admitted reasonable answers to the mystery of giant hairy hominids in North America remained frustratingly elusive, but he elucidated his positions on several qualities and characteristics for Bigfoot, all arrived at from studying available data.

Communication—Walls took features of primates' communication, including a capacity to communicate over large distances and possessing of a broad vocal range, and applied them to Bigfoot. Bigfoot reports contained many examples of loud screams heard across significant distances as well as less intense vocalizations, presumed to correspond to closer, more intimate communication. The latter included whistles, gurgles, grunts, and coughs. Walls believes a whistle's wavelength characteristics permitted maximum penetration through foliage. Whistling also masks, to a degree, the originator's location thereby impeding detection. Bellowing yells and screams are of a lower frequency and therefore able to carry over greater distances. Consequently, the sounds attributed to Bigfoot fit the pattern observed in primates. The intent behind Bigfoot vocalizations was ripe for conjecture; Walls suggested that certain calls could allow different Bigfoot groups to track their respective, disparate locations over great distances or across rough terrain.

Functions of Odor—Walls wrote that only 14% of John Green's Bigfoot incidents contained reference to odor, making it perhaps a more infrequent component of Bigfoot encounters than was widely thought. Walls cited George Schaller's *The Mountain Gorilla: Ecology and Behavior* (1963) in which Schaller notes gorillas' stronger-than-normal odor when agitated or excited. Walls believed Bigfoot might emit a foul stench when confronting another large mammal. Odor emission amounts to an effective communication signal in thick vegetation or varying terrain, and its use at all possibly signals a creature's desire to avoid confrontation.

SEX RATIO—The accumulated data suggested to Walls that most observations were of male Bigfoot—why? Here Walls considered *how* Bigfoot are accorded one gender or another. He mentions Green's speculation that only lactating females have pendulous breasts. But there is no precedent of female Bigfoot breasts among the nonhuman primates . . . only *Homo sapiens* exhibit such features.

> Perhaps female Sasquatch's are more reserved in their daily wanderings, and may therefore rarely stray from the inner reaches of the boreal wilderness. I once thought this to be a likely answer, until a quick check of my files revealed that with sightings deep within forests, where Sasquatch was not aware of a *Homo sapien* observer, males still outnumber females 3.5:1.
>
> How can we account for this unusual ratio of females to males? In no other species of primate do males outnumber females—at best the ratio is 1:1, but more often than not females outnumber males by a 2:1 ratio.
>
> The whole matter of the sex ratio among Sasquatch populations is most disconcerting, and some serious discussion of it is long overdue.[1757]

VEGETATION ZONE PREFERENCE—Most Bigfoot sightings in the Pacific Northwest, according to Walls, occurred in hemlock (*Tsuga heterophylla*) and spruce (*Picea sitchensis*) zones. These are temperate and low altitude zones. The next likely areas to experience a Bigfoot sighting are the subalpine fir (*Abies amabilis*) and mountain hemlock (*Tsugo metensiana*) zones. Northern California's mixed conifer and mixed evergreen zones also ranked high for Bigfoot sightings. Moving east and crossing the Cascades, smaller numbers of sightings occurred in the grand fir (*Abies grandis*), Douglas fir (*Pseudotsugo menziesii*) and ponderosa pine (*Pinus*) zones.

> The explanation for this distribution is quite obvious to those who have lived in the Pacific northwest for any extended period of time. The western side of the Cascades receives far more

> annual precipitation than does the eastern side. Concurrently, the temperature variation (July–January) is not nearly as drastic on the western side of the mountains as it is on the eastern side. It is obvious which zones the Sasquatch prefers—the question remains unanswered is why do they venture into the drier zones at all?[1758]

Creature of the Night—Walls' tabulations showed that 50% of all Bigfoot sightings took place during hours of darkness. Given the 50-50 split of sightings made during night and day, Walls suggested Bigfoot's behavior as arrhythmic.

> The argument that the Sasquatch moves around much more at night than we suspect is based on the premise that the activities of *Homo sapiens* are severely curtailed in darkness, especially in the wilds. While the premise is undoubtedly true, one could counter this argument by asserting that the Sasquatch limits its nocturnal ventures to areas frequented by *Homo sapiens*. An arrhythmic animal's daily behavior is usually based on food accessibility—it will feed either at day or at night, depending on which time of day presents optimal foraging conditions. The Sasquatch, as an arrhythmic animal with an extensive foraging range, might occasionally find itself having to search for food near inhabited areas, compelling it to temporarily adopt nocturnal foraging habits.
>
> Mention should also be made of the Sasquatch's reflected eyeshine, although I hesitate to do so—for it is such a confusing issue. There exists a great contradiction in observations reporting eyeshine—the majority of people see a red reflection, but in a substantial amount of sightings the color green is noted. Now, green is the color reflected off the tapetum, an anatomical feature of the retina found in nocturnal animals. In contrast, the eyes of diurnal animals (which lack a tapetum) will reflect a reddish or white color, and often do not reflect any color whatsoever.[1759]

Survival in Winter—Walls compared Bigfoot's mass to that of a bear, an animal which enters into pseudo-hibernation (body temperature, oxygen consumption, and metabolism levels drop) during the winter season; bears in this state live off their reserves of fat. Those fat stores are built up from gormandizing during the preceding autumn months. But Walls didn't think that Bigfoot adopted a bear-like solution to colder winter months given the number of sightings reported during that season. Walls noted that no known primate can control its metabolic functions on the order of a bear's ability. Walls wrote that one primate, the Japanese snow monkey, appeared to benefit from building up a layer of subcutaneous fat for the winter months. Walls pointed out that this monkey is quite smaller than a Bigfoot, which would have a far greater demand on nutritional requirements. Though the extra fat is a benefit in winter, the snow monkey must continually forage. Walls considered migration, from higher to lower elevations as a survival tactic. Walls added that savanna chimpanzees in Africa migrate short distances, but in the case of Bigfoot, he cautioned more data was required to understand if Bigfoot indeed migrated or not.

Three-Toed Prints—Three-toed tracks were to Walls the most confounding question in his study of Bigfoot. His aversion to the topic was based on the drastic difference between three-toed prints and pentadactyl anatomy of primates (and mammals generally). Walls found no perceived advantage from utilizing three toes vice five and he called for further research and documentation of three-toed prints so their significance could be determined.

New Sasquatch Film?—Walls made reference to the White film. The White film made a splash with researchers but never broke into wider consciousness as it was never released for the general public's viewing. The White film received at least one private showing to a handful of reporters and enjoyed its most significant viewing (which was vehemently panned) at the University of British Columbia's Sasquatch conference. Walls became frustrated after several attempts to work with White to revisit the film site failed to pan out. "White's erratic behavior has done nothing but engender frustration among interested investigators. Until he is able to provide additional evidence supporting the authenticity of his film, I and many others involved must remain very skeptical."[1760]

In his article's wrap up, Walls stated there were no true Bigfoot cognoscenti; voluminous work remained for those devoted to the subject to flesh out Bigfoot's most basic and rudimentary details.

I think though that it is quite safe to say that no one investigator knows *anything* about the general behavior of the Sasquatch. The behaviors we have recorded during our 20 or so years of research are only the behaviors that have been occasionally exhibited in view of a relatively few fortunate observers. Additionally, observations of these behaviors are usually of very short duration, and, of course, are open to subjective interpretations by all.

Think, for a moment, of the history of ethological studies of other feral, non-human primates. It took George Schaller 500 hours and Diane Fossey over 3,000 hours of *direct observation* to determine the true general behavior of the mountain gorilla. It took Jane Goodall and Clarence Carpenter thousands of hours of constant observation and meticulous note taking to even begin to generalize about the behavior of their respective subjects.

But with the Sasquatch we have seen only the minutest portion of its daily activities. If we generalize now, with such meager and dubious data, we will have to suffer the consequences—whatever they may turn out to be, later. Remember, if we had relied on just the accounts (which were then considered to be reliable) given by early explorers observing the mountain gorilla for the first time, and the opportunity to conduct extensive ethological studies had never presented itself, we would still believe the many spurious attributes originally ascribed to the mountain gorilla. Let us not do so with the Sasquatch.[1761]

Ol' Big Foot's Back (Wayne King)

It appeared, as noticed by reporter Fred Garrett, that the Tuscola County Big Foot was back. Four neighbors of County Commissioner Kenneth Kennedy watched a "huge hairy, ape-like creature" walk across his lawn one-half mile west of Millington between 1:30 A.M. and 2:00 A.M. on October 21. The witnesses were Rodney Gouine, George Proctor Sr., George Proctor Jr., and his sister, Tracy. "We had just come home from a date," said Tracy referring to herself and Gouine with whom she was engaged. "We heard a sound like a cow mooing . . . we thought it was. Rod went to the edge of the road and saw it walking around on two legs."[1762]

"Rod came back to get George and they both went across the road, down into a ditch to watch it. It was too big to be a bear," Tracy said.[1763] The creature was aware of the boys' presence. "Then it turned and looked back at them and started walking toward the road and they ran back into the house. But the thing never did come any closer than about 15 feet from the road. It was just walking. It was a big thing—I'll tell you that."[1764]

"I hadn't seen it yet and thought they were only fooling around when they told me," Tracy recalled. She went into the Proctor home and woke her parents. "Mom called the Kennedys. I went into the kitchen to get a drink. Our lights were out. But Mr. Kennedy—who was looking for his gun—turned their lights on . . . then I saw it through our window walking across the Kennedy lawn," Tracy stated. "It was very big in the shoulders . . . but I only saw the upper part of the body."[1765] Eventually George Proctor Sr. found a .22 caliber rifle and joined his son and Gouine outside. "The boys took a flashlight and shined it in his face, and I had my rifle with me, but mostly we just watched it," Proctor Sr. said. "It walked real freely and took steps a lot bigger than a man would take." He noted several physical characteristics of the creature: "It had real big shoulders and walked with them kind of slouched. He didn't have much neck. It was like his head was just plunked down into his shoulders. I could see he was dark in color and his complete body was hair."[1766]

Tracy said Gouine, her father and brother all observed the creature for 15 to 20 minutes. "I'll swear it was something big and hairy," Tracy affirmed. Kennedy said in an interview that his neighbors were "very sensible people, not the kind who would exaggerate." Mrs. Proctor told Kennedy a "big, hairy monster is looking in your east bedroom," when she telephoned him. Kennedy remembered, "After it went away, we sat around in the dark for about an hour waiting for it to come back. The next day, I went looking for cigarettes or something—thinking it was human. My lawn is pretty well packed down and I didn't see any footprints," Kennedy stated. The ground sloped down from his house, Kennedy said, meaning something able to look into the window would have stood about nine feet tall. Kennedy was then in the midst of running for office at the time and decided not to report the incident. "I hadn't seen the creature and I didn't want voters thinking maybe I was nuts," he said.[1767]

The creature disappeared into the darkness behind the Kennedy home. "They don't seem to bother anybody," said Proctor Sr. "We sat quiet and just watched it until it disappeared off into the woods behind the house across the road." Proctor stolidly reflected upon his sighting as well as the possible intent of the creature. "I know it might still be out there, but it doesn't frighten me any," he declared. "It didn't appear to be too aggressive and it wasn't bothering anybody. It seemed to be going about its business. It never endangered us in any way. I don't think we should bother it."[1768]

Wayne King visited the Kennedys and investigated the area about their home in mid-November, giving special attention to a creek behind the Kennedy home. "King lives only seven miles south of here. He said he found what could be possible Big Foot prints . . . sticks crunched right into the ground . . . near that creek," said Kennedy.[1769]

King had investigated another Tuscola County Bigfoot report on Labor Day, 1977. The State Police at Caro initially dismissed the report made by Alice Traster who said a creature had been seen near Kingston on September 5 by her sons, Karl, aged 14, and Steven, aged 10. "My husband was away and the boys were riding their bicycles near our new pond in the back yard," said Traster. Steven told his mother later that he saw a huge, hairy animal standing on two legs behind his brother. "The boys are not afraid of animals . . . a deer or a monkey . . . they've lived in the country most of their lives," Traster stated.

The boys informed their mother that the creature's elbow reached the floor of their treehouse, five feet off the ground. "That would have made it eight or nine feet tall," Traster figured. Steven said the creature had breasts, Karl wasn't sure. When the creature turned and headed into the woods, both boys noticed what they perceived as excretions stuck to its backside and both boys agreed it reeked. "They both said to me, 'Oh mom, it stunk.'"[1770]

Fred Garrett's article for the *Saginaw News* included the police report's indication that the boys had seen something distinctly unusual, "a large creature, humped over with long brown hair, big teeth and long fingernails." But, Garrett wrote, police found no tracks in the dirt or grass at the location and called the incident a "suspicious report."[1771]

The night of the sighting, Traster talked to her sister, Wilma Roose, who suggested calling Bigfoot researcher Wayne King's Michigan Bigfoot Information Center. King and an associate drove to the area around midnight, interviewed the boys, and with others including Wilma's husband Charles Roose, proceeded at an early pre-dawn hour to investigate the scene where the creature had been spotted.

King later described for Garrett the astonishing event of seeing two creatures come out of the dense underbrush to feed on apples. "We saw one large black animal with long arms and all hair . . . we were about 80 yards away

. . . I was afraid. But I went toward it—with caution. I really don't believe they are aggressive," King said. "It had large glowing eyes about the size of golf balls set close together. Later, we figured the eyes were about 10 feet up. . . . I held the lamp on it and the eyes blinked."[1772]

"There was something else about 25 feet to the right," said King who spied a second dark figure in an open field. "It was another creature in a stooped position and bent over. I called out the Indian words I had learned and both animals started cantering . . . back and forth."[1773] King believed he was seeing a Bigfoot mother and her child.

"We got a neighbor to call the police, so that we could have outside confirmation of the sighting, but when the police cars came up with their lights blazing, the two Bigfoot fled into the bushes." Undaunted, King plunged into the darkness, anxious to give chase to his quarry. "We started to follow them into the underbrush, when the mother turned round at bay. Then she began to growl, and the sound was scary, I think it was the first time in my life that I really felt fear. We got out of there fast."[1774]

Follow-on examination of the scene revealed huge boulders had been moved at the base of an apple tree as if used for reaching high fruit. "Those boulders were too big for kids to move," Kind said. While the police were conducting their investigation, King said a "horrible sound" came from the area where the creatures had been seen, but an officer later said he had made the noise. However, Garrett wrote that according to Mrs. Traster the same sound had been heard for three days in a row after the September 5 sightings.

Charles Roose accompanied King and was less sanguine of their possible Bigfoot sighting: "It might have been deer eyes . . . we were too far away to really tell how high they were from the ground. We were 80 yards away. I did not hear any sound. There were at least two sets of eyes, maybe three. . . . I'm not sure." Roose further stated his confidence in the boys' story of encountering something unusual. "Obviously, the kids had been scared. And Karl is very mature for his age. I've never known either to tell lies or make thigs up . . . they believed what they saw . . . and they still have nightmares over it." But what could it have been? Roose suggested a practical, precedent-based answer: "But we used to watch deer all the time in that area. So, with nothing else to go on, I'd have to say they were deer." Roose did add that the eyes seemed "higher up than normal. And," he further explained, "I've only heard of deer standing up on their hind legs for food in the winter near trees to reach food. It wasn't winter and there weren't any trees in that field." Karl had drawn a picture of what he'd seen, an image Roose said looked scary.

"And I see no reason for him to make it up. But what they saw . . . I don't know. I only know what I saw."

Karl described to Garrett what he and his younger brother had seen: "It had hands, hair . . . but not on the face. And it grunted . . . it wasn't a deer, cow or a bear . . . and gorillas aren't that big. It was standing there . . . I saw it and took off. It was there, I swear." Karl concluded: "I think we saw Big Foot . . . I saw something about seven or eight feet tall. It wasn't a bear and it had human ears. I really don't want you to print this because I'll lose a lot of friends . . . they'll think I'm batty. But I know what I saw. And, no, I'm not crazy."[1775]

In an interview conducted by Fred Garrett, King recalled a case he had investigated for a Mrs. Foster of Midland and her daughter, Lori, who both claimed they had witnessed "something strange" while driving toward Midland on the Patterson Road. They were wary of reporting the event for fear of ridicule. They told King they saw "a figure covered with black fur and running on two legs" crossed the road in front of them, covering the asphalt quickly in gigantic hops like a kangaroo.

> The figure was about six feet tall. The two were about 75 or 80 yards away at the time. It hopped—or ran—into a wooded section owned by Dow Chemical Co.
>
> Mr. Foster said he suggested it could have been a deer. But both Mrs. Foster and Lori said it was not a deer. "I had to agree. Deer don't run on [their] hind legs," said Mr. Foster.
>
> "They told me," said King, "it was an animal of some sort but that it was unexplainable. Neither Mrs. Foster nor Lori saw any 'arms.'"
>
> They told King the fur was not coarse but smooth like that of a deer and that it's head was small. It was leaning forward all the time it was running, they said.
>
> Midland County sheriff's deputies said they had not received any other similar report for that area. They did, however, early last year, investigate a possible "sighting" of a Big Foot in the Oil City area. No final determination ever was made on that report.[1776]

"People think Bigfoot is found only in the mountain country of the western U.S. and Canada," King said in an article published in the *Midnight*

Globe. "But they roam across many parts of the country, and there are lots of them as far east as Michigan."

King believed Bigfoot were highly intelligent and especially effective at remaining hidden. "I believe that these creatures, being highly intelligent, have found refuge in areas where hunters are not allowed. And they are human enough to know which humans will harm them, and will retreat."

King, 42 years old in 1978, investigated Bigfoot reports and ran the Michigan Bigfoot Information Center from his home in Millington in his spare time from work as a machine operator in Flint, Michigan. "Seven years ago, I took up the hunt in earnest. I began checking out all the reports of Bigfoot sightings in the Midwest and making a filing system. From the extensive files our group here now has, there's just no doubt that Bigfoot exists." The Michigan Bigfoot Information Center boasted a membership of five—all active researchers. "When we get a report of a sighting, we get there as soon as we can to search for tracks and any other evidence of Bigfoot. If it's reported still in the area, we'll stay out all night, waiting for a glimpse.

"As for a carcass, no one ever finds a carcass of a bear or mountain lion. The scavengers of the wild take care of that." King was aligned in Grover Krantz's camp which advocated a Bigfoot body, or significant part of a body, as necessary to finally convince science of Bigfoot's existence. "And we'll get a specimen one of these days. Not alive, for I don't think we'll be able to capture one. But someone will shoot one, and then we'll realize we're sharing this land with another, man-like creature."[1777]

Wayne King investigated a sighting by Robert Cook of Sears, Michigan, who reported a "large, hairy and gray creature" while on a Sunday drive with his wife on November 12. The couple had been driving near their residence on Big Lake when they saw the creature at a distance of about 350 yards. Cook estimated the animal weighed 500 pounds and observed it stood on its hind legs. It did not look like a bear to Cook given its gray-colored coat. Cook was asked if he believed the creature he saw was Bigfoot. "Well, I wouldn't say it was," he said, "but I wouldn't say it wasn't. It always had been a joke in our family," Cook disclosed.[1778]

According to Norman Nowland, Bigfoot's presence near Sears, Michigan, "might spoil deer hunting in the area for a bit." Nowland, like Robert Cook, also resided in Sears and he was sure in what he hadn't encountered. "It was big and hairy and I could see his arms moving to his side. . . . I'm not exactly sure what it was, but I know what it wasn't and it wasn't a cow or a bear or any other kind of animal."

Nowland estimated the creature's weight at 500 pounds and its height as 7-feet. Nowland encountered the creature on Sunday, November 19th, while he was deer hunting three miles south of Sears. Whatever it was, Nowland said he saw it running out of a wooded area he had hunted in for 12 years. "I spotted it from my car and by the time I got my binoculars out, it had run down to the edge of the swamp 150 yards away," he said. "It was quite frightening in a way, enough so that I'd like to go back there deer hunting, but I'm a little leery of it." Without specifying its convincing details, Wayne King said the sighting was reliable. "This definitely is a valid, credible sighting," he said.

"We are definitely after the [S]asquatch. We are definitely out for a specimen." King stated there may be 300 Bigfoot in Michigan, with an apparent heavy concentration in Livingston County. "We've always had them," said King. "Many people have seen them over the years."

More encounters would come forward into the light, King believed, if witnesses could feel free from ridicule and mockery. "People have to have an assurance from you, a reliance. They're exposing themselves to ridicule."[1779]

Boys Operate Bigfoot Center

> Two Edina boys who operate the year-old Minnesota Bigfoot Center are convinced it's only a matter of time before the elusive creature is found.
>
> The center, based in a closet-sized room in Ted Steiner's home, is dedicated to the proposition that Bigfoot exists.
>
> "We believe there is a Bigfoot," said Ted, 15. "That's all there is to it."
>
> The center's co-owner, 12-year-old Dave Warner, said friends and relatives are skeptical.
>
> "They don't understand," said Dave. "They don't know anything about it. But I guess when we started, we were the same way."
>
> Walls of the room are covered with maps of desolate West Coast areas where the creature has been spotted. Pens and papers wait by the phone for breaking rumors and reports. Paperback books and envelopes crammed with Bigfoot trivia line the bookshelves.

> The center's bi-weekly newsletter, Minnesota Bigfoot Monthly, is pounded out on a small typewriter. At least, it's bi-weekly from March through November. The center is closed the rest of the year.
>
> The center added a UFO specialist, Rich May, 14, to its staff this summer.

Peter Byrne's *The Search for Bigfoot* served to catalyze the boys' interest in Bigfoot. For family vacation-time, Ted and his family made a trip to Bluff Creek in the summer of 1978 "to search for Bigfoot." The boys advocated field study of Bigfoot to learn its habits and behaviors. Should Bigfoot ever be captured, the boys vowed to disband the Minnesota Bigfoot Center. "It wouldn't be a mystery anymore," Dave said. "I mean, you don't see centers keeping tracks of bears and ducks."[1780]

Kirlin Analysis of Audio Tapes

University of Wyoming electrical engineer R. Lynn Kirlin and Lasse Hertel, a graduate student from Norway (who built his Master's Thesis around the Sierra Sounds: "An Application of Speech Processing Techniques to Recordings of Purported Bigfoot Vocalizations to Estimate Physical Parameters," M. S. Thesis, University of Wyoming, 1978), employed a Fourier Analyzer to compare the Sierra Sounds, purported recordings of Bigfoot vocalizations documented by Al Berry and Ron Morehead, with known human speech. "We extract pitch frequency, which is the rate of vocal cord opening and closing," Kirlin told Marcia Zimmer of *Branding Iron,* the University of Wyoming newspaper. "Preliminary findings have shown the pitch frequencies are in the range of a deep-voiced human male. . . . We have found the voice to be proportionately larger for Bigfoot as compared to a human man." Kirlin explained that a human male's vocal tract length—the distance between the vocal cords and the lips—is about 20 centimeters. The taped Bigfoot voices suggest a vocal tract length of about 30 centimeters. "We hope to come up with something conclusive and our main purpose is to determine what kind of animal it is on the recordings."[1781]

Kirlin suggested the tape contained articulation, considered unique to human communication. "Whatever conclusions are made will not verify Bigfoot's existence. That will not happen until one is shot and the carcass brought in," Kirlin said. Kirlin's own interest in Bigfoot was spurred from his visit in June 1977 to Peter Byrne's Bigfoot Information Center at The Dalles, Oregon. Kirlin and Hertel were not completely convinced of the existence of Bigfoot, but did not discount the possibility. "There is no evidence the tapes are fake," Hertel said.[1782]

Vaughn Bryant

Texas A&M University anthropologist Dr. Vaughn Bryant said his interest in Bigfoot started in 1969 after he joined Washington State University where he met Grover Krantz. "Being open minded, I told him I would be glad to listen to his ideas and actually go out with him on several of his investigations of sightings and footprints," Bryant told this author in 2016. "Few others were willing to do that, so we became good friends."[1783] His initial impetus had been to prove the whole thing a hoax. "I figured I'd have reporters calling me, television interviews, even get on the Johnny Carson show," Bryant said of his early interest. But the problem he found himself encountering was difficulty in disproving the legend; actually, much of the evidence was pretty good and the aggregate of data conspired to substantiate the creatures' existence.

Sitting in his A&M office, Bryant puffed a cigar during an interview with *Eagle* (Bryan, Texas) staff writer Jan Bailey in 1977. The space was filled with books, shelves held rocks and fossils, and here and there sat an assorted skull. A collector of Bigfoot news clippings and articles, Bryant had several footprint casts and a single cast of a handprint and had conferred with a biological specialist on what the population of Bigfoot would need to be to propagate the species—they arrived at an estimate of 1,500. Bryant conceded to Bailey that the Bigfoot mystery would likely be solved only by a body submitted to scientific examination.

> Bryant said while he lived in Washington he tried to contact persons who reported sightings to determine if they really had seen a Bigfoot.
>
> And the anthropologist said there were many false alarms. He gave the example of an entire Boy Scout troop who claimed to have seen a Bigfoot while on a campout. After investigating and talking to several in the troop, Bryant determined the boys had not seen anything, only heard a late night noise and thought they saw something moving in the shadows.

> In May, Bryant plans to speak at a conference entitled "Sasquatch and Similar Phenomena." The conference, which will be held at the University of British Columbia in Vancouver, will be the first such conference Bryant has attended and Bryant comments if the Canadian government (which is sponsoring the conference) pays his airfare and accommodations as planned, "This will be the first time in 10 years that I've received any kind of financial support for my research."
>
> Bryant describes his research as being "just like any other hobby." He adds since he's living in Texas, there is little he can do in terms of research since most of the Sasquatch studies are done in the Pacific Northwest.
>
> But Bryant has done a comprehensive study on hair and fecal samples from areas of reported sightings of Bigfoot. He will lecture on his findings at the conference.
>
> The anthropologist who is a recognized authority on prehistoric diet, pollen and fecal analysis said, "The hair and feces are definitely not of human origin. And they do not appear to be from the animal life that usually inhabits such areas."
>
> The hair sample was discovered when a hiker allegedly startled a Sasquatch which hurdled a fence and found hairs near where the Bigfoot had jumped.
>
> The droppings were found lodged in a stream bed. Bryant ruled out wolves, deer, elk, moose and bears from the samples, noting there were no cattle in the area.[1784]

The conference Bailey refers to, which Bryant and other scientists and specialists participated in was the *Anthropology of the Unknown* conference held at the University of British Columbia in May; Bryant contributed a paper on his research of alleged Bigfoot droppings and hair. "I try to objectively examine the information sent me. And I'm in hopes of someday seeing evidence that will either prove or disprove its existence," he said.[1785]

Anthropology of the Unknown—Bigfoot Conference in B.C.

As the '70s progressed, a growing number of scientists, if generally low-key in pursuit of their hobbies and their show of support, had become interested in Bigfoot and mysterious hominids. Dr. Marjorie Halpin, an anthropologist at the University of British Columbia, with help from like-minded scientists like Grover Krantz, organized the first scholarly conference on Bigfoot (first proposed in March 1977), titled "Anthropology of the Unknown, Humanoid Monsters, Sasquatch, and Similar Phenomena," held May 10-13, 1978 at the University of British Columbia at Vancouver.

The conference would be a forum for varying attitudes and viewpoints on Bigfoot. On display would be a spectrum of ideas, each of which was idiosyncratically committed to its own explanation and adduced notion of Bigfoot. Author Rich Louv adeptly summed these viewpoints:

> The creature is known by many names: Sasquatch, Bigfoot, the Abominable Snowman. There are nearly as many brands as there are geographical areas in which the beast has been sighted.
>
> Yet its essential nature remains a mystery. Some say it represents a real, living population of 8-foot tall, 800-pound hairy humanoids; a fellow hominid which has evolved separately and, because of its special senses, has managed to avoid homo sapiens [sic].
>
> Some say the creature is just another higher primate, an upright gorilla-type, which has yet to be discovered. Then there are those who contend the Sasquatch is a psychic phenomenon, a genetic memory, a reminder of what we once were or may yet become. Some say it is Jesus Christ. Others say it is really Howard Jarvis, bringing the great Tax Revolt to the Northwest.[1786]

To some observers, Dr. Marjorie Halpin managed the seemingly impossible: bringing the Bigfoot-interested community, including its warring factions and sparring tribes, together in a professional conference. Bigfoot investigators (René Dahinden, Richard Grumley, Bob Gimlin, etc.), philosophers and scientists—anthropologists, sociologists, psychologists, and naturalists, made up the roster of participants who in their aggregate, as Louv indicated, represented many diverse views and approaches. Writing after the conference ended, reporter Kay Bartlett highlighted some of the challenges which Halpin faced:

> Never again, says Dr. Halpin, who calls herself a "closet believer." The hunters weren't much interested in the role of the

> monster figure in literature, while the English professors didn't care much for the Sasquatch war stories. Besides, Beckjord and Dahinden got into a shoving match. Byrne showed up with a film crew, Dahinden threatened to walk out with his followers if the crew stayed, and one journalist entitled his article on the conference "The Bigfoot Follies."[1787]

Eastern Michigan University's Ron Westrum raised the proposal for the conference in a questionnaire sent to 70 persons to gauge interest in attending such a forum. Of the 70 questionnaires sent out, Westrum received 26 responses.

> Considerable anecdotal evidence indicates that doing research on anomalies like [S]asquatch in an academic environment can be difficult. Hence, one of the questions was "could you characterize the general reaction of your colleagues or work associates to your interest in this area?" For the nonacademics, six out of the eight responses indicated that reaction was favorable. For academics, six indicated "unfavorable" responses. The findings for academics become more significant, however, when we consider the relation between their attitude toward the existence of [S]asquatch and the reaction of their colleagues to their anomaly research.[1788]

Westrum noted that of the three academic respondents who "believe that [S]asquatch-like creatures exist," all perceived their colleagues' reactions as negative.

In an article for *Pursuit,* Patrick Macey recorded an apparently prevalent opinion amongst conference-goers held in regard to a particular attendee, the presence of Peter Byrne (whose presence, by design, was showcased in *Manbeast!*).

> The Conference had some disruptive moments as well: a Hollywood based film crew, attempting to exploit the conference by using it as a "backdrop" for their semi-documentary on monsters and myths, brought along their "star," a Bigfoot hunter from Hood River, Oregon, who otherwise had nothing to contribute to the Conference. After several days of inconvenience, many of the distinguished speakers as well

> as the audience had had enough of the powerful hot glaring lights, the equipment, and the film crew. At the request of many of the researchers and members of the audience, the Conference Chairperson, Dr. Halpin, finally asked the film crew to leave: the "star" left soon after the cameramen stopped taking pictures.[1789]

Several attendees were unhappy with Byrne's presence. In a letter to Dahinden dated August 7, 1978, Krantz held little in reserve regarding Byrne's filming several scenes for his film *Manbeast!* at the conference.

> As to the Landsburg Filming, Yes I'm with you on that. Put my name on the list of those who protest against any use of the film they made in Vancouver. They got some footage of Byrne sitting in the audience with me in the picture, just two rows behind him. I don't want that shown anywhere.[1790]

By 1978, René Dahinden of Vancouver had devoted much of the previous 22 years[1791] to hunting and investigating Bigfoot. Interviewed at the conference, he was asked how he hoped the Sasquatch would be discovered. "By me, by me, of course," he stated emphatically.[1792] Ever outspoken on his opinions, Dahinden offered a stern rebuke on the state of Bigfoot-researching at the time. "Bigfoot research is serious business," he said. "There is no room for some jokers claiming to be researchers who rely on stealing material from serious researchers for their own unethical use. They are liars claiming to be something they are not."

Dahinden and Bob Gimlin screened the Patterson-Gimlin film and Gimlin shared with the audience some of the details leading up to the encounter with Patty. Gimlin said, "Sometimes I wish we had never shot the film." For nearly ten years the film had been largely a source of vexation for Gimlin. "Sometimes I think I should have shot the animal," Gimlin confessed. By the time of the conference, Gimlin had been involved with ongoing legal disputes over the film. "It has only cost me money so far. I'm about $10,000 down in legal fees." Gimlin shared 51% of the film rights with Dahinden.

"I had a gun in my hand as I watched Roger film the creature run for about 500 yards. Shooting it would have saved a lot of bother." The film had not made him rich. "A little money comes in from time to time but we have to pay an attorney for his services." At the time of the conference a Canadian rights infringement case was before the U.S. courts.[1793]

Dr. Vladimir Markotic of the University of Calgary called the conference "speculative."[1794] University of Toronto professor Carole Henderson Carpenter called Bigfoot an evil reflection Canadians saw in themselves. "One could for example, follow Freudian or Jungian theory in suggesting that the negative aspect of Canadian monsters is a reflection of the dark, evil side Canadians see in themselves and therefore, as humans, generally do, project on the environment," she explained.[1795] Dr. Lynn Kirlin and Lasse Hertel from the University of Wyoming's Electrical Engineering Department provided their analysis on the Allan Berry sounds, including estimates of pitch and vocal track length required to make the sounds: "The results indicate more than one speaker present, one or more of which is of larger physical size than an average human adult male." Patrick Macey noted Dahinden was suspicious of the repeated success to record vocalizations over an extended period of time. Dr. Butler of the University of Alberta's Department of Zoology presented a theory that Bigfoot could be possessed of senses devoted to effective avoidance behaviors enabling it to elude official discovery. Science fiction author Judith Merrill, under her pseudonym Eric Thorstein, wrote about one of the conference's more colorful and provocative participants:

> Although his stamp is not universally approved, Carleton Coon (The Origin of Races and Living Races of Man) has a name that still carries weight in scientific circles. Coon is the 74-year-old *éminence terrible* of American anthropology, whose controversial theories of the origin and development of the human race just happen to provide ready evolutionary explanation for a living species of homo erectus [sic].[1796]

"I want the question settled soon," said Grover Krantz during the conference. "I've stuck my neck out and paid a difficult price—not being promoted."[1797]

> There were some humorous moments as well: much to the delight of the audience. Dennis Gates went "ape" over his own personal film of Bigfoot, after warning the audience that the film was under copyright. The first half of the film related the near-convincing hoax of a Bigfoot sighting which took place in Canada and involved a bus full of witnesses. The bus driver's vivid description (including facial features) of a giant creature

> as he chased it after the creature crossed the road into the forest was thought credible until the perpetrators confessed that the incident was a hoax. One of the men involved had dressed in an ape costume while another had severed as a "plant" on the bus to spot the creature as it crossed the designated path. Dahinden and Gates were in the process of investigating the incident and filming the prints when the hoax was exposed. A fuller account of the incident appeared in the Fall, 1977 issue of *Pursuit,* in an article by Dennis Gates entitled "The Mission, B.C., Bigfoot Hoax."
>
> The next scene of the "Gates film" focused on the Canadian forest . . . as a creature came stalking through the trees . . . a creature covered with hair, gigantic in size, walking erect, with ape-like features completely fitting the description of a Bigfoot! (A well known anthropologist has offered similar remarks concerning a movie taken last October near Mount Baker).
>
> Suddenly, the hairy creature posed and curtsied before the cameraman, then disappeared into the bushes, only to return once again, this time without its previous "ape" head—in its place was the terrifying countenance of Dennis Gates. Lon Chaney could not have done a better job; for a finale the Gates Monster swiftly threw Dahinden over his hairy shoulder and lumbered away with his captured prey.
>
> The "Gates film" ended with roaring laughter and applause from the researchers and scientists present as well as the audience. Gates, well known for his Sedro-Wooley, Washington, Bigfoot/Sasquatch Clipping Service, which provides researchers with current nation-wide coverage of the Bigfoot phenomenon, proved that Bigfoot research has it humorous moments.[1798]

Dr. Carole Henderson Carpenter of Toronto's York University presented a paper, "The Cultural Role of Monsters in Canada," at the conference. "The monsters in Canada represent the antithesis of the culture the British sought to foster here—the beasts are negative; civilization is positive." According to Carpenter, the presence of these monsters in the cultural fabric captures the fear and fascination many people feel to their natural environment. "The monsters personify the uncivilized and the underdeveloped in

Canada, and are an indication of beliefs held by Canadians and foreigners alike that the country is, to an extent, primitive or undercivilized." Several Sasquatch legend variants through time were given at the Conference, one such Sasquatch-like creature was the cannibal woman.

> Social conduct of this "wild woman of the woods" was described in a paper by Grant Keddie of the B.C. Provincial Museum delivered at a recent conference on "Sasquatch and Similar Phenomena" at the University of British Columbia:
>
> "The general behavior of a cannibal woman is antisocial; her behavior is the opposite of what is required of human beings. Instead of nurturing and caring for children, she steals and eats them. She also steals corpses from burial grounds."[1799]

A more benign being was Stenwyken, a hairy giant of the Okanagan Valley. An account of this being was recorded in a 1962 report by the Okanagan Historical Society written by Hester White who received the tale from an Indian named Suswap.

> "Stenwyken, the hairy giant who smelled of burning hair, left large tracks near the Indian caches where he helped himself to the dried meat, fish, roots and berries stored for the winter.
>
> "He was often seen at the mouths of creeks catching fish. He was a peaceful man, and never harmed the Indians.
>
> "However, one day in the long ago at berry time an Indian maiden disappeared; it was feared that Stenwyken had carried her away. After a long time she returned to her tribe and said Stenwyken had seized her and carried her to a large cave, the floor of which was covered with skins of bear, deer and sheep.
>
> "Another Indian girl belonging to a north Okanagan Indian tribe vanished from their camp some years later. After three years, she came back and said Stenwyken had captured her and carried her off to a large cave. He had sealed her eyelids with pitch so she could not see where they were going.
>
> "Some time afterwards she gave birth to a Stenwyken baby but it died. Again her eyes were sealed with pitch and she was returned to a place near her people's camp . . . She was released, but Stenwyken watched from a hiding place until she arrived safely in the camp."[1800]

Dr. Carleton Coon, anthropologist and author of the controversial *The Origin of Races* (1962) was one of the better-known scientists to participate in the conference. "A primate other than man, which is either ape or humanoid, is alive in this part of the world," the 71-year-old authority stated during his remarks. Reporter Eric Thorstein interviewed Coon in his Gloucester, Massachusetts office before he departed to attend the conference.

> When he speaks on Friday night [May 12] on "Why There Has to Be a Sasquatch," the scholarly world will listen closely.
>
> Carleton Coon pulls another plaster cast out of the flat drawer file, sets it carefully down on the table, and shuffles back to his kitchen-chair seat. He has been talking about the old days, some 20 years ago up on the roof of the world with Yeti-hunters Tom Slick and Peter Byrne; and about the time, 10 years ago, when Ivan Sanderson and Bernard Huevelmanns [sic] drove across half the continent in midwinter to photograph and measure the Minnesota Iceman, and brought their pictures back to show on this same table in this same chicken-coop-turned-office in Gloucester, Massachusetts, where I am now gingerly examining the Sasquatch foot cast. He has been gossiping about the people he has known through 30 years of background observation and encouragement, since he first heard Eric Shipton speak at the Harvard Travel Club about Yeti footprints. The stories are great, but they all end with, "My God, don't print that!"
>
> I ask him what I *can* print about his Vancouver speech. He replies, "I'm going to say that in my considered judgement, after many years, these things do exist."[1801]

Coon said, "Credible witnesses and visible signs of the elusive creature, including the Patterson film, give credence as to why there has to be a Sasquatch, but the data is rejected by conservative anthropologists." Macey noted that Coon received a standing ovation.

Heeding the Conference's call, 42-year-old Louis Rich Grumley journeyed to Vancouver. By 1978, the six-foot-six-inch, 300-pound Grumley claimed two Bigfoot sightings of his own. "Searching for our hairy friend has cost me everything I held most precious," he told the *Edmonton Journal* during the conference. "I spent so much time searching in the bush that I lost my wife, four children and my home." Despite the changes wrought in his life, Grumley remained adamant that Bigfoot was a reality. "But I won't give up. I'd like to get a team and equipment together to go for an all-out capture." Grumley had some very definite ideas on his dream team's personnel composition and its equipment requirements. "I would like a team of men trained FBI-style to fire tranquillizers from blow-guns or rifles to go for an all-out capture," he said. Grumley had enjoyed a varied tableaux of work experience, including tank driver, military policeman, bouncer, and, at the time of the conference, a disabled explosives driller. "I think an amphibious armored personnel carrier would be an asset in our search. It would be able to move at speed over the rough terrain we are likely to be searching on."

Grumley had founded the California Bigfoot Organization in 1969 (see Chapter 4) which at its peak had 80 members before falling into decline. But at the conference, Grumley maintained CBO membership was "gaining strength once more," and he told the *Edmonton Journal* he was then a veteran of over 800 Bigfoot-hunting expeditions.[1802]

"That there is a Sasquatch is as valid and obligatory to us as the fact that the world is round," wrote Dimitri Bayanov and Igor Bourtsev in their paper presented at the conference. They averred Sasquatch occupied "an intermediate position between ape and man" and that it was to be considered "an original figure not to be confused with any other." Bayanov and Bourtsev's enthusiasm was founded upon the Patterson-Gimlin film, which they concluded portrayed an authentic creature and surely not a mere man in a monkey suit. "We know today that manlike bipedal (two-footed) primates, thought long-extinct, are still walking the earth. . . . We are indebted for this breakthrough to the late Roger Patterson . . ."[1803] Several experts at the conference were unsatisfied with the Soviet's research.

Bourtsev began his study of the film in 1972 by trying to determine the film speed—crucial to establishing the speed and appreciating the style of the film subject's movements. "What it meant," Bourtsev said during an interview in Moscow, "was that I had to study every frame of the 900-odd frames of film." Bourtsev was firm in concluding "beyond the shadow of a doubt" that the film's speed was 16 frames per second. "At 24 frames per second it could have been a man. At 16 frames it would have to be a creature moving totally differently from man, no man capable of imitating it." Bourtsev's study required him to view the film "several thousands of times" during six years of study and enlarge each of the 951 frames for intense scrutiny. "The most significant to me was a particular frame which sharply defined the facial profile of the creature," Bourtsev said. "Somehow, this key frame was overlooked by American investigators. It was never published in America. My enlargement showed that, however close to a human face, it differed from it sufficiently to have its own specific characteristics: protruding jawbones, flattened nose, flat receding forehead, protruding eyebrow bones." Bourtsev's analysis led him to conclude a height of six feet eight inches tall and weighing some 440 pounds. Dr. Dmitri Donskoy, chief of the Chair of Biomechanics at the U.S.S.R. Central Institute of Physical Culture, studied the film subject's movements. "Dr. Donskoy's conclusion was that it (the creature) could not be man. The gait was totally different from man's," said Bourtsev.[1804] Dr. Donskoy concluded, said Bourtsev, that the film subject's gait was "a natural movement without any sign of the artfulness one would see in an imitation. It's gait as seen is absolutely non-typical of man."[1805]

"Then we turned to Nikita Lavinsky," Bourtsev continued, "a Soviet sculptor with profound knowledge of human anatomy and kinetics (motion). And he arrived at the same conclusion after a study of the creature's head, its forward thrust: it could not be a man." An American scientist that Bourtsev didn't need to convince was Krantz who added, "If Patterson faked the film, he also faked the design of the foot, leg and ankle. He knew exactly the right way it was supposed to be for that size animal. And quite frankly that man had no education, no knowledge of this kind of thing—there is no way he could have known what to do. Other things like body proportions, the motions of the arms, the rotating ability of the head . . . no man in a monkey suit would have come out with that design."[1806]

Vaughn Bryant of Texas A & M and Burleigh Trevor-Deutsch of Ontario's Laurentian University did not give the Patterson-Gimlin film the same resounding endorsement, stating that something more substantial than grainy film footage and other evidence like anomalous fecal and hair samples would be necessary to prove Bigfoot's existence. Dr. Charles Reed of the University of Chicago said the Russian pair had failed to provide analysis on the film subject's arm and leg length relative to men and apes. Along with the Patterson-Gimlin film, a movie filmed near Washington's Mount Baker in 1977 was also shown, filmed by retired Seattle civil servant Frank White (see Chapter 8). The White film showed what appeared to be a heavier, "more rumpled" creature than the Patterson-Gimlin film.[1807]

Robert Walls, member of the Society for the Investigation of the Unexplained (SITU), took up the White film in the Fall 1978 edition of *Pursuit* magazine, reporting on the investigation he and others undertook to ascertain the film's veracity.

> In May of 1978, four individuals—Rick Noll and myself from Seattle, Bill Davis from Canada, and Tony Healy from Australia—all conference attendees, made a concerted effort to locate the film site. Although we followed specific directions given by Frank White (the individual who took the film), we were not able to locate the site.
>
> We then made repeated attempts to get Mr. White to personally pinpoint the film site for us. Unfortunately, White never made himself available—which was most curious, especially since he had publicly offered his assistance to do so at the University of British Columbia conference.
>
> White's erratic behavior has done nothing but engender frustration among interested investigators. Until he is able to provide additional evidence supporting the authenticity of his film, I and many others involved must remain very skeptical.[1808]

Modern speculation on the film wonders if a brief clip may have made a cameo-appearance in the movie, *Force Beyond*.[1809]

Vaughn Bryant presented a paper based on research derived from alleged Bigfoot fecal and hair samples. Bigfoot had been Bryant's hobby for ten years. "I try to objectively examine the information sent me. And I'm in hopes of someday seeing evidence that will either prove or disprove its existence," he said. "Out of the three hair samples I've received, two were bear and one was cow," he said. "I haven't been able to completely decide what made the fecal samples."[1810]

"We have raced all over the earth, but some things we just don't know about," Bryant said at the conference.[1811] The persistent and consistent accounts of Bigfoot over the years had made an impression on Bryant. "I've run across a mass of circumstantial evidence during that time. I'm not ready to say it exists, but there is some kind of phenomenon appearing primarily in the Pacific Northwest." Bryant maintained that there were three great unknowns piquing the interest of the cultural body in the 1970s: UFOs, the Loch Ness Monster, and Bigfoot. "The only way the mystery can be truly solved is through the discovery of some hard physical evidence—not fuzzy photos, blurry motion picture film or tape recordings of the animal's supposed sounds," he said. "If we had in our possession one of the creatures thought to be Bigfoot, some bones or even a good hair or blood sample, then we would have the possibility of knowing the truth."[1812]

The conference was an opportunity for an exchange of ideas on the subject as well as a foray into Bigfoot commercialism:

> Ever since the conference opened Thursday, pedlars [sic] have been pushing Sasquatch books, pamphlets, pictures, postcards and—for $40—plaster casts of his footprint.
>
> Despite the lack of Sasquatch buttons, bumper stickers and T-shirts—probably an oversight—it's not a bad showing to honor a creature that might not even exist.[1813]

The Conference's Kill or No Kill Debate: Wanted, Dead or Alive

A conference-sponsored panel discussion on the Kill or No Kill question engendered significant debate and discussion. Panel members included John Green, who at this stage of his life, had accepted the post of executive assistant to Vic Stephens, the B.C. Progressive Conservative Party leader; the venerable Grover Krantz; James Butler of the Alberta Recreation, Parks and Wildlife Ministry; and Robin Ridington, anthropologist from the University of British Columbia.

Ridington and Butler sided with the no-kill position. Butler argued, "We do not know what impact the creature's death or disturbance would have on its own group. It may be a dominant leader and its group may depend on the leadership of that one creature for their survival." Green and Krantz countered that a specimen was necessary for the good of science and to ensure protections are put in place for Bigfoot's survival. "I absolutely advocate shooting one. It's our only final proof," said Krantz.[1814]

Greg Joseph's interview with Grover Krantz prior to the conference's start affirmed the anthropologist's long-held view on (someone) bringing in a specimen for scientific study. "There is no practical way to catch one," Krantz maintained. "The only thing you can believe is a piece of him here on the table. Or, someone could find a skeleton." But ask a bear hunter how many bears he's seen that have died of natural causes, suggested Joseph, and the answer will be zero. "Unless he's killed, an animal will hide himself before he dies. Finding a skeleton would be extraordinary. We could find the skeleton of one that was shot—that's why I've gone public," Krantz explained, "to reach someone who's shot one." To Krantz, the value of scientifically confirming Bigfoot's existence could mean everything to its future: "If it is possible that modern man is doing something to the environment that will destroy Bigfoot, and we have to find him to preserve the environment and save him." Though he had never seen a Bigfoot, Krantz disclosed he had a favorite hotspot in the Pacific Northwest east of Idaho to look for Bigfoot and its tracks. "There is one area I consider prime up there," he said, "but I won't tell you where. People might go up there and cover tracks, or shoot me accidentally."[1815]

From remarks made February 2, three months before the conference started, Krantz stated: "Most of the scientific community is convinced that the Sasquatch is imaginary," he said. "Only 10 to 20 percent of scientists believe they are real and most of those people don't want to acknowledge that belief publicly." Without qualification, Krantz said he *knew* Bigfoot was real, and he was anxious to have its existence proven to the rest of the world. "I think they are real but that it has to be proven. So, I'm trying to establish proof of the existence of these creatures and find out what, in fact, they are."[1816]

During the kill/no-kill debate, the audience's aggregate opinion could be gleaned during Krantz's comments. His arguments met with "a chorus of soft hisses," one article stated. Taking the opposite (and more popular amongst conference goers) standpoint, James Butler suggested a live specimen for study was better than a dead body.

> James Butler, head of the interpretation and education section of the Alberta recreation, parks and wildlife ministry, said it is hypocritical to declare open season on [S]asquatches while trying to protect them.
>
> "Instead of shooting first, we should be trying to communicate with them first. We can capture anything we can shoot."[1817]

"With all the frenzied searching for the Sasquatch the probabilities are fairly high that a human is going to be killed," Robin Ridington said. Butler suggested, "Whoever pulls the trigger would be remembered by history along with such persons as John Wilkes Booth, Lee Harvey Oswald, and James Earl Ray."

John Green did not see Bigfoot as a *pro forma* literal wild man. "There is nothing about it to suggest it has ever had any reason to depend on its brain. Its posture, walking upright, has nothing to do with intelligence. It's strictly animal." Green's acceptance of Bigfoot as an animal stripped away any question of humanity and discarded legal protections as far as collecting a specimen went. "If man makes use of animals, I know of no reason to treat this differently from other animals except we see our reflection in it." Green said he could understand the opposing position. "They really want there to be a noble savage out there, and it's very hard to take that away from them." Green was characteristically straightforward in his assessment of pragmatically obtaining a specimen: "We could spend 500 years and $10 million to catch one alive rather than persuading some little guy to put a .30-06 in his head tomorrow and the result will be exactly the same."[1818]

Green knew accounts of people who had fixed Bigfoot in their crosshairs: "I know many hunters who have had a Sasquatch in their sights and have not fired because of some kind of taboo." Here Green again hammered home the point that since Bigfoot resembles man, it followed to think of it not as an animal but as human. "They thought the Sasquatch had human qualities and could not bring themselves to kill it. But the Sasquatch is an animal and should be treated as such." Researchers in the '70s often proffered estimates of Bigfoot population size—usually in concert with ecological warnings of man's intrusion into its habitat—but Green voiced the rare suggestion that Bigfoot was actually doing quite well and estimated that the Bigfoot population was growing;[1819] deftly countering the notion that Bigfoot's supposed rarity precluded it from being hunted and killed for science. "Quite to the contrary, it is an extremely successful species. The only places we don't get reports are in the Great Plains and the Rocky Mountains. I see no reason to say that these creatures are endangered by man, because, after all, we have no record of anyone successfully hunting a Sasquatch."[1820]

Green avowed his picture of Bigfoot was formed from the many reports he had received and studied over the years. He believed Bigfoot was solitary, omnivorous, possessing night vision, and readily made use of waterways for travel. "Its size and strength have plainly proved to be sufficient both for protection and for obtaining food without reliance on tools or weapons and it has never learned to throw things effectively," said Green. "Hard though it may be to accept, there are reports indicating that it has developed speed of foot sufficient to flee or to catch almost any other animal." Bigfoot was well-adapted to conditions in North America, Green maintained. "Certainly it has never lost its fur coat and is able to get along in cold weather without either clothing or fire."[1821]

> There is no reason why the animal should have developed a brain, and Mr. Green says there would be more [S]asquatch sightings than cougar sightings if cougars weren't hunted by dogs.
>
> He says the biggest argument against there being a [S]asquatch is the lack of remains.[1822]

Green believed the morphological similarity shared between humans and Bigfoot was the source for the former's reticence to the idea of killing the latter. "The only argument for treating this animal in a preferred way is that we see in it a reflection of ourselves because of the way it walks," he stated. "It is not an endangered species. It exists all over North America. There are probably 100,000 of them. If by the sacrifice of one of these animals we can prove they exist, we can then take steps to protect the rest of them."[1823]

Bigfoot seemed to be the perfect mystery caught between two fundamental aspects of human nature—the drive to know and a desire to protect. Green: "We are talking about an animal, not a human being. A lot of people believe in Sasquatch because they like the idea of the innocent savage. But the consistent sightings show that it is not human. It has never even learned to throw a rock in a straight line; in a thousand sightings nobody has ever reported a Sasquatch with the ability to throw overhand. Why should this animal get special treatment? If anybody wants to make a case that man should not kill animals, I'm quite prepared to listen to it and have quite an inclination to be on that side."[1824]

Butler said: "My conflict lies in the fact that I'm both a scientist and an environmentalist, and my feeling is that we should be working together now for a consistent protective ethic, not a killing ethic. If we try to encourage the philosophy of kill-today-and-protect-tomorrow, killing one or six today and then cutting it off there, I'm sorry but that doesn't work. It is highly hypocritical." Butler suggested the ramifications on public opinion and judgment could be disastrous. "It would be very difficult to reverse people's attitudes after the initial killing. Instead of shooting first, we should be trying to communicate first. Instead of developing the ethic of mobs with torches rushing the castle, let's act like the advanced and civilized society we're supposed to be. By continuing to be violent in our contacts with the beast, we may be delaying our chances of communicating with it for years."[1825]

Killing a Bigfoot, Butler maintained, could be the murder of a fellow hominid. "I would hate to think that something would have to be related to us to be granted the necessary asylum." Butler also pointed out that the pro-kill position not only endangered Bigfoot but could imperil people as well. "Some of my colleagues, including Mr. Green, advocate mass education to encourage the killing of a Sasquatch, but I fear the danger that would pose to human beings; first, to practical jokers wearing gorilla suits and secondly to people who happen to be in the woods at the wrong place and wrong time."

Butler further guessed that a wounded Bigfoot, given their supposed difficulty to kill, would pose a danger to people. "I can see a movie coming out of Hollywood soon, called 'The Rogue Sasquatch.'" Bigfoot's inferred low population numbers also begged reconsideration of killing one. "While Mr. Green maintains the Sasquatch population appears to be widespread," Butler said, "I would point out the buffalo, prairie chicken and wolf were once widespread. The greater the distribution of an animal, the more chance there is of fragmentation due to environmental modification." It could be, given the available knowledge on Bigfoot, that even the premature, "unnatural" death of even one specimen could have deleterious effects. "There is in any animal population what we refer to as the 'critical population' level, below which the animal has little chance of recovering. We don't know the 'critical population' level of the Sasquatch. We do know that range fragmentation and environmental stress are contributing factors in reaching a critical population level. In killing one or a few Sasquatches, we may be passing the critical population level."

Bigfoot was a higher primate, Krantz allowed, but not human, and not particularly intelligent. Krantz's advice to a would-be Bigfoot hunter was to "kill the beast, cut off an arm or a leg or anything you can carry, and get the hell out of there." Krantz distilled his position into a moralistic rationalization: "How do you protect an endangered species," he asked, "if you haven't established that the species exists?" Reporter Rich Louv wrote that to some of Krantz's opponents, including Jon Beckjord, his reasoning was reminiscent of a logic expressed during the Vietnam War—destroy a village in order to save it.[1826]

Holding up a jawbone in dramatic fashion before the audience Krantz said: "This is what we need to prove that the Sasquatch exists," he said. "And the best way to obtain a Sasquatch jaw is to kill a Sasquatch."[1827]

"The reason you don't find Sasquatch skeletons is that they probably hide the body like a bear does; like any other animal that dies slowly, the Sasquatch hides itself," Krantz conjectured. "The body is covered by vegetation, eaten by small animals, disappears." Krantz mentioned the oft-repeated argument that Mother Nature performs an exceptional job recycling the old back into the new. "I've talked to hundreds of bear hunters and guides and asked them if they've ever come across the corpse of a bear that has died a natural death. So far, no such corpses have been found. Not one. There are at least a hundred bears to every Sasquatch. After we've found the first hundred bears that have died natural deaths, we ought to be due for a Sasquatch corpse." At this point John Green interrupted to state that the majority of Bigfoot sightings occurred in the Northwest and in British Columbia, an area of high rainfall amounts producing enough moisture to dissolve most bones inside of a month. "The reason I'm willing to talk to the news media and risk my reputation and suffer badly for it is that I'm trying to scare up that hunter who will bring me a jaw or a piece of a Sasquatch corpse. The only practical way to find a jaw like this is to commit a fresh kill. If we wait for a corpse to show up on its own, having died of natural causes, we'll wait forever. And while we wait forever, the Sasquatch will become extinct."

Krantz was dubious as to the efficacy of tranquilizers. "We don't know anything about the body chemistry of a Sasquatch," he said. "If you use too high a dose, you'll kill it. If you use too low a dose, you'll hurt the Sasquatch. I wouldn't want to be a hundred yards from a Sasquatch I've just been rude enough to wound." Krantz offered other impracticalities on attempting capture. "Suppose you are lucky enough to use the right dosage. You're standing there over an unconscious Sasquatch, you're 14 miles from your truck. He might wake up any moment. What are you going to do, throw him over your shoulder and walk home? How are you going to protect him as he lies there? Build a house around him? Tie him up with chains? Give him more drugs, which may kill him? Supposing that you can detain him, you walk back to the nearest pay phone, call the nearest anthropologist, do you know what he's going to say to you?" Louv wrote an unnamed participant said that finding a scientist willing to comment on the existence of Bigfoot was harder to find than the elusive beast itself. Krantz responded: "Unless you call me or one of the other scientists willing to admit the possibility that a Sasquatch exists, you'll be left with an 800-pound animal which, when it awakes, will either never want to see another human being, or will want to kill every human being he encounters. I would not want the blood of those human beings on my hands."[1828]

Ridington walked to the microphone where he stood silently for a few moments. "I speak here tonight," he began, "in behalf of an endangered species: Man. We have seen from this conference that the image of the Sasquatch is definitely a growing cultural phenomenon. This image is being shown on TV, and millions of people have seen this image. An image of something with a human-like gait, something that moves through the mottled woods in a phantom-like way." Next, Ridington echoed what sheriffs and local law officers had often expressed during monster-hunting crazes in their communities and towns. "If the masses of people now familiar with this image are now told to go out into the woods in the early morning or late night and seek this image, with a rifle instead of a camera, we are asking for trouble. I'm not speaking of trouble to the Sasquatch, but to human beings," Ridington said. "We know that in any hunting season human beings are killed. But if hunters begin shooting at a creature with a gait similar to the human gait and shape, hunters who are out in the woods drunk on alcohol or simply intoxicated with the change of being in the woods, then some poor bearded fellow in a heavy coat is going to die. In the frenzy to hunt something in our own image, we may be creating a Greek tragedy. And this tragedy will unfold whether or not a Sasquatch actually exists." Ridington further argued that the best way to determine the intelligence of a creature was not to kill it, but instead study it in its environment and evaluate its behaviors. Ridington thought a creature like Bigfoot, if it existed, could prove to be as smart as a gorilla or a chimpanzee. "We have learned a lot in the last few years about the nature of gorilla and chimpanzee intelligence, from field studies by people like Jane Goodall. Chimps have been taught to communicate with people by using sign language. Studies have indicated that of all the animals, other than man, only chimps are capable of image recognition in mirrors. So we are in the same category as chimps; together we are the only creatures who can recognize our own image."[1829]

Louv posed a soul-searching question in his article: "If the forest can [serve] as a mirror, is man then less effective at image recognition than chimps or Sasquatch? Is the urge to kill Sasquatch evidence of a fatal human flaw, which somehow makes us less humane than our closest relatives?"[1830]

> At the end of the debate, someone in the audience suggested the kill-or-not-to kill question be settled there, at the largest gathering of Sasquatch experts, by democratic vote. Democracy lost.
>
> The group sidestepped taking a vote, and perhaps it is a wise decision. The hunters are going to do what they will do, regardless of any vote or any law. The smell of blood is in the air, whose blood it is remains unclear.[1831]

Writing for *Pursuit,* Patrick Macey summed up the conference:

> In retrospect, the Conference, an important and long overdue event for the field of Sasquatch research, served to instill a common sharing concerning the phenomenon as well as developing deeper respect between field researchers and scientists. The opposing views remain. Where do we go from here? Bigfoot, who may be able to provide the final solution, apparently is not ready to give it up.[1832]

And *Milwaukee Journal* writer Jay Scribna added a denouement of sorts, more on the people at the conference than on the presentations about hairy monsters.

> As for the University of British Columbia conference, including the better-known Bigfoot buffs, an anthropologist was heard muttering to his colleagues, "My, my. We must find some way to study these people. They are a subculture all their own."[1833]

Halpin and Michael M. Ames collected many of the papers given at the conference in their *Manlike Monsters on Trial: Early Records and Modern Evidence* published in 1980. *The Sasquatch and Other Unknown Hominids* by Krantz and Vladimir Markotic published in 1984 included several papers given at the conference not previously published in *Manlike Monsters on Trial.*

Creatures of Legendary

The University of Nebraska at Omaha issued a call for papers for its symposium, *Creatures of Legendary,* to be held September 28 to October 1, 1978, at the Hilton Hotel, Omaha, Nebraska. The University of Nebraska at Omaha (UNO) Folklore Archive, in collaboration with the College of Continuing Studies and the Eppley Conference Center, invited papers on any literary or folkloristic aspect of legendary creatures—ancient or modern. Richard S. Thill, Department of Foreign Languages, offered a listing of suggested topics:

> 1) Legends and myths about the traditional creatures of lower mythology: devils, demons, and demonic beings, elemental powers and spirits; witches and sorcerers; giants; dwarfs. Fairies, elves, "the little folk"; dragons; monsters; trolls, ogres; mermaids, selkies, sea-folk; the Wild Huntsman; will-o'-the-wisps, jack-o'-lanterns; werewolves, lycanthropes, other were-creatures; vampires, blood-and viscera-sucking creatures (incubus and succubus).
> 2) Stories and tales about other supernatural beings; the Devil, ghosts, spirits, poltergeists, revenants, etc.
> 3) Modern variations on older themes: the machine as a demonic figure, robots as symbols of good and evil, Faustian man (the Frankenstein topos), the computer as a threat to or benefactor of man, belief systems and modern technology.[1834]

Reporter Frank Santiago's article on the conference printed several participants' perspectives on Bigfoot.

> Daniel Cohen of Port Jervis, N.Y., a prolific writer of books about monsters and a former editor of *Science Digest* magazine, described himself as "cautious."
>
> "I'd love to believe," he said during a break between one of several sessions on monsters. "I think it would be a marvelous [sic] if there could be something or someone who can escape the world's circumscription." . . .
>
> Chicagoan Jerome Clark, associate editor of *Fate,* a pop magazine dealing with psychic phenomenon and UFOs, leans a little toward believing.
>
> "I'm more open to believing in the existence of Bigfoot in the northwest than elsewhere because of the wilderness there.
>
> "This talk about Bigfoot has produced an incredible body of myths and legends," he said. "Thousands of people have described first-hand experiences. There has to be something going on."[1835]

Print & Media

The Force Beyond

In the vein of popular speculative documentaries in the '70s such as *Chariots of the Gods, The Force Beyond* took on several paranormal subjects while hinting that extraterrestrials were behind them all. A segment of the film focuses on Bigfoot, which includes an interview between William "Rosko" Mercer and Peter Byrne.

> *William (Rosko) Mercer:* It is possible to walk from California to Alaska without ever leaving the forest. Therefore, it is clear how a living creature could remain forever hidden in the dark bowels of this thick and awesome mountainous terrain that has become known as Bigfoot Country. Eyewitnesses report this hairy, elusive giant which we call Bigfoot or Sasquatch, from the Americas to the Himalayas . . .
>
> Throughout history multitudes have maintained that Bigfoot is a myth. Yet a multitude of legends, the Holy Scriptures, and evidence as fresh as this morning's newspaper

prove the existence of a humanoid creature that may well be the ancient brother of man.

I'm visiting with Peter Byrne. Author, former big game hunter, he hunts these days with only a camera. Also, he is the only man in the world to search for the elusive creature known as Bigfoot, full-time.

Peter, we know that the Bigfoot is not the only creature that has failed to gain acceptance by large numbers of the scientific community, and for that matter large segments of the general public.

Byrne: Yes, that's true. There are several other animals in history. I think two good examples are, the giant panda, the Chinese panda and the African gorilla. The panda has been known in Chinese history for a thousand years or more. But scientists did not believe that they were there until the early 1900s. The gorilla, the lowland gorilla, I think first known about in about 1847 and the mountain gorilla not until 1902, which was only a few years ago. And, of course, in the Bigfoot we have something very like that too.

Rosko: So, it's kind of the repetition of an old story.

Byrne: Yes.

Rosko: You tracked the Yeti in the Himalayas, now you're here searching for Bigfoot. What brought you to the United States?

Byrne: I came here to do an investigation of the Bigfoot mystery. I started an expedition, a search if you like, in 1971. We thought it would last about six months, no more. Now we're in our fifth year and we're still working on it.

Rosko: We're pretty high atop the world here, where we're talking. Where exactly are we?

Byrne: We are in the high Cascades of north central Oregon here. It's one of the main mountain ranges that runs from California all the way through to Alaska. Behind us here is Mount Hood, 10,000 feet and right here we're about 4,000 feet, in the pine forests.

Rosko: In this general area where you've made headquarters here there seems to be quite a bit more of Bigfoot activity than anywhere else in the country. What is the reason, is there a particular reason why they center here or why this would be a Bigfoot habitat?

Byrne: I think the main reason is this is the principle mountain range. And these creatures, according to our research, live in the mountains where there is lots of food, lots of water, and lots of dense cover, lots of dense forest and we're in the heart of it right here. So, it's an area that has produced a lot of evidence, a lot of footprint findings, and quite a few sightings.

Keeping with the film's overall theme, Rosko voices the linkage between Bigfoot and visitors from space.

> *Rosko:* Legends from all over the world tell us that gods came down to earth and mingled with mortal man. If this is true, then legends and the Holy Scriptures go hand in hand. Genesis 6:4 tells us, "There were giants in the earth in those days and after that." The sons of god came unto the daughters of men and they bore children to them. Of Esau's birth it says, the first came out red all over like a hairy garment. Many feel the Bible chronicles a mating between terrestrials and extra-terrestrials.

René Dahinden appears in the Bigfoot segment, offering his top-level thoughts on the quarry he had been chasing through three separate decades.

> *Rosko:* René Dahinden, co-author of *The Sasquatch,* is a Swiss-born Canadian adventurer, and a man with a mission.
>
> *Dahinden:* In order to understand what the Sasquatch investigation is all about, one has to understand the four main points, which consist of the Indian legends, reports, which were here before the coming of the white man, the totem poles, the masks, showing the sunaqua, the bukwa and other related creatures, which indicate Sasquatch-type reports. Also, the journals of the explorers which have mentioning of Bigfoot reports, newspaper accounts, et cetera reaching way back in time. So, the Sasquatch is nothing new at all. The second point to consider is that we have about 500, 600 people who claim to have met creatures like the Sasquatch. The third point are the footprints from a 13½-inch track, the 17½-inch track. Then [the fourth point] we have the famous Patterson film which was made October the 20th, 1967, in this area, Bluff Creek,

> tributary to the Klamath River, showing a creature, which looks to be a female, 7-feet tall, hair-covered, upright walking.

The Force Beyond's look at Bigfoot ends with a short, extremely grainy clip from a purported Bigfoot film. It has been suggested in some quarters that the segment could be a clip from the Frank White film.

> *Rosko:* Legends and misidentifications do not leave footprints and bits of hair, and lies and hoaxes are eradicated by electronic voice print analysis, eyewitness sightings, and bits of film. Bits of film that the impartial eye of the camera has managed to capture for the closing of yet another link in the mystery of man. The film you're about to see is the first taken since the now famous Patterson film. It was taken by a young attorney while on a camping trip. Due to the controversial nature of the subject matter he has chosen to remain anonymous. This is the first time that the film has been shown publicly.
>
> *Attorney:* "It was very large and hairy and had a terrible smell—like rotten eggs. The thing that got to me was that the way it walked—smooth and controlled, you know, almost like a gazelle."

Sasquatch Family Workshop Film

> A feature-length children's film on the ever elusive Sasquatch will be filmed in the Spokane area this summer.
>
> Ivan Nachman, owner of the Sasquatch Family Workshop, N1417 Wall, said he will produce the $250,000 movie titled "Mr. Sasquatch Goes to Town."
>
> Nachman's company presently produces and distributes Sasquatch paraphernalia nationwide from T-shirts to plush toys.
>
> He said funding for the project has been provided by private interests in Spokane. Filming, editing, costuming and production will be done by Spokane residents.
>
> Actors will also be from the Spokane area, with an emphasis on untrained "natural" actors, he said.
>
> The story revolves around a boy and a girl who go into the woods, get into trouble and are saved by a Sasquatch. After

> they return safely to town they report their encounter and are subject to criticism and ridicule by disbelievers.
>
> The "key" actors will be the boy and the girl in the 10 to 12-year-old age group.[1836]

Headquartered in Spokane, Washington, the Sasquatch Family Workshop did release a 20-page booklet titled, *The History of the Sasquatch (Bigfoot) in Washington State in 1978* which largely presents brief synopses of sightings from 1847 to 1978. In its preface, the authors state that Bigfoot "lead a normal family life. They have children who are born without hair and drink their mother's milk until they are old enough to eat a balanced diet of meat, fish, fruit and various leaves and roots. They talk with each other by grunts, whistles, yells and piercing screams in times of danger. The Sasquatch is very curious about people and the things they have, so don't be surprised someday to see a Bigfoot standing by the side of a road or train track, as they love the sounds of trains."[1837] Two house ads within the booklet refer to "Operation Bigfoot," an expedition of college students embarking from Spokane, Washington, for a three-month "scientific-photographic" excursion. Donations of canned goods, used camping gear, and funds to defray expenses were requested and notice given that sales of Sasquatch Family Workshop products (posters and Bigfoot dolls) would help support Operation Bigfoot.

Additional Titles

In Marian T. Place's second non-fiction book on Bigfoot, *Bigfoot: All Over the Country,* the author explores the thesis that Bigfoot sightings occur all over North America and are not constrained to specific regional zones. Place writes about 1977's bus passengers' sighting (including an interview with Dennis Gates), Oliver, and sightings from various states. In the book's final chapter, Place shares her recommended approach to Bigfoot:

> You know now there is no single, simple answer to any question concerning "the mystery out there."
>
> So, what do you do . . . or think . . . or say? Here are some suggestions:
>
> *Keep an open mind.*
>
> Listen and learn all you can.
>
> Believe, or disbelieve, but don't ridicule.
>
> Be patient, wait for the truth.

> Some day the mystery will be solved, one way or another. Some day Bigfoot will find its rightful place in the scientists' findings. Or, it will join Paul Bunyan, the *windigo,* and other fabulous fictional characters in North America legends.[1838]

Sasquatch—The Man by E. H. Todd resulted from Todd's wish "to show that the unknown is not always evil." Todd's work of fiction is about one man's determination to legally protect Bigfoot. Jim finds a Bigfoot he names "Sask," whose foot is caught in a bear trap. After helping to free Sask and moving him to his cabin, Jim cares for the creature while it recovers from its wound.

> Jim got two blankets and laid them on the floor near the stove. He had only one pillow; he picked it up, looked at it, looked at the Sasquatch and, deciding that the suffering creature needed it more than himself, placed it on the blankets. Then, as gently as he could, he rolled the Sasquatch onto this makeshift bed arranging his arms and legs in a comfortable position. Jim put the toboggan back outside and then put some water on the stove to heat. If he was going to examine the leg, he would have to wash the matted blood off; and he would also need it for cleansing the wound.[1839]

Jim's relationship with Sask makes him determined to protect him and others of his kind. He finds the Clerk of the Court in Blossomdale and explains, "I want the whole area that you mentioned declared parkland where there would be no hunting or trapping of any animal or Sasquatch. In fact, I would really like to see it illegal for any trespassing of any kind within five miles of any known Sasquatch habitat."[1840]

The author was a retired Canadian Mountie, whose 23-years of service throughout Alberta made him quite familiar with the natural setting of western Canada. "Articles, books and television always depict the Sasquatch as some kind of monster, yet documented accounts of encounters always prove him to be gentle, peaceful and afraid," reads the copy from the book's dustjacket. "None have ever bothered any other human by assault, theft or intimidation."[1841]

Bigfoot and UFO researcher Dennis Pilichis edited the 58-page booklet, *Bigfoot: Tales of Unexpected Creatures* (1978). Articles came from Tim

Church, editor of *Shadows Newsletter* ("Funny Doings in Montana 1975-1976"), Mark Swift and James Rastetter, Tri-County UFO Study Group ("A Report on Recent Bigfoot Type Creatures Seen in Ohio"), and Ron Schaffner, director of Para-Anthropoid Research ("A Report on Ohio Anthropoids and other Strange Creatures"). Schaffner writes:

> Ohio is a very active state, with hundreds of UFO and monster sightings recorded.
>
> Certain anomalies play an important role in these bizarre cases. To the south and east lies the Ohio River Valley, which has in the past, had some of the heaviest flaps in recent years. To the north is one of the nation's magnetic fault lines, which is situated near Ravenna, not to mention the mystery of the great lakes. To the west, is Indiana, which in recent months, has become the center of a local monster flap. All of these regions have numerous UFO, monster sightings, animal mutilations, and missing people.[1842]

Bigfoot & UFOs

Much as Pennsylvania had provided reports of hairy hominid creatures associated with UFOs, Ohio began receiving attention as a hotspot of Bigfoot and unexplained aerial phenomena. Richland County, for example, was the scene for both strange lights in the sky and a large creature lurking in the woods.

> Fourteen residents on Franklin Church Road in Richland County, Ohio, saw a bright yellow light hovering for about thirty minutes. The light then dropped below the skyline for a few seconds, and then raised back up and dimmed, as if taking off. Officials at the Mansfield Airport could not explain the UFO.
>
> Richland County is also being plagued by reports of a seven to nine foot tall creature seen in the hilly wooded area around Mohican State Park. Called "Bighead," the creature has red bulging eyes and a head as wide as a tractor tire.
>
> The creature is usually seen in the woods near Butler, Ohio, on Ohio Route 95. Butler police have stated that the large footprints found indicate that the creature is extremely

> large and heavy. The creature was first reported seen after the June 28th report by fourteen county residents. One wonders if there could be a connection.[1843]

Norman Briazack and Simon Mennick's *The UFO Guidebook* delved into the association between UFOs and Bigfoot, an increasingly popular topic for paranormal researchers.

> One unresolved question about Bigfoot is whether these creatures are permanent inhabitants of the areas of sightings. UFOs have frequently been sighted around the Bigfoot sighting areas, and this has led to the theory that there might be a relationship between UFOs and Bigfoot. The Bigfoot creatures may, for example, be pets of the ufonauts. Another even more bizarre possibility is that the Bigfoot creatures may be the actual occupants of at least some of the UFOs.
>
> The case linking Bigfoot and UFOs possesses one strong argument. If Bigfoot were an earthly creature, then sightings of it ought to be more frequent and one should have been captured by now. But if the creature comes from UFOs or is merely a temporary physical entity resulting from the transmogrification of energy, as has been suggested by some researchers, then this would explain why the creature is so elusive.
>
> No conclusive evidence regarding the Bigfoot creature exists at present. Or has the link between UFOs and Bigfoot, strong as it is, been conclusively established. However, it is inevitable that in time the mystery will be solved.[1844]

Though finding little to recommend serious attention to their linkage, the extent to which UFOs entered the discussion about Bigfoot compelled John Green to touch on the subject.

> Sasquatches are obviously Earth-type animals. Walking like men, looking like apes and living like bears, they fit right in as terrestrial creatures, and they are hardly what anyone would expect to find flying a space vehicle. I greatly doubt that anything should be made out of the fact that a hairy biped might be reported seen at about the same time and place that

> a U.F.O. was reported. If there actually are craft from other places flying around (a subject on which I have no knowledge) and Earth is being studied by some kind of intelligent beings, it seems reasonable to me that they might be having a bit of a problem figuring out why the two-legged creatures that obviously dominate the planet seem to have direct contact with every other kind of creature on it except the one that somewhat resembles themselves. They might very well find the [S]asquatch a fit subject for observation. Also, if there actually are space vehicles being parked here and there from time to time, I see no reason why the occasional [S]asquatch might not feel an urge to look one over, as they have done at times with man-made machinery.[1845]

With too many coincidences in the discussion to ignore, other writers found more cause to logically relate UFOs and Bigfoot.

> Many ufologists discount the theory of earth origin, however, and they believe that Bigfoot was originally deposited here by space aliens. The areas they inhabit have always had a disproportionately high number of UFO sightings, which may well be more than simply a coincidence. Because Bigfoot is remarkably similar to the descriptions of extraterrestials [sic] and he is built to the same scale, it is quite possible that the creature is a servant to his other-wordly masters. It is also quite possible that they somehow have escaped from alien crafts and manage to elude their captors by hiding in the wilderness.[1846]

If It's So Big, Why Can't We Get a Decent Photo?

George E. Condon started his writing career at Cleveland's *Plain Dealer* as a general assignment reporter. In the 1950s he moved to the *Plain Dealer's* editorial page where he wrote a daily column until his retirement in 1985. In January, he turned his attention to looking at photos of paranormal subjects: "Some lucky photographer every now and then happens to be on the scene when a monster lumbers out of the woods, or when a flying saucer zooms overhead, but the photographic result, peculiarly, is almost always the same: a blur. The nice part is that the blurs are interchangeable." Interpretive equivalency between blurry, indistinct images was their common feature. "You could just as easily identify a blur either as (a) a mysterious flying object, or (b) a mysterious monster."

"Because the situation is laughable, it has occurred to me that perhaps what man is grappling with in all these unidentified objects on the ground and in the sky may be creatures with a cosmic sense of humor." To Condon, these strange and inexplicable phenomena could be understood through a comedic lens. "Perhaps they are playing a game of tag with us, tantalizing us deliberately and keeping us in a nervous state, knowing that no matter how hard we try to confirm their existence, the best we can hope for is a flying glimpse, a mysterious, movement in the night, an occasional flash, and a great deal of bewilderment that leaves us with nothing in hand but a blur."[1847]

SIGHTINGS 1978

Brunswick Hunter Find 17-inch Track

Several members of the Town Creek Hunting Club discovered tracks on Friday, December 30, as they searched Green Swamp for deer sign near Town Creek, North Carolina. Other tracks were discovered Sunday and Monday (January 1 and 2) in three separate areas, some four miles apart. "If it's a hoax someone went to an awful lot of work," Charlie Taylor of Winnabow and president of the hunting club said. Taylor had followed the tracks for more than 100 yards along the old CCC road connecting Town Creek to Prosper. The tracks were human-looking in appearance, but unusually large: 17 inches from heel to toe, and six inches across the widest part of the foot. The tracks showed a stride of four feet.

According to the hunters, the deep impressions of the feet in the wet sand indicated a creature of considerable weight. Carter Rabon suggested the track-maker could have weighed between 300 to 400 pounds. "There's been so many deer hunters through here the last few days, this being the last day of the season," Taylor began, "the creature may be heading for the Big Green Swamp. That's the direction deer take when we run them. They seem to know they'll be safer in the deep swamp."

Rabon recalled the first track he spotted on Friday caused him to notice a trail of broken twigs and branches indicating the passage of something large. "I've been hunting here 30 years and it's the first time I ever saw anything like this," Rabon said. "I just thought it was a prank until others found more tracks today." The area where the tracks were spotted is primarily timber land of which the Town Creek Hunting Club leases about 13,000 acres for its members to hunt on. The tracks sparked a collective recall of a 'Swamp Booger Man' in southern Duplin County from mid-1975.[1848]

Iliamna Sighting

Iliamna is a community about 200 miles southwest of Anchorage. A wave of Bigfoot sightings began on January 6, with a substitute teacher's account of a creature across the river from Newhalen, only five miles from Iliamna. A three-day expedition to gather evidence turned up nothing.

Additional reports followed starting on January 8. Postmistress Myrtle Anelion provided an account of a possible thieving Bigfoot. Anelion said her children told her a Bigfoot had ran off with some sheets drying on a clothes line. Anelion admits not seeing any creature but did notice large tracks in the snow near the missing wash. Anelion related an earlier episode when she had in fact seen Bigfoot, describing her sighting involving three Bigfoot creatures in the early 1960s. She said they looked like "People with hair." On January 9, another resident reported seeing a Bigfoot, known locally as "Big Man," through her window.

Reported on January 8, Federal Aviation Administration coordinator Jim Coffee was driving on an icy road when he spotted Bigfoot, describing it as about 8 feet tall and moving on two legs. Coffee slammed on his brakes and fired "a few" shots to scare off the creature. One resident expressed concern that being fired upon could provoke thoughts of vengeance on the creature's part. Some had noted that village dogs seemed to bark more often since the reports of Bigfoot in and around Iliamna started.

Some footprints remained for nearly a week in the snow. Measurements of these prints (it's unclear if the dimensions were taken of partially melted tracks) were reported as one foot across the ball of the foot, two feet long, and the heels were about five inches wide. The residents' reports revealed there may have been two creatures. The bigger "Big Man" had been reported traveling along the road leading to the airport. A smaller creature traveled the other side of that same road and was the fingered culprit for the theft of Anelion's laundry.

Until January 8, only Native residents had seen Big Man. Coffee was the first non-Native resident to see the creature. Restraint had been the common practice on the part of the Native residents when thoughts turned to sharing their experiences with Big Man. "It's sort of a taboo among them," said one young Native woman, referring to her elders' reluctance to entertain and discuss the topic. "They don't even talk about it among themselves much."

An article in the *Daily Sitka Sentinel* reported that area residents believed the creatures appeared when warm weather disrupted their hibernation; unseasonably warm temperatures in early January had been in the 40s. One woman conjectured how she would react if she saw the Big Man. “I’d be scared, but I wouldn’t shoot, that’s for sure,” she said. “That would be much too violent.” Linda Johnson of Iliamna stated Big Man usually traveled in pairs. “They have families just like us. They’re not too smart like people, but they know what is going on. They know.” One resident hoped Big Man and people could enjoy a peaceful coexistence. “Don’t let them be hunted and hounded. They live here too.” Iliamna is known for other legendary creatures including a lake monster in Iliamna Lake capable of overturning boats and little people who dwell underground, reputed to be visible only to children.[1849]

During pioneer fly fisherman Jim Repine’s career he wrote weekly outdoors columns for Alaska newspapers, hosted the “Alaska Outdoors” television show, and edited *Alaska Outdoors* magazine. In early 1978, he also investigated Bigfoot sightings in Iliamna, Alaska.

> January 13, 1978—The *Anchorage Daily News* is mounting an expedition to investigate recent reports of a Bigfoot in the Iliamna area.
>
> *Anchorage Daily News* columnist Jim Repine and Sports Editor Bill Wilson left this morning for Iliamna where they hoped to talk to eye witnesses and local residents [who] have reported the existence of a Sasquatch in the area for years.
>
> The most recent sighting of the Bigfoot was Sunday night when the Federal Aviation Administration (FAA) station coordinator Jim Coffee encountered a creature more than eight feet tall moving quickly through the rain and snow.
>
> “It nearly ran me off the road,” Coffee reported. “I ain’t never seen anything like that before. I don’t believe in those things, but there it was.”
>
> Coffee said he fired several rounds from his revolver at the creature, but he didn’t think he hit it. However, a woman living nearby reported that the Bigfoot had torn down her laundry. She figures that it needed bandages.
>
> A series of 24-inch tracks were found along the road leading to the FAA station. “It looked like a moose walking on its hind legs,” said Coffee, a five year resident of the area. “It looked

> like it was wider at the butt than anywhere else, that's why I say it looks like a moose." But, he said, it definitely wasn't a moose, no horns."
>
> Other reports said the Bigfoot left a trace of "nearly purple" urine.
>
> "I don't go to church too often, but then I don't drink too much on Sunday either," said Coffee avowing that he was sober when he saw the creature.
>
> Repine, who guides in the area has offered a $1,000.00 reward for clear, authentic photos of the beast provided they are accompanied by evidence no harm was done to the Iliamna's [B]igfoot.[1850]

Jersey Devil Connection?

Writing for the *Wall Street Journal,* Douglas Martin contributed an article looking at the past and contemporaneous sightings of the Jersey Devil. Noting the creature's history spanning across three centuries, Martin included recent sightings, which included in their general description, shades of Bigfoot.

> On the evening of Jan. 16, 1978, for example, 14-year-old Dale English and a friend smelled a strong odor "like dead fish" while they were ice skating near their home in Chatsworth, the so-called Capital of the Pine Barrens.
>
> Following their twitching noses, they were suddenly confronted with "two big red eyes staring at us."
>
> They didn't hang around to gather the details. "It was about seven feet tall," Dale remembers.
>
> By morning, snow had blanketed any hope of finding corroborating clues.[1851]

Albany Track Find

Among the many Bigfoot track finds from the 1970s, the Albany, Oregon, prints discovered by two boys while target shooting received relatively broad publicity.[1852]

The tracks were found near Freeway Lake east of Albany on Saturday, March 11. Terry Hayes and Byron Forty were out "plinking," shooting their

.22 rifles at birds and rabbits in a pasture. "I didn't say anything or even think anything," said Byron, describing how he felt when he first noticed the flat tracks with a squared-off heel and five toes. "I just couldn't even talk." The boys said they followed the tracks around a two-acre field near the lake. "It looked like it was trying to find a way out," said Terry who reported the field was surrounded by water. "Then it went across Oak Creek. We found some tracks on the other side." The prints measured 17 inches by 5 ½ inches. "Sometimes the toes are dug in. It is walking and in some of them it's just standing with its feet together like you're standing," said Terry.

The boys returned home and announced their discovery, but family members found their claim humorous. "They just laughed when they first heard it," said Terry. But Terry, in what must have been with a sense of vindication, stated that people stopped laughing when they saw the prints for themselves. Byron's father Ken Forty was the first to go out to the plowed field, curious to see for himself what had so excited the boys. "All five toes were there," said Forty who made plaster casts of both right and left footprints.

Forty was able to follow the footprints across the field, into the woods and across a five-foot deep creek. Along the way he noticed broken tree limbs snapped at heights of five and six feet off the ground, "higher than you can reach." Forty's examination also convinced him that all of the visible tracks were not made at the same time. Some he adjudged to be two weeks old while the most recent were three to four days old. "It's kind of weird for me, being the type of person I am," said Forty. "I was raised in Curry County and I hunted and fished all the time. They (companions) would tell me about Bigfoot and I'd laugh." Forty was a lumber scaler with the Columbia River Scaling & Grading Bureau. But in all his time spent in the wilds, he had never seen anything like the tracks his boys had shown him. "Now, with all the evidence right in front of me—what can I say?"[1853]

Investigating State police officers believed the prints were hoaxed. Trooper Greg Anderson of the Oregon State Police examined the tracks late Saturday afternoon. "He said the tracks look like nice homemade tracks," recalled Trooper Dan Duncan of the Oregon State Police. "He said the tracks are pretty flat with no arch. Somebody must have cut some wood out and stamped around in the mud," Duncan said. "He (Anderson) asked us if we did it. He didn't think it was Bigfoot."

Jeanne Roush of the Bigfoot Information Center intended to make the trip to Albany and take a closer look for herself.

> She's [Roush] not laying bets that the footprints are from Bigfoot, but does say that some believe the creatures migrate, and that Bigfoot sitings [sic] usually increase in warmer weather—either because more Bigfeet are out more or people are out more, she said. Conceivably a Bigfoot might leave a snowy mountain and travel to the Coast Range, following rivers and keeping concealed in underbrush.[1854]

By phone interview with reporter Peggy McMullen, Roush gave her thoughts on Bigfoot tracks: "They are usually quite flat," she said, "from 14 to 24 inches long. Usually they don't resemble a human foot." Roush reserved her judgement on the Albany tracks. "There are characteristics to look for but, even then, it's hard to say." Roush offered that Albany was an unusual setting for Bigfoot. "When they called Saturday, I had to say 'where is Albany?'" she admitted.

> "Everybody is skeptical" about the authenticity of Bigfoot and his footprints, said Rosie Day, a neighbor of the boys. "I don't know if I believe it or not but the footprints were real. It was kind of freaky and kind of scary."
>
> The tracks brought that reaction out in more than one of those who looked over the site this weekend. One teen-age friend of Hayes and Forty got one look at the tracks and took off running. "He ran right through a creek of water up to his waist," said Mrs. Day laughing. The boy didn't stop running until he hit the highway.[1855]

The onsite investigation by Roush in the afternoon of Monday, March 13, left the authenticity of the tracks up in the air. "She said the tracks were pretty old and she couldn't tell if they were real or not," said Byron. Roush had been on site for two hours. "She had to go to Beaverton to look at some other tracks," Byron said who observed Roush make a plaster cast and took "a whole bunch of pictures." She also gave the boys the name and contact information to a "foot expert at the University of North Carolina" to whom the Forty casts could be sent for professional analysis.[1856]

Forty told the *Oregon Statesman* that Albany troopers sent a game warden to examine the tracks. The warden told Forty that Bigfoot was out of his jurisdiction. News of the tracks spread fast and Forty found himself in demand for interviews.

And newspapers and radio stations are beginning to call his home. At one point during this reporter's conversation with Forty, a telephone operator suddenly broke in wanting to know if Forty could accept an emergency message from an Albany radio station.

The emergency—it turns out—was trying to get the Forty story.[1857]

East Brewton Sighting

Luke McDaniel didn't know what he saw, he just knew it was strange to East Brewton, Alabama, and utterly without precedent in his own experience. Officials took the story in stride, finding little to warrant a serious investigation. The *Ledger* reported police were privately saying it was a story of otherwise mundane events blown out of proportion; McDaniel's tale could be a study in the way legends are born.

The events took place in the pinelands along the Conecuh River near East Brewton, Alabama, and began with Mrs. Ruth Mary Gibson, McDaniel's sister, alone in her rural farm home at night on Monday, March 6. She was suddenly startled by a cry sounding like a woman's scream. She telephoned her brother and while McDaniel was on the line, held the receiver out a window but he couldn't hear the screams. "It must be your imagination," he told his sister. "You just got scared." But McDaniel was determined to allay his sibling's fears; he got in his station wagon and "hauled britches over there." After arrival at Gibson's home, McDaniel stood in the yard listening for anything strange for ten to fifteen minutes. When he didn't hear anything unusual, McDaniel contemplated leaving. That's when he heard and felt a scream. "It felt like my cap come up off my head about six inches high," he said. McDaniel walked down the road to see if he could spot what caused the incredible shriek. "The horses were running. The hogs were hollering. But the dogs had left," he said.

When the screams resumed, McDaniel told his sister to call the police. "I thought it might be somebody hurt out there." Lt. Doug McCurdy was the first to arrive followed by Mrs. Gibson's 19-year-old son, Johnny. The four of them were outside when Mrs. Gibson pointed and shouted, "Look there, Johnny, it is somebody." Everybody looked, and Johnny was the first to speak. "Lord have mercy, Mama, get in the house." McCurdy told WALA-TV newswoman Renée Perry he saw something large and unlike any creature he had ever before seen; he was convinced it wasn't human. It crossed the road and disappeared into the woods. Mrs. Gibson believed it was taller than her son Johnny, all six feet of him. Other officers arrived, including Police Chief Don Jackson who later admitted he also heard a scream.

Word of a wreck came over the police radio and the officers left. All became quiet at his sister's house, but when McDaniel finally got back into his car to leave, he saw something in the headlights. "It stood around about six and one-half feet to seven feet tall, weighed about 400 some few pounds and its eyes were solid red," McDaniel said. "I'd say the eyes were about 12 inches apart on its head. It had no neck at all . . . hairy all over. It kind of walked like a person. It was kind of in a hurry," he said. "Its arms seemed a little longer than a human being has. I'm not saying at all it was any 'Bigfoot.' I've seen that on television . . . but I do know what I saw," McDaniel said. "I considered it might be an ape. But I got to thinking about it and it wasn't no ape. There's no ape that high," he said. Could somebody have been trying to pull a hoax which McDaniel fell victim to? "No. It wasn't a prank. There were too many guns out there . . . and a human couldn't move through thick bush like it did."[1858]

> Almost nine months ago a series of bizarre events along the Northwest Florida-Alabama border became the subject of tongue-in-cheek news coverage in both the local and national press.
>
> What most newsmen couldn't bring themselves to treat seriously was that numerous witnesses—including some law enforcement officials—had seen and heard a tall, hairy "monster" in the forested regions between the Blackwater and Conecuh rivers.
>
> The levity accorded the story in the media was not shared, however, by the residents of those parts. To them it was a very serious matter.[1859]

"All I know is what I saw," said McDaniel. "It was 6 ½ to 7 feet tall, hairy all over, and had arms that hung down nearly to the knees. It walked on two legs and when it stepped into the road it turned, stopped and then headed back into the woods. I ain't saying it's a 'Bigfoot' or anything. I'm just saying that's what I saw."

"It smelled like a garbage dump," McDaniel recalled, "and that's why the dogs couldn't stand it."

Two weeks after the Gibson farm incident, the *Daily News* of Fort Walton Beach, Florida, reported that five truckloads of men witnessed a large creature on the Jay pipeline between Flomaton, Alabama, and Jay, Florida. "They said it was so big," stated local radio announcer Jerry Owens, "they just turned and ran. They went home and got their guns but couldn't find anything when they went back." Owens, who had been keeping up with such stories from the area, told the *Daily News* that three weeks after the events at the Gibson farm, a man reported he had seen a similar creature standing in the Conecuh River busy with something underneath the surface. Owens stated that reports of such creatures in the area went back to 1952.[1860]

Dr. Kenneth Turner Investigates Tracks

Two young couples walking near a swampy area of Coaling, Alabama, in July were surprised to suddenly discover three-toed tracks. Dr. Kenneth Turner, an anthropologist with the University of Alabama was contacted. Turner, his wife, and his father-in-law, also an anthropology professor, visited the Tuscaloosa County location. The 31 tracks were inspected and measured resulting in Turner's determination that the tracks were some sort of a joke—they bore evidence of a double-arched foot, a human characteristic. Also, the prints were separated by varying distances between them, one extreme case was six feet apart. Because the prints all had a uniform depth, Turner adjudged a creature hadn't jumped some of the longer observed distances.

> After examining 31 strange footprints at a swamp north of Coaling, a University of Alabama anthropologist has concluded that it is "extremely improbable" that a beast resembling the fabled "Bigfoot" visited the area.
>
> Dr. Kenneth Turner, an assistant professor of anthropology, said of the footprints, "They looked fantastic, but I'm pretty convinced somebody made them as a prank."
>
> The three-toed impressions on the bank of a swamp were first called to Dr. Turner's attention by two young men and their wives who said they discovered the markings while fishing Saturday night.
>
> The anthropologist, along with his wife, father-in-law, and Dr. Earle Smith, a university professor of anthropology and biology, went to the site Sunday afternoon.

By Tuesday, stories of the footprints and even sightings of a nine-foot-tall hairy beast had spread to Brookwood, where town council members joked about "Bigfoot" at an evening meeting.

The creature's reputation comes [from] a variety of reported sightings of "half-men, half-beasts" in wilderness areas around the world.

Dr. Turner said he found 31 footprints at the swamp near Coaling. His group, assisted by the couples who reported the markings, photographed the site and made plaster-of-paris impressions of two of the footprints.

The markings revealed that the "creature" had a double-arched foot (arches running in both directions across the foot), according to Dr. Turner. He said only humans have such a foot.

However, the animal apparently walked in a fashion which does not correspond with the structure of the foot, he said.

In addition, Dr. Turner said, the distances between footprints varied widely, with some strides measuring as long as six feet. He ruled out the possibility that the animal jumped the longer distances because all of the footprints were of the same depth.

The group also found several young trees which had been broken. Dr. Turner said, "I experimented with one myself and found I could break it with only one hand."

In addition to the evidence found in Sunday's four-hour visit to the site, Dr. Turner said it is unlikely that a "Bigfoot" would be found in West Alabama, since nearly all the land has been used at one time for agriculture.

Most other sightings have been reported in remote wilderness areas.[1861]

Ad Hall Bigfoot

Bob and Tommie Throneberry formed the Dallas-based Bigfoot Research Society to further their interest in Bigfoot research. The group received extra-regional attention in 1979 thanks to a long article in *True UFOs & Outer Space Quarterly* which shared several of their early experiences in Bigfoot research. On January 7, 1978, seven members of the Bigfoot Research Society traveled to Paris, Texas, where the researchers met Kenneth Thurman, founder of a local gun powder club. Thurman received the Bigfoot

Research Society of Texas members at his Paris home and shared his unusual experience with them.

About six years before, Thurman was a driver for a butane company in Paris. Every third weekend was his turn to run all three of the county routes. It was late in the fall when the weather was beginning to turn cold at night, and people would call for fuel at night. Thurman got two calls late one Saturday evening. He picked up a friend of his who worked for the same company, and they started out on deliveries. The first stop was to be at a house a few miles from town at the end of a dirt road which cut back at an angle of about thirty degrees off a northeast bound highway.

As Thurman drove up the highway, a large bug flew into the open window of the butane truck. The bug was annoying the two men, so when Thurman turned the truck onto the dirt road he stopped the truck to get the bug out. Leaving the truck motor running, the other man got out of the truck, then noticed a foul odor and mentioned it to Thurman. Thurman commented that he smelled it too.

Thurman's friend then noticed a long shadow being cast in the moonlight moving up to the back of the truck. He shouted to Thurman, "There it is!" Thurman glanced over his shoulder and saw a hairy, upright creature was moving toward him. The men bolted into the truck, and Thurman jerked the truck into gear. The sudden lurch of the truck slammed the truck doors shut, and Thurman got a better look at the creature in the large west coast mirrors that were mounted to the truck doors. Both men were terrified.

Thurman drove the truck at full acceleration to the end of the dirt road where he had to swerve and go through a cattle guard before he could stop the truck. The man who lived in the house where the delivery was to be made, was on the porch with a gun in his hand. Recognizing the butane truck, he laughed saying that the two men had nearly missed him.

They filled the man's butane tank, then turned the truck around to make the run back up the dirt road to the highway. Thurman made it through the encounter area as quickly as possible and veered onto the highway to go toward his second

> stop. As they rounded a bend, Thurman's friend looked out his side window to see the creature running in a field in the same direction as the truck. He brought this to Thurman's attention. Thurman thought that the paths of the truck and the creature would converge at a curve in the road up ahead. He told his friend that he was going to run over it if it got in front of him. The creature disappeared into some trees before it would have reached the curve in the road. The two men didn't see it anymore.[1862]

The Bigfoot Research Society members learned Thurman had reported the incident to his company and they took measurements of a truck similar to the one Thurman said he was driving; the height of the top of the tanks was found to be eight feet and two inches from the ground.[1863]

Another Bigfoot Research Society field investigation occurred on March 4, 1978, as investigators Bob Throneberry, Kenneth Shepherd, Ron Townsend, Jim Maddox, and Tom Adams visited Kiomatia, Texas, a few miles northeast of Paris. The trip was spurred by a Kiomatia man's claim to have shot a Bigfoot about a year prior. Digging into the story, Shepherd learned the man's identity—Louis Hamm. The team interviewed Hamm at his home where he recalled the event took place in the spring of 1977. Hamm said he had heard his daughter screaming out on the family's porch and grabbed his gun to see what the matter was. He found his daughter pointing to a large tree across a dirt road about 100 yards away. There stood a stooped figure which Hamm estimated to be 4 to 4 ½ feet tall and covered in brown hair. The creature had a large chest area. "It looked more like a gorilla than a man," Hamm said. "His arms could have been longer than his legs." Hamm told the researchers that he knocked the creature down with a shot from his .308 rifle. Hamm was transfixed as he watched the creature get up and walk into the woods. Hamm admitted he did not know why he felt compelled to shoot the creature and said he and his family did not stay at their residence that night. When they returned the next morning, family members found tracks in the yard and muddy prints on their porch measuring 12 inches long. Did Hamm know what he had seen that night? "I never saw anything like it," he said matter-of-factly.[1864]

Jeffrey G. Gelner described seeing a large, burly creature covered all over with dark brown hair on Thursday, July 27. The 15-year-old Gelner and his grandfather were combining in a field near dusk when the boy heard a low moaning cry. Gelner was the only one to witness the eight-foot-tall, arm-flailing creature at the edge of his grandfather's maize field in the Little

River bottom.[1865] Jeffrey's father and uncle, Billy and Johnny Gelner kept an overnight vigil in the maize field Friday night. Billy said they heard movements at one point but the firing of a shotgun into the air failed to flush anything into view. Gelner also recounted smelling a sour odor for a few minutes during their overnight vigil. A nearby pig farm was upwind, according to Gelner, and so discounted as the source of the odor.[1866] Canvassing the area yielded about a dozen 22-inch tracks ranging from five to thirteen feet apart.

Milam County Sheriff Leroy Broadus said he believed Jeffrey Gelner had seen something he couldn't explain. "Mr. and Mrs. Gelner and the family were receiving so much publicity, he (Gelner) asked me if there was any type of authority that actually deals with this kind of thing," Broadus said. "He wanted them to look into it." Sheriff Broadus contacted Robert Throneberry and the Bigfoot Research Society was invited to conduct an onsite investigation. After examining the site, including an overnight watch with deputy sheriff John Brooks in the Gelner's maize field on Saturday night, Throneberry said the Gelners and the Cameron community were victims of a hoax. Throneberry issued the following statement: "After completing a thorough investigation of the evidence in the Gelner report in Cameron, Texas, the Bigfoot Research Society of Dallas has concluded that there is not now, nor has there been in recent times, a Bigfoot creature in or near the reported sighting area. The physical evidence of the location was carefully manufactured and skillfully constructed to mislead the people of Milam County. We conclude that a person or persons have attempted to play a dangerous and malicious prank on the Gelners and the Cameron community." Sheriff Broadus accepted The Bigfoot Research Society's findings that Ad Hall was the stomping ground of a mere prankster.

"We didn't have to go out and look around for very long to know that it was a hoax. There were just too many strings left dangling," said Tommie Throneberry who dismissed the idea of a legitimate monster in Milam County. "Just the fact that there was loose soil in the bottom of the alleged tracks was enough to know that no 700-900 pound animal, if any animal at all, had made them," she said.[1867]

Tunnel Monster of Cabbagetown

"I wish you'd never come here," 'Ernest' said to *Toronto Sun* reporter Lorrie Goldstein who had looked him up at his Cabbagetown apartment after hearing his story from a reliable source. Ernest talked to Goldstein on the condition of his anonymity. "If I tell you what I saw, people will think I was drunk or crazy, they'll never believe me." The reactions from strangers could be just as bad as the withholding of approbation from friends and family. "I'm in the phone book," he told his interviewer. "I couldn't stand being called by a bunch of cranks."

While searching a cave for a lost kitten near his Parliament Street apartment in August 1978, Ernest said he saw an anthropoidal creature, the likes of which he'd never encountered before. "It was pitch black in there . . . I saw it with my flashlight. The eyes were orange and red, slanted . . . it was long and thin, almost like a monkey . . . three feet long, large teeth, weighing maybe 30 pounds with slate-grey fur." Initially reluctant to share what happened next, Ernest opted at last to describe to Goldstein how the encounter ended. "I'll never forget it," he stated with conviction. "It said 'Go away, go away,' in a hissing voice. Then it took off down a long tunnel off to the side . . . I got out of there as fast as I could. I was shaking with fear."

Ernest's wife Barbara believed her husband had indeed experienced something highly unusual. "I believe Ernie saw exactly what he says he did," she said. "He was terrified when he came back to the apartment and he doesn't scare easily. Look, he's been known to have a drink in the past—like most people, and to occasionally tie one on, but he's not a drunk and he wasn't drinking at all that day." Goldstein accompanied Ernest to the spot where the encounter took place. It was at the bottom of a long passage between his apartment building and the neighboring one next door. Goldstein was led 15 feet down a fire escape which once served as an exit to the street but was now an access to a narrow chamber with walls on four sides. Peering inside the chamber Goldstein could see that the tunnel broke to the left some ten feet back after leading under a slab of concrete. "I saw it there where the tunnel turns," explained Ernest. "The last I saw it, it was heading off into the dark. The passageway seemed to drop down very quickly and go a long way back." Ernest thought the tunnel could lead to the sewer system beneath Toronto's Metro. A long-time sewer worker told the *Toronto Sun* that he doubted the tunnel led to the sewers and probably had itself resulted from poor drainage which had permitted water to hollow out the passage after long-term erosion.[1868]

Paris Township Monster (Minerva Monster)

> Paris Township, Ohio (A)—A hairy, 6-foot creature was spotted late at night by six area residents as it sat atop a backyard

> chicken coop, according to Stark County sheriff's deputy James Shannon.
>
> Mr. and Mrs. Herbert Cayton and four friends say they saw the creature on the coop and when it peeked through windows in the Cayton home Monday night [August 21]. The [Caytons] maintain they have seen the creature several times over the past several months, Shannon said.
>
> The six also saw two smaller similar creatures with the six-footer.
>
> "When I got there, the people were visibly shaken and some were even afraid to go to sleep," said the deputy. "It was obvious they saw something, but what? I'm skeptical about it myself. There were two footprints—one distinguishable, the other, not so good."
>
> Shannon said he scouted the hilly, heavily wooded area Tuesday, but found no sign of the creature.
>
> Shannon said the Caytons told him one of the witnesses drove a car across the backyard with its headlights on, to get a better look at the creature. When the beast ran towards the car, the five others ran into the house.
>
> "Then, they all were sitting around the kitchen table, waiting for the police to show up," said Shannon. "The creature began looking in the window at them. They couldn't see any facial features because of his bushy hair.
>
> Shannon said the group also heard footsteps on the roof, but when Mrs. Cayton loaded a gun, the creature disappeared into the woods.[1869]

"They heard something in the window, kind of clawing and pawing," Shannon told *Canton Repository* reporter Ed Balint in 2004. Shannon retired from the force in 1997. "From what I remember, I don't think this creature, critter, whatever the hell it was, was trying to get in as much as it was saying, 'Hey look at me.'" Reporter Jim Hillibish did the original reporting for the *Repository* back in 1978. "It was those doldrums between the Hall of Fame (festival) and Labor Day," he told Balint. "It was a good story and we kept it going." The story spread, the creature eventually earned the name Minerva Monster, and its sightings attained national attention.

> A van drove onto the Cayton's front yard one time. A group of hunters hopped out, flanked by Doberman pinschers, trekking into the deep woods and old strip mine behind the property. Bigfoot believers camped out in the woods.
>
> It got so bad that the Caytons posted a fence to keep gawkers out. Evelyn Cayton was on the brink of a nervous breakdown.
>
> "I think the hype lasted into the fall," Shannon recalled.
>
> In 1983, Herbert Cayton, Evelyn's husband, recounted the Bigfoot buzz.
>
> "One day there were 100 to 150 cars . . . in my driveway, on my lawn and lining both sides of the road," he said.
>
> Evelyn and Herbert Cayton are deceased. The remaining Caytons are publicity shy. Howe Cayton, a son, and Rebecca Manley, a daughter, declined to be interviewed about the Bigfoot.
>
> The family took a lot of razzing. At a high school football game, local folks mocked them, chanting, "Bigfoot, Bigfoot." A local eatery spoofed the sighting, advertising on a roadside sign: "Bigfoot ate here."
>
> Herbert Cayton took the skepticism in stride.
>
> "There were doubters," he said. "Those who yelled things from car windows when they passed. It was weird. . . . The way I feel about it is if they don't want to believe, they don't have to."
>
> "I think most people thought of it as a joke, as a lark," said Shannon.
>
> But the Cayton report spurred claims of other sightings.
>
> "Somebody claimed that they saw a Bigfoot running across Route 30 near the Cayton house," Shannon said. "It was a fog-shrouded night and all of a sudden they saw this thing dart out in front of them."
>
> Another sighting was reported on Liberty Church Road SE.
>
> The woman "reported hearing strange noises in the woods surrounding her house since sometime in June," Shannon's August report said. It sounded like a cat fight or a woman's shriek, the woman said. Other neighbors heard the noises.[1870]

Sheriff's deputies searched the forest south of the Cayton home on horseback and in jeeps. They found an animal's skull imbedded in the side of a coal pit. "You could send 100 or 200 men out there to comb the area and not find what you're looking for," admitted Shannon.[1871]

> Shannon took the Bigfoot report seriously, like any other investigation: a stolen car, a drug deal, a barroom scuffle.
>
> On the night of Aug. [21], he spent an hour or two at the Cayton home, then returned when daylight broke.
>
> Shannon and four other deputies scoured the area, searching for six or seven hours in Army surplus Jeeps and on horseback.
>
> "A lot of people thought it was a bear; somebody thought it was a deer," Shannon said. "And I thought, 'These people ought to be able to tell the difference.'"
>
> Cayton, who worked the midnight shift at Diebold, wasn't home that night, but said he had seen the creature twice before.
>
> "It was shaped like a man and it walked like a man," he told the *Repository* in 1983. "When a bear moves away, it goes away on all four feet. This swung up over the (edge of the) strip mine on two."
>
> Part of a skull was found in a pit behind the Cayton home, Shannon said; it appeared to be from a cow or other large animal. Tufts of fur were found on the remains of a chicken coop, where the Caytons had spotted the Bigfoot sitting.
>
> The fur and skull went to Malone College for analysis. The skull also was taken to the pathology laboratory at Aultman Hospital, but the hospital refused to examine it.
>
> Nobody knows what happened to them.
>
> Suzie Thomas, spokeswoman for Malone College, said she's fielded questions about the samples before and has asked those who were on campus then.
>
> "Either their memory is failing them or they're just not admitting they were involved in a hunt for (Bigfoot)," she said, laughing.[1872]

Deputy Sheriff Shannon listened to the witnesses' report and realized that something unusual had happened. "It's obvious to me that these people saw something," he said. "It's now a matter of trying to figure out what they saw."[1873]

> Shannon interviewed residents of the Cayton home, friends, even a professional photographer in quest of a snapshot of Bigfoot.
>
> The Caytons never used the word "Bigfoot."
>
> Mrs. Cayton simply described a creature, more than 6 feet tall with stubby legs and hairy, indistinct features, that at one point turned to protect two "smaller things that were standing beside it," the report said. It eventually walked away into the strip mine.
>
> Manley, 27, and her sister Vicki Keck, 25, were shaken.
>
> Scott Patterson, 18, a family friend, also was shaken up. Skeptical of past sightings, Patterson told Shannon he was now a "believer."
>
> The sightings didn't end on August [21].
>
> Two days later, Mary Ackerman, another Cayton daughter, said she saw the beast standing on the edge of a strip mine when she pulled into her parents' driveway, and five days after the initial report, John Nutter, a photographer from Cuyahoga Falls, said he saw a bear about 30 feet away in a wooded area near Liberty Church Road SE. Nutter took a photo and retreated quickly. A deputy combed the area for 90 minutes and found what appeared to be bear tracks.
>
> But Nutter's color film produced a "fuzzy" image, and he waffled on the bear story.
>
> "I thought it over and now (I) don't think it was a bear," he told *The Repository* a few days later. "It made a sound unlike any bear I've ever heard."[18/4]

After Mary Ackerman witnessed the creature she wished others could have their own glimpse. "I'd give anything so someone else could see it. So it would show up and someone could take a picture," she said.[1875] The creature was seen again near the Cayton residence on August 23. Two more sightings were claimed on September 8 and 9 when Ackerman witnessed two creatures near a strip mine. A man who lived five miles east of Minerva saw a hair-covered creature squatting by a tree; it emitted a sound like a loud cough.[1876] Vicki Keck confirmed her family had "never said it was" Bigfoot, instead the Caytons called the creature "The big, hairy thing," since, as Keck averred, "you can't put a label on something when you don't know what it is."[1877]

Reporter Barbara Mudrak wrote in the August 24 *Akron Beacon Journal* that Evelyn Cayton had mixed feelings about the creature's presence. "I hope someone catches it or takes a picture of it so they know the people of Paris Township aren't imagining things."[1878] The negative tone the publicity had brought to her family left Mary Ackerman concerned with the downside of bringing forward an experience with something unusual and anomalous. "If I'd known my mother was going to get such harassment, I would never have reported it. If I ever see it again, I won't report it."[1879]

Corunna Hoax

As August ended, a Bigfoot prankster was at work in Corunna, Michigan, intending to scare some friends but creating instead a dangerous scenario as people prepared to seriously hunt the nonexistent creature.

> When three townspeople reported seeing a large, upright, growling creature, sheriff's deputies took off in pursuit, thinking maybe they'd get a glimpse of the legendary Bigfoot.
>
> But the creature turned out to be a normal-sized man from Byron decked out in a rented gorilla costume to play a prank on some friends.
>
> The contrite prankster brought the costume to the sheriff's headquarters in Corunna Thursday [August 31] afternoon after hearing that some residents planned to take to the woods—with guns—in search of the hairy beast.
>
> The "monster" was spotted Wednesday [August 30] night. Sheriff's Sgt. Phil Cooley and Deputy Bill Bowman chased it through the woods, but lost it when it jumped into a shallow river channel and ran upstream.[1880]

A prankster caused a massive monster hunt in March after he left faux footprints in the snow of Chetopa, Kansas.

> Chetopa, Kan. (AP)—Chuck Bentley has left his footprints on this tiny southeast Kansas town in a way residents won't quickly forget.
>
> The 20-year-old resident of nearby Oswego fashioned two plywood feet, 17 inches long and 10 inches wide, went

> bounding across the snowy countryside a week ago, and caused a "Big Foot" monster hunt that drew about 5,000 participants.
>
> The case was abruptly solved two days after it began when Bentley, alias "Big Foot," appeared on a newscast of a Pittsburg, Kan., television station.
>
> He said he was trying to add some excitement to life in Chetopa.
>
> W. W. Lancaster, Chetopa police chief said it [sic] as many as 5,000 people—triple the population of Chetopa—visited the area in the last two days.[1881]

Bigfoot Investigations Studies Pennsylvania Sightings

> Allen Hilsmeier and Mike Asselin know, as sure as snow will fall on southern York County and northern Maryland this winter, people will see Bigfoot tracks. And that's what they're after. . . .
>
> They'll stalk the wild, three-toed, three-hundred-pound primate that reportedly has lumbered across York and Harford, Md., counties, and lend an understanding ear to people who have been scared to dickens by an encounter with the thing. Bigfoot Investigations is sort of a Bigfoot crisis center.[1882]

Both men were employed at Aberdeen Proving Grounds in Aberdeen, Maryland; Hilsmeier was a physicist and Asselin was a chemical engineer. *Daily Record* writer Jim Hill said the men "have the unlikeliest occupations for Bigfoot investigating." Hilsmeier was the first of the two to catch the Bigfoot bug, after he and his son found about 2,000 tracks meandering across their Delta, Maryland, farm in January 1978. The tracks were 16-inches long and six-inches wide with a five-foot stride between them.

> Two weeks before [Hilsmeier and his son's] discovery, a Fawn Grove man stumbled onto a 10-foot high creature exuding a powerful stench.
>
> And about a month after Bigfoot visited Hilsmeier, a Baltimore truck driver saw "a whopper of a man" run across the road leading to the Peach Bottom power plant. Two plant guards heard the pig-like screech Bigfoot is supposed to make, and next day a scouting party found huge tracks in the area.

> Bigfoot stories kept coming in, and Hilsmeier's interest infected Asselin. In May, after the snow and the stories had stopped, they decided to try to make some sense of it all and prepare for the snow and stories to come.[1883]

The first story came from a deer hunter in the Holtwood Dam woods on November 27. Hoping to find deer on this, the first day of deer hunting season, the man suddenly heard something heavy moving through the underbrush and coming towards him. When he stopped to listen, the thing stopped too.

> Then the young hunter heard the snap of a big branch, and he knew whatever was coming wasn't a deer. It was crashing through the undergrowth at an amazing speed. As it approached him, it veered off to the left. In the dim light, the hunter saw the image of a seven-foot-tall human, walking too fast to be human.
>
> The hunter returned later and found big tracks, but they were spaced closely together, not like Bigfoot's five-foot stride. They lacked indications of a three-toed foot, but had the characteristic deep heel print and signs of a high arch.
>
> Hilsmeier and Asselin repeatedly questioned the hunter, pointing out how the tracks, the creature's behavior and the absence of a strong odor differed from other Bigfoot encounters. But the young man stuck to his story, adding only that he had a bad cold that dulled his sense of smell.
>
> He remembered also that he heard shots in the direction from which the creature was coming. Hilsmeier said that might explain why the usually cautious creature nearly walked into the hunter: it was fleeing other hunters.[1884]

Hilsmeier and Asselin hoped that if they applied scientific methods to their investigation of Bigfoot, the broader scientific community would eventually be persuaded to join in. For the team behind Bigfoot Investigations, the evidence was worth studying. "If I didn't think there was a possibility that Bigfoot exists, our investigation would end," said Asselin. "I think we ought to keep an open mind about something we can't explain," said Hilsmeier, "and to proceed with the investigation for the sake of research."[1885]

> They have to grin and bear some razzing from their friends. "But you get used to it," Asselin said. "I have fun figuring out what line they're going to use on me next."
>
> Hilsmeier concludes, "I want to go to the ends of the tracks and see what's there. And if it's nothing we'll drop the whole thing.
>
> "I mean, I might just pick up that big 'ol rabbit by the ears and say, 'HERE'S BIGFOOT: END OF STORY.'"[1886]

Big Bigfoot Blow-Up

In Michigan, Shiawassee County Sheriff's deputies said a Byron-area resident, possibly more than one, dressed up in a borrowed ape-suit and portrayed Bigfoot, causing monster sightings in neighboring Livingston County to the south. The owner of the costume became alarmed at the results from the ape-suit romp Wednesday night, August 30—shocked and scared residents, terrified dogs, and an explosive atmosphere as some residents had taken to arming themselves. Concluding the joke had to stop, the suit-owner handed it over to deputies without revealing who perpetrated the nocturnal ape-drag frolics.

Bigfoot reports had been circulating for weeks in Livingston County (Byron is less than three miles north of the Livingston County line). The wife of one of Wednesday's witnesses, Mrs. Jim Copeman, reported that strange smells and noises had been noticed around her Lehring Road residence for several weeks. Sheriff's deputy Otis Little called the ape costume excursions "a joke amongst a few people in the community." Publicized reports of Bigfoot's presence in Livingston County "kind of gave people an idea," he said. But on Wednesday the joke had "got all out of proportion." Deputies said they are not interested in pressing charges and Little said the Sheriff's office had "no reason to disbelieve the person we've been talking to."

> The deputies' admission that they know the identity of at least one subject in the alleged hoax—they said it was personally delivered to them and will be returned in a few days—conflicts with what Byron Chief of Police Joseph Thomas says they told him.
>
> Thomas said sheriff's officials told him they do not know who owns the suit, who wore it Wednesday or who called the sheriff's department to confess to the events.

> Thomas considers the cause of Wednesday night's commotion an unknown.
>
> "The people who saw whatever they saw are insisting that's (a person in a costume) not what they saw," Thomas said. "I don't know if they're right or wrong."[1887]

Thomas confirmed that the reports of Bigfoot were officially a matter of Byron police business. Two deputies from the sheriff's department joined the post-sighting excitement Wednesday. The Livingston County sheriff's department also sent two deputies who were joined later by a sheriff's department sergeant. "We had proof last night that there was something out there," Thomas said on Thursday, referring to wet tracks left in the southern end of the town, near the river.

> No one has reported seeing the creature in question at that point, Thomas said. He posed a question: if the alleged prankster had it in mind to surprise people around town that night, why did he or she, after a successful excursion, wander off to an unpopulated area where he/she would not be spotted, and there walk into and out of the river?
>
> The first call on the sighting was received at about 11:25 P.M., Thomas said, and the tracks were found shortly after midnight.[1888]

Thomas said he had received Bigfoot reports from three witnesses. The route the creature had traveled was easily discernable: starting near Lehring Road in northwest Byron, through town close to the business areas, and eventually tapering off in the southern section of town. Thomas readily acknowledged something capered through town, however, "I'm not talking about a Bigfoot. And I've never talked about a Bigfoot." What would he do if he actually encountered such a creature? "I'll just hand him my gun and say, 'I'm on your side, buddy.'"

Jim Copeman, aroused by the fearful behavior of his 8-week-old puppy, encountered what he said was Bigfoot illuminated by his flashlight about 75 feet away. He stated the creature was at least eight feet tall, standing in the river with the water level about six inches below its knees. At the same spot in the river, Copeman, who was 5 feet, 10 inches tall, asserted the water level would be at his waist. Copeman estimated the creature was four feet across while displaying natural "movements and poise." He said a person in a monkey suit could be believable "if it weren't for the height and the contours of the shoulder area. No one could fill that out with a build like that . . . there's no way they could pad that area and move like that . . . the way it handled itself while walking."

Copeman said that several weeks of strange activity had preceded the sightings. Only the week prior, Copeman's wife reported a prowler to the village police, and two weeks back, a neighbor had experienced the same thing. For the previous three weeks dogs in the area had been barking continually at night, inconsistent with their normal behavior. Lastly, Copeman said many small animals in the area had been disappearing. Two litters of rabbits had gone missing from their nest below a mobile home during the past month and 10 chickens owned by the Copemans had also gone missing. The McCormick family said they had lost two litters of puppies, four adult dogs and several other pets.[1889] Ken McDonough said his German shepherd/collie mix, Queenie, had gone missing two weeks before the sightings.[1890]

McDonough firmly believed that Bigfoot had selected Byron as its stomping ground. Reporter Darlene Jaye wrote in the *Argus-Press* (Owosso, Michigan) of an anonymously reported incident involving area livestock.

> The report goes that an area resident, who apparently chose not to report the matter to police, three years ago found two of his adult pigs brutally torn apart, one of which was half eaten.
>
> The pigs, according to the source, were closed inside a building with a sturdy door, which had been clawed and violently ripped out of its frame. A bear was the suspected culprit.
>
> Several area residents told of an incident a few years ago involving a herd of sheep found dead, the cause of which remains unknown, they say.
>
> Another such story involves a recent mishap on a Livingston County farm, located not far from Byron, say some of those interviewed.
>
> They contend three cows were brutally killed there, but their owner chose not to report the matter, which supposedly included some very strange evidence. The cows were buried on the owner's property, they add.[1891]

A consistent detail among the sightings was a strong odor. Sheriff's deputy Otis Little said his department had not received any complaints of unusual or unnatural activity before the sightings started. Little added that the "Halloween prank" was a one-day affair. Copeman believed that people's hesitation of reporting unusual activity was likely owing to fear of the reactions they would receive.

> He said he knows of six or seven farmers in the area between his home and Stockbridge who have seen Bigfoot shapes, had livestock mutilated mysteriously or otherwise experienced "just weird things happening" but refuse to report their observances officially.[1892]

Two area citizens told Jaye about a rumored Bigfoot appearance in Cohocta on Thursday night, August 31. Jaye's sources said the witnesses had been "strongly requested" by a Livingston County deputy to not discuss the incident further. Sgt. Bill Jonson of Livingston County Sheriff's department responded to the "large and hairy" creature call arriving at the scene within two hours of the incident where he found no evidence of the passing of a large animal.

Wayne King, director of the Michigan Bigfoot Information Center of Millington said he found several unusual signs in the area near the Byron sightings. With assistant Wayne Delo, King found a Bigfoot "laying area" during their on-site investigation. The laying area included a pulverized eight-inch log which was shattered causing King to doubt it could have been done by human feet. King assessed the Byron sightings amounted to "creditable Sasquatch sightings," and promised his team would be back for further investigation. King claimed deputies showed him the apesuit worn by a prankster and he was convinced the suit he saw was not involved in Wednesday night's events.[1893]

Roland Craft and his wife lived near the second sighting area and were convinced there was a Bigfoot in the woods. He had seen the "laying area" commented on by King and was likewise of a mind that human feet could not have stomped and stamped such a clearing. Mrs. Craft recalled the night of the sighting was also strange for its stillness, normally crickets were very busy with their night music.

> Mrs. Craft recalls an incident that happened about two years ago when she lived in the nearby town of Argentine. She says a horse was found in the Shiawassee River there with its throat violently torn out. She notes that citizens of that area suspected the guilty culprit to be a bear, "but I wasn't so sure."[1894]

Cindy Galbraith, a resident of Cohocta who works in Byron completely disregarded the hoax theory. "Police are covering it up to avoid panic," she said.[1895]

Jerry Ernst, *Argus-Press* Area Editor, looked into the Byron reports, specifically comparing the information given out by law enforcement and the information from news media. Taken as two separate accounts of the same events, Ernst found a lack of consistency between them. Shiawassee County sheriff's deputies explained the sightings reported on Wednesday as a hoax. On Thursday, several deputies told Ernst they never gave chase after anything allegedly prowling through Byron.

> The Associated Press reported Friday [September 01], however, that "Sheriff's Sgt. Phil Cooley and Deputy Bill Bowman chased the whatever-it-was Bigfoot through the woods, but lost it when it jumped into a shallow river channel and ran upstream."
>
> This is the account broadcast Thursday over radio station WOAP, as related to The Argus-Press Friday: "Sgt. Phil Cooley and Deputy Bill Bowman said they were able to hear the creature running upstream in the Shiawassee River toward Howell but did not go after it because the area was heavily overgrown."
>
> According to Thursday's *Flint Journal*, the deputies "tried to follow the creature's trail based on information from the witnesses. They said they heard something 'sloshing' in the river, apparently moving south out of the village. Their search was hindered by heavy river foliage they said."[1896]

The *Argus-Press* contacted the Associated Press for clarification and in response an AP reporter said the foundation of the news service's report was a conversation with a sheriff's deputy or deputies. Another contradiction was the deputies' acquisition of an apesuit. Deputy Sheriff Otis Little called The *Argus-Press* Thursday afternoon to state deputies had received a confession from the owner of the apesuit, and a later announcement from Little said the apesuit had been delivered to the department's offices. The *Argus-Press'* assistant managing editor, Joe Peacock, stated Little had told him deputies knew the apesuit-owner's identity and the identity of another individual who dressed up in it for Wednesday's cavorting.

> Byron Chief of Police Joseph Thomas told this reporter [Ernst] Thursday that deputies told him they did not know the owner of the suit, the wearer of the suit or the identity of the individual who had notified deputies of the story.
>
> Asked how deputies came into possession of the suit, Thomas replied "I don't know."
>
> When this reporter Friday asked Little about the apparent discrepancies, he stated he never spoke to Peacock Thursday.
>
> Little also repeated to this reporter, "the owner of the suit, we know. But who was in it, we don't know because the owner refused to say."
>
> Peacock steadfastly maintains the two conversed and discussed the question of the apesuit's owner and wearer.[1897]

Darlene Jaye, reporter for the *Argus-Press* who was present Wednesday night for the deputies' investigation (and writer of the first *Argus-Press* article on the subject), informed Ernst that Little had told her deputies knew the identities of the owner of the suit and the person wearing it during the "Halloween prank."

> However, deputies were quoted in a *Flint Journal* story Friday as identifying those concerned as a Byron woman who made the suit for a male friend. He intended to scare another friend.
>
> Little was quoted as saying the names of the two won't be released because they broke no law.[1898]

Ernst noted the Thursday AP article stated the person inside the suit was "a perfectly normal-sized Byron-area man decked out in a rented gorilla costume to play a prank on some friends, red-faced Shiawassee County sheriff's deputies confess." Concerning the discrepancies in reporting, Little said Friday, September 1, that "as this thing goes around, it's either being added to or deleted from."[1899]

Iowa Town Has Hairy Time with 'Monster'

> On a typical August evening, when the sky is ablaze with stars and the breeze is warm and slight, you can stand near the pop

> machine on Main Street and hear traffic whiz by on the distant highway.
>
> After the lights go out in Twig's Grocery and the post office is long closed, the village of about 100 slips into a soft slumber in the middle of the cornfields that stretch to the horizon.
>
> But lately, Ottosen has been no peaceful, isolated respite. It has been more like Times Square.
>
> Trucks, cars and motorcycles have roared into town, some of the occupants brandishing flashlights—and a few guns.
>
> The visitors have trampled through vacant houses and weedy lots, probing the shadows and knocking on doors asking for directions.
>
> One resident, appalled by the intrusion, called Humboldt County Sheriff Marvin Andersen to complain that she couldn't safely cross the street in front of her home.[1900]

Thusly *World-Herald* staff writer Frank Santiago painted the picture of a classic small American town, quaint and rustic, contrasted with the dramatic change that occurred when a sizeable number of people descended upon Ottosen, three miles east of the Des Moines River. Some of these folks may have been simply curious, but some, as Santiago points out, were armed and ready for the hunt. What brought them was the story of a hairy, smelly, five-foot-high creature that lurked in the shadows about the town. Mrs. Jan Henkins claimed to have seen the ape-like monster twice. "It isn't anything like I've seen before," she said. Henkins believed two of her daughters may have glimpsed the creature. "People think I'm just crazy," she admitted. "But I know what I saw." After her family's experiences, Henkins sent her daughters to stay with a sister in Livermore for several nights. "My oldest daughter would wake up and just be shaking," she said.

> Adding to the drama are assorted stories of dogs and rabbits being mutilated, of cats disappearing, of May Helieseth's grapevines being mysteriously stripped of their fruit and leaves. One resident said, "Every dog in town was barking on the nights when the creature was seen."[1901]

Kevin Cook of Des Moines believed there were pockets of Bigfoot traveling by night through the Midlands, following the Missouri and Mississippi Rivers. Cook, who at the time said he had been researching Bigfoot for 10 years, worked as a customer service officer for United Airlines at the Des Moines airport. He told Santiago that the Ottosen sightings were of creatures from a larger group living in the states of Iowa, South Dakota, and Minnesota. Cook explained that there were actually different species of Bigfoot including a variety that grew to five to six feet, which could be the type seen in Ottosen.

A more cautious attitude was expressed by Sheriff Andersen who said he'd prefer to have "something solid to go on." Interviewed at the Humboldt County Courthouse in Dakota City, Sheriff Andersen said: "I wouldn't rule out the possibility of somebody wearing a costume. I would think he'd get by with it at night. But what has me puzzled is that one of the sightings was during the day. And anybody wearing a costume would be taking an awful chance. They could get shot."

The wife of Ottosen's mayor suggested, "Possibly there is some large animal. It could be a bear, or large bird or some creature." She appreciated that something was going on, that people were seeing something. But a monster? "I don't think you can dismiss what people said they saw, but we don't have to go wild about it."

In the early afternoon on Monday, July 31, three boys aged 10, 11, and 12 were walking near the livestock sale barns at the edge of town. "We were sort of goofing around and chased a cat up a tree. It was scared and it was bleeding," one of the boys said. Then the boys' afternoon of antics changed suddenly. "We heard this scratching noise come from in one of the small buildings like something rubbing up against something. We tossed a rock into the building." In a window there appeared a face, momentarily visible before disappearing. "It was a big head, square-like," the boy added. "He had big eyes and a flat nose and broad shoulders. He was covered by black or dark brown hair." The boys fled. One looked back over his shoulder and witnessed the creature, legs propelling it in big leaps, its body hunched over, as it vanished into a cornfield.[1902] Reporter Dave Brown of the *Des Moines Tribune* reported the sheriff's statement that at least one of the boys said the creature dropped to all four legs when it left the scene.[1903]

Nine-year-old Donette Henkins said she stepped outside her grandmother's home on the night of July 27 and saw the creature. "It had deep-set eyes and fangs," Donette recalled. "It kind of growled and grunted." This event was followed a few days later when Donette's sister, Dawn saw what may have been the same creature while riding her bicycle down Main Street on Sunday, July 30. Like her sister's encounter, Dawn's sighting also came at night and she described a five-foot-tall creature standing near a garage about half a block away from her. "He just stood there. I couldn't see his face because it was in a shadow. But I could he was broad and was covered in hair,' she said.[1904]

> The girl's screams brought her mother and Gina Dahl, 12, and Pat Young, 24.
>
> Riding bikes to where Dawn had been, the trio stopped when they heard a man's voice.
>
> "Somebody asked, 'Does anybody know what time it is?'" Mrs. Henkins said.
>
> "I don't know where the voice came from, but we looked down toward the garage and saw this head looking at us around the corner. It had dazzling eyes, I the dark. They were as big as golfballs. It had a big head covered with hair."
>
> The women bolted.
>
> Mrs. Henkins said the source of the man's voice remains a mystery to her.[1905]

Sheriff Andersen said he didn't know what would happen next. "There really isn't much we can do," he said. Andersen stated he had sent a team of deputies to patrol the village at night and to handle the increase in nocturnal road traffic from the visitors, the curious, and the monster-hunters. "I believe these people saw something but I don't know what," he added.

Cook believed the witnesses and the curious had very likely scared it off to parts unknown. "He is intelligent in the sense he knows how to survive. He is very shy toward people. People have seen him but they either don't believe what they see or they're afraid to speak out because people think they're crazy." And Cook put faith, very much in the vein of Krantz' hopes and beliefs, in the inevitably of the mystery coming to an end. "But it's only a matter of time before he's caught," Cook affirmed. "It may be a hunter or somebody who is out looking for him."[1906]

On August 1, Sheriff Andersen inspected "some real unusual" footprints discovered in a cornfield. "I've never seen any like it before," he said. "There are three 'toes' on the front of the foot and one toward the back. We just don't know what it could be." But the Sheriff was reticent to apply the term 'monster' to the events in town, preferring more prosaic explanations. "It might be a bear, but then it might not. Some of the people said that it walks around on two legs and when it starts to run it gets down on all fours." The reports, the tracks, and the notoriety the town was receiving meant the Bigfoot phenomenon had arrived in Ottosen. "People are scared and mad," said Andersen. "They don't want to go out at night and they're mad because people think they're crazy."[1907]

> A fortnight ago Anna Dodrill froze with fear when she looked up from a load of dishes into the "burning red eyes" of a big-nosed, black-faced, hairy-headed creature staring at her through a window a few feet away.
>
> Terror tied her tongue. Her brother, who earlier that evening thought he had seen a large and hairy arm reach out from behind a cattle shed, sat at a table with a rifle ready. But he knew nothing of the kitchen scene beyond his view.
>
> Seconds passed—slowly, agonizingly. The creature's eyes bored in on Dodrill. Frightened as she had never been before, she blinked but could not look away.
>
> After three minutes, Anna Dodrill screamed. The creature, whatever it was, fled into the darkness outside her farm home three miles northwest of here.
>
> "It was the first time in my life I couldn't move," Dodrill said later.[1908]

On September 12, and about 24 hours after the incident at the Dodrill's home, Robert Newell IV was at home about two miles southeast of Ottosen. Suddenly he heard a whining sound come from the barnyard. "No horse or pig could have made it," Newell said. He glanced out a window toward the barn which was located about 35 feet south of the house and illuminated by yard lights. Newell said he watched a tall, hairy hunchbacked figure dart into the barn. It jumped into a manure spreader, got out and stood for a moment, then got into a grain spreader. As Newell watched, he got the impression the six-to-seven-foot tall creature was looking for food. As Newell watched on, the black-haired creature left the barn, walked around a silo and quickly proceeded south into a recently harvested cornfield, ending the 3 ½ minute-encounter.

Beginning in mid-July the Humboldt and Kossuth County sheriffs' offices received copious complaints from people in the Ottosen, West Bend, and Humboldt areas—complaints comprised of large hairy creatures, strange, eerie screams in the night, stampeded cattle, chewed-up cats, mangled rabbits, and a dog's apparent violent death by broken neck.

By mid-September 25-year-old Kevin Cook had been to Ottosen twice collecting information on what people were experiencing. Cook hadn't found definitive evidence that Bigfoot was responsible for the sightings and other unusual events in Ottosen, but he theorized there could be as many as three Bigfoot in the area—two adults and a child. Ottosen at the time had a population of 135.

> Alberta Bennett, wife of Ottosen Marshall Tom Bennett, said the situation has created a division in town between believers and nonbelievers.
>
> "It's left a strange feeling in town," she said.
>
> There has been the usual humor that accompanies such sightings.
>
> Someone recently tacked a second sign beneath the Ottosen sign on Iowa Highway 222, which skirts the town. The new sign reads, "Big Foot Country." A letter received last week at the post office was addressed to "Big Foot Country." Then there was the fellow who walked into the post office wearing a monkey mask.[1909]

But some of the conversations that took place at Twig's grocery lacked the aforementioned tongue-in-cheek humor. Stories of being awakened at night by chilling screams, strange footprints found in cornfields, unusual feces discovered in Marilyn Schumacher's lean-to, of cattle stampeded by unknown causes, and frightened children unwilling to walk the town's streets were all discussed in serious tones.

Sheriff Andersen listened to the stories. "I tell you, if you're a nonbeliever, after you talk to a few of these people, you have to believe there's something there," Andersen said. "I think those people have seen something, but I don't know if it's this Bigfoot connection they're talking about." Some residents were reluctant to talk to folks from outside the town. "People are afraid to say anything anymore," said Henkins, whose children were not free from ridicule from other kids. But those who saw the creature were firm that they had witnessed something incredible. "They'll [naysayers] ridicule about it until they're unlucky enough to see it themselves," Newell said. Cook believed that the Rock Island railroad tracks parallel to the West Fork of the Des Moines River could play a role in Bigfoot's routes of travel. Many of the sightings in the area occurred near the line's tracks.

Edna Kampen was postmaster in Ottosen and in a position to hear many of the town's thoughts on the subject of a resident Bigfoot on practically a daily basis. Kampen: "At first they thought it was a hoax, I think. But now there's been so many classes of people—farmers, townspeople, etc.—who saw it, that they're taking it more seriously."[1910]

Writing in November, reporters Julie Girres and Jeff Bormann captured the continued unease and concern the Bigfoot sightings had created in Ottosen and the surrounding area.

> It's Friday night after the game and Forsythe's corner is deserted. Where is everybody? Chances are WBHS [West Bend High School] students are somewhere near the river searching for the mysterious night stalker, Bigfoot. . . .
>
> Humboldt and Kossuth [County] sheriff departments, who have done some research, believe that if Bigfoot exists he may follow the Rock Island Railroad that parallels the west fork of the Des Moines River. So far, all reported sightings are only a few miles from this area.
>
> Ottosen, considered to be the home of Bigfoot, is also the home of many WBHS students and their families. Many men, women, and children here have reported seeing the hairy beast.[1911]

"I don't think he'll be back," said one Ottosen resident who believed Bigfoot had mangled his rabbits. "But he could still be in the general area," he concluded. Area resident Julie Biddle said, "I think it's highly unlikely such an animal exists. If something was really out there we would have more substantial evidence."[1912] West Bend High School science teacher Gary Walker said, "I think someone's having a damn good time." Girres and Bormann quoted "Bigfoot hunter" Nick Thilges: "No, I don't believe in Bigfoot, but it sure is fun going Bigfoot hunting."[1913]

> Humboldt County Sheriff Marvin Andersen, who has tracked down dozens of Bigfoot reports this year without success, has come face-to-face with a six-foot-tall, hairy replica of the elusive creature.
>
> Andersen apprehended the stuffed beast in a refrigerator box, to the delight of nearly 200 persons who watched Andersen get his surprise Christmas present.
>
> The gag was set up by Juanita Benton, who operates Benton's Truck Stop with her husband, William. More than 100 county residents chipped in to buy the replica for $95 after Mrs. Benton saw it on display in a Fort Dodge store.[1914]

LaBreque on Iowa Bigfoot

"The animal is here," said Cliff LaBreque of Bigfoot's presence in Iowa after reading the accounts from Ottosen and investigating the reports himself. "All indications point to the fact that they do have Bigfoot there. They have some pretty convincing things to say," he affirmed. "It's here and it's here in big numbers." LaBreque was 39 years old and a truck salesman. He suggested the hardest part of Bigfoot research was getting people to come forward with their encounters. "They are afraid of public criticism—ridicule," LaBreque said. Remarking further on the spate of sightings stemming from Ottosen, LaBreque offered, "They're in the mating season now." LaBreque believed Bigfoot's mating period started in August and ended in early October and could be the reason for the sightings. Though LaBreque said in an interview he had conducted field research in several states including Arkansas, Michigan, Missouri, and Minnesota, he had not been especially active in Iowa field research. "But I'm getting geared up now. I'll start really going to work on this again in the next two or three weeks," he said. At the time, one of LaBreque's interests was to learn more about what Bigfoot did in winter. "We know he doesn't hibernate and I want to find out where the animal stays in wintertime," he said. But for LaBreque, it was an insatiable curiosity that propelled him into the realm of Bigfoot. "I'll never be satisfied until I know one thing. How an animal like this is so smart as to be able to evade being spotted and captured. That is amazing to me," he admitted.[1915]

Mark Thompson Sighting

Mark Thompson was sitting in his pickup truck when he saw a figure he estimated to be seven feet tall and covered all over in brown-black hair in his Hardy, Iowa, soybean field. The creature moved off after Thompson drove closer to the creature and honked his horn and flashed his truck's lights.[1916] Later, footprints were found in the field on Saturday, September 30. The prints, which bore no resemblance to any usual farm animal's tracks, led into a marshy area and disappeared into tall weeds.[1917]

Thompson's encounter occurred as Sheriff Andersen's office was dealing with two other Bigfoot reports. One of Andersen's deputies checked out a report of a creature in a farm field that turned out to be a tandem farm disc with its arms extended upward. The other report came about from some 40 high school students building a homecoming float on Wednesday night, September 27. They reported to authorities they had seen two creatures in a nearby field, one with red eyes, one with blue eyes. Officers investigating the field found no sign or trace of any creatures. "But it had them scared," said Andersen. "It had them scared enough where they went to town and weren't going back out there."

In early September a West Bend fisherman discovered over twenty footprints under a bridge spanning the West Fork of the Des Moines River. Plaster casts made of these tracks were 16 inches long and five inches wide and had the intriguing feature of definite claws measuring three inches.[1918]

"If it is still around here when we get this corn out, it's not going to have as much cover to hide in," Sheriff Andersen said.[1919]

Kinderhook Creature

Kinderhook in Columbia County, New York, is an agricultural community known for its apple orchards. In December 1978, 72-year-old Martha Hallenbeck looked out her window and saw a "big black hairy thing all curled up" in her yard. She later inspected her lawn and found large, human-like footprints pressed into the snow. Worried that no one would believe her, she initially kept mum about her sighting.[1920]

Author Bruce Hallenbeck wrote in *Monsters of the Northwoods,* that strange footprints showed up in the snow around his home and near his parents' home near an area called Cushing's Hill.

> The tracks were three-toed and very large. My cousin, Barry Knights, who was only thirteen at the time, was already an experienced hunter and trapper, and he found a set of three-toed tracks in the snow in December 1978. They were on my own property, crossing a log. I photographed them and sent a copy of the pictures to the [*Hudson River*] *Chronicle,* which promptly lost them—along with my negatives. I was stymied as to what the prints could actually have meant. There were only three, and they seemed to end in the midst of the snow. Unless the creature somehow took flight, that seemed physically impossible.[1921]

Skunk Ape

Tampa native Charlie Robins wrote columns for the *Tampa Tribune* and the *Lakeland Ledger* for over 30 years. In the '70s Robins created the character Nelson Yeti; "Nelson, as you may recall from previous interviews, is a skunk ape who resides in the swamps near the Tamiami Trail, and makes his living picking up tourists by the heels and shaking loose change from their pockets. He is generally regarded as the unofficial spokesyeti for the Florida branch of his species."[1922] With Nelson Yeti, Robins treated the Skunk Ape with whimsy and lightheartedness.

It was not with a light heart that Carolyn Coffey, who stopped short of saying a Skunk Ape had visited the Westwinds Mobile Home Village, found little better explanation. Coffey told the Manatee County Sheriff's Department that a huge footprint was discovered Wednesday morning in a patch of sand outside her trailer. "I'll just let you see it," she told reporters on Wednesday. "I'll tell you one thing, that thing that made that footprint, I don't want to see it." Another resident of Westwinds said that about three months previous, she had seen a creature walking along a road in the mobile home park. Coffey admitted she had never seen a Skunk Ape but had heard strange noises and smelled a terrible odor which she likened to rotting cabbage. Coffey's son, Chip, said he saw the creature one night as he was driving home. The creature was crouched on the roadside as the car's headlights illuminated it, making its eyes shine like jewels, Chip said. Three teenage boys offered their experience—the previous year they looked out a window of their mobile home and saw a Skunk Ape staring back at them. They too were assaulted by a horrendous stench which they used words like "sewer" and "skunk" to describe. As the creature fled the scene it knocked over a bicycle.

> Robert Schuler, owner of the park, says the Skunk-Ape is a lot of hogwash, and told reporters to leave the area Wednesday when they were speaking with Mrs. Coffey.
>
> "It (the footprint) was made by kids," Schuler said. "They do it all the time."
>
> Schuler said he didn't want publicity about the mobile home park being the stomping grounds for Skunk-Apes. He told reporters that in the future they should ask his permission before entering the park.
>
> "Now I'll get 250 telephone calls," he said. News of the creature will scare residents of the park and may prompt them to ask for more security, he complained.[1923]

Mike Corradino's interest in Skunk Apes was fueled by the many calls he received in his work as catcher of runaway and abandoned pet monkeys.

Corradino was founder of the Florida Monkey Sanctuary and served as the official monkey catcher of Sarasota County. "At first I scoffed, too, and said 'impossible,'" Corradino said. "But the physical evidence could not be ignored. Barn doors knocked down. Dead animals, chickens, rabbits, raccoons, with their heads bitten off and always the blood completely drained from the body. Not long ago 25 to 30 rabbits were found that way not far from here," he said. "I figured it could only be one of three things. A crazy man running loose from an asylum. A bear, but none has been seen around here in 75 years and this thing always walks upright. Or a Skunk Ape, which runs 6 to 8 feet tall and can be larger than a gorilla."

Venice, Florida, was the wintering headquarters of the Ringling Brothers & Barnum and Bailey Circus, leading some to conjecture the dead animals could be the result of an escaped predator from the circus. Corradino maintained a list of 74 sightings including a more uncommon type of report wherein two Skunk Apes were seen frolicking in the farmlands outside the city limits. "Some 200 to 300 people have seen it," Corradino insists, "but most are too embarrassed to make a report. They feel they'll be ridiculed and treated as a weirdo at work."

Corradino claimed the stealthy Skunk Ape created little noise to alert people of its presence and rarely left a good set of tracks. The creature had not been photographed because it appeared to be a nocturnal creature. "It can't be a chimpanzee, because chimps do not go out much at night," he said.[1924]

Biltmore Acres' Dave Parks had a dream. "The night before, I had a dream about Bigfoot. This is really strange," he said, "I don't know if the dream carried over and this was just my imagination or what. But I really saw it."

"It" was a large, dark creature Parks glimpsed outside his bedroom window. "It was about 5 A.M., still dark outside, he said. "I was woken up by my dog. There was this whining noise outside my door. I got up and went over to my bedroom window and caught a glimpse of something. It looked like a creature to me.

"It was big and dark. I couldn't tell if it was real hairy. Its back was to me. As it ran west, all these dogs started barking all over the neighborhood. It was about 60 feet away when I saw it, going on to a lot next door where a house is being built." Parks said he could be the owner of an over-active imagination. Parks' wife was home at the time but didn't wake up while the creature was visible. "We both believe in the Skunk Ape. I'm not sure she's going to believe that was it though," he added.[1925]

"I'd say 90 percent of the Skunk Ape sightings are black bears," said Dave Ellis, the executive director of Dreher Park Zoo. Bears in the wild favor high and dry areas of Florida, Ellis maintained, making them susceptible to pressures from encroaching development. Ellis said the resulting compression of bear populations into smaller areas would cause more frequent interactions with people.[1926]

CHAPTER 10
1979

Back in those quiet days of October 1958, it took only a half dozen lines in Redwood Country (then known as RFD) to stir up many years of interest in an unusual "creature," or, at least a living legend. The lines were from a letter by Mrs. Jess Bemis, who now lies at McKinleyville and whose husband was working in the Bluff Creek area. She was truly concerned with what was going on.

The letter was in my basket for a few days, and then finally, with space to spare, I ran it. Until then, no one had apparently heard of the creature—or at least paid much attention to it, even if it had been around for many generations. That column opened a floodgate of interest which continues to this day.

In the first year I received more than 2,000 letters from all over the world, plus hundreds of phone calls and visitors. The Klamath–Trinity Valley to Bluff Creek was flooded with visitors—wanted and unwanted.

The creature had to have a name, so this column dubbed it simply "Bigfoot"—spelled as one word—and it has so remained. Elsewhere it has sometimes been called "Sasquatch" and "Abominable Snowman," and a few other terms not worth mentioning. None of the publicity and business stirred by Bigfoot has been harmful. Smart men came to study the situation, so did fools with elephant guns—but the scene finally calmed to allow Bigfoot his right to move about as he pleases.[1927]

Andrew Genzoli. "Redwood Country,"
Times-Standard (August 17, 1979).

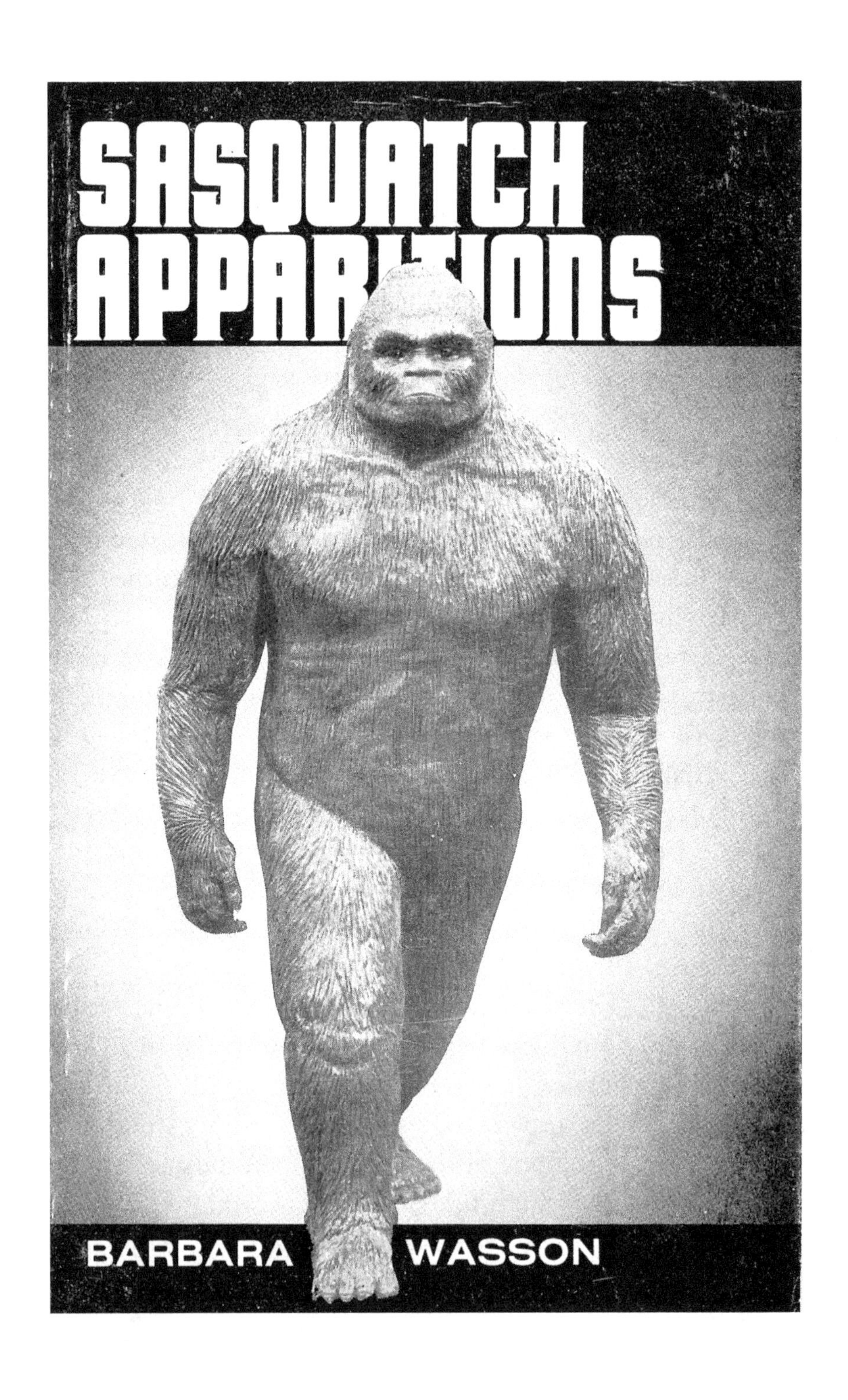
SASQUATCH
APPARITIONS
BARBARA WASSON

Print & Media

At the end of the 1970s, Bigfoot remained a vital incarnation of pop culture—but within the collective psyche cracks appeared, marring its status and indicating an icon whose heyday of popular accession and embrace was beginning to cool. David Coleman's *Bigfoot Filmography* (2012) provides an example of this waning from the standpoint of Bigfoot featured in cinematic offerings. Coleman's exhaustive survey of *Ciné de Sasquatch*[1928] reveals a downward trend in output toward the end of the decade. The five offerings Coleman details for 1979 was the lowest total since the same number was produced for 1975 and less than half of the fictional and documentary appearances that highlighted 1977 as the banner year of Bigfoot in film and television in the '70s.

The year 1979 was not three weeks old when the actor Ted Cassidy, who counted portrayals of Bigfoot in his portfolio, passed away. The 6-foot-8-inch actor, perhaps best-known for his role as Lurch in the television series *The Addams Family,* died at the age of 46 on January 16, 1979. A spokesman at Hollywood's St. Vincent's Hospital said Cassidy suffered complications after open-heart surgery for a non-malignant tumor. Cassidy was not as well-known as the growling voice of Bruce Banner's alter ego on *The Incredible Hulk*. On the latter show's premiere episode, Susan Sullivan's Dr. Elaina Marks asked reporter Jack McGee (played by Jack Colvin) if a large creature (the Hulk) spotted in the area could perhaps be Bigfoot. The question made sense given a large cast of the Hulk's footprint which McGee was holding. Cassidy became the second actor to portray Bigfoot on *The Six Million Dollar Man* and *Bionic Woman* television shows appearing in the episodes: "The Return of Bigfoot" (1976), "The Return of Bigfoot: Part 2" (1976), and "Bigfoot V" (1977).[1929]

Warner Bros.' *Superman* (1978) was one of the most successful movies of the decade which, according to its marketing catchphrase, made millions of people believe that a man could fly. Christopher Reeve donned the blue tights and red cape and left a cinematic portrayal of the Man of Steel that immediately became iconic. Shortly after the blockbuster movie debuted, the original Superman actor, Kirk Alyn, told interviewers about his active role in the search for Bigfoot. Alyn said that three times a year, for two weeks at a stretch, he participated in searching for evidence of Bigfoot's existence as a member of Friends of Bigfoot, "an organization consisting of maybe 100 people, some writers, some scientists and some in various other fields. We have a group of people in the field constantly looking and searching." Alyn remained active in show business at the time, to include a cameo appearance in *Superman;* Alyn played the part of the incredulous Sam Lane, father to Lois Lane who endeavors to convince him that a boy—the young Clark Kent—was outrunning their train.[1930]

Two regional films concerning Bigfoot or Bigfoot-like creatures, *Screams of a Winter Night* and *Revenge of Bigfoot* (originally titled *Rufus J. Pickle and the Indian* for a brief theatrical run), came out in 1979, the latter now considered a lost movie. *Screams of a Winter Night* depicts five young couples who visit a cabin for their holiday, and while a storm rages outside, they gather round the fire to tell ghost stories. *Shreveport Times* reviewer Joe Leydon thought the film's pacing a bit uneven but that it also delivered a "passing shudder."

> There is a great deal more atmosphere than sense to be found in "Screams of a Winter Night," a low-budget chiller filmed on location in Natchitoches Parish. But there are enough unsettling shocks in the film to make one wonder what director James L. Wilson could do with more money and a better script.[1931]

One of the shared tales concerns the Moss Point Man, a smaller-scale Bigfoot-like creature who menaces a young couple parking on a backwoods road. Actor Ray Gaspard, appearing in this film, also had a role in *Return to Boggy Creek.*

Revenge of Bigfoot was produced and directed by Harry Z. Thomason and shot in Texarkana in 1978 and released in 1979. The film was re-released under the title, *Rufus J. Pickle and the Indian.* Actor T. Dan Hopkins had a small part as a Sioux Medicine Man in *Little House on the Prairie* before landing a lead role in *Revenge of Bigfoot.* Hopkins described the movie as a suspense comedy about a small redneck town terrorized by Bigfoot after a local rancher takes in a Native American, Okinagon, played by Hopkins.[1932]

Ito "Bill" Rebane, a Roger Corman-esque producer of science fiction films, lived in a large, old farmhouse nestled in Gleason, Wisconsin. Scenes from movies like *The Great Spider Invasion, Alpha Incident,* and *Invasion from Inner Earth* were filmed in his barn studio, whose nooks and crannies were filled with assorted props such as a replica brain, a giant maggot, enormous spiders, and a cave set festooned with drooping webs. While some special effects were filmed in his barn, Rebane's basement served as his technical workshop where the final steps in film processing occurred. Long strips of film habitually hung near two splicing machines where Rebane and his wife Barbara crafted final edits. His modus operandi (as was with Corman) was to work on a low budget, and Rebane himself served as a jack-of-all-trades, doing everything from writing screenplays to splicing together film.

Capture of Bigfoot was co-written by Rebane and his cousin, Ingrid Neumyer. Bigfoot was played by Canadian Janis Raudkivi. Rebane's 12-year-old son, Randy, made his film debut in the costume of a juvenile Bigfoot.[1933]

Dewey Pfister, staff writer for the Wausau-Merrill *Daily Herald,* reviewed *Capture of Bigfoot:*

> Adventure and suspense prevailed form the opening scene when Bill Dexter of Gleason, cast as trapper Hank Wells, became one of Bigfoot's first victims. Actually a heavy-equipment salesman, Dexter exhibited all the enthusiasm of a Hollywood bit player looking for a bigger role and I settled down to enjoy the hour-and-a-half production.
>
> The pursuit of Bigfoot was marked by fires, explosions, car crashes and flipping snowmobiles, mixed with just enough cursing probably to earn the movie a PG rating.[1934]

Rhinelander writer Dean Hammons wrote the novelization for *Capture of Bigfoot* for which a published book never materialized nor, according to Hammons, was remuneration ever forthcoming.

> "The timing was right, everything was set," Hammons sighs. "The release date [of the book] had been set to coincide with the release of the movie."
>
> "Big Foot," [*Capture of Bigfoot*] much of which was filmed in Rhinelander and Gleason, has not appeared on any movie screen north of Merrill. Hammons' percentage of the take on box office receipts hasn't been seen, either.
>
> Although Hammons has since collaborated on several projects with Bill Rebane, a Gleason area writer-producer whose "Giant Spider Invasion" has grossed over $12 million, screenwriting hasn't been any better to Hammons than novel writing.
>
> "When 'Big Foot' was being filmed up here, I got awfully tired of the food stamp people giving me the fish eye every

time I'd go to pick up my stamps," Hammons says. "The cast and crew on 'Big Foot' got paid, but production costs still haven't been paid. I am one of those production costs."[1935]

The Boy Who Saw Bigfoot, by Marian T. Place focuses on Joey Wilson and his friend Sara who were playing in the woods one day when they were assaulted by a terrible smell followed by their notice of a moving elderberry bush.

> We stared and stared. Pretty soon the branches shook again. A hand and a hairy arm reached for another bunch of berries. But it couldn't reach far enough. Then two hands and two hairy arms parted the branches. Now we could see a dark shiny face, a big mouth full of teeth, and squinty eyes. The face wasn't as big as I expected. It wasn't all that scary looking.
>
> Sara hugged me, and whispered in my ear, "It's a young one!"[1936]

Place's second work of Bigfoot fiction aimed for younger readers was voted the 1982 winner of the Mark Twain award by almost 50,000 Missouri schoolchildren.[1937]

Author Charles Edson documented numerous Bigfoot tales and encounters he claimed to have experienced beginning in 1952 In his book *My Travels with Bigfoot,* published in 1979. Upon the book's release, travel writer and art critic Ted Bredt recalled his acquaintance with Edson and his claims of Bigfoot interaction:

> I first met Charles Edson some years ago when he came to the *California Today* offices to talk about doing an article on Bigfoot. We had done a tongue-in-cheek piece some years back, wishing Bigfoot a happy birthday because it had been the 100th anniversary of Bigfoot's first reported sighting in Santa Clara County.
>
> Charles explained how he had spent 25 years in the wilderness of Siskiyou, Humboldt and Del Norte Counties, first as an occasional hunter and later as a full-time resident and Bigfoot tracker. He'd worked as a logger most of that

> time, taking odd jobs in the off season—he was once a deputy sheriff—to support his family. Nearly all his spare time over those years had been spent searching for Bigfoot and checking out the sightings of others.
>
> He admitted he started as a nonbeliever in the Bigfoot myth, but as evidence piled on evidence—as finding tracks turned into actual sightings of the man-animal—Charlie had become convinced of its reality. He had even gone so far, he said, as to try and establish some kind of communication with his quarry.
>
> The thing that piqued my interest was the fact that Charlie didn't insist on any credit for the story. That caused my natural cynicism to sag a little.[1938]

Bredt encouraged Edson to write his tale down, but Edson demurred, believing he wasn't a very good writer. When Bredt later revisited Bigfoot as the subject for a news story, Charles Edson sprang into his mind. Bredt gave Edson a call. "You must be psychic," Edson told him from his home in Freemont, California. "My book is on the presses right now."

> I've read Charlie Edson's *My Travels with Bigfoot—A True-Life Odyssey,* which we have excerpted here. I was right when I told him to write his story himself. It is an amazing and mystifying chronicle of the Bigfoot phenomenon.
>
> I can't swear to its truth, of course, but perhaps equally important is this: Knowing Charlie Edson, I would refuse to swear that it isn't true.
>
> One thing *is* certain: If you have the slightest leaning toward accepting Bigfoot as a living, breathing resident of our northern high country, this book might very well push you over the edge into the realm of the true believer.[1939]

My Travels with Bigfoot was published by Crescent Publications of Los Angeles, California and has become for collectors a hard-to-find exemplar of 1970s Bigfoot literature, replete with Edson's descriptions of his first-hand experiences with Bigfoot. While promoting the book, Edson stated his 26-year involvement with hairy hominids had produced over 30 sightings. "I shall never forget the first time I saw some Bigfoot tracks in the snow in October, 1952," he said. "I had been on a hunting trip in the Siskiyou country in Northern California when I found myself staring at two huge footprints, nearly five feet apart, trailing off the path into the underbrush."

"Those footprints were at least 18 inches long and seven inches across—larger than any animal I can think off. It had five human toes—and no claws," he said. That surprising discovery started Edson on his journey to learn all he could about Bigfoot, even moving his family into the Siskiyou Mountains to be closer to his passion. On July 24, 1955, Edson experienced his first face-to-face encounter with Bigfoot. "I would leave food out for Bigfoot and the next day, all that was left would be the huge tracks of Bigfoot in the dirt," Edson explained. On one occasion as he was about to leave a research area his attention was drawn to a shadow next to a tree about 200 yards away.

> "I grabbed my binoculars, took a closer look and that tree had legs, arms and a head and it was staring at me!
>
> "I could even see Bigfoot's long arms dangling with hands and fingers.
>
> "He is eight feet tall, of solid muscle and bone and he takes huge, six-foot strides. He has a snout like a hog but with a small mouth like a human, with a large, over-hanging forehead.
>
> "He doesn't talk, but he hums a persistent low groans [sic].
>
> "And he has a pungent, almost over-powering beast stench."[1940]

University of Wisconsin history professor Walker D. Wyman's interest in North American mythical creatures began during his research into the lumberjack frontier stretching from Maine to the Pacific Northwest. Interviews with old lumberjacks exposed Wyman to their tales of strange creatures that populated the dark back woods of the country. Wyman's assemblage of information and stories on these incredible forest denizens culminated with his book, *Mythical Creatures of the U.S.A. and Canada* published by the University of Wisconsin-River Falls Press.

Wyman lists 10 mythical snakes, six insects, 19 birds, 15 fish and water serpents, and 43 assorted strange animals and monsters, including Bigfoot. Each creature is accompanied by a scientific name conjured by the collaborative cogitation between Wyman and his neighbor, Dr. B. H. Kettelkamp, a retired biology professor. "Mostly they (mythical creatures) are the product of imagination, ignorance, or the result of things that happened that couldn't be explained any other way," said Wyman. Wyman's wife, Helen Bryant Wyman provided the book's illustrations.

"I don't think very many people still believe in mythical creatures," Wyman said. "They still talk about them, but more for fun. They are sort of an extension of the tall story." There was one possible exception to his thinking: Bigfoot. "Is the Sasquatch a hoax or a remnant of a race of men that might have migrated here centuries ago from Asia and somehow managed to escape capture?" Wyman asked in his book. "We only know that Bigfoot is one of the great legends of our time and is the mascot of Spokane Community College students."[1941]

Two associate professors at the State University of New York at Buffalo examined a myriad of mysteries such as Atlantis, the Bermuda Triangle, UFOs, and Bigfoot in their book, *Exploring the Unknown: Great Mysteries Re-Examined*. Geologist Joseph Cazeau and archeologist Stuart Scott Jr. wrote their book to assist and prod the layman to question remarkable claims advanced by advocates of the incredible. The need for such a book, the authors argued, was partly the fault of mainstream science.

> Part of the academic silence comes from a "those theories don't deserve consideration" attitude based on some of the poor evidence accompanying them. The Buffalo scientists feel, however, such a posture can lead to problems.
>
> "If someone goes around calling me a 'dirty rat,'" says Cazeau, "and I don't answer, well, then people are going to start believing I'm a rat."
>
> They claim the book is unusual in that "a couple of representatives of the scientific community" seriously consider the more sensational theories on the mysteries mentioned alongside accepted hypotheses.

"We want to make people less gullible," Cazeau said, "to sharpen their critical faculties so that they can spot errors and make valid judgements based on the evidence before them." Eschewing a knuckle-rapping pedagogic style, mysteries such as Bigfoot are presented and explored by the authors in light of various theories devised to explain them. The onus falls to the reader to weigh the evidence.

"We're not a couple of pontificating know-it-alls with PhD's," said Cazeau commenting on the book's lack of didacticism. The authors put faith in the principle of parsimony inherent to Occam's Razor, contending the simpler theory is preferred over more complex speculations propped by innumerable assumptions. "I'm perfectly willing to admit ancient astronauts could have visited Earth 40,000 years ago," added Cazeau. "Some UFO sightings may also be true sightings, but the major evidence is just not strong enough to support the theory."

> Cazeau and Scott say a need for their book was partially created by journalists.
>
> They contend that a reality of successful journalism is that items of marginal news significance need not adhere to strict rules of objectivity.

If unusual, strange stories such as the latest Bigfoot sighting can be written in such a way as to enhance their believability, enticed readers buy more papers, magazines, and books. Cazeau pejoratively summed up this journalistic position as, "So what if the public believes?"[1942]

The authors suggested that "the presumed existence of Bigfoot is based chiefly on the following: (1) eyewitness accounts, (2) tangible evidence, and (3) photographic evidence." Taking up eyewitnesses, the authors draw a parallel between encountering Bigfoot and seeing UFOs:

> Again we have things seen by honest witnesses, but perhaps misinterpreted. Often in the pro-Bigfoot literature we see photographs of eyewitnesses undergoing lie detector tests. This should not be construed as proof that Bigfoot actually exists, but only that the honest witness *thought* he saw something that might have been Bigfoot (or might have been a bear).[1943]

Cazeau and Scott stressed that they did not question the integrity of witnesses, but point out exaggeration, judgement, excitement, and brevity of a sighting as factors bearing on evaluation of reports. Moreover, the growing body of reports in aggregate argued against the outright dismissal of Bigfoot and the authors stated that trends in hair coloration and footprint length from George Gill's "Population Clines of the North American Sasquatch as Evidenced by Track Length and Estimated Stature" delivered at the *Anthropology of the Unknown: Sasquatches and Similar Phenomena* conference in 1978 as supportive of eyewitness credibility.

The most common form of tangible evidence are the large footprints, some of which, Cazeau and Scott rightly point out, are the products of hoaxers. "The most common way to fake the footprints is to carve large feet out of a plank of wood and nail ordinary shoes or boots to them." But other tracks defy easy description of their production: "deep tracks (suggesting heavy weight), a longer than normal human stride, and sometimes seen ascending unusually steep slopes."

> Other kinds of evidence include hair, fecal droppings, bones, and purported sounds made and recorded of the Yeti. The evidence from hair and fecal droppings is a bit shaky. In the first place, few samples of these materials alleged to have been produced by a Bigfoot have been submitted for analyses. Second, there is no basis of comparison. We can obtain samples of bear hair and droppings from such animals in captivity and compare them with samples obtained in the wilderness.[1944]

Cazeau and Scott discuss the different noises that Bigfoot was purported to have made and which had been recorded. These sounds include: grating moans, half-bark half-growls, chattering, whistling, high-pitched screams, and "half-language."

> What is a scientist, or anyone, supposed to make out of such a conglomeration of noises? The whistling and screaming are supposed to be the most common sound. But if all or most of these sounds come from the throat of one kind of creature, it has a remarkable set of vocal cords. Maybe so. However, no scientist would consider these data to be evidence supportive of any conclusion other than that the forest yields a variety of noises.[1945]

Of photographs and movies of Bigfoot, the authors contend that the photos they had seen were inconclusive and amounted to poor evidence. "Fuzzy photos added to recorded noises from a forest do not make a Bigfoot." But the authors summarize their section on Bigfoot stating, "there is sufficient evidence for us to believe these investigations should continue."[1946]

Demands for strong evidence had no stronger proponent than astronomy professor and author Carl Sagan. For Sagan, a vertex of reliability with exoticness underlaid witnesses' claims of extraterrestrial encounters, an apt paradigm suitable for accounts of Bigfoot.

> Sagan puts it this way: to believe somebody who said he had a close encounter, he demands that the witness be credible—and the event be exotic. For example, what he would consider reliable would be the crowd at a World Series game agreeing that a luminous green hexagonal 189-foot-long spaceship had landed at second base at Yankee Stadium, discharging an army of small green men while Ron Guidry was pitching to Davey Lopes. That might be exotic and reliable. But 1,000 people seeing a luminous glow over the hill at a meeting of the Holy Rollers would be reliable, but not exotic. A Cedarhurst, L.I., teenager's report that a flying saucer had swooped down and made off with the family cat would be very exotic, but not reliable. What he would like to see as an example of exotic and reliable proof of visits from beyond, would be artifacts from outer space—tools, for instance for purposes unknown to us, and of materials not known to this galaxy. Take that, carbon chauvinists, he has been understood to say.[1947]

In an article published by the Aerial Phenomena Research Organization (A.P.R.O.) *Bulletin* in October 1979, Jon Beckjord considered the possible linkage between UFOs and Bigfoot.

> A small percentage of reports concerning UFO "landings" and alleged abductions have involved having a crew of ABSMs either on board or in the immediate vicinity. In some cases, witnesses have told such investigators as Indiana's Don Worley, that they have actually seen "Bigfoot" type animals marching out of landed UFOs, bent on some hidden mission. This could be interesting science fiction, unless the midwest can somehow explain why it seems to spawn these type of reports while the Pacific NW, the home range of the alleged Bigfoot creatures, seems to produce relatively fewer, if any reports of direct links between UFOs and these unproven primates. . . .
>
> Perhaps then, if Bigfoot can leave tracks that show an incredible weight, and even tracks that simply "end" in the snow, and if it can possibly disappear, and even have photos taken of it when the photographer didn't see anything, as did Marion Schubert of Pinole, California, then perhaps it has a great

> deal in common with the UFO phenomenon, which is replete with stories of similar paranormal characteristics that seem to indicate a basis for life or existence that is not the same basis on which we exist. Both Bigfoot and the UFOs may come from a time, or a space, that we have not yet evolved into, and simply because we are just beginning to learn that there may be other things than are dreamt of in our philosophy, perhaps we should consider these reports of UFOs and ULOs [Unidentified Land Objects], even UWOs [Unidentified Water Objects], such as the Loch Ness Monster and Ogopogo, as hints of a future to come, and not deny them simply because we have not yet invented the instruments to measure them with.[1948]

Grover Krantz and Roderick Sprague collected several anthropological monographs for publication in a book from the University of Idaho's Department of Sociology/Anthropology. The result was *The Scientist Looks at the Sasquatch,* printed in 1977. Planning and preparation for the book went back as far as the Spring of 1976, as evidenced by the following letter from Krantz to Dahinden, dated April 02, 1976.

> On the use of pictures, I now have a special request of you. Sprague and I are planning to reprint all the Sasquatch articles from *NARN* [Northwest Anthropological Research Notes] in a separate book (there are 6 articles now, none by Byrne, only *real* scientists). What we need is your *written* permission to include the picture of yours that was fussed over before. If we don't get your permission, I will find another to substitute. Before you decide one way or the other there is something you may not know—I don't get any money on these publications, neither does Sprague. Scientific journals don't pay anything. In fact, my publications have *cost* me about $5,000 so far because of delayed promotions and lower than usual pay raises. The public (and academic) attitude is improving, so this book may not hurt me, but I thought you ought to know what this has cost me in the past. Anyway, we would like to use your picture, but the decision is yours.[1949]

An updated version was printed in 1979 which reprinted the original seven papers and included three additional essays: "A Rebuttal of Krantz'

Step Three Approach to Sasquatch Identification" by Jon Beckjord, "Results of a Questionnaire on the Sasquatch" by Ron Westrum, and "The Improbable Primate and Modern Myth" by Richard Beeson.

Sprague, in a book review for *The Sasquatch and Other Unknown Hominids* (1984), stated that *The Scientist Looks at the Sasquatch* did not receive attention from mainstream publications.

> It has never been mentioned in print before, but when the first edition of *The Scientist Looks at the Sasquatch* was published in 1977, review copies were sent to *Science, American Scientist,* and *American Anthropologist.* None of these journals even listed it in their "books received for review" sections. At that time, the review editor of *American Anthropologist* was one of my former graduate professors, one I highly respected for his sense of fair play. Yet, no acknowledgment has ever been received.[1950]

As mentioned in Chapter 7, UFO-themed magazines had largely subsumed the lead publishing role of Bigfoot articles in glossy-covered, monthly and bi-monthly magazine publications. "Sex and the Single Sasquatch" appearing in the Winter 1979 edition of *True's Flying Saucers and UFO Quarterly* was authored by Oklahoma City-based Bigfoot researcher Bob Stamps and Hayden C. Hewes, founder and director of the Unidentified Flying Object Bureau, and who had investigated the Missouri Monster (Momo) sightings in 1972. The authors write on the public's acceptance and familiarity of Bigfoot, suggestive of far-reaching, if not full diffusion into the cultural psyche.

> They live in small groups, raise their young and show aging by the color of their hair. Hardly a day goes by without someone in the United States reporting a Sasquatch. Like UFOs and psychic phenomena, the subject is appearing with amazing rapidity these days. More and more books are appearing on the subject and next year will mark the release of yet another motion picture on the subject, *Yeti.* Now, almost any mention of Sasquatch is understood by the majority of persons as reference to the 8-foot hairy giant that leaves big footprints wherever he goes.[1951]

Hewes and Stamps' article espouses a novel theory for the origins of mankind—as well as Bigfoot.

> According to Zecharia Sitchin who wrote in *The 12th Planet*, ". . . we realize that biblical texts were a condensation of the original Sumerian sources." These sources inform us that after trying to fashion a Primitive Worker by 'mixing' apemen with animals, the gods concluded that the only mixture that would work would be apeman and the Nefilim themselves. After several unsuccessful attempts, a model—Adapa/Adam—was made. Once Adapa/Adam proved to be the right creature, he was used as the genetic model or mold for the creation of duplicates, and these were not only male, but female. Thus from *Homo erectus*, the stargods, whom Sitchin identifies as the Nefilim, created *Homo sapiens*, the man of today.
>
> The authors contend that the solution to the Sasquatch controversy may be simply that the unsuccessful attempts at creation have survived and evolved into a shy, intelligent, peace-loving being, now found in remote areas of the world. Many would find it hard to believe that this being could remain "unknown" in the 20th Century.[1952]

The authors espouse a list of "scientific approaches" integral to their own pursuit of enhancing and increasing the body of Bigfoot knowledge and, as techniques and tools of inquiry, the authors presage their imminent adoption in future analytical research.

> The most significant recent development in Sasquatchology has occurred, in our opinion, in the past year. By that we mean a distinct change in attitude on the part of the scientists and general public. The phenomenon is now treated as a genuine "problem," worthy of our best effort to solve it. The Sasquatch Research Corporation employs the use of the following scientific approaches to the subject.
>
> Computer photographic analysis of photographic evidence;
> Instrumented Sasquatch detection equipment;
> Computer statistical studies;

Psychological stress analysis on sound recordings;
24-hour telephone hotlines[1953]

SIGHTINGS 1979

Knobby, "Definitely Not a Bear!"

Seen in and around Toluca, North Carolina, Knobby became one of the '70s highly-publicized hairy hominids and was named for the location the creature was first spotted: Carpenter's Knob in Appalachia's South Mountains. Knobby was described as manlike in shape, about six feet tall, and covered in jet black hair. Some reports stated the creature had a thin waist and a flat face resembling an ape's. Though often seen walking on its hind legs like a person, at least one report described Knobby ambulating on all fours. Some believed Knobby was innocuous enough; a wandering bear or an invented bogey whose purpose was to scare away those venturing too close to a secret moonshine still.

Featured in numerous newspaper stories, Knobby's doings were in part scribed by author Robert L. Williams. Williams grew up in Statesville, North Carolina, and featured the Tar Heel State in much of his writing. Williams worked for the *Statesville Record and Landmark* and the *Charlotte Observer* before teaching at Gaston College in Dallas, North Carolina, for 30 years. Writing several articles on Knobby, Williams named hunter Taylor Falls as the first person to see the creature. "I won't go back in those woods!" Falls declared in Williams' recounting of Knobby's origins. According to Williams, Falls admitted he had been illegally hunting deer in the summer of 1978 in upper Cleveland County when a buck stepped out from a thicket's shadows and into a clearing in front of him. As Falls raised his rifle for the shot a jet-black *something* running on two legs suddenly broke out of the tree cover and sped across the field, smack between Falls and the buck. "I don't want a deer bad enough to face that thing again!"[1954] Falls estimated the creature stood about six and half feet tall and weighed close to 300 pounds; in stark contrast to a bear it had a flat face. "I don't know what it was," Falls admitted, "and I don't intend to go back to find out. One thing is certain: it wasn't a deer and it wasn't a bear. But he cured me of poaching!"[1955]

Winters in the North Carolina Appalachians can offer up harsh conditions—temperatures routinely below zero and snowfalls accumulating fifteen inches or more. The real publicity started in late December 1978 into early 1979, and the canon of provincial hairy hominids quickly added Knobby to its rolls. Several contemporaneous newspaper stories credited

Minnie Costner Cook as the first to see Knobby when on the cold winter morning of December 21, 1978, she checked on her agitated dog and spotted a dark shape in a pasture near her home. Cook first took the object, about 50 feet away, to be a cow but quickly realized she was looking at an unidentifiable creature which suddenly "rared up on its hind legs" and stared back at Cook and her dog. "It wasn't a bear," Cook insisted. "I've seen many a bear in my time and I know one when I see one. And this wasn't one."[1956] If it resembled anything, it was an ape, she said. "Boy, if you'd see it one time you wouldn't want to see it no more," she said. "These old eyes are 88 years old, but I saw it, that's all there is to it," she said. "I can't name it and I don't want to see it again, but I saw it."

On the same day of Cook's sighting, Williams wrote that a truck driver delivering a load of wood glimpsed something in a field he initially, as others had similarly reported, took to be a bear. He watched the animal for about five minutes as the creature peered back at him while occasionally eating berries from a low-growing bush. The truck driver felt the creature was just as curious about him as he himself was of the highly unusual animal. As news of the sightings spread, Mrs. Clayton Candler, a housewife in her 50s, admitted she too had seen the animal but had been unwilling to share it. "I didn't want people thinking I was crazy," she stated. Mrs. Candler said she had been driving home one day during dusk and saw a cow by the side of the road. Thinking she should get a description of the cow to share with neighbors, for it surely was a lost animal, she rolled down her window to get a better look. The creature rose on its hind legs, startling Mrs. Candler who frantically fumbled her keys to re-start her car. "He walked right over to the car," she said, "but I was too scared to look very hard at him; I was too interested in getting away from there!" In the week following Cook's publicized encounter, Williams wrote that a dozen additional sightings were reported in the Toluca area.[1957]

One of those sightings occurred after Christmas, when bricklayer Sammy Price from Casar, a community located about 10 miles west of Toluca, heard a strange howl from the woods adjacent to his backyard. "It was the awfullest sound you ever heard!" exclaimed Price. "A real high-pitched scream, like a woman being murdered . . . and so loud you could've heard it two or three miles away!" Price stopped what he was doing to peer into the woods, trying to discern through the crowded trees what was out there. Price's attention was suddenly diverted to what looked like a broken tree, about six or seven feet high. "Then that tree started to move! At first I didn't trust my eyes, because it was getting dark, but then I saw it take a dozen steps, and I knew right then it was a big old bear, except I never heard a bear make a noise like that and I been huntin' bears and deer in these mountains for years and years." Price watched the creature for about 15 minutes, and estimated the jet-black creature weighed between 250 to 300 pounds.[1958]

Sleep would be elusive that night for Price and his wife as more screams and howls came from the woods. "I dropped off to sleep one time and it yelled so loud that I was in the middle of the floor before I was completely awake," Price recalled. "I guess we heard it two dozen times altogether." The next morning, and after Price had left for work, his wife was in their driveway when the howl came again. The unnerving daytime scream compelled her retreat back inside the home. Peering out a window she watched the creature in a nearby field eating remnants from the soybean crop. "I watched him while he ate, and then while he crossed the field and came down by the house," said Mrs. Price, "and I can tell you what the others have said is true: he is definitely not a bear!"[1959]

Two days after Price's sighting of the creature, he went into the woods to investigate and found what he believed was Knobby's den, which had been apparently abandoned for several weeks. The entrance was five feet wide and three feet high and was located under an uprooted pine tree. Tendril roots near the opening had snatched an abundance of animal hairs and the ground was full of tracks.

Williams wrote the hairs were glossy and black, about one inch long, and were soft, suggestive of a rabbit or a cat. The tracks were long and slender and sported a thumb-like protrusion extending at almost at right angles to the foot.

The day following Price's discovery of the den, a large goat belonging to Price's brother Forest was killed, and its death became immediately associated with Knobby. "I ain't saying' that Knobby did it," said Price, "but something just killed hell out of old Bill!" Bill's death took place on Sunday morning, January 14,[1960] and when discovered his body was still warm. The goat had died from a broken neck with no other visible signs of violence on the body. "Could be that Old Bill saw Knobby and got scared and tried to jump and broke his neck when he fell," Forest Price offered. "All I know is I got to get me another goat. And I know that my mule broke a grass rope that same night and I couldn't get that mule to go back in that barn no way I tried."

As localized Bigfoot stories had done throughout the '70s, the furor over Knobby evoked memories of other local legends; tales of a lantern-bearing ghost said to haunt the area were recalled and retold. Bigfoot researcher

Jim Hollingsworth thought more mundane subjects could be the basis for Knobby sightings. "I'm reasonably sure some people were seeing a big cat," he said, suggesting a large feline or even a bear prowling the area could have been conflated with the Bigfoot-like image of Knobby.[1961]

Game Warden Lewis Barts lived near Shelby, county seat of Cleveland County, and believed the Knobby business was simply due to an ursine interloper. "All I can tell you is what I think, and I think that it's a bear. There's been a bear in that area for close to a year," Barts said. In early January, Barts searched around Toluca for signs of Knobby. "The first time [searching] I saw bear tracks," Barts said. "Last week I looked again, but I didn't see anything fresh." Barts theorized a bear had wandered into the Smokey Mountain foothills near Toluca in search of food. Some folks organizing searches for Knobby could have had ulterior motives, Barts believed. "It could be an excuse to hunt bear out of season," he said, "or it could be folks spotlighting deer. Either way, hunting any game animal at night is illegal, and if this keeps up I may have to bring some of them in. My fear is that these hunters will get out and shoot at anything that moves. Someone could get hurt."

Sammy Price was adamant that he had not seen a bear. "Whoever saw a bear with a flat face?" he asked. "And whoever saw one with such short, soft hair? And what kind of bear makes a track like Knobby does?" Though Elbert Cook agreed that bears could wander down from higher elevations, he didn't think such an event explained people's Knobby experiences. "I've lived in this area about 40 years, and I've never seen nothing like this," he said. Along with Knobby-hunters, the creature also counted its share of supporters. "I don't want nobody putting it in a cage. It's not a-bothering anybody. Let it roam free," Cook said.[1962]

Jim Hollingsworth drove four hours to Toluca from Pikeville in Wayne County to look into Knobby for himself. Prior to checking in on Knobby, Hollingsworth had been investigating the Green Swamp south of Wilmington, North Carolina, where a five mile stretch of Bigfoot tracks had been discovered. Hollingsworth was not able to make much from the so-called tracks residents showed him and found the ground too frozen to record good prints.[1963] Hollingsworth was very interested in investigating Knobby's vocals. "I interviewed two people who heard something—not this Saturday but the Saturday before (Jan. 6)," he said. "Their descriptions surprised me." Hollingsworth had spent six years collecting information on Bigfoot and at the time he investigated Knobby he counted himself an active member of Ron Olson's North American Research Association. "They describe it as a sound that varies in pitch from a low growl to a high scream, as being like a bull bellowing, but with its own sound. They also say that after it screams for a few seconds it has a yodeling type sound."

Knobby's vocals, Hollingsworth stated, were like "sounds made by a type of creature out west." On his tape recorder, Hollingsworth played sounds recorded from the High Sierras for some interviewees who believed they had heard Knobby. Several witnesses subsequently confirmed the cries and howls they attributed to Knobby sounded very similar to the recording Hollingsworth played for them.

Knobby's shrieks also played a role in the ideas of D. H. Canipe, whose wife claimed to have seen the creature; he believed Knobby was a panther. Canipe said his theory was based on some of the descriptions of the creature's physical and audible characteristics. The thing's vocal cry, he said, "is like a woman in pain."[1964]

The following excerpts from Jennie Palmer's January 21 *Gastonia Gazette* article exemplified the heights Knobby's fame and notoriety achieved:

> TOLUCA—From the back roads that wind through the Smokey Mountain foothills and from the cities that lie below, the masses are converging on this usually quiet Cleveland County community that it's fair week.
>
> And they're all searching for "Knobby", the mysterious ape-like creature folks around here have reported seeing for almost a month now.
>
> Stop at any one of the country stores and many of the homes that dot the hillsides and you'll hear the latest "Knobby" tale. . . .
>
> The Cooks' store lies in the afternoon shadow of Carpenter's Knob, the foothills hill point just west of Toluca and the landmark from which the creature draws its name.
>
> The store and nearby Mountain View Grocery are where area folks gather to swap their "Knobby" stories and where outsiders stop to track down leads to its whereabouts.
>
> "Everybody that comes in here talks about it," Ruby said. "A lot of them are scared to death. Me? Well, I'll just tell you I'm not about to go out looking for it." . . .
>
> Robert Shoup and Butch Craig cut their high school classes to sit all day by a campfire near the top of the knob. "We're just waiting and looking for it," Butch said.
>
> And Russell Cook took a day off work to go "Knobby"

hunting with Rondal Huffman. "We've been all over these woods looking for signs of it but we haven't seen a thing," Rondal said.

Their last trek of the day was through a deep gully that runs behind Sally White's house, the site of one of the most recent "Knobby" reports. . . .

Speculation about the creature's identity ranges from wandering mountain panther to escaped carnival baboon to misplaced bear to Big Foot, the supposed missing link between man and ape.

A state park developer drove from eastern North Carolina to Toluca to check the Big Foot possibility. Two other researchers, working on a project for a Massachusetts university, spent at least one night on Carpenter's Knob checking out their own theories about "Knobby." Area residents say they do not know whether the men have left the area.

At least 16 "Knobby" sightings have been reported since late December in the vicinity of Carpenter's Knob.

An animal den and tracks were found about two miles from the Price houses. Searchers said the tracks were at least as large as a man's hand and similarly shaped with a thumb-like protrusion.

But most people, both hunters and wildlife protectors, are turning up no trace of the mysterious creature as they comb spots where sightings have been reported.

"Most of this talk is just plain old hearsay," said Clyde Price, whose relatives own a large tract of land near the top of Carpenter's Knob. "When something like this gets started it gets bigger and bigger."[1965]

Following on the heels of Knobby's growing popularity came the predictable Knobby merchandising, including t-shirts, towels, and posters.

Inevitably commercialization has come to the rural area where folks are stirred up over sightings of an ape-like monster that's been dubbed "Knobby" for a nearby mountain peak.

"Knobby" posters, showing a critter crouched down, are selling like hotcakes at C. G. Bingham's store at the intersection of N.C. 10 and N. C. 18 in Lincoln County. . . .

> Bingham said he got a batch of the 8- by 10-inch duplications on Sunday and promptly sold them out.
>
> "They sold for a dime which shows you how much everybody thinks of the whole affair," said one customer. "It looks sort of like a bear." . . .
>
> Adding to the spirit of the Knobby craze, Bingham also has a large "Bigfoot" poster on the wall of his store.
>
> "I've seen some hippies that look better than it," Bingham said.[1966]

Shelby radio station WOHS instigated an "all-out," hunt for Knobby that successfully drew a large crowd to Toluca. At least two songs venerating Knobby were recorded and Robert Williams wrote that a "movie company decided to produce a film about the creature and his ostensible threats to the community."[1967] School children even rendered Knobby for class projects.

> In Kinston, Martha Queen Barrett, a Cleveland County native, asked her Westminster Methodist Day School nursery pupils to immaging [sic] Knobby [as] Bongo, the circus bear that broke out of a cage and rode into the woods on a bicycle. Mrs. Barrett sent a sampling of her drawings to the Shelby Daily Star along with a letter from the children. "If you succeed in capturing Knobby, please let us know if it is Bongo," they wrote.
>
> As Knobby's fame grew, so did its dimensions—at least 10 feet tall, according to one story; bloodshot eyes as big as silver dollars. Chased a man into a barn and bit the heads right off a dozen horses. Never even slowed down. Someone claimed he saw a footprint six inches wide and 15 inches long.[1968]

"It's somebody running moonshine," one resident theorized at the Cook's hardware store. "They're trying to scare people away." Eb Cook, son of Minnie who ran a local gas station disagreed. "My mother ain't got no still down on that creek," he countered. "She ain't running moonshine. Why would she say she saw it? I'll tell you why she said it: because she *did* see it," he said. Another sighting was reported by Daniel Cook (no relation to the aforementioned Cook family) who claimed while sawing wood he heard a terrible scream over the chain-whizzing hum of his chainsaw. Cook stopped sawing and went to where he believed the sound emanated from. He didn't find anything and never saw Knobby.

"It's just somebody playing a practical joke," said another resident. "Somebody just wants attention." Sammy Price had little patience for those kinds of reactions: "My house is miles off the highway," he said. "I live at the end of a lonely dead-end road. On the other side of me is more than 100 acres without a building of any kind on the land. The first time I heard Knobby was on a bitter cold night with sleet falling and the ground getting so slick a mountain goat would have had trouble moving around. Now who in his right mind would walk nine miles or so into the woods (there were no cars in the area that night because the roads were impassable) and stand there at three o'clock in the morning and scream to try to get attention? He'd be more likely to get buckshot than attention!"

In January 1979 three sisters rode along Highway 10 on a clear, sunny afternoon. They were west of Casar when one of the girls suddenly screamed and pointed to something outside the car. The 14-year-old buried her head in her hands while her sisters spent the next few minutes trying to console her and ascertain the cause of her shock. When she was able to talk coherently, she said she had just seen a creature standing atop an earthen dam close by the road. The trio agreed to turn their car around and return to the dam. The creature was still there and the first sister to spot it was Gaye Smith, who, acting on a determination to know what she and her sisters were seeing, leapt from the car over her siblings' protestations and ran after the creature as it disappeared into a grove. Gaye carried a small instamatic camera and as she was about to snap a photo, she stepped off an embankment and slid down a 12-foot incline. The developed picture would later reveal she had missed Knobby completely, succeeding only in capturing several trees behind the dam. "He was right in front of me," Gaye said despondently. "I'd have had the only picture of Knobby, and I missed him."[1969]

Though her photography failed, Gaye's close proximity to the creature resulted in one of the best sightings of Knobby. "I was close to him," she recalled, "so close I could see every detail. He was well over six feet tall and he weighed about 300 pounds. I agree with that. But he was not black all over. His chest was sort of rust color, a reddish brown. His face was not hairy at all, but more like a gorilla or a man's. And his chest was broad and shiny where it wasn't hairy." Gaye also noted another detail unique in the descriptions given of Knobby. "He had a slash across his face, like maybe barbed wire had cut him, and I could see the pink flesh where the wound had laid his face open. His legs were much too thin for his body, and his arms were very long, like a chimp's."[1970]

"You say you saw him and the papers will make you look like a fool," one annoyed resident said, according to Williams' *UFO Report* article. "Sure, I saw him not more than 10 minutes ago, and my sister did too, but we're not going to allow anybody to print our names or pictures because I don't enjoy being ridiculed."

Heading toward spring, the fervor over Knobby had begun to die down.

> Cleveland County's mysterious creature some people call Bigfoot Jr. hasn't been spotted lately, and the number of casual sightseers around Carpenter's Knob, which furnished Knobby the name, has diminished.
>
> Gone, too, are the big game hunters, the TV cameras, Florida tourists, and live radio broadcasts. There are still T-shirts for sale depicting Knobby as a Pogo-like animal holding a can of pork and beans, along with Knobby posters and at least one ballad.[1971]

Joe Cook admitted he had thought of capturing, caging, and exploiting Knobby, if indeed it was a real creature. But after the main spate of Knobby reports had run their course, Cook reflected upon the totality of the area's experience with a small-town monster and decided the creature's absence was the more desirable state of affairs.

> Good management would have provided something, real or otherwise, in a sideshow and charged admission. That thought crossed Joe Z. Cooke's mind—having a real live Knobby in a cattle trailer and selling tickets to the attraction.
>
> In reality, all Knobby ever meant to Cooke was an aggravation, he said. The whole episode definitely had a sideshow atmosphere, he thinks.
>
> Cooke owns Carpenter's Knob. He bought the 1,600-foot-high hill in 1950 from his grandfather and lives there on a dead-end road. Knobby-hunters, thinking that the road led to the top of the knob, rambled into Cooke's drive at all hours of the day and night.
>
> A TV camera crew acted like they owned the place, he said.
>
> "The whole country flocked in," he said, adding that he feared someone would get hurt.[1972]

Probably second only to Knobby being a bear, one of the most bandied about explanations was a simple scare tactic adopted to keep folks away from an illicit still. If any kernel of truth could be attributed to this rationale, the results flew in the face of its intent, as the crowds came to search for Knobby. As the Knobby furor died off, an event occurred which rekindled the idea Knobby was meant to ward people away from furtive moonshine production.

> In Casar community, where Knobby was seen most often, an old house caught fire and burned to the ground. The remains of the house contained one of the largest liquor stills ever found in the Carolinas, and it was learned that the fire was caused by an oil burner used in the distilling process. Naturally the die-hards yelled that the Knobby or Bigfoot stories were concocted to keep people away from the site of the illegal still.[1973]

Some of the last Knobby reports from 1979 occurred that spring, just as locals had likely decided the creature—whatever it was or had been—had tied the bow on its adventures in the South Mountains. Robert Williams wrote about some of these last Knobby sightings.

> Then, late in the spring of 1979, a trout fisherman was angling along the banks of a South Mountain vicinity river when a movement behind him caught his eye. According to ensuing reports, the fisherman whirled in time to see a huge black shape, running upright, disappearing into the undergrowth. It was Knobby, the fisherman was certain.
>
> Next day he returned, this time with a 30.30 rifle, it was reported, and he got another look at Knobby. In fact, he shot at it and reportedly wounded the creature.
>
> Now another fear hit the Knobby-hunters: the fear that Knobby was dead—that he had been destroyed by a thoughtless hunter who failed to realize the vast scientific importance of the animal.
>
> Then, near the first of May, one of the oldest residents of the Knobby territory, Annie Maude Barrett, reported that she had heard Knobby screaming, not in pain and not in anger but more in a communicative sense, in her garden. There were the

> telltale tracks in the soft soil, too: again like a human hand except for the acutely angled thumb that jutted out at nearly ninety degrees to the palm. Knobby was back![1974]

Polacca Sightings

A series of Bigfoot sightings occurred in early 1979 in and around the Hopi Indian village of Polacca in northeastern Arizona. According to Kendrick Outah, all the witnesses could be credited as "public figures, reliable people."

> Some call the thing Bigfoot and link it to other stories of mysterious Bigfoot creatures that are said to roam the forest areas of the Pacific Northwest.
>
> Others call it Hairy Harry or the Incredible Hulk. But some elders of the tribe have another, more fearsome name for the apparition—Masau-u—one of the gods of the Hopi pantheon.
>
> For traditional Hopis, that name alone makes the eerie events even more disturbing.
>
> For knowledgeable "bahanas" (the Hopi word for Anglos), the name Masau-u brings a degree of esoteric fascination to the story that far surpasses the Bigfoot legends.[1975]

The Hopi newspaper *Qua Toqti* carried the story of the sightings as related by Outah. The creature first made its appearance at Polacca's Assembly of God Church and its presence "caused every dog in the village to begin barking simultaneously" disrupting church services. As described by Outah, the Hopi Tribal Police found smears of blood on the church bus and located footprints "unusually larger, but otherwise like human footprints." One "sighter" told Outah that he had heard strange, woman-like screams one night, and upon investigating, saw a "very large and hairy living thing" standing beside the shadow of a tree trunk.[1976]

Hopi police followed a series of footprints until they disappeared at the base of sheer sandstone walls rising above Polacca Wash. Investigation into another sighting also turned up footprints which tapered away at the edge of the mesa near the ancient village of Walpi. A third sighting occurred on January 13 which was preceded by the raucous barking of village dogs. A resident peered out a window to see a creature standing near his home; he watched as it ran "toward the West and disappeared from sight."

> Other Hopis have claimed similar experiences (including one who noted that the creature had a head as big a pumpkin), but, said Outah, "these three sightings have been substantiated by police officers who were dispatched at the sighters' requests for assistance."
>
> Now, said Outah, there is an almost tangible feeling in all the Hopi villages—those on Second and Third Mesa, as well as First—that "something weird" is out and about.

"I feel it even over here at New Oraibi," Outah said. "Never before have I heard the village dogs become so disturbed all at the same time. There is a feeling of unease about all this. But for the outside world, we Hopis laugh and say, 'Well, we're a superstitious lot, you know, and maybe we're just seeing things.'"

Masau-u is the Hopi deity of death who controls the Underworld. He is described as a large being, wearing a blood-smeared kachina mask and a rabbit skin robe. His powers allow him to pass between the planes of the living and the dead. Other kachina, or spirit beings, may appear between winter solstice and summer solstice but powerful Masau-u can appear at any time of the year. "There is a certain being at First Mesa whom it could be," suggested a Hopi man, referring to a belief that Masau-u could be serving a warning to the Hopi people. "Because of the way life is now, this being might be showing himself to tell the people to shape up and settle down to living the Hopi way." To many residents, Bigfoot was a term of convenience. "We feel we know what this is all about, but we don't want to become involved in discussing it," the Hopi man told an *Arizona Republic* reporter. "Some bahanas understand it; most don't. So we just grin and say, 'Yeah, they've seen Bigfoot up here.'"

Barton Wright of the San Diego Museum of Man was a renowned authority on Hopi culture. "I laughed too, when I heard they were calling it Bigfoot or Hairy Harry," he said. "They had to have had Masau-u in mind all along because myth has had it for years that Masau-u reappears from time to time and walks around the First Mesa villages in six concentric circuits."

> "Masau-u," said Wright, "is the deity who controls the earth. Those who walk on the land, plant crops in it or build villages atop it, pay homage to him.
>
> "Though the kiva, the underground ceremonial chamber, and the grave are his domain, he is not always the fearsome creature of the night.

"In day, according to legend, he can transform his appearance and can be distinguished from any other handsome young Hopi man only by the incredible length of his feet—roughly the length of a normal man's forearm," he said.

So are the recent Bigfoot sightings in the First Mesa villages really the result of a kiva priest donning Masau-u mask and rabbit-skin robe and taking it upon himself to warn backsliders from the Hopi way? Or a sly little joke perpetrated by young Hopi pranksters? Wright nixes both these ideas.

"In my experience, things aren't done that way among the Hopis," he said. "The manifestation of Masau-u would be regarded more as a divine revelation, though I hate to hazard even that guess.

"Hopis see, do, hear and think things that make complete sense within the framework of their own culture, not ours," Wright said. "I believe when they say they've seen the creature, they believe they've seen the creature. I'll let it go at that."

That, and the admonition to remember that "superstition is always the other fellow's religion."[1977]

Goffs' Sighting

During the nights of March 9-11, less than two weeks before the Spring Equinox, the Goff family said they endured unsettling experiences with a large, smelly creature that had roamed around their home about fifteen miles southwest of Tunica near Clayton, Mississippi. The Goffs claimed the creature scared off or carried away a large black dog the family had adopted.

The family said they had smelled a foul odor and the nights were punctuated by snapping and popping in the darkness around their home—the unmistakable sound of violently broken branches. They also reported deep growls which were similar in sound to a human yodel. One family member claimed he shot at the creature with a .22 rifle on Sunday night, March 11. Later that same night, the creature returned to their home and shattered the front door frame. In the morning, footprints were discovered measuring 16-19 inches long and a quarter-inch in depth leading from the Goffs' home to a levee about 350 yards away.

Both the Tunica County Sheriff's Department and the Mississippi Game and Fish Commission investigated the Goffs' claims of their unusual and unwanted visitor. "The Game Warden (Pat Hawkins) told us that it might be some kind of endangered species," said Rodney Goff. Some of the better prints were cast and a blood sample was taken from the doorframe; reporter Ray Mosby wrote the blood sample was forwarded to the Crime Lab in Jackson.

Mrs. Goff was interviewed at her place of employment, the Blue and White Café on Wednesday, March 14. "I don't know what it was, but it sure did stink, and it scared us to death," she said. Mrs. Goff claimed she and her family were not particularly well-versed in the Bigfoot subject but on the Monday following the harrowing weekend, she checked out two Bigfoot-themed books from the Tunica library.[1978]

Meissner Shoots Bigfoot

Dozens of folks tramped through the backwoods around Barriere, British Columbia, in May, drawn by the claim that a Bigfoot had been shot. Tim Meissner, aged 16, reported that on Saturday, May 5, during a fishing excursion on Dunn Lake, located about 40 miles north of Kamloops, he and three friends were startled by a high-pitched, 30-second scream that suddenly boomed across the water. Meissner said he looked across the lake to the far bank where he saw a creature standing there with upraised arms. It was only a fleeting glimpse as the creature quickly disappeared into the bush.

Two days later, Meissner and his friends returned to Dunn Lake. Meissner saw the creature again, but this time at a much closer distance, only about 50 feet away. "He was about nine feet tall, black and hairy," Meissner said. "He had a human-like face with great big, glaring bright eyes and shoulders four-feet wide." Meissner and the creature stared at each other for several seconds. Then, a "very scared" Meissner raised and fired his Remington rifle. "I was aiming for right between his eyes, and he went down on one knee and one hand. At first, I thought he was dead, but I guess I only grazed him, because he got up and ran away at about 30 miles an hour."

For Meissner, there was no doubt that he had confronted—and shot—a Bigfoot. "It couldn't have been any other animal, and it wasn't a human because no human can run that fast, especially straight up an embankment."

> "Do you want the truth or should I make you up a Sasquatch story?" wildlife official Allan Frisby said in an interview Sunday after Meisser [sic], 16, claimed he had shot and wounded a Sasquatch.

> Frisby said he has not received reports from game wardens who visited the scene in northern British Columbia, but he is convinced the youth shot at a bear.
>
> He said photographs of tracks at the scene look like bear tracks. Royal Canadian Mounted Police said the animal was likely a bear that recently emerged from hibernation.[1979]

Despite the dozens of people lured to Barriere hopeful of finding evidence of a wounded (or even deceased) hairy hominid, not all locals were as convinced that Meissner's monster was Bigfoot. A spokesperson for the Royal Canadian Mounted Police said the 16-year-old likely shot a bear. "The bears are just coming out of hibernation, and they look pretty scruffy this time of year."[1980]

Wayne Lahucik's farm near Dunn Lake became a popular search area for camouflage-wearing groups hunting for Meissner's Bigfoot. "I'm not so much worried about them being on my property, but someone is going to get shot," said Lahucik as people ignored private property signs and fences. Lahucik admitted he had decided to limit his skin diving in Dunn Lake for fear of being mistaken for a Sasquatch. The Royal Canadian Mounted Police's opinion that Meissner likely shot at a bear had Lahucik in full agreement; in fact, he believed he knew the particular bear which Meissner saw: a certain elderly brown bear with tinges of grey to its fur was not unknown to the Dunn Lake area and would even walk on its hind legs at times owing to an injured front paw. "And if there is a wounded bear up there," a concerned Lahucik said, "it's not a very good idea for the kids to be looking for it."[1981]

> The high school student who claims he shot "Bigfoot" after meeting the legendary creature "face to face" says he'll go out hunting for it again soon.
>
> Meanwhile hundreds of tourists and sightseers are jamming roads leading to this community 40 miles north of Kamloops hoping to catch a glimpse of the elusive Sasquatch.[1982]

Two weeks following the publicized encounter, Meissner and a friend returned to Dunn Lake and during their search of the area they discovered a deer partially covered over with brush. "The neck had been crushed and there's no animal which covers its kill like that," said Meissner. His announced plan was to go out hunting for the creature again once the flurry of tourists and monster-seeker activity had died down. "They'll have scared it away by now," he said.[1983]

Mount Vernon Monster

Possible sources for the strange, late-night sounds heard around Mount Vernon in 1979 included Bigfoot, owls, frogs, wild boars, a prankster with a bull horn, and even George Washington's ghost. An AP news story in May said the nightly wailing had been going on for nine months, putting the debut of the Mount Vernon Monster sometime in the second half of 1978.[1984]

Mike Morgan of the National Zoo suggested peacocks, known for their escapes from the zoo when allowed to freely roam the grounds, as a plausible candidate for the nocturnal screeches and wailings. The nighttime noises emanated primarily from a wooded area located close to the historic home of George Washington,[1985] and the mystery would be addressed by police investigations, police helicopters, and volunteer youth patrols, but all to no avail in identifying their cause.[1986]

"The thing seems to know when you leave the woods. Then it starts to holler," said George Stickman, Fairfax County game warden, who conducted several overnight vigils to catch the creature.[1987]

"Maybe it's a wounded animal or bird with damaged vocal cords," said resident Maggie Oyer, who described the creature's sounds as a "low wailing." Another resident, Thelma Crisp, claimed to have seen the monster, which she described as six feet tall; it had lumbered away once spotted, disappearing into the woods.[1988]

A local law enforcement officer, Charlie, took part in one of Stickman's all-night outings. Soon after joining Stickman and others near Hidden Pond, the party heard a "horrible scream." Charlie ran toward the woods and heard a second scream, which caused "every hair on the back of my neck and arms to stand up." Charlie told this author that he and several others could hear something moving in the woods, but no one saw anything. "I've heard every kind of animal in the woods," Charlie averred, "but I never heard a scream like that again." Charlie stated he had been very skeptical of anything beyond wild imaginations or possible pranksters behind the Mount Vernon Monster, "But I heard that . . . and it made me a believer."[1989]

Hoping to finally come to grips with identifying the noise-maker, county police positioned men in the woods, set up two infrared cameras, and called in a U.S. Park Police helicopter. "We hoped that by flying over it, when it started to yell, we could see something," said Maj. Harry S. Sommers from the Fairfax County police headquarters. But the howler didn't oblige officials' efforts and though helicopter blades whirred overhead the night of the combined search, the creature's howling was frustratingly absent. "I'm not really sure it is a police problem anyway," offered Sommers.[1990]

Bigfoot in Lemmon Valley Hills

Footprints measuring 16 to 22 inches long showing the impression of a heel and five round toes were found by three Reno, Nevada, rabbit hunters in the hills northeast of Lemmon Valley about 7 P.M. on Thursday night, July 19. The discovery by teenagers Brian Brady, 19; Patty Carlin, 17; and Mike Wales, 16, came on the heels of a reported Bigfoot sighting at the Pyramid Lake Reservation where authorities also found tracks which an unidentified commenter said evinced a "Sasquatch foot-type."

Wales and Brady took a *Reno Evening Gazette* reporter and photographer to the Lemmon Valley tracks. On the side of a hill overlooking Stead Airport the group inspected and photographed the half dozen prints.

> Leading the newsmen along a narrow dirt road to a spot marked by a fallen tent stake, the two [Wales and Brady] hopped out of a four-wheel drive wagon and traced the footsteps they had taken 13 hours earlier. Within 15 minutes, on the bank of a hill, Wales pointed to an impression that was more than 18 inches long.
>
> Some of the impressions had distinct, rounded toe prints, showing the ball of a foot and heel marks. The finer prints had showed where sand oozed between the toes. Others were vague, showing faint depressions of toes or the heel.
>
> Tracks in a small ravine revealed a stride that was more than a yard long. Other tracks on the hill showed a very short stride, almost one step right after the other.[1991]

"I was following a rabbit when it goes downhill and then I noticed these tracks running down the hill," said Wales. "Heading back, I see all these weird tracks, huge footprints." Though armed with a 12-gauge shotgun, the trio decided to head back to their home in Lemmon Valley. Wales called the Washoe County Sheriff's office and reported their find; Wales recounted his conversation with a skeptical officer. "He said, 'Is this a hoax?' I said, 'If you guys could tell me if it's anything else, I'd be glad to show it to you.'"

"The fact that kids are phoning it in would make me a little suspicious, because of all the publicity. . . . But I am not saying I am questioning the kids. Of course, we would still investigate it. Any calls we get we check out routinely," said Captain Robert Kellerer, of the Sheriff's Department. "I'm not going to say it's a Bigfoot or whatever, but I've never seen anything like this," Brady said. "I don't get goosebumps," he added, "but I got goosebumps last night." Robert Hannuam, a Pyramid Lake Reservation game warden, told Rodney Foo of the *Reno Evening Gazette* on July 20 that prior to Thursday's track find, it had been at least two weeks since the last report of a Bigfoot sighting or track find in the area.[1992]

Bigfoot Walks Again in Martin County

Andy Keith of Martin County, Indiana, claimed a Bigfoot sighting close to his remote, out-of-the-way home in the Hoosier National Forest. Keith, who was employed with the Martin County Highway Department said, "Late last month, on a Monday, I was driving to work about 6:30 (A.M.) and was about a half-mile from home when I came over a hill and seen something coming out of a field and across the road."[1993] The creature's unexpected presence and manner shook Keith. "He was right in the middle of the road when I saw him, and he wasn't looking around or anything, just looking right straight ahead," he said recalling the pulse-quickening incident. "It took just three steps to get across [the road]. It walked straight across." Keith's hands likely tightened into a white-knuckled grip around his truck's steering wheel. "I didn't really believe what I saw at first. But when I got up to the place in the road where he had crossed, I smelled the odor of really strong dead fish. I can still remember that smell and it makes me (sick)," Keith said.[1994] "Sure I was scared. At first I was going to stop and take a look. But then I got to thinking I would be kind of crazy to stop with a thing like that around, so I hit the gas and got out of there," he stated. Keith didn't appear sure what the stalking creature was, but like many witnesses seemed confident regarding what it was not. "A bear wouldn't be walking on his hind legs like that," Keith pointed out.

Keith had a plaster cast made from a footprint which he and two friends found some three weeks after his sighting. The print was about 15 inches long by seven inches wide. The prospect of going out and actively searching for the beast itself didn't particularly interest Keith. "When I got up to the spot where I saw him, it smelled like dead fish," Keith said. "Right after that, every time I'd think about it, I'd almost throw up."

Keith stated he had received no inquiries from scientists or other officials to question him or inspect his cast. "There were a couple reporters around here who asked people in the town if they believed me or not," said Keith, "and they all said they believed I saw something. They just didn't know what." Keith was asked if he had plans for his track cast? "Just keep it, I guess."[1995]

Not far from Keith's home lived his friend William Tharp Jr., also on the payroll of the Martin County Highway Department and who, Keith learned after the publicity from his own sighting, had had his own startling and unforgettable experience. *Courier-Journal* reporter Glenn Rutherford wrote about Keith's description of his friend's experience. "It supposedly happened about three years ago, but I didn't hear about it till recently," Keith stated. "The way I heard it, Bigfoot came right into [Tharp's] house just down the road here and grabbed his sister. When [Tharp] came in, Bigfoot turned her loose and ran off." Tharp shot at the beast with a 16-gauge shotgun and he recalled the creature moaned and ran away into the forest. Interviewed over the incredible event, Tharp confirmed Bigfoot had grabbed his sister's arm. "She was in front of the house when it grabbed her. Jackie started screaming and it freed her and left," Tharp said, and that was the point he took a shot at the creature.[1996] Jackie described the creature's fur like rough hog bristle and later scrutiny of the scene purportedly turned up blood. "I don't think he reported it to anybody," said Keith, "and when I first heard it, I didn't know whether to believe it or not. But after what I saw, I'd say I pretty much have to."[1997]

As receptive as ever to monster stories, newspapers large and small remained the general public's most frequent source for Bigfoot news. A typical article concerning a local Bigfoot sighting, written with a sense of nostalgia, could dependably include reminiscences from previous generations' local monster sightings. The accounts from Keith and Tharp rekindled memories of the Parke County Monster (see Chapter 3), still fresh in people's minds.

> Other curious creatures have been reported in recent state history.
>
> The most noted was a hairy, green, 10-foot-tall monster seen roaming Parke County in 1972. Large bear footprints were found during a search with hunting dogs even though no bears are known to live outside of captivity in Indiana.
>
> But that did not end the mystery in Parke County. A dark, shadowy form about 6 feet tall seen running on hind legs tore up a farmer's 60 chickens and ate half a basket of cucumbers and tomatoes in August, 1972, earning the local name of "furry chicken ripper" according to one report.
>
> That beast eventually was found to be an escaped kangaroo.[1998]

Keith was incredulous that the creature he had seen could have been a kangaroo and dismissive of the suggestion his incredible encounter had been of a mere bear. "Junior [Tharp] has tracked it when they were horseback riding in the hills and found a footprint 13 inches long. Other things have happened, too. My mother found a berry patch with long thorns smashed down like something walked through it," said Keith. "I don't care if anybody else believes me. You may not believe me, that's your opinion," Keith stated. "But I believe what I saw."[1999]

Bigfoot Cause of Scary Incidents?

Despite the fact that no actual creature was seen, frightening incidents in the Uinta Mountains left two men to wonder if their unsettling experiences could have involved Bigfoot. The first man, a 36-year-old Washington Terrace resident, had camped on the north slope of the Uinta Mountains next to Steel Creek west of China Meadows. The oddness started on July 28 when he heard "barking" and "screams" whose source he couldn't identify. "They were like nothing I had ever heard before. It was about 5:30 in the morning and the sounds came from heavy timber nearby," he said. He described the unnerving sounds as starting out like a barking jabber before increasing in volume and pitch.

The second and older incident which came to light in the August 15 *Standard-Examiner* article occurred in 1978 and centered upon a 29-year-old Morgan resident who claimed his camper, situated near Whitney Reservoir below Cuberant Basin, was rocked from side to side by an unknown creature. The events began at about 1 A.M. as the man, his sister-in-law, and a friend, heard noises of something tramping in the woods which were followed by the shaking of the camper. Twice the Morgan man shined a flashlight beam toward the sounds which would then stop, but whatever moved through the woods remained hidden from view. "But I just had that eerie feeling that something was watching us. You just know it," he said.

> Then after the three had retired, two in small pup tents, one 100 yards away from the camper and the other nearby, things really started happening.
>
> The friend said the next morning that something walked around his small tent, stopped and then "slapped it," and walked away.
>
> The sister-in-law said the same thing happened to her and she was "scared to death."
>
> In telling their stories, another group sleeping in a larger tent said they had the same experience, but did not think it was unusual as there were other people at the site.
>
> The Morgan man who told of the experience said "I just froze when the camper started to rock. The camper is an eight-footer on a three-quarter ton truck and there was absolutely no wind. The night was perfectly still," he said.

> In the morning, the party also found that something had torn down a string of fish fastened between two trees but none had been eaten.[2000]

White House Sighting

The city of White House, Tennessee, sits at the intersection of State Highway 76 and Interstate 65, only 20 miles north of Nashville. For a time, White House found itself branded a victim of progress; a community whose economic fortunes changed when Interstate 65 became the main thoroughfare for traffic heading south to Nashville. In pre-Interstate days, when north-south traffic used Highway 31, White House had been the scene of several tourist stands lining the roads, including several caged bears. By 1979, there were only two bears left at the lone remaining souvenir stand.

Some blamed Interstate 65 for not only conferring a level of stagnation upon the small town, but also bringing Bigfoot into its environs. Over Labor Day weekend in 1979, several animals were found slaughtered—a half-dozen dogs, two pigs, and one sheep. An examination of the bodies, found alongside White House roads and in fields, showed no obvious signs of struggle—no claw marks and no broken bones. The animal deaths were followed by large, deep gashes found in a willow tree in Luther Short's backyard. Game warden Larry Harris reportedly labeled the gouges as domain-marking by an unnamed creature. A bear would do that, said Harris, but all were accounted for as either caged at the souvenir stand or previously shipped off to zoos. None were known in the area otherwise.[2001]

"I'm afraid," stated Mizell Broderick whose dog, Major, was one of the casualties of the Labor Day weekend massacre. Two of Major's puppies, gone to neighboring homes, were also killed. "I don't go out around here at night. And, of course, everyone calls 'it' a monster or a creature, but we all know it's a bear," said Broderick. "The old guy who runs that (souvenir) place let him go. We all know he did. 'Course he says that a bear—there used to be three, you know—died. But I don't believe that bear died." But Game Warden Harris knew the bear in question had indeed passed on. "I saw the dead bear myself. Looked at the number inside its mouth." Harris said the bear had died about six months before the Labor Day animal killings.[2002]

Several parties of men organized themselves on September 6 and 7 to get to the bottom of what had been killing animals in White House. One of the groups had the services of two Tennessee Wildlife Research Agency officers. Based on the idea that a bear was to blame, some search efforts ranged down a creek toward a bluff. On Thursday, September 6, searchers discovered unidentifiable tracks. Larry Harris, one of the Wildlife Research Agency officers, stated that about half a dozen tracks in Luther Short's tomato patch appeared to be the hind feet of a bear, but deterioration from weathering and age made a precise determination difficult. He guessed the tracks were left on Monday, April 3, the day three of Short's dogs were killed and the bark gouged off trees in Short's yard.

> But a little farther on, the party came upon dozens of tracks that had them pretty excited for a while. They were like human footprints, about nine inches long, with clearly visible toe, arch and heel imprints, and they zigzagged randomly through the tomato patch and a nearby cornfield before the party lost the trail.
>
> But they sank about three inches deep into the soft ground, while members of the party were leaving footprints no more than half an inch deep. Harris said they obviously were made by something much heavier than a man.
>
> The explanation, when it came, was disappointingly prosaic. Mrs. Joe Rogers said they were hers; she often goes out to the tomato patch and wanders around picking tomatoes barefoot, and she had been walking in soft mud at that time.[2003]

Despite the explanation for those particular tracks found in Short's tomato patch, there was agreement that something had been in the area Thursday night, September 6. Bobby McCormick, a neighbor of Short's, said he heard something behind his house as a search party moved by. "Whatever it was, you were a lot closer to it than you thought," he told a group of searchers. "I could see your flashlights out there in the field, and then I heard this thing coming through the woods."

"At first, I thought it was a cow, but it was moving faster than any cow could have. It was moving right along. And it was making this awful sound. It was a sound I've never heard before. At first, I thought it sounded like a cow, but then it changed and started yapping, something like a dog." McCormick stated that despite being oblivious to the creature's proximity, the party had driven it away. "You-all chased it from the field through the woods to a clearing over there beyond those woods."

Robert Sherborne of Nashville's *The Tennessean* reported that another nearby neighbor said she had also heard an eerie noise as parties were searching the area that was "something like a deer blowing, but somehow different." Fields were checked and an old abandoned house was investigated, but no signs were found. A tracking dog accompanying one of the groups didn't find a scent.

> Many people living in this area said they had heard tales of "Bigfoot" around here for a long time, but discounted them until Short's dogs were killed and his trees scratched up. Now they are frightened. They stay armed, and stick close to their homes.
>
> Some of them want to believe it's a bear. But when they talk about it, they call it "whatever it is . . ."[2004]

The Sumner County Sherriff's office was aware of the stories coming from White House but hadn't taken a direct role. "When we have some eyewitnesses," said Sumner County Sheriff Mayo Wix, "then we'll look into it."[2005]

Don Roberts became an eyewitness after he watched a creature walk across a field on two legs, which he described as about five feet tall and covered in hair except for the face. "There isn't any hair on the top of his head, just dark skin," Roberts said. "And his face is dark brown also." He reported the face as rubber-like and that it sported wide shoulders. "It started to run. It's not a bear, I know."[2006][2007]

Another witness reported a (very) close encounter with a lankier creature than Roberts had described. "He's a little bit taller than I am," said six-foot Bill Cook, of Cummins Lane. "And he looks real wide. He's got hair all over him, except for his head and face." Cook had a good look at the creature because he had the distinction of having wrestled with the monster. According to Cook, he hid behind a tree, spying on Bigfoot when he sprang into action by bear-hugging the creature about the chest. When he did so he noticed the hair compressed, revealing Bigfoot actually had a much thinner torso than looks would lead one to believe. "He was really right poorly," said Cook. "He was real thin underneath all that hair. His body felt like a skinny man's. It had all the same features."[2008] After a struggle, the creature eventually broke free and ran off into the night. Cook said the evening after he wrestled with "Whatever it is," he and his family returned home to find his Alaskan huskie, which had been chained in the yard, dead—apparently crushed to death.[2009]

Milwaukee Sentinel stringer Michael Plemmons captured the prevailing mood at White House:

> The men of White House polished off untold fifths of whiskey and covered scores of footpaths and gullies, tracked every conceivable animal print and some of their own, too. They did it in style, all right. Just like in the movies. Late at night. Under a low hanging, orange moon.[2010]

After the Labor Day animal deaths, things slowly returned to normal in White House. The posses returned home and the diverted traffic bringing the curious and inquisitive resumed its appetite for Interstate 65. Plemmons wrote the at-times raucous monster hunts produced a casualty—one cow had been shot dead, mistaken for a vicious and unwanted animal-killer.[2011]

Ottosen Recalls Bigfoot

Reporter Jack Hovelson solicited Ottosen residents' memories of Bigfoot-related events (see Chapter 9) that had so unnerved the northern Iowa community.

> A year ago parents in this Humboldt County [Iowa] community were gathering in their youngsters at sundown and locking the doors.
>
> The reason was Bigfoot, a big hairy beast that some folk around here said they saw. Others thought it was all a joke. Most didn't know what to think.
>
> Just over a year has passed since the Bigfoot sightings—five or six of them, according to a tally by Humboldt County Sheriff Marvin Andersen.
>
> Bigfoot raised the fear level back then to a fever pitch, but the memory of him today scares up only an over-the-counter comment at Twig's Grocery.
>
> "The whole thing has pretty much died off," said Marilyn Schumacher, proprietor of Twig's. "People joke about it now, but these days, most of the talk around here is about picking corn. [Bigfoot] did one thing, though. He made a lot of strangers aware of this town."
>
> Beginning in July 1978, a lot of people in northern Humboldt County reported weird screams in the night, broken fences, stampeded cattle, and maimed and fatally injured animals.[2012]

"The whole county was spooked for a while," recalled Sheriff Andersen in the *Des Moines Register*. "There were people with loaded guns sitting behind their doors. It was dangerous. I kept thinking that I could run out of gas some night out there and have to walk up to one of those doors." Sheriff Andersen didn't know exactly what people were seeing, but he believed it was not a hoax. "Anyone doing that would have been taking too big a chance," he said. The reports had attracted armed monster-hunters, ready to shoot a Bigfoot. The Sheriff took the reports seriously "because too many reliable people were involved in them."[2013]

Bigfoot investigator Kevin Cook, director of the Iowa Bigfoot Information Center, suggested a theory that a single specimen or group of Bigfoot caused the sightings during their migration from South Dakota to the Mississippi River. "My theory is that it came down the Missouri River, then crossed over in northern Iowa to the Des Moines River and followed it south," Cook said. Cook was not aware of any confirmed Bigfoot reports in Iowa during the autumn of 1979; though he had investigated some Iowa-based reports of possible Bigfoot activity, none had borne out to be genuine.[2014]

Webster City, Iowa, about 60 miles south of Ottosen, was the setting for a Bigfoot encounter that October when a resident came face-to-face with a creature he avowed had to be Bigfoot.

> Bryon Davis, 48, of Webster City was looking for raccoon tracks early Friday [October 26] morning near here in a wooded area by the Boone River. Instead he found a seven-foot animal that he said is Bigfoot.
>
> The creature, which had long, thick, red hair down its shoulders and weighed about 450 pounds, was "just laying there asleep," Davis said.
>
> But he said he must have spooked Bigfoot because "he walked away quite fast in five-foot strides."
>
> Davis said the creature "stands straight like a man," but doesn't look like a human or ape. He shined a flashlight on the departing creature, but only was able to see his backside. He said he was able to get within 10 feet of the animal.
>
> After the creature disappeared into the brush, Davis contacted authorities, who checked the area but found nothing. Meanwhile Davis has volunteered to take a lie-detector test to prove the validity of his claim.[2015]

Reports of Bigfoot Near Adel

Larry Wilson's home was situated in the vicinity of Raccoon River in Minburn, Iowa, some six miles north of Adel and two miles north of Iowa Highway 44. Wilson told Sheriff Deputy Craig Hein his two dogs started barking about 9 P.M. on Thursday, November 15, and after approximately half an hour he decided to see for himself what was ailing them. Sliding open the glass door of his split-foyer home he couldn't see anything in the darkness. But, he did report hearing a deep, raspy rhythmic breathing. "The only way I can describe it is like a horse snorting, only real regular, a second or second and a half apart." Wilson admitted the breathing sounds were outside the bounds of his experience and was something he had never heard before.

"I went in the house, locked the door, and was looking out the living room window when I saw it. It was about 40 yards from the house when it walked under the security light." He immediately knew he was viewing something unusual. "I don't believe in it, and I'm not crazy," Wilson told Hein. He described "it" as a "hunched over, dark thing." Hein related that Wilson would "not commit himself to saying it was hairy," but said it did look like pictures and drawings of Bigfoot which he had seen. Hein and a deputy went to the Wilson home where they found "12- to 13-inch" prints in the frost-covered grass. The stride was measured as "48 inches from toe to toe." Wilson described what he saw stating, "It looked like a man in a gorilla suit, I really couldn't estimate its height. It walked with a fairly long pace, and it had a definite arm swing. It might have had stooped shoulders."

The creature remained illuminated by the security light for two or three seconds before it moved on. "I still don't believe this myself, I'm really shook," he said. "I've always been a skeptic, and had it definitely not scared the living hell out of me, I wouldn't be talking to you now, my friend," he added during his interview with reporter Tom Suk. "I've hunted, fished and been out in the woods a lot, but I never saw or heard anything like that before. It was unnatural." Wilson was the only one of his family home at the time. "Wouldn't you know it," he said.[2016]

Dallas County officials halted their investigation into Wilson's report on Friday, November 16. Deputy Tiedeman said the report was officially on file at headquarters. "If we do get more reports . . . we'll pull the file right back out," he said. Kevin Cook believed the Wilson's sighting was "absolutely legitimate," and he would conduct his own investigation.

On Friday morning before the investigation was halted, Deputy Jerry Tiedeman reexamined the 13-inch tracks outside Wilson's home, but a heavy layer of dew had obliterated any distinguishing features; even locating their fading impressions proved challenging. Deputies explored the possibility of a hoax by looking for tire tracks but none were in evidence. Wilson wasn't alarmed about his family's safety but admitted he was "concerned because it's an unknown to me." Wilson also confessed that his shotgun was sitting with "shells in the loading tubes. They're not in the firing tubes, but they could be kicked in there pretty quick." By his own admission Wilson's experience had triggered concern, adding, "But afraid? Nah."[2017]

Skunk Ape

Cryptozoologist Tony Healy undertook a worldwide "safari" in 1978 looking into accounts of unusual animals across the globe, particularly Bigfoot and lake monsters. After stopping at Flathead Lake in northwestern Montana to look into a lake monster reported there, he traveled to Winnipeg where, as well as making inquiries into reports of monsters in Lakes Manitoba and Winnipegosis, Healy conferred with Brian McNulty, a police reporter with the *Winnipeg Tribune* whom Healy hailed as the "main Sasquatch investigator in Manitoba." Healy spent some time in Easterville in central Manitoba where he collected several stories on Bigfoot. After Manitoba, Healy's further itinerary included stops at Lac Pohenegamook and Lake Champlain, and then a drive south to reach Florida.

> Since I have been in Florida I have interviewed six or seven people who claim to have seen the "Skunk-Ape" as they call the Bigfoot here. The most recent report was three months ago—a lady on a ranch behind Sarasota claimed to have seen an 8-ft. tall ape peering into her barn. The oldest story was told to me by a well known Florida biologist who, like they say in the newspaper, "wishes to remain anonymous," claimed that in 1949, he and six other young students saw a 7-ft. tall ape near Gainesville.
>
> I've encountered a lot of stories from the Miccosokee Indians out in the Everglades and have researched a very solid encounter where 14 people saw a "Skunk Ape" in broad daylight, so I'm pretty sure that if the Sasquatches exist anywhere, they exist here, too.[2018]

Dumas Farm

Skunk Apes may have been on Gerry Mulligan's mind as he mulled over the report that teenagers had spotted an unusual animal north of Inverness in

Citrus County, Florida. "Probably a bear," Mulligan said to reporter Judy Blair-Williams. The editor of Inverness' *Chronicle* took a few additional moments to ruminate on the potential for a story and made a decision. "Why don't you check it out?" As Blair-Williams considered the assignment, Mulligan offered a piece of parting advice: "Try to get close enough to get a picture."

Blair-Williams proceeded to meet and interview the three boys—Tommy Fuller and Matt Bennett, both 13-years-old; and Billy Jones, 16-years old. Their story took place at an old, abandoned dairy farm once owned by Dr. R. L. Dumas. Their story started about mid-August as Tommy's mother had driven him and a friend out to the farm so the boys could try out a new metal detector. Mrs. Fuller parked the car and the boys got out and that's when a loud growl came from the nearby underbrush. Though no creature was seen, the growl was enough to deter all thoughts of metal detecting at that location. "It sounded like a growl only much louder. I'd have to say it made a roar," Mrs. Fuller recalled.

A few days later Tommy Fuller said he had gone alone to the farm and actually saw the creature. He said it was sitting under a tree about 200 yards away. Tommy said he left immediately.

Next came the August 15 sighting shared by Fuller, Bennett, and Jones. As they approached one of the buildings on the farm—a decrepit dairy barn—an ape-like creature suddenly appeared, standing on an old rafter and apparently holding onto a truss. The boys said it was about 150 feet away, covered in black-colored hair, and growled loudly at them. "I was scared," said Billy Jones. "I was closer than the other guys and I was just plain scared. We yelled. We all yelled and boy, we got out of there." The boys went to the Fuller house where they each (and in separate rooms) rendered a drawing of the creature they had seen. "It's amazing how alike the two drawings are," said Mrs. Fuller. "And notice the lack of ears," she said as she showed the boys' pictures to Blair-Williams. "It shows an almost human-like head."

After the boys' sighting on August 15, Tommy's father decided to make a report to authorities at the Citrus County Sherriff's office. Deputy George Simpson thought the animal could have been a black bear. Game and Fresh Water Fish Commission agent Barry White believed the description of the creature made it out as more ape- or monkey-like. Both men inspected the area but didn't find any clues.

On Monday, August 20, *Chronicle* staff writer Norm Swetman joined Judy Blair-Williams and Deputy Simpson for a tour and inspection of the weather-beaten Dumas homestead. "Have you ever heard of the Florida

Skunk-Ape?" Swetman asked Blair-Williams during the drive to the abandoned farm. She answered she hadn't. Swetman then asked, "How about the Yeti or Bigfoot?"

"Wait a minute," Blair-Williams asked, likely with an incredulous tone. "You don't believe . . ." Swetman explained how details from the boys' August 15 encounter dovetailed with the trove of accounts of ape-like somethings in Florida's wildlands. "There have been a lot of stories . . ." he replied to his colleague.

> Getting to the old Dumas' farm off Independence Avenue is a matter of jouncing along a rutted sand road, twisting and turning with high grass scraping the underside of the car. The growth gets thicker as you approach the former homesite [sic] about a mile from the highway. The area is desolate, surrounded by forest and heavy weed growth on the south and eastern side.
>
> Weeds are thick and high in what was once a clearing around the farm buildings. Off to the left are the remains of the dairy barn. Bare, rotted trusses angle upward and stand out stark against the sky. Lathing, with nails sticking out, lie scattered about on the concrete floor and against the concrete walls and window frames.
>
> A hundred feet off to the right of the road are the remains of a three bedroom CBS house guarded by a huge live oak and the ever present weeds.
>
> Deputy George Simpson, who had accompanied us, points out empty beer and whiskey bottles, "Looks like a partying place," he observed. We searched around the buildings and found nothing.
>
> Further down the road from [the] direction we came in we found a pile of white, clean picked bones. Gingerly, Judy extracted two dog collars from the pile. A little distance along the rutted wheel tracks there were more bones from obviously smaller animals.
>
> "Some people probably brought their dogs out here and shot them," Simpson said.
>
> "But why would they leave them in the road?" I questioned. "And what are the bones of these smaller animals nearby?" Simpson shook his head in a puzzled way.[2019]

The following day, Swetman discussed the incidents experienced at the Dumas farm with Citrus County Commissioner Jean Grant. "We need someone who is trained in anthropology or zoology to check into this," he advised. She agreed and began phoning contacts at the University of Florida. On Wednesday morning, August 22, Swetman received a call from county Extension Agent Art Alston who explained that he and marine biologist Mike Oesterling had been appraised of the findings at the Dumas farm. "We had a call from the University," Alston explained to Swetman, "and they asked us to do a little investigating." Swetman shared Deputy Simpson's assurance that a bear would not have been able to climb up into the barn where the boys reported seeing an unknown creature. "A Florida Skunk-Ape!" Alston cried. Swetman could hardly believe he had heard a credentialed scientist use the term. "What did you say?" he asked. "A Florida Skunk-Ape. Sure, we know they exist but we've never been able to capture one so we don't know much about them. We do know they've been seen in Citrus County for years and years. Mostly by hunters and people who live in rural areas." The phone conversation instigated a return trip to the Dumas farm for Swetman, who was there the following day along with Alston, Oesterling, Simspon, and Tommy Fuller.

"Where were you standing when you saw the animal?" Oesterling asked Tommy. "Right here," said Tommy indicating a point in the road about a hundred feet away from the barn. Swetman was satisfied that the view of the barn's framework matched the boys' drawn pictures. Oesterling waded through the weeds and made his way to the barn, got up on the rafters and grabbed hold of a weathered truss. "That's it," affirmed Tommy. Alston and Swetman walked up to the barn. "There's only one way to get up and that's the cement block wall where the windows used to be. Look along near that window frame." A few moments' scrutiny and Alston had found something. "Scratches!" he cried. The scraped gouges stood out against the mildewed stone.

> Two other areas in the barn showed identical markings. Places where an [anthropoid] with hands could have climbed.
>
> One bedroom in the house had a pile of fiberglass insulation piled together like a crude nest. We checked it minutely as we did the places in the barn looking for stands of hair. We had no success.
>
> Both scientists were interested in the bones, their location and they were as puzzled as we had been why they were in

the deserted road. They easily identified the dog bones but they were not too sure about the smaller ones that had been devoured several feet away.

"It would appear," Alston said, "if a man brought his dog here to kill he would have moved it off the road into the trees." I had said the same thing the day before.

"There was a pile of bones behind that big log over there," Tommy pointed. There were only one or two left.

"But there was a big pile of them," Tommy insisted.

"Well now," Mike picked one up, "we have the mystery of the missing bones."[2020]

The party looked for footprints but none were discernable in the heavy leaf matter. After wrapping up their search, Oesterling shared his thoughts about the bones. "The thing that bothers me," he said, "is the fact the bones are not broken or chewed. Just the flesh is gone the way a vulture would have picked it. I'm not too sure the bones have anything to do with what we're looking for."[2021]

With hopes of learning more about the Dumas Farm sightings and investigation, Mr. Gerry Mulligan, the *Chronicle's* editor at the time, graciously responded to my inquiry; from him I learned that the above story by Norm Swetman was a "fantasy piece." *Chronicle* readers in 1979 collectively had a frame of reference in which to place such a fantastic story with the better part of a decade behind them to build the profile of the Skunk Ape. Mr. Mulligan indicated that the story created a high volume of feedback at the time.

Jon Beckjord Lectures about Shy Sasquatch

Jon Beckjord was likely excited as he prepared to present to reporter Jack Pyle photographs taken by Marion Schubert, which he believed were significant evidence in support of Bigfoot. As described in Chapter 9, Beckjord had interviewed Schubert and accompanied her back to the location where she snapped her photos and he shared that experience with Pyle. "One night when a friend of mine, Marion Schubert, 22, of Pinole, Calif., and I were camping out in the Sierras the [S]asquatches set up a howl. It seemed as if they were talking to us.

"This terrific howling went on, and I tried my best to imitate the sounds," said Beckjord. "It was sort of like 'ooga-ga-googa,' and it was pretty easy to imitate, so I did it." To Beckjord, it was as if the creatures were asking, "What the hell are you doing here?"

His revelations came at a "press conference" with *The News Tribune* at Burke Museum on the University of Washington campus.

He was late. The guard hadn't heard of Beckjord, but museum director George Quinby had.

"That's the guy we had to kick out of here yesterday," Quinby explained. "He has nothing to do with the university. He is not a member of the staff. He is not even a student. The museum does not subscribe to his theories."

Beckjord explained that he had called the conference at the museum because there were some Indian-made masks there that resembled the [S]asquatch.

"The Indians didn't make these up," Beckjord said. "This one—Bukuus—is of the creature the Indians called 'the wild man of the woods.'"

He had pictures.

The main photograph in his collection, taken by Miss Schubert, shows a patch of sunlight shining through the trees.

This, said Beckjord, is a whole, blond-haired [S]asquatch family.

Closer examination still showed sunlight shining through the trees.

Not so, said Beckjord, producing a blow-up of a portion of the picture that resembled Card 4 in the Rorschach inkblot test usually given to determine a person's ability to face reality.

He pointed again to the shiny area of the photograph.

Still closer examination indicated sunlight shining through the trees.

Said Beckjord, producing the same photograph with outlines of two ape-like figures carrying two other baby-sized, ape-like figures, is a four-member [S]asquatch family.

Now, he said, you can see it—but not without the drawings made by Beckjord.

He produced another photograph showing, at a distance, Miss Schubert cooking supper—or at least you can believe that is what she is doing.

Behind two trees, he shows, is something of a shadow. In the background—way off—is another shadow.

The one up front, he says, is a [S]asquatch, attracted by the smell of food.

"Where they smell food, they come up to watch," he said.[2022]

Concerning his involvement with Bigfoot, Beckjord stated that his initial objective had been "to prove the [S]asquatch is a hoax, but the joke was on me." Beckjord became convinced that Bigfoot was an extant creature and even came up with his own offering to the crowded field of scientific names for Bigfoot: *Gigantanthropus Pattersoni* in honor of Roger Patterson.[2023] Bigfoot was smart enough, Beckjord believed, to "eliminate their body wastes in the streams so humans won't find them. They're very timid." Despite seeing a Bigfoot near Bellingham ("He was . . . about the size of a man and totally naked, but he wasn't human—I could tell that"), Beckjord said he was overall disappointed with his lack of results in Washington, believing "there are more [S]asquatches near San Francisco than around here."

A significant breakthrough, Beckjord believed, was his communication with Bigfoot creatures during his outing with Schubert. "I think it was because I yelled at them and tried to imitate them that they came down to see us the next day—even though they were hiding behind the trees," he said. "During one night, something opened our truck, and there were no other campers around," Beckjord added. "We tried to attract them by putting out bait—chicken, roast beef, fruit and a lot of other things—but nothing was touched." The ability to communicate with Bigfoot, Beckjord maintained, could easily lead toward establishing trust and breakthroughs for meaningful and measurable encounters. "Before we are through," Beckjord told reporter Don Duncan, "they may come up and knock on my tent flap."[2024]

The Bigfoot tracks he had found in Washington proved to be comparably smaller than tracks typically found by others—only about 13 inches long and ten inches wide. "The Indians really called them the 'sis-quick,' that's the way the word really is pronounced," Beckjord told Pyle.[2025]

> Working from photographs, Beckjord has created a plaster model of the head of a Sasquatch, so heavy he almost needs a Sasquatch to carry it.
>
> Beckjord's favorite photograph from the "Schubert pictures" has been labeled "Little Bruno." It is, he says, a perfect picture of an infant Sasquatch.
>
> It also is not unlike a Rorschach ink-blot test.[2026]

Lee Frank

Lee Frank billed himself as the world's leading investigator of unknown animals and the only person to have actively pursued both the Loch Ness

Monster and Bigfoot. Frank spoke to more than 300 people during a public lecture at Northwest Community College at Powell, Wyoming, telling them modern society took comfort in knowing monsters, such as Bigfoot, simply did not exist. "But the plain fact is," said Frank, "it does." Though Frank conceded such creatures were certainly fantastic, he stressed the resultant volume of claims from thousands of witnesses of encountering Bigfoot creatures over 14 centuries as more incredible. Frank said he has been within five feet of a Bigfoot and in close proximity to the Loch Ness Monster, though he had never actually seen either creature. His close brush with Bigfoot occurred on a Tennessee farm.

> He [Frank] went to the farm late one night and found all of the spotlights he had left there turned on and the hillbilly farmer in the yard waving around a shotgun. Horrible sounds, including screeches, groans and breaking branches, were coming from the nearby woods, he said.
>
> So Frank headed into the woods.
>
> Though it was a moonlit night, Frank said, the woods were so thick he could not see what was making the noise.
>
> He estimated he got within five fee of the beast that was making the noise. "I was close enough that it could have reached out and pecked me on the cheek," he said. "That was a little too close for me so I got out of there."
>
> While investigating the incident the next day, Frank said, hair and 14-inch-long footprints that had been made by a 1,000-pound beast were found.
>
> On another occasion several of the same hillbilly farmers fired guns into the woods at similar noises, Frank said.
>
> Their hospitality was returned in the form of a grapefruit-sized rock. Pathologists have determined that hair samples found on that occasion slightly resemble human hair, but that they fit no known description.

Frank told his audience he had participated in Loch Ness expeditions in '72, '73, and '75. His Northwest Community College presentation included displays of footprint casts he identified as made by Bigfoot and the Abominable Snowman.[2027]

Wayne King

The Michigan Bigfoot Information Center in the basement of Wayne King's home was the repository for King's several footprint casts, a collection of grunt and whistle recordings, hairs that had been caught in a screen door and the so-called crowning jewel of the collection: a pile of scat displayed shrine-like on a velvet platform under a glass dome. King's residence was said to be easy to find; the mailbox out front was held up by a large metal Bigfoot.[2028] King was himself a large man, six feet tall, and a widower with three married daughters.

"We have to end this mystery and the only way this will be done is to take a specimen," King said, announcing what was tantamount to a seismic shift from his advocacy for legislation to protect Bigfoot to a position upheld by Green and Krantz—acquisition of a Bigfoot body, even if by shooting one.

King, a Flint auto worker, and his associates planned a Bigfoot stake-out over the last weekend of September at the farm of John and Virginia Culham in Ingham County, Michigan. Ms. Culham had reported several strange events occurring on the family's farm that September. One of the Culham's cats had been found "with a big hole right through its stomach. It might have been (done by) Bigfoot," Virginia Culham said. Loud, unnerving screaming had been heard by family members, usually between the hours of 1 and 3 A.M. "My son," explained Culham, "says it's the most terrifying scream he's ever heard." Two dozen 50-pound bags of feed and salt had been unceremoniously ripped apart in a grain shed on September 14 leaving "one heck of a mess," possibly the result from a Bigfoot chasing after small prey, King theorized. And a large handprint that measured 11 inches long and seven inches wide was found in the dust atop the Culham's pickup truck. According to Culham, the print bore all the hallmarks of a hand's creases and callouses. The presumed thumb was much closer to the wrist than on a human hand. King believed it was an authentic Bigfoot handprint because it was "close to the foot of a gorilla."[2029]

King gained further attention when his intent to organize a search party to recover the remains of a Bigfoot in northern California became known. The alleged remains were discovered by a woman in 1967. "She and a female companion were wandering an abandoned fire trail in a remote, dense wilderness region when they came upon a large carcass of what was first thought to be a bear," said King. "Closer observation revealed the carcass to have two arms, two legs and an extremely broad chest, a medium head with no noticeable neck, thick black hair 4 to 5 inches in length covering the entire body, large hands, with four digits and a prehensile thumb," reported King. The

Washington State woman was 23 when she told King of the remains in the autumn of 1979, making her approximately 11 years old when she found the body. "We have verified her story through affidavits and depositions," King said. "The witness accurately described color of fingernails as copper in color. She said the carcass was lying on its back with its arms spread and its legs drawn in." King's interview revealed the young woman estimated the creature had a chest about 4 feet across and was about 8 feet in height. The creature's chest had been ripped open, exposing its rib cage.[2030] King said the woman at first believed she was looking at "a bear, then some type of menagerie or freak of nature."[2031] The woman told King "she did have some traumatic experience. She said she felt like something was watching them, she felt menaced," he said. King was interested in raising funds to find the spot, a location which King was confident the woman could "relocate us to the spot within a matter of feet." An expedition to California represented a new venture for King. "We are sincere in our efforts," he said. "We are after the fossil remains; we're certainly not going to quibble about 10 or 12 years [spent conducting research] on a Sasquatch."[2032]

"There are tens of thousands of them throughout the world," the 44-year-old King asserted in an interview with the *National Examiner*, of which 300-500 lived in Michigan. "They are extremely smart and they are dangerous. I know of eight deaths blamed on Bigfeet," King stated, venturing into a seldom-raised Bigfoot topic in the '70s: Bigfoot as a threat to humans. "The most recent one that we know of happened in 1936 in Traverse City, [Michigan]. A man who worked for the Chesapeake and Ohio Railroad told of a co-worker who went to investigate an animal laying across a trestle. He was killed and dragged off by a Sasquatch."[2033]

The *National Examiner* reported King's interest in Bigfoot creatures started in 1951 when announcements of large footprints found on Mt. Everest swept him into the Yeti-craze. "They're carnivorous, live in abandoned buildings, farms or cave dwellings, and are very adaptable," King affirmed. He told the *National Examiner* of a Michigan Bigfoot sighting involving three creatures. "The road was 52 feet wide and they cleared it in three strides," he said. "At top speed they can move as quickly as a deer." Michigan was prime stomping ground for Bigfoot, in King's assessment. "We have 97 different varieties of edible trees, we're 60 percent forest, our climate is damp and we're surrounded by water," he said. "Michigan is also heavy bush country, which is useful to the Sasquatch for keeping concealed." King saw a mother and a juvenile Sasquatch "two years ago," at about 85 yards. "The youngster was 50 to 60 feet away from the mother. Then it walked to her." By the time of his interview with the *National Examiner,* King had concluded that if he should ever get the beast in his sights, he would shoot to kill. "I didn't have my rifle because we didn't expect to see one. But now I'm armed all the time."[2034]

Tranquilizing Bigfoot? Too dangerous, thought King, who with friend Richard Doty, intended to bring one in—dead. The effective range of a tranquilizer gun was about 40 yards or so, King maintained, making it a reckless enterprise. "It would be very foolish for anyone to be within range of the animal without a weapon," he said, espousing a mostly unheard of angle to the kill/no-kill debate: "We aren't hunting, we are defending." Even though a dead specimen would be priceless for science, King supported the passing of legislation to protect Bigfoot after its existence was proven to the world. "We have to end this mystery and the only way this will be done is to take a specimen," said King.

While collecting material for his book, *Bigfoot: A Personal Inquiry into a Phenomenon,* author Kenneth Wylie conducted a three-hour interview with King in the basement headquarters of King's home. Wylie felt the interview assumed the tone of an instructor teaching a pupil.

> "Mr. Wylie, if you are any kind of outdoorsman, you will admit you've seen many strange rock piles in the middle of nowhere; maybe you thought it was from some earlier farm, but not with all those old trees around. Didn't you ever wonder what they were? Well, they are moved there by Sasquatch to trap rodents, snakes, and small edible animals."
>
> Furthermore, he explains, the creature will even attract beavers in special traps set in riverbanks. Seeing my eyebrows raise again, King adds, with asperity, "This can't be denied. We have proof."
>
> King sits back, waiting for my inevitable question, his hands folded across his stomach. So I ask for an example of the proof. Finally, I am becoming accustomed to the rules of the game. I restrain a tendency to grin. But King does not: His broad face breaks into a brilliant smile.
>
> "What can you offer us in return?"
>
> And it doesn't take long to find out what I might offer. There is a great need of money so that King and his associates can buy a "sniper scope," an infrared night detector like those used in Vietnam by the army to detect the movement of enemy

> soldiers. Such a device, he explains, "would be a most valuable asset to our research operation and progress." With it he and his colleagues might be able to spot and shoot a specimen.[2035]

In early October, two reporters accompanied King and Doty during their stakeout on the Culham family's sheep farm in Dansville located some 12 miles southeast of Lansing.

> King picked a spot surprisingly near the farmhouse, in a small area bordered on two sides by trees and underbrush and on a third by cornfields. It was partly illuminated by a large light on a silo about 100 yards away.
>
> King and Doty scattered their special bait—a secret canned substance which they claim is successful in luring the Sasquatch—behind the stakeout near the woods.
>
> "It's either going to come along the cornfields or along the driveway," King said. "He will see us before we see him, but curiosity and the bait will bring him in."[2036]

King's research revealed Michigan to be prime habit for an active population of Bigfoot.[2037]

> In 1978, King said he validated 24 physical sightings and 310 sets of tracks. From that he estimates there are 300 to 500 Bigfoot in the state and tens of thousands throughout the world. There are even, he claims, three to five distinct species.
>
> King discounts people who call him an eccentric.
>
> "The same people who ridicule me and say I'm crazy won't come to my home and see the proof," he complains.[2038]

The investigators and reporters settled into the stakeout by 1:30 A.M. Suddenly a bellow from across the road shot out of the darkness. The cow likely startled those within earshot, given the aim of their vigil. "That's real unusual for a cow to do that," said King. "Once a cow is bedded down it usually stays for the night." Doty agreed with the assessment. "Yeah, something's upsetting it," he said. Occasionally the party could hear grunting sounds. "I wonder if sheep grunt?" King pondered. "I'll have to ask about that."

> About 3:15 A.M. a whistling sound was heard. A minute later it was repeated.
>
> "Hear that?" King asked.
>
> "It's an owl," Doty replied.
>
> Another half hour passed.
>
> Suddenly, sharp crackling sounds were heard in the tree to the left of the camp. The stakeout party stood up and looked intently into the darkness. King grabbed his rifle. Doty's pistol was already on his right hip.
>
> King whispered that an apple or something had been thrown at the tree. He said he heard it going through branches of other trees before it hit.
>
> King said the Bigfoot, if it was out there, was trying to frighten the group.[2039]

The stakeout culminated at about 6:30 in the morning with Doty and King canvassing the immediate area for footprints. Though they didn't turn up any evidence, King told the reporters since his bait was irresistible, Bigfoot had not been lured in because no Bigfoot had been nearby. The specimen that King and Doty believed had been in the area had obviously moved on, he said.[2040]

Grover Krantz

By 1979, Grover Krantz had taught physical anthropology and human evolution classes for 10 years as an associate professor in the Washington State University anthropology department. The mention of Grover Krantz' name on WSU campus would elicit either laughter or expressions of support for a man well-known to believe Bigfoot was an extant animal. Krantz said he had first heard of Sasquatch as a high school student in Salt Lake City. As he matriculated at the University of California at Berkley his curiosity in Bigfoot was still engaged. "I was interested in Sasquatch, but did not necessarily take it seriously until I was here in Pullman for a year, and then I made some serious contacts," he explained.[2041] "I get curious about anything peculiar, UFOs, the Devil's Triangle and this sort of stuff. Most of it I'm satisfied is a bunch of crap. But, I don't want to say something is a bunch of crap until I've looked into it to some degree. And I did look into the Sasquatch thing, fully expecting it to be a bunch of foolishness and I found it was not a bunch of foolishness," he said.

Krantz talked about the price he had paid for his interest. "I did not get flak directly, it took years to accumulate," he said. "I have found out that my promotions and pay raises have very seriously suffered. I have been informed that there are powerful people in this university who are going to see to it that I never get another promotion."[2042] Going public with his research and conclusions was his way of combating the criticism. "Nine years ago I decided to be rather open about it," he stated. "Then people would contact me."[2043] The voluminous correspondence he received contained both recent reports and older sightings. Krantz commented on some of the canonical Bigfoot encounters:

Ostman—probably "got a good look at some Sasquatches," but the kidnapping portion of the story was likely the result of a vivid imagination.

Ape Canyon—Krantz was ready to dismiss the Ape Canyon story: "About half the Sasquatch stories are worthless," he conceded.

Jacko—

> "'Jacko,' as the creature has been called by his captors, is something of the gorilla type standing about four feet seven inches in height and weighing 127 pounds. He has long, black, strong hair and resembles a human being . . . ," noted a June 30, 1884, account of the find in the *Daily British Colonist*. . . .
>
> Krantz said he corresponded with the grandson of a man who saw Jacko. The man verified the account from stories his grandfather had told.[2044]

Patterson Film—"If he [Patterson] could have faked that movie he would have . . . there's no way he could have faked that film. He didn't have the knowledge and he didn't have the equipment."

From his office in the eight-story Johnson Tower, Krantz gave *Union Bulletin* reporter Dodie Wagner a tour of his cast collection. "It's roughly a human foot," Krantz stated as he held a 17-inch long plaster cast. "In my analysis I can show that this is a modification of a human foot designed for one purpose and that is to carry an unusually heavy body," up to eight hundred pounds. Krantz had experimented with trying to produce fake tracks, going so far as to fabricate a wooden foot but found it couldn't match the details of what he considered authentic prints. Krantz had written a paper offering five Sasquatch print characteristics which he had previously lectured on describing how to tell real prints from fakes. "But there are two other characteristics that were not included in the paper," he said. "I think I am the only person who knows them and I haven't told them to anyone. But I can look at a footprint and easily tell if it's real."[2045]

The fossil record supported the existence of Bigfoot, Krantz maintained; *Gigantopithecus* was Bigfoot, "on the button."[2046] Krantz explained the anatomy and behavior of Bigfoot as being close to human beings. "Our ancestors separated from the apes about five million years ago when they became bipeds," Krantz said. "One species, man, got smarter. The other, Sasquatch, got bigger." Krantz noted that the first quarter of ever calendar year—January through March, was the time of fewest Bigfoot sightings. "This could indicate people aren't around in the winter or the Sasquatch is doing something else. How to choose between those I do not know," he said. "Some people say he eats roots, ferns, or steals apples from orchards. Logically, he eats what bears eat—whatever he can lay a hand on. Sasquatch is not designed to bring down game animals like deer. He is primarily a vegetarian," Krantz explained.

"I want to prove they exist and find out what they are," he said. "Sasquatch are not hiding. They avoid people like any animal does. There are very few of them, maybe one Sasquatch for every 100 bears," he explained. "He is primarily nocturnal, active between midnight and dawn. He has eyesight as good as us, or, probably, better. By seeing us they usually can avoid us. They probably can see us at 500 feet, where we couldn't see them."[2047]

Krantz told the *Union Bulletin* that Nature performed exceptionally well in disposing a creature's remains. "I've talked to hunters and game guides and not one of them has ever found a bear that has died a natural death, and we have hundreds of bears for every one Sasquatch."[2048] The subject of remains provided another meaningful comparison between bears and Bigfoot. "When a bear, or Sasquatch, is dying, it hides so it can protect itself while it's in bad shape." Krantz's disposition to quantitative argument asserted itself again: "You'd find one dead Sasquatch for every 100 dead bears, but as I said before, to the best of my knowledge that first bear hasn't been found," he added.[2049]

"Chances are good that people have shot and killed a Sasquatch before and have hidden the bones," Krantz said.[2050] "The person either thinks he has shot a very valuable animal that belongs to somebody or he has shot a very peculiar human being. . . . He hides the body and won't talk." And therein was the mode Krantz hoped he and a Bigfoot carcass would be united. "The only way to get a Sasquatch other than shooting one would be to locate one that already died. That would be my overwhelming preference," Krantz explained.[2051] "While it's valuable, it doesn't belong to anyone, and it's not human. Therefore, shooting a Sasquatch is legal because legally it does not exist," Krantz noted. Krantz hoped that anyone who had killed or knew of the whereabouts of a Bigfoot body would contact him or send him the bones. "But if you don't have bones, don't tell me about it," he said. "The bones are all I want."[2052]

"My first preference is to get somebody who has done that and get him to lead me to the bones. Then we don't have to shoot another one. . . . Bones are all I need." Krantz maintained that concerns of remuneration should not dissuade anyone from coming forward with information about a body. "If there is any money, I'll give him everything I get out of it. I'm not interested in money."[2053] A body was necessarily required to provide the final validation and convince the world of Bigfoot's existence. "Sighting, photos, hair samples are not proof Sasquatch exists. The only proof is to get one. Anyone who doesn't want to get a piece of one does not want Sasquatch to be found," he said. Krantz affirmed that a weapon capable of bringing down a grizzly bear would be sufficient to take down a Sasquatch. "I am in business to kill one," Krantz flatly admitted. "I have the weapon."[2054] A body would be of the greatest utility to science and mankind as well as justify Krantz's support and conviction in Bigfoot's existence. "I've stuck my neck out so much academically that I'm hoping to be vindicated at all costs," he flatly stated.[2055]

Krantz's position on killing a Bigfoot for the benefit of science earned the scorn and contempt from people who did not share his views. In a letter dated February 29, 1979, Donald Linchan of Genesee, Idaho, wrote:

> Mr. Grover Krantz,
> In response to the article about you hunting for Big-Foot in the Lewiston Tribune of Feb 18, 79, I have a few comments for you: First, whether there is a Big Foot or not is immaterial, what right or license do you have to carry an uncased rifle in your vehicle beside you? What right or license do you have to kill one if you should see one? It hasn't harmed or threatened you! You may shoot some prankster who is dressed or camaflagued [sic] like a "Big-Foot" just to tease you and you will have a

> pre-meditated murder charge against you. So if you're going after its body or bones, you had better reconsider, and stick to a camera.
>
> I've been on some back roads in the mountains and around our ranch and have seen a "black hairy" that a fellow like you might think is a Big-Foot, but it is a black angus cow! So you had better do your hunting closer to your tax supported laboratory and you won't get in trouble out on the back roads, because cattlemen don't take kindly to hunters on the back roads at night where those "black hairy" objects are cows. Anyway, what good is a dead Big-Foot—be brave and bring it in alive.
>
> I talked to Latah County Sheriff Mike Goetz and he said you had better not be caught cruising our back roads at night with a rifle by your side, whether you are hunting Big Foot or poaching deer or elk or bear or coyotes or cows, its illegal and your scientific title doesn't mean anything to us if you shoot a "black hairy" cow or man on a black horse. In fact some night patrolling cattlemen might confuse your hairy face for a Big-Foot and take you for a Big-Foot, BOOM! Your story probably makes good reading in New York or Hollywood and good royalty for you, but it doesn't impress me. So it would be best if you put your rifle under your bed and stay off of the back roads especially at night. And just use your camera [and] be a sportsman and catch it by hand![2056]

Wasting little time, Krantz responded on March 3, in a letter seeking to better explain and perhaps ameliorate relations between those with opposing views:

> Your letter of Feb. 26 calls for some comment. I occasionally get letters critical of my approach and generally ignore them. I'm responding to you for several reasons: 1. You gave your name, which most don't do. 2. You went to the trouble to send it to my home address. 3. You seem to have made some assumptions about me that are not correct. 4. I hope to hunt near your area someday and would prefer we understand each other clearly.

First, my rifle is carried openly and unloaded, just like many others do in their pickups—this is legal.

I do not get royalties for articles on my Bigfoot search. Actually it's a bother to talk to reporters—I turn down most requests for interviews. Most of them report it incorrectly, all of them are incomplete. I did write half of a book, published by the University of Idaho, and they do not pay me anything. All profits go to the State of Idaho. In fact, my own pay raises and promotions have been affected by this interest. Between lost pay and personal expenses this is costing me several thousand dollars each year. This may only make me sound like a "nut" with an obsession. Maybe so, but I think this creature can be very important to our understanding both of human evolution and also of mythology and folklore.

Its true that Bigfoot has not harmed me, but neither did the steers I have eaten. On the other hand, we may be harming them—ruining their environment and all that. No politician will risk his reputation calling for protection of a "mythical" animal. If they are proved to exist, then maybe regular primate experts will study them instead of ignoring them. The next concern is how to *prove* they exist.

This proof will only be in the form of a body, or part of one. Photographs can be faked, and all so far have been rejected by the so-called experts. The bones of one (even just a few bones) would be absolute proof. In fact, I would far prefer to find some bones and avoid killing one. Capturing one alive is virtually impossible and would be more cruel to the animal. Also it would be dangerous. You probably know how rarely one finds bones of wild animals who died naturally. My hope is to find someone who shot one in the last few years and chose not to admit it.

Your concern about shooting the wrong thing is valid. Many careless or thoughtless people do shoot up your countryside. I have traveled by night and seen all the things you mentioned, recognizing each for what they were. I have clear tests to be certain of what is there, and have no doubt I would make no mistake. There is no obvious way to convince you of this except to say that I do not enjoy hunting. What else can I say?

> For many years I have hoped that someone like you would shoot the first Bigfoot or discover a skeleton. Some of your neighbors have seen them and only been ridiculed for saying so. They would like very much to be proven right, and strongly encourage me in my efforts. It's not clear how you came to the opposite attitude.
>
> If this letter has helped clear up some misunderstanding perhaps I could meet and talk to you sometime. If possible I would ask your help in all this.[2057]

Rifts Amongst Researchers

Journalist Kay Bartlett wrote an AP article in which she focused on several prominent Bigfoot researchers at the time, specifically the disharmony existing between them. She described the community of Bigfoot hunters as "a network in which nobody seems to like anybody very much." Bartlett's writing confirmed certain expectations many held regarding those involved in studying Bigfoot—that anyone's investment of time and energy toward such pursuits likely denoted that individual as an oddball or crank.

For example, Grover Krantz stood out as one of only a handful, and likely the most prominent of the ivory-towered, accredited scientific community who openly shared his conviction in Bigfoot's existence. Krantz told Bartlett his adult conscience was bothered by a deer he shot when he was 14 but any feelings of guilt or remorse were not enough to dissuade him from occasionally driving lonely back roads with a rifle by his side, all in the hopes of killing a Bigfoot. Bartlett was just one of the many reporters to whom Krantz explained his opinion on the requirement for a physical type specimen. "Even if you photograph them down to their tonsils, it will never convince the scientific community," said Krantz. "We need the body or bones." Krantz estimated he spent a few thousand dollars a year of his own money on Bigfoot. "What else have I got to do with it? I live alone with two dogs."[2058]

Strenuously objecting to killing a Bigfoot was 39-year-old Jon Beckjord of Seattle. "It might be the missing link," he told Bartlett. "We may have a better chance of communicating with this animal than with any other." Bartlett wrote about Beckjord's claims to have seen Bigfoot, perhaps two of the creatures, on the Lummi Island Indian reservation in Washington. But it was some of the evidence Beckjord maintained in his possession that Bartlett called greatest attention to, including a car aerial he claimed was damaged by a Bigfoot.

René Dahinden did not think much of Beckjord's precious artifacts. "I'd need a 60,000 ton truck if I collected everything he thinks is evidence." Again spotlighting researchers' idiosyncrasies, Bartlett wrote of Dahinden's fondness for quoting Chairman Mao and his frequent appearances in court—both suing and being sued. "As Mao would say, there's a time to be in the field and a time to be in the courtroom. And the courtroom is where the excitement is now."[2059]

Illustrating further conflicts and disagreements, the Patterson-Gimlin film, which Bartlett noted was critically important evidence for Krantz and central to Dahinden's presence in the courts, was dismissed by Sydney Anderson, a mammologist at the American Museum of Natural History in New York; it was an example of "show business, not science," he told Bartlett. "It was a man in a monkey suit."

> Dahinden says he's spent some $10,000 in legal fees, and he's being sued by a film company and the widow of a Bigfoot chaser for a total of $200,000 for "malicious harassments" through the courts. . . .
>
> Routine Sasquatcheria: Dahinden demands in a letter that Beckjord stop showing the [Patterson-Gimlin] film, threatens him with the FBI, with legal action, demands a $300 payment . . . Beckjord corrects a score of spelling errors, returns the letter with a red "F-minus" at the top.[2060]

Dahinden, Beckjord confided to Bartlett, "always carries a carbine, gives off bad vibes and besides, the tooth fairy doesn't like him." Bartlett described Beckjord as a "sometime cameraman, oil rigger and mortgage broker," who knew where he'd go to find Bigfoot if he had the money: he'd visit the Sierras rather than, say, the Lummi Indian reservations. "The Lummi Sasquatch are too streetwise," Beckjord explained. "Besides, the Sierra Sasquatch are blond and gentlemen prefer blondes. I am blond. Maybe they'll like me."

Bartlett credited Peter Byrne as a rare standout amongst Bigfoot pursuers for having secured funding for his efforts—some money came from the Academy of Applied Sciences in Boston, which, amongst other provisions, had given funding for the search for the Loch Ness Monster.[2061]

"There is no second prize," John Green said of the effort to prove the existence of Bigfoot. "The man who actually collects one sees a pot of gold and fame out there. And if you pre-select a group of individuals who are willing to fly in the face of society, you tend to get some pretty opinionated individuals."[2062] Dahinden and Beckjord shared an abrasive relationship during the latter '70s. After reading Kay Bartlett's article, Dahinden picked up his pen and wrote a letter to Grover Krantz:

> Dear Grover Richmond, B.C. Feb. 13th. 79
> Re Beckjord. That guy is as nutty as a fruitcake—and I am sorry to see that his name was in that AP report. That woman [Bartlett] who wrote the report did not do such a hot job and I hate to see that Beckjords name got in it. That AP report was carried all over—but the full report was carried only by a few papers. I got [an] article from LA which seems to be a [complete] copy of her report.
>
> "Rene"[2063]

One of René Dahinden's forays into the courts at this time owed to his complaint filed in U.S. District Court accusing Peter Byrne of plagiarism. The suit charged that Byrne, the author of *The Search for Bigfoot: Monster, Myth or Man?* "substantially and blatantly" copied parts of Dahinden's book, *Sasquatch,* without permission from or credit given to Dahinden. With Byrne as defendants were Acropolis Books, publisher of the hardcover edition of *The Search for Bigfoot,* Pocket Books, publisher of the paperback, and Gulf & Western Industries Inc. of Delaware. Dahinden asked that all remaining copies of Byrne's book be turned over to him for destruction, profits of the sale of the book be paid to him, and for $50,000 in punitive damages and general damages for plagiarism.[2064]

John Sinor Helped Invent Bigfoot

John Sinor's daily column on "everyday problems of everyday people," appeared from 1965 to his retirement in 1992. In one of his 1979 columns, Sinor admitted to not knowing much about the Loch Ness Monster or the Abominable Snowman. But Bigfoot, that was a different creature all together.

> I helped invent him.
>
> On a moonless night many years ago in the mountains of Northern California, a little below Pinecrest on the Sonora Pass, two young college men pulled their car to the side of the highway.

> One of them strapped on a pair of 18-inch long plywood boards cut in the shape of feet.
>
> He slipped out of the car, walked about 50 yards off the roadway and tipped over a couple of garbage cans.
>
> Then he threw a couple pieces of raw meat in the snow, circled back to the road and was picked up by his companion, who had driven up the highway a couple hundred feet.
>
> The two young men laughed and drove away into the night.

A Tuolumne County deputy sheriff was on the scene the next morning and radioed in his report. Sinor typed up an article based on the deputy sheriff's findings.

> "Bigfoot may have roamed the Sonora Pass again last night . . ."
>
> The story ran on the front page of my paper and wire services picked it up and sent it around the world.
>
> Two days later a couple of college men were picked up with open bottles of beer in their car—and a couple of big plywood feet.
>
> They admitted their midnight walk in the snow.
>
> My paper used four paragraphs, inside, on their confession. The wire services ignored it.
>
> Nobody seemed to want to NOT believe the monster walked.[2065]

Wetiko

Kamil Pecher wrote *Lonely Voyage by Kayak to Adventure and Discovery* (published in 1978), a book recounting his 600-mile solo kayak trip along the rivers of northern Saskatchewan. Pecher had his own encounter with an inexplicable creature fitting the description of Bigfoot during a solo kayak trip on the Churchill River. Pecher wrote in the Fall 1979 edition of *Pursuit* that he had seen something he couldn't identify and, he admitted, "scared me witless." It also fired him to understand the creature he had seen and investigate if anyone had ever seen something similar in Saskatchewan?

> So I had asked many Cree friends to tell me any story about a giant resembling a monkey, but I didn't have much success. Oh, they told me funny stories about Wisagetchak the Trickster all

> right, but once we got into their legends that are considered sacred, they clammed up.
>
> The problem seemed to be also in the name. The word Sasquatch is a distillation of several Indian names—Seeahtik, Wauk-Wauk, Te Samiel Soquwiam, Saskahevis—attributed to the hairy giant and commonly used by the Chehalis (or Salish) Indians of British Columbia's Frazer Valley, particularly around the area of the villages of Harrison and Agassiz. The names are supposed to mean something like "Wild Man of the Woods."
>
> If I could only find the equivalent Cree name for the creature, I reasoned, I might learn more of what they know about it—but I had no luck.
>
> Then, reading by sheer coincidence a small red booklet entitled "The World of Wetiko," I got my clue word—Wetiko![2066]

The Wetiko as a concept, Pecher learned, covered a litany of subjects—incidents of cannibalism, mentally deranged people, and soul-possessing spirits. Pecher's analysis of these stories led him to conclude that one source of the Wetiko cycle of stories was the "wild man,"—the commonly understood Sasquatch, which Pecher suggested was itself "a puzzling phenomenon even for modern researchers, who also begin to consider the supernatural or parapsychological features of the creature."

Pecher noted that several Wetiko stories bore striking similarities to contemporaneous Bigfoot encounters. The Wetiko has the body and face of a man, dark skin, glaring, protuberant eyes, fang-like teeth and little indication of lips. It leaves large footprints in its wake. Places named Wetiko (or derivations thereof: Wichtigo, Wintego, etc.) could represent historical locations of Wetiko encounters.

Pecher included one of the stories from *The World of Wetiko;* a collection of Cree-narrated stories told by author Marie Merasty's grandmother.

> Not so long ago, when Isabel and Nancy were children, they were left in the care of their blind grandmother at a place called Piskwatsewapasek (Stump Narrows). Their mother was known as Petheses (Bird). One day while the little girls were playing by the river, they noticed someone swimming across towards them, holding something in front of himself to act as camouflage. They ran up to their grandmother and told her what they had just seen.

> 'Get into the house!' she ordered as she took hold of an axe. 'I used to think that when I saw one of them, I would not allow it to make me back down, that perhaps I'd kill it. I guess it must be a Wetiko who is coming, someone insane. A sane person would not be crossing the river holding reeds in front of him and in such cold water.' There was still some ice floating in the river.
>
> So the old lady started towards the shoreline and the moment the Wetiko saw her—just as it was about to wade ashore—back it went into the river in the direction from which it had come. It retreated, thrashing the water with such energy that the wake looked like a rapids behind it. The old woman stood ready, and the children watched, as the Wetiko, upon reaching the opposite bank, seemed to slip under the brush and out of view.[2067]

Vestigia

Vestigia (see Chapter 7 for Vestigia's establishment) investigated Bigfoot sightings outside of New Jersey, including several reports from New York concentrated in an area south of Kingston and north of Poughkeepsie. "As a scientist, I have to take the attitude that these things don't exist. But the conformity of sightings is outstanding," Robert Jones said. "We've got a variety of people in a variety of circumstances at a variety of times—and they all say they saw the same thing." Vestigia members had undertaken field investigations but no team member had spied the beast (as of August, 1981). During these trips into the field, Vestigia collected hair samples, examined footprints, and tape-recorded screams attributed to Bigfoot. "But, it's still a dead end," Jones admitted. "For example, the hair; we've studied it and we know it's not artificially produced. And we know it's not the hair of any other known animal. But we can't make that leap and say 'It's Bigfoot.'" Vestigia hoped government officials would give the subject serious consideration and dared to dream of sufficient funding for more robust search efforts.

By the end of the '70s, Vestigia had 94 Bigfoot sightings on file covering the previous ten years. One of the many questions that Vestigia explored was just how smart was Bigfoot anyway?

> Bigfoot's intelligence is a question mark. The animal does not seem to use any tools, Jones said, although he reportedly was

> once seen near Poughkeepsie carrying stick. No one knows how it might have been used.
>
> "On that basis, he doesn't seem much brighter than a gorilla," Jones said. "On the other hand, he can do remarkable things to stay away from man."
>
> According to Jones, a man in Oregon happened upon a set of Bigfoot prints in the snow one night. He followed the tracks far into the woods, where they went alongside a log, then disappeared.
>
> The man was mystified. He searched the area for a hundred yards around, figuring the creature might have been able to jump away. No tracks. He gave up and was heading back for his jeep when he thought of back-tracking. Was it possible that the big creature re-traced his steps to avoid detection?
>
> The man ran into the woods and found that, yes, Bigfoot had back-tracked his steps on the log and for a few hundred yards. He then ran off into a dense section of the forest.
>
> "Now that's extremely clever," Jones said.[2068]

As the '80s beckoned, Vestigia boasted a membership of 50. "I've been a scientist ever since I left college," Jones said. "But I like to look at new things. Eight or nine years ago I became interested in unexplained phenomena, only I wanted to look at it scientifically. With a few others, I formed the group and we've had a ball ever since." One of Vestigia's benefits was the opportunity for members to network with like-minded folks.

> Yet it is the process of discovery that keeps Jones and like-minded group members together. They are just one link, he said, in a worldwide chain of groups, researchers and scientists who communicate with each other about the "unexplained."[2069]

Members held interests in many areas of strange phenomena and Vestigia developed dedicated teams specializing in and investigating such subjects as "spook lights," the Jersey Devil, and phantom hitchhikers. Team membership depended upon an individual's training, proclivity, and interest. Jones said his area of interest broadly covered anything "that is short-lived or unexplained," which included Bigfoot, haunted houses, and spook lights. "As luck and life would have it, there's a lot of things to work on," he said. The biological-focused Vestigia team concentrated its efforts on Bigfoot and black panthers. A parapsychology team studied UFOs and an earth sciences group examined spook lights, which, like Bigfoot, became an intense subject for research. "That's our hottest item," Jones said in November 1981.

> Jones said the lights, usually three feet in diameter, are generally explained by local residents "with a ghost legend." But in one expedition to Long Valley, the light registered on equipment, and Vestigia members took infra-red photos.
>
> From that evidence, Jones said, the group is working on a theory that may provide some explanation not only for "spook lights," but the Bermuda Triangle, UFOs, ghosts and haunted houses.
>
> He said studies show the light is a special case of air particles ionizing into a ball inside an electrical field and, under certain conditions, causing a glow.
>
> Jones theorizes the phenomenon occurs in areas that are "active seismically," or on a fault line. If subsurface rock happens to contain enough quartz, Jones said, "you have pressure against quartz crystals that causes piezo electricity." If the energy grows large enough, "all kinds of things can happen."[2070]

The Throneberrys & The Bigfoot Research Society of Dallas

Robert and Tommie Throneberry helmed one of the more active Bigfoot research organizations of the latter '70s.

> The legitimate strain of Bigfoot researchers has a motto: "When in doubt—throw it out." We adhere to this at all times. It is a big job to try and find the facts amidst the physical evidence of Bigfoot in spite of all the local folks who would have us think there isn't any evidence. Often local people feel they have stumbled onto a find that will make them wealthy when they run across Bigfoot tracks and they usually try to divert the researchers. The only successful way to deal with this is to be honest with people and let them know we are not trying to pilfer their 'claim'.
>
> Presently, we correspond and exchange with about 18 different researchers. *All* of us finance our own ventures

> without benefit of salary or any other compensation. None of the group has ever been known to [sell] or publish anything sensational about Bigfoot. While everyone openly speculates about the whereabouts and origin of the Bigfeet, the researchers in our circle base their speculation on known fact—not on more speculation or outlandish theories. We all have various reasons for being in the field, but most of us are simply curious and adventurers. . . .
>
> Presently, about 85% of the reports received are completely disregarded as pranks or error. The remaining 15% are questioned at every turn. None of the researchers we know have ever found a single clue to indicate that Bigfoot is from outer space; has ever mutilated a single cow; or has ever performed supernatural feats of any sort including reading people's minds.
>
> Such stories arise as a result of two factors. One is low-key panic in the community where the report originates. Sensation seeking researchers eat up the stories told to them by frightened people. The second factor is called linking. Two strange elements are often connected with one another simply because the person theorizing the connection simply doesn't have an explanation for either. Usually one of the two elements is something quite ordinary that the observer doesn't recognize. He's too busy looking for a monster.[2071]

The Bigfoot Research Society published the *Bigfoot Bulletin,* which was received by about 200 persons including parties in Australia and China. An annual membership fee of $5 covered publication and mailing costs.[2072] The following introduction to the Bigfoot Research Society of Dallas comes from the premiere edition of the *Bigfoot Bulletin:*

> The possibility of the existence of very large man-like creatures in the remote regions of the world is something that has baffled scientists for years. A being that is part man and part ape seems incredible, but there is surprising evidence that such a being does exist. For centuries, a wild, hairy man has been indicated in literature from all over Europe and Asia. Myths and legends abound from places such as Africa, India, Tibet, Nepal, China, South America, as well as throughout most of the North American continent.

> Since the mid-18th century, stories have cropped up from the Pacific coast along an area ranging from Northern California to British Columbia, in Canada. Other reports exist from areas that are scattered through most of the continental United States. There is a concentration of these reports from the regions either side of the Mississippi River, many of which are in excess of one hundred and fifty years old.
>
> In the last half century, numerous reports have sprung up from the heavily wooded areas along the Arkansas River which runs east to west in the southernmost part of that same state. Many people scorn the probable existence of a giant man-like ape (or ape-like man, as you will), but because of the bountiful evidence others feel that a search is well-warranted. We at Bigfoot Research Society of Dallas are among the people who have taken up the search. Our society is dedicated to the protection of the elusive giant so commonly referred to as "Bigfoot". We currently investigate sightings from the immediate four state area. Our search is in earnest, our only motivation is to establish the existence of this creature so seemingly at hand.[2073]

Throneberry thought different Bigfoot species could evince variations of physical characteristics. Throneberry stated a "bear-coated" type of Bigfoot, from the Northwest portion of the country, had apparently migrated from that region to spread across America. Bigfoot descriptions collected during their early days as field investigators left the Throneberrys convinced locals were putting them on.

> The shaggy creature that was described to us was not a Sasquatch. The southern Bigfoot varied in colors from white to silver to gray. In every account he was said to have red reflective eyes. The southern folk weren't telling us what we wanted to hear at all."

The Throneberrys' research uncovered a host of older Bigfoot stories, blowing the dust off some intriguing regional tales dating back as far as 1834. Many of these accounts were localized in an area along the Louisiana-Arkansas line. A large cluster of sightings came from the late 1920s and the Throneberrys noted creature descriptions therein, with some exceptions on the matter of coloring, were largely similar to the most recent sources. One story from 1845 garnered their interest no less for its general description of a shaggy-haired, giant-proportioned creature roaming the bayou regions of Monroe, Louisiana, than for the portrayal of its eyes, "that must surely be as candle flames should they burn red."[2074]

The Bigfoot Research Society cast a huge footprint found near Jerusalem, Arkansas, and a copy was sent to Grover Krantz of the Department of Anthropology at Washington State University, Pullman, Washington. Throneberry hoped Krantz would be able to compare the Jerusalem cast with other casts the professor had in his collection. Krantz wrote the following letter to Throneberry:

> "As promised, here are my thoughts on the footprint. The cast itself looks much like our local [S]asquatch but for two items: the narrow heel and deep toe prints. A heel width of 3 ½ inches would indicate a weight of about 300 pounds. A length of 16 inches or so would call for a body of 8 feet. This works out to a very thin body—the equivalent of a 6-foot man weighing 165 pounds, instead of the actual average (American) of 190. My calculations are only approximations, so a roughly human build seems likely—not the 8-foot, 800-pound monsters of our area. Anyway, that checks with your local descriptions and fits the climate contrast. A separate race, maybe species. Anyway, good luck, good hunting, and write when you can. It was nice of you to drop by and compare notes." *G. S. Krantz*[2075]

Peter Byrne

The Bigfoot Information Center, Peter Byrne's base of operations, was a modest redwood building close by the eponymous river in Hood River, Oregon. The Bigfoot Information Center hosted a Sasquatch Education Exhibit replete with gorilla skulls, plaster casts of foot impressions ranging from 14 to 18 inches long and purported photographs of Bigfoot. The Hood River country was called by some "The Bigfoot Trail," an area with a history of several sightings in that part of the Cascades.

In his March 1979 *Ford Times* article, William Childress wrote that Byrne's goal remained the temporary live-capture of a Bigfoot for scientific study.

Byrne was 54 years old in 1979 and his wife Celia Kileen was 28. "My husband is a very honest man," said Kileen. "Celia worked with me for five years before we got married," Byrne said. "In all that time she never flagged in her enthusiasm for our project, nor in her encouragement when times got tough." Byrne explained his work investigating Bigfoot continued to receive financial support from the Wildlife Conservation Society and the Academy of Applied Science. "We depend on donations for quite a lot of our work," he stated. "Neither of the scientific bodies I am affiliated with can bear the whole burden of outfitting expeditions, purchasing needed equipment, and so forth. The vehicle we drive is donated. Much of our night equipment is loaned, like the NOD, or Night Observation Device. Sasquatches prefer to ramble at night. With the NOD, we can see for 1,000 yards through the process of amplifying starlight."

Byrne was also interested in the Loch Ness Monster, but derided the term 'monster' applied to unknown creatures. "Writers often let their imaginations overflow," Byrne said. "Bigfoot is no more monster than was the giant panda, which by the way no one believed in, either, until a Westerner saw one in China in 1869." Byrne was convinced Bigfoot meant people no harm. "All the creature wants is to be left alone," he said. "I wish people who grab guns and rush into the night every time a Sasquatch is spotted would just try to befriend one. Why assume a thing is dangerous just because it's strange or unknown?"

"I first got interested in Bigfoot when I was a big game hunter," Byrne reminisced. "Naturally, I wanted to kill one. Then one day I belatedly realized that if men didn't stop shooting animals, there would soon be no more wildlife. I got rid of my guns right after. That's been more than a decade ago, and I haven't killed so much as a meadow mouse since." Byrne recalled for Childress his past in India as a tea plantation manager in North Bengal, a post he resigned when India nationalized all the tea planting. "But living in India gave me considerable knowledge about jungle animals, which I hunted in my leisure time," he recalled. "It seemed natural enough to become a white hunter and safari guide."

Starting in 1952, Byrne operated his own Nepal Safaris until he became a conservationist in 1968. He began work on the Sukla Phanta tiger sanctuary supported by the International Wildlife Society of Boston. "We built the only existing sanctuary for Bengal tigers—animals fast-moving toward extinction," Byrne told Childress with pride. As early as 1960, Byrne had been hearing of the strange, manlike creature haunting the Pacific Northwest. "They called it Bigfoot," Byrne recalled, "but it sounded like a Yeti or Abominable Snowman to me. Since I had headed one Yeti expedition in 1958, sponsored by Tom Slick, a San Antonio oilman, I was interested. Tom died in a plane crash the same year. He was a dedicated seeker of Sasquatches, and is greatly missed."

Byrne and Childress discussed a sometime-referred to 'curse' believed to befall those who prominently researched Bigfoot.

> According to Byrne, certain writers of mystical persuasion like to dwell on 'The Bigfoot Curse.' While he labels such talk preposterous, it's nonetheless true that several men prominent in the search for Bigfoot have died in recent years. They include B. F. Porshnev, a Russian scientist; Tom Slick; Clifford Carl, a museum operator; Ivan Sanderson, an author and scientist who wrote a Bigfoot book in 1959; and Roger Patterson, a Washington rancher who is perhaps the most famous of them all in Bigfoot circles. In 1967 Patterson shot the only known footage of a running Bigfoot. It was also the first Bigfoot ever seen in daylight (the film was shot around 1:30 P.M.).[2076]

Curses aside, Byrne was optimistic in young people's attitudes of curiosity and concern.

> Youngsters, whose imaginations are not yet dulled, may be Bigfoot's best friends. When Peter and Celia give lectures, they report keen interest among students, which impelled them to make special "Bigfoot Educational Tapes" narrated in Byrne's careful English tones.
>
> One of the tapes features an eerie, hauntingly sad cry, something from time's primordial depths. It raises the hackles and makes the heart beat fast, but out of sympathy, not fear. It is the wail of a Bigfoot, recorded late one night in the Cascades. Sound-printed, it showed no similarity to any known animal sounds.[2077]

But Byrne's public outreach through the aforementioned educational tapes, lectures, and newsletters as well as his fieldwork to investigate Bigfoot sightings came to an end as the decade drew to a close. After nine years, Peter Byrne decided to close the Bigfoot Information Center and halt his active investigation into the phenomenon. Byrne estimated that over the course of the decade he had interviewed hundreds of people—

Native Americans, outdoorsmen, forest rangers, and tourists—all claiming to have had an experience with Bigfoot. Byrne's conviction in Bigfoot's existence hadn't wavered. "Do you know why I've kept on with the hunt? It's such an incredible damned proposition. It's beyond belief, yet I know it's out there. Nothing could be more fascinating. It's kept me going for all these years."

In point of fact, Byrne hadn't changed many of his views regarding Bigfoot after nearly a decade of full-time searching. "Here in the U.S.-Canadian outback, there are probably 200 or more creatures scattered in small families or colonies." Many particulars and details of Bigfoot's nature and habits remained unclear or only guessed at because of their ability to remain hidden from man. "They're cunning and mobile and very shy, which partly explains why they've never been captured. They see man as a threat, but the evidence indicates that they're not belligerent." And at the end of his multi-year investigation, Byrne had remained faithful to the idea that Bigfoot was more manlike than apelike. "It appears that the creatures make up a small group of primates, definitely humanoid in characteristic. They aren't apes—nothing walks upright but man. I give the creatures an 80 to 90 percent chance of being human."

Byrne was asked if he thought he had wasted years of his life chasing after an elaborate deception. "If it's a hoax, which I'm firmly convinced it's not, then it's a hoax that has been perpetrated for more than 160 years." In a telephone interview with *Beacon Journal* staff writer Bob Downing, Byrne said, "I'm a little frustrated in that there's never been enough money to launch a full program." The lack of proper resources had proven detrimental to creditable Bigfoot study, impugning those involved with the research, and impinging the capability to collect and review evidence. "When you get a report from Northwest Washington, 400 miles away, and you have to worry about having enough money to get there and back, it's time to take stock of things," Byrne said, echoing his almost exact comment to writer James Natal two years previous. Byrne estimated that a full-time, full-scale search would cost between $50,000 and $100,000 per year. He also admitted his frustration toward most scientists' resistance to serious and professional consideration of evidence including footprints, sightings, and the Patterson-Gimlin film. Byrne readily acknowledged that there were few, by his long-held conservative criteria, authentic sightings. "Poor old Bigfoot is likely to end up impaled on the front of a logging truck or shot to death with his carcass serving as proof that he exists. That, I feel, is sad."

As the curtain came down on Byrne's official investigation, he remained opposed to killing a Bigfoot, preferring instead to document or apprehend a specimen by means of camera, nets, and tranquilizers. Closing down operations actually entailed a bit of work—the 24-hour Bigfoot Hotline was shut down, the Bigfoot Information Center nestled in the shadow of 11,000-foot Mt. Hood was shuttered, and the publication of *Bigfoot News* was halted. Bob Downing reported that Byrne's monthly four-page newsletter had 8,000 subscribers at the time. Downing ended his article on the end of Byrne's nine-year effort by describing the adventurer's future: Byrne was to carry on as a "Bigfoot consultant," focused on giving talks and lectures. "What we've been involved in is a search with a layman's approach. What we're talking about in the future is a properly backed, properly financed search with a scientific base."[2078]

CHAPTER 11
1980

> I intend no scorn for the experiences of people that cannot, perhaps, be explained by logic. Certainly, much of what I've written here will be condemned by those who believe that critical objectivity about the Bigfoot phenomenon plays directly into the hands of the "established" professional scientists who have a vested interest—or so it is said—in pooh-poohing the whole matter. It would certainly be naïve to assume that there are no pressures within the scientific community to reject the entire Bigfoot search out of hand. After all, any undue enthusiasm for the unproved and unknown only reinforces the rather scornful attitude that the whole matter is a thorough waste of time, a diversion from more important tasks. This is one reason that the great museums, university departments, and other scientific institutions won't throw their weight behind an organized search for Bigfoot.[2079]
>
> Kenneth Wylie. *Bigfoot: A Personal Inquiry into a Phenomenon* (New York: Viking Press, 1980): 216.

The Kill Debate

The argument for supplying a Bigfoot body for the good of science could depend upon one unwavering champion throughout the '70s and beyond: Grover Krantz. The Washington State University professor who argued a pro-kill position during the *Anthropology of the Unknown: Sasquatch and Similar Phenomena* conference held in 1978, justified killing a Bigfoot for the very benefit of the species. "If we can kill one, the rest of the world including the politicians will finally know that they are real," Krantz said. "Anyone opposed to killing one is taking a stand in favor of their extinction."

In eternal opposition to the pro-kill position were the parties just as adamantly against taking the life of Bigfoot, even for science's sake. One such entity objecting to Krantz's view was the Animal Protection Institute of America. "Murder in the name of science is still murder," said Institute publicist Ted Crail. "Animals do best when they get the least attention from humans," he stated. Crail admitted the availability of a Bigfoot body for study would be of immense benefit to scientists and to the public; but, he also added, "There is something a little berserk about wanting to kill an animal to save it."[2080]

Dmitri Bayanov, Patterson-Gimlin film proponent and Chairman of the Hominoid Research Seminar at the Darwin Museum in Moscow, also advocated against killing Bigfoot to supply a type specimen for scientific study. Bayanov wrote in December 1977: "Modern *Homo sapiens* represents and symbolizes the achievements and failures of civilization. Modern *Homo troglodytes* represents and symbolizes the top achievement and subsequent retreat of nature. Now for the first time in history the two species are going to meet in the limelight of science. Let us make this meeting a happy one for both. Let it be on the credit side of civilization."[2081] Bayanov and John Green sustained a back-and-forth correspondence arguing their respective positions. Bayanov solicited opinions on the kill debate from other scientists, including Jane Goodall who wrote a response to Bayanov on August 22, 1978, from Dar es Salaam, Tanzania:

> Dear Dmitri Bayanov,
> Very many thanks for your letter of 11 July. I am answering it more quickly than usual because of the questions in it. Most particularly the one about the killing of a Sasquatch—or any other form of ape-like or human-like creature. I deeply deplore the killing of animals for museums. I loathe to see a stuffed chimp or gorilla—or monkey—or lion and so on. A photograph is just as good. A film is better. . . . Nor do I look back kindly on what I wrote, which John Green has been able to use to his own ends. I no longer agree with what I said then—I don't think it is at all justifiable to use chimpanzees to find out about a disease which people would not get if they did not eat one another! When I included this (as the book was going to press) I was trying to find out something really useful which scientists had learned from chimps. Something

> which really would alleviate human suffering. The kuru was a bad example, and got into the final book before I had thought about it properly. . . . Anyway—to shoot a creature just to see what it is—well, that is even worse. Most undesirable ethically—and the mark of a poor researcher.[2082]

In 1984, Krantz knew the whereabouts, which he was not disposed to reveal, of a three-man Bigfoot-hunting team led by Mark Keller. The group was in the field for the express purpose to kill a Bigfoot and retrieve its body out of the woods. Though undoubtedly hopeful, Krantz allowed only a 10% success for the Keller expedition.

Commissioners in Skamania County, Washington, voted 3-0 on April 2, 1984, to consider an ordinance making it a misdemeanor to kill Bigfoot within county limits, punishable by up to a year in jail and a $1,000 fine. A public hearing was scheduled two weeks later on April 16. Roy Craft, retired editor of the *Skamania County Pioneer* was the catalyst for the effort. "If indeed they do exist, and I'm 99 percent sure they do, I don't think they ought to be murdered just to have a specimen," he said. Craft, who helped publicize the original Skamania County ordinance in 1969, referred to media reports of Mark Keller's intentions to kill a Bigfoot for the benefit of science as the urging he needed to push for consideration of the ordinance. "These people are planning to come up here with a bunch of sophisticated weaponry and do a lot of hunting at night," Craft stated. "Quite aside from the creature itself, this poses a real danger to a lot of people who might be wandering around loose in the woods."[2083]

"The original ordinance made it a felony to kill a Bigfoot, which really exceeded the jurisdiction of the county commissioners," said County Prosecutor Robert Leick. "We revised that to make it a gross misdemeanor or a misdemeanor, depending on whether or not it is done with malice." Leick, who authored the proposed ordinance, said it would make the Skamania County a preserve for Bigfoot and place it as the first animal on the county's endangered animal list. If a Bigfoot was killed within county limits, then the county coroner would examine the remains to determine if the creature was human, possibly leading to murder charges. At the time, Keller was stating that his expedition to bag a Bigfoot would take place somewhere in the Cascade Range. The Seattle-based National Cryptozoological Society, started by Jon Beckjord, promised to trail Keller into the woods while playing music, banging tin cans together, and otherwise be a distraction during Keller's expedition to kill Bigfoot.[2084]

On April 16, the Skamania County commissioners voted on the revised ordinance.

> It is against the law in Washington State's Skamania County for anyone to kill the legendary ape-like creature said to roam the forests of the Pacific Northwest.
>
> The three commissioners of the largely rural county voted unanimously Monday [April 16, 1984] in Stevenson, Wash., to make it a misdemeanor to kill a Bigfoot, also known as Sasquatch. Violators face up to one year in jail and $5,000 fine.
>
> The commissioners did not try to prove or disprove Bigfoot's existence. But they listened as several people testified about their experiences with the legendary beast.
>
> Datus Perry of Carson, Wash., said he has seen giant apes in Skamania County and in California, but declined to reveal specific locations for fear someone might go there and stalk the creatures.
>
> Perry, 72, a retired diesel engineer, imitated the high-pitched, whistling call he said the creatures make. He said the fine hair on their faces is "like black velvet." He also said they do not smell bad, contrary to some other reports.[2085]

Keller did run afoul of the law, but it was not related to Skamania Country's revised ordinance. Keller's troubles began when he went to Eureka, California, in Humboldt County, to refit his expedition.

> Bigfoot hunter Mark E. Keller was arrested over the weekend on a charge of possession of a nighttime sniper scope on the rifle he plans to use to bring down the legendary creature of the Pacific Northwest.
>
> Keller, who has been hunting for Bigfoot in an undisclosed section of the Cascade Range since May 19, was released on his own recognizance Saturday after he was arrested by a Humboldt County deputy, the sheriff's department said.
>
> He was to appear in Eureka Municipal Court on August 1, deputies said.
>
> "There was an investigation, apparently. It had nothing to do with preventing the Bigfoot operation," Undersheriff Tom Heilmann said Monday.

> Keller claimed his Army-surplus scope, which magnifies available light for use at night, does not violate a state law prohibiting infrared scopes.
>
> Keller said he had been in Eureka to resupply his two-man expedition and get the telescopic sight repaired. He said he planned to return to the mountains as soon as he can get his equipment back from the sheriff's department.
>
> "I'm totally [outraged]," said Keller, a former Army Ranger who quit his job in the U.S. Postal Service to mount an expedition to bring down a Bigfoot.[2086]

Associate Press writer Jeff Barnard wrote in September 1984 that the charges against Keller were ultimately dropped. Keller told Barnard he had spent $9,000 of his own money during his three-month foray into the wilderness. "I'm not disappointed," Keller said. "Obviously, you have the desire to take it 100 percent, which is the acquisition of a Sasquatch." Despite the failure to sight a Bigfoot, let alone shoot one, Keller maintained his expedition had been worthwhile. "But I learned a whole lot," he said, hopeful to produce a journal about his experience in the field. "I have come up with some evidence that satisfies me that I picked the correct target areas. I think now it's just a matter of perseverance. I will keep doing this until I succeed." Keller said he found several sets of tracks and a pile of scat which he believed were left behind by Bigfoot. "The dung I found, which is considered scat, was with two very small tracks with larger tracks beside it, as though left by an adult with its young," Keller claimed. "When I came across it, it was about 10 days old." Keller collected samples of the dung and sent it to the International Society of Cryptozoology in Tucson, Arizona. During his telephone interview with Barnard, Keller was in Hollywood, California, with film producer & editor Tom Boutross (*Legend of Boggy Creek*) to "line up financial backing to return to the wilds next month and mount a better-equipped expedition next summer."[2087]

Peter Byrne

William Childress wrote several stories in the '70s on Bigfoot, including two for auto company magazines: "Tracking the Elusive Bigfoot" for *Friends* (Chevrolet, 1976) and "A Man Who Seeks Bigfoot" in *Ford Times* (Ford, 1979). The latter was recalled by Childress as he revisited the subject of

Bigfoot for a *St. Louis Post-Dispatch* article in August 1984. Would Byrne be amenable to discussing Bigfoot again, five years after their last talk?

> Now 59, he worked out of the Bigfoot Information Center in Hood River, Oregon, when I interviewed him for a *Ford Times* article in 1979.
>
> Since he's still listed, I telephoned Byrne, obtaining his number through Information and mentioning the story I had done earlier.
>
> "I remember vividly," he said, "and I don't want to talk to you."
>
> "Why not?"
>
> "After what you did to us? Putting all that stuff in that *Ford Times* story about a free Bigfoot kit? We got thousands of letters and we've never had a free Bigfoot kit!"
>
> "I don't recall any . . ." *Click!*
>
> The Bigfoot story, dated March 1979, contains no mention of any kit, Bigfoot or otherwise. I re-read it to be certain. But Byrne has had hundreds of stories written about him, and it's easy to get confused in such circumstances.[2088]

Jon Beckjord

Entering the 1980s, one of the newer researchers became one of the most dependable voices for commenting on and contributing to the arena of Bigfoot inquiry. Jon Beckjord brought *Pursuit* readers up to date with a succinct report on contemporary Bigfoot events in the magazine's Spring 1980 edition: Peter Byrne had retired, his Bigfoot information Center and Exhibit at Hood River, Oregon, had closed, and Byrne's *Bigfoot News* had ceased publication; Edd Kaye's Bigfoot Mystery Museum in Seattle, at one time sponsored by the International Sasquatch Society, had shuttered and Kaye's newsletter, *The Bigfoot Newsletter,* had stopped; disappointed subscribers reported they were no longer receiving the *Bigfoot/Sasquatch Clipping Service;* the Bay Area Group's *Bigfoot Bibliography* ("BIB") founded by George Haas still put out editions edited by Warren Thompson; and Beckjord's own Project Bigfoot, formerly known as Project Grendel, was still conducting field research and maintained a hotline for sighting reports.

Beckjord also noted Marcello Truzzi, Sociology Department Chair at Eastern Michigan University in Ypsilanti, Michigan, an original member of the debunking group Committee for the Scientific Investigation of Claims of the Paranormal (CSICOP), had founded a journal for investigating paranormal claims. The *Zetetic Scholar* provided a forum for skeptics and claimants to air both sides of a topic, an editorial and philosophical feature Beckjord found lacking in CSICOP's *Skeptical Inquirer*.[2089]

In the same edition of *Pursuit,* Beckjord presented a methodology for calculating Sasquatch weight based upon soil mechanics and soil-compression formulas. Beckjord believed the depth of tracks aided in calculating Bigfoot's weight; an important factor of which was the settlement of an object in substrate being linearly related to the weight applied. Beckjord provided calculations based on track measurements by Bob Titmus and Harry Halbritter from Bluff Creek which had been recorded within ten days of the Patterson-Gimlin filming in 1967. Given the commonly-reported track depth of 1 ¼ inches and a known subject's average track depth of 3/16 inch, Beckjord ultimately suggested a likely weight of 2,041 pounds for the Patterson-Gimlin film subject. Beckjord recommended upon the discovery of future prints investigators should measure the depth of their own tracks for comparison and proceed to conduct engineering load tests on the same substrate, if conditions permitted.[2090]

In 1983, Beckjord's criticism of three color photographs taken by Ivan Marx gained attention as the Bigfoot community's inner debates again claimed a measure of public interest.

> The photographs taken in 1981 on Snow Cap Mountain in northern California show a large, ape-like creature standing upright and taking what amounts to a streamside bath.
>
> 'The proportions on the photos are all of a human type,' said Beckjord, director of Seattle-based National Cryptozoological Society.
>
> 'A study of as many as 12 other photographs, plus an analysis of 2,000 sightings, indicates Bigfoot has a structure somewhat like a combination of gorilla and human—with gorilla-sized shoulders and chest, small ears close to the head and long hair on the head,' Beckjord said.
>
> 'These pictures show totally human proportions, no barrel chest, the arms are not long, the ears protrude like a teddy bear.'
>
> But Ernest Monteil of Amazing Horizons Co., San Jose, Calif., the company which employs Marx as a photographer

> replied, 'We don't have to defend those photographs' which he said 'stand on their own merits.'[2091]

Amazing Horizons Co. produced Marx and Tom Biscardi's film, *In the Shadow of Bigfoot,* in 1983. This widely-panned, shot-on-video tape offering appeared to many as a profit-making venture with sparse evidence to back up Marx's contention that Bigfoot was a living, breathing creature.

The early '80s was also a time when Beckjord began to explore other cryptozoological interests. The Scottish *Daily Record* of July 25, 1983, stated that Beckjord and Anna Lincoln had started a research effort at Loch Ness called Project Water Monster with the intention of employing a special video camera to cover prospective parts of the Loch.[2092] "The camera can videotape a small area continuously for 240 hours straight, night or day," Beckjord told reporters. "We'll let it go for a couple days straight and then use the fast playback to see if anything has popped up, he said. Beckjord and Lincoln targeted Urquhart Bay as a prime location for their camera. "All due respect to previous attempts, but I think we've got a better chance of seeing something—if there's anything to see—with a robot camera. Not only is it cheaper, it eliminates human error and boredom," Beckjord said.[2093]

For the man who claimed three Bigfoot sightings, good fortune appeared to also attend Beckjord's Nessie-hunting effort. "Things are going fantastic!" Beckjord exclaimed in a transatlantic telephone interview with *Seattle Daily Times* reporter Erik Lacitis. "We were on the BBC. We're going to be on Good Morning America on ABC. CBS is coming up. Germany and Japan called. AP and UPI and Reuters. Every newspaper in Britain is on my tail. I've got 12 people here in the lobby [Clansman Hotel, Loch Ness] waiting for me after I get through talking to you."[2094] The hoopla resulted from Beckjord's claim that he had videotaped not just one, but even three Loch Ness monsters. Not all who viewed Beckjord's tape found the footage compelling.

> It didn't matter that it turned out that Beckjord's evidence, at least judging by the tape shown on yesterday's "Good Morning America," was flimsy. That's the nice thing about stories on monsters. People love them, and you can say anything you want about them. After all, no monster has ever sued for libel.
>
> The images that appeared on yesterday's television segment showed what looked like a bright flash on the water. Beckjord

> said it was created by one of the "Nessies" as it dived into Loch Ness.
>
> Perhaps that's the case, especially if your imagination is fueled by Beckjord's excited description:
>
> "What we have here is for the first time in history a motion recording of one of these creatures on the surface, probably getting air. It makes a very strange and unusual splash, about 30 feet long. It's like a cannon shell was shot through the water.
>
> "Then the splash subsides and you can see three black objects just under the surface of the water. They swim away for about half a minute or a minute. You can see them swimming parallel to each other."[2095]

Much as Beckjord had condemned Marx's color photographs, his video of what he called three Loch Ness monsters met largely with incredulity and doubt. Tony Harmsworth, curator of the Loch Ness Monster Exhibition, referred Beckjord's videotape to an "evidence assessor" with the British Loch Ness and Morar Project Evidence Committee. The assessor reported the images could be explained by several wakes in the water, changes in light conditions, and even waterfowl. "What he said is that it's not necessarily monsters," Harmsworth stated. Beckjord took issue with the pronouncement. "They're soreheads. They're jealous. That 'evidence assessor' they sent out is simply some guy who has a camera and calls himself a photographer. These people don't like me because I'm getting publicity. The objects I taped are big. They're not ducks. They're not little blobs open to interpretation." Harmsworth also noted that should the objects caught on video somehow be validated as Loch Ness cryptids, it would make Beckjord an incredibly lucky man. Others had searched for months, even years and not seen, less capture on video, the Loch's most famous denizen. Beckjord dismissed luck as a factor. "If you want to call it lucky," he said. "I call it applied technology."[2096]

After his foray to Loch Ness and the attendant tumult over his multi-monster videotape, Beckjord was back again to thinking and writing about Bigfoot. Per his letter to *Current Anthropology,* published in that journal's February 1985 edition, Beckjord concluded that despite the fact Bigfoot had successfully defied analysis from conventional, mainstream science, the subject still deserved study. Answers, however, would likely come from the auspices of sources other than anthropologists.

> . . . I would like to say that my "Wildman" (i.e. Sasquatch) field research in the Northwest over the last eight years has led me to conclude that Wildman research is not at all a proper concern of anthropologist or zoologist. Despite some 500 shooting incidents (some with a .357 magnum), 3,000 or more sightings, 2,000-plus track finds, recovery of blood and hair samples that were ultimately found by qualified scientists (Sarich, Rosen, Kurley, Moore) to be from some unknown primate, and the analysis of unknown mammal feces (Von Bryant) [sic], no solid body or bones of any such creature have ever been recovered for analysis. . . .
>
> My conclusion is that while some sort of being may exist in the wilds, it is the proper study of either parapsychologists or Search for Extraterrestrial Intelligence scientists, not anthropologists. . . .
>
> I have also made three brief sightings, from 500 ft., 200 ft., and 150 ft. Our group, the National Cryptozoological Society, has in its files some 15 authentic-seeming photos of the same type of creature, and we have dozens of taped sounds. Yet the physical creature seems not to exist on any basis that can be reliably studied. Let us give the anthropologists a rest, then, and let them do their proper work.[2097]

The author Kim L. Neidigh had already come to a roughly similar interpretation, much as had Bigfoot researchers like B. Ann Slate and Ramona Hibner had during the '70s. Neidigh's article, "Bigfoot as Symbol," published in the Spring 1980 edition of *Pursuit* postulated North America's giant hairy hominid was a product of the unconscious mind reaching out in interaction with the "collective Shadow"—the repressed feelings locked away in people's minds—to manifest Bigfoot into the corporeal world.

> Reports of hairy, man-like creatures continue to increase, leading hunters and scientists on a merry chase to capture the missing link. Although sightings in conjunction with UFOs have raised some doubts, Bigfoot is still commonly considered to be a prehistoric relative of man. Descriptions vary, but recurring features include height 7 to 10 ft., extreme hirsuteness, erect gait, shyness coupled with curiosity, and foul

odor. There are some reports of hostility toward man. So far, so good. It's not too difficult to imagine some primitive throwback possessing these characteristics. But what about red or green glowing eyes, footprints with from 3 to 6 toes, immunity to bullets, and telepathic abilities? These characteristics are also reported but fit no living creature. Any theory of the nature of Bigfoot must explain all the reported facts.

If certain features defy a physical existence, could Bigfoot be some paraphysical denizen of the mind? It will be the thesis of this paper that Bigfoot is a psychokinetically formed representation of the dark, neglected aspects of civilized man's psyche. This would explain such disparate facts as its leaving footprints and droppings while being immune to bullets. Bigfoot is not an imaginary creature although its origins do lie in the imagination. Acting as midwives are the phenomenon of repression and man's neglected PK abilities.

The chain of events that makes Bigfoot possible begins in childhood. As the individual matures he is taught by his parents that "good little boys and girls" do not do certain things. If he persists in these taboo behaviors, whatever they may be, he will be punished. The child learns to avoid pain by not acting out certain impulses. If the parents are really successful the child will learn to deny that these impulses even exist. He has learned to repress them. These unacknowledged parts of his personality continue to seek an outlet. Ideally, these energies would be accepted and channeled into useful activities. But ignored, they fester in the unconscious, transforming themselves into demons and haunting the corridors of his dreams.

C. G. Jung calls these images personifications of the Shadow, which is the totality of all those aspects of an individual that he finds intolerable. By repressing them he does manage to deny responsibility but only by granting them autonomy. They proceed to make themselves known through others. A highly moral man sees all others as criminals; a prude sees hordes of prostitutes and lechers. This mechanism of projection works hand-in-glove with repression.

But suppose the forces of repression are so strong that projection does not occur? The individual does not see his faults in others; he does not see them anywhere. But they have not vanished. They are seething in the unconscious, preparing to erupt. The psyche stumbles; the individual hallucinates. He sees images that personify what he has repressed. They appear to be solid and objective but are mere shadows of the mind.

This is what happens on the individual level, but what about an entire culture which collectively denies certain aspects of human nature? The mechanisms are analogous. If a technologically advanced civilization denies its roots and its kinship to nature, an explosive situation develops. It pollutes the environment. Its citizens lose perspective and become alienated. It works against itself on all levels and, perhaps, its people have visions. Wild men lurk in the forests.

The collective Shadow of our society would be expected to contain just those characteristics attributed to Bigfoot. The foul odor, the body hair, etc., are the direct antithesis of our deodorized, sanitized selves. The huge size compensates for our neglect and also reflects our fear of our darker side.

Having shown how Bigfoot might be a psychic creation, the problem of its obvious corporeality remains. These creatures leave definite physical, albeit inconclusive, evidence behind. If Bigfoot is psychic in origin, then any physical effects can only be the result of psychokinesis. The latent parapsychic forces of the psyche unite with the Shadow elements to make the images more convincing. The unconscious reaches out and utilizes the external environment, giving physical form to the disowned Shadow. Once the emotions of shock and fear grant the image recognition, the forces holding it together abate and the creature vanishes.

To summarize: The author proposes that Bigfoot is the personification of repressed elements of the human psyche given temporary physical existence by latent powers of psychokinesis. These elements take this route because the unconscious mind has left them no alternative.[2098]

Rant Mullens

From his Toledo, Washington, home, 86-year-old Rant Mullens confessed in 1982 that he had hoaxed footprints at Mount St. Helens using carved wooden feet. Mullens said he wanted to get the hoax off his chest and come clean. "If I don't set the record straight now, people will go on believing there really is a hairy monster," said the retired logger. "I tell you, people will believe just about anything." The incident in question occurred in 1924.

> "My uncle, George Ross, and I were fishing in the area (now known as Ape Canyon) in 1924. As we hiked out, we heard some miners talking at the bottom of a canyon. They had fashioned a ladder out of poles to get down the steep cliff.
>
> "George was always playing jokes, so he and I rolled some rocks down over the edge. Then we got out of there fast.
>
> "When we heard that the miners were telling hairy ape stories, we both had a good laugh. We never told anyone the true story."
>
> In 1928, Mullens and fellow Forest Service workers "thought we would have a little fun" while building a trail from Smith Creek to Pine Creek at what is now the upper end of the Swift Reservoir.
>
> With jackknife and hatchet, Mullens whittled out a pair of huge feet from some green alder wood from the banks of the Muddy River, Mullens said.[2099]

Mullens named Ned Packard as the man whose foot Mullens drew and enlarged for the shape and size of the wooden feet he carved. Mullens credited Bill Allen for attaching leather straps onto the feet and stomping around several parked cars belonging to huckleberry pickers. "When the pickers came back and saw the huge footprints, they got out of there fast."[2100]

At the end of the season, Mullens left the carved feet in a Forest Service shed and when he returned the following year he discovered the feet were gone. Almost 20 years later, a friend admitted to Mullens that he had appropriated the feet and returned them to Mullens. Mullens went on to carve a further six sets of wooden feet which were used by several unidentified practical jokers up and down the Pacific coast.

> Mullens has letters from California asking to buy sets of the feet. One, dated March 3, 1958, is from a Willowy Creek, Calif., man who asked, "How much do you want for the feet?"
>
> Mullens says, "I was born within 30 miles of Mount St. Helens and have worked in the woods here almost all my life. I have never seen anything out there that I could not explain."[2101]

Not so fast, said Grover Krantz, who perceived welcome clarity coming out of Mullens' confession; it actually lent credibility to Bigfoot as an extant creature because the Mount St. Helens story, Krantz believed, didn't mesh well with other accounts of Bigfoot. "I always had my doubts about the miners' sighting," he said. "In other sightings, the Bigfoot was solitary, not in a group. And they don't normally attack or throw objects. If anything, (Mullens' disclosure) makes the Bigfoot thing a little cleaner because a very deviant story has dropped out."[2102] Krantz summed up Mullens' fakery as a "particularly dumb hoax."[2103] The first edition of the International Society of Cryptozoology's *Newsletter* carried an editorial suggesting Mullens' revelation had more to answer to if it was to be accepted as the single catalyst for Bigfoot-related incidents in the Mount St. Helens region.

> What Mullens' "confession" does not explain are the footprints found in the area prior to the Ape Canyon incident, both in 1924 and in previous years, by both Spirit Lake rangers, prospectors, and trappers. As to the miners' story of the attack, journalist John Green (author of *Sasquatch: The Apes Among Us,* Saanichton, B.C.; Hancock House) spent an evening with one of them, named Fred Beck, in the 1960s; Beck maintained his version of the events, which he had apparently repeated hundreds of times for about 60 years. Although he tended to accept the reality of the incident, Green concluded that, "as with all the old accounts, there is no prospect of being able to establish now the truth or otherwise of the basic story." . . .
>
> Rene Dahinden, another long-time Sasquatch researcher, doubts the Mullens version, however. In a telephone conversation with the Editor [J. Richard Greenwell], Mr. Dahinden pointed out that several versions of the Ape Canyon events by persons claiming responsibility have surfaced in recent years, including the Mullens claim. Mr. Dahinden feels that Beck's testimony is more reliable than Mullens', and that the footprints found in the Ape Canyon area in 1924 and before were quite unlike the obvious Mullens fakes of 1928 and later.
>
> Fact or fiction, the Ape Canyon incident is destined to remain an integral part of Sasquatch history and lore.[2104]

The Throneberrys

The four-toed footprints found on a Powderly, Texas, farm in early April 1980 left local residents, Game Warden Bill Milling, and Lamar County Sheriff's officers perplexed. "I think it's a hoax, but then there's that doubt in the back of my mind," Milling said. "If it is a hoax, someone went to a lot of work to make them look real." The footprints were found by a Powderly man as he checked fishing lines in a pond on his farm. The prints were 13 inches long and six inches wide and traveled around the man's pond and at one point appeared to enter the water. "I can't really say what I think it is," the man, who asked for his identity to remain anonymous, said. "You want to say it's a joke, but you just can't explain how it was done." The man voiced the familiar refrain of irritation with notoriety caused by the suspected presence of Bigfoot on his property. "I do know they've caused a lot [of] problems for me. Since the prints showed up, people have come trampling through to see them and leaving trash around. I'm almost tempted to make a set of footprints somewhere else to get people's attention off my place."

Milling admitted he was at a loss to explain the tracks. "The stride is consistent and is about 43 inches long," Milling said. "It looks like it wasn't in any hurry. It would have taken someone very tall and heavy to make the tracks." Solutions included the possibility of a youthful prankster, which had a precedent in the area. "I think it was some kids playing a joke, but I have to admit, it's a pretty good one," Sheriff Roger Patterson said. Reporter Celia Laska wrote that many residents reported their cattle had been behaving strangely a few days before the tracks were first discovered. Joe Howard, a resident near the spot where the tracks were found stated he too was perplexed. "The cows apparently caught scent of something in the east," Howard said. "We thought it might have been a panther until the prints were found. Now I'm not really sure."

Tommy Sparks, a local twelve-year-old, said he saw the creature last August and was convinced it was the recent track-maker. "When I told my parents about seeing it then, they just laughed, but I did see it," he said. The footprints gained the attention of two Dallas-based organizations: the Bigfoot Investigation and Research Organization and the Bigfoot Research Society. Several members from each group came to Powderly to investigate the scene. Charles Hignight, a Paris resident taking part in the research, said digging into the area's history had yielded old reports of Bigfoot creatures in the region, but the Powderly report included physical evidence. "We also found the tracks in the woods nearby," he said. "Someone had to go to a lot of trouble to do this if it is a hoax." As usual, not all were convinced. "We've had several reports of odd creatures in the 21 years I've been here," said Game Warden Hill Lawrence. "I'd say about 25 percent of those were legitimate. The circus in Hugo has had animals escape and some of them have ended up down here." Lawrence said he had not personally seen the tracks. "I couldn't really comment on those," he said. "When things like this happen, though, it gets people talking and gets their thoughts off problems. I suppose its newsworthy, but I think it's a hoax."

> Lawrence said several years ago a man reported a strange creature in his tomato patch. "But that turned out to be a bear," he said. "One had escaped from the circus. He ended up being shot in Hughes Springs."
>
> The tracks, however, have almost disappeared and Big Foot investigator Kenneth [Shepherd] of Dallas said he will try to find more evidence in the area in the next few days.
>
> "If someone happens to catch him," Hignight said, "I'm just liable to be out of a hobby."[2105]

The Bigfoot Research Society's investigation culminated with the conclusion that the four-toed Powderly Bigfoot possessed wooden feet. Throneberry determined the tracks were likely made by a wooden foot shaped with a band saw. "Most of the Bigfoot-type footprints that we see in Texas are hoaxes, but we want to check every report just to make sure," he said. "Whenever a report like this comes out, amateur Bigfoot hunters come out and disturb the people living there. We think it's our duty to call a hoax when we see it. Those of us who do serious research on Bigfoot get a bad name from things like that."

"We were skeptical when we heard about it," Throneberry continued. "There's no such thing as a four-toed primate or even a three-toed one." Throneberry stated he believed Bigfoot, if it exists, was a primate. "What we are dealing with is apparently hairy, it's apparently humanlike, it walks upright, it has human structures to its feet and that makes it a mammal, that makes it a primate and that probably makes it a hominid," he said.

To emplace the tracks, Throneberry concluded that the shaped wooden forms were probably pounded into the ground to make it seem as if a heavy creature made them. Game Warden Bill Milling said he was relieved that Throneberry's group considered the tracks a hoax. "I wasn't concerned about the calls I was getting, I was concerned about people coming out here to hunt Bigfoot," Milling said. Milling had the opportunity to see casts of Bigfoot prints made in California and the Ozarks in Arkansas that Throneberry had brought with him. "They had five toes and looked more like a human foot except that they were much longer," Milling said. "They had a little more detail to them." When asked by reporter Celia Laska about his own belief in Bigfoot, Milling was noncommittal. "I really don't know much about all this," he said, "but I do wonder."[2106]

"You deal with direct lies, mistaken identity and facts," said Throneberry, an anthropology student at East Texas University in Commerce, of his experiences researching Bigfoot. "So far, no facts. Nothing backs up any of the stories we've heard in Texas." What the Throneberrys had discovered was that some people (including some researchers) would go to great lengths for publicity. "There are a lot of people who are self-styled Bigfoot researchers that don't have any kind of background or any kind of knowledge about anything that has anything to do with this field who will get out there and make an opinion."

"Back in the '60s, the media gave the researchers a bad time," said Tommie Throneberry. "They couldn't be objective and write a story. They had to put their little one-liners in there. They were indirectly telling the public not to pay any attention to it. And the researchers decided not to talk to the media." Leading the public to believe there was nothing serious at all to the Bigfoot phenomenon instead of objectively reporting the facts behind newsworthy stories was a detrimental practice for all concerned and one the Throneberrys themselves could not fail to take seriously. "We don't think that's funny," Tommie said. "We've got a lot of time and a lot of money invested in this."

The Throneberrys also found fault with what they called the media's penchant for whipping up a needless frenzy through selectively spotlighting fantastic story elements and promoting thrill-seekers' antics. "We try to kill the monster before it gets out of hand." Throneberry said. "People get their guns and hit the bushes and shoot one another. Now to us, that's the monster." He believed responsible researching included an obligation to set the record straight. "When the story gets back in the press that we are in agreement that this thing is a hoax, that kind of discourages the drunk gunslingers from getting out there and shooting up the cows."

"We've run into people that have different ideas about how an investigation ought to be conducted," Tommie said. "We think if a Bigfoot is reported coming out at night to feed, then the best thing to do is to turn the lights out, lay low and keep an all-night watch. At the same time, there's probably going to be a Bigfoot researcher there whose idea of how it ought to be done is to shine floodlights all over the area all night."

"There's one guy who spends probably a minimum of 50 hours a week in the bush," Tommie said. "He's out there trying to see an invisible Bigfoot. He thinks they're invisible and they make themselves visible at will." Tommie averred that one of the biggest controversies in the Bigfoot community was the divisive question of what to do with a Bigfoot specimen. "There are some researchers who say go out take a picture of it or go out and try to communicate with it. On the other side of that line there are researchers who say go out and shoot it. We can see both sides of that issue. Most people would not be inclined to shoot anything that looks that much like a person. You don't know what's under all that hair." Researching Bigfoot, the Throneberrys believed, obligated one to be prepared to conduct responsible and thorough investigation. "Some of those who want to kill a Bigfoot have directed their lives to searching for the creature and have brought in the best physical evidence they could find and it has been rejected out of hand," Tommie stated. "If I get into a situation where I think I'm going to run into a walking, living, breathing Bigfoot then I'm going to be prepared to produce the best physical evidence possible from the situation. If I can't do that nobody will ever know I saw it," she said.

Throneberry said his desire to get into the field came from a need to participate rather than merely observe. "Galileo and Columbus could have sat there and agreed that yes, the Earth is flat," he said. "Somebody has to have the guts and drive to go out and discover things." Upon graduation, Throneberry said he wanted to go to Washington University in Seattle to take Master's and doctorate degrees. Throneberry said he'll continue his Bigfoot research "unless I find one." "If we can prove that every scrap of evidence that has ever been laid down has been falsified, then we'll go out and raise Spanish galleons for a while.[2107]

Eberhart's Book: *A Geo-Biography of Anomalies*

George Eberhart graduated from Ohio State in 1973 with a B.A. in journalism and received his Masters in library science at the University of Chicago in 1976; starting in 1977, Eberhart was employed in the University of Kansas Law Library in Lawrence, Kansas.

> His attitude toward paranormal phenomena is broad-gauge, inquisitive and tolerant, and if he has a preference, it is

> "bibliographic verification of alleged anomalous events." (He translates this from educationalese as "tracking down elusive sources.") Most recent stage in the Eberhart evolution is his appointment, announced in July, as editor of *College and Research Libraries News*, a journal published by the Association of College and Research Libraries in Chicago.[2108]

Eberhart had published a 60-page index of topics and subjects treated within the pages of *Pursuit* from 1967 to 1978. In 1980, Eberhart authored the much larger, 1160-page *A Geo-Biography of Anomalies—Primary Access to Observations of UFOs, Ghosts, and Other Mysteries*. The book reportedly comprises more than 22,000 anomalous events and sites in North America, giving the researcher an imminently usable and thorough tool. The variety of anomalies included covers the gamut of Fortean events: the subject index covers 15 pages. The subject of hairy hominids is covered by Humanoid subject entry which Eberhart defines as, "Hairy, quasi-human creatures seen especially in sparsely populated areas. Their size is ordinarily very large, six to ten feet, although smaller ones are reported occasionally. They are generally thought to be pre-*Homo sapiens* survivals, although some paraphysical theories have been proposed."

A Geo-Bibliography of Anomalies included *Fate, Vestigia Newsletter, Bigfoot News, Page Research Library Bulletin,* and many other Fortean journals in its bibliography. The book was hailed by reviewer Steve Hicks as a boon to researchers, "a reference work easy enough to use and fascinating enough to engage the interest of the most cursory browser."[2109]

Manlike Monsters on Trial

Manlike Monsters on Trial (1980) contains 20 papers presented at the *Anthropology of the Unknown: Sasquatch and Similar Phenomena* conference held in 1978. *The Sasquatch and Other Unknown Hominids* (1985) by Vladimir Markotić and Grover Krantz gave readers eight papers not included by Halpin: "Why There Has to be a Sasquatch" by Dr. Carleton Coon; "Sasquatch Believers vs. Skeptics" by Dr. Grover Krantz; "Theoretical Importance of Higher Sensory Development Toward Avoidance Behavior in the Sasquatch Phenomenon" by James R. Butler; "Analysis of the Patterson-Gimlin Film" by Dmitri Bayanov, Igor Bourtsev, and René Dahinden; "On Creating Un-Humans" by Grant Keddie; "American Humanity and Other Monsters" by Jay Miller; "Brief Ecological Description of the Caucasus Relic" by Marie-Jeanne Koffman; and "The Great Greek God Pan" by Markotić.

Reviewer George W. Earley was disappointed by *Manlike Monsters on Trial's* lack of papers arguing for the existence of Bigfoot. Writing in *Pursuit*, Earley wondered if the conference organizers had actually reached a conclusion before it began. "I looked for an open dialogue, not only on the possibility of the existence of the Sasquatch, but of the mind-set within the scientific establishment that makes searching for such mystery monsters so difficult that it must be the amateurs who do it while the professionals sit home denigrating those in the field."[2110]

Odyssey Research

During the '70s, John Lutz and members of Odyssey Research investigated hundreds of unusual events—Bigfoot, UFOs, and other unexplained phenomena including 1973's Sykesville Monster flap (see Chapter 4). Lutz, who worked as a dispatcher in Baltimore's Transit and Traffic division, told reporter Linda Duffield in 1980 about some of the aggravations he had encountered in his UFO investigations which closely paralleled obstacles Bigfoot researchers described in the '70s.

> Lutz and his cohort often encounter difficulties when trying to investigate UFO reports. Lutz says he feels the government covers up a lot of information it has about aerial spottings. And movies and television shows dealing with subjects such as UFOs "hurt true investigators more than they help."
>
> Lutz says the problem with such shows is that they take a number of reported cases and lump them together rather than deal with separate and specific occurrences.
>
> But perhaps the biggest obstacle, according to Lutz, is the attitude of the people first reporting the sightings. They are embarrassed, he says, "afraid of being ridiculed."[2111]

Whatever strange experiences a witness contacted by Odyssey Research had undergone, Lutz felt it was important to make personal contact and interview people as quickly after the event as possible. "The faster you get back to people, the more accurate the story is going to be," he told Duffield, "because if they think about [their experience] for 24, 48 or 72 hours, they tend to exaggerate a little bit more."[2112]

Enigma

Enigma was started in 1978 by chemist Mike Frizzell and parapsychologist Bob Lazzara to investigate and document claims of unexplained phenomena. Enigma had 10 active members and about a dozen associate members by 1980—many with academic credentials such as meteorology, astronomy, and chemistry. "We're a multi-interest group," Lazzara told a reporter in 1980, "and we usually can find someone with the right background and knowledge for whatever it is we're looking into. One of our members, for example, is a chemist who lives in Charlotte, N.C. A couple of months ago, he was asked to investigate a report of two purple 'blobs' that were found on somebody's front lawn. He tested them and discovered they were caused by residue from battery acid." Enigma divided oddities into three categories: natural, man-made, and purposeful hoaxes. According to Lazzara, only a small proportion of the cases Enigma investigated had no "logical explanation." Enigma investigators assessed the validity of reports by the uniqueness of the experience, the number of witnesses, and the witnesses' credibility.

Along with UFOs, Enigma had a keen organizational interest in Bigfoot. Their very first investigative effort was in Harford County, Maryland, where Lazzara said whatever was being experienced there in a Bigfoot-vein was "normally native to Maryland." During the bitter, blustery winter of '78, police received more than thirty reports of vandalism, strange tracks left in the snow, and eerie cries piercing the night. One of the most disturbing incidents that winter came from a Harford County farmer who claimed an unseen, unheard intruder had entered his chicken coop and dispatched half his flock. A few weeks later the unsettling act appeared to be repeated after a woman's rabbits—seventeen of them—were destroyed. Frizzell and Lazzara put a team together to look into the strange events; Lazzara had initially been skeptical but followed his compulsion to get involved and seek out the truth. "In spite of the sensationalism, there was a lot of sincerity to the witnesses, and some physical evidence, too," Lazzara recalled in 1985. "So we plotted a number of the incidents on a map, and began to see a pattern emerging."[2113]

> "Now, there were about twenty-four sightings that had been made in southern Pennsylvania around this time—all of them moving south in the vicinity of the river, which was packed with ice. Still, when they got into Maryland, I kept thinking that the region was just too populated for a creature like Sasquatch to survive. We studied some military survey maps

> of the terrain, and another member of the group took us up in his plane for an aerial view. That was when we realized that there were these dense, wooded corridors running off the river. Pretty rugged land for Maryland, and empty."
>
> On the basis of the earlier reports and his own research, Lazzara speculated that Rocks State Park, northwest of Bel Air, might be a likely spot for the creature to make an appearance. On the last Monday in February, the Enigma Project members and a few volunteers quietly embarked on their first expedition to the spot, half expecting to find a bear or a bobcat.[2114]

Within hours after entering the park, Enigma team members found a trail of 15-inch footprints in the snow which were followed for two miles before abruptly stopping at the edge of a stream. "They [the tracks] were fresh, made in virgin snow, and the terrain was so difficult I would have been almost impossible for someone to have perpetrated a hoax. The tracks were 15 to 17 inches long and about 6 inches deep. Whatever it was appeared to have three toes, but it's possible it could have been a five-toed animal with close-set toes.

"The most astounding thing was the stride," explained Lazzara. "Each of the tracks was about 5 feet apart. People who have seen the pictures we took of them say they were definitely not bear tracks, and it seems inconceivable that a normal man or woman could have made them running across that terrain. It would have been almost impossible not to fall." Enigma researchers had to go on all fours several times as they followed the tracks over the rough, treacherous ground.

"We think whatever it is may be coming into the state from Pennsylvania in search of food," Lazzara said. "It was seen an incredible number of times in the winter of 1978, and one possible explanation for that is the prolonged cold weather we had that winter. We think the river may have iced up and formed a bridge for the creature to cross into Maryland. There weren't anywhere near the number of unusual animal occurrences last year, and it may be because the winter was a lot milder."[2115]

Ogden Footprints

The Utah Division of Wildlife Resources cast two footprints discovered in a residential area of North Ogden near the home of a family that had reported being awakened early one morning by screams. Later, as the father was doing chores, he spotted the tracks near a ditch. The prints were 13 inches long and four inches wide and pressed over an inch into the wet soil. "I took my own foot and stamped hard into the mud by the ditch and the indentations only measured a half inch," Wildlife Resources official Ralph Blotter said. "We just can't estimate how much weight the animal carried to make such a print," said Blotter who suggested wet conditions when the prints were made might have created a softer substrate.

"If you want my opinion," Blotter said, "I don't think it was an animal because I don't know too many animals that walk around carrying toenail clippers." He referred to indications that the toenails of the print-maker had been clipped. Blotter also said that pad scars such as might be found on a dog print were not visible on the Ogden prints. Lines running through the casts resembled those of a human foot. "No one has ever seen him," Blotter said, referring to Bigfoot, "no droppings have been found and with all the people who go into the mountains and all our people on the job." The lack of acceptable evidence sealed the deal for Blotter. "I just don't see how it would be possible for him to exist," he said. "I guess if you believe in flying saucers, little green men on Mars and ghosts, then you can believe in Bigfoot," he concluded, adding that having some mysteries seemed necessary in modern life. "You don't want everything explained," Blotter said, "we still need to believe in Mickey Mouse."[2116]

Local Group Quietly Investigates Sightings

From his 1980 interview with Bigfoot investigator Kenneth Shepherd, reporter John Mosely wrote the Texas-based Bigfoot Investigation and Research Organization (BIRO) had been operating out of Paris and Dallas for ten years. The group sought a low profile in order to protect the confidentiality of persons filing reports with the organization. Shepherd said BIRO investigators had logged over 100 man-years investigating Bigfoot reports primarily in Texas, Oklahoma, Arkansas, and Louisiana. The most common catalyst for BIRO's field investigation was the examination of suspected Bigfoot footprints.

As mentioned above, in the first week of April 1980, BIRO conducted one of its more high-profile investigations as Shepherd, Charles Hignight, and John R. Shepherd (Kenneth's father) journeyed to Powderly, Texas, where large footprints had been discovered near a stock pond. Property owner and Game Warden Bill Milling assisted the BIRO team with its field work. After making several plaster casts and intensely studying the tracks,

BIRO members determined, as fellow-researchers in the Bigfoot Research Society had concluded, that the prints had been faked.

Reminiscing on his team's investigation, Shepherd told Mosely that the tracks were made by a person weighing less than 200 pounds and that a faint heel mark from a shoe was discernable upon close examination. "Whatever it was that someone used to make that print was made of a flexible material," Shepherd said. "It was especially flexible in the arch area and left a horizontal imprint in the bottom of the track."

In Shepherd's experience investigating Bigfoot reports, he found most witnesses didn't want to have their names associated with sightings of hairy man-like creatures. "We're familiar with such problems," Shepherd said. "That many times causes us to get reports second hand." BIRO was notably involved in the use of hypnosis in uncovering repressed details of a Bigfoot encounter.

> Hignight added that preparations are currently being made to clarify the details of one sighting in Red River County which occurred about six year ago.
>
> The witness, Hignight said, after several years and the resultant ridicule, has subconsciously induced a mild form of amnesia concerning the incident.
>
> Shepherd said the witness will be placed under regressive hypnosis and undergo psychological stress evaluation testing, which is considered more reliable than polygraph (lie detector) tests.[2117]

Bigfoot in Oklahoma (1980)

"I personally don't believe any such creature could exist in the United States today," said Sydney Wilkerson, head of the U.S. Fish and Wildlife Service's Tulsa office. "There's been just too much research, without turning up any real evidence, to give any indication of the existence of these creatures," he added. One resident of southeast Oklahoma said Bigfoot was real because he had seen it twice in his lifetime. Calling the creature "Hattak Lusa Chito" (big black man), the resident said his sightings of the creature occurred in an area bordered by the Yashaua Creek, the Mountain Fork River, and the Little River. *Tulsa World* outdoors writer Sam Powell wrote in his column that many residents in the area due east of Broken Bow who had lived there all their lives, stated flatly there was nothing to the stories other than fun campfire tales.[2118]

Strange Areas—Bridgewater Triangle

The Bermuda Triangle was popular in the 1970s, the mythology of its plane-downing, ship-swallowing characteristics well-known and sensationalized by writers like Charles Berlitz. On October 23, 1980, Loren Coleman and Peter Rodman discussed the strange events that occurred in the Bridgewater Triangle, sponsored by the Friends of the Library in Bridgewater. Slides accompanied their lecture on the defined area that encompassed south of Boston, north of New Bedford, and west of Plymouth; Route 24 runs through the heart of the area. From this area emerged reports of unusual phenomena such as: unidentifiable screeches, glowing balls of light in the air north of Taunton, and large footprints left in the snow from Taunton and Raynham.[2119]

Pennsylvania Prints: Bigfoot or Snowjob?

Scores of people hiked into the state game lands of Towanda, Pennsylvania, in early 1980 looking for the creature that left behind 17-inch tracks in the snow. The tracks were discovered on Wednesday, January 2, and readily fueled the interest of curiosity seekers. "That area was such a mess out there you couldn't see a thing," reported state conservation officer Ed Gallew who estimated that more than 100 people tramped around the forest Sunday, January 6 looking for additional tracks or their originator.[2120]

> TOWANDA, Pa. Giant footprints in the snow have been reported in southern Bradford County by loggers and hunters, but police and game officials are taking a wait-and-see attitude.
>
> "It looked just like human footprints," said Dale E. Vester. Vester, a Towanda logger who saw the prints after two hunters pointed them out, said: "If it was a practical joke, the guy must do it for a living."
>
> The prints turned up for about 100 feet along a road near New Albany, said Charles "Busty" Kellog, who also saw the trail. The prints disappeared into the woods near a spring alongside the road, he said.
>
> Jack Baker, general manager of WTTC radio, saw the footprints and said they had five toes and were flat, indicating that the foot had no arch.
>
> The prints measured 17 inches from heel to toe, Baker said, and the distance between them measured 4 feet, 9 inches.

The tracks turned up about a quarter mile from where he had been working, Vester said. Asked if he was concerned about meeting "Bigfoot" in the woods, he said: "I go out there every day. It doesn't bother me. If it's been out there all this time, it certainly hasn't been a problem."

Kellog also said he wasn't worried about meeting whatever made the tracks.

Ed Gallew, a state game conservation officer in Bradford County, said the only information he had on the prints came from news sources. "It never was officially reported to me at all by anybody," he said, adding that the area of the sighting, near the town of New Albany, is "quite a remote area, really rugged country."

State Game Commission spokesman Ted Godshall was skeptical about the sighting. "Every once in a while, we'll get reports of people finding animals that have been extinct for years—and so on," he said.[2121]

McArthur, Ohio, Sightings & Expedition

The McArthur, Ohio, sightings were probably the most talked about case of 1980.[2122] Based on reports of Bigfoot seen in southern Ohio, including the report of Larry E. Cottrill who said he saw three Bigfoot-like animals near McArthur on August 24 and shot at them (Cottrill believed he may have wounded one in the shoulder), René Debros and members of the North American Sasquatch Research team took to the woods of the Wayne National Forest on Saturday, October 4, 1980, to mount a Bigfoot expedition armed with cameras, "elephant" guns, and, reportedly, illegal sawed-off shotguns. As the weekend expedition progressed, the sheriff's department received calls asking for any updates on Debros' search. "Oh no. Bigfoot again?" moaned one dispatcher. "That's all we hear about. We've hung up a big picture of him here now." Sheriff Ronald Davis seemed to be weary of the Bigfoot flap. "This has been going on for a month. A lot of people from out West, Sasquatch experts and all, have been coming in and searching. We haven't heard a word about anything these people have found."[2123]

Asked about the catalyst for the Debros expedition, Davis admitted that he thought "there's something out there," but said he'd require more evidence in order to identify whatever it was. "A lot of people have been seeing it, but I'm out there a lot and I never saw anything." Davis stated the Debros team was warned they could be arrested for carrying sawed-off weapons. "They think they need them for self-defense," Davis said. "They say once before it (Bigfoot) turned on a tracker. But they also say it never hurts you if it's left alone."[2124]

Robert Gardiner of Columbus, Ohio, and several other hunters entered the Wayne National Forest west of McArthur to search for Bigfoot. After their foray was complete, Gardiner was convinced that at one time, he and his party had been surrounded by several Bigfoot creatures. "We had been to this deserted A-frame . . . and were looking in this ravine for tracks and didn't find anything," Gardiner said. "Later on . . . we came back to the A-frame and there were big tracks. These had to be made within an hour before we got there." Gardiner said the searching had been slow as the party managed through dense woods and underbrush. "We were looking at a specific sign on a tree," he said. "We found something on a tree. I'm not going to divulge what it is, but we were checking it out and we heard one bark." Gardiner said a Bigfoot sounded ape-like. "They have a barking-type growl like a chimpanzee or like a gorilla," Gardiner said. "We listened and then we heard one behind us, and what these two things were doing was communicating back and forth. They couldn't have been over 25 or 30 yards away from us." That was the point when Gardiner realized the creatures were on either side of his party. "One was between us and the other was on the other side of us," he stated. Gardiner thought that Bigfoot would normally pass through McArthur, but perhaps an injury to one of the creatures made them linger in the area.[2125]

In the wake of the McArthur sightings, an Ohio University professor of biological sciences stated Bigfoot sightings could be traced to "some weirdo psychology" as their true cause and averred all so-called evidence he had seen was "totally fake." Professor Gerald Svendsen had gone into the McArthur hills during the excitement in 1980 to see for himself purported Bigfoot tracks. He left unconvinced. "You can see the sand that was dug out alongside the track," he stated, adding there were "so many things wrong with the footprints that anybody with any experience in functional anatomy or zoology would know that." Svendsen said he had been guided to a spot where it was believed Bigfoot had bent down to drink from a stream. "What we have is a small-footed Bigfoot with variable toes," some prints numbering five and others showing six digits. He was also shown scratch marks on a tree which "were not done by any primate," he insisted, but perhaps scored into the bark by an object like a 16- or 20-penny nail.

"The only thing that can't be discounted is the testimonial evidence from people who reported seeing the creatures," he said. "If people want to see something," Svendsen reasoned, "they get it in their mind they are going to see it."[2126]

Vinton County Game Protector James Jamison also examined the evidence. "I'm not saying there is no such thing as a Bigfoot, but I don't think we have a Bigfoot here," he said. "A lot of people believe it. Maybe some are seeing something," Jamison said. "A person would be foolish to call them liars."[2127]

Footprints with Callus

Authorities in Johnstown, Pennsylvania, were perplexed at the discovery of a large footprint found near the home of the James Young family in Conemaugh Township. "If someone did this to play a practical joke, they did one fine job. It's beyond my understanding," said chief of police Kenneth Williamson. The full print measured over 17 inches long and 7 ½ inches wide and left a 3-inch depression behind the Young's home. The family reported recent instances of unexplained noises, foul odors, and fits of fierce, incessant barking from their four dogs. Police made a plaster cast of the print and according to Officer Ronald Pavie from East Conemaugh, it was similar to prints associated with a Bigfoot sighting he investigated three years prior. "What got us was that right behind the big toe on the ball of the foot appears to be a callus," Williamson said. "I'm not going to say this was a hoax, and I'm not going to say it's real. I have to be convinced."[2128]

Cindy Barone Encounter

A large, mysterious creature visited several Yale, Michigan, homes in the latter months of 1981, notably returning on several occasions to William and Cindy Barone's farm.

> Cindy Barone says it's not the torn-down fences nor the barn doors that have been ripped off their hinges, nor is it the high-pitched screaming her family often hears at night. "It's the unknown that scares us," she said. "If I knew what it was, I'd deal with it somehow."
>
> The Barone farm is located in Michigan's "Thumb," properly called the Upper Peninsula. Mrs. Barone, 33, said her

> first encounter with the "unknown" came last September when her neighbor's barn door was ripped off its hinges. "I've had fences torn down and grain barrels dumped over and eaten," she said. Her dogs have raced off into the dark, chasing after a presumed intruder, and the farm animals have been spooked by an unseen presence many times. Then came that Friday night in mid-November:
>
> Tina Barone, 13, and her sister, Roxanne, 12, went to the barn to do chores.[2129]

A story in the tabloid *Weekly World News* provided the details of Tina's extreme, up-close encounter.

> Tina and other members of her family heard the beast's hideous shrieks outside their home several times before the night of her shocking ordeal.
>
> "It was a real high-pitched cry, like nothing I ever heard before," the girl recalled. "It came from one part of the yard and then another part, like something was running around all over the place.
>
> "We never saw it though—until that night I touched it."
>
> Near dusk on that day, Tina and Roxanne were at home with their mother Cindy. Suddenly they heard a wild clamor in the barn. "I went out to check on the horses and goats, and Roxanne was right behind me," Tina said.
>
> "I went into the barn and it was dark in there, so I reached out to turn on the light.
>
> "My hand hit something, so I took off my glove and reached put again."
>
> Then came the moment of horror that Tina will never forget.
>
> "With my bare hand I touched something strange, with fur about an inch thick," she said. "It was all matted down and filthy. I thought at first it was a goat, but then I heard this heavy breathing and something hovered over me—some kind of huge, eerie animal like a huge ape.
>
> "Its eyes were bright red and it glared down at me. It was gigantic.
>
> "I actually had my hands in its fur!"

> The girls ran to the house and told their mom and cousin David, 18, that there was a strange beast in the barn. Mrs. Barone and David then drove to the barn in the family station wagon.
>
> "We dreaded what we might discover, but we had to have a look for ourselves," David said.
>
> "At first we didn't see anything. And then I saw it—a big, furry beast with long arms, hunched over at the back of the barn in the shadows.
>
> "We froze, but it ran away and was gone."
>
> Wayne King, director of the Michigan-Canadian Bigfoot Information Center, said Tina is the first person who's ever touched a savage Bigfoot and survived.
>
> "It's an amazing, historic encounter," he said.[2130]

According to the *Detroit Free Press,* Wayne King referred to his organization as the Michigan-Canadian Bigfoot Information Center by 1981. King was particularly excited by the flesh-to-fur contact between Tina and a presumed Bigfoot, an experience he believed was unprecedented. "It's the first time in Canada and the United States that anyone has touched one of these creatures," he said. "We got a physical encounter. This is what makes this very unique."[2131]

> Cindy Barone wishes those tales would remain in the Himalayas.
>
> "We stated one thing, and everybody's magnifying it," she said, referring to publicity generated by King. "It's a big, hairy animal, and they're adding the rest." Her children were harassed in school, she said, after stories about the big, hairy animal appeared in area newspapers.
>
> King refused to say how he learned of the Barones. "I have a numbers of sources that keep me informed," he said, of animals appearing under "suspicious circumstances, things that can't be explained out. We don't work on phenomena at all—UFOs or Loch Ness monsters. We're dealing with what we believe to be a species of ape, nothing more. . . . People associate this animal with a monster, which it is not.
>
> "From what we've been able to confirm," King said, [S]asquatches "vary between seven to eight feet tall and between 450 and 600 pounds." They walk upright on two feet, King said.

> Cindy Barone says she has seen bears walking upright on two feet at the zoo and contends she never referred to the animal as Bigfoot or a [S]asquatch.
>
> But King, who met with the Barones Nov. 7 and took statements from them, contends they weren't so sure then that the creature in question was a bear. He said he offered to hold "an overnight vigil" on the Barones' property "to lure and bait" the [S]asquatch, but William Barone, Cindy's husband, "refused to give me permission."[2132]

The Barones' encounter continued to make news years after the media's initial suggestions the family had experienced close contact with a Bigfoot. As reported in the June 3, 1983, *Times Herald* of Port Huron, Michigan, Cindy Barone maintained she had never claimed that Bigfoot visited her family's farm; instead she had thought from the start the creature was a bear.

> But after reports of the animal leaked out in September 1981, dozens of newspapers, radio and television stations throughout the country began calling the Barones, wanting to know more about Bigfoot.
>
> They received calls from Bigfoot investigators, scientists and what Barone called "kooks." She said some of the calls were threatening and frightening.
>
> They posted 'No Trespassing' signs on their property to keep the curious out.
>
> The final straw came when a psychic from Ohio tried to hypnotize Barone over the telephone. He believed the animal was supernatural and that she could communicate with it telepathically.
>
> "When I hung up the sweat was pouring off me and I was shaking all over. That was when my husband said, 'That's it, we're getting our number changed,'" she said.[2133]

Booger Legend: Good Fun, Good for Business

> "Run through the bushes and run through the trees.
> "Mr. Bardin Booger, don't get me please."
>
> —Billy Crain, country-Western composer[2134]

"It's a lot of fun. That's what we get out of it, a lot of fun. But I'm not going to say that people don't see what they say they see," said Norma Key, owner and operator with her husband Bud of Bud's Grocery, the only business in Bardin, Florida.[2135]

The Keys styled themselves as Official Bardin Booger Sighting Recorders and sold hats and t-shirts depicting an artist's rendering of the creature, a caricature which carried a lantern which the Keys explained was based on several reports of a light moving through the woods at night.

Bud said he saw something through his porch's screen door that was "big and furry" when he was a child. His father demonstrated to the young Bud that he had been frightened by reflections of leaves rustling in the moonlight. "Sometimes you see what you want to see out there," Bud said.

An AP article stated the Booger sightings increased in February 1981 after an article appeared in the Palatka newspaper.

"Nobody said they leave table scraps out for him," said a critical Doug Crews of an August 1982 article, "We Live with Bigfoot," which appeared in the national tabloid *Weekly World News*. "The stories get bigger and bigger. Some reporters don't stick to the facts," stated Bailey Glisson who was prepared to provide the skinny on the Booger. "I'll tell you what it is. It's all a lot of baloney. The real Bardin Booger is a man I know who likes to fool people, mostly fox hunters," Glisson said. "Either he or another man, I'm not going to tell you their names, get dressed up in a bearskin and let the fox hunters see them."[2136]

René Dahinden—Last Word

For an article cover-featured on the Spring 1985 edition of the International Society of Cryptozoology's *Newsletter,* editor J. Richard Greenwell interviewed René Dahinden, at the time well on his way to starting his fourth decade studying Bigfoot, and who had remained one of the most prominent Bigfoot researchers at any time since the subject's study was taken up in earnest in the 1950s. Herein Dahinden provides insights into his personal search, shares a learned opinion on the state of post-1970s Bigfoot study, and gives us the final word on this closing chapter.

> GREENWELL: You've been studying the whole problem of Sasquatch or Bigfoot since 1956. You've had a lot of information come your way, you've seen it all and heard it all, right?

Dahinden: Close to it.

Greenwell: What's your perception, after all these years, as to where Sasquatch research—if one can it that—stands today? Where are we at?

Dahinden: I think that we need to proceed by stages: one, two, three, four. I think we're past the first stage, which is consideration of the historical evidence found in old newspapers, journals, totem poles, Indian legends, and oral tradition. First, we had to determine if there were, in fact, historical references to Sasquatch. We're now at stage two, which involves present day eye-witness reports, footprints, the Patterson movie, and so forth. We can dissect this stage a little, and address eyewitness reliability, and so forth. Stage three involves getting actual physical evidence.

Greenwell: And how do you propose to go about getting that?

Dahinden: Well, we either wait for a hunter to pop one off, or a truck driver or somebody to run over one, and then have the nerve to step out and pick it up, or we go out ourselves and try to find a dead one or collect a live one.

Greenwell: So it really boils down to a statistical problem; that is, what is the probability, after so many years, with X number of people in the field, hunters and so on, that one would not have been shot or hit by a car? And how long can that last? And also, doesn't that sort of look bad for the case for Sasquatch?

Dahinden: Well, the only argument against the existence of Sasquatch, in my view, is how come one of them hasn't been collected, especially by somebody shooting it? Hunters and so on. Well, I have an argument against that: the emotional shock of seeing something like that could stop a man from actually shooting. I've said often enough that, among the so-called Bigfoot hunters, they go either one way or the other:

they flipflop completely on the side that the creature exists, they get to be believers because, either through emotional commitment or by looking at all the eyewitness accounts and other evidence, they come to the conclusion that it exists.

From then on, they have no doubt that any report coming their way is another piece of evidence. They become believers, and they become very gullible, to put it bluntly. They accept anything, either because they are unable to evaluate it, or because they don't want it, or because they don't want to, because they either want to stick it in a book, or they just like to collect reports. Over the years, I've been going in the opposite direction. I'm getting more cynical and ruthless as time passes, for the very simple reason that, if the damn thing exists, how come in all these years we really have not produced more evidence?

GREENWELL: If you had to assign a probability to a large unknown species, a primate species, surviving like this in North America, what would your probability be? More or less than 50 percent?

DAHINDEN: I would say, looking at all my personal experiences, all the eyewitnesses I've talked to, the footprints I've seen, the Patterson film I investigated, taking everything into consideration, I would say that such animals exist. I have never heard a damn argument, which was based on anything sound, that would indicate to me that Sasquatch does not exist. Some jokers say everybody who claims to see a Sasquatch is a nut, a mental case, he saw a bear or had an hallucination, without, of course, meeting the witness; that the footprints were all faked—of course, they never show how they could be faked in such a realistic manner. I'm not talking about a small number of footprints. I'm talking about hundreds of them. All in a line, straight, where you can see all kinds of variations and toe positions and everything else. Then you have the Patterson film. Nobody has ever shown me how it was faked. I know all about that film. I know as much as Patterson did, except, of course, I don't know for sure if it is real.

Greenwell: So you would assign it a probability of higher than 50 percent?

Dahinden: Everything points to the thing existing. . . .

Greenwell: You must find it exciting, this search. Although you say you don't give a damn about science, it seems that there is a burning curiosity motivating you.

Dahinden: Look, I heard about Sasquatch, I was told it was there, so I thought I'd go and get one. Grab him by the ass and bring him home to mother. Well, that was almost 30 years ago. I didn't know who was telling the truth or who wasn't. Then you collect all this stuff. It was hard to pinpoint what made a sighting good, and what made a witness bad.

There's a mystery to be solved, and I want to help solve it. Let me put it this way. It's not the money as such. I don't walk around with dollar signs in my eyes. I'm speaking of money as a weapon, maybe, because when you have money it opens more doors. Then, you want to know if you are right, and of course I want to be the one who gets it.

You go through various stages in this business. First there was a sense of adventure. Then it got some publicity. Looking back on it, maybe that kind of fueled it a little. Then a certain stubbornness, expectations of a quick glory—I still remember that 1959-1960 Slick expedition, when we thought one of them would be popping from behind a tree any minute. I kept a shell in my gun all the time! Then you kind of get that knocked out of you, and then it's up and down, promises of support which never come, and this and that. So you get yo-yo'd up and down. Finally, I think you get to the point where I am today, where you reach a certain stage where you are an expert. I hate like hell to say that, but it's true. Because you have been at it longer, because you know more. Not because the others are stupid. I think the stage I'm in now is just a dull, unexciting, steady search—it might not sound like it. You went up and down, and now you are just on a steady line, just constantly pushing, just going down this road without really getting emotional. You sometimes get excited a little bit, but not like it was at one time.

Greenwell: Do you see younger people going through those same stages today?

Dahinden: Yes.

Greenwell: Don't you sometimes miss those earlier days, though?

Dahinden: That's just like young people asking you, "Wouldn't you like to be young again?" Would you? Go through all that horse— again?[2137]

APPENDIX I
BIGFOOT GROUPS IN THE 1970S

Group	Contact
Abominable Snowmen Club of America	Roger Patterson
American Anthropological Research	Ted Ernst
American Association of Meta-Science	Tom Bearden
American Yeti Expedition	Robert W. Morgan
Angeles Sasquatch Association	
B-F Enterprises	Tom Biscardi and Findley
Bigfoot Fund, Inc.	Jim McClarin
Bigfoot Investigation and Research Org.	Kenneth Shepherd
Bigfoot Investigations	A. Hilsmeier & M. Asselin
Bigfoot Research, Inc.	Cliff LaBreque
Bigfoot Research Society	
Bigfoot Research Society of Dallas	R. & T. Throneberry
Flora-Fauna Research Corp.	Lee Trippett
High Desert Sasquatch Research Team	Ron Bailey
International Sasquatch Society	Edd Kaye
Michigan Bigfoot Information Center	Wayne King
Minnesota Bigfoot Center	
North American Wildlife Research	Ron Olsen
Odyssey Scientific Research	John A. Lutz
Pacific Coast Primate Research	Gordon Kliewer
Project Discovery	Richard (Dick) Grover**
Project Bigfoot	Jon Eric Beckjord
Project Grendel	Jon Eric Beckjord
Sasquatch Investigation of Mid-America*	H. Hewes & Bob Stamps
Sasquatch Research Corporation	Bob Stamps
Society for the Identification and Protection of Bigfoot	Jon Eric Beckjord

Society for the Investigation of the Unexplained	Ivan T. Sanderson
Southeastern Wildlife Research Association	Jim Vincent
South Mountain Research Group	Ramona Hibner
The Understanding Inc., Unit #85 – Research and Investigation of UFO, Bigfoot and Related Phenomena	Pat Macey
Vanguard	Robert Morgan
Vestigia	Dr. C. Louis Wiedemann & Robert Jones
Western Society for the Explanation of the Unexplained	Terry Albright
Westmoreland County UFO Study Group	Stan Gordon group
Yeti Evaluation and Technological Investigators	Ramona Hibner
Yeti Research Society	Gordon Prescott

* A division of the Sasquatch Research Corporation

** Project Discovery was started in 1973 by Dick Grover. The goals of Project Discovery were: 1. To solve the mystery of the Bigfoot or Sasquatch for the benefit of man. 2. To bring together as a powerful force, investigators and people who wish to specialize in solving the mystery without any thought of monetary gain. 3. To coordinate and deseminate [sic] information for the people at large. 4. To develop a mutual trust between active people in the group and those living in Bigfoot regions. [http://www.bfro.net/gdb/show_article.asp?id=205]

APPENDIX II
MOVIES AND TELEVISION EPISODES WITH BIGFOOT-LIKE CHARACTERS

Title	Year
Bigfoot	1970
Scooby Doo, Where Are You? ["That's Snow Ghost"]	1970
Skullduggery	1970
Trog	1970
El Yeti	1970
Geek	1971
Bigfoot: Man or Beast?	1972
Horror Express	1972
Legend of Boggy Creek	1972
Scooby Doo Meets Laurel and Hardy	1972
Schlock!	1973
Zoo Robbery	1973
Beachcombers "The Sasquatch Walks by Night"	1974
Beauties and the Beast	1974
Kolchak ["The Spanish Moss Murders"]	1974
Land of the Lost ["Ancient Guardian"]	1974
Land of the Lost ["Abominable Snowman"]	1974
Shriek of the Mutilated	1974
Beast	1975
Ghost Busters ["The Abominable Snowman"]	1975

Isis ["Bigfoot"]	1975
Monsters! Mysteries or Myths	1975
Werewolf and the Yeti	1975
Sasqua	1975
Creature from Black Lake	1976
In Search of . . . (Multiple Episodes)	1976
Legend of the Bigfoot	1976
Legend of McCullough's Mountain	1976
Myserious Monsters	1976
Six Million Dollar Man (Multiple Episodes)	1976
Wildman of the Woods	1976
Bigfoot and Wildboy	1977
Bionic Woman ["The Return of Bigfoot Part 2"]	1977
Curse of Bigfoot	1977
Don McCune Library	1977
Forest Story	1977
Mighty Peking Man	1977
Pampalini Lowca Zwierzqt	1977
Return to Boggy Creek	1977
Sasquatch, the Legend of Bigfoot	1977
Snowbeast	1977
Star Wars	1977
Yeti: Giant of the 20th Century	1977
Battle of the Planets ["The Alien Bigfoot"]	1978
Bloodstalkers	1978
The Force Beyond	1978
Godzilla and the Super 90 ["The Sub-Zero Terror"]	1978
Incredible Hulk ["The Antowuk Horror"]	1978
Manbeast! Myth or Monster	1978
Bigfoot Meets the Thing	1979
Capture of Bigfoot	1979

Prophecy	1979
Revenge of Bigfoot	1979
Screams of a Winter's Night	1979
Altered States	1980
Arthur C. Clarke's Mysterious World ["The Missing Ape"]	1980
Berenstein Bears Meet Bigpaw	1980
Bugs Bunny's Bustin' Out All Over ["Spaced Out Bunny"]	1980
Empire Strikes Back	1980
Night of the Demon	1980
Spaced Out Bunny	1980
Tanya's Island	1980

APPENDIX III
BIGFOOT COOKBOOK

Bigfoot 'Happy Camp' Apple Crisp

Preheat oven to 350° F
¼ cup sifted enriched flour
¼ cup margarine or butter
¾ cup raw sugar
1 Tablespoon cinnamon
½ Tablespoon nutmeg
Pinch or three of salt
5 cups chunked apples (Golden Delicious recommended)
1 teaspoon cream cheese (omitted if tastes prefer)

Mix the margarine, raw sugar, flour, spices, and cream cheese.

Over an oiled or greased pan, spread out the apple chunks and press the crumbly mixture firmly into pan.

Bake about 50 minutes.

Serves well with ice cream. Variations include swapping brown sugar for raw sugar.

Source: Brougher, Brad. *The Original Bigfoot Cookbook* (Salem, Oregon: ABC Printers, Inc., 1978): 30.

Boyd Brougher's *The Original Bigfoot Cookbook* contains recipes intended to fit a cast iron Bigfoot pan that came with the book. "I got the idea from doing research on Bigfoot and observing all the casts made of Bigfoot feet," said Brougher. The pan's interior dimensions closely matched the standard 9 x 13 x 2-inch baking pan. Along with Bigfoot 'Happy Camp' Apple Crisp, other recipes included Bigfoot Pizza, Bigfoot Bread Pudding, and Bigfoot 'Stomping Good' Carrot Cake.

Brougher was a former Mr. Oregon (1957) and had contributed to *Logger's World* magazine. A friend of Ron Olson's, Brougher interspersed information about Bigfoot through the recipes. At the time of his cookbook's publishing, Brougher ran a day care, Kandy Kastle, in Salem. It was the day care experience and raising his own four daughters that gave him the idea for the book. "The daycare kids love to cook," he stated. "There is a lot of prestige to helping with the cooking and it is something they really look forward to doing."[2138]

ENDNOTES

1 "Hairy Tribe of Wild Men Found in Vancouver," *Shamokin News-Dispatch* (Shamokin, Pennsylvania) (July 6, 1934): 9.

2 "Hairy Tribe of Wild Men Found in Vancouver," *Shamokin News-Dispatch* (Shamokin, Pennsylvania) (July 6, 1934): 9.

3 MacGillivray, Alex. "Shouldn't Be Captured—'Nothing Monstrous About Sasquatch,' Says Their Pal," *Vancouver Sun* (May 25, 1957): 14.

4 Murphy, Christopher L. *Meet the Sasquatch* (Blaine, Washington: Hancock House Pub., Ltd., 2004): 38.

5 "Report Monster Wild Men Roaming British Columbia," *Racine Journal-Times* (October 7, 1935): 2.

6 Burns, J. W. "The Sasquatch," *Chilliwack Progress* (January 6, 1937): 4.

7 Frank, Scott. "Nestling on the Shores of Harrison Lake," *Arlington Times* (January 23, 2002): C1.

8 "Sasquatch Days, Harrison May 23-24," *Chilliwack Progress* (March 30, 1938): 5.

9 "Bold Fellows at Harrison Lake, Says Torchy Anderson," *Chilliwack Progress* (May 11, 1938): 9.

10 "'Hairy Ones' Honored By Indians—2,000 Tribesmen Gather for Fete," *Daily Argus-Leader* (Sioux Falls, South Dakota) (May 23, 1938): 2.

11 "Indian Ceremonial Honors Hairy Legendary Creatures," *Reading Eagle* (Reading, Pennsylvania) (May 23, 1938): 12.

12 "Thousand Dollar Costume for Hon. Wells Gray as Chief Sasquatch," *Chilliwack Progress* (May 18, 1938): 1.

13 Burns, J. W. "Hon. Wells Gray Now 'Siam Chee'quets Sasquatch'," *Chilliwack Progress* (May 25, 1938): 1.

14 "$10,000 Fire in Harrison Tie Mill," *Chilliwack Progress* (May 25, 1938): 1.

15 "Sasquatch to Belly-Flop at Gala," *Chilliwack Progress* (August 13, 1941): 1.

16 Buhs, Joshua Blu. *Bigfoot: The Life and Times of a Legend* (Chicago: University of Chicago Press, 2009): 57.

17 "1941 Edition of Sasquatch Twice as Big as Predecessors," *Chilliwack Progress* (October 29, 1941): 1.

18 "Publicity," *Chilliwack Progress* (November 26, 1941): 2.
19 Dahinden, René with Don Hunter. *Sasquatch* (New York: Signet, 1975): 74.
20 Greenwell, J. Richard. *ISC Newsletter* (Summer, 1985).
21 Dahinden, René with Don Hunter. *Sasquatch* (New York: Signet, 1975): 75.
22 Dahinden, René with Don Hunter. *Sasquatch* (New York: Signet, 1975): 77.
23 Burns, J. W. "Explorers on Mighty Sasquatch Trail," *Chilliwack Progress* (February 1, 1956): 1.
24 Burns, J. W. "Explorers on Mighty Sasquatch Trail," *Chilliwack Progress* (February 1, 1956): 1.
25 "Sasquatch Sighted? Search Given Impetus," *Chilliwack Progress* (May 9, 1956): 19.
26 "Weather Difficult for Sasquatch Hunt," *Chilliwack Progress* (June 20, 1956): 8.
27 "Harrison," *Chilliwack Progress* (June 27, 1956): 2.
28 "He Wants to Trace Legendary B. C. Giant," *Winnipeg Free Press* (March 5, 1957).
29 "Sasquatch Would be a Problem if Found," *Chilliwack Progress* (March 20, 1957): 2.
30 "Chilliwack Seeks Share in Sasquatch Promotion," *Chilliwack Progress* (March 27, 1957): 2.
31 "Chilliwack Seeks Share in Sasquatch Promotion," *Chilliwack Progress* (March 27, 1957): 2.
32 "Chilliwack Seeks Share in Sasquatch Promotion," *Chilliwack Progress* (March 27, 1957): 2.
33 "Board Claims that Sasquatch Are Human," *Chilliwack Progress* (April 3, 1957): 19.
34 "Sasquatch Call on Commissioner," *Chilliwack Progress* (April 3, 1957): 20.
35 "Community Portrait: Jack Kirkman . . . no Sasquatch," *Chilliwack Progress* (April 3, 1957): 10.
36 "Ontario Woman May Hunt Sasquatch," *Chilliwack Progress* (April 10, 1957): 7.
37 "Sasquatch Like 'Em Pudgy," *Winnipeg Free Press* (April 12, 1957): 6.
38 "Ontario Woman May Hunt Sasquatch," *Chilliwack Progress* (April 10, 1957): 7.
39 "Immigrant Defies Scorn to Seek B. C.'s Lost Race," *Ottawa Citizen* (April 12, 1957): 11.
40 "Immigrant Defies Scorn to Seek B. C.'s Lost Race," *Ottawa Citizen* (April 12, 1957): 11.
41 "Swiss Mountain Climber Leader Sasquatch Hunt," *Medicine Hat News* (April 23, 1957).
42 "Maybe Some of Our Best Friends are Sasquatch," *Winnipeg Free Press* (April 11, 1957): 19.
43 Lampert, Herbert. "Pretty Miss Offers to Trail Sasquatch," *Gazette* (Montreal, Québec) (April 24, 1957): 22.
44 "Ex-Manager Quotes Tales of Sasquatch," *Chilliwack Progress* (April 24, 1957): 15.
45 "What Others Say—West's Own Monster," *Ogden Standard-Examiner* (October 31, 1959): 4.
46 Hutchison, Bruce. "Beware the Sasquatch," *Winnipeg Free Press* (April 24, 1957).

47 Hutchison, Bruce. "Beware the Sasquatch," *Winnipeg Free Press* (April 24, 1957).
48 "Sasquatch Search Cost $15,000," *Chilliwack Progress* (May 1, 1957): 1.
49 "No Centennial Funds for Giant Hunt," *Chilliwack Progress* (May 8, 1957): 9.
50 MacGillivray, Alex. "Shouldn't Be Captured—'Nothing Monstrous About Sasquatch,' Says Their Pal," *Vancouver Sun* (May 25, 1957): 14.
51 "Giants Real? Certainly, Says Reeve," *Chilliwack Progress* (May 29, 1957): 15.
52 "Cave Merely Indian Lookout," *Chilliwack Progress* (June 26, 1957): 7.
53 "Still Search for Sasquatch Sponsors," *Chilliwack Progress* (July 3, 1957): 7.
54 "Sasquatch Gets His Price Cut," *Winnipeg Free Press* (October 12, 1957): 2.
55 "Ex-Logger Claims He Was Held Six Days by Sasquatch Family," *Chilliwack Progress* (March 26, 1958): 11.
56 Downton, Eric. "Canadian Version of 'Snowman'," *Steubenville Herald-Star* (August 18, 1959): 6.
57 "Ivan Sanderson, Naturalist, Dies," *New York Times* (February 21, 1973): 46.
58 Kirkpatrick, Dick. "The Search for Bigfoot," *National Wildlife* (April-May 1968): 45.
59 Pendergast, Tom. *Creating the Modern Man: American Magazines and Consumer Culture*, 1900-1950 (Columbia: University of Missouri Press, 2000): 238.
60 Sanderson, Ivan T. "What Could UFOs Be," (Introduction to *Uninvited Visitors*: A Biologist Looks at UFOs (1967)) accessed September 7, 2017 at www.noufors.com/Documents/sanderson.pdf
61 Sanderson, Ivan T. "What Could UFOs Be," (Introduction to *Uninvited Visitors*: A Biologist Looks at UFOs (1967)) accessed September 7, 2017 at www.noufors.com/Documents/sanderson.pdf
62 "Huge Monster Stalks Wilds of California, Loggers Say," *Milwaukee Journal* (October 6, 1958): 10.
63 Davis, Don. "Bigfoot and Betty Allen," BigfootEncounters.com. http://www.bigfootencounters.com/articles/bettyallen.htm
64 Place, Marian T. *On the Track of Bigfoot* (New York: Dodd, Mead & Company, 1974): 21.
65 Place, Marian T. *On the Track of Bigfoot* (New York: Dodd, Mead & Company, 1974): 22.
66 Place, Marian T. *On the Track of Bigfoot* (New York: Dodd, Mead & Company, 1974): 23.
67 Place, Marian T. *On the Track of Bigfoot* (New York: Dodd, Mead & Company, 1974): 23.
68 Davis, Don. "Bigfoot and Betty Allen," BigfootEncounters.com. http://www.bigfootencounters.com/articles/bettyallen.htm
69 Place, Marian T. *On the Track of Bigfoot* (New York: Dodd, Mead & Company, 1974): 21.
70 Sanderson, Ivan T. "The Strange Story of America's Abominable Snowman," *True* (December 1959): 42.
71 Davis, Don. "Bigfoot and Betty Allen," BigfootEncounters.com. http://www.bigfootencounters.com/articles/bettyallen.htm
72 Place, Marian T. *On the Track of Bigfoot* (New York: Dodd, Mead & Company, 1974): 23-24.
73 Place, Marian T. *On the Track of Bigfoot* (New York: Dodd, Mead & Company, 1974): 24.
74 Place, Marian T. *On the Track of Bigfoot* (New York: Dodd, Mead & Company, 1974): 24-25.

75 "Huge Monster Stalks Wilds of California, Loggers Say," *Milwaukee Journal* (October 6, 1958): 10.

76 Place, Marian T. *On the Track of Bigfoot* (New York: Dodd, Mead & Company, 1974): 25.

77 "Huge Monster Stalks Wilds of California, Loggers Say," *Milwaukee Journal* (October 6, 1958): 10.

78 Place, Marian T. *On the Track of Bigfoot* (New York: Dodd, Mead & Company, 1974): 25.

79 "Huge Monster Stalks Wilds of California, Loggers Say," *Milwaukee Journal* (October 6, 1958): 10.

80 Knutson, Ted. "They Counted Calories by the Thousands," *Pittsburgh Press Sunday Magazine* (February 12, 1984): 2.

81 Knutson, Ted. "They Counted Calories by the Thousands," *Pittsburgh Press Sunday Magazine* (February 12, 1984): 3.

82 Carranco, Links. "The Humboldt Historian," Humboldt.edu. http://library.humboldt.edu/humco/holdings/carranco.htm.

83 Carranco, Links. "The Humboldt Historian," Humboldt.edu. http://library.humboldt.edu/humco/holdings/carranco.htm.

84 Carranco, Links. "The Humboldt Historian," Humboldt.edu. http://library.humboldt.edu/humco/holdings/carranco.htm.

85 "Lakewood One-Man Army Routs 100 Japs, Kills 20," *Youngstown Vindicator* (September 30, 1943).

86 Carranco, Links. "The Humboldt Historian," Humboldt.edu. http://library.humboldt.edu/humco/holdings/carranco.htm.

87 Carranco, Links. "The Humboldt Historian," Humboldt.edu. http://library.humboldt.edu/humco/holdings/carranco.htm.

88 Carranco, Links. "The Humboldt Historian," Humboldt.edu. http://library.humboldt.edu/humco/holdings/carranco.htm.

89 Carranco, Links. "The Humboldt Historian," Humboldt.edu. http://library.humboldt.edu/humco/holdings/carranco.htm.

90 Bemis, Rocky. "The Rocky Bemis Story with Old Articles," BigfootEncounters.com. http://www.bigfootencounters.com/stories/rocky.htm

91 Place, Marian T. *On the Track of Bigfoot* (New York: Dodd, Mead & Company, 1974): 40.

92 Driscoll, John. "Birth of Bigfoot," *Times-Standard* (Eureka, California). Times-Standard.com. http://www.times-standard.com/ci_10853838.

93 Genzoli, Andrew. "RFD," *Humboldt Times* (October 1, 1961): 5.

94 Chambers, Bill. "Eye-Witnesses See Bigfoot," *Humboldt Standard* (October 15, 1958): 1.

95 "Bigfoot Tracks Through Ages Says UC Professor," *Humboldt Standard* (October 14, 1958): 1.

96 Allen, Betty. "Bigfoot Still on March as Experts Try Explanations," *Humboldt Times* (October 31, 1958). BigfootEncounters.com. http://www.bigfootencounters.com/articles/humboldt_times1958.htm.

97 Carranco, Links. "The Humboldt Historian," Humboldt.edu. http://library.humboldt.edu/humco/holdings/carranco.htm.

98 Murphy, Christopher L. *Meet the Sasquatch* (Blaine, Washington: Hancock House Pub. Ltd., 2004): 38-39.

99 "Nicholas Man in Area of Search for Giant," *Beckley Post-Herald* (December 23, 1959): 6.

100 "Nicholas Man in Area of Search for Giant," *Beckley Post-Herald* (December 23, 1958): 6.

101 Holmstrom, David. "Search for 'Bigfoot' Goes On," *Oakland Tribune* (March 24, 1973): E9.

102 Green John. *Sasquatch: The Apes Among Us* (Blaine, Washington: Hancock House, 1979): 69-70.

103 "Humboldt's 'Bigfoot' Tracks Seen Again," *Medford Mail Tribune* (Medford, Oregon) (June 29, 1960): 5.

104 "Big Foot Stomps Around Again Near Bluff Creek," *Humboldt Standard* (June 23, 1960): 32.

105 "Big Foot Stomps Around Again Near Bluff Creek," *Humboldt Standard* (June 23, 1960): 32.

106 "Big Foot Stomps Around Again Near Bluff Creek," *Humboldt Standard* (June 23, 1960): 32.

107 Genzoli, Andrew. "RFD," *Humboldt Times* (February 11, 1961): 11.

108 Wright, Glen. "Bigfoot Legend Persists," *Kansas City Times* (November 22, 1973): G2.

109 Genzoli, Andrew. "Redwood Country," *Times-Standard* (Eureka, California) (April 19, 1974): 11.

110 "'Bigfoot Daze' at Willow Creek on Labor Day," *Humboldt Standard* (July 25, 1960): 13.

111 "'Big Foot Daze' Coming to Willow Creek," *Humboldt Standard* (August 26, 1965): 9.

112 Genzoli, Andrew. "Redwood Country," *Times-Standard* (Eureka, California) (August 14, 1970).

113 "Western Mountain 'Ape' Legend Growing," *Daily Messenger* (Canandaigua, New York) (July 1, 1964): 12.

114 "Western Mountain 'Ape' Legend Growing," *Daily Messenger* (Canandaigua, New York) (July 1, 1964): 12.

115 Beck, Fred. *I Fought the Apemen of Mt. St. Helens* (1967): 10.

116 Beck, Fred. *I Fought the Apemen of Mt. St. Helens* (1967): 2.

117 Beck, Fred. *I Fought the Apemen of Mt. St. Helens* (1967): 2.

118 Beck, Fred. *I Fought the Apemen of Mt. St. Helens* (1967): 2.

119 Beck, Fred. *I Fought the Apemen of Mt. St. Helens* (1967): 3.

120 Beck, Fred. *I Fought the Apemen of Mt. St. Helens* (1967): 4.

121 Beck, Fred. *I Fought the Apemen of Mt. St. Helens* (1967): 7.

122 Beck, Fred. *I Fought the Apemen of Mt. St. Helens* (1967): 10.

123 Kidder, Karl M. "McLane Teacher Finds Trail of Elusive 'Bigfoot' in Siskiyous," *Fresno Bee* (September 15, 1964): 4.

124 Kidder, Karl M. "McLane Teacher Finds Trail of Elusive 'Bigfoot' in Siskiyous," *Fresno Bee* (September 15, 1964): 4.

125 Kirkpatrick, Dick "The Search for Bigfoot," *National Wildlife* (April-May 1968): 45.

126 Daegling, David. *Bigfoot Exposed: An Anthropologist Examines America's Enduring Legend* (Walnut Creek, California: AltaMira Press, 2004): 105.

127 Hancock, David. "The Sasquatch Returns," *Weekend Magazine* (No. 2, 1968): 9, 10

128 Kirkpatrick, Dick "The Search for Bigfoot," *National Wildlife* (April-May 1968): 46.

129 "Washington Man Vows to Catch Big-Footed Abominable Snowman," *Idaho State Journal* (February 2, 1969): A7.

130 "Sasquatch Film Said a 'Hoax'," *Ottawa Journal* (December 10, 1969): 28.

131 Fritts, Bill. "Is There an Abominable Woodsman," *Herald-Tribune* (Sarasota, Florida) (March 3, 1968): C2.

132 Hugli, Paul. "Bigfoot—Darwin's 'Missing Link'," *Beyond Reality* (July-August 1976): 25.

133 Hancock, David. "The Sasquatch Returns," *Weekend Magazine* (No. 2, 1968): 9, 10

134 Frazier, Joe. "Bigfoot Still Has Lots of Believers," *Spokane Daily Chronicle* (March 12, 1973): 12.

135 Genzoli, Andrew. "Redwood Country," *Times-Standard* (Eureka, California) March 27, 1973): 22.

136 "The Sasquatch Lives in B.C.," *Medicine Hat News* (October 24, 1967): 3.

137 Wiesenfeld, Joe. "Sasquatch Sleuth Sets Sights on North Trek," *Winnipeg Free Press* (November 2, 1968): 18.

138 Wiesenfeld, Joe. "Sasquatch Sleuth Sets Sights on North Trek," *Winnipeg Free Press* (November 2, 1968): 18.

139 Wiesenfeld, Joe. "Sasquatch Sleuth Sets Sights on North Trek," *Winnipeg Free Press* (November 2, 1968): 18.

140 Wiesenfeld, Joe. "Sasquatch Sleuth Sets Sights on North Trek," *Winnipeg Free Press* (November 2, 1968): 18.

141 Wiesenfeld, Joe. "Sasquatch Sleuth Sets Sights on North Trek," *Winnipeg Free Press* (November 2, 1968): 18.

142 "He Still Wants a Sasquatch," *Brandon Sun* (Brandon, Manitoba) (September 18, 1968): 17.

143 "Sasquatch Hunter off to Nordegg," *Lethbridge Herald* (October 18, 1969): 12.

144 Soberanes, Bill. "Bigfoot Stories," *Argus-Courier* (Petaluma, California) (May 27, 1976): 12.

145 Soberanes, Bill. "Flying Saucers and Bigfoot," *Argus-Courier* (Petaluma, California) (April 28, 1986): 14.

146 Klobuchar, Jim. "Does 'Bigfoot' Beast Really Exist," *Minneapolis Star* (April 22, 1968): 4.

147 "Zoo Reviver John Fletcher Dies; Helped Transform Como Zoo into Modern Showcase," Highbeam.com. https://www.highbeam.com/doc/1G1-62577143.html.

148 Klobuchar, Jim. "Does 'Bigfoot' Beast Really Exist," *Minneapolis Star* (April 22, 1968): 4.

149 Klobuchar, Jim. "'Snowman' Country is Abominably Wild, Hostile," *Minneapolis Star* (April 23, 1968): 1.

150 Klobuchar, Jim. "'Snowman' Country is Abominably Wild, Hostile," *Minneapolis Star* (April 23, 1968): 4.

151 Klobuchar, Jim. "'Footprint' Recalls Stories & Sparks Speculation," *Minneapolis Star* (April 24, 1968): 1.

152 Klobuchar, Jim. "'Footprint' Recalls Stories & Sparks Speculation, ," *Minneapolis Star* (April 24, 1968): 5.

153 Klobuchar, Jim. "Did Searcher See Snowman in Dimly Lit Ravine," *Minneapolis Star* (April 25, 1968): 1.

154 Klobuchar, Jim. "Did Searcher See Snowman in Dimly Lit Ravine," *Minneapolis Star* (April 25, 1968): 4.

155 Klobuchar, Jim. "You Can't Blame Bigfoot for Hiding," *Minneapolis Star* (April 26, 1968): 4.

156 Klobuchar, Jim. "Snowman Arguments End in Stalemate," *Minneapolis Star* (April 27, 1968): 3.

157 "Klobuchar, Jim. "Your Man Friday," *Minneapolis Star* (May 3, 1968): 15.

158 James Klobuchar, telephone interview by author, July 6, 2015.

159 Sanderson, Ivan T. "The Patterson Affair," *Pursuit* (June, 1968): 10.

160 Rylander, Janice. "New Yorkers Hunt for Bigfoot," *Times-Standard* (Eureka, California) (July 13, 1968): 11.

161 Seginski, John. "Bigfoot: Man or Ape," *Western Treasures* (March 1970): 27.

162 Seginski, John. "Bigfoot: Man or Ape," *Western Treasures* (March 1970): 27.

163 Seginski, John. "Bigfoot: Man or Ape," *Western Treasures* (March 1970): 27.

164 Seginski, John. "Bigfoot: Man or Ape," *Western Treasures* (March 1970): 27.

165 "Gigantic Man Back," *Daily Chronicle* (March 27, 1969): 2.

166 Spehner, Norbert. "Strange, Strange World . . ." *Pursuit* (October 1975): 83.

167 Morin, Bonnie. "Man's Stubborness [sic] Leads to Sasquatch Investigation," *Lynnwood Enterprise* (July 16, 1969): 1.

168 Morin, Bonnie. "Man's Stubborness [sic] Leads to Sasquatch Investigation," *Lynnwood Enterprise* (July 16, 1969): 6.

169 Green, John. *Year of the Sasquatch* (Agassiz, British Columbia: Cheam Publishing, Ltd. (1970): 3.

170 Davies, Dave. "Sasquatch? More I Dug, More I Found, Man Says," *Winnipeg Free Press* (November 26, 1969): 36.

171 Boyce, Wayne. "I am Curious (Hairy)," *Brandon Sun* (Brandon, Manitoba) (November 29, 1969).

172 Norman, Eric. *The Abominable Snowmen* (New York: Award Books, 1969): 120-121.

173 Evans, Christopher. "History of the Lake Worth Monster," *Fort Worth Star-Telegram* (June 4, 1989): 100.

174 "'Bigfoot' Leaves Doubt About Hairy Creature," *Omaha World-Herald* (January 15, 1970): 17.

175 Mahar, Ted. "'Bigfoot' Presents Only Known Film," *Oregonian* (March 13, 1969): 35.

176 Mahar, Ted. "'Bigfoot' Presents Only Known Film," *Oregonian* (March 13, 1969): 35.

177 Woolheater, Craig. "Jim McClarin: The Formative Years," Cryptomundo.com. http://cryptomundo.com/bigfoot-report/jim-mcclarin-the-formative-years/

178 Woolheater, Craig. "Jim McClarin: The Formative Years," Cryptomundo.com http://cryptomundo.com/bigfoot-report/jim-mcclarin-the-formative-years/

179 Norman, Eric. *The Abominable Snowmen* (New York: Award Books, 1969): 111.

180 "Expeditioner to Speak on 'Bigfoot'," *Pony Express* (Sacramento City College, Sacramento, California) (March 1, 1968): 3.

181 Green, John. *Year of the Sasquatch*. (Agassiz, British Columbia: Cheam Publishing, Ltd., 1970): 23.

182 Hancock, David. "The Sasquatch Returns," *Weekend Magazine* (No. 2, 1968): 9, 10.

183 Patterson, Roger. *Bigfoot: Volume 1* (1968): 68.

184 Barry, W. E. "Life in Lumber Camp," *Ludington Daily News* (Ludington, Michigan) (July 6, 1951): 4.

185 "Posse Learns Great Ape Only Small Monkey," *Daily Republican* (Belvidere, Illinois) (July 26, 1929): 8.

186 Patterson, Roger. *Bigfoot: Volume 1* (1968): 22-26.

187 "Is Braxton Monster Back? Truck Driver Believes So," *Charleston Daily Mail* (December 31, 1960): 1, 3.

188 "'Monster' Branches Out, New Sightings Reported," *Raleigh Register* (January 5, 1961): 1.

189 "Three Chased by Hairy, Huge Monster," *Daily Herald* (Provo, Utah) (February 15, 1962): A4.

190 "Deputies Push Search for Lode Monster," *Lodi News Sentinel* (July 26, 1963): 1.

191 "Michigan Community Ready to Track Down 'The Thing'," *Lexington Herald* (Lexington, Kentucky) (June 11, 1964): 1.

192 Caesar, Gene. "The Hellzapoppin' Hunt for the Michigan Monster," *True* (June 1966): 60.

193 Nottingham, Ben. "Monster is Huge and Hairy—Also Bashful," *News-Palladium* (Benton Harbor, Michigan) (June 11, 1964): 1.

194 "'Monster' Causes Big Traffic Jam," *Wilmington News* (June 11, 1964): 1.

195 Caesar, Gene. "The Hellzapoppin' Hunt for the Michigan Monster," *True* (June 1966): 84.

196 "3 Girls Report Seeing 'Monster'," *Port Huron Times Herald* (June 11, 1964): 1.

197 "'Monster' Appears in Daylight," *Pittsburgh Press* (June 11, 1964): 6.

198 Caesar, Gene. "The Hellzapoppin' Hunt for the Michigan Monster," *True* (June 1966): 84.

199 Norman, Eric. *The Abominable Snowmen* (New York: Award Books, 1969): 132.

200 Norman, Eric. *The Abominable Snowmen* (New York: Award Books, 1969): 132.

201 Caesar, Gene. "The Hellzapoppin' Hunt for the Michigan Monster," *True* (June 1966): 84.

202 Caesar, Gene. “The Hellzapoppin’ Hunt for the Michigan Monster,” *True* (June 1966): 84.
203 Putnam, Stan. “Monster Days Are Here Again,” *Detroit Free Press* (August 17, 1965): 3.
204 “17 Year Old Beauty School Student Meets Monster—Help,” *Fresno Bee* (August 18, 1965): E5.
205 Putnam, Stan. “Monster Days Are Here Again,” *Detroit Free Press* (August 17, 1965): 3.
206 Caesar, Gene. “The Hellzapoppin’ Hunt for the Michigan Monster,” *True* (June 1966): 85.
207 Caesar, Gene. “The Hellzapoppin’ Hunt for the Michigan Monster,” *True* (June 1966): 85.
208 Caesar, Gene. “The Hellzapoppin’ Hunt for the Michigan Monster,” *True* (June 1966): 85.
209 “Monroe Beast Teenage Hoax,” *Gadsden Times* (August 25, 1965): 10.
210 Caesar, Gene. “The Hellzapoppin’ Hunt for the Michigan Monster,” *True* (June 1966): 85.
211 Bruce, Bob. “’Critter Talk’ Takes Heat Off Caddo Conversations,” *Abilene Reporter-News* (July 22, 1964): A3.
212 Baumann, Elwood D. *Bigfoot* (New York: Franklin Watts, Inc., 1975): 46-48.
213 “Now Everyone’s After Hairy Monster,” *Tuscaloosa News* (September 3, 1966): 1.
214 Steiger, Brad and Joan Whritenour. “Abominable Spacemen,” *Saga* (February 1968): 34.
215 “’Werewolf’ is Hunted by Teens Near Zoo,” *Plain Dealer* (Cleveland, Ohio) (April 24, 1968): 15.
216 Baldwin, Arthur. “New Proof America’s Abominable Snowmen Exist,” *Male* (January 1969):16-17, 74.
217 “Tracks on Mt. Etna,” *Pursuit* (January 1971): 11.
218 Green, John. *Sasquatch: The Apes Among Us* (Seattle, WA: Hancock House Publishers, 1978): 161.
219 Dahinden, René and Don Hunter. *Sasquatch* (New York: Signet, 1975): 152.
220 Dahinden, René and Don Hunter. *Sasquatch* (New York: Signet, 1975): 153-154.
221 Dahinden, René and Don Hunter. *Sasquatch* (New York: Signet, 1975): 155.
222 Green John. *Year of the Sasquatch* (Agassiz, British Columbia: Cheam Publishing Ltd., 1970): 50.
223 Bowman, Joan. “Sasquatch: Reality or Hoax,” *Lethbridge Herald* (February 15, 1971): 14
224 Green, John. *Year of the Sasquatch* (Agassiz, British Columbia: Cheam Publishing Ltd., 1970): 50-51.
225 Dahinden, René and Don Hunter. *Sasquatch* (New York: Signet, 1975): 158.
226 Regal, Brian. *Searching for Sasquatch* (New York: Palgrave Macmillan, 2013): 90.
227 Dahinden, René and Don Hunter. *Sasquatch* (New York: Signet, 1975): 160.
228 Dahinden, René and Don Hunter. *Sasquatch* (New York: Signet, 1975): 163.
229 Dahinden, René and Don Hunter. *Sasquatch* (New York: Signet, 1975): 163-164.
230 “Shaggy ‘Bigfoot’ Seen Feeding on Snowy Ferns,” *Montana Standard* (February 1, 1970): 1.
231 Dahinden, René and Don Hunter. *Sasquatch* (New York: Signet, 1975): 166-168.
232 “Hunting Guide Films Sasquatch,” *Walla Wall Union-Bulletin* (November 15, 1970): 2.
233 “Hunting Guide Films Sasquatch,” *Walla Wall Union-Bulletin* (November 15, 1970): 2.
234 Dahinden, René and Don Hunter. *Sasquatch* (New York: Signet, 1975): 166-168.
235 “Hunting Guide Films Sasquatch,” *Walla Wall Union-Bulletin* (November 15, 1970): 2.
236 “Hunting Guide Films Sasquatch,” *Walla Wall Union-Bulletin* (November 15, 1970): 2.

237 "Hunting Guide Films Sasquatch," *Walla Wall Union-Bulletin* (November 15, 1970): 2.

238 Haas, George F. "Reports from Our Correspondents," *Bigfoot Bulletin* (November 30, 1970): 2.

239 Haas, George F. "Reports from Our Correspondents," *Bigfoot Bulletin* (November 30, 1970): 3.

240 Dahinden, René and Don Hunter. *Sasquatch* (New York: Signet, 1975): 169.

241 "Guide is Tracking Creature Called 'Bigfoot' in Legend," *Bridgeport Post* (February 20, 1971): 3.

242 "Sasquatch is Top Attraction for Tourists," *Bulletin* (Bend, Oregon) (February 18, 1971): 24.

243 "Footprints Add to Tale of Giant Creature Living in Washington," *Idaho State Journal* (February 17, 1971): 8B.

244 "Footprints Add to Tale of Giant Creature Living in Washington," *Idaho State Journal* (February 17, 1971): 8B.

245 "Sasquatch is Top Attraction for Tourists," *Bulletin* (Bend, Oregon) (February 18, 1971): 24.

246 "Footprints Add to Tale of Giant Creature Living in Washington," *Idaho State Journal* (February 17, 1971): 8B.

247 "Footprints Add to Tale of Giant Creature Living in Washington," *Idaho State Journal* (February 17, 1971): 8B.

248 Dent, James. "The Gazetteer," *Charleston Gazette* (March 12, 1971): 17.

249 Dahinden, René and Don Hunter. *Sasquatch* (New York: Signet, 1975): 169.

250 "Legend of Sasquatch Diminished by 'Fake,'" *Centralia Daily Chronicle* (April 9, 1971): 2.

251 "Legend of Sasquatch Diminished by 'Fake,'" *Centralia Daily Chronicle* (April 9, 1971): 2.

252 "The Bossberg [sic] Sasquatch," *Pursuit* (April 1971): 48.

253 "Ivan Marx's Film," *Pursuit* (July 1971): 65-66.

254 "Ivan Marx's Film," *Pursuit* (July 1971): 65-66.

255 Genzoli, Andrew. "Redwood Country," *Times-Standard* (Eureka, California) (April 9, 1971): 13.

256 Genzoli, Andrew. "Redwood Country," *Times-Standard* (Eureka, California) (April 9, 1971): 13.

257 "Colville Man Faked Sasquatch Footprints," *Spokane-Review* (April 1, 1971): 1.

258 Regal, Brian. *Searching for Sasquatch* (New York: Palgrave Macmillan, 2013): 88.

259 Chou, Rose and Keeley Kerrins. "Register to the Papers of Grover Sanders Krantz," (April 2012). Anthropology.si.edu. https://anthropology.si.edu/naa/fa/krantz.pdf.

260 Chou, Rose and Keeley Kerrins. "Register to the Papers of Grover Sanders Krantz," (April 2012). Anthropology.si.edu. https://anthropology.si.edu/naa/fa/krantz.pdf.

261 Regal, Brian. "Amateur Versus Professional: The Search for Bigfoot," *Endeavor* (Vol.32 No. 2): 55.

262 Folder 0343, box 10, Grover Krantz Papers Collection, National Anthropological Archive, Smithsonian Institution.

263 "Prof Says Sasquatch Footprints Real," *Statesman* (Salem, Oregon) (April 18, 1971): 14.

264 "Sasquatch Still Lives, Says Prof.," *Idaho State Journal* (April 19, 1971): B1.

265 Bowman, Joan. "Sasquatch: Reality or Hoax," *Lethbridge Herald* (February 15, 1971): 14.

266 Bowman, Joan. "Sasquatch: Reality or Hoax," *Lethbridge Herald* (February 15, 1971): 14.

267 "B. C. Man Won't Give up Search," *Lethbridge Herald* (January 29, 1970): 2.

268 Russians Asked to Help Track Down 'Snowman'," *Beaver County Times* (December 21, 1971).

269 Bowman, Joan. "Sasquatch: Reality or Hoax," *Lethbridge Herald* (February 15, 1971): 14.

270 Bowman, Joan. "Sasquatch: Reality or Hoax," *Lethbridge Herald* (February 15, 1971): 14.

271 Halpin, James. "Sasquatch," *Seattle* (August 1970). BigfootEncounters.com. http://www.bigfootencounters.com/articles/seattlemag70.htm.

272 Halpin, James. "Sasquatch," *Seattle* (August 1970). BigfootEncounters.com. http://www.bigfootencounters.com/articles/seattlemag70.htm.

273 Bowman, Joan. "Sasquatch: Reality or Hoax," *Lethbridge Herald* (February 15, 1971): 14.

274 Baert, Renee. "Canadian Pursues 'Sasquatch'," *Pantagraph* (Bloomington, Illinois) (December 5, 1971): A15.

275 Baert, Renee. "Canadian Pursues 'Sasquatch'," *Pantagraph* (Bloomington, Illinois) (December 5, 1971): A15.

276 "Sasquatch Hunter Hoping to Find Answer in Europe," *Brandon Sun* (Brandon, Manitoba) (October 27, 1971): 3.

277 Dahinden, René. "René Dahinden's Eurasian Trip," *Manimals Newsletter* (August 12, 1972): 1-3.

278 "Check Existence of B. C.'s Hairy Giant," *Lethbridge Herald* (November 11, 1971): 31.

279 "Sasquatch Interests Europeans," *Brandon Sun* (Brandon, Manitoba) (March 15, 1972).

280 "Sasquatch Interests Europeans," *Brandon Sun* (Brandon, Manitoba) (March 15, 1972).

281 Russians Asked to Help Track Down 'Snowman'," *Beaver County Times* (December 21, 1971): 2.

282 "Russians Asked to Help Track Down 'Snowman'," *Beaver County Times* (December 21, 1971): 2.

283 Brooks, Jack. "Snowman or Maybe Snow Job," *New York Post* (November 10, 1971): 26 as cited in Keel, John Ed., *Anomaly* (Fall, 1971): 112.

284 "Sasquatch Interests Europeans," *Brandon Sun* (Brandon, Manitoba) (March 15, 1972).

285 Byrne, Peter. *The Search for Bigfoot* (New York: Pocket Books, 1976): 107.

286 Byrne, Peter. *A Fortunate Life* (San Bernardino, California, CreateSpace, 2017): 271.

287 Byrne, Peter. *A Fortunate Life* (San Bernardino, California, CreateSpace, 2017): 274.

288 Byrne, Peter. *A Fortunate Life* (San Bernardino, California, CreateSpace, 2017): 282.

289 Byrne, Peter. *A Fortunate Life* (San Bernardino, California, CreateSpace, 2017): 286.

290 Byrne, Peter. *A Fortunate Life* (San Bernardino, California, CreateSpace, 2017): 288.

291 Byrne, Peter. *A Fortunate Life* (San Bernardino, California, CreateSpace, 2017): 290.

292 Mitchell, John G. "Bigfoot and Yeti" *Sports Afield* (February 1977): 127.

293 Beale, Betty. "Socialite Stalks Snowman," *News Journal* (Mansfield, Ohio) (August 15, 1971): 18.

294 Hill, Bill. "To Track "Monster"," *Lowell Sun* (May 13, 1971): 6.

295 Beale, Betty. "Socialite Stalks Snowman," *News Journal* (Mansfield, Ohio) (August 15, 1971): 18.

296 Beale, Betty. "Around Miami," *Cedar Rapids Gazette* (July 23, 1972): 8C.
297 Byrne, Peter. *The Search for Bigfoot* (New York: Pocket Books, 1976): 75-76.
298 "British Climber Tracks Illusive 'Apeman' of Northwest," *Cincinnati Enquirer* (December 10, 1972): 4M.
299 Holmstrom, David. "Search for 'Bigfoot' Goes On," *Oakland Tribune* (March 24, 1973): 9E.
300 Fradkin, Philip "Has Bigfoot Been Sighted in Oregon," *Anniston Star* (December 7, 1972): 1D.
301 Bylin, James. "Bigfoot: Legend or Reality," *Pocono Record* (September 8, 1972): 11.
302 Fradkin, Philip. "Lonely Hunt for Bigfoot," *Express and News* (San Antonio, Texas) (December 10, 1972).
303 Genzoli, Andrew. "Redwood Country," *Times-Standard* (Eureka, California) (April 9, 1971): 13.
304 Hill, Bill. "Wildlife Group Tracks Legendary Giant Creature Called 'Bigfoot'," *Waco News-Tribune* (March 4, 1971): 10D.
305 Hill, Bill. "Sasquatch . . . Does Mysterious 'Bigfoot' Exist," *Deseret News* (March 20, 1971): 2T.
306 Hill, Bill. "Wildlife Group Tracks Legendary Giant Creature Called 'Bigfoot'," *Waco News-Tribune* (March 4, 1971): 10D.
307 Hill, Bill. "To Track "Monster"," *Lowell Sun* (May 13, 1971): 6.
308 Steiger, Brad "The Strange World of Brad Steiger—Monsters Along the Mississippi," *Daily Democrat* (December 6, 1971): 10.
309 Steiger, Brad "The Strange World of Brad Steiger—Monsters Along the Mississippi," *Daily Democrat* (December 6, 1971): 10.
310 Burroughs, Betty. "Once Upon Paper," *Morning News* (Wilmington, Delaware) (October 31, 1970): 13.
311 Harrison, George H. "On the Trail of Bigfoot," *National Wildlife* (October-November 1970): 5.
312 McPhee, Penelope. "Man Against Myth: The Search for Bigfoot," *Spokesman-Review Sunday Magazine* (September 8, 1974): 14.
313 McPhee, Penelope. "Man Against Myth: The Search for Bigfoot," *Spokesman-Review Sunday Magazine* (September 8, 1974): 14.
314 "American 'Abominable Snowman' found by Florida Scientists," *Boca Raton News* (July 8, 1970): 16.
315 "Five Seek U.S. 'Abominable Snowman'," *St. Petersburg Times* (June 9, 1970): 10B.
316 "Five Seek U.S. 'Abominable Snowman'," *St. Petersburg Times* (June 9, 1970): 10B.
317 "Five Seek U.S. 'Abominable Snowman'," *St. Petersburg Times* (June 9, 1970): 10B.
318 Harrison, George H. "On the Trail of Bigfoot," *National Wildlife* (October-November 1970): 9.
319 "Floridians Search Country for Clues About Bigfoot," *Spokane Daily Chronicle* (July 9, 1970): B3.

320 Harrison, George H. “On the Trail of Bigfoot,” *National Wildlife* (October-November 1970): 9.

321 “Floridians Search Country for Clues About Bigfoot”, *Spokane Daily Chronicle* (July 9, 1970): B3.

322 Harrison, George H. “On the Trail of Bigfoot,” *National Wildlife* (October-November 1970): 7, 9.

323 “Floridians Search Country for Clues About Bigfoot,” *Spokane Daily Chronicle* (July 9, 1970).

324 Harrison, George H. “On the Trail of Bigfoot,” *National Wildlife* (October-November 1970): 9.

325 “American ‘Abominable Snowman’ found by Florida scientists,” *Boca Raton News* (July 8, 1970): 16.

326 “Floridians Search Country for Clues About Bigfoot,” *Spokane Daily Chronicle* (July 9, 1970): B3.

327 Harrison, George H. “On the Trail of Bigfoot,” *National Wildlife* (October-November 1970): 9.

328 “Florida Firm Scouring Cascades for Bigfoot,” *St. Petersburg Times* (July 2, 1971): 10B.

329 “The ‘Bigfoot’ Hunt—New Style,” *Pursuit* (April 1971): 44.

330 “The ‘Bigfoot’ Hunt—New Style,” *Pursuit* (April 1971): 44.

331 “The ‘Bigfoot’ Hunt—New Style,” *Pursuit* (April 1971): 44.

332 Harrison, George H. “On the Trail of Bigfoot,” *National Wildlife* (October-November 1970): 7.

333 Pyle, Robert Michael. *Where Bigfoot Walks* (New York: Houghton Mifflin Company, 1995): 278.

334 Harrison, George H. “On the Trail of Bigfoot,” *National Wildlife* (October-November 1970): 6.

335 Hunter, Don and René Dahinden. *Sasquatch* (New York: Signet, 1975): 139.

336 “Will Stand up for Sasquatch,” *Evening News* (Port Angeles, Washington) (August 26, 1970): 12.

337 “‘Protect Bigfoot’ Campaign Starts,” *Times-Standard* (Eureka, California.) (July 25, 1970): 9.

338 Castle, Ken. “The Search for Bigfoot,” *Outdoor Outlook* (February 3, 1974).

339 Genzoli, Andrew. “Redwood Country,” *Times-Standard* (Eureka, California) (February 17, 1970): 9.

340 Haas, George F. *Bigfoot Bulletin* (January 2, 1969): 1.

341 Genzoli, Andrew. “Redwood Country,” *Times-Standard* (Eureka, California) (August 7, 1970): 11.

342 Genzoli, Andrew. “Redwood Country,” *Times-Standard* (Eureka, California) (February 24, 1971): 21.

343 Shutt, David. “Sasquatch Hunt Makes ‘Believers’,” *Blade* (Toledo, Ohio) (March 1, 1971): 6.

344 “Report Places in ‘Y’ Caravan for Boys 12-15,” *Valley News* (Van Nuys, California) (June 25, 1970).

345 'Y' Boys to Hunt 'Bigfoot' in Wilds of Northern California," *Van Nuys News* (June 14, 1970).
346 "Bigfoot Coming," *Red Bluff Daily News* (September 13, 1971): 3.
347 Keel, John A. "Incredible Monster-Man Sighting in the U.S.," *Male* (August 1970): 28-29.
348 Keel, John A. "Incredible Monster-Man Sighting in the U.S.," *Male* (August 1970): 82.
349 Keel, John A. *Strange Creatures from Time and Space* (Point Pleasant, West Virginia: New Saucerian Books, 2014): 63.
350 Smith, Warren. *Strange Abominable Snowmen* (New York: Popular Library, 1970): 10-11.
351 Cooper, Gary. "Showmen Come to Rescue of Fever Victims," *Edmonton Journal* (January 15, 1971): 18.
352 "Scooby's Back," *Palladium-Item* (Richmond, Indiana) (March 26, 2004): C1.
353 Simms, David. "Twisted Concepts, Ideas Cloud 'Skullduggery'," *Palm Beach Post* (May 21, 1970): C11.
354 Champlin, Charles. "'Skullduggery' Satire that Fails to Click," *Los Angeles Times* (March 26, 1970).
355 Thomas, Kevin. "'Bigfoot' Leader of a Cast of Monsters," *Los Angeles Times* (January 21, 1972): 15.
356 Siskel, Gene. "'Trog!'," *Chicago Tribune* (October 1, 1970): (Section 2) 13.
357 Orchard, Vance. "Has Bigfoot Again Made Area Visit," *Walla Walla Union-Bulletin* (August 30, 1970) as cited in McClean, Scott. *Big News Prints* (2006): 241.
358 Brimeyer, Jack. "The Benton 'Monster': Some Scoff, Some Worry," *Telegraph Herald* (September 3, 1970): 1.
359 Clark, Jerome, and Loren Coleman. "Anthropoids, Monsters and UFOs," *INFO Journal* (January-February 1973).
360 Bingaman, Frances. "UFO, Huge Footprints Puzzle Vader Family," *Centralia Daily Chronicle* (December 16, 1970): 1
361 Clark, Jerome, and Loren Coleman. "Anthropoids, Monsters and UFOs," *INFO Journal* (January-February 1973).
362 Clark, Jerome, and Loren Coleman. "Anthropoids, Monsters and UFOs," *INFO Journal* (January-February 1973).
363 Clark, Jerome, and Loren Coleman. "Anthropoids, Monsters and UFOs," *INFO Journal* (January-February 1973).
364 Bingaman, Frances. "UFO, Huge Footprints Puzzle Vader Family," *Centralia Daily Chronicle* (December 16, 1970): 1.
365 "Halloween Mask Offers Clue," *Ada Evening News* (March 3, 1971).
366 "Witnesses See 'Wolfman' Running Loose in Lawton," *Wichita Falls Times* (March 2, 1971) as cited in *Anomaly, Interim Newsletter—Supplement to #7* (Fall, 1971).
367 "Halloween Mask Offers Clue," *Ada Evening News* (March 3, 1971).
368 "'Wolfman' is Just Prankster," *Favorite* (Bonham, Tex.) (March 4, 1971): 7.
369Clark, Jerome. "'Manimals' Make Tracks in Oklahoma," *Fate* (September 1971): 63.

370 "You Never Know About Those Mysterious Happenings," *Ada Evening News* (March 10, 1971): 4.

371 McCombs, Philip. "Chicken Man at War," *Pacific Stars and Stripes* (January 25, 1970).

372 Clark, Jerome. "'Manimals' Make Tracks in Oklahoma," *Fate* (September 1971): 63.

373 Montgomery, Dennis. "Farmers Hunt Chicken Man," *Spokesman-Review* (March 1, 1971): 6.

374 Montgomery, Dennis. "Chicken Man Stirs 'Critter' Memos," *Atchison Globe* (March 10, 1971): 18.

375 Montgomery, Dennis. "Chicken Man Stirs 'Critter' Memos," *Atchison Globe* (March 10, 1971): 18.

376 Montgomery, Dennis. "Farmers Hunt Chicken Man," *Spokesman-Review* (March 1, 1971): 6.

377 Clark, Jerome. "Manimals' Make Tracks in Oklahoma," *Fate* (September 1971): 63-64.

378 "Pemiscot 'Monster' Travels to Bernie," *Daily Standard* (Sikeston, Missouri) (May 27, 1971): 18.

379 Gust, Suzy. "Lee Township has a 'Monster'," *Marshall Evening Chronicle* (October 6, 1971): 1.

380 Gust, Suzy. "Where's Monster? Lee Residents Don't Know," *Marshall Evening Chronicle* (October 8, 1971): 1.

381 Gust, Suzy. "Where's Monster? Lee Residents Don't Know," *Marshall Evening Chronicle* (October 8, 1971): 1.

382 Martin, Bernard. "On the Trail of the Elusive Bigfoot," *Kansas City Times* (May 1, 1971): 14C.

383 Tiede, Tom. ". . . A Visit by 'Bigfoot,'," *Tuscaloosa News* (June 23, 1971): 35.

384 Hansen, Frank. "I Killed the Ape-Man Creature of Whiteface," *Saga* (July 1970): 55-56.

385 Hansen, Frank. "I Killed the Ape-Man Creature of Whiteface," *Saga* (July 1970): 56.

386 Hansen, Frank. "I Killed the Ape-Man Creature of Whiteface," *Saga* (July 1970): 56.

387 Hansen, Frank. "I Killed the Ape-Man Creature of Whiteface," *Saga* (July 1970): 58.

388 Hansen, Frank. "I Killed the Ape-Man Creature of Whiteface," *Saga* (July 1970): 58.

389 Hansen, Frank. "I Killed the Ape-Man Creature of Whiteface," *Saga* (July 1970): 58.

390 Hansen, Frank. "I Killed the Ape-Man Creature of Whiteface," *Saga* (July 1970): 58, 60.

391 Hansen, Frank. "I Killed the Ape-Man Creature of Whiteface," *Saga* (July 1970): 60.

392 "Editorial," *Pursuit* (April 1969): 22.

393 "Editorial," *Pursuit* (April 1969): 22.

394 Sanderson, Ivan. "The Missing Link," *Argosy* (May 1969): 23.

395 Sanderson, Ivan. "The Missing Link," *Argosy* (May 1969): 28.

396 "Genuine Article," *Argosy* (September 1969): 12.

397 Regal, Brian. *Searching for Sasquatch* (New York: Palgrave Macmillan, 2013): 72.

398 Regal, Brian. *Searching for Sasquatch* (New York: Palgrave Macmillan, 2013): 74.

399 "Editorial," *Pursuit* (April 1969): 22.

400 Regal, Brian. *Searching for Sasquatch* (New York: Palgrave Macmillan, 2013): 75-76.

401 Regal, Brian. *Searching for Sasquatch* (New York: Palgrave Macmillan, 2013): 77.

402 Hansen, Frank. "I Killed the Ape-Man Creature of Whiteface," *Saga* (July 1970): 60.

403 "Ends "Bozo"—We Think," *Pursuit* (July 1969): 55.

404 Tchernine, Odette. *In Pursuit of the Abominable Snowman* (New York: Taplinger Publishing Company, 1970): 11.

405 "Book Reviews," *Pursuit* (July 1971): 72.

406 Steiger, Brad "The Strange World of Brad Steiger—Monsters Along the Mississippi," *Daily Democrat* (December 6, 1971): 10.

407 Hansen, Frank. "I Killed the Ape-Man Creature of Whiteface," *Saga* (July 1970): 60.

408 Bothwell, Dick. "Ape Hunt in the Everglades," *Gazette* (Emporia, Kansas) (August 20, 1971): 4

409 Bothwell, Dick. "It's No Hoax, Says Archeology Leader, 'Skunk Ape' in the Everglades—A Hairy Giant That Smells Bad," *National Observer* (August 16, 1971) as published in *Anomaly* (April 1974): 216.

410 Beckley, Timothy Green. "America's Abominable Swamp Man," *Saga* (March 1975).

411 "Pyramids in Florida and Georgia Constructed by Mayans," MayaInAmerica.com. http://www.mayainamerica.com/2012/01/pyramids-in-florida-and-georgia.html

412 "Big Cypress 'Skunk Ape' Object of Forthcoming Hunt," *Miami News* (August 9, 1971): 3.

413 Beckley, Timothy Green. "America's Abominable Swamp Man," *Saga* (March 1975): 72.

414 "Big Cypress 'Skunk Ape' Object of Forthcoming Hunt," *Miami News* (August 9, 1971): 3.

415 Bothwell, Dick. "It's No Hoax, Says Archeology Leader, 'Skunk Ape' in the Everglades—A Hairy Giant That Smells Bad," *National Observer* (August 16, 1971) as published in *Anomaly* (April 1974): 216.

416 Beckley, Timothy Green. "America's Abominable Swamp Man," *Saga* (March 1975): 37.

417 Beckley, Timothy Green. "America's Abominable Swamp Man," *Saga* (March 1975): 37.

418 "Big Cypress 'Skunk Ape' Object of Forthcoming Hunt," *Miami News* (August 9, 1971): 3.

419 Beckley, Timothy Green. "America's Abominable Swamp Man," *Saga* (March 1975): 66.

420 Bothwell, Dick. "Ape Hunt in the Everglades," *Gazette* (Emporia, Kansas) (August 20, 1971): 4.

421 Beckley, Timothy Green. "America's Abominable Swamp Man," *Saga* (March 1975): 72, 74.

422 "'Skunk Ape' Reported in Swamp," *Tucson Daily Citizen* (August 11, 1971): 15.

423 Cardozo, Yvette. "Posse Set to Hunt Two 'Ape Critters'," *Fort Lauderdale News* (August 13, 1971): B1.

424 Putnam, Pat. "He's Big! He's Bashful! He Smells Bad," *Sports Illustrated* (August 30, 1971). SI.com. http://www.si.com/vault/1971/08/30/612120/hes-big-hes-bashful-he-smells-bad

425 "'Skunk Apes' Sighted," *Boca Raton News* (August 3, 1971). BFRO.net. http://www.bfro.net/gdb/show_report.asp?ID=44837

426 "Posse Hunts Everglades Ape," *St. Petersburg Independent* (August 13, 1971): 2.

427 "2 Ape-Like Creatures Spotted, Hunted by Posse in Everglades," *Miami News* (August 13, 1971): 2.

428 "Posse Hunts Everglades Ape," *St. Petersburg Independent* (August 13, 1971): 2.

429 "Posse Hunts Everglades Ape," *St. Petersburg Independent* (August 13, 1971): 2.

430 "2 Ape-Like Creatures Spotted, Hunted by Posse in Everglades," *Miami News* (August 13, 1971): 2.

431 "What's Weirder than Fiction? The Factual Doings of Man," *Naples Daily News* (August 18, 1971): 4B.

432 "What's Weirder than Fiction? The Factual Doings of Man," *Naples Daily News* (August 18, 1971): 4B.

433 "What's Weirder than Fiction? The Factual Doings of Man," *Naples Daily News* (August 18, 1971): 4B.

434 Putnam, Pat. "He's Big! He's Bashful! He Smells Bad," *Sports Illustrated* (August 30, 1971). SI.com. http://www.si.com/vault/1971/08/30/612120/hes-big-hes-bashful-he-smells-bad

435 Putnam, Pat. "He's Big! He's Bashful! He Smells Bad," *Sports Illustrated* (August 30, 1971). SI.com. http://www.si.com/vault/1971/08/30/612120/hes-big-hes-bashful-he-smells-bad

436 Putnam, Pat. "He's Big! He's Bashful! He Smells Bad," *Sports Illustrated* (August 30, 1971). SI.com. http://www.si.com/vault/1971/08/30/612120/hes-big-hes-bashful-he-smells-bad

437 "What's Weirder than Fiction? The Factual Doings of Man," *Naples Daily News* (August 18, 1971): 4B.

438 "What's Weirder than Fiction? The Factual Doings of Man," *Naples Daily News* (August 18, 1971): 4B.

439 Sharp, Greg. "Great Ape Hunt Grows Weirder," *Florida Today* (August 18, 1971): 6B.

440 "What's Weirder than Fiction? The Factual Doings of Man," *Naples Daily News* (August 18, 1971): 4B.

441 Richardson, Norman. "Memories of 'It' Rekindled by New Incident at Fouke," *Shreveport Times* (May 4, 1971): 10.

442 "Archeologist, Citing Toe Number, Thinks Monster Track a Hoax," *Arkansas Gazette* (Little Rock, Arkansas) (June 17, 1971).
443 "Fouke 'Monster' Seen Again," *Courier News* (Blytheville, Arkansas) (May 25, 1971): 1.
444 "Archeologist, Citing Toe Number, Thinks Monster Track a Hoax," *Arkansas Gazette* (Little Rock, Arkansas) (June 17, 1971).
445 "Archeologist, Citing Toe Number, Thinks Monster Track a Hoax," *Arkansas Gazette* (Little Rock, Arkansas) (June 17, 1971).
446 Allin, Richard. "Hope for the Monster," *Arkansas Gazette* (Little Rock, Arkansas) (June 17, 1971).
447 McKinsey, Dala. "'Monster' Draws the Curious," *Blytheville Courier News* (Blytheville, Arkansas) (May 8, 1971): 1.
448 Brown, Donald C. Jr., "Arkansas Claims to Harbor Two Monsters," *Altoona Mirror* (October 21, 1971): 19.
449 Brown, Donald C. Jr., "Arkansas Claims to Harbor Two Monsters," *Altoona Mirror* (October 21, 1971): 19.
450 Childress, William. "The Most Sensational Bigfoot Pictures Ever Taken," *Saga* (December 1973): 69-70.
451 Genzoli, Andrew. "Redwood Country," *Times-Standard* (Eureka, California) (July 21, 1972): 34.
452 "Gorilla Costumes are Big Item for this Halloween," *Dixon Evening Telegraph* (Dixon, Illinois) (October 30, 1972): 1.
453 Hale, Debra. "Boggy Creek Monster Flick Puts Fouke, Ark., on Map," *Amarillo Globe-Times* (September 5, 1973): 60.
454 "Full-Length Film Planned About Fouke's 'Monster'," *Vernon Daily Record* (Vernon, Texas) (February 4, 1972): 8.
455 Richardson, Norman. "Doubt, 'Maybe So' Greet E-Texas Monster Reports," *Shreveport Times* (September 5, 1965): 4.
456 Richardson, Norman. "Pear-Loving Etex 'Monster' Subject of Scorn, Mystery," *Shreveport Times* (September 19, 1965): 12.
457 Richardson, Norman. "Pear-Loving Etex 'Monster' Subject of Scorn, Mystery," *Shreveport Times* (September 19, 1965): 12.
458 Richardson, Norman. "Pear-Loving Etex 'Monster' Subject of Scorn, Mystery," *Shreveport Times* (September 19, 1965): 12.
459 Spehner, Norbert. "Strange, Strange World . . ." *Pursuit* (October 1975): 86.
460 Bylin, James E. "Does 'Bigfoot' Stalk Wilds of Northwest? That's Good Question," *Wall Street Journal* (August 10, 1972).
461 Crowley, Lawrence, dir. 1972. *Bigfoot: Man or Beast.* American National Enterprises.
462 Crowley, Lawrence, dir. 1972. *Bigfoot: Man or Beast.* American National Enterprises.
463 Crowley, Lawrence, dir. 1972. *Bigfoot: Man or Beast.* American National Enterprises.

464 Crowley, Lawrence, dir. 1972. *Bigfoot: Man or Beast*. American National Enterprises.
465 Crowley, Lawrence, dir. 1972. *Bigfoot: Man or Beast*. American National Enterprises.
466 Crowley, Lawrence, dir. 1972. *Bigfoot: Man or Beast*. American National Enterprises.
467 Crowley, Lawrence, dir. 1972. *Bigfoot: Man or Beast*. American National Enterprises.
468 Crowley, Lawrence, dir. 1972. *Bigfoot: Man or Beast*. American National Enterprises.
469 Crowley, Lawrence, dir. 1972. *Bigfoot: Man or Beast*. American National Enterprises.
470 Crowley, Lawrence, dir. 1972. *Bigfoot: Man or Beast*. American National Enterprises.
471 Crowley, Lawrence, dir. 1972. *Bigfoot: Man or Beast*. American National Enterprises.
472 Crowley, Lawrence, dir. 1972. *Bigfoot: Man or Beast*. American National Enterprises.
473 Bates, Doug. "Big Foot Hunters Using Technology," *Register-Guard* (Eugene, Oregon) (May 21, 1972): 10A.
474 Bylin, James E. "Does 'Bigfoot' Stalk Wilds of Northwest? That's Good Question," *Wall Street Journal* (August 10, 1972).
475 Bates, Doug. "Big Foot Hunters Using Technology," *Register-Guard* (Eugene, Oregon) (May 21, 1972): 10A.
476 "Letters in the Editor's Mailbag," *Register-Guard* (Eugene, Oregon) (May 23, 1972): 14A.
477 Cahill, Tim. "Giant Hairy Apes in the North Woods: A Bigfoot Study," *Rolling Stone* (May 10, 1973).
478 "Hunt Halted Because of Weather," *Times-Standard* (Eureka, California) (December 19, 1972): 9.
479 "Rescue Party Reaches L. A. Bigfoot Hunter," *Times-Standard* (Eureka, California) (December 20, 1972): 2.
480 McClarin, Jim. *Manimals Newsletter* (August 12, 1972): 1.
481 McClarin, Jim. *Manimals Newsletter* (August 12, 1972): 1.
482 "Jim McClarin. "*Manimals Newsletter*," *Pursuit* (October 1972): 96.
483 Fradkin, Philip. "Hunters Pressing 'Bigfoot' Search," *Los Angeles Times* (November 26, 1972): 23.
484 Fradkin, Philip. "Hunters Pressing 'Bigfoot' Search," *Los Angeles Times* (November 26, 1972): 23.
485 Fradkin, Philip. "Hunters Pressing 'Bigfoot' Search," *Los Angeles Times* (November 26, 1972): 23.
486 Fradkin, Philip. "Hunters Pressing 'Bigfoot' Search," *Los Angeles Times* (November 26, 1972): 23.
487 Fradkin, Philip. "Hunters Pressing 'Bigfoot' Search," *Los Angeles Times* (November 26, 1972): 23.
488 Morris, Tom. *California's Bigfoot/Sasquatch* (1994).
489 "Determined Scientist Tracks Mysterious Loch Ness Monster with All Types of Equipment," *Lawton Constitution* (Lawton, Oklahoma) (May 5, 1972): 33.
490 Byrne, Peter "'Bigfoot Bed' Investigated in No. California," *Manimals Newsletter* (September 27, 1972): 2-3.

491 Bylin, James E. "Does 'Bigfoot' Stalk Wilds of Northwest? That's Good Question," *Wall Street Journal* (August 10, 1972).

492 Bylin, James E. "Does 'Bigfoot' Stalk Wilds of Northwest? That's Good Question," *Wall Street Journal* (August 10, 1972).

493 Stevens, Scott. "Bigfoot," *Southland Sunday* (September 17, 1972): 8-9.

494 Bylin, James E. "Does 'Bigfoot' Stalk Wilds of Northwest? That's Good Question," *Wall Street Journal* (August 10, 1972).

495 Bylin, James E. "Does 'Bigfoot' Stalk Wilds of Northwest? That's Good Question," *Wall Street Journal* (August 10, 1972).

496 Bylin, James E. "Does 'Bigfoot' Stalk Wilds of Northwest? That's Good Question," *Wall Street Journal* (August 10, 1972).

497 Bylin, James E. "Does 'Bigfoot' Stalk Wilds of Northwest? That's Good Question," *Wall Street Journal* (August 10, 1972).

498 Coleman, Margo. "Some of My Friends Are Very Imaginative," *Derrick* (Oil City, Pennsylvania) (December 6, 1972): 5.

499 Bell, John. "Sasquatch Researcher Taking Things 1 Footprint at a Time," *Seattle Times* (February 13, 1972): 6C.

500 Bell, John. "Sasquatch Researcher Taking Things 1 Footprint at a Time," *Seattle Times* (February 13, 1972): 6C.

501 Bell, John. "Sasquatch Researcher Taking Things 1 Footprint at a Time," *Seattle Times* (February 13, 1972): 6C.

502 Bell, John. "Sasquatch Researcher Taking Things 1 Footprint at a Time," *Seattle Times* (February 13, 1972): 6C.

503 Bell, John. "Sasquatch Researcher Taking Things 1 Footprint at a Time," *Seattle Times* (February 13, 1972): 6C.

504 Coleman, Margo. "Some of My Friends Are Very Imaginative," *Derrick* (Oil City, Pennsylvania) (December 6, 1972): 5.

505 Coleman, Margo. "Some of My Friends Are Very Imaginative," *Derrick* (Oil City, Pennsylvania) (December 6, 1972): 5.

506 Bell, John. "Sasquatch Researcher Taking Things 1 Footprint at a Time," *Seattle Times* (February 13, 1972): 6C.

507 Bell, John. "Sasquatch Researcher Taking Things 1 Footprint at a Time," *Seattle Times* (February 13, 1972): 6C.

508 Bell, John. "Sasquatch Researcher Taking Things 1 Footprint at a Time," *Seattle Times* (February 13, 1972): 6C.

509 Ostlind, Emilene. "John Mionczynski: A Biologist Revered and Ridiculed," WyoFile.com. http://wyofile.com/emilene_ostlind/john-mionczynski/

510John Mionczynski, telephone interview by author, December 15, 2015.

511 Neavoll, George. "Bigfoot's Home in Ape Canyon," *Idaho State Journal* (Pocatello, Idaho) (February 25, 1972).

512 Jorgenson, Mica Amy Royer. *"It Happened to Me in Barkerville": Aboriginal Identity, Economy, and Law in the Cariboo Gold Rush, 1862-1900* (University of Northern British Columbia, 2009): 35-36.

513 Stockand, Dave. "Sasquatch Cave Sealed by Water," *Vancouver Sun* (September 6, 1972).

514 Stockand, Dave. "Sasquatch Cave Sealed by Water," *Vancouver Sun* (September 6, 1972).

515 "The Silent Companion," *Salmon Trout Steelheader* (March-April 1972): 14.

516 "Wallace Court Monster Frightens Loma Lindans," *San Bernardino County Sun* (August 7, 1972): 3B.

517 Caffery, Bethia. "But He's There . . . Monster Search Fruitless," *St. Petersburg Independent* (October 14, 1972): 2B.

518 "Bigfoot is Back; People Not Happy," *Lebanon Daily News* (Lebanon, Pennsylvania) (August 24, 1972): 52.

519 "An Unbeliever," *Gaffney Ledger* (August 25, 1972): 10A.

520 "2 Campers Claim Encounter with Hairy 'Bigfoot'," *Palo Alto Times* (October 12, 1972).

521 "Folks Still See Monster," *Blade* (Toledo, Ohio) (August 10, 1972): 34.

522 "Defiance Residents Suspicious of their Werewolf," *Blade* (Toledo, Ohio) (August 4, 1972): 1.

523 Stegall, James. "Werewolf Case in Defiance Not Viewed Lightly by Police," *Blade* (Toledo, Ohio) (August 3, 1972): 1.

524 "Defiance Residents Suspicious of their Werewolf," *Blade* (Toledo, Ohio) (August 4, 1972): 4.

525 Stegall, James. "Werewolf Case in Defiance Not Viewed Lightly by Police," *Blade* (Toledo, Ohio) (August 3, 1972): 1.

526 "Defiance Residents Suspicious of their Werewolf," *Blade* (Toledo, Ohio) (August 4, 1972): 4.

527 Stegall, James. "Werewolf Case in Defiance Not Viewed Lightly by Police," *Blade* (Toledo, Ohio) (August 3, 1972): 4.

528 "Defiance Residents Suspicious of their Werewolf," *Blade* (Toledo, Ohio) (August 4, 1972): 4.

529 Clark, Jerome. "On the Trail of Unidentified Furry Objects," *Fate* (August 1973): 58.

530 Clark, Jerome. "On the Trail of Unidentified Furry Objects," *Fate* (August 1973): 58-59.

531 Clark, Jerome. "On the Trail of Unidentified Furry Objects," *Fate* (August 1973): 59-60.

532 Clark, Jerome. "On the Trail of Unidentified Furry Objects," *Fate* (August 1973): 60.

533 Clark, Jerome. "On the Trail of Unidentified Furry Objects," *Fate* (August 1973): 62.

534 "Cooper Lays to Rest Tale of Parke County Monster," *Star* (Indianapolis, Indiana) (September 22, 1972): 7.

535 "Parke Sheriff Checks on Report of Monster," *Terre Haute Tribune* (September 20, 1972): 1.

536 "Parke Officials Conducting a Bear Hunt," *Brazil Daily Times* (Brazil, Indiana) (September 22, 1972): 1.

537 "Cooper Lays to Rest Tale of Parke County Monster," *Star* (Indianapolis, Indiana) (September 22, 1972): 7.

538 "2 Counties Hunt for 'Monster'," *Star* (Indianapolis, Indiana) (September 22, 1972): 47.

539 "Cleveland Suburb Residents Scared by 'Monster Animal'," *Logan Daily News* (Logan, Ohio) (August 14, 1972): 2.

540 "UFOs—Those Saucers in the Sky are Coming Back Once Again," *Morning Herald* (Hagerstown, Maryland) (February 14, 1972): 3.

541 "UFOs—Those Saucers in the Sky are Coming Back Once Again," *Morning Herald* (Hagerstown, Maryland) (February 14, 1972): 3.

542 "Several Patterns Apparent in UFO Sightings," *Sarasota Journal* (December 11, 1972): 4B.

543 Steiger, Brad. "Missouri's Mystifying 'Momo' Monster," *Saga* (March 1973): 75.

544 Sexton, Kim. "Some Believe in Monster," *Nevada Daily Mail* (Nevada, Missouri) (July 31, 1972): 2.

545 Steiger, Brad. "Missouri's Mystifying 'Momo' Monster," *Saga* (March 1973): 75.

546 Sexton, Kim. "Louisianians Believe in Momo So Do Many Newspapermen," *Nevada Daily Mail* (Nevada, Missouri) (August 6, 1972): 9.

547 Clark, Jerome, and Loren Coleman. "Anthropoids, Monsters and UFOs," *Flying Saucer Review* (January/February 1973): 19.

548 Kiss, Mary. "City Man Saw Monster," *Kingsport Times News* (Kingsport, Tennessee) (July 23, 1972): 1, 10.

549 Clark, Jerome, and Loren Coleman. "Anthropoids, Monsters and UFOs," *Flying Saucer Review* (January-February 1973): 24.

550 Coleman, Loren. "Eastern Bigfoot," *Fate* (November 2000). FateMag.com. http://www.fatemag.com/eastern-bigfoot-of-Momo-and-the-marked-hominids/

551 Clark, Jerome, and Loren Coleman. "Anthropoids, Monsters and UFOs," *Flying Saucer Review* (January/February 1973): 23.

552 Steiger, Brad. "Missouri's Mystifying 'Momo' Monster," *Saga* (March 1973): 72.

553 Eisele, Dana. "Predicts Campers Threaten to Turn State Parks into Slums," *Southeast Missourian* (July 1, 1971): 1.

554 Steiger, Brad. "Missouri's Mystifying 'Momo' Monster," *Saga* (March 1973): 72, 74.

555 "UFO Members Get Lowdown on Missouri Monster Cases," *Centralia Sentinel* (Centralia, Illinois) (July 24, 1972): 1.

556 "Mo Mo—That Missouri Monster," *Skylook* (September 1972): 5.

557 Sexton, Kim. "Many See Missouri Monster," *Nevada Daily Mail* (Nevada, Missouri) (August 2, 1972): 9.

558 Wilks, Ed. "Visit From Hairy Creature Sends Louisiana, Mo., Family Packing," *St. Louis Dispatch* (July 20, 1972): 3.
559 Crowe, Richard. "Missouri Monster," *Fate* (December 1972): 59.
560 Steiger, Brad. "Missouri's Mystifying 'Momo' Monster," *Saga* (March 1973): 24-25.
561 "Gruesome Missouri Monster Sets Sleepy Hamlet Agog," *Pittsburgh Press* (July 28, 1972): 17.
562 Steiger, Brad. "Missouri's Mystifying 'Momo' Monster," *Saga* (March 1973): 24-25, 68.
563 Clark, Jerome, and Loren Coleman. "Anthropoids, Monsters and UFOs," *Flying Saucer Review* (January-February 1973): 20.
564 Steiger, Brad. "Missouri's Mystifying 'Momo' Monster," *Saga* (March 1973): 70.
565 Sexton, Kim. "Many See Missouri Monster," *Nevada Daily Mail* (Nevada, Missouri) (August 2, 1972): 9.
566 "There's Something on Marzolf Hill," *Mexico Daily Ledger* (Mexico, Missouri) (July 19, 1972): 1.
567 Sexton, Kim. "Many See Missouri Monster," *Nevada Daily Mail* (Nevada, Missouri) (August 2, 1972): 9.
568 "UFO Members Get Lowdown on Missouri Monster Cases," *Centralia Sentinel* (July 24, 1972): 1.
569 Clark, Jerome, and Loren Coleman. "Anthropoids, Monsters and UFOs," *Flying Saucer Review* (January-February 1973): 21.
570 Clark, Jerome, and Loren Coleman. "Anthropoids, Monsters and UFOs," *Flying Saucer Review* (January-February 1973): 21.
571 Steiger, Brad. "Missouri's Mystifying 'Momo' Monster," *Saga* (March 1973): 70.
572 "There's Something on Marzolf Hill," *Mexico Daily Ledger* (Mexico, Missouri) (July 19, 1972): 5.
573 Sexton, Kim. "Many See Missouri Monster," *Nevada Daily Mail* (Nevada, Missouri) (August 2, 1972): 9.
574 "Gruesome Missouri Monster Sets Sleepy Hamlet Agog," *Pittsburgh Press* (July 28, 1972): 17.
575 "UFO Members Get Lowdown on Missouri Monster Cases," *Centralia Sentinel* (July 24, 1972): 1.
576 Clark, Jerome, and Loren Coleman. "Anthropoids, Monsters and UFOs," *Flying Saucer Review* (January-February 1973): 22.
577 Sexton, Kim. "Many See Missouri Monster," *Nevada Daily Mail* (Nevada, Missouri) (August 2, 1972): 9.
578 Crowe, Richard. "Missouri Monster," *Fate* (December 1972): 61.
579 Smith, Warren. *The Secret Origins of Bigfoot* (New York: Zebra Books, 1977): 95.
580 "There's Something on Marzolf Hill," *Mexico Daily Ledger* (Mexico, Missouri) (July 19, 1972): 1.

581 Steiger, Brad. "Missouri's Mystifying 'Momo' Monster," *Saga* (March 1973): 70.

582 "There's Something on Marzolf Hill," *Mexico Daily Ledger* (Mexico, Missouri) (July 19, 1972): 1.

583 Wilks, Ed. "Visit From Hairy Creature Sends Louisiana, Mo., Family Packing," *St. Louis Dispatch* (July 20, 1972): 3.

584 Wilks, Ed. "Visit From Hairy Creature Sends Louisiana, Mo., Family Packing," *St. Louis Dispatch* (July 20, 1972): 3.

585 Sexton, Kim. "Many See Missouri Monster," *Nevada Daily Mail* (Nevada, Missouri) (August 2, 1972): 9.

586 Steiger, Brad. "Missouri's Mystifying 'Momo' Monster," *Saga* (March 1973): 70.

587 Wilks, Ed. "Visit from Hairy Creature Sends Louisiana, Mo., Family Packing," *St. Louis Dispatch* (July 20, 1972): 3.

588 Steiger, Brad. "Missouri's Mystifying 'Momo' Monster," *Saga* (March 1973): 70, 72.

589 "Around Town," *Mexico Daily Ledger* (Mexico, Missouri) (July 20, 1972): 5.

590 "Sheriff Says Monster is Hoax & Rumor," *Mexico Daily Ledger* (Mexico, Missouri) (July 20, 1972): 5.

591 Crowe, Richard. "Missouri Monster," *Fate* (December 1972): 61.

592 Clark, Jerome, and Loren Coleman. "Anthropoids, Monsters and UFOs," *Flying Saucer Review* (January-February 1973): 22.

593 Steiger, Brad. "Missouri's Mystifying 'Momo' Monster," *Saga* (March 1973): 72.

594 "Is Foul-Smelling Monster Creature from Outer Space," *News-Herald* (Panama City, Florida) (July 23, 1972): 3A.

595 Steiger, Brad. "Missouri's Mystifying 'Momo' Monster," *Saga* (March 1973): 72.

596 Uhlenbrock, Thomas. "Strange 'Monster' Has Area Agog," *Ogden Standard-Examiner* (July 28, 1972): 16.

597 "Gruesome Missouri Monster Sets Sleepy Hamlet Agog," *Pittsburgh Press* (July 28, 1972): 17.

598 Steiger, Brad. "Missouri's Mystifying 'Momo' Monster," *Saga* (March 1973): 72.

599 Steiger, Brad. "Missouri's Mystifying 'Momo' Monster," *Saga* (March 1973): 72.

600 Sexton, Kim. "Many See Missouri Monster," *Nevada Daily Mail* (Nevada, Missouri) (August 2, 1972): 9.

601 "Is Momo a Creature from Another Planet," *Sarasota Herald-Tribune* (July 23, 1972): 4.

602 "UFO Researcher Awaits Return of Momo Monster," *Sarasota Journal* (July 24, 1972): 3.

603 "Is Momo a Creature from Another Planet," *Sarasota Herald-Tribune* (July 23, 1972): 4.

604 "Furry Missouri Monster is Really Hairy Biped: IUFOB," *Galesburg Register-Mail* (July 21, 1972): 2.

605 "UFO Members Get Lowdown on Missouri Monster Cases," *Centralia Sentinel* (July 24, 1972): 1.

606 "UFO Members Get Lowdown on Missouri Monster Cases," *Centralia Sentinel* (July 24, 1972): 1.

607 Warman, S. C. "'Expert' Doubts Monster, UFO Link," *Tucson Daily Citizen* (August 1, 1972): 23.

608 Crowe, Richard. "Missouri Monster," *Fate* (December 1972): 63-64.

609 Warman, S. C. "'Expert' Doubts Monster, UFO Link," *Tucson Daily Citizen* (August 1, 1972): 23.

610 Clark, Jerome, and Loren Coleman. "Anthropoids, Monsters and UFOs," *Flying Saucer Review* (January-February 1973): 23-24.

611 Crowe, Richard. "Missouri Monster," *Fate* (December 1972): 64-66.

612 Sexton, Kim. "Some Believe in Monster," *Nevada Daily Mail* (Nevada, Missouri) (July 31, 1972): 2.

613 Sexton, Kim. "Some Believe in Monster," *Nevada Daily Mail* (Nevada, Missouri) (July 31, 1972): 2.

614 "Shaggy Monster (Possibly from Outer Space!) Haunts Community," *Bonham Daily Favorite* (July 23, 1972): 6.

615 "Hairy Creature Sighted in Missouri Town," *Jefferson City News and Tribune* (July 23, 1972): 2.

616 Steiger, Brad. "Missouri's Mystifying 'Momo' Monster," *Saga* (March 1973): 74.

617 Power, John. "Louisiana Residents Continue to Report Monster 'Evidence'," *Jacksonville Journal* (July 25, 1972): 18.

618 Power, John. "Louisiana Residents Continue to Report Monster 'Evidence'," *Jacksonville Journal* (July 25, 1972): 18.

619 Clark, Jerome, and Loren Coleman. "Anthropoids, Monsters and UFOs," *Flying Saucer Review* (January-February 1973): 23.

620 Clark, Jerome, and Loren Coleman. "Anthropoids, Monsters and UFOs," *Flying Saucer Review* (January-February 1973): 23.

621 "Woman Tells Police Hairy Tale of Monster in Garden," *Joplin Globe* (July 27, 1972): 1.

622 "Search Finds No Monster on Cuivre," *Mexico Daily Ledger* (Mexico, Missouri) (July 22, 1972): 2.

623 "'Monster' Sighted in Illinois," *St. Joseph News-Press* (July 29, 1972): 2A.

624 Clark, Jerome, and Loren Coleman. "Anthropoids, Monsters and UFOs," *Flying Saucer Review* (January-February 1973): 22.

625 "3 Chicago Youths to Form Stakeout for Hairy Monster," *Arkansas Gazette* (Little Rock, Arkansas) (July 22, 1972): 6B.

626 "Costume Found; May Be Monster," *Panama City News Herald* (July 30, 1972): 81.

627 Thurman, Pennie Sue. "Search for Monster is at Least Fun," *Lewiston Morning Tribune* (July 31, 1972): 1.

628 Clark, Jerome, and Loren Coleman. "Anthropoids, Monsters and UFOs," *Flying Saucer Review* (January-February 1973): 23.

629 "Gruesome Missouri Monster Sets Sleepy Hamlet Agog," *Pittsburgh Press* (July 28, 1972): 17.

630 "Gruesome Missouri Monster Sets Sleepy Hamlet Agog," *Pittsburgh Press* (July 28, 1972): 17.

631 "'Monster' Sighted in Illinois," *St. Joseph News-Press* (July 29, 1972): 2.

632 Clark, Jerome, and Loren Coleman. "Anthropoids, Monsters and UFOs," *Flying Saucer Review* (January-February 1973): 22.

633 Sexton, Kim. "Some Believe in Monster," *Nevada Daily Mail* (Nevada, Missouri) (July 31, 1972): 2.

634 Thurman, Pennie Sue. "Search for Monster is at Least Fun," *Lewiston Morning Tribune* (Lewiston, Idaho) (July 31, 1972): 1.

635 "The Monster Moves to East Peoria," *Kingsport Times* (Kingsport, Tennessee) (July 27, 1972): 2A.

636 Clark, Jerome, and Loren Coleman. "Anthropoids, Monsters and UFOs," *Flying Saucer Review* (January/February 1973): 23.

637 Steiger, Brad. "Missouri's Mystifying 'Momo' Monster," *Saga* (March 1973): 74-75.

638 "Two-State Phenomenon," *Morning Star* (Rockford, Illinois) (August 1, 1972): 6.

639 "Big Foot Still Alive," *Hartford Courant* (August 17, 1972): 22.

640 Crowe, Richard. "Missouri Monster," *Fate* (December 1972): 64.

641 "Gruesome Missouri Monster Sets Sleepy Hamlet Agog," *Pittsburgh Press* (July 28, 1972): 17.

642 "Gruesome Missouri Monster Sets Sleepy Hamlet Agog," *Pittsburgh Press* (July 28, 1972): 17.

643 "Louisiana Jokes About Its Monster," *Mexico Daily Ledger* (Mexico, Missouri) (July 21, 1972): 1.

644 "From Local Newspapers," *St. Joseph News-Press* (August 12, 1972): 4.

645 Steiger, Brad. "Missouri's Mystifying 'Momo' Monster," *Saga* (March 1973): 68.

646 Steiger, Brad. "Missouri's Mystifying 'Momo' Monster," *Saga* (March 1973): 68.

647 Steiger, Brad. "Missouri's Mystifying 'Momo' Monster," *Saga* (March 1973): 70.

648 Steiger, Brad. "Missouri's Mystifying 'Momo' Monster," *Saga* (March 1973): 75.

649 "Mo Mo—That Missouri Monster," *Skylook* (September 1972).

650 Steiger, Brad. "Missouri's Mystifying 'Momo' Monster," *Saga* (March 1973): 75.

651 Steiger, Brad. "Missouri's Mystifying 'Momo' Monster," *Saga* (March 1973): 75.

652 "Mo Mo—That Missouri Monster," *Skylook* (September 1972).

653 "Monster Space Pledged by Zoo," *Lawrence Journal-World* (July 26, 1972): 12.

654 "Do Monsters Still Roam the Earth? Some Professional Think They Do," *Pottstown Mercury* (Pottstown, Pennsylvania) (July 29, 1972): 10.

655 Steiger, Brad. "Missouri's Mystifying 'Momo' Monster," *Saga* (March 1973): 75.

656 Steiger, Brad. "Missouri's Mystifying 'Momo' Monster," *Saga* (March 1973): 75.

657 "From Hairy Monster to Eerie Lights," *Southeast Missourian* (April 12, 1973): 7.

658 "From Hairy Monster to Eerie Lights," *Southeast Missourian* (April 12, 1973): 7.

659 "Is Mo Mo Still Around," *Skylook* (August 1973): 13.

660 Noe, Allen V. "And Still the Reports Roll In," *Pursuit* (January 1974): 16.

661 Hunter, Don and René Dahinden. *Sasquatch* (New York: Signet, 1975): 197-198.

662 Russell, Andy. "New Sasquatch Hunter," *Lethbridge Herald* (December 6, 1973): 5.

663 Folder 0348, box 10, Grover Krantz Papers Collection, National Anthropological Archive, Smithsonian Institution.

664 Napier John. *Bigfoot: The Yeti and Sasquatch in Myth and Reality* (New York: E. P. Dutton & Co., 1974): 18.

665 Napier John. *Bigfoot: The Yeti and Sasquatch in Myth and Reality* (New York: E. P. Dutton & Co., 1974): 19.

666 Umland, Rudolph. "Does Bigfoot Exist Beyond the Myth," *Kansas City Times* (April 10, 1973): 15.

667 Regal, Brian. *Searching for Sasquatch* (New York: Palgrave Macmillan, 2013): 64.

668 Regal, Brian. *Searching for Sasquatch* (New York: Palgrave Macmillan, 2013): 64.

669 Cowen, Robert C. "Is Bigfoot Real," *Salina Journal* (Salina, Kansas) (April 22, 1973): 18.

670 "Bigfoot Beyond the Myth," *Mexico Ledger* (Mexico, Missouri) (May 18, 1973): 4.

671 "Child-Oriented TV Spots," *Longview Morning Journal* (Longview, Texas) (November 11, 1973): 12.

672 Daniel Perez, email message to author, June 6, 2016.

673 Butler, Tom. "It's Scary, Funny, and True . . . 'Legend' Made on a Budget, Is Grossing Millions," *Spartanburg Herald* (February 22, 1973): 3.

674 Butler, Tom. "It's Scary, Funny, and True . . . 'Legend' Made on a Budget, Is Grossing Millions," *Spartanburg Herald* (February 22, 1973): 3.

675 White, Ron. "Success Comes on First Try at Filmmaking," *Express and News* (San Antonio, Texas) (March 18, 1972): 5.

676 Butler, Tom. "It's Scary, Funny, and True . . . 'Legend' Made on a Budget, is Grossing Millions," *Spartanburg Herald* (February 22, 1973): 3.

677 "'Legend of Boggy Creek' to Debut in Shreveport," *State-Times* (Baton Rouge, Louisiana) (August 5, 1972)

678 "Area Documentary Opens," *Camden Daily News* (Camden, Arkansas) (August 12, 1972).

679 Sexton, Ruby. "'The Legend of Boggy Creek' Breaking Box-Office Records," *Brownsville Herald* (Brownsville, Texas) (May 11, 1973).

680 Blackburn, Lyle. *The Beast of Boggy Creek* (San Antonio: Anomalist Books, 2012): 89.

681 Butler, Tom. "It's Scary, Funny, and True . . . 'Legend' Made on a Budget, is Grossing Millions," *Spartanburg Herald* (February 22, 1973): 3.

682 Harp, Jack. "Director Believes There's Something to Fouke Creature," *Alexandria Daily Town Talk* (Alexandria, Louisiana) (December 2, 1972): 14.

683 Harp, Jack. "Director Believes There's Something to Fouke Creature," *Alexandria Daily Town Talk* (Alexandria, Louisiana) (December 2, 1972): 14.

684 "Boggy Creek Legend Monstrous Success," *Journal-News* (Hamilton, Ohio) (June 14, 1973): 24.

685 Harp, Jack. "Director Believes There's Something to Fouke Creature," *Alexandria Daily Town Talk* (Alexandria, Louisiana) (December 2, 1972): 14.

686 Wright, Fred. "Home-Spun Tale Child's Delight," *St. Petersburg Independent* (March 27, 1973): 5B.

687 Toles, Tommy. "'Boggy Creek' Movie Ruins Documentary," *Rome News-Tribune* (Rome, Georgia) (June 14, 1973): 5.

688 Richardson, Norman. "Latest Monster Hunt Also Failure," *Shreveport Times* (November 10, 1972): 10.

689 Hale, Debra. "Fouke Monster Film Does Good," *Childress Index* (Childress, Texas) (August 21, 1973): 2.

690 Hale, Debra. "Fouke Monster Film Does Good," *Childress Index* (Childress, Texas) (August 21, 1973): 2.

691 Hale, Debra. "Fouke Monster Film Does Good," *Childress Index* (Childress, Texas) (August 21, 1973): 2.

692 Harp, Jack. "Director Believes There's Something to Fouke Creature," *Alexandria Daily Town Talk* (Alexandria, Louisiana) (December 2, 1972): 14.

693 Richardson, Norman. "Fouke Monster Shows Up Again," *Shreveport Times* (November 27, 1973): 8.

694 "Fouke Monster Makes Believer of Skeptic," *El Dorado Times* (El Dorado, Arkansas) (November 27, 1973): 6.

695 "Bigfoot Still Has Lots of Believers," *Spokane Daily Chronicle* (March 12, 1973): 12.

696 Childress, William. "The Most Sensational Bigfoot Pictures Ever Taken," *Saga* (December 1973): 30, 31.

697 Folder 0340, box 9, Grover Krantz Papers Collection, National Anthropological Archive, Smithsonian Institution.

698 Folder 0340, box 9, Grover Krantz Papers Collection, National Anthropological Archive, Smithsonian Institution.

699 Folder 0340, box 9, Grover Krantz Papers Collection, National Anthropological Archive, Smithsonian Institution.

700 Reiffel, Leonard. "Computers Join Hunt for Bigfoot Wild 'Man'," *Dallas Morning News* (March 18, 1973): 64D.

701 The given math works out to Olson hearing about Bigfoot in 1954. If in fact Olson (through Bates) refers to the Gerald Crew story from 1958, Olson would have been about 16 years old vice 12.

702 An interesting comment coming from one who procured the rights to the film.

703 Bates, Doug. "The Man Who Chases Bigfoot," *Eugene Register-Guard* (October 21, 1973).

704 "Oregon Man Searches for Ape-Like 'Bigfoot'," *Beaver County Times* (Beaver County, Pennsylvania.) (April 18, 1973).

705 "Oregon Man Searches for Ape-Like 'Bigfoot'," *Beaver County Times* (Beaver, Pennsylvania) (April 18, 1973).

706 "Oregon Man Searches for Ape-Like 'Bigfoot'," *Beaver County Times* (Beaver, Pennsylvania) (April 18, 1973).

707 "Oregon Man Searches for Ape-Like 'Bigfoot'," *Beaver County Times* (Beaver, Pennsylvania) (April 18, 1973).

708 Keel, John A., ed. *Anomaly* (June 1973): 167.

709 "In Memoriam—Ivan T. Sanderson," *Pursuit* (April 1973): 26.

710 Taylor, Charles S. "'Big Foot' Like UFOs—Not Enough Evidence," *Chronicle-Telegram* (December 23, 1973): 4B.

711 "Bigfoot: Too Much Evidence That Can't Be Explained Any Other Way," *Walla Walla Union Bulletin* (March 12, 1973): 10.

712 Holmstrom, David. "Search for 'Bigfoot' Goes On," *Oakland Tribune* (March 24, 1973): 9E.

713 Childress, William. "The Most Sensational Bigfoot Pictures Ever Taken," *Saga* (December 1973): 70.

714 Harris, Richard. "The Bigfoot: Fact, Fiction or Flim-Flam," *Times-Standard* (Eureka, California) (June 8, 1973): 13.

715 "Bigfoot Legends Varied," *Times-Standard* (Eureka, California) (June 8, 1973): 13.

716 "On the Trail of 'Old Bigfoot'," *Fairbanks Daily News-Miner* (July 28, 1973): 3.

717 Harris, Richard. "The Bigfoot: Fact, Fiction or Flim-Flam," *Times-Standard* (Eureka, California) (June 8, 1973): 13.

718 "The Searching for Bigfoot Live Capture Team," SearchingForBigfoot.com http://searchingforbigfoot.com/Tom_Biscardi/.

719 Wheeler, Chuck. "Bigfoot Sightings in the Antelope Valley Are Just About Over for 1973," *Daily Ledger Gazette* (May 22, 1973). BFRO.net. http://www.bfro.net/gdb/show_article.asp?id=102.

720 "Tracking Down Bigfoot," *Pocono Record* (Stroudsburg, Pennsylvania) (May 18, 1973): 21.

721 Harris, Richard. "The Bigfoot: Fact, Fiction or Flim-Flam," *Times-Standard* (Eureka, California) (June 8, 1973): 13.

722 Harris, Richard. "The Bigfoot: Fact, Fiction or Flim-Flam," *Times-Standard* (Eureka, California) (June 8, 1973): 13.

723 Harris, Richard. "The Bigfoot: Fact, Fiction or Flim-Flam," *Times-Standard* (Eureka, California) (June 8, 1973): 13.

724 Harris, Richard. "The Bigfoot: Fact, Fiction or Flim-Flam," *Times-Standard* (Eureka, California) (June 8, 1973): 13.

725 Harris, Richard. "The Bigfoot: Fact, Fiction or Flim-Flam," *Times-Standard* (Eureka, California) (June 8, 1973): 13.

726 Childress, William. "The Most Sensational Bigfoot Pictures Ever Taken," *Saga* (December 1973): 30.

727 Harris, Richard. "The Bigfoot: Fact, Fiction or Flim-Flam," *Times-Standard* (Eureka, California) (June 8, 1973): 13.

728 "'Big Foot' Capture Opposed," *Reno Evening Gazette* (December 12, 1973): 20.

729 Childress, William. "The Most Sensational Bigfoot Pictures Ever Taken," *Saga* (December 1973): 70, 72.

730 Leavitt, Carrick. "ESP Hunters Pay to Track Bigfoot," *Times-Standard* (Eureka, California) (September 29, 1974): 8.

731 "'Big Foot' Capture Opposed," *Reno Evening Gazette* (December 12, 1973): 20.

732 "Eastside Students Hear Bigfoot Talk," *Antelope Valley Ledger Gazette* (April 11, 1973). BigfootEncounters.com. http://www.bigfootencounters.com/articles/grumley.htm.

733 Wheeler, Chuck. "Bigfoot Searchers Scramble for Cover as Gunfire Breaks up Local Hunt," *Daily Ledger Gazette* (Lancaster, California) (May 17, 1973). BFRO.net. http://www.bfro.net/gdb/show_article.asp?id=101.

734 Wheeler, Chuck. "Bigfoot Surfaces Again in Palmdale, Nine-Mile Canyon," *Daily Ledger Gazette* (Lancaster, California) (June 1, 1973). BFRO.net. http://www.bfro.net/gdb/show_article.asp?id=103.

735 Wheeler, Chuck. "Bigfoot Surfaces Again in Palmdale, Nine-Mile Canyon," *Daily Ledger Gazette* (Lancaster, California) (June 1, 1973). BFRO.net. http://www.bfro.net/gdb/show_article.asp?id=103.

736 Bostwick, Charles. "Bigfoot Visits Antelope Valley—Or Does He," *Antelope Valley Press* (August 28, 2007). BFRO.net. http://www.bfro.net/gdb/show_article.asp?id=537.

737 Bostwick, Charles. "Bigfoot Visits Antelope Valley—Or Does He," *Antelope Valley Press* (August 28, 2007). BFRO.net. http://www.bfro.net/gdb/show_article.asp?id=537.

738 Bostwick, Charles. "Bigfoot Visits Antelope Valley—Or Does He," *Antelope Valley Press* (August 28, 2007). BFRO.net. http://www.bfro.net/gdb/show_article.asp?id=537.

739 Wheeler, Chuck. "Bigfoot Searchers Scramble for Cover as Gunfire Breaks up Local Hunt," *Daily Ledger Gazette* (Lancaster, Ca) (May 17, 1973). BFRO.net. http://www.bfro.net/gdb/show_article.asp?id=101.

740 Bostwick, Charles. "Bigfoot Visits Antelope Valley—Or Does He," *Antelope Valley Press* (August 28, 2007). BFRO.net. http://www.bfro.net/gdb/show_article.asp?id=537.

741 "Bell-Jars and Gargoyles," *Canadian UFO Report* (No. 20, 1975):5-6.

742 "Bell-Jars and Gargoyles," *Canadian UFO Report* (No. 20, 1975):6.

743 "Stations Deluged," *Daily Herald* (Provo, Utah) (November 8, 1973): 4.

744 "Little Monster Breaks Fishing Poles of Women," *Northwest Arkansas Times* (May 28, 1973): 2.

745 "Sykesville Hunts for Hairy Monster 7ft. Tall," *Baltimore Afro-American* (June 9, 1973): 1.

746 The surname should be Dorsey, not Norris. Anthony Dorsey lived on Norris Avenue, Sykesville.

747 "Mystery Monster Reappears," *Morning Herald* (Hagerstown, Maryland) (June 12, 1973): 1.

748 Opsasnick, Mark. "Monsters of Maryland: An Occasional Series Part I" *Strange Magazine*, no. 3: 19.

749 Opsasnick, Mark. "Monsters of Maryland: An Occasional Series Part I" *Strange Magazine*, no. 3: 19.

750 "Sykesville Hunts for Hairy Monster 7 Ft. Tall," *Baltimore Afro-American* (June 9, 1973): 1.

751 "Similar Monster Seen Last Year in Missouri," *Baltimore Afro-American* (June 16, 1973): 16B.

752 Stover, S. "Does Maryland Have a Sasquatch," *INFO Journal* (March-April 1979): 3.

753 "Local Citizen Saw Monster, Joins Hunt in Sykesville," *Baltimore Afro-American* (June 19, 1973): 26.

754 "Local Citizen Saw Monster, Joins Hunt in Sykesville," *Baltimore Afro-American* (June 19, 1973): 26.

755 Rhoden, Bill. "Sykesville Monster Interest Spreads," *Baltimore Afro-American* (June 12, 1973): 26.

756 "Transit Worker Moonlights in Quest for UFOs," *St. Petersburg Independent* (March 1, 1980): 3.

757 "UFOs—Those Saucers in the Sky are Coming Back Once Again," *Morning Herald* (Hagerstown, Maryland) (February 14, 1972): 3.

758 "Sykesville Monster Relatives of Abominable Snowman," *Baltimore Afro-American* (July 3, 1973): 26.

759 Sherwood, John. "Sykesville Beastie is Still Mystery," *Evening Star and Daily News* (Washington, D.C.) (June 13, 1973): A-3.

760 Rhoden, Bill. "Hunt Still in Progress—Sykesville Monster Interest Spreads," *Baltimore Afro-American* (June 12, 1973): 26.

761 Rhoden, Bill. "Hunt Still in Progress—Sykesville Monster Interest Spreads," *Baltimore Afro-American* (June 12, 1973): 26.

762 Dr. Pokrass told the *Baltimore Afro-American* that within the last two weeks, "10 or 12 people have taken unauthorized leaves," including one or two individuals considered "dangerous to themselves or to others."

763 "Movin' Down the Line," *Baltimore Afro-American* (June 30, 1973): 16B.

764 "Sykesville Monster Relatives of Abominable Snowman," *Baltimore Afro-American* (July 3, 1973): 26.

765 "Sykesville Monster Relatives of Abominable Snowman," *Baltimore Afro-American* (July 3, 1973): 26.

766 "Sykesville Monster Relatives of Abominable Snowman," *Baltimore Afro-American* (July 3, 1973): 26.

767 "Baltimore Man Says He Can Solve Monster Mystery but Quick," *Baltimore Afro-American* (July 10, 1973): 3.

768 "Sykesville Monster Joins the Urban Set," *Baltimore Afro-American* (July 14, 1973): 10B.

769 "Sykesville Monster Joins the Urban Set," *Baltimore Afro-American* (July 14, 1973): 10B.

770 "Quick Look at Bigfoot is Claimed," *Spokane Daily Chronicle* (June 8, 1973): 6.

771 "Bigfoot 'Hunt' Slated," *Spokesman-Review* (July 20, 1973).

772 Strang, Jim. "Lorain Seeks Red-Eyed 'Monster' That Screams," *Plain Dealer* (Cleveland, Ohio) (August 16, 1973).

773 "Oberlin Hit with Claims of 'Monster'," *Steubenville Herald Star* (August 10, 1973): 9.

774 "Monster Seen Near Oberlin," *Plain Dealer* (Cleveland, Ohio) (August 5, 1973): 8.

775 "Oberlin Hit with Claims of 'Monster'," *Steubenville Herald Star* (August 10, 1973): 9.

776 Strang, Jim. "Lorain Seeks Red-Eyed 'Monster' That Screams," *Plain Dealer* (Cleveland, Ohio) (August 16, 1973).

777 "Oberlin Hit with Claims of 'Monster'," *Steubenville Herald Star* (August 10, 1973): 9.

778 "Oberlin Hit with Claims of 'Monster'," *Steubenville Herald Star* (August 10, 1973): 9.

779 *In Search of The Swamp Monster* produced by Robert L. Long (Alan Landsburg Productions, 1978).

780 "New Monster in Bayou," *Ruston Daily Leader* ((October 23, 1973): 3.

781 Stan Gordon, telephone interview by author, June 22, 2016.

782 Fawcett, George. "1973—Big for UFO's," *Skylook* (February 1974): 10.

783 "UFO Reports from Pennsylvania—From Stan Gordon's Files," *Skylook* (May 1972).

784 "Stan Gordon, Director of Pennsylvania UFO Study Group, A Busy Man," *Skylook* (July 1972).

785 "Are Creatures & UFOs Related," *Skylook* (February 1974): 6.

786 "Are Creatures & UFOs Related," *Skylook* (February 1974): 6.

787 "UFO, 'Bigfoot' Report Here Similar to Other Sightings," *Uniontown Evening Standard* (October 27, 1973): 3.

788 "Bigfoot Shook Couple's Auto," *Grit* (October 30, 1977) as cited in *Mysteries of the World Supplement* (December 1977).

789 "'Bigfoot' Wreaking Havoc in Westmoreland," *Observer-Reporter* (Washington, Pennsylvania) (August 31, 1973): 5.

790 "'Bigfoot' Wreaking Havoc in Westmoreland," *Observer-Reporter* (Washington, Pennsylvania) (August 31, 1973): 5.

791 "'Big Foot' Mystery In Blairsville Area," *Indiana Evening Gazette* (August 28, 1973): 13.

792 "Are Creatures & UFOs Related," *Skylook* (February 1974): 6.

793 Tippins, John. "Skunk Ape May Have Kissin' Kin," *Naples Daily News* (December 29, 1974): 1F.

794 Morrison, Pat. "Woman Describes 'Bigfoot'," *The Derrick* (Oil City, Pennsylvania) (May 13, 1977): 5

795 "Are Creatures & UFOs Related," *Skylook* (February 1974).

796 "Are Creatures & UFOs Related," *Skylook* (February 1974).

797 Schwarz, Berthold Eric. "Berserk! A UFO-Creature Encounter," *UFO Report* (July 1980): 78.

798 "UFO, 'Bigfoot' Report Here Similar to Other Sightings," *Uniontown Evening Standard* (October 27, 1973): 3.

799 Dvorchak, Bob. "Across the Desk," *Morning Herald* (Uniontown, Pennsylvania) (November 2, 1973): 4.

800 Quinlan, James. "Dr. Hynek—Rock in 'Wilderness' of UFOs," *Palm Beach Post-Times* (November 4, 1973): 1C.

801 Taylor, Charles S. "'Big Foot' Like UFOs—Not Enough Evidence," *Chronicle-Telegram* (December 23, 1973): 4B.

802 "Hairy Monster Sighted, Shot at," *Daily Sentinel* (Pomeroy, Ohio) (May 7, 1973): 1.

803 Dettro, Chris. "Henry's Grey-Haired Critter Puts Village in a Dither," *Lima News* (August 26, 1973): C11.

804 "Hairy Monster Sighted, Shot at," *Daily Sentinel* (Pomeroy, Ohio) (May 7, 1973): 1.

805 "Three Elwood Men Hunt 'Monster,' Two Are Arrested," *Call Leader* (Elwood, Indiana) (May 9, 1973): 1.

806 Dettro, Chris. "Henry's Grey-Haired Critter Puts Village in a Dither," *Lima News* (August 26, 1973): 11C.

807 Taylor, Troy. *Monsters of Illinois: Mysterious Creatures in the Prairie State* (Mechanicsburg, Pennsylvania: Stackpole Books, 2011).

808 Dettro, Chris. "Henry's Grey-Haired Critter Puts Village in a Dither," *Lima News* (August 26, 1973): 11C.

809 Dettro, Chris. "Henry's Grey-Haired Critter Puts Village in a Dither," *Lima News* (August 26, 1973): 11C.

810 Dettro, Chris. "Henry's Grey-Haired Critter Puts Village in a Dither," *Lima News* (August 26, 1973): 11C.

811 Taylor, Troy. *Monsters of Illinois: Mysterious Creatures in the Prairie State* (Mechanicsburg, Pennsylvania: Stackpole Books, 2011).

812 Taylor, Troy. *Monsters of Illinois: Mysterious Creatures in the Prairie State* (Mechanicsburg, Pennsylvania: Stackpole Books, 2011).

813 Clark, Jerome, and Loren Coleman. "Anthropoids, Monsters and UFOs," *INFO Journal* (January-February 1973).

814 Guttilla, Peter. "Bigfoot: 3 Tales of Terror," *UFO Report* (October 1976): 49.

815 Guttilla, Peter. "Bigfoot: 3 Tales of Terror," *UFO Report* (October 1976): 63.

816 Guttilla, Peter. "Bigfoot: 3 Tales of Terror," *UFO Report* (October 1976): 64.
817 Guttilla, Peter. "Bigfoot: 3 Tales of Terror," *UFO Report* (October 1976): 64.
818 Guttilla, Peter. "Bigfoot: 3 Tales of Terror," *UFO Report* (October 1976): 64-66.
819 Guttilla, Peter. "Bigfoot: 3 Tales of Terror," *UFO Report* (October 1976): 66.
820 Malcolm, Andrew H. "Mysterious 'It' Frightens Town," *Ocala-Star Banner* (November 6, 1973): 1.
821 Malcolm, Andrew H. "Mysterious 'It' Frightens Town," *Ocala-Star Banner* (November 6, 1973): 1.
822 Malcolm, Andrew H. "Mysterious 'It' Frightens Town," *Ocala-Star Banner* (November 6, 1973): 1.
823 Malcolm, Andrew H. "Mysterious 'It' Frightens Town," *Ocala-Star Banner* (November 6, 1973): 10.
824 Taylor, Troy. *Monsters of Illinois: Mysterious Creatures in the Prairie State* (Mechanicsburg, Pennsylvania: Stackpole Books, 2011).
825 "More Meanderings for the Murphysboro Monster," *Carbondale Southern Illinoisan* (June 27, 1973). StanCourtney.com. http://www.stancourtney.com/wordpress/media-article-jackson-county-illinois-5/.
826 "Monster Watching Popular," *Southern Illinoisan* (Carbondale, Illinois) (June 28, 1973).
827 Malcolm, Andrew H. "Mysterious 'It' Frightens Town," *Ocala-Star Banner* (November 6, 1973): 10.
828 "Bear Wasn't There, Neither Was Monster," *Southern Illinoisan* Carbondale, Illinois) (July 2, 1973): 3.
829 Malcolm, Andrew H. "Gorilla-Like 'Monster' Gives Staid Town in Illinois a Fright," *Bennington Banner* (November 2, 1973): 10.
830 "Tracking Down the Abominable Big Foot," *Sun-Herald* (Sydney, Australia) (November 23, 1975): 137.
831 Taylor, Troy. *Monsters of Illinois: Mysterious Creatures in the Prairie State* (2011).
832 Taylor, Troy. *Monsters of Illinois: Mysterious Creatures in the Prairie State* (Mechanicsburg, Pennsylvania: Stackpole Books, 2011): 33.
833 "Leigh Van Valen, Evolutionary Theorist and Paleobiology Pioneer, 1935-2010," News.UChicago.edu. https://news.uchicago.edu/article/2010/10/19/leigh-van-valen-evolutionary-theorist-and-paleobiology-pioneer-1935-2010.
834 Lee, John and Barbara Moore. *Monsters Among Us: Journey to the Unexplained* (New York: Pyramid Communications, Inc., 1975): 14.
835 Gusewelle, C. W. "Stalking Sasquatch," *Milwaukee Journal* (August 5, 1979) as cited in *Mysteries of the World Supplement* (September 1979).
836 Noe, Allan V. "And Still the Reports Roll In," *Pursuit* (January 1974): 17.
837 Noe, Allan V. "And Still the Reports Roll In," *Pursuit* (January 1974): 16.
838 Noe, Allan V. "And Still the Reports Roll In," *Pursuit* (January 1974): 18.

839 "Search on for Monkey Man," *Lewiston Daily Sun* (April 20, 1973): 8.

840 "Search on for Monkey Man," *Lewiston Daily Sun* (April 20, 1973): 8.

841 "Rented Gorilla Costume has not been Returned," *Lewiston Daily Sun* (July 30, 1973): 28

842 Coleman, Loren. "Series of Sightings Taking Place Over Three Days," BFRO.net. http://www.bfro.net/GDB/show_report.asp?ID=1186.

843 Coleman, Loren. "Series of Sightings Taking Place Over Three Days," BFRO.net. http://www.bfro.net/GDB/show_report.asp?ID=1186.

844 Skelton, Kathryn. "Durham's 'Gorilla'," Weird, Wicked Weird. *Lewiston Sun Journal* (August 2, 2008).

845 "Anyone Lose an Ape at Durham," *Lewiston Daily Sun* (July 27, 1973): 2.

846 "Anyone Lose an Ape at Durham," *Lewiston Daily Sun* (July 27, 1973): 2.

847 "Beast Reported Prowling in Durham Area," *Bangor Daily News* (July 27, 1973): 19.

848 "Anyone Lose an Ape at Durham," *Lewiston Daily Sun* (July 27, 1973): 2.

849 "Anyone Lose an Ape at Durham," *Lewiston Daily Sun* (July 27, 1973): 2.

850 "Gorilla is Back," *Lewiston Evening Journal* (August 13, 1973): 22.

851 "Gorilla is Back," *Lewiston Evening Journal* (August 13, 1973): 22.

852 "Gorilla Spectators Cause Durham Property Damage," *Lewiston Daily Sun* (August 15, 1973): 28.

853 "Gorilla Spectators Cause Durham Property Damage," *Lewiston Daily Sun* (August 15, 1973): 28.

854 "Gorilla Spectators Cause Durham Property Damage," *Lewiston Daily Sun* (August 15, 1973): 28.

855 Day, John S. "Ford may Make N. H. Gains by Handling Hecklers Better than Reagan," *Bangor Daily News* (February 12, 1976): 1.

856 Slate, B. Ann. "Man-Ape's Reign of Terror," *UFO Report* (August 1977): 22.

857 Estes, Bruce. "City Group After Brooksville Beast," *St. Petersburg Independent* (October 26, 1973): 8A.

858 "Swamp Expedition to Seek Out Skunk Apes," *Florida Today* (September 19, 1973): 6B.

859 Estes, Bruce. "Is Big Cypress Yeti Land," *Evening Independent* (St. Petersburg, Florida) (September 19, 1973): 1.

860 Estes, Bruce. "City Group After Brooksville Beast," *St. Petersburg Independent* (October 26, 1973): 8A.

861 Estes, Bruce. "City Group After Brooksville Beast," *St. Petersburg Independent* (October 26, 1973): 8A.

862 Estes, Bruce. "City Group After Brooksville Beast," *St. Petersburg Independent* (October 26, 1973): 8A.

863 Estes, Bruce. "City Group After Brooksville Beast," *St. Petersburg Independent* (October 26, 1973): 8A.

864 "Yeti Winters in Florida," *News-Herald* (Panama City, Florida) (November 25, 1973): 2.

865 White, Randy. "You Might Scoff Him Aside, But the Swamp Ape Laughs Last," *News-Press* (Ft. Myers, Florida) (September 4, 1974): 2D.

866 "Highlights," *St. Louis Post-Dispatch* (December 9, 1973): 6I.

867 Genzoli, Andrew. "Redwood Country," *Times-Standard* (Eureka, California) (February 20, 1974): 17.

868 Anderson, David C. "The Mystery of "Big Foot," *Courier-Journal & Times Magazine* (Louisville, Kentucky) (February 24, 1974): 30.

869 Castle, Ken. "The Search for Bigfoot," *Outdoor Outlook* (February 3, 1974): 8.

870 Genzoli, Andrew. "Redwood Country," *Times-Standard* (Eureka, California) (April 19, 1974): 11.

871 "NABS Interview of the Bay Area Bigfoot Group Co-Founder Warren Thompson," NABigfootSearch.com. http://www.nabigfootsearch.com/Guestcolumnist.html

872 "The Bay Area Group," NABigfootSearch.com. http://www.nabigfootsearch.com/Bigfootbulletin.html.

873 Castle, Ken. "The Search for Bigfoot," *Outdoor Outlook* (February 3, 1974): 9-10.

874 Castle, Ken. "The Search for Bigfoot," *Outdoor Outlook* (February 3, 1974): 10.

875 Castle, Ken. "The Search for Bigfoot," *Outdoor Outlook* (February 3, 1974): 10.

876 Castle, Ken. "The Search for Bigfoot," *Outdoor Outlook* (February 3, 1974): 10.

877 Castle, Ken. "The Search for Bigfoot," *Outdoor Outlook* (February 3, 1974): 9.

878 Castle, Ken. "The Search for Bigfoot," *Outdoor Outlook* (February 3, 1974): 11.

879 Green, John. *The Sasquatch File* (Agassiz, British Columbia: Cheam Publishing Ltd., 1973): 71.

880 Castle, Ken. "The Search for Bigfoot," *Outdoor Outlook* (February 3, 1974): 11.

881 Castle, Ken. "The Search for Bigfoot," *Outdoor Outlook* (February 3, 1974): 11.

882 Castle, Ken. "The Search for Bigfoot," *Outdoor Outlook* (February 3, 1974): 11.

883 Genzoli, Andrew. "Redwood Country," *Times-Standard* (Eureka, California) (October 21, 1974): 6.

884 Brisso, Paul. "Bigfoot Hunter Still Believes Creature Not Just Legend," *Times-Standard* (Eureka, California.) (September 29, 1974): 8.

885 Brisso, Paul. "Bigfoot Hunter Still Believes Creature Not Just Legend," *Times-Standard* (Eureka, California.) (September 29, 1974): 8.

886 Wright, Glen. "Bigfoot Legend Persists," *Kansas City Times* (November 22, 1973): 2G.

887 Trabing, Wally. "Bigfoot—Endangered Species," *Santa Cruz Sentinel* (October 30, 1974): 35.

888 Genzoli, Andrew. "Redwood Country," *Times-Standard* (Eureka, California) (May 21, 1973): 18.

889 Castle, Ken. "The Search for Bigfoot," *Outdoor Outlook* (February 3, 1974): 10.

890 Castle, Ken. "The Search for Bigfoot," *Outdoor Outlook* (February 3, 1974): 11.

891 Downing, Bob. "One Man's Search for Bigfoot," *Akron Beacon Journal* (January 27, 1974): 14.

892 Downing, Bob. "One Man's Search for Bigfoot," *Akron Beacon Journal* (January 27, 1974): 15, 17.

893 Downing, Bob. "One Man's Search for Bigfoot," *Akron Beacon Journal* (January 27, 1974): 17.

894 Downing, Bob. "One Man's Search for Bigfoot," *Akron Beacon Journal* (January 27, 1974): 20.

895 Heerwald, Martin. "Fisherman Hunting Snowman," *Gaffney Ledger* (December 19, 1973): 4B.

896 Byrne, Peter. "All Quiet on the Western Front: Bigfoot, April 1974," *Pursuit* (April 1974): 41.

897 Green, John. "Not All Quiet on the Western Front," *Pursuit* (October 1974): 98.

898 Green, John. "Not All Quiet on the Western Front," *Pursuit* (October 1974): 98-99.

899 Donskoy, Dmitri D. "The Patterson Film: An Analysis," *Pursuit* (October 1974): 97-98.

900 Sanderson, Ivan T. "Composite Reconstructions of Sasquatch and Yeti," *Pursuit* (October 1974): 95.

901 "Pennsylvania ABSMery," *Pursuit* (October 1974): 94.

902 "Pennsylvania ABSMery," *Pursuit* (October 1974): 94.

903 Klobuchar, Jim. "Support Your Local Wildmen," *Minneapolis Star* (January 28, 1974): 9.

904 *Rosemary's Baby* (1968) and the *Exorcist* (1973) ushered in a wave of books and movies on the occult.

905 Genzoli, Andrew. "Redwood Country," *Times-Standard* (Eureka, California) (March 11, 1974): 16.

906 McPhee, Penelope. "Man Against Myth: The Search for Bigfoot," *Spokesman-Review Sunday Magazine* (September 8, 1974): 12.

907 McPhee, Penelope. "Man Against Myth: The Search for Bigfoot," *Spokesman-Review Sunday Magazine* (September 8, 1974): 14.

908 McPhee, Penelope. "Man Against Myth: The Search for Bigfoot," *Spokesman-Review Sunday Magazine* (September 8, 1974): 14.

909 McPhee, Penelope. "Man Against Myth: The Search for Bigfoot," *Spokesman-Review Sunday Magazine* (September 8, 1974): 12.

910 McPhee, Penelope. "Man Against Myth: The Search for Bigfoot," *Spokesman-Review Sunday Magazine* (September 8, 1974): 15.

911 McPhee, Penelope. "Man Against Myth: The Search for Bigfoot," *Spokesman-Review Sunday Magazine* (September 8, 1974): 15.

912 McPhee, Penelope. "Man Against Myth: The Search for Bigfoot," *Spokesman-Review Sunday Magazine* (September 8, 1974): 16.

913 "Human-Like Hair Found Near Man-Beast's Tracks," *Evening Journal* (Wilmington, Delaware) (September 24, 1974): 33.

914 "Human-Like Hair Found Near Man-Beast's Tracks," *Evening Journal* (Wilmington, Delaware) (September 24, 1974): 33.

915 "Sasquatch Hunters Find Strands of Human Hair," *Bulletin* (Bend, Ore.) (September 24, 1974): 8.

916 "Scientists Also Hunt Legendary Creature," *Times-Standard* (Eureka, California) (September 29, 1974): 8.

917 "Bigfoot Tracks Discovered by Loggers," *Ukiah Daily Journal* (Ukiah, California) (October 16, 1974): 5.

918 "Bigfoot Tracks Discovered by Loggers," *Ukiah Daily Journal* (Ukiah, California) (October 16, 1974): 5

919 "Bigfoot Tracks Discovered by Loggers," *Ukiah Daily Journal* (Ukiah, Calif.) (October 16, 1974): 5.

920 "Sasquatch—'Not Again!'," *Daily Record* (Ellensburg, Wash.) (October 17, 1974): 3.

921 "Sasquatch—'Not Again!'," *Daily Record* (Ellensburg, Wash.) (October 17, 1974): 3.

922 "Serling Narrates 'Monsters'," *Times-News* (Burlington, N.C.) (November 2, 1974): 7A.

923 Coleman, David. *The Bigfoot Filmography* (North Carolina: McFarland & Company, 2012): 197.

924 "Serling to Narrate Monster Special," *Abilene Reporter-News* (November 24, 1974): 11-E.

925 Fanning, Win. "On the Air," *Pittsburgh Post-Gazette* (November 27, 1974): 23.

926 Ripley, Dillon. "Mythical Monsters Are a Scientific Quest," *Nevada Daily Mail* (December 3, 1974): 4.

927 Genzoli, Andrew. "Redwood Country," *Times-Standard* (Eureka, California) (February 20, 1974): 17.

928 Davis, Beau R. *Bigfoot is Alive!* (Beverly Hills, California: Tambarlee International, Inc., 1974): 54.

929 Slate, A.B. "The Ex-Marine Being Stalked by a Bigfoot," *Saga* (June 1976): 54.

930 Slate, A.B. "The Ex-Marine Being Stalked by a Bigfoot," *Saga* (June 1976): 79.

931 Slate, A.B. "The Ex-Marine Being Stalked by a Bigfoot," *Saga* (June 1976): 79.

932 Slate, A.B. "The Ex-Marine Being Stalked by a Bigfoot," *Saga* (June 1976): 80.

933 Slate, A.B. "The Ex-Marine Being Stalked by a Bigfoot," *Saga* (June 1976): 80.

934 Slate, A.B. "The Ex-Marine Being Stalked by a Bigfoot," *Saga* (June 1976): 80.

935 Slate, A.B. "The Ex-Marine Being Stalked by a Bigfoot," *Saga* (June 1976): 80-81.

936 Slate, A.B. "The Ex-Marine Being Stalked by a Bigfoot," *Saga* (June 1976): 81.

937 Slate, A.B. "The Ex-Marine Being Stalked by a Bigfoot," *Saga* (June 1976): 81.

938 Guttilla, Peter. "UFO Nights of Terror," *UFO Report* (July 1978): 70.

939 "Occupant Case in Wisconsin (William Bosak Encounter)," UFOEvidence.com. http://www.ufoevidence.org/cases/case360.htm

940 "Another Gargoyle and Bell-Jar," *Canadian UFO Report* (No. 21, 1975):1.
941 "Another Gargoyle and Bell-Jar," *Canadian UFO Report* (No. 21, 1975):3.
942 Guttilla, Peter. "UFO Nights of Terror," UFO Report (July 1978): 72.
943 Lubas, Kenneth. "Group Feels Bigfoot is Canyon Monster," *Los Angeles Times* (November 18, 1974). BigfootEncounters.com. www.bigfootencounters.com/articles/ esper.htm
944 Guttilla, Peter. "Bigfoot: 3 Tales of Terror," *UFO Report* (October 1976): 48.
945 Guttilla, Peter. "Bigfoot: Three Tales of Terror," *UFO Report* (October 1976): 49.
946 Guttilla, Peter. "Bigfoot: Three Tales of Terror," *UFO Report* (October 1976).
947 Guttilla, Peter. "Bigfoot: Advance Guard from Outer Space," *UFO Report* (June 1977): 22, 24.
948 Guttilla, Peter. "Bigfoot: Advance Guard from Outer Space," *UFO Report* (June 1977): 24.
949 Guttilla, Peter. "Bigfoot: Advance Guard from Outer Space," *UFO Report* (June 1977): 48.
950 Guttilla, Peter. "Bigfoot: Advance Guard from Outer Space," *UFO Report* (June 1977): 48.
951 Guttilla, Peter. "Bigfoot: Advance Guard from Outer Space," *UFO Report* (June,1977): 48.
952 Guttilla, Peter. "Bigfoot: Advance Guard from Outer Space," *UFO Report* (June 1977): 48.
953 Guttilla, Peter. "Bigfoot: Advance Guard from Outer Space," *UFO Report* (June 1977): 48.
954 George, Jim. "Frisbees Shaped like UFOs," *Independent* (Long Beach, California) (November 2, 1974).
955 Marston, Red. "In S. C., Bigfoot is Making Tracks," *St. Petersburg Times* (July 8, 1974): D1.
956 Fawcett, George D. "On The Trail of Big Foot," *Mount Airy News* (September 13, 1974): 14B.
957 Stump, Al. "The Man Who Tracks 'Bigfoot'," *True* (May 1975): 28.
958 "Is Bigfoot For Real," *Danville Register* (November 20, 1975): 8C.
959 "Sightings of Bigfoot Becoming More Common," *Ledger* (Lakeland, Florida) (November 27, 1975): 19A.
960 "Report of Hairy Beast at Youth Camp Probed," *Ocala Star-Banner* (July 23, 1974): 8A.
961 "Unidentified Monster Keeps Sooners Jumpy," *Lawton Constitution* (August 2, 1974): 2A.
962 "Unidentified Monster Keeps Sooners Jumpy," *Lawton Constitution* (August 2, 1974): 2A.
963 "Just a Wolf of Different Color," *Victoria Advocate* (August 3, 1974): 2A.
964 "Unidentified Monster Keeps Sooners Jumpy," *Lawton Constitution* (August 2, 1974): 2A.

965 Jones, Robert E. "Pennsylvania ABSMery: A Report," *Pursuit* (January 1975): 20.

966 Jones, Robert E. "Pennsylvania ABSMery: A Report," *Pursuit* (January 1975).

967 "Monster," *Republic* (Columbus, Indiana) (November 2, 1974): 1.

968 "Mill Race Monster Makes Appearance After Voting," *Republic* (Columbus, Indiana) (November 6, 1974): 18.

969 "Mill Race Monster Hunt out of Hand," *Republic* (Columbus, Indiana) (November 8, 1974): 1.

970 "Columbus Jaycees Plan Haunted House," *Republic* (Columbus, Indiana) (October 18, 1975): 11.

971 Genzoli, Andrew. "Redwood Country," *Times-Standard* (Eureka, California) (December 18, 1974): 32.

972 Schneidman, Dave. "Carol Stream's Bigfoot: Is Monster Really Out There," *Chicago Tribune* (October 6, 1974).

973 Parsons, Don. "Bigfoot—Was He in Lakeland," *Ledger* (Lakeland, Florida) (December 1, 1974).

974 Parsons, Don. "Bigfoot—Was He in Lakeland," *Ledger* (Lakeland, Florida) (December 1, 1974).

975 "'Ape' Afoot," *Bangor Daily News* (January 10, 1974): 1, 2.

976 "'Ape' Afoot," *Bangor Daily News* (January 10, 1974): 1, 2.

977 Glass, Ian, and Jon Hall. "'Skunk Ape' on Prowl? Glades Creature Sought," *Miami News* (January 9, 1974).

978 "'Ape' Afoot," *Bangor Daily News* (January 10, 1974): 1, 2

979 "'Ape' Startles Motorists," *South Mississippi Sun* (January 10, 1974): 7.

980 Glass, Ian and Jon Hall. "Skunk Ape on Prowl? Glade Creature Sought," *Miami News* (January 9, 1974): 1A.

981 Glass, Ian and Jon Hall. "Skunk Ape on Prowl? Glade Creature Sought," *Miami News* (January 9, 1974): 1A.

982 Wilson, Jon. "Swamp Creature," *Evening Independent* (January 9, 1974).

983 "Everglades 'skunk ape' lurks again," *Pocono Record* (January 10, 1974): 1.

984 "'The Thing' is Sought," *Naples Daily News* (January 9, 1974): 6B.

985 Allen, Joe. "Candid Comment is Skunk-Ape Real," *News-Herald* (January 13, 1974): 1D.

986 Glass, Ian. "'Skunk Ape? I've Seen it 3 Times," *Miami News* (January 12, 1974)

987 "Yeti Winters in Florida," *News-Herald* (Panama City, Florida) (November 25, 1973): 2A.

988 "Yeti Winters in Florida," *News-Herald* (Panama City, Florida) (November 25, 1973): 2A.

989 Slate, Barabra Ann. "Does Earth Really Belong to Man? *Saga UFO Report* (October 1977): 34-35.

990 Denley, Susan. "Yeti Hunters Form Their Own Group in Hernando," *St. Petersburg Times* (March 27, 1974).

991 Denley, Susan. "Yeti Hunters Form Their Own Group in Hernando," *St. Petersburg Times* (March 27, 1974).

992 Denley, Susan. "Yeti Hunters Form Their Own Group in Hernando," *St. Petersburg Times* (March 27, 1974).

993 Denley, Susan. "Yeti Hunters Form Their Own Group in Hernando," *St. Petersburg Times* (March 27, 1974).

994 Slate, B. Ann. "Man-Ape's Reign of Terror," *UFO Report* (August 1977): 20-23, 54-58.

995 Slate, B. Ann. "Man-Ape's Reign of Terror," *UFO Report* (August 1977): 20-23, 54-58.

996 Slate, B. Ann. "Man-Ape's Reign of Terror," *UFO Report* (August 1977): 20-23, 54-58.

997 Slate, B. Ann. "Man-Ape's Reign of Terror," *UFO Report* (August 1977): 20-23, 54-58.

998 Slate, B. Ann. "Man-Ape's Reign of Terror," *UFO Report* (August 1977): 54.

999 Slate, B. Ann. "Man-Ape's Reign of Terror," *UFO Report* (August 1977): 54.

1000 Slate, B. Ann. "Man-Ape's Reign of Terror," *UFO Report* (August 1977): 54.

1001 Slate, Barbara Ann. "Does Earth Really Belong to Man? *Saga UFO Report* (October 1977): 35.

1002 Marzella, Michael. "Society Aims to Capture Elusive Yeti," *St. Petersburg Times* (July 8, 1974): D-1.

1003 Marzella, Michael. "Society Aims to Capture Elusive Yeti," *St. Petersburg Times* (July 8, 1974): D-1.

1004 Marzella, Michael. "Society Aims to Capture Elusive Yeti," *St. Petersburg Times* (July 8, 1974): D-1.

1005 Marzella, Michael. "Society Aims to Capture Elusive Yeti," *St. Petersburg Times* (July 8, 1974): D-1.

1006 Slate, B. Ann. "Florida's Rampaging Man-Ape," *UFO Report* (July 1977): 35.

1007 Brink, Bob. "A Noise, a Shape, 6 Shots, a Scream...," *Palm Beach Post* (September 26, 1974): C2.

1008 White, Randy. "You Might Scoff Him Aside, But the Swamp Ape Laughs Last," *News-Press* (Ft. Myers, Florida) (September 4, 1974).

1009 White, Randy. "You Might Scoff Him Aside, But the Swamp Ape Laughs Last," *News-Press* (Ft. Myers, Florida) (September 4, 1974).

1010 White, Randy. "You Might Scoff Him Aside, But the Swamp Ape Laughs Last," *News-Press* (Ft. Myers, Florida) (September 4, 1974): 2D.

1011 Crouch, Paula. "Skunk Ape Festival," *News-Press* (Fort Myers, Florida) (December 15, 1974): B1.

1012 Leiren, Hall. "It's Sasquatch Time Again in B.C.," *Ottawa Journal* (November 15, 1975): 8.

1013 Genzoli, Andrew. "Redwood Country," *Times-Standard* (Eureka, California) (September 17, 1975): 12.

1014 "Information About Bigfoot Sought," *Daily Inter Lake* (Kalispell, Montana) (December 16, 1975): 14.
1015 Butler, Robert. "Hunter-Filmmaker Hot on Bigfoot's Trail," *Kansas City Times* (December 19, 1975): 6D.
1016 Butler, Robert. "Hunter-Filmmaker Hot on Bigfoot's Trail," *Kansas City Times* (December 19, 1975): 6D.
1017 Scott, Jim. "Tracking Bigfoot," *Argosy* (April 1975): 16.
1018 Scott, Jim. "Tracking Bigfoot," *Argosy* (April 1975): 16.
1019 Butler, Robert. "Hunter-Filmmaker Hot on Bigfoot's Trail," *Kansas City Times* (December 19, 1975): 6D.
1020 Scott, Jim. "Tracking Bigfoot," *Argosy* (April 1975): 17.
1021 Cohea, Carol. "'Legends of Bigfoot': Film Recounts Beast Search," *Albuquerque Journal* (October 30, 1975): C1.
1022 Scott, Jim. "Tracking Bigfoot," *Argosy* (April 1975): 17.
1023 Cohea, Carol. "'Legends of Bigfoot': Film Recounts Beast Search," *Albuquerque Journal* (October 30, 1975): C1.
1024 Butler, Robert. "Hunter-Filmmaker Hot on Bigfoot's Trail," *Kansas City Times* (December 19, 1975): 6D.
1025 Butler, Robert. "Hunter-Filmmaker Hot on Bigfoot's Trail," *Kansas City Times* (December 19, 1975): 6D.
1026 Scott, Jim. "Tracking Bigfoot," *Argosy* (April 1975): 17.
1027 Scott, Jim. "Tracking Bigfoot," *Argosy* (April 1975): 17.
1028 Scott, Jim. "Tracking Bigfoot," *Argosy* (April 1975): 17.
1029 Scott, Jim. "Tracking Bigfoot," *Argosy* (April 1975): 17.
1030 Scott, Jim. "Tracking Bigfoot," *Argosy* (April 1975): 17.
1031 Scott, Jim. "Tracking Bigfoot," *Argosy* (April 1975): 17.
1032 Scott, Jim. "Tracking Bigfoot," *Argosy* (April 1975): 17, 30.
1033 Scott, Jim. "Tracking Bigfoot," *Argosy* (April 1975): 30.
1034 Butler, Robert. "Hunter-Filmmaker Hot on Bigfoot's Trail," *Kansas City Times* (December 19, 1975): 6D.
1035 Butler, Robert. "Hunter-Filmmaker Hot on Bigfoot's Trail," *Kansas City Times* (December 19, 1975): 6D.
1036 Scott, Jim. "Tracking Bigfoot," *Argosy* (April 1975): 30.
1037 Scott, Jim. "Tracking Bigfoot," *Argosy* (April 1975): 30.
1038 Cohea, Carol. "'Legends of Bigfoot': Film Recounts Beast Search," *Albuquerque Journal* (October 30, 1975): C1.
1039 Cohea, Carol. "'Legends of Bigfoot': Film Recounts Beast Search," *Albuquerque Journal* (October 30, 1975): C1.
1040 Butler, Robert. "Hunter-Filmmaker Hot on Bigfoot's Trail," *Kansas City Times* (December 19, 1975): 6D.

1041 Cohea, Carol. "'Legends of Bigfoot': Film Recounts Beast Search," *Albuquerque Journal* (October 30, 1975): C1.

1042 Butler, Robert. "Hunter-Filmmaker Hot on Bigfoot's Trail," *Kansas City Times* (December 19, 1975): 6D.

1043 Cohea, Carol. "'Legends of Bigfoot': Film Recounts Beast Search," *Albuquerque Journal* (October 30, 1975): C1.

1044 Butler, Robert. "Hunter-Filmmaker Hot on Bigfoot's Trail," *Kansas City Times* (December 19, 1975): 6D

1045 Cohea, Carol. "'Legends of Bigfoot': Film Recounts Beast Search," *Albuquerque Journal* (October 30, 1975): C1.

1046 Butler, Robert. "Hunter-Filmmaker Hot on Bigfoot's Trail," *Kansas City Times* (December 19, 1975): 6D.

1047 Cook, Richard. "'Sasqua' Lurked in Area Woods," *Lowell Sun Sunday Magazine* (November 24, 1974): 6.

1048 Wood, Lee. "Local 'Actors' Hailed as 'Sasqua' Premieres," *Lowell Sun* (August 14, 1975): 4.

1049 Graham, Cuck. "Bigfoot Still Tiptoeing Through the Tules," *Tucson Daily Citizen* (November 6, 1975): 18.

1050 Graham, Cuck. "Bigfoot Still Tiptoeing Through the Tules," *Tucson Daily Citizen* (November 6, 1975): 18.

1051 Graham, Cuck. "Bigfoot Still Tiptoeing Through the Tules," *Tucson Daily Citizen* (November 6, 1975): 18.

1052 Perkins, Ron. "He Finds the Audience, Then Makes the Picture," *Arizona Daily Star* (November 9, 1975): 9G.

1053 "'Big Foot' Ads," *Record Eagle* (November 15, 1975): 4.

1054 "Bigfoot Action," *Record Eagle* (November 22, 1975): 4.

1055 Sinor, John. "Snowtime Monsters," *Times* (San Mateo, California) (February 2, 1977): 6.

1056 Guenette, Robert and Frances. *The Mysterious Monsters* (Sun Classic Pictures Book, 1975): 1-2.

1057 "Book Reviews," *Pursuit* (April 1976): 46.

1058 Keel, John A. *The Eighth Tower* (San Antonio, Texas: Anomalist Books, 2013): 108.

1059 Keel, John A. *The Eighth Tower* (San Antonio, Texas: Anomalist Books, 2013): 120-121.

1060 Keel, John A. *The Eighth Tower* Anomalist Books (2013): 121.

1061 Keel, John A. "No News is Bad News," *Pursuit* (Summer, 1976): 50.

1062 Keel, John A. "No News is Bad News," *Pursuit* (Summer, 1976): 50.

1063 Keel, John A. "Can Science and Scientists Help," *Pursuit* (Fall, 1977): 120.

1064 Byrne, Peter. *A Fortunate Life* (San Bernardino, California, CreateSpace, 2017): 293.

1065 Byrne, Peter. *The Search for Bigfoot* (New York: Pocket Books, 1976): xiii.

1066 Byrne, Peter. *The Search for Bigfoot* (New York: Pocket Books, 1976): 135.

1067 Felgenhauer, Neil. "Atlas Lists Sasquatch," *Spokane Daily Chronicle* (July 4, 1975): 3.

1068 "Tracking Down the Abominable Big Foot," *Sun-Herald* (November 23, 1975): 123.

1069 Raborg, Frederick A. "Short Trips Suggested," *Bakersfield Californian* (August 29, 1975).

1070 Baumann, Elwood D. *Bigfoot: America's Abominable Snowman* (New York: Franklin Watts, Inc. 1975): 94.

1071 Byrne, Peter. *The Search for Bigfoot* (New York: Pocket Books, 1976): 186.

1072 Guttilla, Peter. "Bigfoot: Advance Guard from Outer Space," *UFO Report* (June 1977).

1073 Guttilla, Peter. "Bigfoot: Advance Guard from Outer Space," *UFO Report* (June 1977).

1074 Guttilla, Peter. "Bigfoot: Advance Guard from Outer Space," *UFO Report* (June 1977).

1075 Jones, Robert E. "Oliver—An Unusual Ape," *Pursuit* (October 1975): 92.

1076 Jones, Robert E. "Oliver—An Unusual Ape," *Pursuit* (October 1975): 93.

1077 Shreeve, James. "Oliver's Travels," *Atlantic* (October 2003). TheAtlantic.com. http://www.theatlantic.com/magazine/archive/2003/10/olivers-travels/302808/.

1078 Marsh, Ron. "Notes From a Member," *Pursuit* (July 1975): 77.

1079 Jones, Robert E. "The Jersey Devil," *Pursuit* (July 1974): 68.

1080 Jones, Robert E. "Bigfoot in New Jersey," *Pursuit* (July 1975): 68.

1081 Jones, Robert E. "Bigfoot in New Jersey," *Pursuit* (July 1975): 69.

1082 Jones, Robert E. "Bigfoot in New Jersey," *Pursuit* (October 1975): 101-102.

1083 Cocking, Clive. "The Magical, Mystical, Mythical Sasquatch," *Ottawa Journal* (May 10, 1975): 10.

1084 Cocking, Clive. "The Magical, Mystical, Mythical Sasquatch," *Ottawa Journal* (May 10, 1975): 10.

1085 Cocking, Clive. "The Magical, Mystical, Mythical Sasquatch," *Ottawa Journal* (May 10, 1975): 10.

1086 Cocking, Clive. "The Magical, Mystical, Mythical Sasquatch," *Ottawa Journal* (May 10, 1975): 10.

1087 Cocking, Clive. "The Magical, Mystical, Mythical Sasquatch," *Ottawa Journal* (May 10, 1975): 10, 12.

1088 Cocking, Clive. "The Magical, Mystical, Mythical Sasquatch," *Ottawa Journal* (May 10, 1975): 12.

1089 Stump, Al. "The Man Who Tracks 'Bigfoot'," *True* (May 1975): 28-31.

1090 Stump, Al. "The Man Who Tracks 'Bigfoot'," *True* (May 1975): 74.

1091 Stump, Al. "The Man Who Tracks 'Bigfoot'," *True* (May 1975): 76.

1092 Stump, Al. "The Man Who Tracks 'Bigfoot'," *True* (May 1975): 74-75

1093 Discovered by Ivan Marx.

1094 Stump, Al. "The Man Who Tracks 'Bigfoot'," *True* (May 1975): 75

1095 Stump, Al. "The Man Who Tracks 'Bigfoot'," *True* (May 1975): 75

1096 Stump, Al. "The Man Who Tracks 'Bigfoot'," *True* (May 1975): 76-77.

1097 Stump, Al. "The Man Who Tracks 'Bigfoot'," *True* (May 1975): 77.

1098 Stump, Al. "The Man Who Tracks 'Bigfoot'," *True* (May 1975): 77.

1099 Stump, Al. "The Man Who Tracks 'Bigfoot'," *True* (May 1975): 30.

1100 Cruickshauk, Ken. "In Search of the Elusive 'Bigfoot' Out West," *Hartford Courant* (October 24, 1975): 8.

1101 Stump, Al. "The Man Who Tracks 'Bigfoot'," *True* (May 1975): 30.

1102 Stump, Al. "The Man Who Tracks 'Bigfoot'," *True* (May 1975): 77.

1103 Stump, Al. "The Man Who Tracks 'Bigfoot'," *True* (May 1975): 77.

1104 Stingley, Jim. "Adventurer Trying to Smoke Out 'Big Foot' *Anderson Sunday Herald* (October 19, 1975): 5.

1105 Stingley, Jim. "Adventurer Trying to Smoke Out 'Big Foot' *Anderson Sunday Herald* (October 19, 1975): 5.

1106 Wolf, Marty. "An Interview with Bob Morgan," *Pursuit* (July 1975): 70.

1107 Wolf, Marty. "An Interview with Bob Morgan," *Pursuit* (July 1975): 70-71.

1108 Miller, Bill. "Game Commission in Pursuit, Stalking the Wild Skunk Ape," *News-Press* (Fort Myers, Florida) (February 13, 1975): 5C.

1109 Wolf, Marty. "An Interview with Bob Morgan," *Pursuit* (July 1975): 70-71

1110 Wolf, Marty. "An Interview with Bob Morgan," *Pursuit* (July 1975): 71.

1111 Wolf, Marty. "An Interview with Bob Morgan," *Pursuit* (July 1975): 72.

1112 "Scientists Plan Study of the Elusive Yeti," *Daily News* (Port Angeles, Washington) (30 October 1975): 10.

1113 "A Renewed Search for 'Bigfoot'," *Argus-Courier* (Petaluma, California) (October 30, 1975): 3.

1114 Greer, Jeff. "'Bigfoot' Moved to Marin? Musician Believes He Saw it," *Independent Journal* (San Rafael, California) (September 29, 1975): 11.

1115 Quast, Mike. *Big Footage: A History of Claims for the Sasquatch on Film* (2001):80.

1116 Berry, A. R. "The Voice of Bigfoot," *Probe the Unknown* (November 1975): 37.

1117 Berry, A. R. "The Voice of Bigfoot," *Probe the Unknown* (November 1975): 38.

1118 Berry, A. R. "The Voice of Bigfoot," *Probe the Unknown* (November 1975): 38.

1119 Berry, A. R. "The Voice of Bigfoot," *Probe the Unknown* (November 1975): 38-39.

1120 Berry, A. R. "The Voice of Bigfoot," *Probe the Unknown* (November 1975): 39-40.

1121 Berry, A. R. "The Voice of Bigfoot," *Probe the Unknown* (November 1975): 40.

1122 "Bigfoot Legend . . . Spellbinder Around Campfire for Le Mars Folks," *Daily Sentinel* (Le Mars, Iowa) (July 9, 1975): 15.

1123 Berry, A. R. "The Voice of Bigfoot," *Probe the Unknown* (November 1975): 40.

1124 "More Evidence Claims Existence of Bigfoot," *Eagle* (Bryan-College Station) (June 18, 1975): 9C.

1125 "More Evidence Claims Existence of Bigfoot," *Eagle* (Bryan-College Station) (June 18, 1975): 9C.

1126 Berry, A. R. "The Voice of Bigfoot," *Probe the Unknown* (November 1975): 38.

1127 Berry, A. R. "The Voice of Bigfoot," *Probe the Unknown* (November 1975): 38.

1128 Berry, A. R. "The Voice of Bigfoot," *Probe the Unknown* (November 1975): 40.

1129 Alexander, Sue. "Creature Comforts," *Lexington Leader* (June 8, 1976).

1130 Fulkerson, Perry. "Creature: A Mystery Kept on Ice," *Evening Independent* (St. Petersburg, Florida) (April 19, 1975): 1-B.

1131 Harris, Jerry. "Is Man in Ice Real? Only Few Persons Know," *Gadsen Times* (Gadsen, Alabama) (May 18, 1975): 2.

1132 Harris, Jerry. "Is Man in Ice Real? Only Few Persons Know," *Gadsen Times* (Gadsen, Alabama) (May 18, 1975): 2.

1133 Durant, Robert J. "Epilogue on Bozo," *Pursuit* (July 1975): 66.

1134 "Big, Monkey-Like 'Monster' Seen by Oklahomans," *Victoria Advocate* (September 18, 1975): 7C.

1135 "In Aid of the 'Bigfoot'," *Kingston Daily Freeman* (November 21, 1975): 18.

1136 Grishman, Milton. "UA Student Leads a Hunt for Bigfoot," *Tuscaloosa News* (April 6, 1975): 1, 3.

1137 "A Hairy Monster in Corona," *Sun-Telegram* (San Bernardino, California) (August 21, 1975): B9.

1138 Slate, B. Ann "Does Earth Really Belong to Man," *Saga UFO Report* (October 1977): 32.

1139 "Hunters Worry Sheriff More Than Monster Does," *Telegraph* (Nashua, New Hampshire) (September 10, 1975): 20.

1140 "'Noxie Monster' Causing Stir," *Sarasota Herald-Tribune* (September 5, 1975): 7B.

1141 Clark, Jerome. *Unexplained! Strange Sightings, Incredible Occurrences & Puzzling Physical Phenomena* (Canton, Michigan: Visible Ink Press, 1999): 92.

1142 Clark, Jerome. *Unexplained! Strange Sightings, Incredible Occurrences & Puzzling Physical Phenomena* (Canton, Michigan: Visible Ink Press, 1999): 92.

1143 "'Noxie Monster' Causing Stir," *Sarasota Herald-Tribune* (September 5, 1975): 7B.

1144 "Hairy Creature Haunts Town," *Kansas City Times* (September 6, 1975): 9B.

1145 "'Noxie Monster' Causing Stir," *Sarasota Herald-Tribune* (September 5, 1975): 7B.

1146 "Hollywood Producer Offers $10,000 for Home Movies of Noxie Monster," *Ludington Daily News* (September 12, 1975): 2.

1147 "'Noxie Monster' Causing Stir," *Sarasota Herald-Tribune* (September 5, 1975): 7B.

1148 "Does a Monster Prowl Farmville's Gardens," *Index-Journal* (Greenwood, South Carolina) (September 18, 1975): 21.

1149 "Big Foot," *Spartanburg Herald* (September 19, 1975): B1.

1150 "Hairy Monster Scares Town—Until Costumed Youth Caught," *Ogden Standard-Examiner* (October 1, 1975): 7A.

1151 "Youth Use a Gorilla Suit to Terrify Missouri Town," *Nashua Telegraph* (October 3, 1975): 26.

1152 "Hairy Monster Hoax Revealed," *Dispatch* (Lexington, North Carolina) (October 1, 1975): 1.

1153 "Red-Eyed Hairy Monster Turns out to be Costume," *Greeley Daily Tribune* (Greeley, Colorado) (October 1, 1975): 17.

1154 Koonse, Alan. "Iowa's Own Lockridge Monster," *Des Moines Register* (December 15, 1975): 1.

1155 "Monster is Stalking Cornfields," *Palm Beach Post-Times* (November 16, 1975): G9.

1156 Koonse, Alan. "Iowa's Own Lockridge Monster," *Des Moines Register* (December 15, 1975): 1.

1157 "Bigfoot Lies Low Sightings Fewer," *Ottawa Journal* (October 14, 1975): 36.

1158 Gosney, J. and D. Grover. "Bigfoot," *Beyond Reality* (July-August 1976): 21.

1159 Gosney, J. and D. Grover. "Bigfoot," *Beyond Reality* (July-August 1976): 21.

1160 Gosney, J. and D. Grover. "Bigfoot," *Beyond Reality* (July-August 1976): 22-23.

1161 Penn, John. "Residents Report Spottsville Monster," *Evansville Press* (Evansville, Indiana) (November 10, 1975): 13.

1162 Penn, John. "Residents Report Spottsville Monster," *Evansville Press* (Evansville, Indiana) (November 10, 1975): 13.

1163 Lawrence, Keith. "Simply Monstrous," *Messenger-Inquirer* (Owensboro, Kentucky) (November 14, 1975): B1.

1164 Love, Thomas. "Al, Curious 'Bigfoot' Stared at Each Other Over Campfire," *Spokesman Review* (August 8, 1976): A24.

1165 Denley, Susan. "Does a Yeti Live in the Woods Near Safety Harbor, Oldsmar," *Manatee Times* (May 16, 1975): 5.

1166 Denley, Susan. "Does a Yeti Live in the Woods Near Safety Harbor, Oldsmar," *Manatee Times* (May 16, 1975): 5.

1167 Denley, Susan. "Does a Yeti Live in the Woods Near Safety Harbor, Oldsmar," *Manatee Times* (May 16, 1975): 5.

1168 "Yeti," *Manatee Times* (January 1, 1976).

1169 "Yeti," *Manatee Times* (January 1, 1976).

1170 Denley, Susan. "Does a Yeti Live in the Woods Near Safety Harbor, Oldsmar," *Manatee Times* (May 16, 1975): 5.

1171 Stanfield, Jeff. "12-Year-Old Reports Sighting of Strange Apelike Creature," *Sarasota Herald-Tribune* (June 9, 1975): 2B.

1172 Slate, B. Ann. "Florida's Rampaging Man-Ape," *UFO Report* (July 1977): 65.

1173 Dobens, Peter. "Skunkape 'Something' Lurks in Area Woods," *Sarasota Journal* (March 3, 1977) as cited in *Mysteries of the World Supplement* (April 1977).

1174 Slate, B. Ann. "Florida's Rampaging Man-Ape," *UFO Report* (July 1977): 67.

1175 Griffiths, Patti. "Bigfoot," *Star-Banner* (Ocala, Florida) (June 8, 1975): 7B.

1176 Griffiths, Patti. "Bigfoot," *Star-Banner* (Ocala, Florida) (June 8, 1975): 7B.

1177 Braun, William H. "Large Footprints Found; Mystery Creature Hunted," *St. Petersburg Times* (June 14, 1975): 1, 5.

1178 Braun, William H. "Large Footprints Found; Mystery Creature Hunted," *St. Petersburg Times* (June 14, 1975): 1, 5.

1179 Braun, William H. "Skeptics May be Wrong about Ape-Like Creature," *St. Petersburg Times* (June 27, 1975): 2.

1180 Braun, William H. "Skeptics May be Wrong about Ape-Like Creature," *St. Petersburg Times* (June 27, 1975): 2

1181 "Yeti," *Manatee Times* (January 1, 1976).

1182 Slate, B. Ann. "Florida's Rampaging Man-Ape," *UFO Report* (July 1977): 34.

1183 Slate, B. Ann. "Florida's Rampaging Man-Ape," *UFO Report* (July 1977): 34.

1184 Slate, B. Ann. "Florida's Rampaging Man-Ape," *UFO Report* (July 1977): 34.

1185 Slate, B. Ann. "Florida's Rampaging Man-Ape," *UFO Report* (July 1977): 35.

1186 Slate, B. Ann. "Florida's Rampaging Man-Ape," *UFO Report* (July 1977): 35.

1187 Alva, Marilyn. "Waiting for Skunk Ape to Surface Again," *Palm Beach Post* (November 19, 1975): B1.

1188 Slate, B. Ann. "Man-Ape's Reign of Terror," *UFO Report* (August 1977): 22-23.

1189 "Yeti," *Manatee Times* (January 1, 1976).

1190 "Yeti," *Manatee Times* (January 1, 1976).

1191 Hall, Mark A. "Contemporary Stories or 'Taku He' or 'Bigfoot' in South Dakota as Drawn from Newspaper Accounts," *Minnesota Archaeologist* (May 1978).

1192 "Editorial," *Bigfoot News* (May 1976): 1,

1193 "Bigfoot Search is On," *Spokane Daily Chronicle* (January 27, 1976): 6.

1194 The Bigfoot Information Center's examination of the tracks determined they evinced three toes.

1195 "Investigator Following Trail of Legendary Ape-Man Bigfoot," *Daily News-Miner* (Fairfax, Alaska) (January 27, 1976): 2.

1196 "Bigfoot Hunter Trailing Tracks," *Tri City Herald* (January 23, 1976).

1197 "'Bigfoot Prints' Faked," *Daily News-Miner* (Fairbanks, Alaska) (January 30, 1976): A-2.

1198 Jones, Robert E. "Peter Byrne. The Search for Bigfoot," *Pursuit* (January 1976): 24.

1199 "Biography," SasquatchSummit.com. http://sasquatchsummit.com/speaker/richard-noll/.

1200 "Latest News," *Bigfoot News* (May 1976): 1.

1201 Byrne, Peter. "II. Bigfoot, Homo Nocturnis, Update for 1976," *Pursuit* (Summer 1976): 66.

1202 Hevia, Fred. "'Bigfoot' is for Real, Monessen Rotary Told," *Monessen Valley Independent* (August 5, 1976): 19.

1203 Childress, William. "A Man Who Seeks Bigfoot," *Ford Times* (March 1979):57.

1204 Childress, William. "Tracking the Elusive Bigfoot," *Friends* (November 1976): 17.

1205 Childress, William. "Tracking the Elusive Bigfoot," *Friends* (November 1976): 19.

1206 Childress, William. "Tracking the Elusive Bigfoot," *Friends* (November 1976): 19, 31.

1207 Childress, William. "Tracking the Elusive Bigfoot," *Friends* (November 1976): 31.

1208 Childress, William. "Tracking the Elusive Bigfoot," *Friends* (November 1976): 31.

1209 Genzoli, Andrew. "Redwood Country," *Times-Standard* (Eureka, California) (November 3, 1975): 6.

1210 Green, John. "Fossil Tracks at Glen Rose," *Pursuit* (Fall 1976): 83-84.

1211 "Two Decade Search for the Sasquatch," *Ottawa Journal* (December 20, 1976): 15.

1212 "7 Day Program Highlights," *Portage Leader* (August 4, 1976).

1213 "Vancouverite Devotes Years to Searching for Sasquatch," *Winnipeg Free Press* (February 28, 1976): 26.

1214 "Ex-Local Man Headed Search for Bigfoot," *Massillon Evening Independent* (October 29, 1976): 17.

1215 Beck, Peter. "Hoax or Real? Group Searches for 'Bigfoot'," Richardgrigonis.com. http://richardgrigonis.com/CollegeHijinx.html.

1216 McCloy, James F. and Ray Miller Jr. *Phantom of the Pines* (Moorestown, New Jersey, Middle Atlantic Press, 1998): 62.

1217 Grigonis, Richard. "The Bigfoot 'Expedition'," RichardGrigonis.com. http://richardgrigonis.com/CollegeHijinx.html.

1218 "Bigfoot Expeditions," *Pursuit* (Summer 1976): 70.

1219 "A Baby Bigfoot," *Spokesman Review* (January 3, 1976): 6.

1220 "Bigfoot," *Kingsport Times-News* (January 6, 1976): 6.

1221 "Attorney Owns Creature Which May Be a Bigfoot," *Nashua Telegraph* (Nashua, New Hampshire) (January 3, 1976): 10.

1222 "'Half Ape, Half Human' Purchased by Attorney," *Playground Daily News* (Fort Walton Beach, Florida) (January 4, 1976): 2A.

1223 "'Half Ape, Half Human' Purchased by Attorney," *Playground Daily News* (Fort Walton Beach, Florida) (January 4, 1976): 2A.

1224 Walsh, Lee. "Strange and Unknown," *Beyond Reality* (July/August 1976): 10, 27.

1225 Williams, Pat. *Ahead of the Game: The Pat Williams Story* (Grand Rapids, Michigan, Revell, 2014).

1226 "Genetic Tests Show Oliver, the Chimp, is Just a Chimp," *Daily News* (Galveston, Texas) (January 2, 1997): 3.

1227 Cuny, Marty. "Reader Comments on Bigfoot," *Montana Standard* (February 29, 1976): 6.

1228 "'Bigfoot' Theory Hit," *Times-Standard* (Eureka, California) (January 9, 1976): 2.

1229 Craighead, John. "Studying Grizzly Bear Habitat by Satellite," *National Geographic* (July 1976): 148.

1230 Craighead, John. "Studying Grizzly Bear Habitat by Satellite," *National Geographic* (July 1976): 150.

1231 Craighead, John. "Studying Grizzly Bear Habitat by Satellite," *National Geographic* (July 1976): 157.

1232 Craighead, John. "Studying Grizzly Bear Habitat by Satellite," *National Geographic* (July 1976): 158.

1233 Craighead, John. "Studying Grizzly Bear Habitat by Satellite," *National Geographic* (July 1976): 150.

1234 Wyma, Mike. "Stepping in Bigfoot's Toes," *Valley News* (Van Nuys, California) (August 15, 1976): 2.

1235 Holden, John C. "Taxonomic Description of Bigfoot & The Abominable Snowman," *INFO Journal* (July 1976): 14-15.

1236 "Sasquatch Books Become 'Hot' Items at Libraries," *Daily Chronicle* (Centralia, Washington) (January 24, 1976): W1.

1237 "Sasquatch Books Become 'Hot' Items at Libraries," *Daily Chronicle* (Centralia, Washington) (January 24, 1976): W1.

1238 Goldbloom, Shelley. "Bigfoot Lives in the Pages of Student Press," *La Crosse Tribune* (December 16, 1976): 9.

1239 Genzoli, Andrew. "Redwood Country," *Times-Standard* (Eureka, California) (March 29, 1976): 2.

1240 Klement, Jan. *The Creature* (Pittsburgh, Pennsylvania, Allegheny Press, 1976): 3.

1241 Bush, Ed and Terry Gaston. *Wildman of the Woods* (1976): 20.

1242 Bush, Ed and Terry Gaston. *Wildman of the Woods* (1976): 98.

1243 Bush, Ed and Terry Gaston. *Wildman of the Woods* (1976): 109.

1244 "Big Foot," *Oelwein Daily Register* (May 24, 1976): 1.

1245 "Missing Woman Returns Safe, but Screaming," *Gadsden Times* (May 25, 1976): 14.

1246 "'Kidnapped by Big Foot'," *Telegraph-Herald* (May 24, 1976).

1247 "Woman Carried Off by 'Large Animal?'," *Racine Journal Times* (May 24, 1976): 2.

1248 Bush, Ed and Terry Gaston. *Wildman of the Woods* (1976): 102-103.

1249 "Big Foot," *Oelwein Daily Register* (May 24, 1976): 1.

1250 "Woman Carried Off by 'Large Animal?'," *Racine Journal Times* (May 24, 1976): 2.

1251 "Big Foot Seen Again," *Altus Times-Democrat* (May 24, 1976): 2.

1252 "Big Foot," *Oelwein Daily Register* (May 24, 1976): 1.

1253 "Big Foot Victim Located," *Daily Union Democrat* (May 25, 1976): 2.

1254 "Big Foot Victim Located," *Daily Union Democrat* (May 25, 1976): 2.

1255 "Shasta Board Ordered by Judge to Explain Refusal of Payback," *Times-Standard* (Eureka, California) (September 14, 1977): 13.

1256 "Missing Woman Returns Safe, but Screaming," *Gadsden Times*, (May 25, 1976): 14.

1257 "Big Foot Seen Again," *Altus Times-Democrat* (May 24, 1976): 2.

1258 "Big Foot Seen Again," *Altus Times-Democrat* (May 24, 1976): 2.

1259 "Missing Woman Returns Safe, but Screaming," *Gadsden Times* (May 25, 1976): 14.

1260 "Bigfoot Abduction Regarded as Hoax," *Leader-Post* (May 26, 1976): 58.

1261 "Kidnapped by Bigfoot? Search Continues," *Spokesman-Review* (May 25, 1976): 12.

1262 "Women Taken by 'Bigfoot'," *Kennebec Journal* (May 25, 1976): 2.

1263 "Alleged Bigfoot Victim Wants Lie Test," *Press Telegram* (Long Beach, California) (May 28, 1976): 3.

1264 "Alleged Bigfoot Victim Wants Lie Test," *Press Telegram* (Long Beach, California) (May 28, 1976): 3.

1265 "Alleged Bigfoot Victim Wants Lie Test," *Press Telegram* (Long Beach, California) (May 28, 1976): 3.

1266 "Screaming Girl Mum on Bigfoot 'Kidnap'," *Charleston Daily Mail* (May 25, 1976): 1.

1267 "Some Screams But No Bigfoot," *Deseret News* (May 25, 1976): 2A.

1268 "Missing Woman Returns Safe, but Screaming," *Gadsden Times* (May 25, 1976): 14.

1269 "Missing Woman Returns Safe, but Screaming," *Gadsden Times* (May 25, 1976): 14.

1270 "Big Foot Kidnapping Tale Smells," *Lodi News-Sentinel* (May 26, 1976): 5.

1271 "Big Foot Kidnapping Tale Smells," *Lodi News-Sentinel* (May 26, 1976): 5.

1272 "Victim Won't Talk—Bigfoot Story Called Garbage," *Spokesman-Review* (May 26, 1976).

1273 "'Bigfoot' Case Charges Possible—Cox," *Times-Standard* (Eureka, California) (May 26, 1976): 1, 2.

1274 McDonough, Mac. "Expert: If Bigfoot Only Weighs 350 Pounds He's Emaciated," *Bakersfield Californian* (May 26, 1976): 26.

1275 "D. A. Eyes 'Bigfoot' Case Action," *Times-Standard* (Eureka, California) (May 27, 1976): 1, 2.

1276 "Humboldt Bills Shasta for $11,613 for Bigfoot 'Kidnapping' Search," *Modesto Bee* (August 19, 1976).

1277 "Bigfoot Hunt Brings Bill," *Daily Union Democrat* (August 18, 1976): 2.

1278 "Bigfoot Hunt Brings Bill," *Daily Union Democrat* (August 18, 1976): 2.

1279 Bishoff, Don. "Hot on the Trail of Big Foot Once Again," *Eugene Register-Guard* (July 11, 1976).

1280 "Bigfoot Flicker Interests DA," *Times-Standard* (Eureka, California) (November 16, 1977): 6.

1281 "Big Foot Kidnapping Tale Smells," *Lodi News-Sentinel* (May 26, 1976): 5.

1282 "Bigfoot Flicker Interests DA," *Times-Standard* (Eureka, California) (November 16, 1977): 6.

1283 "Shasta Board Ordered by Judge to Explain Refusal of Payback," *Times-Standard* (Eureka, California) (September 14, 1977): 13.

1284"Bigfoot Search Costs Humboldt," *Record-Searchlight* (February 8, 1978) as cited in *Mysteries of the World Supplement* (April 1978).

1285 "Judge Refuses to Allow Bigfoot Search Payment," *Bulletin* (Bend, Oregon) (February 8, 1978): 20.

1286 "Bigfoot Search Costs Humboldt," *Record-Searchlight* (February 8, 1978) as cited in *Mysteries of the World Supplement* (April 1978).

1287 "Judge 'Pooh-Poohs' Bigfoot," *Times-Herald* (Vallejo, California) (February 9, 1978) as cited in *Mysteries of the World Supplement* (April 1978).

1288 "Humboldt Will Not Appeal Bigfoot Ruling," *Times-Standard* (February 15, 1978) as cited in *Mysteries of the World Supplement* (April 1978).

1289 "Humboldt Will Not Appeal Bigfoot Ruling," *Times-Standard* (February 15, 1978) as cited in *Mysteries of the World Supplement* (April 1978).

1290 Genzoli, Andrew. "Redwood Country," *Times-Standard* (Eureka, California) (May 26, 1976): 15.

1291 The term Ciné du Sasquatch was created by David Coleman, author of *The Bigfoot Filmography.*

1292 Smiljanich, Dorothy. "Hunt for 'Creature from Black Lake' Stops at Dead End," *St. Petersburg Times* (August 25, 1976): 3D.

1293 Murray, Noel. "Pre-Star Wars, Six Million Dollar Man and Bionic Woman were Beacons for Young Nerds," AVClub.com. http://www.avclub.com/article/pre-istar-warsii-six-million-dollar-mani-and-ibion-92782.

1294 "Andre the Giant vs . . . The Six Million Dollar Man," *Inside Wrestling* (May 1976): 34-35; 58-59.

1295 O'Brien, Mike. "Lights . . . Cameras . . . Sasquatch," *Eugene Register-Guard* (January 25, 1976): 11B.

1296 "Bigfoot Film Called a First for Oregon," *Eugene Register-Guard* (August 19, 1975): 12A.

1297 "You Can't Say: 'Let Me Do It Again'," *Eugene Register-Guard* (January 25, 1976): 11B.

1298 "Filming of Bigfoot Drama Moves to Blue River Area," *Eugene Register-Guard* (August 11, 1975): B1.

1299 O'Brien, Mike. "On Location," *Eugene Register-Guard* (August 31, 1975): 2C.

1300 "Big Foot Film Subject of Suit," *Eugene Register-Guard* (November 30, 1975): 7A.

1301 Taylor, Brett. "George Lauris," *Filmfax* (Fall, 2010): 102.

1302 "Computer Set to Sasquatch Hunting in Spring," *Sarasota Herald Tribune* (January 30, 1976): 9C.

1303 "Bigfoot Print Reported Found Near Medford," *Eugene Register-Guard* (April 19, 1976): 3B.

1304 "Bigfoot Hunters," *Reading Eagle* (July 7, 1976): 15.

1305 "Secret Expedition Hunts Bigfoot in Forests of British Columbia," *Sunday Journal and Star* (Lincoln, Nebraska) (July 11, 1976): 1E.

1306 Bishoff, Don. "Hot on the Trail of Big Foot Once Again," *Eugene Register-Guard* (July 11, 1976): C1.

1307 "Secret Expedition Hunts Bigfoot in Forests of British Columbia," *Sunday Journal and Star* (Lincoln, Nebraska) (July 11, 1976): 1E.

1308 "Bigfoot Sighting Prompts Search," *Tri-City Herald* (July 7, 1976).

1309 "Bigfoot Sighting Prompts Search," *Tri-City Herald* (July 7, 1976).

1310 McFarland, B. J. "'Bigfoot' Evades Researchers," *Syracuse Herald-Journal* (August 25, 1976): 48.

1311 Bishoff, Don. "Hot on the Trail of Big Foot Once Again," *Eugene Register-Guard* (July 11, 1976): C1.

1312 Barnes, Harper. "On Heels of Bigfoot," *St. Louis Post-Dispatch* (December 3, 1976): 3H.

1313 "Secret Expedition Hunts Bigfoot in Forests of British Columbia," *Sunday Journal and Star* (Lincoln, Nebraska) (July 11, 1976): 1E.

1314 Bishoff, Don. "The Joke Left Ron and the Sheriff Cold," *Eugene Register-Guard* (September 21, 1976): 1B.

1315 "Something Lurking in Corinth Hills," *Waxahachie Daily Light* (March 24, 1976).

1316 Fisher, Gene. "Youth Says Creatures Lurking Near Helena," *Independent Record* (Helena, Montana) (April 12, 1976): 1, 2.

1317 "Creature Sets off 'Bigfoot' Buzzing," *Idaho Free Press & The News Tribune* (April 23, 1976): 15.

1318 Floyd, E. Randall. "Bigfoot-Like Beast Terrorizes Quiet Tennessee Farming Community," *Spartanburg Herald-Journal* (June 28, 1992): C1, C9.

1319 Raynes, Brent. "Bigfoot in Lincoln County," *Alternate Perceptions Magazine* (November 2010). Mysterious-America.com. http://mysterious-america.com/encounters1110.html.

1320 Raynes, Brent. "Bigfoot in Lincoln County," *Alternate Perceptions Magazine* (November 2010). Mysterious-America.com. http://mysterious-america.com/encounters1110.html.

1321 Auvil, Dennis. "Bigfoot in Packwood Area," *Daily Chronicle* (Centralia, Washington) (June 19, 1976): W-6.

1322 "Bigfoot Authority Says Packwood Tracks Faked," *Daily Chronicle* (Centralia, Washington) (June 26, 1976): W3.

1323 Palmer, Jennie. "The Hunt is On for Beast of Lincoln," *Gastonia Gazette* (July 20, 1976): 1.

1324 "Report Sighting Bigfoot Near Ocheyedan," *Index Reporter* (Hull, Iowa) (September 9, 1976): 2.

1325 "Dixon Park Stroll by Bigfoot Doubted," *Morning Star* (Rockford, Illinois) (July 15, 1976).

1326 Bartholomew, Paul, and Robert Bartholomew, William Brann, and Bruce Hallenbeck. *Monsters of the Northwoods* (Utica, New York, North Country Books, Inc. 1992): 22-23.

1327 Gosselin, Brian and Sue Gosselin. *Abair Road: The True Story* (Middletown, Delaware, CreateSpace, 2018): 11-12.

1328 Gosselin, Brian and Sue Gosselin. *Abair Road: The True Story* (Middletown, Delaware, CreateSpace, 2018): 14.

1329 "Officers Track Creature," *Post-Star* (Glen Falls, New York) (August 30, 1976): 1.

1330 Berry, Rick. *Bigfoot on the East Coast* (Harrisonburg, Virginia, Campbell Copy Center, Inc., 1993): 25.

1331 Gosselin, Brian and Sue Gosselin. *Abair Road: The True Story* (Middletown, Delaware, CreateSpace, 2018): 21.

1332 Gosselin, Brian and Sue Gosselin. *Abair Road: The True Story* (Middletown, Delaware, CreateSpace, 2018): 22.

1333 Burt, Terry. "Bigfoot was a Big Story in Cashton," *La Crosse Tribune* (July 28, 2004). BFRO.net. http://www.bfro.net/gdb/show_article.asp?id=408.

1334 Stokes, Bill. "Cats Come, Cats Go at Cashton Depot," *Milwaukee Journal Sunday Accent* (January 14, 1979): 1, 4.

1335 "Maybe He's Tired," *La Crosse Tribune* (La Crosse, Wisconsin) (October 28, 1976): 4.

1336 Burt, Terry. "Bigfoot was a Big Story in Cashton," *La Crosse Tribune* (La Crosse, Wisconsin) (July 28, 2004). BFRO.net. http://www.bfro.net/gdb/show_article.asp?id=408.

1337 Cavadini, Bud. "Cashton's Bigfoot: He's a Stinker," *La Crosse Tribune* (La Crosse, Wisconsin) (October 28, 1976): 1.

1338 Burt, Terry. "Bigfoot Gone, Rumors Linger," *La Crosse Tribune* (La Crosse, Wisconsin) (November 17, 1976): 23.

1339 "Big Foot is Showing up in Wisconsin," *Capital Journal* (Salem, Oregon) (October 25, 1976): 6B.

1340 "'Bigfoot' Sighted in Sterling Area," *Sentinel* (Burnett County, Wisconsin) (1976). BigfootEncounters.com. http://www.bigfootencounters.com/articles/grantsburgWI.htm.

1341 Spavin, Don. "'Bigfoot' Big Publicity for Little Town," *Independent* (Long Beach, California) (November 18, 1976).

1342 Spavin, Don. "'Bigfoot' Big Publicity for Little Town," *Independent* (Long Beach, California) (November 18, 1976).

1343 Spavin, Don. "'Bigfoot' Big Publicity for Little Town," *Independent* (Long Beach, California) (November 18, 1976).

1344 Migliore, Mary. "'Bigfoot' Eludes Team on Overnight Campout," *Morning Union* (December 31, 1976). BFRO.net. http://www.bfro.net/gdb/show_article.asp?id=48

1345 Migliore, Mary. "'Bigfoot' Eludes Team on Overnight Campout," *Morning Union* (December 31, 1976). BFRO.net. http://www.bfro.net/gdb/show_article.asp?id=48.

1346 "'Big Foot' Hoaxer Says Joke Went Too Far," *Sun* (Lowell, Massachusetts) (January 3, 1977).

1347 Earley, George W. "Some Aren't Hoaxes," *Morning Union* (Springfield, Massachusetts) (January 8, 1977): 10.

1348 "Bigfoot Tracks," *Argus* (Fremont, California) (September 4, 1976): 2.

1349 "Sasquatch-Like Creatures Spotted," *Independent Record* (Helena, Montana) (August 1, 1976): 15.

1350 "Search for 'The Thing'," *Playground Daily News* (September 19, 1976): 9C.

1351 Opsasnick, Mark. "Monsters of Maryland: An Occasional Series Part I" *Strange Magazine*, no. 3: 21.

1352 Opsasnick, Mark. "Monsters of Maryland: An Occasional Series Part I" *Strange Magazine*, no. 3: 60.

1353 Opsasnick, Mark. "Monsters of Maryland: An Occasional Series Part II" *Strange Magazine*, no. 4: 53.

1354 Opsasnick, Mark. "Monsters of Maryland: An Occasional Series Part II" *Strange Magazine*, no. 4: 53.

1355 "Hunter 'Bags' Strange Tracks," *Morning Herald* (Hagerstown, Maryland) (November 15, 1976): 11.

1356 Opsasnick, Mark. "Monsters of Maryland: An Occasional Series Part II" *Strange Magazine*, no. 4: 28.

1357 Slate, B. Ann. "Man-Ape's Reign of Terror," *UFO Report* (August 1977): 56.

1358 Slate, B. Ann. "Man-Ape's Reign of Terror," *UFO Report* (August 1977): 56.

1359 Slate, B. Ann. "Man-Ape's Reign of Terror," *UFO Report* (August 1977): 56.

1360 Slate, B. Ann. "Man-Ape's Reign of Terror," *UFO Report* (August 1977): 56.

1361 LaSalle, Milton. "Bigfoot and Water," *Pursuit* (Fall 1976): 89.

1362 LaSalle, Milton. "Bigfoot and Water," *Pursuit* (Fall 1976): 89-90.

1363 Slate, B. Ann. "Man-Ape's Reign of Terror," *UFO Report* (August 1977): 56.

1364 Slate, B. Ann. "Man-Ape's Reign of Terror," *UFO Report* (August 1977): 58

1365 Slate, B. Ann. "Man-Ape's Reign of Terror," *UFO Report* (August 1977): 57.

1366 Slate, B. Ann. "Man-Ape's Reign of Terror," *UFO Report* (August 1977): 58.

1367 Slate, B. Ann. "Man-Ape's Reign of Terror," *UFO Report* (August 1977): 57-58.

1368 Slate, B. Ann. "Florida's Rampaging Man-Ape," *UFO Report* (July 1977): 34.

1369 Slate, B. Ann. "Florida's Rampaging Man-Ape," UFO Report (July 1977): 34.

1370 Slate, B. Ann. "Florida's Rampaging Man-Ape," UFO Report (July 1977): 67.

1371 Also known as the Bimini Wall, the Bimini Road is an undersea rock formation off the Bahamas which consists of a half-mile long linear feature of limestone blocks.

1372 "Skunk Ape Hair Studied," *Delta Democrat-Times* (June 9, 1976): 3.

1373 Dobens, Peter. "Skunkape 'Something' Lurks in Area Woods," *Sarasota Journal* (March 3, 1977) as cited in *Mysteries of the World Supplement* (April 1977).

1374 Miller, Gene. "Former Sailor Has Some Bigfoot Ideas," *Charleston Daily Mail* (November 10, 1976): 2.

1375 Miller, Gene. "Former Sailor Has Some Bigfoot Ideas," *Charleston Daily Mail* (November 10, 1976): 2.

1376 Enns, Bob. "Views from the Newsroom," *News Tribune* (May 16, 1976): 20.

1377 Whited, Charles. "'Bigfoot' Tracker 'Reforms'," *San Antonio Light* (May 25, 1977): 9-C.

1378 McDonough, Mac. "Bigfoot Tippy-Toes Down Near Kern—for Spud Bowl," *Bakersfield Californian* (December 3, 1976): 14.

1379 "Santa's Sasquatch," *Atlanta Journal and Constitution* (December 26, 1976): 8B.

1380 Bradford, William R. "No Foolin'," *Fort Mill Times* (February 28, 1977) as cited in *Mysteries of the World Supplement* (April 1977).

1381 Genzoli, Andrew. "Redwood Country," *Times-Standard* (Eureka, California) (October 21, 1977): 11.

1382 "Clayfoot," *Greensboro Daily News* (May 30, 1977): 4.

1383 "Jerry Crew Named 'Bigfoot'," *Escalon Times* (October 26, 1977). NorthAmericanBigfoot.com. http://www.northamericanbigfoot.com/2013/10/historical-1977-article-featuring-jerry.html.

1384 "Sasquatch Search Takes Times, Money," *Bakersfield Californian* (June 16, 1977): 13.

1385 "Bigfoot Find," *Columbia Press* (July 28, 1977) as cited in *Mysteries of the World Supplement* (September 1977).

1386 Williams, T. Jeff. "Bigfoot: Man, Beast or Myth," *Argosy* (December/January 1977): 40.

1387 Folder 0321, box 8, Grover Krantz Papers Collection, National Anthropological Archive, Smithsonian Institution.

1388 Gross, Melodie Ann. "Proof Needed—Speaker Would Shoot 'Bigfoot'," *News-Journal* (Mansfield, Ohio) (April 9, 1977): 3.

1389 Hinterberger, John. "Sasquatch Clues Raise Big Stink," *Seattle Times* (October 15, 1977): 10.

1390 Hinterberger, John. "Sasquatch Clues Raise Big Stink," *Seattle Times* (October 15, 1977): 10.

1391 "Tests Might Prove Sasquatch is Real," *Bulletin* (Bend, Oregon) (September 24, 1977): 10.

1392 "Big Foot Kin Found Throughout U.S.," *Modern People* (December 11, 1977) as cited in *Mysteries of the World Supplement* (December 1977).

1393 "Tests Might Prove Sasquatch is Real," *Bulletin* (Bend, Oregon) (September 24, 1977): 10.

1394 "Bigfoot Hunter now After 'Nessie'," *Daily Record* (Ellensburg, Washington) (July 20, 1983): 10.

1395 "Hair Samples May Prove Existence of Sasquatch," *Daily Record* (Ellensburg, Washington) (September 23, 1977): 4.

1396 "Bigfoot Hunter now After 'Nessie'," *Daily Record* (Ellensburg, Washington) (July 20, 1983): 10.

1397 "Sasquatch like Yowling Coyotes," *Register-Guard* (Eugene, Oregon) (December 25, 1977): 15F.

1398 "Logo Mark Trademark Information: Pacific National Bank of Washington," Trademarkia.com. http://www.trademarkia.com/logo-73087879.html.

1399 "Bank Declines to Help Bigfoot," *Daily Herald* (Arlington Heights, Illinois) (December 21, 1977).

1400 "Bigfoot Appeal Rejected," *Daily Chronicle* (Centralia, Washington) (December 20, 1977).

1401 "Bigfoot Meets His Match," *Spokane Daily Chronicle* (October 16, 1980): 6.

1402 York, Max. "Tracking Bigfoot in Middle Tennessee," *Tennessean Magazine* (November 6, 1977): 53.

1403 York, Max. "Tracking Bigfoot in Middle Tennessee," *Tennessean Magazine* (November 6, 1977): 54-55.

1404 Montgomery, Robert. "Man is Hot After Monsters," *Tallahassee Democrat* (April 11, 1977): 10.

1405 Glidewell, Jan. "Curiosity Has Drawn this Man in Search of Bigfoot and Nessie," *Pasco Times* (March 2, 1977): 1.

1406 "'Monsters' to be Discussed at USC," *State* (Columbia, South Carolina) (April 27, 1977): 7C.

1407 Montgomery, Robert. "Man is Hot After Monsters," *Tallahassee Democrat* (April 11, 1977): 10.

1408 Glidewell, Jan. "Curiosity Has Drawn This Man in Search of Bigfoot and Nessie," *Pasco Times* (March 2, 1977): 3.

1409 May be Davisville, Missouri however, reporter Peter Genovese gave the state as Tennessee in his October 18, 1978 article, "Bigfoot, Nessie Are No Fairy Tales, 'Monster-Watcher Says," in *Home News* (New Brunswick, New Jersey).

1410 Frank, Lee. "Stalking Bigfoot in the Land of Cotton," *High Times* (January 1977): 91.

1411 Frank, Lee. "Stalking Bigfoot in the Land of Cotton," *High Times* (January 1977): 130.

1412 Frank, Lee. "Stalking Bigfoot in the Land of Cotton," *High Times* (January 1977): 93, 130.

1413 Frank, Lee. "Stalking Bigfoot in the Land of Cotton," *High Times* (January 1977): 131, 142.

1414 Frank, Lee. "Stalking Bigfoot in the Land of Cotton," *High Times* (January 1977): 142.

1415 "'Bigfoot' Again Stirs Interest," *Waukesha Daily Freeman* (May 24, 1977): 6.

1416 Rhein, Dave. "Stalking 'Bigfoot' Across Iowa—to the State Fair," *Des Moines Sunday Register* (August 7, 1977): 12A.

1417 Mitchell, John G. "Bigfoot and Yeti," *Sports Afield* (February 1977): 45.

1418 Mitchell, John G. "Bigfoot and Yeti," *Sports Afield* (February 1977): 127.

1419 Mitchell, John G. "Bigfoot and Yeti," *Sports Afield* (February 1977): 127.

1420 Williams, T. Jeff. "Bigfoot: Man, Beast or Myth," *Argosy* (December/January 1977): 40.

1421 "'Bigfoot' Again Stirs Interest," *Waukesha Daily Freeman* (May 24, 1977): 6.

1422 "Four Men Tell How They Engineered Sasquatch Hoax," *Lethbridge Herald* (May 27, 1977): 1.

1423 "Driver Shaken After Chasing 'Bigfoot'," *Lawrence Journal World* (May 18, 1977): 20.

1424 "'Bigfoot' Seen by Bus Group," *New Castle News* (New Castle, Pennsylvania) (May 16, 1977): 40.

1425 "Brush with 'Bigfoot' Startles Bus Driver," *Daily Times* (St. Cloud, Minnesota) (May 21, 1977): 7.

1426 "Sightseers Turn out to Hunt 'Sasquatch'," *Medicine Hat News* (May 17, 1977): 3.

1427 Gates, Dennis. "The Mission, B.C. Bigfoot Hoax," *Pursuit* (Fall, 1977): 127.

1428 "Sighting Said to be Hoax," *Medicine Hat News* (May 24, 1977): 3.

1429 'Bigfoot' Yarn Admitted Hoax," *Evening News* (Newburgh, New York) (May 28, 1977): 10A.

1430 "Gorilla Suits," *Circus Report* (November 14, 1977): 6.

1431 DollarTimes.com. https://www.dollartimes.com/inflation/inflation.php?amount=10&year=1977.

1432 "Bigfoot Devotee Jarred at Hoax," *Watertown Daily Times* (May 28, 1977) as cited in *Mysteries of the World Supplement* (July 1977).

1433 "Bigfoot Devotee Jarred at Hoax," *Watertown Daily Times* (May 28, 1977) as cited in *Mysteries of the World Supplement* (July 1977).

1434 Gates, Dennis. "The Mission, B.C. Bigfoot Hoax," *Pursuit* (Fall, 1977): 127-128.

1435 "Brush with 'Bigfoot' Startles Bus Driver," *Daily Times* (St. Cloud, Minnesota) (May 21, 1977): 7.

1436 Ode, Kim. "Big Foot—Many Sightings but No One Knows for Sure," *Argus Leader* (September 30, 1977) as cited in *Mysteries of the World Supplement* (November 1977).

1437 "Bigfoot Watcher Says He has Sasquatch Films," *Lewiston Morning Tribune* (October 18, 1977).

1438 "Huge Ape Reported in Seattle Area Forest," *Bakersfield Californian* (October 18, 1977).

1439 "Huge Ape Reported in Seattle Area Forest," *Bakersfield Californian* (October 18, 1977).

1440 "Man Films 'Sasquatch'," *Spokesman-Review* (October 18, 1977): 10.

1441 O'Ryan, John. "Quest for the Elusive Sasquatch," *Post Intelligencer* (November 4, 1977) as cited *in Mysteries of the World Supplement* (December 1977).

1442 Folder 0342, box 10, Grover Krantz Papers Collection, National Anthropological Archive, Smithsonian Institution.

1443 Gates, Dennis. "Another Bigfoot Hoax," *Pursuit* (Spring 1978): 78.
1444 Gordon, Tom. "Tales of Bigfoot Spawn Pitter-Patter of Mischievousness," *Anniston Star* (August 11, 1977): 7.
1445 Purnell, Florestine. "Monster Tracks, Beastly Joke," *Morning-Star* (Rockford, Illinois) (January 21, 1977): 4.
1446 "Family Finds Tracks and Has Close Visual Encounter," BFRO.net. http://www.bfro.net/GDB/show_report.asp?id=7473.
1447 "Big Foot Hunter Here Inspects Claw Marks," *Stilwell Democrat Journal* (August 25, 1977): 20.
1448 "Search Continues for Bigfoot," *Southeast Missourian* (August 23, 1977): 8.
1449 "Claw Marks, Prints of 'Monster' Found at Farm," *Stilwell Democrat Journal* (August 18, 1977) as cited in *Mysteries of the World Supplement* (October, 1977).
1450 Crow, Ray. "Hairy Monster Real to Stilwell Clan," *Phoenix & Times-Democrat* (August 11, 1977) as cited in *Mysteries of the World Supplement* (September 1977).
1451 "Mystery Creature May Be Big Foot," *Big Spring Herald* (August 10, 1977): 3B.
1452 "Search Continues for Bigfoot," *Southeast Missourian* (August 23, 1977): 8.
1453 "'Bigfoot' Hair Probably Bear," *Corsicana Daily Sun* (August 18, 1977): 3A.
1454 "Bigfoot or Bear," *Big Spring Herald* (August 18, 1977): 18.
1455 "Claw Marks, Prints of 'Monster' Found at Farm," *Stilwell Democrat Journal* (August 18, 1977): 1.
1456 "Claw Marks, Prints of 'Monster' Found at Farm," *Stilwell Democrat Journal* (August 18, 1977): 16.
1457 "Reward Offered for Beast Alive," *Stilwell Democrat Journal* (August 25, 1977): 1.
1458 "Monster Story Hoax Youth Tells Sheriff," *Stilwell Democrat Journal* (August 25, 1977): 1.
1459 "Search Continues for Bigfoot," *Southeast Missourian* (August 23, 1977): 8.
1460 "Search Continues for Bigfoot," *Southeast Missourian* (August 23, 1977): 8.
1461 Phillips, Kevin. "Politicians and Yetis," *Naugatuck Daily News* (September 21, 1977): 4.
1462 "'Protect Bigfoot' Campaign Starts," *Times-Standard* (Eureka, California) (July 25, 1970): 9.
1463 "Oregon Panel Votes to Protect Bigfoot," *Nashua Telegraph* (June 9, 1977): 20.
1464 Bishoff, Don. "Bigfoot Sought Dead or Alive," *Register-Guard* (Eugene, Oregon) (February 25, 1988): B1.
1465 Bishoff, Don. "Bigfoot Sought Dead or Alive," *Register-Guard* (Eugene, Oregon) (February 25, 1988): B1.
1466 "To Ted with Love from Sasquatch," *Register-Guard* (Eugene, Oregon) (February 15, 1977): A10.
1467 "Skunk Apes Protected," *News* (Frederick, Maryland) (May 21, 1977): A10.
1468 "Pranks Relieve Tedium," *Naples Daily News* (May 23, 1977): 4B.
1469 "'Skunk Ape' Shouted Down," *Playground Daily News* (June 3, 1977): 8B.

1470 Baygents, Ron. "Bigfoot," *Ocala Star-Banner* (November 17, 1977): 10A.
1471 "Are We Ready for 'Bigfoot' or the Loch Ness Monster," FWS.gov. https://www.fws.gov/news/ShowNews.cfm?ID=HNR-5618.
1472 "What if Bigfoot is Located? Call Out the National Guard," *Daily Chronicle* (Centralia, Washington) (December 20, 1977).
1473 "What if Bigfoot is Located? Call Out the National Guard," *Daily Chronicle* (Centralia, Washington) (December 20, 1977).
1474 "Government Won't Let Bigfoot Undergo 'King Kong' Exploitation," *Walla Walla Union Bulletin* (January 24, 1978): 15.
1475 Hartz, Sam. "No Monkeying with Bigfoot," *Free Lance-Star* (Fredericksburg, Virginia) (January 28, 1978): 1, 10.
1476 Wyman, Mike. "Bigfoot to Find Taxman at Hand," *Valley News* (Van Nuys, California) (December 23, 1977): 2.
1477 Delay, Jim. "Bigfoot Walks Tall, But is Out of Step with Civilization," *Boston Herald American* (May 26, 1977): 3.
1478 "Pardon my Fingers," *Morning Union* (Springfield, Massachusetts) (April 2, 1977): 2.
1479 "What a Beast," *Seattle Times* (May 7, 1977): 10.
1480 Burlingame, Burl. "At the Movies," *Honolulu Star-Bulletin* (December 19, 1980): D10.
1481 Poe, Stephanie. "Bigfoot Returns for Kids in 'Boggy'," *Tallahassee Democrat* (October 1, 1977): 8.
1482 "La. Natives Cast in Family Movie," *Town Talk* (Alexandria-Pineville, Louisiana) (June 12, 1977): A3.
1483 Smith, Fred L. "TV Talk," *News and Courier* (Charleston, South Carolina) (February 10, 1978): 3A.
1484 Heilemann, Michael. "The Complete Conceptual History of Chewbacca," Kitbashed.com https://kitbashed.com/blog/chewbacca.
1485 Thomas, Bob. "'Beverly Hillbillies' Movie Could Lead to Another Stint as Weekly Series," *News-Press Airwaves* (Fort Myers, Florida) (October 4, 1981): 45.
1486 Roe, Jon. "New this Season," *Minneapolis Tribune* (September 4, 1977): 27.
1487 "Bigfoot's Feeding Ground: We Hid a Case of Canadian Club Here, Then Ran Like Crazy," *Playboy* (March 1977): 154-155.
1488 Fulton, Ben. "On Publicity and the 'Bigfoot'," *Augusta Chronicle* (March 25, 1977): 4.
1489 Bumiller, Elisabeth. "The Case of the Buried Booze," Washingtonpost.com. https://www.washingtonpost.com/archive/lifestyle/1980/08/27/the-case-of-the-buried-booze/6c8a79db-abaf-439e-a88f-e84973372442/?utm_term=.1dea8fe2df4d.
1490 Sellers, Mary. *Night Shadows* (New York, NY: Berkley Medallion Books, 1977): 8
1491 Knerr, M. E. *Sasquatch: Monster of the Northwest Woods* (New York: Tower Publications, 1977): 202-203.

1492 Jones, Marianna. "Artist Continues to Think Big for Series of 12 Bronze Sculptures," *Walla Wall Union-Bulletin* (March 20, 1977) as cited in McClean, Scott. *Big News Prints* (2006): 55.

1493 "Big Foot is Missing," *Ironwood Daily Globe* (December 27, 1977): 6.

1494 "Bigfoot Back," *Kokomo Tribune* (April 2, 1977): 9.

1495 'Bigfoot' is Found," *Gastonia Gazette* (December 28, 1977): 3A.

1496 "'Monster' Missing," *Statesville Record & Landmark* (December 27, 1977).

1497 "Bigfoot Back," *Kokomo Tribune* (April 2, 1977): 9.

1498 "'Bigfoot' Search," *Wilmington Morning Star* (August 30, 1977): 16.

1499 Rhein, Dave. "Stalking 'Bigfoot' Across Iowa—to the State Fair," *Des Moines Sunday Register* (August 7, 1977): 1A, 12A.

1500 "Bigfoot in Iowa," *Mt. Pleasant News* (August 27, 1977): 1.

1501 "Terrifying Eyewitness Report of a Life and Death Encounter with a Monster in the U.S. Forest," BigfootEncounters.com. www.bigfootencounters.com/articles/desmoines1977.htm.

1502 "Not all Believe in Bigfoot," *Daily Republic* (Mitchell, South Dakota) (October 7, 1977): 1.

1503 Lake, Bonnie. "Dakota's Bigfoot," *Horizons* (Spring, 1978): 27.

1504 Hasner, Tom. "Monster No Illusion to South Dakotans Who Claim Sightings," *Argus-Leader* (Sioux Falls, South Dakota) (September 30, 1977): 1.

1505 Hasner, Tom. Monster No Illusion to South Dakotans Who Claim Sightings," *Argus-Leader* (Sioux Falls, South Dakota) (September 30, 1977): 1

1506 Hasner, Tom. "McLaughlin Monster Has Become a Part of Life," *Argus-Leader* (Sioux Falls, South Dakota) (October 23, 1977): 1D.

1507 Hasner, Tom. "McLaughlin Monster Has Become a Part of Life," *Argus-Leader* (Sioux Falls, South Dakota) (October 23, 1977): 1D.

1508 Edman, Mary. "They're Scared—Something's Out There," *Sioux Falls Argus-Leader* (September 30, 1977): C1.

1509 Hasner, Tom. "McLaughlin Monster Has Become a Part of Life," *Argus-Leader* (Sioux Falls, South Dakota) (October 23, 1977): 1D.

1510 "Dakotans Seek Elusive Monster," *Sioux City Journal* (September 30, 1977): 5.

1511 "Not all Believe in Bigfoot," *Daily Republic* (Mitchell, South Dakota) (October 7, 1977): 1.

1512 Lake, Bonnie. "Dakota's Bigfoot," *Horizons* (Spring 1978): 27.

1513 Lofgren, Merle E. "Newsman Finds Signs of Something," *Sioux Falls Argus-Leader* (September 30, 1977): C1.

1514 Tucker, Bob. "'Big Foot' Sighted Again at Little Eagle," *Rapid City Journal* (Rapid City, South Dakota) (October 11, 1981): 1.

1515 "More Monster Tracks Found," *Argus Leader* (October 3, 1977) as cited in *Mysteries of the World Supplement* (November 1977).

1516 "Elusive Monster Reportedly Seen in South Dakota," *Bulletin* (Bend, Oregon]) (September 30, 1977): 22.

1517 "Elusive Monster Reportedly Seen in South Dakota," *Bulletin* (Bend, Oregon) (September 30, 1977): 22.

1518 Lake, Bonnie. "Dakota's Bigfoot," *Horizons* (Spring 1978): 28-29.

1519 "Not all Believe in Bigfoot," *Daily Republic* (Mitchell, South Dakota) (October 7, 1977): 1.

1520 Lake, Bonnie. "Dakota's Bigfoot," *Horizons* (Spring 1978): 28.

1521 Tucker, Bob. "'Big Foot' Sighted Again at Little Eagle," *Rapid City Journal* (Rapid City, South Dakota) (October 11, 1981): 1.

1522 "Two Bigfoots Sighted Near Little Eagle," *Mclaughlin Messenger* (November 3, 1977) as cited in *Mysteries of the World Supplement* (January 1978).

1523 Lowe, Sam. "Sam Lowe's Valley," *Phoenix Gazette* (December 15, 1977) as cited in *Mysteries of the World Supplement* (February 1978).

1524 Lake, Bonnie. "Dakota's Bigfoot," *Horizons* (Spring 1978): 30.

1525 Lowe, Sam. "Sam Lowe's Valley," *Phoenix Gazette* (December 15, 1977) as cited in *Mysteries of the World Supplement* (February 1978).

1526 Hasner, Tom. "Monster Publicity Floods Little Eagle," *Argus Leader* (October 17, 1977) as cited in *Mysteries of the World* (December 1977).

1527 "Two Bigfoots Sighted Near Little Eagle," *Mclaughlin Messenger* (November 3, 1977) as cited in *Mysteries of the World Supplement* (January 1978).

1528 "Two Bigfoots Sighted Near Little Eagle," *McIntosh News* (November 3, 1977) as cited in *Mysteries of the World Supplement* (December 1977).

1529 "'Big Foot' Stories Bring an Appeal," *Bismarck Tribune* (November 10, 1977) as cited in *Mysteries of the World Supplement* (December 1977).

1530 "Two Bigfoots Sighted Near Little Eagle," *Mclaughlin Messenger* (November 3, 1977) as cited in *Mysteries of the World Supplement* (January 1978).

1531 "Bigfoot's Shrieks Driving Indians off Reservation," *Independent* (Long Beach, California) (December 8, 1977): 25.

1532 "'Big Foot' Stories Bring an Appeal," *Bismarck Tribune* (November 10, 1977) as cited in *Mysteries of the World Supplement* (December 1977).

1533 "Standing Rock Tribe Calls off Big Foot Hunt," *Timber Lake Topic* (November 10, 1977) as cited in *Mysteries of the World Supplement* (January 1978).

1534 Katus, Ralph. "Writer Invades Lair of Big Foot Seeking Answers," *McLaughlin Messenger* (November 17, 1977) as cited in *Mysteries of the World Supplement* (January 1978).

1535 Katus, Ralph. "Writer Invades Lair of Big Foot Seeking Answers," *McLaughlin Messenger* (November 17, 1977) as cited in *Mysteries of the World Supplement* (January 1978).

1536 "Indians Leave S.D. Hamlet in Bigfoot Scare," *Honolulu Star-Bulletin* (November 29, 1977): C14.

1537 Kinders, Mark. "Bigfoot Fear Hits Little Eagle," *Huron Daily Plainsman* (November 28, 1977): 7.

1538 "Bigfoot Scares Many Indians," *Fort Scott Tribune* (Kansas) (November 30, 1977): 6.

1539 Lowe, Sam. "Sam Lowe's Valley," *Phoenix Gazette* (December 15, 1977) as cited in *Mysteries of the World Supplement* (February 1978).

1540 Lowe, Sam. "Sam Lowe's Valley," *Phoenix Gazette* (December 15, 1977) as cited in *Mysteries of the World Supplement* (February 1978).

1541 Lake, Bonnie. "Dakota's Bigfoot," *Horizons* (Spring 1978): 29.

1542 "Bigfoot Hasn't Been Seen Lately," *Aberdeen Daily News* (Aberdeen, South Dakota) (January 8, 1978): 3.

1543 Lowe, Sam. "Sam Lowe's Valley," *Phoenix Gazette* (December 15, 1977) as cited in *Mysteries of the World Supplement* (February 1978).

1544 Lake, Bonnie. "Dakota's Bigfoot," *Horizons* (Spring 1978): 29.

1545 Lake, Bonnie. "Dakota's Bigfoot," *Horizons* (Spring 1978): 30.

1546 Lake, Bonnie. "Dakota's Bigfoot," *Horizons* (Spring 1978): 30.

1547 Lake, Bonnie. "Dakota's Bigfoot," *Horizons* (Spring 1978): 30.

1548 Lake, Bonnie. "Dakota's Bigfoot," *Horizons* (Spring 1978): 30.

1549 Tucker, Bob. "'Big Foot' Sighted Again at Little Eagle," *Rapid City Journal* (Rapid City, South Dakota) (October 11, 1981): 2.

1550 "Big Foot Hunter Here Inspects Claw Marks," *Stilwell Democrat Journal* (August 25, 1977): 1, 20.

1551 "Claw Marks, Prints of 'Monster' Found at Farm," *Stilwell Democrat Journal* (August 18, 1977) as cited in *Mysteries of the World Supplement* (October 1977).

1552 Pritchard, Bill. "Bigfoot? Sasquatch Hunter Plies the Platte," *Traverse City Record-Eagle* (April 12, 1977): 1.

1553 "Bigfoot Search Started," *Galesburg Register-Mail* (May 7, 1977): 12.

1554 Pritchard, Bill. "Bigfoot Hunter Convinced He's on Right Track," *Traverse City Record-Eagle* (May 23, 1977): 5.

1555 Sheler, Jeffrey. "Bigfoot Continues to Elude Searchers," *Delta Democrat-Times* (Greenville, Mississippi) (June 1, 1977): 8.

1556 Sheler, Jeffrey. "Hunt for 'Bigfoot' in Western Michigan," *Ludington Daily News* (May 31, 1977): 20.

1557 "Bigfoot a Big Laugh to Most," *Traverse City Record* (May 23, 1977): 5.

1558 Orr, Steve. "A Bigfoot for Michigan," *Detroit Free Press* (July 11, 1977).

1559 Orr, Steve. "A Bigfoot for Michigan," *Detroit Free Press* (July 11, 1977).

1560 Charles, Gordon. "Bigfoot? Story May Be True," *Traverse City Record-Eagle* (September 9, 1977): 1.

1561 Charles, Gordon. "Bigfoot? Story May Be True," *Traverse City Record-Eagle* (September 9, 1977): 1.

1562 Charles, Gordon. "Bigfoot? Story May Be True," *Traverse City Record-Eagle* (September 9, 1977): 8.

1563 Charles, Gordon. "Bigfoot? Story May Be True," *Traverse City Record-Eagle* (September 9, 1977): 8.

1564 MacClean, Scott. *Big News Prints* (2006): 189.

1565 Hogan, Brian. *National Enquirer* (November 15, 1977) as cited in *Mysteries of the World Supplement* (December 1977).

1566 "Science Group Hits 'Cult of Unreason'," *Chicago Sun-Times* (August 10, 1977) as cited in *Mysteries of the World Supplement* (September 1977).

1567 Hospodar, June, and Paul Hospodar. "Sasquatch, Big Foot or Yeti, He's Known Around the World," *Valley News* (May 19, 1977): 7.

1568 Hospodar, June, and Paul Hospodar. "Sasquatch, Big Foot or Yeti, He's Known Around the World," *Valley News* (May 19, 1977): 7.

1569 Hospodar, June, and Paul Hospodar. "A Tough Marine Tells Story of a Hairy Hippie," *Valley News* (May 26, 1977): 16.

1570 Hospodar, June, and Paul Hospodar. "A Tough Marine Tells Story of a Hairy Hippie," *Valley News* (May 26, 1977): 16.

1571 Hospodar, June, and Paul Hospodar. "A Tough Marine Tells Story of a Hairy Hippie," *Valley News* (May 26, 1977): 16.

1572 Hospodar, June, and Paul Hospodar. "Fear Grips 'Daring' Trio in Search for Bigfoot," *Valley News* (June 2, 1977): 6.

1573 Hospodar, June, and Paul Hospodar. "Fear Grips 'Daring' Trio in Search for Bigfoot," *Valley News* (June 2, 1977): 6.

1574 Hospodar, June, and Paul Hospodar. "Psychic Aids Bigfoot Hunters," *Valley News* (June 9, 1977): 10.

1575 Zogg, Ivan. "Bigfoot: Born in the Bermuda Triangle," *National Spotlite* (August 1977).

1576 Saxty, Dick. "Top Psychics Predict We're About to Solve Three of World's Most Baffling Mysteries," *National Enquirer* (December 20, 1977) as cited in *Mysteries of the World Supplement* (January 1978).

1577 "Astronomers Want UFOs Probed," *Derrick* (Oily City, Pennsylvania) (May 4, 1977).

1578 Slate, Barbara Ann. "Does Earth Really Belong to Man," *Saga UFO Report* (October 1977): 34.

1579 Guttilla, Peter. "Bigfoot: Advance Guard from Outer Space," *UFO Report* (June 1977).

1580 Guttilla, Peter. "Bigfoot: Advance Guard from Outer Space," *UFO Report* (June 1977).

1581 Pruett, Cheryl. "OC Man Says UFOs, Bigfoot May be Connected," *Register* (October 2, 1977): C7.

1582 Pruett, Cheryl. "OC Man Says UFOs, Bigfoot May be Connected," *Register* (October 2, 1977): C7.

1583 "'I Saw a Monster'," *Binghamton Press* (Binghamton, New York) (November 10, 1958): 9.

1584 Barker, Gray. "UFO Creatures on the Prowl," *UFO Report* (March 1977): 23-24.

1585 "Riverside 'Monster' On Loose, He's Inhuman," *Redlands Daily Facts* (Redlands, California) (November 11, 1958): 4.

1586 "Charlie Wetzel Meets Earless, Long-Armed, Gurgling Monster," *Greenville News* (Greenville, South Carolina) (November 10, 1958): 1.

1587 Barker, Gray. "UFO Creatures on the Prowl," *UFO Report* (March 1977): 48.

1588 Cato, Sid. "Is the Monster of Wilder Creek Fact or Fiction," *Marshall Evening Chronicle* (Marshall, Michigan) (June 14, 1956): 1.

1589 Cato, Sid. "Is the Monster of Wilder Creek Fact or Fiction," *Marshall Evening Chronicle* (Marshall, Michigan) (June 14, 1956): 1.

1590 Cato, Sid. "Is the Monster of Wilder Creek Fact or Fiction," *Marshall Evening Chronicle* (Marshall, Michigan) (June 14, 1956): 1.

1591 Cato, Sid. "Is the Monster of Wilder Creek Fact or Fiction," *Marshall Evening Chronicle* (Marshall, Michigan) (June 14, 1956): 1, 5.

1592 Cato, Sid. "Is the Monster of Wilder Creek Fact or Fiction," *Marshall Evening Chronicle* (Marshall, Michigan) (June 14, 1956): 5.

1593 Barker, Gray. "UFO Creatures on the Prowl," *UFO Report* (March 1977): 48.

1594 Cato, Sid. "Is the Monster of Wilder Creek Fact or Fiction," *Marshall Evening Chronicle* (Marshall, Michigan) (June 14, 1956): 5.

1595 Barker, Gray. "UFO Creatures on the Prowl," *UFO Report* (March 1977): 48.

1596 Cato, Sid. "Is the Monster of Wilder Creek Fact or Fiction," *Marshall Evening Chronicle* (Marshall, Michigan) (June 14, 1956): 5.

1597 Barker, Gray. "UFO Creatures on the Prowl," *UFO Report* (March 1977): 48.

1598 Barker, Gray. "UFO Creatures on the Prowl," *UFO Report* (March 1977): 52.

1599 Barker, Gray. "UFO Creatures on the Prowl," *UFO Report* (March 1977): 52.

1600 Barker, Gray. "UFO Creatures on the Prowl," *UFO Report* (March 1977): 52.

1601 "'Bigfoot,' UFOs are Discussed," *Salem News* (Salem, Ohio) (March 17, 1977): 5.

1602 Cowen, Robert C. "Why the UFOs Won't Go Away," *Derrick* (Oil City, Pennsylvania) (May 4, 1977).

1603 Morrison, Pam. "Adventures into the Unexplained," *Derrick* (Oil City, Pennsylvania) (May 4, 1977).

1604 Godwin, Julian. "Local Men Study 'Paranormal' Events," *Athens News Courier* (December 18, 1977): 7A.

1605 Sutherly, Curt. "Bigfoot in Jersey Kills Farm Rabbits," *Lebanon Daily News* (June 30, 1977): 15

1606 Sutherly, Curt. "Group Probes Bigfoot, UFO Sightings," *Lebanon Daily News* (September 23, 1976): 42.

1607 "The Journal Previews Tonight's TV," *Jersey Journal* (October 26, 1976): 15.
1608 Sutherly, Curt. "Group Probes Bigfoot, UFO Sightings," *Lebanon Daily News* (September 23, 1976): 42
1609 Sutherly, Curt. "Bigfoot in Jersey Kills Farm Rabbits," *Lebanon Daily News* (June 30, 1977): 15.
1610 Sutherly, Curt. "Bigfoot in Jersey Kills Farm Rabbits," *Lebanon Daily News* (June 30, 1977): 15.
1611 Mayne, S.N. "The Wantage Event," *Pursuit* (Fall 1977): 124.
1612 Mayne, S.N. "The Wantage Event," *Pursuit* (Fall 1977): 125.
1613 Mayne, S.N. "The Wantage Event," *Pursuit* (Fall 1977): 126-127.
1614 Mayne, S.N. "The Wantage Event," *Pursuit* (Fall 1977): 127.
1615 "Does Carolina Have Bigfoot on the Loose," *Free-Lance Star* (January 4, 1978): 24.
1616 "'Booger' Search Fruitless," *Wilmington Morning Star* (January 11, 1977): 9.
1617 "'Booger' Search Fruitless," *Wilmington Morning Star* (January 11, 1977): 9.
1618 "Man, 'Booger' Meet in Swamp," *Wilmington Morning Star* (January 8, 1977): 12.
1619 "Man, 'Booger' Meet in Swamp," *Wilmington Morning Star* (January 8, 1977): 12.
1620 "Booger Tales are Told," *Wilmington Morning Star* (January 15, 1977): 5.
1621 "Man, 'Booger' Meet in Swamp," *Wilmington Morning Star* (January 8, 1977): 12.
1622 "Booger Tales are Told," *Wilmington Morning Star* (January 15, 1977): 5.
1623 "Man, 'Booger' Meet in Swamp," *Wilmington Morning Star* (January 8, 1977): 12.
1624 "Booger Tales are Told," *Wilmington Morning Star* (January 15, 1977): 5.
1625 "Marines May Have 'Big Foot' of Their Own," *Sunday Times* (February 6, 1977) as cited in McClean, Scott. *Big News Prints* (2006): 234.
1626 "Marines May Have 'Big Foot' of Their Own," *Sunday Times* (February 6, 1977) as cited in McClean, Scott. *Big News Prints* (2006): 234.
1627 "Footprints Look Real to Farmer," *News and Courier* (February 20, 1977): 14-A.
1628 "Mystery Printmaker Still Unknown," *Rock Hill Herald* (February 15, 1977).
1629 "Man Reportedly in Shock After Seeing 'Bigfoot'," *Bulletin* (Bend, Oregon) (March 24, 1977): 15.
1630 "Soldier in Shock After Seeing 'Big Hairy Thing'," *Tri-City Herald* (Washington: Pasco, Kennewick, and Richland) (March 24, 1977).
1631 Churchhill, Marlowe. "Do NW Trek Visitors Include a Bigfoot," *Tacoma News Tribune* (March 22, 1977) as cited in *Mysteries of the World Supplement* (April 1977).
1632 Lewis, Greg. "Could Bigfoot be Scouting GGO Turf," *Greensboro Daily News* (March 16, 1977): B2.
1633 Benowitz, Sam. "Is Sasquatch Roaming in Packwood Region," *Daily Chronicle* (Centralia-Chehalis, Washington) (May 3, 1977): 1.
1634 "Bigfoot in the News Again," *Brownsville Telegraph* (May 21, 1977): 3.
1635 Downing, John. "'Bigfoot' is Sighted in Stoneridge Plan," *News Record* (North Hills, Pennsylvania) (June 18, 1977): 2.

1636 Downing, Roger. "Youths Report Attack by the 'Hawley Him'," *Abilene Reporter-News* (July 7, 1977): 1, 8A.

1637 "Monster's Capture Sought," *Las Cruces Sun-News* (August 17, 1977): 6.

1638 "Hunters Seek Sniff of 'Hawley Him'," *Abilene Reporter-News* (July 8, 1977): 1.

1639 Duff, Katharyn. "Page One," *Abilene Reporter-News* (July 15, 1977): 1.

1640 Duff, Katharyn. "Page One," Abilene Reporter-News (July 8, 1977): 1.

1641 Duff, Katharyn. "Page One," Abilene Reporter News (June 10, 1970): 1.

1642 "Bigfoot Trods Again," *Independent Record* (Helena, Montana) (August 26, 1977): 3.

1643 "People in the News," *Ottawa Journal* (August 29, 1977): 12.

1644 "Disbelieving Men to Check Report on Sighting Bigfoot," *Register-Guard* (August 31, 1977): 7C.

1645 "Disbelieving Men to Check Report on Sighting Bigfoot," *Register-Guard* (August 31, 1977): 7C.

1646 "Bigfoot Sightings Spur Utah Search," *Detroit Free Press* (September 2, 1977): 12B.

1647 "New Search for Bigfoot Mounted," *Day* (New London, Connecticut.) (September 3, 1977): 18.

1648 "Big Foot in Uintas: Nothing Conclusive," *Reflex* (Kaysville, Utah) (September 15, 1977) as cited in *Mysteries of the World Supplement* (November 1977).

1649 Fement, Jack. "No Dream, Says Beaverton Woman—It Was Bigfoot," *Oregon Journal* (January 12, 1978) as cited in *Mysteries of the World Supplement* (February 1978).

1650 "A Renewed Search for 'Bigfoot'," *Argus-Courier* (Petaluma, California) (October 30, 1975): 3.

1651 Lawrence, Keith. "In Search of Bigfoot," *Messenger-Inquirer* (Owensboro, Kentucky) (February 9, 1977): 1C.

1652 Lawrence, Keith. "In Search of Bigfoot," *Messenger-Inquirer* (Owensboro, Kentucky) (February 9, 1977): 1C.

1653 Lawrence, Keith. "In Search of Bigfoot," *Messenger-Inquirer* (Owensboro, Kentucky) (February 9, 1977): 1C.

1654 Lindley, Tom. "Bigfoot—Search for Elusive 'Creature' Continues," *Sunday Courier and Press* (Evansville, Indiana) (February 13, 1977): 1.

1655 Lindley, Tom. "Bigfoot—Search for Elusive 'Creature' Continues," *Sunday Courier and Press* (Evansville, Indiana) (February 13, 1977): 5.

1656 Dobens, Peter. "Skunkape 'Something' Lurks in Area Woods," *Sarasota Journal* (March 3, 1977) as cited in *Mysteries of the World Supplement* (April 1977).

1657 "Believe It, or Not," *Ocala Star-Banner* (November 17, 1977): 10A.

1658 Baygents, Ron. "Bigfoot," *Ocala Star-Banner* (November 17, 1977): 10A.

1659 Klinger, Rafe. "Florida's Skunk Ape," *Palm Beach Post-Times* (September 15, 1977) as cited in *Mysteries of the World Supplement* (November 1977).

1660 Brink, Bob. "UFOs from Another Dimension," *Palm Beach Post-Times* (February 20, 1977): B1.

1661 Klinger, Rafe. "'Skunk Ape' Seen at Golf Course," *Palm Beach Post* (February 11, 1977): C1.

1662 White, Randy. "Search Ends in Mystery," *News-Press* (Fort Myers, Florida) (March 2, 1977) as cited in *Mysteries of the World Supplement* (April 1977).

1663 White, Randy. "Expert Convinced We Saw Skunk Ape," *News-Press* (Fort Myers, Florida) (February 28, 1977) as cited in *Mysteries of the World Supplement* (April 1977).

1664 White, Randy. "Search Ends in Mystery," *News-Press* (Fort Myers, Florida) (March 2, 1977) as cited in *Mysteries of the World Supplement* (April 1977).

1665 "8-Foot 'Thing' Unnerves Florida Family," *Pittsburgh Press* (July 27, 1977).

1666 "'Skunk Ape' Frightens Florida Family," *Salina Journal* (July 27, 1977): 27.

1667 Sloan, Phillip. "Skunk-Ape Seer Moves Out Takes Photograph with Him," *Keynoter* (Marathon, Florida) (August 04, 1977) as cited in *Mysteries of the World Supplement* (October 1977): 11.

1668 Sloan, Phillip. "Skunk-Ape Seer Moves Out Takes Photograph with Him" *Keynoter* (Marathon, Florida) (August 04, 1977) as cited in *Mysteries of the World Supplement* (October 1977): 11.

1669 Sloan, Phillip. "Skunk-Ape Seer Moves Out Takes Photograph with Him," *Keynoter* (Marathon, Florida) (August 4, 1977) as cited in *Mysteries of the World Supplement* (October 1977): 11.

1670 "Officials Label Big Foot Attack Hoax," *Apopka Chief* (October 7, 1977) as cited in *Mysteries of the World Supplement* (November 1977).

1671 Burt, Al. "A Creature? No Way My Man," *Gazette Telegraph* (May 28, 1978): 8B.

1672 Meiten, Don. [no title provided] *Florida Times-Union* (November 11, 1977) as cited in *Mysteries of the World Supplement* (December 1977).

1673 Lounsberry, Alyse. "Was it Bigfoot? Preacher Says Story No Lie," *Ocala Star-Banner* (November 16, 1977): 1, 8.

1674 Burt, Al. "A Creature? No Way My Man," *Gazette Telegraph* (May 28, 1978): 8B.

1675 Woodcock, Nell. "'I Know What I Saw (A Hairy Monster)," *St. Petersburg Times —Pasco Times* (October 28, 1977): 1, 3.

1676 "Little Bigfoot," *Palatka Daily News* (October 4, 1977) as cited in *Mysteries of the World Supplement* (November 1977).

1677 Connelly, Joel. "The Mysterious Monsters of B.C.," *Post-Intelligencer* (Seattle, Washington) (September 17, 1978) as cited in *Mysteries of the World Supplement* (November 1978).

1678 Louv, Rich. "Bigfoot: To Kill or Not to Kill," *Star-News* (Chula Vista, California) (June 22, 1978): B1.

1679 "Obituaries," *Oakland Tribune* (February 23, 1978).

1680 Natal, James. "Peter Byrne and the Ultimate Hunt," *UFO Annual 1980* (Volume 6, 1980): 45.

1681 Natal, James. "Peter Byrne and the Ultimate Hunt," *UFO Annual 1980* (Volume 6, 1980): 45-46.

1682 "Sukla Phanta Wildlife Reserve," Roughguides.com. http://www.roughguides.com/destinations/asia/nepal/the-western-terai/the-far-west/west-of-the-karnali-river/sukla-phanta-wildlife-reserve/.

1683 Natal, James. "Peter Byrne and the Ultimate Hunt," *UFO Annual 1980* (Volume 6, 1980): 46.

1684 Natal, James. "Peter Byrne and the Ultimate Hunt," *UFO Annual 1980* (Volume 6, 1980): 46.

1685 Natal, James. "Peter Byrne and the Ultimate Hunt," *UFO Annual 1980* (Volume 6, 1980): 46.

1686 Natal, James. "Peter Byrne and the Ultimate Hunt," *UFO Annual 1980* (Volume 6, 1980): 46.

1687 Natal, James. "Peter Byrne and the Ultimate Hunt," *UFO Annual 1980* (Volume 6, 1980): 47.

1688 Natal, James. "Peter Byrne and the Ultimate Hunt," *UFO Annual 1980* (Volume 6, 1980): 47.

1689 Natal, James. "Peter Byrne and the Ultimate Hunt," *UFO Annual 1980* (Volume 6, 1980): 47.

1690 Natal, James. "Peter Byrne and the Ultimate Hunt," *UFO Annual 1980* (Volume 6, 1980): 47.

1691 Natal, James. "Peter Byrne and the Ultimate Hunt," *UFO Annual 1980* (Volume 6, 1980): 86.

1692 Natal, James. "Peter Byrne and the Ultimate Hunt," *UFO Annual 1980* (Volume 6, 1980): 86.

1693 Natal, James. "Peter Byrne and the Ultimate Hunt," *UFO Annual 1980* (Volume 6, 1980): 86.

1694 Smark, Peter. "Amiable Monster Keeps the Scientists Guessing," *Age* (Melbourne, Victoria, Australia) (July 8, 1978): 16.

1695 Smark, Peter. "Amiable Monster Keeps the Scientists Guessing," *Age* (Melbourne, Victoria, Australia) (July 8, 1978): 16.

1696 Smark, Peter. "Amiable Monster Keeps the Scientists Guessing," *Age* (Melbourne, Victoria, Australia) (July 8, 1978): 16.

1697 Beckjord, Jon. "Fact or Fiction," *Anthropology Newsletter* (March 1978).

1698 Haley, Jim. "If You See Bigfoot, Call Him Up," *Herald* (Everett, Washington) (January 20, 1978) as cited in *Mysteries of the World Supplement* (March 1978).

1699 Porterfield, Bob. "Iliamna's Bigfoot Near Record Size," *Anchorage Daily News* (January 17, 1978): 1.

1700 Haley, Jim. "If You See Bigfoot, Call Him Up," *Herald* (Everett, Washington) (January 20, 1978) as cited in *Mysteries of the World Supplement* (March 1978).

1701 "Warning: Sasquatch Crossing," *Montana Gazette* (June 1978) as cited in *Mysteries of the World Supplement* (October 1978).

1702 Singer, Sam. "She Fids Bigfoot in Her Photo," *San Pablo News* (October 11, 1978) as cited in *Mysteries of the World* (December 1978).

1703 DeMain, Don. "She Took Tahoe Picture and Maybe Bigfoot Too," *Oakland Tribune* (October 6, 1978) as cited in *Mysteries of the World Supplement* (November 1978).

1704 Dolan, Maura. "How About Mr. and Mrs. Bigfoot and Family," *San Francisco Examiner* (October 6, 1978) as cited in *Mysteries of the World Supplement* (November 1978).

1705 Singer, Sam. "She Finds Bigfoot in Her Photo," *San Pablo News* (October 11, 1978) as cited in *Mysteries of the World* (December 1978).

1706 Duncan, Don. "High Adventure on Sasquatch Trail," *Seattle Times* (April 1, 1979): A17.

1707 Duncan, Don. "High Adventure on Sasquatch Trail," *Seattle Times* (April 1, 1979): A17.

1708 Singer, Sam. "She Finds Bigfoot in Her Photo," *San Pablo News* (October 11, 1978) as cited in *Mysteries of the World* (December 1978).

1709 Genovese, Peter. "Bigfoot, Nessie Are No Fairy Tales, 'Monster-Watcher' Says," *Home News* (New Brunswick, New Jersey) (October 18, 1978): 26.

1710 Loughran, Edward. "Notes on the Origin of Bigfoot," *INFO Journal* (March-April 1978): 12.

1711 Loughran, Edward. "Notes on the Origin of Bigfoot," *INFO Journal* (March-April 1978): 12.

1712 Cahoon, Delwin D. "The Psychological Hypothesis Defended: Comment on 'Notes on the Origin of Bigfoot'," *INFO Journal* (July-August 1978): 11, 12.

1713 Greenwell, Richard J. "Further Notes on the Origin of Bigfoot," *INFO Journal* (July-August 1978): 15-16.

1714 Michals, Bob. "Obsession: Tracking the Sasquatch Legend," *Palm Beach Post* (February 7, 1978): B1.

1715 Moorhead, Jim. "Sasquatches: Do They Really Exist," *Evening Independent* (February 2, 1978): B3.

1716 Michals, Bob. "Obsession: Tracking the Sasquatch Legend," *Palm Beach Post* (February 7, 1978): B1, B3.

1717 Otto, Steve. "Sasquatch's Big Foot Leaves a Deep Impression on Ron Olson," *Tampa Times* (February 8, 1978): B1, B2.

1718 Michals, Bob. "Obsession: Tracking the Sasquatch Legend," *Palm Beach Post* (February 7, 1978): B3.

1719 Michals, Bob. "Sasquatch the Legend Flops as a Movie Star," *Palm Beach Post* (February 7, 1978): B3.

1720 Maslin, Janet. "Film: 'Sasquatch' Roams Northwest: Monster Search," *New York Times* (January 12, 1978). NYTimes.com. http://www.nytimes.com/movie/review?res=9D05E1DD103EE632A25751C1A9679C946990D6CF).

1721 North American Film Enterprises, Inc. "Sasquatch," *Boxoffice* (January 30, 1978): 2.

1722 Crafts, Fred. "How 'Sasquatch' Slickered New York City," *Eugene Register-Guard* (April 6, 1978): 1D, 2D.

1723 Moorhead, Jim. "Sasquatches: Do They Really Exist," *Evening Independent* (February 2, 1978): 3B.

1724 "'Big Foot' Producer Makes Tracks for Film," *St. Petersburg Times* (February 3, 1978).

1725 Moorhead, Jim. "Not Bad, But No Documentary," *St. Petersburg Independent* (February 7, 1978): 6B.

1726 Otto, Steve. "Movie Attempts to Ape Bigfoot," *Tampa Times* (February 8, 1978): B1.

1727 "Monday TV," *Aberdeen American News* (Aberdeen, South Dakota) (March 28, 1978): 2.

1728 Sharbutt, Jay. "NBC Creates Parody on CBS's 60 Minutes," *Desert Sun* (January 25, 1978): B4.

1729 Harper, Timothy. "'Manbeast!' More Abominable than Snowman," *Beaver County Times* (Beaver, Pennsylvania) (August 5, 1983): B10.

1730 McLeod, Mike. "Producer Stalks Man-Beast Myth," *Pensacola Journal* (November 25, 1978): D1.

1731 "Big Foot Caper," *Calgary Herald* (July 20, 1978).

1732 "Sasquatch: The Apes Among Us," *Pursuit* (Fall, 1978): 175-176.

1733 Banks, William H. "Creatures on the Outer Edge," *Pursuit* (Fall, 1978): 176.

1734 Burt, Terry. "Stalking the Wild Big Foot Report," *La Crosse Tribune* (October 20, 1978) as cited in *Mysteries of the World Supplement* (December 1978).

1735 Burt, Terry. "Stalking the Wild Big Foot Report," *La Crosse Tribune* (October 20, 1978) as cited in *Mysteries of the World Supplement* (December 1978).

1736 Polesnek, Michael Jr., "Bigfoot Hunter Back in Mount St. Helens," *Lewis River News* (August 17, 1978) as cited in *Mysteries of the World Supplement* (September 1978).

1737 Smith, Cliff. "Scientists Blame NBC on Psychic Programs," *San Diego Union* (April 27, 1978) as cited in *Mysteries of the World Supplement* (July 1978).

1738 Anderson, Ed. "Bigfoot Scare Reported, But Nothing Bears Up," *New Orleans Times* (June 7, 1978) as cited in *Mysteries of the World Supplement* (July 1978).

1739 "Man Has Second 'Bigfoot' Sighting," *Cleveland Press* (October 18, 1978) as cited in *Mysteries of the World Supplement* (December 1978).

1740 McRee, Tim. "'Big Foot' Only a Big Bear," *Picayune Item* (March 26, 1978) as cited in *Mysteries of the World Supplement* (June 1978).

1741 McRee, Tim. "'Big Foot' Only a Big Bear," *Picayune Item* (March 26, 1978) as cited in *Mysteries of the World Supplement* (June 1978).

1742 McRee, Tim. "'Big Foot' Only a Big Bear," *Picayune Item* (March 26, 1978) as cited in *Mysteries of the World Supplement* (June 1978).

1743 "Waiting in the Woods for Brush to Move," *University of Washington Daily* (October 11, 1978) as cited in *Mysteries of the World Supplement* (December 1978).

1744 Miletich, Steve. "Bigfoot Follow-up: Expert Tracker Finds 8 Possible Prints Along Willow Road," *Journal-American* (Bellevue, Washington) (January 10, 1978). BFRO.net. http://www.bfro.net/gdb/show_article.asp?id=148.

1745 Tisher, Bill. "Friends Discover Evidence of Bigfoot," *Tribune* (South Lake Tahoe, California) (March 3, 1978) as cited in *Mysteries of the World Supplement* (May 1978).

1746 Parsons, Larry. "Bigfoot's in Trouble if He's Alive, Teacher Says," *Record-Searchlight* (Redding, California) (February 25, 1978) as cited in *Mysteries of the World Supplement* (April 1978).

1747 Parsons, Larry. "Bigfoot's in Trouble if He's Alive, Teacher Says," *Record-Searchlight* (Redding, California) (February 25, 1978) as cited in *Mysteries of the World Supplement* (April 1978).

1748 Dougherty, Terri. "Bigfoot is it Myth or Reality," *Chico Enterprise* (August 26, 1978) as cited in *Mysteries of the World Supplement* (September 1978).

1749 Greenwell, Richard J. and James E. King. "Scientists and Anomalous Phenomena: Preliminary Results of a Survey," *Zetetic Scholar* (July 1980): 18.

1750 Greenwell, Richard J. and James E. King. "Scientists and Anomalous Phenomena: Preliminary Results of a Survey," *Zetetic Scholar* (July 1980): 19.

1751 "The Weekend Poll—The Supernatural," *Ottawa Journal Weekend Magazine* (May 6, 1978): 3.

1752 Gallup, George. "Many Believe in Supernatural," *San Diego Union* (June 15, 1978): 14.

1753 "Bigfoot Lives in Pennsylvania," *Gettysburg Times* (July 24, 1978): 1.

1754 "Bigfoot Lives in Pennsylvania," *Gettysburg Times* (July 24, 1978): 2.

1755 "Bigfoot Lives in Pennsylvania," *Gettysburg Times* (July 24, 1978): 2.

1756 "Bigfoot Lives in Pennsylvania," *Gettysburg Times* (July 24, 1978): 2.

1757 Walls, Robert E. "Comments and Queries on the Observed Ecology and anatomy of an Unclassified Species of Primate," *Pursuit* (Fall 1978): 132.

1758 Walls, Robert E. "Comments and Queries on the Observed Ecology and anatomy of an Unclassified Species of Primate," *Pursuit* (Fall 1978): 132.

1759 Walls, Robert E. "Comments and Queries on the Observed Ecology and anatomy of an Unclassified Species of Primate," *Pursuit* (Fall 1978): 132-133.

1760 Walls, Robert E. "Comments and Queries on the Observed Ecology and anatomy of an Unclassified Species of Primate," *Pursuit* (Fall 1978): 132-134.

1761 Walls, Robert E. "Comments and Queries on the Observed Ecology and anatomy of an Unclassified Species of Primate," *Pursuit* (Fall 1978): 134.

1762 Garrett, Fred E. "Ol' Big Foot's Back," *Saginaw News* (November 23, 1978) as cited in *Mysteries of the World Supplement* (January 1979).

1763 Garrett, Fred E. "Ol' Big Foot's Back," *Saginaw News* (November 23, 1978) as cited in *Mysteries of the World Supplement* (January 1979).

1764 Walker-Tyson, Joyce. "Life is Not Easy for Bigfoot," *Detroit Free Press* (November 13, 1978): A19.

1765 Garrett, Fred E. "Ol' Big Foot's Back," *Saginaw News* (November 23, 1978) as cited in *Mysteries of the World Supplement* (January 1979).

1766 Walker-Tyson, Joyce. "Life is Not Easy for Bigfoot," *Detroit Free Press* (November 13, 1978): A19.

1767 Garrett, Fred E. "Ol' Big Foot's Back," *Saginaw News* (November 23, 1978) as cited in *Mysteries of the World Supplement* (January 1979).

1768 Walker-Tyson, Joyce. "Life is Not Easy for Bigfoot," *Detroit Free Press* (November 13, 1978): A19.

1769 Garrett, Fred E. "Ol' Big Foot's Back," *Saginaw News* (November 23, 1978) as cited in *Mysteries of the World Supplement* (January 1979).

1770 Garrett, Fred E. "Ol' Big Foot's Back," *Saginaw News* (November 23, 1978) as cited in *Mysteries of the World Supplement* (January 1979).

1771 Garrett, Fred E. "Ol' Big Foot's Back," *Saginaw News* (November 23, 1978) as cited in *Mysteries of the World Supplement* (January 1979).

1772 Garrett, Fred E. "Ol' Big Foot's Back," *Saginaw News* (November 23, 1978) as cited in *Mysteries of the World Supplement* (January 1979).

1773 Garrett, Fred E. "Ol' Big Foot's Back," *Saginaw News* (November 23, 1978) as cited in *Mysteries of the World Supplement* (January 1979).

1774 "Bigfoot Hunter Says—We Must Seize This Monster," *Mysteries of the World Supplement* (September 1978).

1775 Garrett, Fred E. "Ol' Big Foot's Back," *Saginaw News* (November 23, 1978) as cited in *Mysteries of the World Supplement* (January 1979).

1776 Garrett, Fred E. "Big Foot in Midland? *Saginaw News* (November 23, 1978) as cited in *Mysteries of the World Supplement* (January 1979).

1777 "Bigfoot Hunter Says—We Must Seize This Monster," as cited in *Mysteries of the World Supplement* (September 1978).

1778 "Sears Man Steps Forward to Say He Saw Bigfoot in Area, Too," *Cadillac News* (Cadillac, Michigan) (December 18, 1978) as cited in *Mysteries of the World Supplement* (February, 1979).

1779 Shubitowksi, Janet and Andrew Angelo. "Bigfoot in Osceola? Don't Laugh one Hunter Isn't," *Cadillac News* (Cadillac, Michigan) (November 25, 1978) as cited in *Mysteries of the World Supplement* (January 1979).

1780 "Boys Operate Bigfoot Center," *Aberdeen American News* (Aberdeen, South Dakota) (November 4, 1978): 5.

1781 Clark, Jerome. "UFO Update—Proof of Bigfoot," *UFO Report* (October 1978): 13.

1782 "Researchers Think Tape May be That of Bigfoot," *Bulletin* (Bend, Oregon) (April 6, 1978): 22.

1783 Vaughn Bryant, email message to author, January 12, 2016.

1784 Bailey, Jan. "Researcher Looks for True Bigfoot," *Eagle* (Bryan, Texas) (November 14, 1977): 11.

1785 "Bryant Gives Bigfoot Paper," *Eagle* (Bryan-College Station, Texas) (May 10, 1978): 6D.

1786 Louv, Rich. "Bigfoot: To Kill or Not to Kill," *Star-News* (Chula Vista, California) (June 22, 1978): B1.

1787 Bartlett, Kay. "Sasquatch Hunters Find Each Other 'Fair Game'," *Albuquerque Journal* (January 28, 1979): B8.

1788 Sprague, Roderick (Ed.) and Grover Krantz. *The Scientist Looks at the Sasquatch (II)* (Moscow, Idaho: University Press of Idaho, 1979): 164.

1789 Macey, Patrick J. "Anthropology of the Unknown: A Conference on Sasquatch and Similar Humanoid Monsters," *Pursuit* (Fall 1978): 130.

1790 Folder 0342, box 10, Grover Krantz Papers Collection, National Anthropological Archive, Smithsonian Institution.

1791 "Bigfoot Meeting Draws Scientists," *Ocala Star Banner* (May 13, 1978): 8A.

1792 "Scientists Compare Notes on 'Bigfoot'," *Daily Sitka Sentinel* (May 15, 1978): 6.

1793 "Sasquatch Film Has Brought only Money Woes to Owner," *Edmonton Journal* (May 13, 1978) as cited in *Mysteries of the World Supplement* (July 1978).

1794 "Bigfoot Takes Center Stage in Drama of World's Unknown," *Evening Journal* (Wilmington, Delaware) (May 12, 1978): 6.

1795 "Bigfoot Takes Center Stage in Drama of World's Unknown," *Evening Journal* [Wilmington, Delaware] (May 12, 1978): 6.

1796 Thorstein, Eric. "Close Encounters of a Monstrous Kind," *Ottawa Journal Weekend Magazine* (May 6, 1978): 16.

1797 "Scientists Compare Notes on 'Bigfoot'," *Daily Sitka Sentinel* (May 15, 1978): 6.

1798 Macey, Patrick J. "Anthropology of the Unknown: A Conference on Sasquatch and Similar Humanoid Monsters," *Pursuit* (Fall 1978): 130-131.

1799 Connelly, Joel. "The Mysterious Monsters of B.C.," *Post-Intelligencer* (Seattle, Washington) (September 17, 1978) as cited in *Mysteries of the World Supplement* (November 1978).

1800 Connelly, Joel. "The Mysterious Monsters of B.C.," *Post-Intelligencer* (Seattle, Washington) (September 17, 1978) as cited in *Mysteries of the World Supplement* (November 1978).

1801 Thorstein, Eric. "Close Encounters of a Monstrous Kind," *Ottawa Journal Weekend Magazine* (May 6, 1978): 16.

1802 "Hunting the Beast Cost Him His Wife and Family," *Edmonton Journal* (May 13, 1978) as cited in *Mysteries of the World Supplement* (July 1978).

1803 "I'm 100% Certain American Film of Bigfoot is No Hoax," as cited in *Mysteries of the World Supplement* (October 1978): 4.

1804 "I'm 100% Certain American Film of Bigfoot is No Hoax," as cited in *Mysteries of the World Supplement* (October 1978): 4.

1805 Thorstein, Eric. "Close Encounters of a Monstrous Kind," *Ottawa Journal Weekend Magazine* (May 6, 1978): 16.

1806 "I'm 100% Certain American Film of Bigfoot is No Hoax," as cited in *Mysteries of the World Supplement* (October 1978): 4.

1807 "Soviet Scientists Emphatic: Sasquatch is for Real," *Spokesman-Review* (Spokane, Washington) (May 14, 1978): A16.

1808 Walls, Robert E. "Comments and Queries on the Observed Ecology and Anatomy of an Unclassified Species of Primate," *Pursuit* (Fall, 1978): 133-134.

1809 Poulsen, Jonathan. "Bigfoot Caught on Film Ten Years after Patterson-Gimlin Film," BigfootEvidence.blogspot.com. http://bigfootevidence.blogspot.com/2012/05/bigfoot-caught-on-film-ten-years-after.html.

1810 "Bryant Gives Bigfoot Paper," *Eagle* (Bryan, Texas) (May 10, 1978): 6D.

1811 "Scientists Compare Notes on 'Bigfoot'," *Daily Sitka Sentinel* (May 15, 1978): 6.

1812 "Bryant Gives Bigfoot Paper," *Eagle* (Bryan, Texas) (May 10, 1978): 6D.

1813 Doney, Stef. "It's Beastly," *Toronto Star* (May 13, 1978) as cited in *Mysteries of the World Supplement* (June 1978).

1814 "Shooting Sasquatch Debated," *St. Louis Post-Dispatch* (May 14, 1978): 6A.

1815 Joseph, Greg. "Bigfoot: Wanted Dead or Alive," *Advocate* (Newark, Ohio) (February 18, 1978): 10.

1816 "Professor Says Kill Bigfoot for Proof," *Ukiah Daily Journal* (February 6, 1978): 11.

1817 "Shooting to Kill Would Help Solve Sasquatch Mystery," *Lethbridge Herald* (May 15, 1978).

1818 Williamson, Robert. "Ape-Like Creature Wanted: Dead or Alive," *Globe & Mail* (May 15, 1978) as cited in Mysteries of the World Supplement (June 1978).

1819 "It's Not Endangered: Expert," *Edmonton Journal* (May 13, 1978) as cited in *Mysteries of the World Supplement* (July 1978).

1820 Louv, Rich. "Bigfoot: To Kill or Not to Kill," *Star-News* (Chula Vista, California) (June 22, 1978): B1.

1821 "It's Not Endangered: Expert," *Edmonton Journal* (May 13, 1978) as cited in *Mysteries of the World Supplement* (July 1978).

1822 "It's Not Endangered: Expert," *Edmonton Journal* (May 13, 1978) as cited in *Mysteries of the World Supplement* (July 1978).

1823 "Shooting to Kill Would Help Solve Sasquatch Mystery," *The Lethbridge Herald* (May 15, 1978).

1824 Louv, Rich. "Bigfoot: To Kill or Not to Kill," *Star-News* (Chula Vista, California) (June 22, 1978): B1.

1825 Louv, Rich. "Bigfoot: To Kill or Not to Kill," *Star-News* (Chula Vista, California) (June 22, 1978): B1.

1826 Louv, Rich. "Bigfoot: To Kill or Not to Kill," *Star-News* (Chula Vista, California) (June 22, 1978): B1.

1827 Louv, Rich. "Bigfoot: To Kill or Not to Kill," *Star-News* (Chula Vista, California) (June 22, 1978): B1.

1828 Louv, Rich. "Bigfoot: To Kill or Not to Kill," *Star-News* (Chula Vista, California) (June 22, 1978): B1.

1829 Louv, Rich. "Bigfoot: To Kill or Not to Kill," *Star-News* (Chula Vista, California) (June 22, 1978): B1.

1830 Louv, Rich. "Bigfoot: To Kill or Not to Kill," *Star-News* (Chula Vista, California) (June 22, 1978): B1

1831 Louv, Rich. "Bigfoot: To Kill or Not to Kill," *Star-News* (Chula Vista, California) (June 22, 1978): B1.

1832 Macey, Patrick J. "Anthropology of the Unknown: A Conference on Sasquatch and Similar Humanoid Monsters," *Pursuit* (Fall 1978): 130-131.

1833 Scriba, Jay. "Bigfoot Basher," *Milwaukee Journal* (January 16, 1981): 14.

1834 Pennsylvania Folklore Society. *Keystone Folklore* (vol. 21, 1976): 63.

1835 Santiago, Frank. "Bigfoot Tale Leaves Heckuva Impression," *Omaha World News* (October 1, 1978) as cited in *Mysteries of the World Supplement* (November 1978).

1836 "Sasquatch Kid's Film Planned," *Spokesman-Review* (Spokane, Washington) (April 10, 1978): 9.

1837 *The History of the Sasquatch (Bigfoot) in Washington* State (Spokane, Washington: Nachman-McCallister Advertising, 1978): 2.

1838 Place, Marian T. *Bigfoot: All Over the Country* (New York: Dodd, Mead & Company, 1978): 185.

1839 Todd, E.H. *Sasquatch—The Man* (New York: Carlton Press, 1978): 20.

1840 Todd, E.H. *Sasquatch—The Man* (New York: Carlton Press, 1978): 52.

1841 Todd, E.H. *Sasquatch—The Man* (New York: Carlton Press, 1978).

1842 Pilichis, Dennis. (Ed.) *Bigfoot: Tales of Unexplained Creatures.* (Rome, Ohio: Page Research Library, 1978): 40.

1843 "Recent UFO Sightings," *UFO Magazine: News Bulletin* (October 1978): 2-3.

1844 Briazack, Norman J. and Simon Mennick. *The UFO Guidebook* (Citadel Press, 1978): 47-48.

1845 Green, John. Sasquatch: *The Apes Among Us* (Seattle, WA: Hancock House Publishers, 1978): 256.

1846 Williams, Gorney. "The Riddle of Bigfoot," *UFO Encounters* (April 1978): 71-72.

1847 Condon, George E. "If It's So Big, Why Can't We Get a Decent Photo," *Plain Dealer* (Cleveland, Ohio) (January 20, 1978): 15.

1848 Gruber, Leslie. "'Bigfoot'—Brunswick Hunters Find 17-Inch Tracks," *Wilmington Morning Star* (January 3, 1978): 2.

1849 "Iliamna Residents Report Seeing 'Bigfoot'," *Daily Sitka Sentinel* (January 16, 1978): 6.

1850 "Sighting of Iliamna Bigfoot Sparks Expedition," *Anchorage Daily News* (January 1978). BigfootEncounters.com. http://www.bigfootencounters.com/articles/iliamna.htm.

1851 Martin, Douglas. "'Hideous' Devil Does Live in New Jersey," (*The Wall Street Journal*) *Beaver County Times* (Beaver, Pennsylvania) (December 2, 1979): A-19.

1852 Wheeler, Cheryl. "Is Albany a Bigfoot Hangout? Tracks in Field Cited as Evidence," *Oregon Statesman* (March 13, 1978) as cited in *Mysteries of the World Supplement* (May 1978).

1853 Wheeler, Cheryl. "Is Albany a Bigfoot Hangout? Tracks in Field Cited as Evidence," *Oregon Statesman* (March 13, 1978) as cited in *Mysteries of the World Supplement* (May 1978).

1854 Wheeler, Cheryl. "Is Albany a Bigfoot Hangout? Tracks in Field Cited as Evidence," *Oregon Statesman* (March 13, 1978) as cited in *Mysteries of the World Supplement* (May 1978).

1855 McMullen, Peggy. "'Bigfoot' Tracks Near Albany Get Residents Wondering . . ." *Democrat-Herald* (Albany, New York) (March 13, 1978) as cited in Mysteries of the World Supplement (May 1978).

1856 "Are Bigfoot Tracks Real? Prober Shed Little Light," *Democrat-Herald* (Albany, New York) (March 14, 1978) as cited *in Mysteries of the World Supplement* (June 1978).

1857 Wheeler, Cheryl. "Is Albany a Bigfoot Hangout? Tracks in Field Cited as Evidence," *Oregon Statesman* (March 13, 1978) as cited in *Mysteries of the World Supplement* (May 1978).

1858 "May Not be Bigfoot, But it was Strange," *Ledger* (Lakeland, Florida) (March 13, 1978): 6B.

1859 Goetsch, Ron. "Beware of Mysterious Blackwater Bigfoot," *Daily News* (Fort Walton Beach, Florida) (November 26, 1978) as cited in *Mysteries of the World Supplement* (January 1979): 10.

1860 Goetsch, Ron. "Beware of Mysterious Blackwater Bigfoot," *Daily News* (Fort Walton Beach, Florida) (November 26, 1978) as cited in *Mysteries of the World Supplement* (January 1979): 10.

1861 Simpson, David Jr., "'Footprints' from Bigfoot Determined to be Prank," *Tuscaloosa News* (July 13, 1978): 1.

1862 "A Dallas Group is Following in the Footsteps of Bigfoot," *True UFOs & Outer Space Quarterly* (Fall, 1979): 56-57.

1863 "A Dallas Group is Following in the Footsteps of Bigfoot," *True UFOs & Outer Space Quarterly* (Fall, 1979): 57.

1864 "A Dallas Group is Following in the Footsteps of Bigfoot," *True UFOs & Outer Space Quarterly* (Fall, 1979): 57-59.

1865 "Bigfoot Rumor Surfaces," *Eagle* (Bryan, Texas) (July 30, 1978): 2E.

1866 Cumings, Tim. "Milam Sheriff Says Bigfoot Sighting Result of Prankster," *Eagle* (Bryan, Texas) (July 31, 1978): 11.

1867 Cox, Mike. "Big Foot Sighting is Called a Hoax," *American Statesman* (Austin, Texas) (July 31, 1978) as cited in *Mysteries of the World Supplement* (September 1978).

1868 Goldstein, Lorrie. "Tunnel Monster of Cabbagetown," *Sunday Sun (Toronto)* (March 25, 1979) as cited in *Mysteries of the World Supplement* (May 1979).

1869 "Hairy Creature Spotted," *Greenville Daily Advocate* (August 24, 1978): 2.

1870 Balint, Ed. "1978 'Bigfoot' Sighting Local Legend," BigfootEncounters.com. http://www.bigfootencounters.com/articles/minerva_1978.htm

1871 Mudrak, Barbara, and Bob Downing. "Curious Bring Guns, Beer to Search for 'Creature'," *Akron Beacon Journal* (August 27, 1978): 9.

1872 Balint, Ed. "1978 'Bigfoot' Sighting Local Legend," BigfootEncounters.com http://www.bigfootencounters.com/articles/minerva_1978.htm

1873 Mudrak, Barbara, and Bob Downing. "Curious Bring Guns, Beer to Search for 'Creature'," *Akron Beacon Journal* (August 27, 1978): 9.

1874 Balint, Ed. "1978 'Bigfoot' Sighting Local Legend," BigfootEncounters.com http://www.bigfootencounters.com/articles/minerva_1978.htm

1875 Mudrak, Barbara, and Bob Downing. "Curious Bring Guns, Beer to Search for 'Creature'," *Akron Beacon Journal* (August 27, 1978): 9.

1876 Woolheater, Craig. "Did Bigfoot Really Visit Minerva in 1978," (January 22, 2015) Cryptomundo.com http://cryptomundo.com/bigfoot-report/did-bigfoot-really-visit-minerva-in-1978/

1877 Mudrak, Barbara, and Bob Downing. "Curious Bring Guns, Beer to Search for 'Creature'," *Akron Beacon Journal* (August 27, 1978): 1.

1878 Mudrak, Barbara. "Crickets Quiet When the 'Creature' Prowls," *Akron Beacon Journal* (August 24, 1978): 1.

1879 Mudrak, Barbara, and Bob Downing. "Curious Bring Guns, Beer to Search for 'Creature'," *Akron Beacon Journal* (August 27, 1978): 9.

1880 "Suspected Bigfoot Quite Harmless," *Morning Advocate* (Baton Rouge, Louisiana) (September 2, 1978): 10A.

1881 "Big Foot Hoax," *Leader-Post* (Regina, Saskatchewan) (March 16, 1978): 48.

1882 Hill, Jim. "Stalking Bigfoot: Pair Study Sightings," *Daily Record* (York, Pennsylvania) (January 15, 1979) as cited in *Bigfoot-Sasquatch Information Service* (February 1979).

1883 Hill, Jim. "Stalking Bigfoot: Pair Study Sightings," *Daily Record* (York, Pennsylvania) (January 15, 1979) as cited in *Bigfoot-Sasquatch Information Service* (February 1979).

1884 Hill, Jim. "Stalking Bigfoot: Pair Study Sightings," *Daily Record* (York, Pennsylvania) (January 15, 1979) as cited in *Bigfoot-Sasquatch Information Service* (February 1979).

1885 Hill, Jim. "Stalking Bigfoot: Pair Study Sightings," *Daily Record* (York, Pennsylvania) (January 15, 1979) as cited in *Bigfoot-Sasquatch Information Service* (February 1979).

1886 Hill, Jim. "Stalking Bigfoot: Pair Study Sightings," *Daily Record* (York, Pennsylvania) (January 15, 1979) as cited in *Bigfoot-Sasquatch Information Service* (February 1979).

1887 Ernst, Jerry. "Bigfoot Big Hoax," *Argus-Press* (Owosso, Michigan) (September 1, 1978): 16.

1888 Ernst, Jerry. "Bigfoot Big Hoax," *Argus-Press* (Owosso, Michigan) (September 1, 1978): 16.

1889 Jaye, Darlene. "Who Knows What Lurks in the Shadows," *Argus-Press* (Owosso, Michigan) (September 6, 1978): 13.

1890 Jaye, Darlene. "Who Knows What Lurks in the Shadows," *Argus-Press* (Owosso, Michigan) (September 6, 1978): 13.

1891 Jaye, Darlene. "Who Knows What Lurks in the Shadows," *Argus-Press* (Owosso, Michigan) (September 6, 1978): 13.

1892 Ernst, Jerry. "Bigfoot Big Hoax," *Argus-Press* (Owosso, Michigan) (September 1, 1978): 16.

1893 Ernst, Jerry. "Bigfoot Remains Elusive in More Ways Than One," *Argus-Press* (Owosso, Michigan) (September 2, 1978): 7.

1894 Jaye, Darlene. "Who Knows What Lurks in the Shadows," *Argus-Press* (Owosso, Michigan) (September 6, 1978): 13.

1895 Jaye, Darlene. "Who Knows What Lurks in the Shadows," *Argus-Press* (Owosso, Michigan) (September 6, 1978): 13.

1896 Ernst, Jerry. "Bigfoot Remains Elusive in More Ways Than One," *Argus-Press* (Owosso, Michigan) (September 2, 1978): 7.

1897 Ernst, Jerry. "Bigfoot Remains Elusive in More Ways Than One," *Argus-Press* (Owosso, Michigan) (September 2, 1978): 7.

1898 Ernst, Jerry. "Bigfoot Remains Elusive in More Ways Than One," *Argus-Press* (Owosso, Michigan) (September 2, 1978): 7.

1899 Ernst, Jerry. "Bigfoot Remains Elusive in More Ways Than One," *Argus-Press* [Owosso, Michigan] (September 2, 1978): 7.

1900 Santiago, Frank. "Town has Hairy Time with 'Monster'," *Detroit Free Press* (August 6, 1978) as cited in *Mysteries of the World Supplement* (September 1978).

1901 Santiago, Frank. "Town has Hairy Time with 'Monster'," *Detroit Free Press* (August 6, 1978) as cited in *Mysteries of the World Supplement* (September 1978).

1902 Santiago, Frank. "Town has Hairy Time with 'Monster'," *Detroit Free Press* (August 6, 1978) as cited in *Mysteries of the World Supplement* (September 1978).

1903 Brown, Dave. "Ape-like 'Creature' Scaring Ottosen," *Des Moines Register* (August 2, 1978): 1.

1904 Santiago, Frank. "Town has Hairy Time with 'Monster'," *Detroit Free Press* (August 6, 1978) as cited in *Mysteries of the World Supplement* (September 1978).

1905 Santiago, Frank. "Town has Hairy Time with 'Monster'," *Detroit Free Press* (August 6, 1978) as cited in *Mysteries of the World Supplement* (September 1978).

1906 Santiago, Frank. "Town has Hairy Time with 'Monster'," *Detroit Free Press* (August 6, 1978) as cited in *Mysteries of the World Supplement* (September 1978).

1907 "'Creature' Scaring Iowa Town," *Omaha World-Herald* (August 2, 1978) as cited in *Mysteries of the World Supplement* (October 1978).

1908 Klaus, Steven. "Reports of Hairy Beast, Night Screams Have Iowa Town on Edge," *Des Moines Register* (September 24, 1978) as cited in *Mysteries of the World Supplement* (November 1978): 5.

1909 Klaus, Steven. "Reports of Hairy Beast, Night Screams Have Iowa Town on Edge," *Des Moines Register* (September 24, 1978) as cited in *Mysteries of the World Supplement* (November 1978): 5-6.

1910 Klaus, Steven. "Reports of Hairy Beast, Night Screams Have Iowa Town on Edge," *Des Moines Register* (September 24, 1978) as cited in *Mysteries of the World Supplement* (November 1978): 5.

1911 Girres, Julie and Jeff Bormann. "Is Bigfoot Really Out There," *West Bend Journal* (November 9, 1978) as cited in *Mysteries of the World* (December 1978).

1912 Girres, Julie, and Jeff Bormann. "Is Bigfoot Really Out There," *West Bend Journal* (November 9, 1978) as cited in *Mysteries of the World* (December 1978).

1913 Girres, Julie, and Jeff Bormann. "Is Bigfoot Really Out There," *West Bend Journal* (November 9, 1978) as cited in *Mysteries of the World* (December 1978).

1914 "Sheriff, Meet Your Hairy Present," *Omaha World-Herald* (December 24, 1978) as cited in *Mysteries of the World Supplement* (February 1979).

1915 "Man Convinced Bigfoot is in Northwest Iowa," *West Bend Daily News* (September 21, 1978) as cited in *Mysteries of the World Supplement* (November 1978).

1916 Klaus, Steve. "Omah Gosh! Yeti Another Bigfoot Seen," *Des Moines Register* (October 1, 1978) as cited in *Mysteries of the World Supplement* (November 1978).

1917 "Bigfoot-Type Creature Spotted," *Tampa Times* (October 2, 1978) as cited in *Mysteries of the World Supplement* (November 1978).

1918 Klaus, Steve. "Omah Gosh! Yeti Another Bigfoot Seen," *Des Moines Register* (October 1, 1978) as cited in *Mysteries of the World Supplement* (November 1978).

1919 "'Bigfoot' on Iowa Farm," *Antigo Daily Journal* (October 2, 1978) as cited in *Mysteries of the World Supplement* (November 1978).

1920 Bartholomew, Paul B., and Robert E. Bartholomew. *Bigfoot: Encounters in New York & New England* (Blaine, Washington: Hancock House Publishers, 2008): 40.

1921 Bartholomew, Paul, and Robert Bartholomew, William Brann, and Bruce Hallenbeck. *Monsters of the Northwoods* (Utica, New York: North Country Books, Inc. 1992): 51.

1922 Robins, Charlie. "For a Florida Yeti, This is Snow Place Like Home," *Tampa Times* (February 8, 1978): B1.

1923 Roberts, Russ. "Little Stink is Raised Over Skunk-Ape Report," *Herald-Tribune* (April 6, 1978) as cited in *Mysteries of the World Supplement* (June 1978).

1924 Mulligan, Hugh A. "The Skunk Ape," *St. Petersburg Independent* (February 27, 1978): 15A.

1925 Kahn, Jeffrey. "Man Sights Skunk Ape," *Palm Beach Post and Times* (April 20, 1978): S14.

1926 Burns, Robert. "Limelight Not New to Bears," *Palm Beach Post and Times* (February 22, 1979): CZ1, CZ4.

1927 Genzoli, Andrew. "Redwood Country: Bigfoot Inspires Willow Creek," *Times-Standard* (Eureka, California) (August 17, 1979): 11.

1928 *Ciné de Sasquatch* is author David Coleman's term for the hairy hominids genre in television and film.

1929 "Ted 'Lurch' Cassidy Dies After Surgery," *Ocala Star-Banner* (January 24, 1979): 6A.

1930 "A Dallas Group is Following in the Footsteps of Bigfoot," *True UFOs & Outer Space Quarterly* (Fall, 1979): 57.

1931 Leydon, Joe. "'Screams' film Pacing Found Sluggish in Spots," *Shreveport Times* (February 1, 1979): 11C.

1932 Hill, Martin. "On the Road to Fame," *Desert Sun* (Palm Springs, California) (February 16, 1980): 3.

1933 Thatcher, S. "Filmed Where? Gleason, Wis.," *Milwaukee Sentinel* (April 7, 1979).

1934 Pfister, Dewey. "Lots of Action in 'Bigfoot'," *Daily Herald* (Merrill, Wisconsin) (July 28, 1979).

1935 Stowers, Bonnie. "Fantastic Doesn't Pay for Rhinelander Novelist," *Green Bay Press-Gazette* (June 21, 1981): B-4.

1936 Place, Marian T. *The Boy Who Saw Bigfoot* (New York: Dodd, Mead & Co., 1979): 55.

1937 "Twain Winner," *Kansas City-Star* (September 19, 1982): I10.

1938 Bredt, Ted. "Face to Face with Bigfoot," *San Jose Mercury-News* (May 20, 1979) as cited in *Mysteries of the Word Supplement* (July 1979).

1939 Bredt, Ted. "Face to Face with Bigfoot," *San Jose Mercury-News* (May 20, 1979) as cited in *Mysteries of the Word Supplement* (July 1979).

1940 "I Stood Face to Face with Bigfoot," *Midnight Globe* (June 26, 1979) as cited in *Mysteries of the World Supplement* (July 1979).

1941 Enstad, Robert. "Bigfoot, Make Way for the Agropelter," *Detroit Free Press* (May 18, 1979): 2B.

1942 Conroy, Thomas. "Some Other Answers to Myths, Monsters," *Rochester Democrat and Chronicle* (October 7, 1979): 10C.

1943 Cazeau, Charles D., and Stuart D. Scott Jr. *Exploring the Unknown* (New York: Plenium Press) (1979): 212-213.

1944 Cazeau, Charles D., and Stuart D. Scott Jr. *Exploring the Unknown* (New York: Plenium Press) (1979): 215.

1945 Cazeau, Charles D., and Stuart D. Scott Jr. *Exploring the Unknown* (New York: Plenium Press) (1979): 216.

1946 Cazeau, Charles D., and Stuart D. Scott Jr. *Exploring the Unknown* (New York: Plenium Press) (1979): 217.

1947 Hanchett, Jim. "The Human Mind on Earth, and in Space," *True UFOs & Outer Space Quarterly* (Fall 1979): 36.

1948 Beckjord, Jon. "UFOs & America's Abominable Snowman," *APRO Bulletin* (October 1979).

1949 Folder 0342, box 10, Grover Krantz Papers Collection, National Anthropological Archive, Smithsonian Institution.

1950 Sprague, Roderick. "The Sasquatch and Other Unknown Hominoids," Bigfootencounters.com. http://www.bigfootencounters.com/reviews/sprague.htm.

1951 Hewes, Hayden, and Bob Stamps. "Sex and the Single Sasquatch," *True Flying Saucers & UFOs Quarterly* (Winter 1979): 44.

1952 Hewes, Hayden, and Bob Stamps. "Sex and the Single Sasquatch," *True Flying Saucers & UFOs Quarterly* (Winter 1979): 44.

1953 Hewes, Hayden, and Bob Stamps. "Sex and the Single Sasquatch," *True Flying Saucers & UFOs Quarterly* (Winter 1979): 44.

1954 Williams, Robert L. "'Knobby' North Carolina's Bigfoot," *UFO Report* (September 1979).

1955 Williams, Robert L. "Cousin of Big Foot," *State* (November 1979).

1956 "Bigfoot May Be Prowling Carolina," *Wilmington Morning Star* (January 4, 1979): 7C.

1957 Williams, Robert L. "'Knobby' North Carolina's Bigfoot," *UFO Report* (September 1979): 24.

1958 Williams, Robert L. "'Knobby' North Carolina's Bigfoot," *UFO Report* (September 1979): 24.

1959 Williams, Robert L. "'Knobby' North Carolina's Bigfoot," *UFO Report* (September 1979): 24.

1960 "N.C. Creature," *Asheville Citizen* (January 17, 1979): 1.

1961 DePriest, Joe. "Knobby Remains Elusive 'Thing'," *Daily Independent* (Kannapolis, North Carolina) (March 14, 1979): 2-E.

1962 DePriest, Joe. "Knobby Remains Elusive 'Thing'," *Daily Independent* (Kannapolis, North Carolina) (March 14, 1979): 2-E.

1963 DePriest, Joe. "Knobby Remains Elusive 'Thing'," *Daily Independent* (Kannapolis, N.C.) (March 14, 1979): 2-E.

1964 Palmer, Jennie. "Bear or Bigfoot: Knobby's Got 'Em Buzzin'," *Gastonia Gazette* (January 17, 1979). BFRO.net. http://www.bfro.net/gdb/show_article.asp?id=290.

1965 Palmer, Jennie. "Knobby: Where is He? What is He," *Gastonia Gazette* (January 21, 1979). BFRO.net. http://www.bfro.net/GDB/show_article.asp?id=292.

1966 "And Now—'Knobby' Posters," *Charlotte News* (undated) as cited in *Bigfoot-Sasquatch Information Service* (March 1979).

1967 Williams, Robert L. "Cousin of Big Foot," *State* (November 1979): 16-18.

1968 "Knobby's' Popularity Diminishes," *Rocky Mount Telegram* (Rocky Mount, North Carolina) (March 13, 1979): 2.
1969 Williams, Robert L. "'Knobby' North Carolina's Bigfoot," *UFO Report* (September 1979): 26.
1970 Williams, Robert L. "'Knobby' North Carolina's Bigfoot," *UFO Report* (September 1979): 26.
1971 DePriest, Joe. "Bigfoot Jr. Not Seen Recently," *Daily Independent* (Kannapolis, North Carolina) (March 14, 1979): 2E.
1972 DePriest, Joe. "Bigfoot Jr. Not Seen Recently," *Daily Independent* (Kannapolis, North Carolina) (March 14, 1979): 2E.
1973 Williams, Robert L. "'Knobby' North Carolina's Bigfoot," *UFO Report* (September 1979): 27.
1974 Williams, Robert L. "'Knobby' North Carolina's Bigfoot," *UFO Report* (September 1979): 27, 70.
1975 Wilson, Maggie. "Bigfoot," *Arizona Republic* (February 11, 1979) as cited in *Mysteries of the World Supplement* (March 1979).
1976 Wilson, Maggie. "Bigfoot," *Arizona Republic* (February 11, 1979) as cited in *Mysteries of the World Supplement* (March 1979).
1977 Wilson, Maggie. "Bigfoot," *Arizona Republic* (February 11, 1979) as cited in *Mysteries of the World Supplement* (March 1979).
1978 Mosby, Ray. "Tunica County Family Sights 'Bigfoot'," *Clarksdale Press-Register* (March 16, 1979) as cited in *Mysteries of the World Supplement* (May 1979).
1979 "High School Student Shoots Sasquatch," *Daily Sitka Sentinel* (Sitka, Alaska) (May 7, 1979): 2.
1980 "Canada Town Hunts for Injured 'Bigfoot'," *Daily Herald* (May 7, 1979) as cited in McClean, Scott *Big News Prints* (2006): 57.
1981 "Hunt for Big-Foot," *Iola Register* (May 8, 1979): 10.
1982 Harvey, Ian. "The Return of Bigfoot," *Toronto Sun* (May 1979) as cited in *Mysteries of the World Supplement* (June 1979).
1983 Harvey, Ian. "The Return of Bigfoot," *Toronto Sun* (May 1979) as cited in *Mysteries of the World Supplement* (June 1979).
1984 Hartz, Sam. "Mount Vernon Monster: Stranger in the Night," *Free Lance-Star* (May 18, 1979): 1.
1985 "Strange 'Thing' Screams Nightly at Mt. Vernon," *Free Lance-Star* (May 12, 1979): 5.
1986 Hartz, Sam. "Mount Vernon Monster: Stranger in the Night," *Free Lance-Star* (May 18, 1979): 1.
1987 Hartz, Sam. "Mount Vernon Monster: Stranger in the Night," *Free Lance-Star* (May 18, 1979): 1.
1988 Hartz, Sam. "Mount Vernon Monster: Stranger in the Night," *Free Lance-Star* (May 18, 1979): 1.

1989 Telephone interview with retired law enforcement officer by author, January 18, 2016.

1990 "The Mount Vernon Monster: George Washington or Bigfoot," *Pursuit* (Fall, 1979): 192.

1991 Foo, Rodney. "Another Bigfoot Report," *Reno Evening Gazette* (July 20, 1979): 1.

1992 Foo, Rodney. "Another Bigfoot Report," *Reno Evening Gazette* (July 20, 1979): 3.

1993 "Bigfoot Walks Again in Martin County," *Indianapolis Star* (August 10, 1979): 6.

1994 "Bigfoot Walks Again in Martin County," *Indianapolis Star* (August 10, 1979): 6.

1995 Rutherford, Glenn. "Silverman Man Says His Bigfoot Story is No Song and Dance," *Courier-Journal* (October 8, 1979): B1.

1996 "Bigfoot Walks Again in Martin County," *Indianapolis Star* (August 10, 1979): 6.

1997 Rutherford, Glenn. "Silverman Man Says His Bigfoot Story is No Song and Dance," *Courier-Journal* (October 8, 1979): B1

1998 "Bigfoot Walks Again in Martin County," *Indianapolis Star* (August 10, 1979): 6

1999 "Bigfoot Walks Again in Martin County," *Indianapolis Star* (August 10, 1979): 6.

2000 "Did 'Big Foot' Cause Scary Experience," *Standard-Examiner* (August 15, 1979) as cited in *Mysteries of the World Supplement* (September 1979).

2001 Plemmons, Michael. "Legends Puts 'Bigfoot' in White House (Tenn.)," *Milwaukee Sentinel* (September 28, 1979) as cited in *Mysteries of the World Supplement* (November 1979).

2002 Plemmons, Michael. "Legends Puts 'Bigfoot' in White House (Tenn.)," *Milwaukee Sentinel* (September 28, 1979) as cited in *Mysteries of the World Supplement* (November 1979).

2003 Sherborne, Robert. "Armed Men Seek 'Bigfoot'—Or . . ." *Tennessean* (September 8, 1979): 1.

2004 Sherborne, Robert. "Armed Men Seek 'Bigfoot'—Or . . ." *Tennessean* (September 8, 1979): 6.

2005 Sherborne, Robert. "Armed Men Seek 'Bigfoot'—Or . . ." *Tennessean* (September 8, 1979): 6.

2006 Sherborne, Robert. "Armed Men Seek 'Bigfoot'—Or . . ." *Tennessean* (September 8, 1979): 6.

2007 "White House Area Beast Sighters in Agreement Upon Descriptions," *Tennessean* (September 11, 1979).

2008 "White House Area Beast Sighters in Agreement Upon Descriptions," *Tennessean* (September 11, 1979).

2009 Sherborne, Robert. "Armed Men Seek 'Bigfoot'—Or . . ." *Tennessean* ((September 8, 1979).

2010 Plemmons, Michael. "Legends Puts 'Bigfoot' in White House (Tenn.)," *Milwaukee Sentinel* (September 28, 1979) as cited in *Mysteries of the World Supplement* (November 1979).

2011 Plemmons, Michael. "Legends Puts 'Bigfoot' in White House (Tenn.)," *Milwaukee Sentinel* (September 28, 1979) as cited in *Mysteries of the World Supplement* (November 1979).

2012 Hovelson, Jack. "Ottosen Residents Recall Terrifying Visits Last Year," *Des Moines Sunday Register* (October 28, 1979): B1.

2013 Hovelson, Jack. "Ottosen Residents Recall Terrifying Visits Last Year," *Des Moines Sunday Register* (October 28, 1979): B6.

2014 Hovelson, Jack. "Ottosen Residents Recall Terrifying Visits Last Year," *Des Moines Sunday Register* (October 28, 1979): B6.

2015 "Webster City Man Lets Sleeping Creature Flee," *Des Moines Sunday Register* (October 28, 1979): B1.

2016 Suk, Tom. "Officials Probe Reports of Bigfoot Near Adel," *Des Moines Register* (November 16, 1979): 1, 4.

2017 Graham, Diane. "Dallas County Calls Off its Search for 'Bigfoot'," *Des Moines Register* (November 17, 1979): 1.

2018 "Report on 'Monster' Safari," *Flathead Courier* (February 15, 1979) as cited in *Mysteries of the World Supplement* (April 1979).

2019 Swetman, Norm. "What is that Creature in the Highlands," *Chronicle* (September 6, 1979) as cited in *Mysteries of the World Supplement* (November 1979): 11.

2020 Swetman, Norm. "What is that Creature in the Highlands," *Chronicle* (September 6, 1979) as cited in *Mysteries of the World Supplement* (November 1979).

2021 Swetman, Norm. "What is that Creature in the Highlands," *Chronicle* (September 6, 1979) as cited in *Mysteries of the World Supplement* (November 1979).

2022 Pyle, Jack. "'Lecturer Talked to Shy Sasquatch," *Tacoma News Tribune* (March 21, 1979) as cited in *Mysteries of the World Supplement* (May 1979).

2023 Duncan, Don. "High Adventure on Sasquatch Trail," *Seattle Times* (April 1, 1979): A17.

2024 Duncan, Don. "High Adventure on Sasquatch Trail," *Seattle Times* (April 1, 1979): A17.

2025 Pyle, Jack. "'Lecturer Talked to Shy Sasquatch," *Tacoma News Tribune* (March 21, 1979) as cited in *Mysteries of the World Supplement* (May 1979).

2026 Duncan, Don. "High Adventure on Sasquatch Trail," *Seattle Times* (April 1, 1979): A17.

2027 Gibson, Robert C. "Tracking Monsters Can Be Fun," *Billings Gazette* (March 30, 1979) as cited in *Mysteries of the World Supplement* (June 1979).

2028 "Bigfoot—Superstar Monster of the 70's!!," Monsterkidclassichorrorforum.yuku.com. http://monsterkidclassichorrorforum.yuku.com/topic/3107#.VHja38mSxkg.

2029 "Bigfoot Stakeout Planned," *Day* (New London, Connecticut) (September 25, 1979): 11.

2030 "Bigfoot Search Planned," *Daily Record* (Ellensburg, Washington) (December 14, 1979): 9.

2031 Yang, Iris. "Bigfoot Search," *Sacramento Bee* (December 15, 1979) as cited in *Mysteries of the World Supplement* (January 1980).

2032 Yang, Iris. "Bigfoot Search," *Sacramento Bee* (December 15, 1979) as cited in *Mysteries of the World Supplement* (January 1980).

2033 Tibbett, Ron. "Man Who Hunts for Bigfoot," *National Examiner* (January 1, 1980) as cited in *Mysteries of the World Supplement* (January, 1980).

2034 Tibbett, Ron. "Man Who Hunts for Bigfoot," *National Examiner* (January 1, 1980) as cited in *Mysteries of the World Supplement* (January, 1980).

2035 Wylie, Kenneth. *Bigfoot: A Personal Inquiry into a Phenomenon* (New York: Viking Press, 1980): 126.

2036 Sharn, Lori. "Bigfoot Hunter Wants One Kill," *Detroit Free Press* (October 8, 1979): A3.

2037 Wylie, Kenneth. *Bigfoot: A Personal Inquiry into a Phenomenon* (New York: Viking Press, 1980): 123.

2038 Sharn, Lori. "Bigfoot Hunter Wants One Kill," *Detroit Free Press* (October 8, 1979): A5.

2039 Sharn, Lori. "Bigfoot Hunter Wants One Kill," *Detroit Free Press* (October 8, 1979): A5.

2040 "Hunters Try to Bag Bigfoot," *Poughkeepsie Journal* (September 26, 1979): 8.

2041 Wagner, Dodie. "Professor Says Yes, Sasquatch Does Exist," *Spokane Daily Chronicle* (March 6, 1979): 10.

2042 "Strange and Unknown," *Beyond Reality* (November-December 1979): 62.

2043 "In Search of Sasquatch," *Union Bulletin* (Walla Walla, Washington) (March 4, 1979) as cited in *Mysteries of the World Supplement* (April 1979).

2044 "In Search of Sasquatch," *Union Bulletin* (Walla Walla, Washington) (March 4, 1979) as cited in *Mysteries of the World Supplement* (April 1979).

2045 Wagner, Dodie. "Professor Says Yes, Sasquatch Does Exist," *Spokane Daily Chronicle* (March 6, 1979): 10.

2046 "In Search of Sasquatch," *Union Bulletin* (March 4, 1979) as cited in *Mysteries of the World Supplement* (April 1979).

2047 Wagner, Dodie. "Professor Says Yes, Sasquatch Does Exist," *Spokane Daily Chronicle* (March 6, 1979): 10.

2048 "In Search of Sasquatch," *Union Bulletin* (March 4, 1979) as cited in *Mysteries of the World Supplement* (April 1979).

2049 Wagner, Dodie. "Professor Says Yes, Sasquatch Does Exist," *Spokane Daily Chronicle* (March 6, 1979): 10.

2050 Wagner, Dodie. "Professor Says Yes, Sasquatch Does Exist," *Spokane Daily Chronicle* (March 6, 1979): 10.

2051 Wagner, Dodie. "Professor Says Yes, Sasquatch Does Exist," *Spokane Daily Chronicle* (March 6, 1979): 10.

2052 Wagner, Dodie. "Professor Says Yes, Sasquatch Does Exist," *Spokane Daily Chronicle* (March 6, 1979): 10.

2053 "In Search of Sasquatch," *Union Bulletin* (March 4, 1979) as cited in *Mysteries of the World Supplement* (April 1979).

2054 Wagner, Dodie. "Professor Says Yes, Sasquatch Does Exist," *Spokane Daily Chronicle* (March 6, 1979): 10.

2055 "In Search of Sasquatch," *Union Bulletin* (March 4, 1979) as cited in *Mysteries of the World Supplement* (April 1979).

2056 Folder 0348, box 10, Grover Krantz Papers Collection, National Anthropological Archive, Smithsonian Institution.

2057 Folder 0348, box 10, Grover Krantz Papers Collection, National Anthropological Archive, Smithsonian Institution.

2058 Bartlett, Kay. "Bigfoot Pursued in Pacific Northwest," *Evening News* (January 28, 1979): 4C.

2059 Bartlett, Kay. "Bigfoot Pursued in Pacific Northwest," *Evening News* (January 28, 1979): 4C.

2060 Bartlett, Kay. "Bigfoot Pursued in Pacific Northwest," *Evening News* (January 28, 1979): 4C.

2061 Bartlett, Kay. "Hunt Goes On," *Modesto Bee* (January 28, 1979): A7.

2062 Bartlett, Kay. "Hunt Goes On," *Modesto Bee* (January 28, 1979): A6.

2063 Folder 0343, box 10, Grover Krantz Papers Collection, National Anthropological Archive, Smithsonian Institution.

2064 "Canadian Files Suit Over Bigfoot," *Bulletin* (Bend, Oregon) (August 24, 1979): 9.

2065 Sinor, John. "How Bigfoot Made the Big Time," *Call-Leader* (December 19, 1979): 15.

2066 Pecher, Kamil. "What is our Northern Wetiko," *Pursuit* (Fall 1979): 156.

2067 Merasty, Marie. *The World of Wetiko: Tales from the Woodland Cree* (Saskatoon, Saskatchewan: The Saskatchewan Indian Cultural College, 1974): 7.

2068 Ferullo, Joe. "Does Bigfoot Roam the Hudson Valley," *Schenectady Gazette* (August 27, 1981): 13.

2069 Burke, Cathy. "Computer Analyst Probes Unknown," *Schenectady Gazette* (November 26, 1981): E4.

2070 Burke, Cathy. "Computer Analyst Probes Unknown," *Schenectady Gazette* (November 26, 1981): E4.

2071 "A Dallas Group is Following in the Footsteps of Bigfoot," *True UFOs & Outer Space Quarterly* (Fall 1979): 53.

2072 "Bigfoot Researchers Undaunted," *Victoria Advocate* (May 27, 1980): 3A.

2073 "A Dallas Group is Following in the Footsteps of Bigfoot," *True UFOs & Outer Space Quarterly* (Fall 1979): 53.

2074 "A Dallas Group is Following in the Footsteps of Bigfoot," *True UFOs & Outer Space Quarterly* (Fall 1979): 54.

2075 "A Dallas Group is Following in the Footsteps of Bigfoot," *True UFOs & Outer Space Quarterly* (Fall 1979): 53.

2076 Childress, William. "A Man Who Seeks Bigfoot," *Ford Times* (March 1979): 54-57.

2077 Childress, William. "A Man Who Seeks Bigfoot," *Ford Times* (March 1979): 58-59.

2078 Downing, Bob. "Last of Big Time Bigfoot Hunters Calls It Quits," *Akron Beacon Journal* (August 26, 1979): G1.

2079 Wylie, Kenneth. *Bigfoot: A Personal Inquiry into a Phenomenon* (New York: Viking Press, 1980): 216.

2080 "Killing Sasquatch Way to Save it," *Daily Sitka Sentinel* (Sitka, Alaska) (July 12, 1984): 6.

2081 Bayanov, Dmitri. "Why it is Not Right to Kill a Gentle Giant," *Pursuit* (Fall, 1980): 141.

2082 Bayanov, Dmitri. "Why it is not Right to Kill a Gentle Giant," *Pursuit* (Fall, 1980): 140-141.

2083 "County May Outlaw Killing of Sasquatch," *Spokane Chronicle* (April 3, 1984): C8.

2084 "Bigfoot Protection Ordinance Pondered," *Spokesman-Review* (Spokane, Washington) (April 3, 1984).

2085 Bigfoot Can Step Forward Now," *Courier News* (Bridgewater, New Jersey) (April 18, 1984): 2.

2086 "Bigfoot Hunter Arrested," *Gazette-Times* (Corvallis, Oregon) (July 17, 1984): 7.

2087 Barnard, Jeff. "On the Trail of Bigfoot," *Missoulian* (Missoula, Missouri) (September 20, 1984): 16.

2088 Childress, William. "Bigfoot," *Post-Dispatch* (St. Louis, Missouri) (August 10, 1984): E1.

2089 Beckjord, Jon. "Letters to the Editor," *Pursuit* (Spring, 1980): 96.

2090 Beckjord, Jon. "A New Method for Calculating Sasquatch Weight," *Pursuit* (Spring 1980): 67-71.

2091 "The Legendary Phantom of the Pacific Northwest Backwoods," UPI.com. https://www.upi.com/Archives/1983/07/05/The-legendary-phantom-of-the-Pacific-Northwest-backwoods/2223426225600/.

2092 "New Loch Ness Monster Hunt Begins," *Sioux City Journal* (July 26, 1983): B7.

2093 "Americans Begin Effort to Find Lake Monster," *Evening Journal* (Lubbock, Texas) (July 25, 1983): C16.

2094 Lacitis, Erik. "Elusive Nessie," *Seattle Daily Times* (August 12, 1983): D1.

2095 Lacitis, Erik. "Elusive Nessie," *Seattle Daily Times* (August 12, 1983): D1.

2096 Lacitis, Erik. "Elusive Nessie," *Seattle Daily Times* (August 12, 1983): D1.

2097 "Our Readers Write," *Current Anthropology;* volume 26 no. 1 (February 1985).

2098 Neidigh, Kim L. "Bigfoot as Symbol," *Pursuit* (Spring, 1980): 66.

2099 "Mr. Bigfoot," *Statesman-Journal* (Salem, Oregon) (April 13, 1982): B1.

2100 "Mr. Bigfoot," *Statesman-Journal* (Salem, Oregon) (April 13, 1982): B1.

2101 "Mr. Bigfoot," *Statesman-Journal* (Salem, Oregon) (April 13, 1982): B1.

2102 "Mr. Bigfoot," *Statesman-Journal* (Salem, Oregon) (April 13, 1982): B1.

2103 "Logger 'Fesses Up: He Was Bigfoot'," *Gazette* (Indiana, Pennsylvania) (April 13, 1982): 7.

2104 *ISC Newsletter*; volume 1 no. 1 (Spring, 1982): 8.

2105 Laska, Celia. "Big Footprints Seen on Powderly Farm," *Paris News* (Paris, Texas) April 10, 1980): 6.

2106 Laska, Celia. "Big Footprints are Called Hoax," *Paris News* (Paris, Texas) (April 13, 1980): 8.

2107 "Bigfoot Researchers Undaunted," *Victoria Advocate* (May 27, 1980): A3.

2108 "Authors in Pursuit," *Pursuit* (Summer 1980): 98.

2109 Hicks, Steve. "A Geo-Bibliography of Anomalies," *Pursuit* (Summer, 1980): 130-131.

2110 Earley, George W. "Manlike monsters on Trial," *Pursuit* (Fourth Quarter, 1981): 180.

2111 Duffield, Linda. "UFOs—A Mushrooming Hobby," *Poughkeepsie Journal* (March 6, 1980): 7.

2112 Duffield, Linda. "UFOs—A Mushrooming Hobby," *Poughkeepsie Journal* (March 6, 1980): 7.

2113 Denny, Carol. "Mr. Enigma," *Baltimore Magazine* (October 1985): 83, 161.

2114 Denny, Carol. "Mr. Enigma," *Baltimore Magazine* (October 1985): 83, 161.

2115 "Enigma—They Won't Laugh at Your Strange Tale," *Baltimore Sun* (January 13, 1980) as cited in *Mysteries of the World Supplement* (February 1980).

2116 Baur, Margaret. "Footprints Big—But Are They Bigfoot's," *Deseret News* (May 1, 1980) as cited in *Mysteries of the World Supplement* (May 1980).

2117 Moseley, John. "Local Group Quietly Investigates Sightings, Reports of Bigfoot," *Paris News* (Paris, Texas) (July 6, 1980): A3.

2118 Powell, Sam. "The 'Bigfoot' Legend," *Tulsa World* (May 21, 1980) as cited in *Mysteries of the World Supplement* (June 1980).

2119 "Phenomena in Focus," *Pursuit* (Fall, 1980): 177.

2120 "Folks Make Tracks to Find a 'Bigfoot'," *Star-Gazette* (Elmira, New York) (January 9, 1980): 13.

2121 "Pennsylvania Prints: Bigfoot or Snowjob," *Pursuit* (Summer 1980): 116-117.

2122 "R. Schaffner's Case Report About the Vinton County Incidents in Fall of 1980," BFRO.net. http://www.bfro.net/gdb/show_article.asp?id=322.

2123 "Trackers Fail to Spot Bigfoot in Ohio," *Post* (Palm Beach, Florida) (October 6, 1980): 2.

2124 "Trackers Fail to Spot Bigfoot in Ohio," *Post* (Palm Beach, Florida) (October 6, 1980): 2.

2125 "Tracker Claims 'Bigfoot' Sighting," *Salina Journal* (Salina, Kansas) (October 8, 1980): 3.

2126 "Bigfoot a Fake, Zoologist Says," *Times-Picayune/States-Item* (October 14, 1980): 5.

2127 "Bigfoot a Fake, Zoologist Says," *Times-Picayune/States-Item* (October 14, 1980): 5.

2128 "This Bigfoot Apparently Has a Callus," *Paris News* (Paris, Texas) (September 3, 1980).

2129 "Bigfoot in 'Thumb'," *Pursuit* (Fourth Quarter, 1981): 187.

2130 Berger, Joe. "I Touched Bigfoot. . . ," *Weekly World News* (December 29, 1981): 37.

2131 Kohn, Martin F. "Is it Bear or Beast Stalking Town? No One Can Be Sure," *Detroit Free Press* (November 29, 1981): 3.

2132 Kohn, Martin F. "Is it Bear or Beast Stalking Town? No One Can Be Sure," *Detroit Free Press* (November 29, 1981): 6.

2133 "Bigfoot Tale Stalks Family," *Times Herald* (Port Huron, Michigan) (June 3, 1983): B6.

2134 "Monster, Hermit or Ghost, It's Called the Bardin Booger," *Sentinel Star* (Orlando, Florida) (May 29, 1981): C5.

2135 "Monster, Hermit or Ghost, It's Called the Bardin Booger," *Sentinel Star* (Orlando, Florida) (May 29, 1981): C5.

2136 "Bardin Booger Good for Business, Fun," *Florida Today* (November 1, 1983): B4.

2137 Greenwell, J. Richard. *ISC Newsletter* (Summer, 1985).

2138 Grim, Ann. "Bake the Recipes from Bigfoot Cookbook in Pan Shaped like Bigfoot's Foot," *Oregon Statesman and Capital Journal* (Salem, Oregon) (February 28, 1979) as cited in *Bigfoot-Sasquatch Information Service* (March 1979).

INDEX

ABOUT THE AUTHOR

Author Dan Green is himself a child of the '70s, and well remembers Bigfoot's rise to cultural stardom during those years. He completed undergraduate studies in History at the University of Maine and is the author of Shadows in the Woods, also from Coachwhip Publications, about Bigfoot in the state of Maine. Dan is married to his best friend, Holly, and they have two wonderful sons.

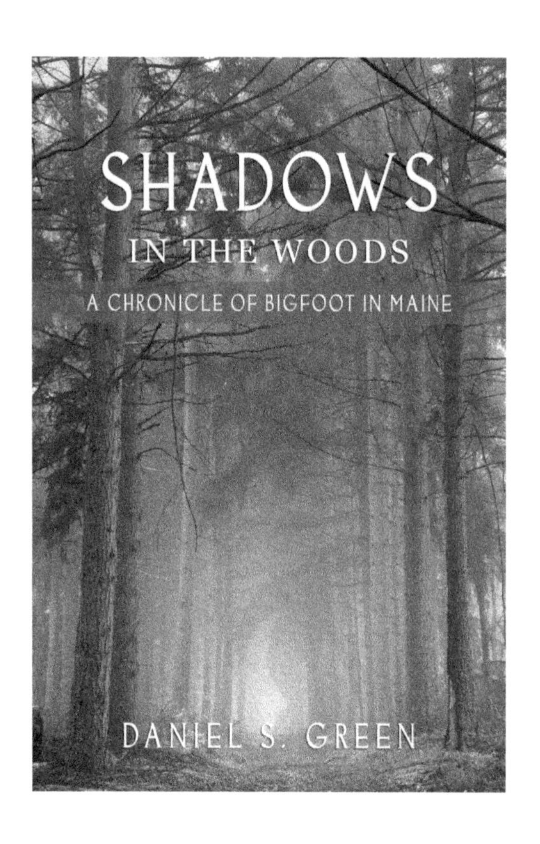

ALSO AVAILABLE
FROM
COACHWHIP
PUBLICATIONS

COACHWHIPBOOKS.COM

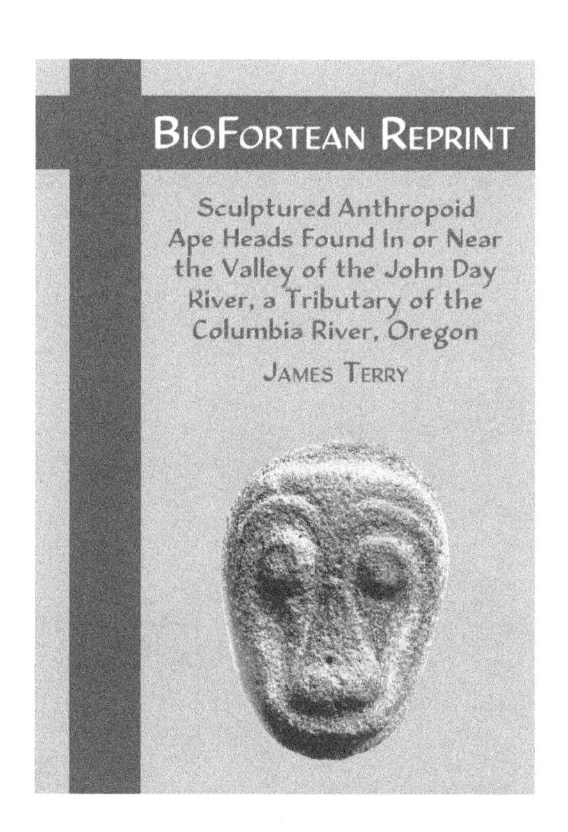

Investigating
Tales of
Strange
Creatures
Around the
World

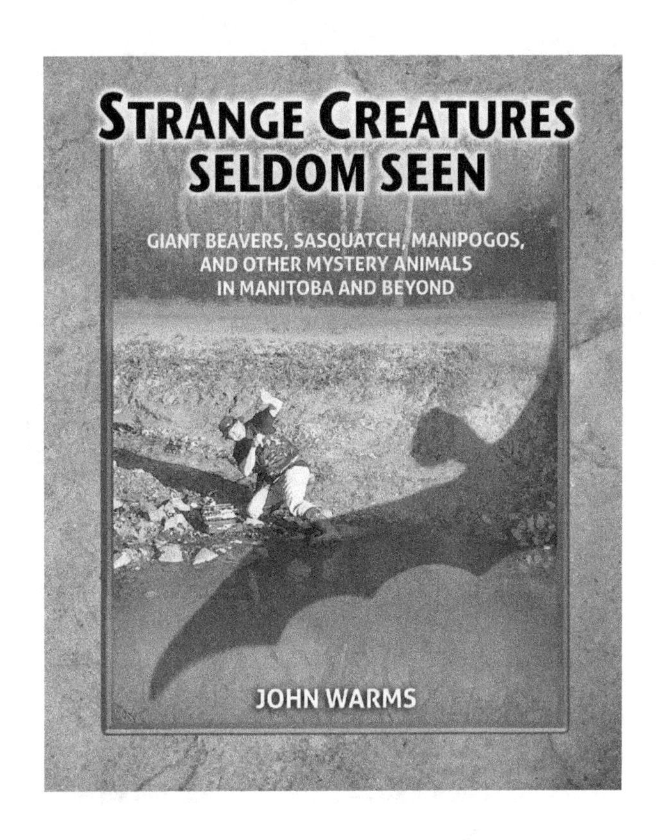

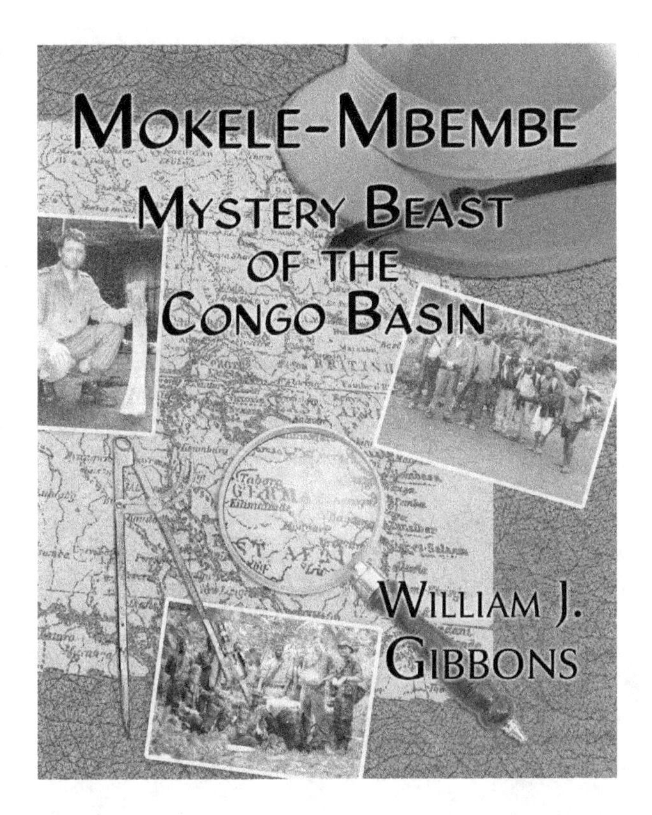

Exploring
Forgotten
Landscapes
for Hidden
Species

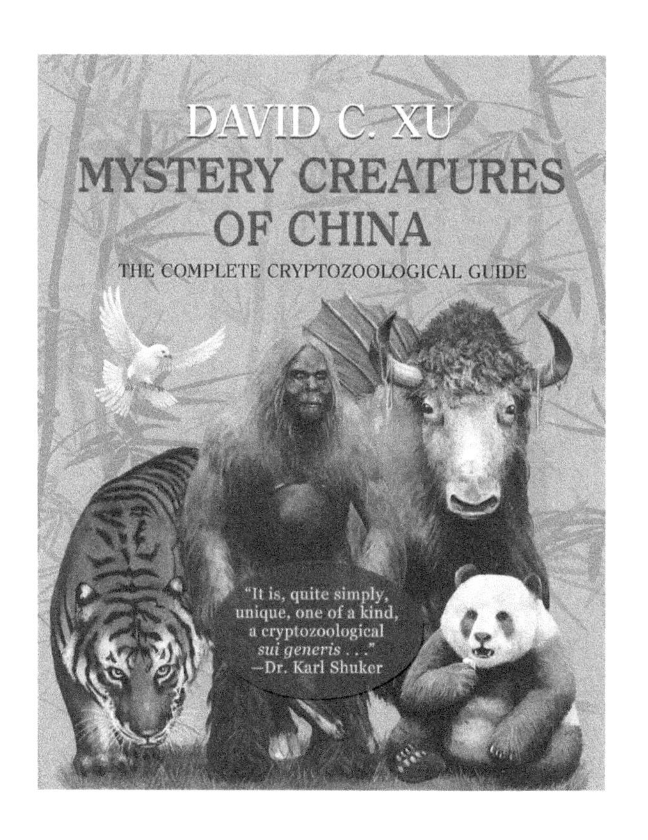

Uncovering Legends from the Remote Corners of the Globe

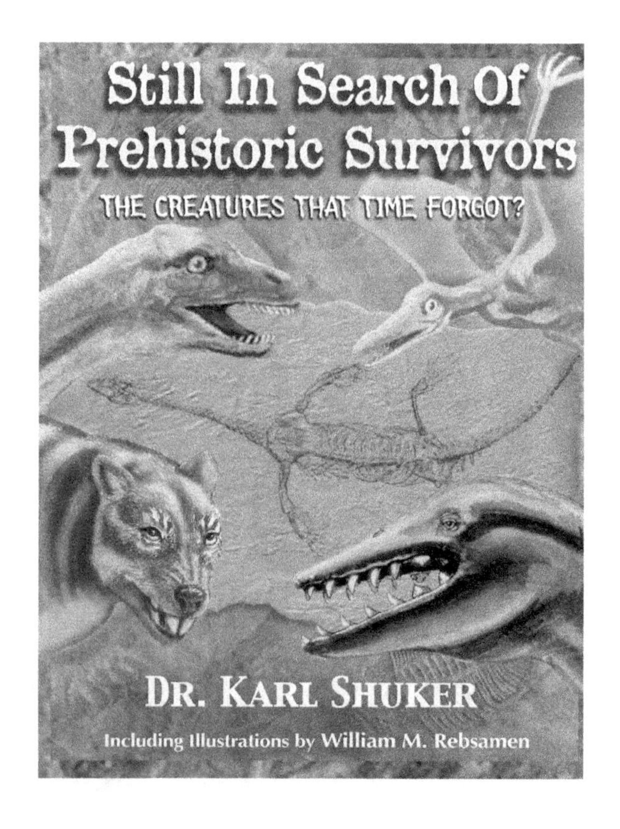

Digging into Stories of Cryptozoological Beasts and the Possibility of Existence

Researching
the Past
for Clues to
Zoological
Mysteries

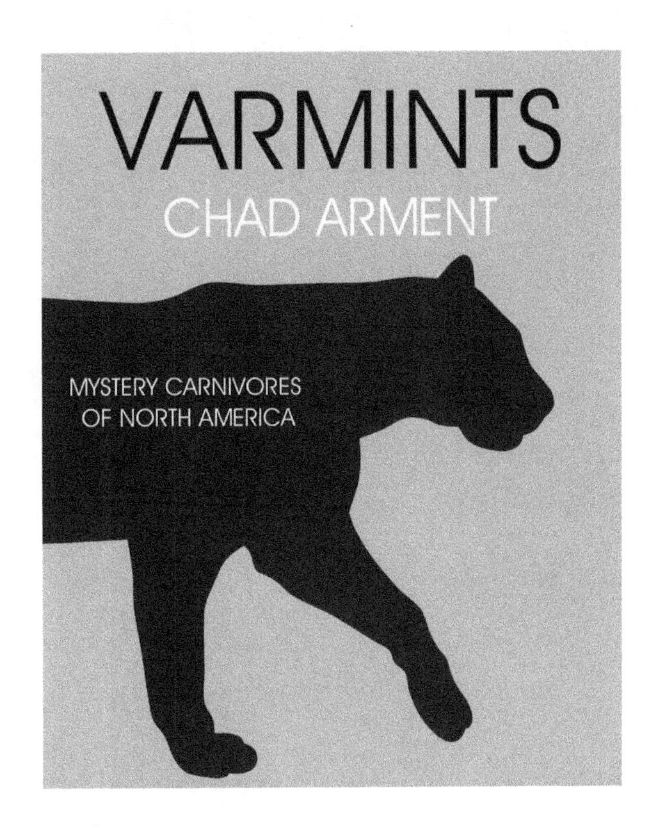

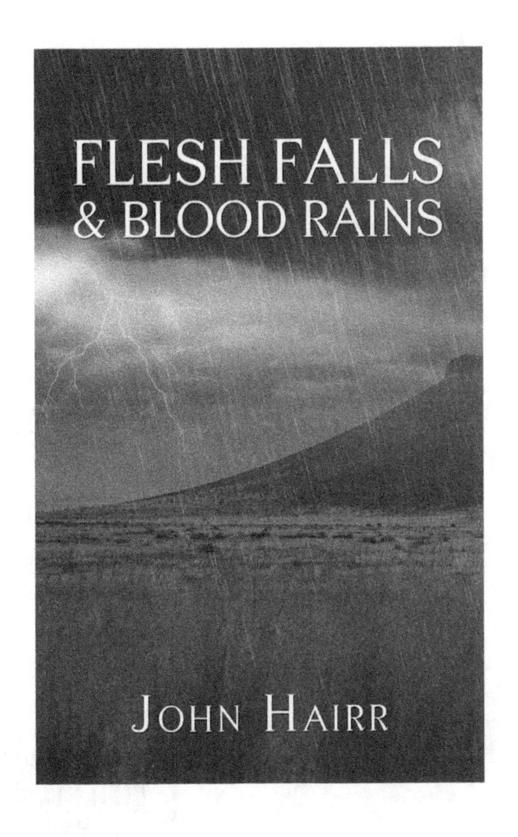

Discovering
the Amazing
Breadth of
Natural
Phenomena

CPSIA information can be obtained
at www.ICGtesting.com
Printed in the USA
BVHW091403100719
553058BV00012B/382/P

9 781616 464578